Country Music

THE ROUGH GUIDE

Other Rough Guides music titles:

Music Reference Series

Classical Music • Drum'n'bass • House • Jazz
Music USA • Opera • Reggae • Rock • Techno
World Music 1 (Africa, Europe and the Middle East)
World Music 2 (Americas, Asia, Pacific)

100 Essential CDs

Classical Music • Opera • Reggae • Rock

Forthcoming

Blues • Soul • World Music

www.roughguides.com

Credits

Editor: Orla Duane
Proofreading: Matthew Teller, Derek Wilde
Design and image scanning: Henry Iles
Typesetting: Katie Pringle
Production: Susanne Hillen, Julia Bovis and Michelle Draycott

Author's acknowledgements

Many people contributed generous amounts of time and energy to the creation of this book. Some gave by way of personal encouragement, others helped with research and/or lent records and CDs essential to this project's completion. Among these friends and supporters, I'd especially like to thank Robert Shepard, Richie Unterberger, Madeleine Budnick, Jan Van Der Zwaag, Tom Armstrong, Brian Gordon, Denise Sullivan, Mike Ryan, Woody Chancy, Tom Heyman, Liz Gazzano, and Margaret Phelps.

For providing crucial promotional materials and digging up hard-to-find information, quite a few people went out of their way to help, among them Lisa Shively at the Press Network; Kent Henderson, Alan Stoker, Paul Kingsbury, and the staff of the Country Music Foundation in Nashville; Ken Irwin, Bing Broderick, and Steve Burton at Rounder Records; Stacey Studebaker at MCA Nashville; Jenny Alford at Mercury Nashville; Greg McGraw and Chris King at County/Rebel; Nancy Cardwell at the IBMA; Mike Seeger; Richard Nevins at Shanachie; Peter Blackstock and Grant Alden at *No Depression*; Cary Mansfield at Varese Sarabande; Randy Haecker at Sony Legacy Recordings; Annie Johnston at Arhoolie; Jason Catz at Network Ink; Rebekah Radisch at Sugar Hill; Brenda Dunlap at Smithsonian Folkways; Julia Honeywell at Ace Records; Gina Williams at RCA; Marc Fenton and Andy Kotowicz at Razor & Tie; Chris Melancon at Arista Nashville; Kelly Hogan and Stacey Earley at Bloodshot Records; Nancy Henderson at Capitol Nashville; Bettina and Howard at Thrill Jockey; Bryan Thomas at Del-Fi Records; Mark Pucci; Lance Cowan; John McCord at Down Home Music in El Cerrito, California; Mark and Jeff at Flat Plastic Sound in San Francisco, California.

A big thanks goes out to all the contributing writers and photographers, including Jonny Whiteside, Bill Friskics-Warren, Nick Tangborn, Candi Strecker, Tom Erikson, Dan Dion, Virginia Lee Hunter, and Ron Scofield.

And thanks to Orla Duane and Mark Ellingham at the Rough Guides for their support (and patience) through this project.

Publishing details

Published 2000 by Rough Guides Ltd, 62-70 Shorts Gardens, London WC2H 9AB.
Distributed by the Penguin Group:
Penguin Books Ltd, 27 Wrights Lane, London W8 5TZ.
Penguin Putnam, Inc. 375 Hudson Street, New York, NY 10014, USA.
Penguin Books Australia Ltd, 487 Maroondah Highway, PO Box 257, Ringwood,
    Victoria 3134, Australia.
Penguin Books Canada Ltd, 10 Alcorn Avenue, Toronto, Ontario M4V 1E4, Canada.
Penguin Books (NZ) Ltd, 182–190 Wairau Road, Auckland 10, New Zealand.

Typeset in Bembo and Helvetica to an original design by Henry Iles.
Printed in Spain by Graphy Cems.

A catalogue record for this book is available from the British Library.
ISBN 1-85828-534-8

Country Music

THE ROUGH GUIDE

Written by
Kurt Wolff

Edited by
Orla Duane

ROUGH GUIDES

Contents

Introduction

ountry is a music that's frequently misunderstood. It's got a reputation for being simple and homespun, a style defined by twangy untrained voices, the lonesome moan of a steel guitar, and songs that deal in such stock subjects as faithful dogs, loving mothers, shattered love affairs, empty bottles, and the little old log cabin in the lane. Some dislike country music because it sounds crusty and creaky, while others define it by the homogenized pop-country sounds that emanate from most contemporary radio stations. Which is really no surprise, given that, during the 1990s, superstars like Garth Brooks and Shania Twain sold more records than any country artist before them, crossing to the *Billboard* pop charts many times over. But these country-music stereotypes are poor representations, only scratching the surface of what country music is all about. Contrary to what many have always assumed, country is not just a singular style with an easily defined set of musical parameters. It's a broad, overriding term for a rich and varied musical world—one that, once you start to take a look beneath that surface, quickly shoots off in all sorts of strange directions.

At its commercial inception in the early '20s, country emerged from a folk-music tradition that was chiefly rural, white, and southern—hillbilly string bands who entertained at community gatherings; fiddlers who showed off their skills at contests all over the South; blind balladeers who sang of trouble and strife on street corners for spare change. Blues was the music's close cousin, but within a surprisingly short time, country (or 'hillbilly,' or just plain 'folk' music, as it was then often known) also began absorbing and reflecting such influences as urban jazz, western songs, big-band swing, and sentimental Tin Pan Alley balladry (not to mention, several decades later, rock'n'roll). Jimmie Rodgers, the "father of country music," rolled many of these diverse influences into his catchy little songs, which is largely why he was so popular then and is so well remembered today.

Rodgers was just the beginning. There was also Hank Williams, who's still the most famous figure in the music's history. Yet the world of country music as we know it today would not be the same if it weren't for such equally significant innovators as bluegrass patriarch Bill Monroe, western swing bandleader Bob Wills, and honky-tonk pioneer Ernest Tubb. The music that these artists created was widely different, as were the audiences who were attracted to the various styles. Yet all of this music falls under the 'country' banner.

And, of course, the country music of today is a very different animal from the one it was back in Rodgers' or Wills' time. The industry has grown from one centered on homespun radio broadcasts and programs such as the *Grand Ole*

Opry and the *National Barn Dance* to a record-selling machine that pulls in many millions, even billions, of dollars each year. Superstars such as Brooks, Twain, Reba McEntire, and Tim McGraw have taken major cues from rock'n'roll, and their concert tours are often just as flashy and extravagant. The country fans these days, too, are a different breed, driving Land Rovers and Jeep Grand Cherokees as often as John Deeres and International Harvesters. The music's roots may be rural, but country is no longer the exclusive property of farmers, cowboys, and mountain dwellers: it's one of the most popular genres of contemporary American music.

The Rough Guide to Country Music is designed to guide listeners—newcomers as well as seasoned fans—through the myriad roots and branches of the music, exploring both its complex past and its present state. The bulk of the book consists of biographical entries on individual artists, but *The Rough Guide to Country Music* is not just a straight A–Z encyclopedia. The book has been divided into fourteen chapters, which lay out the entire history of the music, from the early '20s to the turn of the twenty-first century, in an easily accessible format. The chapters progress more or less in chronological order, starting with fiddle, banjo, and string-band music; running through genres like western swing, honky tonk, countrypolitan, and new traditionalism; and winding up in contemporary times with chapters on both 'young country' stars (Brooks, the Dixie Chicks) and the artists who inhabit the fringes, the world of 'alternative country.'

Each chapter begins with an overview essay that sets the scene, laying out the important figures, influential songs, and significant social and cultural events—the proliferation of cowboy movies during the '30s; the onslaught of rock'n'roll in the '50s; the sexual revolution of the '60s and '70s. An important focus of this book is to help reinvigorate the music's historical thread—to show connections from one era to the next, whether you're starting with the Carter Family and looking forward, or with Alan Jackson and winding your way back to the dawn of the honky-tonk era.

The essays are followed by a series of biographical entries of artists from that particular period, bringing together innovators, pioneers, and major radio stars as well as more offbeat and curious types who, in typical country-music books and magazine articles over the years, have frequently fallen by the wayside. Artists like Jimmie Skinner, the Farmer Boys, Texas Ruby, and Dick Curless, for example, might not be legends on a par with Hank, Lefty, and Merle, yet they made some stunning music that many would be thrilled to discover.

Obviously, it would have been impossible to include every country artist. This book could have run on for thousands of pages—and taken countless years more to research and complete—but at some point the line had to be drawn. In some cases the decisions were easy: legends like Willie Nelson or Tammy Wynette, unavoidable superstars like Garth Brooks or Kenny Rogers are all featured. Other times it came down to which artist helped best illustrate the story of that particular era. Olivia Newton-John and Lee Greenwood might not be personal favorites, yet they were significant figures during the '70s and early '80s.

The reviews, too, had to be selective. Compiling a complete discography on many country artists would be a monumental task. Many albums and 'greatest hits' collections, too, turn out to be cheap budget packages with bottom-barrel fidelity. A careful effort was therefore made to choose CD collections that best reflect the artists in their prime periods. Thankfully, country music is lately better represented on compact disc. Classic albums are being reissued in their entirety—Dolly Parton's COAT OF MANY COLORS, Waylon Jennings' HONKY TONK HEROES, the Louvin Brothers' TRAGIC SONGS OF LIFE—and substantial collections are surfacing, some in lavish box sets, others on well-mastered single CDs, that do the artist justice. In some cases, vinyl LPs are also listed and marked with a ●. These were included either because the original album is a classic in that artists' repertoire (and has not yet made it onto CD), or because the vinyl release remains the best representation of their work. These albums often show up in used record store bins, and in many cases they're still cheaper than a comparable CD. Of course, there's nothing like hearing a classic older recording in its original format—be it 45 or 78 rpm—but that's another story.

So dig in and enjoy—you just might make some new musical discoveries that will stay with you for years to come.

Kurt Wolff

Ranging, Roaming, Traveling: Hillbilly Music Takes Shape

Country is a music that plays like it's been around for centuries. In some ways it has—at least the roots of the music have. The old-timey lyrics and melodies that are the foundation for much early country music often originated hundreds and even thousands of years ago, many of them crossing the Atlantic in the heads and hearts of immigrants from Ireland, England, Scotland and other nations. Performed regularly in the company of family and friends, passed on from generation to generation like a treasured heirloom—and altered slightly with each passing—this is the stuff we call 'folk music', and it's an integral part of the American heritage.

In the southeastern United States in the 1920s, though, it wasn't called folk (an urban term for the older music, though by the '60s folk came to denote newly written and often politicized songs), but 'old-time' or simply 'fiddle and banjo' music—songs and tunes that had just always been around. When southern musicians began performing this generations-old music on radio and even recording it, the line between between 'folk' and 'country' (another moniker that wouldn't come into use for many years) was drawn. What differentiated the two was commercialism—no longer were musicians simply performing for friends and family at casual community gatherings, they were attempting to capture increasingly greater audiences. The old-fashioned songs were still played for fun, but now they represented a 'style' that was being marketed via records and radio—in other words, the stakes were higher, and that changed the scenery (the inspiration and the motivation) dramatically.

If country history officially began the first time the music made it onto record, then the date is specific: 30 June, 1922. That's when the Victor Talking Machine Company became the first to record a southern rural white musician—champion Texas fiddler **Eck Robertson**. Over two days (30 June–1 July) he recorded twelve sides for Victor, some solo, and others with his pal, Oklahoma fiddler and Civil War veteran Henry Gilliland.

The recording industry had been operating since the late 1800s, and the bulk of the songs making it onto commercially released wax cylinders and, later, 78 rpm discs, were classical compositions and popular Tin Pan Alley, Broadway and dance-band numbers—most of them geared toward urban, middle-class audiences. The first jazz records were released during the late Teens, and the blues era began a few years later when the OKeh label released Mamie Smith's "Crazy Blues" in 1920 (and coined the term 'race music' as a way of marketing records to blacks).

Though the folks at Victor had taken the time to record Robertson and Gilliland, they didn't do much with the music at first—the songs weren't even released until almost a year later. Ditto for the two 'audition' songs recorded in early 1923 by Virginia textile worker Henry Whitter, which made him technically the second country artist to record (though nothing was released for another ten months). At this point, these recordings were little more than rural curiosities to the big-city company men.

That's exactly why the first record by **Fiddlin' John Carson** is such a milestone. When OKeh began marketing the Georgia-born fiddling contest champion's 1923 recordings (and advertising the songs in its catalog), it was the first time any company had specifically made music by a country

(rural, southern, and white) artist specifically for sale to a country audience. Ralph Peer, then working for OKeh as a producer and talent scout who regularly traveled the South seeking out and recording rural artists, gets the credit for first putting Carson's music on wax; he only did so at the insistence of Atlanta businessman Polk Brockman, who ran the phonograph department at his grandfather's furniture store (and doubled as OKeh's Atlanta distributor). Brockman was familiar with a wide assortment of southern music, and knew discs by Carson would be a sure sell. When Carson's first record, "The Little Old Log Cabin In The Lane" coupled with "The Old Hen Cackled And The Rooster's Going To Crow," quickly sold from the bins at Brockman's store, OKeh gave the disc a series number and began advertising the Carson songs in its catalog—which set off a new rural music trend. It's at this point that the country music industry as we know it was officially born.

Records and Radio

The recording industry was certainly instrumental in popularizing southern rural music, but an invention that played an even bigger role—at least in terms of reaching a greater number of country fans—was radio. Quite simply, radio changed the landscape. When commercial broadcasting took off after World War I, it brought people of varying locales and economic classes together in a way that no product of the increasingly industrialized American society had previously managed.

Rather like early record company executives, owners of the first radio stations (which were largely urban-based) quickly realized that many of their listeners lived not just in cities, but in outlying areas as far as the station's signal could reach.

For these people, radio was a means of connecting with the modern world. And when they began hearing 'their' music coming over the airwaves from hundreds of miles away—especially via programs like the WLS *National Barn Dance* in Chicago and the WSM *Barn Dance* in Nashville (see box p.18)—they were thrilled that their heritage, too, was a part of that world.

Radio was so popular that for a while it caused record sales to dip, creating an element of competition between the two fledgling industries. Early radio programs, for instance, hardly ever featured records—the 78s were often even stamped with the warning "not licensed for radio broadcast". Many stations hired hillbilly acts to perform live on daily programs instead. Overall, however, the dip in record sales had a positive impact on the industry, spurring the phonograph companies to explore new territory outside the safety zone of the pop-music market.

Once the Carson records hit the stores, country music was off and running. Inspired by the early recordings of Fiddlin' John and Henry Whitter, hillbilly musicians drifted out of the hills, factories and farms, all wanting to try their hand at recording. In rare cases, and at their own expense, artists made the journey to New York City (then, as now, one of the major recording centers) to audition and hopefully secure a contract. Such do-it-yourselfers included **Kelly Harrell** (a friend of Whitter) and **Ernest Stoneman**, the latter one of country music's great patriarchs whose career lasted into the 1960s.

In most cases, however—and certainly as methods and procedures became more standardized—the record companies sent representatives to cities throughout the South to seek out new blood. The talent scout who pioneered this type of field work, and in the process jolted the country recording and publishing industry into action, was Ralph Peer. During the '20s this dapper New Yorker traveled to cities large and small recording all sorts of rural artists and music—black and white, gospel and secular. He first worked for OKeh (owned by the General Phonograph Corporation) and later Victor. Peer initially sought black singers (for example, Mamie Smith), but following the success of Fiddlin' John Carson (and encouraged by local reps like Brockman) he recorded whites more frequently. Always a keen businessman, Peer later created his own song-publishing empire, Southern Music Company and Peer International. These two companies came to control a huge number of songs, including those by **Jimmie Rodgers** and the **Carter Family**.

The process of recording hillbilly artists usually began with a regional call for auditions; the artists who passed this hurdle were then invited to record in a formal studio setting. In some cases this meant a trip to New York City. Often as not, though, the A&R man set up a temporary studio in a centrally located southern city (Atlanta was a popular spot, but many sessions took place in smaller towns) and cut the wax masters on the spot. The 1927 sessions conducted by Peer over a two-week period in Bristol, a town on the Virginia/Tennessee border, are today among the most legendary moments in country music history, since they yielded the very first recordings by both the Carter Family and Jimmie Rodgers. Most early hillbilly recording artists, however, had nowhere near that kind of longevity, and only recorded a handful of tunes in their lifetime.

String Bands and Balladeers

Country music of the 1920s was a different breed from the music we know today. The majority of it was string-band music with the focus almost always on the fiddle—the chief rural American instrument for the past two or more centuries—but it could also include banjo, guitar, mandolin, and assorted oddball elements like the kazoo, banjo-uke, or Jew's harp. Groups like Gid Tanner And His **Skillet Lickers**, **Charlie Poole** And His North Carolina Ramblers, and Ernest V. Stoneman And His Dixie Mountaineers were among the best-known acts. Some did feature vocalists, though singing wasn't the main attraction, and besides, the voices were

Promo for the Purina - sponsored portion of the *Grand Ole Opry*

often creaky and downright crude (vocal technique became much more refined by the '30s). Local bands might be tossed together for a Saturday-night dance party, but as recording prospects grew they often embraced the task more seriously. The players themselves may have been conservative and to some degree God-fearing (at least on major religious holidays), but their music reeked of late-night shindigs and homemade corn liquor. It's one of the great dichotomies of the American South that hardcore traditionalism and good-ole-boy partying are equal parts of a single heritage. All of this contributed to music that, even by today's standards, is among the most raucous in the country canon.

Solo artists were common enough, although no single style was yet established (the concept of a lone singer-guitarist wouldn't become standard until after the heyday of Jimmie Rodgers). Smooth-voiced **Bradley Kincaid** sentimentalized the past in old-fashioned tunes; harmonica whiz DeFord Bailey, country music's first African-American star, wowed *Grand Ole Opry* audiences with his famous "Pan-American Blues," which replicated the sound of a steam train; and blind balladeers like Riley Puckett, **Blind Alfred Reed**, and Richard Burnett sang material that ranged from event songs (Reed's "The Wreck Of The Virginian") to sad and tragic personal sagas (Bur-

nett's "Farewell Song," later popularized as "A Man Of Constant Sorrow").

After the fiddle, the banjo was among the most popular instruments, and personal styles varied greatly—from the vaudeville showmanship of *Opry* icon **Uncle Dave Macon**, to the haunting country blues of **Dock Boggs** and the three-finger style of Charlie Poole (a style that would later evolve into the mind-bending moves of Earl Scruggs). The guitar was also a favorite, although the instrument itself had only come into fashion among southern performers during the late 1800s (partly because fiddle playing was considered sinful, the instrument itself being a tool of the Devil). The weepy steel-guitar sound so closely associated with country music nowadays was only in its infancy during the '20s. It's actually a direct descendant of Hawaiian guitar playing (popularized by stylists like Frank Ferera), though it was certainly related to slide techniques developed by black blues performers (and the blues men were likely influenced by the Hawaiians as well). Where blues players usually held the instrument to their chest in picking position, country artists laid it flat on their lap; all used a bottleneck, knife, or thick piece of metal for a slide. The guitars themselves were acoustic (amplification wouldn't come around for another couple of decades) and a far cry from the sit-down, pedal-steel consoles that would become a Nashville Sound staple in the '50s and '60s. Among the pioneering steel players were **Jimmie Tarlton** (who also had a weirdly spooky yodel when he sang in harmony with his partner, **Tom Darby**) and **Cliff Carlisle**.

The term 'country' wouldn't be commonly applied to the music for another few decades. During the '20s, record companies alternated between such generic terms as 'old-time,' 'old-fashioned,' or 'old familiar' songs as well as 'Hill Country Tunes,' 'Music from Dixie,' and even 'Native American' music. The most common name, however, and the one that would stick around for years to come, was 'hillbilly.' The word caught on after Ralph Peer gave the name "Al Hopkins And The Hill Billies" to a group he was working with in 1925 (a Georgia group, George Daniell's Hill Billies, also adopted the name around the same time; and Uncle Dave Macon had, in 1924, cut a song called "Hill Billie Blues"). While some artists and fans liked the term, others considered 'hillbilly' derogatory and despised it (Bradley Kincaid felt it cheapened the music). Opinions also depended on who was using the term and in what capacity. Either way, the name stuck.

Some artists, it seemed, worried little about perpetuating crude southern stereotypes, as they gleefully took on silly band names such as the Fruit Jar Drinkers and the Possum Hunters. Many of these names appeared courtesy of George D. Hay, founder and emcee of the *Grand Ole Opry*, who felt that they would attract more attention to the bands, and to his show. Some of the musicians were country folks who initially appeared in Sunday suits and ties before Hay dressed them down in overalls and straw hats. Others were city-dwellers who'd probably never eaten possum (slugging moonshine was likely a different story; this was, after all, the height of Prohibition). Though the names contributed to a dopey 'backwoods' schtick that some (including the Nashville city fathers) found embarrassing, at heart it was all good fun, and fans ate it up like homemade biscuits.

The success of early rural musicians such as Charlie Poole and Ernest Stoneman, though substantial (they toured and recorded regularly), was largely regional. The man who had the first national country hit was **Vernon Dalhart**, a pop singer who 'switched' to hillbilly music, meeting with widespread success almost immediately. "The Wreck Of The Old '97" and "The Prisoner's Song" were the two songs that made his reputation. Released in 1924, the record (the songs were on either side) became country's first million-seller. Dalhart's musical approach, however, was definitely more rural-styled than authentically 'country'—his delivery, for one thing, was stiff and mannered—but his success did bring country music into the national spotlight, boosting the industry as a viable money-making enterprise.

The First Country Stars

With pop singers like Dalhart and **Carson Jay Robison** (first a collaborator and then a rival of Dalhart's) taking almost exclusive advantage of the virginal hillbilly market, it's no wonder that Jimmie Rodgers became such a huge sensation. 'Discovered' in 1927 by Ralph Peer during the legendary Bristol Sessions, Rodgers captivated the American public during his brief career (he died of tuberculosis in 1933). He was the first full-fledged country music star and truly deserves his moniker, the Father Of Country Music.

Though marketed as a hillbilly singer, Rodgers' approach was far more contemporary than his string-band and ballad-singing peers. Apart from his pleasant voice and magnetic personality (he glowed in the spotlight and couldn't keep away from stage or studio, despite his illness), Rodgers earned his

COUNTRY MUSIC FOUNDATION

Ralph Peer

reputation by deftly blending musical styles, marrying his rural/southern foundation with a sophisticated presentation. Traveling the country as a young man he had learned all sorts of songs, but he didn't sing strictly blues, popular, western, or mountain folk material. He blended all of these styles instead, effectively giving old-fashioned music a brand-new spin. Songs like "In The Jailhouse Now" and "My Rough And Rowdy Ways" had a sophistication in their melodic twists and turns; at the same time they were far more down-to-earth than the starched and pressed urban ditties of Vernon Dalhart.

Right from the outset, Rodgers was frequently imitated, especially his trademark blue-yodeling style. Cliff Carlisle and Gene Autry were just two prominent singers who began their careers emulating Rodgers—his laid-back bluesy rhythms, his mix of song styles and material, and his fascination with the West (Rodgers was among the first country artists to wear a cowboy hat, not to mention introducing western-themed songs into a hillbilly repertoire). Over the years the adulation has continued, as tribute records have been made by the likes of Lefty Frizzell, Merle Haggard, and, most recently, Bob Dylan. Probably no other artist in country music (even Hank Williams) has had such profound and long-lasting impact.

The Carter Family (A.P. Carter, his wife Sara, and their sister-in-law Maybelle) emerged at the same as Rodgers because they, too, were first recorded during the Bristol Sessions. A different breed entirely, they were more professionally modest and emotionally reserved than the flamboyant Rodgers. No matter, because the Carters were consistently popular, and in their heyday, as now, they enjoyed tremendous respect. The beautiful close harmonies and keen instrumental skills (especially Maybelle's guitar playing) were a source of inspiration to many. Their incredible song repertoire—most tunes dug up, pieced together, and then copyrighted by A.P.—has become one of the major foundations upon which modern country music is built. It's hard to imagine the genre without songs like "Wabash Cannonball" and "Will The Circle Be Unbroken."

The Depression

Everything changed when the Depression hit. After the 1929 US stock market crash and resulting economic upheaval, the phonograph business was just one of many industries to feel the impact. Record sales dropped to a fraction of what they'd been in the late '20s, and hillbilly artists of all sorts and styles began losing their recording contracts—most of them part-time players with limited popularity.

Major artists such as the Carter Family, Jimmie Rodgers, and Bradley Kincaid managed to survive, but the list of performers who quit the business post-Depression is a long one. Most went back to day jobs in order to pay mounting bills; many even pawned or packed away their instruments, though some, such as Dock Boggs and Jimmie Tarlton, would return to their music decades later when urban folk revivalists sought them out.

The Depression dented the country music industry but it didn't kill it. Radio prospered as a direct result—it was free, after all, since most people had already invested in a radio set. And with so many new fans listening, the barn dance concept really took off during the '30s. The Wheeling Jamboree (WWVA in Wheeling), The Boone County Jamboree (WLW in Cincinnati), and the Old Dominion Barn Dance (WRVA in Richmond) were among the biggest, but stations as distant as Tulsa, Des Moines, and Shreveport—not to mention New York City and, later, Los Angeles—also hosted them. These and many more stations also hired hillbilly musicians for short daily programs sponsored by the makers of such products as Black Draught and Crazy Water Crystals. And down along the Rio Grande, just across the Texas border in Mexico, Dr. John R. Brinkley began hawking his dubious wares from super-powered 'border radio' stations, at the same time bringing music by hillbilly and western artists (including the Carter Family) to listeners far beyond the Texas state line.

The string-band tradition continued with bands like **J.E. Mainer's Mountaineers**, the Coon Creek Girls, Byron Parker's Mountaineers (which featured three-finger banjoist Snuffy Jenkins), Roy Hall And His Blue Ridge Entertainers, and the Prairie Ramblers (who developed a western edge and worked with both Patsy Montana and Gene Autry). As a whole, though, the music of the '30s was increasingly more refined compared to the rough-hewn mountain sounds that had typified hillbilly music a decade earlier. Emerging artists had had time to study the work of their pioneering brethren—listening to radio and records religiously, memorizing melodies and solos note-for-note—and now they were coming into their own. The **Delmore Brothers**, the Monroe Brothers (pre-bluegrass Bill Monroe and his older brother Charlie), the Shelton Brothers, the Callahan Brothers, and the **Blue Sky Boys** led a trend of 'brother acts' typified by tight, pretty harmonies and simple acoustic instrumentation (though the playing was often intricate). It's beautiful stuff that would culminate years later in the popular harmonies of the Louvins and Everlys.

The recording industry eventually bounced back, of course. In 1934 a brand-new label, Decca (which grew out of its British parent company of the same name), was launched in the US, and one of the first things it did was cut the price of records to 35 cents (from an average of 75 cents), forcing other American companies to match the price. Records, too, were now sold through the popular Sears and Roebuck catalog. As President Roosevelt's New Deal progressed, people's attitudes grew sunnier, their pocketbooks more liberal, and the country music industry was once again swinging.

When the *Grand Ole Opry* gained national syndication via NBC in 1939, it emerged as the nation's single most important country radio program. It also signaled that country music was a national phenomenon here to stay. Uncle Dave Macon was still a major attraction on the program, but at this point he (and the older musical styles he represented) was about to become eclipsed by brand-new stars like Roy Acuff and Ernest Tubb—the latter sporting a cowboy hat, performing with an electric guitar, and leading a trend soon to be known as honky tonk.

Anthologies

Jumping into this music head-first can be difficult. Much of it is rough stuff in terms of musicianship and recording techniques. So many artists recorded the same basic song (with slightly altered lyrics and/or melody probably learned from family, friends or associates), and the differences from song to song, even artist to artist, can be subtle for unaccustomed ears. But once you know something of who these folks are—where they were coming from and what their world was like at the time—individual songs and voices take shape and the music begins to come alive. It's fascinating stuff, as lively and raw and honest, and in the best instances as exciting, as anything country music has experienced since.

⊙ **Anthology Of American Folk Music** (1952; Folkways; reissued 1997; Smithsonian Folkways). The motherlode of early American music, this massive 6-CD collection (put together by the late filmmaker Harry Smith) covers a huge range of songs and artists, many of whom might be forgotten if not for Smith's diligence. The collection's influence when first released was phenomenal, and it helped kick off the urban folk revival and, thus, a renewed national interest in early country music.

⊙ **Are You From Dixie? Great Country Brother Teams Of The 1930s** (1988; RCA). Sadly out-of-print at the time of writing, this CD collection includes songs (all RCA Victor recordings) by the Blue Sky Boys, the Lone Star Cowboys, and the Delmore, Monroe, Allen and Dixon Brothers. The companion collection, RAGGED BUT RIGHT: GREAT COUNTRY STRING BANDS OF THE 1930S, is equally wonderful (and equally out-of-print).

⊙ **The Bristol Sessions** (1991; Country Music Foundation). Containing 35 tracks from the 76 Ralph Peer recorded in 1927 during his legendary recording session in Bristol, this collection gives an excellent range of the type of music that typified mid-'20s 'country'—a jumble of folk, gospel, blues and sentimental Tin Pan Alley-type numbers. The singers are some of the early greats: the Carter Family and Jimmie Rodgers, of course, but also Ernest Stoneman, Blind Alfred Reed and gospel singers Ernest Phipps and Alfred G. Karnes.

⊙ **White Country Blues: 1926–1938, A Lighter Shade Of Blue** (1993; Columbia/Legacy). The spotlight here is on white hillbilly artists with a pronounced blues influence, and it shows how closely related the two worlds were at the time. The album includes cuts by Frank Hutchison, Charlie Poole, Riley Puckett, Cliff and Bill Carlisle, the Prairie Ramblers, W. Lee O'Daniel, and Roy Acuff, among others. Another excellent compilation.

⊙ **Old-Time Mountain Ballads** (1995; County). A great single-CD collection of early country ballads by the likes of Blind Alfred Reed, Kelly Harrell, Grayson and Whitter, Burnett and Rutherford, and Uncle Dave Macon. Other County Records collections of early hillbilly material include RURAL STRING BANDS OF TENNESSEE (mixing vocal and instrumental numbers from the Tennessee Ramblers, Weems String Band, Vance's Tennessee Breakdowners, and others) and OLD TIME MOUNTAIN GUITAR (which emphasizes early guitar whizes like Roy Harvey and Sam McGee).

⊙ **Times Ain't Like They Used To Be** (1997; Yazoo). The mostly blues-oriented label Yazoo now has several collections of early American hillbilly music, including two single-disc volumes under this title. It's great stuff, painstakingly remastered, and would be near-impossible to find anywhere else. Other Yazoo collections include THE MUSIC OF KENTUCKY and ROSES GROW ROUND THE BRIAR.

Hillbilly: The Artists

Allen Brothers

Austin and Lee Allen were one of the more popular brother duets of the 1920s and '30s. Their songs, many of them upbeat with a good-natured blues feeling, aren't as well known as those of other brother teams such as the Delmores and the Blue Sky Boys (who specialized in more sombre, melancholy numbers), but the Allen Brothers' music retains a well-executed, vivacious character that helps it stand out from the pack and hold up well over time.

The Allens recorded between 1927 and 1934, but couldn't sustain a music career in the wake of the Depression. Both sang, and Austin chiefly played banjo (and sometimes a tenor banjo) while his brother Lee played guitar and kazoo. Hardly a professional 'instrument' by today's standards, the kazoo adds a strange, almost kooky edge to the Allens' music. They had a few sentimental numbers in their bag, but most of their songs were upbeat blues with vaudevillian overtones. Many were topical songs, though the tone varied: "New Deal Blues" was serious in its support for F.D.R.'s Depression cure, while "Jake Walk Blues" told of a crude but serious ailment—'jake leg,' a poisoning courtesy of Jamaican Ginger, an ingredient in some illegal liquors during Prohibition—with an almost mocking tone. Other songs were spirited and fun: "Ain't That Skippin' And Flyin';" an early version of "Molly And Tenbrooks" (later a bluegrass standard); the surly "Rough Neck Blues;" "Chattanooga Mama" (one of their bawdier numbers); and a variation of "Deep Elem Blues" (which referred to a Dallas red-light district). A wacko standout is "Drunk And Nutty Blues" (found on Columbia's excellent WHITE COUNTRY BLUES compilation), which features Lee alternately crying and laughing as Austin loudly complains.

Both brothers hailed from Sewanee, Tennessee, a small town just west of Chattanooga. Austin Allen was born in 1901 and his brother in 1905. Absorbing all sorts of music as children, by the early '20s the two were playing gigs throughout the South, in tiny coal-mining towns, as part of medicine shows and on vaudeville stages. They first recorded for Columbia in 1927, but one of the songs mistakenly ended up on the label's 'race' series instead of its 'hillbilly' series. The brothers threatened a lawsuit but ultimately left Columbia for Victor, where they worked with pioneering producer/A&R man Ralph Peer (who that same year had made his famous Bristol recordings). One of the Allen Brothers' biggest hits was "A New Salty Dog," by far the most popular of several 'salty dog' songs they recorded (including "Salty Dog Blues," one of their first, and "Salty Dog Hey Hey Hey"). They also regularly mentioned Chattanooga in song titles, which earned them the nickname Chattanooga Boys.

Like so many groups of only limited popularity, however, the Depression ended the brothers' musical career. As record sales faltered, recording opportunities dried up, and the brothers didn't make enough on performance fees alone to feed their families. Austin moved to New York looking for work while Lee stayed in Tennessee. They entered the studio one last time in 1934, recording this time for Vocalion, but none of the tracks brought them much success. After that, both men picked up jobs in the construction business. Austin died in South Carolina in 1959. During the '60s, folk revivalists discovered the Allens Brothers' music, and Lee eventually made a few public appearances around his home town in Tennessee. He died in the '80s.

⊙ **1927–1930** (1999; Document). The first of 3 CD collections presenting all the Allen Brothers' recordings in chronological order. It's the best volume to start with, as among the 24 cuts are such gems as "Ain't That Skippin' And Flyin'," "Jake Walk Blues," and "Price Of Cotton Blues."

Blue Sky Boys

"Never did I think that we were good, but I did realize that we were different."

—Bill Bolick

Along with the Delmores and the Monroes, the Blue Sky Boys (Bill and Earl Bolick) were one of the finest of the many close-harmony brother duets to emerge in the 1930s. They weren't so much songwriters—their repertoire instead was a carefully honed mix of traditional ballads, gospel songs and sentimental standards which they sang with tight, delicately phrased harmonies and only minimal instrumental accompaniment (guitar and mandolin). It's hard to imagine a more organic blend of two voices. This simple style became their musical trademark, and they adhered to it throughout their career, only occasionally adding fiddle and stand-up bass. They were also about the only close-harmony group not to use their own surname, choosing instead to name themselves after the Blue Ridge Mountains (the area was also known as the "Land of the Sky") of their North Carolina homeland.

William Bolick was born on 28 October, 1917 in Hickory, a medium-sized town in North Carolina's Piedmont—a high, flat region of the state east of the Appalachians possessing a rich heritage in old-time music. Earl was born two years later on 16 November, 1919. They began singing together from an early age, settling on an instrumental accompaniment of just guitar and mandolin. Both played briefly in a local outfit known as the Crazy Hickory Nuts, and in 1935 they began singing on the radio in North Carolina under various names, finally settling on the Blue Sky Boys. A year later they recorded their first songs for RCA Victor, and these were released on the budget Bluebird line. The brothers' style proved popular, and they maintained their association with the label for fifteen years, cutting more than one hundred songs (nearly ninety of which were released). Most of these records were simple duets, though some of the later songs included a fiddler, often Curly Parker.

As it did for nearly every country music performer, World War II interrupted the radio and recording career of the Blue Sky Boys. The fact that they never regained the popularity they'd enjoyed earlier was largely beyond their control, as after the war the commercial country music climate had altered considerably—honky-tonk songs, western-swing dance numbers and loud electric guitars dominated the airwaves where previously folk ballads, close-harmony singing and quiet acoustic instrumentation were in demand. The Delmore Brothers reinvigorated their career by shifting into hillbilly boogie territory. The Bolicks, however, while they did record more contemporary material (such as "Rainbow At Midnight"), chose to stick to their familiar and near-perfect close-harmony sound. As their popularity declined, it was getting harder to book personal appearances, and they decided to retire from professional music in 1951.

By the early '60s, however, the urban folk revival had created renewed interest in old-time folk music, and the Blue Sky Boys emerged from retirement. Starday issued an album of early radio transcriptions, prompting the brothers to record two new albums, one for Starday and, later, one for Capitol. These recordings showed the Bolicks in almost finer voice than ever before. In 1964, encouraged by folklorist Archie Green, they gave their first concert in over a decade, which was recorded and eventually issued by Rounder Records. A decade later, Rounder brought the brothers back in the studio for more recordings. Since then, Copper Creek has also issued a series of fascinating live radio transcriptions from the '40s. There's plenty of Blue Sky Boys to be heard—all except their classic Bluebird recordings, which are currently, and shamefully, out-of-print (they most recently showed up on ARE YOU FROM DIXIE? GREAT BROTHER TEAMS OF THE 1930S—an excellent CD compilation if you can find it).

BLUE SKY Boys
(BILL & EARL BOLICK)

RARE RADIO TRANSCRIPTIONS RECORDED IN ATLANTA, GEORGIA IN 1946 AND 1947

ON RADIO VOLUME FOUR

⊙ **The Blue Sky Boys** (1976; Rounder; reissued 1996). Brought out of retirement once again in the 1970s by Ken Irwin of Rounder, the Bolicks run through 14 traditional songs that they'd often played but had not previously recorded. Titles include "Tramp On The Street," "Let Me Be Your Salty Dog," and "When I Take My Vacation In Heaven."

⊙ **In Concert, 1964** (1989; Rounder). Recorded at the University of Illinois, this was the brothers' first concert appearance in over a decade, offering an enjoyable overview of their repertoire, from "I'm Just Here To Get My Baby Out Of Jail" and "Kentucky" to "If I Could Hear My Mother Pray Again."

⊙ **On Radio—Volumes 1–4** (1993–1997; Copper Creek). The Blue Sky Boys were one of many old-time groups who were more popular on radio than as recording artists. Thus, each of these 4 individual CDs is an important collection, not only for the music they contain, but for their preservation of their classic country radio programs. The transcriptions date from Georgia in the late 1940s, and they're peppered with introductions, station announcements, humorous skits and advertisements for Willy's Jeeps as well as plenty of traditional balladry—a greater range of material, in fact, than on their RCA recordings. The sound quality is surprisingly good, and Bill Bolick's liner notes offer fascinating insight.

Dock Boggs

"Boggs' music accepted death, sympathized with its mission, embraced its seductions, and traveled with its wiles."

—Greil Marcus

Like his West Virginian contemporaries, Frank Hutchison and Dick Justice, Virginian banjoist Dock Boggs bridged the worlds of black blues and white folk music. He did so, too, on the banjo—an unusual choice for a bluesman. Today, the music he created sounds as chilling, raw, and thoroughly mesmerizing as nearly anything that emerged from Appalachia in the 1920s. Boggs' voice, just a few steps away from primitive, conjures up images of hard-labor days and dark, dark nights burdened by spirits—good and bad, but mostly bad. This is a man who first saw the blackness of a coal mine as a child, who had to dodge bullets on the streets of his hometown, and for whom a ten-day drunken binge was a spiritual retreat. It's the twentieth century, but it's also a time and place far, far away.

Boggs' banjo is his guide post, his walking stick, leading him through the dense overgrowth of lyrics and melodies. At this point, the banjo was rarely (if at all) played the way Boggs played it—picking the melody note-for-note as opposed to flailing fingers against the strings, or playing it in the popular clawhammer style. His banjo playing was, of course, a far cry from the rolls and swirls of three-finger guru Earl Scruggs, but in its own country-blues way it still resonates many decades later.

Moran Lee "Dock" Boggs (he was named after a doctor, hence his nickname) was born in 1898 in Wise County, Virginia—a remote area in the southwestern sliver of the state close to where both the Stanley Brothers and the Carter Family hailed from. It was rough coal-mining territory and young Boggs began working in mines at the age of twelve. He also started playing banjo, piecing together his style from watching local black musicians pick the blues. It was a talent he'd nurture well into his twenties and one that would—at least on a historical level if not in actual day-to-day experience—ultimately release him from the ragged obscurity of a poor miner's life.

Boggs first recorded in 1927 for Brunswick Records, and these eight sides are still his most compelling. In February of that year, the label had held auditions for mountain folk musicians at the hotel in Norton, the small Wise County town where Boggs spent much of his life. He and the Dykes Magic City Trio had been the only two acts to win recording contracts with Brunswick that day (A.P. Carter of the Carter Family didn't make the cut). A month later, Boggs was in a New York City studio recording those eight songs, some featuring just his voice and banjo, others with the accompaniment of guitarist "Hub" Mahaffey from the Magic City Trio. After that Boggs quit his job in the mine, formed a band, and began playing more regularly. The four 78 records released by Brunswick, however, never gave him anything close to a hit.

Boggs' second recording session was in Chicago in 1929. The four songs were released on Lonesome Ace, a tiny label run by Virginian W.E. Myer (who also wrote the lyrics). At this point, however, the Depression set in, Lonesome Ace folded, and recording opportunities with other labels failed to materialize. Boggs had suddenly run out of money—not to mention luck and, ultimately, steam. During the early '30s—and encouraged by his wife, Sara—he quit playing music altogether and pawned his banjo.

For the next few decades, Boggs worked at various mines in the area where he'd grown up. He eventually even found religion, which must have helped him through the lean times when the mines closed in 1954 and Social Security had not yet kicked in. In 1963, musician Mike Seeger—who like countless other folk and old-time music enthusiasts had heard Boggs on the influential ANTHOLOGY OF AMERICAN FOLK MUSIC and been enthralled—sought out the banjoist, finding him still living in Norton. Boggs had recently retrieved his banjo and had started playing music again despite objections from his local church, and with Seeger's help was suddenly recording once

Dock Boggs

Dock Boggs

1970. All 50 of the recordings were made on a portable Nagra by Mike Seeger, who played a vital role in bringing Boggs into the folk-revival limelight. Though not as gritty as his '20s recordings, the music is nonetheless moving and expands Boggs' repertoire. Excellent liner notes.

Cliff Carlisle

"Even Hawaiian music has a sort of blues to it."

—Cliff Carlisle

One of the many Jimmie Rodgers stylists of the 1930s was Kentucky singer and guitarist Cliff Carlisle. But like fellow up-and-coming performers **Jimmie Davis** and Gene Autry, Carlisle was much more than just a blue-yodel copycat. He was an innovative guitarist as well as a talented singer and yodeler, and one of the first hillbilly artists to play the Hawaiian steel guitar exclusively. The instrument had only been recently introduced to American shores, and since his childhood Carlisle had been enamored with it. Whether he was singing the bawdy novelty "Tom Cat Blues" or a standard-issue hobo song like "Rambling Yodeler," the expressive moans and shivers of the steel guitar gave his many recordings (he was a popular and prolific artist, recording more than three hundred songs) an engaging, haunting tone.

Clifford Raymond Carlisle was born on 6 May, 1904 in Spencer County, Kentucky. His younger brother, Bill Carlisle, would go on to be a well-known country musician himself and a star on the *Grand Ole Opry* during the '50s. During his childhood Cliff heard plenty of blues, as well as a typical assortment of string-band and gospel music, but from an early age he was also completely fascinated with the Hawaiian steel guitar— a sound that was sweeping the nation thanks to guitarists such as Frank Ferara and Sol Hoopi. When he was twenty, he teamed up with Louisville guitarist Wilbur Ball. The two young men gained much experience touring the country

more (albums were released on Folkways and Asch) and performing at folk festivals and colleges as something of an old-time musical hero, until his death in 1971.

⊙ **Country Blues** (1997; Revenant). Featuring 21 tracks, extensive liner notes (64 pages!) by writers like Greil Marcus, Jon Pankake and Barry O'Connell, and beautiful book-like packaging, this is a superb collection of Boggs' 1920s recordings that does his music (and his heritage) justice. The tracks include the 8 sides Boggs recorded for Brunswick, his 4 Lonesome Ace sides, and 5 previously unreleased alternate takes. As a bonus, the set finishes up with 4 haunting tracks by Bill and Hayes Shepard, contemporaries of Boggs who also recorded for Lonesome Ace.

⊙ **Dock Boggs: His Folkways Years 1963–1968** (1998; Smithsonian Folkways). This double CD reissues 3 Boggs LPs released by Folkways between 1963 and

Dock Boggs • Cliff Carlisle

Cliff (left) and Bill Carlisle with Shannon Grayson (center)

Cliff's music appeared on all sorts of ARC-owned labels—Vocalion, Supertone, Oriole, and Conqueror. He later recorded for Decca, Victor and King, among other labels. His repertoire was wide and grew to include standard-style train and hobo songs (he even earned the nickname "The Wandering Hobo"); silly feminist-baiting ditties ("Seven Years With The Wrong Woman"); songs that took a light-hearted view of domestic violence ("A Wild Cat Woman And A Tom Cat Man," "Pay Day Fight"); and sentimental numbers like "Rainbow At Midnight" and "Footprints In The Snow." All of these subjects, including domestic violence, were pretty standard hillbilly and blues fare during the '30s. Cliff also recorded a healthy number of smutty songs rife with double entendres ("That Nasty Swing," "Ash Can Blues"), often using pseudonyms like Bob Clifford and Amos Greene.

In addition to his hundreds of recordings, he published several songbooks (often a lucrative venture for early hillbilly artists) and performed on stations all over the east through the '40s. By the '50s he'd more or less retired, though he did contribute songs to his brother Bill's family group, the Carlisles, who made the country charts during the '50s with twisted novelty songs like "Too Old To Cut The Mustard," "Is Zat You Myrtle," and "Knothole." During the '60s the folk revival group, the Rooftop Singers, cut Cliff's "Tom Cat Blues," which brought renewed attention and led to some live performances here and there and even some recording for the Rem label. He died on 2 April, 1983 in Lexington, Kentucky.

with vaudeville shows, which were still very active at the time, alternating their styles (depending on the venue) between hillbilly and Hawaiian music. Carlisle and Ball first played on the radio in Louisville in 1930, and that same year they made their first recordings for the Gennett and Champion labels. One of the first songs they cut was "Memphis Yodel," which was previously recorded by Jimmie Rodgers; it's clearly performed in a Rodgers blue-yodel style, though the Hawaiian influence (not to mention the guitar) is far more pronounced, and Carlisle's versatile voice has its own set of unique dips, yips and moans. Rodgers obviously liked what Carlisle and Ball were doing, for in 1931 he asked the duo to back him up on a couple of recordings (including "When The Cactus Is In Bloom") and for some shows as well.

As a result of the Depression, Carlisle's recordings didn't sell as well as they probably could have, but considering the circumstances they did quite well—selling enough, at least, to get him signed to the American Record Corporation (ARC) in 1931. Sometime around 1934 younger brother Bill Carlisle became Cliff's new partner, taking the place of Wilbur Ball. During this time Cliff also sometimes brought his son Tommy into the studio and on stage as a duet partner.

⊙ **Blues Yodeler And Steel Guitar Wizard** (1996; Arhoolie). An excellent sampler of Carlisle's 1930s recordings, which show off some of the era's finest steel guitar. It includes early Rodgers-style numbers like "No Daddy Blues" and the quirky "Shanghai Rooster Yodel" alongside "That Nasty Swing," the rough-and-tumble "Pay Day Fight," and standards like "Columbus Stockade Blues" (popularized by Darby And Tarlton) and "Black Jack David."

Cliff Carlisle

Fiddlin' John Carson

Georgia fiddle-contest champion John Carson wasn't the first southern white rural musician to make a commercial recording—that honor belongs to Texas fiddler Eck Robertson. Still, the records Carson cut for OKeh in 1923 proved to be milestones, representing a record company's direct marketing of country music to a country audience for the first time. The surprise popularity of these records opened the gates to a new and previously ignored market of rural music fans. Unlike Robertson, Carson not only fiddled but also sang. His voice was creaky and weathered, but that crude, unadorned quality was full of personality and definitely part of his appeal—rural folks had finally found a recording artist they could relate to.

Fiddlin' John Carson

Carson was born on 23 March, 1868 in Fannin County, Georgia, and learned to play on a fiddle his grandfather had brought with him from Ireland. Carson did an assortment of jobs but also earned a reputation for his fiddling, often playing as a hired gun during political campaigns, as well as at community dances, medicine shows and fiddle contests. He gained significant notoriety in Atlanta when he performed for crowds during the trial of accused murderer Leo Frank—a sensational

event at the time. In 1922 he became a featured performer on WSB in Atlanta, making him one of the earliest country artists to perform on radio. And in June 1923 he made his first recordings for the OKeh label, with Ralph Peer at the helm. The five hundred copies they pressed of Carson's "The Little Old Log Cabin In The Lane" coupled with "The Old Hen Cackled And The Rooster's Going To Crow" quickly sold out. Impressed by this, and smelling an untapped musical market, OKeh gave the Carson songs a series number and began advertising them in its catalog. It's these two significant, deliberate steps that mark the true official beginning of the commercial country music industry.

Carson recorded more than 120 songs for OKeh during the '20s, some solo, others with his daughter Rosa Lee (a guitarist who frequently worked under the moniker Moonshine Kate), and some with a band dubbed the Virginia Reelers. He frequently sang, too, to the accompaniment of his own fiddling. He was no longer a young man by the time he started recording, and so his songs—fiddle melodies, minstrel songs, sentimental tunes, old-time hill-country reels—offer a rare glimpse of hand-me-down nineteenth-century musical styles in as close to their natural state as just about any that made it onto record. This is country music in its infancy, raw and unadorned. As simple as they are, however, these songs are also entirely refreshing, especially when compared to the slick recording standards employed today.

After the Depression put a stop to his regular recording schedule, Carson stepped into the studio once more in 1934, this time for RCA Victor's Bluebird label. But country music had evolved considerably in only a decade, moving from primitive string-band music and fiddle tunes to the slicker sounds of Jimmie Rodgers, Gene Autry, brother acts like the Monroes and the Delmores and the western swing music of Bob Wills, and Milton Brown—all artists for whom music was a full-time profession, not just a sideline activity. Carson remained a celebrity in his native Georgia, however. He was even given a position as an elevator operator in the state capitol building—more an honorary appointment than a 'job'—which he held with dignity until his death on 11 December, 1949.

○ **The Old Hen Cackled And The Rooster's Going To Crow** (1973; Rounder). Too bad this collection has fallen out-of-print, because it's a solid round-up of Carson's OKeh recordings, both solo and with assorted musicians. Titles run from his earliest numbers ("Little

Fiddlin' John Carson

Old Log Cabin" and the title track) through an assortment of classic fiddle tunes like "Sugar In The Gourd" and such old-fashioned satires as "It's A Shame To Whip Your Wife On Sunday"—quite an eye-opener, that one!

⊙ **Complete Recorded Works In Chronological Order** (1998; Document). As they have done for several other hillbilly (and countless blues and gospel) artists, the folks at the Austrian label Document have meticulously assembled Carson's complete works, which fill up 7 individually sold CDs. Obviously, it's far more Fiddlin' John than any but the most ardent fan or historian needs, but it's nice to know these historic recordings are out there. If you're going to dive in, you might as well start at the beginning with "Little Old Log Cabin In The Lane" on the very first disc.

Carter Family

> "They look[ed] like hillbillies. But as soon as I heard Sara's voice, that was it. I knew it was going to be wonderful."

> —Ralph Peer

The Carter Family—A.P., Sara and Maybelle Carter—deserve pretty much every rousing accolade and reverential dose of praise they've received. Strong, simple and spiritually haunting, their songs are among modern country music's most crucial foundations, and their influence continues to widen and extend into new territory with each coming generation. It's no exaggeration to say that without their mountain-born harmonies and rich repertoire of traditional melodies, country music would be a whole different beast from the one we know today.

The heritage starts with the songs "Will The Circle Be Unbroken," "Wabash Cannonball," "Wildwood Flower," and "Keep On The Sunny Side" (which became the group's radio theme song) that top the roster as some of country's universally known and loved melodies. Others include "Jimmie Brown The Newsboy" (later popularized by Flatt & Scruggs), "I'm Thinking Tonight Of My Blue Eyes" (which shares the same tune as Roy Acuff's "The Great Speckled Bird" and Hank Thompson's "The Wild Side Of Life"), and "Little Darling, Pal Of Mine." The list of all they recorded is some three hundred titles longer.

In addition to their material, the group's strong, tight harmonies and keen instrumental talent have been an inspiration to many. The music was built around the voices, as opposed to fiddles and other string-band instruments, the more standard focus at the time. Sara's sturdy, clear voice is deservedly out front on most of the songs, with Maybelle's signature thumb-brush guitar style (played after 1928 on her huge black Gibson) keeping the rhythm steady and strong. Faced with such raw talent and unequivocal skill, it's no wonder that New York producer Ralph Peer—presiding over the Bristol sessions—was so quickly bowled over.

Held in August of 1927 in the Virginia/Tennessee border town of Bristol, those sessions were a magical event from which emerged both the Carter Family and Jimmie Rodgers. But the Carters were a different breed entirely from the great Blue Yodeler. Where Rodgers was a flamboyant entertainer with fancy clothes and a mile-wide smile, A.P., Sara, and Maybelle were proudly reserved in every way save the emotional truths that rang through their songs. When not recording, Rodgers strengthened his appeal by touring with major vaudeville troupes; the Carters played mostly informal, regional gigs and tended to chores back home on the farm. Nevertheless, the Carter Family was well loved and highly revered throughout their seventeen-plus-year career. They never sold records to the extent that Rodgers did—they never had a major commercial 'hit'—but they did sell them steadily, even during the Depression.

The Carter Family was a group effort from beginning to end, but A.P. was clearly the main driving force. He was the one who dug up the songs—some he'd written, others he'd found, though at times he had only bits of lyrics and/or melodies to go on. 'Working up' these songs, as he called it, had been his passion (or more accurately, the biggest of his many odd passions) since he was young. With encouragement from Ralph Peer, A.P. then copyrighted them in his own name (he was one of the first artists to do so), which even if he didn't write the songs at least helped preserve them for future generations. Never mind that his fiddling was mediocre at best, and that he harmonized only occasionally, his presence alone—seated in suit and tie between Sara and Maybelle in a promotional photo, presiding over a local concert—lent their music an extra air of authority. Without his energy and persistence, Sara and Maybelle's talents would likely have remained a local phenomenon, and so many songs we know and love today would have languished in obscurity.

Alvin Pleasant Delaney "Doc" Carter was born on 15 December, 1891 near Maces Springs, Virginia, a small town in the Clinch Mountains close to the Tennessee state line and not far from both Kingsport and Bristol. He traveled a little as a young man, and began writing and collecting songs during this time, but he eventually settled back in Maces Springs and sold fruit trees (one of many money-making schemes he'd dabble in during his lifetime). It was at this point that he met and began courting Sara Dougherty (born on 21 July, 1898 in Wise County, Virginia) who, legend has it, was playing an autoharp and singing "Engine 143" when A.P. encountered her during a sales trip to Copper Creek. The pair married in 1915 and played music together regularly—Sara the autoharp and A.P. the fiddle, which they'd each learned as children.

Maybelle Addington was born on 10 May, 1909 in Nickelsville, Virginia. Like

Carter Family (left to right) Maybelle, Sara, and A.P.

Sara (her older cousin) she learned the autoharp as a girl, but she also took up the guitar and banjo and soon had a local reputation as a stellar instrumentalist. She'd already played with A.P. and Sara by the time she married A.P.'s brother Ezra Carter in 1926, but this coupling cemented the 'family' and also brought Maybelle to Maces Springs, where they could practice together more often. They played community functions regularly and were soon quite popular.

In addition to booking performances, A.P. Carter worked during this time to get the group greater attention and, hopefully, signed and recorded. It's unclear what precise steps led to an audition with Ralph Peer, but as soon as Sara opened her mouth and let her clear, full-bodied voice fly forth, Peer knew he'd stumbled upon something incredible. The Carter Family ended up recording six sides in Bristol, and history was made.

The following spring they journeyed to Camden, New Jersey to record again for the Victor Talking Machine Company, with Peer once again

at the helm. Victor was the biggest label of the '20s, and it was the label for whom the Carters would record most often during their career (Decca and Columbia were two others). Even during the Depression, and without ever achieving a 'hit' of any kind, they were in the studio at least once or twice a year, and their fans were in the stores soon after to pick up the latest discs.

Given the conservative reputation the group is often saddled with, it's interesting to discover that the Carter family continued to play together regularly through the early '40s, despite the fact that A.P. and Sara Carter suffered through years of marriage troubles, separating in 1933 and finally divorcing in 1939. A separated couple working together is a not-unheard-of arrangement today, but at the time—and especially in their mountain community—it must have been difficult, to say the least. To top matters off, Sara remarried a cousin of A.P.'s named Coy Bayes.

Another curious twist in the family saga took place when they moved to Texas in the winter of

1938. The reason: a steady gig on the super-powered Mexican radio station XERA, located just across the border from Del Rio, Texas. It was a major upheaval for these Appalachian natives, but Ralph Peer, who managed the group throughout their career, had figured that through the station (whose broadcast signal was far larger than any allowed in the US) the Carters could gain nationwide exposure without the trouble and expense of a major tour. Being consummate professionals, they agreed. In addition to performing live on the radio, the Carters also recorded transcription discs that were distributed to a variety of border stations. The whole family went to Texas with them, including A.P. and Sara's children Janette, Joe and Gladys, and Maybelle and Ezra's daughters Helen, June and Anita. Only a few years later, however, they'd tired of Texas (plus the international laws regarding border stations had changed) and moved back east, landing in Charlotte, North Carolina. The magic was obviously waning, and in 1943 the group split up. A.P. returned to Maces Springs and opened a store, while Sara headed to California with her new husband and more or less retired. Only Maybelle continued to pursue music full-time, beginning a successful career with her three daughters as Mother Maybelle and the Carter Sisters. They played various radio and barn dance programs until finally joining the *Grand Ole Opry* in 1950 (with none other than Chet Atkins on guitar). They recorded for a couple of different labels and even opened for Elvis Presley in the mid-'50s.

A.P. briefly reformed the Carter Family in 1952 with Sara, Janette and Joe, and they even recorded for a small label, Acme. A.P. also opened Summer Park, an outdoor performing space in Maces Springs. But with honky tonk the current rage and rockabilly just on the horizon, the reunion was shortlived. At the time of A.P.'s death in 1960 there wasn't yet a Country Music Hall of Fame to honor the family name, and there were no LP collections of their music for young music fans to explore (though a few songs were included on Folkways' groundbreaking ANTHOLOGY OF AMERICAN FOLK MUSIC, and both Flatt & Scruggs and singer-folklorist Bill Clifton recorded albums of Carter Family songs released just after A.P.'s death). A decade later the situation was far different—the Original Carter Family entered the Country Music Hall of Fame in 1970, and stars like Johnny Cash (who married June Carter in 1968) sung their praises regularly—but during his final years A.P. must have felt more than slightly forgotten.

Maybelle enjoyed a thriving career that lasted until her death in 1978. During the '60s she often performed alone, and as the great matriarch of country music, her very presence added prestige to projects like Merle Haggard's LAND OF MANY CHURCHES and the Nitty Gritty Dirt Band's ice-breaking country-rock collaboration WILL THE CIRCLE BE UNBROKEN. Maybelle and Sara reunited occasionally, performing at folk festivals and even recording an album for Columbia.

June, Anita and Helen, too, kept the Carter Family's musical heritage alive. Anita recorded regularly (including duets with Hank Snow and Waylon Jennings), Helen concentrated more on songwriting, and June—after two previous marriages (her first was to singer Carl Smith)—finally tied the knot with Johnny Cash, which brought the two major musical entourages together. Cash and the Carters had recorded together prior to their marriage, and in 1967 the Carters had left the *Opry* to join Cash's TV show. June, Helen and Anita were still touring with Cash in the '90s (Helen died in 1998). June's daughter Carlene and Johnny's daughter Rosanne both started their careers singing alongside the children of Helen and Anita as the next generation of the Carter Family.

Fourteen years after A.P.'s death, Janette Carter began holding Saturday-night old-time country shows at her father's former country store in Maces Springs. These proved popular, and soon she, Joe and Gladys built the Carter Family Fold (officially the Carter Family Memorial Museum Center), a venue that still holds regular traditional country showcases (no electric instruments or drinking allowed). The store sits nearby and is now the Carter Family Museum. A festival is also held here each August commemorating the group's first 1927 recordings.

○ **Keep On The Sunny Side** (1964; Columbia). Johnny Cash joins Mother Maybelle and the Carter Sisters (Helen, June, and Anita) on a dozen songs made famous by the original Carters. The album is bright and lively, though its tone is folkier (in the reborn 1960s sense of the word) and lacks a certain intensity that A.P. and Sara brought to the group's music.

☉ **An Historic Reunion: Sara And Maybelle, The Original Carters** (1966; Columbia; reissued 1997; Koch). This moving collection marked the first time in two decades that Sara and Maybelle Carter recorded together. Spending only half a day in the studio, they came up with 11 spare and achingly pure songs, many written by Sara Carter during her 'retirement' years in California. The acoustic arrangements ring with simple country beauty, and Sara's voice, though deeper and older, is firm and full of conviction—perhaps even more so than during her heyday.

⊙ **Country Music Hall Of Fame** (1991; MCA). Sixteen selections from the 60 the Carters cut for Decca between 1936 and 1938. The material might not be as historically significant as their early Victor sides, but songs like "Dixie Darling," "You Are My Flower," "Hello Stranger," and "Oh Take Me Back" are beautiful, strong, and as 'classic' as they've ever sounded, thanks to Maybelle's mature guitar work and especially their rich vocal harmonies. A very satisfying collection.

⊙ **The Carter Family: Their Complete Victor Recordings** (1993–1998; Rounder). From the late 1920s through to the early '40s, A.P., Sara and Maybelle Carter recorded the bulk of their material for Victor. It's a crime that for decades this incredible music remained out-of-print, locked away in RCA's vaults. Thankfully, the entire Victor collection has now been reissued, and the results are superb—raw in spirit, but smooth in tone, haunting yet entirely beautiful. Divided into 9 individual CD volumes (organized and presented in chronological order), it's hard to go wrong with any of them, but the earlier collections, packed as they are with so many classic songs, make a great place to start.

⊙ **The Carter Family On Border Radio** (1995–1999; Arhoolie). Released individually in 3 volumes, this music is culled from radio transcription discs the Carters recorded for their popular Mexican border radio broadcasts in the late 1930s. More so than their studio recordings, these programs (complete with song medleys, introductory remarks, and station breaks) give us a broader picture of the Carter Family—and a taste of hillbilly music as it was heard by thousands of fans and casual listeners alike all over the country. The Carter children are featured on many of the songs, lending the material a real 'family' feel.

Crook Brothers

The Crook Brothers were the longest-running band in country music history. They were first on the WSM's weeky radio barn dance in 1926, when the program was less than a year old (it hadn't even yet been named the *Grand Ole Opry*), and they stayed put on that show continuously (albeit in various configurations) through to 1988, when Herman Crook passed away.

That's a total of 62 years on the program—more than twice as long as Hank Williams was even breathing on this earth. Curiously, while they were mainstays on the *Opry*—and toured a bit with Uncle Dave Macon and others—they recorded very few songs.

The core of the original group consisted of Herman and Matthew Crook, born in 1899 and 1896 respectively in Scottsboro, Tennessee. Both brothers played harmonica, and it's this double-barreled sound that was their trademark—the harmonicas taking the lead melody, normally played by a fiddler. Herman and Matthew first played on Nashville radio station WDAD in 1925, then a year later they began playing on WSM as well. By day they worked at the American Tobacco Company. In 1928 they recorded four songs for Ralph Peer, but those were the only recordings the group (which also included two guitarists and a banjoist) made until the '60s.

Sometime in the late '20s, Herman and Matthew met Lewis Crook (no relation), a mean banjo player who agreed to join the group. Around 1930 Matthew left to join the police force, and so it was Herman and Lewis who helmed the Crook Brothers for those next fifty-odd years. Lewis did a bit of singing, too, which expanded the group's purely instrumental repertoire to include songs by Jimmie Rodgers, Charlie Poole, the Carter Family, and other favorites of that era.

During the '50s, Herman and Lewis (the group's only consistent bandmembers) joined forces with the surviving members of Dr. Humphrey Bate's Possum Hunters to play square dance music on the *Opry*. In 1962, the Crooks recorded an album for Starday—it was released as a joint effort with fellow *Opry* regulars Sam And Kirk McGee. The Crooks' music was heard on the *Opry* on a weekly basis all the way until 1988. Herman Crook's death that year marked the end of an incredible legacy that ran from the very first years of commercial country history right up through the dawn of the 'young country' era.

⦿ **Sam And Kirk McGee And The Crook Brothers** (1962; Starday). Though out-of-print, this album represents the only Crook Brothers songs that are even vaguely available to modern audiences. It's a joint release with another long-running *Opry* act, Sam And Kirk McGee, with each group featured on alternating tracks. The 7 Crook Brothers' songs are old-time standards (mostly instrumental) such as "Soldier's Joy" and "John Henry." Interesting and pleasant, though not exactly earth-shattering.

Rural Radio: The Grand Ole Opry And Radio Barn Dance Shows

Radio was one of the most socially significant inventions of the early twentieth century. Along with the automobile, it was a technology that transformed the lives of millions of people—young and old, rich and poor—linking the nation together like never before. Even in rural areas folks could now hear what others around their home state—and around the country and even the world—were talking about and listening to.

The rise of commercial hillbilly and old-time music coincided with the onslaught of radio, and many rural artists performed over the airwaves even in the early 1920s. This became an important means for them to spread the word about their live performances in the region. As records increased in popularity, they added the potential of greater prestige and fame, but in terms of practical payoff, radio exposure was more useful. For their part, radio station programmers understood straight away that many rural folks were tuning in. Designing a program aimed at their tastes—and gathering advertisers looking to sell products to that market—made sense. Out of these ideas arose the concept of the radio barn dance, which was designed to re-create the feel and flavor of a community gathering or dance.

An early version of a barn dance program cropped up in Fort Worth, Texas in 1923, but the first station to create one on a large and long-lasting scale was WLS in Chicago. (The station was owned at the time by Chicago-based Sears, Roebuck and Company; the call letters stood for "World's Largest Store.") Beginning in 1924, the station began broadcasting a weekly variety program with a rural slant that was eventually dubbed the **National Barn Dance**. Its programming was a mix of pop and rural music, blending sentimental singers and novelty acts (the Hoosier Hot Shots) with old-time balladeers like Bradley Kincaid and string bands like the Cumberland Ridge Runners. The program gained national syndication via NBC in 1933 under the sponsorship of Alka-Seltzer, and remained on the air (later the network affiliation changed to ABC) through the '60s.

The one country music radio program that has by far been the most influential, however, is the **Grand Ole Opry**. The *Opry* was broadcast from Memphis, Tennessee by WSM, a new station owned by the National Life and Accident Insurance Company (whose motto, "We Shield Millions," gave the station its call letters). Begun in 1925, the program grew into an institution whose name was synonymous with that of country music as a whole. Where many of today's Tim McGraw and Shania Twain fans wouldn't know the *National Barn Dance* from *The Dukes Of Hazzard*, the *Grand Ole Opry* remains world-renowned—even if its influence is no longer even close to what it was during the '40s and '50s.

The man behind the Opry concept was George D. Hay (aka the "Solemn Old Judge"), a radio announcer who'd been hired away from WLS in the fall of 1925 to work at WSM. He brought with him a concept of a radio music program aimed at rural listeners. The show's beginnings were humble. On 28 November, 1925, Hay invited fiddler Uncle Jimmy Thompson to perform a handful of old-time tunes over the airwaves. Response from listeners was immediate and large, and the program became a weekly Saturday night event. It showcased mostly local musicians and string bands but eventually took on better-known performers such

Vernon Dalhart

"There is no burlesquing in Mr Dalhart's singing ... he simply imagines he's 'back home' again and sings as the spirit dictates."

Victor catalog, 1920s

Until Jimmie Rodgers hit the airwaves, Vernon Dalhart was the most popular 'hillbilly' singer. The word hillbilly is in quotes for a reason, however, because Dalhart—though possessing rural Texas roots—was actually an aspiring opera singer who spent most his career in New York City, recording pop tunes for several years before switching to hill-billy. He made this move in an attempt to jump-start his ailing singing career by capitalizing on the new market, and for six or seven years the plan worked beautifully. Less a 'sell-out' than a 'buy-in,' he was country's first nationally recognized 'star.'

Listening to Dalhart sing "The Wreck Of The Old '97", however—his initial hillbilly recording and country music's first million-seller—it's clear he's a completely different bird from rural contemporaries such as Henry Whitter, Dock Boggs and Charlie Poole. Dalhart's pretty tenor voice is obviously trained, and his style is stiff, formal and overburdened by vibrato. He even affects a hillbilly accent. Like that of Carson Robison (a frequent collaborator of his), Dalhart's music is missing the rough-hewn edges that give so much early hillbilly

as Uncle Dave Macon, the Crook Brothers and DeFord Bailey. Even so, the tone under Hay's command remained homespun and informal. Initially the program was known simply as the *WSM Barn Dance*, but in 1927 Hay came up with its more famous name.

Beginning in the early '30s, the *Opry* broadened its scope from a regional program to a national one with a greater commercial emphasis. Now under the guidance of Harry Stone, it gained larger sponsors and attracted bigger names. The Delmore Brothers joined in 1933, followed over the next several years by Pee Wee King, Roy Acuff, Bill Monroe, Ernest Tubb, and

Minnie Pearl. These artists in turn brought a star quality to the program that widened the listenership. Further corporate support came from the likes of Purina and Prince Albert Smoking Tobacco, two companies, in particular, that came to sponsor individual segments of the *Opry*. In 1939, NBC began broadcasting a half-hour segment of the program nationwide.

As a result of its national syndication, Chicago's *National Barn Dance* remained the most popular program of its kind in the country throughout the '30s. Along with regulars like Kincaid and Lulu Belle & Scotty, it was home (at varying times) to such stars as Gene Autry, Patsy Montana, Red Foley, and the Girls of the Golden West. Its popularity (and eventually that of the *Opry* as well) prompted many further barn dances to crop up in cities large and small throughout the nation. Among the bigger were the *Wheeling Jamboree* (Wheeling, West Virginia), the *Renfro Valley Barn Dance* (Cincinnati, Ohio and later Renfro Valley, Kentucky), the *Big D Jamboree* (Dallas, Texas), the *Mid-Day Merry-Go-Round* (Knoxville, Tennessee) and, beginning in 1948, the *Louisiana Hayride* (Shreveport, Louisiana).

Live audiences were a feature of these programs almost from the very beginning, and in several cases the venues themselves took on special meaning. The *Renfro Valley Barn Dance*, for instance, was famous for originating (beginning in 1939) out of an actual barn in rural Kentucky. As for the *Opry*, it had been broadcast out of various studios and theaters during its first couple of decades before, in the early '40s, it settled into the building with which it has been closely linked ever since: the Ryman Auditorium. This onetime tabernacle (dubbed the "mother church of country music") served as the program's home for three decades. In 1974, however, and amidst much tear-shedding and media attention, the program moved to the brand-new Opryland complex on the east side of Nashville. Country music had seen dramatic changes by that stage, and the *Opry* had already been losing the influence it once held. Still, when the show left its longtime downtown base for a home in the suburbs, a major era came to an end.

music its haunting, mesmerizing emotions and red-raw energy (play Dalhart's "Wreck" next to Poole's "Ramblin' Blues" and you'll soon get the picture).

Dalhart was born Marion Try Slaughter in 1883 in Jefferson, Texas. He grew up working as a cowboy in northern Texas (the towns of Vernon and Dalhart inspired his stage name), but he eventually moved to Dallas, married, and attended the Dallas Conservatory of Music. He moved to New York City about 1910, where he studied opera and eventually landed parts in local productions. In 1916 he made his first recordings for Edison, including one of his earliest, "Can't Yo' Heah Me Callin', Caroline?"

Despite his efforts, Dalhart never had much real success as either an opera performer or pop recording artist. In 1924, he got the bright idea to try his luck with material from the brand-new hill-billy market. His first release was "The Wreck Of The Old '97," a song previously recorded (and according to some claims written) by Henry Whitter. One of country music's best-known standards today, it was based on a real-life event: the wreck of a Virginia mail train in 1903 that killed about a dozen people. Dalhart first recorded the song for Edison, but it was when Victor re-released "Wreck" paired with "The Prisoner's Song" that the record truly took off. The simple and deliberately sentimental "Prisoner's Song" (which Dalhart would re-record many times over for various labels) was attributed to a writer named Guy Massey, and the issue has never been settled as to whether this

Vernon Dalhart

hit the scene in the late '20s, his intense popularity worked to Dalhart's detriment. By the early '30s, Dalhart's career was petering out, and he was no longer in demand as a recording artist. A decade later he was living in Bridgeport, Connecticut, giving singing lessons and working as a night clerk in a hotel. When he died in 1948 he'd been more or less forgotten by the public despite the huge impact he'd had on the growing country music industry. After much lobbying, his fans finally won him a spot in the Country Music Hall of Fame in 1981.

◉ **The Many Faces Of Vernon Dalhart** (no date; Cowgirlboy Records). It's ironic but not entirely surprising that the songs of Dalhart, one of the most popular early country singers, are difficult to find on record these days. This European compilation includes 16 songs he recorded under various pseudonyms.

⊙ **25 Hillbilly All-Time Greats** (1995; ASV). This compilation of hillbilly music from the 1920s, '30s and '40s includes two Dalhart songs, "The Wreck Of The Old '97" (1924) and "The Runaway Train" (1931). About half of the collection is pop-oriented hillbilly material by the likes of Carson Robison and Wendell Hall, but the rest includes excellent cuts from Jimmie Rodgers, the Carter Family, Patsy Montana, Roy Acuff, Ernest Tubb, and others.

was Dalhart under a pseudonym (he used over one hundred, including Bob Ash, Sam White, and Mr. X) or a cousin of his, or whether it was a false claim altogether. Whatever the case, the two songs propelled Dalhart into the national spotlight. They also greatly boosted Victor's hillbilly sales and helped country music as a whole attain national popularity.

During the '20s and into the early '30s, Dalhart recorded thousands of songs on all sorts of different labels (and under various pseudonyms). His repertoire ranged about as far as the imagination of his southern fans and included event songs ("The Death Of Floyd Collins," "The John T. Scopes Trial"), as well as sentimental numbers such as "The Dying Girl's Message." For several years (until the two eventually had a falling out), he recorded duets with Carson Robison, another pop-oriented singer who'd discovered the then virgin territory of the hillbilly market. Though prolific in the studio, Dalhart didn't tour much or perform very often on the radio, as most country stars tended to.

Perhaps as a result of failing to play the part of an 'authentic' hillbilly singer, it was inevitable that Dalhart's career was overtaken by someone more true to the genre. When Jimmie Rodgers

Darby And Tarlton

Between the almost spiritual vocal harmonies and the shimmering moan of the steel guitar, the music of Tom Darby and Jimmie Tarlton is some of the most hauntingly beautiful, not just of country's first decade, but of the entire genre. It is a music owing as much to country blues as white folk traditions, but in the short time the two men played together it evolved into something wholly original. Their vocal harmonies blend and give the music a loose, comfortable feeling: Darby generally takes the lead with a clear, gently warbling tenor, while Tarlton's voice rises above the melody in a spooky falsetto yodel that's more Hawaiian than western. Underneath this is Tarlton's steel guitar, whining and moaning like a restless breeze, while Darby's rhythm guitar maintains a steady beat and gives the music its grounding. Add it all up and you've got a sound that's like something from a faraway world.

Vernon Dalhart • Darby and Tarlton

Darby And Tarlton recorded numerous songs for three different labels between 1927 and 1933. By far their biggest and best-remembered hits were "Columbus Stockade Blues" and its flip side, "Birmingham Jail"—songs that have since been covered regularly. Their other popular songs included "Lonesome Railroad" (a version of "The Longest Train"), "Sweet Sarah Blues" (a fairly straightforward blues tune), and "The Rainbow Division." Some of their best recordings are sentimental numbers like "Little Bessie," worked up with an other-worldly glow.

Details of Tom Darby's early life are sketchy. He was born in the 1880s in the vicinity of Columbus, Georgia, where he lived nearly all his life. He picked up guitar at about the age of ten and was writing songs not long after. Johnny James Rimbert Tarlton was born in 1892 in Chesterfield County, South Carolina, but the family moved regularly all over the southeast in search of work. Although he started on banjo, he soon moved on to the steel guitar, picking it in typical fashion to begin with, but soon graduating to open tunings and the use of a bottleneck as a slide. Tarlton left home early and traveled extensively, working in mills and oil fields throughout the South and West. While in California, he learned Hawaiian steel guitar techniques from Frank Ferera, a well-known player who helped popularize the Hawaiian steel sound on the US mainland. In the mid-'20s Tarlton returned to the East Coast and married. He and his wife eventually landed in Columbus, Georgia, where a local music store owner hooked him up with Darby.

Darby And Tarlton first recorded together on 5 April, 1927. It was during November of that year, however, that they cut the songs that made their reputation—"Columbus Stockade Blues" and "Birmingham Jail." Paired together the two songs became the biggest record Columbia had at the time, selling upwards of 200,000 copies. Rather than take a risk on royalties, however, Darby insisted they get paid a safe, flat rate ($75) for the songs, a common enough decision especially among lesser-known artists at the time—they were still regretting it decades later.

The pair's music career eventually ground to a halt, thanks in part to the Depression and also the rising popularity of 'brother acts' like the Blue Sky Boys, the Delmore Brothers, and the Monroe Brothers, whose harmonies were tighter and whose music was cleaner-sounding overall. What we find 'haunting' in Darby And Tarlton's songs today was considered old-fashioned and out of date in the mid-'30s—at least by the record company bosses signing the checks. Before the end of the decade the two musicians had slipped out of the music business and back into civilian life.

During the early '60s, when urban folk enthusiasts were reviving interests in old-time, folk and bluegrass music, Robert Nobley and Emory Ward tracked down the two artists. Darby was still living in Columbus and Tarlton was in Phenix City, Alabama. The latter eventually appeared regularly at folk festivals and clubs (including a week at LA's famed Ash Grove) and recorded some songs for the Testament label. Tarlton died in 1979; Darby died eight years earlier in 1971.

⊙ **On The Banks Of A Lonely River** (1994; County). This collection of songs, recorded for Columbia between 1927 and 1930, is one of the highlights of this era. "Little Bessie" and "Roy Dixon" are sentimental songs recast in a manner that'll make you believe in ghosts and spirits, "Frankie Dean" is a shimmering version of the popular "Frankie And Johnny" ballad, and "Lonesome In The Pines" is a swift and sleek song that's been re-recorded many times since under the shortened title "In The Pines." Tarlton's steel playing is some of the era's greatest, and if his falsetto doesn't give you chills nothing will.

⊙ **Complete Recordings** (1995; Bear Family). This is one occasion where shelling out for a 3-disc collection (84 selections from the 1920s and '30s) is worth it. It's hard to get too much of this duo's mesmerizing sound. The collection includes a few songs Tarlton recorded solo in 1930 and others Darby made with Jesse Pitts a year later.

Darby and Tarlton

Jimmie Davis

Jimmie Davis is a strange one. He was a hugely popular gospel and pop recording star from the mid-1930s on through to the '50s and '60s. Much of this success was due to his association with "You Are My Sunshine," one of those innocuous songs that nearly everybody, country fan or not, can hum in their sleep. On top of that he was a government worker and politician who landed the Louisiana governorship in 1944 (during his second term in the '60s he earned further recognition as a proponent of segregationism). But before all this mainstream notoriety there was another Jimmie Davis—a man who started his career as a Jimmie Rodgers imitator and who also sang some of the era's bawdiest material. Can you imagine a governor today recording ditties like "Tom Cat And Pussy Blues," "She's A Hum-Dum Dinger (from Dingersville)," "High Behind Blues," and "The Keyhole In The Door"? Davis, too, had a hard time choking down that thought. It's no wonder that during his political campaign he concentrated on exploiting "You Are My Sunshine" while suppressing the seedier aspects of his colorful past.

It's exactly this material, however, that makes Davis such an interesting artist. His later recordings for Decca like "You Are My Sunshine," "Nobody's Darlin' But Mine," "There's A New Moon Over My Shoulder," and countless gospel tunes may have gained him national fame, yet these songs and hundreds more like them, which make up the bulk of his musical output, are a mixed bag of western swing, pop and gospel—pleasant, 'nice' melodies that are too often bland and innocuous. But the dark and dirty blues he cut for Victor during the late '20s and early '30s is where the real flavor lies.

Jimmie was born James Houston Davis on 11 September, 1899 in Beech Springs, Louisiana. He attended Louisiana College in Pineville, where he sang in the glee club and also in a local quartet. After earning his master's degree from Louisiana State University, he taught history at Dodd College before landing a job with the Shreveport Criminal Court. He also began singing on Shreveport radio station KWKH (future home of the *Louisiana Hayride*) and recording pop and sentimental songs for the station's Doggone label (the self-penned "Where The Old Red River Flows" was one that endured throughout his career).

In 1929 Davis signed with Victor, and his music quickly became juicier. At first he copied the blue yodeling style of Jimmie Rodgers (as did

countless singers in the late '20s and '30s), while also tending toward a dirtier, grittier sound. Some of the credit for this goes to local black blues artists such as guitarists Oscar Woods and Ed Schaffer, whom Davis hired for more than a few of the seven sessions he did for Victor. It was this hot playing that gave such bluesy songs as "Barnyard Stomp" and "Bear Cat Mama From Horner's Corners" their visceral character. Another Rodgers protégé, Gene Autry, counted himself a Davis fan when he covered "Hum Dum Dinger" in 1931.

Davis recorded for Victor from 1929–1933 before signing with the newly formed US Decca label in 1934 (the label had been founded a few years earlier in England). One of his first hits was "Nobody's Darlin' But Mine," a straightforward cowboy-styled number, and it set the tone for the smooth pop he'd concentrate on ever after. He did

record a few more risqué songs, but by the late '30s, when his political career was heating up, these had suddenly disappeared not only from his recording rosters, but from most public accounts of his career. He recorded "It Makes No Difference Now" (which he'd purchased from its writer, Floyd Tillman, for a few hundred easy dollars), and turned it into a decent-sized hit. And in 1940 he cut "You Are My Sunshine" (which he supposedly co-wrote with Charles Mitchell), and this pushed his musical career into overdrive. It became not only the signature hit of his musical career, recorded by such big names as Autry and Bing Crosby, but his campaign theme song as well—it probably did as much as anything to help him get elected first as public safety commissioner and, later, as democratic governor of Louisiana. His band the Sunshine Boys

Jimmie Davis

was led by Joe Shelton of the Shelton Brothers during the mid-'40s and for a time included honky-tonk pianist Moon Mullican.

Davis' musical career continued to blossom even while he was in office, with songs like "There's A New Moon Over My Shoulder" and "Is It Too Late Now" hitting the charts one after another. He also appeared in several movies, including *Louisiana*, which was based to some degree on his life story. After his term ended in 1948 he dived into music full-time, recording songs like "Suppertime," but also turning frequently to gospel material. He was elected to a second term as governor in 1960. Davis continued to record steadily through the '60s for Decca and later for various smaller labels. He was inducted into the Nashville Songwriters Hall of Fame in 1971 and the Country Music Hall of Fame in 1972. He also tried for a third term as Louisiana's governor but lost. He continued performing occasionally even past the age of ninety. At the end of the millennium, in his hundredth year, Davis was the oldest living country music artist.

The Delmore Brothers

⊙ **Rockin' Blues** (1988; Bear Family). An LP collection of Davis' Victor recordings, which are among his earliest and by far his most interesting. Not only are they Jimmie Rodgers-styled blue yodels laced with truly hot Louisiana bluesmen, the songs are some of his raunchiest. The companion volume, BARNYARD STOMP, is equally juicy.

⊙ **Country Music Hall Of Fame** (1991; MCA). A solid sampler of Davis' original recordings for Decca, from the 1930s onwards, including the big hits "Sunshine," "Nobody's Darlin' But Mine," and "Suppertime." Unfortunately, the disc has fallen out-of-print, and it was the label's only Davis CD. Hopefully this oversight will soon be rectified.

⊙ **Nobody's Darlin' But Mine, 1928–1937** (1998; Bear Family). This 5-CD box begins with Davis' first recordings from 1928 on KWKH's label Doggone Records followed by Victor recordings from the late '20s and early '30s and his earliest Decca and World recordings.

Delmore Brothers

O f all the close-harmony brother duets to emerge during the 1930s, Alton and Rabon Delmore were among the finest and most influential. When

woven together, their voices were exceptionally tight, pure and beautiful, and their guitar playing—often the only accompaniment they used, especially in their early years—was subtle but well crafted. As well as being excellent musicians, they also wrote much of their own material, and several songs—most notably "Blues Stay Away From Me," "Brown's Ferry Blues," and "Gonna Lay Down My Old Guitar"—are now classics. Song credit was usually given to both brothers, but Alton was the chief writer, penning upward of one thousand songs during his lifetime.

Throughout the '30s, the Delmores were one of the first star acts on the *Grand Ole Opry*, joining the fledgling radio program several years before Roy Acuff, Bill Monroe and Ernest Tubb. In the '40s, when close-harmony duet singing was fading in popularity—and old-time music as a whole was giving way to honky tonk and more R&B-based material—the Delmore Brothers proved their resilience, shifting to a somewhat denser and more rhythmically oriented boogie-woogie sound. Their harmonies translated amazingly well to this new up-tempo style; because of this, the Delmores' music served as a bridge between early hillbilly and postwar country and western—and foreshadowed the rise of rockabilly a decade later. Hillbilly boogie tunes became very popular during the '40s and '50s, cut by such artists as Red Foley, the Maddox Brothers, and Rose and Arthur "Guitar Boogie" Smith, but the catchphrase itself comes from a 1946 Delmore Brothers tune titled, you guessed it, "Hillbilly Boogie."

Alton Delmore was born on 25 December, 1908 in the northern Alabama town of Elkmont. His brother Rabon was born in the same town eight years later, on 3 December, 1916. They grew up poor, but in a strong musical environment, attending singing schools and also listening to their mother, who sang and wrote gospel songs. The brothers thus developed their soft-voiced, delicately phrased and tightly woven singing style from an early age, and Alton wrote his first songs under his mother's guidance. The Delmores began singing regularly at fiddling contests, and in 1931 they traveled to Atlanta to record a mere two songs for Columbia, "Got The Kansas City Blues" and "Alabama Lullaby." This

WAYNE RANEY

in turn helped them win a spot on the *Grand Ole Opry* in 1933. That same year they also began recording for Victor, which released the brothers' songs on its newly formed budget label, Bluebird. Between 1933 and early 1940 they cut more than one hundred songs for the label, both originals like "Brown's Ferry Blues," and popular songs of the era such as "More Pretty Girls Than One"—a composition by fellow *Opry* star and Bluebird artist Fiddlin' Arthur Smith, with whom the Delmores sometimes recorded.

The Delmore Brothers were the *Opry*'s most popular act in the mid-'30s, but in 1938 they quit the show, allegedly over a dispute with *Opry* management. They continued recording for Bluebird and, in late 1940 and 1941, for Decca (the latter stint ended with the Petrillo recording ban—a year-long strike during which record manufacturing virtually halted). Finding another radio outlet, however, wasn't so easy for the Delmores.

They flitted from station to station until they finally landed in 1943 on Cincinnati, Ohio's 50,000-watt WLW, home to the *Boone County Jamboree* (later called the *Midwestern Hayride*). Here they hooked up with Grandpa Jones and Merle Travis to form the gospel group the Brown's Ferry Four and also signed their own deal as a duo with the brand-new Cincinnati label, King.

After hooking up with King owner Syd Nathan, the Delmores settled into the second wave of their career. Nathan pushed them further in the direction of the blues-based boogie-woogie sound, and this resulted in a spate of catchy up-tempo songs, many with 'boogie' ("Freight Train Boogie," "Peach Tree Street Boogie," "Pan American Boogie") and 'blues' ("Used Car Blues," "Sand Mountain Blues," "Blues Stay Away From Me") in the title. The brothers' harmonies and acoustic guitar playing was still the foundation of their songs, but now their sound was filled out by additional guitar work (Merle Travis and Zeke Turner were among the hired guns), a string bass, and occasionally drums and a steel guitar. The most significant new addition to their arrangements, however, was the harmonica work of Wayne Raney. This young mouth-harp whiz played with them regularly from 1946 onwards, and his sturdy, exciting fills pushed the Delmores more firmly into modern musical territory.

During World War II Alton was briefly drafted into the Navy, and Rabon worked in a defense plant. After the war each worked solo for a short period (WLW refused to re-hire the brothers due to an earlier dispute with Rabon) before reuniting and relocating to WMC in Memphis—a town that responded very well to their new blues and boogie sound. They continued recording for King, but they never settled in any one place again for very long, moving from station to station throughout the South and as far west as Del Rio, Texas. By the '50s, the endless traveling had grown tiresome, and the brothers split up—though they did record together as late as August, 1952. Sadly, Rabon developed lung cancer and died on 4 December that same year. Suddenly alone, Alton drifted through odd jobs and recorded as a solo artist for Acme and Linco. He also worked as a DJ, taught guitar, dabbled in prose writing (both journalism and short stories), and continued writing songs. The most significant project of his later years was the autobiography he almost completed before his death on 8 June, 1964. Published posthumously by the Country Music Foundation under the title *Truth*

Is Stranger Than Publicity, the book is a smooth read and a fascinating insight into country music's early years.

⊙ **Freight Train Boogie** (1993; Ace). The focus here is entirely on the brothers' hillbilly boogie tunes cut for King during the late 1940s and early '50s, most featuring harmonica whiz Wayne Raney. Songs like "Hillbilly Boogie" and "Blues Stay Away From Me" are some of the era's finest—an essential collection.

⊙ **Browns Ferry Blues** (1995; County). An 18-track collection of their Bluebird recordings from 1933–1940, including "Gonna Lay Down My Old Guitar," "Blue Railroad Train," "The Frozen Girl," and the title track. Quieter in tone than their later boogie material, the delicate, precise beauty of their harmonies is stunning.

Kelly Harrell

Right up there with country music's earliest artists was Virginia singer Kelly Harrell. He may not be as well remembered as pioneers such as Fiddlin' John Carson or string-band strong men like Charlie Poole, but Harrell did record on a steady basis through the 1920s, earning a decent reputation at the time. Unlike almost all of his peers, Harrell couldn't play an instrument; instead he hired (or had hired for him) accompanists of all sorts, from a simple guitarist or fiddler to, later, a full-on string band. His voice was no great shakes either, though at the time such a nasal mountain tone was pretty standard. What really made Harrell stand out was his undeniable talent as an entertainer with a true knack for digging up and writing some pretty interesting songs.

The closest Harrell ever had to a hit was "Charles Guiteau," a song about the man who assassinated US President James Garfield; his most famous song, however, was probably "Away Out On The Mountain," which Jimmie Rodgers covered on the flip side to "Blue Yodel" ("T For Texas"). The rest of Harrell's songs deal in such subjects as drinking, courtship, souring marriages (sometimes taking a female point of view), and the difficult day-to-day life of the working classes (Harrell was one of many musicians who emerged from the South's rough textile-mill culture). Some of his songs poke fun (the kooky "The Henpecked Man," the positively weird "Cave Love Has Gained The Day"), while others are dark and dour ("Nobody's Darling On Earth," "I Have No Loving Mother Now"). Songs like "The Cuckoo She's A Fine Bird" show Harrell at his best, however. Strange, silly and sad all at once, the simple veneer of this song (and others, including semi-sweet "I Want A Nice Little Fellow") belies a deep and almost existential understanding of humanity's ticks and foibles.

Crockett Kelly Harrell was born in 1889 in Wythe County, Virginia—the same region that was home to recording pioneer Henry Whitter and longstanding musical patriarch Ernest "Pop" Stoneman. The area had a rich musical heritage, and Harrell learned many tunes and ballads growing up. But he also got stuck in the textile-mill rut at an early age, landing a job in a Fries, Virginia mill when he was only about fourteen. The upside was that through one job he met Whitter—a man who would eventually inspire Harrell (and others) to try his luck at recording.

In 1925, Harrell traveled to New York City and won the chance to record for Victor, accompanied by some local players on songs like "New River Train" and "I Wish I Was A Single Girl Again." Later that year he recorded in Asheville, North Carolina for OKeh, with Whitter backing him on guitar and harmonica. He recorded again the following year before hooking up with the Virginia String Band, which included fiddler Posey Rorer from Charlie Poole's band. He recorded twice with this band as his backing group, and these recordings proved to be his best-selling songs.

Harrell recorded his final session in 1929 at the Victor studio in Camden, New Jersey. When the Depression hit, his career came to a dead end; his record company refused to pay for studio musicians anymore, and Harrell stubbornly refused to pay for them himself. He soon fell back into full-time mill work, although he did perform locally around Fieldale, Virginia (where he'd settled a few years earlier). He finally died of a heart attack in 1942.

⊙ **Complete Recorded Works In Chronological Order: Volume 1, 1925–1926; Volume 2, 1926–1929** (1998; Document). All of Harrell's recordings are meticulously assembled by the Austrian label Document on these 2 CDs, which together replace the triple-LP box set that Germany's Bear Family label released in the mid-1970s. All 43 songs are more Harrell than most people need, so thankfully the CDs are sold separately. Both contain excellent material, but VOLUME 2 is a better starting place for songs alone: "Charles Guiteau" (one of several with the Virginia String Band), "The Cuckoo She's A Fine Bird," and "Cave Love Has Gained The Day" are all here.

Frank Hutchison

As much a blues artist as a hillbilly, West Virginia singer/guitarist Frank Hutchison is a fine example of how closely related those two styles were during the early part of the twentieth century. Along with his neighbor Dick Justice (who recorded ten songs for Brunswick and, like Hutchison, appeared on Harry Smith's influential ANTHOLOGY OF AMERICAN FOLK MUSIC collection) and Virginia banjoist Dock Boggs, Hutchison was deeply influenced by the black-blues music he heard growing up, and his playing style reflects this heritage. Songs like "The Train That Carried The Girl From Town" and "Coney Isle" (referring to a now defunct theme park in Cincinnati), which are among his best-known works, showcase an incredible slide-guitar style, one which Hutchison accomplished with a pocket knife while holding the instrument on his lap.

Hutchison was born in 1897 in Raleigh County, West Virginia but grew up in rural Logan County, a coal-mining region in the state's southwestern corner. As a child he first learned harmonica and later guitar. A good deal of Hutchison's musical inspiration, including his slide-guitar technique, came from local black musicians such as Henry Vaughan and Bill Hunt. The latter, in particular, taught him many blues songs, including

"Worried Blues" and "The Train That Carried The Girl From Town"—the two songs he'd eventually record at his first session for OKeh in 1926.

During his early adulthood Hutchison did odd jobs, including working in the West Virginia coal mines. He also played at schoolhouse dances and in movie houses, building up a decent regional following. By the time of his first OKeh session, he'd developed a fluid, confident guitar sound, which accompanied his roughshod singing and made even those crude early recordings ring with beauty. Both his slide playing and picking only got better with time. During his 1927 sessions, songs such as "Coney Isle" (modified by Cowboy Copas in the '50s and retitled "Alabam"), "Logan County Blues," "The Last Scene Of The Titanic," and especially his re-recording of "The Train That Carried The Girl From Town," showcased his playing to even greater extent. It's these hillbilly-blues songs that Hutchison excelled at, and overall they're far more exciting than standard old-time fare like "Lightening Express" (also recorded in 1927), which didn't allow Hutchison's guitar talent the room it needed to breathe.

Hutchison recorded for OKeh between 1926 and 1929, mostly in New York City. Except for one session in 1928, when he was accompanied by fiddler Sherman Lawson, he recorded alone, singing and playing guitar and harmonica. His voice, while hardly 'pretty' in the classical sense, had a rural charm that marked a good sense of humor and a knack for Saturday-night entertaining. His final recordings in 1929 were part of a six-part series of medicine show skits. After that, the Depression set in hard and Hutchison's recording and performing career dried up. He and his wife moved to Chesapeake, Ohio and then to Lake, West Virginia, where they ran a store (which eventually burned down). Hutchison spent his final years back in Ohio, finally succumbing to liver cancer in 1940.

⊙ **Complete Recorded Works In Chronological Order: Volume 1, 1926–1929** (1997; Document). This well-researched compilation contains Hutchison's first 24 recordings, presented in chronological order and with sound quality that ranges from fair to excellent. It kicks off with his initial recordings of "Worried Blues" and "The Train That Carried The Girl From Town," which are scratchy and raw but still vibrant (versions of both recorded a year later are far brighter in recording technique and performance). Hutchison's slide-guitar is superb throughout, and the moods run between the lively "West Virginia Rag" and the spooky, but mesmerizing instrumental "Logan County Blues."

Making Records In The 1920s

In an age when recording studios are measured by digital doohickeys and multitrack sensationalism, it's hard to imagine how the mavens of the phonograph industry managed before the advent of something as fundamental as magnetic tape—or, indeed, microphones. But that was exactly the reality during the earliest days of country. The technology was certainly crude and primitive, but it's all that was available, and, mikes or no mikes, it proved more than capable of capturing some truly mind-blowing music.

Until around 1926, all music—from pop and classical to blues and hillbilly—was recorded acoustically. Instead of playing or singing into a microphone, the musicians let rip directly into an acoustic horn. "It was identical to what you see on old wind-up machines that played back records through a horn," says Richard Nevins, president of Shanachie Records and a "superb remasterer" (in the words of old-time musician Mike Seeger) of early 78 recordings. Inside the horn sound waves hit a diaphragm causing it to vibrate, and this moved a cutter head that cut grooves into a spinning wax disc. "When microphones came along they did the same thing but better, more efficiently," says Nevins.

About as close to hi-fi as a clock radio, the original discs of early '20s acoustic recordings have more surface noise than actual music. Frank Hutchison's first recordings of "Worried Blues" and "The Train That Carried The Girl From Town," for instance, have a soft, mildly muffled sound that lacks depth. By comparison, on electrical versions of both songs he recorded a year later, Hutchison's voice and especially his slide-guitar playing are louder, crisper, and far brighter around the edges. The acoustic recordings do have a certain appeal, but the sound quality and tonal distinctions on the electrical ones are so improved there's little contest.

While phonograph companies recorded their pop and classical acts in formal studios in New York, Chicago, and other cities, most early country acts were, at least initially, cut by producers and A&R men (Ralph Peer being the pioneer in this) during recording excursions all over the South. Hotels, furniture stores, or warehouses in cities large and small—"convenient places to congregate local talent," says Nevins—were turned into temporary studios. Auditions were held, and the chosen few came back a few days or weeks later to lay their songs onto wax. The Bristol Sessions (when both Jimmie Rodgers and the Carter Family were discovered) were the most famous example of this process.

The set-up was pretty simple, continues Nevins: "A guy played a fiddle, or a blues guy played guitar and sang. The microphone was in front of him. The signal went directly to a lathe that cut the disc." These discs had a wax surface that allowed the needle to cut grooves into it. After recording, the discs were shipped back to the home office in cold storage, where they were plated as soon as possible. The resulting metal parts were then used to stamp out the actual 78 records.

After the advent of electrical technology, the recording process changed little until after World War II, when performers started to record on tape rather than direct to disc. From this point, it evolved into a system of 12-, 16-, 24-track facilities and high-paid producers.

⊙ **Old-Time Music From West Virginia** (1997; Document). The final 8 songs of Hutchison's recorded output (from 1929) are on this compilation CD, which also includes 10 songs by Hutchison's neighbor Dick Justice and 6 by the Williamson Brothers and Curry.

Bradley Kincaid

"**O**ld-fashioned" is a term that fits Bradley Kincaid better than any other rural artist in this chapter. An educated singer with a smooth, warm, relaxing voice, Kincaid's music was all about memorializing the past—the country homestead, mama, family values—through his large repertoire of traditional ballads and sentimental songs, many of which he'd known since childhood. His success as a folksinger in turn proved just how popular rural and old-time music such as this really was. Kincaid usually performed alone, accompanying himself on guitar. Many of the songs he sang were hand-me-down standards in rural communities, but through the voice of the "Kentucky Mountain Boy" (his nickname) they reached much wider audiences.

Kincaid began recording in the late 1920s, but more important than his records were his songbooks. These were a lucrative product for musicians at the time, as records were still fairly new—and meant a person had to purchase an expensive player. Kincaid's greatest fame of all, though, was as a radio performer. He was a regular on WLS *National Barn Dance* for a few years during the late '20s, and went on to perform on stations

Bradley Kincaid

Bradley Kincaid

The C&O Road" (decades later Townes Van Zandt sang a re-arranged version of this railroad song on DELTA MAMA BLUES), and "Sweet Kitty Wells" (a nineteenth-century blackface song penned by Thomas Sloan) proved immensely popular.

To capitalize on his radio success, and because listeners kept requesting Kincaid's songs, WLS sponsor Sears, Roebuck Co. published a songbook collection of Kincaid's material in 1928, making him the first rural radio star to see his material in such a format. The book proved hugely popular, selling more than 100,000 copies and inspiring several more Kincaid collections. At the same time the Kentucky folk artist (a term he greatly prefered to 'hillbilly') also began recording, and labels like Gennett, Brunswick, Silvertone and Montgomery Ward went on to release well over one hundred of his songs. Sears even began marketing a 'hound dog' guitar that bore Kincaid's name. The story went that Kincaid's father had traded a fox hound to give his son his first guitar, hence the cute moniker.

In 1930 Kincaid moved to WLW in Cincinnati, and then for the rest of the decade and into the next he hopped from station to station throughout the East. He also assembled a touring show, and one of his bandmembers was an up-and-coming singer named Louis Marshall Jones. Kincaid is credited with naming the young singer "Grandpa" Jones.

Kincaid returned to WLW in the early '40s, and later that same decade he was a regular on the *Grand Ole Opry*. He then bought an interest in a radio station in Springfield, Ohio, where he performed until semi-retirement in the mid-'50s while also running a music store. He continued recording into the '60s and '70s, however, mostly for the Bluebonnet label. Many of these recordings were later reissued by Old Homestead, along with col-

and programs throughout the eastern US, including the *Grand Ole Opry* in Nashville.

Kincaid was born on 13 July, 1895 in the rural Garrard County, Kentucky. His family regularly sang hymns as well as popular songs, laying the musical foundation for his later repertoire. At the age of nineteen, he entered a new school in Berea, Kentucky, that was dedicated to giving rural people a decent education while at the same time preserving and celebrating Appalachian arts and culture. (One of Kincaid's schoolmates here was Scott Wiseman, later half of the popular duo Lulu Belle And Scotty.) At Berea, Kincaid earned his high school degree, which wasn't exactly a regular occurence in his part of the country at the time. He also served briefly in World War I.

Having graduated from Berea, Kincaid moved to Chicago to attend a YMCA college, and it was singing with a YMCA quartet that landed him his first appearance on WLS. The young radio station was home to a brand-new show soon to be dubbed the *National Barn Dance*, and when programmers discovered Kincaid's vast knowledge of traditional Kentucky ballads, he soon won a Saturday night solo spot. During his run on the show, his renditions of classic rural folk songs like "Barbara Allen," "The Letter Edged In Black," "The Wreck On

lections of his earlier material. Kincaid died on 23 September, 1989 in a nursing home in Springfield, Ohio, at the age of ninety-four.

⊙ **Memories Of Jimmie Rodgers** (1997; Bear Family). A collection of various artists who recorded songs in tribute to the late, great Jimmie Rodgers. The Kincaid contributions include "Jimmie Rodgers' Life," "Death Of Jimmie Rodgers," and "Mrs. Jimmie Rodgers' Lament." There are also songs by Gene Autry, Ernest Tubb, Hank Snow, and others.

⊙ **Old Time Songs And Hymns** (1998; Old Homestead). A collection of some of Kincaid's best-known titles, including "Barbara Allen," "Letter Edged In Black," "Footprints In The Snow," "Methodist Pie," and "The Legend Of Red Robin."

Lulu Belle And Scotty

One of the most popular radio acts of the 1930s was the husband-and-wife team of Lulu Belle and Scotty Wiseman. For a quarter of a century they were fixtures on Chicago station WLS's weekly *National Barn Dance* program, where they earned the nickname the "Sweethearts of Country Music." Cornball skits, downhome humor, and good-natured bickering were a big part of their regular routine, but their musical repertoire was diverse, including traditional ballads, sentimental songs, gospel tunes and Tin Pan Alley pop songs. Lulu Belle had a bright and bubbly personality that was a big part of the duo's wide appeal. As for Wiseman, he earned his reputation not only from his vocal and banjo work, but for his knowledge of traditional folk balladry—and for his songwriting. He was a prolific writer, and he's credited with such well-known titles as "Have I Told You Lately That I Love You," "Mountain Dew" (written with Bascomb Lamar Lunsford, an early influence on Wiseman), and "Remember Me" (later sung by both T. Texas Tyler and Willie Nelson). He also occa-

sionally dabbled in topical material, such as "I'm No Communist"—which, contrary to the lively, grinning melody, was deadly serious ("I like this private ownership, I want to be left alone/Let the government run its business, and let me run my own").

Lulu Belle was born Myrtle Eleanor Cooper on 24 December, 1913 in Boone, North Carolina in the Blue Ridge Mountains. A guitarist and singer, she joined the cast of the *National Barn Dance* at the age of eighteen, where she took on the name "Lulu Belle." She first played the hillbilly girlfriend of singer Red Foley, with whom she sang old-time songs and performed comedy routines, quickly earning herself a strong following. In 1934 she was paired with Scotty, himself a recent addition to the show, and by the end of the year they were married.

Scott Greene Wiseman was born on 8 November, 1909 near Spruce Pine, North Carolina—only about thirty miles from Lulu Belle's birthplace, though the two never knew each other

Lulu Belle And Scotty

growing up. Early on Wiseman learned guitar and banjo and also began collecting folk songs much in the manner of his hero, Bradley Kincaid. During the late '20s and early '30s Wiseman attended college and worked on several radio stations, and in 1933 he joined the cast of the *National Barn Dance*.

Lulu Belle And Scotty were mostly popular through their radio work; Lulu Belle was even named "National Radio Queen" in 1936. They did record for a few different labels, however. When he first came to Chicago, Wiseman had recorded a handful of songs for RCA subsidiary Bluebird under the name Skyland Scotty; Lulu Belle in turn cut her first few sides with Foley for the American Record Corporation (ARC). As a duo, Lulu Belle And Scotty continued recording for ARC, and their records were released on such imprints as Conqueror and Vocalion. During the '60s they recorded three albums' worth of their classic songs for Starday-King; a decade later they cut further songs for Old Homestead.

The couple remained with WLS through the '50s, breaking their Chicago streak only once during the early '40s when they worked on WLW in Cincinnati for eighteen months. After retiring from radio they headed back to North Carolina. Though no longer in the music business, they didn't sit still: Scotty earned himself a master's degree from Northwestern University, and during the '70s Lulu Belle was elected to the North Carolina House of Representatives.

⊙ **Early And Great, Vol. 1** (1999; Old Homestead). This CD brings together 24 of Lulu Belle And Scotty's original recordings, including "The Wampus Cat," "That Crazy War," "Yoo-Hoo In The Valley," and "Remember Me."

Uncle Dave Macon

"He wasn't happy 'til he made you happy ..."

—Archie Macon

The music of Uncle Dave Macon might be rough around the edges and considered a little wacky by today's standards, but that's precisely it's appeal—there's enough gut-level charm and good-natured hillbilly spirit in Macon's songs to raise the dead as well as just the plain lazy. Macon, who was nicknamed the "Dixie Dewdrop," didn't have much of a singing voice, and was hardly a virtuoso on the banjo, his chosen instrument; but that never stopped him from barnstorming his way through old-fashioned tunes like "Keep My Skillet Good And Greasy," "Carve That Possum," "Go Long

Mule," "Bully Of The Town," "Rock About My Saro Jane," and "Way Down The Old Plank Road."

Macon was the *Grand Ole Opry*'s first 'star' performer, though that fledgling radio show wasn't what made his career; by the time he joined he was already well established on the vaudeville circuit. His professionalism showed in his confident, fearless approach both to performing and to the business that took place behind the scenes. Whether on stage, singing for a radio audience, or belting a song in a makeshift recording studio, Macon was at the ready with a huge assortment of old-time songs, an endless stream of jokes, and even, when the time was right, a serious tune or two. And he was fast approaching sixty before his performing career started—a fact that makes his music and his performing style an important link between the nineteenth-century American music and folk entertainment styles he grew up with and the hillbilly music business that was just getting off the ground in the 1920s and '30s.

Uncle Dave was born David Harrison Macon to a relatively well-to-do family on 7 October, 1870 in Warren County, Tennessee. The whole flock later moved to Nashville, where they ran a hotel frequented by vaudeville performers. Dave gained loads of inspiration from these folks, and before long he was learning to play the banjo and entertain anyone who might listen. When his father was stabbed to death in front of the hotel, the family moved back to the country, where his mother ran a stagecoach rest stop in a small town called Readyville. It's here that Dave began entertaining travelers from a little stage he built by the watering hole.

Macon didn't go into the professional entertainment business, however, until much later in life. He married local, inherited the family farm, had a brood of children, and ran a mule-driven hauling business between Murfreesboro and Woodbury in middle Tennessee. This life was all well and good until the '20s, when trucks gave his mule trains serious competition. He was on the brink of retirement when a vaudeville talent scout heard him singing by chance and signed him up. Accompanied by fiddler Sid Harkreader, Macon proved to be quite popular, and the pair toured all over the eastern US. In 1924, Macon recorded his first sides for Vocalion in New York City, and these included "Keep My Skillet Good And Greasy" and "Chewing Gum." A year later he joined the WSM *Barn Dance*, which had yet to be titled the *Grand Ole Opry*. He was one of the show's first cast members and the only one with a national reputation.

Macon recorded throughout the '20s and '30s for all sorts of labels, toured regularly, and played on the *Opry* past the age of eighty. His band went by the name the Fruit Jar Drinkers, though this is not the string band with the same name that played regularly on the *Opry*. Other artists Macon paired himself with over the years included the Delmore Brothers, Roy Acuff and guitarist Sam McGee. He died on 22 March, 1952.

⊙ **Go Long Mule** (1994; County). Macon cut these 18 old-time and novelty tunes between 1926 and 1934. Raucous and wild, loose in structure and often silly in spirit, titles like "I'm Goin' Away In The Morn," "Way Down The Old Plank Road," "Rock About Saro Jane," and "Carve That Possum" are packed with history, humor and huge helpings of Macon's boisterous, downhome personality.

⊙ **Travelin' Down The Road** (1995; County). Eighteen recordings from 1935–1938, which represent selections of Macon's final recordings, all made for the Bluebird label. A few are recorded with the Delmore Brothers and possibly Arthur Smith. While slightly more refined than his earlier work, Macon's spirit is well intact on titles like "Country Ham And Red Gravy" and "The Gayest Old Dude That's Out."

J.E. Mainer's Mountaineers

One of the few old-time string bands to find a successful career in the years following the Depression was J.E. Mainer's Mountaineers. They had their heyday in the 1930s, but the band actually survived, in one form or another, into the '60s. Leading the pack was fiddler and former cotton-mill worker Joseph Emmett Mainer, a native of Buncombe County, North Carolina, where he was born on 20 July, 1898. Mainer began playing locally in the '20s, and a decade later he and his band had landed a respectable gig on WBT in Charlotte, North Carolina, playing on the popular *Crazy Water Crystals Barn Dance.*

Mainer's music was a full-bodied, downhome and often rambunctious mix of old-time dance tunes and sentimental numbers that centered around fiddle, banjo, guitar, string bass, and mandolin. The classic line-up during the band's heyday included guitarists Zeke Morris and Daddy John Love and J.E.'s younger brother Wade Mainer on banjo. Both Wade and Zeke left the Mountaineers in the mid-'30s, first to play as a duo and then to form their own groups—Wade with the Sons Of The Mountaineers, and Zeke with the Morris Brothers (whose rendition of "Let Me Be Your Salty Dog," aka "Salty Dog Blues," later became a bluegrass standard). After that, membership of Mainer's Mountaineers changed regularly, at times including fiddler Homer Sherrill, guitarist Leonard Stokes, three-finger banjoist Snuffy Jenkins (an influence on Earl Scruggs), and Clyde Moody (an early member of Bill Monroe's Blue Grass Boys).

The Mountaineers played on more than 190 radio stations throughout the South, Midwest, and as far west as border station XERF in Monterrey, Mexico—their shows sponsored by the likes of Crazy Water Crystals and Black Draught. They also recorded for Bluebird, starting in 1935. Though the music of Mainer and his band was an early influence on future bluegrass artists such as Bill Monroe and the Stanley Brothers, by the time bluegrass had caught on, Mainer's music (and that of other surviving string bands such as Roy Hall and his Blue Ridge Entertainers and Byron Parker and His Mountaineers) was considered old-fashioned and out of date. Despite his influence on bluegrass, Mainer never steered his music fully into that genre—though stylistically he came fairly close.

After World War II Mainer recorded for King, but by the '50s his popularity had pretty much disappeared. That is, until the folk revival spawned new interest in his music. Mainer's Mountaineers were brought out of semi-retirement in 1963 by folklorist Chris Strachwitz to record for his label, Arhoolie, and the music was as fresh, loose and lively as it had been decades earlier. Mainer performed at festivals during the '60s and later cut a few more sessions for other small labels. He died on 12 June, 1971.

⊙ **Run Mountain** (1997; Arhoolie). In 1963, Arhoolie founder Chris Strachwitz brought Mainer into the studio for the first time in well over a decade. The CD version expands upon the original LP issue and includes a total of 23 songs—familiar old-time numbers, fiddle tunes and gospel numbers, all played in a classic string-band style with a band that includes his children Glenn, J.E., Jr. and Carolyn Mainer. The music isn't quite as rowdy as his earlier recordings, but the homespun, hill-country vibe is intact and genuine.

Worth Searching For: Nine Far-Out Favorites

Even country's earliest singers and songwriters had some pretty far-out imaginations, as these nine songs will attest. Some are dark and spooky, others are just plain crazy. Strangeness aside, they also represent a decent smattering of typical hillbilly subjects and musical styles, from 'event songs' based on real-life occurrences (a popular and plentiful concept of the 1920s) to old-time hand-me-downs to sentimental Tin Pan Alley nuggets.

Allen Brothers "Drunk And Nutty Blues" (WHITE COUNTRY BLUES).
Between the drunken whining, laughing and crying of Lee Allen and the chiding, unsympathetic comments from his brother Austin ("I think I'll just kill you right here on the spot"), this wacko wonder will bust you up.

Dock Boggs "Country Blues" (COUNTRY BLUES).
Boggs' voice freely wanders up and down the scale, telling of a man haunted by corn-liquor dreams and fair-weather friends. Like too many people Boggs likely knew, the life of the "poor rounder" is a dark, downhill slide toward the grave, where he hopes he'll touch redemption, however briefly.

Darby And Tarlton "Little Bessie" (ON THE BANKS OF A LONELY RIVER).
The song itself was a popular parlor tune of the time, but the vocal harmonies and Tarlton's haunting steel guitar (not to mention his quivering falsetto yodel) send it to a faraway world no mere songwriting sentimentalist could ever dare hope to comprehend.

Dixon Brothers "Intoxicated Rat" (ARE YOU FROM DIXIE? GREAT COUNTRY BROTHER TEAMS OF THE 1930S).
Stumbling home drunk one night, our hero watches a rat get itself in hot water when it dabbles in some spilled booze.

Kelly Harrell "All My Sins Are Taken Away" (COMPLETE RECORDED WORKS IN CHRONOLOGICAL ORDER, VOLUME 2).
Full of Prohibitionist tomfoolery and absurdist conundrums ("Here's the gate and there's the latch/And on the other side is a watermelon patch"), you'll drive yourself crazy trying to figure what it all means.

Hickory Nuts "Louisville Burgler" (OLD TIME MOUNTAIN BALLADS).
A 'moral' tale told in first person of a fellow "raised up by honest parents" who turns to burglary and winds up in the clink, causing his family great shame. Regretting his naughty ways, he lectures listeners not to "break the laws of man" or risk a life behind bars.

Frank Hutchison "The Last Scene Of The Titanic" (COMPLETE RECORDED WORKS IN CHRONOLOGICAL ORDER, VOLUME 1).
One of many Titanic songs of the day, it's marked by Hutchison's excellent slide-guitar playing, which works like magic to fire up his lively, rambling story of the ship's tragic journey.

Charlie Poole "Ramblin' Blues" (WHITE COUNTRY BLUES).
Just hearing the way Poole pronounces "Paris, France" in his thick, deliberately raw North Carolina dialect is enough to endear this song for good. The playing is tight and tasty, and the good-time energy is hard to resist.

Tennessee Ramblers "Preacher Got Drunk And Laid His Bible Down" (RURAL STRING BANDS OF TENNESSEE).
The Tennessee Ramblers were a family string band from the Knoxville area. The song is a wound-up version of "Alabama Bound," complete with donkey brays and some knockout fiddling.

Sam And Kirk McGee

"What we play ain't wrote down in books."

—Sam McGee

While the Crook Brothers win the prize as the longest-running group in country music, brothers Sam And Kirk McGee ("from Sunny Tennessee") were also longtime favorites on the *Grand Ole Opry,* playing that show for nearly fifty years until 1975, when guitarist Sam was killed at the age of eighty-one. As well as honing their own underrated act, the brothers also worked as accompanists with fellow *Opry* stars such as Uncle Dave Macon and Fiddlin' Arthur Smith.

Sam (born 1 May, 1894) was a gifted and innovative guitar player, one of country music's earliest

Sam and Kirk McGee

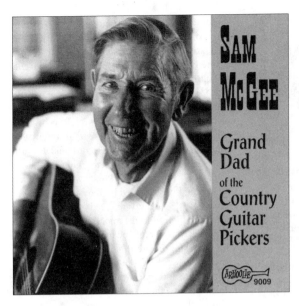

SAM McGEE

Grand Dad of the Country Guitar Pickers

ARHOOLIE 9009

impressed visiting journalist Garrison Keillor to such a degree that they helped inspire his own radio show, *A Prairie Home Companion*. A year later, Sam was killed in a tractor accident. Kirk continued as a solo act on and off until his death in 1983.

⊙ **Sam McGee: Grand Dad Of The Country Guitar Pickers** (1971; Arhoolie; reissued 1997). A beautiful collection of mostly instrumentals that feature Sam's excellent picking on guitar, banjo and the intriguing banjo-guitar. He's joined by guitarist Clifton McGee and bassist Goldie Stewart. Recorded in 1969 and 1970, the songs are a mix of old-time favorites ("Franklin Blues," "Wayfaring Stranger") along with some McGee originals ("Fuller Blues," "Buckdancer's Choice"). On each one of these tracks, McGee's virtuosity as an instrumentalist is stunningly clear.

⊙ **Old-Time Songs And Guitar Tunes, Vol. 1** (1999; Old Homestead). These 24 recordings feature both Sam and Kirk McGee, including "Railroad Blues," "Only One Step To The Grave," "Salty Dog Blues," "Chevrolet Car," "Buckdancer's Choice," and "If I Could Only Blot Out The Past."

virtuosos. As a child he first played banjo, but soon also learned to pick and play slide guitar from black blues musicians around Williamson County, Tennessee, where he grew up with his brother Kirk (born 4 November, 1899). The latter focused on fiddling and singing, and both could play blues as well as jazz, novelty songs and string-band music. Sam was working as a blacksmith and farmer and picking on the side when he began playing in the band of Uncle Dave Macon around 1918. Macon claimed at the time he had never before heard anyone pick out a melody on the guitar (the instrument was usually relegated to an accompanying role). During a 1926 session with Macon, Sam made his first solo recordings for Vocalion—guitar instrumentals (including "Buckdancer's Choice" and "Franklin Blues") that are country music's earliest. That year he also began playing on the weekly WSM barn dance (which wasn't yet called the *Grand Ole Opry*). Kirk eventually joined the Macon outfit as well, and not long after Sam And Kirk McGee (who adopted the catchy tagline "from Sunny Tennessee") began also working as a team, cutting their first sides together in 1928.

During the '30s, the brothers worked with Fiddlin' Arthur Smith, though the three of them never recorded. The two brothers remained together for decades afterward, and during the '50s and '60s were rewarded with new sparks of interest from eager folk revivalists. Together they recorded for Starday and Folkways, and Sam also recorded as a soloist. He also launched a label called MBA. During the final *Grand Ole Opry* performance at the Ryman Auditorium in 1974, Sam and Kirk

Charlie Poole

"He talked 90 miles an hour and patted his foot the whole time."

—Niece of Charlie Poole

Banjoist Charlie Poole and his group the North Carolina Ramblers were, during their short existence, one of the most exciting string bands of the pre-Depression hillbilly era. Poole, who was barely literate, let alone musically trained, makes a good case that 'pure talent' does indeed exist. His voice was unmistakably rural and in its own way had charm. His music overall had a rough energy—matching the hard, textile-mill lifestyle he and so many others from his region of North Carolina endured—though at the same time it was brimming with humor and charm.

Poole also had a knack for digging up good material, and his repertoire combined folk and minstrel songs, sentimental ballads and lively instrumentals. These came from earlier generations as

Sam and Kirk McGee • Charlie Poole

THE LEGEND OF CHARLIE **Poole** VOLUME 3

ORIGINAL RECORDINGS 1926-1930

often as they did from contemporary Tin Pan Alley writers (the silly "It's Moving Day" was written in 1906 by Andrew Sterling and Harry von Tilzer), and all the material ended up 'personalized' to some degree by Poole and his bandmates. "If The River Was Whiskey" is his take on the 1915 W.C. Handy blues standard "Hesitating Blues," while the excellent "Ramblin' Blues" (hands down one of Poole's best recordings) is Handy's "Beale Street Blues;" "Leaving Home" is Poole's kooky, fun-filled reworking of "Frankie And Johnny;" "Bill Mason" was inspired by a Bret Harte poem. The origins of further numbers may never be known, but like these they were probably passed down through friends and people he met during his travels.

Poole was an influential figure for his three-finger banjo picking—a style prevalent in and around the Piedmont region of North Carolina where he grew up (three-finger stylists Snuffy Jenkins and Earl Scruggs also hailed from the Piedmont). Though Poole's technique is far simpler than that of Scruggs, he and other local players were certainly inspirational to the soon-to-be blue-grass banjo star. Thanks in large part to the well-crafted music Poole made with his North Carolina Ramblers, the banjo became a standout instrument in early country music.

Charles Cleveland Poole was born on 22 March, 1892 in Randolph County, North Carolina. His childhood and the early part of his adult life centered on the region's many textile mills and the family traveled from city to city in search of employment. Nevertheless, it was a popular occupation among poor southern whites, and several other early hillbilly artists (including Henry Whitter and Kelly Harrell) also emerged from this world.

Poole had traveled around a little as a young man, and also played music regularly with friends—he'd started playing the banjo as a child. Music became his ticket to freedom from the dead-end mill culture, and in 1925 he quit his factory job and headed for New York City to try his luck at making records. With fiddler Posey Rorer (his brother-in-law) and guitarist Norman Woodlieff in tow, he soon wound up recording several tracks for Columbia. One of their earliest records sold upwards of 100,000 copies, quickly establishing Poole and company as a force to be reckoned with. Woodlieff soon left and was replaced by Roy Harvey. Rorer then left in 1928 and was replaced by fiddler Lonnie Austin, who introduced a smoother, cleaner sound. Austin was in turn replaced by fiddler Odell Smith, who joined for the group's final two recording sessions. Smith was barely in his twenties at the time, and his tone and style were smoother still. All of Poole's players, though, were excellent, and each had his individual charm.

Poole recorded plenty over the years, mostly for Columbia but also for Paramount and Brunswick. Sadly, however, he didn't live very long. He was a heavy drinker, and he ran through life with fast, reckless energy. In 1931, after an incredible thirteen-week celebratory drinking binge (he'd been offered a job playing music for a western film), he reached the end of the line just a few months after his thirty-ninth birthday. Thankfully, his legend and especially his music have been well preserved. Poole had a knack for communicating and stirring up good times through music, and he definitely touched the lives of many people lucky enough to hear him play. It's a power that still resonates in his recordings today.

⊙ **Charlie Poole And The North Carolina Ramblers, Volumes 1–3** (1993–1998; County). These 3 individual CDs compile Poole's Columbia recordings from the mid-1920s through to 1930, and contain some of the most visceral and at the same time well-crafted string-band music of the early hillbilly era. Few could play this well and keep their music so tight, yet never lose that wild and playful feeling that makes it so moving.

Blind Alfred Reed

Alfred Reed was a blind singer, songwriter and fiddler with an attractive baritone voice that was smoother and fuller than the scratchy, rough-hewn singing of so many of his hill-country peers in the 1920s. Born on 15 June, 1880 in Floyd, Virginia, Reed learned to sing, write songs and play a variety of instruments from an early age— a common occupation of blind people at the time, stuck for ways to earn a living. He played at local dances and community events as well as on the streets, where he often sold little 'ballet cards,' or broadsides of his songs for extra money. Though this was hardly a gravy train, he did make enough to support his wife, Nettie, and their six children.

Reed's songs included gospel numbers and sentimental ballads, but he was best remembered for his social commentary songs—from the unusual "Why Do You Bob Your Hair Girls" (referring to a popular hairstyle that obviously unsettled him) to the stark "How Can A Poor Man Stand Such Times And Live," a plainspoken ballad that conveyed the hardships of rural life (Ry Cooder revived it in the '70s). The song that landed Reed his first recording opportunity was "The Wreck Of The Virginian," a standard-issue 'event song' based on a train wreck that happened in May, 1927. When talent scout Ralph Peer got wind of the song, he invited Reed to a marathon recording session, sponsored by the Victor Talking Machine Company, in Bristol later that summer. Reed cut four songs with Peer, and the resulting records sold well enough to warrant an invitation to Victor headquarters in Camden, New Jersey in December, 1927 for a second session. Along for the ride this time were his son, guitarist Arville Reed, and fiddler Fred Pendleton. Alfred and Arville then recorded twelve more songs at a third and final session in New York City in 1929. Pendelton, by the way, also recorded in 1931 with a group of his own that he called the West Virginia Melody Boys.

The Depression effectively ended Reed's recording career. He continued to perform around Mercer County, West Virginia, where he'd lived most of his life. By the end of the '30s, however, new laws regarding street musicians put a damper on his public performances. Reed died on 17 January, 1956.

⊙ **Complete Recorded Works In Chronological Order: 1927–1930** (1998; Document). All Reed's recordings are gathered on this single CD. His style is primitive but his voice is sturdy, and songs like "How Can A Poor Man Stand Such Times And Live," "Why Do You Bob Your Hair Girls," and "Beware" ring with rural morality and truth.

Eck Robertson

"It's awfully hard to get Eck to toe the mark of any kind."

—J.B. Cranfill, 1929

When Texas fiddler Eck Robertson traveled to New York City in 1922 with his buddy (and fellow fiddler) Henry Gilliland and was given the opportunity to record a handful of his fiddle tunes, it might not have been such a dramatic event but for one little detail: it was the first time a white southern rural folk musician had put his music onto wax. Laying down those tracks for the Victor Talking Machine Company puts Robertson at the front door of the entire era of commercial country music. He wasn't a big-selling artist by any means, but he was the first.

By the time Robertson came to record for Victor, he was already a champion fiddler in and around Texas and it's his reputation as a fiddle-contest champion—earned before and after that famous New York session—that sustained him through a long professional career, performing at concerts (often with his family band) and countless fiddle contests throughout the South. Listen to his stellar playing on the 1922 recording of "Sallie Gooden"—with its complex melody and lively rhythm—and it's apparent even to non-fiddlers that Robertson is completely at ease on his instrument. That this comes across despite the crude acoustic recording methods of the time (microphones wouldn't be used until about 1926— see box p.27) is testament to his phenomenal talent. "Sallie Gooden" has since been cut many times over, yet it's this 1922 recording—scratchy and rough as it is—that's considered the benchmark of Texas-style fiddling even by contemporary players.

Alexander Campbell "Eck" Robertson was born on 20 November, 1887 in Delaney, Arkansas. His family moved to the Texas Panhandle when Eck was three years old, and it's this state that he called home ever after. Eck's father was a farmer and a preacher and had once been a serious fiddler himself. Eck first learned to play on a crude instrument made from a gourd neck and cat hide. When he obtained a real fiddle he began attending local contests and meeting veteran players like Polk Harris and Matt Brown (the latter is credited with writing "Ragtime Annie" and "Done Gone," both of which Robertson later recorded). During his teens Robertson joined a traveling medicine show, where he learned some rudimentary showman's tricks. In 1906 he married childhood sweetheart

Nettie (Jenetta Belle Levy), who was also a guitarist; the two began a music career together accompanying their own magic lantern shows and, later, silent films.

By the end of World War I, Robertson was well known throughout the Southwest for his fiddling skills. He also played regularly at Confederate soldiers' reunions—he was allowed to attend since he was the son of a veteran. It's at one of these conventions that he met Oklahoma fiddler and former Confederate soldier Gilliland.

It's never been precisely clear what inspired Robertson and Gilliland to make the journey to New York City in 1922, but it certainly had to do with the enthusiasm he received at contests and gatherings, and to some further degree with the big-time media interest (he'd performed for a newsreel film crew earlier that year). Perhaps this, coupled with the fact that Gilliland knew someone who did legal work for Victor, was enough to send them on the hunt. Whatever the case, after a Confederate veterans' reunion in Richmond, Virginia in the late spring of 1922, the two fiddlers headed north to New York City to try their luck.

Legend has it that the two men appeared at the Victor offices dressed in Confederate uniforms insisting they be allowed to audition. A 1924 Victor catalog, however, describes them as wearing "the garb of western plainsmen." The story goes on to say that the Victor people recorded a few songs mostly as a way to get rid of them and then promptly shelved the discs (they were unreleased for almost another year). It's more likely, however, that the Victor executives were curious enough to listen and, once they heard the music, registered right away it was valuable (with radio cutting into their sales at the time, record companies were on the lookout for new music and markets). The same Victor catalog actually describes the producers as being impressed with Robertson and Gilliland's playing, and later interviews with Robertson confirm this. Whatever the case, Robertson recorded ten sides over two days, 30 June–1 July—some by himself, some duets with Gilliland, and a few with studio piano accompaniment.

The music wasn't released until the spring of 1923—maybe there was some truth in the idea that the Victor folks didn't know what to do with it. The first record paired the Robertson/Gilliland duet "Arkansas Traveler" with the solo piece "Sallie Gooden," and though its sales never made anyone rich it remained in print for many years. All but four of the ten songs were eventually released.

Robertson—although his recordings were a historical milestone and although a popular draw at fiddle contests—never achieved the wider fame

Eck Robertson

of his fellow country pioneers, including Fiddlin' John Carson. Perhaps it was because he lived far away in Texas (Carson lived in Georgia) rather than in the Southeast, the main focus of the record company A&R men during the '20s. Or perhaps it was because Victor, to which he remained furiously loyal, was holding up the promotional work. OKeh, Carson's label, had far better distribution in the South.

During the '20s Robertson played frequently and even got some members of his large family involved, including his daughter Daphne on guitar and son Eck Jr. on banjo, and his music had more of a string-band sound. It wasn't until 1929, however, that he recorded again. The setting this time was Texas during one of Ralph Peer's recording trips. The Robertson family traveled down from the Panhandle and recorded a few songs in Dallas on 12 August (Peer wanted brand-new songs so he could copyright them). That October, Robertson journeyed to Dallas once again, and this session included his "Brilliancy Medley" (which ended up on the ANTHOLOGY OF AMERICAN FOLK MUSIC) and a peculiar ballad called "The Island Unknown," which he and his wife sang to their own fiddle and guitar accompaniment.

Those 1929 sessions (the latter finished only weeks before the stock market crash) turned out to be Robertson's last commercial recordings. During the '30s he tried to get Victor to record him again, but they refused, judging his old-time fiddle music out of date (this was the heyday of brother duets and western-swing dance bands). Robertson kept his family band going until the 40s, and apparently recorded some one hundred sides for the Sellers Transcription service, which were then supposedly sold to radio stations for broadcast. To date, however, none of these recordings has turned up. Robertson recorded one more time in 1963, when members of the New Lost City Ramblers sought him out; the songs were later released on the album ECK ROBERTSON: FAMOUS COWBOY FIDDLER. In the '60s he was still playing Texas fiddle contests, and he also began appearing at folk festivals. He died on 17 February, 1975 and was buried in Fritch, Texas.

⊙ **Old Time Texas Fiddler** (1998; County). These 16 historically important recordings may not be essential listening for casual country fans, but they are interesting and revealing. And, of course, fiddlers will find them invaluable. Included are all the released sides from Robertson's Victor sessions in 1922 and 1929, from "Sallie Gooden" (still a knockout performance,

despite even the poor acoustic recording quality) and "Arkansas Traveler" to the strange vocal piece "The Island Unknown."

Carson Robison

Carson Jay Robison was a 'citybilly,' a pop-oriented singer who successfully adapted his urban-trained style to the burgeoning hillbilly market, not unlike Vernon Dalhart. Though raised in rural Kansas, his smooth, pretty voice had little in common with the raw tones of his southern contemporaries. Robison was actually much closer in style to the Hollywood cowboys or crooners like Bing Crosby than artists like Charlie Poole, Riley Puckett, or even Jimmie Rodgers. Perhaps more importantly, Robison was also a prolific songwriter, and this coupled with his pleasant voice helped him enjoy a popular career that lasted more than thirty years.

Robison was born on 4 August, 1890 in Oswego, Kansas, a small town in the far southeastern corner of the state. His father was a fiddler and his mother sang and played piano. Carson himself picked up the guitar, and by his teens was playing and singing professionally. He moved to Kansas City, where he got work with a local orchestra and performed on radio station WDAF. In 1924, encouraged by singer Wendell Hall (who was then enjoying a hit with "It Ain't Gonna Rain No Mo"), Robison moved again, this time to New York City. There he first sang (and whistled) back-up with singers such as Hall, Gene Austin and Vernon Dalhart. Robison, who had been writing songs for years and had a storehouse of them at

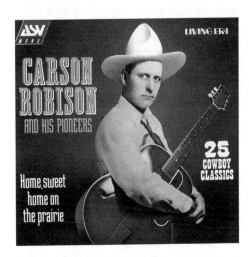

Carson Robison

this point, formed a partnership with Dalhart, and the pair sang and recorded numerous duets during the mid- to late '20s.

Many of Robison's songs, such as "My Blue Ridge Mountain Home," were nostalgic numbers about country life sung in a sentimental pop manner and sometimes featuring orchestral accompaniment. Others such as "The Wreck Of Number Nine" and "The Santa Barbara Earthquake" were 'event songs', a type widely popular at the time.

After Dalhart and Robison split, Robison found a new partner in Frank Luther Crowe. They wrote songs together (such as "My Blue Ridge Mountain Home") and sang duets in the late '20s and early '30s. Where Dalhart's career was by this point fading, Robison found new life with Luther. Their songs together include "Barnacle Bill The Sailor" (recorded for Victor under the names Bub and Joe Billings) and "Missouri Valley." They also recorded under the name Carson Robison Trio, a group that included Luther's brother Phil Crowe and occasionally Luther's wife Zora Layman.

Robison soon formed his own band, which he called the Pioneers and then later the Buckaroos. They were popular on radio and toured widely throughout the decade, including internationally. In 1932 Robison toured Great Britain, even recording during his stay there.

With the outbreak of World War II, Robison was writing again, and many of his songs (recorded for RCA Victor and Bluebird) took an aggressively patriotic approach: "1942 Turkey In The Straw," "Hirohito's Letter To Hitler," "Hitler's Last Letter To Hirohito," "1945 Mother Goose Rhymes," and the notorious "We're Gonna Have To Slap that Dirty Little Jap." He also penned a gasoline rationing song, "The Old Gray Mare Is Back Where She Used To Be." After the war he signed with MGM; his 1947 song "Life Gets Tee-Jus Don't It" made the Top 3 and became one of the biggest songs of his career. He followed this with "More And More Teejus" before getting topical again with "Ike's Letter To Harry" and "I'm No Communist." Robison remained active until his death in Pleasant Valley, New York, on 24 March, 1957. In his final years he lived on a farm near Poughkeepsie, New York and did some radio programs. One of his last songs was "Rockin' And Rollin' With Grandma."

⊙ **Home Sweet Home On The Prairie** (1996; ASV). Subtitled "25 Cowboy Classics" and sporting a cover photo of Robison in a cowboy hat, this British collection consists of cowboy-oriented material, most of it recorded in London during the 1930s. There are a few duets with Vernon Dalhart and Frank Luther, and a handful of solo numbers, but most of it features Robison's band the Pioneers. Overall it's pretty tame stuff—but not unpleasant.

Jimmie Rodgers

"I thought his yodel alone might spell success."

—Ralph Peer

James Charles Rodgers is not called "the Father of Country Music" for nothing. He was the music's first superstar, and it would be fair to say that no other single artist, before or since, has had more impact on its development. A white Texan who could play the blues as deftly as western numbers and popular songs, he mingled song styles together with a seemingly effortless showmanship. Added to this, he had an easygoing presence that was as evident during live performances as it was on his recordings. His popularity, especially among (but not limited to) southerners, was huge even during the onslaught of the Depression. "Country music's evolution as a star-oriented phenomenon is largely the legacy of Jimmie Rodgers," wrote Bill Malone in his seminal *Country Music USA*. In a career that was cut short in 1933 by tuberculosis, Rodgers had not only made a place for himself in country music songbooks as a writer and arranger—contributing songs like "Waiting For A Train," "T For Texas," "In The Jailhouse Now," "Miss The Mississippi And You," and "My Rough And Rowdy Ways"—he'd fired the genre with new energy and pointed the industry toward its future.

Rodgers' country roots were a big part of his appeal: he grew up in rural Mississippi; as a railroader he roamed the country, which had romantic appeal for many country fans, and even at the height of stardom (and the depths of the Depression) he retained a connection with his fans at all economic levels, from dirt-poor to Hollywood-spoiled. But while Jimmie Rodgers was marketed as a hillbilly singer (and it was working-class southerners who comprised his, and country music's, largest fan base), his approach was contemporary—he gave old-fashioned music a brand-new spin. Compare him to singers like Charlie Poole or Ernest Stoneman and his delivery and arrangements are much more sophisticated and uptown; at the same time he's far more down to

Carson Robison • Jimmie Rodgers

earth, and much more a man of the people, than New York studio musician Vernon Dalhart (who'd earlier given country music its first million-seller, "The Wreck Of The Old '97"). When Rodgers hoisted his guitar (often his only accompaniment), cocked his hat, smiled and started to sing, his fans throughout the South and all over the world were captivated.

From the point of his first hit, "Blue Yodel" (known today as "T For Texas"), until years after his death, Rodgers' style was widely copied by up-and-coming singers, many of whom gave their songs the 'blue yodel' vocal tag that had been a Rodgers signature (even Sara Carter of the Carter Family occasionally tried it). Cliff Carlisle, Jimmie Davis, and Gene Autry were just three of the more prominent singers who copped the Rodgers approach early in their careers. After Rodgers' death, Ernest Tubb was one of many more who picked up the Rodgers mantle; Tubb, however, won the support of Rodgers' widow Carrie and even inherited the master's guitar. And nearly seventy years after Rodgers made his debut at the Bristol Sessions, Bob Dylan acknowledged the "Singing Brakeman"'s influence with the album THE SONGS OF JIMMIE RODGERS: A TRIBUTE. Released on Dylan's Egyptian label (via Columbia), it features such contemporary artists as Bono, John Mellencamp, Dickey Betts, and Van Morrison performing Rodgers' material.

Rodgers was born on 8 September, 1897 near Meridian, Mississippi. His father was a railroad man and farmer, and his mother died when he was a child. He grew up listening to vaudeville performers and popular singers such as Al Jolson as well as the black blues common throughout the region. Rodgers wanted to be a professional singer, but his father persuaded him to take a railroad job (though he continued to play music and in some ways railroading was the 'side' work). Often employed as a brakeman (hence his nickname), he traveled extensively, mostly in the Southwest, but his railroading career ended in 1925 after he was diagnosed with tuberculosis. The upside was that he could now devote the bulk of his attention to music.

Rodgers worked as a blackface entertainer with a touring medicine show before moving with his second wife Carrie (his first marriage had barely lasted a few months) to Alabama and finally, in 1927, to Asheville, North Carolina. He performed on a local radio station and hooked up with a string band called the Tenneva Ramblers, who were then temporarily renamed the Jimmie Rodgers Entertainers. That summer the group got wind of Victor A&R man Ralph Peer's upcoming recording session in Bristol, on the Virginia/Tennessee border. Rodgers and his bandmates were among the many groups and artists who traveled to Bristol and won the chance to record for Peer. Because they'd had a fight the night before, Rodgers and the Tenneva Rambers ended up performing separately. Rodgers recorded two songs with just his own guitar as accompaniment: "The Soldier's Sweetheart," a straightforward sentimental number, and "Sleep Baby, Sleep," which was equally pretty but also allowed Rodgers the chance to show off his yodeling.

Neither song sold all that well when first released, but Rodgers did win a second chance with Victor, this time recording one of his signature songs, "T For Texas." It was released under the title "Blue Yodel," the first in a streak of 'blue yodel' songs Rodgers would record at various points in his career (the flip side was "Away Out On The Mountain" written by hillbilly singer Kelly Harrell). Sales this time picked up tremendously, and "Blue Yodel" eventually sold a million copies, still a rare feat at that time.

Rodgers' career was now off and running and over six very full years he recorded more than 110 songs for Victor. Stylistically, these ranged widely, from sentimental Tin Pan Alley numbers to folk, blues and western songs, all sung with an uptown flair. Rodgers' tunes covered familiar territory such as unrequited love and romance, but he also wrote frequently of the rambling lifestyle he'd only partly enjoyed himself (but which his fans passionately believed in); his song subjects included cowboys, railroaders, gamblers, and all sorts of unfortunate and/or misguided souls. Rodgers wrote the majority of these tunes, often alone, but sometimes with others (a frequent co-writer was his sister-in-law, Elsie McWilliams). His popularity also attracted aspiring songwriters, and some were lucky enough to enjoy the royalties a Rodgers rendition of their tune could bring.

In the studio, Rodgers' accompaniment varied from jazz and Hawaiian bands (usually at the suggestion of Ralph Peer) to just his own guitar. When he toured, however, he almost always played alone. His illness regularly interfered with grand plans for national concert tours (he never played any farther north than Washington, DC), but he did play throughout the South, often starring in major vaudeville shows. Many of these appearances were in Texas, a state that he more or less adopted as his own (he was even made an honorary Texas Ranger). In 1929 he built a huge home in Kerrville, Texas that he dubbed the Blue Yodeler's Paradise.

Rodgers was briefly touched by Hollywood when in 1929 he was the subject of a short film, *The Singing Brakeman*. The only known footage of him, the film is now part of an excellent video compilation of early country singers, *Times Ain't Like They Used to Be*, released by the Yazoo label in 1992.

He had weathered the early years of the Depression well enough, but eventually the economic downturn began to affect his record sales and his income. This, coupled with medical costs and his high-flying lifestyle, meant he eventually had to sell the Blue Yodeler's Paradise—though it wasn't as significant a loss as other hillbilly singers suffered, many of whom were forced out of the business entirely. By 1933, Rodgers' illness was far worse. Despite this, he agreed to do a recording session for Victor that May—perhaps he knew it'd be his last. During the session in New York City, Victor set up a cot in the studio so he could rest between takes. These songs proved to be almost literally his last breath. He died two days later.

Rodgers' legacy, however, has not quit. In 1961, he became the very first inductee (along with Fred Rose) into the Country Music Hall of Fame; he was also inducted into the Rock and Roll Hall of Fame in 1986. Years after his heyday, artists like Chet Atkins and Hank Snow (in a duet) and Crystal Gayle had hits with his songs. And in 1997 the Dylan-assembled tribute album brought his name into the spotlight once again.

⊙ **Train Whistle Blues** (1957; RCA; reissued 1998; Koch). A varied and surprisingly solid assemblage of some of Rodgers' better-than-average (even grittier)

material, including "Train Whistle Blues," "Let Me Be Your Sidetrack," "Somewhere Down Below The Dixie Line," and "My Good Gal's Gone—Blues," the last song pairing him with the Louisville Jug Band.

⊙ **First Sessions, 1927–1928** (1990; Rounder). This is the initial volume of an 8-CD series (each sold separately, which keeps it affordable) that covers Rodgers' entire recording career. Like the Carter Family series also released by Rounder, the CDs present the beautifully remastered songs in chronological order, include a few alternate versions here and there (but not enough to get in the way), and are enhanced by excellent liner notes from Rodgers biographer Nolan Porterfield. Frankly, it's hard to go wrong with any of the individual collections, but if you're looking for a starting place, try FIRST SESSIONS—on which you can hear Rodgers' confidence grow—RIDING HIGH, 1929–1930, and NO HARD TIMES, 1932. This music is a vital part of country music's foundation, and even decades later it's still solid and full of life.

⊙ **The Singing Brakeman** (1992; Bear Family). For serious Rodgers fans only, this collection contains basically the same material as the individual Rounder CDs, but it does so in one neat package (though it condenses the material onto 6 discs). Some of the alternate takes are different, and it comes (as is typical of Bear Family box sets) with a beautiful large-format booklet.

Skillet Lickers

One of the most popular string bands of the 1920s was North Georgia's the Skillet Lickers. Basically a fiddle band—with sometimes three players sawing at once, and not always quite in synch—they were always augmented with guitar, often banjo, and occasionally mandolin or harmonica thrown in for good measure. The music was on the whole loose and raucous, like something you might have heard at a Saturday-night dance party where the bootleg hooch was flowing and the dancing fast and furious. The bandmembers liked to cultivate this image of moonshining, good-timing hill-country folks (some of them later lived to regret it). But for all the fun they were having, they were actually, for the most part, quite skilled musicians, and the rhythms and melodies they created together—traditional dance tunes, old-time ballads, even a few Tin Pan Alley pop songs—were catchy, ripe and hard to resist.

Jimmie Rodgers • Skillet Lickers

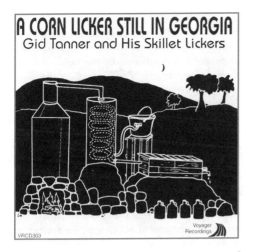

A CORN LICKER STILL IN GEORGIA
Gid Tanner and His Skillet Lickers

Voyager
Recordings

VRCD303

The Skillet Lickers were a supergroup of sorts—a quartet of North Georgia musicians who'd both recorded and performed on the radio before they hooked up as a full unit. The man often placed at the center of the band was fiddler and lifelong chicken farmer James Gideon "Gid" Tanner, a gritty-voiced showman who was responsible for much of the band's rowdy, downhome vibe. Though he was a well-known fiddler, Tanner earned his reputation at least as much from his comedy routines and crazy stage antics.

But while Tanner was often given top billing (the group's records were regularly credited to Gid Tanner And His Skillet Lickers), he was not the bandleader in the traditional sense—nor the group's most talented musician by any means. That glory was shared by guitarist George Riley Puckett and fiddler Clayton McMichen. The latter was a fiddling champion who'd been leading his own groups since the Teens. More than anyone else, McMichen was the one who assumed leadership of the group—his musical skills were solid, as was his ambition; he also does much of the talking on the intros to the group's recordings. Even McMichen admits, though, that Puckett was probably the band's star attraction. Blind since childhood, Puckett had a smooth, inviting voice and an intricate guitar style that drew in listeners. Over the years, in fact, he grew to be one of the era's finest and most popular balladeers. Rounding out the quartet's core was banjoist Fate Norris.

The group first came together in the mid-'20s. Tanner, a regular participant in fiddle contests and musical conventions, was invited to New York for a recording session in 1924. Fiddlin' John Carson's records were fast catching on, and the record labels were itching for more rural music to pour

into the market. Tanner brought along his friend and frequent musical partner Puckett, and the pair cut a handful of songs together for Columbia— making them the label's first hillbilly act, about a year before bandleader Charlie Poole made his Columbia recording debut.

Two years later, Columbia A&R man Frank Walker came to Atlanta, and he looked up Tanner and Puckett. Wanting a bigger sound this time, Walker paired Tanner and Puckett with two more North Georgia musicians, McMichen and Norris. An earlier band of McMichen's had been called the Lick The Skillet Band—which in 1922 had become one of the very first bands to perform on radio, only nine days after Carson made history with his debut on the same station, Atlanta's WSB—and it's from this group that the Skillet Lickers derived their name.

The first Skillet Lickers records hit the stores in 1926 and were immediately popular, selling hundreds of thousands of copies. Over the next several years the group cut 88 sides together with titles like "Sal's Gone To The Cider Mill," "Hell Broke Loose In Georgia," "Pass Around The Bottle," and "Bully Of The Town." Beginning in 1927, they recorded the first instalments of a fourteen-part skit titled "A Corn Licker Still In Georgia," a comedy and music routine about struggling moonshiners and backwoods pickers. On all their recordings Puckett was the lead vocalist (his singing was one of the group's most attractive qualities) and McMichen the chief fiddler, with Tanner adopting a secondary instrumental role—and piping in once in a while with laughter or his crazed falsetto. From time to time the four main players were joined by such musicians as fiddlers Lowe Stokes and Bert Layne and mandolinist Ted Hawkins.

The original Skillet Lickers recorded their last songs together for Columbia in 1931. The one semi-official 'reunion' came in 1934, when Tanner recorded again under the Skillet Lickers name for the Bluebird label, bringing Puckett and Hawkins (but not McMichen) into the studio with him. One song from this session, "Down Yonder," became the group's final hit.

McMichen recorded on his own here and there during his Skillet Lickers reign, and worked also as a studio musician (even playing on some Jimmie Rodgers sides). During the '30s he organized a group he called the Georgia Wildcats. He'd been as much drawn to pop and jazz styles as hillbilly music, and his Wildcat recordings emphasized this new direction more than ever. He continued recording for many years under that name, and he also earned a stellar reputation for his fiddling and was nominated national champion many times over.

Puckett had recorded and worked on the radio as a balladeer before hooking up with Tanner and McMichen, and he continued his own singing career both during the group's heyday in the '20s, and for a couple of decades after they disbanded. He was quite a successful artist during this time, recording a wide-ranging mixture of old-time and contemporary pop-styled songs for Columbia, Bluebird and Decca, all featuring his smooth voice and intricate guitar runs. Along with Jimmie Rodgers and Bradley Kincaid he was among the most popular (not to mention skilled) balladeers of the period—one deserving of far more attention than he's generally received since his death in 1946.

⊙ **A Corn Licker Still In Georgia** (1970; Voyager; reissued 1997). All 14 sides (originally released on 7 individual 78 records) of this comedy and music skit are presented in chronological order. The routines are silly, but the music is no less lively and fun than on the County compilation (below); and besides, all the banter between bandmembers allows priceless insight into the Skillet Lickers' inner world.

⊙ **Old Time Fiddle Tunes And Songs From North Georgia** (1996; County). "Red Hot And Rarin' To Go" is how Clayton McMichen describes the band on the introduction to "Soldier's Joy," and that's what we get on this excellent overview of the Skillet Lickers' career. The CD is a 16-song compilation of 2 earlier LP releases by County.

⊙ **Old-Time Greats (Riley Puckett)** (1999; Old Homestead). Puckett's solo recordings are well worth the trouble to track down, as his voice and guitar playing are some of the period's best. This CD is an assortment of old-time and Tin Pan Alley songs he recorded, including "Short Life Of Trouble," "The Boston Burglar," "I Only Want A Buddy," and "Back On The Texas Plains."

Ernest "Pop" Stoneman

Country pioneer Ernest Stoneman actually enjoyed two separate musical careers in the twentieth century. During the 1920s he rose to fame as one the genre's earliest recording artists,

singing hillbilly and gospel songs on record, radio and at concerts throughout the South, and leading a string band that included some of the top players of the Galax, Virginia area. By the '60s he'd transformed into patriarch "Pop" Stoneman, presiding this time over a band of his musical children, the Stonemans, who played a progressive brand of country and bluegrass and were popular at festivals. Though several early musicians came out of retirement during the heady days of the folk revival, few were able to bridge the generation gap to the degree that Stoneman did.

Stoneman's voice was as creaky as the Clinch Mountain pines, but it was also firm and proud; his musicianship (he was a virtuoso on the autoharp) and that of his various bandmembers was excellent, the string-band arrangements succinct and bright. His repertoire was a broad and bountiful mix of gospel tunes, social and sentimental ballads, and 'event songs', from "Remember The Poor Tramp Has To Live" (one of his signature songs) to "The Unlucky Road To Washington" (aka "White House Blues") to "Are You Washed In The Blood?" He recorded more than two hundred songs at the time for labels such as Edison, Gennett, Victor, Vocalion, and OKeh, and was a major participant in the legendary Bristol Sessions (by which point he was already an established recording artist). Stoneman, who lived in the area, was in fact one of the chief reasons Ralph Peer chose Bristol as a location to begin with.

The area around Galax has a strong musical heritage (it claims to be the old-time music capital and hosts an annual music festival), and it's in this environment that Ernest Van Stoneman was born on 25 May, 1893. As a child he quickly picked up all sorts of gospel songs, ballads and string-band tunes and learned the harmonica and autoharp. The latter is a simple-to-strum instrument that a few daring musicians, Stoneman and Maybelle Carter among them, picked and played with greater complexity. After marrying Hattie Frost (herself a fiddler) in 1918, the pair moved just across the state line to Bluefield, West Virginia.

At this point, music was just a way of kicking back and letting off steam. This relaxed philosophy changed in 1924, however, when Stoneman heard the early recordings of Henry Whitter, another musician from the Galax region. Whitter's songs inspired Stoneman, who figured he was a better player and singer. He wrote to Columbia and OKeh requesting auditions, and both replied that their doors were open. In the summer of 1924 he made the trip to New York, first visiting Columbia

ERNEST V. STONEMAN

EDISON RECORDINGS

1928

but eventually choosing to record with Ralph Peer at OKeh. A second session in 1925 led to his first commercial single, "The Titanic" and "The Face That Never Returned."

Stoneman recorded for the next several years both as a solo artist and with various incarnations of his string band, the Dixie Mountaineers. Among the excellent players he gathered were Galax-area friends and family members Kahle Brewer, Eck Dunford, his wife Hattie and her brother Bolen Frost. By the time of the Bristol Sessions, he'd recorded some one hundred songs, the most of any hillbilly artist at the time (that's the equivalent of ten albums in less than three years).

When the Depression set in, the Stoneman family, like many southerners, hit hard times. By 1932 Ernest, Hattie and their huge brood of nine children (they would later have several more) had moved east to the Washington, DC area in search of work and better living. Stoneman recorded a session for Vocalion in 1934, but economics had seriously wounded his once proud musical career.

The Depression didn't destroy his spirit entirely, however; by the '40s he was working a decent job at the Naval Gun Factory, and Ernest (who began calling himself "Pop" Stoneman) and his family were becoming known for their music again. This came initially through talent contests and TV appearances (Ernest won $10,000 on a quiz show in the '50s and got to sing a bit on screen; some of his children, in a group called the Bluegrass Champs—founded by Scotty Stoneman and Jimmy Case—appeared on Arthur Godfrey's *Talent Scouts*). Daughter Roni Stoneman became the first female banjoist to record when she played on the groundbreaking

AMERICAN BANJO SCRUGGS STYLE, a Folkways album that helped bring bluegrass to a younger generation of folk revivalists. Ernest and Hattie were also recorded by old-time musician Mike Seeger for Folkways.

By the 1960s, the family was making records and touring all over the country as the Stonemans—which had evolved out of the Bluegrass Champs—with "Pop" singing and playing the autoharp alongside his children Scotty, Donna, Jimmy, Roni and Van. Their repertoire mixed country and progressive bluegrass with an updated vibe that caught the ears of '60s folk- and rock-bred audiences (the gals' miniskirts didn't hurt their appeal, either). They eventually landed a recording contract with MGM in Nashville (working with producer Jack Clement), hosted their own television show, and in 1967 won the CMA's Vocal Group of the Year award. Pop Stoneman performed with the group until early 1968 when he fell sick. He died on 14 June of that year.

After Pop's passing, the Stonemans continued to perform and record, though the mediocre chart hits they'd enjoyed a few years earlier ("Tupelo County Jail," "West Canterbury Subdivision Blues") would come around no more. During the '70s the line-up began shifting further. Roni landed a gig performing comedy routines on *Hee-Haw*, Donna left and turned to gospel music, and Scotty died in 1973. The remaining members and a few new players scuttled their way through a few small labels during the '70s and '80s, with the original family members regrouping in 1982 to record a reunion album (THE FIRST FAMILY OF COUNTRY MUSIC). Roni and Donna eventually picked up the Stoneman mantle but by the late '80s were performing only occasionally. In 1993 the Ivan Tribe book *The Stonemans: An Appalachian Family And The Music That Shaped Their Lives* hit the stores to tell the long and winding Stoneman story.

Ernest "Pop" Stoneman

⊙ **Edison Recordings—1928** (1996; County). This is a superb collection showcasing not only Stoneman at the height of his powers but some of the finest pre-Depression string-band music on record. Stoneman recorded 50 sides for the Edison label between 1926 and 1928, and these 22 cuts are from the latter sessions with fiddler Hattie Stoneman, banjoist Bolen Frost, and others backing him up. Old-time folk and gospel songs like "Remember The Poor Tramp Has To Live," "Down On The Banks Of The Ohio," "Midnight

On The Stormy Deep," and "I Remember Calvary" may sound old-fashioned to some ears, but at the same time they're warm and inviting.

The Stonemans

O The Stonemans (1970; MGM). The Stoneman family band of the 1960s and '70s belongs in the folk-revival camp. Arrangements of songs like "In The Early Morning Rain," "Nine Pound Hammer," and "Blue Ridge Mountain Blues" sound dated now—a whole different breed from Pop Stoneman's classic '20s material. This collection (part of MGM's Golden Archive Series) is culled from 5 of their mid-'60s MGM records.

⊙ **Country Hospitality (The Stonemans)** (1999; My Father's Business). The only Stonemans album that has made it to CD so far is this collection of 12 mountain-flavored bluegrass recordings from 1978; curiously, the album wasn't commercially released until 21 years later. The bandmembers include Van, Patsy, and Jimmy Stoneman, David Dougherty and Johnny Bellar.

Ernest "Pop" Stoneman

Beyond the Sunset: Singing Cowboys and Western Fantasies

2

To most Americans, cowboys are, and always have been, fascinating figures. They've long been symbols of freedom and individuality, two ingredients at the country's very foundation. During their late nineteenth-century heyday, cowboys roamed the wide open spaces of the American West in a free-spirited manner that many people only dreamed of doing. At the same time, they were more than simple drifters, and lived by an unspoken code of honor that invited the respect of most people they encountered. As well as all of this, they possessed a fearless sense of adventure coupled with the courage to follow their dreams.

From its very birth, country music revered cowboys as a noble race. The image of the hillbilly, on the other hand, was burdened by negative stereotypes from bootlegging to shotgun marriages; too many people, especially urbanites, saw these sturdy southern mountain folk as little more than backwood buffoons. Neither of these stereotypes, of course, represents how southerners or westerners actually lived. But stereotypes, once established, can stick long after the reality has disappeared.

It was during the late nineteenth and early twentieth centuries that cowboys made their great migration from the cattle ranges of the Southwest to the fictionalized landscape of stories, songs, and movies. The American frontier was closed, and the long dusty trail rides that had once defined the cowboy lifestyle were a thing of history. But the legends of that western heyday were still alive and well—more so, in fact, than they'd ever been.

As modern America drifted further and further from the days of the wild frontier, nostalgia grew stronger and cowboy legends grew taller. Many of the West's best-known figures (Wild Bill Hickock, Jesse James) and most famous stories (the gunfight at the O.K. Corral) had been sensationalized and hopelessly romanticized by pulp writers and journalists in magazines, newspapers, and dime-store novels. The public, for their part, ate it up, and by the turn of the century the appetite for all things western was raging. Owen Wister's novel, *The Virginian*, was an instant best-seller when first published in 1902; also immensely popular was Edwin S. Porter's *The Great Train Robbery* (1903), one of the first narrative films and an inspiration for countless westerns to come.

Singing cowboys grew out of this western fever. Much of the cowboy image revolved more around good-natured kitsch—big hats, matching six-guns and faithful horses—than range-riding realism. But neither Hollywood stars like **Gene**

Autry and **Roy Rogers**, nor for that matter camped-up contemporary groups like **Riders In The Sky**, have ever pretended any different.

The First Singing Cowboys

Working nineteenth-century cowboys might not have burst into joyous song at the drop of a ten-gallon hat the way Roy Rogers did at the Saturday afternoon matinee, but they regularly sang to lull their cattle at night and to ease the boredom of long trail rides. As is the case with Appalachian folk music, the origins of many cowboy songs can be traced back hundreds of years. "Streets Of Laredo," for instance, a well-known ballad about a dying cowboy, is a derivation of a British song "The Unfortunate Rake" about a soldier dying of syphilis.

It wasn't until the early twentieth century, however, that cowboy music developed as a genre people could actually get their hands on. A key turning point was the publication in 1908 of Nathan Howard Thorp's *Songs Of The Cowboy* and John Lomax's *Cowboy Songs And Other Frontier Ballads* in 1910. (John is the father of Alan Lomax, who continued the family tradition of song collecting and field recording well into the '60s.) Cowboy and country singers, not to mention budding Tin Pan Alley songwriters, often first learned western songs like "The Dying Cowboy" ("Bury Me Not On The Lone Prairie") from these books.

Cowboy singers were first recorded commercially in the mid-'20s, around the same time that Eck Robertson, Fiddlin' John Carson and other rural southern musicians were entering the music marketplace. The first cowboy singer to record commercially was **Carl Sprague**. Sprague had worked as a cowboy as a young man and was inspired by the success of Vernon Dalhart to try his luck at recording some of the songs he'd learned as a child. He traveled to New York in 1925 and cut ten records with Victor. When one of these songs, "When The Work's All Done This Fall," sold close to 100,000 copies, the singing cowboy trend was begun.

Other singers followed Sprague's lead during the '20s and into the '30s. Jules Verne Allen was a cowboy who knew quite a few songs; he later published many of them along with some historical essays in his book, *Cowboy Lore*. The Arizona Wranglers, one of the earliest cowboy bands, also featured some 'real' cowboy bandmembers. One of the wildest and most diverse cowboys of the time, though, was balladeer **Harry "Haywire Mac" McClintock**, an extensive world traveler and a Wobblie (IWW—Industrial Workers of the World) member, whose repertoire mixed classic cowboy material ("Sam Bass," "The Old Chisolm Trail") with union songs and even a few of his own, the best-known being "Big Rock Candy Mountain." Still other singers of the era included Charles Nabell, the Cartwright Brothers, and Powder River Jack (who hailed from the far-away town of Deer Lodge, Montana) and his wife Kitty Lee.

Early cowboy songs were stories about work ("Long Side Of The Santa Fe Trail"), legendary horses ("Strawberry Roan"), heroic figures ("Utah Carroll"), or the wandering lifestyle ("Wild West Rambler"). The singers had a rougher sound than their soon-to-come Hollywood counterparts, but on the other hand their voices lacked the nasal tones of hillbilly singers like Ernest Stoneman or Charlie Poole. The music was quieter, dreamier and prettier than Poole's string-band tunes or the haunting blues of Dock Boggs. It was simple stuff intended to tell you a story, crack you a smile, or shed you a sad little tear.

Some sang a cappella, while others were accompanied by just a guitar, fiddle, or harmonica. In many ways this minimal instrumentation marked the transition between the unaccompanied singing of the 'true' nineteenth-century cowboys (who couldn't possibly carry instruments while riding the range) and the full studio bands that backed the Hollywood cowboy stars of the '30s. Since singers like Sprague and Allen had actually worked as cowboys, it makes sense they'd retain a certain degree of authenticity. Their music may not sound exactly like that of the men who followed the cattle on the Santa Fe Trail, but it's as close as we can get.

A few early cowboy records such as "When The Work's All Done This Fall" met with success, but there were no great blockbusters to really turn

WHEN I WAS A COWBOY Vol. 1

Early American Songs of the West

Classic Recordings from the 1920s and 30s.

heads. The singer who deserves the most credit for introducing western music into the mainstream is actually Jimmie Rodgers. Sporting a cowboy hat as frequently as a brakeman's cap, Rodgers was afflicted with western fever as were so many of his fans. He wrote and sang numbers like "When The Cactus Is In Bloom" and "Cowhand's Last Ride," and tagged many more with his trademark blue yodel. He toured regularly in Texas and even fancied himself an honorary Texan. Rodgers was also chiefly responsible for introducing the yodel to millions of listeners and singers.

Hollywood Stars

The 1930s was the golden era of the singing cowboys, when Hollywood discovered just how appealing the voices of Gene Autry and other crooning cowboys could be. Westerns had been popular ever since film was first introduced; when Ken Maynard sang and played the fiddle in the 1929 film *The Wagon Master*, the singing-cowboy concept was born. It was Autry, however, who sent the concept into orbit. He'd actually begun his recording career emulating the blue-yodeling style of Jimmie Rodgers, and during the early '30s was regularly making the charts with a mixture of country and cowboy material. Encouraged by a record company executive with contacts in Hollywood, Autry made his film debut in the 1934 Maynard vehicle, *In Old Santa Fe*. He was an immediate hit, and by 1935 he was cranking out films on a regular basis.

Following Autry's success, cowboys who could both sing and ride cropped up regularly in films, among them Dick Foran, Eddie Dean, and Ray Whitley (who wrote the original "Back In The Saddle Again"). Even John Wayne 'sang' a few times in his early westerns as "Singing Sandy," though his voice was dubbed over. **Tex Ritter**, who had earlier cut a handful of cowboy songs—some of the era's grittiest—debuted in the 1936 film *Song Of The Gringo* and went on to star in over fifty more.

The only true rival to Autry's star power, however, was Roy Rogers. Born Leonard Slye and hailing from Ohio, Rogers got his start singing with the **Sons Of The Pioneers**, a group that has remained remarkably popular over the years for its easygoing pop style and western-sunset romanticism. The Sons appeared in movies, too, during the mid-'30s, some opposite Autry; Rogers was finally pulled to become a star on his own in *Under Western Skies*.

Autry, Rogers, and the majority of the singing cowboys did not have parched, dusty, or otherwise trail-weary voices. Their songs, too—often written

by Tin Pan Alley writers who didn't know Cheyenne from Shanghai—turned western exploits into happy-go-lucky fantasies. But it was exactly these qualities, not hard-bitten authenticity, that made cowboy stars so appealing to the '30s mainstream.

Not all the singing cowboys were screen stars. Canadian **Wilf Carter** (aka Montana Slim), a superb yodeler, had a voice that was pretty, though far from slick—a sort of happy medium between early cowboy singers like Sprague and Hollywood versions like Autry and **Rex Allen**. One unusual group, the Beverly Hill Billies, was put together by enterprising staff members at Los Angeles station KMPC who claimed the band were simpleton singers discovered in Beverly Hills (the '60s TV show of the same name wasn't based on that exact story, but it was close enough for surviving band-members to eventually sue the show's producers). While the Beverly Hill Billies began as something of a joke, the group did launch the serious musical careers of **Stuart Hamblen** and Elton Britt. Hamblen was a singer and West Coast radio star well known for his songwriting ("This Ole House," "Texas Plains"). Britt enjoyed a long career as a singer and yodeler, and his 1942 hit "There's A Star-Spangled Banner Waving Somewhere" was country's first certified gold record.

The Beverly Hill Billies weren't the only group with a manufactured past. **The Girls Of The Golden West** claimed to be from Muleshoe, Texas, but were actually Illinois farm girls who worked out of St. Louis, Chicago, and Cincinnati.

The most popular cowgirl of the era, though, was easily **Patsy Montana**. Her 1935 song "I Want To Be A Cowboy's Sweetheart" alone made her country's first major female star. She was a regular on the WLS *National Barn Dance*, and her lively yodeling and spunky demeanor inspired all sorts of up-and-coming singers. Montana spent much of the '30s fronting the Prairie Ramblers, a string band formerly known as the Kentucky Ramblers who had changed their name (and smoothed out their sound) after western fever broke.

Assimilation

By the time World War II had come and gone, the musical landscape was far different. Honky tonk music was taking shape and gaining popularity, and the heyday of singing-cowboy movies was fading. Autry and Rogers continued to star in a string of films, though at the same time they (very successfully) made the leap to television. And there was still enough of an audience to support newer stars such as **Jimmy Wakely**, Rex Allen, and Foy Willing And The Riders Of The Purple Sage. Willing's group rivaled the still-strong Sons Of The Pioneers in popularity. Wakely, who later

---

Anthologies

☉ **Back In The Saddle Again** (1983; New World). A double-CD set of mostly classic 1920s and '30s recordings that's probably the best starting point if you're curious about the evolution of cowboy music. There's a song each from Patsy Montana, Stuart Hamblen, Rex Allen, Tex Owens, Powder River Jack and Kitty Lee, Jules Verne Allen, Ken Maynard, and many others—all of them classic recordings from their heydays. Tagged on the end are a handful of contemporary cowboy recordings by the likes of Riders In The Sky and former rodeo star Chris LeDoux.

☉ **Cowboy Songs On Folkways** (1991; Smithsonian Folkways). Twenty-six songs pulled together from the Folkways archives that straddle the cowboy-folk music borderline. The artists include Harry McClintock, Woody Guthrie, Cisco Houston, Peter LaFarge, Rosalie Sorrels and Leadbelly, and the songs are a wild and varied bunch, from an a cappella version of the "Chisolm Trail" (sung by the Tex-I-An Boys) to Guthrie and Houston singing Guthrie's composition "Philadelphia Lawyer" (which was made famous by the Maddox Brothers and Rose).

☉ **Songs Of The West** (1993; Rhino). With 72 songs on 4 CDs, this is the next step if you're seriously into cowboys and want the whole story of the development of western music in one neat package. It starts in the mid-1920s, takes its time moving through the singing-cowboy era, and winds up with a disc of theme songs from shows like *Gunsmoke* and *Rawhide*.

☉ **Howdy! 25 Hillbilly All-Time Greats** (1995; ASV). Although not a thorough cowboy collection by any means, this British-issue disc is nonetheless noteworthy because it places singers like Patsy Montana and Montana Slim in context with western-influenced artists who came before (Jimmie Rodgers, the Carter Family, Carson Robison) and after (Bob Wills, Roy Acuff and Ernest Tubb).

☉ **When I Was A Cowboy, Vols. 1 & 2** (1996; Yazoo). If cowboy music turns you on, but the Hollywood version makes you cringe, these 2 CDs (sold individually) are your ticket. Each concentrates on classic 1920s and '30s material by the likes of Harry McClintock, Carl Sprague, the Cartwright Brothers, the Arkansas Woodchopper, and others. Many of the songs are quite rare, and all are much earthier than anything Gene Autry or Roy Rogers ever recorded.

☉ **Singing In The Saddle** (1996; Rounder). This is actually a 4-CD series (each sold individually), and like RHINO'S SONGS OF THE WEST covers the history of cowboy music from its first recordings in the 1920s through to the present day.

☉ **Deep River Of Song: Black Texicans** (1999; Rounder). If the idea of a black cowboy singer seems like an oxymoron, it's not surprising, since the role played by black cowboys in the settling of the West is rarely given due historical treatment. But many cowboys were indeed men of color, and, as this CD proves, more than a few could sing. These 29 field recordings from the 1930s show a fascinating crossover between cowboy and blues traditions, and, while the music is raw, rough and close to the ground, the spirit is mighty high. Most of the singers aren't well known, though the name Leadbelly should be familiar—as might be titles like "The Old Chisolm Trail" and "Boll Weevil." The CD is part of the Alan Lomax Collection, a large and impressive series of CD reissues that is bringing Lomax's historic field recordings back into public view.

---

crossed over to straight country singing, had a voice with an uncanny resemblance to Dean Martin's. Allen, the last of the classic singing-cowboy stars, went on to become a narrator for numerous Disney cartoons and TV programs. Continuing the family legacy, his son Rex Allen, Jr. became a popular country singer in the 1970s.

Just as cowboy stars like Wakely and Tex Ritter were 'going straight' and crossing into mainstream country, Nashville was latching onto the western concept with both hands. Ernest Tubb didn't sing cowboy material per se, but he debuted on the *Opry* wearing a cowboy hat and boots. Soon hats, boots and western outfits by designers like Nudie and Turk were *de rigueur* for *Opry* stars. Western fever didn't show up in fashion alone. Hank Williams had named his band the Drifting Cowboys, Hank Snow was known as the Singing Ranger, and Faron Young was the Young Sheriff. The centerpoint of Marty Robbins' career was his GUNFIGHTER BALLADS AND TRAIL SONGS album, and even the crooners jumped on the bandwagon: Eddie Arnold's version of "Cattle Call" (a song written and originally recorded by **Tex Owens** in 1935) was one of the biggest hits of his career.

Early on, western music had been a genre separate from hillbilly. By the '30s cowboys were entering the country mainstream, and by the '40s the two genres were linked as one under the moniker 'hillbilly and western.' This soon evolved into 'country and western.' Nowadays, musicians as diverse as Loretta Lynn, George Strait, **Don Walser**, and Sawyer Brown—whether they hail from Poteet, Texas or Dayton, Ohio; whether they wear a gingham dress or Tony Lamas—are simply called 'country.'

The 'western' half of the moniker may have faded from popular terminology, but cowboys are indelible symbols of country music today. They continue to show up regularly in songs from "Mamas Don't Let Your Babies Grow Up To Be Cowboys" (Willie Nelson) to "Amarillo By Morning" (George Strait) to "Rolling Stone From Texas" (Don Walser). While Walser can yodel like the dickens, and contemporary western artists such as singer-cum-poet Red Steagall and born-again cowboy **Ian Tyson** keep the hardscrabble buckaroo lifestyle within view, about the only old-school 'singing cowboys' left are Riders In The Sky — and they play into that campy market with an impressive degree of relish. If still in doubt about the continuing extent of the cowboy's influence, just look at what's on the head of just about every 'young country' star gracing the pages of *Music City News*. It sure ain't a fedora.

Singing Cowboys: The Artists

Rex Allen

A mong the final generation of singing cowboys was Rex Allen, an Arizona native whose on-screen career was limited to the early 1950s, but whose voice carried him a few decades further. And it wasn't just the singing that made this man: during the latter half of his career he became a regular narrator on all sorts of Walt Disney nature and animal films and even on a few cartoons.

Allen's popularity hit about the same time the uptown Nashville Sound was coming into fashion, and his arrangements reflected this heavier-handed,

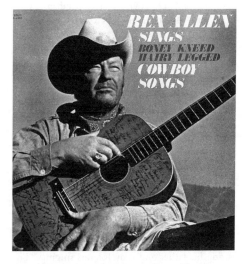

'sophisticated' style. His '50s and '60s recordings today sound about as far from 'true' working-man's western music as any of his singing cowboy brethren, maybe with the exception of Jimmy

Rex Allen

Wakely. But nearly all the cowboys were turning to pop at the time, and besides, it's not to say Allen's songs weren't pleasant: he's got one of the sweetest voices in country and western music, a friendly public persona, and his tunes (at least the western ones) speak directly to our well-traveled Old West romanticisms. But if you're looking for cracked-leather authenticity in your cowboy, you'd better seek it elsewhere.

Rex Allen was born on 1 January, 1920 on a ranch near Willcox, Arizona. Early on he worked in radio and did some rodeo riding, though he quit the latter after an injury. During the '40s he was based in New Jersey and Pennsylvania; after a performance in 1945, WLS *National Barn Dance* stars Lulu Belle And Scotty heard him and suggested he try out for the show. He did, and soon he was a favorite (he later had a popular radio show of his own on CBS). In 1946 he signed to Mercury, becoming one of the label's first country artists. His first chart hit was "Afraid" in 1949 and he also cut some duets with Patti Page.

In 1950 Allen moved to Los Angeles and kicked off his motion-picture career. His first feature was *Arizona Cowboy* (which was his nickname), and through 1954 he appeared in over two dozen pictures. He continued recording as well, eventually switching to Decca, which released his big hit "Crying In The Chapel" in 1953. After his filmmaking streak ended, he cut western albums (he returned to Mercury at the end of the decade) and pop-country crossover songs like "Marines Let's Go" and "Don't Go Near The Indians." One of Allen's oddest records of all has to have been "Slap Her Down Again, Paw," a crude novelty song about a husband reprimanding his philandering wife that was meant as good old-fashioned humor. Bet he's pretty embarrassed about it today.

During the '60s, Allen recorded pop songs like "Honey," "Little Green Apples," and "Tiny Bubbles" (a minor hit and his last), syrupy and highly orchestrated stuff that was a distant cry from his cowboy past, though his voice fit it like a glove. He also worked a steady gig as narrator for the Walt Disney corporation during this period, and it's this that gave him probably his biggest audience of all.

Meanwhile his son, Rex Allen, Jr., rose during the '70s to become a country hitmaker himself. One of the highlights of Rex Jr.'s career was a 1982 concept album THE SINGING COWBOY, featuring his father and Roy Rogers singing "The Last Of The Silver Screen Cowboys." That same year, Rex Jr.'s song "Arizona" became the Arizona state song. The senior Allen continued to appear at festivals and fairs, and during the '80s his hometown of Willcox opened a museum in his honor.

⊙ **Voice Of The West** (1986; Bear Family). Ten of the 16 songs here originally appeared on REX ALLEN SINGS BONY KNEED HAIRY LEGGED COWBOY SONGS, an album recorded in the early 1970s with producer Jack Clement (the back cover featured a letter of support from his pal John Wayne). Allen sings and tells stories about such "hairy legged" subjects as homemade booze ("Moonshine Steer"), trail-riding heroics ("Little Joe The Wrangler"), and gunfights ("Tyin' Knots In The Devil's Tail")—but he just can't shake the jovial Walt Disney tone from his smooth voice. The arrangements, though, are nicely pared-down and even gritty. The 6 bonus tracks include "Today I Started Loving You Again," "Catfish John," and the Clement original "Gone Girl" (previously a hit for Tompall And The Glaser Brothers).

⊙ **The Last Of The Great Singing Cowboys** (1999; Soundies/Bloodshot). Finding early, original Rex Allen recordings on CD hasn't been easy, at least until this collection came along. It consists of 22 previously unreleased radio transcription recordings that Allen cut in Chicago for the M.M. Cole Company during the late 1940s—the dawn of his recording career. The sound is clean and the arrangements warm and cozy on such titles as "My Dear Old Arizona Home," "Way Out West Is Calling," and "Dude Ranch Polka."

Gene Autry

G ene Autry wasn't the first singing cowboy, but had this Texan not drifted down the Hollywood trail, the concept might never have achieved such massive popularity. His sweet, gentle voice and nice-guy demeanor appealed to the widest range of fans possible—from hero-worshipping kids to nostalgic adults. During the Depression-rattled 1930s, movies were cheap escapist entertainment, and Autry was a welcome sight: smiling from the screen all adorned in his white hat, snazzy duds, and matching six-guns. Autry also kept his persona clean, sticking closely to a personal moral code (he didn't drink, smoke, kiss the leading ladies, or shoot first) so that no one save 'bad guys' took offense. Bursting from the back of his horse Champion with jolly tunes like "Don't Fence Me In" and "Back In The Saddle Again," his pretty voice was much closer in style to pop crooner Bing Crosby than 'authentic' cowboy singers like Carl Sprague or Jules Verne

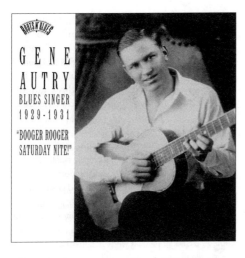

GENE AUTRY
BLUES SINGER
1929-1931
"BOOGER ROOGER SATURDAY NITE!"

Allen. Yet Autry wasn't a history-book cowpoke; he was all about fantasy.

By the time he made his first screen appearance in 1934, Autry was already a popular singing star who had sold millions of records. His repertoire then was a mix of hillbilly, blues, sentimental, novelty and western numbers—not that unusual for a country singer in the wake of Jimmie Rodgers, whom Autry emulated on his first recordings. Before his movie career, Autry's most popular song was a home-and-hearth duet with Jimmy Long, "Silver-Haired Daddy Of Mine." But he had toyed with a few cowboy numbers like "Empty Cot In The Bunkhouse Tonight" and even begun calling himself Oklahoma's Yodeling Cowboy. It wasn't until the dawn of his movie career that Autry's identity as a cowboy truly solidified. From that point onwards he was on his way to becoming one of the most popular and financially successful entertainers in all of country music.

Orvon Gene Autry was born on 29 September, 1907 in Tioga, Texas and raised on a cattle ranch. His mother taught him guitar, and while he grew to love music immensely he didn't think of it as a serious career until years later when he was working as a telegraph operator in Oklahoma. Autry sang on the job all the time and, as the famous story goes, one day Will Rogers (who had a sister living nearby) happened to visit, heard Autry, and told him he ought to try singing professionally. He took Rogers' advice and made a trip to New York City; his auditions the first time there were unsuccessful, but returning in 1929—and thanks in part to the contacts he made on his initial visit—he ended up recording. Convincing arguments from Art Satherley (a British-born producer who also worked with Roy Acuff,

Lefty Frizzell, Ma Rainey, Bessie Smith and Bob Wills, among many others) led to Autry's signing with the American Recording Corporation (ARC), which controlled a huge stable of budget labels.

For his first couple of years on record, Autry's style was—like so many up-and-coming singers at the time—a direct imitation of Jimmie Rodgers. He had the blue yodel down pat and cut plenty of Rodgers' material, too, like "Waiting For A Train" and "California Blues." The CD BLUES SINGER, 1929–1931 collects 23 of these songs, in a far more loping blues style than anything Autry would record again; if you didn't know it was Autry singing, you'd almost certainly mistake him for Rodgers.

Autry's popularity increased dramatically after he began his association with radio station WLS in 1931. He appeared regularly on the *National Barn Dance,* then the most popular radio barn dance in the country, and even hosted his own program, *Conqueror Record Time.* The Sears and Roebuck catalog (Sears owned WLS) now sold Autry's records and eventually also "Roundup" guitars with his name on them; cheap and easily obtained through the mail, these would be the first instruments for countless musicians in generations to come.

The big turning point in Autry's career came almost out of the blue. Hollywood was looking to bring new life to the oversaturated western movie market, and the small studio Mascot had ties to Autry's label, ARC. Singing had been tested a few years back in westerns, but never with a professional, and so Mascot hired Autry to sing a tune in the Ken Maynard vehicle, *In Old Santa Fe.* The response to Autry's performance was so phenomenal that the studio signed him up for further projects, and suddenly he was a Saturday-matinee leading man. His first starring project, a real oddball, was the science-fiction serial *The Phantom Empire.* After that (and now working for the newly formed Republic Pictures), Autry cranked out cowboy films at a rate that would make today's Hollywood stars wither in fear. By the time of his final feature, 1953's *Last Of The Pony Riders*, he'd made over ninety films.

And this wasn't all: Autry continued to record steadily, his repertoire a mixture of more standard pop and hillbilly fare like "Blueberry Hill," "You Are My Sunshine," and the wartime weeper "At Mail Call Today" alongside a generous helping of western numbers ("Mexicali Rose," "El Rancho Grande," "Rhythm Of The Range," "One Hundred And Sixty Acres"). As well as this, he

Gene Autry

began a hugely popular radio program, *Melody Ranch*, in 1939. With "Back In The Saddle Again" as its theme song, the show featured an assortment of music, fireside-type chatter and even a short western radio drama.

Autry's success turned cowboy culture into an industry, and all sorts of newcomers coveted an association with him. One of his earliest backing bands was the Jimmy Wakely Trio, which featured soon-to-be cowboy star Wakely as well as Mr. "Ten Little Bottles" himself, Johnny Bond. Bond stayed with Autry for years, playing music and performing comedy routines on *Melody Ranch*. Autry's cinematic sidekick for years was Smiley Burnette, who later worked with Roy Rogers and also had a recording career of his own. Another Autry hire was teenage guitarist Merle Travis. And songwriters like Ray Whitley (who wrote the initial version of "Back In The Saddle Again") and Fred Rose (a frequent Autry collaborator) benefited tremendously from the singing cowboy's success.

Feeling the pull of patriotism after the Pearl Harbor bombing, Autry enlisted in the US Army Air Corps in 1942 and was sworn in on air during a *Melody Ranch* broadcast. After the war, however, he found he had a screen rival in Roy Rogers, who'd come to prominence in his absence. In reality it didn't matter because the singing cowboy era was almost at an end. Autry, shocked by the next-to-nothing salary the Army paid him, had already begun to invest his money in interests outside the film and music world—a smart business tactic that would ultimately make him a very rich man. He came to own hotels, radio and TV stations, oil wells, record companies, and even the California Angels baseball team. Until the arrival of Garth Brooks, Autry almost certainly owned the fattest wallet of any country music star.

The best-selling recordings of his career also came after the war, and both were children's songs: "Here Comes Santa Claus" and "Rudolph The Red-Nosed Reindeer." He went on to cut others, too, like "Peter Cottontail" and "Frosty The Snowman." These came alongside orchestrated pop numbers such as "Buttons And Bows" and western songs like "(Ghost) Riders In The Sky," the latter from the pen of National Park ranger Stan Jones.

During the early '50s Autry made the big leap from film to television—which happened to be one of his new business interests. Eventually, however, business affairs became his primary focus: he made his last feature film in 1953, and the final *Melody Ranch* broadcast followed three years later. Even his TV productions ceased and his touring schedule dwindled. By the early '60s, he'd pretty much retired, making only rare public or TV appearances. He was inducted into the Country Music Hall of Fame in 1969. In the '80s he opened the Autry Museum of Western Heritage in Los Angeles. Autry died in 1998, just three months after the death of his singing-cowboy rival, Roy Rogers.

⊙ **Essential Gene Autry, 1933–1946** (1992; Columbia/Legacy). The 18 tracks on this single CD collection are culled from Autry's vast recordings for such labels as Oriole, Vocalion, OKeh and Columbia (the rights to all of which are now owned by Sony Music). Included here are the popular studio versions of songs like "Mexicali Rose" and "Take Me Back To My Boots And Saddle" (which were also featured in his movies) along with hits such as Floyd Tillman's "It Makes No Difference Now," the Carter Family's "I'm Thinking Tonight Of My Blue Eyes," and the traditional cowboy number "Red River Valley."

⊙ **Blues Singer, 1929–1931** (1996; Columbia/Legacy). America's Favorite Singing Cowboy was basically a Jimmie Rodgers rip-off on his earliest recordings, right down to the blue yodels and laid-back phrasing, which makes this collection one of the best examples of just how powerful Rodgers' influence was. The songs (some by Rodgers, others by Autry) show a bluesy side of Autry that had been largely forgotten up to this point.

⊙ **Sing Cowboy Sing! The Gene Autry Collection** (1997; Rhino). Gene Autry's music may seem to have mostly kitsch appeal at first, but his gentle voice and smooth style have actually grown more and more likeable with age. This 3-CD collection is definitely pleasant listening, though it's admittedly a lot of Autry for the average curiosity seeker. The well-put-together box includes *Melody Ranch* radio transcripts (songs and chit-chat) along with music from Autry's golden years.

⊙ **The Singing Cowboy, Chapter One** (1997; Varèse Sarabande). Collects 16 songs from the actual soundtracks to Autry's movies during the 1930s and '40s. The sound quality is muddy at times (some songs are from original Republic Pictures acetates), but the music itself—from mid-'30s titles such as "Take Me Back To My Boots And Saddle" and "Guns And Guitars" to later, more orchestrated cuts like "Sioux City Sue" and the spooky "Ghost Riders In The Sky"—are very enjoyable for those seeking a nostalgic Autry experience. CHAPTER TWO, released in 1998, continues to explore the vast world of Autry's soundtrack recordings, including duets with Smiley Burnette, Mary Lee, and the Cass County Boys.

Wilf Carter

Canadian cowboy star Wilf Carter, who went by the moniker Montana Slim in the US, was not only a fine singer but one of the best yodelers in the business. His had a rich, pure style that was beautiful and soaring on the one hand, but was also much more grounded than the smooth, pop-influenced voices of the silver-screen cowboys. Because of this, Carter's recordings clearly illustrate the transition in song and performance styles between reality-based cowboys like Carl Sprague and Hollywood stars like Gene Autry.

Born on 18 December, 1904 in Guysboro, Nova Scotia, young Wilf was initially inspired by the singing and yodeling of Jimmie Rodgers. He left home to ride the rodeos and work as a cowboy in the Canadian West, and it was in Calgary, Alberta in the early '30s that he first started performing on the radio. Like fellow Nova Scotian Hank Snow, Carter began his recording career on RCA Victor in the '30s. He took on the nickname Montana Slim when he began crossing over into the US market. He wrote somewhere in the vicinity of five hundred songs and enjoyed a recording career that lasted half a century. These songs included all sorts of cowboy material—from classic western folksongs like "Strawberry Roan" to nostalgic numbers like his own "Little Old Log Shack I Always Call My Home"—as well as assorted country and pop material. Carter's

yodeling was often featured prominently on his records, and for good reason, as few came even close to matching his ability. He didn't have much in the way of *Billboard* country chart hits, but he remained a popular performer. He died on 5 December, 1996.

⊙ **The Dynamite Trail: The Decca Years 1954–58** (1994; Bear Family). This 23-song CD of Carter's recordings from midway through his career may not be as classic as his early RCA material, but it's the most easily accessible and affordable single-disc collection on the current market. The songs are a mixed bag, as evidenced by curious titles such as "The Alpine Milkman," "I'm Gonna Tear Down The Mailbox," and "Ragged But Right" alongside cowboy numbers like "Strawberry Roan." More serious Carter fans might consider shelling out for the 4-CD Bear Family box set A PRAIRIE LEGEND.

Girls Of The Golden West

A lively, cheerful duo, the Girls Of The Golden West (aka Millie and Dolly Good) were a popular cowgirl outfit during most of the 1930s and '40s. Publicity at the time claimed their roots lay in Muleshoe, Texas, but in reality they were farm girls who grew up in rural southeastern Illinois. Their fictitious background—a story they stuck to throughout their career—was their way of appealing to the western craze sweeping the nation during the '30s in film and music. Cowboys and cowgirls carried an automatic cache of exoticism and awe—the western "mystique"—that most hillbilly singers lacked. Ironically, the duo's stage name came from an opera by Puccini, *The Girl Of The Golden West*.

With their crisp harmonies and engaging voices, the Good sisters had more in common stylistically with brother duets like the Delmores, the Monroes, and the Blue Sky Boys. But instead of wearing suits and ties or checked shirts, they dressed in cowgirl duds (white hats and fringe outfits). And though they did sing familiar eastern ballads like "My Sweet Kitty Wells" and "Put My Little Shoes Away," the bulk of their repertoire was western fare such as "Ragtime Cowboy Joe," "Lonesome Cowgirl," "Silvery Moon On The Golden Gate" (one of their signature tunes), and "When It's Round-up Time In Texas." Their arrangements were simple and pleasant: vocal harmonies with only guitar accompaniment.

Mildred Fern Good and Dorothy Laverne Goad (the original family spelling of their last name, which was Americanized to "Good") were born in Mt. Carmel, Illinois in 1913 and 1915 respectively. They first worked in radio on a St. Louis station before moving to the WLS *National Barn Dance* in 1933—home base during that time for both Gene Autry and Patsy Montana. Another WLS stalwart, the warm-voiced balladeer Bradley Kincaid, would later record with the Girls. The pair's first recordings were for Bluebird in 1933; they'd go on to record over sixty sides.

Toward the end of the decade, the Good sisters moved from WLS to WLW in Cincinnati, Ohio. They first played on the *Renfro Valley Barn Dance*, then switched to the *Boone County Jamboree*. Either way, they were one of WLW's most popular acts, staying active through to the end of the '40s. They did perform occasionally afterwards, and even recorded again in the early '60s for the Bluebonnet label. Dolly died in 1967, Millie in 1993.

○ **Songs Of The West** (1981; Old Homestead). The 18 songs on this collection give a good overview of the Girls Of The Golden West—folk ballads like "My Sweet Kitty Wells" (a 1963 duet with Bradley Kincaid), western numbers like "Ragtime Cowboy Joe," their popular sentimental song "Silvery Moon On The Golden Gate," and assorted ditties like "When The Bees Are In The Hive" and "Roamin' In The Gloamin'."

Stuart Hamblen

"**I** want to drink my java from an old tin cup as the moon goes climbing high," sings Stuart Hamblen in one of his earliest compositions, "Texas Plains." It's easy to see why this enticing ditty's been copied so much over the years. Not only is it catchy, it speaks as directly to America's romantic western fantasies as just about any cowboy song out there.

When Hamblen first recorded that song in 1934, the singing-cowboy era was in full swing. Though he did have a film career (often playing the bad guy), he was best known for his singing, songwriting and radio work—he was one of the West Coast's earliest, and most popular, cowboy radio personalities. He wrote quite a few of his most popular tunes early in his career, including "Texas Plains" and "My Mary." But if Hamblen's lyrics were romantic, vocally he was no Son Of A Pioneer. Where the Sons played things smooth and easy, Hamblen's voice was big, bold and bellowing—becoming even more so round the time he sobered up, found God, and recorded "This Ole House." That and other later recordings like "Remember Me" make the tall, burly cowboy singer sound as if he was struggling to contain some boyish excitement. On the whole his earlier recordings are more vocally subdued and, frankly, easier to take.

Hamblen was raised among cowboys and lived a rough lifestyle that was anything but subtle. He was "a man's man" wrote his wife Suzy in the liner notes to his 1960 album REMEMBER ME. A heavy boozer and gambler in his younger days (before evangelist Billy Graham got hold of him), he also owned a stable of racehorses and a couple of dozen hounds, and he was proud of the fact that he'd hunted and killed over one hundred bears and some fifty mountain lions. ("On our honeymoon camping in New Mexico," wrote Suzy, "he ran down and roped 28 head of wild horses.")

Carl Stuart Hamblen was born in 1908 in Kellyville, Texas. His father was a preacher who passed on his love of the outdoors. The young Hamblen rode in rodeos but later studied to be a teacher. While working his way through college he was learning western ballads and beginning to write songs, and eventually took his music interest more seriously.

His first radio gig was as "Cowboy Joe" in Dallas and Fort Worth. In the late '20s he recorded a few songs in New Jersey for Victor, then joined a touring vocal group and landed in California where his career really began to blossom. In 1930 he joined the Beverly Hill Billies, a 'manufactured' West Coast country act with a large regional following. During the '30s and into the '40s he gained a huge reputation as a radio personality, with "Texas Plains" becoming his radio theme song. Other hits from this time include "Little Old Rag Doll," "Brown Eyed Texas Rose," and the sentimental love song "My Mary."

Stuart's 'manly' lifestyle (booze, fights and even a spell in jail) inevitably propelled him towards breaking point. His big turnaround came in 1949 when, attending a Billy Graham Crusade in Los Angeles, he was suddenly 'saved.' He gave up drinking and gambling, and he sold his race-horses. He was still a prolific songwriter, and he began churning out songs like "It Is No Secret (What

Stuart Hamblen

Stuart Hamblen

God Can Do)," "This Ole House," "His Hands," "Open Up Your Heart And Let The Sun Shine In," and "Remember Me (I'm The One Who Loves You)." "This Ole House" became a popular standard, though "It Is No Secret" (the title track of his first LP) was no slouch either, and "Remember Me" was recorded by the likes of Elvis Presley and Pat Boone. Wanting to spread his personal gospel even wider, in 1952 he ran for President of the United States on the (what else?) Prohibitionist ticket.

Hamblen continued to record through the '60s and '70s. His 1961 album THE SPELL OF THE YUKON put Robert Service poems to music, and the title track of a subsequent album, THIS OLE HOUSE HAS GOT TO GO (THERE'S A FREEWAY COMIN' THRU) (1966)—a sort of sequel to his most popular tune—was about suburban encroachment on a once idyllic, old-fashioned lifestyle (frankly, it's not as interesting a song as it sounds). He also recorded sacred albums for labels like Word and Lamb & Lion. In 1970 Hamblen was inducted into the Nashville Songwriters Hall of Fame, and a year later the Academy of Country

Music bestowed him with their Pioneer Award. He died in 1989.

⊙ **Remember Me** (1960; Coral). Hamblen's big, brash, bold voice sounds rather like a bellowing grandfather, and it's all a bit much. The music is highly orchestrated as well—even his versions of "Texas Plains" and the cowboy classic "The Strawberry Roan" sound more like Broadway show tunes than anything you'd hum on a long and dusty trail ride.

Harry "Haywire Mac" McClintock

Harry McClintock wasn't your average cowboy singer. He wasn't your average anything, in fact. Born in Knoxville, Tennessee in 1882, he left home as a teenager to ride the rails and see the world. His travels took him from the Philippines (during the Spanish-American War) and China to Africa, Australia, South America, Alaska, and all points across the contintental US. In addition to making music, he held an assortment of odd jobs during his lifetime, including cowboy, mule driver, seaman and journalist. "Haywire Mac," a nickname he picked up along the way, recorded more than forty sides for Victor, but he became well known as a pioneering radio personality. From 1926, he worked on the San Francisco station KFRC, one of the earliest hillbilly radio programs on the West Coast.

Mac picked up all sorts of classic old-time cowboy songs while working as a cow puncher, and he recorded quite a few, such as "The Old Chisolm Trail" and "Sam Bass." But he was also an active member of the Industrial Workers of the World and wrote and sang many songs with labor and social themes. McClintock is best remembered, however, for a pair of hobo songs, "Hallelujah! I'm A Bum" and "Big Rock Candy Mountain." Both became hobo-camp mainstays and survived in folk circles for decades afterwards; the latter was also borrowed for the title of a Wallace Stegner novel.

Mac's hobo songs (another was titled "The Bum Song") were gritty and unflinching on the one hand, yet also presented a good-natured view of the wanderer's lifestyle—which was a common experience at the time, as many young men rode the rails both as a way to see the world and as a means to travel between jobs. "Hallelujah" isn't so much a ballad on the perils of homelessness as it is a celebration of the hobo lifestyle—something the protagonist has adopted by choice. "I don't like work, and work don't like me," sings McClintock, "and that is the reason I am so hungry."

McClintock was a popular entertainer all his life, both on stage and on the radio. In addition to his records for Victor (and later, Decca), he published a songbook, *Songs Of The Road And Range*. Folkways Records caught up with him during the early '50s and had him record a series of his classic songs. McClintock worked on various radio programs and continued to write and perform through the mid-'50s, when he retired. He died in San Francisco on 24 April, 1957.

⊙ **Hallelujah! I'm A Bum** (1980; Rounder). A selection of cowboy, hobo and even a few novelty songs that "Haywire Mac" recorded for Victor in Oakland, California in 1928 and 1929. Unfortunately, the disc is out-of-print, but it's been the only collection of McClintock's Victor recordings to hit the market so far.

⊙ **Back In The Saddle Again** (1983; New World). This double-CD set of 1920s and '30s cowboy songs

includes one McClintock number, the cowboy classic "The Old Chisolm Trail." It's a lively, fun rendition thanks to McClintock's lively vocals and the whoops and hollers of his buddy in the background.

Patsy Montana

Spunky, good-natured cowgirl Patsy Montana was country music's first female star and a pioneering figure in early twentieth-century American music. Her notoriety is largely based around her song "I Want To Be A Cowboy's Sweetheart," a million-seller that she wrote and recorded in 1935, though her career was already well off the ground at that stage. Many more of her songs were equally bursting with life, but "Cowboy's Sweetheart" easily stands out as a classic of early country and western recording.

Montana played the cowgirl role to the hilt. She dressed in fancy western-styled duds, wore a wide-brimmed hat, and on recordings regularly showed off her keen knack for yodeling. During the '30s she played mostly with the Prairie Ramblers, a string band formerly known as the Kentucky Ramblers. Their earlier recordings betrayed their hillbilly roots, but by the mid-'30s their sound had smoothed out and was definitely more uptown-swinging than mountain-bred. Whether working with Montana or Gene Autry (the Ramblers were his original back-up outfit), or playing just on their own, their musicianship was always top-notch.

Patsy Montana was born Rubye Blevins near Hot Springs, Arkansas in 1914. During the '20s she moved to Los Angeles with some family members, and it's here she was fully exposed to the singing cowboys, whose popularity was about to soar. She formed the Montana Cowgirls with two other women and, as was the order of the day among western wannabes, adopted a catchy stage name—Patsy Montana.

In the early '30s, Montana cut some sides with Jimmie Davis and a few on her own. During a trip to Chicago in 1933, she hooked up with the Prairie Ramblers, a band she'd stay with on and off until the early '40s. She and the Ramblers had a regular gig on the WLS *National Barn Dance*, and from 1933 onward they began recording together for the American Recording Corporation. Montana's first signature tune was "Montana Plains," a reworking of Stuart Hamblen's cowboy standard "Texas Plains." Most of her songs played on cowgirl themes ("The She Buckaroo," "Shy Anne From Old Cheyenne"), and after "Cowboy's Sweetheart" became a sweep-away hit Montana followed it with take-offs such as "I Want To Be A Cowboy's Dream Girl" and "I Want A Buddy Not A Sweetheart."

During the '30s Montana worked briefly at a New York station and also took time away from WLS to appear in a few movies, including *Colorado Sunset* with Gene Autry (a former WLS star himself). She switched to Decca Records during the early '40s and later jumped again to RCA Victor. She also worked on some Mexican border radio stations. She moved briefly back to Arkansas before finally landing, once again, in California.

Montana's career ran for decades after her heyday, much longer than most of her contemporaries. Until her death in 1996 (the same year she was inducted into the Country Music Hall of Fame) she recorded for several independent labels (Sims, Flying Fish) and played shows and festivals wherever she could. Dressed in an impressive cowgirl outfit, she'd sit on a stool and belt out her classics, happy to sing and tell stories to a whole new generation of listeners.

⊙ **The Cowboy's Sweetheart** (1988; Flying Fish). Produced by folk and children's singer Cathy Fink, this album contains Montana's final studio recordings, most of them familiar western songs like "That Silver-Haired Daddy Of Mine," "Cool Water," and inevitably "I Want To Be A Cowboy's Sweetheart."

⊙ **The Golden Age Of The Late Patsy Montana** (1998; Cattle). Collects original recordings from the mid-1930s through the mid-'40s of Montana titles—some true classics, others not as well known—such as "I Want To Be A Cowboy's Sweetheart," "I Want A Buddy Not A Sweetheart," "Have I Told You Lately That I Love You," "Two Seated Saddle And A One Gaited Horse," and "Smile And Drive Your Blues Away."

Patsy Montana with the Prairie Ramblers

Tex Owens

T he name Tex Owens may not ring many bells these days, but the song "Cattle Call" is a whole different story. Written by Owens, it was a huge hit for Eddy Arnold in 1955, twenty years after Owens first recorded it himself. With its loping rhythm and yodeling chorus, it's now something of a country music classic.

Among the western singers who came of age in the '30s, Owens was also one of the few who'd actually worked as a cowboy in his younger days. The song "Cattle Call" itself grew out of his working experience, capturing a cowboy's attempts to sooth his herd at night with sweet, mellow singing. Owens' voice may not be as pretty and smooth as Arnold's, but his version is much simpler and closer to the ground—you can imagine him lying under the stars at night singing it to the animals, not standing in a studio crooning for the housewives in Peoria.

Doye "Tex" Owens was born in 1892 in Killeen, Texas. His sister was burly-voiced country singer Texas Ruby, who went on to become an *Opry* star with her husband Curly Fox. (One of Owens' daughters, too, Laura Lee, would later achieve fame of her own singing with Bob Wills.) Owens worked a series of odd jobs—he was even

Patsy Montana • Tex Owens

Tom Russell On Cowboy Songs And Songwriters

As a songwriter, performer and even project co-ordinator (he and Dave Alvin compiled Tulare Dust: A Songwriters' Tribute To Merle Haggard), Tom Russell has been a good friend to country, folk and cowboy music. His 1997 album SONG OF THE WEST: THE COWBOY COLLECTION is his personal take on cowboy songs—the traditional "Rambler, Gambler" and originals like "Gallo Del Cielo," "The John Bull Tin," and "Navajo Rug," the latter written with his friend Ian Tyson. "I grew up listening to cowboy records in the '50s," Russell explains, "early Marty Robbins, and the traditional stuff like Carl Sprague, Gene Autry and Woody Guthrie, who also wrote some cowboy songs."

and there was a big controversy over 'Ira Hayes.' DJs wouldn't play it, and Johnny Cash took a big ad out in *Billboard* blasting them. LaFarge was very important in the '60s as a cowboy songwriter. He used to be a rodeo rider and he knew what he was talking about. Jack also toured with rodeos as a kid and so he used to pal around with him. I think Jack turned a lot of people on to cowboy music. And still does. For many years, through the late '60s and '70s, a lot of folkies and country people didn't care much for cowboy songs. It's just become reborn in the last ten years."

For more of Russell's own story, check out his 1999 album THE MAN FROM GOD KNOWS WHERE, which documents his personal family history in song, with vocal help from Iris Dement and folk legend Dave Van Ronk. Below are Russell's Top 5 cowboy albums:

EBET ROBERTS

⊙ Ian Tyson, COWBOYOGRAPHY (1986; Stony Plain; reissued 1994; Vanguard).
"Tyson redefined cowboy song in the 1980s and '90s," says Russell.

⊙ Buck Ramsey, ROLLIN' UP HILL FROM TEXAS (1992; Fiel Publications).
"An epic cowboy poet and a great traditional singer."

In addition to these artists, Russell discussed the careers and influence of two more singers whose work he admires, Ramblin' Jack Elliot and Peter LaFarge.

"I've been seeing Jack Elliot since the '60s at the Ash Grove in LA. Back then, he had—and he still has—a categorical knowledge of old folk/cowboy songs, from 'The Hills Of Mexico' to 'Strawberry Roan,' because he's such a lover of cowboy culture. As Jack is primarily a song interpreter rather than a songwriter, he did them in his inimitable style. People like Bob Dylan learned a lot from the repertoire of Jack and Peter LaFarge. LaFarge was a Native American from New Mexico, and he was the first folksinger signed to a major label in the '60s. Before he died in 1965, he made five records of mostly cowboy songs and also songs about Indians. He wrote 'The Ballad Of Ira Hayes.' Johnny Cash did an entire record of Peter's songs called BITTER TEARS,

⊙ Don Edwards
"Any of his are equal—just pick one. He carries the torch of Marty Robbins."

⊙ Marty Robbins, GUNFIGHTER BALLADS & TRAIL SONGS (1959; Columbia; reissued 1999; Columbia/Legacy).
"Really top of the line. It combines great cowboy lyrics with almost pop production. 'El Paso' was the first big cowboy crossover hit."

⊙ Paul Zarzyski, WORDS GROWING WILD (1999; Four Winds Trading Company).
"Cowboy poetry mixed with music by people like Duane Eddy. It's experimental cowboy poetry and song."

—Denise Sullivan

a deputy sheriff—before getting involved in music seriously. He eventually ended up on radio station KMBC in Kansas City, Missouri, where he performed regularly with his band and co-hosted the *Brush Creek Follies*. "Cattle Call" wasn't his only recording, but it was by far his most famous; he earned a far wider reputation as a radio personality. He also occasionally appeared in films (including a small role in the classic Howard Hawks western *Red River*). Owens died in 1962 from a heart attack.

⊙ **Back In The Saddle Again** (1983; New World). Owens' "Cattle Call" is one of 28 tracks on this great 2-CD compilation of assorted western singers. His sister, Texas Ruby, also sings "Dim Narrow Trail."

⊙ **Cattle Call** (1994; Bear Family). The title track is one of western music's classic songs. It's also by far the best-known of Owens' recordings, 20 of which are included on this single-CD collection. Owens had a pretty voice (and a beautiful yodel), and his arrangements were far simpler than almost every one of the silver-screen cowboys (who were his contemporaries)—though at the same time not as primitive as early western singers like Carl Sprague.

Riders In The Sky

There aren't many true singing cowboy outfits in country music circles today, but there are a few, and Riders In The Sky leads the pack. Sure they're campy, sure they're kind of silly, but it's all deliberate; if you dig kitschy campfire songs sung gallantly by a trio of cowboys in colorful duds, you've found your Holy Grail in the music of Riders In The Sky.

Core members Ranger Doug, Too Slim and Woody Paul are not only fun-loving gents having a grand time, they're also excellent singers and musicians who look to the beautiful harmonies of the Sons Of The Pioneers for inspiration as often as they do to the cheesy B-westerns of the 1930s. Frankly, without such musical skills Riders In The Sky couldn't come close to pulling this act off. And they have a deep love and an excellent sense for old-time cowboy and western tunes—whether classic songs (David Kapp's "A Hundred And Sixty Acres") or originals like the pretty "Cimarron Moon," or the playful song-cum-radio drama "The Ballad Of Palindrome."

Riders In The Sky formed in Nashville in the mid-'70s, where they played weekly gigs and began building what's now a strong cult following. Each member has a substantial background: lead vocalist Ranger Doug is Douglas Green, who once played with Bill Monroe's Blue Grass Boys and was also editor of the *Journal Of Country Music* and the *Country Music Foundation Press*; fiddler Woody Paul is Dr. Paul Chrisman, former physics professor at MIT who previously played with Loggins and Messina; and Too Slim, the group's 'sidekick' character and comic relief, is Fred LaBour, songwriter and former member of Dickey Lee's band.

The group began recording for Rounder in the late '70s, and they've been cranking out cowboy music on a regular basis ever since. Most of their albums have been released on Rounder, though during the '80s and early '90s they recorded for MCA and Columbia. Always playful, their albums sported titles like Riders Go Commercial and Horse Opera. They also recorded children's albums, and during the mid-'80s hosted *Tumbleweed Theater* on The Nashville Network. Their 1988 album Riders Radio Theater helped inspire a true radio show of the same name on National Public Radio. In the '90s they were back on Rounder and still going strong.

⊙ **The Best Of The West** (1988; Rounder). Highlights from the group's previous several albums on Rounder, stretching back to 1979's Three On The Trail. It's a fine sampler of their style, which is to mix over-the-top cowboy yucks (songs as well as skits) with under-the-western-stars ballads that emphasize the boys' pretty harmonies.

⊙ **A Great Big Western Howdy From Riders In The Sky** (1998; Rounder). Like most Riders In The Sky albums, this one is full of cowboy tunes both silly and serious. The singing is pretty, but the humor will be far too corny for anyone who doesn't get a kick out of grown men overplaying every cowboy cliché in the book.

Tex Ritter

Among Hollywood's top-drawer singing cowboys, Tex Ritter had the biggest, boomingest voice of them all. He was a college-educated Texan whose style was more scholarly and practiced than dirty and raw, but his interest in western music and its roots was genuine, and his voice commanded attention and packed an awesome punch. He had a drawl that wrapped and

curled itself around every word of his many tales—whether the hiccupping "Rye Whiskey" (about as psychedelic as any prewar cowboy song ever got), the gruesome "Blood On The Saddle," the cutesy "(I've Got Spurs That) Jingle Jangle Jingle," or the flag-waving "God Bless America Again." He was a God-loving patriot on the one hand, with a belief in America's wholesome heritage; yet he wasn't the type either to pull a protective blanket over humanity's seedier elements. Even "High Noon (Do Not Foresake Me)"—the theme song from one of the last great westerns—seethes with lurid texture.

Ritter was, along with Gene Autry and Roy Rogers, one of the biggest western movie stars with more than fifty films to his credit. And when the sun began setting on the glory days of the singing-cowboy era, he made a smooth leap to mainstream country with hits like "I'm Wasting My Time On You" and "Deck Of Cards." Ritter was also quite active in the country community, as president of the Country Music Association and later as a patriarch on the *Grand Ole Opry*. In 1964 he won a spot in the Country Music Hall of Fame, five years ahead of even Autry.

Tex was born Maurice Woodward Ritter in 1905 in Murvaul, a small town in east Texas. He sang in the glee club while attending the University of Texas and later tried law school for a year. But it was the cowboy and folk music he'd learned as a child that eventually captured his full attention; he started singing on a Houston radio station and within two years he'd gone to New York City. His acting career also took off at this point, with roles in Broadway plays like *Green Grow The Lilacs*. New Yorkers were in general much more receptive to western singers than they were to

southerners—cowboys were noble and free creatures, while hillbillies were little more than moonshining simpletons—and Ritter's full-bodied, Texas-fueled voice went over big. His baritone was so expressive you could almost taste the arid landscape; on top of that there was conviction and authority in his voice that captivated his listeners. In 1933 he cut four sides for the American Record Corporation; "Rye Whiskey" turned into one of his standards, and all were among the grittiest cowboy songs of the decade. In 1935 he switched to Decca.

Ritter made his first movie appearance in *Song Of The Gringo* in 1936. He moved to California and, although he continued recording, it's his singing cowboy roles that gave him a national identity during these years. In the early '40s, he began to focus more seriously on music again. He signed with LA-based Capitol Records in 1942, becoming the newly formed label's first country artist and remaining with Capitol for the rest of his career. He had all sorts of hits during the '40s and early '50s, some western-oriented ("Pecos Bill"), but many covering standard ground like lost love ("I'm Wasting My Tears Over You") and, well, more lost love ("When You Leave Don't Slam The Door"). Then there were the spoken-word soldier songs such as "Daddy's Last Letter" and, the most famous of all, "Deck Of Cards," a sentimental religious number about how a young soldier's playing cards keep him in touch with his Lord (it was an old folksong rearranged and earlier recorded by T. Texas Tyler). One of Ritter's masterpieces was "High Noon," his voice treating each line as if it were a Biblical pronouncement, vividly conjuring up a dark scenario of stubborn morality, honest dread and blood-thirsty western vengeance.

During the '50s Ritter evolved yet again, from country hitmaker to one of country music's elder statesmen. He'd hosted Southern California's *Town Hall Party* for most of the decade, and in 1963 and 1964 he served as CMA president. He ultimately moved to Nashville and joined the *Opry* and even ran for US Senate as a republican. He continued to record right up until his death in 1974, and his later songs revealed his still-adventurous spirit; there were plenty of sentimental recitations such as "Growin' Up" or "Papa," but these came side-by-side with works by left-of-center songwriters like Billy Joe Shaver ("Willie The Wandering Gypsy And Me"). Carrying on the Ritter legacy was Tex's son John: anyone who grew up in the '70s remembers him from the sitcom *Three's Company*.

⦿ **Blood On The Saddle** (1960; Capitol). Some of these songs, including the title track and the cowboy narrative "Samuel Hall" (a sort of western version of the classic murder ballad "Stagger Lee"), are surprisingly violent and at times downright nasty. Ritter, the patriarch, may have represented old-fashioned family values, but as a cowboy singer he sure knew how to roll in the dirt.

⦿ **Country Music Hall Of Fame** (1991; MCA). Ritter cut these 16 recordings for Decca between 1935 and 1939, when he was trying to get his movie career off the ground. Though they weren't his very first sides (those were cut for ARC in 1933), titles like "Get Along Little Dogies," "Bill The Bar Fly," "Sing, Cowboy, Sing," and "When It's Lamplighting Time In The Valley" pre-date this legendary singer's hitmaking period and are among the earliest of his long recording career.

⦿ **Capitol Collector's Series** (1992; Capitol). Twenty-five tracks that are classic Ritter, culled from his long tenure at Capitol, mostly from the 1940s and early '50s. Ritter was a master vocalist and storyteller, and titles like "High Noon" and "Blood On The Saddle" are some of the most intense and emotionally expressive cowboy songs you'll find. Even the harmlessly sentimental "Jingle Jangle Jingle" (his first Capitol single) and "I Dreamed Of A Hillbilly Heaven" are hard to resist—though recitations like "Deck Of Cards" and "The Americans (A Canadian's Opinion)" are best avoided.

Roy Rogers

Before he was given the name Roy Rogers by a Hollywood studio executive, this "King of the Cowboys" was known as Leonard Franklin Slye, born 5 November, 1911 in Cincinnati, Ohio. His family moved west to Los Angeles in 1930, and a year later—just days after appearing on the *Midnight Frolic* radio program—he joined a vocal group called the Rocky Mountaineers. Tim Spencer and Bob Nolan also drifted into (and out of) the group, and by 1933 Slye, Nolan and Spencer were singing together in a group they first called the Pioneer Trio and then the Sons Of The Pioneers. The group rose in popularity and even starred in a couple movies opposite Gene Autry.

In 1937 Slye heard by chance that Republic Pictures was auditioning for a new singing cowboy. Autry was threatening to quit the company because of a contract dispute, and Republic wanted a back-up. Slye won the auditon and signed a seven-year contract. He first appeared in the film *Wild Horse Rodeo* under the name Dick Weston, and then—when Autry made good on his threat—took the lead role in *Under Western Stars*, this time billed under his new moniker, Roy Rogers.

The film was released in 1938, and Rogers was an immediate on-screen success. He left the Pioneers and jumped full-on into his newfound Hollywood career. Unlike Autry, who was a million-selling pop and country singer (and radio star) as much as he was a leading man, Rogers focused mostly on his film career, cranking out more than eighty films over almost fifteen years in the business. He did record western-pop songs for RCA Victor (sometimes reuniting with his old pals the Sons Of The Pioneers), and he did have a few Top 10 hits, but his recording career was nowhere near as significant as Autry's. His movie career, however, was a powerhouse, and by 1943 he was the top box-office draw, the new "King of the Cowboys." Alongside his movie roles, another commercial industry quickly sprouted, marketing guitars, comic books, bedspreads and lunch boxes, each plastered with Roy's name and image.

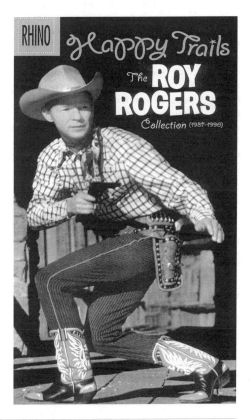

For the latter half of his life, Rogers was closely associated with film star, songwriter, and one-time jazz/pop vocalist Dale Evans (aka Frances Octavia Smith). She first starred opposite him in the 1944 film *The Cowboy And The Señorita*, and the pair worked together in nineteen more films over the next five years. Rogers was married when he first met Dale, but in 1946 his wife, Arline, died of an embolism. He and Evans married a year later. Though the famous couple only had one child together (Robin, who was born with Down's syndrome and died before reaching the age of two), they assembled a huge family consisting of Rogers' three children from his previous marriage and several more of varying ethnic backgrounds whom they adopted. Tragically, they lost two of their adopted children as well, each in separate accidents. The couple became deeply religious partly as a means of dealing with the recurring trauma. Evans also wrote a book, *Angel Unaware*, about their daughter Robin and the impact her short life, and death, had on the family.

In 1951, after his Republic Pictures contract ended, Rogers made the move to television and began the weekly program that ran for six years, *The Roy Rogers Show,* with Dale by his side—along with his sidekick Pat Brady (who had replaced "Gabby" Hayes), his horse Trigger, and Bullet the Wonder Dog. Dale wrote the TV show's closing theme song, "Happy Trails." During the '60s Roy opened a museum to exhibit all the memorabilia he'd collected over the years, and in 1976 he moved it to a bigger facility in Victorville, California. Among all manner of Roy Rogers costumes, commercial items and Hollywood paraphernalia on display at the Roy Rogers-Dale Evans Museum is Roy's old palomino pal Trigger, who died in 1965, but lives on now, stuffed and mounted, at the museum. In the late '60s, Rogers also allowed his name to be used on a national chain of fast-food 'family' restaurants, which thrived and survived for decades afterwards.

Rogers has been elected twice to the Country Music Hall of Fame—in 1980 as an original member of the Sons Of The Pioneers, and in 1988 as a solo performer. He recorded country and gospel albums during the '60s, '70s and into the '80s, often for Capitol, and in 1990 he cut the ROY ROGERS TRIBUTE album for RCA, which featured a series of duets with such Nashville stars as Randy Travis, Emmylou Harris and Clint Black. Rogers died on 6 July, 1998 at the age of eighty-six.

⊙ **Country Music Hall Of Fame** (1992; MCA). Covers the years 1934–1942, from Leonard Slye's years with the Sons Of The Pioneers through his intial period as a rising motion-picture star and cowboy icon.

⊙ **A&E Biography—A Musical Tribute** (1998; Capitol). The compilation claims to span Roy's career, and, while it does contain such classics as "Stampede" and "Happy Trails," the focus is on the songs he cut for Capitol during the 1970s (4 of them previously unreleased). His voice isn't bad, but he's well past his prime, and the material is more contemporary pop than classic cowboy—which makes this a less appealing starter CD.

⊙ **Happy Trails: The Roy Rogers Collection** (1999; Rhino). Rogers' fans probably know all about this box set already. It's a full-bodied, 3-disc collection that begins with Sons Of The Pioneers recordings from the late 1930s and early '40s, runs through all manner of Roy and Dale's film and TV songs, and finishes up with some Capitol cuts from the '70s, and one song, "Alive And Kickin'," from 1990.

Sons Of The Pioneers

If asked to nominate the most classic of western sounds, the Sons Of The Pioneers would stand as strong candidates. Defined by smooth vocal harmonies and soothing, creamy-textured arrangements, the Sons were the great vocal and instrumental group of the singing-cowboy era, and their long career (still going!) reflects their enduring popularity. Despite numerous shifts in personnel over the years, the group's sound has remained amazingly consistent—even after the departure

The mania for all things cowboy and western permeated American culture during the early to mid-twentieth century; musically, it wasn't just the hillbilly world that was affected. Bing Crosby was the biggest pop star to jump on the bandwagon, recording many western songs and even dressing the part. Plenty of others, though, such as white gospel group the Stamps Quartet, were equally enamored with the "wide open spaces" of the American West—an image they cultivated even if the sacred songs inside weren't exactly tailored toward campfires and trail rides.

during the 1950s of core members like Tim Spencer, the Farr brothers, and most especially Bob Nolan.

The Sons Of The Pioneers had a healthy appetite for Old West nostalgia, but they weren't just a bunch of crusty-minded cowboys sharing old-fashioned campfire tunes. Their music was beautifully and at times intricately arranged, with their trademark three- and four-part harmonies at the forefront where they belonged. Despite the obvious trappings—the romantic yearning for days of yore and, most especially, the orchestration that cropped up on later recordings—it's highly likeable stuff and difficult to resist.

The group was formed in the Los Angeles area in 1931 when a young Ohio man named Leonard Slye (soon to be Roy Rogers) was invited to join a group called the Rocky Mountaineers. He was soon followed by Canadian Bob Nolan, though Nolan quit only a few months later. His place was taken by Missouri musician Tim Spencer.

When Slye and Spencer quit the Mountaineers, they drifted through an assortment of western groups before getting serious with their own music. Slye convinced Nolan to join them, and the newly christened Pioneer Trio debuted on a local radio station. One of their earliest songs was the Nolan composition "Way Out There." Their popularity grew, and in 1934 a fourth member, Texas fiddler Hugh Farr, rounded out the line-up. All four of them sang, and right from

the start their carefully crafted harmonies were a large part of their appeal.

Changing their name to the Sons Of The Pioneers, they signed with the nascent (in the US at least) Decca record company in 1934, recording nearly three dozen songs for the label over two years. "Tumbling Tumbleweeds" (originally titled "Tumbling Leaves") was one of the first releases and quickly became their theme song. Another Nolan composition, it gave the group's music a moody western-desert vibe that would define them for decades to come. In 1935 Hugh's brother Karl Farr joined the Sons as a guitarist. That same year they also made the first of many feature film appearances in *The Old Homestead*. Movies were also the reason for Slye's leaving the Sons in 1938; he was offered the lead role in a picture for Republic, a competing studio (the Sons were exclusively Columbia boys). In his starring debut, *Under Western Stars*, Slye was billed under his new name, Roy Rogers.

The Sons now embarked on a game of musical chairs that would continue for decades to come. By the time Slye quit, Spencer had also left the group and Lloyd Perryman had taken his place. Slye's slot was filled by Pat Brady. Spencer rejoined two years later, and the line-up—Nolan, Spencer, Perryman, Brady, and the Farr brothers—is considered the 'classic' Sons Of The Pioneers. During the late 1930s and early '40s they appeared in numerous films and recorded some of their tastiest

Sons Of The Pioneers

material—for OKeh, Vocalion, and then once again for Decca. Their 1941 recording of Nolan's hallucinatory masterpiece "Cool Water" is especially haunting. In 1944 (after more line-up changes, partly due to the war) they landed a contract with RCA Victor, where they remained for some two dozen years.

During their RCA tenure, the Sons music took on a more orchestral texture, as studio musicians were brought in to give the once self-contained group a fuller, rounder sound. Flowing with the times toward a more suburban, middle-class appeal is part of the reason the Sons survived so long. Their popular titles at the time were not just western-themed, but also included the likes of "Stars And Stripes On Iwo Jima" and "Room Full Of Roses," the latter written by Spencer just before leaving the group for good in 1949. His departure was bombshell enough, but when Bob Nolan announced that he was also quitting, the golden era of the Sons Of The Pioneers was suddenly ended. Nolan did continue to sing on studio recordings, though by the late '50s he'd abandoned that as well. Fiddler Hugh Farr left the group in 1958, and his brother Karl tragically died on stage three years later. This left Perryman as the group's longest-running member.

Nolan and Spencer were both elected to the Nashville Songwriters Hall of Fame in 1971, and in 1976 the Sons Of The Pioneers were inducted into the Country Music Hall of Fame. The induction came just in time, as Spencer died that same year, followed by Perryman in 1977, and both Nolan and Hugh Farr in 1980. Roy Rogers died in 1998. The Sons Of The Pioneers have also been designated a 'national treasure' by the Smithsonian Institute.

Even after the death of longtime member Perryman, the group have continued to record and perform well into the '90s, with Dale Warren (who joined in 1952) assuming leadership. As of 1998 they could be found performing in places like Branson, Missouri and Tucson, Arizona.

○ **Cool Water** (1959; RCA Victor). The Sons' late 1950s material is far more orchestrated than anything they'd previously done, though that comes as little surprise since it was the heyday of the Nashville Sound. Yet even with all the heavy-handed trimmings, it's still amazingly beautiful music. COOL WATER was the most popular of the group's later RCA releases and features new versions of classic titles like "Cool Water," "Riders In The Sky," and "Tumbling Tumbleweeds." If you can find it, the "Living Stereo" edition of the album is

particularly gorgeous. The CD reissue with this same title, by the way, features different songs and lesser versions.

⊙ **Columbia Historic Edition** (1982; Columbia). The Sons recorded these 10 songs in 1937 during their brief tenure with the American Record Corporation and producer Art Satherley. The arrangements on songs like "At The Rainbow's End," "You Must Come In At The Door," and the fiery instrumental "Cajon Stomp" are far more spare than their later orchestrated recordings, but they're bursting with the energy and excitement of musicians who know they're in their prime and on a roll.

⊙ **Country Music Hall Of Fame** (1991; MCA). About half of the 16 tracks here were cut during the 1930s for Decca and feature the original Sons line-up (including vocalist Roy Rogers). It includes their first recording, "Way Out There" (1934), as well as the initial recorded versions of classics like "Tumbling Tumbleweeds" and "Cool Water." Further songs were cut during the '40s and '50s, when the Sons returned briefly to the Decca fold. Its sweeping coverage alone makes this the best single-disc Sons collection on the market.

⊙ **Wagons West** (1993; Bear Family). Serious Sons fans likely already own or at least know about this 4-CD box set, which contains over one hundred classic songs.

Carl Sprague

Carl Sprague was a budding athletic coach when he decided to make a trip to New York City and try his hand at recording some old cowboy songs—tunes he'd known since he was a child working on ranches in Texas. The year was 1925, and the songs he cut for the Victor Talking Machine Company became the first commercial western recordings. When one of them, "When The Work's All Done This Fall," became a major hit, selling nearly 100,000 copies, the saddle-manic era of singing cowboys and horseback poets was under way.

Sprague's voice isn't exactly gritty—compared to hillbilly contemporaries like Ernest Stoneman and Dock Boggs, it's almost pretty. At the same time, though, Sprague was a much cruder singer than later cowboys like Gene Autry and Jimmy Wakely, but it's precisely this quality that gives his music an authenticity the Hollywood cowboys could never touch. Sprague didn't record all that much—four sessions in four years—and none of his other songs sold as well as "When The Work's All Done," but he was a significant pioneer, and his music has an earthy strength that endures.

Carl T. Sprague was born near Houston, Texas in 1895. He grew up among cowboys and worked on a ranch as a child, learning from fellow workers the songs he'd later record. He attended Texas A&M University before a stint in the Army during World War I. After the war, he finished his studies and then took a job with the university's athletic department.

Music hadn't entirely drifted out of Sprague's life, however. He played a weekly radio show with a local band, and when he heard Vernon Dalhart's million-selling record "The Prisoner's Song," he was inspired to attempt some recording himself, hoping he'd have some success with a few of the old cowboy songs he'd known from his youth. In 1925 he contacted Victor, won an audition, and traveled to Camden, New Jersey where he made his initial recordings of cowboy ballads. He returned to Camden a year later for his second session; his third and fourth were held in Savannah, Georgia and Dallas, Texas respectively.

After his final Victor session in 1929, Sprague more or less retired from music, concentrating on his coaching and, later, an assortment of business and government work. He resurfaced at a few folk festivals and university concerts during the '60s, and in the early '70s he even made some recordings for Germany's Bear Family label.

⊙ **Classic Cowboy Songs** (1988; Bear Family). A CD collection dedicated to Sprague's 1920s recordings has yet to hit the market, so this will have to do. Sprague cut these songs for Bear Family in the '70s, and they include classic titles like "When The Work's All Done This Fall" and "Red River Valley," as well as more

Ian Tyson

recent material such as Stuart Hamblen's "It Is No Secret."

Ian Tyson

As half of the duo Ian And Sylvia, Canadian singer-songwriter Ian Tyson was one of the most popular and influential artists on the urban folk scene during the 1960s. After he and his longtime partner (and wife) Sylvia Fricker split up, however, he turned back toward to his western roots—settling on a ranch in Alberta and renewing his interest in western music and cowboy songs. Since releasing his 1983 album OLD CORRALS AND SAGEBRUSH, Tyson has found a new calling as a modern-day western balladeer. His timing was right, too, as cowboy music and poetry were in the early stages of a revival at the time, and few modern singer-songwriters had truly embraced the genre.

Tyson's interest in cowboy culture didn't come out of the blue. His father had worked with horses before he turned to business, and Tyson—who was born on 23 September, 1933 in Victoria, British Columbia—grew up learning to rope and

Carl Sprague • Ian Tyson

ride. His dream of being a rodeo star, however, was sidelined due to injury, and he veered into music instead. A strong folk scene was building in urban clubs and coffee-houses across Canada and the US, and this drew Tyson in. He soon moved to Toronto, where he met Sylvia, and the pair got their career off the ground. During the early '60s they were an established part of the Greenwich Village folk scene in New York City alongside such artists as Bob Dylan and Judy Collins. As well as assorted folk standards, both Fricker and Tyson wrote numerous originals such as "You Were On My Mind," "Four Strong Winds," and "Someday Soon." The duo were also among the first to cut songs by fellow Canadian Gordon Lightfoot, helping to launch his career.

Ian and Sylvia slowly drifted apart towards the late '60s, and eventually divorced in 1975. Tyson hosted a country TV show in Canada through the mid-'70s. He then moved west to Alberta, where he bought a ranch that he continues to run to this day. Inspired in part by a cowboy poetry gathering he attended in Elko, Nevada, Tyson began singing and writing cowboy songs. He's stuck with the genre ever since, cutting a series of albums for Columbia, Stony Plain, Vanguard, and other labels. His warm, dusty baritone voice is well suited to the material, which includes dance songs played with a full electric band, late-night ballads steeped in western melancholy, and songs that tell it like it is about the life and times of contemporary working cowboys.

⊙ **Cowboyography** (1986; Stony Plain; reissued 1994; Vanguard). Tyson's fans almost unanimously consider this the finest of his cowboy collections, thanks to songs like "Navaho Rug" (co-written with Tom Russell) and "Cowboy Pride."

⊙ **Eighteen Inches Of Rain** (1994; Vanguard). Another solid collection of western originals like "Horsethief Moon," "Heartaches Are Stealin'" (another collaboration with Tom Russell), and "Chasin' The Moon" (co-written with cowboy poet Baxter Black). This time, though, Tyson recorded in Nashville rather than Alberta.

⊙ **All the Good'uns** (1996; Vanguard). A greatest hits (well, he hasn't really had any *hits*) package that includes songs from his previous western-music solo albums—"Navajo Rug," "Springtime in Alberta," "The Old Double Diamond," and 14 others—as well as 2 new songs, "The Wonder Of It All" and "Barrel Racing Angel."

Jimmy Wakely

Along with Rex Allen, Jimmy Wakely was one of the last of the classic singing cowboy movie and recording stars. He made his first screen appearance in 1939, and went on to star in over two dozen films. He also had one of the smoothest country voices of his day, which enabled him to pursue a second-wind career as a pop-country crooner. At the time people called him the Bing Crosby of country (hard to say whether that was a compliment or not), though his lazy, sweet, cocktail-suave voice actually sounds amazingly like Dean Martin. If Wakely turned more toward pop in his '50s recordings, his fans for the most part didn't mind, and besides, the whole country and western world was on its way uptown. Wakely's crooning qualities only gave him even greater crossover charm.

James Clarence Wakely was born on 16 February, 1914 near Mineola, Arkansas, but he grew up in Oklahoma. His first professional music gig was on a local radio program with Johnny Bond and Scotty Harrell. Known first as the Bell Trio and later as the Jimmy Wakely Trio, they were big fans of the Sons Of The Pioneers and in 1939 made an appearance in the Roy Rogers picture *Saga Of Death Valley*. A year after that, Wakely, Bond, and new member Dick Reinhart had moved to California and were working for Gene Autry on his *Melody Ranch* radio show.

Wakely began recording for Decca during the early '40s (he'd later switch to Capitol), and he played a mixture of western ("Cimarron") and pop ("I'm Sending You Red Roses") material right from the start. At the same time, his small film appearances continued (often as a musician with Bond, Reinhart and later Harrell again) and eventually led to some bigger roles. In 1944 Monogram Pictures offered him a lead role in *Song Of The Range*, and suddenly he, too, was a big-screen singing cowboy star. Wakely went on to make several more films before the genre petered out.

His movie roles may have cemented Wakely's cowboy persona in most people's minds, but a more pop-country sound dominated his recordings, especially during the late '40s and '50s. The cheating song "One Has My Name (The Other Has My Heart)"—written by a fellow cowboy star, Eddie Dean—was a major hit for him in 1949. He also had a hit with Floyd Tillman's "I Love You So Much It Hurts." His biggest successes, however, were a series of duets with pop singer Margaret Whiting, including a version of Tillman's "Slippin'

Around," which reached #1 on both the pop and country charts in *Billboard*.

Wakely's chart success tapered off during the '50s, but he continued to record for Coral, Decca (including a popular album of cowboy songs, SANTA FE TRAIL), and later his own Shasta imprint. He had his own radio show and also co-hosted the TV program *Five Star Jubilee* with Tex Ritter. Wakely performed regularly through the '60s and '70s, up until his death from emphysema in 1982.

⊙ **Vintage Collection** (1996; Capitol). A decent 20-track overview of Wakely's tenure on Capitol in the late 1940s and early '50s. The emphasis is on Wakely's pop material—which he handles with smooth, easygoing style—but the music does run the gamut from his hit versions of Floyd Tillman's "I Love You So Much It Hurts" and "Slipping Around" (a duet with Margaret Whiting) to lively swing numbers ("Don't Lay The Blame On Me") and a few cowboy songs ("Moon Over Montana").

⊙ **Jimmy Wakely** (1998; Simitar/Pickwick). Wakely cut these songs during the 1940s, though unfortunately the liner notes lack specific details. Nonetheless, the recordings are clean and the arrangements are much more swing- and country-based than Wakely's later

Capitol material. Songs include Kokomo Arnold's "Milk Cow Blues," Jimmie Rodgers' "For The Sake Of Days Gone By," and Wakely's own "Oklahoma City Blues" and "I'm Sorry I Met You."

Don Walser

S weet-voiced Texas crooner Don Walser may be the best contemporary example of a singing cowboy we currently have. He yodels like the dickens, his songs have a distinct western flavor, and he imbues his music with such a warm, friendly spirit you can't help but catch his strain of cowboy fever. Walser doesn't dress in fringe costumes, nor does he have a handlebar moustache, but he does wear a wide-brimmed hat and boots, looking like a typical customer you'd find at a George Jones show or the Texas State Fair. Instead of playing up the camp element in the manner of Riders In The Sky, Walser's cowboyness is simply a part of who he's always been: a country singer with a voice as pure and pretty as any sound that's swept across the plains since the days of Jimmie Rodgers.

Don Walser

Born on 14 September, 1934 in Brownfied, Texas, for years Walser was a National Guardsman who played country music on the side with his Pure Texas Band. Though singing was a hobby, he did take it seriously enough, so that by the time he reached retirement age he was ready for a professional career. Recognition at the Austin Music Awards (not to mention a kind word or two from the Butthole Surfers' Gibby Haynes) led to greater recognition outside the V.A. Hall circuit and, eventually, a contract with the independent label Watermelon. Walser has since won widespread acclaim and continues to woo fans with public appearances, recordings, and yodeling demonstrations on radio programs like National Public Radio's *Fresh Air*.

⊙ **Rolling Stone From Texas** (1994; Watermelon). One listen to Walser's stellar tenor voice and you'll understand why he earned his nickname "the Pavarotti of the Plains." His yodeling alone will knock your socks off. Like the bulk of his singing-cowboy forbears, Walser sticks to nostalgic themes (the classic "Cowpoke" and the down-home "John Deere Tractor"—not to be confused with the Larry Sparks song of the same name) and maintains an up-beat vibe. You won't find much grit under his fingernails, in other words.

⊙ **The Archive Series, Vols. 1 & 2** (1995; Watermelon). These two individual CDs feature music Walser recorded in the years before his 'discovery.'

⊙ **Texas Top Hand** (1996; Watermelon). Walser's second studio album collects a handful of originals along with classics like "Tumbling Tumbleweeds" and traditional country favorites such as Faron Young's "Wind Me Up." Walser's versatile voice shifts effortlessly between the lonesome "Whispering Pines" and the dance-friendly "Signposts of Life." This is country music that greets you with open arms.

⊙ **Down At The Sky-Vue Drive-In** (1998; Sire/Watermelon). Another fine collection of country cuts from a man whose voice just won't quit. Songs include Cindy Walker's western swing-flavored "Cherokee Maiden" and the Sons Of The Pioneers number "The Devil's Great Grandson," another yodeling showcase. Like Walser's previous albums, this one's produced by Ray Benson of Asleep At The Wheel.

⊙ **Here's To Country Music** (1999; Watermelon/Sire). On his fourth proper album, Walser dives head-first into country music's glorious golden years. The album is (almost) all cover songs from honky-tonk days of yore, including Hank Thompson's "Here's To Country Music," Damon Black's "Arkansas" (a hit for the Wilburn Brothers that Walser remembers well from his childhood), and Johnny Tyler's "Oakie Boogie."

Don Walser

3

Big Balls in Cowtown: Western Swing From Fort Worth to Fresno

A s cowboy singers like Gene Autry and Tex Ritter were strumming their way across the silver screen, another western-styled music was developing back in Texas. But where the music of the singing cowboys was dreamy, folky and nostalgic, the hot dance music that would come to be called western swing was fired up and ready for action.

Western swing is a music that inspires passion not only in the players but in the fans, who speak of the music's two biggies, **Bob Wills** and **Milton Brown**, with a reverence normally reserved for the likes of Abe Lincoln. Western swing's Texas roots, perhaps, have something to do with the incredible loyalty the genre inspires. This unique musical hybrid that blended fiddles, horns, steel guitars and clarinets—'cowboy jazz' it was often called— was unlike anything that has fallen under the 'country' banner before or since.

Western swing wasn't invented by one single person in the way that bluegrass, for example, was invented by Bill Monroe. But it does in many ways have a 'father' figure, a man who put his heart and soul—his whole life—into the music, bringing it out of Texas and Oklahoma and transforming it into a national phenomenon. That man is bandleader and fiddler Bob Wills. The music itself is not solely

his: there were others involved in its creation, most notably singer and bandleader Milton Brown, whose group the Musical Brownies predated Wills' Texas Playboys by about a year (though the pair had worked together before that in the Light Crust Doughboys). Brown, though, died tragically at the age of thirty-two, leaving western swing fans to wonder ever after how the genre might have changed had the talented Texan survived.

Despite their shared role in the music's invention, it is Wills who has stood out from the pack ever since. Not only were his compositions and increasingly complex arrangements exciting and head-turning, he had the sort of burning energy necessary to maintain the intensity he'd started out with—energy to record newer and better songs; to take the band around the state and, eventually, all over the West; and to play the part of the star, even appearing in movies. West Coast bandleader **Spade Cooley** may have billed himself as the "King of Western Swing," but that crown will always belong to Wills, whose name is forever associated with the music and who ranks among such musical innovators as Jimmie Rodgers, Bill Monroe and Hank Williams.

If it wasn't for Wills, it's very possible that western swing would never have reached a national audience. The ice was truly broken when his 1940 recording "New San Antonio Rose"—a vocal version of one of his earliest compositions—became a major national hit. For years afterwards, it rivaled songs like Ernest Tubb's "Walking The Floor Over You" and Al Dexter's "Pistol Packin' Mama" for jukebox nickels. While Wills never attained the popularity of a star like Gene Autry—few did—he was far more than just a big fish in a Texas pond. Wills was invited to play the *Grand Ole Opry* in 1944, though when he unveiled a drummer—an act of sacrilege in the mother church of country—he killed his future on that show. Which was fine with him anyway, as he never considered himself a 'country' artist. He was 'western.' The *Opry* may have shunned him, but he appeared in quite a few movies and out West his popularity as a concert draw was hard to beat. On the huge California dance-hall circuit that sprouted during the '40s, only Cooley came close to matching Wills' following.

Hillbilly It Ain't

Western swing was a curious hybrid of musical styles. At its most basic level it was a blend of Texas fiddle music and uptown jazz. The whole package also had a western flavor that set it apart from Dixieland and communicated to folks that this music was born and bred in Texas. Fiddle music, for instance, had a long tradition in Texas (country music's first recording artist, Eck Robertson, was a Texas fiddle contest champion), and fiddling has remained at the centre of the music. At the same time, folks in urban areas were hot to trot for up-tempo jazz sounds—one of the biggest musical trends of the 1920s and '30s. Two great tastes that taste great together? It sounds like a funny mix, but it certainly worked.

Of course, there's a lot more to it than that. Texas was a state where cultures mixed and mingled—Mexican, Cajun, Bohemian, African-American—and it's out of this background that western swing arose. The list of influences is a large one: blues, Cajun and Norteño sounds; Bohemian polka music; and healthy inspirations from Jimmie Rodgers, minstrel performers like Emmett Miller and all sorts of Tin Pan Alley pop songs. Hillbilly is definitely a part of the music, too, but Wills hated the term; he deliberately fashioned himself as a bandleader in the manner of Tommy Dorsey, not Charlie Poole.

Perhaps the key factor at the heart of the music, the one thing that drove it from the very beginning, was dancing. When they started their own groups in the mid-'30s, Wills and Brown both wanted to create a sound that could fill a large hall and keep people on their feet all night long. Though in Texas an oil boom had partially relieved the hardship of the Depression, people were still yearning for release from their day-to-day woes, and dancing—whether in a dingy roadhouse or an upscale downtown ballroom—was a perfect antidote. The mix of musical flavors that western swing brought with it only added to the fun. By the end of the '30s, Wills' band, in particular, had grown incredibly diverse in its instrumentation and song repertoire. It truly was 'hot dance music,' as the music was then popularly called ('western swing' didn't come into use until after World War II).

On the surface the music had an air of sophistication; at its core was an untamed spirit. The earliest recordings of both Brown and Wills had a loose and unruly feel—a sense of musical freedom that was inspiring and refreshing. The playing was tasty and packed with flavor, and it always stayed close to the ground. The music may have been classy on one level, but it was never stuffy. Western swing was all about good times, and the players, Wills included, gave it a sense of fun. Most of the songs had happy, joyful themes like Cliff Bruner's recording of the pop gem "When You're Smiling" and Wills' famous anthem of western pride, "Take Me Back To Tulsa;" others veered into good-natured risqué territory, most famously the Light Crust Doughboys' "Pussy, Pussy, Pussy." In the end the music was almost impossible to resist; urban audiences as well as ranch folk flocked to the dance halls and turned it into the major music of the American Southwest.

The Founding Fathers

In Fort Worth in 1929, Bob Wills and guitarist Herman Arnspiger were playing around town as the Wills Fiddle Band. When Wills asked vocalist and out-of-work cigar salesman Milton Brown and his brother Durwood to join the group, the story of western swing truly began. The boys changed their name first to the Aladdin Laddies (named after their sponsor, the Aladdin Lamp Company) and, finally, to the Light Crust Doughboys (their new sponsor, Burrus Mill and Elevator Company, made Light Crust Flour). The latter group fell under the leadership of Burrus company man (and aspiring politico) W. Lee O'Daniel, who acted as their emcee and manager. The group did gain a decent reputation, but O'Daniel's insistence that they concentrate on radio appearances—where they hawked Light Crust Flour—at the expense of concerts became more and more of a problem. Brown soon quit and formed the Musical Brownies; Wills left a year later and formed the Texas Playboys.

Brown was taking a gamble—he'd left a steady gig in the middle of the Depression—but it paid off. Before long he was a huge sensation throughout the state, leading the biggest western swing band of his time, until his career was abruptly cut short.

When Wills left the Doughboys, he brought vocalist Tommy Duncan and his brother Johnny Lee Wills with him to form his own group. Like the Brownies, the Texas Playboys were an immediate success. If anything, Wills' jazzy elements were even more pronounced than Brown's, with vocalist Duncan giving the Playboys an enticing smooth vocal finish. As Wills' music developed over the years, he'd add to it further by bringing in horns and reeds to fill out the melodies, and drums to beef up the rhythm. He'd eventually have nearly twenty players, a monumental number for any band, let alone of the country and western variety; his Texas Playboys during the late '30s and early '40s certainly rivaled the size and complexity of any big jazz bands of the era.

The Playing's the Thing

Fiddling was at the center of western swing from the start—Wills himself was a fiddler—but that was only one element. The instrumentation of both Brown's and Wills' bands, in fact, was one of the major distinctions that set their music apart from either straight hillbilly or jazz. For starters, the Brownies featured Bob Dunn, a steel guitarist who is credited as the first country artist on record to use an electric string instrument (see box p.78). Wills had his answer to Dunn in Leon McAuliffe, whose "Steel Guitar Rag" became hugely popular and brought the new amplified sound to the public's attention. Later, Cliff Bruner (himself a Brownie alumnus) employed electric mandolinist Leo Raley in his group the Texas Wanderers. The new amplified sound gave the music a bright new edge and foreshadowed the arrival of honky tonk, which was only several years down the road.

Instrumental prowess was the focus of western swing music in its early years. As in jazz, solo breaks from the individual players were enticing highlights. Vocals were, of course, a part of the instrumental mix from the beginning, but as the music evolved from a regional 'hot dance' phenomenon to a nationally popular style of music, singing took on more importance—it was how most people related to the music, especially songs with such complex instrumentation and arrangements. This was true of country music as a whole: hillbilly music during the 1930s had itself been moving away from string bands and more toward vocal duets like the Blue Sky Boys and Delmore Brothers. During the '40s Wills added lyrics to several instrumental favorites, including "New San Antonio Rose" and "Faded Love," which helped them make the national charts. These and other Wills songs like "Bubbles In My Beer" and "Roly Poly" signaled a new pop-oriented 'maturity' of the music. The trend culminated in the '50s with songs like **Pee Wee King**'s "Slow Poke," and **Hank Thompson**'s "The Wild Side Of Life."

Once the music of Brown and Wills had caught on, other groups began appearing throughout the region. Wills had settled in Tulsa, Oklahoma, making Cain's Ballroom his home base for the next decade. Another Tulsa-based group was the Alabama Boys; they had a strong following that rivaled Wills' but recorded only once before sliding into oblivion.

The Light Crust Doughboys continued to roll onward without their former star members and remained, in fact, one of the biggest western swing groups of the decade. Their base was still Fort Worth, home also to the Crystal Springs Ramblers (house band at the Crystal Springs Ballroom) and Roy Newman And His Boys (who actually recorded before Wills). Leon Selph's Blue Ridge Playboys, Cliff Bruner's Texas Wanderers, and **Smokey Wood** worked out of Houston, while San Antonio had the Tune Wranglers and **Jimmie Revard** And His Oklahoma Playboys. Revard's group was the starting point for another future bandleader, **Adolph Hofner**—interesting in that he played Bohemian polka music as well as western swing and country. And we can't forget the more string-band-flavored **Bill Boyd** And His Cowboy Ramblers, a contemporary of the Playboys and the Brownies and the group who gave us the classic "Under The Double Eagle."

Westward Expansion

As the music evolved, its popularity continued to spread, most of it westward towards California. By the 1940s Wills and the Texas Playboys had begun appearing in cowboy films with the likes of Tex Ritter, which helped increase their national popularity. During trips to Hollywood, they also played gigs at such major West Coast ballrooms as Venice Pier and the Riverside Rancho. Wills' presence in California fueled an already growing western swing movement up and down the state. California was by this point inundated with displaced

Okies and other drifters who, thanks to the Dust Bowl and the Depression, had come West in search of work and better living conditions in the "Golden State". Many wound up as migrant farm workers, while others joined the service or worked in factories and shipyards. They may have arrived penniless, but they brought with them a love for country and western music; so when western swing bands like those of Wills, Spade Cooley and **Tex Williams** appeared, they turned out in droves. Wills obviously had this in mind when he moved to California in 1943. The Texas Playboys had split up at the start of World War II with several members, including Tommy Duncan, joining the armed forces. Wills himself enlisted but couldn't cut it physically. Returning to music, he decided to try his luck in California, where the live music scene was bigger and stronger at the time than anywhere else in the country.

With western swing now a hot ticket in California, regional bands soon cropped up. The biggest and most influential artist by far was fiddler Spade Cooley, whose massive 'orchestra' was even larger than the Playboys in their heyday and just might have been the biggest group ever in country music. Cooley was billed as a 'western swing' band, probably the first wide use of the term. His sound was smoother and somewhat flashier than Wills or any of his Texas and Oklahoma cohorts had been—not surprising considering Cooley's home base was LA. In a tragic twist, two decades later, after his popularity had burned out, Cooley would make headlines for brutally murdering his wife.

One of Cooley's chief vocalists during the '40s was Tex Williams. In 1946 he was fired by Cooley but quickly formed his own group with several other Cooley sidemen. Tex Williams And His Western Caravan went on to achieve fame of their own thanks especially to his hit "Smoke! Smoke! Smoke! (That Cigarette)," a song co-written by one of the biggest West Coast country stars at the time, Merle Travis. Another popular California band during the '40s, the Maddox Brothers And Rose, didn't exactly play western swing—it was more 'hillbilly boogie'—but their music shared similarities and they certainly played the same concert circuit.

Still other artists moved West to capitalize on the exploding swing dance scene. *Opry* singers and other groups based in and around Appalachia could play school rooms and community halls and attract a few hundred souls; in the major dance halls that cropped up across California and the West, however, audiences attended in the thousands. It didn't take a genius to figure out where the money was. Texas-based Adolph Hofner and *Opry* star Curley Williams both moved to California to try their luck.

Hank Penny was one of the few western swing artists to complete much of his formative work in the East, playing in his native Alabama as well as New Orleans, Atlanta, Cincinnati and Nashville. His band, the Radio Cowboys, included for a time noted steel player Noel Boggs and songwriter Boudleaux Bryant. Penny eventually came to California and met with mixed results, never quite achieving the success he deserved. Another eastern-based artist was **Louise Massey** (who wrote the standard "My Adobe Hacienda"); with her band the Westerners she mostly worked out of Chicago.

By the '50s, California's massive love affair with western swing was fading, as it soon would all over the country. Wills had moved back to Tulsa in 1949, and though he remained a popular live draw his national popularity waned —partly due to his failing health. The last of the great western swing bands was Hank Thompson And The Brazos Valley Boys, who came to prominence during the '50s with a slightly sharper, more honky-tonk-infused sound ('honky tonk swing' he called it) and a healthy batch of good-natured songs ("Humpty Dumpty Heart," "Six Pack To Go"). The secret of Thompson's long-lasting success was his propensity for touring ballrooms and dance halls all over the country, east as well as west. Bob Wills, says Thompson, didn't like to tour to that degree: "He'd rather play Tulsa than Detroit."

Revival

By the late 1960s and early '70s, the popularity of western swing as a musical style had long since abated, though the faith was still strong among believers, and Wills was still held in great esteem. He was honored with tribute albums by both George Jones (GEORGE JONES SINGS BOB WILLS) and Merle Haggard (A TRIBUTE TO THE BEST DAMN FIDDLE PLAYER IN THE WORLD, see box p.95), as well as being inducted into the Country Music Hall of Fame. Despite a debilitating stroke, he did manage a final recording session in 1973 that resulted in the excellent album FOR THE LAST TIME (Haggard helped organize the project). Waylon Jennings wrote the song "Bob Wills Is Still The King," a #1 hit in 1975, but it was thanks to western swing revivalists like Dan Hicks and especially **Asleep At The Wheel** that the music truly found a newer (and younger) audience, working its way into the country fabric as more than just an act of nostalgia. Like Waylon and Willie Nelson, the Wheel was a hip alternative to the glitzy material Nashville was churning out. A decade later came new traditionalist George Strait, a big western swing fan who turned "Right Or Wrong" (recorded by Wills, Brown, and before them Emmett Miller) into a #1 hit in 1984. By the '90s, a reinvigorated rockabilly and swing dance scene led to a new wave of revivalist bands and a crop of fans who dressed in fancy western duds and knew all the right dance moves by heart. Among the best of the bunch are LA's Big Sandy And The Fly-Rite Boys and the Austin, Texas-based **Hot Club Of Cowtown**.

Anthologies

⊙ **OKeh Western Swing** (1982; Epic). A compilation of western swing from the OKeh label, mostly from the 1930s–'40s. Early influences are evident, including that of blackface artists like Al Bernard ("Hesitation Blues") and Emmett Miller ("Lovesick Blues"—yes, the very song Hank Williams later recorded). The jazz element is very pronounced here: this wasn't campfire music, it was all about swingin' rhythms and truly was 'cowboy jazz.' A lot of it is instrumental, too. The excellent liner notes by John Morthland are a bonus. The album is sadly out-of-print, but worth looking for.

⊙ **Hillbilly Boogie!** (1994; Columbia/Legacy). Twenty warm and wired tunes that blur the lines between western swing, blues-based boogie music and honky tonk. It's a great compilation of lesser-known but thoroughly juicy material from the Columbia vaults, including songs by Louise Massey, Curley Williams, Leon McAuliffe, Paul Howard, Spade Cooley and honky tonkers Al Dexter, Johnny Bond, and Lefty Frizzell. The mood is upbeat—though these folks were pretty easy to please. As Smiley Maxedon declared, "Give Me A Red Hot Mama And An Ice Cold Beer" ("and I can sorta get along").

⊙ **Texas Music, Vol. 2: Western Swing And Honky Tonk** (1994; Rhino). From Wills, Brown, and Bruner through to Hank Thompson, Alvin Crow, and Asleep At The Wheel, this 18-song CD covers the whole gamut of western swing's development. Honky tonkers like Al Dexter, Ernest Tubb and Floyd Tillman broaden the picture.

⊙ **Heroes Of Country Music, Vol. 1: Legends Of Western Swing** (1995; Rhino). Eighteen songs mostly by familar singers like Milton Brown, Bob Wills, Cliff Bruner, Hank Thompson, and Spade Cooley alongside a few lesser-knowns like the Fort Worth Doughboys. Begins with "Sunbonnet Sue" by the Forth Worth Doughboys, a song recorded in 1932

and featuring Wills and Brown. Rhino's 5-part series of classic country was originally titled "Hillbilly Fever."

⊙ **Stompin' At The Honky Tonk: The Roots Of Rock And Roll, Vol. 7** (1997; President). A decent cowboy and western swing sampler with slightly off-the-beaten-path cuts by Smokey Wood, Adolph Hofner, Luke Wills, and the Sweet Violet Boys (doing the classic "I Love My Fruit").

⊙ **Jitterbug Jive: Hot Texas Swing 1940–1941** (1997; Krazy Kat). British label Krazy Kat compiled these 25 recordings that were cut for Bluebird (an RCA subsidiary) during the early 1940s. The songs feature such legendary artists as Moon Mullican, Jerry Irby (who wrote "Driving Nails In My Coffin"), Bill Boyd, Leon Payne, and Cliff Bruner, who are playing with such groups as the Cowboy Ramblers, the Modern Mountaineers, and the Bar-X Cowboys. And steel-guitar pioneer Bob Dunn plays on nearly half the songs.

⊙ **Jive And Smile: Kings Of Western Swing** (1998; Charly). As far as western swing overviews go, this British-issued double-CD collection is as substantial as they come—a great way to throw yourself head-on into the music. Sure there are songs by Wills and Brown, but you also get Cliff Bruner, Hank Penny, Smokey Wood, and Jimmie Revard, among many others—50 in all, which should keep you busy for quite a while.

⊙ **Swing West! Volume 3, Western Swing** (1999; Razor & Tie). Yet another fine western swing compilation, this one focuses on the West Coast scene. Includes big stars like Wills, Spade Cooley, and Tex Williams along with Tommy Duncan ("Gambling Polka Dot Blues"), Ole Rasmussen ("C Jam Blues"), Jack Guthrie ("Oakie Boogie"), and Hank Thompson ("Total Strangers").

Western Swing: The Artists

Asleep At The Wheel

Asleep At The Wheel were not just a long-haired western swing revival outfit paying tribute to their idol, Bob Wills. They were one of the most popular country-rock bands of the 1970s, a group that attracted young and restless freedom rockers as well as older Texas Playboys fans, putting them side-by-side at festivals and in clubs and pretending it was no big deal. The Wheel was as adept at straight country weepers and Louis Jordan jump-blues material as it was at western swing. The group played plenty of classics but also wrote quite a few themselves, including "My Baby Thinks She's A Train," "Bump Bounce Boogie," and "The Letter That Johnny Walker Read," their first sizeable hit. In short, they were a diverse bunch with impeccable musical credentials that earned them wide and well-deserved appeal.

Asleep At The Wheel was formed in 1969 and has been centered ever since around singer and guitarist Ray Benson, whose smooth baritone echoes great singers like Tommy Duncan with a little Ernest Tubb thrown on top. The other two founding members are drummer/guitarist Leroy Preston and steel guitarist Lucky Oceans. The three young players got their start with a series of local gigs around Benson's farm in Paw Paw, West Virginia. Guitarist and singer Chris O'Connell was the next to join, after which they moved west to San Francisco. Staying in the Bay Area for a few years, they added pianist Floyd Domino and played a steady gig at Berkeley's Long Branch Saloon. Their following finally grew and they landed a contract with United Artists, who released their first album, COMIN' RIGHT AT YA, in 1973. A year later they moved to Austin, Texas, where they've been based ever since. Their next album, self-titled and released this time by Epic, was a diverse bag of styles that ran from Louis Jordan's "Choo Choo Ch'Boogie" (a minor hit for them), to a slow and weepy version of Rex Griffin's "The Last Letter."

The band was already running strong and had an excellent reputation as a live outfit, but their records finally began catching up with them following the release of the 1975 album TEXAS GOLD. Their first for Capitol, it again showcased a lively mix of swing, blues and honky tonk; as a bonus the catchy Benson original "The Letter That Johnny Walker Read" made the Top 10. Other albums like THE WHEEL and WHEELIN' AND DEALIN' kept them kicking their way through the '70s. They wrapped up the decade by winning a Grammy for the instrumental "One O'Clock Jump."

As was typical of long-running groups like the Texas Playboys, the Wheel (which at one point reached eleven members) saw its share of personnel changes over the years. Founding member Oceans and guitarist O'Connell quit in the 1980s. Benson, however, remained the focal point, the man who then, as now, kept the group alive through a career of ups and downs that's so far spanned three decades. He's also managed to introduce a steady stream of special guests: former Texas Playboys Johnny Gimble, Leon Rausch, Tiny Moore, and Eldon Shamblin have all lent a hand on various recordings, as have trumpeter Bobby Womack, guitarist Linda Hargrove, Bonnie Raitt, and Willie Nelson.

The group's heyday was clearly the '70s. After that, membership changes and financial crises led to kinks in the pipeline. Still, by the late '80s they were in the charts again, and in 1992 the album LIVE AND KICKIN' (recorded in Austin) brought them renewed interest. Since then, the group has cut not one but two albums paying homage to their hero, Bob Wills. Both A TRIBUTE TO THE MUSIC OF BOB WILLS AND THE TEXAS PLAYBOYS (1993) and RIDE WITH BOB (1999) are packed with specials guests from both country and pop music (see box p.95).

⊙ **Texas Gold** (1975; Capitol). A mix of western swing, honky tonk, blues and God knows what else, this album is packed full of energy and charm and is definitely one of the Wheel's standout achievements on record. It's hard to argue with songs like "Let Me Go Home, Whiskey," "The Letter That Johnny Walker Read," and "Tonight The Bartender Is On The Wrong Side Of The Bar," not to mention the Bob Wills standard "Trouble In Mind."

⊙ **Live And Kickin': Greatest Hits** (1992; Arista). An album recorded live in Austin, Texas, and featuring an impressive array of their classic songs.

⊙ **The Swinging Best Of Asleep At The Wheel** (1992; Epic). A compilation of tracks from their two periods on Epic Records, the early 1970s (the album ASLEEP AT THE WHEEL which includes the cool and catchy "Choo Choo Ch'Boogie") and the late '80s (WESTERN STANDARD TIME AND 10).

Bill And Jim Boyd

Along with Bob Wills and Milton Brown, Bill Boyd was one of the pioneering bandleaders of western swing. His group, the Dallas-based Cowboy Ramblers, was one of the first Texas swing bands to record, in 1934, and while Boyd never achieved national fame on a par with Wills, he and the group carved out a decent reputation for themselves, thanks in large part to a popular Dallas radio program and a performing and recording career that lasted for decades.

Boyd's music definitely fell into the western swing camp, but many of his songs had more of a string-band flavor than contemporary artists like Wills, Brown and Jimmie Revard. On the Ramblers' 1935 recording of their classic "Under The Double Eagle," for instance, the instrumentation was close to that of a standard string band—guitar, bass, fiddle, banjo—with piano being the only new addition. The melody and rhythm, however, have an unmistakably jazzed-up swing. As Boyd and his band evolved over the next several years, the number of players would rise to ten and the jazz elements increase.

William Lemuel Boyd was born in 1910 in Fannin County, Texas, and was raised on a ranch northwest of Dallas near the Oklahoma border. He and his brother Jim played on the radio and later, after the family moved to Dallas, with local bands. Bill formed his first incarnation of the Cowboy Ramblers in 1932, featuring his brother Jim on bass, Art Davis on fiddle, Walter Kirkes on tenor banjo and himself on guitar. They played a regular radio show, the *Bill Boyd Ranch House*, which would continue on the same station for decades; two years later they recorded their first sides for Bluebird. Among the songs were a few cowboy classics such as "Strawberry Roan," which showed the Boyd brothers' lingering attachment to their childhood ranching days. The next year, in 1935, their western swing reputation was sealed when they recorded "Under The Double Eagle," a fleet-footed instrumental that's become a standard of the genre.

Like many singers of the '30s and '40s with any hint of western in their character, Boyd ended up appearing in a few movies. This brought him and the band to Hollywood for a time. There he continued to perform and record, and during World War II he also joined a group called the Western Minute Men who toured the country promoting the sale of War Bonds.

Boyd kept the Cowboy Ramblers running steadily for several decades. Over the years the group has included notable players like fiddlers Cecil Brower and Jesse Ashlock, pianist John "Knocky" Parker, steel guitarist "Lefty" Perkins, and banjoist Marvin Montgomery. Noted West Coast steel maestro Noel Boggs also played with Boyd in the late '40s. Jim Boyd worked as Bill's substitute director when the boss was otherwise occupied; during the late '40s and early '50s he formed his own group, the Men Of The West, adding a catchy hillbilly-boogie sound to the western swing mix. Bill Boyd recorded into the early '50s. By the middle of the decade, however, both brothers gave up their long-running live-music radio show and became DJs. Bill died in 1977 and Jim in 1993.

⊙ **Under The Double Eagle** (1990; RCA). This single-CD collection has 9 cuts each from Bill Boyd And His Cowboy Ramblers and Milton Brown And His Musical Brownies. A shame it has fallen out-of-print so quickly.

⊙ **Western Swing, Honky Tonk, And Blues Favorites** (1995; Bronco Buster). Boyd songs show up on several western swing compilations, and this excellent CD includes 2 from his postwar period—the Jenny Lou Carson song "You Laughing Up Your Sleeve" and the Noel Boggs instrumental "Southern Steel Guitar" (recorded in 1947 and prominently featuring Boggs on steel). Adding to the disc's appeal are two Jim Boyd recordings, the silly but solidly rendered "Mule Boogie" and the fiddle-and-steel-fueled "Truck Driver's Boogie."

⊙ **Eyes Of Texas** (1998; Bronco Buster). This is a nice German-issue collection of 20 recordings Boyd and the Cowboy Ramblers cut from 1935 onward, including the sentimental "Tell My Why Daddy Won't Come Home," the silly "Poison Ivy," and the Spade Cooley hit "Shame On You."

Milton Brown And His Musical Brownies

Bandleader and vocalist Milton Brown was, along with Bob Wills, one of the creators of the western swing sound. The main reason he's not as well remembered and revered as his one-time musical partner Wills, however, is because

he was tragically killed when he was only thirty-two years old and just beginning to enjoy the thriving popularity of this new 'hot dance' music. Luckily for his admirers, Brown was a prolific artist and managed to lay down more than one hundred sides during a bright and promising career that lasted only a few short years.

Brown and Wills were actually good friends, having played together in the Light Crust Doughboys. Brown was the first to leave the Doughboys to start his own group, the Musical Brownies, which quickly became one of the most popular dance bands in Texas. Considering the musical innovations he introduced during that short time, the number of songs he recorded, and the fact that the Brownies were a hugely popular dance band—this man certainly had energy and drive to spare—there's little doubt that Brown, had he lived longer, would almost certainly have equaled the popularity of western swing's chief ambassador, Bob Wills.

Brown was born on 8 September, 1903 in Stephensville, Texas, a small town southwest of Forth Worth. The family eventually moved to Forth Worth when he was in his teens, a city he'd call home for the rest of his life. After graduating, Brown got a job as a cigar salesman, but the ambition to lead his own dance band had remained with him since childhood. One night in 1930 he attended a dance where the Wills Fiddle Band was playing. Perhaps he sensed his cigar-selling job was unstable (which was true as he'd eventually lose it), or perhaps he was completely taken by the music he heard; whatever the case he approached Wills and asked to sing one song. Before Brown knew it he was the group's new vocalist (Brown's brother Durwood also eventually joined).

The group first landed a radio gig sponsored by the Aladdin Lamp Company and named themselves the Aladdin Laddies. Their next sponsor was the Burrus Mill and Elevator Company, makers of Light Crust Flour. The group became the Light Crust Doughboys, with Burrus manager O'Daniel as their emcee, and by day they worked for the company. They had a popular radio show, played dances, and even recorded once in 1932 as the Fort Worth Doughboys, but soon it was all too clear the group's chief purpose was to sell flour. When later that year O'Daniel insisted they cut back on dances and play only on the radio, Brown quit.

And thank goodness he did, as he quickly formed the Musical Brownies and got down to some serious jamming. The band initially included his brother Durwood on guitar, fiddler Jesse Ashlock, bassist Wanna Coffman, and tenor banjoist Ocie Stockard. Later, pianist Fred Calhoun and fiddler Cecil Brower were added, both seasoned musicians, giving the group a bigger and more versatile sound. The instrumentation really fell into place when steel guitarist Bob Dunn joined the group. Dunn is generally acknowledged as the first country musician to amplify his instrument, and his electric steel guitar gave a new and biting edge to the band's repertoire of dance-oriented jazz and pop songs.

The Brownies' hot, swinging dance music struck a chord with people all over the state who were suffering through the Depression. The music was hot and loose, with a mixture of fiddle, piano and guitar playing, a Dixieland-style rhythm, Dunn's amplified steel and Brown's smooth lead vocals. They played familiar jazz tunes like "St. Louis Blues," sentimental ditties ("My Mary"), novelty songs ("Somebody's Been Using That Thing"), and steaming-hot Mexican-flavored numbers like "In El Rancho Grande." At his peak Brown's songs were wild, juicy and almost out of control—the instrumentalists firmly tethered to the rhythm, yet at the same time appearing to barely hang on.

The Brownies cut their first songs for Bluebird in 1934 and a year later switched to the newly formed US Decca label. By this time they were one of the biggest dance bands in the state, with Bill Boyd's Cowboy Ramblers, Roy Newman And His Boys, and the still-ticking Light Crust Doughboys as their chief competition (Wills' Texas Playboys had yet to really get off the ground). Brown's final session was in March of 1936, when the group recorded a whopping fifty songs with a line-up that this time included fiddler Cliff Bruner. A few weeks after this session Brown was involved in a fatal car crash. The wreck didn't kill him instantly, but he died of his injuries only days later.

Milton Brown And His Musical Brownies

Milton's brother Durwood kept the Brownies together for about a year, recording once more in 1937, but the momentum that was so strong at the time of Milton's death was lost. They eventually split up, and within a year Bruner, Stockard and Dunn had formed their own groups.

◉ **Country And Western Dance-O-Rama** (1955; Decca; reissued by Western). This reissue of an original 1955 Decca 10″ album is short but sweet, giving a quick taste of the Brownies at their peak. A fun and affordable item if you can find it.

⊙ **Under The Double Eagle** (1990; RCA). This single CD featuring 9 cuts each by Brown and fellow bandleader Bill Boyd was in print far too briefly.

⊙ **Complete Recordings Of The Father Of Western Swing** (1996; Texas Rose). A few single-album Brown collections were issued during the 1980s by Texas Rose, Charly and MCA, but all have unfortunately fallen out-of-print. Which leaves this 5-CD box set as the only Brown package currently available. It's a great one, mind you, so if you're into Brown and the classic western swing sound you won't be disappointed. Compiled by Brown biographer Cary Ginell, it includes all 102 Brownies sides for Bluebird and Decca plus the Fort Worth Doughboys recordings, the material Durwood Brown recorded in 1937, and a few later songs featuring Roy Lee Brown.

Cliff Bruner

Fiddler Cliff Bruner went from working alongside western swing pioneer Milton Brown to forming his own band, the Texas Wanderers, and cutting two early honky-tonk classics, "It Makes No Difference Now" (written by Floyd Tillman) and "Truck Driver's Blues" (by Ted Daffan). The former was a slow-paced down-and-outer, an unusual choice for a dance band. Though songs like this helped illustrate the transition from swing to honky tonk (it was also their best-selling number), the Texas Wanderers were primarily a western swing outfit with a typical mix of pop, blues and especially jazz in their sound. Key players like steel-guitar maestro Bob Dunn and pianist Moon Mullican helped the group rule the dance-band scene in Houston during the late 1930s.

Bruner was born in 1915 in Texas City, Texas, a Gulf Coast town just south of Houston. He started playing fiddle as a child, and in his teens he did some train-hopping, playing a dance or two wherever he could, before settling into a regular gig with a medicine show. By the time he was barely twenty years old Milton Brown had snapped him up to fiddle with his pioneering western swing group the Musical Brownies. Bruner was present for their final recording sessions in March 1936, helping the group lay down some fifty tracks.

When Brown was killed only a few weeks after those sessions, Bruner moved to Houston and put together his own group, the Texas Wanderers. By 1937 they'd signed with Decca and were one of the most popular bands in Houston and along the Gulf Coast. A year later they recorded the seminal "It Makes No Difference Now," a prototype honky-tonk weeper written by Floyd Tillman. At that point the band's impressive line-up included Dunn, Mullican, vocalist Dickie McBride, and mandolinist Leo Raley. Along with Dunn, Raley was one of the first to amplify his instrument, having had his guitar customized in honky-tonker Ted Daffan's radio repair shop. The amplification improved Raley's sound in large halls, and the fans ate it up.

In addition to running his own show, Bruner also played in McBride's band the Village Boys. Sharing bandmembers was common practice, and several of the Texas Wanderers played in each other's outfits—the Village Boys, Bob Dunn's Vagabonds, and so on. It's pretty confusing if you're trying to keep track, but it also reflects the fun, friendly, and sometimes silly nature of the music itself. Bruner recorded for Decca into the early '40s and then switched to the Ayo label. Though he'd quit playing professionally by the '50s, he continued to perform around the Houston area for many years.

◉ **Cliff Bruner's Texas Wanderers: Western Swing Music 1937–1944** (1983; Texas Rose). For several years Texas Rose was a dedicated western swing reissue label in the US. Unfortunately, this compilation of Bruner recordings was issued on LP only and has long since fallen out-of-print—as have most Texas Rose collections at this point. They're worth looking out for.

⊙ **Cliff Bruner And His Texas Wanderers** (1997; Bear Family). A 5-CD box of classic Bruner recordings that's probably more than the average western swing fan needs. Other than this, the only place to find Bruner's songs in print on CD are the various western swing compilations listed in the chapter introduction.

Amplified Steel

It comes as a surprise to many people that the deepest roots of the steel guitar in country music lie not in the American South but in the blue Pacific. Ninteenth-century Hawaiian musicians picked up the guitar from the Spanish and adapted it to their own taste, playing it flat on their laps and fretting it with a slide instead of their fingers. In the 1910s and '20s, recording and touring by Hawaiian musicians was tremendously popular throughout the continental US, and it wasn't long before hillbilly musicians like Jimmie Tarlton and Cliff Carlisle began imitating what they heard and saw.

It's probably impossible to determine who the first person was to mount an electric pick-up on a Hawaiian guitar, but **Bob Dunn** comes close. Milton Brown's Musical Brownies were one of the pioneering groups of the crazy mix of country fiddle tunes and hot jazz that eventually became known as western swing, and Dunn was a key member of the group. More than anyone else, Dunn furthered the initial spread of the amplified steel guitar in his recording and touring with Brown in the mid-'30s.

Not to be outdone, Brown's rival Bob Wills soon discovered a youngster with an unparalleled speed and dexterity on the amplified steel. **Leon McAuliffe** could play hot swing with the best of them, but he could also play sweet. Over the years, Wills' massive popularity

and steady work allowed him to hire the best, and he was to introduce many other fine players including Herb Remington, Noel Boggs and Joaquin Murphy.

As the instrument became a mainstay of western acts, its sound also took hold in southeastern country music and the Nashville mainstream. Country singers of all different styles began to rely on different steel players to give them a distinctive, signature sound. Eddy Arnold looked to Little Roy Wiggins, whose famous 'ting-a-ling' style dripped Hawaiian sweetness and closely matched Arnold's warm, smooth voice. Hank Williams, on the other hand, found his musical soulmate in the harsh, bluesy tone and high, keening simplicity of Don Helms.

Meanwhile, in California, the next revolution in steel guitar was brewing. **Speedy West**, the flashy, flamboyant virtuoso whose brilliant '50s work with guitarist Jimmy Bryant marked one of the highest points in instrumental country music, began fooling around with using foot pedals to bend the pitch of the strings. Custom guitar companies like Bigsby and Fender studied Speedy's experiments and began to manufacture the new pedal steel guitars. In 1954, Nashville musician Bud Isaacs played one on Webb Pierce's monster hit "Slowly." The sound caught on, and the revolution was complete: the pedal steel had arrived.

Don Helms adapted brilliantly to the new instrument, playing the crying chords heard on many of Ray Price's classic '50s hits. **Pete Drake** arrived on the studio scene and helped to define the Nashville sound of the late '50s, '60s and '70s (he also contributed "incredibly strange" experiments like his series of "talking steel guitar" records). On the west coast, **Ralph Mooney** created a rolling chord style in his work with singer Wynn Stewart that became a signature of the Bakersfield sound of the '60s. And the great **Lloyd Green**'s distinctive tumbling, descending licks helped to make Johnny Paycheck's early recordings for the Little Darlin' label shine.

For sheer dexterity, virtuosity and musical acumen, however, it would be hard to beat **Buddy Emmons**. Emmons hit the scene in the mid-'50s with Little Jimmie Dickens and went on to work for some of the best touring bands of the era, including Ernest Tubb's Texas Troubadours and Ray Price's Cherokee Cowboys. His varied career included forming his own guitar company, recording an album of straightahead jazz, and eventually moving to LA where his studio work graced the recordings of artists as varied as Ray Charles and Henry Mancini.

Pete Drake

—Tom Armstrong

Spade Cooley

> "We used to finish a dance with Spade and then get in the car and they'd take us to what they called a Swing Shift dance. It'd be like three in the morning. It took a rugged constitution."
>
> —Carolina Cotton,
> member of Spade Cooley's orchestra

Cheery-faced bandleader and fiddler Spade Cooley may not have been the "King of Western Swing", but he was certainly the cream of the West Coast bandleaders. He led a massive western swing orchestra that was likely the biggest group in all of country music, and his popularity during the postwar era in ballrooms up and down California was matched only by Wills' Texas Playboys.

Cooley took western swing's concept of sophistication a few steps further. The Hollywood socialite and his orchestra were nowhere near as rowdy and loose around the edges as the great Texas swing bands of the 1930s; Cooley perfected a smoother, cooler, and in many ways slicker sound that was far more orchestrated than the music of Wills or Brown. The electric guitar tone, for instance, had a rounder sound, the strings were denser and arranged in a 'section' compared to the bright twin-fiddle sound of the Texas Playboys. Fronted by Tex Williams, songs like "Shame On You" and "You'll Rue The Day" professed a gentle, easygoing atmosphere, but always maintained just enough rhythmic energy to keep folks spinning on the dance floor. In his heyday Cooley's music was pleasant and engaging, and he proved himself a master at straddling the divide between the world of the factory workers (he played many late-night 'swing shift' dances in LA) and the classy vibe of LA's uptown and celebrity crowds.

Donnell Clyde Cooley was born on 17 December, 1910 in Grand, Oklahoma, his family soon moving west to Oregon and years later resettling in Modesto, California. Spade, who'd been classically trained on violin as a child, played occasional gigs and worked a little in LA as a movie extra. He eventually became a Roy Rogers stand-in, which led to membership of Roy's touring band as a fiddler. He also performed with Foy Willing's Riders Of The Purple Sage and with Cal Shrum. His biggest break came in the early '40s when he was hired to fiddle in Jimmy Wakely's band. The singing cowboy star eventually turned the band over to Cooley, who expanded on the already large line-up by hiring three fiddlers and three vocalists, one of them Tex Williams. Definitely the standout crooner of the bunch, Williams added a beautifully warm western glow.

During the World War II era, when swing dance music was just reaching its peak (thanks in part to the large numbers of Southern California defense-plant employees who crowded the dance halls after work), Cooley's reputation soared. He shifted his operation's home base between the Venice Pier, Riverside Rancho, and Santa Monica ballrooms, and wherever he went he drew thousands of fans. Cooley signed first to OKeh Records in 1945, who released his #1 hit "Shame On You," then switched to Columbia in 1946. Later that same year Cooley, in a fit of arrogance, fired Williams for supposedly demanding too much money; when the smooth stylist left to form his own group he took many of Cooley's bandmembers with him. Spade responded by hiring a new crew and creating an orchestra that was bigger than ever.

In 1947 Cooley's popularity increased again as a result of movie appearances and the television show *The Hoffman Hayride* which he hosted. He signed with Decca in 1950 and his hit singles continued. By the late '50s, however, his career, once so successful, was on the wane. Western swing itself was drifting out of popularity (Cooley's orchestra had already been moving in a more Lawrence Welk-ish direction), and on top of that Cooley had a series of heart attacks. His television show was cancelled, his marriage began to crumble, and one of his business ventures—an entertainment complex in the Mojave Desert called Winter Wonderland—was faltering.

In 1961, liquored to the gills and burning mad with lewd fantasies that his wife was having affairs and looking to join a sex cult, Spade beat Ella Mae to death in their home outside Bakersfield. As if that wasn't enough, he forced their fourteen-year-old daughter Melody to watch. He was sentenced to life imprisonment on the strength of Melody's testimony. He turned out to be a model prisoner, and in 1969 he was given a three-day furlough to perform at a sheriff's benefit in Oakland, California. After receiving a standing ovation he walked backstage, was suddenly struck with another heart attack, and died on the spot.

⊙ **Spadella: The Essential Spade Cooley** (1994; Columbia/Legacy). This 20-track CD highlights Spade's recordings for OKeh and Columbia from his mid-1940s heyday (both before and after the departure of Tex Williams). Polished on the surface, but lively as hell

Spade Cooley And His Orchestra

underneath, with accordions, fiddles and steel guitars popping in from all sides.

⊙ **Shame On You** (1999; Bloodshot Revival/Soundies). Twenty-five previously unreleased radio transcriptions from the mid-1940s—instrumentals that skip and fly at a ready clip as well as ballads featuring the great Tex Williams, whose lead voice is as warm, rich and soothing as buttered rum. It's similar turf to SPADELLA, and, while the sound isn't quite as crisp, the spirit and tone are slightly looser.

Adolph Hofner

"A man ain't no better than his rhythm section."

—J.R. Chatwell,
fiddler in Hofner's band

Western swing evolved out of a huge mishmash of musical sources, among them the Bohemian polka music of the German and Czech communities that have been a part of Texas culture since the 1800s. Of all the western swing greats, south Texan Adolph Hofner is probably the bandleader who best exemplifies this particular heritage. Over a more than fifty-year career, Adolph Hofner And His San Antonians (who've also been known as His Texans, His Orchestra, and the Pearl Wranglers) have divided their time between western swing, polka music, and country music, all of it buttered with Hofner's smooth lead vocals. Hofner's music has always been anything but straightforward, his influences dripping into one another constantly—which is a big part of what makes his music so enticing.

Adolph Hofner was born on 8 June, 1916 in Moulton, Texas, a small town halfway between San Antonio and Houston. He had a German-Czech heritage, which meant he spoke Czech around the house and also listened to plenty of polka, but he also had a fondness for Hawaiian guitar music and the vocal stylings of both Bing Crosby and Jimmie Rodgers. As teenagers Adolph and his brother Emil, on guitar and steel respectively, played the San Antonio nightclubs. When Adolph heard the music of Milton Brown, he knew the direction he wanted to take. Brown's singing, the full band sound, and the fact that dance music was a potential moneymaker added up to a very attractive musical prospect.

In 1935 Adolph joined bandleader Jimmie Revard to form the Oklahoma Playboys, a group also based in San Antonio. He performed regularly and recorded sessions with them, playing guitar and singing lead (with brother Emil alongside him on steel), but he also appeared under his own name as well. He began recording as Adolph Hofner And His Texans in the late '30s and early '40s (for Bluebird, OKeh and Columbia), leaving Revard's group behind in order to go it alone full-time. Emil (who also went by the name of "Bash" Hofner) joined him once again.

Hofner enjoyed a fair amount of success in Texas and also in California, where he moved for a time during World War II (changing his name to Dolph or "Dub" Hofner for obvious reasons) to catch the western swing wave that rolled up and down the West Coast during the '40s. Later in the decade he settled back in Texas and also began playing a lot more polka music—thanks in large part to a polka craze that spread across the US during the postwar period. He'd played a bit of polka and even some Hawaiian-style music with Revard, but it was during the late '40s and '50s that the diversity and full potential of Hofner and his group truly revealed itself. From one gig to the next the San Antonians shifted focus from swing to country to polka without blinking, Hofner singing in Czech as well as English. If their recordings are any indication, they were having as much fun as possible. In 1949 Hofner nabbed Pearl Beer as a sponsor and changed the name of his group to the Pearl Wranglers (a common practice at the time, though these days a band would certainly lose face). Regular fixtures on the Texas dance hall scene from then on, Hofner and his group (whether Wranglers, Texans, or San Anto-

nians) have continued to play steadily well into the '90s.

⊙ **South Texas Swing** (1980; Arhoolie). An excellent collection of early Hofner cuts from the 1930s and '40s, some with Revard but most with various incarnations of his own group. There's even a Pearl Beer radio spot tacked on the end. Great stuff.

Hot Club Of Cowtown

An Austin, Texas band, Hot Club Of Cowtown is one of the most authentic western swing outfits to emerge since Asleep At The Wheel hit the scene a quarter-century ago. The playing is lively and exciting and the music fresh—which is a key for a band that could otherwise be filed away as 'retro' and passed over. At the group's core are guitarist Whit Smith, fiddler Elana Fremerman and bassist Billy Horton who've been playing together as a trio since December, 1997. Smith is a New Englander who met Kansas native Fremerman in New York City when he was forming a much larger swing band, the Western Caravan. After the band split, the two moved around a bit before landing in Austin, where they met Horton, a native Texan.

The Hot Club Of Cowtown's sound is unmistakably western swing with its hot fiddling, jazzy arrangements, danceable rhythms and a repertoire that mixes Tin Pan Alley songs with Bob Wills and Spade Cooley numbers. The arrangements are tastefully streamlined to fit the trio, though accordion, piano, steel guitar and a second fiddle (played by Texas Playboys alumnus Johnny Gimble) do add color and texture to the group's debut album. The sound isn't huge but it sure is tasty.

⊙ **Swingin' Stampede** (1998; High Tone). A promising debut from a group that brings a fresh and exciting edge to a traditional Texas-brand western swing sound. These three can really play—they don't need fancy western outfits to get your attention. Songs include classic sentimental numbers like "Silver Dew On The Blue Grass Tonight," alongside the great western swing standard "Sweet Jennie Lee" and others by Bob Wills, Johnny Gimble (who adds his fiddling to 4 of the songs), and Spade Cooley.

⊙ **Tall Tales** (1999; High Tone). The Hot Club dishes up 4 original songs on their sophomore CD (produced

Adolph Hofner • Hot Club Of Cowtown

by Dave Stuckey, formerly of the cool Dave And Deke Combo), and they fit well alongside vintage titles like Pee Wee King's "Bonaparte's Retreat," Bob Wills' "I Laugh When I Think How I Cried Over You," and the classic fiddle tune "Sallie Gooden." This is straight-up stuff from a hot trio that likes to laugh but isn't just fooling around.

Pee Wee King And The Golden West Cowboys

"Few entertainers have done more to define the look and sound of modern country music."

—Bill Malone

Pee Wee King is the main man behind the song "Tennessee Waltz," a dreamy-sweet number (despite being a song about a guy ripping off his best friend's gal) that he and his band, the Golden West Cowboys, first recorded in 1947. Thanks to a pop version by Patti Page released soon after, the song became a goldmine for its composers, King and his regular vocalist Redd Stewart, and for its publisher, the Nashville-based Acuff-Rose. Recorded again and again by all sorts of singers, "Tennessee Waltz" went on to sell many millions of copies over the years, rivaling Jimmie Davis' "You Are My Sunshine" as the most valuable song in country music. King's romantic little ditty wasn't single-handedly responsible for Nashville becoming the centerpoint of the country music industry, but it was about as significant as any single piece of music could have been.

King's music was not easily categorized. Despite his western outfits and the name of his band, he himself was no trail-riding, rye whiskey-slugging cowboy. He was a milk-fed accordion player from Wisconsin, and he grew up with far more polka in his blood than anything 'western.' Of course, mid-western roots had never stopped a singing cowboy before—think of Ohio native Roy Rogers. King was never a singing cowboy per se, but he did pick up a western aura from his days working alongside Gene Autry—and from the fact that cowboys were simply the 'in' thing during the '30s. When he joined the *Grand Ole Opry* later in 1937, he was one of the very first to bring cowboy style to that decidedly southern hillbilly showcase. He also brought a new degree of organization and profes-sional showmanship to the show, something that had more in common with the big western swing bands in Texas than the mountain string bands of east Tennessee.

King and his Cowboys were best known for gently swaying tunes, many featuring the warm, glowing voice of Redd Stewart (whom he hired in 1940 and who took the lead vocal spot formerly occupied by Eddy Arnold and Cowboy Copas). When Stewart did step front and center, he ended up singing on King's most popular cuts in the late '40s and early '50s including "Tennessee Waltz," "Slow Poke" (#1 for King on both the country and pop charts), "Bonaparte's Retreat," "Changing Partners," and "Bimbo." The pair also wrote together frequently. King wasn't all schmaltz, however: other titles he recorded include the more up-tempo "Birmingham Bounce," "Quit Honkin' That Horn," "Keep Them Icy Cold Fingers Off Of Me," "The Red Deck Of Cards," "Bull Fiddle Boogie," and even "Blue Suede Shoes."

Pee Wee King was also one of the first *Opry* stars to emerge not from the South but the Midwest. He was born Julius Frank Kuczynski in 1914 in Milwaukee, Wisconsin. His father played in a polka band, the Midnight Four, and soon young Julius joined him. He picked up the fiddle, harmonica and finally the accordion and also spent time memorizing cowboy and pop songs he heard on the radio. When Kuczynski was a teenager Gene Autry heard him and hired him to play accordion in his group. For clarity's sake he gave Kuczynski, the shortest player in the band, his nickname.

King moved with Autry to a radio job in Louisville, Kentucky in 1934. When Autry departed for Hollywood, King worked briefly with Frankie More's Log Cabin Boys before forming his own group, the Golden West Cowboys. The sound he developed was tightly arranged and more uptown in sound than the average hillbilly string bands of the day. It wasn't jazzed-up dance music à la western swing bandleaders such as Bob Wills and Milton Brown, but showcased instead a sophisticated pop-western sound similar to that which Louise Massey and the Westerners were developing about the same time. (Massey's big hit was the smooth romantic tune "My Adobe Hacienda," a precursor to "Tennessee Waltz.")

Wanting to get more involved in television, King left the *Opry* after a decade and turned his attention once again to Louisville, where he landed his own weekly television and radio shows. His TV exposure later expanded to Chicago, Cincinnati and other cities. He remained a popular figure on TV and radio, and as a touring act, well into the '60s. In 1965, "Tennessee Waltz" became the official state song of Tennessee, and during the '70s King was inducted first into the Nashville Songwriters Hall of Fame and finally, in 1974, into the Country Music Hall of Fame.

⊙ **Rompin' Stompin' Singin' Swingin'** (1983; Bear Family). A manageable, single-LP collection of up-tempo King material including "Birmingham Bounce," "The Ghost And Honest Joe," "Keep Them Icy Cold Fingers Off Of Me," "I Hear You Knockin'," "Mop Rag Boogie," and "Juke Box Blues."

⊙ **Pee Wee King And His Golden West Cowboys** (1995; Bear Family). If you're seriously into Pee Wee's music, check out this massive 6-CD box set of his recordings.

⊙ **Pee Wee King's Country Hoedown** (1999; Bloodshot Revival/Soundies). Considering how popular and influential a bandleader he was during the 1940s and '50s, it's sure been slim pickings when it comes to King material in today's CD bins. Which makes this double-disc collection a blessing. King, vocalist Redd Stewart, and the rest of the Golden West Cowboys cut these 51 songs for Standard Transcriptions in 1952. Great stuff that really hops and swings. A bonus feature are the detailed liner notes by country historian Bill Malone.

Louise Massey And The Westerners

Louise Massey wasn't strictly a cowgirl singer in the manner of Patsy Montana, nor was she a Bob Wills-type bandleader either, despite a leaning towards swing. The music she played with her band, the Westerners, may not be simple to categorize; what is certain, however, is Massey's importance as one of the few female western music stars of the music's first few decades.

Massey had a smooth and slightly dusky voice, and her stylish outfits, beautiful smile and knockout good looks gave the Westerners a glamorous appeal. Massey was also a songwriter, her most famous tune being "My Adobe Hacienda" (co-written with Lee Penny). A sentimental and gently romantic song celebrating the joys of home life, "My Adobe Hacienda" was covered by all sorts of country and pop singers during the 1940s, from Pee Wee King to Bob Wills to the Dinning Sisters.

The music of Massey and the Westerners fits somewhere between cowboy and cowgirl tunes ("Home On The Range," "I Only Want A Buddy [Not A Sweetheart]") and swinging pop numbers ("Gals Don't Mean A Thing [In My Young Life]," featuring lead vocals by younger brother Curt Massey), though their repertoire was wide open and included polkas, waltzes and quite a few Mexican songs (the Masseys had learned Spanish as children). The band had the standard guitar, banjo and fiddle but also featured swing-oriented instruments like the clarinet; each of the members, in fact, could play more than one instrument. The Westerners may have given their music a sophisticated flair, but at the same time they brought a distinct southwestern flavor to the world of hillbilly and western music, thanks to their upbringing in rural New Mexico.

Massey herself dressed the part of a stylish southwestern star—her boots were made of satin, her cowgirl outfits adorned in beads and sequins. Whoever called her "the original rhinestone cowgirl" was definitely an astute publicist.

Unlike many singing cowboys and cowgirls of the era, Victoria Louise Massey had authentic western roots—she was born on 10 August, 1902 in Hart County, Texas. Her father, a fiddler as well as a rancher, moved the family to rural New Mexico when she was still a child. Louise learned to rope and ride, but she also learned to play piano and sing. Together with their father, Louise and her younger brothers Curt and Allen formed a family band (which later included Louise's new husband Milt Mabie) and played mainly for fun. That is, until a local talent scout got to see them. First they toured the US and Canada, after which they landed a radio gig in Kansas City and began calling themselves the Westerners. Papa Massey eventually went back to New Mexico, leaving Louise, Milt, Curt, and Allen to their newfound

trayed in Massey's signature song. Massey died in 1983. Her brother Curt went on to become, among other things, musical director of the *Beverly Hillbillies* TV show, even writing the theme song.

⊙ **Swing West** (1997; Bronco Buster). A collection of the Massey and family's 1940s recordings including "Rancho Grande," "I'm Thinking Tonight Of My Blue Eyes," "I Only Want A Buddy (Not A Sweetheart)," and of course "My Adobe Hacienda."

Hank Penny

A popular bandleader first in the Southeast and later on the California dance-hall circuit, Hank Penny was an anomaly—a western swing artist who emerged from the Deep South and earned his chops east of the Mississippi. When he formed his first group, the Radio Cowboys in 1936, he modeled them on the Musical Brownies and their pioneering bandleader Milton Brown. Penny's career didn't stop when that band broke up, and a decade later he had moved to California and become a popular bandleader on the West Coast live music scene. Penny's friendly, laid-back vocal approach, coupled with his keen sense of humor, was instantly appealing, and it lent itself not only to some excellent western swing recordings but also to work as a DJ and comedy performer.

Hank was born Herbert Clayton Penny on 18 September, 1918 in Birmingham, Alabama. He played on a local station as a teenager and later moved to New Orleans, where he was first turned on to the music of Brown and Bob Wills. Returning to Birmingham, he formed the Radio Cowboys with fiddler Sheldon Bennett (who'd later join the Hi-Flyers), banjoist Louis Dumont, bassist Carl Stewart, and steel guitarist Sammy Forsmark. A year later they cut their first sides for ARC with producer Art Satherley who was working with Bob Wills at the time and knew

Louise Massey and the Westerners

career. Louise was the group's chief vocalist and front person, but Curt sang a few on his own, too, and the rest of them shared instrumental duties. By 1933 the Westerners were regulars on the WLS *National Barn Dance* (arriving the same year as Patsy Montana and just in time to share the airwaves with Gene Autry, who was still a year away from his Hollywood debut).

Louise and the Westerners left Chicago in 1936 for New York City, landing a weekly show on NBC called *The Log Cabin Dude Ranch*. Hillbilly music still lacked respect in the urban world, but western music like that of the Westerners (along with cowboy singers like Tex Ritter and Texas Jim Robertson) helped open the doors for country in cities like New York. After this they headed west to Hollywood, appearing in a few movies before returning to Chicago. Ironically, in the late '40s, just when Massey had earned a national reputation via her song "My Adobe Hacienda" (which made it to the pop charts), she and Milt decided to retire. The couple returned to New Mexico, determined to enjoy the home life ("soft desert stars and the strum of guitars") so pleasantly por-

something about western swing. The session produced a couple of hot Penny originals, "Flamin' Mamie" and "Back Up A Little Bit" ("I'm stepping right in to tear your little playhouse down"). In 1939 the Radio Cowboys moved to Atlanta's Crossroads Follies, and Penny replaced Forsmark with steel guitarist Noel Boggs, and brought fiddler Boudleaux Bryant on board. (Bryant and his wife Felice would go on to be country's top songwriting couple, penning "Bye Bye Love" and "Rocky Top" among many others.) An audition for the *Opry* was unsuccessful, but Penny and the band continued to cut records with Satherley. Titles include "It Ain't Gonna Rain No Mo," an old Tin Pan Alley ditty that Penny revved right up; "All Night And All Day Long," which starts out with him peeping through the keyhole at his baby's house and finding "another mule in my stall;" and the sweet "Won't You Ride In My Little Red Wagon," which became his theme song.

With the outbreak of World War II, the Radio Cowboys split up, though Penny did assemble Stewart and some others for a final session with Satherley in 1941. After that, he was employed as a DJ in Atlanta before moving to Cincinnati, where he began an association first with WLW and later with King Records. Merle Travis, however, convinced Penny the time was right to move to California, and in the mid-'40s he made the leap. He led bands at the Venice Pier and Riverside Rancho ballrooms, among others, and formed a band, the Penny Serenaders. He also continued to record for

King, including such kooky songs as "Get Yourself A Redhead" and "My Inlaws Made An Outlaw Out Of Me." In 1950 one of his compositions, "Bloodshot Eyes" ("don't roll those bloodshot eyes at me"), a catchy misogynist ditty that blues shouter Wynonie Harris later recorded, climbed high in the charts.

During the late '40s Penny became involved in the nightclub business, and in 1950 he co-founded LA's famous Palomino. He continued to play and record (for RCA Victor and Decca) in the '50s, but he worked regularly as a DJ and was smitten with television (he even briefly had his own show). He had also set his sights more on comedy, an interest that had been evident since the '30s. One of his most classic novelty recordings has to be "The Freckle Song" ("she's got freckles on her butt," Penny sings, "she's nice").

Penny was a regular at the Golden Nugget in Las Vegas during the late '50s, and later tried out for *Hee-Haw* but didn't make the grade. He continued in his later years, as he pretty much had all his life, to move from city to city and coast to coast, and he finally settled in Southern California. He died of a heart attack in 1992.

⦿ Tobacco State Swing (1980; Rambler). It's a real shame that no decent Hank Penny compilation is currently available. The only Penny collection so far has been this LP, and it's sadly out-of-print. If you can find it, though, you'll be treated to 14 songs Penny recorded with the Radio Cowboys between 1938–1941, including "Back Up A Little Bit," "Mama's Getting Young," and his initial recording of "Won't You Ride In My Little Red Wagon."

⊙ **Smile And Jive: Kings Of Western Swing** (1997; Charly). This excellent British-issue double-CD western swing compilation contains 5 Penny cuts, 2 from his early days with the Radio Cowboys ("Chill Tonic," "Peach Tree Shuffle") and King recordings from the mid-1940s: "Talkin' Bout You," "Flamin' Mamie," and "These Wild Wild Women."

⊙ **Hollywood Western Swing: The Best Of Hank Penny (1944–1947)** (1999; Krazy Kat). Twenty-six cuts Penny made for the King label, including "Back Up A Little Bit," "Texas In My Soul," "Wildcat Mama," "My Inlaws Made An Outlaw Out Of Me," and "Get Yourself A Redhead."

Hank Penny

Hank Penny

Jimmie Revard And His Oklahoma Playboys

J immie Revard and His Oklahoma Playboys hit the south Texas dance-hall scene when western swing was just stepping out into the limelight. They quickly became one of the biggest draws in the San Antonio area, rivaled only by the Tune Wranglers (who shared several bandmembers). The Oklahoma Playboys didn't last long—their heyday was the mid- to late 1930s, after which point they pretty much dissolved—but the recordings they've left behind were substantial and hold up well.

The group's bandleader was James Revard, who was born on 26 November, 1909 in Pawhuska, Oklahoma. His father, who was a fiddler, moved the family to the San Antonio area when Jimmie was a child, and despite the group's name it's here that the Oklahoma Playboys were based. Jimmie had first played fiddle but eventually switched to bass, a choice later reflected in his group's emphasis on a strong, dance-friendly rhythm. (On "It's My Time Now" and the lively "Oh! Swing It," for instance, the piano, guitar, bass and banjo play almost in unison creating a tight and steady beat.) It was a full band sound— one inspired by jazz bandleaders like Benny Goodman and created by a variety of instruments, not just fiddle and guitar—that Revard wished to develop when he began forming the Oklahoma Playboys in the mid-'30s. The story has it that he happened upon his initial recruits, brothers Adolph (guitar and lead vocals) and Emil Hofner (steel

Dirty Swing

Like any other music, western swing reflected the mores and attitudes of the musicians and their fans set against the social backdrop of the day. At the same time that this raucous hybrid of jazz, blues, hillbilly, and everything else was shaping up, the country also happened to be immersed in the Depression. The nation's economic impotency thus threatened the virility of the millions of unemployed laborers, and these feelings came to be expressed in western swing through endearing, boastful songs of abnormal male sexuality. With that chug-chug beat that no doubt inspired chugging of another sort (and not always with one's mate), male braggadocio and all manner of sexual innuendo were right at home.

Doing it once was just not enough. In Bob Wills' "Four Or Five Times," Tommy Duncan matter-of-factly suggests to his girl dropping by to "do things right" a few times that evening. One gal is not always enough, either: Milton Brown's "Easy Ridin' Papa" needs seven to stay healthy. After Brown's death his band backed Jimmie Davis who, before coming up with "You Are My Sunshine" and pursuing a political career, crooned the ditty "High-Geared Daddy"and suggested that his woman feel his knee and thigh, "but if you feel my thigh you better ride me high." Of course, you need the corresponding equipment. In the version of "Pipeliner Blues" by Cliff Bruner's Texas Wanderers, vocalist Moon Mullican sings about laying pipe all day long and then coming home to his mean mama where he no doubt laid it there, too. And Daddy sure liked variety. Jimmie Revard, with the encouragement of a delightfully naughty steel guitar solo from Emil Hofner, imagines himself an ever-lovin', aggravatin', cookie-pushin' "Cake Eatin' Man."

Naturally enough, other songs were equally obsessed with and grateful for "that thing." It's clear when the Tune Wranglers sing "It makes me laugh and it makes me sing, give it to me mama, I'm wild about that thing" what the source of all that pleasure is. "That thing" isn't always available, either. The Brownies express such frustrations in "Somebody's Been Using That Thing" (underscored with Bob Dunn's wild steel guitar solo after the first verse—was it that limber, wild, flexible instrument that encouraged all this carrying on?). The subject of the Light Crust Doughboys' "Pussy, Pussy, Pussy" appears to be a stray feline; the owner does find one, but it doesn't smell like his, and, well ... enough said.

The Modern Mountaineers summed it all up when they had the brilliance to deduce that "Everybody's Truckin'." The folks in Harlem are doin' it, everybody's doin' it now, and against a great swinging beat vocalist Smokey Wood slurs "truckin'" to such a degree that it sounds like he's saying something else. It was a little too much back in 1937, as the record got yanked off many a jukebox in Texas.

Such songs—a mere smidgen of western swing's dirty ditties—are classics in their own way, taking their rightful places alongside the genre's innocent love songs, blues tunes and great instrumentals. In these modern times, their misogynist message may inspire a comment or two from some. The rest of us, however, can be grateful for their existence—for documenting the times, expressing a little innocent fun, and providing irresistible music that was great for dancing ... and other things, too.

—Brian Gordon

guitar), when they were playing at a drive-in restaurant in Laredo. Other bandmembers followed, and by 1936 the group had recorded its first sessions for the Bluebird label.

Along with the Tune Wranglers, the Oklahoma Playboys were one of the top groups in south Texas during the late '30s. Their heyday was short-lived, however. In 1938 Revard tried moving the group to a new home base on a Pittsburgh, Kansas radio station, but this didn't last very long. By the end of the year the band was disbanding, with several players joining a new group led by Adolph Hofner. Revard recorded again in 1940, but this time without his former bandmates. He joined the San Antonio police force and continued playing in various local outfits for the next several decades.

⊙ **South Texas Swing** (1980; Arhoolie). This is an Adolph Hofner collection, but it does include 5 tasty Jimmie Revard cuts with Hofner on lead vocals. One of the most unusual (and most beautiful) is "Star Kovarna," a laid-back waltz recorded in 1936 and credited to Jimmie Revard's band that's a curious multicultural mix of fiddle, Hawaiian-style steel guitar, a simple and slow rhythm, and Adolph and Emil Hofner's mournful harmony vocals (sung in Czech).

⊙ **Smile And Jive: Kings Of Western Swing** (1997; Charly). Revard and the Oklahoma Playboys have 2 songs on this excellent 2-CD compilation, "It's A Long Way To Tipperary" and the jazzed-up "Oh! Swing It," recorded in 1938 and featuring Revard on clarinet and lead vocals (Adolph Hofner was busy recording his own session that same day).

Hank Thompson

"I believed in the band dressing in colorful outfits. It was showbiz, so let's be showbiz people."

—Hank Thompson

Hank Thompson And The Brazos Valley Boys were the last of the great western swing bands to sweep the nation at the tail end of the music's golden era. Songs like "Whoa Sailor," "The Wild Side Of Life," "A Six Pack To Go," "Where Is The Circus," and "Smoky The Bar" were appealing mixes of good-natured humor, catchy melodies and rhythms that catered to rooms full of dancers. Western swing may have been on the way out before he was even ten years into his career, but that didn't seem to faze Thompson, who hit the fifty-year mark as a recording artist and bandleader in the mid-1990s.

Thompson managed to make a long and prosperous career out of a music he dubbed 'honky tonk swing'—a little brighter and sharper than the typical western swing sound of the '40s. One key factor to his success was his decision to take his band to nightclubs and ballrooms all over the US, not just around western swing's home turf of Texas, Oklahoma and California. Another important element was better sound quality. When he was getting started, the sound and electrical systems in many of the smaller clubs he played were, in his words, "pathetically inadequate." He'd trained as an electrical engineer during his college years (including a stint at Princeton) and in the Navy, and this helped him quickly figure out ways to devise a quality portable light and sound system for touring.

As a songwriter, Thompson's trademarks were clever wordplays and lively melodies. In songs like "Humpty Dumpty Heart," "A Six Pack To Go," and "How Cold-Hearted Can You Get" ("I know that you'd be satisfied if I took strychnine and croaked"), he took on subjects like bitter heartaches and hard drinking and livened them up with a good-natured spin. His songs had the essence of honky-tonk down-and-outers at their core, but Thompson's music was all about making people dance and smile, not drop their faces on the counter and sob.

While Thompson was clearly going for a clever and gently comic spin when he penned songs like "A Six Pack To Go," "Where Is The Circus," and "Mark Of A Heel," it's to his credit as a writer that none comes off as a mere novelty number—the sentiments are real, and their complexity gives his work life beyond a few simple chuckles. In "Where Is The Circus," for instance, a jilted lover thinks all the local townspeople are laughing at him ("Where is the circus?" he imagines them shouting, "Here comes the clown"). The fact that Thompson can communicate these disturbing emotions, yet at the same time keep listeners smiling with a witty turn of phrase and a solid melody—not to mention his warm voice—reveals precisely why he's long stood out from the pack as a songwriter.

Hank was born Henry William Thompson in Waco, Texas, on 3 September, 1925. As a teenager he performed on a local station as Hank The Hired Hand. A stint in the Navy during World War II enabled him to hone his skills as a writer, as he penned songs to entertain his buddies. When he returned he studied at Princeton, Southern Methodist Univesity, and the University of Texas at Austin. He began playing again on a Waco radio station and soon put together a band for some live gigs. They recorded a few songs for

Hank Thompson in Hollywood, 1953

some local labels; but when cowboy star Tex Ritter heard Thompson and told his label, Capitol, about him, Hank's career took a great leap forward.

Thompson's heyday on Capitol lasted from 1947–1965 (with guitarist Merle Travis playing on almost every session since the early '50s), and his many hits for the label included "Humpty Dumpty Heart," "Swing Wide Your Gate Of Love," "A Six Pack To Go," and the Jack and Woody Guthrie song "Oklahoma Hills." Of all his recordings, however, it was the 1952 song "The Wild Side Of Life" that really boosted his career. Written by William Warren and Arlie Carter, the song had been wildly popular on juke-boxes back in Texas in a version by Jimmy Heap and the Melody Masters. Thompson was initially wary of the song—as was his producer at Capitol, Ken Nelson—mostly because the melody was the

same as both "The Great Speckled Bird" (made famous by Roy Acuff) and "I'm Thinking Tonight Of My Blue Eyes" (a Carter Family standard). But since it had been so popular in Texas they tried it as a B-side. It soon shot to #1 and stayed there for fifteen weeks. The song gained legendary status soon after when Kitty Wells recorded an answer song, "It Wasn't God Who Made Honky Tonk Angels," which became one of the biggest-selling songs ever recorded by a female artist. The impact Wells made was so great, in fact, that record companies began paying more attention to women artists (among them Wanda Jackson, whose career Thompson personally helped get off the ground).

In the mid-'60s Thompson moved to Warner Brothers (for whom he recorded the crafty and frequently overlooked album WHERE IS THE CIRCUS) before jumping labels again to Dot, where he stayed for twelve years. Hits recorded during the '60s and '70s included "Mark Of A Heel," "He's Got A Way With Women" ("and he just got away with mine"), "The Older The Violin, The Sweeter The Music," and "On Tap, In The Can, Or In The Bottle." Many of these show Thompson and his producers experimenting with the Nashville Sound, but the songs themselves are frequently as strong as his '50s Capitol classics.

Though his hits had thinned out by the late '70s and '80s, he continued to maintain a heavy touring schedule and to record as often as a label would allow him. In 1997, Curb Records released the album HANK THOMPSON AND FRIENDS featuring Thompson alongside big-name duet partners like Vince Gill, George Jones and Lyle Lovett. By the time this album was released his career had run about as long as that of anyone else in country music—and remarkably, Thompson was still playing some one hundred concert dates every year.

⊙ **At The Golden Nugget** (1961; Capitol; reissued 1995; Liberty). This was the first live country album ever recorded by a single artist (not a group road show or barn dance compilation), and the sound quality is really pretty decent. As are the song choices: Thompson sings "Honky Tonk Girl" and "A Six Pack To Go" alongside covers of "Orange Blossom Special," "Lost Highway," and Merle Travis' "Nine Pound Hammer." Travis, by the way, is in the band on lead guitar.

⊙ **The Best of Hank Thompson, 1966–1979** (1996; Varese Sarabande). Don't stop at Thompson's 1940s and '50s Capitol material: these later recordings (especially the Warner Bros. and Dot singles) are excellent. Songs like "Where Is The Circus," "Smoky The Bar," "Mark Of A Heel," and "The Older The Violin, The Sweeter The Music" are still grounded in the same 'honky-tonk swing' as his earlier sides.

⊙ **Vintage Collections** (1996; Capitol). This collection's your best Hank Thompson starting point as it's here you'll find his all-time classics, from "Humpty Dumpty Heart" to "The Wild Side Of Life" to "A Six Pack To Go." Other gems include the talking blues-styled "Total Stranger" and the incredible "I Cast A Lonesome Shadow," which has got to be the darkest song Thompson ever recorded.

⊙ **Hank Thompson And Friends** (1997; Curb). Mixing new versions of his classics with brand-new material, this was one of the freshest and most traditional-sounding country records to come out of Nashville in years. Most of the songs are duets, and the star-studded list of Thompson's partners includes Vince Gill, George Jones, Lyle Lovett, Brooks & Dunn, Marty Stuart, David Ball and Kitty Wells. From new recordings of "A Six Pack To Go" and "Total Stranger" to brand-new songs like "Gotta' Sell Them Chickens" (with Junior Brown who's a near-perfect stylistic match to Thompson), this is no simple tribute album to a onetime great, it's a firm collection of big-boned country that stands on its own merits.

⊙ **Dance Ranch/Songs For Rounders** (1999; Koch). A single-CD package containing 2 full Thompson albums from 1958 and 1959 respectively. They don't contain his most classic singles, but they do catch the singer, songwriter and bandleader in his prime—and they work as albums, the songs moving one into another like a solid night at the Trianon Ballroom.

⊙ **Hank World** (1999; Bloodshot Revival/Soundies). A fine collection of 23 recordings from the early 1950s that Thompson made in his state-of-the-art home studio in Oklahoma City for the World Transcription Library, which were used only for radio broadcast. Includes lots of lesser-known Thompson originals like the forlorn "I Find You Cheatin' On Me" and the corny "California Women."

Tex Williams

Along with the orchestra led by his former boss, Spade Cooley, smooth-toned vocalist Tex Williams and his band the Western Caravan were one of the most popular western swing bands on the hopping California scene in the late 1940s. They were a stylish lot with a gentle but dance-friendly rhythm at their foundation and Williams' affable showmanship and wonderful voice out front. Williams was best known for "Smoke! Smoke! Smoke! (That Cigarette)," a catchy novelty song written by Merle Travis about the travails of nicotine addiction. Not only was it the group's first hit, it was the first million-seller for his label, the LA-based indie Capitol, which had jumped into the record business only a few years earlier. Williams followed up "Smoke!" with similarly styled talking-blues songs like "Wild Card," "Never Trust A Woman" (written by Jenny Lou Carson, in case you were wondering), "That's What I Like About The West," and "Suspicion." These folky narratives were full of good-natured spousal ribbing or warnings about shady characters and steeped in corny humor. That's all well and good, but Williams was actually at his best on more straightfoward ballads like "Won't You Ride In My Little Red Wagon," "Texas In My Soul," and "The Leaf Of Love," which focused rightfully on his soothing vocal style.

Tex was born Sollie Paul Williams on 23 August, 1917 in Ramsey, Illinois into a family of ten children. During his teens he sang on a local station and joined a band under the name Jack Williams before moving west to pick apples in Washington. He finally made it to Los Angeles in 1942, just in time for the western swing fever that was sweeping the state. He ended up as one of three vocalists in Spade Cooley's 'orchestra,' and his voice added depth and warmth to the group's already smooth western sound. He sang lead on some of Cooley's top hit singles, including "Shame On You" and "Detour," vocal performances that still stand as some of Williams' best. The band was initially based at the Venice Pier ballroom, and it was club owner Bert "Foreman" Phillips who gave Williams his nickname "Tex."

Cooley could turn nasty when drunk and was difficult to work with in any state. Capitol had offered Williams a chance to record on his own, which ticked off Cooley; in 1946 he fired the best singer he ever had. Most of Cooley's band followed Williams out the door. Almost immediately they regrouped as Tex Williams And His Western Caravan, and a month later they recorded their first session for Capitol. It took almost a year before the group had their first hit with "Smoke!", which became a country and even pop standard.

Williams and band toured the state regularly and even ventured across the nation, though their

Tex Williams And His Western Caravan

home base was LA's Riverside Rancho. Williams also became the first to suit up with tailor Nudie Cohen, who with his wife was then just working out of his garage. Williams soon told fellow bandleader Hank Thompson about Nudie, who was much cheaper than the popular tailor Nathan Turk, and from that point on word of Nudie's prowess spread like wildfire and country music never looked the same again.

The success of "Smoke!" left Williams concentrating on the talking-blues songs. When the hits stopped coming in the early '50s, Capitol dropped him. He signed up with RCA Victor and then Decca, but had no more hit songs. Finally in 1957 the Western Caravan split up. Williams turned his attention to his new nightclub, the Tex Williams Village in Newhall, California. During the '60s he recorded a live album for Liberty, TEX WILLIAMS AT THE MINT, and a few more for smaller labels. His final semi-hit song was "The Night Miss Nancy Ann's Hotel For Single Girls Burned Down" in 1971. Ironically, considering the subject of his biggest hit song, Williams died of lung cancer in 1985.

⊙ Vintage Collections (1996; Capitol). A decent sampling of Williams' Capitol material, most of it from the 1940s and early '50s. The majority of the songs (including "Smoke!" and the previously unreleased

"Brother, Drop Dead") are of the talking-blues variety. Though fun and certainly instrumentally sound, they tend toward novelty. Ballads like "The Leaf Of Love" and "I Got Texas In My Soul" are the songs that really show off the band's smooth style and Williams' stellar baritone voice.

Billy Jack Wills

"I thought our band was a lot like Bill Haley and the Comets. [Haley] just had better exposure."

—Tiny Moore

Bob Wills' youngest brother was overshadowed by his famous sibling to the point of becoming barely a footnote in the history of western swing. On the other hand the older Wills' success was certainly a great inspiration to young Billy Jack, allowing him to step into the industry gracefully and come of age without too great a struggle.

Billy Jack Wills was born in 1926 in Memphis, Texas, a small town in the Panhandle. By that year Bob (twenty-one years his senior) had already left home, and when Billy Jack was in his late teens "New San Antonio Rose" was high on the charts and Bob's national reputation was solid. Billy Jack first played in the band of another brother, Johnny Lee Wills, before joining the Texas Playboys after World War II as a bassist, drummer and vocalist. He wrote several songs for the Playboys including the lyrics to one of their best-known songs, "Faded Love."

Billy Jack formed his own band in 1952 and set up shop at Wills Point, the Sacramento, California nightclub owned by brother Bob. By the time he'd formed this group, however, western swing was beginning to fade from popularity and a stronger, louder sound was on the horizon. Billy Jack's music reflected this changing sentiment. His songs had familiar and still-prominent big-band elements like trumpet, fiddle and warm lead vocals (shared by Billy Jack and mandolinist Tiny Moore), but reflected the influence of honky tonk and especially R&B and also anticipated the coming rockabilly revolution by introducing harder rhythms, bigger drumbeats (with Billy Jack wielding the sticks) and the visceral steel playing of West Coast sensation Vance Terry into the foreground. Billy Jack's arrangements could still swing and sway like the good old days but the music had an exciting new edge.

The group tore up the Sacramento scene for a few years, packing Wills Point each weekend and also recording singles for MGM and Four Star

Los Angeles Dance Halls And Nightclubs

The big boom for live country music in Southern California—the golden heyday of sold-out dance jobs—came with World War II, and the whole shebang can be laid at the door of an ambitious Texas hustler known as Bert "Foreman" Phillips. Prior to Phillips, who alternated between radio DJ, personal management, booking agent and promoter duties, the rodeo and fair circuit was the mainstay for country and western performers, although the public could make the scene at numerous live radio broadcasts by the likes of Stuart Hamblen and the Beverly Hill Billies (who appeared barefoot and clad in rags). The Hollywood Barndance, adjacent to Grauman's Chinese Theater, featured a dance floor and all sorts of local hillbilly and string bands, but hardly set a trend for urban country venues.

After Phillips realized he could capitalize on the defense industry crowd, he began promoting his fabled Swing Shift dances at the Venice Pier in the summer of 1942, hiring bandleaders like Spade Cooley, Jimmy Wakely, Tex Williams, and later, Hank Penny (who tended towards elliptical jazz-style guitar solos, prompting Phillips to unceremoniously fire him and post a large backstage sign asking "Where's the melody?"). Business was phenomenal and in no time Phillips was promoting concurrent dances at both the Venice and Santa Monica piers, as well as Compton's Town Hall Ballroom, Culver City's Plantation and various venues from Long Beach to Baldwin Park. At the peak of these all-night dance events—Phillips ran five to seven at a time— he was using fourteen bands nightly, and was drawing crowds that ranged between five and seven thousand people on average. A correspondent from *Time* magazine visited when Bob Wills and the Texas Playboys were performing and expressed fears that the pier itself might collapse.

After the war, country nightclubs sprouted all over the area: Dave Ming's 97th Street Corral in South Central Los Angeles; the legendary Riverside Rancho in East Hollywood's Los Feliz district, top spot from the late '40s on, booking the likes of Hank Williams and home for years to the Squeakin' Deacon and Tex Williams Western Caravan radio shows; in the San Fernando Valley where cowboy star Hoot Gibson's Painted Post featured Capitol Records star Wesley Tuttle as bandleader and proudly bore the motto, "Where the sidewalk ends and the West begins."

But it was that feisty, jazz-bent Alabaman Hank Penny who opened the most notorious spot of all, the Palomino, in 1949. Located on North Hollywood's Lankershim Avenue, the Pal had one of the longest and most spectacular runs of any California country nitery. Booking local stars and national touring talent, Penny also instituted a Monday night jazz jam featuring the likes of Barney Kessel and Woody Herman, who dubbed Penny "the Hip Hick." At Penny's request, there was always a couple of undercover narco squad men from the LAPD's Van Nuys division to ensure no jazz cats were burning reefer.

None of these venues remains, although the decaying Palomino hung on until 1995. There is one hillbilly classic location intact, the Foothill Club, which opened in Long Beach adjacent Signal Hill in the mid-'50s, and regularly featured the likes of Wynn Stewart and Billy Mize. Almost every stick of furniture and fixture is original, as are the spectacular Western mural behind the bar and charmingly primitive oil portraits of Hank Thompson, Johnny Western, the Collins Kids, Cash, and Haggard. Unfortunately, the booking policy runs toward double-dipped rockabilly phonies, who provide a most pathetic coda for this once magnificent dance hall.

—Jonny Whiteside

Billy Jack Wills

along with some radio transcriptions. But after a while the crowds at the club started thinning out and the Billy Jack Wills band's short, but successful, run had come to an end. Bandmember Tiny Moore blamed televison. After that Bob Wills poached most of the bandmembers. Billy Jack made a few attempts to re-establish his musical foothold in northern California, and also worked on and off as a Texas Playboy again, but eventually retired from music altogether. He died in 1991. Tiny Moore went on to play with Merle Haggard and several ex-Playboys before his death in 1987. Vance Terry turned up the heat playing steel for Jimmie Rivers, who led the house band during the '50s and '60s at the still-surviving 23 Club in downtown Brisbane, California.

⊙ **Billy Jack Wills And His Western Swing Band** (1982; Western; reissued 1996; Joaquin). These 19 tracks are radio transcriptions recorded in Sacramento, California between 1952 and 1954. Thankfully they've been rescued and reissued by the Joaquin label. The songs are a mix of R&B, swing, and bopping jazz, and the heavy rhythm foundation and strong steel playing rock the room as hard as almost any western group did before rockabilly tore the pants off the unsuspecting.

Bob Wills And His Texas Playboys

"I can't think of a country artist we ever listened to and learned their tunes. We listened to Benny Goodman, Glenn Miller, Louis Armstrong ..."
—Leon McAuliffe

If any single person deserves to be considered the 'father' of western swing, it must be Bob Wills. Along with fellow bandleader (and former bandmate) Milton Brown, Wills was one of the originators of western swing in the early 1930s, and with his band of Texas Playboys he turned what was at first a regionally popular brand of 'hot dance' music, a hybrid form of 'Texas jazz,' into a phenomenon that swept the Southwest and, ultimately, the nation. His name came to be synonymous with western swing, and the evolution of the genre itself in many ways echoed the development of Wills' career. Thanks to his seemingly boundless energy as a bandleader and his undying belief in the musical style itself—to say nothing of his talents as a fiddler, songwriter, arranger and

spokesman—Wills is one of the true innovators in the history of country music, a man who has since earned legendary status.

If it wasn't for Wills, it's possible western swing would never have reached as widespread an audience as it ultimately did. When his 1940 recording of "New San Antonio Rose," a vocal version of one of his earliest compositions, became a major hit, western swing music jumped out of the southwestern dance-hall circuit and into the national consciousness. Wills had always considered his music 'western' and not 'country' (and definitely not 'hillbilly'). Yet the country mainstream did eventually embrace him. They basically had little choice: before his career was half over he had several movies under his belt, he was a bona fide hitmaker, and he packed clubs and ballrooms wherever he toured. Wills only played the *Grand Ole Opry* once in 1944 (bringing—gasp!— a drummer onto the program, which certainly irked the Founding Fathers), but his place in the country pantheon was sealed when in 1968 he was inducted into the Country Music Hall of Fame.

James Robert Wills was born on 6 March, 1905 in Limestone County, Texas just east of Waco. His family was large, and he was one of the several (including Johnny Lee, Luke and Billy Jack Wills) who'd eventually take on music as a profession. Fiddling had a long tradition in his family, and young Bob, or "Jim Rob" as he was called back then, soon started it as well. The family later moved to a farm in the Texas Panhandle near the town of Turkey. It was here that Jim Rob got his professional start at the tender age of ten playing a square dance one night when his Daddy got drunk and failed to show up.

As Wills grew older he continued to play music, but also dabbled in various other careers, including preaching the Gospel and cutting hair (he even went to barber college). The scissors suited him better than the Bible, and he soon moved to Fort Worth looking for work. By luck, however, he landed a gig with a medicine show instead. He performed music and comedy sketches and at times even did so in blackface. Minstrel entertainers like Emmett Miller and Al Bernard were quite popular at the time, and their jazzy singing style and vaudevillian showmanship definitely played a crucial role in western swing's development. Wills, for instance, was as big a fan of the sassy-voiced Miller (who sang the original version of "Lovesick Blues" in a manner that would later entrance Hank Williams) as he was of blues belter Bessie Smith (whose huge repertoire included the awesome "St. Louis Blues," a soon-to-be western swing standard). Wills' own singing style, not to mention his hoots and hollers, came from this minstrel tradition and Miller in particular.

Wills and the medicine show's guitarist Herman Arnspiger eventually formed a duo, the Wills Fiddle Band. They were soon joined by Milton and Durwood Brown, brothers who'd later go on to form the Musical Brownies. For a few short years in the early '30s, however, these four young fellows worked together and set the stage for the great western swing dance bands that would soon barnstorm the Southwest. As many bands at the time did, the Wills Fiddle Band sought out a radio-program sponsor and soon nabbed the Aladdin Lamp Company, renaming themselves the Aladdin Laddies in the process. Their biggest break came soon after when they won the support of the Burrus Mill and Elevator Company, makers of Light Crust Flour. They now worked under a new moniker, the Light Crust Doughboys, and it's in this context that Wills, Brown and company began developing their unique mix of Dixieland jazz, folk, blues and Tin Pan Alley styles. The Doughboys played dance halls as well as a regular radio program, and even recorded two songs in 1932 (as the Fort Worth Doughboys). Though instrumentally they were a simple string band at this point, these two songs do exhibit the jazzed-up melodies and dance-friendly rhythms that are now western swing trademarks.

When they began working for Burrus, the Doughboys inherited company man W. Lee O'Daniel as their emcee and manager (a man whose slick way with words later landed him the governorship of Texas). Problems arose finally after O'Daniel insisted they cut back on concerts and focus on selling flour on radio. Brown was the first to leave, taking Durwood with him to form the Musical Brownies in 1932. Wills stayed another year, after which he was booted out of the group for drinking and missing performances. When Wills left, he took his brother Johnny Lee and the Doughboys' latest lead vocalist, Tommy Duncan

Bob Wills And His Texas Playboys

(who'd been hired as Brown's replacement), with him.

Wills named his new group the Playboys and set up shop in Waco, Texas. The powerful and obviously jilted O'Daniel, however, harassed the Playboys right out of Texas and, in early 1934, into Oklahoma, where Wills modified their name to the Texas Playboys. They finally settled in Tulsa at Cain's Dancing Academy, which would be the group's home base for the rest of the decade.

With O'Daniel finally off his back, Wills had a chance to really spread out. He began beefing up his sound with a slew of mighty instrumentalists, among them pianist Al Stricklin, steel player Leon McAuliffe (who like the Musical Brownies' Bob Dunn played an amplified steel guitar), drummer Smokey Dacus, and second fiddler Jesse Ashlock, who'd previously played with the Brownies. Wills also added horns, saxophone and clarinet, punching the jazz quotient up another couple of notches. And of course there was lead crooner Tommy Duncan, whose smooth voice beamed a warm glow across the whole beautiful musical foundation. The line-up was bigger than average from the start, and it would keep growing throughout the decade. Hundreds of players would pass through the band's ranks over the years— mandolinist Tiny Moore, steel players Herb Remington and Noel Boggs, vocalist Laura Lee Owens, fiddler Johnny Gimble, Bob's brothers Billy Jack, Luke, and Johnny Lee, and so many more. Many of these Playboys would then move on to form their own bands, two of the most notable being McAuliffe and Duncan.

Fiddles were definitely at the center of the music, but right from the start the sound as a whole was far more eclectic than the average string band. Which was exactly what Wills was after: he didn't want anything to do with 'hillbilly,' he wanted his music to maintain an air of sophistication. It was dance music, but it was classy. The band played a jazzed-up urban sound and its repertoire included blues ("Sittin' On Top Of The World"), Jimmie Rodgers songs ("Blue Yodel #1"), and others like "Who Walks In When I Walk Out" and "Osage Stomp" that were almost full-on jazz if not for the western overtones (namely the fiddle and steel guitar). The matching western shirts and crisp-brimmed stetsons that Wills dressed his bandmenbers in also let folks know that this was a Texas outfit, and that the Playboys were gentlemen, not some rowdy band of good ole boys.

For all its sophistication, the Playboys' music was also wild, loose and free of stylistic constraints. When the twin fiddles, guitars, horns and drums fired into song, 'rowdy' was definitely part of the agenda. The players were superb, and one by one each would take solos that boggled the minds of the spectators and dancers. Western swing was all about fun and good times, and Wills' whoops, "ahh-haa"'s, and interjections of "play that trombone, boy" or "take it away, Leon" when each man stepped to the mike gave the whole experience a playful feeling. Wills wasn't opposed to singing a few numbers himself, either, his voice squishy and almost girlish (sounding more than anything like Emmett Miller). To the public all this tomfoolery and brazen showing-off gave the proceedings familiarity. Cindy Walker even wrote a song for the Playboys titled "What Makes Bob Holler?" that poked gentle fun at Wills' uninhibited commentary; it became a Playboys standard.

Wills And The Texas Playboys hit the deck running in the mid-'30s and didn't stop for breath until the advent of World War II. At night they played dances in clubs throughout Texas and Oklahoma, including twice a week at Cain's, then turned around and maintained a noon broadcast each weekday on Tulsa station KVOO. The Playboys recorded plenty of material as well, beginning in 1935 for ARC (which was later bought out by Columbia), and famed A&R man Art Satherley became Wills' producer. The band's concentration during this period, however, was on their radio and concert appearances. They were a top-rate live music sensation and they knew it.

The focus began to change in the '40s. Wills had begun appearing in western movies, which furthered his national stardom; and the band had found they could sell out large ballrooms in Los Angeles. One of the key turning points was "New San Antonio Rose," the Playboys' first national hit. The record sold over a million and was a jukebox favorite. With "New San Antonio Rose" on every country fan's lips, this new nationwide acceptance marked a shift in Wills' music, and the climate of western swing in general, toward a more pop- and vocal-oriented sound. The Playboys' repertoire became more song-focused, and such familiar Wills classics as "Bubbles In My Beer," "Roly Poly," and "Faded Love" all made the charts in the '40s and '50s. With his list of hits growing, his popularity was now bigger than ever.

The biggest change of all for the Texas Playboys came as a result of Pearl Harbor. When the US joined the war, many of the bandmembers signed up for duty, one of the first being Tommy Duncan. With his once towering band suddenly reduced to rubble, even Wills decided to enlist. He only lasted a few months, however, and upon returning to civilian life he opted for a change of pace and moved to California. A huge live music scene had burst open there in recent years, from the massive Venice Pier and Santa Monica ballrooms in LA to assorted nightclubs and dance halls in cities up and down the state. Western swing and hillbilly boogie were the musical styles for thousands of Californians at the time (many newly transplanted from Texas and Oklahoma), and so Wills put together a new, though much smaller, version of the Texas Playboys and jumped right in. He even opened a club of his own, Wills Point, in Sacramento.

When Duncan returned from duty he rejoined Wills in California; in 1948, however, he decided to leave again, this time to form his own band. A year later Wills returned to Oklahoma and had dreams of settling into a more regular home life with his new wife Betty. But settling wasn't easy for a man who'd been on the go since leaving Turkey, Texas twenty years earlier. He continued to move around, maintaining a heavy tour schedule. On top of some bad financial investments—most notably the Bob Wills Ranch House in Dallas— Wills' health began to give him problems. He had his first heart attack in 1962 and a second one not long after. Still, he kept on performing and recording throughout the '60s (for labels like Liberty, Kapp, and Longhorn). Not long after his induction into the Country Music Hall of Fame, however, he suffered a stroke that left him partially paralyzed and confined to a wheelchair.

Western swing had been fading from popular view since the '50s, and though it was never

entirely forgotten it was far from the spotlight. Merle Haggard, a big-time Wills fan, became one of the instigators of the music's resurgence, thanks first to a Wills tribute album he recorded

Bob Wills Tribute Albums

Being one of country music's seminal figures, a key innovator of a musical style with which his name is forever associated, Bob Wills has inspired numerous tribute songs and albums. Here's a few worth looking for:

⊙ **Asleep At The Wheel,** A TRIBUTE TO THE MUSIC OF BOB WILLS AND THE TEXAS PLAYBOYS (1993; Liberty). An array of special guests—Chet Atkins, Dolly Parton, George Strait, Garth Brooks, Suzy Bogguss, Huey Lewis (a friend of the Wheel from their San Francisco days), Marty Stuart, Lyle Lovett, Johnny Rodriguez, Brooks & Dunn, Merle Haggard, Willie Nelson and ex-Playboys Shamblin, Rausch, and Gimble—are all a part of this solid, fun-filled take on the Bob Wills legacy.

⊙ **Asleep At The Wheel,** RIDE WITH BOB (1999; Dreamworks). The Wheel members must really love ole Bob to dish out a *second* tribute album in less than a single decade. But they pull it off with perhaps even more enthusiasm and loose energy than the first time around. The tracks are thick with high-profile guests like Merle Haggard, Tim McGraw, Willie Nelson, Dwight Yoakam, and the Dixie Chicks, but it's Wheel bandleader Ray Benson who remains at center-stage during this 17-song celebration.

⊙ **Merle Haggard,** A TRIBUTE TO THE BEST DAMN FIDDLE PLAYER IN THE WORLD (or, MY SALUTE TO BOB WILLS) (1970; Capitol; reissued 1995; Koch). By the late 1960s Merle Haggard was a fresh country superstar with a string of hits lined up behind him. So when he offered tribute albums to his musical influences—first Jimmie Rodgers, then Wills—his fans sat up and paid attention. For his SALUTE TO BOB WILLS, Haggard assembled an impressive line-up of former Texas Playboys (Tiny Moore, Johnny Gimble, Johnny Lee Wills, and others), coupled them with his own band the Strangers, and laid down a series of Wills material with a spirit of both reverence and loose-collared good times. Haggard's voice fits songs like "Time Changes Everything," "Right Or Wrong," and "Roly Poly" beautifully, and the playing is lovingly crafted.

⊙ **George Jones,** GEORGE JONES SINGS BOB WILLS (1962; United Artists; reissued 1994; Razor & Tie). Honky-tonk icon George Jones was in the midst of his initial popularity surge when he cut this album of songs written or made famous by Bob Wills. The arrangements are straightfoward and solid, virtually ignoring (as early Jones records typically did) the Nashville Sound that was permeating the country charts at the time. His trademark vocal rolls, dips, and slurs were only beginning to break the surface at this time, but he sure is playful on the great "Trouble In Mind," and his rendition of Cindy Walker's "Warm Red Wine" will leave you flat on the bar-room floor.

⊙ **The Pine Valley Cosmonauts,** THE PINE VALLEY COSMONAUTS SALUTE THE MAJESTY OF BOB WILLS (1998; Bloodshot). Bob Wills made some rowdy music in his day, and that's exactly the spirit this tribute album projects. The Cosmonauts are a loose group of Chicago musicians captained by Mekons/Waco Brothers singer and guitarist Jon Langford, and they do a spot-on job with the famous Texan's cowboy-jazz songs, giving them a healthy shot of rock'n'roll hoochie-coo in the process. The 19 songs also boast guest vocal turns from Jimmie Dale Gilmore, Robbie Fulks, Edith Frost, Alejandro Escovedo, Sally Timms, and lots more from the indie-rock/alt.country side of the fence.

⊙ **Ray Price,** SAN ANTONIO ROSE (1961; Columbia; reissued 1996; Koch). Price was at the peak of his popularity when he cut what became the very first Bob Wills tribute album. "We hope you like our version of them," Price gracefully intones in the record's introduction, before kicking into such Wills songs as "Whose Heart Are You Breaking Now," "Roly Poly," and "Hang Your Head In Shame." Price has arranged the songs in his own 4/4 shuffle style, which works beautifully to give them his personal stamp without losing touch with the music's original spirit. The album was cut in one day, and the musicians included Grady Martin, Jimmy Day, Tommy Jackson, and a young Willie Nelson.

Bob Wills And His Texas Playboys

in 1970 (A TRIBUTE TO THE BEST DAMN FIDDLE PLAYER IN THE WORLD) with several Texas Playboys alumni, and secondly to a Wills recording session he organized three years later. With McAuliffe, Dacus, Stricklin, Gimble, and other former Playboys on hand alongside Wills (who could still holler it up), it resulted in Wills' final album, FOR THE LAST TIME. Wills never saw its release, however. He had another stroke and fell into a coma, finally passing away on 13 May, 1975.

⊙ **The Bob Wills Anthology** (1973; Columbia). This single-CD collection of what was originally a double-LP set is a good one and quite diverse, covering most the 1930s and early '40s. It reaches back to instrumentals like "Spanish Two Step" and "Maiden's Prayer" as well as the Jimmie Rodgers song "Blue Yodel #1" and Wills himself singing "Sittin' On Top Of The World." Many of the songs, in fact, are instrumental (if you don't count Wills' frequent interjections), but there are also familiar vocal titles like "Time Changes Everything," "Take Me Back To Tulsa," and "New San Antonio Rose."

⊙ **For The Last Time** (1974; United Artists; reissued 1994; Liberty). This former 2-album box set and booklet have since been issued on a single CD. Organized by Wills fan Merle Haggard, and featuring an assortment of former Playboys, these were Wills' final studio sessions. The playing is sharp, the repertoire packed with classics like "Big Balls In Cowtown," "Roly Poly," Emmett Miller's "Right Or Wrong," and the beautiful "Faded Love." Haggard plays the Tommy Duncan role, taking many of the lead vocals.

⊙ **Fiddle** (1987; Country Music Foundation/CBS). As you might guess, the fiddle is the focus here, and the songs are a mix of old-time tunes (some just simple duets) as well as swing, jazz and blues. All were cut between 1935–1942 and show Wills, in addition to being a born bandleader, was also quite skilled on the old 'devil's box.'

⊙ **Anthology, 1935–1973** (1991; Rhino). Spanning his entire recording career and spread out over 2 CDs, this compilation is the most complete overview and introduction to Wills that's currently available.

⊙ **Tiffany Transcriptions** (1983–1991; Kaleidoscope). Nine individual volumes of radio transcriptions Wills and the Texas Playboys cut in Oakland, California during the mid-1940s. Nearly all of it is solid stuff. Reissued on CD by Rhino.

Johnnie Lee Wills

Though his music career was always over-shadowed by that of his brother Bob, Johnnie Lee Wills nonetheless led a successful western swing band through the 1940s and '50s, producing music that stands well on its own feet. Records he made such as "Milk Cow Blues," "Peter Cottontail," and "Rag Mop" were popular during the '40s, and his daily broadcasts out of Tulsa, Oklahoma reached far across the Southwest and Midwest. His instrumentation was fairly basic and emphasized twin-fiddle leads (played by the likes of Cotton Thompson and Curly Lewis), the arrangements generally retaining a smooth, sophisticated edge representative of late-period western swing.

Wills was born in 1912 in east Texas. He grew up in an environment rich with traditional American music, thanks to the influence of his father, John Wills, a renowned fiddler. Johnny Lee learned fiddle, guitar and banjo, and during the '30s played tenor banjo as a member of his brother Bob's Texas Playboys. In 1940, with Bob's blessing and encouragement, he formed his own band, Johnnie Lee Wills And His Boys, and began recording for Decca. "Milk Cow Blues" was a hit for him in 1941. When Bob relocated to California during World War II, Johnny Lee kept the Wills legacy alive in Tulsa, broadcasting daily over radio station KVOO. His band membership grew to include some men who'd originally played with Bob's Texas Playboys, such as vocalist/guitarist Leon Huff, saxophonist/clarinetist Don Harlan, and fiddler Henry Boatman.

Johnny Lee remained a fixture on the Tulsa scene throughout the '40s and '50s, continuing his daily broadcasts and also recording a series of radio transcriptions that were sent out nationally. He recorded for Bullet in the late '40s (including the popular "Rag Mop") and RCA in the early '50s. In the '60s he pretty much retired from performing, choosing instead to focus on a Tulsa western-wear store he owned and a local rodeo he helped put together called the Tulsa Stampede. He did, however, manage to cut a couple of albums for the Sims label in the early '60s. When the western swing revival took hold during the '70s, he began playing shows regularly with fiddler Curley Lewis and recorded a reunion album for Flying Fish that featured many great western swing instrumentalists. He died in 1984.

○ **Tulsa Swing** (1978; Rounder). A sampling of the two hundred radio transcriptions Wills and his band recorded in the early 1950s. The recordings are relatively clear, and vocalist Leon Huff keeps a smooth edge on the lively melodies. Song choices include the lively "Boogie Woogie Highball," a gentle version of Floyd Tillman's "I Love You So Much It Hurts," and the famous Texas fiddle tune "Sallie Gooden."

○ **Rompin' Stompin' Singin' Swingin'** (1983; Bear Family). A great collection of Wills' recordings for RCA in the early 1950s. Songs include "Hot Check Baby," "Bees In My Bonny," "There Are Just Two Is In Dixie," and "Blackberry Boogie" with Leon Huff, Curley Lewis and even Wills himself sharing lead vocal duties.

☉ **The Band's A-Rockin'** (1996; Krazy Kat). A British-issued, 27-track CD of recordings Wills made during the 1940s for Decca and Bullet.

Smokey Wood

They really didn't make 'em much like Smokey Wood, then or now. This tea-smokin', good-humored bundle of wit and charm might con you out of your best suit or your last buck, but quick as you heard him banging hard jazz and lowdown blues from a bar-room piano—singing about dirty dogs, sweet mamas and the Oklahoma moonlight—you'd forget the trouble and start smiling all over again. His voice wasn't anything you'd call pretty, but he sure knew how to sing and play that old piano in a style so loose and spirited it could almost stop time. He was certainly a little crazy—writer John Morthland calls him an "all-around, all-American smart-ass" which seems right on the money—but his stints with Houston band the Modern Mountaineers and later his own dashed-together outfit the Wood Chips resulted in some of the wildest, grittiest, and most beautifully jazzed-up Texas swing recordings of the 1930s.

Smokey was born John Bryce Wood on 16 September, 1918 in Harrison, Arkansas. He grew up in Oklahoma and arrived ready for action on the Houston music scene in 1935, primed on Fats Waller jazz and homegrown grass. He played here and there before pulling together the Modern Mountaineers, a loose band of hot young players who loved to drink (and in Wood's case, smoke) as much as pick and blow their way through a frazzled blend of jazz, blues, and hillbilly boogie. When they recorded in early 1937 the line-up included Smokey on lead vocals and piano, Hal Herbert on saxophone and clarinet, fiddler J.R. Chatwell, guitarist Lefty Groves, steel player J.C. Way, banjoist Johnny Thames, and bassist Rip Ramsey. The songs were as dirty in sound as they were in lyrics—or at least the implied lyrics, especially the single word that was not-so-hidden below the surface on the great "Everybody's Truckin'." The music overall was as gritty as a backyard brawl and as tasty as a freshly barbecued hog. On "Dirty Dog Blues," the way the musicians roll and tumble behind Smokey's vocals ("I got rocks in my coffee, gravel in my bed") is so beautiful you want to lay your head right down and cry.

Wood left the group after they hired another singer, and the Mountaineers continued for a couple of years without him, giving some competition to fellow Houston outfit Cliff Bruner And His Texas Wanderers. Wood, however, ended up in the studio again before the year was out, this

Smokey Wood

time under the name Smokey Wood And The Wood Chips. The songs this time included the sentimental "Carry Me Back To Virginny" and a Woodsian update of Jimmie Rodgers' "Traveling Blues," all of it again a grinning creation as loosely structured as it was magnetic.

Wood took his music seriously, and it shows in these recordings, but he couldn't sit still very long. He drifted from job to job, playing with bandleaders such as Cliff Bruner, Adolph Hofner, Spade Cooley, and later a Dixieland bandleader named Joe Sanchez. He lived like a hobo one minute, played in nightclubs the next, and took up hobbies like raising fighting cocks in the meantime. Later in life he gained a lot of weight and finally died in 1975.

⊙ The Houston Hipster (1982; Rambler). Smokey Wood's recordings do occasionally show up on compilations (including JIVE AND SMILE and STOMPIN' AT THE HONKY TONK—see the chapter introduction), but this 16-song album is the only Wood compilation to have (briefly) made it onto the market thus far. One side is dedicated to Wood's work with the Modern Mountaineers, the other to his Wood Chips. And the liner notes are quite extensive and thoroughly amusing.

Smokey Wood

4

The Lost and the Found:
Honky-Tonk Hearts
and Great Speckled Birds

When it pulled into town like a ragged old truck that had lost its way down a long and rambling road, honky tonk brought country music out of the woods and into the modern age. This was music that needed to shout to be heard, the searing electric guitar leads and chuck-a-chuck 'sock' rhythms rising over the din of the taverns and roadhouses on the nasty side of the tracks—the infamous 'honky tonks' themselves, joints where workaday folks, many of them displaced country people, gathered to let off steam. There was drinking, there was dancing, there was flirting, fighting, laughing, and more and more drinking, all of it in an atmosphere rife with broken glass, broken arms, broken minds and folks who were just plain broke. And the music, coming from a Wurlitzer Jukebox, or a live in-the-flesh country band, powered the whole beautiful mess like a rebuilt tractor engine leaking fumes and filling the place to its rickety rafters with one good reason after another to stay put and lap it up.

The melodies themselves were certainly attractive, some even pretty, but the music was no longer 'nice.' "Born to lose, I've lived my life in vain," moaned Leon Seago on **Ted Daffan**'s "Born To Lose", one of the starkest country songs ever written, and legions of grown men, the mud still fresh on their boots, bowed their heads and wept bitter tears. **Ernest Tubb** plugged in his guitar and sang about leaning on the bar and "driving nails in my coffin," while **Al Dexter** (in a curiously jovial first-person voice) waxed about his gun-toting girlfriend who "kicked out my windshield," "hit me over the head," and then filled him full of lead.

When Dexter's "Pistol Packin' Mama" hit the jukes for a nickel a spin, everyone loved it, even Bing Crosby, who turned out a version of his own with the Andrew Sisters at his side. Dexter's song became one of the anthems of the early honky-tonk era. From here on out the sound became even more rippled with raw, bitter energy. Honky tonk was heaven and hell wrapped together, good time Charleys and blue eyes crying in the rain, crazy love and long black veils. 'You're a self-destructive lot,' the music seemed to say, 'you can't help yourselves.' At the same time, it offered up saucy melodies and catchy rhymes that caught fans' ears and perhaps showed them they weren't so alone in their troubles.

In the end, this new kind of country music would prove itself the meat and potatoes of the genre for ever afterwards. The songs would only get tastier, moving from **Floyd Tillman**'s remorseless cheating masterpiece "Slipping

Around" through **Lefty Frizzell**'s "Always Late (With Your Kisses)" and **Webb Pierce**'s "Wondering." Of course it was the mighty songbook of **Hank Williams** that really set the woods on fire. "No matter how I struggle and strive," sang ol' Hank, only six months before his crude death in the back seat of his new Cadillac, "I'll never get out of this world alive." Thankfully, honky tonk didn't take flight to the heavens with Hank, it continued right on into the 1960s, Nashville Sound be damned, thanks to singers like **Ray Price**, **Hank Snow**, **George Jones**, and Johnny Paycheck. And that wasn't all: it was reinvigorated in the '70s by Moe Bandy and Gary Stewart and in the '80s and '90s by Randy Travis, Marty Stuart, and Alan Jackson. Even in a contemporary world overloaded with 'young country,' the spare rhythms and haunting melodies that are the very soul of honky tonk remain at the core of the music.

The Wild Side Of Life

A dim-lit tavern, a rollicking party, or the darkest end of the street—all these things have been 'honky tonk' at some point. The word's been around since before the turn of the twentieth century—though where it actually came from, and what exactly it meant, is still a mystery—and by the 1920s it had even shown up in the titles of pop tunes and Broadway productions. It wasn't until Al Dexter recorded "Honky Tonk Blues" in 1936, however, that the term entered the country music vernacular.

Unlike country music of the previous couple of decades, honky tonk grew out of an urban world—that of displaced country people who'd come to the cities to find work and a 'better' life. During the '30s the Depression had knocked many rural families flat onto the ground, taking the final pennies from their pockets, and now the impending World War II was stealing whatever innocence still lingered. The war would lead to greater industrialization—factory and defense jobs—and a migration out of the hills, as people not only moved to the cities to find work, but also traveled overseas to fight. The idyllic rural lifestyle—the one symbolized by Mama's cooking, the family Bible, and the little old log cabin down the lane—was disappearing fast. The change was exciting on one level, but it was also regrettable.

That honky tonk music originated in Texas is significant, and no accident. Folk-based singers like **Roy Acuff**, brother duos like the Blue Sky Boys, and string bands like Mainer's Mountaineers were popular all over the Southeast. But in Texas, a place far enough removed from Appalachia to be a different world, the landscape was different—big, wide

open and wild. An oil boom had given the economy an unexpected boost during the Depression, and when Prohibition was repealed in 1933 people were itching to let loose. Nightclubs, beer joints and dance halls sprouted up all over, with bands like the Texas Playboys, the Musical Brownies, and the Texas Wanderers filling them to capacity. Some of the in-town joints had inklings of class, but it was on the outskirts of town, where the taverns were seedier and the clientele as dubious as the quality of the liquor, that the moods darkened and the music of singers like Dexter and Tubb (both bar owners themselves) took shape.

Electric instruments were a key ingredient to the sound. The trend toward electricity had been pioneered by the western swing bands of Milton Brown, Bob Wills, and Cliff Bruner, and by the end of the '30s Daffan, Dexter, and Tillman had all experimented with electric guitars. But it was Ernest Tubb, a onetime Jimmie Rodgers protégé, who signaled the upheaval of country's folk-based acoustic heritage and spurred the electric revolution. His band may not have been the first to plug in, but his were the songs that truly popularized the sound.

Tubb was already a hitmaking Decca recording artist in 1941 when he stepped into the studio with guitarist Fay "Smitty" Smith to lay down "Walking The Floor Over You." Jukebox operators had complained that his previous recordings had been difficult to hear over the din of the nightclubs, so this time the lead guitar was electrified. It worked, turning the song into a million-seller and landed Tubb a slot on the *Grand Ole Opry*. The arrangement was simple, yet the song's piercing guitar licks coupled with Tubb's rich, slightly off-kilter, but always neighborly vocals set the tone for honky-tonk songs for decades to come, from Hank Williams to Junior Brown.

At the time, though, with **Roy Acuff** creaking out "The Precious Jewel," **Red Foley** weeping about "Old Shep," and Jimmie Davis hammering "You Are My Sunshine" down the throats of his soon-to-be constituents, honky tonk struck the conservative world of hillbilly music like one big fat sour note. But of course, like it or not, the time was right, and there was little even the establishment could do to stop the slaughter.

After Tubb and his Texas brethren had picked the locks, the doors swung wide open and honky tonk was on its way to being the central focus of the country music world. Electric guitars were commonplace by the mid-'40s. And singers like Lefty Frizzell, Webb Pierce, and Hank Williams would soon take the music to new heights of both pleasure and pain. Country music had lost its virginity, and when Hank belted "Lovesick Blues" on the *Opry* in 1949 it was more obvious than ever that things would never be the same again.

Here Comes Nashville

Radio barn dances had sprouted up all over the nation, in cities large and small, during the 1930s and '40s. Initially, the most popular was the WLS *National Barn Dance* in Chicago, where during the '30s you could have caught Gene Autry, Patsy Montana, Louise Massey and the popular duet of Lulu Belle And Scotty. By the '40s, however, it was becoming clear that Nashville's *Grand Ole Opry* would predominate. The *Opry* had gained national syndication under the sponsorship of Prince Albert Tobacco in 1939, and it was hard to argue with a roster of heavies like Acuff, Tubb, Bill Monroe, and comedian **Minnie Pearl**. As the *Opry* grew, alongside it sprouted music publishers, studios and booking agencies, all of which helped turn Nashville into the bustling center of a burgeoning country music industry.

The proclaimed "King Of Country Music" was Roy Acuff, whose star had been on the rise since 1936 when he recorded the deeply serious Church of God number "The Great Speckled Bird." He soon signed to the *Opry* and became one of the show's top draws. Acuff knew how to have good clean fun ("The Wabash Cannonball"), but overall he exuded a moralistic aura so entrenched in old-time religion that it sometimes verged on the macabre—like his fascination with the "whiskey and blood" and the "groans of the dying" on "Wreck On The Highway." For Acuff, however, the climax of that tragic tale was that no one cared enough to get down on their knees and pray. All this staunch sincerity, of course, only makes his music more appealing.

Acuff was one of the biggest figures in country music to come along since Jimmie Rodgers, but his influence was not just as an *Opry* star. In 1942 Acuff and partner Fred Rose opened a music publishing house, Acuff-Rose, that not only controlled Acuff's songs but eventually nabbed the rights to material by such giants as Hank Williams, the **Louvin Brothers**, Roy Orbison, and the Everly Brothers. Rose himself was a highly influential behind-the-scenes songwriter and businessman. He wrote a large number of familiar tunes, including "Roly Poly," "Blue Eyes Crying In The Rain," and "We Live In Two Different Worlds." He also worked closely with **Molly O'Day**, **Leon Payne**, Pee Wee King, and most importantly of all Hank Williams, guiding the Drifting Cowboy's career through its ups and downs. Along with Rodgers

and Williams, Rose was one of the first three inductees into the Country Music Hall of Fame.

Acuff was signed and produced by British-born A&R man Arthur Satherley. Since 1929, smartly dressed "Uncle Art" had been working for the American Record Corporation (ARC)—which was later bought by the Columbia Broadcasting Company—and he'd been responsible for signing Gene Autry. Like Ralph Peer in the '20s (the man who'd discovered both Jimmie Rodgers and the Carter Family at the Bristol Sessions), Satherley was an influential presence during country music's formative years, and he helped guide the music's future. He'd go on to sign Hank Penny, Lefty Frizzell, **Little Jimmy Dickens**, and **Carl Smith,** and have a hand in the careers of Tex Ritter, Red Foley and Bob Wills, among others.

One of the biggest names in country music during the '30s was Jimmie Davis. The future governor of Louisiana got his start singing risqué blues in a Jimmie Rodgers style, graduating to more upstanding numbers like "Nobody's Darlin' But Mine" and the Floyd Tillman song "It Makes No Difference Now," and finally arriving into pop music glory with the heinous "You Are My Sunshine." That song put Davis into a sophisticated league with the likes of Red Foley—longtime host of the Prince Albert portion of the *Grand Ole Opry* and later the television series *Ozark Jubilee.*

Golden Years

Although World War II clearly affected fans and players as it did everyone else, the 1940s actually proved to be a time of steady growth and development for country music. Disputes between the American Society of Composers, Authors, and Publishers (ASCAP) and the National Association of Broadcasters in 1941—which led to the formation of Broadcast Music, Inc. (BMI)—and a year later between record companies and the American Federation of Musicians (which led to a year-long recording ban instigated by AFM president James Petrillo) were in the end more help than hindrance. Both disputes created an opening for underdog labels and previously ignored artists, who were able to record and get their songs broadcast while the big boys were battling over money. Even the wartime rationing of shellac couldn't stop "Pistol Packin' Mama" and "Born To Lose" becoming major hits. On top of all this, the superpowered border radio broadcasts brought country into more homes than ever, and beginning in 1944, industry magazine *Billboard* finally devoted a regular column to country (under the title "Juke Box Folk Records"). By the time the war was over, country and western—which is what people were beginning to call it, 'hillbilly' finally falling into the dustbin—was bigger and better than ever.

This postwar period, from the mid-'40s to the mid-'50s, is country's golden era. The list of icons who entered the spotlight at this time is enormous: Lefty Frizzell, **Faron Young**, Webb Pierce, Ray Price, **Kitty Wells**, Eddy Arnold, Minnie Pearl, George Jones, Carl Smith, **Johnny Horton**, and Hank Snow are just the heavyweights, with lesser-knowns like Leon Payne, **Texas Ruby**, Tibby Edwards, **Jimmie Skinner**, Melvin Endsley, **Marvin Rainwater**, Harry Choates, **Frankie Miller**, and **James O'Gwynn** filling in some of the cracks. Every one of these singers and songwriters was substantial, but the era truly peaked with the arrival of a lanky, cowboy-hatted Alabama boy Hank Williams.

Hank was "a mixture of whiskey, lamb's blood, and grave dirt," writes Nick Tosches in his honky-tonk essay in *Country: The Music And The Musicians*, and it's hard to beat a description as visceral as that. Hank's voice expressed everything honky tonk had been alluding to for the past decade. Though he was a crude singer he was incredibly expressive, his voice yipping, breaking, moaning and almost choking on the words. His thick nasal twang has been closely associated with country ever since—present in mid-'50s Hank-styled singers like Frankie Miller and Tibby Edwards (who even recorded with the Drifting Cowboys after Hank's death) all the way up to Marty Brown and Wayne Hancock in the '90s.

On top of that Hank was a prolific writer, penning (often under the watchful gaze of Fred Rose) song after song that would almost instantly turn classic: "Your Cheating Heart," "I'm So Lonesome I Could Cry," "Honky Tonk Blues," etc., etc. His songs could hit a raw nerve with spine-chilling effect, yet at the same time were often so beautiful a person could sit down and weep from the sheer joy of their simple but awesome power. Hank embodied all the beauty and sadness of modern country music—literally so, as the words of his songs echoed the harsh realities of his turbulent personal life. In the end he raised the stakes almost beyond reach.

Hank's voice had beauty in its cracks and dips, but from his chart-topping cohort Lefty Frizzell came a sound that was close to divine. Lefty had an alluring way of slurring and breaking up words that gave songs like "I Love You A Thousand Ways" and "I Want To Be With You Always" a lusciousness country music had only rarely seen previously. In the process Lefty created an entire new starting point for country singers to come. Just ask Merle Haggard: virtually everyone singing today owes a debt to Lefty.

Or George Jones. A Texan (but of course), Jones was another honky-tonk strong man who came of age in the '50s and '60s singing hard-ass material like "Why Baby Why" and weepers like "The Window Up Above." By the time of his massive '70s hits with producer Billy Sherrill ("He Stopped Loving Her Today" should be declared a national treasure), Jones had proven himself to be among the most extraordinary vocal stylists of the genre—hell, of American music on the whole.

Honky tonk was full of turmoil and troubled lives, and neither Hank, Lefty, George, nor countless other singers could fully escape its grip. Though not a honky-tonker per se, the same sort of deep-welled trouble also haunted Ira Louvin. Ira was half of the Louvin Brothers, one in a decades-long tradition of harmonizing brother duets stretching back to the Delmores, Monroes and the Blue Sky Boys in the '30s. He and his brother Charlie developed an amazing repertoire that mixed secular and sacred material, and though all of it was absolutely gorgeous it's the latter songs that have the spookiest edge. When the brothers warn that "Satan Is Real," you better believe it. The pair split in 1963 and each went solo, but Ira was killed in a car wreck in 1965.

The Next Step

Honky tonk remained center-stage through the mid-1950s, until it was usurped by a music that in many ways took its energy several steps further: rockabilly, the bastard cousin of rock-'n'roll. If Hank Williams was the picture of turmoil, Elvis Presley and Jerry Lee Lewis showed a whole new generation how to let the anguish out. The rollicking boogie-woogie piano of **Moon Mullican** (another Texan who once played in a western swing band, the Blue Ridge Playboys, with Daffan and Tillman) came close to blurring the lines between honky tonk and rockabilly. Mullican never dived into the genre himself, though he did remain on its cusp.

Rockabilly wasn't the only trend bringing change in the new decade. Back in Nashville, as the music industry flourished and grew more settled in its new home—as the whole beautiful country and western mess 'matured'—the sound of the music itself softened into an uptown, pop-friendly style that would come to be known as the Nashville Sound. This was the 'adult' answer to the wild-haired world of rock 'n' roll, and it left honky tonk caught in the middle. Thank the Lord, then, for George Jones and Ray Price—and out on the West Coast Wynn Stewart, Buck Owens and Merle Haggard—mighty singers who would keep honky-tonk fever alive and push the music into the next decade and beyond.

Anthologies

⊙ **Columbia Country Classics, Vol. 1: The Golden Age** (1990; Columbia). This excellent 27-track compilation gives strong coverage mostly to artists outside the honky-tonk guidelines such as Roy Acuff, Molly O'Day and Wilma Lee And Stoney Cooper. It also brings Spade Cooley, Gene Autry, Bill Monroe and Texas Ruby into the picture.

⊙ **Columbia Country Classics, Vol. 2: Honky Tonk Heroes** (1990; Columbia). The Columbia roster had some definite classic honky-tonkers, including Floyd Tillman, Lefty Frizzell, Marty Robbins, Ray Price, Carl Butler and Little Jimmy Dickens, who all make appearances on this generous 27-track sampler. Songs by Bob Wills, Stuart Hamblen and George Morgan are thrown in for good measure, too.

⊙ **Cat'n Around** (1992; Krazy Kat). A British collection of hillbilly-boogie and honky-tonk bands who recorded for the Houston label, Macy's Recordings. Harry Choates and the Bar X Cowboys are about the only recognizable names, but that's exactly the point—to unearth such lesser-known greats as Ramblin' Tommy Scott ("Tennessee"), the Vance Brothers ("Draftboard Blues"), and Woody Carter ("Who's Gonna Chop My Baby's Firewood"). The CD's packed with incredible stuff from the late 1940s/early '50s era that transcends categories and swings, rocks and honky-tonks like crazy.

⊙ **Texas Music, Vol. 2: Western Swing And Honky Tonk** (1994; Rhino). An album that places the classic early honky-tonk Texans (Ernest Tubb, Ted Daffan, Al Dexter, Lefty Frizzell) alongside western swing bands (Milton Brown, Bob Wills, the Blue Ridge Playboys) and later artists like Asleep At The Wheel and Alvin Crow, which helps widen the big picture. Though it only scratches the surface, it's not bad for a starter package.

⊙ **Heroes Of Country Music, Vol. 2: Legends Of Honky Tonk** (1995; Rhino). This 18-song collection is quite a good sample of the honky-tonk years, as it runs from Al Dexter's "Honky Tonk Blues" through Hank, Lefty, Ernest and George before winding up with Jim Ed Brown's "Pop A Top," a wonderful ditty worth the purchase price all on its own.

⊙ **Heroes Of Country Music, Vol. 3: Legends Of Nashville** (1995; Rhino). This gives a wide view of Nashville in the 1950s, from Red Foley and Eddy Arnold to Webb Pierce, Faron Young, the Louvin Brothers, Kitty Wells and Slim Whitman.

Honky Tonk: The Artists

Roy Acuff

When Roy Acuff died on 23 November, 1992, country music lost one of its most important, longstanding icons. Acuff was much more than a country singer and fiddler with a few golden-age hits under his belt: he was an artist whose sixty-year career paralleled the development and growth of modern country music as it evolved from a homespun hillbilly phenomenon into a massive worldwide industry—a man who was able to witness and experience some of the music's biggest changes. Acuff was a popular recording star known by every country music fan for such songs as "The Great Speckled Bird" and "Wabash Cannonball;" and as a founding partner in the Acuff-Rose publishing company he was also a major player in the business side of the music. Formed in conjunction with songwriter Fred Rose in 1942, Acuff-Rose was the first music publisher based in Nashville and the first devoted exclusively to country (their motto: "songs for home folks"). Its presence definitely helped define Nashville as the future capital city of the country music industry.

Acuff's chief association, however, was with the *Grand Ole Opry*. For almost his entire career, through hit records, business ventures and political aspirations, the *Opry* remained Acuff's central focus. He'd been a star on the show almost from the moment he joined in 1938; his presence, in fact, marked the show's turning point from an old-time radio program into the industry-leading showcase for country music. Acuff's name has been almost inseparable from the *Opry* ever since. "The King of Country Music," a nickname first given him by Dizzy Dean in the '40s, stuck around for the duration of his career. In 1962 he was inducted into the Country Music Hall of Fame, the fourth artist to be so honored, and the first living artist.

When fans speak today of 'young country,' the flashy, fresh-faced world that

Roy Acuff

springs to mind is not one that includes Roy Acuff. Quite the opposite: Acuff's craggy, home-schooled voice and his many songs about freight trains, evening prayers and old-fashioned romances virtually embodied everything 'traditional' about country—an aura he maintained and nurtured for the duration of his career. He resisted electric guitars and amplification at the same time that his *Opry* compatriot, Ernest Tubb, was turning the honky-tonk sound into a national phenomenon.

Acuff did have his kooky side: he had a passion for the yo-yo and loved to balance objects on his nose, and during his first recording session he even cut a couple of risqué numbers. But for the most part, this Tennessee native adhered to an old-time religious and socially conservative moral code, one that had been deeply entrenched in him since

childhood. It's a sincerity that was, and is, refreshing. When he sang about the lack of prayer in "Wreck Of The Highway" or his broken heart in "The Precious Jewel," there's no doubt he meant every word.

Roy Claxton Acuff was born on 15 September, 1903 in Maynardville, Tennessee, a small Appalachian town in the eastern half of the state just north of Knoxville. His father was a Baptist preacher and lawyer, and the community was brimming with old-time religious fervor and traditional Anglo-American folk music. Acuff learned to sing in church, but he was also passionate about sport. When his family moved to a suburb of Knoxville, he concentrated more on baseball, eventually winning a chance to try out at a Yankees rookie camp in Florida. Before the big game, however, he suffered severe sunstroke and afterwards had a nervous breakdown. During a long convalescence back home he rediscovered singing and fiddle playing, and once recovered, was invited by his neighbor Dr. Hauer to join his medicine show, giving the young Tennessean his first experience as a public entertainer. He sang, played his fiddle, and performed skits, some of them in blackface.

Returning to Knoxville, Acuff hooked up with a local band, the Tennessee Crackerjacks, and the group landed a series of local radio shows. A local announcer one day inadvertently called them the Crazy Tennesseans, and the name stuck. Though crazy on the one hand, Acuff and his boys also revealed their spiritual leanings when they began covering "The Great Speckled Bird" (sometimes spelled "Speckle"). This was a religious hymn associated with hardline religious outfits, that had fascinated Acuff since boyhood, and he finally obtained the lyrics from another musician, Charlie Swain. The song shared its melody with the Carter Family's "I'm Thinking Tonight Of My Blue Eyes" and later Hank Thompson's honky-tonk hit "The Wild Side Of Life." Rendered with Acuff's craggy, mountain-aged voice, it was mysterious and captivating, and it eventually landed him a recording contract with ARC (soon to be bought out by Columbia). "The Bird" would become Acuff's signature song, and he'd sing it many more thousands of times before his death.

Acuff's first recording session also included "Wabash Cannonball" (another song tied to the Carter Family), the pop tune "My Gal Sal," and even the dirty-minded songs "When Lulu's Gone" and "Doin' It The Old Fashioned Way" (which were released under the name the Bang Boys). Acuff didn't always sing: that first recording of "Wabash Cannonball," for instance, featured lead vocalist Dynamite Hatcher, with Acuff providing the train whistle sound effects. Acuff had first signed with A&R man William Calaway, but a couple of years later he began working with British-born producer Art Satherley (whose other charges included Gene Autry and Bob Wills).

Acuff had long wanted a spot on the *Opry*; he'd tried out before and been rejected. But thanks to some insider support, he tried out once again in 1938; his rendition of "Great Speckled Bird" earned him enough fan letters to persuade the *Opry* to keep him on. Until that point the show mainly featured instrumental acts and comedy, and Uncle Dave Macon was its star attraction. The Delmore Brothers and Pee Wee King were already *Opry* members with strong vocal repertoires, but it was

Acuff who gave the *Opry* a single singing star to focus on; his popularity changed the tone of the show permanently, and helped win it far greater attention. In 1939 NBC began broadcasting a half-hour segment nationally with Acuff as host.

This national exposure cemented Acuff's position as the primary spokesperson for, and icon of, hillbilly (ie non-western) music. Despite the popularity of Gene Autry and other singing cowboys at the time, Acuff never sang a western song; it's testament to his strength and integrity that he was able to keep the traditional mountain-bred, string-band style of hillbilly music alive during a time when honky tonk and western swing were flourishing. While Ted Daffan, Ernest Tubb, and Bob Wills were featuring electric steel guitars and even drums, Acuff hired acoustic Dobro player Pete Kirby (Bashful Brother Oswald). Kirby's proficiency on the recently invented instrument—an acoustic guitar fitted with a metal disc to amplify the sound, which was played Hawaiian-style—became the instrumental signature of Acuff's band (who now called themselves the Smoky Mountain Boys because *Opry* officials felt Crazy Tennesseans was derogatory).

Acuff's star rose quickly during the '40s, thanks in large part to a string of hit records ("The Precious Jewel," "Wreck On The Highway," "Night Train To Memphis," "Waltz Of The Wind") and his close association with the *Opry*. He also ran (unsuccessfully) for governor of Tennessee in 1948. And thanks to his publishing company, Acuff-Rose, his position as a country music businessman was equally strong and influential.

Acuff stayed with Columbia until 1952, when he and the label had a falling out. After that he recorded for Capitol, MGM, Decca, and beginning in 1957 Hickory, an offshoot of Acuff-Rose. He dabbled in electric instrumentation at various points during the '50s and '60s, trying to keep his head above water in the age of rock'n'roll, but he never felt quite comfortable. Later recordings did incorporate electric guitars and even drums, but the basis of his sound remained acoustic. He had a chart hit as late as 1973 (aged seventy) with "Back In The Country," a lively song celebrating old-time values written by Eddy Raven. More important was his participation (albeit with some hesitation) in the Nitty Gritty Dirt Band's WILL THE CIRCLE BE UNBROKEN album project, which united older country icons like Acuff, Doc Watson and Mother Maybelle Carter with the Dirt Band and, subsequently, their younger (and longer-haired) fans in a celebration of traditional country music.

Having been on the *Opry* when it moved from east Nashville's Dixie Tabernacle to the downtown

Roy Acuff

Ryman Auditorium in 1943, Acuff was witness to another major shift when in 1974 it relocated to the Opryland entertainment complex just outside of Nashville. President Nixon attended the opening on 16 March, even taking the stage and getting a now infamous lesson in how to operate a yo-yo. Nixon went home and resigned, while Acuff stayed put and settled comfortably into his role as *Opry* patriarch. In his final years he greeted fans from the porch of a specially built house on the Opryland grounds. He was given national artistic honors in 1991 with the Kennedy Center's Lifetime Achievement Award. His death a year later signaled the closing of an era in country music history.

⊙ **The Essential Roy Acuff (1936–1949)** (1992; Columbia/Legacy). This is an excellent Acuff starting point, and probably the only collection you'll need and want, as it contains the classic recordings of his best-known material. Two songs, "Great Speckled Bird" (1936) and "Steel Guitar Blues" (1937), feature the Crazy Tennesseans; the rest were recorded in the '40s with the Smoky Mountain Boys. The big-name titles include "Wreck On The Highway," "Precious Jewel," "Night Train To Memphis," "Wabash Cannonball" (the first featuring Acuff's lead vocals), "Jole Blon," and Acuff's rendition of "Tennessee Waltz."

⊙ **The King Of Country Music** (1993; Bear Family). This double-CD collection includes songs from Acuff's middle, post-Columbia period that were produced by Ken Nelson (Capitol), Paul Cohen (Decca), and Jim Vienneau (MGM).

⊙ **The King Of Country Music** (1998; ASV). This single CD has 25 tracks recorded between 1936 and 1947. It covers the same basic terrain as the Columbia/Legacy collection, but with slightly different titles. It includes three songs with the Crazy Tennesseans ("Wabash Cannonball," "Great Speckled Bird," and "Freight Train Blues").

Carl And Pearl Butler

"Carl And Pearl Butler are pure country and have stuck to it."

—Ernest Tubb

During the 1950s warbly-voiced Tennessee native Carl Butler was a successful songwriter, having penned an assortment of tunes ("If Teardrops Were Pennies," "Guilty Conscience," "Loving Arms," "Cryin' My Heart Out Over You") that were covered by the likes of Carl Smith, Roy Acuff, Lefty Frizzell and Bill Monroe. He finally cracked the charts on his own with "Honky Tonkitis" in 1961, then a year later made an even more indelible mark with "Don't Let Me Cross Over." The latter song became his signature, staying at #1 on the *Billboard* country charts for nearly three months. It also featured the vocal work of his wife Pearl, who became his musical partner for rest of his career.

Carl Roberts Butler was born on 2 June, 1927 in Knoxville, Tennessee. He played on various radio programs as a young man, and after World War II sang briefly with local groups the Bailey Brothers and the Sauceman Brothers. He first recorded for Capitol in the early '50s, then switched to Columbia, where he remained for about two decades. He met his wife-to-be Pearl (born Pearl Dee Jones on 20 September, 1927) in Nashville, her home town. She, too, was a songwriter, one of her songs being "Kisses Don't Lie," a Top 5 hit for Carl Smith in 1955. Carl didn't have a chart hit until "Honky Tonkitis" in 1961—a beauty marked by its sharp-edged twin-fiddle intro and Ray Price-style shuffle beat. "Don't Let Me Cross Over" was another unabashedly raw-flavored gem—about a desperate man on the verge of crossing over "love's cheating line." It was also the first Carl Butler recording to feature Pearl, who sang harmony on the chorus. After that, they were a team, earning nine more chart successes during the '60s.

Carl had been on the *Grand Ole Opry* since the late '50s, and in 1962 Pearl joined as well. In 1967 they appeared in the film *Second Fiddle To A Steel Guitar*. Their chart hits stopped by the end of the '60s, but in the years following they continued to record on small labels such as CMH, Chart, and Pedaca. Pearl Butler died on 1 March, 1989, and Carl Butler passed away on 4 September, 1992.

⊙ **Crying My Heart Out Over You** (1993; Bear Family). The German label Bear Family dug up and reissued these 12 recordings, which were originally recorded between 1974 and 1976 and released as the album COUNTRY WE LOVE on the small Pedaca label. Some are new songs ("Blue Eyes And Waltzes"), others re-recordings of hits they had as recording artists ("Don't Let Me Cross Over") and as writers ("Cryin' My Heart Out Over You," "If Teardrops Were Pennies"). Though the late-period releases of too many honky-tonk greats tend to be mushy re-treads of past glory days, this collection is surprisingly healthy. Their voices sound a bit aged, but the arrangements are bright and their spirits high.

Wilma Lee And Stoney Cooper

Along with artists like Roy Acuff, Bill Monroe, and Mother Maybelle Carter, the team of Stoney and Wilma Lee Cooper helped carry the old-time Appalachian music traditions out of the mountains and into contemporary country music circles. There's nothing fancy about Wilma Lee's bold, pure and deeply rough-hewn voice; you can feel the mountain air and wet, raw soil of her West Virginia homeland in every curl and twist. At the same time, singer and fiddler Stoney and their band, the Clinch Mountain Clan, created a tight, sturdy foundation on the recordings they made together from the late 1940s through to 1977, the year Stoney passed away.

Wilma Leigh Leary was born on 7 February, 1921 in Valley Head, West Virginia and grew up as a member of the singing gospel group the Leary Family. One of the group's fiddlers was Dale Troy "Stoney" Cooper, born 16 October, 1918 in Harman, West Virginia. The two were married in 1941. After working at an assortment of radio stations, they made their first recordings for the small Tennessee label Rich-R-Tone beginning in 1947. With their band the Clinch Mountain Boys (aka the Clinch Mountain Clan), they sang standards like "The Little Rosewood Casket" as well as then current material such as Roy Acuff's "This World Can't Stand Long" and Bill Monroe's "Wicked Path Of Sin"—raw and earthy recordings that are highlighted by excellent mountain-bred harmonies, deeply serious gospel themes, and a couple of prominently placed mandolin solos.

The duo signed to Columbia in 1949, and they remained with the label through the mid-'50s, cutting further traditional songs like "Sunny Side Of The Mountain" and several gospel numbers such as "Legend Of The Dogwood Tree" and "He Will Save Your Soul (From The Burning Fire)," which they wrote themselves. Their instrumentation maintained a traditional feel and included fiddle, banjo, mandolin and Dobro. Beginning in 1955 they recorded for Hickory, an association that yielded a handful of *Billboard* chart hits ("Come Walk With Me," "Big Midnight Special") in the late '50s and early '60s. Later they made records for Decca, Rounder, Starday, and other small labels.

Wilma Lee and Stoney had been associated with the *Wheeling Jamboree* in Wheeling, West Virginia since 1947, and a decade later they arrived at the *Grand Ole Opry*. They performed on the show together for the next twenty years, until Stoney passed away on 22 March, 1977. Since then Wilma Lee has persevered as a solo artist, performing on the *Opry* and recording for labels like Rounder and Rebel—her voice and spirit still firm and strong. Wilma Lee and Stoney's daughter, Carol Lee, who'd been singing with their group since she was a little girl, also began performing on her own beginning in the '70s.

◉ **Early Recordings** (1979; County). A collection of their Columbia masters cut between the late 1940s and mid-'50s. The old-time flavor is absolutely genuine, a rarity these days, making this a collection worth searching for.

◉ **Wilma Lee Cooper** (1981; Rounder). Five of the 11 songs here were cut in 1976 and are Wilma Lee's final recordings with Stoney. The playing on all of them is solid and steady, and Wilma Lee's voice, though older, has lost none of its raw power.

⊙ **Classic Country Favorites (Wilma Lee Cooper)** (1996; Rebel). Though not as classic as their Columbia material, these recordings that Wilma Lee made in 1979 and 1981 do maintain the hard-country traditions and feature great acoustic instrumental work.

Cowboy Copas

Cowboy Copas was an Ohio-born singer with a warm, smooth, full-bodied voice that was marked by a slightly gritty, ground-level education but at the same time possessed the pleasant tone of a crooner. During his twenty-year professional career, he was most frequently associated with the song "Filipino Baby," a late nineteenth-century composition that he updated and first recorded in the mid-1940s (Ernest Tubb also covered it), and "Alabam," a rewritten version of the song "Coney Isle," which Frank Hutchison cut back in the '20s. Copas' career lasted into the early '60s but was tragically cut short—he lost his life in the same 1963 plane crash that killed singers Patsy Cline and Hawkshaw Hawkins and pilot Randy Hughes.

Lloyd Estel Copas was born on 15 July, 1913 in Blue Creek, Ohio. As a teenager he performed in tent shows and at local contests, teaming up first with his brother and then with Lester Vernon Storer, a local fiddler. Storer was known as Natchee the Indian, so Copas took on the moniker

"Cowboy"—although, ironically, he didn't sing much western material. In the early '40s he took a job with WLW in Cincinnati, and he also hooked up with the locally based King Records, a newly formed independent label. Cowboy's first release was "Filipino Baby," about a soldier dreaming of a woman he met during a tour of duty in Asia. With lines like "she's my treasure and my pet," it's hardly the most enlightened song in the Copas canon, yet it's pretty obvious he meant no harm. The charm quotient on the song was high enough, and when finally released in 1946 it became a Top 5 hit. It also gained him entry to the *Grand Ole Opry*, where he remained a fixture for the rest of his career.

Copas joined Pee Wee King's Golden West Cowboys for a short time during the mid-'40s, and he also had a series of hits on his own with King's career-topping song "Tennessee Waltz," "Tragic Romance" (a Grandpa Jones composition), "Signed, Sealed And Delivered," "Tennessee Moon," and George Morgan's "Candy Kisses," among others. Several of these were covers, yet he did write much of his own material. He remained with King through the late '50s, though he temporarily lost momentum on the charts thanks to the advent of rockabilly. Signing with Starday in 1959, he soon had the biggest hit of his career with "Alabam." Unfortunately, right in the midst of that career revival, he was killed in that fateful plane crash near Camden, Tennessee on 5 March, 1963.

⊙ **Tragic Tales Of Love And Life** (1960; King; reissued 1994). Though this collection does contain original recordings from 1946 through to 1955, it's hardly the Cowboy's best stuff from that period.

⊙ **Opry Star Spotlight** (1962; Starday; reissued 1994). Includes mostly late-period cover songs such as "Loose Talk," "Wings Of A Dove," "The Rebel—Johnny Yuma," and "Mental Cruelty"—which is a shame, since Copas wrote so many worthwhile originals. He deserves far better representation on CD.

Ted Daffan

Like Floyd Tillman ("It Makes No Difference Now") and Al Dexter ("Pistol Packin' Mama"), bandleader and steel guitarist Ted Daffan penned one of the enduring classics of early honky tonk, "Born To Lose." Slow and mournful with lyrics

that verge on the suicidal ("every dream has only brought me pain"), "Born To Lose" set the pattern for countless cry-in-your-beer songs to come, and cleared the stage for the mighty creations of Hank Williams. "Born To Lose" is definitely Daffan's best-known, but there were others, too. Among the songs he wrote and recorded over the years (often using the pen name Frankie Brown) are "Truck Driver's Blues" (considered the first truck-driving song), "No Letter Today," "Worried Mind," and "Headin' Down The Wrong Highway."

Daffan didn't sing—he left that task to band-members such as Chuck Keeshan ("Worried Mind") and Leon Seago ("Born To Lose") and concentrated instead on writing songs, leading the band and playing the steel guitar. Inspired by the work of the pioneering western swing steel player Bob Dunn (who first recorded with an electric steel guitar in 1935), Daffan became fascinated with electric instruments and amplification. He didn't play an electric steel on record until 1939, but he experimented with it very often before that. He owned a radio repair shop in Houston that was the source for much of the equipment used by fellow players like Tillman and Leo Raley (who played an electric mandolin with Cliff Bruner's Texas Wanderers).

Ted was born Theron Eugene Daffan on 21 September, 1912 in Beauregarde Parish, Louisiana. His family moved to Houston when he was a boy, and this became his home base for most of his musical career. Before turning to country music, Daffan was dazzled by the Hawaiian steel guitar style—so much so that the first band he fronted was a Hawaiian outfit called the Blue Islanders. With western swing sweeping the state, though, it wasn't long before Daffan was caught in the whirlwind. In 1934 he joined the Blue Ridge Playboys, a somewhat jazzed-up hillbilly group led by fiddler Leon "Pappy" Selph that also included two other soon-to-be honky-tonk giants, guitarist Floyd Tillman and pianist Moon Mullican. From there Daffan moved to the Bar X Cowboys and then joined Shelly Lee Alley And His Alley Cats. At the same time he also ran his Houston radio repair shop, where he and his musician friends experimented with amplification and homemade electric pick-ups for guitars and other acoustic instruments—a more and more necessary modification if a player wanted to be heard in the big dance halls. Finally, around 1940, Daffan rounded up a few of the Alley Cats (including vocalist and guitarist Chuck Keeshan) and formed his own group, Ted Daffan's Texans.

Ted Daffan

Cliff Bruner had had a hit with Daffan's song "Truck Driver's Blues" in 1939, and this helped Daffan and his Texans gain a recording contract on OKeh (and later Columbia). One of their first recordings was "Worried Mind" in 1940; it was an instant hit and a country standard not long after. "No Letter Today" and "Born To Lose" were released on either side of the same record in 1943, and within a year that record had sold even better—over a million. Daffan and his Texans had many more hits through the rest of the decade, including "Look Who's Talkin'," "Headin' Down The Wrong Highway," "Shut That Gate," and, in 1950, "I've Got Five Dollars And Its Saturday Night." He took his band out to California in the mid-'40s where they played the Venice Pier ballroom, and a couple of years later they returned for a regular slot on the *Town Hall Party* in Compton.

By the early '50s Daffan had split up the Texans and relocated back to Houston. He still played with some local musicians, but he also got to enjoy the fruits of his labors when Faron Young, Les Paul and Mary Ford, Hank Snow and other artists recorded his songs. The biggest by far was Ray Charles' recording of "Born To Lose" for his hugely popular 1962 album MODERN SOUNDS IN COUNTRY AND WESTERN MUSIC. Daffan also started his own record label, Daffan Records, in 1955, and over the next sixteen years it released music by such artists as Eddie Noack, Floyd Tillman, Jerry Irby, and William Penix that straddled the borders of country, blues and rock'n'roll. In 1970 Daffan was among the first batch of artists inducted into the Nashville Songwriters Hall of Fame. He died on 6 October, 1996.

⊙ **The Daffan Records Story** (1995; Bear Family). A 2-CD set of singles released between 1955 and 1971 on the Daffan label. Artists include Floyd Tillman (playing acoustic blues), Dickie and Laura Lee McBride, pianist Johnny Bundrick, the Pickering Brothers, and Jerry Jericho.

⊙ **Country Hit Maker Of The 1940s** (1999; Cattle). It took a small German label to issue these classic OKeh and Columbia sides, even though Daffan was quite a hitmaker in his day. This is, in fact, the first (and only) CD collection on this influential artist to date—Columbia never even issued an LP on Daffan. The 22 cuts here all date from the 1940s, and all are culled from cleaned-up 78s—apparently the masters were destroyed or lost.

Al Dexter

"Pistol Packin' Mama" made Al Dexter, who both wrote the song and sang the original recording, a household name in the 1940s. A bouncy little number about a gal who barges into a tavern looking to gun down her cheating man, it sold a million well before the year was out and also became the first country song to top the pop-music charts. It boiled out of nearly every jukebox in the nation for far too long and was covered by some of the biggest pop singers of the day, including Bing Crosby and Frank Sinatra.

His "Mama" wasn't kidding around when she "filled him full of lead," but Dexter sure sounded like he was having a jolly good time recording "Pistol Packin' Mama." Despite the bitterness and violence that burns through the song's lyrics ("she kicked out my windshield and hit me over the head"), Dexter delivered them with a smile on his face. Then again, this was the era that produced the Three Stooges, who showed us just how funny a smack in the face could be.

Novelty tunes with a gnarlier subtext, "Pistol Packin' Mama," "You've Been Cheating Baby"— perhaps a better example of his personal philosophy

Al Dexter

("I'm not the kind to get a gun, I'll go out and have some fun")—and other Dexter ditties were the middle ground between vaudeville and the grittier honky tonk that was emerging at the time. Setting "Pistol Packin' Mama" in a tavern (Dexter called it a "cabaret") and talking openly of (gasp) beer-drinking even caused a minor uproar. It wasn't long, however, before such lascivious references became as commonplace as the überpatriotism of Elton Britt's "There's A Star Spangled Banner Waving Somewhere" and the squeaky-clean morals of Jimmie Davis' "You Are My Sunshine." Like it or not, "Pistol Packin' Mama" was a milestone.

Al Dexter was born Clarence Albert Poindexter on 4 May, 1905 near Jacksonville, Texas. He came of age during the oil boom that hit east Texas during the '20s and '30s, playing parties and dances for the workers and writing songs, too. He worked with an all-black dance band for a while before forming his own group, the Troopers. They first recorded in 1934 for a local label and a couple years later were signed to ARC. One of Dexter's first recordings, "New Jelly Roll Blues," clearly showed the black-blues side of his musical influences, and was much more raw than any of his '40s sides. Another song, "Honky Tonk Blues," brought the term 'honky tonk' into the country music vernacular for the first time. Dexter himself didn't know honky tonk from hop-scotch until his songwriting pal, James Paris, clued him in.

Dexter first recorded "Pistol Packin' Mama" in early 1942; it was released by OKeh in 1943 and was a smash shortly after. He followed it up with further songs alluding to guns and gals such as "Calamity Jane" ("She don't have to pack any pistols around/She just looks at me and she mows me down"), but also recorded instrumentals ("Guitar Polka") and sentimental songs ("So Long Pal," "I'll Wait For You Dear"). His 1946 hit "Wine Women And Song" was a pretty straight-forward arrangement, but others like "Down At The Roadside Inn" added trumpet and accordion for an extra jazzy bounce.

Dexter's heady chart success continued through the end of the '40s. After his Columbia contract expired he recorded for King, Decca and Dot before forming his own Aldex label. In the early '60s he signed briefly with Capitol, then opened the Bridgeport Club in Dallas, where he played until his retirement (he'd owned a beer joint once before in the '30s). In 1971 Dexter was inducted into the Nashville Songwriters Hall of Fame along with Jimmie Davis, Bradley Kincaid, Tex Ritter, and others. He died in 1984.

⊙ **White Country Blues** (1993; Columbia/Legacy). This excellent 2-CD compilation of early hillbilly and blues music has one Dexter cut, "New Jelly Roll Blues," from 1936. The song's worth noting because its laid-back, bluesy feeling is so different to the jovial sound of Dexter's better-known recordings. Other artists on the collection include Frank Hutchison, Darby And Tarlton, W. Lee O'Daniel And His Hillbilly Boys, Charlie Poole, and many more from the couple of decades before honky tonk's heyday.

⊙ **The Original 'Pistol Packin' Mama'** (1997; Bronco Buster). This German-issue CD includes Dexter's recordings from the 1940s and '50s, among them "So Long Pal," "Calamity Jane," "You've Been Cheating Baby," and, as the title states, his original 1942 recording of "Pistol Packin' Mama."

Little Jimmy Dickens

A stalwart on the *Grand Ole Opry* who first appeared on the show in 1948, singer and gui-tarist Jimmy Dickens had a solid country repu-tation that he built during the '50s and '60s mostly on novelty tunes like "Take An Old Cold Tater (And Wait)," "Out Behind The Barn," "When The Ship Hit The Sand," "Bessie The Heifer," and the silly "May The Bird Of Paradise Fly Up Your Nose." But as much as he joked around and played the role of the feisty 'little guy' (he stood under five feet tall), he was at the same time a hard-working, deeply committed musician who stuck to his hard-country arrangements even after the arrival of the lush Nashville Sound. Songs like "A-Sleepin' At The Foot Of The Bed" and especially "Take An Old Cold Tater (And Wait)" were played for laughs, but they also spoke of the dif-ficult realities of growing up in a large rural family with little money. Dickens presented these and other songs with a healthy dose of country charm, which was the root of his wide appeal.

The thirteenth child in a family of farmers, Jimmy was born James Cecil Dickens on 19 December, 1920 in Bolt, West Virginia. He started working at a local West Virginia station as Jimmy The Kid, then later attended the University of West Virginia. After that he performed on stations all over the Midwest. Roy Acuff heard him on the radio in Saginaw, Michigan, and he helped Dickens get a spot on the *Opry* and a contract with Columbia. His first session was in 1949, and among the songs he recorded was "Take An Old Cold

Tater," written by Eugene M. Bartlett, which he'd picked up while living in Indiana. It was the first of several hits for Dickens during the next decade, and one in a long line of hugely popular comic and novelty songs that formed the foundation of his repertoire. Over the years he also mixed in heart songs (see box p.112) and ballads (an underrated side of his music) and later some rockabilly-tinged material as well ("I've Got A Hole In My Pocket").

Dickens had the biggest hit of his career in 1965 with "May The Bird Of Paradise Fly Up Your Nose," a dumb but catchy song about a tightfisted man who's repeatedly cursed with that insulting refrain. Dickens had a few more hits, his last, in 1967, being "Country Music Lover." That same year he switched to the Decca label, then moved to United Artists and finally to a succession of smaller labels. He was inducted into the Country Music Hall of Fame in 1983.

◉ **Straight From The Heart** (1985; Rounder). This collection focuses on Dickens' heart songs and ballads—though unfortunately it's fallen out-of-print.

◉ **I'm Little But I'm Loud** (1996; Razor & Tie). This is a respectable Dickens collection covering his Columbia years from 1949's "Take An Old Cold Tater" to 1967's "Country Music Lover."

◉ **Country Boy** (1997; Bear Family). If Dickens tickles your fancy more than just a little, Bear Family's box set is your ticket to paradise.

Jimmie Driftwood

"When I was very small, my grandmother, she'd say, 'I'm going to tell you a tale and I want you to make a song about it,' and I'd make up a little old song and she'd clap and make me some molasses muffins."

—Jimmie Driftwood

Ozark native Jimmie Driftwood knew a thing or two about history as well as country singing and songwriting. Driftwood was actually James Corbett Morris, a schoolteacher from Snowball, Arkansas, who began writing songs as a way to liven up the history lessons in his classroom. During class, and subsequently on his records, he made the past come alive—playing a strange-looking one-string mouth bow, a 'leafola,' and a homemade

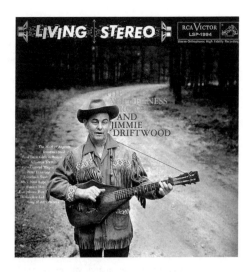

guitar crafted by his grandfather over a century before. Dressing like a frontiersman, he sang a huge repertoire of traditional tunes ("Sweet Betsy From Pike," "Run Johnny Run") and self-penned 'folk' songs like "The Battle Of New Orleans" and "The Widders Of Bowling Green." Driftwood's voice is rural and a bit sandy, but his albums could not be classed as field recordings by any means. Whether he's singing a legend about the Revolutionary War ("The Giant Of The Thunderhead") or a slice of backwoods cornpone like "Razorback Steak," he's got a professional's sense of showmanship and panache.

Morris was born on 20 June, 1907 in Richwood, Arkansas, a tiny town near the only slightly larger Mountain View and tucked deep in the Ozark mountains. His father was a folksinger, and he grew up playing music. He first began teaching school while still a teenager (with only an eighth-grade education!), but continued his learning through high school and then various colleges and universities until he finally earned a degree in education when he was forty-one years old. He soon figured out that his students responded well to music, and started teaching history lessons via songs. Luckily he was good at it. He composed "The Battle Of New Orleans" as early as 1936 (it was set to the tune of an old fiddle number "The Eighth Of January"), but it wasn't until the '50s, when the folk revival began taking shape, that anyone outside his immediate circle of students, friends and family recognized his talent. Through a mutual friend, Driftwood hooked up with Don Warden in 1957, a steel player for Porter Wagoner and a budding song publisher looking for new material. Warden immediately liked "The Battle Of New Orleans,"

Heart Songs

What is a 'heart song?' It's not simply a song with the word 'heart' in it – that would make just about every country song ever written a heart song! Like all of country music, the heart song emerged from diverse sources, many of them sentimental: the tugging on heartstrings of dying child ballads; the cheesy moon/june/spoon wooing of Tin Pan Alley; the bittersweet freedom of blues. A bit of the feeling of all of these resides in the heart song, which really came into its own in the 1940s and '50s.

Usually taking the form of a slow or mid-tempo declaration of eternal love, happy or sad, heart songs were not limited to one particular style of country music. Artists associated with honky tonk, western swing, the Nashville Sound and southeastern country music all sang them. **Ray Price**'s first Columbia LP, RAY PRICE SINGS HEART SONGS, is a perfect illustration of this, and a quick rundown on the diverse sources for the tunes that make up this LP gives a clear illustration of the heart song's range.

Leon Payne wrote and recorded "I Love You Because" in 1949, and it quickly became a country standard. A sweet and straightforward pledge of undying and unpretentious love (for all the right reasons), its unabashed sentimentality, casual mid-tempo and pleasing melody with a hint of drama make it a quintessential heart song.

Never a huge hit, "Let Me Talk To You" was nonetheless a longtime steady favorite of Ray Price's own repertoire. Written by veteran Nashville songwriters Danny Dill and Danny Davis, this bittersweet plea for reconcilliation has a touch of honky tonk to it as Ray warns his lover "don't go too far/with that crowd at the bar."

The **Delmore Brothers** were successful radio and recording stars during the '30s. After World War II, most acts of their ilk faded away, but the Delmores updated their style by adding an electric guitar and playing hot boogie-woogie and stone blues. "Blues Stay Away From Me" was their greatest success yet, and illustrates how even a straightforward blues can come to be considered a heart song.

In many ways, **Ernest Tubb** was the absolute embodiment of honky tonk, and he sang of drink, infidelity, divorce and plain old heartbreak. "Letters Have No Arms" was one of his most successful songs during the '40s when so many husbands and wives were separated by the war, and it's this quality of enduring love and yearning that makes this a true heart song.

"Faded Love" is a standard now, widely recognized by most people from Patsy Cline's early '60s recording, but the song's roots go much deeper. It originated with western swing pioneer **Bob Wills**, who grew up in the 1910s and '20s fiddling in rural Texas with his father, John Wills. They wrote the melody together when Bob was very young; it wasn't until 1950 that the song gained lyrics, courtesy of Bob's younger brother, Billy Jack. The melody has an inherently relaxed, lilting feel but climaxes in a dramatic reach for plaintive high notes at the end of the verse.

The slow weeper "I Saw My Castles Fall Today" was a tune Price co-wrote with Rex Griffin early in his career. It expresses nothing but the immediate sadness and disappointment of a lost love, unencumbered by recriminations, blame, or bitterness, with a high, wailing melody that gives the song a relentless, almost claustrophobic feel.

A more versatile stylist than **Moon Mullican** would be hard to imagine. One of his biggest hits, "I'll Sail My Ship Alone" takes a simple nautical metaphor for a broken romance and runs with it, offsetting the self-pity of a directionless soul with a catchy, perky melody and an easy tempo that hints at a carefree attitude.

Price's honky-tonk credentials are unquestionable, largely as a result of the direct tutorship he received as a young performer from **Hank Williams**. Hank's confessional and emotional songs like "I Can't Help It" seem to emerge so directly from his own personal experiences that to call them heart songs seems like an understatement.

The forthright expressiveness of Roy Acuff's singing was a huge influence on Hank's own musical direction, and it garnered Acuff enormous success in the World War II era and beyond. "Pins And Needles" was penned by Floyd Jenkins and remained one of Acuff's most popular numbers for years. The song's melody is simple and forlorn, the lyrics plain and mournful. Longing and loss are all over this number, with only the faintest dash of desperate hope; and yet it's delivered with a bouncy feel at a brisk tempo, adding a note of cathartic release to this classic heart song.

— Tom Armstrong

and before the year was out Jimmie had signed not only a publishing contract but a recording deal with RCA Victor. His first album, NEWLY DISCOVERED EARLY AMERICAN FOLK SONGS, was released in 1958 and included originals like "New Orleans" alongside others Driftwood had collected over the years. A year later Johnny Horton recorded a version of "New Orleans" and turned it into a #1 country and pop hit—pretty amazing for a song that was at heart a history lesson for elementary-school kids.

Another of Driftwood's famous songs was "Tennessee Stud," which was cut by Eddie Arnold in 1959 and later became a Doc Watson standard. Driftwood had further success in 1959, with versions of his songs "Sal's Got A Sugar Lip," "Sailor Man," "Soldier's Joy," and others, all making the *Billboard* charts. He appeared on the *Louisiana Hayride* and the *Grand Ole Opry* and as a result of all the attention even gave up teaching to concentrate on music. He recorded six albums for RCA, picking his grandfather's guitar on each and every one. His producer, Chet Atkins, had kept the arrangements simple and traditional at first—with only minimal accompaniment that allowed Driftwood's songs and stories to stand and shine on their own—but as time wore on he added background choruses that were unnecessary and at times intrusive.

The growing commercialization of songs was a little too much for Driftwood, who began losing interest in the bright lights of Nashville and the *Opry*. The folk revival that had originally fueled his career was also waning. Driftwood didn't give up recording entirely— he switched to Monument in 1963—but he did shift his focus back to his beloved Ozarks. His first major accomplishment was turning a local arts and crafts fair in Mountain View, Arkansas into the nationally recognized Arkansas Folk Festival. Ten years later the tiny town was home to the Ozark Folk Center, the Rackensack Folklore Society, and his own Driftwood Barn, where he performed regularly (for free). Driftwood worked as a conservationist and also filled a variety of prestigious national appointments (including program director for the Smithsonian's National Folk Festival). He died of a heart attack in 1998 at the age of ninety-one.

○ **Down In The Arkansas** (1964; Monument). A fun album that mixes traditional Ozark lore with kooky stories about wild hogs and shotgun weddings. The title track is a real beauty and one of his catchiest.

⊙ **Americana** (1991; Bear Family). This 3-CD box set contains all Driftwood's RCA recordings. The earlier stuff is best, when producer Chet Atkins had sense enough to keep the arrangements simple and allow Driftwood's voice and stories to speak for themselves. Taken in large doses, Driftwood's music does get repetitive, but a few at a time are very gratifying.

Werly Fairburn

The career of Werly Fairburn may be a mere footnote in country music history, but a good portion of the few dozen recordings he made in the 1950s and '60s for Trumpet, Capitol, Columbia, and other labels are actually quite heady, strong-willed and refreshingly dirty around the edges. Standing with one foot kicking its way into the burgeoning territory of rockabilly and the other stubbornly planted knee-deep in hillbilly, Fairburn may have come across as a man who couldn't get his story straight, but for fans, he's a fascinating singer and songwriter with a handful of sturdy, memorable songs worth more than just a casual listen.

Fairburn was born in New Orleans on 27 November, 1924 and grew up playing guitar. After serving in the Navy during World War II he took a job in New Orleans as a barber—though he also wrote songs and played music on the side, leading local fans to dub him the Singing Barber. The tiny regional label Trumpet released his first record, the Cajun-flavored honky-tonker "Camping With Marie" (b/w "Let's Live It Over"), in the early '50s. Soon after he was picked up by Capitol, which released only a few more records before deciding Fairburn wasn't much of a moneymaking prospect. He next recorded for Columbia, including the mournful "I Guess I'm Crazy (For Loving You)"—cut at Castle Studios in Nashville—and the up-tempo "Everybody's Rockin'," one of four songs he recorded at Jim Beck's legendary honky-tonk studio in Dallas (where Lefty Frizzell and Ray Price, among others, cut their early hits).

Fairburn wrote most of his own material, and a few of his songs were picked up by other artists. "I Guess I'm Crazy" turned into a small gold mine for Fairburn when Tommy Collins first cut it in 1955 and then, in 1964, Jim Reeves. Reeves was killed in a plane crash soon after, rocketing the song to #1 for seven weeks. Fairburn's own recordings, however, never once charted. He

Jimmie Driftwood • Werly Fairburn

recorded further songs for the R&B label Savoy (including what some consider a rockabilly classic, "All The Time") and later for Milestone, a label he founded after moving to California. In the '60s he cut his final few songs for Fair-Lew (another of his label ventures) and the LA-based Best in Country. He contracted Reynauld's Syndrome in the '70s, and a decade later he discovered a tumor in his lung. He continued singing until his voice gave out completely, finally passing away on 18 January, 1985.

⊙ **Everybody's Rockin'** (1993; Bear Family). A sturdy 29-song collection covering the bulk of Fairburn's recording career, from his early Trumpet single ("Camping With Marie") through spare rock'n'roll gems like "I'm Jealous" and "All The Time" and hard-edged, no-frills honky-tonk greats such as his 1954 Capitol recordings "Prison Cell Of Love" and "It's A Cold Weary World."

Red Foley

Red Foley

"Nobody was ever able to put into a song, wistful or gay, more of his own true self. Quite a fellow, this Foley."
—Don Richardson

Red Foley was one of the biggest stars in country music during the 1940s and '50s. He had a smooth, pleasant voice and a straight-man persona that helped inch country that much closer to the pop style of Bing Crosby, but musically Foley was actually quite versatile—jumping beautifully between hot-tempoed hillbilly boogie songs ("Chattanoogie Shoe Shine Boy," "Tennessee Saturday Night," "Sugarfoot Rag"), sentimental numbers ("Old Shep"), feel-good family tunes ("Methodist Pie," "Company's Comin'"), and sacred material ("Peace In The Valley"). His records, which sold by the millions, helped country music achieve its postwar glory years. Foley himself, however, was less an instrumental virtuoso than he was a masterful entertainer with significant leadership qualities. He was a major star on such radio programs as the WLS *National Barn Dance*, the *Renfro Valley Barn Dance*, and the *Grand Ole Opry*. During the '50s, he ventured into new territory, stepping into the world of television to host the *Ozark Jubilee*, a program based out of Springfield, Missouri that proved hugely successful.

Clyde Julian Foley was born on 17 June, 1910 in Blue Lick, Kentucky and grew up near Berea. He sang locally, and continued to sing while briefly at college, eventually signing on with Chicago station WLS in 1931. There he quickly became one of the leading figures on the *National Barn Dance*, performing alone as well as with the Cumberland Ridge Runners and soon-to-be star Lulu Belle Stamey (who had yet to marry Scotty Wiseman). During the late '30s Foley moved to Cincinnati, Ohio, where he helped John Lair get his radio show the *Renfro Valley Barn Dance* off the ground. He switched between various radio shows after that, including a stint back in Chicago.

Foley recorded some tracks for the American Record Corporation (ARC) with the Cumberland Ridge Runners, but his recordings didn't start making noise until 1941, when he signed as a solo artist with Decca. One of his earliest hits was "Old Shep," a sappy tune he wrote about his dog, Hoover, that has become a country standard (it was a favorite of Elvis Presley's, among others). Throughout the next couple of decades he was on the *Billboard* charts regularly. His peppy, lively recording "Chattanoogie Shoe Shine Boy" was his biggest hit by far, topping the country charts for three months in 1950 and hitting the #1 slot in the pop charts as well.

In 1946 Foley was hired to host the Prince Albert Hour on the *Grand Ole Opry*, a prestigious post he maintained for the next seven years. During the mid-'40s, Foley and his producer, Paul Cohen, also began cutting his records in Nashville—a pioneering move that helped establish that city as a noteworthy recording center. In 1953 Foley quit his Prince Albert duties and a year later was hired to headline the ABC network show *Ozark Jubilee,* a radio show broadcast out of KWTO in Springfield, Missouri. In 1955 the show made its television debut with Foley as host. It ran for another five years and was later renamed *Ozark Jubilee USA.*

Many of Foley's later recordings, from the mid-'50s onward, were cut in a soothing pop style that made grand use of the Nashville Sound machine, including the Owen Bradley Orchestra and background vocalists the Anita Kerr Singers. Foley appeared on television once more for a couple of years in the early '60s as part of the show *Mr. Smith Goes To Washington,* which starred Fess Parker, and in 1967 he was elected to the Country Music Hall of Fame. He toured regularly throughout his career and right up until his death on 19 September, 1968 in Fort Wayne, Indiana.

⊙ **Hot Country Boogies** (1982; Rocketeer). A 31-song single-CD collection of Decca sides and Radiozark transcriptions.

⊙ **Country Music Hall Of Fame** (1991; MCA). An excellent 16-song compilation of Foley's biggest and most classic material. Along with sacred material and a few cool bluesy tunes ("Midnight," "Deep Blues"), many of his great boogie tunes are packed in here, including "Tennessee Border," "Tennessee Saturday Night," and of course "Chattanoogie Shoe Shine Boy."

Lefty Frizzell

"Just being around him was a lesson in life."

—David Frizzell

Hank had the songs, but Lefty had the voice. You could say it as simply as that and not be far off the mark, as Lefty Frizzell was certainly a profound vocal stylist whose influence is still prevalent fifty years after he first cut "If You've Got The Money I've Got The Time." But the story of this legendary honky-tonk artist actually stretches wider and deeper. To begin with, Lefty had songs of his own—beautiful ones like "I Love You A Thousand Ways," "Always Late (With Your Kisses)," and "I'm An Old, Old Man (Tryin' To Live While I Can)." Some like "Give Me More More More (Of Your Kisses)" and "I Want

To Be With You Always" were as happy as the flowers, while others such as "I Never Go Around Mirrors" made him sound two steps away from the gutter. And during a performing and recording career that spanned four decades—from the honky-tonks of Texas to the big studios of Nashville—he cut some 240 commercial recordings.

Lefty really made his mark with his voice rather than his songwriting. He had an endearing way of slurring and breaking up words that gave songs like "Always Late" and "I Want To Be With You Always" a lusciousness country music hadn't yet experienced. Eddie Arnold and Bing Crosby were smoothies, but Lefty zigzagged through the valleys and soared into the mountains. He warbled, rippled and curled around each word with incredible dexterity. He broke syllables; he held notes like he never wanted to let go. And his singing was not simply about showing off, it was about conveying genuine emotions and feelings. Hank Williams was certainly an expressive singer, but Lefty's voice was infused with pure, warm beauty. More than any other singer in country music, he set the pace and the tone for the next generation of vocalists.

"Every kid that's singing right now is either mimicking Lefty Frizzell or George Jones," remarked Mickey Newbury, a beautiful vocalist himself, in a 1997 interview. "He was the first country singer to do little vocal twists. And that style, and the clenched-jaw style of George Jones, are basically what everybody is doing now." Lefty protégés include Keith Whitley, Randy Travis, and John Anderson—and even to some degree in his earliest days George Jones himself—though the singer who inherited Lefty's vocal style to the fullest is Merle Haggard. During the '60s Merle was among the first to acknowledge the debt that he—and country music as a whole—owed to this legendary Texan.

Maybe if his career had burst into a fireball, as Hank Williams' had done, Lefty might be spoken of more often today. But his career progressed into the modern country era in fits and starts, the short bursts of commercial interest counterbalanced by popular indifference. Fame on the level that he enjoyed in the '50s (at one point he had an unprecedented four songs in the Top 10 of *Billboard*'s country charts at once!) was simply impossible to maintain. Sadly, by his later years, Lefty had deteriorated both physically and emotionally. All his life he was plagued with personal problems centering on his alcoholism and infidelity. By the '70s they'd caught up with him and in 1975 he finally succumbed to a stroke.

Lefty Frizzell

called the Ace of Clubs. His break came when he took his songs to Dallas to audition for maverick sound engineer Jim Beck, whose complex but entirely homemade recording studio (most country records up to that point were cut either in the big city studios or in field recordings) would soon become the early stomping ground for several honky-tonk greats, including Marty Robbins and Ray Price. Beck cut some demos of Lefty, and during a trip to Nashville (when he was trying to shop Lefty's song "If You've Got The Money I've Got The Time" to Little Jimmy Dickens), Columbia producer Don Law heard the song and soon signed the twenty-two-year-old to a regular contract.

Lefty's first recordings—"If You've Got The Money" and "I Love You A Thousand Ways"—were cut at Beck's studio with Law in the producer's chair. The latter song had been one of many love letters he'd written to his wife from his New Mexico jail cell. The back-to-back songs were an instant hit and walked off the shelves. Hit after hit followed in quick succession—among them the cute come-on "Give Me More More More (Of Your Kisses)," the gently sentimental "Mom And Dad's Waltz," and the almost existential-sounding "Look What Thoughts Will Do." All of these were excellent showcases for Lefty's amazing vocal styles, though one of his best has to be "Always Late (With Your Kisses)," his voice echoing the shifting-sand ripple of Curly Chalker's steel guitar introduction. Lefty also recorded some Jimmie Rodgers' songs like "Travellin' Blues" and "My Rough And Rowdy Ways," his voice well suited to the laid-back bluesy style of Rodgers' material. Columbia made the unusual decision to release a whole album's worth—and this at a time when the Singing Brakeman's songs were barely even in print.

Having practically ruled the country charts between 1950 and 1952, Lefty stumbled upon a roadblock. Climbing to the top of the charts was suddenly more difficult, partly due to the rise of

Lefty was born William Orville Frizzell on 31 March, 1928 in Corsicana, Texas, an oil town about fifty miles south of Dallas. He was one of eight children and not the only one to take on a career in music—another was his brother David, who cut a series of slick duets with Shelly West in the '80s. His family moved from Texas to Oklahoma and then Arkansas, eventually settling in El Dorado. It's here that Lefty got his nickname during a schoolyard brawl, and it was here also that he began singing on local radio programs, initially influenced by Jimmie Rodgers. Lefty spent the '40s singing on radio shows and playing dances and eventually a string of bars and clubs throughout the Southwest. By this time such honky-tonk heroes as Ernest Tubb, Ted Daffan, and Floyd Tillman were popular, and their influence crept into Lefty's music as well. He also got married young, at the age of sixteen, to a girl named Alice, also sixteen. They even had a child, though this didn't prevent him from fooling around. One such tryst even landed him in jail for statutory rape! He was nineteen, the girl was fourteen.

In 1949 and 1950, Lefty enjoyed a steady gig at a hardcore honky-tonk in Big Spring, Texas

rockabilly and rock'n'roll, which cut seriously into country's record-buying youth market, and partly due to the fact that his huge burst of fame had come at such an early age and he was now perhaps burning out. One solution was a change of scene: in 1954 he and his family left Texas and moved to California.

Lefty continued recording steadily through the '50s—at Beck's studio in Dallas and later in Nashville and Hollywood. One difference was that he began recording fewer original songs and picking up more outside material. This wasn't a bad thing, it was only natural, and besides he made great work out of songs by the likes of Onie Wheeler ("Run 'em Off"), Marty Robbins ("Cigarettes And Coffee Blues"), and Harlan Howard (the utterly bleak "How Far Down Can I Go"). He also created a masterpiece out of "Long Black Veil," a song by Marijohn Wilkins and Danny Dill about murder, mistaken identity and a mysterious woman who spends her nights at the graveside of a former lover. This not only generated the hit necessary to put Lefty's name back in lights, but it became one of his signatures. Many have since covered the song, but none has matched his spooky subtleties. His career suddenly rejuvenated, Lefty and family moved east, this time to Nashville. Soon he was blessed with another major country hit, "Saginaw, Michigan." Despite the heavier Nashville production on this and other recordings from the '60s and '70s, Lefty's voice proved itself able to transcend the changes. "Saginaw, Michigan" was another beauty.

Though he drifted in and out of creative periods in the '60s and '70s, Lefty did continue to write. One of his late-period standouts was "I Never Go Around Mirrors," co-written with up-and-coming Nashville songwriter Whitey Shafer. He cut it in 1973 for ABC (he'd been dropped by Columbia the previous year), and that and two other Shafer/Frizzell songs, "Lucky Arms" and "That's The Way Love Goes," demonstrated how well he could still express himself with a pen. As was the case with much of his '60s Columbia material, the production (by Don Gant) on his ABC debut THE LEGENDARY LEFTY FRIZZELL was heavy. Nonetheless, his performance revealed him to be back in business as a singer and songwriter—and besides, no chorus or string section could kill the deep, dark mood of a song like "Mirrors." Merle Haggard later adopted both "Mirrors" and "Love Goes" as standards in his repertoire. The connection between the two singers ran both ways: on his second ABC album, THE CLASSIC STYLE OF LEFTY FRIZZELL, Lefty recorded Haggard's

"Life's Like Poetry." It turned out to be his final recording.

During his later years Lefty was regularly acknowledged as a 'living legend.' Physically, however, he was a wreck. His blood pressure was high, he'd gained a lot of weight, he continued to drink heavily and his marriage to Alice was on the rocks. After suffering two strokes, he fell into a coma and died on 19 July, 1975. He was only forty-seven years old. He finally earned his rightful place in the Country Music Hall of Fame in 1982.

⊙ **The Best Of Lefty Frizzell** (1991; Rhino). These 18 songs represent the choicest highlights from Lefty's hitmaking years. The song choices are great, even if they only scratch the surface of his long career.

⊙ **Life's Like Poetry** (1992; Bear Family). This massive 12-CD box set is more than a straight reissue of the German label's previous 14-LP set (which was titled HIS LIFE, HIS MUSIC) as it includes recently uncovered pre-Columbia demos and more and better master recordings. The booklet, written by Charles Wolfe, was also expanded.

⊙ **Final Recordings Of Lefty Frizzell** (1996; Varese Sarabande). A collection of Lefty's 1970s sessions for ABC Records produced by Don Gant. The production threatens sweetness but never overwhelms, and songs like "That's The Way Love Goes," "I Never Go Around Mirrors," and the pleasantly optimistic "Life's Like Poetry" are a strong and vital final chapter to Lefty's story.

⊙ **Look What Thoughts Will Do** (1997; Columbia/Legacy). At 34 songs, all from Frizzell's Columbia catalog, this excellent 2-CD set digs a bit deeper into Lefty's world than the single-disc Rhino collection, and it's clearly worth the extra pennies. Consider it the best 'starter' collection.

Rex Griffin

"In my opinion his singing was second only to that of Jimmie Rodgers."
—Ernest Tubb

S ongwriter and singer Rex Griffin wasn't exactly an icon of honky tonk, but he was a significant and too-often-neglected artist whose career is a great example of country music's transition from the world of Jimmie Rodgers to that of Hank Williams.

Of particular note was Griffin's 1937 near-suicidal hit song about lost love, "The Last Letter," which came just a few years before Ted Daffan's "Born To Lose" and which helped set the stage for the darker songs of honky tonk to come. It has since been covered by countless artists, though it's not the only Griffin song to have been picked up: "Won't You Ride In My Little Red Wagon" and "Just Call Me Lonesome," although never recorded by Griffin himself, were hits for Hank Penny and Eddy Arnold respectively, and the lively "Everybody's Trying To Be My Baby" was later recorded by both Carl Perkins and the Beatles. Even Griffin's 1939 version of "Lovesick Blues," a Tin Pan Alley song initially recorded by minstrel singer Emmett Miller in the '20s, proved influential, as it inspired the major hit version by Hank Williams.

Griffin's late '30s recordings for Decca were simple and straightforward with just his acoustic guitar and sometimes one other instrument (banjo, steel guitar) as accompaniment. His voice wasn't exactly pretty, but it was sturdy and charming. Early recordings showed the direct influence of Griffin's hero Jimmie Rodgers, but before long his darker side was showing more and more. Though Griffin's acoustic arrangement on "The Last Letter" lacked the amplified instrumental edge of artists like Ted Daffan ("Born To Lose") and Floyd Tillman ("Slippin' Around"), it clearly foreshadowed honky tonk with its atmospheric purity and its unadorned darkness, and was definitely one of the significant country songs of its time.

Rex was born Alsie Griffin on 12 August, 1912 in Sand Valley, Alabama. His father was a farmer but also a fiddler who taught his son to appreciate music, and when Jimmie Rodgers hit the scene young Alsie was hooked. He latched onto Rodgers' blue-yodeling style and never completely gave it up. As a teenager he'd taken a job at a local foundry, but before long he was heading for Birmingham and a professional life as a musician. It was also the start of a drifting lifestyle that would take him to radio station showcases and musical appearances all over the South and Midwest.

Griffin made his first recordings in Chicago for Decca in 1935. Many were often cute and romantic ("I Don't Love Anybody But You"), and like his hero Rodgers he proved a fine yodeler ("Love Call Yodel"). He did, however, indulge his darker side when he cut songs like "Why Should I Care If You're Blue." It was "The Last Letter" that showed Griffin taking himself more seriously and truly maturing as a writer and performer. The lyrics, which offered one man's perspective on a romantic break-up, were stark and

deeply personal ("what have I done that has made you so different and cold"). Rumor had it that Griffin wrote "The Last Letter" following the departure of his first wife, Margaret. Whatever the case, the sad, painful, and bitter end of a romance had never been so realistically portrayed in song.

"The Last Letter" won Griffin a fair amount of attention. Ernest Tubb wrote him a fan letter (and later helped him financially), and Jimmie Davis was just one who covered the song, turning it into a hit all over again in 1939 (repeating the deed in 1941 with Griffin's "I Told You So"). Griffin himself made another highly influential recording with "Lovesick Blues" at a 1939 session, but that proved his last for Decca; despite his popularity as a songwriter and radio personality, the label dumped him. He continued to perform on radio and also in an all-female (except, obviously, for Griffin) group led by Billie Walker. In 1944 he recorded another couple of dozen songs in Chicago for World, a radio transcriptions company owned by Decca. These were his first sessions with a full band, which suited him just fine, and he drew on most of the material he'd previously recorded for Decca. He recorded a final studio sesson for King in 1946, after which his health began to deteriorate. He had a reputation as a drifter, but was also diabetic and a notorious drinker (when he'd sung "I'm Ready To Reform" in 1944 he obviously wasn't telling the whole truth). Griffin never made any more records himself, although Ray Price recorded some of his songs in the early '50s (including the morbid masterpiece "Beyond The Last Mile"), bandleader Leo Teel cut the oddity "He's Gazin' At Daisy Roots Now," and Eddy Arnold and Red Foley both turned "Just Call Me Lonesome" into a big hit. Griffin, however, never got to enjoy the financial fruits of his career. Struck by tuberculosis on top of his diabetes, he finally died in 1958 at the age of forty-six.

⊙ **The Last Letter** (1996; Bear Family). This 3-disc box includes all of Rex Griffin's recordings for Decca, World, and King plus 16 songs of his recorded by his brother Buddy in the 1950s. It's a pretty interesting look at the growth of a yodeling Jimmie Rodgers protégé into a more full-bodied songwriter with his own voice. Early songs have an attractive quaintness, but later recordings like "The Last Letter," "Over The River," and "Beyond The Last Mile" are more full-bodied—honestly rendered and wonderfully dark. Even "I'm As Free As The Breeze" cuts like a knife ("I'm as free as the breeze and happy as you please while you're singing the blues in the rain").

Suicide Songs

Death and dying have long provided fertile fodder for country songsmiths. From Victorian murder ballads to paeans to dying mothers, from epic remembrances of great tragedies to the personal pain of losing a beloved child, country music has gained a reputation as a rather morbid form of expression. With this in mind, it should be clear that even that most intimate and loaded means of passing, suicide, has been a favorite subject among many prominent country artists.

In the 1930s, the brother duet of Bill and Earl Bollick (the **Blue Sky Boys**) popularized "Katie Dear," a story of star-crossed young lovers who make a suicide pact when the girl's parents refuse to allow their union. This classic tune tells a timeless story that closely resembles *Romeo And Juliet*. The archaic imagery and third-person delivery gives the song a somewhat emotionally remote quality peculiar to early commercial country music.

By the '40s, the rise of honky-tonk music was creating a more personal approach to songwriting. One of the innovators of this trend was the great **Floyd Tillman**, whose "You Made Me Live, Love, And Die" tackles the subject from an altogether different perspective. Sung from the point of view of the doomed man, in Tillman's hands it becomes the ultimate vengeful guilt trip to be laid on an unfaithful lover.

Furthering this trend in personal singing and songwriting with much greater renown than Tillman was **Hank Williams**. Of course, his self-destruction in the early '50s is the stuff of legend and almost qualifies as a kind of suicide in and of itself. But "Long Gone Lonesome Blues" makes light of a man's desire to drown himself with the kind of gritty dark humor that made Hank famous.

The underrated Bakersfield honky-tonker **Wynn Stewart** gave one of his most chilling performances in 1962 on a tune called "One Way To Go." Recorded as an afterthought merely to round out a session, it tells the story of a man who sees plunging himself headlong off a rooftop as the only way to release himself from his loneliness. An understated arrangement complements an over-the-top theme to make a memorable record.

The '70s saw the rise of another stellar songwriting talent with a penchant for self-destructive behavior. One of **Townes Van Zandt**'s most haunting compositions was "Waiting Around To Die," which cast narcotics addiction as a form of slow suicide. The little-seen film *Heartworn Highways* features an amazing performance of this song, captured in Townes' living room while his tough-as-nails neighbor openly weeps. It's a moment not to be missed.

—Tom Armstrong

Hawkshaw Hawkins

Hawkshaw Hawkins racked up a handful of country chart hits during the late 1940s, and throughout the '50s he was a mighty *Grand Ole Opry* star. After his tragic death in a plane crash in 1963, however (the same crash that killed Patsy Cline, Cowboy Copas, and Randy Hughes), his fame faded. These days, few country fans know much about him—if they know his name at all.

And that's a shame, because musically Hawkins was a sturdy, reliable recording artist. Despite his colorful western attire and commanding tall figure, he wasn't a flashy singer, which was part of his appeal. He had a smooth, attractive voice and a honky-tonk style that remained more or less consistent as he jumped back and forth between three labels (King, RCA Victor, and Columbia) during his fifteen years as a recording artist.

Harold Franklin Hawkins was born on 22 December, 1921 in Huntington, West Virginia. He played locally on the radio and traveled a bit on the East Coast before joining the military during World War II. After the war, he became a member of the WWVA *Wheeling Jamboree* in Wheeling, West Virginia, and also had a program on CBS radio. During this time he also developed a following not only for his excellent singing but for his colorful stage shows which often involved trained horses and tricks performed with rope and bullwhip. In 1955 he joined the *Grand Ole Opry*.

Hawkins recorded his first singles, "Pan American" and "Doghouse Boogie," for King Records in 1948, and both made the Top 10 on *Billboard*'s country charts. He stayed with King until 1953, earning four more chart hits—a minor streak that dried up when he switched to RCA Victor. At a time when the Nashville Sound was turning many country singers to mush, it was to Hawkins' credit that he never succumbed to that suburban trend, though he dabbled now and again in modern production styles and the occasional background chorus. In 1959 he moved to Columbia, and again his material retained a refreshing edge. He had a small hit with "Soldier's Joy," but that was the end of his chart success,

⊙ **22 Greatest Hits** (1997; Deluxe/Highland). A substantial disc that brings together recordings from thoughout his career, such as "I Wasted A Nickel," "Dog House Boogie," "Slow Poke," "Little White Washed Chimney," and "Lonesome 7-7203."

Hawkshaw Hawkins

although he remained a popular *Opry* star. In 1960 he married singer Jean Shepard.

Hawkins left Columbia in 1962 and returned to his old home base, King. He scored his only #1 for them with the Justin Tubb composition "Lonesome 7-7203," but sadly wasn't able to capitalize on that new success. On 5 March, 1963, returning from a benefit gig in Kansas City, he lost his life in that fatal plane crash.

⊙ **Hawkshaw Hawkins, Vol. 1** (1958; King; reissued 1988). Contains many of his earliest recordings from the late 1940s and early '50s. The only hit here is his 1951 cover of Pee Wee King's "Slow Poke," but that doesn't matter: the rest is a lively mix of old-time standards ("Barbara Allen") and well-rendered heart songs ("I Am Slowly Dying Of A Broken Heart").

⊙ **Hawk 1953–1961** (1991; Bear Family). If you're a honky-tonk fan who's never heard Hawkins' music, this 3-CD box set will be a fabulous surprise. The set contains Hawk's RCA and Columbia recordings, which are as strong and reliable as his early King material. In typical Bear Family fashion, too, it contains an excellent biographical booklet.

Goldie Hill

Texas-born singer Goldie Hill might well have had a long and lucrative career in country music if she'd stuck with it longer than a few years. Instead, after one big hit ("I Let The Stars Get In My Eyes") and a few solid follow-ups, she got married to singer Carl Smith in 1957 and more or less retired from the business, choosing to spend her time at home on their horse farm south of Nashville. A shame, really, because Hill was a strong, firm singer with a rich, full voice. She also helped open doors: along with Kitty Wells' "It Wasn't God Who Made Honky Tonk Angels," Hill's "I Let The Stars" showed the conservative Nashville music industry that female artists could indeed sell a large number of records.

Goldie was born Angolda Voncile Hill on 11 January, 1933 in Karnes City, Texas, a small town southeast of San Antonio. In 1952 she started performing on the *Louisiana Hayride* and after that landed a record contract with Decca (thanks in part to the success of Wells). There weren't many female singers on the country charts at the time, so when Goldie's song "I Let The Stars Get In My Eyes" made it to the top in early 1953, it got her noticed. It was an answer song to "Don't Let The Stars Get In Your Eyes," a recent hit by its writer, Slim Willet, and also a hit for Perry Como and

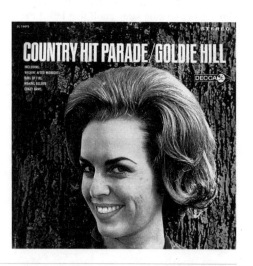

Skeets McDonald. Willet, in a flash of inspiration (and knowing an opportunity when he saw one), wrote the answer song as well. The next year Hill cut a couple of excellent duets with singer Justin Tubb (son of Ernest), "Looking Back To See" and "Sure Fire Kisses," then sang with Red Sovine on "Are You Mine." She continued to record songs on her own, too, such as the bold and bright "I'm Beginning To Feel Mistreated." Her musical career, though, which had plenty of life left in it, came to an end after she married Smith. She did record two albums for Epic in the late '60s as Goldie Hill Smith, but they failed to make a substantial impact and she returned to home life on the farm.

◗ Goldie Hill (1960; Decca). The first of several albums Decca released that collected Hill's singles from the 1950s. Not all Hill's recordings were standouts, but at her high points the music soared. She's well-deserving of a CD compilation.

Johnny Horton

S inger and songwriter Johnny Horton was at the peak of country success when his career was tragically halted by a drunk driver. Hits such as "Honky Tonk Man" and "North To Alaska," however, left a lasting impression. They were not only popular in their day but have endured: George Jones made great work out of Horton's "I'm A One Woman Man," for instance, and "Honky Tonk Man," Horton's first hit, was revived three decades later by Dwight Yoakam (it was his breakthrough song as well).

Toward the end of his career Horton cut a series of historical story songs for which he is most remembered, including "Johnny Reb," "Sink The Bismark," and "The Battle Of New Orleans". But Horton was diverse, drifting in and out of assorted musical interests and styles—western music, rockabilly, hard-edged honky tonk. During the last few years of his life he shifted between the dark-edged fable "When It's Springtime In Alaska," a beautifully loping version of "Lost Highway," the romantic "Whispering Pines," and the syrupy "The Mansion You Stole"—with all sorts of excellent boogie tunes like "Bull By The Horns," "The Electrified Donkey," and "Honky Tonk Man" scattered in among them.

Horton was born John Gale Horton on 30 April, 1925 in Los Angeles, California. He often claimed he came from Tyler, Texas and did indeed spend part of his childhood in Tyler. He attended several different colleges, though none for long, and drifted around the country taking odd jobs. At one point he headed north, to Alaska, where he worked in the fishing industry and also began to write songs. In 1950 he moved to Texas and then back out to Los Angeles. Fabor Robison—a notoriously shady record man who'd later handle Jim Reeves and the Browns until their relationship soured—spotted Horton and offered his services as manager. He persuaded his young client to sign to Cormac Records, and when that small label folded Robison started his own label, Abbott, specifically to release Horton's western-influenced music. Later he managed to get Horton a contract with Mercury. Horton also had his own TV show on a Pasadena station, on which he began calling himself the "Singing Fisherman." He then moved back east to Shreveport, Louisiana and started playing the *Louisiana Hayride*, where he met Hank Williams, who'd just been fired from the *Opry*. In 1953, less than a year after Hank's death, Horton married his widow Billie Jean Jones.

Johnny Horton, toupee firmly in place

Horton was not entirely driven toward music, and if it hadn't been for the encouragement of his new bride he might have quit the business altogether and headed for the fishing hole. None of his early records made any noise in the charts, but with Billie Jean in mind he decided to keep trying. He took on a new manager, Tillman Franks (Robison had by this point dumped Horton to focus on Jim Reeves) and before long he had a new contract with Columbia. At his first session he cut "Honky Tonk Man," a high-energy song that skirted the edges of rockabilly, and which turned Horton's career to gold. Two years later his direction shifted again when he got hold of Jimmie Driftwood's song "The Battle Of New Orleans." It hit the top of both the country and pop charts and made Horton a major star. The song also set him in a more historical and folky direction, one defined by songs like "Johnny Freedom," "Jim Bridger," "Sink The Bismark," and "North To Alaska." These fitted in well with the then thriving urban folk revival (which was also fueling Driftwood's career). Just as "Alaska" was hitting the charts, however, Horton was mowed down by a drunk driver on 5 November, 1960 while returning from a gig in Austin, Texas.

⊙ **The Early Years** (1991; Bear Family; reissued 1998). This set collects all Horton's hard-to-find pre-Columbia sides for the Cormac, Abbott and Mercury labels. There are also overdubs he did for Briar and Dot and some early publishing demos of songs like "Why Did It Happen To Me" and "All For The Love Of A Girl," which, performed solo, are that much more haunting.

⊙ **1956–1960** (1991; Bear Family). For those who feel the Columbia/Legacy collection isn't enough, this 4-CD box set contains all Horton's Columbia recordings.

⊙ **Honky Tonk Man: The Essential Johnny Horton (1956–1960)** (1996; Columbia/Legacy). This substantial 2-CD compilation covers the highlights of Horton's 5 years with Columbia. A few songs like "The Mansion You Stole" are drowned in strings, and beauties like "Whispering Pines" are sadly missing, but there's still plenty to love—from spare and edgy early cuts ("Honky Tonk Hardwood Floor") to later greats like "Bull By The Horns" and "North To Alaska."

Johnnie And Jack

With their up-beat and tangy 1951 hit "Poison Love," vocal and guitar team Johnnie And

Jack introduced hints of Latin rhythms into the Nashville consciousness. The duo's name implies they were a brother act, but in actuality they were brothers-in-law, brought together on a full-time basis in 1938 when Jack Anglin (born 13 May, 1916 in Franklin, Tennessee) married the singing sister (Louise) of Johnnie Wright (born 13 May, 1914 in Mount Juliet, Tennessee). Wright himself was married to Muriel Ellen Deason, aka Kitty Wells, who sang with the two men from the late '30s until she hit the charts as a solo artist with her landmark 1952 single "It Wasn't God Who Made Honky Tonk Angels."

Johnnie, Jack, Muriel, and their Tennessee Hillbillies band toured the South and played on various radio stations throughout the '40s, their music and travels briefly interrupted by World War II service. Johnnie And Jack first recorded for Apollo and King in the late '40s, and soon after they earned a spot on the *Grand Ole Opry*—which insisted they drop the term "hillbillies" from their name (they opted for Tennessee Mountain Boys instead). From 1948–52 they shifted their home base to Shreveport, Louisiana and station KWKH, home of the *Louisiana Hayride*—they were even part of that program's first broadcast on 3 April, 1948.

The duo signed to RCA in 1949, and had their first chart hit with "Poison Love" in 1951. Their vocal harmonies and arrangements maintain an old-time hillbilly flavor, yet their songs are often up-beat, lively, and full of rhythmic curls, showing the influence of Latin, Cajun and calypso music ("The Banana Boat Song") as well as R&B (their 1954 #1 hit "Oh Baby Mine"). They returned to the *Grand Ole Opry* in 1953, and continued recording for RCA throughout the rest of the decade. They next jumped over to Decca, which issued their 1962 recording "Slow Poison" (their only Decca hit) under the name Johnny And Jack—a misspelling that Wright, even as a solo artist, adhered to for the rest of his career.

The duo's career ended sadly on 7 March, 1963 when Jack Anglin died in a car wreck. Ironically, he was on his way to the funeral of Patsy Cline, Hawkshaw Hawkins, Cowboy Copas, and Randy Hughes, who'd been killed in a plane crash only days earlier. Wright continued performing as a solo artist, and in 1965 he earned a #1 chart hit with "Hello Vietnam." A loping call-to-duty song ("We must end communism in that land/or freedom will start slipping through our hands") wherein a soldier kisses his sweetheart goodbye before heading off to war, it was one of Tom T.

Johnnie (aka "Johnny") And Jack

Hall's earliest lucky breaks as a songwriter—well before he matured into more socially conscious material like "Mama Bake A Pie" and "America The Ugly." Wright had a few other solo hits during the '60s, but without Jack Anglin his voice felt naked and unstable. From 1969 onward he and Kitty Wells formed a touring Family Show (which for a while also took the form of a syndicated TV program) that they've maintained into the new millennium.

⊙ **All The Best Of Johnnie And Jack** (1970; RCA). A great and quite substantial double-LP collection of the duo's RCA material, from "Poison Love" to "The Banana Boat Song," in their original mono versions (as a rule, beware of "reprocessed" or "rechanneled" stereo versions of historic mono recordings). Too bad RCA hasn't kept this (and countless more of its awesome stash of vault recordings) in print.

⊙ **At KWKH** (1994; Bear Family). A live radio recording from the group's days at Shreveport station KWKH (home of the *Louisiana Hayride*), this single-CD set features Kitty Wells trading lead vocals with Johnnie And Jack on a mixture of old-time favorites and country hits such as "Orange Blossom Special," "The Singing Waterfall," "My Bucket's Got A Hole In It," and "Cotton-Eyed Joe."

⊙ **Johnnie And Jack And The Tennessee Mountain Boys** (1992; Bear Family). As is often the case with Bear Family's bigger collections, this 6-CD box set of Johnnie And Jack recordings is more than the average fan will care to handle, but a godsend to those who can't get enough of this rurally flavored duo.

⊙ **Greatest Hits** (1997; King). A slim 10-song CD, it nonetheless includes such chart-hit highlights as "Poison Love," "Cryin' Hear Blues," "I Get So Lonely (Oh Baby Mine)," and "Slow Poison."

Johnnie And Jack

George Jones

> "Jones' voice, when he unleashes it, has the power of a great primal scream of sorrow, conjuring up a bottomless pathos that is the essence of honky tonk desperation."
>
> —Billy Sherrill

George Jones is not just one of country music's master vocalists, he's one of the greatest American song stylists of the twentieth century. Care to argue? Listen to a sampling of his hundreds of recordings, and it's obvious: his rich, buttery vocal tone coupled with his penchant for turning words and syllables into taffy, pulling them apart and gnawing them into pieces, give his songs a feeling of truth that's impossible to capture and define. Jones doesn't just sing, he gets inside the lyrics—whether of sorrow, pain, or tenderness—and loses himself almost blindly. Hank Williams, Ernest Tubb, and Lefty Frizzell created the honky-tonk setting that Jones grew up in and around, but when the young Texas singer got hold of it he took the music where it had never been before. In turn, he helped country stay honest, alive, and emotionally raw even as the world (and the recording studios) grew increasingly modern.

Jones has written songs himself ("The Window Up Above," "Life To Go"), but his vocal performances are what stand out more than anything. It doesn't matter that George Richey penned "The Grand Tour" or that James Taylor wrote the vocal *tour de force* "Bartender's Blues:" when George sings, the song is his. In a career spanning five decades and counting, he's covered all shades of fragile human emotions—romantic optimism ("We Can Make It"), loneliness ("These Days I Barely Get By"), drunken shame ("Still Doin' Time") and unrequited love ("He Stopped Loving Her Today"). He can get silly ("I'm A People") and sappy ("The Ceremony"), but it's the down-and-out portraits of people scraping bottom that he does best of all. Which is why such mindblowing songs as "The Grand Tour," "If Drinking Don't Kill Me," and most especially "A Good Year For The Roses" will bring you right to your knees.

Like so many country music greats, George Glenn Jones came from a small town and a working-class background. He was born on 12 September, 1931 in Saratoga, Texas, a rough-hewn pinprick in a southeastern region of the state known as the Big Thickets. As a child he sang in church, and though his father was a notorious drunk he was intuitive enough to buy young George a guitar. By the age of twelve George was playing for money on the streets of nearby Beaumont, where his father now worked in the shipyards. Several years later he had a show on a local radio station and was playing clubs with a local duo, Eddie & Pearl. He married in 1950 (it quickly soured), served a couple of years in the Marines, then returned to Texas, where in 1953 he gained the attention of budding producer and label honcho Harold "Pappy" Daily. The pair began a business relationship that would last for many years—a bond not unlike that between Hank Williams and his producer, Fred Rose.

Daily co-owned (with Jack Starnes and later Don Pierce) a brand-new label, Starday, and Jones was quickly signed to it. His first singles were hardly standouts—it's amazing how close he sounds to his hero Hank Williams, for instance, on "No Money In This Deal," one of his first recordings. Jones' own personality and style began to trickle through in 1955 when he cut the sharp and quick "Why Baby Why." Stylistically, it was still in the Williams camp, but it sounded fresh and turned heads—including those of Webb Pierce and Red Sovine, who covered it as a duet and took it to #1 in 1956. Jones had already appeared on the *Louisiana Hayride*, but later that year, thanks to a string of hits that began with "Why Baby Why" and included "I'm Ragged But I'm Right," he made his *Grand Ole Opry* debut. Around this same time George also knocked out some rockabilly songs under the pseudonym Thumper Jones.

In early 1957 Starday and Mercury joined forces, which brought Jones into the Mercury fold. When the two labels then parted ways a year and a half later, Daily and Jones stayed on at Mercury and Don Pierce went on to run Starday alone. Following the split, Jones had his first #1 hit with "White Lightning," a goofy song about moonshining written by J.P. Richardson (aka the Big Bopper) that showed off Jones' vocal playfulness. On the other side of the fence was "The Window Up Above," a mournful cheating song that—along with his #1 follow-up, the sweeping "Tender Years"—indicated the more ballad-oriented style that would define Jones' sound over the next couple of decades. The vocal chorus on "Window," "Family Bible," and other late-period Mercury material also marks the entry of the Nashville Sound into Jones' arrangements.

Jones' Mercury contract expired in 1962, and when Mercury executive Art Talmadge made the leap over to United Artists, Daily brought George there as well. That year his new label released "She Thinks I Still Care," another stellar ballad of pain. Jones stayed with United Artists for two years, cutting further gems like "The Race Is On" and some sturdy duets with Melba Montgomery. Then he switched labels once again, following Talmadge over to Musicor, with Daily still working as his producer and manager.

Jones had recorded some odd material before—"Slave Lover," "Open Pit Mine"—but his Musicor period produced some truly strange tracks, including "Love Bug," "I'm A People," and the truly pitiful "Unwanted Babies," a 'protest' song of sorts written by his friend, Peanut Montgomery, meant to captivate the Bob Dylan generation.

By 1968, George's marriage to his wife Shirley was over, thanks in no small part to his incessant drinking. He'd met hairdresser-turned-country singer Tammy Wynette previously, but when he moved to Nashville after his divorce he fell in love with her. Their marriage and reign as "Mr. and Mrs. Country Music" was tabloid fodder from its glamorous start in 1969 to its bitter end six years later. Along the way they cut several albums together, with many of the songs (from the gooey "The Ceremony" to the pessimistic "Golden Rings") reminiscent of their own relationship.

When his Musicor contract came to an end in 1971, Jones moved to Tammy's label, Epic. He also had a falling out with Daily—a man who'd been a father figure to him for almost two decades—and began working instead with Tammy's producer, Billy Sherrill. Jones' first single for Epic was the optimistic "We Can Make It." As a producer, Sherrill's hand was heavy, and for this reason Jones' Epic work is frequently criticized. It's true that some songs were sickly sweet (George's version of Rex Griffin's "The Last Letter" is hard to bear), but when the vibe was right Jones' voice fit Sherrill's lush, melodramatic approach amazingly well. In many ways, his singing never sounded better. Strings and choruses had shown up in Jones' songs since the early '60s, and frankly, Sherrill was much more savvy with such accoutrements than Pappy Daily.

Over the next decade, Sherrill helped Jones create some of his most intense music: "Loving You Could Never Be Better," "The Grand Tour," "The Door," "Memories Of Us," "If Drinking Don't Kill Me (Her Memory Will)," and "These Days I Barely Get By." The climax of his relationship with Sherrill came in 1980 with "He Stopped Loving Her Today," which stormed the charts, sold in the millions, and won all manner of awards. It also rescued him back from some of his roughest years. During the late '70s he'd divorced Tammy, declared bankruptcy, tried (and failed) to quit drinking, battled with drug abuse, and earned his reputation as "No-Show Jones" for missing gigs regularly. In the years following "He Stopped Loving Her Today" his life began turning back around. The biggest news was that by the mid-'80s he'd finally (with help from his new wife, Nancy) given up drugs and drink.

Jones recorded for Epic until the end of the '80s, then switched labels yet again to MCA. His hits were no longer big or frequent, but he was adored by music stars young and old, country and rock, who were lining up to sing his praises, and to sing with him. Among those who dueted with him during the '80s and '90s were: Randy Travis, Shelby Lynne, Ricky Van Shelton, James Taylor, Emmylou Harris, Merle Haggard, Mark Chesnutt, B.B. King, Elvis Costello, and Patty Loveless. Jones was inducted into the Country Music Hall of Fame in 1992, and has continued to release solo albums regular as clockwork. Some songs like "High-Tech Redneck" were pretty dumb, but others such as 1996's "Hundred Proof Memories" and 1998's "Wild Irish Rose" show he's still very much a contender. Even in his later years his voice is far richer and stronger than almost anyone else's on the market.

"Wild Irish Rose" appeared on the album It Don't Get Any Better Than This, which turned out to be George's last for MCA — the label dropped him not long afterward. And, speaking of tragedies, in the spring of 1999, he came close to meeting his creator when he slammed his Lexus sport-utility vehicle into a bridge abutment near his Franklin, Tennessee home. He was talking on a cell phone at the time, didn't have his seat belt on, and, as if those two acts weren't sin enough, it turned out he'd been drinking again. Incredibly (and after some shame-faced apologizing), Jones was back on the touring circuit that very summer to support his new album, COLD HARD TRUTH, which was released on his new label, Asylum.

⦿ If My Heart Had Windows (1968; Musicor). The source for both "Unwanted Babies" and "Poor Chinee," probably the crassest songs of Jones' recording career. Other songs on the album, however, including the title track, are typically beautiful.

⊙ The Great Songs Of Leon Payne (1971; Musicor; reissued 1987; Highland). Jones had previously recorded entire albums of songs by Bob Wills, Hank Williams, and Dallas Frazier, among others, but this tribute to the great honky-tonk songwriter (author of "I Love You Because") is a cut above, mostly because Payne's writing is so stellar—and a great match for Jones' voice.

⊙ Don't Stop The Music (1987; Ace). An excellent collection covering Jones' years with producer Pappy Daily, beginning in the 1950s and running through Jones' first decade. It concentrates on his hard and solid honky-tonk material, especially lesser-known titles like "Mr. Fool," "Giveaway Girl," and "Boogie Woogie Mexican Boy."

⊙ Cup Of Loneliness: The Classic Mercury Years (1994; Mercury Nashville). A double-CD collection of the first decade of his career, covering his years on Starday and Mercury. An excellent package if you're looking for Jones' purer honky-tonk arrangements, stuff that's more spare than lush.

⊙ The Essential George Jones: The Spirit Of Country (1994; Sony Legacy/Epic). This 2-CD collection is the most comprehensive overview of Jones' career, containing songs from his Starday years in the 1950s through his lush work with Billy Sherrill two decades later. Though it hits earlier high points like "Why Baby Why" and "A Good Year For The Roses," most of it is dedicated to Jones' years on Epic in the '70s and '80s—which is great stuff, mind you.

⊙ Vintage Collection (1996; Capitol). Jones had been paired with singing partners since the 1950s—Sonny Burns, Virginia Spurlock, Margie Singleton—but Melba Montgomery was one of the most successful, as the duo made a great match in voice and style. This

collection contains most of the duets they cut for United Artists.

⊙ The Battle/Memories Of Us (1999; Koch). A single CD packed with two great mid-1970s Sherrill-produced beauties. "The Battle" likens love to a wartime skirmish—the good stuff as well as the troubles, which makes the song doubly disturbing. Ditto for "Wean Me," a self-deprecating drinking song with a baby-bottle analogy. "I Still Sing The Old Songs" (penned by David Allan Coe) is a powerhouse, "Memories Of Us" is dark and lonely, while "Have You Seen My Chicken" is one of those twisted, near-nonsensical oddities that George does so well.

⊙ The George Jones Collection (1999; MCA). If you want to hear what George was up to during the 1990s, MCA dashed together a 12-song collection (released, by the way, just after he was dumped from the roster) that gives a halfway decent picture. There are a few low points ("High-Tech Redneck"), but also some highlights—the "Honky Tonk Song," in which George gently mocks his old booze-induced habits, the moving "Wild Irish Rose," and the long-winded but still intriguing "Patches," a duet with B.B. King. Not bad for a late-period collection.

Grandpa Jones

A popular singer and showman on both the *Grand Ole Opry* and *Hee-Haw*, Grandpa Jones made a career out of writing and playing old-time novelty tunes with the voice and personality of a man who (at least when he started the act) was easily three times his age. A quirky idea, for sure, but it was obviously well thought out and earned him a hearty following. Everything about him was deliberately 'old,' in fact. His repertoire was filled with folksongs like "Brown Girl And Fair Ellender" and "Mountain Dew" (his first hit); others were originals that spoke fondly of coon hunts and made cranky fun of new-fangled ideas like "Daylight Savings Time." He learned to frail the banjo at the same time that Earl Scruggs was dazzling *Opry* audiences with his three-finger runs and swirls. And as modern pop and rock influences crept further into country music, Jones turned and made a hit out of a Jimmie Rodgers song ("T For Texas") and maintained a traditional spirit in his music. By the time he actually did become a grandpa, his recording career had spanned five decades, he'd earned a place in the Country Music

Hall of Fame, and was one of country's most universally loved performers.

Grandpa was born Louis Marshall Jones on 20 October, 1913 in Niagra, Kentucky. Like many rural children he had a musical background: his mother sang ballads and his father fiddled. As a teenager Jones began performing on the radio in Akron, Ohio, playing songs inspired by Jimmie Rodgers (who was then still alive). After that he began working with balladeer Bradley Kincaid, and by 1935 the two singers had a radio show in Boston playing traditional songs (like other northern cities, Boston was filling up with transplanted southerners pining for a taste of home). Kincaid began calling Jones "Grandpa" because of his early-morning grumpiness, and the name stuck. With the help of Kincaid and a couple of Boston vaudevillians, Jones concocted an old man's costume to match his newfound character.

During the late '30s "Grandpa" Jones started playing radio shows on his own around the West Virginia and Ohio region and also publishing songbooks, which won him further public attention. While at Cincinnati's WLW during the '40s he met the Delmore Brothers and Merle Travis, and the group began playing gospel music together as the Brown's Ferry Four. Cincinnati was also home to a new independent record label, King, and it's here that Jones first recorded. He cut a few songs in the early '40s, but after World War II—about the same time he started playing banjo instead of guitar—King released his versions of "Mountain Dew" and "Old Rattler." His lively readings of these two old-time songs really took off and gained him a wider reputation.

Jones first joined the *Grand Ole Opry* in 1946. A couple of years later he moved to Washington, DC, but by 1952 he was back on the *Opry* and living in Nashville. During the '50s he recorded for RCA Victor and then Decca. In 1960 he began a long tenure with Monument, staying with that label into the early '70s. One of his Monument albums was GRANDPA JONES SINGS REAL FOLK SONGS, his answer to the growing folk music revival. In the mid-'70s he finally switched to the CMH label.

Contemporary country fans probably know Jones best from his *Hee-Haw* days. By the time he started on that show in 1969 he was in his late fifties and, if not quite a senior citizen, at least he was beginning to gray for real around the edges. He was inducted into the Country Music Hall of Fame in 1978, and in 1984 the University of Tennessee published his autobiography *Everybody's Grandpa*. He performed regularly on the *Grand Ole Opry* right up until his death in early 1998.

⊙ **Country Music Hall Of Fame** (1991; MCA). A collection of all 15 studio tracks Jones cut for Decca in the late 1950s plus one live recording ("Cindy"). Many are straight-up novelty songs like "Rattler's Pup," but "Fallen Leaves" is a nice original ballad (strange it was previously unreleased) and "All American Boy" (written by a young Bobby Bare) is a mildly humorous talking-blues in the soon-to-come Bob Dylan style.

⊙ **Everybody's Grandpa** (1996; Bear Family). A 5-CD box set of all Jones' recordings for Monument from 1960–1973. Many of the arrangements are simple and traditional, others feature drums, choruses and other Nashville Sound accoutrements.

⊙ **An American Original** (1998; CMH). Thirty songs from Jones' days on the CMH label in the 1970s and '80s.

⊙ **28 Greatest Hits** (1998; King). A collection of Grandpa's classic King sides on a CD that updates and nearly doubles the earlier 16 GREATEST HITS collection. There are even liner notes this time.

Louvin Brothers

When Ira and Charlie Louvin sang together, the sound they created was otherworldly. It sounds corny, and it's difficult to explain, but the delicate, subtle harmonies produced by these two Alabama boys were and are like no other sound in country music. The Louvin Brothers actually represent the culmination—the epitome—of a tradition of close-harmony brother groups stretching back to the 1930s. Like their forebears the Blue Sky Boys, the Delmore Brothers, and the Monroe Brothers, they played stripped-down, acoustic-based music—Charlie on guitar, Ira on mandolin—that emphasized their singing. The mandolin, combined with the high-tenor harmonies, created similarities to bluegrass, though the brothers chose not to associate themselves with that musically furious world. Instead they split their time between straighter and simply arranged country and gospel songs, many of them originals.

Throughout their career together, the Louvins' music embraced all sorts of styles and subjects: sentimental love ("If I Could Only Win Your Love," later a hit for Emmylou Harris); murder ("Knoxville Girl"); war tragedies ("From Mother's Arms To Korea"); up-tempo novelties ("Cash On The Barrelhead"); philosophical rants ("Broad

Minded," which features the mind-boggling line "the word 'broad-minded' is spelled s-i-n"); and fundamentalist politics ("Don't Let Them Take The Bible Out Of Our School Rooms"). A few songs such as "Red Hen Hop" even toyed with rockabilly. And then there's the gospel material, which possesses an intensity, a deep-welled sincerity, that can't be matched. Both brothers grew up in a staunchly religious part of the country, but perhaps Ira—who was plagued all his adult life by an addiction to drink—also saw gospel singing as a means to redeem his darker side. Whatever the case, when they sing such fiery numbers as "Are You Washed In The Blood" and "Satan Is Real," the fear of God drips from every word. Even on the paranoid "They've Got The Church Outnumbered" they're not kidding around. No irony here: this stuff is absolutely real.

Ira was born Ira Lonnie Loudermilk on 21 April, 1924; Charlie was born three years later on 7 July. (Future songwriter and singer John D. Loudermilk, born in 1934, was their first cousin.) They were both born near Henagar, Alabama, a small town in the San Mountain region in the state's northeastern corner. Taken with the close-harmony singing style of groups like the Delmores and the Monroe Brothers, Ira and Charlie began performing together on a local station. When Charlie entered the service during World War II, Ira sang briefly in Charlie Monroe's band (the Monroe Brothers had split in the late '30s, and Bill Monroe had by that point already formed the Blue Grass Boys). When Charlie returned he and Ira began singing at various stations, mostly in Knoxville.

The Louvins first recorded in 1947 with singer-guitarist Eddie Hill for the small Apollo label. One of the four songs they cut together, "Alabama"—a pleasantly sentimental song of love for their home state—was the only one that featured them on lead vocals. Hill put them in touch with the publishing house Acuff-Rose, and founding partner Fred Rose helped them get a session with Decca (they cut two songs in supposedly under ten minutes), then a deal with MGM (Hank Williams' label). Here the brothers first cut some of their classic numbers, including "Weapon Of Prayer" and "Great Atomic Power." Their early Capitol sides were superbly crafted, but these MGM sessions were among the purest-sounding of their career, partly because they stuck exclusively to the acoustic guitar/mandolin arrangements. Finally, in 1952, Rose landed them a better contract with Los Angeles-based Capitol,

Ira (left) and Charlie Louvin, Newburgh, NY, 1960

Louvin Brothers

which remained their label from then on. Their first session produced their first hit, "The Family Who Prays," and featured a young Chet Atkins on electric guitar.

After Charlie briefly served in the Korean War, the brothers regrouped and in 1955 began appearing on the *Grand Ole Opry* (thanks to some serious string-pulling from their producer, Ken Nelson). That same year they released "When I Stop Dreaming," their first secular hit and a big one at that. The Louvins had more chart hits, including "I Don't Believe You've Met My Baby" and "Cash On The Barrelhead" (which Gram Parsons later revived), and in 1956 Capitol released their first long-play album, TRAGIC SONGS OF LIFE. (MGM also released one, THE LOUVIN BROTHERS, a collection of their earlier sides.) They even toured with Elvis Presley. As the decade wore on, however, and rock'n'roll took its toll on the country market, the Louvins' promising popularity reached only moderate level. The success of a traditional, harmony-based duet was simply hard to maintain in the face of the rockabilly assault—even with the addition of electric guitar and further leanings toward a mainstream country sound. Turbulence was also building on a personal level, and fights between the two brothers became as famous as Ira's drinking bouts (not to mention his scuffle with his third wife, during which she pulled a gun on him).

The brothers persevered into the '60s, recording their usual mixture of traditional and original material as well as tribute albums to both the Delmore Brothers and Roy Acuff. Later recordings also saw far more modern instrumentation—drums, piano, electric guitars—mixed in with their harmonies. Finally in 1963, the feuding came to a head and the brothers split up, each moving on to a solo career. Ira, the eternally troubled genius, didn't fare so well on his own. He retreated to Alabama with his fourth wife, Anne, but he did record for Capitol and eventually emerged to begin performing again. However, in 1965, returning from a gig in Kansas City with his wife and two friends, they were hit head-on by a drunk driver and killed.

Charlie was a successful solo artist almost right off the bat, his voice and style adapting to the modern sounds and songs of Nashville quite comfortably. He maintained a Capitol contract into the '70s and had hits with such songs as "See The Big Man Cry," "I Don't Love You Anymore," "Will You Visit Me On Sundays," and "Something To Brag About" (the latter a duet with Melba Montgomery). His solo material isn't as gorgeous

and haunting as his recordings with Ira, but it's attractive in its own right. He continues to appear on the *Opry* and record and tour occasionally. He also presides over the homespun Louvin Brothers Museum near his home in Bell Buckle, Tennessee.

Louvin Brothers

⊙ **Tragic Songs Of Life** (1956; Capitol; reissued 1996). A beauty and a classic, this album (their first and now finally reissued on CD) contains such gems as "Knoxville Girl" and "Alabama," most (but not all) with sadness and tragedy as their theme.

⊙ **Satan Is Real** (1960; Capitol; reissued 1996). Sporting a notorious cover of the brothers in white suits being chased through the flames of Hell by Satan himself! It's not just a novelty, though, as the music inside is sung with pure, haunted passion. Songs include "The Christian Life," covered later by the Byrds.

⊙ **A Tribute To The Delmore Brothers** (1960; Capitol; reissued 1996). A concept album the Louvin Brothers were destined to record, as the Delmores were one of their inspirations and also hailed from the same region of Alabama. Beautiful music, without question.

⊙ **Radio Favorites 1951–1957** (1987; Country Music Foundation; reissued 1993). Contains 14 live versions, many from various *Grand Ole Opry* performances, of the brothers singing such greats as "You're Running Wild," "They've Got The Church Outnumbered," and "When I Stop Dreaming." The sound quality is excellent, and they're both in fine voice and spirit.

⊙ **Close Harmony** (1992; Bear Family). A massive 8-CD box set of all the Louvins' recordings. Expensive, but hard to resist.

⊙ **When I Stop Dreaming: The Best Of The Louvin Brothers** (1995; Razor & Tie). Here's your best bet for a single sampler CD of Louvin Brothers material—one that contains both secular and gospel material from throughout their career.

Charlie Louvin

⊙ **The Longest Train** (1996; Watermelon). Charlie's voice is unfortunately no longer what it once was, but still there's an endearing warmth to these songs.

Louvin Brothers

This Cold War With You: Skunks, Reds And Atom Bombs

For the first few decades especially, the content of many country songs really stuck close to home—love for mother, desire for another, despair over unrequited passion, even the inevitability of death. Songs of soldiers were common enough and most were sentimental in tone, telling of death in the line of duty ("A Soldier's Last Letter") or the pain of separated lovers ("At Mail Call Today"). But the advent of World War II also offered a prime opportunity for well-mannered singers to shed their skins of politeness and get a little vicious. Carson Robison, a songwriting giant from the 1920s who was no stranger to 'event songs,' invited listeners to "Get Your Gun And Come Along (We're Fixin' To Kill A Skunk)" before declaring, in even blunter fashion, that "We've Gotta Slap That Dirty Little Jap." Zeke Clements gave the enemy a stern warning in "Smoke On The Water," and Johnny Bond suggested (with appropriate 'novelty' sound effects) hurling a wad of spit right in "Der Fuehrer's Face." Texas Jim Robertson assured fans that "You'll Never Be Blue In A Blue Uniform," and Elton Britt maintained a sentimental but still stately demeanor in "There's A Star-Spangled Banner Waving Somewhere," a song about a crippled boy's yearning to fight for his country. Britt's song in particular proved hugely popular, racking up millions in sales and becoming country's first gold record.

After the war ended, the threats didn't entirely disappear. Just ask Lulu Belle And Scotty, who wrote and recorded the self-righteous "I'm No Communist." The lyrics refer to the joys of "private ownership" ("I believe a man should own his own") and even give kudos to the McCarthy-led House Un-American Activities Committee for attempting to sort out "who's American and who's a low-down Red." Scotty's song wasn't the only piece of Commie bait to make the market. Little Jimmie Dickens moaned about how "They Locked God Outside The Iron Curtain," while both Pee Wee King and Red River Dave sang about the "Red Deck Of Cards" (a sort of answer song to the Bible-minded T. Texas Tyler hit "Deck Of Cards"). Roy Acuff offered some dead-serious "Advice To Joe"—meaning Stalin. And even Hank Williams (as Luke the Drifter) chimed in with "No, No Joe," a Fred Rose composition that adopted a more good-natured tone ("you're acting like a clown," Hank

said of the Soviet dictator). As for Ray Anderson, he could hardly contain his glee when "Stalin Kicked The Bucket."

The titles themselves may seem dated, but the messages at their core have by no means disappeared—in fact, patriotism has been a recurring theme in country music ever since. Just take a listen to Merle Haggard's "The Fightin' Side Of Me," Moe Bandy's "Americana," and especially Lee Greenwood's "God Bless The USA" (in which the onetime lounge singer intones "I'm proud to be an American, where at least I know I'm free").

While we're on the subject of evil menaces, we can't ignore the big bad Bomb. Atomic weapons, power and energy brought images of Armageddon into many folks' heads, and so it made sense that the subject often attached itself to religous-based material. In "The Great Atomic Power," the Louvin Brothers asked listeners whether they were truly prepared for the potential of "horrible destruction." The answer? "Give your heart and soul to Jesus, he will be your shielding sword." Johnnie And Jack saw God's only son in a different light, singing that "Jesus Hits Like An Atom Bomb." And the Buchanan Brothers took a far sterner attitude, reminding us that "There Is A Power Greater Than Atomic"—and that "if He [ie God] strikes us with His mighty power, not just some but everyone must die."

The reality of atomic catastrophe is dealt with in further songs like Marvin Rainwater's "Down In The Cellar," in which he's "holding my baby's hand" in what sounds like (if the menacing guitar leads and reference to "red hot sand" are any indication) a bomb shelter. During the '60s, Johnny Paycheck turned the spookiness up a few notches with "The Cave," about a man getting lost in a cave, hearing thunder up above, and then emerging to face the aftermath of a nuclear holocaust. And in "Revelation" (written by Bobby Braddock), singer Waylon Jennings recounts the terror of what appears to be nuclear annihilation in vivid melodramatic detail. That the song's protagonist is in a "cheap motel" with "someone else's woman" when the darkness comes just makes the end of the world that much more sordid.

Frankie Miller

Texas honky-tonker Frankie Miller may not be that well known, but he cut some excellent material during the 1950s and '60s that holds up

well. Hank Williams was clearly an influence: you can hear that in his vocals and arrangements, especially on his Columbia sides. But on songs he cut for Starday like "Too Hot To Handle," "Blackland Farmer," and "Mean Old Greyhound Bus" (written by Hank Cochran and Willie Nelson), he showed an intriguing, craftier approach that was more hillbilly in sound and proved he was much more than just a decent Hank copycat. As much as he loved playing, however, Miller was apparently plagued by stage fright which kept him from breaking bigger as a star.

Frank Miller was born on 17 December, 1931 in Victoria, Texas. He attended a local junior college on a football scholarship, formed a band he called the Drifting Texans (obviously in honor of Hank Williams' band the Drifting Cowboys), and began playing on a local radio station. In Houston he met Hank Locklin, who helped win him a contract with the small Gilt-Edge record label, a subsidiary of the somewhat larger Four Star (where Webb Pierce and the Maddox Brothers And Rose first recorded). Miller cut a handful of singles for Gilt Edge, then after a short stint in the military he signed with Columbia. Working at Jim Beck's studio in Dallas (where Lefty Frizzell recorded his classic early-'50s sides), Miller cut a series of singles between 1954 and 1956 that clearly showed the influence of Williams. When none charted, however, Columbia dropped him.

Miller performed locally for a few years until he was picked up by the Texas label Starday in 1959, at that point owned by Don Pierce (Starday co-founder "Pappy" Daily was by then busy at Mercury keeping tabs on his young charge, George Jones). That year Miller cut the self-penned "Blackland Farmer," which quickly became his best-known song and the biggest hit of his career. (Sleepy LaBeef also had a minor hit with it a decade later.) Other songs that gained some renown included "Family Man" and "Baby Rocked Her Dolly." He appeared for a while on the *Louisiana Hayride* and guested a few times on the *Grand Ole Opry*. Miller recorded for Starday until 1964, then a year later cut some material for United Artists. At this point, although much of his material had been excellent, he hadn't proved himself a lasting hitmaker—part of the reason being that his thick hillbilly sound was well out of fashion. Frustrated with Nashville he returned to Texas. In 1968 he cut a few more sides for Stop, but then took a management job at a Chrysler dealership in Arlington, Texas.

⊙ **Rockin' Rollin' Frankie Miller** (1983; Bear Family). His Starday sides from 1959–1964, the most musically interesting and stylistically original songs of his career, including "Blackland Farmer."

⊙ **Sugar Coated Baby** (1996; Bear Family). A hot single-CD collection of Miller's earliest recordings, beginning with 13 songs he cut for Gilt Edge in 1951 and 1952 and then including another dozen he cut in Jim Beck's studio for Columbia a few years later. Of the latter, "Hey! Where Ya Goin'?" and the sassy "It's No Big Thing To Me" are particularly tasty. The last 5 cuts are demos Miller made in 1956.

⊙ **Sugar Coated Baby** (1996; Bear Family). A single-CD collection of Miller's mid-1960s recordings.

George Morgan

"I never heard him hit a bad note."
—Lorrie Morgan

Eddy Arnold may have been the king of the countrypolitan singers in the 1950s and '60s, but country crooner George Morgan was, at least for a few years, hot on his tail. Morgan had an equally smooth and warm voice, a delicate sense of phrasing, and over the years retained a greater degree of traditional-country appeal. A Country Music Hall of Famer (elected in 1998), *Opry* regular, and the father of '90s country star Lorrie Morgan, George had quite a few hits during his nearly thirty-year career, though the biggest number came in one year, 1949. Still, Morgan is well remembered for one song that became his lifelong signature, "Candy Kisses." Built around heart-tugging lyrics and his warm, golden voice, the song foreshadowed the coming country-pop trends, yet at its core it was really just a down-to-earth tune with a simple arrangement and an endearing, unadorned melody.

George Thomas Morgan was born on 28 June, 1924 in Waverly, Tennessee and grew up in Barberton, Ohio. During his teens he gained experience on local radio programs, and his career was further strengthened when he began playing on the WWVA *Wheeling Jamboree* during the '40s. He joined the *Grand Ole Opry* in 1948, replacing Eddy Arnold, and signed to Columbia Records. His first session in early 1949 included his classic rendition of "Candy Kisses," and it eventually hit #1 on the country charts, remaining there for three weeks. Six more of his songs were country hits that year, including another of his own compositions, "Rainbow In My Heart," the Leon Payne song "Cry Baby Heart," and "Room Full Of Roses," written by Tim Spencer, a founding member of the Sons of the Pioneers.

Frankie Miller • George Morgan

Morgan left the *Opry* in 1956 to host a television program, but after a few years he returned, remaining with the show for the rest of his life. He enjoyed further hits through the '50s and into the '60s, including a duet with pop singer Marion Worth ("Slipping Around"), but toward the end most were barely cracking the country Top 40. He stayed with Columbia through the mid-'60s, then recorded for Starday, Stop, Decca/MCA, and Four Star. Some of his later recordings featured Little Roy Wiggins, formerly Eddy Arnold's steel guitarist, and retained a traditional feel in the midst of an increasingly glitz-oriented Nashville music scene. In the '70s Morgan joined with several dozen other country stars to form the Association of Country Entertainers, whose purpose was to defend the traditional aspects of country music in the modern era. He briefly served as chairman of the group. Unfortunately, however, complications from open-heart surgery eventually led to his death on 7 July, 1975.

⊙ **Room Full Of Roses: The George Morgan Collection** (1996; Razor & Tie). An excellent compilation of Morgan's original recordings, highlighted by such delicate, melancholy beauties as "Rainbow In My Heart," "Cry Baby Heart," and of course "Candy Kisses." Later songs like "Mr. Ting-a-Ling" (a tribute to Little Roy Wiggins) and Morgan's 1973 hit "Red Rose From The Blue Side Of Town" retain a refreshing simple-hearted quality.

Moon Mullican

Pianist and singer Moon Mullican was a multi-talented showman who crossed genre lines and today stands as one of the heroes of mid-period country music. Few artists can claim such a long and varied career—one that began in the earliest days of western swing, drove right into the heart of the honky-tonk world, and left Mullican standing just on the verge of rockabilly. An original in the country music world, Mullican the piano-playing honky-tonker was not only a top-notch instrumentalist but also a fine lead vocalist and songwriter—the only hillbilly pianist of his generation to emerge as a true country star.

Mullican's repertoire ran from "Sweeter Than The Flowers," an old-time sentimental ballad about the death of dear old Mom, to far more wild-haired numbers like "Cherokee Boogie" and the raunchy "Pipeliners Blues." Through it all Mullican

developed and maintained a rollicking hillbilly-boogie piano style that was loose, rowdy and thrilling—and in the end entirely his own. It wasn't until the arrival of Jerry Lee Lewis in the mid-1950s that another artist would use the piano to create such a roisterous country sound.

Moon was born Aubrey Wilson Mullican on 29 March, 1909 in Corrigan, a small town in the Piney Woods region of east Texas. His family was deeply religious, but Moon soon found himself more drawn to blues and juke-joint music. He first played guitar but eventually discovered the piano, and by the age of sixteen had left home to begin a career banging the keys in assorted bars, clubs, and probably brothels in Houston. During the early '30s western swing began to emerge as a popular new dance music, and Mullican found himself caught up in it. He first joined Leon "Pappy" Selph's Blue Ridge Playboys, a hillbilly dance band with a jazzy overbite. His bandmates there included future honky-tonk heroes Floyd Tillman and Ted Daffan. But Mullican's big break came when fiddler Cliff Bruner (a former member of Milton Brown's Brownies) tapped him as pianist and singer for his new western swing outfit, the Texas Wanderers. One of the songs Mullican performed with Bruner was his composition "Pipeliners Blues," a good-natured but raunchy number in which he spoke of laying pipe

Moon Mullican

As honky tonk was taking hold, country music opened its doors to yet another genre, boogie-woogie, which had debuted in the blues world in the 1920s courtesy of **Clarence "Pinetop" Smith**'s rollicking piano. **Albert Ammons** and **Pete Johnson** were the best of numerous pianists who continued the craze into the '30s. It was only a matter of time before the rest of the country (ie white folks) caught on, and in 1938 **Tommy Dorsey** had a hit with Smith's "Pinetop's Boogie Woogie." The next year country singer **Johnny Barfield** recorded "Boogie Woogie," and though it's boogie-woogie in name only it indicated that country folks were ready to shuffle and boogie on the dance floor, too (or at least now it was officially sanctioned). After the war, boogie was ready to occupy its rightful place in the hallowed honky-tonks.

It's not surprising that western swing bands, already possessing a seemingly endless amalgamation of musical genres and always ready for something new, would be the first to take a crack at boogie tunes. **Bob Wills** did it in 1946 with the energizing "Bob Wills' Boogie," and **Moon Mullican**—piano maestro for Cliff Bruner who possessed a 'three-finger' barrelhouse piano style meant for shaking the bottles—fronted a hot band on the boogie instrumental "Shoot The Moon" in 1946. Mullican's 1947 recording "Cherokee Boogie" was a big hit for Cincinnati's King label.

Another early country boogieman was **Merle Travis**, whose tasty licks were the driving force behind rhythm guitarist Porky Freeman's eight-to-the-bar "Boogie Woogie Boy" in 1945. Travis signed on with King a year later and continued his role, playing on

some early King sides of country brother duet the **Delmore Brothers**. Alton and Rabon Delmore recorded some classic tunes for Bluebird in the '30s, but in 1946 the boogie bug bit them big, and they hit back with "Hillbilly Boogie" (creating a new musical term in the process). They continued with such hits as "Freight Train Boogie" and the slower "Blues Stay Away From Me," both featuring a seductive low-end, wall-shaking electric guitar sound. They did some old-style tunes for King, too, very beautiful ones indeed, but as the boogie craze got bigger these songs were relegated to B-sides or the shelf.

And so it went. Country audiences did the boogie to such tunes as Arthur Smith's "Guitar Boogie," Speedy West and Jimmy Bryant's "Stratosphere Boogie," Jack Guthrie's "Oakie Boogie," Tennessee Ernie Ford's innumerable boogie numbers, Merle Travis' Capitol sides, Big Jim De Noone's "E Ramble," Lucky Boggs' "Drilling Rig Boogie," the Milo Twins' "Baby Buggy Boogie," Spade Cooley's "Three Way Boogie," and countless others. Even Hank Williams got into the act with the boogie-beat "Fly Trouble." And let's not forget the **Maddox Brothers And Rose**, who combined honky tonk, reckless abandon, good times and great costumes with that driving boogie beat to create a boogie style unto their own—and who, with the Delmore Brothers and Mullican's immeasurable influence on a young Jerry Lee Lewis, initiated the formation of yet another hybrid that would eventually be known as rockabilly.

—Brian Gordon

in the field all day (this was oil-rich east Texas), then doing the same at home with his gal. It was a favorite with Mullican's fans for the rest of his career.

Mullican stayed with Bruner's band for several years until about 1943, when he joined Jimmie Davis' group the Sunshine Boys just as Davis was running for governor of Louisiana. Later Mullican worked again with Bruner, this time calling themselves the Showboys. He finally ventured out under his own name in 1946, signing a recording contract with King Records, a newly formed label run by Syd Nathan in Cincinnati, Ohio. Mullican's years with King, which lasted through to the mid-'50s, produced about one hundred sides, most of it solid honky-tonk and hillbilly boogie material. Over the years he developed a wide-ranging repertoire that included Leadbelly's "Goodnight Irene," the sentimental "Sweeter Than The Flowers," and

the straight-up love song "All I Need Is You" alongside up-tempo boogie-blues numbers like "Cherokee Boogie," "Good Deal Lucille," and "Rocket To The Moon." His singing and piano playing were at the forefront of the mix, but the instrumentation also featured steel guitar, horns and drums.

Moon scored hits—beginning with "New Jole Blon," a parody of Harry Choates' popular "Jole Blon"—that made good-natured nonsense out of the original's hard-to-decipher Cajun lyrics. Others that made it high on the charts included "Sweeter Than The Flowers" and the excellent "I'll Sail My Ship Alone," two of his more straightforward ballads. He later even covered the pop standard "Mona Lisa." Mullican joined the *Grand Ole Opry* for a bit; later he ventured more toward rock'n'roll territory, a world he'd certainly have slotted right

Moon Mullican

into if he'd been a generation younger. In the late '50s he signed with Decca and then moved to Kapp, Starday, and other smaller labels. His health, however, began to slow him down, especially after he had a heart attack on stage in 1962. He continued to perform but finally died of another heart attack on New Year's Day, 1967.

⊙ **Moonshine Jamboree** (1993; Ace). At his best Mullican's music is absolutely thrilling, and this album has plenty of that good stuff. The playing and Mullican's energy level are consistent throughout, but the songs are varied enough that they never fall into a rut. The groovy "Hey Mr. Cotton Picker" and "What's The Matter With The Mill" are absolute highlights alongside the bitter lost-love song "I'll Sail My Ship Alone," the piano showcase piece "Cherokee Boogie," and songs like "Good Deal Lucille", which are, for all intents and purposes, rock'n'roll.

Molly O'Day

"Molly was, without a doubt, the female Hank Williams."

—Mac Wiseman

Singer and guitarist Molly O'Day was a pioneering female artist at a time (the mid-1940s) when few women were taking the lead—and even fewer were doing so fronting an acoustic string band playing southern folk and gospel ballads. O'Day didn't cultivate the cowgirl aesthetic of her girlhood idol Patsy Montana. Women singers in the '30s and '40s usually opted for the western motif (Girls Of The Golden West, Louise Massey) or were part of a larger family band (the Carter Family, the Maddox Brothers And Rose). O'Day did partner up with her husband, vocalist/guitarist Lynn Davis, much as Lulu Belle Wiseman (half of the hugely popular husband and wife duo Lulu Belle & Scotty) and Wilma Lee Cooper (who sang with husband Stoney Cooper) had done. And she wasn't a band 'leader' the way most male singers were. Still, it was O'Day's name, personality and voice that stood out front and center when the group played and recorded. It wasn't until the arrival of Kitty Wells a decade later that female country singers would finally begin breaking down the country world's sexist stereotypes—and another several years before the arrival of such bold personalities as Wanda Jackson, Patsy Cline, and Dolly Parton.

The Appalachian mountain heritage that O'Day grew up with in eastern Kentucky rang through every word she sang. Her voice was untrained but powerful, ringing loud and clear with raw, honest beauty. Backing O'Day and her husband during the five short years she recorded for Columbia was a solid string band that at various points included her fiddling brother Skeets Williamson, Dobro player Speedy Krise, and two young bass players who'd soon move on to fame of their own: Mac Wiseman and Carl Smith. O'Day loved traditional ballads and especially gospel numbers (which she'd later turn to exclusively), yet many of her older-sounding songs were actually penned by contemporary writers (and in a few cases by O'Day herself). "Poor Ellen Smith" was a familiar turn-of-the-century murder ballad, but "Tramp On The Street" was written by Grady and Hazel Cole, "The Black Sheep Returned To The Fold" by Fred Rose, and "At The First Fall Of Snow" by Rose's wife Lorene. She also sang material from Roy Acuff ("Lonely Mound Of Clay"), Jimmie Rodgers ("Fifteen Years Ago Today"), and harmonizing family group the Bailes Brothers ("Traveling The Highway Home"), but most notable of all were the songs that came from Hank Williams. O'Day was the first to record the work of Williams, who was just getting his start in the business. For Columbia she cut "The Singing Waterfall," "Six More Miles To The Graveyard," "When God Comes And Gathers His Jewels," and "I Don't Care If Tomorrow Never Comes."

Despite the fact that the amplified honky-tonk sound was top dog on the nation's airwaves, O'Day stuck to her acoustic string-band sound and no one seemed to mind at all. Whether moralistic tales of tragedy like "The Drunken Driver" and "Don't Sell Daddy Any More Whiskey" (doubly disturbing thanks to the sounds of a crying baby, which were added later), sentimental songs like "Put My Rubber Doll Away" and "At The First Fall Of Snow," or gospel numbers like "Heaven's Radio" and "When We See Our Redeemer's Face," her voice and energetic approach kept things fresh. Though bluegrass was coming to the fore at the same time, O'Day never dabbled in it—though she certainly shared similar musical roots with Bill Monroe. Instead her closest contemporary was probably *Opry* icon Roy Acuff.

Molly was born Lois Laverne Williamson on 9 July, 1923 in Pike County, Kentucky. She grew up on traditional Appalachian music, and soon became enamored with singers like Patsy Montana and Lulu Belle Wiseman, both of whom she heard

Molly O'Day

regularly on the *National Barn Dance*. When Molly's brother Skeets began performing on a West Virginia station, he invited Molly to join him. She sang first under the name Mountain Fern, later Dixie Lee, and finally settled on Molly O'Day in the early '40s. By this point she'd married guitarist Leonard "Lynn" Davis; the pair performed together for the rest of her life. They played around the South for several years before Fred Rose (songwriter and co-founder of the Acuff-Rose publishing house) heard them on a Knoxville station in 1946. He was struck by the strength and beauty of O'Day's voice. Rose got the band signed to Columbia, and over the next five years they recorded three dozen songs for the label. Some of her first were penned by Hank Williams, whom Rose had also started working with. Ironically, Molly and the group had already met Hank during a stint in Birmingham; it was Hank, in fact, who'd turned her attention to what would be her best-known song, "Tramp On The Street."

O'Day had always sung a good deal of gospel material, but by the early '50s she figured it was time to offer her talent exclusively to the Lord. That wasn't entirely her reason for quitting the music business, however: she also suffered from stress and poor health. After their 1951 Columbia session (six fired-up gospel songs, with O'Day's voice in top form), Davis entered the ministry and O'Day sang only in church. We can only guess where her career might have led if she'd stuck with secular music—and if she'd had the physical and mental stamina that stardom requires. Would she have rivaled Kitty Wells as the "Queen of Country Music"? Or lived up to Mac Wiseman's declaration that she was "the female Hank Williams"? We'll never know. Instead O'Day stuck to a steady gospel path. She recorded a couple more albums during the '60s, and in 1973 she and Davis began a gospel radio program in West Virginia, which they maintained together until O'Day's death in 1987.

⊙ **Molly O'Day And The Cumberland Mountain Folks** (1992; Bear Family). This 2-CD set contains all 36 songs O'Day recorded for Columbia between 1946 and 1951. Her music stands on the border between the old-time ballads and gospel of decades past and the honky-tonk artistry of songwriters like Hank Williams—4 of whose songs she covers. Her voice is an awesome instrument, classically raw but stunning for its earthy richness and strength. Gospel or secular, the songs are moving and genuine.

James O'Gwynn

One of producer and label honcho Harold "Pappy" Daily's first signings to his Starday and D labels, James O'Gwynn was a vibrant honky-tonk singer who landed a string of respectable hits during the 1950s and early '60s. His voice was sharp and almost piercing at times, but it was also rich and expressive—at its best on fired-up honky-tonkers like "Losing Game," "If You Don't Want To Hold Me," and "I'm Tired," but also capable of handling a mournful ballad like the beautiful "Talk To Me Lonesome Heart." A star of the *Louisiana Hayride* and later the *Grand Ole Opry*, his hit streak in the end didn't give him the longevity enjoyed by his contemporaries, most notably George Jones. O'Gwynn's best material, though, has a whipped-up energy that holds its own with the best of late '50s honky tonk.

James Leroy O'Gwynn was born on 26 January, 1928 in Winchester, Mississippi. He joined the *Houston Jamboree* in 1954, where he met George Jones, who'd started recording that same year for Starday. The label had been founded in Beaumont, Texas in 1953 by Daily and Jack Starnes. Through the Jones connection Daily was introduced to O'Gwynn and ended up signing him. O'Gwynn's first single, "Losing Game/I'll Never Get To Heaven," hit the streets in 1956. Two years later Daily shifted O'Gwynn to his Houston-based D label, another start-up, this time with the vision of promoting mostly regional artists. It was on the D label that O'Gwynn's hits started to roll out. They were never huge, but songs like "Talk To Me Lonesome Heart" and "Blue Memories" did make themselves known on the country charts.

In 1959 O'Gwynn joined the Mercury roster, where he stayed put for several years. This time he was produced by Shelby Singleton (who'd later start the Plantation label and produce Jeannie C. Riley's hit "Harper Valley P.T.A."). O'Gwynn had already been making a name for himself on the *Louisiana Hayride* since the late '50s, and after a couple of Mercury hits, "My Name Is Mud" and "Down On The Corner Of Love," he made the final leap to the *Grand Ole Opry*, where he stayed for a couple of years. Mercury also released two albums of O'Gwynn's material. After Singleton left Mercury, O'Gwynn's career began its downward slide. He jumped to United Artists, where Daily was working at the time and was still as preoccupied as ever with Jones, his increasingly famous charge. O'Gwynn hopped labels a few more times before landing on Plantation, which released two of his albums in the late '70s.

● **The Smiling Irishman Of Country Music** (1982; Cattle). Two volumes on two individual LPs of O'Gwynn's Starday, Mercury, D and United Artists material from 1956–1959, all produced by Pappy Daily. This is definitely O'Gwynn's best material.

Leon Payne

Texas songwriter and singer Leon Payne wrote a couple of bona fide classics, "I Love You Because" and "Lost Highway," and a heaping handful more that are strong runners-up: "Take Me" (co-written with George Jones), "Cry Baby Heart," "They'll Never Take Her Love from Me," "You Are The One" and "The Blue Side Of Lonesome." Payne's reputation is chiefly for his writing, and giants like Hank Williams, George Jones, Patti Page and even Elvis Presley all recorded his material. Payne was also a recording artist himself, however, with a smooth and easygoing tenor voice that worked nicely on songs like "I Love You Because" (written for his wife) and "Wouldn't It Be Wonderful." On other songs, such as "I Need Your Love," his vocal limitations were evident. What he mainly lacked, no matter how good his songs, was the rich and confident character that made singers like Williams, Floyd Tillman, Lefty Frizzell, and even mister off-key himself, Ernest Tubb, stand out so brightly.

Leon Roger Payne was born on 15 June, 1917 in Alba, Texas. Blind from childhood, he studied music while attending the Texas School for the Blind in Austin. After graduating, he started on a local Texas station, hitchhiked all over the state to play in various clubs, and began writing songs on a more serious basis. His first recordings were in 1939 and 1940, but it wasn't until about a decade later, when he formed his group the Lone Star Buddies, that he made much of a splash. In 1949 two of his songs became major hits for George Morgan ("Cry Baby Heart") and Hank Williams ("Lost Highway"). The latter has gone on to be one of the signature songs of honky tonk. That year he also signed with Capitol Records, and his own recording of "I Love You Because"

went all the way to #1 in 1950. He cut further songs for Capitol but switched to Starday in 1955, where he stayed for the better part of a decade. As he was also a prolific songwriter, his work continued to appear in the charts recorded by stars like Hank Snow, Carl Smith, and Jim Reeves. Jones did some especially fine work with Payne's songs, even co-writing a couple with him ("Things Have Gone To Pieces" and the gorgeous "Take Me") and recording an entire album of Payne material. A heart attack in 1965 cut Payne's performing career short, and four years later he died. "I Love You Because" lived on in versions by Don Gibson (1978) and Roger Whittaker (1983). "You Are The One" ended up on a Carlene Carter album, and one of Payne's strangest and darkest songs, "Psycho," found him an entirely new audience when Elvis Costello cut a version (it's on his 1987 B-sides collection, OUT OF OUR IDIOT).

⊙ **The Great Songs Of Leon Payne** (1971; Musicor; reissued 1987; Highland). This is a George Jones album, but all the material was written or co-written by Payne. It's also one of the few places to find any Payne material on CD. The background choruses get a bit overwrought at times, but Jones' performance on songs like "Brothers Of The Bottle," "Things Have Gone To Pieces," and the absolutely gorgeous "Take Me"— which Payne co-wrote with Jones—easily transcends any production shortcomings.

Leon Payne

⊙ **I Love You Because** (1999; Bear Family). A 30-song, single-disc set that collects Payne's recordings for Capitol from 1949–1953. Includes "I Love You

Because," Payne's biggest hit, as well as such intriguing titles as "Polk Salad Greens," "Find Them, Fool Them, And Leave Them," "I'm A Lone Wolf," "I Just Said Goodbye To My Dreams," "Lolita," and "Farewell Waltz."

Minnie Pearl

Like her friend and longtime professional partner Roy Acuff, comedienne, actress, and sometime singer Minnie Pearl (aka Sarah Ophelia Colley) was an icon of the *Grand Ole Opry*—and of country music as a whole. Her costume always included her trademark straw hat with his dangling price tag, and her bellowed greeting "How-DEE! I'm just so proud to be here!" was a phrase *Opry* fans heard every week for fifty years.

Ophelia (as she was often known in her younger days) was born on 25 October, 1912 in Centerville, Tennessee, a small town not far from Nashville. She hoped to become an actress, and during her early twenties worked for a small traveling theater company. While traveling with this group, she met a woman who inspired her to create the character later known by millions as Minnie Pearl. She first performed the character at a hotel function in South Carolina in 1939, and in November, 1940 "Minnie Pearl" made her debut on the *Grand Ole Opry*. She was an immediate sensation.

The character whom Ophelia honed was a gossiping spinster who lived in the fictional small town of Grinder's Switch. In 1942 she added the "How-DEE!" greeting, a distinctive element of her act—and personality—that she maintained for the rest of her career. On the *Opry* she performed monologues full of down-home, corn-fed (and sometimes gently racy) humor about small-town scandals and the folks who fuel them. She also regularly worked with another comic, Rod Brasfield. During the '60s Minnie branched out into TV, performing on various programs including the Carol Burnett and Jonathan Winters shows, but most especially *Hee-Haw*. Her appearances on the latter program, which expanded on the Minnie Pearl repertoire by putting her in all manner of silly scenarios, gained her an even bigger audience. Sarah Cannon (she'd modified her 'real' name after marrying pilot Henry Cannon in 1947) also recorded several albums' worth of material over the years, but she only had one charting country hit, "Giddyup Go—Answer." It was a tear-choked

and decidedly un-funny answer to Red Sovine's sappy 1965 hit recitation "Giddyup Go," about a truck-driving father and his long-lost son.

Sarah Ophelia Colley Cannon was inducted into the Country Music Hall of Fame in 1975, appeared on TNN's *Nashville Now* program in the '80s, and continued performing regularly on the *Opry* into the early '90s. Following a show in Illinois in 1991, however, she suffered a stroke that sadly ended her performing career and left her bedridden for the next five years. After another series of strokes, she died on 4 March, 1996, and fans around the world mourned the passing of this good-natured, universally loved personality—an irreplaceable force in country music history.

The many moods of Minnie Pearl

⊙ **Country Music Hall Of Fame 1975** (1998; King/Highland). This 14-track CD is a decent and fairly well-rounded introduction to Minnie Pearl's recorded history. It collects songs such as "How To Catch A Man" and "Alabam" (a duet with Red Sovine), recitations (her 'hit' recording "Giddyup Go—Answer"), and of course several good-natured, freewheeling monologues that give the lowdown on life in Grinder's Switch.

Webb Pierce

During the 1950s, the country artist who racked up the most #1 hits was not Hank Williams, Lefty Frizzell, or even the hugely popular Eddy Arnold. It was Webb Pierce, a Louisiana native with a sharp nasal voice. Songs he recorded such as "Slowly," "Wondering," "There Stands The Glass," and "Back Street Affair" were awesome nuggets of purebred honky tonk that have since become standards of the genre.

Pierce was no crooner like Arnold or Red Foley; he had a sharply toned, piercing tenor voice, but it was always pretty and never shrill. His classic Decca recordings were based around the standard honky-tonk instrumentation of guitar, bass, fiddle and steel, a spare and bright sound that was irresistible to country fans fresh off a Hank Williams high. Pierce was also a pioneer—the first major Nashville artist to use pedal steel guitar, played by Bud Isaacs, on his recordings (the instrument had already debuted out west). First heard to full effect on "Slowly," the instrument's sweeping, mournful sound has come to denote country music ever since. Though in later years Webb became best known for his symbols of excess—a pair of silver-dollar-studded Pontiacs, a guitar-shaped swimming pool—the streak of success he enjoyed during his heyday has proven difficult to beat. Though he has yet to be inducted into the Country Music Hall of Fame, he was easily among the most influential honky-tonkers of the '50s.

Webb Pierce was born on 8 August, 1921 near West Monroe, Louisiana. He learned guitar growing up, listened to a lot of Jimmie Rodgers, and by his mid-teens had his own radio show. He spent three years in the Army, then moved to Shreveport and worked as a shoe salesman for Sears, playing music on the side. Shreveport was home to radio station KWKH and the recently formed *Louisiana Hayride*, and eventually Webb caught the ear of KWKH's program director. By early 1950 he'd joined the *Hayride*, and he also cut his first records about this same time. Historical details are foggy, but he probably recorded his first sides for the independent label Four Star before joining the *Hayride*, then later cut a few more for Pacemaker, a label he partially owned. Finally in early 1951 he was signed to Decca.

Webb's first few releases didn't do much, but a song from his second session, "Wondering"—written and previously recorded in the '30s by Joe Warner—hit #1 and set him up as an exciting new country star. He followed this hit with two more chart-topping songs, "That Heart Belongs To Me" and "Back Street Affair," the latter written and previously recorded by Billy Wallace. With all this success in his pocket he finally moved to Nashville and joined the *Grand Ole Opry* (though he quit the show a couple years later). His hits continued at a strong and steady pace—"There Stands The Glass" in 1953, "Slowly" and "More And More" in 1954, "I Don't Care" (which Ricky Skaggs would later record) and a cover of Jimmie Rodgers' "In The Jailhouse Now" in 1955. There were, of course, many more than just these few, including duets with Kitty Wells and Red Sovine. Virtually all of Webb's singles, in fact, made the country charts (which then had only ten to twenty places each week) between 1952 and 1958. In 1953 Webb and Jim Denny, manager of the *Opry*, founded the Cedarwood song publishing company.

Webb's success as a hitmaker continued into the '60s. But when rock'n'roll began eating into the country music fan base, things slowed a bit and his pure honky-tonk sound began to change. He first attempted to incorporate rock rhythms into songs like "Teenage Boogie;" not long after that he turned the other direction, smoothing his sound with gentler arrangements and background choruses typical of the increasingly popular Nashville Sound. One of his last chart hits was "Fool Fool Fool" in 1967, though he continued recording for Decca until 1975. He made a few albums for the Plantation label after that, then in 1982 was back in the charts, singing a duet version of "In The Jailhouse Now" with Willie Nelson. During the '70s, though, Pierce was more notorious for causing a public nuisance than rattling the honky-tonk rafters. Each week tour buses brought thousands of fans to his sedate suburban neighborhood to get a gander at his guitar-shaped swimming

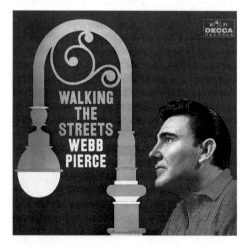

pool—which infuriated his neighbors, who ultimately stopped the madness with a court order.
By the mid-'80s, well after the dust from this
debacle had settled, Pierce had pretty much stopped
recording and performing. He lived long enough
to see Ricky Skaggs bring back to life a couple of
his early hits ("I Don't Care" and "I'm Tired"),
but on 24 February, 1991 he died of pancreatic
cancer.

⊙ **1951–1958** (1990; Bear Family). A 4-CD box set
containing 113 songs covering the best years of
Webb's association with Decca. It's great stuff for
hardcore Webb fans, but overkill for the merely curious.

⊙ **King Of The Honky Tonk: From The Original
Master Tapes** (1994; CMF). The cream of Webb's
crop, this is a collection of his classic Decca sides from
the early to mid-1950s. It's essential honky tonk
listening.

⊙ **Unavailable Sides (1950–1951)** (1994; Krazy Kat).
A CD collecting together some of Webb's earliest
recordings for the small Pacemaker label.

Ray Price

Ray Price was one of the great honky-tonk song
stylists, vocalists, and bandleaders of the 1950s
and '60s. Recordings such as "Crazy Arms," "Invitation To The Blues," "City Lights," and "Night
Life" are undeniable classics, with their innovative
arrangements mixing honky-tonk fiddles and steel
guitar with a steady, pronounced rhythm borrowed
from western swing. Unfortunately, however, the
depth of Price's achievements has been over-
shadowed by the lushly orchestrated, urban-pop
sound he turned to during the mid-'60s and '70s
as a countrypolitan balladeer on songs like "Danny
Boy" and "For The Good Times."

Early on, Price played in a pared-down style
(albeit one that borrowed liberally from Hank
Williams) that was jukebox honky tonk at its most
gut-level gorgeous. Songs like "I'll Be There"
(1953) and "You Done Me Wrong" (1956) grab
hard and don't let go. As Price's personality
matured, his arrangements grew more complex.
By the mid-'50s western swing's popularity was
far short of its massive postwar peak, but Price was
able to blend the dance-hall rhythms of that Texas-
born style with the classic line-up of guitar, fiddle
and steel to create a whole new sound in country

music: the honky-tonk shuffle. Soon known as
simply the "Ray Price Beat," this 4/4 shuffle
became his trademark, thanks to the strength and
huge popularity of such hits as "My Shoes Keep
Walking Back To You," "Invitation To The
Blues," "City Lights," and especially "Crazy
Arms," which spent a mighty twenty weeks at the
top of *Billboard*'s country-music charts in 1956.
For these now classic shuffle songs alone, Price is
more than deserving of his place in the Country
Music Hall of Fame, to which he was elected in
1996.

Ray Noble Price was born on 12 January,
1926 near the East Texas town of Perryville. He
served in the Marines during World War II, then
attended North Texas Agricultural College near
Dallas, where he studied veterinary medicine. At
the same time he started singing at local clubs,
and by about 1949 he had dropped out of college
and was singing on the *Big D Jamboree*, a well-
known barn dance based in Dallas. He also cut a
single for the independent Bullet label in Jim
Beck's recording studio, a honky-tonk hot spot
in Dallas that Columbia producer Don Law was
fond of using (Lefty Frizzell and Marty Robbins
also recorded many of their early classics there).
In 1951 Price was signed to Columbia. His first
single for his new label, "If You're Ever Lonely
Darling," was written by Frizzell; the two had
become friends during the time they spent
hanging out at Beck's studio. In 1952 Price
moved to Nashville and joined the *Grand Ole
Opry*.

Price's early honky tonk is heady stuff, but at
the time it didn't help him stand out much from
the pack of Hank Williams wannabes. Price met
Williams in the early '50s—the two even roomed

together later when Price first arrived in Nashville (and Hank was freshly divorced from Miss Audrey). It's clear the young Texan considered the great Alabama songwriter his mentor, as several of his early recordings have a clear Hank Williams stamp. But others such as "I'll Be There" and "You Done Me Wrong" show Price breaking out of the mold and asserting his individuality. Both songs have a delicious edge: you can hear him chomping at the bit, ready to bust out the gate. Another song, "Release Me" (yes, the very same song that Englebert Humperdinck would record fourteen years later), was the first to foreshadow the countrypolitan direction Price would later take. The arrangements were spare and sharp (surprisingly so for anyone who knows only pop versions of the song), but nonetheless they served as proof that, vocally, Price was well suited to handle soaring tear-jerkers.

The song that really broke Price out of the honky-tonk sidelines and into the mainstream was "Crazy Arms." A bold fiddle line charged the melody right from the beginning, but the rhythmic foundation was based around a fresh and entirely irresistible shuffle beat. This gently driving rhythm, with its emphasis on drums and a walking bass line, grew more and more prominent in Price's music over the next several years.

In his quest for new material, Price ended up giving several soon-to-be prominent songwriters their first big breaks. The song credits of his classic late '50s, early '60s hits read like a who's who of country music's up-and-coming generation: Bill Anderson ("City Lights"), Roger Miller ("Invitation To The Blues"), Harlan Howard

("Heartaches By The Number"), Willie Nelson ("Night Life"), Mel Tillis ("Burning Memories"), and Hank Cochran ("Make The World Go Away"). Miller, Nelson, and another young Nashville upstart, Donny Young (aka Johnny Paycheck), also played in Price's band, the Cherokee Cowboys, before striking out on their own.

As far as albums go, Price's 1963 album NIGHT LIFE is one of his finest achievements, a well-conceived, beautifully blue and moody collection. It's also an album that suggests the changes in his style that were soon to come. Compared to his earlier honky-tonk singles, the arrangements here are lusher and softer around the edges; Price's voice, too, has a more laid-back (and less reedy) tone. His first true foray into Nashville Sound territory came on his 1965 album BURNING MEMORIES. It's here that his producers, Don Law and Frank Jones, added strings and background singers to numbers like "Make The World Go Away" (another #1 hit for Price), and Price allowed his voice to sweeten further and, especially on the title track, soar straight into the clouds.

After this point there was no turning back, as Price was hooked on the smoother pop sound, which he felt was a natural progression from his earlier style. Besides, this was the trend in country music: to ignore it would mean being stuck once again back on those lonely sidelines. And so came "Danny Boy," a 1967 hit that showed Price at his lushest and most fully orchestrated, and then, in 1970, "For The Good Times." Price's new uptown style redefined him in many listeners' minds. It alienated many of his hardcore country fans, but it gave him a newer, broader pop audience and kept him at or near the top of the charts well into the '70s.

Price continued to record for Columbia through 1974, after which he cut records for such labels as Myrrh, ABC/Dot, Monument and Step One. During the '70s he also moved back to Texas. In 1977 he cut a reunion album with several of his former Cherokee Cowboys that was as straight-up country as anything he'd done in years. In 1980 a duet album with Willie Nelson (SAN ANTONIO ROSE, which was also the name of a 1961 Price album) yielded him another short burst of attention.

Price continued recording, though less steadily, through the '80s and into the '90s. He also opened a theater in Branson, Missouri. By the mid-'90s he was discovered all over again by alternative country fans, who recognized him as a true honky-tonk innovator and one of country music's living legends. In his seventies by this point, his musicianship was still sharp: at a 1998 performance in Austin, Texas—backed by a large band that included a half-dozen sweeping violins—his voice sounded beautiful and strong as he ran through hits from both his honky-tonk and pop years. A new album, too, was rumored to be in the works.

⊙ **San Antonio Rose** (1961; Columbia; reissued 1996; Koch). Price's tribute to the music of Bob Wills is more than just a noble gesture: the rhythms and arrangements of western swing were a major influence of Price's honky-tonk shuffle sound. Recorded in just one afternoon and evening, this was country music's first Wills tribute album. It's also an excellent, enjoyable collection that captures Price at his peak.

⊙ **Night Life** (1963; Columbia; reissued 1996; Koch). Smooth, easygoing, and blue around the edges, but still touched by real fiddles and steel guitars, this album is a genuine work of art. The pace might be slower and the mood more late-night and laid-back than Price's earlier material, but the sound is not yet countrypolitan—songs like "Pride," "Lonely Street," "Sittin' And Thinkin'" (written by Charlie Rich), and the title track (a Willie Nelson classic) still speak straight from the gut.

⊙ **Essential Ray Price (1951–1962)** (1991; Columbia/Legacy). An absolutely fantastic 20-song collection that covers Price's early years. It begins with pared-down honky-tonkers like 1951's "If You're Ever Lonely Darling" (written by Lefty Frizzell) and his first Top 10 single, "Talk To Your Heart," before moving into the standout "You Done Me Wrong" and, of course, his string of prime-period shuffles, among them "Crazy Arms," "City Lights," "Invitation To The Blues," and "Heartaches By The Number." This is top-quality material, so don't miss out.

⊙ **Honky Tonk Years (1950–1966)** (1996; Bear Family). A massive 10-CD set that brings together (in chronological order) the better half of Price's recorded history. This collection not only covers Price's creative development but gives us a picture of country music as a whole, moving from hardcore 1950s honky tonk to the urban pop influences that took over during the '60s.

Marvin Rainwater

Whether decked out in a Native American-style buckskin jacket, or a plain ole suit and tie, Marvin Rainwater was an eccentric—a fabulous singer and songwriter who never quite found his niche. He was a country balladeer on the one

Marvin Rainwater

hand, but he was drawn to rockabilly, and had also been trained as a classical pianist. With all that swirling in his head at once, it's no wonder he never quite fitted into the trends of his time. The Native American regalia might have made him stand out at first (he was one-quarter Cherokee), but in the end it only confused matters—adding 'novelty' to his already hard-to-decipher persona. Rainwater's burly baritone voice and playful approach to songs that cross the country-rockabilly borderline was not only unique, but downright thrilling.

He was born Marvin Karlton Percy Rainwater on 2 July, 1925 in Wichita, Kansas. Rather than listen to the *Grand Ole Opry* with his father, Marvin took piano lessons and studied the classics. That came to an end, however, after he lost a thumb in a work accident as a teenager. After short stints in college and with the Navy, he took up guitar. He discovered Roy Acuff and began playing and writing country songs. He joined his brothers in northern Virginia and played clubs in and around the Washington, DC area, sometimes dressing in a buckskin jacket and headband. A young Roy Clark was Rainwater's lead guitarist. They cut some demos which were shopped around by Four Star Records owner Bill Crandall. Teresa Brewer ended up turning Rainwater's "I Gotta Go Get My Baby Back" into a pop hit. Others were later heavily overdubbed and released on budget labels.

Rainwater's real break, however, came via a popular talent show hosted by Arthur Godfrey. His performance there was enough to win him a spot on Red Foley's *Ozark Jubilee* in Springfield, Missouri. This led to a recording contract with MGM, which had been Hank Williams' label. He tried country, he tried recitations, but the standout songs were two 'pepped-up' numbers, "Mr. Blues" and "Hot And Cold." The former was a great showcase for Rainwater's acrobatic vocal style, while the latter had a crazier sound with the instruments (including Clark's lead guitar) flying in from all directions and really shaking up the landscape. While revealing Rainwater's amazing energy and versatility as a performer, these songs also alienated many of his country fans, who felt he was 'selling out' to rock 'n'roll. Perhaps that's what prompted him to cut "Gonna Find Me A Bluebird" later that year. It worked like a charm, becoming a big country and pop hit. After this, Rainwater relocated from Missouri to the New Jersey-New York area.

Despite glimmers of success, his career couldn't hold a steady pace. Quirky, rocked-up songs like "Whole Lotta Woman" and "I Dig You Baby" were exciting enough, but they never got far off the ground (though "Woman," which barely made the charts in the US, did reach #1 in England). Rainwater performed relentlessly, but he never seemed to be doing the right thing at the right time. Finally his voice began to give out—he developed calluses on his vocal cords—which led to the termination of his MGM contract in 1960. After a brief rest he then cut some songs for the Warwick label, but as good as these sides sounded they still didn't chart. During the '60s Rainwater recorded here and there for a series of labels, including United Artists, Warner Brothers, Sonet and his own Brave Records. After that he appeared occasionally on rockabilly revival tours in Europe, before eventually retiring to northern Minnesota.

⊙ **Classic Recordings** (1992; Bear Family). A big 4-CD box set covering Rainwater's entire recording career. It starts with his early demos, runs through all his MGM sides, includes his various 1960s recordings, and concludes with a live 1962 radio performance from The *Wheeling Jamboree*, West Virginia.

⊙ **Whole Lotta Woman** (1994; Bear Family). This superb 26-song collection is culled mostly from Rainwater's MGM and Warwick recordings in the late 1950s and early '60s. Hearing all these fired-up songs packed tightly together, it's hard to imagine why Rainwater wasn't a smash in his day. Songs like "I Dig You Baby" and "Whole Lotta Woman" are absolutely irresistible.

Marty Robbins

Few country singers have enjoyed such a long and steady career as Marty Robbins. Few, too, have been as diverse, covering the range of material he did over his thirty-year recording career. As a vocalist, Robbins had a smooth, attractive tenor voice that had none of the deep southern twang of his honky-tonk contemporaries and was more in line with the pop-country stylings of Eddy Arnold, whom he admired. Not only was Robbins' voice one of the prettiest in modern country music, it was also incredibly versatile—he could handle tearful ballads (his early trademark, which earned him the nickname Mr. Teardrop), cowboy songs (his 1959 album GUNFIGHTER BALLADS AND TRAIL SONGS is a classic), Hawaiian music, pop standards and tightly wound rockabilly numbers with equal skill.

As a songwriter, Robbins was responsible for such classics as "A White Sport Coat (And A Pink Carnation)," "You Gave Me A Mountain," and the great western saga "El Paso." Over the years he was also a film actor, radio and TV show host and NASCAR stock-car driver. And as a recording artist his career lasted from the early '50s through to the '80s, during which time he racked up more than ninety chart hits (including sixteen #1s and several pop crossovers)—right up through "Some Memories Just Won't Die," which made the country Top 10 in 1982.

Martin David Robinson was born on 26 September, 1925 near Glendale, Arizona, a town on the west side of Phoenix. His family was poor, his father mean, but his grandfather, a onetime Texas Ranger named Texas Bob Heckle, left a lasting impression on young Marty by regaling him with tales of the Old West. Marty also adored Gene Autry—as did millions of other young film and music fans during the '30s. After some rough teenage years, he joined the Navy during World War II, and it's here that he first learned to play guitar and write songs. He also developed an interest in Hawaiian music. Back in Arizona after the war, he played guitar with local singer Frankie Starr, then landed his own radio show in the town of Mesa. A series of radio shows followed as well as his TV debut on the Phoenix program *Country Caravan*. When Little Jimmy Dickens came through town in 1951, the *Opry* star appeared on the show and liked Robbins' singing. He then recommended Robbins to Columbia producer Art Satherley, who flew to Phoenix to hear the young man sing. In May of 1951 Robbins signed to Columbia, a contract he maintained (apart from a brief stint with Decca/MCA in the early '70s) through the duration of his career.

Robbins first recorded in LA that same year, and he caused a stir because he chose to record his own compositions instead of a selection that had been picked out for him. He next recorded at Jim Beck's studio in Dallas, where Lefty Frizzell and Ray Price cut some of their most classic material. His producer this time was Don Law, a Satherley protégé. One of the songs from the Dallas session, an original titled "I'll Go On Alone," made it to #1 on the *Billboard* country charts. It gained Robbins a publishing contract with Acuff-Rose and an appearance on the *Grand Ole Opry*. In 1953 he joined the *Opry* and moved to Nashville with his wife and two children.

Throughout the '50s Marty's recording career was extremely active, versatile and successful. He hit #1 with songs as diverse as Melvin Endsley's "Singing The Blues" (1956), the teen pop song "A White Sport Coat (And A Pink Carnation)" (cut in New York in 1957 with the Ray Coniff Singers and pop producer Mitch Miller), and "El Paso" (1959). The latter was revolutionary in that it broke the three-minute limit, running to a grand total of four and a half minutes. Surprisingly, the full-length version of the song crossed over to the pop charts and also won Robbins a Grammy (the first ever awarded for a country song). "El Paso" again appeared on Robbins'

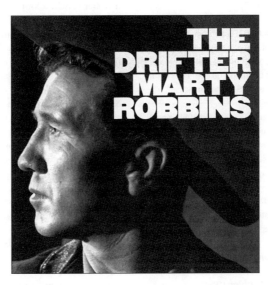

1959 concept album GUNFIGHTER BALLADS AND TRAIL SONGS, which included originals inspired by his grandfather's stories as well as several cowboy classics. He released further western-themed albums such as RETURN OF THE GUNFIGHTER, THE DRIFTER, and ALL AROUND COWBOY. Other thematic territory he ventured into on album included rock'n'roll (ROCK'N ROLL'N ROBBINS), jazz and pop standards with a moody, late-night vibe (MARTY AFTER MIDNIGHT), and Hawaiian material (SONGS OF THE ISLANDS, HAWAII'S CALLING ME).

Robbins' songs continued to make the charts through the '60s and '70s, and he maintained a busy schedule of recording, touring and acting (*Hell On Wheels, The Road To Nashville, A Man And A Train*), not to mention his weekly *Opry* appearances and frequent stock-car races. He suffered a heart attack in 1969, but early the following year underwent successful bypass surgery. He received the Artist of the Decade award in 1970 from the Academy of Country Music for his achievements during the '60s (later recipients were Loretta Lynn, Alabama, and Garth Brooks), and in 1971 his song "My Woman, My Woman, My Wife" won him a second Grammy.

Robbins briefly switched to Decca/MCA in 1972, then returned to Columbia in 1975. He returned to the charts, as well, with such songs as the sentimental Tin Pan Alley number "Among My Souvenirs," "Return To Me," and "El Paso City." This last song was another sequel to "El Paso"—"Feleena (From El Paso)" had appeared a decade earlier on THE DRIFTER—only this time it was about a man flying over the city and remembering "each and every word" of Robbins' famous song. He was elected to the Nashville Songwriters Hall of Fame in 1975 and the Country Music Hall of Fame in 1982, only seven weeks before he was again struck by a heart attack. He died on 11 December. Early the following year, he was posthumously honored when his recording of "Honkytonk Man," the title song from the Clint

Eastwood movie of the same name, became his final Top 10 country hit.

⊙ **Rock'n Roll'n Robbins** (1957; Columbia; reissued 1996; Koch). This was Marty's very first album, and it collects his rockabilly sides from the mid- to late 1950s.

⊙ **Gunfighter Ballads And Trail Songs** (1959; Columbia; ; reissued 1999; Columbia/Legacy). Robbins' first western-themed album mixes originals such as "El Paso" and "Big Iron" (some inspired by his grandfather's stories) with traditional cowboy songs like "Strawberry Roan" and contemporary western classics like Bob Nolan's "Cool Water."

⊙ **Marty After Midnight** (1962; Columbia; reissued 1996; Koch). Robbins ventures (successfully) into Sinatra territory on this concept album that features slow and moody versions of standards like "I'm In The Mood For Love," "Misty," and "Summertime."

⊙ **The Drifter** (1966; Columbia; reissued 1996; Koch). The songs here were all culled from a TV series of the same name that Robbins starred in during the early 1960s. Like GUNFIGHTER BALLADS, it's another well-paced collection of cowboy and western material.

◉ **Just Me And My Guitar** (1983; Bear Family). Recordings cut in 1956 with producer Owen Bradley that are just what the titles says—Robbins alone with his acoustic guitar. Pretty, yes, though they all maintain a similar gentle, low-key tone.

⊙ **The Essential Marty Robbins** (1991; Columbia/Legacy). This is an excellent retrospective of one of the most substantial artists in modern country music. And being a double-CD set, it's far more substantial than the average 'best of' collection. Disc one starts with one of his 1951 LA recordings ("Tomorrow You'll Be Gone") and his first #1 ("I'll Go On Alone") before running through such '50s gems as "Singing The Blues," "That's All Right," "Mister Teardrop," "White Sport Coat," "Big Iron," and "El Paso." The second dishes up beauties like "Devil Woman" and "Smokin' Cigarettes And Drinkin' Coffee Blues", as well as some Hawaiian material ("Beyond The Reef") and later hits like "You Gave Me A Mountain," and "El Paso City."

⊙ **Country 1951–1958** (1991; Bear Family). Five CDs covering all but his New York and Hollywood pop hits from this time period. Includes outtakes from New York and Nashville sessions.

Jimmie Skinner

"It's hard to get in the top forty once you get in the top fifties."

—Jimmie Skinner

Jimmie Skinner was a distinctive figure in country music who was never hugely popular, yet he managed to maintain a thirty-year music career by deftly straddling the worlds of hillbilly, honky tonk and bluegrass. His voice was reedy but warm, his phrasing quirky but genuine, and these gave his music an individual stamp—as did the lead electric mandolin playing of his longtime band-member Ray Lunsford. Skinner recorded for several different labels from the 1940s through to the '70s, producing a handful of minor hits himself and quite a few honky-tonk songs that other artists picked up over the years. Ernest Tubb was among the first, taking Skinner's composition "Let's Say Goodbye Like We Said Hello" to the Top 5 in 1948; Flatt & Scruggs helped turned "Doin' My Time" into a bluegrass standard (it was later cut by Jimmy Martin and Johnny Cash, among others). Almost half a century later, "Don't Give Your Heart To A Rambler" was covered by Travis Tritt on his album IT'S ALL ABOUT TO CHANGE; and Marty Stuart included a version of "Doin' My Time" on his 1992 outing THIS ONE'S GONNA HURT YOU.

Another unique and important aspect of Skinner's career was the record store that proudly bore his name for more than twenty years, the Jimmie Skinner Music Center. Through this hugely popular retail and mail-order outlet, founded in Cincinnati, Ohio, in the early '50s, Skinner helped distribute bluegrass and hillbilly music to rural music fans craving the records they heard on their favorite country music radio programs.

Born on 27 April, 1909, Skinner hailed from Blue Lick, a small community near Berea, Kentucky. It was a region thick with a rural music heritage, and quite a few notable players also emerged from the area over the years, among them Red Foley, Karl And Harty and Bradley Kincaid. When Jimmie was a teenager his family moved to Hamilton, Ohio, near Cincinnati, and it's there that he began playing on local radio stations. With his brother Esmer he cut a couple of songs for Gennett in the '30s, but they were never issued. During the '40s he made some records for the label Red Barn, and one of these, "Will You Be Satisfied That Way," became popular in Knoxville, Tennessee. He moved there for a while but was soon back in southwestern Ohio, a region that remained his home base for most of his life.

In Cincinnati Skinner hooked up with manager Lou Epstein, and together they gained control of the small label, Radio Artists. During the late '40s the label released a series of Skinner recordings, including such songs as "Don't Give Your Heart To A Rambler," "You Don't Know My Mind," and "Doin' My Time." The arrangements were simple, based essentially around Skinner's lead vocals and guitar and the electric mandolin playing of Ray Lunsford, a local picker he'd worked with earlier. In 1950 Skinner was signed to Capitol, for whom he cut another thirteen records; three years later he switched to Decca, and then in 1956 he shifted over to Mercury. He'd had a minor *Billboard* chart hit in 1949 with "Tennessee Border," but with Mercury he reached the Top 10 with the Bill Browning composition "Dark Hollow" (now a modern folk standard), "What Makes A Man Wander," and the song that became Skinner's signature, "I Found My Girl In The USA"—a patriotic ditty about loving the ladies in one's own backyard. Connie Hall even released an answer song, "I'm The Girl In The USA," and then went on to cut a handful of duets with Skinner. In 1961 he cut the beautifully moody and low-key JIMMIE SKINNER SINGS JIMMIE RODGERS, a tribute album to one of his earliest musical influences.

During the '60s Skinner switched to Starday Records, and he also began concentrating more specifically on bluegrass music. He'd given the genre tremendous support via his Music Center

in Ohio, and, now that older styles were dropping from public view, bluegrass fans began coming out of the woodwork in support of his spare, rural style. He continued cutting records into the '70s for further small labels such as Vetco, Stop, QCA and Rich-R-Tone. In 1974 he moved to Nashville, and five years later, in October 1979, he passed away.

⊙ **Another Saturday Night** (1988; Bear Family). An LP collection of Skinner's Mercury recordings, including "I Found My Girl In The USA," "Another Saturday Night," "John Wesley Hardin," and 4 duets with Connie Hall.

⊙ **From The Beginning To Fame** (1997; Bronco Buster). Contains 22 singles that Skinner cut between 1949 and 1961 for Radio Artists, Capitol and Mercury. Titles include "Yesterday's Winner Is A Loser Today," "Dreaming My Weary Life Away," "'Tis Sweet To Be Remembered," "Don't Let Your Love Get You Down," and the Jimmie Rodgers tribute "Jimmie's Yodel Blues." Great original recordings from an artist who deserves to be far better remembered.

Carl Smith

The 1950s was an era of honky-tonk greats, but few had the voice, songs and style—not to mention the chiseled good looks—of Tennessee native Carl Smith. Combining his smooth voice with a basic, Hank Williams-type honky-tonk sound, Smith carved a solid career as one of the finest singers and country stylists of the period. He was great at handling high-energy songs like "Hey Joe!" and "Loose Talk," two standouts that flew surprisingly close to rockabilly territory. More frequently, however, he opted for a crooner's pace, making beautiful work out of "I Just Dropped In To Say Goodbye," "If Teardrops Were Pennies," "This Orchid Means Goodbye," and many others from his early '50s heyday. Always, he kept the arrangements honest and down to earth—even as many of his peers were sweetening their sound with strings. His voice may have been pretty, but Smith was a honky-tonker at heart; he smoothed his edges but never let go of the music's spare and sturdy foundation. Even such late '60s Smith albums as THE COUNTRY GENTLEMAN and TAKE IT LIKE A MAN show him sticking to his guns. Smith's was a simple formula, but it helped him hold his own during the late '50s, when rock'n'roll

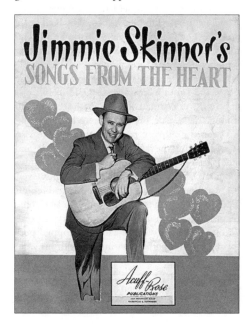

Carl Smith

written with Carl Story), but he also attracted some stellar young songwriters, among them Boudleaux and Felice Bryant ("Just Wait Till I Get You Alone," "Hey Joe!") and Porter Wagoner ("Trademark"). The more romantic songs matched his voice beautifully, but Smith wasn't just a crooner. His music had sharp edges, too, as proved by his sassy take on Bryant's "Hey Joe!," Leon Payne's "You Are The One," and Freddie Hart's "Loose Talk." The last of the three—full of fast words, strong drumbeats and a quick-paced rhythm—set him closer to rock'n'roll than any of his previous recordings, though that was a musical line he never crossed. He didn't need to: there was already a fiery burn to his music, a pretty curl in his voice and a twinkle in his eye.

Wanting a change of pace, Smith quit the *Opry* in 1956 and headed for California to appear in a couple of movies. After that he joined the Phillip Morris Country Music Show and spent over a year touring the nation. He settled for a while on the *Ozark Jubilee* television show (hosted by Red Foley and the *Opry*'s prime competitor). Smith had married June Carter in 1955 and had a daughter with her, Carlene Carter, but by 1957 the couple had divorced. June went on to become Mrs Johnny Cash, and Smith married singer Goldie Hill.

Smith continued having mediocre hits all through the decade, enough to keep both him and his record company relatively happy. He also started hosting the TV series *Four Star Jubilee* and after that a popular show in Canada, Carl Smith's Country Music Hall. By the mid-'70s,however, he was heading toward retirement. He left Columbia after almost 25 years with the label, only recording a few more times for Hickory Records and, in 1983, for Gusto. He also stopped performing, spending his days instead with his wife, Goldie, on their horse farm outside of Nashville.

was eating into much of the country music market. And it earned him a hitmaking career that lasted into the '70s.

Carl Smith was born on 15 March, 1927 in Maynardsville, Tennessee, the same birthplace as Roy Acuff. In his teens he played on the radio in Knoxville, and after serving briefly in the Navy he began playing in the surrounding area as well. He played bass in Molly O'Day's band for a while and after that with Archie Campbell. While with Campbell, Smith caught the attention of Troy Martin, a representative for music publisher Peer International, who helped get him an audition for both the *Grand Ole Opry* and Columbia Records. He made his *Opry* debut in 1950 singing Jimmie Davis' slow and sad "I Just Dropped In To Say Goodbye." Columbia producer Don Law signed him soon after.

Smith's career took off quickly in the early '50s. He cut songs by Carl Butler ("Guilty Conscience"), Ernest Tubb ("[When You're In Love] Don't Just Stand There"), the Louvin Brothers ("Are You Teasing Me"), among others, and within a year he'd made a good showing on the charts. Over the next several years, which were Smith's heyday as a performer and recording artist, he produced a strong and consistent body of work. He occasionally wrote himself ("I Overlooked An Orchid," co-

○ **The Country Gentleman** (1967; Columbia). Smith's 1960s Columbia albums are remarkably consistent and true to form, thankfully avoiding the heavy, overly saccharine production style of the Nashville Sound. Maybe the songs here aren't as vibrant as his best early-'50s sides, but the music is solid to the core and all the way through.

⊙ **The Essential Carl Smith (1950–1956)** (1991; Columbia/Legacy). An excellent compilation from Smith's heyday, this CD packs in 20 songs that run from crooner specials like "Let's Live A Little" to the sharp and tasty "Hey Joe!," one of his standouts. Smith was among the decade's finest honky-tonk stylists, and this compilation is the proof.

⊙ **Satisfaction Guaranteed** (1996; Bear Family). If you want more Smith than just 1 CD can hold, this set has 5, bringing together all of Smith's 1950s recordings.

Hank Snow

The honky-tonker with one of the longest-running careers in country music was Canadian singer and songwriter Hank Snow. He cut his first sides as early as 1936, and went on to record hundreds of songs for RCA Victor through the early '80s. He began as a yodeling Jimmie Rodgers fan and singing-cowboy hopeful, but he soon came into his own as a versatile singer with a crisp, pretty, nasal-tinged tenor and a penchant for spare honky-tonk arrangements. It was a distinct style that made up-tempo songs like "I'm Movin' On" and "The Rhumba Boogie," as well as weepers like "I Don't Hurt Anymore" and "Down The Trail Of Aching Hearts" (a duet with Anita Carter), standouts of '50s country. When Snow parted ways with RCA decades later, he left behind a huge repertoire of songs and recordings that is among country music's most substantial.

The story of Hank's rise to fame is a colorful, but not entirely happy one. Hank was born Clarence Eugene Snow on 9 May, 1914 in Brooklyn, Nova Scotia. Sadly, his childhood turned traumatic when his parents divorced and his mother remarried a fisherman who was prone to violence. (Years later he'd found the Hank Snow Fund for the Prevention of Child Abuse and Neglect in America.) Hank's escape from this trouble was the sea, and between the ages of twelve and sixteen he worked as a cabin boy. Later in his teens he worked an assortment of odd jobs. At the same time, he was busy singing, playing guitar and listening to records, especially those by

Vernon Dalhart and Jimmie Rodgers. His musical studies finally paid off when he landed a radio show in Halifax, where he was billed first as the "Yodeling Ranger" and then the "Singing Ranger."

Snow cut his first sides for Bluebird (a subsidiary of RCA) in 1936. He had success with them in Canada, though they weren't released in the US for another decade. During this time Snow's radio work widened in Canada, and by the mid-'40s he was ready to try and break into the American market. He played some shows in Philadelphia stations, then appeared on the WWVA *Wheeling Jamboree* in Wheeling, West Virginia. Later in Dallas on the *Big D Jamboree* he met Ernest Tubb, another bigtime Jimmie Rodgers fan. Around 1949 Snow finally started cutting sides in the US for RCA Victor with his band, the Rainbow Ranch Boys. One of them was "I'm Movin' On" which, when released in 1950, hit #1 in the *Billboard* country charts and stayed there for five months. That same year Snow finally made it (with Tubb's help) onto the *Grand Ole Opry*.

The next several years were Snow's heyday. He followed the success of "I'm Movin' On" with titles like "Golden Rocket," "The Rhumba Boogie," "The Gal Who Invented Kissin'," and "Married By The Bible, Divorced By The Law." Snow wrote many of these himself, though not all. The gentle and pretty "I Don't Hurt Anymore," for instance, was penned by Don Robertson (a master songwriter who wrote many more country classics) and Jack Rollins. The song was another chart-topping smash for Snow in 1954 and led to steady success as a recording artist over the next decade. He charted many times,

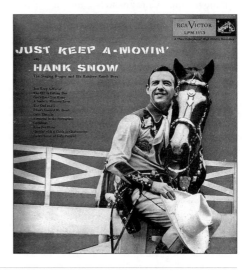

Hank Snow

recorded duets with singer Anita Carter (daughter of Maybelle) and guitarist Chet Atkins, and his live shows, too, were popular events (often including stunts with his pony, Shawnee). By the '60s he also owned a publishing company, talent agency and radio station. He wasn't writing as frequently as he had done earlier, but the material he covered on his many albums was all over the map: older songs like "Wreck Of The Old '97" and assorted Jimmie Rodgers songs, and more recent titles like "Miller's Cave" and "I've Been Everywhere." The latter was penned by Australian songwriter Geoff Mack and was another major hit for Snow.

His career was still kicking in the '70s. "Hello Love"—an easygoing, thoroughly pleasant song—took him again to #1 in 1974, an incredible feat for a man who'd at that point recorded for 38 long and steady years. "Hello Love" aside, though, Snow and other *Grand Ole Opry* stalwarts were finding their songs edged out of radio playlists during the '70s by a younger generation of country artists—pop crooners like Kenny Rogers on the one hand, 'outlaws' like Waylon and Willie on the other. In response came the Association of Country Entertainers (ACE), a group that spoke out against pop trends in country music. Snow served briefly as president, though soon he was dabbling in some of those same trends himself. "If you can't beat them, join them," he reasoned. On the title track to his 1977 album STILL MOVIN' ON (produced by Chuck Glaser of the Glaser Brothers) he admits that "outlaw music has a real good beat and the new kind of pop I got to say it is sweet"—though in the end he warns "when it's all disappeared you're gonna find me right here still movin' on." Unfortunately, "movin' on" for him at that point meant covering himself in sticky pop-syrup on his 1981 duet album with Kelly Foxton, WIN SOME, LOSE SOME, LONESOME. It also meant the end, after some 45 years, of his RCA recording contract.

Pop mistakes aside, Snow's career was easily one of the most persistent and successful in all of country music. No matter that his heyday was in the '50s; his voice and spirit were still strong twenty years later. Never mind that he toyed with string sections; the main thrust of his sound was always traditional at its core. When he was inducted into the Country Music Hall of Fame in 1979, it was a well-deserved honor. Sadly, Snow died at his home in Tennessee on 20 December, 1999. For further details on his life and times, read the essay on him in Peter Guralnick's excellent book *Lost Highway*; his autobiography, *The Hank Snow Story*, is also worth a read.

◉ Hank Snow #104: Still Movin' On (1977; RCA). Produced by Chuck Glaser of the Glaser Brothers, this album is driven with a contemporary outlaw-style rhythm, a sound that Snow fits into just fine. The songs may not equal his 1950s classics, but the album is crammed with personality.

☉ The Yodeling Ranger (1936–1947) (1993; Bear Family). These 5 CDs gather Snow's Canadian recordings for Bluebird and its parent company, RCA Victor, from the first decade of his career.

☉ The Singing Ranger (1949–1953) (1994; Bear Family). The 4 CDs here cover Snow's initial years on RCA in the US. Bear Family is apparently quite enamored with Snow, and has released 3 further box sets, each picking up where the last left off and chronicling his career at RCA. Some previously unreleased tidbits await the curious Snow fanatic.

☉ The Thesaurus Transcriptions (1994; Bear Family). Five CDs containing 140 transcriptions Snow made between 1950 and 1956 for radio airplay only, many of which have an informal atmosphere different from his studio recordings.

☉ The Essential Hank Snow (1997; RCA). Twenty tracks of solid Snow, and the best single-disc collection on this *Opry* icon that's currently on the market. Obvious classics like "I'm Movin' On" and "I Don't Hurt Anymore" are included, but all the songs here were Top 10 hits from the early 1950s through to the '70s.

Texas Ruby And Curly Fox

R uby Agnes Owens was a strong-willed singer with a confident, no-pussyfooting style and a big, deep voice. She and her husband, fiddler Curly Fox, were a popular team on Cincinnati's *Boone County Jamboree* and the *Grand Ole Opry* during the 1930s and '40s, well loved for songs like "Blue Love (In My Heart)" and "Don't Let That Man Get You Down." The latter had a swing-fed, old-time showmanship quality, yet at the same time it possessed a biting, quasi-feminist undercurrent. Ruby was also one of the few nationally recognized female country stars in the days before singers like Kitty Wells, Goldie Hill, Jean Shepard, and, later, Patsy Cline opened up the market, and so it's unfortunate that since her death in 1963 she's fallen between the cracks of country music history.

Curly was a well-known fiddler in his own right before joining forces with Ruby. Born Arnim LeRoy Fox on 9 November, 1910 in Graysville, Tennessee, he made his first recordings with the Roane County Ramblers and the Shelton Brothers in the late '20s and early '30s. Clayton McMichen, a top-notch fiddler and former member of the Skillet Lickers, helped him gain entry to the fiddle contest circuit, and it was during a trip to Texas that he met his wife-to-be, Ruby. Born on 4 June, 1909, in Decatur, Texas, Ruby was the younger sister of cowboy singer Tex Owens (the composer of "Cattle Call"). The duo began performing together on the *Opry* in 1936, switched to WLW's *Boone County Jamboree* in the early '40s, then were back on the *Opry* for several more years after that. They cut records together for Columbia in the '40s and later for King and Starday. Fox also cut a series of fiddle instrumentals that proved popular. During much of the '50s the couple appeared regularly on television programs in New York and Houston, returning to the *Opry* once again in the early '60s. Tragically, Ruby died on 29 March, 1963 in a trailer fire while Fox was playing a radio show. Fox continued playing into the early '90s until his death in 1995.

⊙ **A Memorial Tribute To Texas Ruby And Curly Fox** (1996; Bronco Buster). This 20-song CD collection is a mix of commercial recordings the pair made during the 1940s along with some rare radio transcription material.

⊙ **18 Old Time Country Favorites (Curly Fox)** (1998; Rural Rhythm). A collection of fiddle tunes like "Sittin' On Top Of The World," "Mountain Dew," and "Floatin' Down To Cotton Town" that give well-deserved focus to the instrumental talents of Mr. Fox.

Floyd Tillman

Though he rarely strayed from his home base in Houston, Texas, Floyd Tillman was one of the prime movers in honky tonk, a man whose songwriting and singing helped define the genre and give it depth. He did finally earn a rightful place in the Country Music Hall of Fame, though

HILLBILLY · FOLK · WESTERN Picture Magazine

COUNTRY SONG ROUNDUP

A CHARLTON PUBLICATION

FP1 No. 5

TWENTY-FIVE CENTS

Exclusive! Your Favorite Songs

BLUES STAY AWAY FROM ME
I GOTTA HAVE MY BABY BACK
I'LL NEVER SLIP AROUND AGAIN
HANGMAN'S BOOGIE
I LOVE YOU BECAUSE
CRY BABY HEART
LOST HIGHWAY
MY BUCKET'S GOT A HOLE IN IT
MULE TRAIN
I LOVE EVERYTHING ABOUT YOU
WHY DON'T YOU HAUL OFF AND LOVE ME?
DEAR HEARTS AND GENTLE PEOPLE
YOU'RE GONNA CHANGE
I WASTED A NICKEL LAST NIGHT
BONAPARTE'S RETREAT
MAMA WHAT'LL I DO
THE WALTZ OF REGRET
SMOKEY MT. BOOGIE
TENNESSEE WALTZ
THE GRASS LOOKS GREENER (OVER YONDER)

FLOYD TILLMAN

PICTURES and **STORIES** of **Your Favorite Stars**

KENNY ROBERTS
OFF TO A GOOD START

JIMMY RODGERS
THE BLUE YODELER

EDDY ARNOLD
"HOEDOWN"

JIMMY DICKENS
STORY OF A "LITTLE" GUY

MEET MISS MARGE
MAUMEE VALLEY JAMBOREE

SMILEY BURNETTE
"I'VE MADE 80 MOVIES WITH GENE AUTRY"

HAWKSHAW HAWKINS
RABBITS TO GUITAR

RED RIVER DAVE
SPEED SONG WRITER

SLIM CARTER
SINGIN' COUNTRY BOY

CANDID ROUNDUP
TEX FLETCHER
WAYNE RANEY
MERVIN SHINER
RAY SMITH

he'll never be as well remembered as his cowboy-hatted contemporary, Ernest Tubb. The chief difference is self-promotion: Tubb became an *Opry* icon and toured the country regularly, while Tillman preferred to stick close to home, working as his own manager and booking agent. He did appear on the *Opry*, but mostly he left Nashville to its own devices and let his fans come find him in Texas.

Tillman's voice is an oddity. He sings in a rich Texan drawl, and as the words rise from deep within his chest he pulls them apart like they were hunks of caramel stuck to his molars. It's a style that's drawn-out and chewy, not to mention slightly lazy and behind the beat, and it makes him one of the more distinct vocalists in country music. Though Tillman did have hits himself, his singing was a little too off-kilter to really make him a mainstream star. No matter, really, because he was also a first-class songwriter, having penned such honky-tonk standards as "It Makes No Difference Now" and "Slipping Around." The latter dealt openly with sexual temptation and infidelity—it was country's first cheating song and it made no apologies for being so. Eyebrows rose, sure, but the song also nailed a longing that even country fans knew all too well. When the 'respectable' duo of Jimmy

Floyd Tillman

Wakely and Margaret Whiting recorded it in 1949, the song stayed on top of the country charts for a whopping four months.

In song, Tillman was the master of pain. "It Makes No Difference Now," about a man who shrugs his shoulders at unrequited love ("let things happen as they will and I'll get by somehow," he drawls in a voice of empty surrender), was another early smash, covered first by Cliff Bruner in 1938 and later by Jimmie Davis (who bought it outright from Tillman for $300—a common practice at the time), Gene Autry and even Bing Crosby. Tillman had many more hurt-filled tunes where that came from. "I'll Take What I Can Get" again covers loneliness, only this time there's a quickie cure: "I'll go down to the old dance hall and find a girl to pet," he sings. And if he can't find the perfect woman, well, he'll take what he can get—a sentiment echoed three decades later in Mickey Gilley's bleary-eyed barroom jewel "Don't The Girls All Look Prettier At Closing Time." Tillman's genius didn't stop with lost-love sagas, however: "A Small Little Town" is a curio that conveys the disappointment and sadness of returning to one's old home town to find life there has grown tired and bleak (even "the taverns close early," he moans, leaving "no wine for my heartaches"). The steel guitar even sounds like howling cats. And when love comes knocking, Tillman still can't help himself: "I love you so much it hurts me," he cries, his voice dripping with angst despite his apparent good fortune.

Tillman was born across the border in Ryan, Oklahoma in 1914, but his family moved south to Post, Texas only a year later and he's been a proud Texan ever since. He learned guitar as a child and started playing it publicly as a teenager. By the mid-'30s he'd found himself in San Antonio, playing first in Adolph Hofner's swing band before joining the Blue Ridge Playboys in Houston under the leadership of fiddler Leon "Pappy" Selph. Along with Tillman, the Playboys included two other honky-tonk innovators, pianist Moon Mullican and steel guitarist Ted Daffan. Amplified instruments were catching on fast in Texas at the time, and Daffan—who owned a radio repair shop—helped fit Tillman's guitar with a simple electric pickup.

Tillman began recording during the late '30s and eventually landed at Decca. He had some luck a few years later with "They Took The Stars Out Of Heaven" and "Each Night At Nine." After a stint in the Army he signed with Columbia and hit the charts again with "Driving Nails In My Coffin," "Slipping Around," and "I Love You So Much It Hurts." Wakely and Whiting had started covering his songs in the late '40s, climbing high in the charts with the latter two as well as the answer song "I'll Never Slip Around Again" (a sort of atonement for their previous sin).

By the '50s Tillman had a fistful of memorable honky-tonk hits under his belt. He continued to record through the '60s for RCA Victor, Liberty and Musicor, and by the '70s he was a legend not only among traditional country fans—he won a spot in the Nashville Songwriters Hall of Fame—but also among the progressive-country crowd in Austin, Texas. He recorded an album with "Crazy Cajun" producer Huey P. Meaux, known for his work with both Freddy Fender and the late Doug Sahm, and, while you might think that matching Tillman with a bunch of young hippie-cowboy musicians was a good idea, the results were nothing to go out of your way for. (As a general rule, in fact, you're better off avoiding Tillman's '60s and '70s releases, as they attempt to give him a 'contemporary' vibe with heavier drumbeats and beefier instrumentation—which is absolutely unnecessary and at times even insulting.) In 1984 Tillman finally earned a much deserved spot in the Country Music Hall of Fame.

○ **The Best Of Floyd Tillman** (1976; Columbia). The best and most classic Tillman tracks are the ones he cut for Columbia in the late 1940s and early '50s. This album is sadly out-of-print, but keep your eyes peeled for it and other Columbia collections like the out-of-print Columbia Historic Edition.

⊙ **Country Music Hall Of Fame Series** (1991; MCA). Contains his early singles for Decca, from 1939–1944, including both his initial solo recordings and a couple he made as lead vocalist with the Blue Ridge Playboys. These pre-date his big Columbia hits and are more western swing in style—and pretty darn tasty at that.

⊙ **The Best Of Floyd Tillman** (1998; Collector's Choice). Finally, a CD collection of Tillman's Columbia material has arrived, and it's a healthy-sized one at that, containing an impressive 24 cuts from the mid-1940s and '50s. It's here that you'll find such classic titles as "Slipping Around," "I Love You So Much It Hurts," "This Cold War With You," "I Almost Lost My Mind," and the biggest downer of the bunch, the flat-out suicide song "You Made Me Live, Love, And Die."

Floyd Tillman

Ernest Tubb

"I want my music to be simple enough, so that the boy out there on the farm can learn it and practice it and try to play it."

—Ernest Tubb

If there's one country singer who symbolizes the heart and soul of 1940s honky tonk, it's Ernest Tubb. His repertoire and career were both huge, spanning four decades and including such undisputed classics as "Walking The Floor Over You," "Driving Nails In My Coffin," "Thanks A Lot," and "Waltz Across Texas." A onetime Jimmie Rodgers protégé, he helped usher in the honky-tonk era, then worked all his life to keep country's traditional core alive and kicking—this despite the onslaught of first rockabilly and then the slick Nashville Sound. Tubb didn't just represent the 'old ways' like a golden statuette; even in his later years he was a robust and active performer, out on the road playing more than two hundred dates a year and still making the *Opry* (and his own *Midnight Jamboree*) each Saturday night.

Tubb's style was firmly grounded in Texas honky tonk, yet the most outstanding quality was how informal and all-out friendly his songs always sounded. His voice was distinct—deep and gravelly but also warm and inviting. He sang out of tune now and again, but that was all part of his charm. He was no pretty-voiced Bing Crosby, he was the guy next door. He sang with feeling and from the heart, and it's this gusto that made his music so genuine.

Aside from fueling country's down-home vibe—which included greeting fans and signing autographs for hours after a show—Tubb was also a revolutionary of sorts, thanks to his early use of an electric lead guitar. Electric instruments had been pioneered in the western swing bands of Milton Brown, Bob Wills, and Cliff Bruner during the '30s, as well as by honky-tonk axemen like Ted Daffan and Floyd Tillman, so Tubb certainly wasn't the first when he asked his lead guitarist to plug in on "Walking The Floor Over You." But more than almost any other country and western artist, Tubb was the man who popularized the sound—bringing it onto the stages of the *Grand Ole Opry* and, by turn, into the hearts and homes of hillbilly fans across the nation—and made it the new industry standard.

Ernest Dale Tubb was born on 9 February, 1914 near the tiny farming community of Crisp in Ellis County, Texas. As a child he listened to cowboy singers like Jules Verne Allen; later, like most aspiring young musicians of his day, he was bowled over by the singing, yodeling and picking of Jimmie Rodgers. When Tubb began his career on the radio in San Antonio, playing the songs and imitating the style of his musical hero, he

Ernest Tubb

Ernest Tubb

was just one of many youngsters with a Rodgers fixation. That changed the day he opened the San Antonio phone book and found the name and number of Carrie Rodgers, his idol's widow. He called her on a lark, and that conversation instigated a lifelong friendship. She helped him get off the ground—loaning him Jimmie's tuxedo and guitar for a promotional photo session (she later gave him the guitar as a gift), setting him up on his first tour, even getting him an audition with RCA Victor. He recorded a handful of sides that were released on the RCA subsidiary, Bluebird, but, despite the assistance of Mrs Rodgers (which included some original songs penned by her sister, Elsie McWilliams, who'd written songs with Jimmie), Tubb didn't get much notice. Instead he continued to pay his dues, playing various radio stations and working odd jobs.

The crucial turning point in Tubb's musical development, aside from that phone call to Mrs Rodgers, came again by accident: he had his tonsils removed. Suddenly he could no longer yodel like Rodgers—his voice had changed, it was no longer 'pretty.' Although devastating for him, at the same time it turned him into something different, giving him a sound that was far more original and fresh. He began not only singing differently but writing songs with a new perspective. In 1940 he won a chance to record again, this time for Decca. He showed up for the session in Jimmie Rodgers' limousine and cut four songs including "Blue Eyed Elaine"—a tender love song written to his first wife ("I couldn't find a sweeter pal if I search the whole world round")—and "I'll Get Along Somehow." And lo and behold he made the charts.

It was another year before he cut "Walking The Floor Over You" and made honky-tonk history. Jukebox operators had complained that his first recordings were difficult to hear over the din of the nightclub crowds, so this time the lead guitar—with Fay "Smitty" Smith taking the place of Tubb's usual picker, Jimmie Short—was electrified. It worked. The song sold 400,000 in a matter of months. As a result Tubb landed a few movie roles, but more importantly he won the attention of the *Grand Ole Opry*, becoming a full-fledged member in 1943. His weekly appearance on that show coupled with his heavy touring schedule set a routine—and a lifestyle—he'd maintain with dignity for the rest of his life.

In 1947 Tubb opened his now famous Ernest Tubb's Record Shop in downtown Nashville across the street from the Ryman Auditorium, home (at the time) to the *Grand Ole Opry*. He also instigated the tradition of the *Midnight Jamboree*, an informal post-*Opry* broadcast of stars and special guests gathered on a small stage in his store. He hosted it all his life, and it continues to this day, though now it's held at the Opryland branch of the growing chain of Tubb's stores (which, of course, no longer sell 'records'). The store, by the way, does a thriving mail-order business.

Tubb enjoyed a long and steady stream of hit songs from the '40s well into the '50s. Among his hundreds of recordings were originals like "Our Baby's Book" (about the death of his young son), "Let's Say Goodbye Like We Said Hello," and "Soldier's Last Letter;" songs by such writers as Lost John Miller ("Rainbow At Midnight") and Jerry Irby ("Driving Nails In My Coffin"); and duets with pop group the Andrews Sisters ("I'm Bitin' My Fingernails And Thinking Of You") and crooner Red Foley (the parody "Tennessee Border No. 2"). His hits slowed down during the late '50s when rockabilly began raiding the honky-tonk market, but his recordings continued. During the '60s, in fact, he cut two of his best-remembered songs, "Waltz Across Texas" and "Thanks A Lot." He also recorded albums with Loretta Lynn, whose rich, rural voice was a good match on songs like "Who's Gonna Take The Garbage Out." Then in 1975, after 35 long years with the same label, Decca (which by then had become MCA) dumped him. It wasn't personal—many older artists lost their longstanding contracts during the '70s due to unspectacular sales figures—but it was rather indelicate.

Tubb was inducted into the Country Music Hall of Fame in 1965. Unfortunately, he was also diagnosed with emphysema a year or so later. He chose to maintain a heavy touring schedule anyway, playing cards and sleeping in the back of his bus all through the '70s and into the early '80s. After leaving Decca he signed with First Generation, a label run by steel guitarist Pete Drake. One of the Tubb albums Drake released was THE LEGEND AND THE LEGACY, which featured guest vocals by George Jones, Charlie Rich, Johnny Paycheck, and others overdubbed onto Tubb's recordings (it's not as bad, really, as the concept may seem). Tubb finally retired from touring in 1982, and on 6 September, 1984 he passed away. With him went an entire generation of country music.

❂ Honky Tonk Classics (1983; Rounder). A great sampling of 14 Tubb songs cut between 1940 and 1954 that mostly avoids the obvious songs, which is refreshing. It's one of a series of classic country albums Rounder put out during the '80s. They're now out-of-print, but worth grabbing if you see them.

Ernest Tubb

⊙ **Country Music Hall Of Fame** (1991; MCA). A great single-CD set of original recordings, 16 in all from 1941's "Walking The Floor" through to 1965's "Waltz Across Texas."

⊙ **Walking The Floor Over You** (1996; Bear Family). This is Bear Family's earliest Tubb collection: 8 CDs in all, from his earliest Bluebird recordings in 1936 to his hitmaking heyday in 1947. There are also some rare radio transciptions. It's a massive set, but it should be—after all, this is the birth of honky tonk. Bear Family also offers 4 further Tubb box sets that follow, in chronological order, his years at Decca/MCA up through 1975.

⊙ **The Last Sessions—All Time Greatest Hits** (1997; First Generation). This double CD compiles Tubb's final 47 recordings from the late 1970s and early '80s, completely undubbed this time. Vocalists and instrumentalists who appeared on THE LEGEND AND THE LEGACY are now absent. It's just pure Tubb.

⊙ **The Complete Live 1965 Show** (1998; Lost Gold). This double-disc live set from the Spanish Castle Ballroom in Seattle was previously issued by Rhino in an abbreviated (single-CD) form under the title LIVE, 1965. This release restores the entire set, and it's a well-rounded, full-bodied performance (not to mention a clear and crisp recording) that gives us a taste of his down-home concert style.

Justin Tubb

The eldest son of honky-tonk legend Ernest Tubb was a fine country singer and songwriter in his own right, penning hits for more than a few country stars and making the charts several times himself during the 1950s and '60s as a solo artist and in duet with Goldie Hill. It's no secret that Justin Wayne Tubb (born 20 August, 1935 in San Antonio, Texas) had a massive legacy to uphold. He first appeared on the *Opry* at the age of nine, joined the program at twenty, and when he was first signed to his father's label, Decca, in 1953, Ernest was still making plenty of waves in the country charts. Yet Justin never simply cashed in on his father's name; the honky-tonk style he chose was originally modeled on that of his hero, Hank Williams, and his natural vocal tone was decidedly smoother, and prettier, than that of his deep-voiced father.

Admittedly, Justin did have his first song, "My Mother Must Have Been A Girl Like You,"

recorded by his father in 1951. In the years following, however, he proved his mettle when his songs were cut by George Jones ("Big Fool Of The Year"), Hawkshaw Hawkins ("Lonesome 7-7203"), Patsy Cline ("Imagine That"), Willie Nelson ("Feed It A Memory"), and Del Reeves ("Be Glad"), among others. As a singer, Justin had his first hit in 1954 with "Looking Back To See," written by Jim Ed and Maxine Brown (aka The Browns). Lively and full of country spirit, the song was one of several excellent duets Tubb recorded with fellow Decca artist Goldie Hill. As a solo artist, Tubb's only '50s hit was with the Marvin Rainwater song "I've Gotta Go Get My Baby." He didn't strike again until his 1963 original "Take A Letter, Miss Gray" brought him back into the Top 10. It was cut for Groove, one of several labels he recorded for after leaving Decca in 1959. Tubb made the *Billboard* charts one more time in 1965 with "Hurry, Mr. Peters," a duet with Lorene Mann. In addition to Groove, he cut records for RCA and Starday and concentrated on his songwriting. During the '70s he raised a few eyebrows with his song "What's Wrong With The Way We're Doin' It Now," a commentary on the state of contemporary country music, and in 1985 he cut a tribute album to his father for MCA-Dot. He also took over the job of hosting the *Midnight Jamboree*, a post-*Opry* program begun by his father in 1947. He died on 24 January, 1998.

⊙ **Rock It On Down To My House** (1994; Bear Family). A substantial 2-CD set of Justin Tubb's Decca material from the 1950s, showcasing the fine work of one of country music's most famous (and undervalued) sons. The arrangements begin on the spare side and eventually fill out; a few toy with rockabilly, while others take on elements of the Nashville Sound, though they never lose their core honky-tonk flavor. Several excellent duets Tubb made with Goldie Hill are highlights.

Kitty Wells

"There's no way I could pretend to be Kitty Wells."

—Emmylou Harris

The artist who almost single-handedly established the commercial worth of female country singers was Kitty Wells. It happened largely as a result of her 1952 recording of "It Wasn't God

Who Made Honky Tonk Angels," an answer song to Hank Thompson's hugely popular "The Wild Side Of Life" (which contained the line "I didn't know God made honky tonk angels ... "). Almost as soon as Wells' recording left the studio and hit the charts, record company men were scrambling to find additional women singers to match Kitty's surprise success—and songs that approached life from a woman's point of view.

As for Kitty herself, she was far more than a one-hit wonder, going on to chart again and again throughout the '50s and '60s. Her deeply rural voice, with its Tennessee twang, and her myriad songs that spoke openly and honestly of heartache hardship, earned her the well-deserved title Queen of Country Music. She almost retired to her home life (as so many talented women musicians commonly did at the time) before "Honky Tonk Angels" hit the airwaves, but since then she's given her singing career a lifelong commitment, and more than four decades after her breakthrough she continues to perform.

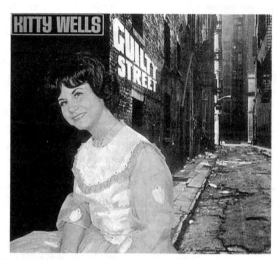

Despite the revolutionary nature of her 1952 song, Kitty was not a 'feminist' or 'liberated' in the manner we think of today. She was actually quite modest—the "wonderful woman in gingham" is how the liner notes to Decca's THE KITTY WELLS STORY described her, referring to her comfortable cotton dresses. She sang about drinking (the grim "Death At The Bar") and cheating ("Paying For That Back Street Affair"), and proved more than willing to stand up to chauvinism ("Broken Marriage Vows"), but in both her singing style and stage manner she was nowhere near as bold and brazen as soon-to-come female stars like, say, Wanda Jackson or Patsy Cline. And no matter what she might be singing, or how big a star she was on the *Grand Ole Opry*, she always maintained the image of a good wife and mother.

Kitty was born Ellen Muriel Deason on 30 August, 1919 in Nashville, Tennessee, well before that town gained its musical reputation. At the age of eighteen she married Johnnie Wright, a cabinet-maker who aspired to country-music stardom

(which he'd eventually achieve as half of the duo Johnnie And Jack). She sang with Johnnie and his sister Louise Wright as Johnnie Wright And The Harmony Girls. When Wright teamed up with Jack Anglin (who married Louise) to form the harmony duo Johnnie And Jack, the 'girls' some-times performed with them. The war temporarily split up the band, but afterwards they regrouped, with Muriel (who was now a mother of two children) becoming more of a featured singer. At the instigation of a radio announcer (Lowell Blanchard of the popular *Mid-Day Merry-Go-Round*), Wright gave his wife her stage name, taking it from an old sentimental folksong, "My Sweet Kitty Wells." Johnnie And Jack eventually worked their way up to per-forming regularly on the newly founded *Louisiana Hayride* and recording for a couple of small labels. Though she sang on the *Hayride*, Kitty didn't sing on their records until they signed to RCA in 1949. At their first session she not only accompanied Johnnie And Jack but also cut four sides on her own. Her records got some notice, but at that time promoters were not so keen on female singers. RCA decided to keep Johnnie And Jack (who had a strong career with songs like "Poison Love") but dropped Kitty.

Wright had sent a demo tape of Kitty's singing to Paul Cohen at Decca Records, but at that point Kitty was ready to retire and turn to motherhood full-time. Fate intervened, however, in the guise of the song "It Wasn't God Who Made Honky Tonk Angels." It was written by J.D. Miller and was being shopped around; Cohen liked it, and he also liked Kitty's tape and thought the two would be a good match. Kitty was less than enthu-siastic about the song, but went ahead anyway and cut it for Decca in May of 1952, with Owen Bradley producing (though Cohen would be her regular producer). The session also featured the electric steel-guitar work of Shot Jackson, who'd play with Kitty for years to come. The song made it to #1, stayed put for six weeks, and turned Kitty into a bright new star. A long and steady stream of hits followed, including "Making Believe," "Lonely Side Of Town," and "Whose Shoulder Will You Cry On." She sang further answer songs to hits by Lefty Frizzell ("I Don't Want Your Money, I Want Your Time"), Webb Pierce ("Paying For That Back Street Affair"), and Bobby Helms ("I'll Always Be Your Fraulein"); duets with Red Foley ("You And Me"), Pierce ("One Week Later"), and Roy Acuff ("Goodbye Mr Brown"); and gospel material ("Dust On The Bible"). Her repertoire was rich and varied, and it kept her fans enthralled.

Kitty's hits slowed down during the '60s and she finally left Decca (now MCA) in 1973. After that she recorded for Capricorn, her husband's own Rubaca label, and Step One. Even though her hitmaking years were well behind her, Kitty and Johnnie (Jack was killed in an auto accident) have continued touring, playing festivals and concerts well into the '90s. Kitty was inducted into the Country Music Hall of Fame in 1976 (the same year as her longtime producer Paul Cohen), and won a lifetime achievement Grammy award in 1991.

◐ **The Golden Years (1949–1957)** (1987; Bear Family). The original LP version of Bear Family's box set on Wells contains 5 albums' worth of material, each beautifully packaged with a colorful album cover. It's still a nice way to listen to the music—one side at a time—as you're not bombarded with quite so much music all at once, as is the case with the later CD version (which, reissued in 1992, goes by the title QUEEN OF COUNTRY MUSIC and packs 10 years of her music onto 4 CDs).

☉ **Country Music Hall Of Fame Series** (1991; MCA). Sixteen original recordings from the 1950s and early '60s, many of them an essential part of the '50s honky-tonk picture.

☉ **At KWKH** (1994; Bear Family). This is a Johnnie And Jack live radio concert that features Kitty sharing lead vocal duties with Paul Warren.

Onie Wheeler

Singer, songwriter and harmonica player Onie Wheeler was one of the unsung heroes of the honky-tonk era. He wasn't all that well known even in his day, which is strange, since his sound was definitely original and so many of his recordings absolutely thrilling. The supercharged "Jump Right Out Of This Jukebox" and the more low-key "Run 'em Off," in fact, are some of the best honky-tonk–infused numbers that came out in the post-Hank 1950s. Wheeler's deep voice owes a debt to Ernest Tubb, but he's actually a more versatile singer than the Texas Troubadour, beautifully rolling, dipping and yelping his way around his songs (most of which he wrote). The mix of fiddle, guitar and harmonica, and the curious lack of steel guitar (apparently Wheeler just didn't like it), give his music a different tone from the average arrangements of the day. The clear presence of the drums adds a nice kick. Wheeler did dabble in rockabilly, but his best songs like "Run 'em Off" and "No, I Don't Guess I Will" were cut to be country.

Onie Daniel Wheeler was born on 10 November, 1921 in Senath, Missouri, a small town in the southeastern toe of the state. He was first a fan of the Delmore Brothers and later Ernest Tubb, whose influence is pretty evident. After the war he played music in the Missouri and Arkansas area, got married to a singer named Betty Jean Crowe, and moved with her to Detroit—following the job trail north to find work in the auto plants (a bit of history Steve Earle sang about on "Hillbilly Highway"). Onie and Jean were soon back in Missouri, where Onie hooked up with local musicians Ernest Thompson and Doyal and A.J. Nelson and landed a spot on a small radio station. Onie couldn't play much guitar because of an injury, so he stuck to singing and playing harmonica, which he'd learned as a child. He and the Nelson brothers then spent time playing in Texas before heading for Nashville, where an audition of Wheeler's song "Mother Prays Loud In Her Sleep" landed them a recording contract with OKeh. It was a classic 'mother' song that verged close to bluegrass (as did several of Wheeler's tunes), though Wheeler's distinct voice and harmonica hinted he was looking elsewhere for inspiration.

Wheeler's first recording session, in 1953, not only yielded "Mother Prays" but "Run 'em Off," one of his stellar recordings. "Run 'em Off" didn't chart, but it did sell well over time, and by the end of the year Lefty Frizzell had covered it. (Flatt & Scruggs also covered "Mother Prays".) In 1955 Wheeler went on tour with Elvis Presley, and this experience coupled with the onslaught of rock 'n'roll affected his style, which already had a touch of the wild side. The amusing "Onie's Bop" is based around that familiar boogie kind of rhythm, but it's also twisted through with plenty of Wheeler charm.

When his Columbia contract ended in 1957, Wheeler jumped over to Sun (he'd met Jerry Lee Lewis, Johnny Cash and other Sun kings during a recent tour) and recorded "Jump Right Out Of This Jukebox." It was an easy standout and undoubtedly among his best songs to date—too bad, then, that it got lost in the ether (thanks in part to Sun's mishandling of it). His career faltering, Wheeler briefly tried California but mostly stuck it out playing around Missouri. In 1962 he recorded "Sandyland Farmer," an answer song to Frankie Miller's superb "Blackland Farmer," for Epic (another division of Columbia); he also recorded for United Artists and Musicor. During the mid-'60s he played harmonica in Roy Acuff's band and in the early '70s cut "John's Been Shucking My Corn," a minor hit on the Royal American. After that Wheeler continued to play and record a little, but things had pretty much slowed down. He had an aneurysm in early 1984, and in May he died during a gig with Reverend Jimmie Snow at Opryland USA.

⊙ **Onie's Bop** (1991; Bear Family). This jam-packed 31-song collection brings together Wheeler's OKeh, Columbia and Sun recordings from 1953–1957. He moves back and forth between straight honky tonk, bluegrass, bluesy shuffles and semi-rockabilly numbers (interestingly, the songs are not presented in chronological order). Not every cut is a standout, but a good deal of them are truly mind-blowing.

Slim Whitman

"They call me a western tenor."
—Slim Whitman

With his soaring range, trembling falsetto and almost freakish yodeling style, mustachioed singer Slim Whitman possessed one of the oddest voices in country (and pop) music. Contemporary listeners may find him an acquired taste at best; and the fact that stylistically he comes off more like Wayne Newton than Hank Williams may explain why he's been such a magnet for anti-country ridicule. A series of TV ads in the late 1970s induced a wave of Whitman mockery, including silly Slim Whitman lookalike kits you could buy from smartass radio jocks. And in the 1996 movie *Mars Attacks!* his soaring yodel on his signature hit "Indian Love Call" proved the only thing deadly enough to halt the savage Martian invaders. Now how's that for a legacy?

But Whitman actually has a substantial musical history, and during his decades-long career he's sold millions of records and amassed a huge fan base. During the '50s, his recordings such as "Love Song Of The Waterfall," "Indian Love Call," "Rose Marie," and "Secret Love" attracted a sturdy following among country as well as pop audiences. Later, a good portion of his enduring success came from Europe. During the '50s he pioneered the pathway to success overseas, achieving quite a few chart hits in England and winning many new Whitman converts during international tours.

Ottis Dewey Whitman, Jr. was born on 20 January, 1924 in Tampa, Florida. As a child he learned to yodel from cowboy records, and he picked up the guitar while in the Navy during World War II. He played the instrument left-handed, as he'd lost a finger during a previous job in a meat-packing plant. It took a lot of courage to overcome his childhood shyness, but when postwar shipyard work dried up he slowly moved toward a singing career. He sang a repertoire of older pop ballads and western songs, all marked by his delicate, almost operatic vocal style. His break in the music business came when Colonel Tom Parker, then managing Eddy Arnold (and later Elvis Presley), heard him on a local station and alerted RCA's Steve Sholes. He cut a handful of records for RCA, one being "I'm Casting My Lasso Toward The Sky," which became a theme song during his shows. Guitarist Chet Atkins and mandolinist Jethro Burns were among the pickers on the records, but ultimately they didn't sell well, and in 1950 Whitman was dropped by his record company. By that time, though, he'd earned a spot as a regular on the *Louisiana Hayride*. In 1951 the California indie label Imperial picked him up, and it's with this company that he cut his most classic songs.

Whitman's first Imperial single, "Love Song Of The Waterfall" (co-written by Sons Of The Pioneers founder Bob Nolan), edged into the country Top 10 in 1952. It's a strange yet haunting piece of work, marked by the eerie interplay between Whitman's falsetto and Hoot Rains' steel guitar. Though the arrangements are spare and traditional, the feeling is more that of an old-fashioned parlor song than the kind of beer-joint ballad Hank or Lefty might have sung. Ditto for "Indian Love Call," a gentle, sentimental number that crossed into the pop charts and earned Whitman his first gold record. Several more of Whitman's singles charted in the US during the '50s, but a major turning point came when his 1954 recording of "Rose Marie" topped the music charts in England. His hitmaking streak dried up in the US during the late '50s—thanks in good part to the advent of rock'n'roll, which stifled the careers of many traditional country singers—but in England and Europe his popularity remained strong. He sang at the London Palladium in 1956 and a year later returned for a full British tour.

Whitman had a few more hits in the US from the mid-'60s through to the early '70s, including soft-edged sentimental songs like "The Twelfth Of Never," "More Than Yesterday," and "Guess Who." United Artists eventually absorbed Imperial (and was in turn later gobbled up by Capitol), and Whitman continued recording for United Artists until 1974. Four years later, a hits package titled ALL MY BEST was assembled by Suffolk Marketing and given a vigorous late-night television campaign. It provoked all sorts of teenage mockery from high-school kids who had no idea who this yodeler was; yet the cruelty of this experience was entirely overshadowed by the fact that the album sold several million copies. Another TV collection followed, and soon Whitman was signed to the Cleveland International label, and even dented the country Top 20 one final time in 1980 with the song "When."

⊙ **Rose Marie** (1996; Bear Family). A 6-disc box set that features all of Whitman's recordings from 1949–1959, for both RCA and Imperial. Make sure that you indulge moderately at a single sitting: this is strange stuff that just might induce hallucinations before knocking you flat out.

⊙ **Vintage Collections** (1996; Capitol). There's little in country music that compares to the interplay between Whitman's innocently trembling tenor and the spooky steel guitar of Hoot Rains on numbers like "Love Song Of The Waterfall" and "Song Of The Old Waterwheel" (the latter backdropped by the sounds of a gurgling brook). This hearty 15-song collection concentrates on his early 1950s Imperial material but includes several later songs like the up-beat, Dean Martin-ish "Rainbows Are Back In Style" and the more saccharine "Guess Who."

Hank Williams

"Hank was a mixture of whiskey, lamb's blood, and grave dirt."

—Nick Tosches

If any single artist captures the essence of country music—has the ability to conjure its emotional turmoil and rustic, earthy beauty in a handful of notes and a few turns of phrase—it must surely be Hank Williams. Country music was already in the midst of a honky-tonk revolution lead by conquistadors like Ernest Tubb and Floyd Tillman, but when this wiry young Alabama singer arrived on the stage of the *Grand Ole Opry* in 1949, the music burst its seams, foamed at the mouth, and was never the same beast again.

Though Hank was on the surface a raw and untrained singer, he was also an incredibly expressive one, his voice yipping, breaking, moaning and almost choking on each word, big or small. Locked into each crack and dip of his southern twang was a beauty and truth, pure and very real. Hank was a miracle of a writer at the same time, penning (often with the help of his producer and mentor Fred Rose) song after song that would almost instantly turn classic: "Your Cheating Heart," "I'm So Lonesome I Could Cry," "Honky Tonk Blues," "Hey, Good Lookin'," "You Win Again," "Cold, Cold Heart," etc., etc., etc. During his short recording career he cut some fifty original songs, many of which are still the best-known in all of country music even half a century later. His songs hit raw nerves with spine-chilling effect, yet at the same time they were so beautiful a person could sit down and weep from the sheer joy of their simple but awesome power. Never had pain and sadness sounded so damn good. Yet there was a harsh reality to much of what Hank sang, as the words of his songs echoed the ups and downs of his turbulent personal life. He often gave his hurt a self-deprecating comic spin ("I'll Never Get Out Of This World Alive"), but on other songs like "Cold, Cold Heart" and "You Win Again" the pain drips like ice under the Alabama sun. Another, "Ramblin' Man," is so haunting it seems as if he's already crooning from beyond the grave.

Hank's tragic and untimely death only added fuel to the legends and stories that had already been building during his lifetime. Hank himself, from his childhood onward, was as deeply troubled as he was ambitious. He was plagued with recurring back pain and he was a serious alcoholic. The women in his life were also a source of ongoing turmoil—on the one hand his mother, on the other his first wife, Audrey, who was an obsession he couldn't shake off. And finally there was the

Hank Williams

from his deathbed. And on his final studio recording, "Take These Chains From My Heart," he literally begged to be set free.

If Hank (the first country singer to win the honor of first-name-only recognition) was revered in his lifetime, he achieved the stature of an icon afterwards. Many authors have attempted to decipher his personality—the joy and the darkness, the incredible driving force—among them Chet Flippo (*Your Cheatin' Heart: A Biography of Hank Williams*) and Colin Escott (whose 1994 biography, *Hank Williams*, is at this point the definitive tome). And all sorts of singers—Waylon Jennings and Hank Jr. ("The Conversation"), David Allan Coe ("The Ride"), and Alan Jackson ("Midnight in Montgomery")—have stumbled over themselves singing his praises.

Hank's childhood wasn't picture-perfect by a long shot, but it's the sort salivating fans would expect and hope for from this icon of all things 'country.' Hank was born Hiram Williams on 17 September, 1923 in rural Butler County, Alabama. When he was only six, his father was admitted to a V.A. hospital following a World War I injury. He stayed there for the next seven years, leaving Hank and his older sister Irene in the care of their mother, Lillie, a strong-willed, hard-shelled woman. The family first moved to the tiny town of Georgiana, where Hank discovered he could earn money playing music on the street. There, too, he met Rufus "Tee-Tot" Payne, a black street musician who gave young Hank some rudimentary, but apparently invaluable music lessons. Later the family moved to nearby Greenville and finally to the state capital, Montgomery, site of numerous Civil Rights confrontations in the mid-'50s. Lillie began running a boarding house. Hank briefly attended high school (pictures of him in glasses make him look almost scholarly) and also started performing on local radio station WSFA. Before he was eighteen years old he'd pulled together a local band and—a vision of his idol Roy Acuff and those western skies passing briefly through his head—named it the Drifting Cowboys.

Hank first met Audrey Mae Sheppard while he was touring with a medicine show in southern Alabama. A year later they were married, and almost just as quickly the arguing began, usually

pressure to perform. Hank was a poor southern kid who by his mid-twenties had suddenly landed more fame and fortune than he may ever have dreamed of. After the massive success of "Lovesick Blues" in 1949, all eyes were upon him, and those same eyes also demanded hit after hit. Hank delivered right to the end, spewing forth "I'll Never Get Out Of This World Alive" practically fueled by Hank's appetite for booze. Drinking was a habit that would land Hank in jail, dry-docked in a sanatorium, and face down in the gutter many times over. Even in Montgomery he'd gained a drinker's reputation. And neither Audrey, nor Hank's mother Lillie, could keep him sober when beer was on his mind.

A year before his marriage, Hank had performed in Montgomery with Pee Wee King, and the *Opry* star decided to buy a share of Hank's song "(I'm Praying For The Day That) Peace Will Come." Hank had been writing almost since he'd started playing music, and this marked his first sale. In 1946 he and Audrey traveled to Nashville and met in person with Acuff-Rose partner (and former Tin Pan Alley songsmith) Fred Rose, with whom Hank had previously corresponded. The invitation had almost certainly something to do with the fact that Rose was responsible for finding song material for singer Molly O'Day, who'd just been signed to Columbia. Hank and Molly already knew each other from the touring circuit, and now Molly became the first to record his work. Rose, for his part, may have spent his days in a suit, but he knew country when he heard it. When later that year he was asked to produce country records for the New York indie label Sterling, he saw to it that the label signed Hank. By December Rose was presiding over Hank's first recording session. Among the songs cut were "When God Comes And Gathers His Jewels" and "Calling You," with another new Sterling act, the Oklahoma Wranglers (aka the Willis Brothers), backing him up. Rose was most impressed with a song called "Honky Tonkin'" from Hank's second Sterling session, held two months later. From here on out he began assuming the role of Hank's mentor and advisor—not only offering business advice, but producing his records and helping him write and rewrite his famous songs. In early 1947 he won Hank a much better contract with the much bigger start-up label, MGM, owned by the Loews corporation (Carson Robison and Bob Wills were also signed to the label that year). Hank recorded his first MGM session on 21 April, 1947—with Red Foley's band backing him up—and by June "Move It On Over" had become his first hit song, albeit a minor one.

Hank had been based in Montgomery during this time, still playing regional clubs and local station WSFA. Rose wanted a larger audience for him, and in 1948 secured him a slot on the *Louisiana Hayride*, a radio show that had begun broadcasting just months before as a rival to the *Grand Ole Opry*. Johnny And Jack, Kitty Wells,

Fred Rose

and the Bailes Brothers were already fixtures on the program; others who later got their break on it included Jim Reeves, Johnny Horton, Webb Pierce, and Elvis Presley.

Hank re-recorded "Honky Tonkin'" for MGM in 1948, and again it was a minor hit. All this was well and good, but it wasn't until he cut "Lovesick Blues" in December that his career really took off. It was an old Tin Pan Alley song that minstrel singer Emmett Miller had cut in the '20s and Rex Griffin had waxed a decade later. Now it was Hank's turn, and he yanked and cranked it, giving it a fully energized and inspired country reading. Rose hated the song at first, but the *Hayride* audiences loved it, and before anyone could blink the song was climbing the country charts. It landed smack at #1 and stayed there for four long, beautiful months, even crossing over to the pop charts. When Hank debuted the song on the *Grand Ole Opry* on 11 June, 1949, the audience went crazy. Needless to say, the *Opry* wanted him badly, and he quickly left the *Louisiana Hayride* and entered the Nashville fold. Little did the establishment know what they were getting themselves into.

The hits came pretty steadily from this point onwards. "Lost Highway" (written by Leon Payne), "Mind Your Own Business," and the gorgeous "I'm So Lonesome I Could Cry" were released in 1949; "Long Gone Lonesome Blues," "Why Don't You Love Me," and "Moanin' The Blues" were all #1 hits in 1950. Hank was now

Hank Williams

the best-selling country artist this side of crooner Eddy Arnold. It was at this time that he also began recording spoken-word recitations under the moniker Luke The Drifter—not that it was any big secret who "Luke" was, but Rose felt Hank's fans, especially the jukebox junkies, might balk. Hank's 'sermons' included "The Funeral" (a crude stab at interracial understanding), the stark and chilling "Men With Broken Hearts" (for whom "a living death is all that's left"), and the warning "Be Careful Of Stones That You Throw." He was troubled, but he wasn't without his sense of morality. He was reaching out, offering guidance, though how many lost souls actually grabbed his meager lifeline we'll never know.

The person who really needed that lifeline was Hank himself. He may have been an *Opry* star, he may have enjoyed the huge royalty checks from his record sales, but his personal life was deeply troubled. He stopped drinking briefly after his *Opry* debut, but not for long. His back pain (an ailment since childhood) was getting worse, and his already turbulent relationship with Audrey was souring to the point of divorce—which the couple had done for the first time in 1948 and would do again in 1952.

Audrey was an integral part of the Hank Williams story. She was the love of his life and as such had a powerful influence on her husband, even persuading him that they should record together although she had little or no talent as a singer. Some songs they cut together are tolerable, but on their 1951 duet "The Pale Horse And His Rider" Audrey's out-of-tune vocal (singing lead!) was not just irritating, but turned an otherwise decent song into an unlistenable farce. It's no wonder that this and its flipside, the not-quite-as-distressing "A Home In Heaven," were held back and after Hank's death became his last studio recordings to be released. Interestingly, Hank never sang openly of his drinking problem, but it's pretty obvious that songs like "Your Cheatin' Heart," "You Win Again," and "Cold, Cold Heart" ("you're afraid each thing I do is just some evil scheme") were directed at Audrey.

Despite his private trauma, Hank's popularity seemed unstoppable. His version of "Cold, Cold Heart"—a stark ballad of hurt and pain—made the #1 slot in mid-1951. But the song became even more deeply embedded in the national consciousness when pop singer Tony Bennett (himself just getting a go in the business) hit the top of the pop charts six months later with a version arranged by Percy Faith featuring a full orchestra. Bennett's success started a trend, prompting other pop artists

to cover Hank's songs, among them "Window Shopping" (Art Mooney), "Settin' The Woods On Fire" (Fran Warren), and "Jambalaya" (Jo Stafford). Toward the end of the year, however, Hank entered a hospital for back surgery; he'd recently taken a bad fall that aggravated the problem. He and Audrey also split again, this time for good. He spent his recovery time with his mother in Montgomery, then moved in with singer Ray Price in Nashville.

The final year of his life, 1952, was eventful to say the least. He recorded three final sessions that resulted in some of his best-known songs—among them "Jambalaya" (co-written with Moon Mullican and another smash), "Kaw-Liga" (a kooky song about a wooden Indian who falls in love), and "Your Cheatin' Heart," one of the definitive country songs of all time. His divorce became final in May, and in August he was fired from the *Opry* for excessive drinking. Rose, however, got him back on the *Louisiana Hayride*. That fall he acknowledged and agreed to support an as-yet-unborn child he'd fathered by another girlfriend, Bobbie Jett (the girl, later known as Jett Williams, was born just days after Hank's death). At the same time he married a young beauty named Billie Jean Jones he'd met through singer Faron Young. The wedding was made a public spectacle: the couple had been officially joined privately, but that night they had not one, but two, public ceremonies in New Orleans' Municipal Auditorium, with folks paying between one and three dollars a head to see Hank kiss his new bride.

Shortly after the marriage, Hank began having heart problems. He hooked up with a dubious doctor (Toby Marshall, who'd previously done time for armed robbery) who prescribed him even more dubious 'medication'—chloral hydrate—to ease his suffering. This was on top of a regular diet of morphine, pills and booze. By the end of the year Hank had two gigs scheduled—31 December in Charleston, West Virginia and 1 January in Canton, Ohio. Bad weather prevented him from flying, so Hank hired a chauffeur to drive him to the venue in his new Cadillac. During a rest in a Knoxville hotel, a local doctor shot him up with painkillers. He was then piled into the back seat, and the two men left for Canton. There's a great deal of speculation surrounding the circumstances of Hank's death—some claim he was dead before leaving the Knoxville hotel—but whatever the case, by 7 am on New Year's Day, 1953, he was officially declared dead in Oak Hill Hospital in West Virginia.

His funeral was held three days later in Montgomery, and thousands of people turned out to pay their respects. "Jambalaya" was still #1 and not long after "I'll Never Get Out Of This World Alive" took its place. Both songs had been recorded the previous June. Hank's memory lived on as songs continued to soar on the charts for months after his death, among them his final recordings "Your Cheatin' Heart," "Kaw-Liga," and "Take These Chains From My Heart." His legacy also lived on in the budding career of his and Audrey's only son, Hank Williams, Jr. Dubbed "Bocephus" by his father (after a ventriloquist's dummy popular on the *Opry*), Hank Jr. barely knew his father (he was only three years old when Hank died), but by the age of eight he was being trotted out on stage by his mother as the living embodiment of his late and great Daddy.

⊙ **Rare Demos: First To Last** (1990; Country Music Foundation). A collection bringing together 24 demos the CMF previously released on 2 LPs as THE FIRST RECORDINGS and JUST ME AND MY GUITAR.

⊙ **Original Singles Collection ... Plus** (1992; Polydor). Countless album issues and reissues of Hank Williams' recordings have surfaced since his death, many of them marred by electronic stereo effects, strings, and even the overdubbed voice of his son, Hank Jr. This sizeable box set wasn't the first to go back to the original mono masters, but it stands as one of the purest collections on the market today. It's not cheap, but it's far more affordable than the 10-CD COMPLETE box.

⊙ **Health And Happiness Shows** (1993; Mercury Nashville). A well-mastered compilation of radio transcriptions Hank cut in 1949, just after "Lovesick Blues" had hit. The sponsor of these shows was Hadacol, a 'dubious' 'medicine' popular among country folk. The songs have a casual old-fashioned flavor, and the set includes titles like "Tramp On The Street" that he never officially recorded. It's an intriguing addition to collections of his studio tracks.

⊙ **The Legend Of Hank Williams** (1996; Mercury Nashville). Colin Escott's excellent biography of Hank is abridged to fit on 2 CDs, the text read by Sammy Kershaw. If you want more details about Hank's life and times, this is a great place to get it (as is Escott's actual book). The one thing the CDs have over the book is that they include several songs to help illustrate Hank's story.

⊙ **The Complete Hank Williams** (1998; Mercury Nashville). Packed with 10 CDs, a hardcover book (with writing by Escott and Daniel Cooper), lots of gorgeous

photos, and even some colorful postcards, this is a massive and in some ways overwhelming collection. But it's also a superbly well-crafted creation—all of country's great singers deserve such loving treatment. Includes all studio recordings plus various demos, transcriptions and radio performances from throughout his career.

Jimmy Work

He wrote two classics from the 1940s and '50s, "Tennessee Border" and "Making Believe," but Jimmy Work never had more than mediocre success as a recording artist himself, which must have been frustrating. His voice wasn't as expressive as that of Hank or Lefty, but his rural and slightly nasal tone was certainly solid, especially on beautiful downers like "Hands Away From My Heart" and "That's What Makes The Jukebox Play"— the latter a forgotten mid-'50s honky-tonk gem.

Jimmy Work was born in Akron, Ohio in 1924 but grew up on a farm near the town of Dukedom on the Kentucky/Tennessee border (the inspiration, obviously, for his breakthrough song). Around 1945 he moved to Pontiac, Michigan and began playing country music for the defense- and automobile-industry workers. Many of these men and women were displaced southerners who'd come north seeking factory work, and as a result country music thrived in the Detroit area. Work landed a show on WCAR and even made his first recordings for a small local label, Trophy. It was for another local label, Alben, that he first cut "Tennessee Border" in 1948. The song caught people's attention and a year later Red Foley and Tennessee Ernie Ford were among those who covered it; Homer And Jethro even did a parody version. On the strength of "Tennessee Border" Work cut a few sides for Decca and appeared on the *Grand Ole Opry*, but the songs didn't chart. He label-hopped a few more times, from Nashville-based Bullet to Capitol, finally landing on Dot Records in 1954. It was with this label that he first cut "That's What Makes The Jukebox Play" and "Making Believe." The latter made a decent showing on the country charts, and a version by Kitty Wells, released about the same time, was even more successful. Work's moment may have arrived, but rockabilly had begun to emerge, and country musicians were having a hard time competing for the public's attention. Work toured for a couple years in the South, but his final Dot session was in 1956. He moved to California, cut two songs for the small All label, then moved back to the town of Dukedom and gave up recording and performing (though he continued writing). If Work's name hasn't exactly remained in lights, his songs have survived. During the '70s, Emmylou Harris, the Kendalls and Merle Haggard all cut "Making Believe," and Moe Bandy recorded "That's What Makes The Jukebox Play."

⊙ **Making Believe** (1994; Bear Family). A double-CD collection (compiling the label's earlier LP releases) that includes all Work's great recordings such as "Making Believe," "That's What Makes The Jukebox Play," and "Tennessee Border," plus lesser-knowns like the weeper "Hands Away From My Heart" to the up-tempo (and slightly silly) "When She Said You All."

Faron Young

Louisiana native Faron Young had a bold, occasionally curly, but always attractive (even pretty) voice that, coupled with his neo-honky-tonk style, was packed with spirit. Musically, though, he wasn't so easily pinned down. Even in his 1950s prime, when Hank, Lefty, and Ray Price were hogging jukebox dimes, Young wasn't content to ape his contemporaries, choosing instead to mix stomping honky-tonk songs like "I've Got Five Dollars And It's Saturday Night" (an old Ted Daffan classic) with gentle-faced balladry ("In the Chapel in the Moonlight," "Sweet Dreams") and quasi-rockabilly ("I'm Gonna Live Some Before I Die"). Another example of Young's ability to straddle different worlds revealed itself during the '50s when he signed to Capitol Records, the focal point of a thriving West Coast country scene, yet chose to record and live (at least during his professional life) in Nashville. The fact that he wasn't easily marked by a single scene or style, however, wasn't much of an issue as far as the public was concerned—Young's hitmaking career ran steady and solid for three decades.

Young was born on 25 February, 1932 in Shreveport, Louisiana. Pop music was his first love, but his high-school football coach, who also played in a country band, encouraged his singing talents and helped him land some local gigs. Meeting Webb Pierce, who was then based in Shreveport, was a bonus. Pierce was a top star on local station KWKH and its weekend barn dance, the *Louisiana Hayride*—which was then only a few years old but already quite popular. Pierce helped Young get his first appearances on KWKH and the *Hayride*, and soon after Young was recording for the Philadelphia-based label Gotham. In 1952, however, Young signed with Capitol Records, an association he'd keep for the next decade. His signing was something of a fluke: Capitol producer Ken Nelson happened to be in town for a recording session when he was captivated by a singer on his car radio. Unidentified by the DJ, Nelson drove to the station to find out who the voice belonged to. Young was signed shortly after.

Young didn't write all that much, but his first charting single, the wily honky-tonk ballad "Goin' Steady," was one of his own compositions. The song hit #2 on *Billboard*'s country charts in early 1953 and heralded a long, steady stream of hits that continued for nearly three decades. Young was drafted into the Army in late 1952, but the experience actually worked to his advantage. During his two-year stint, he performed on radio recruitment programs and even continued recording. His version of "If You Ain't Livin'" (one of several songs he recorded by West Coast hitmaker Tommy Collins) climbed high in the charts just as he returned to civilian life, and early in 1955 he finally hit #1 with the sassy, hot-tempoed "Live Fast, Love Hard, Die Young." Further hits followed, including his bare-bones rendition of Don Gibson's "Sweet Dreams" (later made famous by Patsy Cline) and the catchy Roy Drusky composition "Alone With You." The biggest and best-remembered hit of Young's career, however, was "Hello Walls," written by Willie Nelson, a recent Nashville transplant, who was then still relatively unknown. The song made it to #1 in 1961 and crossed into the pop charts as well, boosting Nelson's career tremendously.

A fine-looking man with a smooth, pleasant face, Young also landed several movie roles in the '50s and '60s, including *Raiders Of Old California* (with Lee Van Cleef), *Daniel Boone, Trail Blazer* (with Lon Chaney), and later *Nashville Rebel* (with Waylon Jennings). It was a '50s TV series called *The Young Sheriff*, though (a spin-off of his early westerns), that earned him his nickname.

Young switched from Capitol Records to Mercury in 1963, and many of his subsequent recordings during that decade veered into Nashville Sound territory, marked by a more heavy-handed production. Still, even as contemporaries such as Ray Price left their honky-tonk past behind, Young never entirely forgot his roots. And neither did his fans, who made "Wine Me Up" a major hit in 1969 and then did the same for "It's Four In The Morning" in 1971. By that time Young had also earned a business reputation for the Nashville real estate he owned and also for the *Music City News,* a trade publication he founded in 1963 that has long been one of Nashville's most popular fan-oriented, star-centered magazines. Young also became increasingly notorious for his outspoken beliefs and opinions—and sometimes his actions, which included spanking a little girl on stage during a concert in 1972.

In 1979 he switched to MCA but only stayed for two years. Later he recorded for Step One. Despite his long hitmaking career and his status as one of country music's top stars, Young grew increasingly frustrated with the country music industry during the final years of his life, feeling he was being ignored and undervalued. He was also beginning to have health problems. Tragically, these and possibly other personal problems led to his suicide. On 9 December, 1996, Young shot himself, and a day later he passed away.

⊙ **The Classic Years, 1952–1962** (1994; Bear Family). If a single CD of Young's Capitol material is insufficient, this 5-CD box set from Young's most classic period should satisfy your craving. It's a lot for the novice, but serious fans shouldn't be disappointed.

⊙ **Live Fast, Love Hard: Original Capitol Recordings, 1952–1962** (1995; Country Music Foundation). After years of half-baked, 'best of' collections and CDs full of unspectacular late-period re-recordings, this superb 24-track collection has emerged to spotlight Faron Young in all his honky-tonking, rocking'n'rolling, and occasionally tear-stained glory.

⊙ **Faron Young And The Circle A Wranglers** (1997; Bronco Buster). A collection of recordings Young made during the 1950s for the US Army Recruiting Service— taken from radio programs such as *Town And Country Time* and *Navy Country Hoedown*.

Faron Young

Bakersfield Bound: Country on the West Coast

W hile the history of country music is closely associated with the Southeast, and Nashville has monopolized the business side of things since the 1950s, the music itself actually developed all over the nation, in small towns and other cracks and crevices from North Carolina to as far away as California. The West Coast is too often left out of the discussion of the genre's overall development, when, in fact, it has played a very important part, with California providing a bustling country scene for much of the twentieth century. The first major country presence arrived with the singing cowboys of the '30s, who poured into town to appear in films, forging a path for a steady stream of Hollywood wannabes. California's true country music foundations, however, were laid down even before that, thanks to the Dust Bowl and the Depression, which saw a huge influx of Okies, midwesterners, southerners and all manner of migrant workers to the Golden State with dreams of milk and honey clouding their road-weary minds. They brought with them their love of hillbilly, honky tonk and Texas-style swing dance music, and as they settled into jobs in the shipyards, defense factories, oil fields, or the countless orchards and farms up and down the San Joaquin Valley, they created a huge market for country music of all shapes and styles.

The West Coast country music scene tends to conjure up images of one town—Bakersfield—and the two singers—**Buck Owens** and **Merle Haggard**—who put it on the map. Bakersfield, though, was only part of the picture. Country music in California was initially centered more around Los Angeles. The city was not only home to cowboy stars like Tex Ritter, Gene Autry, Ray Whitley and Jimmy Wakely, it was the center-point of the western swing craze that swept the state in the '40s. The 'cowboy jazz' pioneered by Bob Wills and Milton Brown spread like wildfire throughout the Southwest, from Texas and Oklahoma all the way out to California. By the '40s—when the economy was active again in anticipation of World War II—Californians were packing ballrooms and nightclubs not only in LA but in towns throughout the state. They simply couldn't get enough of bands like Spade Cooley And His Orchestra, Tex Williams And His Western Caravan, and Bob Wills And His Texas Playboys (Wills had moved to California in 1943).

Owing to the intense live music scene that developed in California, it almost seemed for a time that Los Angeles could be tapped as the nation's centerpoint for country music. New York had been the major business and recording center since the '20s, but with so many singers, bands, cowboys and hillbillys flocking west, thanks to the film industry, by the late '30s LA, too, had developed a sizeable music industry. Groups like the Sons Of The Pioneers and singers like Tex Ritter and especially Gene Autry (who was among the decade's most popular vocalists) recorded here, and hillbillies with any vestige of 'West' in their soul (including Ernest Tubb and even Roy Acuff) showed up in town for some sort of B-movie appearance. By the '40s a majority of western swing stars were also calling LA home—their loyalty to the region fueled by the fans who packed the massive Venice Pier and Riverside Rancho ballrooms. If Hollywood had made Los Angeles a legitimate business town, the big-wig country music players quickly recognized this; during the '40s, more than a dozen record labels—including the majors, Decca, Columbia, and RCA—opened offices in the LA area.

Most important of all, however, was the founding of Capitol Records, an independent label set up in 1942 by pop singer Johnny Mercer, businessman Glenn Wallichs, and movie producer Buddy De Sylva. The founders first concentrated on pop singers like Ella Mae Morse, Jo Stafford and Nat King Cole, but being in LA they knew enough not to shy away from country music. A sturdy country department was established under the guidance of Lee Gillette, Cliffie Stone and, most especially, Ken Nelson, and as the label itself came to rival the big boys—RCA, Columbia, Decca—its country roster also grew. Tex Ritter was the first country artist to record for Capitol ("Jingle Jangle Jingle" in 1942), and by the '50s the label's roster was bulging with now legendary names: Buck Owens, Merle Haggard, **Wynn Stewart**, **Merle Travis**, Faron Young, the Louvin Brothers, Hank Thompson, **Jean Shepard**, Wanda Jackson, **Tommy Collins**, **Skeets McDonald**, and **Ferlin Husky** are just some of the bigger names to call Capitol home.

The Capitol Tower

It was no mere coincidence, no simple twist of fate, that the music coming out of Southern California sounded louder and more free-spirited than the sort being made two thousand miles away in Nashville. While the *Opry* had all sorts of strict rules about noise and what country 'should' sound like (Bob Wills caused a stir when he used a drummer on the *Opry* in 1944 and was never invited back), country music out west had a dif-

ferent attitude. Western swing was designed to be played in front of big crowds who loved to dance. It was also intended to be heard loud and clear in the cavernous dance hall or rowdy roadhouse, not listened to politely in the schoolhouse, church, or theater where chit-chat (not to mention beer) was frowned upon. Thus the big western swing bands of Cooley, Williams, and Hank Thompson were hugely popular—as was the sharp guitar sound of Wynn Stewart and Buck Owens, a sound that would become a signature of West Coast country music by the late '50s and early '60s.

The so-called Bakersfield Sound largely exists as a result of the open-mindedness of Capitol A&R man Nelson, who gave his artists (Buck, Merle, Jean Shepard, and even countrypolitan crooner Husky) an unusual amount of freedom in the studio. Many of these Capitol artists were encouraged to follow their own artistic vision, and were also allowed to use their road bands in the studio (a move that predated the 'Outlaw' recordings of Waylon and Willie by a good quarter-century). Guitars could be loud, pedal steel and fiddle sharp as tacks, and drums were generally not a problem. One great song after another poured out of the Capitol recording studios, and more than a few turned into nationwide #1 hits.

As Capitol grew, Los Angeles continued to build on its decent-sized country and western music industry of nightclubs, radio and TV programs, independent labels (such as Four Star and Challenge), and a talented pool of songwriters and studio musicians. The list of the region's session guitarists alone is phenomenal: Merle Travis, Buck Owens, **Joe Maphis**, **Jimmy Bryant**, and later James Burton and **Glen Campbell** were all highly sought-after pickers.

When Merle Travis moved to LA in 1946, he became one of the most influential and sought-after songwriters and guitarists in town. His songs are some of the classics of modern country music, and are quite a diverse bunch, from the jokey "So Round, So Firm, So Fully Packed" to the haunting coal-mining ballad "Dark As A Dungeon." Songs like "Nine Pound Hammer" and "Sixteen Tons" are considered folksongs, but they were penned not by some anonymous balladeer of bygone days, but by a man playing a solid-body electric guitar (Travis was one of the first to do so) and cruising the streets of hip, modern LA on a motorbike. These songs foreshadowed the folk revival movement, which redefined the term 'folk' to mean modern songs written in an older, acoustic style. That movement ultimately 'discovered' and embraced Travis, too, in the '60s.

Travis was one of many regulars on the region's radio shows, including the *Town Hall Party* and the *Dinner Bell Roundup*. The latter was a daily variety show hosted by musician, bandleader, and later Capitol Records executive Cliffie Stone. Through the *Dinner Bell* and its later incarnation the *Hometown Jamboree*, Stone helped bring the music of Travis, **Tennessee Ernie Ford**, Skeets McDonald and other country and pop performers into households all over Southern California. Ford, a radio announcer-turned-singer who truly was from Tennessee, recorded and sold a couple of million copies of Travis' "Sixteen Tons" before turning much of his attention to gospel recordings and TV programs.

When making their grand entrance onto the Riverside Rancho or *Town Hall Party* stages, many performers in the '40s and '50s wore increasingly outrageous western-styled outfits, a look that was soon commonplace among country stars everywhere, even those on the *Opry*. A man in Philadelphia named Rodeo Ben made some western costumes, but the two big-name tailors who turned out the best stuff were Southern Californians Nathan Turk and Nudie Cohen (see box p.194). The **Maddox Brothers And Rose**, in particular, flashed their Turk outfits everywhere they went, earning their nickname as "the most colorful hillbilly band in America."

Dance Halls and Honky-Tonks

The heyday of the large dance hall or ballroom was in the 1940s, and its success was largely down to the ingenuity of one man, Bert "Foreman" Phillips, who opened the Venice Pier ballroom in 1942 and later ran several others as well. Alongside these rose the Santa Monica Ballroom and Riverside Rancho in the LA area, and clubs in the San Joaquin Valley like the Big Barn in Fresno and Bob Wills' Wills Point in Sacramento. During the '40s and into the early '50s, Spade Cooley, Hank Penny, Tex Williams, Ray Whitley, Ted Daffan, **T. Texas Tyler**, and the Maddox Brothers And Rose were fixtures in these and other nightspots.

One of the greatest live bands at the time has to have been the Maddox Brothers And Rose. Having traveled the Okie Highway from Alabama to California in 1933, hitching rides and hopping freights, the Maddoxes proved themselves a miracle of perseverance. The energy and intensity in their music reflected the deadly serious dreams that had brought them west, and had made them one of the most authentic country bands to emerge from that or any period. Rose Maddox, who went from singing in honky-tonks at the age of twelve to a solo contract with Capitol three decades later—

and who recorded and performed up until her death in 1998—is long overdue for a spot in the Country Music Hall of Fame.

The Maddoxes literally rose to fame from the dirt of a cotton patch, and long before they played anywhere as classy as the Riverside Rancho they burned up the stages at assorted rodeos, country fairs and nightclubs up and down the state. The heart of this circuit was an assortment of honky-tonks and dance halls—some decent, others as crude as the inside of an old shoe—scattered through California's agriculturally rich San Joaquin Valley. One of the biggest concentrations of musical activity was in Bakersfield, a hot and dusty blue-collar burg about a hundred miles northeast of LA and about as classic a honky-tonk town as anywhere in the world. It was an agricultural and shipping center for the region, as well as an oil town, and the people who packed the bars and nightclubs looking for a break from their routine were not often a pretty sight. This is exactly why Bakersfield, not LA, gained the reputation as the honky-tonk capital of the West.

The Bakersfield Sound

The so-called Bakersfield Sound probably wouldn't be remembered so well, or even exist at all under that name, were it not for the huge and lasting success of Merle Haggard and Buck Owens. But it's also likely that those two might not be the superstars they are today were it not for the rich music scene that thrived in the city before they rose to the top.

While the clubs and clientele in LA were often urban and swanky, Bakersfield's crowds appreciated things a little more raw and gritty. The music that developed here and in other San Joaquin working-class towns came to be marked by the sharp, loud, high-end sound of the electric guitar (often a Fender Telecaster), a prominence of pedal steel and fiddle, and strong vocals—all of it influenced by rock'n'roll and rockabilly as well as country. Like the honky tonk that emerged in Texas two decades before, it was simple in structure and designed to be heard over the din of the average bar-room crowd. But this was the 1950s, not the '30s or '40s, and back east the country music industry was rallying around the then innovative Nashville Sound, a production technique marked by crooning voices, lush string arrangements and background choruses.

It was in their own raw and gritty context that Bakersfield artists such as Tommy Collins ("You Better Not Do That"), the **Farmer Boys**, Wynn Stewart, **Red** "I'm A Truck" **Simpson** and Ferlin Husky, and bandleaders like Bill

Woods and Billy Mize played regularly and earned reputations as solid acts with large appeal. It's here also, in Bakersfield, that young guitarist Buck Owens and ex-con songwriter Merle Haggard (the only artist of the bunch actually born in Bakersfield) got their start—Haggard in Stewart's band, Owens playing on '50s sessions with Tommy Collins and countless others on the Capitol roster. When in the Capitol studios Nelson helped translate the honky-tonk influences of artists like Owens and Haggard into hit records, the West Coast ended up with a nationally recognized country sound all its own.

If anyone deserves to be called the "King of Bakersfield", it must be Buck Owens. He and his then wife, Bonnie Owens, moved to Bakersfield in 1951, and soon Buck was playing in a house band at the Blackboard with bandleader Bill Woods. Owens' guitar playing (on his Fender Telecaster) stood out for its sharp, punchy sound, and after recording with Tommy Collins on a Capitol session in the mid-'50s he landed plenty of session work and was finally signed himself. His 1960 version of his friend Harlan Howard's song "Above And Beyond"—a lively, up-beat rendition that was cut to be noticed—shot him into the national spotlight.

One of Nashville's top songwriters, Howard got his start while living in LA in the '50s. His songs are loosely tied to the Bakersfield crowd via Owens and, to a lesser degree, Wynn Stewart, who recorded a version of "Above And Beyond" six months before Owens. Stewart's recordings failed to make him much of a household name, yet today they stand out as some of the era's classics. "Wishful Thinking", in particular, is a clear-minded, hard-driving song that grabs hold from the very first notes. That he recorded this and other outstanding songs for Challenge was proof enough that Capitol wasn't the only influential California label.

Stewart was a mainstay and highly successful performer on the region's club circuit. He was also responsible for giving a job to another up-and-coming musician, Merle Haggard, who played in his band for a year. In 1963, Haggard recorded a version of Stewart's "Sing A Sad Song" for the Bakersfield-based Tally label, and it became his first record to chart; Haggard's 1964 hit "(My Friends Are Gonna Be) Strangers" led to a contract with Capitol. The pen behind that song belonged to Liz Anderson (Lynn Anderson's mother), who lived for a while in California and also wrote the Haggard hit "I'm A Lonesome Fugitive."

Haggard's style matured into something far more personal and individualistic than his honky-tonk surroundings, yet his San Joaquin roots remained in his soul, and he's never forgotten them. He wrote a song paying tribute to his friend, Bakersfield mainstay Tommy Collins ("Leonard"), and covered that artist's material many times ("High On A Hilltop," "Carolyn"). One of Haggard's finest albums, SOMEDAY WE'LL LOOK BACK, recalls the field work of his youth (his parents were Okies), and includes the Dallas Frazier song "California Cotton Fields," probably the best picture of the migrant workers' life ever put into song.

Frazier grew up in Bakersfield and got his start in the business after entering a talent contest run by Ferlin Husky, who was working as a DJ and playing the club circuit under the name Terry Preston. Frazier soon moved to Nashville, however, where he became another of Music Row's top songwriters from the '60s onwards (his song "Elvira" was a smash for the Oak Ridge Boys). Husky was the anomaly of the Bakersfield bunch. Instead of embracing honky tonk, his country-pop crossover hit "Gone" was marked by his smooth tenor and a lush background chorus. It's a song some claim inspired the Nashville Sound.

Many hoped the success of these and other artists might make Bakersfield a neck-and-neck rival to Nashville, but such dreams never materialized. It was simply too late in the game for the bulk of the industry to pull up roots and move elsewhere. And besides, the Nashville Sound was selling plenty of records and doing just fine on its own.

A Town Called Trouble

Bakersfield might have run out of steam, but country music certainly continued to play a role on the LA music scene. The Academy of Country Music had been formed there in 1964 to give greater acknowledgement to western-based singers (see box p.173), but as the '60s progressed the city became more and more a major recording and business center for pop and especially rock'n'roll. One success story of all this development was Glen Campbell, a guitarist who, like Owens, rose from sought-after session man to nationwide singing sensation. At his peak Campbell was basically a middle-of-the-road pop singer, but he revealed his country leanings with tunes like "Gentle On My Mind" and "Burning Bridges." The Nashville establishment eventually embraced him, the Country Music Association naming him Entertainer of the Year in 1968. Campbell's success was an early sign of the glitzy music that would hit Nashville in the mid-'70s. His hit song "Rhinestone Cowboy" even became one of that period's anthems.

And then there was Lee Hazlewood, definitely one of LA's oddest music-biz characters and also one of its true geniuses. Beginning his career as a DJ in Phoenix, he made his mark as a producer and songwriter first with Duane Eddy and later with Nancy Sinatra (he wrote and produced "These Boots Are Made For Walkin'"). The true Hazlewood gems, however, are the duets he recorded with Sinatra (for example, the kooky "Some Velvet Morning") and his solo albums from the '60s and '70s (such as TROUBLE IS A LONESOME TOWN, LEE HAZLE-WOODISM: ITS CAUSE AND CURE and POET, FOOL OR BUM). His style was a truly weird country-pop fusion of cowboy fantasies, small-town corniness, a lurking sexual tension and an existential perspective that, while thought-provoking, was not exactly something to set your clocks by. He didn't always blow people's minds, but Hazlewood certainly made them sit up and take notice.

During the '60s, the rock'n'roll and the growing folk-rock movement introduced all sorts of new ideas and a mix of musical styles to Southern California. Soon bluegrass and then honky-tonk-style country became part of the mix. Artists like Gram Parsons, Chris Hillman and Gene Clark helped kick off a country-rock trend that ultimately gave us bands like Poco and the Eagles.

The country scene in Bakersfield is pretty minimal these days, though the 'sound' has lived on in contemporary country music, most notably in the music of Dwight Yoakam. He was a country singer from Kentucky who moved west to be closer to his hero Buck Owens. He even coaxed Buck out of retirement to sing with him on Buck's song "Streets Of Bakersfield," a duet that went to #1 in 1988. Owens has since been playing regularly and even recording, and in 1996 he opened his Crystal Palace nightclub, restaurant and museum. Not exactly a throwback to the city's gnarly past, it's a brand-new Branson-like structure located just north of Bakersfield, right off the freeway and across the road from Denny's.

Anthologies

⊙ **A Town South Of Bakersfield, Vols. 1 & 2** (1988; Restless). The first 2 volumes of this 3-album series are now together on one CD, and it's a decent compilation of 1980s-era LA country and country-rock artists. The roster is mostly made up of unknowns but does include recordings by Dwight Yoakam, Jim Lauderdale, Rosie Flores, Lucinda Williams, and Katy Moffatt. Production is by Yoakam's guitarist and business partner Pete Anderson.

⊙ **Hillbilly Music ... Thank God!** (1989; Capitol/Bug). Compiled by singer-songwriter Marshall Crenshaw, this single CD packs together 24 Capitol sides from the late 1940s through to the early '50s. Most, though not all, are West Coast artists, including Tommy Collins, Jean Shepard, Tennessee Ernie Ford, Rose Maddox, Gene O'Quin, and the Farmer Boys.

⊙ **A Town South Of Bakersfield, Vol. 3** (1992; Restless). The series continues, this time produced by Dan Fredman, and while it's not quite as strong as the first 2 volumes it does come through with tracks by Dale Watson, Wylie And The Wild West Show, former Long Ryder Sid Griffin, and even Harry Dean Stanton.

⊙ **Heroes Of Country Music, Vol. 4: Legends Of The West Coast** (1995; Rhino). This is a very decent sampler of classic West Coast country music, starting with Jack Guthrie's "Oklahoma Hills" and running through Gene Autry, Sons Of The Pioneers, the Maddox Brothers And Rose, Wynn Stewart and Jean Shepard, all the way up to Haggard's "Sing A Sad Song."

⊙ **Swing West! Volume 1, Bakersfield** (1999; Razor & Tie). Now this is more like it, a Bakersfield-centric compilation that digs into the Capitol vaults and pulls out some gems and even a few genuine surprises. Not only do we get respectable songs from classic artists like Wynn Stewart, Rose Maddox and Tommy Collins, but also overlooked greats like Bobby Austin's "Apartment #9," the Farmer Boys' "Humdinger," and the original 1953 "Gone" by Terry Preston (aka Ferlin Husky), which is far superior to the later hit version, a Nashville Sound prototype.

⊙ **Swing West! Volume 2, Guitar Slingers** (1999; Razor & Tie). The emphasis here is, like the title says, on the guitar giants of the West Coast—men like Merle Travis, Tut Taylor and Clarence White, Speedy West and Jimmy Bryant, Joe Maphis, Roy Clark, Glen Campbell, and even Les Paul. A nice lesson in classic country styles, and a smooth listen throughout.

West Coast:
The Artists

Kay Adams

Trucking songs were almost strictly the domain of male singers, but Kay Adams boldly stepped into that pie-and-coffee territory when she cut her single "Little Pink Mack." A minor hit for her in 1966, the song was about the sought-after female driver of a snazzy, pink-colored Mack truck—it was cute, good-natured and a little bit sassy. A native of Knox City, Texas (she was born in 1941), Adams became associated with the Bakersfield scene after moving there in 1964. She met Capitol A&R man Cliffie Stone soon after, and before she knew it she'd landed a recording contract. A year later she won the Most Promising Female Vocalist award from the newly formed West Coast-based Academy of Country Music. Adams' 1966 album WHEELS & TEARS was a collection of truck-driving songs presented from the female perspective, and "Little Pink Mack" was one of its highlights. The song only reached #30 in the *Billboard* country charts, but it has continued to resonate mostly for its unique take on a familiar genre. Adams recorded for Capitol and its subsidiary, Tower (including a half-baked duet album with the otherwise excellent singer Dick Curless), as well as other small labels. She also toured with fellow Bakersfield stars Buck Owens and Merle Haggard. Her career eventually fizzled out, but in 1996 she emerged from retirement (and semi-obscurity) to cut a duet with BR-549, "Mama Was A Rock (Daddy Was A Rolling Stone)," for the alternative-country truck-driving compilation RIG ROCK DELUXE.

○ **Wheels & Tears** (1966; Tower). "This is the first time that the girl's side of the truck-driving songs has been offered," wrote producer Cliffie Stone in the liner notes to this album, which includes tracks such as "Little Pink Mack," "Big Mack," "Six Days A-Waiting" (sung to the tune of "Six Days On The Road"), "The Worst Is Yet To Come" (penned by Liz Anderson), and "Second Fiddle." The latter is a Buck Owens song that's not exactly about life on the nation's highways, but at least fits the album's honky-tonk tone quite well.

Bobby Austin

Bobby Austin was a West Coast singer with a warbly, pleasant voice who made the first of his two brief dents on the country charts in 1966. The song that brought him his first taste of national attention was "Apartment #9," a pure and beautiful downer he co-wrote with Johnny Paycheck (whom he'd hung around with while living in Las Vegas). It was even named Song of the Year by the Academy of Country Music in 1966. A year later Tammy Wynette made it her very first single, and that same year Paycheck cut what's easily the definitive version, but it was Austin's recording that grabbed the highest *Billboard* chart position—and made him a singer to watch on the California music radar.

Austin had actually been working the Southern California scene for over a decade at that point. A native of Wenatchee, Washington (born 1933), he moved to LA in the mid-'50s. He played bass in Wynn Stewart's band, and he was with Stewart when he set up residence in the Nashville Nevada club in Las Vegas. In fact, it was Austin's decision to quit that band in 1962 that led Stewart to hire a young Merle Haggard to replace him. The reason Austin left was because he finally obtained a prized Capitol Records contract. The Capitol singles, however—decent as they were—went nowhere, and in fact "Apartment #9" was actually initially released on Tally, a Bakersfield label that previously had released Haggard's first recordings. Once the song hit, though, Austin was back on the Capitol roster. Songs such as "Cupid's Last Arrow," "This Song Is Just For You," and "I Wouldn't Know Where To Begin" were released on Capitol and Tower, but they barely charted. In 1972 Austin squeaked into the Top 40 for the second and final

Kay Adams • Bobby Austin

time with "Knoxville Station," which was initially released on a small independent label but was picked up by Atlantic. After that, Austin pretty much faded from public view.

○ **Apartment #9** (1967; Capitol). The title song of this out-of-print collection is well worth tracking down—though Johnny Paycheck, the song's co-writer (with Austin), cut the definitive version. Austin's voice is pleasant enough, marked by a little vibrato trail he leaves at the end of each line.

Johnny Bond

"**B**oozers never fear, Johnny Bond is here," begin the liner notes to Johnny Bond's 1965 album TEN LITTLE BOTTLES. The hard-boozing persona he created through material like the woozy comedic recitation "Ten Little Bottles" and the dopey "Sick, Sober, And Sorry" is what many people remember him by. Others will always define him as a cowboy: he got his professional start thanks to the support of Gene Autry, and for more than fifteen years he was Autry's sidekick on the *Melody Ranch* radio program. Truth is, however, Bond was actually a versatile performer whose long recording career traversed the genres of honky tonk, cowboy music, hillbilly boogie, western swing and even rock'n'roll (his version of "Hot Rod Lincoln" made the pop charts in 1960) with little hassle. Bond was also a talented guitarist, comedian and songwriter—his pen was responsible for such titles as "Tomorrow Never Comes," "I Wonder Where You Are Tonight," "Your Old Love Letters," and the western classic "Cimarron."

Cyrus Whitfield Bond was born on 1 June, 1915 in Enville, Oklahoma. During his early twenties he lived in Oklahoma City, and it's there that he began performing with Jimmy Wakely and Scotty Harrell as the Bell Boys. Later the group changed its name to the Jimmy Wakely Trio, and Dick Reinhart replaced Harrell. Gene Autry got wind of the group, invited them to California, and in 1940 the three young musicians were newfound res-idents of the Golden State. They worked as Autry's backing band on his *Melody Ranch* radio show, but it wasn't long before each of them had solo contracts of their own. Bond began recording for Columbia in 1941 and stayed with the label until 1958. During that time he recorded on a steady basis—western swing, boogie songs and even strange period curios like "Der Fuehrer's Face" —and he made the country charts several times with "Divorce Me C.O.D.," "The Daughter Of Jole Blon," and "Oklahoma Waltz," among others. He also appeared in quite a few western films (albeit usually in small roles), was a regular on the *Town Hall Party,* worked as a session guitarist, entered into the music publishing business with Tex Ritter, and stayed put on Autry's *Melody Ranch* right up through the show's final airing in 1956.

Bond first cut "Ten Little Bottles" for Columbia in 1954, but it was a version released on Starday eleven years later that became the hit, giving his recording and performing career new juice. In the meantime, however, he had continued to experiment stylistically, recording

Johnny Bond

cowboy songs as well as the rockabilly-inspired "Hot Rod Lincoln," released on Republic. He had been label-jumping since leaving Columbia, and this pattern continued through the '70s. He also served for a while as president of the Academy of Country Music, a newly formed trade organization whose initial focus was to promote West Coast country music. He died in 1978.

⊙ **The Very Best Of Johnny Bond** (1998; Varese Sarabande). Though a few Columbia sides are included, this 17-song set consists mostly of Bond's later recordings for various indie labels, including Republic ("Hot Rod Lincoln"), Ditto ("The Tijuana Jail"), Starday ("Ten Little Bottles"), and Lamb and Lion (a 1974 version of "Cimarron").

Buddy Cagle

B uddy Cagle was a smooth-voiced stylist who racked up a handful of hit songs during the 1960s, but since then he's more or less faded into the backdrop. Born Walter Cagle in Concord, North Carolina in 1936, Buddy made his entrée into the country music scene after moving to Southern California in the late '50s. There he met with the encouragement of such artists as Don Sessions and Wynn Stewart, who helped him win the attention of the right ears at Capitol Records. Buddy was signed up and his first single, "Your Mother's Prayer," slightly dented the *Billboard* charts in 1963. He made the charts a second time with Stewart's "Sing A Sad Song" (which Merle Haggard also cut around that same time) before switching to Mercury for yet another minor hit with "Honky Tonkin' Again" in 1965. After that he recorded a string of albums for Imperial that matched his easygoing vocal style with pop-influenced material such as "Tonight I'm Coming Home," "Shutters And Boards," and "Mi Casa, Tu Casa." The songs were decent and friendly, if at times a little bland, and Cagle's tenor voice was clearly reaching into Marty Robbins territory—croonerish at times but still retaining a solid country underpinning. The arrangements mixed Nashville Sound touches with prominently placed guitar and pedal-steel solos. Cagle toured frequently with Hank Thompson and worked up a solid following during the '60s, but by the end of the decade his recording career had all but dried up.

⊙ **The Way You Like It** (1966; Imperial). "Tonight I'm Coming Home" was Cagle's final Top 40 chart hit, and it's the lead track on this album, his first of several for Imperial. Like most of the songs here—and Cagle's style in general—it's marked by a casual, unchallenging style.

Glen Campbell

> "I just find a good song and do it like I want to, and if country fans gripe or pop fans gripe, I can't help it."
> —Glen Campbell

D uring the late 1960s and '70s, guitarist Glen Campbell was one of the hottest singers on the market. Ever since his days as an LA session guitarist he'd felt the pull from both sides of the fence, pop and country, and some of his biggest hits—"Rhinestone Cowboy," "Southern Nights," and especially "Gentle On My Mind"—effectively bridged the gap between the two musical worlds. Other songs like "Galveston" and "Wichita Lineman" (two Jimmy Webb songs that were among his finest achievements) had scarcely a hint of country. Yet in live appearances and on his TV show, *Glen Campbell's Goodtime Hour*, the one-time Arkansas farm boy could turn on the down-home charm just enough to keep Nashville riveted, and he won numerous awards from the Country Music Association and especially the Academy of Country Music as a result. His smooth voice and handsome features were impossible to resist, and the Nashville establishment—busy swinging uptown and looking to class up its image—wasn't about to turn its back on such a cash cow.

Campbell actually had some real good ole country in his background, more than many of his highly orchestrated hit songs indicated. He was born Glen Travis Campbell on 22 April, 1936 in Delight, Arkansas. He got his first guitar at the age of four and less than a decade later was playing in his uncle's western swing band. He toured with his own group, the Western Wranglers, before landing in Los Angeles and finding work as a session musician with Bobby Darin, Rick Nelson, and later with the Monkees. He also briefly joined the Champs, one-hit wonders who'd earlier charted with the instrumental "Tequila."

In addition to his guitar work, Campbell made demo recordings—used by songwriters and pub-

The Versatile Glen Campbell

lishers to peddle songs to producers and singers—and it was through these tapes that his voice was first noticed, landing him the opportunity to cut an album for Capitol. Campbell's was a voice "as warm and pure as a southern breeze," or so said producer Nick Venet in the liner notes to his debut solo album TOO LATE TO WORRY—TOO BLUE TO CRY. Venet went on to describe his young charge as "a handsome fellow raised on pork and guitar chords, hominy and Hank Williams." Whatever the opinion, the country angle was there, at least in the song choices, which included three by Ernest Tubb and one (the title track) by Al Dexter. His version of Tubb's "Tomorrow Never Comes" and "Walking The Floor Over You," however, were so strangely rearranged and so heavily orchestrated they were almost unrecognizable. Campbell also cut BIG BLUEGRASS SPECIAL around the same time with the one-off Green River Boys, and later recorded guitar records (including THE ASTOUNDING 12-STRING GUITAR OF GLEN CAMPBELL) as well as a couple of old-time albums with the Dillards and Tut Taylor as the Folkswingers.

Campbell's session work increased, and he backed up such giants as Frank Sinatra, Merle Haggard, Dean Martin and Elvis Presley. He toured with the Beach Boys, and in 1966 he was paraded out again as a solo vocalist with the album

BURNING BRIDGES. Songs by Leon Payne and Buck Owens kept the flavor country, though again the orchestration was impenetrable. The next year Campbell's big breakthrough arrived via "Gentle On My Mind," a pleasant little number written by folkie John Hartford that romanticized the rambling-man lifestyle ("I dip my cup of soup back from a gurgling, crackling cauldron in some trainyard"—ah the sweet joys of the hobo jungle). It turned both Campbell and Hartford into stars. Campbell followed it with "By The Time I Get To Phoenix," a now tired and over-covered Jimmy Webb song, but it was his biggest hit to date. Next came "I Wanna Live," "Dreams Of An Everyday Housewife," and "Wichita Lineman." Yet despite the pure-pop sound of these and other hits, Campbell was named the ACM's Male Vocalist of the Year and the CMA's Entertainer of the Year.

Campbell's popularity soared when *Glen Campbell's Goodtime Hour*, his TV variety show, hit the airwaves in 1969. He appeared on the show until 1972 and also dabbled in movies—starring opposite John Wayne in *True Grit* and alongside Joe Namath and a dancing chicken in *Norwood*. He recorded duets with Bobbie Gentry and Anne Murray, and though his solo recordings were mostly safe, middle-of-the-road pop he did flirt with adventurous country material like Kinky

Friedman's "I Knew Jesus (Before He Was A Star)." In 1975 he stormed the charts once again with the "Rhinestone Cowboy," a bombastic anthem embraced by the same generation of glitz-obsessed performers that its lyrics criticized. Two years later came "Southern Nights," his last major hit, though he maintained a presence in the charts into the next decade. By the '90s his stormy relationship with Tanya Tucker (detailed in Randall Reise's amusing book *Nashville Babylon*) had come and gone out of the tabloids, and he was recording Christian albums as well as pop-country material—religion and new marriage having superseded the booze and pills that plagued his personal life for years (a time that Campbell now refers to simply as "the doldrums"). In 1999 the ACM honored Campbell once again with its Pioneer Award for a lifetime's worth of musical achievement.

○ **Galveston** (1969; Capitol). The rousing title track (with the enticing line "I clean my gun and dream of Galveston") was a huge hit for Campbell, and it's one of his finest pop achievements. The guitar solo at the end alone is worth the 50 cents you'll likely pay for the album, one of thousands of discarded Campbell LPs clogging thrift-store record bins from coast to coast. It also includes another curious Jimmy Webb song, "Where's The Playground Susie."

The Academy Of Country Music

While today's Academy of Country Music awards show broadcasts are examples of slick wall-to-wall commercial pandering at its most crass, it didn't start out that way. When the Los Angeles-based organization began in 1964, it was not only overseen by some of the big wheels of California country music (Tex Williams, Johnny Bond, and Cliffie Stone are among the Academy's past presidents, and singing cowboys Jimmy Wakely and Eddie Dean were also active), it also put together the very first public presentation of its kind—preceding by two years Nashville's CMA (Country Music Association), which operated on a strict insiders' basis in conjunction with the annual DJ convention. The ongoing grudge between the two bodies has frequently taken on the characteristics of a Sicilian blood feud.

The ACM's voting body then included both fans and performers—another significant difference from the rival CMA—and slowly rose from a distinctly humble start at a Pomona honky-tonk to roaring good time at the Hollywood Palladium and finally an annual network television gala. Formed in 1964 as the Country & Western Music Academy, the organization's stated end ("to enhance and promote the growth of country music") initially focused almost exclusively on West Coast stars. The members gave nods to Bakersfield's Merle Haggard, Bonnie Owens and Buck Owens right off the bat, and their voting tended to concentrate, almost anachronistically (some might say incestuously), on western, traditional and hard country artists, rather than crossover successes, for most of the ACM's first ten years. Bonnie Guitar was 1966's top female vocalist; Sons Of The Pioneers were 1967's top vocal group; North Hollywood's Palomino was voted top nightclub for sixteen straight years.

Operating out of a small office located in Sunset Boulevard's Crossroads of the World—with donated office furniture (Wakely contributed a three-legged desk), shoeboxes full of three-by-five index cards, and, courtesy of Johnny "Hot Rod Lincoln" Bond, a barely operable typewriter—many Hollywood insiders initially derided the organization as a corny, overdone mutual-admiration society and cringed at such early profile-raising efforts as an Academy float in the 1967 Hollywood Christmas parade.

The arrival, shortly thereafter, of Tennessee-born disc jockey Bill Boyd (who cut his teeth driving boyhood friend Carl Perkins to Sun Records package dates, spinning R&B on Nashville's WLAC, and who went on to head Armed Forces Radio country programming) was a key addition to the ACM's increasingly aggressive stance. It was Boyd (not to be confused with the Texas-based western swing bandleader of the same name) who helped the Academy get a weekly country radio show, hosted by Tex Williams, in production and on the air courtesy of Armed Forces Radio. It was Boyd who first roped Dick Clark into the ACM, getting the world's oldest teenager to emcee the awards show in 1969. And by 1974 (when the organization officially changed its name to the Academy of Country Music), with Clark, producer Gene Weed and Cliffie Stone, it was Boyd who hustled up the first network airing of an awards show. Along with his wife, Fran Boyd, Bill put the ACM into overdrive, annually raising more than $100,000 for a variety of charitable causes. The ACM's Pioneer award, too, kept the legacy of 'Coast Country''s trailblazers in the forefront. Since Boyd passed away in the mid-'90s, however, there's been, sadly, less and less of a discernible difference between the ACM and Nashville's CMA.

— Jonny Whiteside

Glen Campbell

⊙ **Gentle On My Mind: The Collection** (1997; Razor & Tie). If you don't want to load up on used vinyl, then this 2-CD set is the only Campbell collection you'll need. The big hits "Gentle On My Mind," "Wichita Lineman," and "Galveston" are attractive pop songs, but be warned that Campbell's smarmy, watered-down sound gets old and tired faster than you think.

Jenks "Tex" Carman

Even during his heyday in the 1940s and '50s, Jenks "Tex" Carman was an oddball performer, and for many people an acquired taste. Known as the "Dixie Cowboy," his music and personality was part western, part Hawaiian (his songs showcased his rambunctious steel-guitar playing), and part American-Indian (he claimed to have Cherokee blood and sometimes dressed in native costumes). His voice was strangely pinched and shrill, his arrangements pushed the boundaries of a modern concept of harmonics, and his songs ("The Possum Twist," "Indian Polka," and his best-known number "Hillbilly Hula") bopped along at a quirky gait that left folks scratching their heads yet tapping their feet at the same time. "I'm gonna build a highway to your heart so I can drive right in," he sings on "Highway To Your Heart." Sure it's novelty material, but while Carman was smiling for his audience he wasn't just playing for laughs. His style was actually, when you think about it, rather innovative.

Born in Breckenridge County, Kentucky in 1903, Carman sang with a local glee club before jumping on the vaudeville circuit and touring the country. He learned to play Hawaiian steel guitar from Frank Plada, a popular Hawaiian guitarist from the '20s. Carman eventually drifted west to Los Angeles, where he began billing himself as the Dixie Cowboy (singing cowboys were, after all, still in fashion at the time). He played on Southern California programs such as the *Hometown Jamboree* and *Town Hall Party,* recorded for the indie label Four Star beginning in the late '40s, and actually worked up a decent following. During the early '50s he landed a Capitol recording contract and cut about twenty sides for the label, but none of them was a hit (frankly, it's a wonder anyone even thought the Top 40 was a possibility). He later recorded for labels such as Sage & Sand and Rem, but eventually settled into retirement. He died in 1968.

⊙ **Chippeha! The Essential Dixie Cowboy** (1998; Revenant). This retrospective of Carman's recording history covers the bulk of his studio recordings from 1947–1953, cut for both Four Star and Capitol sessions (including three versions of the semi-popular "Hillbilly Hula"), and then throws in some US Air Force *Country Music Time* recruitment ads for good measure. His vaudeville roots are clear in his often goofy, yet still solidly entertaining presentation, and his steel-guitar playing—not to mention his singing, which will probably send most folks packing—is a curious mix of old-fashioned traditionalism, western boogie-making, and tropical hallucination. Ain't nothing quite like it, that's for sure.

Tommy Collins

If you want a crash course in the life and career of Bakersfield honky-tonker Tommy Collins, give a listen to Merle Haggard's 1980 hit "Leonard." The song is a tribute to Collins (his real name is Leonard Raymond Sipes), who was one of Haggard's musical heroes and an early star of the then up-and-coming Bakersfield music scene. Haggard has cut numerous Collins songs during his career ("Sam Hill," "Carolyn," "The Roots Of My Raising"), and fellow Bakersfield star Buck Owens also recorded quite a few (one of his first albums, in fact, was BUCK OWENS SINGS TOMMY COLLINS).

Collins himself was best known for novelty songs like "You Better Not Do That," "I Got Mine," "You Gotta Have A License," and "If You Can't Bite, Don't Growl," but he also mixed in straightforward numbers such as "High On A Hilltop" and "You're For Me", as well as strange birds like "You Oughta See Pickles Now" and the dour "I Wish I Had Died In My Cradle" ("before I grew up to love you"). No matter what type of song he played, though, he approached it with a smart and spirited style that was pure honky tonk and honest to the core. Most of his initial recordings in the '50s even featured the guitar work of Buck Owens, who was just getting his start at the time. Buck's sharp Telecaster guitar sound eventually became a trademark on his own recordings, but it was also a distinct element of the otherwise sparse arrangements of many Collins' hits. Ever since artists like Owens and Haggard became superstars, they've been quick to credit Tommy Collins as one of the key architects of the Bakersfield country music scene—thanks to his

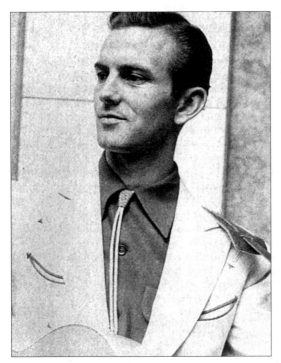

Tommy Collins

the Gospel, though he did continue recording for Capitol until his contract ran out in 1960. A few years later, however, the ministry no longer captivated him and he returned to Bakersfield, signed up with Capitol once more, and got back into the country music business all over again. In 1965, after switching to Columbia, he made the charts with "If You Can't Bite, Don't Growl," another oddball song in the manner of his earlier hits. "I'm a wampus kitty," declared the ex-preacherman as a big, beefy rhythm chugged behind him. This time the arrangement and even Collins' voice brought to mind Lee Hazlewood rather than Buck Owens.

Collins toured during the '60s with his former protégés Owens and Haggard, who were by this time major country stars and stiff competition for him. He continued to write and record into the '70s, but he also increasingly mired himself in alcohol and pills. Writing further hits for Haggard helped get him off this treadmill. He moved to Nashville and cut an album for Starday. The success of Haggard's song "Leonard" brought him newfound attention, and Mel Tillis and George Strait recorded a few of his songs—Strait even taking a version of "If You Ain't Lovin'" to #1 in 1988 (Faron Young had recorded it three decades earlier). In the '90s Collins was concentrating on songwriting and touring Europe occasionally.

◉ **Words And Music Country Style** (1957; Capitol). Collins' first full-length album, capturing him in his youthful pre-gospel prime, is now a prized collector's item.

◉ **Leonard** (1992; Bear Family). A 5-disc box set covering all the material he recorded for Capitol. This is a worthwhile investment for serious Collins fans, but for the merely curious it's a shame no single-disc CD collection of Collins' work is currently available.

strong songwriting skills and unadorned honky-tonk sound.

Leonard Sipes was born on 28 September, 1930 in Bethany, Oklahoma just outside Oklahoma City. He first appeared on a few local radio programs, and while he was attending college he cut his first singles for Morgan, a small label based in Fresno, California. After serving in the Marines, he headed west to California on a tour with Wanda Jackson, another native Oklahoman. Sipes remained behind in Bakersfield, where he met and became pals with rising star Ferlin Husky. He wrote a few songs for Husky, who helped Sipes get a recording contract with Capitol. One of his first releases (under his new professional name, Tommy Collins) was the self-penned "You Better Not Do That," a gently risqué novelty song that shot high in the charts and got him noticed fast.

The mid-'50s was Collins' heyday, as he achieved hit after hit with songs like "It Tickles," "All Of The Monkees Ain't In The Zoo," "High On A Hilltop" (later cut by both Owens and Haggard), and the kooky "You Oughta See Pickles Now." It was profoundly bad timing, then (at least in terms of his music career), when in 1956 he found God and enrolled in a Baptist seminary. By the end of the decade he was actively preaching

The Farmer Boys

Because their time in the spotlight was so brief, and they never had a chart hit to speak of, the Farmer Boys have never made the 'A' list of Bakersfield Sound progenitors. But the sixteen songs singer-guitarists Bobby Adamson and Woody

Wayne Murray cut for Capitol during the mid-1950s were excellent examples of high-energy, sharp-edged West Coast honky tonk.

Though Adamson (born 20 September, 1933) and Murray (born 11 September, 1933) both hailed from rural Arkansas, they didn't hook up until they were eighteen and living in Farmersville, California in Tulare County—an agricultural region just north of Bakersfield. Their families had come west during the great Okie migration. The two boys met in a Farmersville café: the story goes that Adamson was harmonizing along with the jukebox and Murray, sitting across the room, joined in. They quickly became friends and began singing together in local clubs. During a gig at the Happy-Go-Lucky Club in Tulare, television personality "Cousin" Herb Henson heard them and invited the duo to perform on his *Trading Post Show,* a regionally popular TV program based out of Bakersfield. Henson dubbed them the Farmer Boys after the town they lived in, Farmersville, and they became regulars on his show.

Henson next helped them get a contract with Capitol Records. They'd tried out with MGM, but the deal never came through. Capitol's A&R man Ken Nelson, however, was immediately impressed and inked them to a three-year contract. They cut their first session in LA in 1955 with a band that included guitarist Roy Nichols (who'd later be an integral member of Merle Haggard's band), Bill Woods (who helped kickstart the career of Buck Owens) and Lewis Talley. During that time they also toured with such established stars as Carl Smith, Webb Pierce and Elvis Presley. Their up-tempo honky-tonk sound was sharp, tight, and built around the boys' piercing harmonies. They cut novelty titles ("Onions, Onions" and the Tommy Collins song "You're A Humdinger") and later some quasi-rockabilly material, but on the whole they maintained a hard country approach right through to their final session on 21 February, 1957. That session, incidentally, featured steel player Norm Hamlet and guitarist Buck Owens, who also wrote or co-wrote each of the four songs they cut that day.

The Farmer Boys never had a hit song, and perhaps that was part of the reason why they parted ways with Capitol in 1957. Another factor was certainly the rise of rock'n'roll, which cut sharply into the country music market. A Columbia deal was discussed, but it didn't materialize, and the Farmer Boys never recorded again. They did, however, continue playing around California with a band until 1964, when they finally called it quits.

⊙ **Flash, Crash And Thunder** (1991; Bear Family). The Farmer Boys are one of the great lost bands of the Bakersfield saga, and thankfully the Bear Family folks figured that out and have collected all 16 songs they cut during the mid-1950s onto a single CD. The boys dabble in novelty songs ("It Pays To Advertise," "You're A Humdinger") and flirt with rockabilly ("Cool Down Mame"), but their sound—with some of the great Southern California instrumentalists backing them up, including Roy Nichols and Norm Hamlet—remains cutting-edge honky tonk all the way through.

The Farmer Boys

Tennessee Ernie Ford

Tennessee Ernie Ford had a voice as warm, rich and deeply flavored as Belgian chocolate. Though he recorded more than his share of mediocre pop and gospel material (the record bins at Salvation Army are usually full of such offerings), his range of material was actually much greater. His signature hit, "Sixteen Tons," was a catchy sensation, but Ford was at his rockin'n' rollin' best on "Milk 'Em In The Mornin' Blues" and "Shotgun Boogie," two of the many boogie tunes he cut in his early years. And just as deftly he could take the tempo way, way down on a Nashville standard like "Don't Rob Another Man's Castle" (found on his excellent album COUNTRY HITS ... FEELIN' BLUE). His voice was so burly and full-bodied that he hardly needed accompaniment.

Ford may have liked to rock things up, but he was no stone-cold honky-tonker. His voice was infused with a generous amount of natural energy, but it was smooth, not edgy. So for him to jump from hopped-up tunes like "Shotgun Boogie" to unabashed pop ditties like "Talk To The Animals" and "My Favorite Things" a decade later was actually not much of a surprise. Still, his renditions of songs like "Sixteen Tons," "Milk 'Em In The Mornin' Blues," and "Catfish Boogie" are classic.

Ernest Jennings Ford was born on 13 February, 1919 in Fordtown, Tennessee. He was raised in nearby Bristol, where he first worked in radio. He also studied voice in Cincinnati. After serving in World War II he and his wife settled in Southern California, and it's here that he built his reputation. He worked as a radio announcer (taking the moniker "Tennessee Ernie" Ford), and it's on the radio that Capitol Records A&R man Cliffie Stone first heard him. Stone became his manager and began featuring him on his own influential show the *Dinner Bell Roundup* (later known as the *Hometown Jamboree*). Stone also got Ford signed to Capitol, which released his first singles in 1949. Titles like "Tennessee Border" and "Smokey Mountain Boogie" made *Billboard*'s country charts that year, and "Mule Train" became his first #1. Ford wrote many of his early tunes, with Stone often listed as co-writer. In 1950 he debuted on the *Grand Ole Opry*, though he never joined the show, keeping his career based on the West Coast instead—a smart move considering the wide appeal he soon achieved in pop as well as country. Riding the success of subsequent hits like "Shotgun Boogie" and a couple of duets with Kay Starr (including hot-tempoed goofball "Ain't Nobody's Business But My Own"), he played both in Las Vegas and at the London Palladium.

Ford's reputation as a well-rounded entertainer really crossed borders into the big time when he began hosting the TV game show *The College Of Musical Knowledge* in 1954. The show was also the stage for his music, and he debuted "Sixteen Tons" there soon after. Written by West Coast guitarist and songwriter Merle Travis, it was a smash hit and became not only Ford's signature but one of country music's best-known songs. Beginning in 1956 he took a prime-time TV gig on *The Ford Show*, where he instigated the time-worn phrase "Bless your pea-pickin' hearts." Further TV shows followed during the '60s. By this stage Ford was cutting far more gospel and highly orchestrated pop music than boogie songs, his voice exuding a more majestic quality. His 1956 album, HYMNS, had become the first gospel album to be certified gold, and it kicked off the gospel-album trend among country artists from George Jones to Ricky Van Shelton. For the next decade Ford cut many more albums—his total was around a hundred—and enjoyed distinction as a stately vocalist who brought an image of uptown class to country music, though much of this later music had more in common with Jim Nabors than anyone on the *Opry*. Still, Ford occasionally cut worthwhile gems like COUNTRY HITS ... FEELIN' BLUE and ERNIE SINGS AND GLEN PICKS (a duet album with Glen Campbell), both of which feature minimal acoustic accompaniment and allow Ford's voice the freedom it deserves to truly shine. In 1990 Ford was inducted into the Country Music Hall of Fame. A year later, however, he died of liver failure in a hospital in Reston, Virginia.

⊙ **Country Hits ... Feelin' Blue** (1964; Capitol). This album is a great surprise and an easy standout in the Ford catalog. He sings quiet, minimalist renditions of classic country songs like "Born To Lose," "I Don't Hurt Anymore," and "Funny How Time Slips Away" with acoustic guitar (courtesy of LA session regular Billy Strange) and standup bass (played by John Mosher) his only accompaniment. It proves how strong a singer Ford really was.

⊙ **Vintage Collection** (1996; Capitol). A concise single-CD collection of well-known Ford titles like "Milk 'Em In The Mornin' Blues," "Smokey Mountain Boogie," "Sixteen Tons," and "Hey Mister Cotton Picker," as well as duets with Kay Starr, the Dinning Sisters, and others.

⊙ **The Ultimate Tennessee Ernie Ford Collection**
(1997; Razor & Tie). A substantial 2-disc set that
contains 40 songs from throughout Ford's career at
Capitol. It begins with early songs like "Tennessee
Border" and "Mule Train", runs his classic boogie
period ("Blackberry Boogie," "Kissin' Bug Boogie"),
tosses in assorted duets (including one with Glen
Campbell), and even pays respects to his massive
gospel repertoire ("The Old Rugged Cross," "Just A
Little Talk With Jesus").

Bobbie Gentry

"Billie Joe McAllister and the narrator
walked out on that old bridge, and
what they ceremoniously dropped into
the muddy water below was our innocence."

—Ron Carlson

She may not have had the career longevity of
Dolly Parton or Loretta Lynn, but Mississippi
native Bobbie Gentry wrote and performed two
of the most powerful songs of late 1960s country:
"Ode To Billie Joe" and "Fancy." The former, in
particular, was an amazing accomplishment. Gentry's very first single, it rocketed into the pop and
country charts in 1967, becoming a song almost
anyone listening to the radio at that time can still
sing. The lyrics unraveled such an intriguing story
that in 1976 the song was made into a movie
(starring Robby Benson). The storyline centers
around the suicide of young Billie Joe McAllister,
but the details leading to the tragedy (let alone the
event itself) are never entirely divulged. Instead,
they emerge in little pieces during a long dinner
conversation at the home of the narrator, who was
apparently Billie Joe's girlfriend. Questions arise:
Were the two adolescents actually lovers? Was the
young girl who was seen with Billie Joe up on
Choctaw Ridge our beloved narrator? What was
in that package that Preacher Taylor saw Billie Joe
and his companion subsequently toss off the Tal-
lahatchie Bridge? And why aren't the parents asking
these very questions of their daughter point-blank?
With a sultry, blues-inflected voice and a swampy,
humid rhythm that makes the sweat run thick down
the back of the neck, Gentry beautifully captures
the deep-welled repression that was uncomfortably
rampant throughout the South (and America in
general) at the time.

Gentry was born Roberta Streeter in
Chickasaw County, Mississippi on 27 July, 1944.
As a teenager her family moved to Palm Springs,
California, and later she attended UCLA and the
Los Angeles Conservatory of Music. She also sang
in local clubs and worked as a Las Vegas dancer.
In 1967 she landed a deal with Capitol Records,
recorded and released "Billie Joe," and before the
year was out she was practically a household name.
The song spent a month at #1 in the pop charts,
and she eventually won three Grammys, among
other awards. It wasn't just her writing that stood
out, though, as Gentry had a dusky, sexy voice—
closer to Dusty Springfield than Patsy Cline—that
wrapped itself around the words like toffee on a
stick.

None of Gentry's follow-ups ("I Saw An
Angel Die," "Louisiana Man") came even close
to the runaway success of "Billie Joe," though
that's hardly unusual. Nonetheless, "Fancy"—
which Capitol released in late 1969—has proven
itself to be another resilient piece of writing. This
time the protaganist is a poor southern girl who,
with her mother's prodding, rises triumphantly
above her "plain white trash" background to
"charm" kings, congressmen and aristocrats, and
generally live the good life. Basically, we're talking
prostitution—and at an unspecified and highly
questionable age, too. "Lord, forgive me for what
I do," cries the mother as she sacrifices daughter

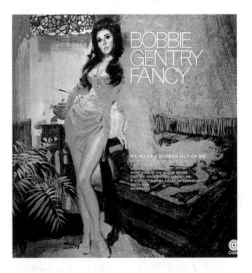

Fancy—tarting her up and sending her out the
door—so that they both might enjoy a better
future. The subject matter may have had sordid
underpinnings, but the song was at heart one of
personal triumph in the face of immense hardship.

Like "Billie Joe," the arrangements (swells of strings and all) were swampy and thick enough to soak right through the skin. A quarter-century later, the song was enthusiastically revived by both the indie rock group Geraldine Fibbers and Reba McEntire—the latter taking her version to the country Top 10 in 1991 (and also onto TV as part of a Doritos commercial).

Beginning in the late '60s Gentry cut a series of duets with Glen Campbell, and two of them ("Let It Be Me" and a remake of the Everly Brothers song "All I Have To Do Is Dream") made the charts. During the '70s she tried inching her way into television, but her *Bobbie Gentry Show* didn't make it past a handful of episodes. She re-recorded "Ode To Billie Joe" for the movie soundtrack, released in 1976, and two years later married singer Jim Stafford ("Spiders And Snakes")—a marriage that lasted less than a year. She became popular in England during the late '70s, but since then has basically dropped out of the music spotlight.

⊙ **The Golden Classics Of Bobbie Gentry** (1998; Collectibles). This is a reissue of Gentry's debut album, ODE TO BILLIE JOE, with 8 bonus tracks tacked on at the end, including "Fancy," "Louisiana Man," and the Campbell duets "Let It Be Me" and "All I Have To Do Is Dream." Though not technically a greatest hits package, it basically functions as such and makes as good a CD introduction to Gentry's work as you'll find.

Jack Guthrie

Jack Guthrie is best known for two classic songs he cut in the 1940s, "Oklahoma Hills" and "Oakie Boogie." The latter was a high-charged hillbilly boogie song that the Maddox Brothers And Rose later covered, but "Oklahoma Hills" proved even more famous. It was written by Jack's cousin, folksinger Woody Guthrie, and was a major #1 hit for Jack in 1945. Jack Guthrie himself died at an early age from tuberculosis (eerily echoing the death of Jimmie Rodgers fifteen years earlier), but the song has endured for decades afterwards in numerous versions by artists from Hank Thompson to Charlie Feathers. Woody Guthrie's son, Arlo, has also recorded Jack's songs more than once.

Jack was born Leon Jerry Guthrie in Olive, Oklahoma on 13 November, 1915. His family migrated west to California during the Dust Bowl

days. He performed in rodeos and worked for the forest service before marrying Ruth Henderson, with whom he developed a western novelty act. His cousin, Woody, came to California in the late '30s and the two began performing together on a Hollywood radio station. During this time, Woody wrote "Oklahoma Hills," and when he took off for New York City in 1939 he left the song in cousin Jack's hands. In 1944 Jack won a contract with Capitol Records and cut "Oklahoma Hills" at his first session. Unfortunately, he was drafted soon after, and by the time the song made #1 in 1945 he was overseas and extremely frustrated that he couldn't enjoy his new-found fame. He finally made it back in 1946, and over the next couple of years played with a band in Tacoma, Washington and recorded further tracks for Capitol. "Oakie Boogie" hit the charts in 1947, but by this time Jack's health was beginning to fail. He was eventually assigned to a veterans' hospital, although he continued to record, as Rodgers had done, even in his final days. He died in early 1948.

⊙ **Oklahoma Hills** (1991; Bear Family). A single-disc collection of Guthrie's recordings for Capitol in the late 1940s. "Oklahoma Hills" is a hands-down classic, with the catchy "Oakie Boogie" not far behind. Other memorable songs include "When The Cactus Is In Bloom" (a happy-go-lucky Jimmie Rodgers tune), the sassy "The Clouds Rained Trouble Down," and the sad "You Laughed And I Cried." Guthrie's voice has an attractive nasal quality, the guitar playing is hot to trot, and even the downer songs have a lively, swing-styled beat.

Merle Haggard

"You have to move beyond your heroes to find your own voice."

—Merle Haggard

Throughout a career that's spanned four decades and counting, Merle Haggard has built a musical reputation that's hard to rival. He's one of country music's best vocalists, with a warm baritone that took cues early on from Lefty Frizzell, but has since gained a richness few country singers this side of George Jones can touch. At the same time Merle (another of the country élite who's earned first-name-only recognition) has created a songbook that's as rich and varied as that of almost any twentieth-century American songwriter, country or otherwise. He's recorded tender love songs ("I Started Loving You Again"), painful songs ("Going Where The Lonely Go"), western swing, folk, blues, jazz, and, of course, unabashed hard-shell honky tonk. Not even Hank Williams can boast a repertoire as rich, wide, strong and enduring.

Merle has seen the top of the charts many times over, yet he has always kept his music down to earth. Much of the appeal of his songs is that they reflect life as Merle has seen it. They're not always the truth verbatim, but many lyrics are taken from his experiences: turning twenty-one in prison, going to bed hungry, learning the tricks of the 'hobo jungle,' hearing his grandma's stories, feeling empty inside when love has disappeared.

Over the years Merle's style and approach have varied, reflecting both his own fluctuating moods and the times that keep changing all around him. He likes to have fun, but he's also unafraid to plunge deep into the American psyche to see what makes things tick. Thus we get blue-collar anthems like "Fightin' Side Of Me" and "Working Man's Blues" alongside the folk-inspired "They're Tearing The Labor Camps Down" and "Tulare Dust," and self-reflective numbers like "Footlights." Finally, there are gems like "If We Make It Through December" and "I Take A Lot Of Pride In What I Am," everyman songs that only blur the boundaries that much further. And, of course, Merle's never forgotten his roots, cutting tribute albums to Jimmie Rodgers and Bob Wills,

and recording numerous songs written by one of his early supporters, Tommy Collins ("High On A Hilltop," "Carolyn"). He even paid Collins the ultimate tribute when he wrote "Leonard" (Collins' real name was Leonard Sipes), a song that told his friend's life story.

Merle Ronald Haggard was born on 6 April, 1937 in Oildale, California, a town immediately north of Bakersfield. His family was living at the time in an old railroad car, which his father had converted into half-decent living quarters. Both his parents were Okie migrants, his father a fiddler and his mother a fundamentalist. Merle's father died when he was only nine, and despite his mother's attempts to keep him on the straight and narrow, her son headed down a path of trouble. "No one could steer me right but Mama tried," he later sang. He did learn to play guitar and sing as a teenager, even taking the stage once with his hero Lefty Frizzell. But he also dabbled in assorted crimes that grew from petty to felonious. The turning point in his young life came after he and a buddy were picked up for trying to crowbar their way into a restaurant—they were drunk and thought it was 3 am, but actually the place was still open! During the subsequent term he served at San Quentin (he really did turn twenty-one in prison, as his song "Mama Tried" tells it), he realized he was heading down a dead-end street and turned his attention to music. Once released in 1960, he began playing the nightclubs in Bakersfield, which was in the thick of its

The young and pensive Merle Haggard

Merle Haggard

honky-tonk boom period. Here he met musicians Lewis Talley and Fuzzy Owen, cousins who were working the Bakersfield scene and who'd also founded a small record label, Tally. Owen eventually jumped on board as Merle's manager, and all three men became lifelong friends and business associates.

Merle's first release on Tally was "Skid Row," but it was "Sing A Sad Song" that gained him widespread attention for the first time. The song was written by Wynn Stewart, and Merle learned it during the year (1962) he spent playing with Stewart's band in Las Vegas. Released in 1963, it made the national charts. Merle followed it with "Sam Hill," written by Tommy Collins, whom he'd only just met, and then cut a duet, "Just Between The Two Of Us," with singer Bonnie Owens. Bonnie was another Bakersfield singer who'd previously been married to Buck Owens, and it wouldn't be long before she and Merle were hitched as well. "Two Of Us" was written by Liz Anderson, a singer and songwriter then living in Sacramento. Anderson also penned "(My Friends Are Gonna Be) Strangers," which made the Top 10, and "The Fugitive" (aka "I'm A Lonesome Fugitive"), Merle's first recording to mention prison.

After the success of "Two Of Us" and "Strangers," Capitol Records signed Merle in 1965. He and Bonnie married that summer and then hit the road with a band they christened the Strangers. "Swinging Doors" was the first of Merle's own songs to become a major hit, and it made folks aware of his talent as a writer as well as a singer. "Swinging Doors" and its follow-up "The Bottle Let Me Down" are two of Merle's most classic honky-tonkers, and they were also the first of a long line of chart hits (including "Branded Man," "I Threw Away The Rose," "Sing Me Back Home," "Mama Tried," and "I Take A Lot Of Pride In What I Am"). His life story started to show through with each passing song: "Branded Man" spoke of the shame he felt about his prison record; "Mama Tried" of his troubled youth; "Hungry Eyes" of his upbringing among migrant families. He became a working-class hero, looking at social issues from a blue-collar viewpoint ("I ain't never been on welfare and that's one place I won't be 'cause I'll be working," he blustered on "Workin' Man Blues"); yet he also wrote touching love songs like "Silver Wings" and "I Started Loving You Again."

Two songs pushed Merle into the realm of the superstar: the notorious "Okie From Muskogee" and its follow-up, "The Fightin' Side Of Me." He claims he always meant "Okie" as a spoof; these days his fans—even the "hippies out in San Francisco"—giggle right back at lines like "leather boots are still in style for manly footwear." At the time, though, the song's hippie-baiting lyrics ("we don't let our hair grow long and shaggy") were taken quite seriously. The country was in the midst of the Vietnam era, after all. "Okie"'s follow-up, "The Fightin' Side Of Me," seemed to firm things up that much more: "I read about some squirrely guy who claims that he just don't believe in fighting," Merle sings, "And I wonder just how long the rest of us can count on being free." It's doubtful Merle himself ever came to blows with anyone over their political views (or long hair), but he sure sounded like he meant business. Whether he wanted it or not—and by most accounts he didn't—both songs thrust an image on Merle as a flag-waving spokesman for the hardhat generation. Talk about a "branded man." The trade-off was that he sold millions of records, won accolades like the CMA's Entertainer of the Year award, and could charge large sums of money for concert appearances.

A deal with the devil? Not exactly. Merle could have recorded albums full of right-wing fire and brimstone songs; instead he came back down to earth and cut a tribute album to one of his musical heroes, Bob Wills. And a month before "Fightin' Side" he'd cut "Irma Jackson," a sympathetic song about an interracial love affair that made his record label nervous enough to hold it back. He also cut "Big Time Annie's Square," a song about love between an Oklahoma farm boy and a California hippie gal ("We don't agree on nothing, but I'll be danged if we don't make a pair"). If anything, each one of these songs shows that Merle was simply trying to understand multiple points of view—to reach the hearts and minds of all kinds of people. And the fact that he did so with the utmost sincerity largely explains why he's such a revered artist today.

Through the first half of the '70s Merle recorded further hits like the joyous "Daddy Frank (The Guitar Man)," the pensive "If We Make It Through December," "Movin' On" (the theme song for a mid-'70s TV show about truckers), and "The Way It Was In '51," a tribute to his idol Lefty Frizzell, who died in 1975. He performed on, and helped organize, Bob Wills' final recording session, and even employed several members of Wills' Texas Playboys in his own band, the Strangers. He also divorced Bonnie Owens. (Bonnie has remained a part of the band, though, and when Merle married singer Leona

Williams she even served as a bridesmaid!) In 1977 Merle signed a new contract with MCA—it wasn't that he'd had a falling out with Capitol, more that MCA had made him a decent offer and besides, he felt a change of pace couldn't hurt. It's between late-period Capitol songs like "It's All In The Movies" and MCA recordings like "Ramblin' Fever" (a nod, however intentional, to Outlaw country) and the gorgeous bar-room melodrama "Misery And Gin" that Merle's songs began to take on a more contemporary feel, slotting him comfortably into the late '70s country landscape. At the same time age seemed to be leading to deeper introspection, as heard in such overlooked recordings as "Always On A Mountain When I Fall" and "Footlights" ("I'm 41 years old and I ain't got no place to go when it's over ..."). "Footlights", in particular, is as humbling and revealing as any song in Merle's catalog.

In the early '80s Merle switched labels again, this time to Epic. He got things rolling with the excellent "Big City," a song about taking that city job, shoving it, and then heading off to "somewhere in the middle of Montana." (The cranky side of Merle still works in a dig at big government with his reference to "so-called Social Security.") The death of Lewis Talley and the disintegration of his marriage to Leona, however, made this new decade less than pretty. But Merle did manage to record the sad and beautiful "Kern River" (which Dave Alvin cut for the TULARE DUST tribute and has since adopted into his own repertoire), the downer "Going Where The Lonely Go," and the gentle "Twinkle Twinkle Lucky Star."

In 1990 he moved from Epic to Curb, where he revisited patriotism in "Me And Crippled Soldiers" (at the height of an anti-flag-burning frenzy) and then got back down to earth with "In My Next Life" (from his album 1994), in which an ageing farmer reflects on his personal accomplishments. In 1994 Merle was also inducted into the Country Music Hall of Fame; on top of that two tribute albums of his songs hit the market, TULARE DUST and MAMA'S HUNGRY EYES. Two years later Curb released another studio album with another uncreative title, 1996, which appeared to indicate the label's lack of enthusiasm for him. Whatever the case, Merle adopted the theme of his earlier blue-collar songs and simply kept on working. At the end of the '90s he was still playing nightclub shows and making county fair appearances all over the nation, his voice as rich as ever and his spirit still very much alive and determined.

⊙ **Sing Me Back Home** (1967; Capitol; reissued 1995; Koch). Reissued on CD with original artwork. Includes songs by Buck Owens ("Where Does The Good Times Go"), Dallas Frazier ("Son Of Hickory Holler's Tramp"), and Lefty Frizzell ("Mom And Dad's Waltz"), as well as Haggard originals like "Seeing Eye Dog," "Good Times," and the monumental title track, which is one of his most moving songs.

● **Someday We'll Look Back** (1971; Capitol). Compiled from two years' worth of studio sessions, this is an amazingly cohesive picture of Merle at his peak. The migrant workers' ballad "Tulare Dust" and the hard-edged prison anthem "Huntsville" are overlooked gems. The album also includes "Big Time Annie's Square," an excellent rendition of Dallas Frazier's song "California Cottonfields," and Tommy Collins' "Carolyn," a sad and innovative song speaking openly of why men seek solace with prostitutes.

⊙ **Serving 190 Proof** (1979; MCA; reissued 1994). After 1978's "Always On A Mountain When I Fall," Merle got even more existential on "Footlights," a song about a singer filled with self-doubt and one he was still performing in the late '90s. It's definitely the album's standout, but "Red Bandana" and "My Own Kind Of Hat" aren't too shabby, either.

⊙ **Big City** (1981; Epic; reissued 1999; Epic/Legacy). The years (and the labels) go by, but the Hag just keeps on ticking. The title track here is another classic, this time fueled by a take-this-job-and-shove-it attitude ("keep your retirement and your so-called Social Security"). "You Don't Have Very Far To Go" is a sad beauty, while "Are The Good Times Really Over (I Wish A Buck Was Still Silver)" is a smart blend of nostalgia, bitterness and honest-to-god hope. The CD reissue includes 2 bonus cuts, "Call Me" and "I Won't Give Up My Train."

⊙ **Capitol Collectors Series** (1990; Capitol). A solid 20-song retrospective of Merle's Capitol recordings, from "Swingin' Doors" to "Okie" to "Emptiest Arms In The World."

⊙ **Tulare Dust: A Songwriters' Tribute To Merle Haggard** (1994; High Tone). Great renditions of Haggard classics by such artists as Tom Russell, Steve Young, Billy Joe Shaver, John Doe, Iris Dement and Dave Alvin make this one of the better tribute albums on the market. (Another Haggard tribute, MAMA'S HUNGRY EYES, features more mainstream country singers.)

⊙ **The Lonesome Fugitive: The Merle Haggard Anthology (1963–1977)** (1995; Razor & Tie). Two CDs of Merle's Tally and Capitol material. Admittedly, this covers much of the same ground as DOWN EVERY ROAD, but it's a good middle ground if you can't afford the bigger box set.

⊙ **Down Every Road (1962–1994)** (1996; Capitol). Four-CD box set concentrating on Merle's Capitol period, but also including early Tally recordings and later MCA and Epic releases like "Footlights," "Ramblin' Fever," "Big City," and "Pancho And Lefty" (a duet with Willie Nelson on a song by Townes Van Zandt). There are only a few surprises, such as a previously unreleased version of "White Line Fever" that's quieter and more introspective, but as a compilation of Merle's long career it's substantial and superb.

⊙ **For The Record: 43 Legendary Hits** (1999; BMG). They're hits, and they're legendary, but they're not the original recordings, so be forewarned. On the other hand, there's a natural graying in Haggard's voice that gives the versions of "Mama Tried," "Hungry Eyes," "Kern River," "If We Make It Through December," "I'm Always On A Mountain When I Fall," "A Place To Fall Apart," and others a true warmth. As much as you might want to write this collection off, it's not that easy. Oh, and there are guest appearances from stars like Willie Nelson, Brooks & Dunn, and, believe it or not, Jewel.

Freddie Hart

Though he didn't blossom on the country charts until later in life, Freddie Hart was quite a hit-maker for a few years in the early 1970s. The song that finally broke the ice for him was "Easy Loving," an oozy, quasi-erotic country-pop crossover smash. Amazingly enough, the crooning Hart was nearly fifty years old at the time of his success—something that would be almost unheard of today. Hart's early records had a more gutsy honky-tonk style but, as with '50s-era compatriots like Ray Price and Don Gibson, he drifted with the changing times into a more pop-oriented atmosphere as the decades progressed. And ultimately, it was his countrypolitan material that yielded him his highest-charting singles.

Hart was born Frederick Segrest on 21 December, 1926 in Lochapoka, Alabama—one of fifteen children. He joined the Marines during World War II (while underage), and afterwards worked odd jobs in Texas and New York. He'd done some entertaining while in the service, and in 1949 moved to Nashville with his eye on the music business. A budding songwriter as well as a singer, Hart earned his first taste of success when George Morgan recorded "Every Little Thing Rolled Into One" in 1952. Later Hart moved to Phoenix, where he met and finally toured with Lefty Frizzell before drifting west to Los Angeles, where he became a regular on the *Town Hall Party* between 1953 and 1956. He also played on other southern and central California shows including the rival LA show *Home Town Jamboree*.

Hart first recorded for Capitol, and his uppity honky-tonker "Loose Talk" was released in 1954. Singer Carl Smith got to hear it and cut the song that same year, taking it to #1 in the country charts and staying there for seven weeks. Hart left Capitol for Columbia a couple of years later, and finally began making minor dents in the *Billboard* country charts in 1959 and 1960 with "The Wall," "Chain Gang," and "The Key's In The Mailbox." He switched to the Kapp label midway through the decade, then by the early '70s he was back on Capitol. In 1971 he struck paydirt with "Easy Loving," and over the next two years had five #1 hits in a row with titles like "My Hang–Up Is You," "Got The All Overs For You (All Over Me)," and "Super Kind Of Woman." Some were positive ("Every day's Thanksgiving" he crooned to his lover in "Easy Loving"), while other titles, though equally steeped in fleshy imagery, were told from a loser's perspective ("If Fingerprints Showed Up On Skin," "Write It All In [Put It All In]").

Hart remained a steady presence in the Top 40 into the following decade, then he drifted out of the charts—and out of the average listener's consciousness, as indicated by the fact that few of his recordings have made it to the CD age. He continued to record for small labels like Sunbird and El Dorado, and in 1996 boldly declared I WILL NEVER DIE, the title of an album he released on the Branson Gold label.

⊙ **The Neon And The Rain** (1968; Kapp). In the title track of Hart's mid-1960s album, a cuckolded man, with gun in hand, awaits the appearance of his wife and her lover at a local motel. Despite being an obvious take-off on the Porter Wagoner hit "Cold Hard Facts Of Life" (which Hart also covers on this very album), the song is a black-handed gem from an era when country dared to be dark.

⊙ **The Best Of Freddie Hart** (1996; EMI-Capitol). Despite a sparse content of only 10 songs, this CD serves as a decent overview—OK, the *only* overview— of Hart's hitmaking period. It's also dirt cheap. Titles include "Easy Loving," "My Hang-Up Is You," "Super Kind Of Woman," "Trip To Heaven," and other hits from Hart's gold-record years.

Ferlin Husky

Ferlin Husky was an anomaly: a smooth-voiced crooner with a cry-baby curl in his voice who emerged from the gritty, working-class honky-tonks of California's San Joaquin Valley. Husky (who early on went by the name Terry Preston) was playing the clubs of Bakersfield during the late 1940s and early '50s when Telecaster cowboys like Tommy Collins, Wynn Stewart, and Buck Owens were just getting their start. In this environment Husky developed honky-tonk roots, but by the time of his massive pop and country hit "Gone" in 1957, his music was heading more uptown. Husky's stage personality also included a popular comic alter ego named Simon Crum, but it's lushly produced songs like "Gone" and such follow-ups as "True True Loving," "Just For You," and "On The Wings Of A Dove" that defined his style.

Ferlin Husky, believe it or not, is his real name. The singer was born on 3 December, 1927 and raised on a farm in Missouri. After serving in World War II, he got his start playing clubs around St. Louis before moving west to Bakersfield. He worked as a DJ, played bass for Big Jim De Noone And The Melody Rangers (who recorded for Four Star), and also performed with cowboy singer Smiley Burnette, Gene Autry's famous movie

sidekick. Feeling his given name was too rural-sounding, Husky first used the pseudonym Tex Terry, then changed it to Terry Preston. He cut his first sides as a solo artist for Four Star under the Preston moniker. When bandleader and *Hometown Jamboree* host Cliffie Stone heard Husky, he invited the young singer to perform on the *Jamboree* and also helped him get a contract with Capitol. Ferlin cut songs as both Husky and Preston for a couple of years before finally dropping the pseudonym.

One of the earliest numbers to win him attention was "Hank's Song," a tribute written by Tommy Collins. It was "A Dear John Letter," though—a half-spoken duet with Jean Shepard about a romance that fizzled during a soldier's duty in Korea—that earned Husky his first major hit. Husky also cut cornball comic songs like "Cuzz You're So Sweet" under the name Simon Crum. In 1957, Husky's career really hit the big time when "Gone" (which he'd first cut back in 1953 in a version that's far less melodramtic and surprisingly more visceral) became a smash country and pop hit. Though released on LA-based Capitol Records, the song was actually recorded in Nashville. Husky was living in Tennessee at this point (he'd moved east to perform on Red Foley's *Ozark Jubilee* television show). Produced by Ken Nelson at Owen Bradley's studio, "Gone" featured background vocals by the Jordanaires— a smooth-making technique quickly adopted as part of the burgeoning Nashville Sound—and also featured a makeshift echo chamber, one of the first of its kind. The sound produced was one that Husky stayed with for years afterwards.

Over the next decade, Husky nurtured the popularity of hits like "Gone" and "Wings Of A Dove" (a 1960 #1) by touring regularly with his band, the Hush Puppies, and appearing on TV

shows like *Kraft Television Theatre*, and in movies such as *Las Vegas Hillbillys* (with a cast including Jayne Mansfield, Sonny James, Connie Smith, and Bill Anderson) and its one-of-a-kind follow-up, *Hillbillys In A Haunted House*. He stayed with Capitol until 1972, by which time his career had slowed considerably. He later cut records for ABC, Cachet and MCA, and he also underwent heart surgery more than once. During the '90s he still made *Opry* appearances and played occasional shows in Branson, Missouri.

⊙ **Vintage Collection** (1996; Capitol). This may be the only Husky collection you need, as it contains all his major hits including "A Dear John Letter," "Wings Of A Dove," and both versions (1953 and 1957) of "Gone."

Rose Maddox

"We were a live group, even on records—singin', hollerin', cuttin' up, and the people would just go wild over it."

—Rose Maddox

The Maddox Brothers And Rose were one of a kind. Among the most exciting bands to ever hit the country and western scene, these onetime "fruit tramps" tore the roof off countless dance halls and honky-tonks up and down the West Coast from the 1930s through to the '50s. Fronted by teenage singer Rose Maddox, the group played a homegrown and hugely eclectic mix of hillbilly swing, old-time country, cowboy, gospel, and fired-up boogie songs. Alongside Rose were her older brothers Fred, Cal, Henry and Don, and behind the scenes at every performance was their mother, Lulu, keeping a tight grip not only on the cash box, but also the personal life of her young daughter, the group's charming center of attention. With their intricate western costumes (designed by Nathan Turk), lively stage antics and goofball humor, they filled the dance halls with rip-roaring, wacked-out energy and earned their moniker "The Most Colorful Hillbilly Band in America" many times over.

The Maddox Brothers would never have been as successful as they were without Rose (the subject, by the way, of an excellent 1997 biography by Jonny Whiteside, *Ramblin' Rose*). Known as "the Sweetheart of Hillbilly Swing," she was a powerhouse of a vocalist with a strong, unrelenting

spirit, and when the band broke up in the '50s she moved onward with a dynamic solo career. Recording a series of albums for Capitol and dueting with the likes of Bill Monroe and Buck Owens, Rose strengthened her reputation as one of country music's finest performers. As a female lead vocalist in what was still largely a man's world, she had fashioned herself into an important female role model while still very young, laying into songs like "I Wish I Was A Single Girl Again" and "Sally Let Your Bangs Hang Down" with unabashed gusto. Though she never considered herself a feminist, she was a vital inspiration to women singers for generations to come. Despite a series of heart attacks during the '80s, Rose persevered as always, continuing to record and perform right up until her death in 1998. Today she stands as one of the true giants of country music.

The Maddoxes literally rose to fame from the dirt of a cotton patch. Roselea Arbana Maddox (born 15 August, 1925) and her brothers all hailed from Boaz, Alabama, but when they were still children their parents—in deep financial straits due to the Depression—moved the family west to California, hitching rides and hopping freights with dreams of milk and honey swirling in their heads. (Ironically, they were ahead of their time even then, arriving just before thousands of Okies flooded the state.) The Maddoxes realized quickly that the streets were not paved with gold, and soon settled into a life of fruit and vegetable harvesting up and down the San Joaquin Valley, eating and sleeping on the ground.

Modesto became their home base, and it's here that the family's musical aspirations first came to fruition. Dabbling in music for years, Fred Maddox—the smooth talker of the family—convinced a local furniture store owner to sponsor a Maddox Brothers radio program. The one stipulation was that they had to include a 'girl' singer, and so they brought along sister Rose, who was not yet twelve years old but who loved to sing. Debuting on the air in 1937, it wasn't long before letters of support flooded in. Soon the family was playing live shows, too—small-town rodeos, county fairs, wherever they could get an audience—leaving the fruit fields behind forever.

The band won a statewide talent contest in 1939, which led to wider radio exposure and bigger (and more lucrative) nightclub dates. Outfitting themselves in fancy western duds brought them further attention. They toured relentlessly up and down the state, night after night, yet always returned to Modesto (and later Stockton and Sacramento) to make their daily radio broadcasts. Not

Rose Maddox

just the most colorful, they had to be one of the hardest-working bands in America, too.

As it did for hillbilly bands all across the nation, World War II temporarily split the Maddox Brothers And Rose just as their star was shining. When the war ended, though, they regrouped and their fans flocked right back. Their music began taking on a harder, louder, and faster-paced personality as they added electric instruments and even a few additional non-family bandmembers, among them guitarist Roy Nichols (who'd later play with Merle Haggard) and steel player Bud Duncan. Boogie tunes now entered their repertoire, and Fred's slap-bass style (a foreshadowing of rockabilly) became a prominent part of their sound.

Beginning in 1946 the Maddoxes started recording as well, choosing the small LA-based Four Star label partly because the man in charge at Capitol, Lee Gillette, was off sick the day they came calling (with only a couple of days between show dates to take care of this record label business, they didn't have the patience to wait around). It was hardly the best deal for them financially, but Four Star did promote their records and let them record in a wild, free-form style that matched their live shows. Up to now they'd been huge in California but little known back east; through recordings like "Sally Let Your Bangs Hang Down," "Philadelphia Lawyer" (written by Woody Guthrie and long one of their signature songs), and "Gathering Flowers For The Masters Bouquet" they finally began gaining ground nationally. They played the *Grand Ole Opry* once in 1949 and then began regular appearances during the '50s on the rival *Louisiana Hayride*. Their home base, however, remained on the West Coast where they played LA's *Town Hall Party* and *Hometown Jamboree*.

In 1951 the group finally left Four Star behind and started recording for Columbia. Rose was also signed as a solo artist, experimenting with pop ("When The Sun Goes Down") as well as country ("Tall Men"). Her increasing solo success, coupled with the onslaught of rock'n'roll, the waning popularity of the great dance halls, and the national focus on singers as opposed to bands, led to the break-up of the Maddox Brothers And Rose. Their final session together was in 1957. Fred, Don, and Henry continued on as a unit for a short while but the spark had disappeared. Fred later opened three different nightclubs in Southern California. Cal accompanied Rose on her budding solo venture.

Rose recorded for Columbia until 1958 (including one full-length gospel album, PRECIOUS MEMORIES), then switched to Capitol. Beginning

with her first single, the dynamic "Gambler's Love," and running through the mid-'60s, she had a string of medium-sized hits like "Kissing My Pillow" and "Sing A Little Song Of Heartache." "Mental Cruelty" and "Loose Talk" (written by Freddie Hart and a '50s hit for Carl Smith) were duets with Buck Owens, a longtime Maddox Brothers And Rose fan. Much of her music now had a sharper honky-tonk edge, though she also mixed in pretty pop songs and others that rocked and rolled hard and fast. During this fruitful period Capitol released several excellent Rose Maddox albums, beginning with THE ONE ROSE in 1960. Two years later, at Bill Monroe's instigation, Rose broke new ground when she cut ROSE MADDOX SINGS BLUEGRASS, the first bluegrass album by a female artist.

Rose's Capitol contract expired in 1965, after which the label let her go, feeling that despite her respectable popularity she wasn't selling enough records. She toured with Buck Owens and Merle Haggard (as she had previously done with Johnny Cash) and cut an album, ROSIE!, for Starday in 1967. After the deaths of her brother Cal and her mother Lulu, Rose dabbled in some long overdue wild living, which included hanging around Las Vegas with Jerry Lee Lewis. During the '70s, though, her life quietened down. She performed at smaller clubs and folk festivals and recorded for a succession of small labels—Cathay, Portland, Takoma, Varrick. The Arhoolie reissues of the Maddox Brothers And Rose's Four Star recordings fueled her reputation further. The Nashville establishment had forgotten her, but newer generations discovered her, and she played punk and rockabilly clubs in LA and the annual gay rodeo in

Reno. She also sang regularly with the Vern Williams Band, a California bluegrass outfit, and occasionally reunited to perform with brother Fred. She suffered several heart attacks during the '80s, one of which left her in a coma for three months. But even after this brush with death she continued working the clubs up and down the West Coast. At a San Francisco appearance with Merle Haggard in early 1998 she was frail but still smiling brightly, singing hard, and cracking dirty jokes. She died just a few months later.

⊙ **Rose Maddox Sings Bluegrass** (1962; Capitol; reissued 1996). Bill Monroe, who inspired the project, performs with Rose, as do bluegrass stalwarts Reno & Smiley and their band the Tennessee Cut Ups.

⊙ **Rose Of The West Coast Country** (1990; Arhoolie). A dynamic collection of country, gospel and bluegrass songs that Rose cut in 1980 and 1982 with the Vern Williams Band (they were previously released on separate LPs). It's a lively collection, the bright bluegrass arrangements fitting her still-strong voice incredibly well.

⊙ **The Maddox Brothers & Rose—Vol. 1** (1993; Arhoolie). This is your starting place, a 27-song collection of their original Four Star recordings, cut between 1946 and 1951. Songs like "George's Playhouse Boogie," "Whoa Sailor," "Honky Tonkin'," and "Philadelphia Lawyer" are wild-natured examples of what this band was all about. Their crazy antics and fun-loving spirit translated amazingly well onto record.

⊙ **The One Rose** (1994; Bear Family). A 4-CD box set of everything Rose recorded for Capitol from the late 1950s through the mid-'60s. For fans, this set makes perfect sense, because once you get hooked on Rose's voice you won't want to let go.

⊙ **$35 And A Dream** (1994; Arhoolie). On this Grammy-nominated collection, Rose gets instrumental support from Byron Berline, John Jorgenson, Herb Pedersen, Norm Hamlet and her grandson Donny, among many others. Not as vital as earlier recordings, and her voice is hardly as crisp, but it's pleasant and bright.

⊙ **The Maddox Brothers & Rose—Vol. 2** (1995; Arhoolie). More original Four Star recordings made between 1947 and 1951, some of which were previously unreleased. Another excellent collection.

⊙ **On The Air** (1996; Arhoolie). Includes their first radio recordings from 1940, when Rose was only a teenager.

Her voice is young and the arrangements are simple (just Fred and Cal), but the music is captivating. Also includes further radio recordings and two songs they performed live on the *Grand Ole Opry*. All told, it's a great slice of '40s country.

⊙ **Maddox Brothers & Rose: The Most Colorful Hillbilly Band In America** (1998; Bear Family). This 4-disc box focuses on Rose and her brothers' years at Columbia during the 1950s. Their major-label recordings may not have the same untamed and innocent vigor of their Four Star sides, but as a trade-off they give us increased sharpness and maturity. The set also includes Rose's solo recordings for Columbia.

⊙ **Live—On the Radio** (1998; Arhoolie). Contains excerpts from various radio broadcasts in 1953—covers of current songs like Lefty Frizzell's "I'm An Old, Old Man" and silly comedy routines like "Mr. Know It All." While not essential Maddox listening for casual fans, it is a lot of fun and fills out the picture of their career.

Joe And Rose Lee Maphis

"[Joe could] hoe-down on a guitar just as fast as you please, and never miss a lick."

—Merle Travis

West Coast guitar slinger Joe Maphis (the "King of the Strings") and his wife Rose Lee were the artists behind one of the all-time honky-tonk classics, "Dim Lights, Thick Smoke (And Loud, Loud Music)"—a song that wraps up the sound and the atmosphere of the genre, as well as its moralistic backlash, into one neat, three-minute package. Like many songs of the period, the lyrics were actually meant as a warning to would-be bar hoppers—specifically the women. "You'll never make a wife to a home-loving man," cautioned Joe and Rose Lee, "I'm sorry for you and your honky-tonk heart." On the other hand, the music itself was enticing, thanks to an arrangement that emphasizes fiddle, steel guitar and Joe's own lead guitar work (played on an eye-opening, double-neck Moserite monster that was his trademark).

Joe And Rose Lee Maphis were favorites on the West Coast country scene during the 1950s and '60s. In addition to their own recordings, both

Four Star Records

When ex-serviceman Dick Nelson returned to Southern California in 1945 and decided to try the record business, it was no small gamble. Initially, his Pasadena-based Gilt Edge label enjoyed success with R&B's Cecil Gant (the "Sepia Sinatra") and gospel boy-wonder Solomon Burke, and so Nelson launched a sister label, Four Star Records. This new venture led to pop flops by the likes of dance-band leader Ted Fio Rito. Within months, a series of similar misfires brought the label to the brink of receivership.

Enter Bill McCall, a Texas hustler who coughed up five grand, saved the company, took over, and promptly signed T. Texas Tyler, the marijuana-smoking "Man with a Million Friends." Tyler specialized in folksy laments, and by the spring of 1946 his archaic recitation "Deck Of Cards" was selling so fast that Four Star's Larchmont Avenue pressing plant could not keep up with consumer demand. McCall realized, as a con-

temporary headline trumpeted, "There's Gold in Them There Hillbillies"; as a result, Four Star became one of the first California indie labels to successfully exploit the postwar country market.

In 1948, the label also pioneered a new marketing innovation that foreshadowed the coming LP era. Discouraged by the costly necessities of packaging fragile 78 rpm records to service radio stations, Four Star introduced semi-flexible vinylite records, pressing four songs by different artists onto 10" discs.

McCall, along with Nelson and fledgling A&R man Don Pierce (who went on to co-found Starday Records), steadily built an impressive roster of country up-and-comers: the Maddox Brothers And Rose,

former Sears-Roebuck accountant Webb Pierce, Slim Willet, Ferlin Husky, Carl Belew (who wrote the country standards "Lonely Street," "Stop The World And Let Me Off," and "Am I That Easy To Forget?"), and later a young Patsy Cline (whom McCall insisted record nothing but songs from the overwhelmingly mediocre Four Star publishing catalog, licensing the masters to Coral and Decca—some of the worst country records ever made, and a huge hindrance to her early career). Four Star also released discs by an army of lesser-knowns such as "Rocky" Bill Ford and Sammy Masters.

All of them, however—from name talent like Pierce and the Maddoxes to the starving young local aspirants—quickly realized they'd been screwed. McCall, Pierce said, "felt it was a sin to pay anybody." Rose Maddox recalled very distinctly that at the close of every session, McCall would write out a check, hand it over, then insist it immediately be given back—he preferred they take crates of their latest releases, to be sold at personal appearances. Naively, most of McCall's artists agreed.

By 1952, it was clear that McCall's exploitation of the roster was poisonous. The Maddoxes, characteristically, became the first to rebel, threatening union intervention. After Pierce asked how they'd managed it, he followed suit (and went so far as to buy back all his own masters). Slim Willet, whose "Don't Let The Stars Get In Your Eyes" was a monster hit in 1952 (for himself as well as artists like Skeets McDonald and Perry Como), made anecdotal history as the only person ever to receive full royalties—after the 250-pound singer burst into McCall's office with a six-shooter, demanding his money. Willet got it, returned to Abilene, and bought, among other things, the town's only ice-cream factory. McCall slithered off to Nashville to concentrate on the publishing racket; he eventually sold the label to Gene Autry, and by the early '60s he seemed to have dropped off the face of the earth.

—Jonny Whiteside

Four Star Records

solo and as a team, Joe played guitar and various other stringed instruments on numerous recording sessions (including records by Wanda Jackson and Ricky Nelson), as well as on the soundtracks for assorted movies and television series. They won plenty of fans via their live shows, but Joe and Rose Lee were probably most widely known as regulars on the popular Southern California television program *Town Hall Party*.

Like many of their West Coast country compatriots, the couple actually hailed from the eastern half of the country. Joe was born Otis Wilson Maphis on 12 May, 1921 in Suffolk, Virginia; Rose Lee Schetrompf was born on 29 December, 1922 in Hagerstown, Maryland. They each played on various radio programs throughout the East and Midwest before meeting as members of the *Old Dominion Barn Dance* in Richmond, Virginia in 1948. A few years later they moved to California and got married, and by 1953 they were cast-members of the brand-new *Town Hall Party* (Joe led the *Town Hall* band). Joe quickly earned a reputation for his lightning-fast picking, and his recording "Fire On The Strings" (an adaption of the fiddle tune "Fire On The Mountain") is certainly an impressive piece of work. His doubleneck guitar was built for him by Semie Moseley, the man behind the Moserite guitar brand. Joe and Rose Lee spent more than three decades together as a musical team, recording for Capitol, Columbia, Starday, Chart and CMH. During the '60s, "Cousin" Herb Henson brought them onto his Bakersfield-based show *Trading Post* as co-hosts, though at the same time they still performed around LA. Their partnership ended when Joe died on 27 June, 1986.

⊙ **Flying Fingers** (1997; Bear Family). A hot collection of guitar instrumentals that showcase Joe Maphis' lightning-fast fingers—and why he was such an in-demand session player in his day. The recordings are mostly from the Columbia archives dating from the late 1950s. The song roster includes his trademark "Fire On The Strings" and several duets with his young guitar-slinging protégé, Larry Collins (of the Collins Kids).

⊙ **Live At Town Hall Party** (1997; Interstate/Country Routes). A Czech-issue single-CD collection of *Town Hall Party* broadcasts that feature Joe And Rose Lee Maphis performing with various guests and regulars on the program, including Skeets McDonald, George Jones, Johnny Bond, Tommy Duncan, the Carlisles, and Texas Ruby.

Skeets McDonald

Skeets McDonald is hardly considered a household name these days, but during the 1950s he was an influential presence on the West Coast's burgeoning country music scene. His 1952 recording of "Don't Let The Stars Get In Your Eyes" was a #1 national hit, and it gained McDonald prominent slots on popular California shows like the *Hometown Jamboree* and the *Town Hall Party*. Skeets was a benevolent star, giving a hand to up-and-coming artists like Wynn Stewart and Harlan Howard. At the same time he was creating inspired honky-tonk songs like "Smoke Comes Out of My Chimney Just The Same" that took cues from blues and even rockabilly—and this at a time when Nashville artists were busy declaring rock'n'roll the enemy of the state.

Skeets was a childhood nickname for Enos William McDonald, who was born on 1 October, 1915 near Rector, Arkansas. The story has it that he traded a hound dog for a guitar at the age of twelve, which set his farm-bred music career off and running. When he was older Skeets moved to Michigan, following in the footsteps of an elder brother, and started playing the clubs and radio stations around Detroit, Flint, and Pontiac. The area had a large country music following at the time thanks to all the southern transplants, most of whom had followed the hillbilly highway north to find factory work. After serving overseas in World War II, Skeets returned to Michigan where he continued to play in the clubs and on television. Soon he had a decent local reputation, and in 1950 he cut his first songs for the small Fortune label. After that he recorded some sides for London and Mercury and then moved west, landing in Los Angeles. When

talent seeker Cliffie Stone caught wind of him, he signed him up for his TV show the *Hometown Jamboree* and also got him a record contract with Capitol. Skeets also appeared in several movies, including *The Glenn Miller Story* and *Hud*.

Almost as soon as "Don't Let The Stars Get In Your Eyes" hit the airwaves and topped the country charts, it was picked up by Perry Como and turned into a pop hit as well; it also inspired an answer song, "I Let The Stars Get In My Eyes," a hit for Goldie Hill (like the original, it was written by Texas singer and DJ Slim Willet). Many of Skeets' early '50s sides had a classic honky-tonk sound, but as the decade wore on a much rawer and more distinct sound crept into his music. By the mid-'50s he was demonstrating the courage to rock things up: the novelty song "You Ought To See Grandma Rock" was a fiery rockabilly number that even featured Eddie Cochran on lead guitar. Other songs took cues from the blues like the awesome 1956 single "Smoke Comes Out Of My Chimney Just The Same," a sassy song with a gritty up-tempo beat.

Skeets' Capitol years culminated with the album GOIN' STEADY WITH THE BLUES, a smart mix of blues, rockabilly and honky-tonk influences. Following its release, he switched to Columbia and shifted back to a more straightforward country sound. For his Columbia recordings Skeets adopted some uptown aspects of the Nashville Sound; yet his music remained strongly rooted in '50s country, never succumbing entirely to the saccharine trends that had become the norm in Nashville. During the '60s he performed on the *Grand Ole Opry* as well as the *Big D Jamboree* in Dallas, and eventually left California for Nashville. He had only one more significant hit, "Call Me Mr. Brown" in 1963, but he recorded throughout the decade. In 1968 his career was suddenly cut short when he suffered a major heart attack and died.

◐ **Goin' Steady With The Blues** (1958; Capitol). The bright, exciting energy Skeets created in his 1950s recordings came to a head on this album, a true classic of West Coast country. The arrangements (guitar, bass, piano, drums) are simple yet firm, and the rhythms have a fresh, rockabilly-inspired urgency. Skeets' Arkansas drawl, though, keeps the music rooted in country. The excellent title track is a Harlan Howard song.

☉ **Don't Let The Stars Get In Your Eyes** (1998; Bear Family). If you want Skeets, you got it here, as this big box set contains all 143 songs he cut between 1949 and 1967.

Bonnie Owens

"Every cowgirl singer on the West Coast owes a debt of thanks to Bonnie Owens."

—Rosie Flores

Bonnie Owens is known to most country fans as the onetime wife of first Buck Owens and then Merle Haggard. And for much of her career, she's been content to work in Haggard's shadow—which lately entailed singing back-up in his touring band, only stepping to the front once during the show to run through a song on her own. But during the 1950s and '60s, Owens was a promising singer and songwriter in her own right—the most influential and steadfast female artist to emerge out of the Bakersfield music scene (and stick with it), and a lifelong musician who has gone on to encourage and lend her support to further West Coast women artists.

Owens was born Bonnie Campbell in Blanchard, Oklahoma in 1932, and met a then unknown Buck Owens when she was only fifteen. They played in a band together in Mesa, Arizona, got married, and in 1951 moved to Bakersfield in the hope of cracking that town's burgeoning live-music scene. Their marriage didn't last much longer, but at least it got them both up and running in the West Coast music market.

Bonnie's first recording was a duet of "A Dear John Letter" with Fuzzy Owen, a local musician who later co-founded the Bakersfield-based Tally label with Lewis Talley, his cousin and frequent musical partner. Tally was the label that launched Haggard's career, and Bonnie recorded a pair of songs for it as well, "Why Don't Daddy Live Here Anymore" and "Don't Take Advantage Of Me." Both made the *Billboard* Top 40 in 1963 and 1964, but it was Bonnie's subsequent duet with Haggard, "Just Between The Two Of Us," that garnered her the most attention. In 1965 she was named Female Vocalist of the Year by the newly formed Academy of Country Music, and from 1965–1968 she and Haggard also won as the top Vocal Duet. She married Haggard in 1965, and ever since has pretty much devoted all her musical energy to his career—touring with his band and, later, helping run the business end of things. They divorced in 1978 but have remained friends and musical associates ever since. She continues to tour with Haggard to this day, and on stage her bright, down-home personality frequently lends a welcome kick in the pants to the deeply serious (and often dour) Haggard.

● **Just Between The Two of Us** (1966; Capitol). A duet album of Owens and Haggard with material that they cut right around the time they were married.

Buck Owens

"One of the great things my music had was energy."

—Buck Owens

If there's one artist who symbolizes country music in Bakersfield, it's Buck Owens. The fresh-faced singer with the big boyish grin wasn't actually born and raised in that Southern California working-class city, but he has made it his home ever since settling there in the early 1950s. At the height of Owens' popularity, fans even took to calling it "Buckersfield" for all the attention he brought to the town—not to mention the fact that he owned numerous local businesses and plenty of real estate. But financial investments aside, Buck's music was true and genuine, and frankly the Bakersfield Sound might not have become such a phenomenon without Owens' huge country success.

Like his friend Wynn Stewart, Buck Owens had a sharp and exciting Telecaster-driven guitar sound around which he based much of his music. As had been the case with his Texas honky-tonk predecessors Ernest Tubb and Floyd Tillman, Owens and his lead guitarist and partner-in-crime, Don Rich, simply wanted to make themselves heard above the noise of the honky-tonks. Another factor that made Owens' music stand out was his timing: he hit the scene at the same time as Nashville was going soft with string sec-

tions, syrupy arrangements and adult-contemporary song material (more "Make The World Go Away" than "Lovesick Blues"). When Buck came along with high-energy material like "Act Naturally," "I've Got A Tiger By The Tail," and "Under Your Spell Again"—"freight train" songs he called them—it took Music Row by surprise and delighted honky-tonk fans. The West Coast was far enough away to remain independent from lofty *Opry* ideals, yet strong enough to stand on its own feet and reach out to a national audience craving stronger stuff. His success was considerable: during his mid-'60s heyday he racked up more than fifteen #1 hits.

Buck was born Alvis Edgar Owens, Jr. on 12 August, 1929 in Sherman, Texas. His parents were sharecroppers and during the Depression they migrated to Arizona. Buck (he earned the nickname as a child) only had a ninth-grade education; he preferred to concentrate on his music. In his late teens he was playing in area honky-tonks and on a local radio station. He married aspiring singer Bonnie Campbell (better known as Bonnie Owens and, more than a decade later, as the wife of Merle Haggard) and fathered two children, then in 1951 moved his family out to Bakersfield, California, to find work in that city's active nightclub scene. Soon he was playing with bandleader Bill Woods and singing for the first time at a club called the Blackboard, which would remain his home

VIRGINIA LEE HUNTER

Buck Owens

Dwight Yoakam and Buck Owens on the "Streets of Bakerfield" video set

base for most of the '50s. He also took up the Fender Telecaster solid-body guitar, a brand-new instrument developed in Southern California that had a much sharper, and louder, sound.

Buck's Bakersfield gigs led to some session work for Capitol Records, based in nearby Los Angeles. One of his first assignments was as guest guitarist on the song "You Better Not Do That" for singer Tommy Collins, another Bakersfield regular. While in the Capitol studios with producer Ken Nelson, Buck really honed his guitar style, playing on all sorts of sessions with the likes of Collins, Wanda Jackson, Faron Young, the Farmer Boys, and Gene Vincent. In 1956 he cut his first singles for the small Pep label, including "Down On The Corner Of Love," "Sweethearts In Heaven," and "Hot Dog." The latter was released under the name Corky Jones because it was feared the rockabilly sound would tarnish Owens' country reputation.

With his popularity growing, Columbia Records displayed an interest in signing Owens, which in turn prompted Capitol to ink him first. His initial session as a solo artist happened in 1957, but he really made his mark a year later when he laid down "Second Fiddle," a hard honky-tonk song with a Ray Price-style shuffle beat. At this time he was living in Tacoma, Washington, where he'd bought an interest in a small radio station and landed a job hosting a local TV show. Most importantly, Tacoma is where he met Don Rich, who would become his musical alter ego. Rich played fiddle on Buck's early sessions before switching to guitar, and his solos and rhythmic leads became as much a part of the Owens sound as Buck's voice. (The Country Music Association gave him a well-deserved nod in 1974, naming him Musician of the Year.)

After his follow-up recording "Under Your Spell Again" made *Billboard*'s Top 10, Buck returned to Bakersfield. His next hit was "Above And Beyond," a song written by Harlan Howard, who was living on the West Coast at the time (he'd later move on to an illustrious career as Nashville's most beloved songwriter). Howard and Owens were pals and had been introduced through another friend, Wynn Stewart. An excellent singer and songwriter himself, Stewart actually cut the song first but had only minor success with it. Stewart's version was solid and full of passion, but Buck's had a sharper sound and rhythm, and it pounced into the heads of DJs and fans with eager ferocity.

"Above And Beyond" kicked off a phenomenal hitmaking streak for Buck that included such classics as "Excuse Me (I Think I've Got A

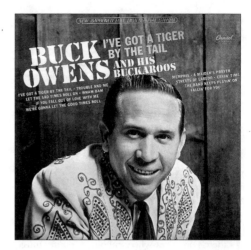

Heartache)," "You're For Me," "Act Naturally," "Cryin' Time," "Love's Gonna Live Here," "Together Again," "I've Got A Tiger By The Tail," and "Waitin' In Your Welfare Line." Buck penned most of these songs himself and continued to write regularly throughout his recording career. By 1965, when the brand-new Academy of Country Music named him their first Male Vocalist of the Year, he was one of the top stars in country music. He appeared at Carnegie Hall (and Capitol released a live album of the event) and starred on his own TV show *Buck Owens Ranch*. He sang duets with his son, Buddy Alan, and nurtured the career of Susan Raye, with whom he cut a couple of albums. His business ventures grew, and among them were a publishing company, a music studio (Buck Owens Studios in Bakersfield), and a couple of radio stations, KUZZ-AM and KKXX-FM. And in the March, 1965 issue of *Music City News* he printed his "Pledge to Country Music," in which he stated he'd never sing or record a song that wasn't country. "I refuse to be known as anything but a country singer," he wrote. (What foul play would Buck's fans have cried if they had known he'd be covering "The Macarena" three decades later?)

As the decade rolled on, Buck's hits piled up: "Sweet Rosie Jones," "Who's Gonna Mow Your Grass," "Tall Dark Stranger," the melodramatic "Big In Vegas," and "The Great White Horse," a duet with Susan Raye. But he also wanted to branch out from his winning honky-tonk formula: he tried folksongs (the throwaway "Bridge Over Troubled Water"—hello, "Pledge to Country Music"?) and bluegrass (the fired-up "Ruby"), and cut some oddballs like "Big Game Hunter" and "Made In Japan." His career really took a turn, though, in 1968 when he began co-hosting (with

Roy Clark) the country music comedy show *Hee-Haw*. The show was immensely popular for the next decade and a half (Buck stayed with it until 1986), and it plastered his toothy grin and trademark red, white and blue guitar onto TV screens everywhere. For a generation of music fans just coming of age, however, this was the Buck Owens they got to know—the show transformed him from a high-energy honky-tonker into a goofball comic in a cardboard cornfield.

The event that shook Buck's world to the core was the death of Don Rich, who was tragically killed in a motorcycle accident in 1974. Rich had been Buck's musical partner and close friend, and without him Buck's enthusiasm drained. A year later he and Capitol Records parted ways, and Buck signed to Warner Brothers, recording in Nashville with producer Norro Wilson. Without Rich, however, the spark that had driven Buck for so many years had simply vanished. His records weren't selling that well either and *Hee-Haw* continued to eat away at his creative energy. In the early '80s he stepped out of the performing spotlight and into a life of semi-retirement.

He might have never risen from his easy chair had it not been for Dwight Yoakam. A fan of Buck's for many years, Yoakam had chosen LA as his home partly because of his love of the music of Owens and other Bakersfield artists. In 1987 he coaxed Buck out of retirement to perform with him on stage. The following year they recorded "Streets Of Bakersfield" together, a song written by Homer Joy that Buck had originally cut in 1972. The new duet appeared on Dwight's BUENAS NOCHES FROM A LONELY ROOM album and was a #1 hit. Buck toured with Dwight that year, and with his energy suddenly revived he turned around and cut a new album of his own, HOT DOG, for Capitol. He followed that up in 1989 with ACT NATURALLY, which featured a duet with Ringo Starr on the title track (the Beatles had covered the song in 1965). In 1993 Buck had part of his tongue removed due to cancer. He recovered amazingly well, however, and while his speech is a bit slurred his singing voice is intact. In 1996 he opened his own club, The Crystal Palace, in Bakersfield, which serves as one of the few reminders of Bakersfield's once thriving country music community, and Buck And His Buckeroos have played there nearly every weekend since it opened.

⊙ **Buck Owens** (1961; Capitol; reissued 1995; Sundazed). Owens' first album for Capitol (there was one earlier release on the small La Brea label) includes early greats like "Second Fiddle," "Excuse Me (I Think

I've Got A Heartache)," "Above And Beyond," and "Under Your Spell Again."

⊙ **Sings Harlan Howard** (1961; Capitol; reissued 1997; Sundazed). Includes "Heartaches By The Number," "I Don't Believe I'll Fall In Love Today," and "Pick Me Up On Your Way Down" among other Howard classics.

⊙ **Sings Tommy Collins** (1963; Capitol; reissued 1997; Sundazed). Buck began his recording career playing guitar on Collins' mid-1950s hits, so it was only natural he'd turn and record an album of his songs— among them "You Gotta Have A License," "It Tickles," and "High On A Hilltop" (which Merle Haggard, another Collins fan and supporter, also later covered).

⊙ **I've Got A Tiger By The Tail** (1965; Capitol; reissued 1995; Sundazed). The title track is a Buck classic, as bright, spunky and catchy as anything he's done. "Trouble And Me" maintains a lighthearted attitude—"trouble and me are old buddies you see"— while the great "Cryin' Time" is a slower and more traditional cry-in-your-beer ballad. The CD reissue includes a couple of bonus live cuts, "This Ol' Heart" and "Act Naturally."

⊙ **Buck Owens And His Buckaroos In Japan** (1967; Capitol; reissued 1997; Sundazed). One of several live albums Buck and his band cut all over the globe. Aside from the songs, highlights are the spoken Japanese intro and Buck's own corny banter ("I apologize that I cannot speak Japanese very good... ").

⊙ **The Buck Owens Collection (1959–1990)** (1992; Rhino). An excellent 3-CD set covering almost the whole of Buck's career. Later songs like "Bridge Over Troubled Water" and the silly "On The Cover Of The Music City News" can be skipped, but the first half is essential honky-tonk listening.

⊙ **The Very Best Of Buck Owens, Vol. 1** (1994; Rhino). A pared-down, single-disc collection for those wanting only a beginners' sampler of Buckaroo heaven.

Susan Raye

Susan Raye first gained national fame during the late 1960s dueting with Buck Owens, and later she earned further attention as a regular on *Hee-Haw,* but during that time she also enjoyed a successful solo recording career. She wasn't

"Dress for success" means something different on Music Row from what it does on Wall Street. While top business executives prefer subdued gray flannel suits, country music stars have often reached into their closets for something a bit louder—like an electric-turquoise suit with matching stetson and boots, studded with rhinestones and embroidered with big gold coins and dollar bills. These flamboyantly decorated outfits in peacock colors are generically called "Nudie suits," after Ukrainian-born, Brooklyn-bred tailor Nutya Kotlyrenko (aka Nudie Cohn or Cohen), the western-wear specialist best known for creating them.

Serving as both performance costumes and status symbols, Nudie-style suits are typically embroidered, studded, sequined and spangled with motifs big enough to be seen in the back row of any auditorium. The simplest are trimmed with names, initials, or a pattern of musical notes and guitars. Western images such as cactuses, six-shooters, prairie flowers, or arrows and teepees are also popular. Some outfits play off a performer's name: Porter Wagoner's suits are decked out with wagon wheels, Ferlin Husky's with husky dogs. Other costumes plug hit songs. Nudie made a "Humpty Dumpty Heart" suit for Hank Thompson, and a suit covered with locks, keys and prison bars for Webb Pierce when "In The Jailhouse Now" topped the charts.

This 'rhinestone cowboy' look is rooted in cowboy culture. The fun began when turn-of-the-century rodeo and Wild West Show performers ordered practical styles sewn up in high-visibility colors, with eye-catching trim and fringe. During the 1920s, Rodeo Ben of Philadelphia was famed for the costumes he created for traveling rodeo and circus folk, and soon orders poured in from cowboy movie stars like Tom Mix, Gene Autry, Roy Rogers and Dale Evans. After gaining attention with the flashy costumes he crafted for Rose Bowl Parade riders, Nathan Turk of Los Angeles (aka Polish immigrant Nathan Tieg) became another favorite tailor for Hollywood's western stars. The matching outfits he designed for the Maddox Brothers And Rose in the late '40s, covered with exuberant flowers, are his most famous creations.

Nudie's initial customers in the country-western department were western swing bandleaders Tex Williams and Hank Thompson. In 1947, Nudie was able to open his own shop in Hollywood. By that stage, the fashions worn by silver-screen cowboys had been adopted by many hillbilly performers who'd never been west of the Mississippi. These country stars loved Nudie's show-biz flair (he'd once sewn g-strings and costumes for strippers in New York), and each custom suit from his shop seemed more outrageous than the last. Over the years, Nudie has put sparkles and spangles on Lefty Frizzell, Hank Williams, Little Jimmy Dickens, Ernest Tubb, Kitty Wells, Buck Owens, Conway Twitty, George Jones, Tammy Wynette, Merle Haggard, and Dolly Parton. His customers also included such non-country performers as Diana Ross, Michael Jackson, Liberace, Elton John, and members of the Rolling Stones and the Beatles. Among his best-known creations are the $10,000 24-karat gold lamé tuxedo worn by Elvis Presley on the cover of the album 50,000,000 ELVIS FANS CAN'T BE WRONG, and the suits decked in marijuana leaves and opium poppies for country-rock pioneers the Flying Burrito Brothers (as seen on the cover of their album THE GILDED PALACE OF SIN).

Ben, Turk and Nudie are sewing sequins onto angels' robes now, but one of Nudie's top designers continues to provide fine and flashy western tailoring to a new generation of country music stars. At his Nashville shop, Manuel (last name Cuevas, but like Nudie he prefers to keep things simple) has helped performers like Linda Ronstadt, Dwight Yoakam, Wynonna Judd, Alan Jackson, and Travis Tritt look like a million onstage.

Museums with vintage western wear by Nudie, N. Turk and Rodeo Ben on display include the Gene Autry Western Heritage Museum in Los Angeles; the Roy Rogers and Dale Evans Museum in Victorville, California; the National Cowboy Hall of Fame Museum in Oklahoma City; and the Country Music Hall of Fame and Opryland USA Museum in Nashville. Many of the privately owned museums run by individual performers in and around Nashville also display flamboyant costumes from their owners' glory days, as does Buck Owens' Crystal Palace in Bakersfield.

—Candi Strecker

much of a songwriter, and she generally stayed out of the decision-making process when it came to cutting records and choosing material—quite the opposite of one of her contemporaries, Dolly Parton—but Raye did possess a pretty voice and knew how to use it. Her striking good looks certainly didn't hurt either when it came to winning fans.

Raye was born in Eugene, Oregon in 1944. She performed on a Portland TV show as well as

Susan Raye

at local clubs, and during one performance met Buck Owens' manager, who landed her an audition with the country star. She moved to Bakersfield and began singing with Owens in 1968, and soon after she also cut her first recordings. One of these songs, "Put A Little Love In Your Heart," made the country Top 30 in 1970, and within a month she was back on the charts for a series of duets with Owens, including the cutesy "We're Gonna Get Together" and "The Great White Horse"—the latter a fantasy-laden, but nonetheless delicately beautiful song that was one of their finest works together. In late 1970 and 1971 she had her biggest chart successes with "Willy Jones" (one of many Buck Owens compositions she recorded), "LA International Airport," "Pitty Pitty Patter," and "(I've Got A) Happy Heart." Much of her material was light-hearted in tone and colored by scenes of domestic life, but a handful of songs (most notably the Owens material and the lonesome, grey-specked "Airport") have an intriguing edge to them. In the late '70s, Raye dropped out of the music business, citing family and religion as her reasons. She did record again during the '80s, but by that time her turn in the country music spotlight had come and gone.

⊙ **16 Greatest Hits** (1999; Varese Sarabande). A solid overview of Raye's hitmaking career, this collection starts with "Put A Little Love In Your Heart" and runs through such popular 1970s-era songs as "Willy Jones," "LA International Airport," "Cheating Game," and "Stop The World (And Let Me Off)."

Jean Shepard

J ean Shepard was a singer who cut her own path, and during the 1950s there weren't many like her. She had a firm voice, one that could growl as well as yelp, yodel and cry. She was also a strong-willed, independently minded artist who hit the charts with a purebred honky-tonk style and a unique (and absolutely refreshing) female point of view. She may have looked like a sweet little country gal, but she certainly wasn't afraid to speak her mind. Songs like "Don't Fall In Love With A Married Man," "Sad Singin' And Slow Ridin'," "The Root Of All Evil (Is A Man)," and "Second Fiddle (To An Old Guitar)," were proto-feminist and downright bold. Men can "smoke and drink" and even "step out on their wives" with little backlash, sang an incensed Shepard in "Two

Whoops And A Holler," but if a woman does the same "she's the lowest thing in town." Shepard didn't write her material (many of her songs were in fact written by men), but she sure grabbed hold and made them her own.

Though she wasn't kidding around or cracking jokes, Shepard's vitriol was sung with a (mostly) good-natured flair. And not every song, of course, declared that "women ought to rule the world" as did "Two Whoops." Whatever she sang, it was clear she was a top-notch musician. And like many other California-based singers of the '50s and '60s—Rose Maddox, Buck Owens, Wynn Stewart—Shepard created a pure, clean, straight-ahead honky-tonk sound that was hard to resist. She stuck by it dutifully for years afterwards, too, even as more and more of her contemporaries softened their music and turned to pop. Her hits lasted from the '50s through the '70s, and even during the late '90s she was still performing regularly on the *Opry*.

Jean was born Ollie Imogene Shepard on 21 November, 1933 in Paul's Valley, Oklahoma. During World War II her family moved west in search of a better life, landing in the central California town of Visalia. While at high school Jean formed the Melody Ranch Girls, and they developed a decent regional following. Bandleader Hank Thompson heard her during a show at Noble's Melody Ranch, and with his help she landed a recording contract with Capitol in 1952. She cut four songs at her first session with big guns Jimmy Bryant, Speedy West, Cliffie Stone, and Billy Strange backing her up. Despite being just eighteen years old, on the no-nonsense honky-tonker "Twice The Lovin' (In Half The Time)" Shepard's voice sounds seasoned and her attitude worldly ("I'm gonna tear your playhouse down,"

Susan Raye • Jean Shepard

she warns). The song that broke her onto the charts, however, was "A Dear John Letter," a hokey half-spoken duet with another up-and-coming West Coast singer, Ferlin Husky. It was a #1 smash.

On later sessions Shepard was backed by a studio band featuring future Merle Haggard cohorts Fuzzy Owen and Lewis Talley, as well as guitarist Buck Owens. Her next big hit was "A Satisfied Mind" in 1955, which entered the charts about the same time as versions by Red Foley and Porter Wagoner. By this time Shepard was living in Missouri and working on the upstart *Ozark Jubilee* television show, which was hosted by Foley. Soon after, she moved to Nashville and joined the *Grand Ole Opry*, and she's been an active member on the show ever since. Continuing to record for Capitol until the '70s, she dabbled a bit in the Nashville Sound but for the most part didn't stray far from the gutsy honky-tonk sound she'd developed on the West Coast. As her acclaim grew she sang with even more confidence and fervor.

In 1960 Shepard married fellow *Opry* star Hawkshaw Hawkins. Tragically, however, Hawkins was killed three years later in the same plane crash that killed Patsy Cline and Cowboy Copas. She recorded steadily through the '60s and into the '70s—"Second Fiddle (To An Old Guitar)," "Many Happy Hangovers To You," "If Teardrops Were Silver," "I'll Take The Dog" (the title track from her duet album with Ray Pillow)—and her Capitol recordings were remarkably consistent and maintained a traditionalist edge. She stayed with the label until 1973, when she signed with United Artists. During the '70s she openly criticized pop influences in country music, and in 1979 served as president of the controversial Association of Country Entertainers (ACE). Over the past couple of decades she hasn't recorded so much, but she has remained a regular on the *Opry*.

⊙ **Honky-Tonk Heroine** (1995; Country Music Foundation). A superb compilation of Shepard's early Capitol material, both hits and obscurities cut between 1952 and 1964. The CD's packed with gutsy proto-feminist titles like "Two Whoops And A Holler" and "Sad Singin' And Slow Ridin'," as well as goodies like the rocked-up "He's My Baby" (a live radio transcription) and the mournfully beautiful "Crying Steel Guitar Waltz" (featuring Speedy West).

⊙ **Melody Ranch Girl** (1996; Bear Family). Five CDs of Shepard's prime Capitol material that show just

how substantial a recording artist she really was. The CMF collection is a better starting place, but this collection puts the great song nuggets found on that CD in a much wider context. Dig deep, she's worth the effort.

⊙ **Songs Of A Love Affair/Heartaches And Tears** (1998; EMI). Two classic Shepard albums from 1958 and 1962 respectively, released on a single CD. The first is a concept album that deals with "the moods and experiences of a young girl in love"—a theme that could prove saccharine in the wrong hands, but in the care of Shepard (and producer Ken Nelson) it comes out as clean, hard honky tonk. Together they're a fine companion to the compilation HONKY-TONK HEROINE.

Red Simpson

A regular on the Bakersfield club scene during the 1960s and a prolific songwriter, Red Simpson made his mark with a spate of big-rig songs like "Roll, Truck, Roll" and "I'm A Truck." The latter, a kooky, partially spoken number from the point of view of a truck, was his biggest hit as a recording artist. But Simpson also wrote a bunch of songs with Buck Owens, among them Owens' greatest hits "Sam's Place," "Gonna Have Love," and "The Kansas City Song." Merle Haggard also cut some of Simpson's songs, including "You Don't Have Very Far To Go", and "Bill Woods Of Bakersfield," about the bandleader who hired both Owens and Simpson. Both Charlie Walker and Gram Parsons cut versions of Simpson's "Close Up The Honky Tonks," and a couple of decades later his

"Highway Patrol" was brought back to life in a beefed-up version by Junior Brown.

Red was born Joseph Simpson in Arizona on 6 March, 1934 and brought up in Bakersfield. He played in a country band while serving in Korea, then played the clubs around Bakersfield where he met and played with folks like Fuzzy Owen (Haggard's future manager), bandleader Bill Woods, and rising star Buck Owens. Back east Dave Dudley had a huge hit in 1963 with the truckers' anthem "Six Days On The Road," and so Capitol Records, sensing an opportunity, also wanted to record trucking songs. This resulted in Simpson cutting Tommy Collins' "Roll, Truck, Roll" for Capitol in 1966, a pleasant song sympathetic to a trucker's loneliness. When it charted he recorded a full-length album under the same title, and further albums followed with similar road-ravaged themes—THE MAN BEHIND THE BADGE, TRUCK DRIVIN' FOOL. "I'm A Truck" became Simpson's biggest hit to date in 1972 and won him awards and accolades as a promising 'new' artist. Not every song of Red's looked at the world through a windshield, however: one of his best and most distinct was "Party Girl," a catchy song with an offbeat rhythm and vocal line.

Red couldn't quite leave the truck-driving theme alone, and he cut songs throughout the '70s such as "Awful Lot To Learn About Truck Drivin'," "Truck Driver Man And Wife" (a duet with Lorraine Walden), and "The Flying Saucer Man And The Truck Driver." He later underwent cancer surgery, but as of the '90s he was still writing songs and performing around Southern California. Junior Brown included "Highway Patrol" on his GUIT WITH IT album, after which Simpson and Brown cut the duet "Semi Crazy," the title track to Brown's follow-up album.

○ **The Man Behind The Badge** (1967; Capitol). A cool concept album sympathetic to the patrolman's plight. Includes Red's original version of "Highway Patrol."

⊙ **The Best Of Red Simpson: Country Western Truck Drivin' Singer** (1999; Razor & Tie). It's about time a Simpson collection finally hit the market. Here we get 20 of Simpson's big and burly Capitol recordings, including "Highway Patrol," "Roll, Truck Roll," "I'm A Truck," "Jeannie With The Light Brown Cadillac," "Truckin' Trees For Christmas," and "Mini Skirt Minnie" (though that song's original flip side, "Party Girl," is unfortunately missing).

Wynn Stewart

Wynn Stewart is one of the great unsung heroes of West Coast country music. A contemporary of Buck Owens, his music was built around a similar sharp-edged Telecaster guitar sound, much of it with a hard-driving rhythm that made it difficult to resist. Despite a dynamic sound and a strong repertoire of songs (many of which he wrote himself), Stewart's name is not that well remembered. Part of the reason lies in the fact that he lacked the same relentless drive that kept Owens and Haggard constantly in the spotlight. The fact that Stewart's name isn't better known is really something of a crime, particularly when songs like "Wishful Thinking," "Playboy," "It's Such A Pretty World Today," "She Just Tears Me Up," and "Wrong Company" (one of his many duets with Jan Howard) stand out as some of the period's strongest.

Wynnford Lindsey Stewart was born on 7 June, 1934 in Morrisville, Missouri. As a teenager he played on a radio station in nearby Springfield, but soon the family moved west to Los Angeles (they'd briefly lived in California once before during World War II). There he started playing the nightclubs, which were booming all over the state at the time. He met steel player Ralph Mooney (who'd stick with him for years to come and later play with Waylon Jennings) at a local talent contest, and in 1954 he made his first recordings for the tiny Intro label. His big break, however, was a meeting with honky-tonker Skeets McDonald, who helped him secure a recording contract with LA-based Capitol Records. Stewart had a minor hit with "Waltz Of The Angels" but was dropped after only a year. In 1958 he was signed to the indie label Jackpot, a subsidiary of Challenge, which was originally owned by Gene Autry. Stewart's first singles included "Come On" and "She Just Tears Me Up," both of which had a deliciously edgy tension and a hot tempo that veered into rock'n'roll territory. He also cut duets such as "How The Other Half Lives" and "Wrong Company" with Jan Howard, who'd been signed about the same time. Jan's husband was Harlan Howard, who in a few years would begin his reign as king of the Nashville songwriters. Stewart cut one of Harlan's earliest songs, "Above And Beyond" in 1959; it gained some attention, but it was Buck Owens' subsequent version that turned into a major national hit and helped put Bakersfield on the map.

Wynn had his first sizeable hit in 1960 with "Wishful Thinking," which featured a female voice

(Wynn's sister Beverly) rising in spooky harmony behind his lead vocals and the sharp sound of the fiddle (Gordon Terry) and steel guitar (Mooney). As dreamy as it is mournful, and as musically refreshing and alive as anything Buck Owens ever cut, the song is one of the true classics of West Coast country. Unfortunately, Stewart wasn't too good at backing up his hits with frequent public appearances or immediate follow-up singles, and as a result his name never stayed in lights for long.

He did, however, earn a reputation as a solid club performer. Having played in the Southern California region for years, Wynn ended up partial owner of a Las Vegas club called the Nashville Nevada. He set up shop there, playing six nights a week with a band that included Mooney and Roy Nichols, Merle Haggard's soon-to-be lead guitarist. Stewart hired Haggard himself, in fact, when his original bass player Bobby Austin (later a minor singing star himself) quit the band. Haggard stayed with Stewart for about a year, then returned to Bakersfield and had his first hit with Stewart's "Sing A Sad Song."

Stewart cut his final Challenge session in 1963, after which the label folded. He also left Vegas and moved first to Bakersfield and then LA. A couple of years later he had formed a new band he called the Tourists and had won another contract with Capitol, which this time lasted much longer. He nabbed his first #1 single in 1967 with "It's Such A Pretty World Today" and recorded several albums for Capitol. Wynn also had some serious West Coast competition at the time, as Buck and Merle were at, or near, the peak of their popularity. By the end of the decade Wynn had moved to a ranch in Texas, and a few years later he was living in Nashville. He'd also left Capitol and later recorded for RCA, Playboy (including the sappy hit "After The Storm" and a decent, but kooky number called "Don't Monkey With My Widder"), and finally his own Pretty World label. Plagued by marital as well as drinking problems over the years, he was living with his mother and sister Beverly when he died of a heart attack in 1985.

---

❶ It's Such A Pretty World Today (1967; Capitol). Stewart's mid-1960s work didn't have the same urgency and high-charged energy of his classic Challenge material, but his first few albums for Capitol, including this one, show his musicianship (and songwriting, ie "The Tourist") to be solid as ever. Capitol needs to open its vaults and get this material on CD.

⊙ Best Of The Challenge Masters (1995; AVI). With 29 songs from Stewart's prime period recording for Jackpot and Challenge, this is an incredible collection of top-shelf West Coast country, with knockout songs like "Playboy" and "Wishful Thinking" edging between honky tonk and rockabilly. It's one of the most exciting collections in this book—really. The German label Bear Family previously issued a double-LP version of this material, too.

Merle Travis

B y far one of the most influential and in-demand country guitarists of the 1940s and '50s, Merle Travis was also a superb songwriter, a jolly humorist, and a decent singer, too. He penned such classics as "Sixteen Tons" and "Dark As A Dungeon" that tell of life as a Kentucky coal miner, but he also wrote novelty songs—silly and good-natured, yet at the same time a bit twisted—such as "I Like My Chicken Fryin' Size," "So Round, So Firm, So Fully Packed," "Divorce Me C.O.D," "Fat Gal," and "Smoke! Smoke! Smoke! (That Cigarette)." This last song he conjured with a little help from bandleader Tex Williams (who had a million-selling hit with it), while he penned further songs with Capitol Records' talent maven Cliffie Stone. Ernest Tubb, Hank Thompson, and Tennessee Ernie Ford were just a few of the artists who recorded excellent versions of Travis' songs.

Merle Robert Travis was born on 29 November, 1917 in Muhlenberg County, Kentucky, right in the heart of coal-mining territory and just down the road from Bill Monroe's birthplace. He learned the basics of his trademark thumb-style guitar technique—known as 'Travis picking,' where the thumb keeps time and the forefingers walk the strings—as a child from a handful of influential local players including Mose Rager (who taught him the song "I Am A Pilgrim") and Kennedy Jones. During the mid-'30s he landed a spot on a station in Evansville, Indiana, then made his way over to the powerful WLW in Cincinnati, Ohio. He played with Clayton McMichen in the Georgia Wildcats and later with the Delmore Brothers and Grandpa Jones in the gospel quartet the Brown's Ferry Four. Working under the name the Sheppard Brothers, Jones and Travis cut the very first record for the budding Cincinnati label King in 1943.

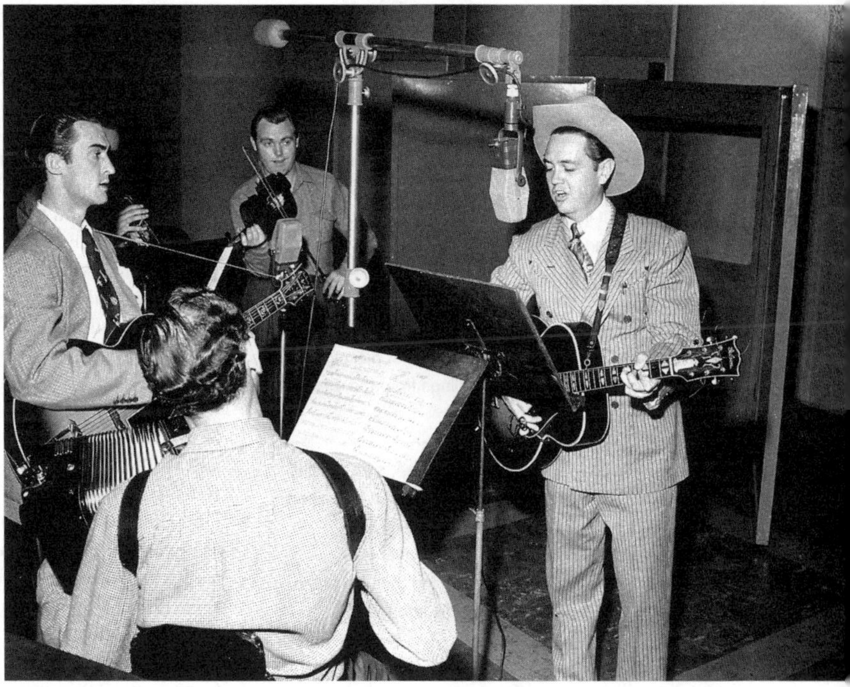
MICHAEL OCHS ARCHIVES

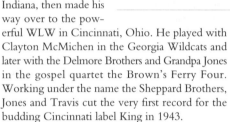

Merle Travis in studio

After serving briefly in World War II, Travis made his way out to Los Angeles, where the live music scene was red-hot and a recording industry (mostly centered around Capitol Records) was beginning to blossom. Travis worked as a session guitarist, appeared in a few movies, and in 1946 cut his first solo recordings for Capitol. Over the next several years he racked up a string of national hits including "Cincinnati Lou," "No Vacancy," "So Round, So Firm, So Fully Packed," "Divorce Me C.O.D.," and "Steel Guitar Rag" (which updated and added lyrics to the instrumental version by Bob Wills' steel player Leon McAuliffe). Answering a request to record some Appalachian-style folksongs, Travis came up with his own—"Dark As A Dungeon," "Sixteen Tons"—and rearranged more to fit his style, including "I Am A Pilgrim," "John Henry," and "Nine Pound Hammer."

Amplified steel guitars had been around for about a decade, but during the mid-'40s electric solid-body guitars became a new West Coast phenomenon. Travis was one of the first to pick on one, a custom model made by Paul Bigsby. It was an early version of the type of guitar that would later be widely used by Buck Owens, Wynn Stewart, Roy Nichols, and other Bakersfield pickers—not to mention countless rock'n'rollers. During the '50s he performed regularly on the *Town Hall Party* and *Hometown Jamboree*, appeared in the 1953 movie *From Here To Eternity*, and played on most of the Capitol recordings by his friend Hank Thompson. (He later even married Thompson's ex-wife, Dorothy.) Chet Atkins was a huge Travis disciple, and brought Travis-style picking deeper into the country and pop mainstream. During the '60s Travis was a hero to the new generation of urban folk revivalists, with several of his songs (alongside those of Woody Guthrie and others) serving as prototypes for contemporary socially oriented 'folk' music. His 1963 album SONGS OF THE COAL MINES was geared to this audience. Travis apparently lived a wild lifestyle that prevented him, in part, from making the charts much even during the '50s. He did continue to record for the next couple of decades, however. During the '70s he re-recorded many of his early hits for the CMH label and even worked again with Grandpa Jones. He also moved to Oklahoma

and settled down. He died in 1983 following a heart attack.

⊙ **Folk Songs Of The Hills** (1947; Capitol; reissued 1996). Originally released in an album of four 78 records, then reissued on LP in 1957, this landmark concept album has now been reissued on CD with 5 extra tracks. It includes his initial recordings of "Sixteen Tons" and "Dark As A Dungeon."

⊙ **Walkin' The Strings** (1960; Capitol; reissued 1996). Instead of the folksong angle of the above collection, this album concentrates on Travis' guitar picking, presenting 22 unadorned recordings from the 1940s and '50s.

⊙ **Unreleased Radio Transcriptions, 1944–1949** (1991; Country Routes/Interstate). A British collection and one of several CDs of Travis' early radio recordings. Culled from shows like *Dinner Bell Roundup*, *Hollywood Barn Dance* and the *Grand Ole Opry*, these cuts have an enjoyable informality.

⊙ **Guitar Rags And A Too-Fast Past** (1994; Bear Family). A 5-CD box set that pulls together songs from the first dozen years of Travis' recording career—his early King sides; radio transcriptions; material with bandleaders like Wesley Tuttle and Hank Penny; tons of Captiol recordings, including his classic 'folk' songs and novelties like "Divorce Me C.O.D." and "A Fool At The Steering Wheel;" and loads more songs and instrumentals that show what a genius this guy was as both a songwriter and guitarist.

T. Texas Tyler

Singer and bandleader T. Texas Tyler was a hot ticket on the Southern California dance-hall circuit during the 1940s. Songs like "Remember Me" and "Gals Don't Mean A Thing," two of his best recordings, were more honky tonk than western swing, but they did have a cowboy flavor, helped along by a cool vocal growl Tyler developed during his early years playing radio stations around West Virginia. And then there was "Deck Of Cards," a recitation about a soldier who uses playing cards not for poker, but for Bible lessons. An old folksong that Tyler rearranged, it was a major hit for him in 1948. His career, however, shouldn't be judged on that hokey religious number alone but on the wilder and more fun-filled songs he cut like "Remember Me," "Filipino Baby," and "Oklahoma Hills."

Tex was born David Luke Myrick on 20 June, 1916 in Mena, Arkansas. His first radio appearances were in Newport, Rhode Island where his brother was stationed for Navy duty. After that he hit the road, playing hillbilly radio shows around West Virginia and in other eastern cities. He also adopted the name Tex Tyler, which was hardly an unusual move: with cowboy singers at the peak of their popularity, countless artists gave themselves names like "Tex," "Cowboy," and "Slim." After serving in World War II Tyler landed in California and began playing the local clubs and radio stations. He won a recording contract with Four Star, the same label that later signed Webb Pierce and the Maddox Brothers And Rose. "Filipino Baby," a song first cut by Billy Cox in the '30s (and later by Ernest Tubb), hit the charts in 1946, followed by "Remember Me"—a great showpiece for his growl—and "Oklahoma Hills." The last of these songs was written by Woody Guthrie and previously a hit for his cousin, Jack Guthrie.

Tyler's biggest hit, however, was "Deck Of Cards" in 1948, foreshadowing his turn toward the Lord. He also sang in the 1949 movie *Horsemen Of The Sierras*, and in the '50s cut "Bumming Around" and a few other singles for Decca. Tyler joined the *Grand Ole Opry* in 1957, but soon after he found religion and turned to gospel music, even becoming an Assembly of God minister. He recorded a gospel album, SALVATION, for Capitol in 1962, but by the end of the decade he'd returned to playing at least some country music—he cut a secular album for Starday (THE MAN WITH A MILLION FRIENDS) and even resettled on the West Coast. Finally, he moved to Springfield, Missouri, though shortly after he was diagnosed with stomach cancer. He died in January of 1972.

⊙ **T. Texas Tyler** (1961; King; reissued 1987; King/Highland). One of several King albums compiling Tyler's Four Star singles, the 12 songs include greats like "Remember Me," "Filipino Baby," "Gals Don't Mean A Thing," and "Careless Love." Some liner notes would be useful, but musically it's a worthwhile purchase.

⊙ **The Best Of T. Texas Tyler** (1998; Collector's Choice). With 18 songs this is an even better bargain. Tyler standards like "Remember Me," "Filipino Baby," "Oklahoma Hills," and "Deck Of Cards" are included, as well as his version of "My Bucket's Got A Hole In It" and the bluegrass-style number "Courtin' In The Rain."

Speedy West And Jimmy Bryant

"We just let our minds run rampant."
—Speedy West

On the whole, the country scene on the West Coast was far more tolerant of progressive musical ideas than Nashville. One listen to the hot-wired instrumentals that pedal-steel virtuoso Speedy West and Telecaster genius Jimmy Bryant cut together during the 1950s, and you'll have to agree: nothing like that had ever crossed the WSM airwaves or blared from the hallowed halls of the Ryman Auditorium. Goodness knows, such a sound might have led to someone's arrest.

During the '50s, West and Bryant were a practically unbeatable guitar team who played together not just on their own mind-blowing recordings, but on countless gun-for-hire sessions, many of them in the studios of Capitol Records. The sounds introduced by West, in particular, on his pedal steel (then a brand-new instrument) are like nothing country music had ever heard before—or has ever heard since. While an amplified steel guitar had been used to add color and depth to country music since the '30s, West's pedal-steel work was from another galaxy entirely—his solos a wild, unchained, and sometimes zany torrent of sonic loops, leaps, curves, hums and gallops. As for Bryant, he was a bright, energetic and lightning-fast stylist in his own right—a man even West often struggled to keep pace with.

Both men originally hailed from points east. Wesley Webb West was born on 25 January, 1924 in Springfield, Missouri. Early on he became enamored with the work of Bob Wills' steel man Leon McAuliffe and Roy Acuff's Dobro master

"Bashful Brother" Oswald Kirby, among others; later he was a huge fan of Joaquin Murphy, who played steel with Tex Williams. West married early, worked on his family's farm, and played music on the side. A local musician nicknamed him "Speedy," and it stuck. After the war, he and his family moved to Los Angeles, looking for a change and better, brighter opportunities.

As for Speedy's soon-to-be partner, he was born Ivy J. Bryant, Jr. on 5 March, 1925 in Pavo, Georgia. He first played the fiddle; later, while recovering from a World War II injury in Washington, DC, he learned guitar and became a big jazz fan—one of his heroes being jazz guitarist Django Reinhardt. He played jazz clubs around

MICHAEL OCHS ARCHIVES

Jimmy Bryant

DC before getting married and, in 1946, moving west to LA.

The pair first met in 1947 during a jam session at a place called Murphy's Bar, although they didn't unite as a team until a few years later. In the meantime, Speedy made his name first with Hank Penny and Spade Cooley and then on the *Dinner Bell Roundup* radio program and the TV show it eventually became, the *Hometown Jamboree*. Both programs were hosted by Capitol A&R man Cliffie Stone, who was instrumental in bringing West together with Bryant (who had been playing in

Speedy West and Jimmy Bryant

Tex Williams' band). Stone hired Bryant to lead the *Hometown Jamboree* band, and once they began working as a team he dubbed the pair the "Flaming Guitars." West and Bryant were soon also playing on Capitol sessions; among their first recordings were Tennessee Ernie Ford's "Shot Gun Boogie" and his hit duet with Kay Starr, "I'll Never Be Free."

West played a three-neck pedal steel that had been custom made for him by Paul Bigsby. He had started playing the instrument in 1948, making him the first country artist to regularly use a pedal-steel guitar. (Nashville didn't jump on the band-wagon until Webb Pierce's "Slowly," featuring the mournful pedal-steel work of Bud Isaacs, became a hit in 1954.) As for Bryant, he, too, was a pioneer. Since about 1950 he'd been playing a solid-body electric guitar made by Leo Fender; initially called a Broadcaster, it was the prototype of the Fender Telecaster—the lead instrument with the sharp, edgy sound that became a defining characteristic of the West Coast honky-tonk sound.

West was initially signed as a solo artist to Capitol, but he convinced the label to sign Bryant as his partner. They churned out more than fifty instrumentals together between 1951 and 1956, much of it self-penned material with titles like "Stratosphere Boogie," "Flippin' The Lid," "Whistle Stop," "Pickin' Peppers," and "Caffeine Patrol." The only album they released under both their names, TWO GUITARS COUNTRY STYLE (1954), is a highly sought-after item among record collectors. They also played on thousands of sessions with artists from Jean Shepard and Ferlin Husky to Bing Crosby and Spike Jones. West and Bryant remained a team on the *Hometown Jamboree* until Bryant quit in 1955 (he was replaced by Roy

Lanham), though the pair continued to play together on recording sessions.

West maintained his Capitol contract into the '60s and kept busy with session work, though that eventually tapered off. In 1960 he produced Loretta Lynn's very first single and then took a job with the Fender corporation in Tulsa, Oklahoma. Bryant continued playing on sessions through the '60s, recorded some solo albums for Imperial, and also concentrated on his songwriting (one of his most memorable songs was Waylon Jennings' hit "Only Daddy That'll Walk The Line"). In 1975 the two guitar devils recorded a reunion album together, produced by Pete Drake, though it wasn't released until 1990 by the Nashville indie label Step One. Bryant died of lung cancer on 22 September, 1980. A year later, Speedy suffered a stroke, which ended his playing career, though he has continued to appear at special functions.

⊙ **Stratosphere Boogie: The Flaming Guitars Of Speedy West And Jimmy Bryant** (1995; Razor & Tie). This excellent 16-track CD collects songs these two maestros cut during the early 1950s for Capitol. Call it jazz, country, rock, swing, or blues: elements of each of these styles are there in melodies that are as outlandish, freewheeling and off-the-charts as they are tight, subtly crafted and mind-bogglingly imaginative. A superb introduction to their work.

⊙ **Swingin' On The Strings: The Speedy West And Jimmy Bryant Collection, Volume 2** (1999; Razor & Tie). If one CD's worth of this guitar team's skull-busting virtuosity isn't enough, this second volume of 20 further Capitol recordings should suffice. Including the exotic steel-guitar atmospherics of "West Of Samoa" and the fleet-fingered rush that is "China Boy" (more than six minutes long).

Speedy West and Jimmy Bryant

6

On My Journey Home: The Story Of Bluegrass

Bluegrass is a rare music. Its foundations are conservative, but at its heart is a wild amalgamation of styles—from blues and jazz to old-time and gospel—that makes it almost a closer kin to rock'n'roll than the Appalachian folk or hillbilly string-band music it's typically associated with. The development of bluegrass also reflects the shifting lifestyles of country fans and musicians, many of whom were grappling with a fast-changing world while trying to hang on to the culture of their past.

Contrary to what many people believe, bluegrass is not "as old as the hills." Relative to the commercial country music industry, which was born during the 1920s, and certainly the vast world of American folk music, which stretches back centuries, bluegrass is a fairly modern invention, having only been around since 1939—the year **Bill Monroe** and the Blue Grass Boys auditioned for the *Grand Ole Opry* with their revved-up rendition of "Mule Skinner Blues." And that's another unique point about bluegrass: this is a style created by one man, Bill Monroe—the "father of bluegrass." The name bluegrass, in fact, comes directly from Monroe's band, the Blue Grass Boys—which he'd in turn named in honor of his home state, Kentucky (the Blue Grass State).

Bluegrass is often thought of as Appalachian music, which is a misnomer. To begin with, much of the old-time folk music of Appalachia, while beautiful in its own right, lacks the instrumental complexity and speedy tempos that define classic bluegrass; furthermore, Monroe grew up in the coal mining country of western Kentucky, half a state away from the Appalachian Mountains. To be fair, though, bluegrass does retain an "old-fashioned" esthetic. It has strong roots in southern fiddle, string band and hillbilly music; and downhome images of family, the old homestead, the landscape and other rural memories—some romantic, some tragic—are woven into its lyrics. Kentucky after all is a "Southern" state (the thick accents and numerous tobacco farms are proof enough of that), and so the culture and traditions Monroe grew up with were shared by rural people in much of Appalachia and throughout the southeastern United States (including Carter and Ralph Stanley in Virginia, Don Reno in North Carolina, and Jimmy Martin in Tennessee).

Like many families, Monroe's parents and siblings danced, played instruments, and sang both at home and at church. Community dances were held regularly, usually featuring a local fiddler (such as Monroe's Uncle Pen Vandiver) whose repertoire had been handed down by generations of players before him. Few people could afford phonographs, so radio shows were an important venue. Bands and singers competed for cherished spots playing live on local stations (the concept of DJs spinning records didn't catch on until the '50s), and nearly everybody whose radio could pick up Nashville's WSM listened to the *Grand Ole Opry* on Saturday night.

Those were the music's (and Monroe's) roots. But bluegrass wasn't just string-band music: Its influences also came from jazz bands, haunting blues artists, commercial hillbilly singers (most notably Jimmie Rodgers), and black R&B dance music—stuff you'd sooner hear in cities. Which is just where many young, rurally raised men had moved during the '30s—they'd left the farm to find work, traveling the "hillbilly highway" to northern cities like Detroit and Chicago, and in the process were exposed to a whole new set of cultural influences.

Under Monroe's leadership, hillbilly string-band music moved out of the barn. During the early days of the Blue Grass Boys, Monroe brought a symphony of influences into the rehearsal space— fiddle tunes, gospel quartets, tight-knit jazz music, lonesome Jimmie Rodgers blues songs, and memories of his mother singing around the house while doing chores— and let the sparks fly. To country audiences in the late '30s and early '40s, Monroe's version of "Mule Skinner Blues," his first signature tune, was a mind-blower. The vocals soared as high as the roofbeams (a sound described countless times since as "high lonesome"); the playing was virtuosic, intricate and tightly knit; and the tempo was fast and furious. Monroe arranged his music in atypical keys, which added tension, and he allowed his instrumentalists brief solos, spotlighting them in the manner of modern jazz bands. He also demanded a high level of musicianship—and he got it with a succession of highly skilled players, many of whom came out of the hills to knock on the back door of the *Opry* every Saturday night, begging for a chance to audition.

At the same time, however, the music often retained a mournful quality that took listeners back home—a familiar and conservative feeling. These were folks whose livelihood and culture had been tied to the land ever since Daniel Boone crossed the Cumberland Gap, so while the music was new, to them the lyrics brimming with images of southern rural life were anything but foreign. This was their music, it spoke their language. And it's a quality that's remained with the music right to the present day.

The fundamental characteristics of Monroe's style were in evidence on his recordings from 1940 and 1941—music that rightfully deserves the name "bluegrass." But it wasn't until 1946—when Monroe was backed by the quintessential Blue Grass Boys line-up of Lester Flatt, Earl Scruggs, Chubby Wise, and Cedric Rainwater—that the music truly gelled. If country fans hadn't already been convinced of the music's power and ferocity,

five-string banjoist Earl Scruggs changed their tune. This young whiz kid played complex lines and rolls with apparent ease, thrilling *Opry* fans and turning him into a star almost overnight. Ever since his debut, three-finger banjo playing (also known as "Scruggs style") has been closely associated with bluegrass. Often the sound of a three-finger banjo roll alone is enough to give a song a "bluegrass" feel.

By the late '40s, young players were already copying Monroe's music. Yet it would be several years before people began speaking of bluegrass as a style of its own. When **Flatt & Scruggs** quit the Blue Grass Boys and formed their own band, describing their music as "Blue Grass style" was a way for fans and DJs to invoke the Monroe tradition without using the master's name. The **Stanley Brothers** were the first to actually copy Monroe's style on record—a version of the Monroe song "Molly And Tenbrooks"—though they soon developed their own approach to become another of the genre's most revered groups. During the mid-'50s bluegrass achieved its "golden age," a time when the Stanleys, the **Foggy Mountain Boys**, **Reno & Smiley**, **Mac Wiseman**, the **Osborne Brothers**, **Jim & Jesse**, **Jimmy Martin**, and others gained significant popularity and pushed the music in new and different directions. By this time, too, DJs, fans and record distributors were arguing over who had been the first to use the term bluegrass.

The '50s was also a decade of change for the world of country music as a whole. During the '30s and '40s, rural lifestyles—which had once defined the music and its audience—were fading as folks left the hills to escape the Depression and to seek better-paying jobs. In the process they brought country music to cities like Detroit, Boston and Washington, DC—which in turn developed strong communities of bluegrass and country musicians and fans. By the '50s, the means of hearing new music was also changing, as records and radio DJ shows grew even more popular.

On top of all this came rock'n'roll, which practically flipped the country music industry on its head. The initial instigator was, of course, Elvis Presley. Bluegrass was involved in the onslaught right from the start, as the flip side of Presley's first Sun single was an uptempo cover of Bill Monroe's "Blue Moon Of Kentucky." Presley's music—and that of others following in his wake—opened up new territory for record sales. Teenagers who'd once bought country records now wanted rock'n'roll and rockabilly, and the major record companies were quick to comply.

Where rockabilly thrust country into the teenage market, the Nashville Sound was designed to widen country's appeal among the easy-listening crowd. In Nashville (which by the '50s had become country music's centerpoint), recording studios were popping up all over town, and along with them came session players hired by producers to give their labels' records a uniform sheen.

In the wake of all this change, bluegrass began losing its industry support. The fiddle, for instance, once the chief instrument in hillbilly music, was deemed outmoded—even an embarrassment—in the "modern" music world. It remained a key element of bluegrass, however, which only added to a growing feeling that the music was becoming too "old-fashioned." Established artists with strong followings like Monroe, Flatt & Scruggs and the Stanley Brothers weathered these years with less trouble. In fact, sticking to acoustic instruments and a traditional repertoire worked to their benefit, as older fans, disgusted with country's kowtowing to pop trends, turned to bluegrass as the last bastion of "real" country. (In the process, it further reinforced "bluegrass" as a stylistic moniker.) Other acts like the Osborne Brothers and Mac Wiseman took a different approach, modifying their sound to survive and compete. They toyed with drums and electric and steel guitars, and they worked contemporary country songs (even some rockabilly) into their repertoires.

Revival and Progression

If rock'n'roll threatened to destroy bluegrass, the genre's saviour came in the form of another youth-based movement: the urban folk revival. Consisting mostly of young, college-educated music lovers, many of them from New York City (where they frequently gathered in Washington Square to pick and sing), they were turned off by teen-oriented rock'n'roll and at the same time almost entirely ignorant of mainstream country. What they sought was the "pure" music of years gone by—songs and sounds unadulterated by the modern world and its trendy, often fly-by-night tastes. By the end of the decade, they'd discovered bluegrass, which they considered one of the last true "folk" styles.

Most revivalists initially focused on the banjo. They'd first heard Pete Seeger play the instrument but eventually hit upon Scruggs (by 1962, the folk magazine *Sing Out!* was declaring Scruggs "the undisputed master of bluegrass music"). Slowly, the folk and bluegrass worlds began to intersect: Scruggs (without Flatt) and the Stanley Brothers were invited to play at the first Newport Folk

Festival in 1959; and just a month earlier, folklorist Alan Lomax had organized a folk concert at New York's Carnegie Hall that featured, along with Muddy Waters, Jimmie Driftwood, and Pete Seeger, Virginia bluegrass singer Earl Taylor and his Stoney Mountain Boys. (Monroe apparently turned Lomax down, put off by his leftist politics.) New York critics were baffled by Taylor's music, but he was a hit with the audience. A year later, the Osborne Brothers became the first bluegrass band to play a concert on a college campus (Antioch College in Yellow Springs, Ohio).

In the late '50s, the Folkways label released two influential bluegrass compilation albums that helped young folkies digest and understand the music. The first, AMERICAN BANJO SCRUGGS STYLE—which, released in 1957, was the first bluegrass LP—featured fifteen banjoists performing variations on the three-finger picking style Scruggs had popularized. It also included liner notes by Ralph Rinzler (a traditional music historian and member of the Greenbriar Boys) that detailed the history of bluegrass—one of the first times the word "bluegrass" was used in print. The second, MOUNTAIN MUSIC BLUEGRASS STYLE, came out two years later with more songs and further information that was again marketed toward the music's hungry new fans.

As the bluegrass fan base evolved, so did the players and, finally, the music itself. Through the '50s, the major bluegrass acts were almost exclusively southerners from rural backgrounds. But now college kids and even northerners were studying and playing the music. **Mike Seeger** (who co-founded the old-time group New Lost City Ramblers in 1958) and Eric Weissberg (later one of the players on "Dueling Banjos," the theme from *Deliverance* and probably the most famous banjo tune) are two instrumentalists who participated in the Washington Square scene. The new bluegrass band that made the biggest impact during this time, however, was the **Country Gentlemen**, who formed in Washington, DC in 1957. They played in a classic acoustic bluegrass style, but their approach was more studied and their repertoire mixed contemporary folk material with traditional songs. Fast and exciting players, the Gentlemen appealed to country and folk fans alike, and they were soon touted as the first "progressive bluegrass" band. They were also the flagship band of a newly thriving bluegrass scene in Washington, DC.

It soon became clear that "progressive" influences (which included up-to-date material and even electric instruments) were a boon to stunted bluegrass record sales. Monroe refused to alter his traditional sound, but Jim & Jesse, the Osborne Brothers, and eventually even Flatt & Scruggs modified their repertoires (a move that ultimately led to Flatt's split with Scruggs in 1969). At the same time, new bands and players such as the **Dillards**, John Hartford, the Hillmen, and the **Kentucky Colonels** began cropping up, bringing an even more open-minded approach to bluegrass and pushing the music into closer proximity with folk, country and even rock. Chris Hillman (of the Hillmen) and Clarence White (of the Kentucky Colonels) later became members of California country-rockers the Byrds.

By the '70s, progressive bands like Red, White & Blue (Grass) and New Grass Revival were playing music that was more hippie than high lonesome. The latter band was also the source of the term "newgrass," another moniker for progressive bluegrass—which by this point regularly featured long instrumental jams and more electric instruments than acoustic ones. Even Earl Scruggs, newly split from his longtime partner, was now playing country-rock in a band with his sons.

Since its inception, bluegrass had almost entirely remained a male domain. Wilma Lee Cooper and her husband Stoney had skirted the periphery of bluegrass since their days on the Rich-R-Tone label in the '40s, and hillbilly singer Molly O'Day (with whom Mac Wiseman once played) was another strong voice of the era, but more frequently these and other female musicians ended up playing folk, old-time, or straight country music. A notable exception was accordionist Wilene "Sally Ann" Forrester, who was a Blue Grass Boy during the early '40s (as was her husband, fiddler Howdy Forrester). There was also husky-voiced Margie Sullivan, who founded the gospel-bluegrass Sullivan Family (with husband Enoch) in 1949. And Roni Stoneman (daughter of '20s hillbilly singer Ernest Stoneman) played on AMERICAN BANJO SCRUGGS STYLE in 1957.

Until the folk revival movement came along, however, no female artist had been given the spotlight. That changed beginning in the '60s and '70s as singers such as Lilimae, **Hazel Dickens** and Alice Gerrard, Betty Fisher, **Delia Bell**, and Ginger Boatwright—along with groups like the Buffalo Gals (fronted by Susie Monick) and the Good Ol' Persons (the latter a product of the Berkeley folk scene and featuring singer Kathy Kallick and fiddler Laurie Lewis)—entered the scene. By the '90s, singer, fiddler and bandleader **Alison Krauss** would become the top-selling bluegrass artist of all time—and the first to make a country music video.

More than any single phenomena of the era, bluegrass festivals were a key element to helping bluegrass music (especially the traditional variety) win a permanent place in the modern world. Folk festivals had gained popularity by the late '50s, but it was still rare for bluegrass acts to share the same bill. In 1961, guitarist **Bill Clifton** organized a daylong all-bluegrass concert at a Luray, Virginia music park featuring Monroe, the Stanley Brothers, the Country Gentlemen, Jim & Jesse, and others. The first multiday bluegrass festival, however—the one most fans refer to as "the first festival"—was put together in Roanoke, Virginia in 1965 (the same year Dylan went electric at Newport) by promoter Carlton Haney. Assisting Haney was Ralph Rinzler, who'd by that point served as Monroe's manager and become a leading bluegrass, old-time, and folk music historian. (Rinzler also helped organize the Newport Folk Festival, then later founded the Smithsonian's Festival of American Folklife.) Modeled after Newport, the three-day Roanoke festival was capped by a special presentation, "The Story of Bluegrass," which paid tribute to Monroe's legacy by having previous sidemen (Flatt & Scruggs excluded) take the stage with him, in chronological order, to show how he'd developed his music over the years. It was a major turning point for Monroe and for bluegrass as a whole—one that eventually led to Monroe's recognition as the true "father of bluegrass" and his induction into the Country Music Hall of Fame in 1970.

Festivals began popping up regularly in the late '60s, and really took off in the '70s. They often mixed traditional and progressive bands (not to mention audiences of both conservative farmers and pot-smoking hippies). The point, though, was the music: at festivals bluegrass bands were the main event, not just a side attraction as they had been at folk festivals or on country music package tours. Because of this, festivals became the one place where traditional bands could relax and even thrive, unworried about satisfying their labels' demands for more contemporary sounds and songs. Artists like Mac Wiseman and the Osborne Brothers, for instance, returned to playing traditional bluegrass at these gatherings, much to the delight of older fans. The popularity of bluegrass festivals has continued, unabated, well into the '90s, and in their guard the music itself has grown stronger.

Bluegrass magazines also first appeared in the '60s and had significant impact. Along with the aforementioned Folkways compilation albums and their long liner notes, magazines like *Bluegrass Unlimited* (founded by Pete Kuykendall, who once played with the Country Gentlemen) and

Muleskinner News (founded by Carlton Haney) documented the music's history and current directions by publishing interviews with legendary and contemporary players, numerous album reviews, and up-to-date festival listings.

Independent labels were another saving grace, as most major record companies had dropped their remaining classic bluegrass artists by the mid-'70s (Monroe being the exception). Two labels founded in the '50s, Starday and King, had long been bluegrass strongholds; their ownership has since changed hands more than once, but a good deal of their classic material has remained in print. During the '70s, small indie labels like County, Rebel, CMH, Rounder, Flying Fish, and Sugar Hill cropped up and eventually became home to numerous bluegrass artists, both progressive and traditional. Some also reissued older material that had dropped out-of-print. Selling bluegrass records by mail order had proven a successful method for reaching rural audiences (Jimmie Skinner's Music Center in Cincinnati was a leading distributor during the '50s and '60s), and many of these younger labels continued the practice.

During the '80s, newgrass evolved into "supergrass" and "spacegrass" as artists like Sam Bush and **Béla Fleck** continued to branch further into pop, jazz, world music, and even borderline New Age. At the same time and at the opposite end of the spectrum, that decade witnessed a resurgence of traditional bluegrass—music built, as it had been since the '40s, around acoustic instruments, high lonesome harmonies, and tight, intricate arrangements. Groups like the **Johnson**

Anthologies

⊙ **The Bluegrass Hall Of Fame** (1987; Highland). A collection of Starday and King singles by some classic artists (Reno & Smiley, the Stanley Brothers, Jim & Jessie, Carl Story) as well as others whose relationship to bluegrass was only part-time (Jimmie Skinner) or peripheral (Hylo Brown, Grandpa Jones)—but who share qualities with the genre nonetheless.

⊙ **The Best Of Bluegrass, Vol. 1: Standards** (1991; Mercury). Mercury was home to many bluegrass greats over the years including the Stanley Brothers, Flatt & Scruggs, the Osborne Brothers, the Country Gentlemen, and Carl Story. Their inclusion here (along with several others) makes this an excellent compilation of classic material.

⊙ **High Lonesome: The Story Of Bluegrass Music** (1994; CMH). The soundtrack to the documentary *High Lonesome*—a film directed by Rachel Liebling that is, by the way, a superb introduction to bluegrass music and history—is an excellent compilation of classic bluegrass tracks and a nice beginner CD. Artists represented include Bill Monroe, Ralph Stanley, Mac Wiseman, Jimmy Martin, and the Seldom Scene.

⊙ **Hand-Picked: 25 Years Of Bluegrass Music On Rounder Records** (1995; Rounder). Honoring their company's silver anniversary, the folks at Rounder compiled this excellent 2-CD set featuring a wide range of traditional and progressive bluegrass—from Del McCoury, Joe Val, Wilma Lee Cooper, and Lynn Morris to Tony Rice, J.D. Crowe, Laurie Lewis, and David Grisman. A full-bodied picture of the genre in its recent incarnation(s).

⊙ **Top Of The Hill Bluegrass** (1995; Sugar Hill). A 20-song collection of modern bluegrass sounds from the Sugar Hill roster. Participants include Peter Rowan, Doc Watson, the Nashville Bluegrass Band, Lonesome Standard Time, New Grass Revival, Tim O'Brien, and Doyle Lawson.

⊙ **Appalachian Stomp: Bluegrass Classics** (1995; Rhino). Eighteen tracks covering a half-century of bluegrass, from Bill Monroe, Flatt & Scruggs, and Jimmy Martin to Del McCoury, the Kentucky Colonels, and Alison Krauss. Like the HIGH LONESOME CD, it's a nice beginner's collection, as it contains many of the genre's most classic tracks like "Uncle Pen," "Foggy Mountain Breakdown," "Rocky Top," and even "Dueling Banjos."

⊙ **Live Again! WCYB Bristol Farm And Fun Time** (1997; Rebel). Excellent and fun-to-listen-to double-CD collection of radio programs featuring several songs each from the Stanley Brothers, Carl and J.P. Sauceman, Flatt & Scruggs, Curly King, and Mac Wiseman. For many groups during the 1940s and '50s, radio was much more important than recording, which makes this collection a great way to get a sense of working musicians in action.

Mountain Boys and the Del McCoury Band (formerly the Dixie Pals) have proven just how powerful and dynamic traditional bluegrass can be in the hands of contemporary musicians who speak its language. Other standouts include Doyle Lawson, who developed a beautiful bluegrass-gospel sound with his band Quicksilver; the late Joe Val, who took tenor singing to new heights; and Larry Sparks, whose earthy, wholesome sound echoes traditional country as well as blue-grass influences. The biggest success story in recent years, though, is certainly that of Alison Krauss. A child prodigy (she was signed to Rounder when only fourteen), this talented singer, songwriter, fiddler and bandleader has even crossed over into the country charts (her 1995 album achieved multiplatinum sales). In 1993 she was also the first bluegrass artist for 29 years to be invited to join the *Grand Ole Opry*.

While bluegrass has branched in all sorts of directions since its founding more than half a century ago, the core of the music has remained stable. It's the strength of bluegrass's conservative foundation, in fact, that has helped it survive largely intact in a contemporary music world where singers are too often signed based on their youthful good looks and/or how well they can wiggle their way through a music video. With festivals going strong summer after summer, a fan base that continues to widen, and a bevy of new artists (Chris Jones, James King, Claire Lynch) who continue to captivate the public, bluegrass has a bright future.

Bluegrass: The Artists

Delia Bell And Bill Grant

When Emmylou Harris titled her 1980 album ROSES IN THE SNOW after a song she'd heard sung by Delia Bell, and then convinced Warner Brothers to sign Bell, it seemed this child of the Great Depression was finally going to get her due. Born in Bonham, Texas in the 1930s and raised in Oklahoma, Bell was of the few women in blue-grass when she started singing in 1959 with man-dolinist and songwriter Bill Grant, a childhood friend of her husband's. After visiting (and per-forming at) Bill Monroe's Bean Blossom festival in 1969, the pair had become regular favorites at blue-grass festivals all over the country; by the late '70s they'd toured England and Ireland several times and released a series of albums and singles on Grant's own label, Kiamichi. Bell's (and Grant's) talents deserved wider recognition, and gaining the support of country star Harris—who called Bell one of the best singers in country music—seemed just the ticket. Warner Brothers released DELIA BELL, the singer's second solo album (her first being 1978's BLUER THAN MIDNIGHT), in 1983.

But alas, a voice as pure, earthy and lonesome-sounding as Bell's is rarely the stuff of major label marketing campaigns—especially in an age when video was just beginning to take off. And Bell herself—who had been deeply shy when she first played with Grant—was simply not all that comfortable in the Nashvillian world of soaring sales charts and publicity protocol. Her Warner Brothers album gained her one minor hit—a duet with John Anderson on the old George Jones song "Flame In My Heart"—but the big label eventually dropped Bell, and she and Grant began once again playing bluegrass and old-time country songs (both classics and originals written by Grant) mostly as a duet. They've since recorded several duet albums for Rounder Records that feature the Johnson Mountain Boys and Del and Jerry McCoury, among others, as their back-up band. Other labels they've worked with include Rebel and Old Homestead, the latter releasing the pair's 1992 album DREAMING OF THE TIMES. Since the late '60s, Grant has also kept busy running an annual bluegrass festival in Hugo, Oklahoma.

⊙ Delia Bell (1983; Warner Bros.). Emmylou Harris once raved that Bell's strong, wonderfully rural voice sounded like the product of a marriage between Hank Williams and Kitty Wells. Further comparisons might include Loretta Lynn and Hazel Dickens. Harris produced this album and kept the hybrid bluegrass-country arrangements reasonably spare, giving the Oklahoma singer plenty of room. Songs include the Wells classic "Backstreet Affair," the Carter Family's "Wildwood Flower," Carter Stanley's "Weary Heart," and Bell's duet with John Anderson, "Flame In My Heart."

⊙ **Dreaming** (1997; Rounder). This 14-song collection is culled from the three albums Bell and Grant recorded for Rounder in the 1980s: CHEER OF THE HOME FIRES, A FEW DOLLARS MORE, and FOLLOWING A FEELING. The song list includes works by Marty Robbins, Hugh Moffatt, and Hazel Dickens.

Bill Clifton

While Bill Clifton may not have emerged straight from the folk revivalist movement, he was certainly among the first of the college-educated set to become a major player in the world of bluegrass. He was born into a wealthy Baltimore-area family—hardly a typical bluegrass background, yet his love for rural music was strong and unquestionably sincere. A folklorist as well as an accomplished guitarist, singer, and songwriter, Clifton's musical approach is more studied than that of the average southern picker—his vocals are cleaner, his instrumentation somewhat tidier than that of Monroe or the Stanley Brothers—but his songs and arrangements are traditional to the core.

Aside from his musical talent, Clifton has also been a major supporter of bluegrass and old-time music in other capacities. He's long been a song collector, and in 1953 he first published an influential songbook, *150 Old-Time Folk And Gospel Songs*, that's since been dubbed the "Bluegrass Bible"; on 4 July, 1961 he organized the very first bluegrass festival, a one-day affair at a Luray, Virginia music park (an event "ahead of its time," wrote historian Ralph Rinzler); he championed the music throughout Europe and the Pacific Rim while living abroad during the '60s and '70s; and he helped re-organize the Newport Folk Festival.

Clifton was born William August Marburg on 5 April, 1931 and grew up on a farm outside Baltimore. He attended private schools, and in 1949 he enrolled in the University of Virginia, from which he eventually earned a business degree. He had listened to plenty of country and folk music growing up, and at college he formed the Dixie Mountain Boys—taking the stage name "Bill Clifton" to avoid embarrassing his family, who didn't appreciate his country-boy leanings. The group recorded for the Blue Ridge label in 1953 and 1954 and eventually won a spot on the *Wheeling Jamboree*.

In the mid-'50s Clifton spent two years in the Marines (during which time he published his songbook); after returning to civilian life he cut sides for Mercury and Starday (he financed the initial sessions himself). Many of his songs were older public domain numbers that Clifton was determined to prevent fading away; others he wrote or co-wrote himself. One, "Springhill Disaster," was written in 1958 following the Springhill Mine explosion in Nova Scotia (two hundred men were trapped underground, 81 of them later rescued), and it was based on one survivor's words: "Give me a drink of water and I'll sing you a song." Half the song's proceeds went to the miners' relief fund. In 1961, following the death (in 1960) of A.P. Carter, Clifton paid tribute to his friend and biggest influence by recording the CARTER FAMILY MEMORIAL ALBUM for Starday.

In 1961, while working as the producer of summer music shows at Oak Leaf Park in Luray, Virginia near Washington, DC, Clifton felt it was time for an all-day bluegrass event. His Bluegrass Day at Luray featured the Country Gentlemen, Mac Wiseman, Monroe, Jim & Jesse, the Stanley Brothers, and himself. It wasn't hugely successful—the next bluegrass festival wouldn't happen until 1965—but it was certainly memorable, as it brought the broad network of bluegrass bands and fans together for the first time. The next year, instead of booking a second Bluegrass Day, Clifton was hired by the Newport Folk Foundation to help re-organize their infamous folk festival.

In 1963 Clifton moved to England, where he played folk clubs and toured throughout Europe and, later, Asia, Australia, and New Zealand. He stayed abroad for fifteen years, visiting the US only occasionally to perform or record. Finally resettling in America during the late '70s, Clifton recorded for County Records and formed the group First Generation with Red Rector and Don Stover. He's since continued to record (including an instrumental autoharp album in 1980 for his own Elf label) and perform at festivals.

⊙ **The Early Years 1957–1958** (1992; Rounder). Culled from the prime of Clifton's recording career, these 19 tracks also feature notable guests such as Ralph Stanley, Benny Martin, Curley Lambert, John Duffey, and Mike Seeger. Though he lacks the haunting presence of classic singers like Carter Stanley and Bill Monroe, Clifton's voice is warm, and his songs—beautiful folk and hillbilly melodies that even at the time were quickly being forgotten—ring with rural truth and beauty.

Bill Clifton

Larry Cordle And Lonesome Standard Time

Fronted by guitarist and singer Larry Cordle, Lonesome Standard Time is one of the finest traditional bluegrass bands to emerge in the 1990s. The name of the band came from a song Cordle wrote for Kathy Mattea. Cordle, in fact, has done rather well as a country songwriter, placing his material with several Nashville stars, among them Trisha Yearwood ("Lonesome Dove"), John Anderson ("Lower On The Hog"), Ricky Skaggs ("You Can't Take It With You When You Go"), and even Garth Brooks ("Against The Grain"). Cordle's crossover success as a writer helps fuel his own music, which he's been making since the early '90s. His albums include several excellent originals ("Anything Southbound," "You Can't Do Wrong And Get By") as well as classic country (Jimmie Rodgers) and traditional bluegrass (Stanley Brothers, Flatt & Scruggs).

Cordle's voice is earthy and warm, even if his range is limited and his tone a bit plain. The players he's hired over the years (fiddler and tenor singer Glen Duncan, mandolinist Butch Baldassari, and banjoist Mike Bub, among many others) have turned out to be top-notch talents, yet Cordle and Lonesome Standard Time are not a flashy band by any means; instead, when they pick up their instruments and start to play, they wow their audiences with a spirited show that's easygoing, down-home and good fun.

⊙ **Larry Cordle, Glen Duncan, And Lonesome Standard Time** (1992; Sugar Hill). Cordle's debut is packed with great playing (most notably that of much-in-demand Nashville session fiddler Duncan) and excellent material, including "Lonesome Standard Time" (a hit for Kathy Mattea), the mournful but gorgeous "Lonesome Dove" and "The Fields Of Home," the lively "Lower On The Hog," and the common-sense song "You Can't Do Wrong And Get By." Cordle wrote all but one song—an instrumental called "Castillon Springs" penned by Duncan. The album was also nominated for a Grammy.

⊙ **Mighty Lonesome** (1993; Sugar Hill). An excellent follow-up to Cordle's superb debut. Duncan's name was dropped from the bill, but his fiddle is still an integral part of the band's hearty sound. Along with Cordle's originals are the traditional instrumental "Sugar In The Gourd" and songs by the Stanley Brothers and Flatt & Scruggs.

⊙ **Lonesome As It Gets** (1995; Sugar Hill). Cordle wrote or co-wrote half of this album's 12 tracks, the rest coming from Jimmie Rodgers ("Mother, The Queen Of My Heart"), John Prine ("Grandpa Was A Carpenter"), and LST fiddler Glen Duncan (the instrumental "Blue Field"), among others.

⊙ **Murder On Music Row** (1999; Shell Point Records). The title track is sort of a cornball concept, but it does ring with truth. As for the playing, it's hot from start to finish. And the songs—from originals like "Black Diamond Strings" and "Jesus And Bartenders" to the moving Bert Colwell recitation "Old Kentucky Miners"—are excellent, showing that Cordle and company are making some of the finest neo-traditional country and bluegrass in Nashville these days.

The Country Gentlemen

Progressive bluegrass got its full-fledged start with the Country Gentlemen, the first major band to kick off with a mix of bluegrass, folk, country, and rock material. The musical credentials of Charlie Waller and company are certainly sound, as was their love and respect for traditional music, but the new element was their progressive attitude and open-minded sense of adventure towards bluegrass; as a result, they attracted a large audience of urban intellectuals, many of whom were unfamiliar with the music's roots. In the process of all this, however, the Gentlemen helped create a new beginning for bluegrass, which during the late 1950s was being labeled "old-fashioned" and rapidly fading from country radio playlists. They also became the flagship band for a bluegrass scene building around the Washington, DC area—one that would continue to flourish for years to come, with the Gentlemen right there in the front line.

Guitarist and singer Charlie Waller is the lone founding member who's stuck with the band through its many incarnations. Other significant Gentlemen have gone on to form well-received bands of their own: John Duffey put together the DC-based Seldom Scene in 1971, and it quickly became one of the most popular bluegrass bands of its generation; Eddie Adcock, who quit the Gentlemen in 1970, headed for California and formed II (Second) Generation, a jazzy, decidedly electric bluegrass-rock outfit.

Waller, who was born in Texas and raised in Louisiana and DC, played with Earl Taylor in

Baltimore before joining mandolinist, singer and bandleader Buzz Busby's Bayou Boys, a bluegrass band that jumped between Shreveport, Louisiana (where they played the *Louisiana Hayride*) and the busy DC club scene. The Country Gentlemen were formed on the spur of the moment in 1957—Busby's group had been involved in a car accident, and Waller and banjoist Bill Emerson filled in for a Bayou Boys gig in Virginia—but the band didn't stabilize and fully kick into gear until 1959. By that stage, band membership had shifted and settled into the quartet of Waller, mandolinist and tenor vocalist John Duffey, banjoist Eddie Adcock, and bassist Tom Gray. Earlier Gentlemen incarnations had recorded a few singles and one album for Starday, but this band, which remained solid for five years (pretty good for bluegrass), recorded the band's first three albums for Folkways. These proved landmarks in the genre for their mix of old and new material (bluegrass, contemporary country, and old hillbilly songs), all of it played bluegrass style.

Though they'd omitted a fiddle player, the Gentlemen nonetheless had crafted themselves as a traditional acoustic bluegrass band. The music they created was bright, fast, strong, and perhaps even more revved up than usual ("hyper-bluegrass," historian Bill Malone called it)—a technique that served to showcase the musicians' talents and heighten the excitement at their concerts. Young, mostly collegiate folk revivalists were becoming more and more attracted to bluegrass for the mind-boggling playing of people like Earl Scruggs, and were less interested in a band's hard-earned country credentials (Scruggs played

Newport in 1959, but Flatt was left at home). The Gentlemen went for this audience and soon won them over. They played Dylan songs alongside traditional bluegrass numbers, eventually dabbling in pop material as well. Even their comedy (a standard segment of most bluegrass shows) was geared toward a younger, college-educated generation.

The Gentlemen did experiment with outside influences in their solos and arrangements, but because they basically remained true to the music's acoustic roots at a time when even traditional bands were toying with electric instruments—and because their top-notch playing was hard to resist—they won the support of young and old fans alike.

Waller and his gang continued to experiment with more eclectic material (such as a bluegrass version of the "Theme From Exodus") through the '60s and into the '70s. Among their most popular songs were "Bringing Mary Home" in 1965 and, from the 1970 album SOUND OFF, re-arranged versions of Manfred Mann's "Fox On The Run" and Crosby, Stills, and Nash's "Teach Your Children." The latter was voted Song of the Year in a *Muleskinner News* poll.

The Gentlemen's line-up has changed regularly over the years, though the mellow, soulful-voiced Waller has always remained at the helm. In the early '70s, the line-up included the talented Doyle Lawson, Bill Emerson and Bill Yates. Other notable members who've passed through the group over the years include Pete Kuykendall (founder of the magazine *Bluegrass Unlimited*), Ricky Skaggs, Jerry Douglas, Jimmy Gaudreau, and Norman Wright. The band continued to record through the '80s and into the '90s.

⊙ **Country Songs Old And New** (1960; Smithsonian/Folkways). Though technically not the Gentlemen's debut album (which had been released by Starday in 1959), the group's first for the Folkways label was the one that got them noticed on the folk revival and bluegrass scene. The mix of traditional and then-contemporary folk and country material was innovative at the time, and the group proved themselves solid players from the start.

⊙ **25 Years** (1986; Rebel). The 24 songs on this compilation—which celebrates the band's 25th anniversary—are culled from the various records they made during their long tenure on Rebel Records, to which they first signed in 1964. It's a great sampler of the different line-ups the band experienced during that time—and of the huge variety of material they covered, from "The Fields Have Turned Brown" and "Aunt

Dinah's Quilting Party" to "Teach Your Children" and "500 Miles." It's too bad the liner notes are minimal (no recording dates or song credits), but that hardly detracts from the high quality of the music inside. An excellent collection to start with.

⊙ **Sugar Hill Collection** (1995; Sugar Hill). This CD compiles 10 tracks each from two late-'80s releases on the Sugar Hill label: SIT DOWN YOUNG STRANGER and RIVER BOTTOM. Waller's voice is mellow and aged—a warm breath of country air—and the song choices include two by Kris Kristofferson and one each by Gordon Lightfoot and Dolly Parton. Not their most classic stuff, but pleasant enough.

J.D. Crowe

Laid-back bandleader and banjoist J.D. Crowe is a progressive bluegrass artist who got his start as a teenager in the 1950s playing with one of the greats, Jimmy Martin. He's since led a successful solo career that's lasted well into the '90s, making him a big-league player on the contemporary scene.

Crowe was born in Lexington, Kentucky on 27 August, 1937. Early on he was a big fan of Flatt & Scruggs, often attending the local *Kentucky Barn Dance*, where the duo regularly played. During his teenage years he played in various local bands as well as with Pee Wee Lambert and Curly Parker. His big break came in 1956, when Jimmy Martin was driving through Lexington and heard the young banjoist playing on the radio. The story goes that Martin drove straight to the station and offered Crowe a job on the spot.

In addition to traditional bluegrass, Crowe, like a growing number of younger pickers, was also interested in blues, R&B and rock'n'roll—influences that would eventually creep into his own music. With Martin, he even took to singing Little Richard songs.

Crowe stayed with Martin until 1962. During the next several years he played in various joints around Lexington, eventually forming his own band, the Kentucky Mountain Boys. One of his bandmembers during this time was Doyle Lawson, who's since gone on to sing a good deal of gospel bluegrass with his own group, Quicksilver. In a vein similar to the Country Gentlemen, Crowe and the Boys mixed traditional bluegrass with a more modern rock and country sound. They recorded three albums for the Lemco label,

including the excellent gospel album THE MODEL CHURCH.

In 1971, Crowe changed his band's name to the New South, a move intended to reflect his more solid commitment to progressive music, which was winning wider acceptance. (At the same time, and following the Osborne Brothers' lead, Crowe also made the transition from an all-acoustic band to one that included electric instruments.) The band that recorded with him on his 1975 album for Rounder, J.D. CROWE AND THE NEW SOUTH, featured a stellar cast of new-generation players, Ricky Skaggs, Jerry Douglas, Bobby Slone and Tony Rice, all of whom were members of Crowe's touring band at the time. The New South had first recorded for Starday, but thanks to the impeccable musicianship, the release on Rounder (an upstart indie "collective" label just getting its feet wet in progressive bluegrass) is today regarded as one of the standout bluegrass albums of the decade.

Crowe drifted even further toward progressive shores with subsequent albums, which continued to aggravate traditional fans, who had bristled already at Crowe's New South direction. At the same time, however, it brought him a wider audience. In 1980, he hooked up with Lawson, Rice, Bobby Hicks, and Todd Phillips; a year later they recorded an album for Rounder entitled simply THE BLUEGRASS ALBUM, which dug out old '50s bluegrass material and gave it a new polish. It sold well, and the group went on to record several more together—though the line-up eventually evolved to include Crowe, Rice, Lawson, Jerry Douglas, Mark Schatz, and Vassar Clements.

During the late '70s and early '80s, Crowe's own band included lead singer and guitarist Keith Whitley, then on the verge of his mainstream country career. In 1983, Crowe and the New South won a Grammy for their instrumental "Fireball." By 1988, Crowe had quit touring, though in the '90s he returned to it part-time.

⊙ **The Model Church** (1969; Lemco; reissued 1992; Rebel). Not only is THE MODEL CHURCH one of the first progressive gospel albums, but it's one of the best of Crowe's career. The line-up features Crowe and his Kentucky Mountain Boys: Doyle Lawson, Larry Rice, and Bobby Slone. The album's 11 all-acoustic songs are also the first gospel recordings of lead singer and guitarist Lawson, who later went on to record many more with his own group, Quicksilver. Lawson is largely responsible, too, for finding and arranging these songs.

⊙ **J.D. Crowe And The New South** (1975; Rounder). One of the seminal albums of the progressive bluegrass era. Crowe's New South band at this point included Ricky Skaggs, Jerry Douglas, and Tony Rice.

⊙ **The Bluegrass Album** (1981; Rounder). Tight, pretty four-part harmonies and fiery acoustic instrumental skills mark the debut album by this all-star group, which was conceived by guitarist and lead vocalist Tony Rice to let traditionalists know these progressive players still cared about their music's roots. Billing themselves simply as The Bluegrass Album Band, Rice, Crowe, Bobby Hicks, Doyle Lawson, and Todd Phillips shoot through an excellent collection of traditional material, from several songs by Monroe (including the haunting "River Of Death") to Lawson's arrangement of "Model Church." Due to this album's popularity, the group (with varied line-ups) went on to record several more together.

Hazel Dickens

> "This role of being the chief cook and bottle washer, have the kids and stay at home—I think it's just too much to expect of a human being."
>
> —Hazel Dickens

W hile most of her folk-music peers of the 1960s and '70s were raised and educated in urban areas, Hazel Dickens hailed from deep in West Virginia's coal-mining territory. Her rural roots are as genuine as they come—a heritage that's reflected in her strong, earthy voice and heartstopping original songs like "Will Jesus Wash The Bloodstains From Your Hands," "West Virginia My Home," "Mama's Hand," and the devastating "Black Lung" (two of her brothers would eventually die from the disease). Like Doc Watson, another rural artist embraced by urban folkies, Dickens is no country innocent. Her musicianship is sturdy and confident, her voice vibrant and original, and her personality—both on stage and off—is as intelligent as it is warm and easygoing. Social concerns, especially those of mine workers, are an important element of her music; in 1976 several of her songs were used in Barbara Kopples' *Harlan County, USA*, an excellent Academy Award-winning documentary about struggling coal miners. She also championed feminist issues in her songs ("Working Girl

Blues," "Don't Put Her Down, You Helped Put Her There"), which came on top of the fact that when she started out, she and her frequent duet partner, Alice Gerrard, were among the few female singer-songwriters on the bluegrass and old-time circuits.

Hazel Jane Dickens was born on 1 June, 1935 in Mercer County, West Virginia. She was one of eleven children in a family so poor that finding enough food to eat was often a struggle. She learned music from her father, a banjo-playing Baptist preacher, and from the radio, where she soaked up the music of the Carter Family, Uncle Dave Macon, Wilma Lee and Stoney Cooper, Molly O'Day, and plenty of others. At the age of sixteen she and three of her siblings moved to Baltimore to find work, and Hazel wound up in a series of odd jobs, from cleaning houses to working in a tin-can factory. Baltimore and Washington were fast becoming havens for displaced country people, and bluegrass and old-time music thrived here. It was in this new urban world that Hazel was exposed to music through festivals and picking parties, and it's where she first started singing publicly. She eventually met Mike Seeger, a musician and avid old-time music fan, and with him she formed a band that also included two of her brothers. They played shows around the Baltimore and Washington, DC area. After that Hazel sang and played bass with groups such as the Greenbriar Boys and the Pike County Boys.

During the '60s she became good friends with Alice Gerrard (who would later marry Mike Seeger), a classically trained, college-educated musician from California, and a musical partnership developed that has lasted on and off ever since. They were soon writing and singing together— Alice's smoother voice blending surprisingly well with Hazel's sharper, grittier tones. The pair were also enamored with early feminist songs, many found after hours of digging through the Library of Congress archives. In 1965 Folkways released an album of their material titled WHO'S THAT KNOCKING (AND OTHER BLUEGRASS COUNTRY MUSIC). She and Alice recorded one further album for Folkways, WON'T YOU COME & SING FOR ME?, which was recorded around the same time, though not released until 1973. They also collaborated with Mike Seeger, Tracy Schwartz, and Lamar Grief as the Strange Creek Singers, releasing one album in 1972 (see Mike Seeger entry). Hazel and Alice toured together all over the country during this time and became regulars at bluegrass and folk festivals, clubs and rallies. Rounder Records then released two further Hazel and Alice

Hazel Dickens (left) and Alice Gerrard, Berkeley, California, 1997

⊙ **Hazel Dickens And Alice Gerrard** (1976; Rounder; reissued 1998). An excellent collaboration between these two influential country artists. In terms of both songs and arrangements it's also a much more mature piece of work than their previous Folkways efforts (makes sense, since they were cut a decade earlier). Highlights include Bill Monroe's "True Life Blues" and the Dickens compositions "Working Girl Blues" as well as the hauntingly beautiful "West Virginia My Home."

⊙ **A Few Old Memories** (1995; Rounder). Compiles 18 songs from Hazel's 1980s albums. Perhaps even more succinctly than her previous collections with Alice, Hazel's solo work mixes her political and social ideals with her love of honky tonk, old-time, bluegrass, and contemporary folk music. Some of her most enduring original songs, including "It's Hard To Tell The Singer From The Song" and "Old Calloused Hands," are included here. It's a superb starting point.

⊙ **Pioneering Women Of Bluegrass** (1996; Smithsonian/Folkways). This collection brings together the 2 landmark albums Hazel and Alice recorded in the mid-'60s for Folkways, WHO'S THAT KNOCKING and WON'T YOU COME & SING FOR ME? Two women harmonizing together (as so many men had previously done) on songs they'd fiercely compiled on their own was a rarity in the bluegrass world. Musically this collection has more of a retro vibe than Hazel's later, more mature material. But their harmonies on songs by the Delmore Brothers ("Gonna Lay Down My Old Guitar"), Bill Monroe ("The One I Love Is Gone"), and the Carter Family, among others, are fine-tuned and hauntingly gorgeous. Musicians include fiddler Chubby Wise and mandolinist Dave Grisman.

⊙ **Heart Of A Singer** (1998; Rounder). Hazel's first new recording in more than a decade is a collaboration with Ginny Hawker and Carol Elizabeth Jones. The two- and three-part harmonies between the women are the heart and soul of this album, while the musical roots remain firmly grounded in Appalachian soil. Standout songs include Woody Guthrie's "Forsaken Lover," Steve Young's "Old Memories Mean Nothing To Me," and Jenny Lou Carson's "Jealous Heart."

albums during the early '70s, HAZEL & ALICE and HAZEL DICKENS AND ALICE GERRARD, which expanded their musical horizons beyond bluegrass and old-time music and showed a deeper, more mature musical sensibility.

In 1976, however, the duo split. Alice went on to perform with the all-female band the Harmony Sisters, and she also began publishing the quarterly music journal *Old Time Herald*. Hazel's solo career picked up almost immediately, thanks in part to her songs appearing in *Harlan County, USA*. Rounder maintained her recording contract, and in 1980 she cut her first solo album for the label, HARD HITTING SONGS FOR HARD HIT PEOPLE. She's remained associated with Rounder ever since, recording several more albums including BY THE SWEAT OF MY BROW and IT'S HARD TO TELL THE SINGER FROM THE SONG. She's such a strong songwriter, and her voice has held up so beautifully over the years, that it's hard to go wrong with any of them. In 1994 Hazel received the Merit Award from the International Bluegrass Music Association, becoming the first female artist so honored. In the mid-'90s she teamed up again with Alice Gerrard for a national tour—their first in two decades—and together they sounded as fresh and inspiring as ever. The impact Dickens has had on younger generations is probably impossible to measure, but it's popped up in groups from the Judds to rising bluegrass star Lynn Morris (who cut a beautiful rendition of Hazel's "Mama's Hand") to alt.country groups Hazeldine and Freakwater.

Hazel Dickens

The Dillards

The Dillards were one of the most popular and influential progressive bluegrass bands to crop up during the early 1960s; along with the Kentucky Colonels and the Hillmen, they were also one of the chief bluegrass elements of a burgeoning West Coast folk-rock scene. With a progressive outlook toward the music they grew up playing, the Dillards acted as a bridge between generations, bringing young people into the world of bluegrass and at the same time opening up that largely conservative community to new musical ideas. Focused initially around singer-guitarist Rodney Dillard and his banjo-playing brother Doug, the Dillards at first mixed bluegrass with folk influences ("coffeehouse bluegrass" writes Neil Rosenberg in his excellent book *Bluegrass: A History*), which appealed to revivalist audiences; when Doug left the band, their sound evolved into easygoing country-rock. Hillbilly humor was also a big part of their act, which gave the band a corny veneer and probably translated better when heard at festivals and clubs back then. That aside, plenty of Dillards songs have endured over the years, thanks in no small part to the bandmembers' instrumental prowess.

The hillbilly image the Dillards adopted wasn't entirely fabricated: Doug and Rodney Dillard did indeed hail from the Ozark mountains, both having grown up in Salem, Missouri. They played bluegrass together as boys, and landed a gig on the *Ozark Jubilee* radio program. They recorded a couple of singles and played with a few different bluegrass outfits in the area before forming the first incarnation of the Dillards with mandolinist Dean Webb and bassist Mitch Jayne (who helped shape the group's image and became its spokesperson). In 1962, the band moved to Southern California with big dreams of making it in the music business. Immediately after arriving in LA they set up in the lobby of the folk club, Ash Grove, during a Greenbriar Boys gig and gathered a crowd. Elektra producer Jim Dickson (who'd soon be busy producing the Byrds) heard the band and quickly signed them. In 1963 Elektra released BACK PORCH BLUEGRASS, the first of five albums the Dillards recorded for the label.

The Dillards were a hit with young folk revivalists, who had only recently discovered bluegrass through the likes of Flatt & Scruggs and the Country Gentlemen. The Dillards appealed to their audience by mixing the bluegrass styles they'd played back in Missouri with folk, country, and eventually some rock influences as well. (Their second album, LIVE!!! ALMOST!!!, included the first bluegrass cover of a Bob Dylan song, "Walking Down The Line.") Dillards bassist/spokesperson Jayne played up the band's country-boy background, which further appealed to folk audiences.

Bluegrass revivalists the Dillards

ANDREW PUTLER

The Dillards

The boys also played folk festivals regularly and gained national exposure by appearing on the *Andy Griffith Show* as members of the Darling Family. In addition to their Elektra albums, producer Dickson also recorded the Dillards, Dobro player Tut Taylor, and an up-and-coming guitarist named Glen Campbell on the World Pacific label under the name the Folkswingers.

The Dillards' third album, PICKIN' AND FIDDLIN', featured fiddler Byron Berline, whom they'd met in Oklahoma a couple of years earlier— a bold move since fiddle music had been out of fashion for nearly a decade. (Berline would later join the Blue Grass Boys and then go on to become one of the premier fiddlers on the progressive side of bluegrass.) Doug and Rodney also played on the soundtrack to *Bonnie And Clyde*. By 1967, however, Doug had left the Dillards, and he eventually hooked up with Gene Clark, who'd recently quit the Byrds. He played on GENE CLARK AND THE GOSDIN BROTHERS and then the pair released two albums as Dillard & Clark. Doug also recorded THE BANJO ALBUM in 1968 which featured Clark, Bernie Leadon and Dillard's pal John Hartford (who'd grown up in St Louis). From the '70s onward Doug recorded further solo and group material and did session work for the likes of the Beach Boys and Glen Campbell.

Banjo player, singer and songwriter Herb Pedersen (who'd just finished a stint with Flatt & Scruggs) took Doug's spot in the Dillards, and with his input the band's sound shifted even further from the familiar bluegrass-folk mixture and more toward country-rock (thanks in part to the popularity of the Byrds). In 1968 Elektra released WHEATSTRAW SUITE, which included drums, steel guitars and countrified covers of popular songs like Tim Hardin's "Reason To Believe" and the Beatles' "I've Just Seen A Face." They followed it up with COPPERFIELDS in 1971, the highly orchestrated title track of which is a far cry from the staunch bluegrass and folk roots that shine brightly on early songs like "Dooley" or "Polly Vaughn." Purism aside, though, some of this later Elektra material—"She Sang Hymns Out Of Tune" and the pretty "Lemon Chimes"—are among the most fully realized and enduring songs the Dillards recorded.

During the '70s the Dillards roster changed frequently—Pedersen was replaced by banjoist Billy Ray Lathum, Jayne by bassist Jeff Gilkinson, and so on. The Dillards recorded for Anthem and Poppy, then finally landed on Flying Fish in 1977. Old bandmembers began returning for reunion performances and recordings, the culmination of which was the 1980 album HOMECOMING &

FAMILY REUNION, recorded in Salem on what the town had declared "Dillard Day" (8 August). The band's line-up continued to evolve well into the next decade. The core membership for their 1990 album LET IT FLY (released on Vanguard) consisted of Rodney Dillard, Webb, Jayne, and banjoist Steve Cooley (with Berline and Pedersen, among others, as guests). Doug, Rodney and John Hartford also released albums together as Dillard Hartford Dillard, and during the '80s Rodney formed his own Rodney Dillard Band. Jayne also moonlighted fairly successfully as a writer; his 1969 book *The Fish Hawk* was even adapted for film in 1980.

⊙ **There Is A Time (1963–70)** (1991; Vanguard). An excellent round-up of classic Dillards material culled from the band's 5 Elektra albums, this is the only Dillards album most casual fans need. It captures the band's shifting styles very well—from the bluegrass-folk of "Dooley" to the lush country-rock of "Copperfields." There's plenty of Ozark cornpone to sift through, and some uninteresting covers, but standout songs such as "She Sang Hymns Out Of Tune," "Lemon Chimes," Dylan's "Walkin' Down The Line," and Harry Nilsson's "Rainmaker" are reason enough to see why this band made such an indelible mark.

Jim Eanes

Virginia native Homer Robert Eanes, Jr. was a bluegrass and country recording artist from the early 1950s all the way into the '90s. His baritone voice is smooth and warm, and his musical approach was even-keeled and pleasantly down-home. As well as a singer and guitarist he was an accomplished songwriter. Born on 6 December, 1923 in Mountain Valley, Virginia, Eanes began his career as a member of Roy Hall And The Blue Ridge Entertainers in the early '40s. Later he worked with Flatt & Scruggs, Bill Monroe, and other artists. He began performing under his own name in 1949, appearing on the WWVA *Wheeling Jamboree* soon after with his band the Shenandoah Valley Boys. He also cut his first records for the Rich-R-Tone and Blue Ridge labels. Decca signed him in 1952 and released more than a dozen sides that tried to sell him as a country artist—even bringing him to Nashville to record with studio musicians—though he did cut some mountain-bred bluegrass songs as well. In the mid-'50s he assembled a new version of his Shenandoah Valley Boys and began recording for Starday. After that he worked with several different smaller labels and began concentrating more closely on bluegrass. During the late '60s Eanes briefly took the leadership reins of the Bluegrass Cut-Ups, which had been Red Smiley's group after the great Reno & Smiley duo parted ways. Under his own name he continued cutting records and touring through the next couple of decades. In the early '90s he celebrated half a century in the music business with his 50TH ANNIVERSARY album. He died on 21 November, 1995.

⊙ **Classic Bluegrass** (1992; Rebel). This collection is a mix of mid- to late-1970s and even late-'80s recordings—perhaps not as "classic" as the title implies. Nonetheless, Eanes' aging voice is still in quite nice shape, and the songs (many of them Eanes originals such as "Baby Blue Eyes," "I'll Pretend It's Raining," and "Rose Garden Waltz") have a warm, folky spirit that goes down slow and easy.

⊙ **Your Old Standby: Complete Starday Recordings** (1998; Starday). A 2-CD collection of the recordings Eanes and his Shenandoah Valley Boys made during the late '50s and early '60s for Starday.

⊙ **The Complete Decca Recordings** (1999; Bear Family). All the recordings Eanes cut for Decca in the early '50s, including some unreleased tracks, are packed onto this single CD. Save for a handful of songs, the music is more country than bluegrass; titles include "I Cried Again," which Hank Williams often sang, "Rose Garden Waltz," "Wiggle Worm Wiggle," and a couple of Red-baiting beauties: "They Locked God Outside The Iron Curtain" and Scotty Wiseman's "I'm No Communist."

Flatt & Scruggs

"Elvis was for the girls. Earl Scruggs was for the men."

—Del McCoury

B ill Monroe may be the father of bluegrass, but Flatt & Scruggs have done more to popularize the music than anyone else. Flatt's guitar picking and strong lead voice, coupled with the mighty banjo playing of Earl Scruggs, have become defining characteristics of the music. The pair's songs and performances are some of the best-known songs in bluegrass—most especially their far-too-overplayed recordings for the soundtracks to *The Beverly Hillbillies* ("The Ballad Of Jed Clampett") and *Bonnie And Clyde* ("Foggy Mountain Breakdown").

Flatt & Scruggs' popularity began in 1945 during their tenure with Monroe's Blue Grass Boys. It was here—on the *Opry* stage, during the group's long tours through the East, and on recordings like "Heavy Traffic Ahead," "Mollie And Tenbrooks," and "Blue Grass Breakdown"—that country fans were first bowled over by the prowess and professionalism of these two musical wizards. Flatt, who joined the group first, was soon established as Monroe's emcee and "first lieutenant," a moniker given him by *Opry* founder George D. Hay. And the speed and complexity of Scruggs' three-finger banjo playing turned him almost overnight into the shining star of Monroe's band—and at the same time made thousands of WSM listeners sit up and take notice of Monroe's new musical style. Because of these two players' popularity, it's no surprise that, once they figured out they could make far more money as headliners than as sidemen, they quit Monroe's band to strike out on their own as Lester Flatt, Earl Scruggs, and the Foggy Mountain Boys. It's also no big shocker that, with his stellar band suddenly dissolved, Monroe would refuse to speak to his former partners for decades to come.

Lester Flatt was born on 14 June, 1914 in Overton County, Tennessee, in the Cumberland Mountains. When he was twelve, his family moved to the vicinity of Sparta, Tennessee, and he dropped out of school to work in the sawmill with his father. He married Gladys Lee Stacy in 1931, worked a series of textile-mill jobs, and played music on the side. He was a big fan of the Monroe Brothers and of fiddler Arthur Smith, who approached old-time tunes with new, exciting energy. In 1939 Flatt joined the Charlie Scott Harmonizers, and then he moved to North Carolina and played with Clyde Moody under the name the Carolina Woodchoppers. Flatt was living again in Sparta when in 1942 Charlie Monroe asked both Gladys and him to join his band, the Kentucky Pardners (Gladys sang under the name Bobbie Jean). Then he got another call, this time from Bill Monroe, who'd heard his work with Charlie and wanted Lester to join the Blue Grass Boys. By 1945 Flatt was Monroe's new guitarist and lead singer.

Flatt and Scruggs didn't know each other until they began working together in Monroe's band. They were hired several months apart; in fact, before Scruggs' audition, Flatt even suggested that Monroe omit the banjo from the Blue Grass Boys' line-up. As soon as he heard young Scruggs play, however, he changed his tune.

Flatt & Scruggs on the *Opry* stage

Earl Scruggs didn't invent the three-finger banjo style itself; the technique was fairly familiar throughout the North Carolina region where Scruggs grew up. Snuffy Jenkins (who'd worked with Byron Parker's Mountaineers, and whom Scruggs had heard as a child) and string-band leader Charlie Poole are among the better-known players who employed three-finger playing in their music. What Scruggs did, though, was start with that basic technique and use it to create his own fast and fluid style. In the process he not only popularized three-finger playing (which quickly became known as "Scruggs style") among a whole new generation of musicians and fans, but also the instrument itself. In addition, he was not a comedian, a role that traditionally went hand-in-hand with the banjo.

Scruggs was born on 6 January, 1924 in Cleveland County, North Carolina. It was an area rich in traditional music, and local banjo players like Mack Woolbright and Smith Hammett were early influences. Scruggs picked up banjo early on, and by the age of ten he could play a three-finger roll. Soon he was on the radio with the Carolina Wildcats and, later, the Morris Brothers (a group that, coincidentally, banjoist Don Reno also played with early on).

After high school Scruggs worked in a mill supporting his widowed mother and sister, which allowed him exemption from the draft. In 1945 he was working in Knoxville as a full-time member of "Lost" John Miller's band. When Miller quit

performing, Scruggs' friend, fiddler Jim Shumate, set up an audition for him with Monroe's Blue Grass Boys. When Scruggs joined the group he was only twenty-one years old. More than any other of Monroe's sidemen, his mindblowing banjo picking fueled the fire and fanned the flames of the master's music, inspiring the work of the other players—including Monroe.

Flatt, Scruggs and bassist/comedian Cedric Rainwater left Monroe's band in early 1948. They initially claimed individual reasons for leaving— they were tired of the road—but it's also clear they knew they'd make big money as headliners themselves. Flatt, too, had written lots of songs during his tenure with Monroe, on top of being the group's emcee, so he and Scruggs were well seasoned musicians. They soon began performing together along with Shumate and up-and-coming singer Mac Wiseman. They played in North Carolina and then Bristol, Virginia, calling themselves the Foggy Mountain Boys. Later in 1948, they signed with Mercury Records. Before the year was out, Shumate and Wiseman were gone (the latter to Monroe's band), and mandolin player and vocalist Curley Seckler—a former Blue Grass Boy—was in. He remained with Flatt & Scruggs on and off until 1962.

During these early years, many of the Foggy Mountain Boys were alumni of Monroe's band; this further contributed to the idea that what the Foggy Mountain Boys played was "blue grass style" music. The differences in styles between the two acts, however, were growing. Though Monroe continued to employ "Scruggs style" banjoists, Earl's banjo playing was far more prominent in the Foggy Mountain Boys' arrangements—and the mandolin less so. And where Monroe's voice grew higher and sharper during the '50s, Flatt's voice mellowed and stayed within a more moderate range.

Flatt & Scruggs signed with Columbia Records (Monroe's former label) in late 1950. They had a Top 10 single in 1952 with "'Tis Sweet To Be Remembered," but thanks in no small part to the Opry's refusal to let them join (they'd quit one of the show's top acts, after all), Flatt & Scruggs struggled during this period, playing shows on small radio stations in the Southeast as well as gigs in odd places like furniture stores and drive-in movie theaters. (Drive-ins had just become popular, and they frequently also hosted live music—the stage was the top of the concession stand, and applause came by way of car horns).

In 1953 Flatt & Scruggs were offered a job by the Martha White Flour Company to play a morning show on WSM in Nashville. With this new sponsor, the band reached a turning point in terms of getting their name out on a much larger scale. The association with Martha White lasted more than fifteen years.

With their popularity growing steadily, the Opry was unable to ignore Flatt & Scruggs anymore; in 1955 they were finally invited to join the cast. They also began a series of television programs (sponsored by Martha White) in various Appalachian towns; by 1959, the shows entered syndication. Songs like "Foggy Mountain Breakdown," "Earl's Breakdown," and "Cabin On The Hill" gained Flatt & Scruggs further acclaim. Their 1957 release FOGGY MOUNTAIN JAMBOREE was the first bluegrass LP devoted to a single band—further proof of their popularity at the time, since albums were initially only issued by a label's biggest groups. Bandmembers during the '50s included, along with Seckler, fiddler Paul Warren, bassist Jake Tullock, and Dobro player Josh Graves—the last of the list adding a new and different element to the group's sound.

During the '50s, the urban folk revival had been building, and by the end of the decade many revivalists were turning to bluegrass for its "authentic" sound. Scruggs' playing, in particular, stood out from the crowd, and he became the initial focus for many of these new fans (a point that likely also irked Monroe). Folk music journals like Sing Out ran articles praising Scruggs, and he was asked to play (without Flatt) at the first Newport Folk Festival in 1959. Two years earlier, Folkways had

even issued a bluegrass compilation album entitled AMERICAN BANJO SCRUGGS STYLE. Suddenly, bluegrass was reaching entire new audiences, who were acknowledging it as authentic "folk" music.

Flatt & Scruggs continued to chart during the '60s, more so than any other bluegrass band, with songs like "Crying My Heart Out Over You," "Go Home," "New York Town," "Petticoat Junction," and "You Are My Flower." When "The Ballad Of Jed Clampett" was chosen as the theme song to the TV show The Beverly Hillbillies, it shot to #1, the first bluegrass song to do so; it even crossed over to the pop charts. As Flatt & Scruggs' popularity grew, however, so did the rift between them. Flatt detested the "modernization" of their traditional sound—which Columbia had pushed on them in order to satisfy the younger market—while Scruggs was more than willing to experiment with folk and rock songs and new instrumentation (including drums). The two men eventually parted ways in February, 1969, each forming his own band.

Flatt gathered former bandmembers Warren, Graves' and Tullock—as well as Vic Jordan and Roland White—and returned to playing more traditional music under the name Nashville Grass. A young mandolinist named Marty Stuart was one of several subsequent players who passed through Flatt's band. Flatt also cut three albums with Mac Wiseman for RCA that are well worth a listen. In the latter half of the '70s Flatt recorded for the Flying Fish, Canaan and CMH labels.

Scruggs, meanwhile, teamed up with his long-haired sons Randy, Gary and Steve, drummer Jody Maphis and, eventually, Josh Graves (who'd first played with Flatt for two years). Signing with Columbia and calling themselves the Earl Scruggs Revue, they shifted further away from bluegrass, recording songs by Bob Dylan, Rod Stewart, and Shel Silverstein, for instance (along with material written by Gary and Earl); they ultimately developed a fairly straightforward, electrified country-rock sound that was augmented by Earl's banjo and Graves' Dobro. In addition to recording steadily with the Revue throughout the '70s, Scruggs also helped the Nitty Gritty Dirt Band assemble its all-star cast of older musicians for the 1972 album WILL THE CIRCLE BE UNBROKEN? Other artists Scruggs recorded with during the '70s and '80s included Dylan, Doc Watson, Joan Baez, and the Byrds (EARL SCRUGGS—HIS FAMILY AND FRIENDS, 1971), Tom T. Hall (THE STORYTELLER AND THE BANJO MAN, 1982), and Ricky Skaggs, Lacy J. Dalton, and others (TOP OF THE WORLD, 1983). In the '90s Scruggs retired, mainly for health reasons.

Flatt & Scruggs

Flatt & Scruggs did play together again shortly before Lester Flatt's death in 1979. In 1985, the duo was inducted into the Country Music Hall of Fame, the second bluegrass act to be so honored after Bill Monroe. In 1991, each was inducted individually into the Bluegrass Hall of Honor.

⊙ **You Can Feel It In Your Soul** (1988; County). Thirteen gospel songs from Flatt & Scruggs' repertoire offer a slightly different perspective on this seminal group.

⊙ **1949–1959** (1992; Bear Family). For the completist, Bear Family has compiled a 4-CD box set of Flatt & Scruggs songs recorded during the golden years of their first decade together. Still not satisfied? Two more box sets, 1959–1963 (5 CDs) and 1964–1969 (6 CDs), pick up where this one leaves off.

⊙ **The Complete Mercury Sessions** (1992; Mercury). Flatt & Scruggs recorded for Mercury between 1948 and 1950, and the songs from those years include "Foggy Mountain Breakdown" and "Roll In My Sweet Baby's Arms." Essential early material.

⊙ **The Essential Flatt & Scruggs** (1997; Sony Legacy). There are many worthwhile Flatt & Scruggs compilations on the market, but this one makes a great starting point: a double-disc collection of the pair's Columbia material from both the 1950s and '60s.

Béla Fleck

Named after composer Béla Bartók, Fleck is a New York City boy who grew up to become one of the top banjo players in modern bluegrass. However, with the New Grass Revival and, later, his own band the Flecktones, he put plenty of distance between his kind of grass and the traditional turf once ruled by Earl Scruggs and Don Reno. Flatt & Scruggs were an early influence on Fleck, who didn't get his first banjo until the age of fifteen. But, studying at an art and music high school in New York, he became equally versed in the work of jazz greats like Charlie Parker, John Coltrane, and Chick Corea, whose music Fleck reworked for banjo. After high school, he played with the Boston band, Tasty Licks, before moving to Kentucky and joining Spectrum. By the age of twenty, he'd recorded his first solo album, CROSSING THE TRACKS, which was extremely well received, especially considering Fleck had only been playing banjo for five years.

In 1982, Fleck left Spectrum and joined New Grass Revival, the progressive bluegrass band that inspired the "newgrass" tag. At that point New Grass Revival (which had been around for ten years) included mandolin player Sam Bush, bassist John Cowan and guitarist Pat Flynn, and it was teetering on the borderline between folky grass and pop. Fleck played with that band until it broke up in 1990, during which time his song "Drive" from the 1988 album NEW GRASS REVIVAL was nominated for a Grammy. As a side project in 1989, under the name Strength In Numbers, Fleck, Bush, fiddler Mark O'Connor, bassist Edgar Meyer, and Dobroist Jerry Douglas recorded the album THE TELLURIDE SESSIONS.

After New Grass Revival split up, Fleck finally formed his own band, the Flecktones, who released their debut on Warner Brothers in 1990. By this stage, however, any trace of traditional bluegrass was far in the distance. One of Fleck's bandmates, Roy Wooten (aka "Futureman"), played a guitar-shaped drum contraption called a synth-ax-drumitar; another, Howard Levy, played harmonica, piano, synthesizer and pennywhistle. Their albums took on kooky names like FLIGHT OF THE COSMIC HIPPO and UFO TOFU and featured a well-honed but slick and thoroughly electronified mix of bluegrass, jazz and world beat. Though greats like Scruggs have praised Fleck's playing in the past (and there's no question the man knows the ups and downs of his axe), these days Fleck's music—and his audience—is as pop as any that's ever passed through the world of bluegrass.

⊙ **Crossing The Tracks** (1979; Rounder). Fleck's first solo album, made when he'd been playing the banjo for only five years.

⊙ **Greatest Hits Of The 20th Century** (1999; Warner Brothers). Collects material that has appeared on such Warner Brothers albums as FLIGHT OF THE COSMIC HIPPO, UFO TOFU, THREE FLEW OVER THE CUCKOO'S NEST and TALKES FROM THE ACOUSTIC PLANET. Depending on how green you like your grass, you'll either lap up this material like a dog in the desert or want to keep a healthy distance.

Jim & Jesse

Sweet, mountain-home harmonies and an easy-going, folk-inspired sound are qualities permeating the music of Jim & Jesse McReynolds.

Gathering Momentum: The IBMA Comes Of Age

The quick growth and rising popularity of the International Bluegrass Music Association (IBMA) is yet another indication of just how strong the worldwide bluegrass community is even half a century past the music's so-called "golden era"—and how that community continues to look after its own.

A non-profit professional trade organization, the IBMA was formed to help promote bluegrass music and to bring professional and amateur musicians, industry executives and employees (promoters, agents, record companies, retailers, talent buyers), journalists, DJs, fans, and other bluegrass-oriented folks together under a single roof. "We're like the chamber of commerce for the worldwide bluegrass family," explains Nancy Cardwell, special projects co-ordinator for the IBMA since 1994 and one of the group's three fulltime staffers.

Conceived in a Nashville board room in 1985 by a handful of industry professionals, the IBMA has grown from a founding membership of 57 to one that in 1997 exceeded 2600 and included people from all fifty states and thirty different countries. In 1986 the IBMA set up permanent headquarters in Owensboro, a Kentucky town set on a deep bend in the Ohio River between Louisville and Evansville, Indiana (and about 50 miles from Rosine, the birthplace of Bill Monroe). The group chose Owensboro because, at the same time the IBMA was forming, the Owensboro-Davies County Tourist Commission was busy with bluegrass plans of its own, which included a museum, a trade show, a professional organization, and a festival (the commission staged its first festival, called Bluegrass With Class, in 1985). When the commission got wind of the IBMA, the two groups quickly joined forces.

Among the resources the IBMA offers its members are consultation services, an event liability insurance plan, a bimonthly newsletter called *International Bluegrass*, the Bluegrass Trust Fund (which gives financial assistance to members during emergencies), and a database of specialized information (talent buyers, clubs, media contacts, regional associations, etc.). The IBMA has also "given those within the community a single place to deal with issues," says Ken Irwin, co-founder and co-owner of Rounder Records, whose label has released bluegrass records since 1971. And, he notes, it's become a vital point of contact between the bluegrass community and outsiders looking for information about the music. Cardwell agrees. "One of our main purposes is to be a source for networking. Someone calls up and wants to pitch a bluegrass radio show to their local station. We can give them demographic information, offer marketing tools, and put them in touch with someone who's done it successfully somewhere else."

The IBMA is most visible each fall, when it holds its annual World of Bluegrass trade show and Fan Fest bluegrass festival. The trade show was first held in 1986 in conjunction with the tourist commission's second Bluegrass With Class festival; a year later the IBMA had taken over festival duties, renaming it the Bluegrass Fan Fest.

Both Owensboro and Louisville have hosted the week-long gathering, which is no simple backyard barbecue: in 1996 attendance topped 20,000. Major bluegrass acts perform each year at Fan Fest, and all of them donate their services. Half of the money raised during the festival and related events then goes toward promoting IBMA projects (this event coupled with annual membership dues are the IBMA's chief sources of income), and rest is dropped into the Bluegrass Trust Fund.

Since 1990, the centerpoint of the event has been the annual International Bluegrass Music Awards. Similar in structure to the Grammys and Country Music Association awards, the categories include entertainer of the year, male and female vocalists of the year, song and album of the year, instrumental performers of the year, and so on.

The IBMA's ultimate honor, however—which is given each year during the awards ceremony—is induction into the Bluegrass Hall of Honor. This prestigious pantheon—modeled after Nashville's Country Music Hall of Fame—was established in 1991, and the first person inducted was, of course, Bill Monroe. Inductees since then include Flatt & Scruggs, the Stanley Brothers, Reno & Smiley, Mac Wiseman, Jim & Jesse, the Osborne Brothers, Jimmy Martin, the "classic" Country Gentlemen, Bluegrass Unlimited editor Peter Kuykendall, and Josh Graves.

The Hall of Honor itself is housed in the International Bluegrass Music Museum in Owensboro. The museum, says Cardwell, is "a separate entity. They have a separate board of directors and a different mission statement. We're more industry focused, interested in promoting the music; their goal is to preserve the history and develop a place for people to remember bluegrass music."

To contact the IBMA, write them at 207 East Second Street, Owensboro, KY 42303, or check their Web site (Ⓦ www.ibma.org).

These two brothers were among the first wave of bluegrass bands to crop up in the early 1950s—the genre's golden era—but their sound was notably different from classic acts like Flatt & Scruggs. Instead of following closely in the footsteps of the master, Bill Monroe, Jim & Jesse deftly blended

Jim & Jesse

the instrumentation and arrangements of traditional bluegrass with the haunting country harmonies of brother duos like Ira and Charlie Louvin. Instead of a speeding musical freight train, Jim & Jesse's songs (usually) moved at a more moderate pace. Their vocals could and did reach the high registers, but the brothers tended to avoid sharp, piercing edges, singing instead in warmer, gentler tones—Jesse's mellow-bodied lead voice blending beautifully with Jim's tenor.

By the mid-'60s, Jim & Jesse had gained national acclaim. The only drawback to their success, however, at least in the minds of many traditionalists, was that the brothers achieved it by marrying their beautiful harmonies to the Nashville Sound and bending more and more toward country, pop and rock numbers, such as the trucker's anthem "Diesel On My Tail." This has led them to be underrated today, at least in relation to other bluegrass acts from the '50s. However, their early material was some of the loveliest and most moving rural music made during that era, and to overlook it is a crime.

The McReynolds brothers were born in the farm and coal mining country of Wise County, Virginia—James Monroe on 13 February, 1927 and Jesse Lester on 9 July, 1929. Among their musical family members was a fiddling grandfather who'd recorded for Victor in 1927. The boys played and sang with their family regularly, and like many young musicians during the '30s, they were enamored with popular brother acts like the Delmores and the Monroes.

Jim & Jesse didn't take the possibilities of a musical career seriously until after World War II. In 1947 they won a spot on WNVA in Norton, Virginia—the same station where the Stanley Brothers had started only a few months earlier. After this they played a series of local stations, some as far away as Iowa and Kansas.

While working a Middletown, Ohio radio gig in 1951, they cut their first sides in nearby Cincinnati for Kentucky Records—ten gospel songs that also featured vocalist Larry Roll. In 1952, they joined the *Kentucky Barn Dance*, and soon after landed a record contract with Capitol. The band, newly christened the Virginia Boys, included banjoist Hoke Jenkins (nephew of Snuffy Jenkins, one of the earliest three-finger stylists) and guitarist Curley Seckler—both of whom the brothers had played with earlier—along with bassist Bob Moore and fiddler James Loden (who'd soon be known as country star Sonny James). Jim played a steady rhythm guitar, but it's Jesse's skills on mandolin that were the standout feature of the group's

sound—a flat-picking style modeled after Scruggs' banjo playing.

Their first Capitol single was the Louvin Brothers song "Are You Missing Me." Just when it started to show chart promise, however, Jesse was drafted into the army. They rushed through another recording session before he was shipped to Korea (where for a time he played in a band with Charlie Louvin). After his return, Jim & Jesse recorded once more for Capitol and played on a series of radio programs. By the end of 1955, however, which was a critical time in their young career, the brothers met with another obstacle: Capitol dropped them. The burgeoning teen music market was now the focus of most major labels, and Jim & Jesse's traditional acoustic sound just didn't fit into the business plan. It would be another three years before they were signed again.

Jim & Jesse persevered through these lean times, eventually updating their traditional sound with more modern country material, a survival tactic that other traditional bluegrass acts had also employed. By the end of the decade things began to turn around. They found success in Florida on the *Swanee River Jamboree*, which helped them build a following in the South, and in 1958 they recorded for Starday. A year later, they gained the sponsorship of Martha White Mills, the same company sponsoring Flatt & Scruggs. In 1960 they signed with Columbia, and soon began guesting regularly on the *Grand Ole Opry*. In 1963 they played the Newport Folk Festival, and in 1964, they became *Opry* members.

Columbia popped the brothers over to its subsidiary label, Epic, where they stayed for the rest of the decade. Their mid-'60s songs "Cotton Mill Man" (which some southern radio stations perceived as a protest song) and "Better Times A-Comin'" made the charts; among their albums was BERRY PICKIN IN THE COUNTRY, a 1965 collection of Chuck Berry covers performed bluegrass style. By the end of the decade, they were playing more country than traditional bluegrass, and using electric and steel guitars. Songs like "Diesel On My Tail" (produced by none other than Billy Sherrill) and "Ballad Of Thunder Road" may have won them chart points and a wider fan base, but that material is no match for the pure, bright mountain bluegrass sound of their '50s Capitol recordings.

As bluegrass festivals began catching on, Jim & Jesse's live appearances increased, and they eventually swung back around to a traditional acoustic bluegrass sound, which, along with their strong harmony vocals, would remain an integral part of

Jim & Jesse

their music from then onwards. Over the next couple of decades, they released albums on several different labels, including two (in 1982) with Charlie Louvin. By the late '80s they were recording for Rounder; the 1991 album MUSIC AMONG FRIENDS features such guests as Ricky Skaggs, Emmylou Harris and Mac Wiseman.

⊙ **The Jim & Jesse Story** (1990; CMH). A 24-track compilation of many of their best-known songs, including "Diesel On My Tail" and "Are You Missing Me," recorded during the 1970s.

⊙ **Jim & Jesse: 1952–1955** (1992; Bear Family). This is without question the Jim & Jesse collection of choice, compiling onto one CD the 20 tracks they recorded for Capitol during the mid-'50s. Jim & Jesse's soulful, haunting vocal work alone makes this some of the most beautiful, moving music the bluegrass genre has to offer.

⊙ **Y'All Come: The Essential Jim & Jesse** (1998; Epic/Legacy). Collects the pair's Epic recordings from the '60s, which showed them delving into some modern song material ("Maybelline," "Truck Drivin' Man") and adding drums and electric guitars. Their earlier Capitol sides are the true bluegrass classics, but the brothers' harmonies here are still lovely.

Johnson Mountain Boys

"I'm kind of a rock'n'roller at heart. That's one reason I got involved in traditional bluegrass in the first place. It has sort of a rock'n'roll attitude about it."
—Dudley Connell

One of the great neo-traditional bluegrass bands to crop up in recent years, the Johnson Mountain Boys couldn't have hit the scene at a better time. They formed in 1978, when progressive bluegrass was at its peak and the music was, in the opinion of many long and loyal bluegrass fans, becoming too hippie, too radical, too loud, too pop and/or too forgetful of its roots. It was time to get back to basics, and the Johnson Mountain Boys had the skill and the gumption to bring a fresh, new and thoroughly invigorating spirit to traditional grass.

Aside from singer–guitarist Dudley Connell, who hails from West Virginia, the original bandmembers

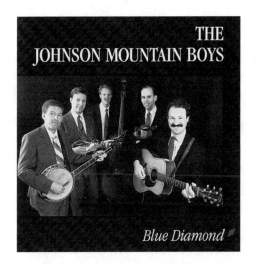

THE JOHNSON MOUNTAIN BOYS

Blue Diamond

came from Washington, DC and the surrounding area; couple these suburban roots with a deliberate choice to play traditional music—not to mention the fact that bandmembers wore suits and cowboy hats and kept their hair short—and you have a safe middle ground between "old" and "new." Thus, the Johnson Mountain Boys won acceptance by both urban-hip grass fans in DC clubs and conservative audiences weary of modern trappings.

Right from the start, the combination of Connell's strong tenor voice, Eddie Stubbs' furious fiddle, David McLaughlin's mandolin, Richard Underwood's banjo, and Larry Robbins' bass was superb, and the group's song choices were innovative and exciting. Their repertoire was thick with old-time traditional songs by folks like Wilma Lee Cooper or Jimmie Rodgers, and bluegrass classics by Monroe or Carter Stanley, but they also worked up bluegrass arrangements of songs by the likes of Bob Dylan and Harlan Howard. In addition to handling lead vocal duties, Connell was also a strong writer, and he contributed quite a few originals. But no matter what they were singing, the keen arrangements—which alternated between gently meandering and fast and furious—reflected their deep love of rich, earthy acoustic music. The excitement with which they played was immediately felt by fans, and their popularity quickly grew.

After Connell formed the band in 1978, the Boys played clubs in the DC area for a few years before recording their self-titled debut album for Rounder in 1981. After this, festival bookers became interested in them, and their career took off. The line-up remained more or less stable through 1986, when banjoist Tom Adams took Underwood's slot and Robbins was replaced by Marshall Wilborn. Two years later, however, the

Johnson Mountain Boys

band announced it was to split. In actual fact they went part-time, playing occasional dates over the next few years. In 1993 they released a superb new album, BLUE DIAMOND, that included Connell, McLaughlin, Stubbs, Adams, and bassist Earl Yager. In the years since, however, the Boys have slipped out of view again. Stubbs became a regular DJ on Nashville's WSM (home of the *Grand Ole Opry*), and his evening radio show is easily one of the most exciting and informative country music programs on the air. Connell joined another DC favorite, the Seldom Scene, in 1996, and he sings on their album DREAM SCENE. He is also a member of Longview, a bluegrass supergroup that's so far released two excellent albums. As for the future of the Johnson Mountain Boys, it's not necessarily all over yet—only time will tell.

⊙ **Johnson Mountain Boys** (1981; Rounder). The band's debut album includes a healthy number of originals alongside traditional songs such as "John Henry, The Steel Drivin' Man."

⊙ **Live At The Old Schoolhouse** (1988; Rounder). Their second live album (the first being 1984's LIVE AT THE BIRCHMERE), this 23-song collection documents their "farewell" performance just before they temporarily retired. Recorded at the Lucketts, Virginia Community Center, it won Record of the Year from the IBMA as well as a Grammy nomination.

⊙ **Blue Diamond** (1993; Rounder). This album contains some of the most exciting bluegrass music that's been put on record in the last few decades— from a group of players who are clearly among the genre's top talents. Connell's lead vocals are bright, crisp and honest, and the tight-knit instrumental work of McLaughlin, Stubbs, Adams, and Yager—which alternates between understated and all-out raging—is stellar. They're as rooted in traditional styles as they are progressive in the way they approach the material—by songwriters from Hazel Dickens to Buck Owens to Carter Stanley. Their intensely moving rendition of Jean Ritchie's "Blue Diamond Mines" is one of the standout songs of their career.

Bill Keith

When Bill Keith joined Bill Monroe's band in 1963, the bluegrass world took notice. Here was a man who could play his banjo like no one before him—even Scruggs. With a method that's been since dubbed "chromatic" (or sometimes "melodic," "Yankee picking," or simply "Keith style"), Bill Keith redefined bluegrass banjo playing for a whole new generation of players.

What Keith had managed to do was invent a way to play fiddle-style leads note-for-note on the banjo; in fact, Monroe hired Keith based on hearing him play a banjo rendition of the old fiddle tune "Devil's Dream" on the *Grand Ole Opry*. Where Scruggs' famous three-finger style involved runs and riffs of syncopated notes that didn't follow a song's melody entirely, Keith's style was more chromatic and chordal. It was a different language entirely, as opposed to the unique inflections and accents that had given players like Don Reno and J.D. Crowe their individuality in a Scruggs-dominated world. Keith knew his music theory up and down, too, and it's this background that had helped this precision-oriented player break the chromatic barrier.

Keith was a full-fledged product of the folk revival, and a Yankee to boot. Born in 1939 and raised near Boston, he was educated at Exeter Academy and Amherst College, and like many of his generation, he first came to the banjo through Pete Seeger—learning from Seeger's manual *How To Play The Five-String Banjo* (Keith would later help Earl Scruggs write his own manual). He was familiar with bluegrass music, however; during the '50s, thanks to the large number of Appalachian migrants (and folks from Canada, too) who'd moved to the area looking for work, a strong traditional music scene had blossomed in the Boston area, with Don Stover and the Lilly Brothers at the center of the bluegrass contingent.

In the early '60s, Keith and his college roommate Jim Rooney (later the author of *Bossmen*, a book on Monroe and Muddy Waters) were playing folk and country at joints like Club 47, one of the most famous coffeehouses of the folky era. In 1962 Keith moved to Washington, DC where he played in the Kentuckians with singer/guitarist Red Allen and mandolinist/banjoist Frank Wakefield. He soon met Earl Scruggs, who was so impressed with how the young player had methodically transcribed his solos that he hired Keith to help him write his first banjo-playing manual. This brought Keith to Nashville in 1963, where he ended up playing "Devil's Dream" on the *Opry* and landing the prestigious position with Monroe. That song, in fact, became one of several from Keith's repertoire that Monroe released as singles later that year—recordings that placed Keith's stop-and-stare playing at the forefront. With Keith and Del McCoury (who'd joined about the same time) now in his band—and a smart new manager, Ralph Rinzler—Monroe began rising out of a creative slump and readying his re-entry into the bluegrass spotlight.

Despite Monroe's wide praises, Keith stayed with the master less than a year. He began doing session work, and in 1964 he joined Jim Kwesin's Jug Band. Four years later he was playing with Eric Weissberg, Richard Greene and Jim Rooney in the Blue Velvet Band. Soon after, however, he began playing pedal steel and moving more in folk-rock circles with the likes of Ian and Sylvia, Jonathan Edwards and Judy Collins. By the '70s he was living in Woodstock, New York, where he eventually played banjo with a community of musicians called the Woodstock Mountain Review. In 1977, he began writing a music theory column for *Frets* magazine.

Keith recorded his first solo banjo album for Rounder, SOMETHING AULD, SOMETHING NEW-GRASS, SOMETHING BORROWED, SOMETHING BLUE-GRASS, in 1976, following it up five years later with FIDDLE TUNES FOR THE BANJO (with Tony Trischka and Béla Fleck) and, in 1984, BANJOISTICS. By the end of the '80s, Keith, Rooney, and Weissberg were back together as the New Blue Velvet Band.

⊙ **Something Auld, Something Newgrass, Something Borrowed, Something Bluegrass** (1976; Rounder). This was Keith's first album devoted exclusively to his adventurous banjo playing. Featured soloists include Vassar Clements, David Grisman and Tony Rice, and the broad range of tunes runs from traditional material ("Richett's Hornpipe," "Auld Lang Syne") to interpretations of the Rolling Stones' "No Expectations" and Duke Ellington's "Caravan."

Kentucky Colonels

"Clarence had wonderful control over the guitar. He's the first guy I heard who really knocked me out."

—Jerry Garcia

The Kentucky Colonels were a short-lived band who left a memorable impact on the progressive bluegrass scene in the early 1960s. The initial line-up centered around two brothers—Roland (mandolin, banjo) and Clarence (lead guitar, vocals) White. Other members included at various times their brother Eric White (bass), fiddler Bobby Slone, Dobro player LeRoy Mack, bassist Roger Bush, banjoist Billy Ray Lathum and fiddler Scott Stoneman.

Clarence White

The Whites were born in Lewiston, Maine, but in 1954 the family moved to Los Angeles. There Clarence, Roland and Eric played on local TV shows, calling themselves the Three Little Country Boys. In 1958 they added banjoist Billy Ray Lathum, and the name shortened to the Country Boys. Still only teenagers, they became regulars on the *Town Hall Party* (a popular LA country music TV show) and recorded a few singles. Eric quit in 1961, and was replaced by Roger Bush. By 1963 the group's name was changed again to the Kentucky Colonels (by request of the Briar label, who released their first album, NEW SOUNDS OF BLUEGRASS AMERICA).

A turning point for the band came when Clarence heard Doc Watson flat-picking leads on his guitar during a stint at Hollywood's Ash Grove, a famous folk-music coffeehouse. He was inspired by Watson's combination of rhythm and lead playing—not a regular feature in bluegrass—and strove to improve upon that style and incorporate it into the Colonels' music. His guitar became a defining element of their sound.

The Kentucky Colonels became regulars at the Ash Grove and on the national folk music circuit during the '60s, appearing at the Newport Folk Festival in 1964, and their album APPALACHIAN SWING (released for the World Pacific label, which had recently tasted success with two instrumental Glen Campbell albums) was considered an underground classic. Commercial success continued to elude them, however, and the band finally split in 1965.

The two White brothers' careers didn't stop there. Roland played with a succession of groups,

Kentucky Colonels

from the bands of Bill Monroe and Flatt & Scruggs to Country Gazette (a progressive bluegrass band founded in the '70s) and, most recently, the Nashville Bluegrass Band. Clarence began by doing session work for various LA artists, which would soon make him one of the top players on the West Coast country-rock scene. He joined the Gene Clark Group, formed after Clark quit the Byrds in 1966, and played on one Clark album, GENE CLARK AND THE GOSDIN BROTHERS. In 1968, White was playing in a group called Nashville West with Gene Parsons, Gib Gilbeau, Wayne Moore, Sneaky Pete Kleinow, and Glen D. Hardin. Later that year he joined the Byrds, playing guitar with them until 1973, after which he continued his busy session schedule playing with such artists as Joe Cocker, Delaney & Bonnie, the Everly Brothers, Arlo Guthrie, Jackson Browne, Wynn Stewart, and Ricky Nelson. He also played with a band called the Muleskinners that included Bill Keith, David Grisman and Peter Rowan. He was working on a solo record and playing some shows with the Kentucky Colonels again when he met a tragic death: on 14 July, 1973 he was hit and killed by a drunk driver while loading a tour bus.

⊙ **Appalachian Swing** (1964; World Pacific; reissued 1993; Rounder). Recorded completely live in just one evening, this all-instrumental showed the folk music world (the Colonels' main audience) that these boys were serious and profoundly innovative players. It's exciting stuff, with each player shining on solos while also holding up a firm rhythmic foundation; and even though many of these songs were originally vocal tunes ("Nine Pound Hammer," "Faded Love"), the playing is so strong you never miss the voices.

⊙ **Livin' In The Past** (1976; Briar; reissued 1997; Sierra). A live album that deliberately includes between-song patter and bits of comedy, LIVIN' IN THE PAST does a fine job re-creating the concert experience.

James King

"He finds a good song, and he tells a good story. Even Carter Stanley could not have asked for more."

—Charles Wolfe

Since the early 1990s, Virginia native James King has risen to a well-deserved spot at the forefront of the traditional bluegrass circuit. He's

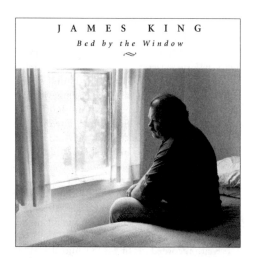

J A M E S   K I N G
Bed by the Window

done so thanks to a superb lead voice and a great repertoire of songs—and a little help from Dudley Connell and other members of the Johnson Mountain Boys, who played on his first two albums, THESE OLD PICTURES (1993) and LONESOME AND THEN SOME (1995). "Lonesome" is definitely a theme that runs through all of King's recordings—a mixture of melancholy, gritty emotional truths and pastoral images of a hard country past that's slowly drifting away.

Though it may have seemed that way, King didn't exactly come out of nowhere. During the early '80s he played with Bobby and T.J. Lundy—sons of renowned banjoist and singer Ted Lundy—and later he cut a couple of records with Ralph Stanley and his Clinch Mountain Boys. King first formed his own band in 1988, recording the album JAMES KING SINGS COLD, COLD WORLD for the Webco label. And it was out of a desire to perform some duets with Connell that led King to his breakthrough 1993 album THESE OLD PICTURES, released by Rounder.

The Stanley Brothers were definitely among the many old-time and bluegrass artists who made an impression on King when he was growing up. He was born on 9 September, 1958 in Henry County, Virginia and raised in Carroll County, a nearby region with about as strong an old-time music heritage as anywhere in the nation (the annual fiddler's convention in Galax, Virginia is a decades-old event). Both King's uncle, a fiddler, and his father, a singer and guitarist, played with a locally renowned group the Country Cousins. With all this musical heritage thick in the air, it's no wonder that the pure truth of bluegrass comes so naturally to King. When he empties his soul into a song, it's like the hills are coming to life and talking right back. Few contemporary country artists, bluegrass or otherwise, can speak with that kind of rural authority. Whether singing on his own records or as a member of the highly regarded "supergroup" Longview, King is a bluegrass artist to keep watch on. His style is entirely organic, his arrangements steeped in a century's worth of musical tradition, and his songs are some of the most heart-wrenchingly beautiful on the country circuit today.

⊙ **Lonesome And Then Some** (1995; Rounder). King dishes up another excellent bluegrass collection that showcases not only his stellar lead voice, but also the excellent instrumental work of his back-up band (which includes a few Johnson Mountain Boys). Songs include Hazel Dickens' "A Few Old Memories," Vince Gill's "When I Call Your Name," and Ernest Tubb's "Letters Have No Arms."

⊙ **Bed By The Window** (1998; Rounder). King's third album for Rounder is his most musically mature, and most achingly beautiful, to date—a showcase of melancholy material juxtaposed with top-notch instrumental work that's anything but down. It's also the first to feature his road band: Kevin Prater, Jason Moore, Adam Poindexter, Bobby Hicks, and Owen Saunders. A real knockout.

Alison Krauss

"She's absolutely brilliant, I'm just crazy about her."
—Dolly Parton

W ho could ever have imagined that the top-selling bluegrass artist of all time would turn out to be a female fiddler from the Midwest who hadn't even celebrated her twentieth birthday at the turn of the 1990s? That, however, is the story behind Alison Krauss, a gifted singer, instrumentalist and bandleader from Champaign, Illinois who's almost single-handedly brought bluegrass back within sight of mainstream country fans. Her list of achievements is impressive for any country music artist, let alone one working in the sidelines of bluegrass: she was signed to Rounder Records when only fourteen; five years later she won her first Grammy; when invited to join the *Grand Ole Opry* in 1993, she was the first bluegrass artist to do so in twenty-nine years; and by 1996 her album NOW THAT I'VE FOUND YOU: A COLLECTION

had sold more than two million copies—an unprecedented feat for an indie-label country artist (she was, and still is, signed to Rounder). Krauss is living proof that even in the great wide world of modern country music, bluegrass is a long way from forgotten.

Traditional bluegrass is a rich part of Krauss' music, but she hasn't strictly tied herself to that or any other particular style; over the years she has—both as a solo artist and with her band Union Station—deftly blended contemporary folk, country and even hints of rock and pop (songs by the Beatles, Gregg Allman, and Shawn Colvin, for instance) into her acoustic-based repertoire. Her high, strong voice rings with the spirit of Bill Monroe but also brings to mind singers like Dolly Parton and Emmylou Harris. She plays clubs and festivals, but also has made country music videos (her first was "I've Got That Old Feeling" in 1990). But even at the peak of her popularity,

PETER NASH

Alison Krauss

Alison Krauss

Krauss' grass-roots, ground-level integrity has remained an integral part of her persona: she's refused to budge from Rounder, the small New England label that gave her her start (even though a move to a major label would likely give her the radio hits her music so obviously deserves). "I'd never want the kind of fame Garth [Brooks] has," she told the *New York Times* in 1994, when she was busy opening for Brooks' national tour. "It's not music anymore. I couldn't play on stages that big, night after night." Financial temptation must lurk around every corner, but Krauss chooses instead to sing and play simply what feels right to her and her band alone.

Born on 23 July, 1971 in Champaign, a university town in east-central Illinois, Krauss took up classical violin at the age of five, then entered and began winning a series of regional fiddle contests. At twelve she was introduced to bluegrass by the man she calls her mentor, songwriter John Pennell. Two years later she was playing with the local bluegrass band Union Station. The band's line-up has since evolved (past members include Pennell, Krauss' brother Viktor, and banjoist Alison Brown), but Krauss' support for the group she literally grew up with has remained firm. That same year she also won her recording contract with Rounder who released her first solo album, TOO LATE TO CRY, in 1987 (she'd previously appeared with her brother on a compilation, DIFFERENT STROKES).

In 1989 Krauss and Union Station released TWO HIGHWAYS, which won a Grammy nomination. Her next album, I'VE GOT THAT OLD FEELING, finally won her a Grammy—as did her 1992 album with Union Station, EVERY TIME YOU SAY GOODBYE. The awards didn't stop there: among other accolades, the International Bluegrass Music Association named her Entertainer of the Year in 1991. They repeated the honor in 1995, the same year she also won Female Vocalist of the Year, the Horizon Award, Single of the Year (for "When You Say Nothing At All" from KEITH WHITLEY: A TRIBUTE ALBUM), and Vocal Event of the Year (for her duet with Shenandoah) from the Country Music Association. And she became the *Opry*'s newest and youngest member when inducted on 3 July, 1993.

Over the years Krauss has sung and played on sessions for numerous other artists, among them Dolly Parton, Michelle Shocked (on ARKANSAS TRAVELER, Shocked's 1992 country album), Nanci Griffith, Ralph Stanley, Bad Company, and Mandy Barnett. She's dueted with Alan Jackson, Vince Gill, and Shenandoah, and toured nationally with

Brooks, Jackson, Amy Grant, and Bob Dylan, among others. She has also recorded one album with the gospel-bluegrass group the Cox Family (the Grammy-winning I KNOW WHO HOLDS TOMORROW) and produced three others. Obviously, with all this work in recent years (and the accompanying industry and media attention), Krauss is on a roll. But in other ways she's just getting started: after all, she was still a couple of years shy of thirty when her eighth album was released in 1999, the low-key and delicately toned FORGET ABOUT IT. Clearly, Krauss is one of modern country music's strongest and most distinct talents.

⊙ **Too Late To Cry** (1987; Rounder). John Pennell wrote most of the material on Krauss' debut. Her band includes Sam Bush, Jerry Douglas, Tony Trischka, and Roy Husky, Jr.

⊙ **Every Time You Say Goodbye** (1992; Rounder). A strong and solid collection of songs written by John Pennell, Sidney Cox, Karla Bonoff, Shawn Colvin, Union Station banjoist Ron Block, and others.

⊙ **Now That I've Found You: A Collection** (1995; Rounder). Not a best-of album per se, this CD gathers several of Krauss and the band's personal favorites from previous albums along with a few new songs and unreleased takes.

⊙ **So Long So Wrong** (1997; Rounder). Despite her burgeoning popularity, Krauss has deftly avoided the saccharine trappings of some of her contemporaries. Instead, this album is an invigorating showcase of 14 acoustic songs that swing, pick, shiver, and roll between bluegrass, country, and contemporary folk.

Doyle Lawson And Quicksilver

"So they were trying to decide on a name. I said, 'What about Quicksilver? There's no stopping Quicksilver.'"
—Doyle Lawson's mother

Singer-mandolinist Doyle Lawson first won the attention of bluegrass fans during the 1960s when he sang with first Jimmy Martin, then J.D. Crowe, and ultimately the Country Gentlemen, but since then he has gone on to become a strong bandleader in his own right. Despite a progressive background, especially during his stint with the Gentlemen, Lawson's band Quicksilver maintains a relatively conservative sound (electric bass being one of the few exceptions). They've built a solid reputation on gospel music—featuring pristine trio and quartet singing, much of it a cappella—but Lawson also handles secular material with equal depth and clarity.

Born in Kingsport, Tennessee in 1944, Lawson was raised on traditional bluegrass. His father sang in a gospel quartet, and one of the singers gave him his first mandolin at the age of eleven; he also learned banjo and guitar. Jimmy Martin was a neighbor of Lawson's, and in 1963 Lawson joined his band, the Sunny Mountain Boys. He played banjo with Martin, but stayed only seven months before moving to Louisville. Here he eventually hooked up with Crowe, with whom he played for several years, recording two albums. In 1971, he moved on to join the Country Gentlemen, playing with that pioneering progressive band at a time when its popularity was peaking.

Lawson quit the Gentlemen in 1979 and founded his own band, Quicksilver, with banjoist Terry Baucom, guitarist Jimmy Haley, and electric bassist Lou Reid. Their first album, DOYLE LAWSON AND QUICKSILVER, released by the North Carolina label Sugar Hill in 1979, focused on secular material, but in 1981 they recorded ROCK MY SOUL, an album of stellar gospel material that launched Lawson's career proper. Since then he's alternated between secular and gospel albums, although his gospel music continues to sell better. Like most bluegrass bands, Quicksilver's line-up has changed frequently, but the group's sound has remained consistent. Lawson briefly jumped ship and recorded two albums for Brentwood in the early '90s, but soon he and Quicksilver were back on Sugar Hill, their longtime home base.

⊙ **Rock My Soul** (1981; Sugar Hill). Lawson's first gospel album and the first also to win him widespread acclaim, based largely on his ability to bring southern sacred and secular musical traditions under one roof.

⊙ **Never Walk Away** (1995; Sugar Hill). A strong collection of country-flavored bluegrass, this (mostly) secular music includes songs by Buck Owens, Bill Carlisle, Dallas Frazier, Hylo Brown, and even Glen Campbell and Jeannie Seely ("Senses"). In many ways it's more rootsy and earthbound than his sacred albums and no less emotive.

⊙ **There's A Light Guiding Me** (1996; Sugar Hill). If an album packed full of impeccably arranged

gospel quartet singing is what you're looking for, this one—Lawson's 11th all-gospel album—is a perfect choice. More gorgeous music—much of it sung a cappella or with minimal instrumentation—from one of bluegrass and gospel's top bandleaders, arrangers and singers.

⊙ **The Original Band** (1999; Sugar Hill). A 2-for-1 CD that combines the group's eponymously titled debut album with its third, QUICKSILVER RIDES AGAIN, originally released in 1982. Both albums feature mostly secular material played by the original line-up of Lawson, Haley, Baucom and Reid and show the group coming out of a progressive background but leaning toward a more traditional sound. RIDES AGAIN, in particular, shows the band firming its voice with songs like "Georgia Girl," "Yellow River," and "Heart Of A Little Mountain Girl."

Laurie Lewis

There's no denying that Laurie Lewis' heart has strong roots in bluegrass music, but like many folk-revival musicians who grew up in the 1960s and '70s, her music is not so easily categorized. Throughout her career, this singer, songwriter, fiddler and bandleader has proven herself equally adept at writing and playing country, folk, old-time, Cajun and acoustic New Age, comfortably and deftly mixing these and other musical influences together.

Though she spent some of her "formative years" in Michigan, Lewis is a native of Berkeley, California, and that folk-friendly university town has more or less been her home base for most of her life. It's in Berkeley—with its folk music festivals, eager students, political activism and frequent concerts by legendary performers such as Doc Watson and Mississippi John Hurt—that Lewis began playing music seriously. Her fiddling won her awards, and soon she was playing in bands: first with the Phantoms Of The Opry (with Pat Enright, now of the Nashville Bluegrass Band) and eventually with the Good Ol' Persons. The latter was a strong, versatile group that played a mixture of bluegrass, folk and old-time music; it was also one of the first bands to spotlight female bluegrass players (fiddler Lewis, lead singer Kathy Kallick, and Dobro player Sally Van Meter among them).

Since her departure from the Persons in 1979, Lewis has fronted her own string band, Grant

Street, honing her vocal, instrumental and song-writing skills. Like many contemporary bluegrass artists, she's not afraid to mix traditional and contemporary influences, and her repertoire of strong originals reflects her widespread taste. Her music can get a little sweet at times, but it can also be rather rootsy: she is a well-seasoned, adventurous and spirited musician who can write, sing, and play fiddle with skill and grace. There's no doubt this multitalented woman knows her way around a song, whether it's a rousing bluegrass number, an old-time fiddle tune, or a gentle "new acoustic" ballad.

As a solo artist and with Grant Street, Lewis recorded three albums for Flying Fish, beginning with RESTLESS RAMBLING HEART, released in 1986. The title track to her 1989 album, LOVE CHOOSES YOU, was recorded by Nashville singer Kathy Mattea. Since 1993 Lewis has been signed to Rounder. In addition to all this, she has recorded collaborative albums with Kathy Kallick (TOGETHER), Cathy Fink, Sally Van Meter, Marcy Marxer and Molly Manson (BLUE ROSE), and Grant Street mandolinist Tom Rozum (THE OAK AND THE LAUREL). In 1992, and again in 1994, Lewis won the International Bluegrass Music Association's female vocalist of the year award. During much of the '90s Lewis drifted away from bluegrass and more toward singer-songwriter material. After 1998's folky SEEING THINGS, however, she did dive back into traditionalism with LAURIE LEWIS AND HER BLUEGRASS PALS a year later. She also cut the album WINTER'S GRACE, which branched out from the standard Christmas-album concept to embrace such cold-season material as Merle Haggard's "If We Make It Through December."

⊙ **Together** (1991; Kaleidoscope). An album of duets with Kathy Kallick, Lewis' onetime Good Ol' Persons partner, that includes some great old country material like the Delmore Brothers' "Don't You See That Train."

⊙ **True Stories** (1993; Rounder). The playing is excellent, and for the most part the songs are strong, but there's an overt sweetness that knocks much of the edge off this collection.

⊙ **The Oak And The Laurel** (1995; Rounder). A duet album with Tom Rozum (a mandolinist who joined Grant Street in 1987), this is a great collection of old-time songs—both instrumental and vocal tunes—that are among Lewis' rootsiest to date.

⊙ **Earth & Sky: Songs Of Laurie Lewis** (1997; Rounder). Culled from Lewis' 3 Flying Fish albums (plus 4 unreleased tracks), this album was designed to spotlight Lewis' songwriting talent. It also makes a nice introduction to her oeuvre.

The Lilly Brothers And Don Stover

During the 1950s, country and bluegrass music was spreading from the southern countryside to the nation's urban centers, many of them in the North. One such locale was Boston, Massachusetts, which was a new home not just to an Appalachian contingent, but all sorts of folk musicians, many from Canada. Bluegrass was definitely strong, though, and the musicians at the center of the region's burgeoning community—the ones who helped inspire an entire generation of New England players, including Joe Val and Bill Keith—were West Virginia transplants Charles Everett and Mitchell Burt ("B.") Lilly and their frequent bandmate, banjoist Don Stover.

Like Jim & Jesse, the Lilly Brothers sang their rich, mountain-flavored bluegrass in a harmony style closely related to the brother duets they grew up listening to. B. played rhythm guitar, Everett the mandolin and, later, fiddle and lead guitar. Some songs were more in the vein of the old-time material they played on West Virginia radio programs during the '40s. Others, with their haunting vocal leads and simmering mandolin and fiddle lines—and the lively banjo work of Stover who, like Don Reno and Sonny Osborne, was one of the great players working in the wake of Scruggs—left no doubt that these players' hearts were devoted to bluegrass.

Everett and B. grew up in the rural mountain community of Clear Creek, West Virginia. They listened intently to radio acts like the Monroe Brothers and the Delmore Brothers, and played their first radio show in this brother-duet style in Charleston in 1938. Throughout the late '30s and '40s, they played radio shows in the area and performed with the likes of Lynn Davis, Molly O'Day and Speedy Krise. By 1948 they were on the WWVA *Wheeling Jamboree* as part of Red Belcher's Kentucky Ridge Runners. Here they met fiddler Benjamin "Tex" Logan, who would work with them again a few years down the road in Boston.

After two years with Belcher, the brothers split, and in 1951 Everett joined Flatt & Scruggs, playing on two of their Columbia sessions. In 1952, with Logan's encouragement (who was studying

Laurie Lewis • The Lilly Brothers And Don Stover

electrical engineering at MIT at the time), they headed for Boston, bringing their brand of southern folk and mountain bluegrass straight into the heart of urban New England. Stover, another West Virginian who'd played with the Lillys previously, joined them in Boston that same year. ("Those guys hit town like a bombshell," Joe Val once remarked. "Nobody'd ever heard anything like that before.") The group played at various spots around town, but settled into a regular gig at a popular downtown country music club called the Hillbilly Ranch. It's here, amongst a crowd of hard-drinking hillbillies and sailors—with a few folk-music scholars thrown in—that they gained their following and cemented their reputation.

During the '50s, Stover briefly played with Bill Monroe and Buzz Busby, while Everett spent another year with Flatt & Scruggs; yet despite these interruptions, the Lillys and Stover played together more or less regularly through the end of the '60s, working mostly in the Boston area. They recorded for Event Records in the mid-'50s and also for Folkways and Prestige; these latter albums became popular in folk revivalist circles.

In 1970, Everett's son Jiles was killed in a car accident, and he and his wife moved back to West Virginia, which effectively ended the Lilly Brothers' music career. The brothers and Stover hooked up occasionally over the next several years playing festivals, touring Japan, and recording one gospel and three live albums. Stover has since recorded solo albums (his first was 1972's THINGS IN LIFE) and done some session work. By the '80s, Everett was driving a school bus and playing part-time with his other son, Mark. Despite their semi-retirement, however, the brothers haven't been forgotten: their albums have been reissued and their career was even covered in a 1979 documentary film, *True Facts In A Country Song*.

⊙ **Early Recordings** (1971; Rebel). The 11 songs on this excellent collection are the two sessions the Lilly Brothers and Stover recorded for Event Records during 1956 and '57—and only 4 were previously issued. This is the real, worthwhile stuff.

⊙ **Live At Hillbilly Ranch** (1996; Hay Holler). On 4 July, 1967, bluegrass fan Fred Pement brought a portable deck to the Hillbilly Ranch and recorded a performance by the Lilly Brothers and Stover. Though recorded toward the end of the group's career, the music is still haunting and earthy. The sound, too, is remarkably clean, resulting in an incredible document of an old-time bluegrass show.

Longview

Longview is a "supergroup" of contemporary bluegrass singers and pickers and one of the freshest and most exciting projects to pop up in the bluegrass world in recent years. The membership roster consists of singer and guitarist Dudley Connell of the Johnson Mountain Boys (and, more recently, the Seldom Scene); Glen Duncan, fiddler with Larry Cordle and Lonesome Standard Time; guitarist James King, a solo recording artist in his own right; banjoist Joe Mullins, co-founder of Traditional Grass; mandolinist Don Rigsby, who's played with J.D. Crowe, the Bluegrass Cardinals and the Lonesome River Band, among others; and bassist Marshall Wilborn, who has played with Jimmy Martin, the Johnson Mountain Boys and the Lynn Morris Band.

The initial spark for the project came during a North Carolina bluegrass festival in 1994, when Connell, King and Rigsby found themselves on stage harmonizing together on the Stanley Brothers song "The Angels Are Singing In Heaven Tonight"—and were inspired by the results. A few weeks later Connell performed at a festival in Ohio with Duncan and Mullins and before long the five of them (along with bassist Wilborn) were holed up for a week-long session in the Long View recording studio in central Massachusetts. It was the first time they'd all worked together as a group—though you'd never know it judging from the stunning harmonies (four of the six players trade vocal duties) and instrumental interplay. The band was initially only conceived as a one-off project, but their debut album turned out so well—and public response was so enthusiastic—that they went back in the studio two years later and put together a follow-up collection. It remains to be seen whether they'll hang onto the concept and take it further.

⊙ **Longview** (1997; Rounder). Even during its most low-key and introspective moments, the arrangements on Longview's debut have a sharp and lively edge that give the songs an up-to-date vibe, yet these top-flight bluegrass veterans never lose sight of the music's first-generation roots. Superb solo, duo and trio vocals highlight one of the finest bluegrass albums—heck, finest *country music* albums—to come down the pike in ages.

⊙ **High Lonesome** (1999; Rounder). The title track is a Randy Travis song from 1991, one of many standouts included on the second album from this still-active supergroup (the same six pickers as on the original release). Other songs are a mix of classic (the Carter Family) and contemporary (Larry Sparks) sources. Another highlight is the Stanley Brothers' "The Angels Are Singing In Heaven Tonight" the very song that inspired the group to begin with.

Claire Lynch

Though a member of the Front Porch String Band since the 1970s, it took another two decades before singer, songwriter and rhythm guitarist Claire Lynch began putting serious energy into her solo career. You might wonder what took her so long, given the fact that she soon won widespread recognition: her 1995 album MOONLIGHTER was nominated for a Grammy, and a year later the IBMA named her Female Vocalist of the Year (they repeated the honor in 1997). With a high, pretty voice that brings to mind Texas singer-songwriter Nanci Griffith, Lynch has the feel of a folksinger. Some of her songs verge on the fragile, but overall her music is laced with the spirit of traditional bluegrass, both in her acoustic instrumentation (which includes fiddle, banjo, mandolin) and her overall approach—whether she's singing her own songs or others penned by the likes of Kostas, Gretchen Peters, or Guy Clark.

Born in Poughkeepsie, New York, Lynch moved to Alabama with her family when she was twelve. She was living in the Alabama town of Hazel Green when she first began playing professionally with the Front Porch String Band (originally named Hickory Wind), which had been formed by Larry Lynch, a mandolinist who eventually became Claire's husband. The group recorded three albums before splitting in 1981, and Claire released one solo album, BREAKIN' IT. Over the next decade, she found work in Nashville as a session vocalist and songwriter (her work has been recorded by Kathy Mattea, Patty Loveless and Tanya Tucker, among others). In the early '90s Claire and Larry regrouped the Front Porch String Band for LINES AND TRACES (1991); two years later, Claire recorded her second solo album, the gospel collection FRIENDS FOR A LIFETIME. It was the 1995 release of MOONLIGHTER, however, that gained Lynch her most widespread attention yet. She followed it up two years later with SILVER AND GOLD.

⊙ **Moonlighter** (1995; Rounder). Lynch penned more than half the songs on this album, her third solo effort and her debut for Rounder Records.

⊙ **Silver And Gold** (1997; Rounder). The haunting "Death Angel"—one of several songs written or co-written by Lynch—is a standout on an album of folk- and country-inspired bluegrass that's pretty almost to the point of delicate. Musicians include mandolinist Larry Lynch, guitarist Jim Hurst, bassist Missy Raines, and banjoist Michael McLain.

Jimmy Martin

Jimmy Martin's voice has almost all the qualities a bluegrass singer dreams of. His high tenor is piercing and sharp, yet at the same time it's full-bodied, richly textured with character and conviction, and strong enough to carry the lead melody alone, or in harmony. Which is just what Martin has done for more than fifty years, both as a member of Monroe's Blue Grass Boys and as a solo artist fronting his own band, the Sunny Mountain Boys.

As for personality, Martin's got plenty of it. He's full of deep country pride for the musical legacy he helps uphold—"(I'm Proud To Be A) Bluegrass Singin' Man" is one of the stellar songs in his repertoire. Never mind that he may have grown a bit full of himself en route: when this Tennessee boy starts to pick his guitar and sing with the Sunny Mountain Boys, the music is so pure and rich and full of life—the energy intense, the feelings genuine, the musicianship superb—that all his quirks are soon forgotten.

James Henry Martin was born in 1927 in Sneedville, Tennessee, a small town in the Cumberland Mountains, northeast of Knoxville. He sang and played traditional music as a child, and was especially taken with Bill Monroe's music. He played on various radio programs in the region until he finally got up the nerve to head for Nashville and audition for Monroe's band. The trip paid off when he ended up replacing Mac Wiseman as Monroe's singer and guitarist.

Martin stayed with the Blue Grass Boys on and off from late 1949 to early 1954, helping inspire Monroe's vocal and instrumental growth during what became one of the master's most productive periods, when he was fine tuning the bluegrass sound he'd recently invented and, in the process, recording some of his most enduring music. Martin cut 46 songs with Monroe, including "Uncle Pen," "I'm On My Way To The Old Home," and "Walking In Jerusalem," and his strong-willed lead vocals and piercing

Jimmy Martin (right) and his Sunny Mountain Boys

excellent players who would later strike out on their own as well.

Martin's career thrived well into the '60s. He concentrated on bluegrass vocal songs more than instrumentals, recording such favorites as "Free Born Man" and "Sunny Side Of The Mountain" and even scoring hits with the trucker's song "Widow Maker" and "I Can't Quit Cigarettes." When bluegrass festivals took off, Martin was a mainstay; he also performed regularly on the *Louisiana Hayride* and *Wheeling Jamboree*. By the '70s, his recording and performing career still going strong, he was guesting on the *Opry* regularly, though he was never invited to become a member. He was, however, asked to sing on the Nitty Gritty Dirt Band's landmark 1973 album WILL THE CIRCLE BE UNBROKEN?. Later, he even started his own label, King of Bluegrass.

Martin has performed and recorded a variety of music throughout his long career, covering such traditional bluegrass themes as tragically lost love ("Beautiful Blue Eyes"), death (the Louvins' "Knoxville Girl"), family, and the old-time religion ("Water The Flowers") with unshakable conviction. He's sung his share of oddball numbers as well, yet they're a lot of fun and even endearing because they belie his quirky personality. "Run Pete Run" and "Pete, The Best Coon Dog In The State Of Tennessee," for instance, show that Martin's as obsessed with coon hunting and his hounds (one of which is named George Jones) as he is with traditional music. As clownish as it seems, letting his hound dog howl on record ("Run Pete Run") doesn't break the song's (or the album's) mood of downhome sincerity, but rather adds to it—which is testament to Martin's ingrained musical sensibility. Call him what you want, but you can't ever say that Jimmy Martin isn't country.

harmonies helped define these Monroe songs as true classics.

During this time Martin had also recorded a few songs with Bobby Osborne, and in 1954 he and Bobby, along with Bobby's younger brother Sonny, formed a partnership and headed for a radio gig in Detroit—one of several northern outposts that was fast becoming a bluegrass centerpoint as a result of rural immigration. Songs the trio recorded include "20/20 Vision" and "That's How I Can Count On You," two bluegrass classics.

In 1955 the group split up, and Martin began calling his band the Sunny Mountain Boys (a name previously associated with the Osbornes). A year later he was recording with Decca. Among the numbers he cut during the late '50s were "Hit Parade Of Love," "Ocean Of Diamonds," and "Rock Hearts." By the end of the decade, he'd assembled a crack band that included banjoist J.D. Crowe and vocalist and mandolin player Paul Williams—both

◉ **20 Greatest Hits** (1988; Highland). These recordings were made in the mid-1970s after Martin switched labels from Decca to Gusto. They're not as "classic" as his earlier material, but they're pretty great. Songs include the boastful "Bluegrass Singin' Man," the gorgeous "Beautiful Brown Eyes," and the hound-dog howler "Run Pete Run." They're packaged on a budget CD, making this introduction to Martin's music very affordable.

Jimmy Martin

⊙ **You Don't Know My Mind (1956–1966)** (1990; Rounder). A 14-song collection of Martin's most classic material. The songs and the playing are tight, steeped in tradition and teeming with vitality. His style is fairly straightforward, but his soul and songs are as brisk and pure as a mountain breeze.

⊙ **Jimmy Martin And The Sunny Mountain Boys** (1994; Bear Family). This incredible 6-CD box set compiles Martin's Decca recordings from the late '50s and '60s.

Del McCoury

"His band is really the essence of blue-grass."

—Pat Enright

With his pure, clear, mountain-flavored tenor voice that practically defines the term "high lonesome," and an instinct for excellent songs and traditional arrangements, Del McCoury has, over the course of a musical career that's lasted more than three decades, become one of the most highly regarded (and popular) singers and bandleaders on the late-twentieth-century bluegrass scene.

McCoury sings closer to the range of Bill Monroe than nearly anyone in contemporary bluegrass, but at the same time his voice is completely his own. He's got a profoundly blue and melancholy tone that's immediately striking, and his delivery is tight and energetic; he can speed along as part of an intricate harmony, or pin a melody to the wall while singing alone. But as precise as McCoury's voice can be, it's also got an immediate warmth to it, revealing that this man obviously loves his work. When he lets go on a ripe piece of blues (hardly an album goes by without at least one song with "blue" in the title), the emotions he communicates are nothing short of genuine—when the hair stands up on the back of your neck, you've got your proof. Yet at the same time, there's so much joy in the simple act of making good music that you can almost hear McCoury smiling.

Like the Johnson Mountain Boys' Eddie Stubbs and Dudley Connell, McCoury's got a knack for picking excellent songs that work well in a traditional bluegrass context; along with his own original songs, he deftly mixes classic bluegrass, country, blues and contemporary material on his albums. Never just retreads, his takes are always adventurous and bold. His 1996 album THE COLD HARD FACTS, for instance, included an arrangement of Robert Cray's "Smoking Gun" that's a standout for its tension-building mix of mandolin, fiddle and Dobro breaks alongside Del's intense and high-reaching lead vocals. McCoury's also made excellent work of songs by Tom Petty, Steve Earle, and Kevin Welch, among other contemporaries. And all this is in addition to classic numbers by Monroe, Ernest Tubb and Ray Price—not to mention originals written by Del and, recently, his son Ronnie.

Del McCoury had a classic "country" upbringing—even if he spent much of his childhood north of the Mason-Dixon Line. He was born in North Carolina, but when he was still a child his family moved to a farm in southeastern Pennsylvania. His family was musical; they played and sang regularly at home and in church. Del was initially inspired by Earl Scruggs, and for years he concentrated on the banjo, playing in a number of different groups. In 1963 he joined Monroe's band; he was hired as a banjoist, but Monroe had also hired banjoist Bill Keith at the same time, and so to straighten matters out he switched Del to the role of guitarist and lead vocalist. Del recorded only one session with Monroe for Decca.

Leaving the Blue Grass Boys in 1964 with a newly minted reputation as a stellar vocalist, Del spent the next few years playing in an assortment of bands with fiddler (and former Blue Grass Boy) Billy Baker, including the Golden State Boys and a regrouped version of Baker's Shady Valley Boys. McCoury recorded his first album in 1967 for Arhoolie with the help of Baker, Bill Emerson (an ex-Country Gentleman), and Wayne Yates. Two years later he formed his own band, the Dixie Pals; the original line-up consisted of mandolinist Dick Laird, banjoist Larry Smith, and Del's brother Jerry (also a professional musician) on bass. Later players included mandolinist Dick Staber, bassist Dewey Renfro, banjoist Bill Runkle, and fiddlers Bill Sage and Baker. The Dixie Pals' first album came out in 1972, and over a twenty-year span they recorded for Rebel, Rounder and other small labels. In 1987 Del and Jerry recorded an album as the McCoury Brothers for Rounder.

In 1987, Del restyled his group around his two sons, Rob (banjo) and Ronnie (mandolin), changing the name from Dixie Pals to the Del McCoury Band. Both Rob and Ronnie have grown to be top-rated players in their own right who, like their father, are continuing the musical heritage of Bill Monroe. The band's sound is well-honed and tight, and through plenty of touring

Del McCoury

The Adventures of Del McCoury and his band

and a series of excellent albums, they've cemented their reputation as one of the hardest working and most highly respected bands in bluegrass (and perhaps country music as a whole) today. Getting the Country Music Association to take notice is still obviously going to take time, but the IBMA is on top of things, having honored McCoury and band with more than two dozen awards ... so far. Del teamed up with Doc Watson and Mac Wiseman for the enjoyable MAC, DOC & DEL collaboration in 1998, and a year later the Del McCoury Band joined Steve Earle to create THE MOUNTAIN, a successful project that offered new perspectives on each artist and some tasty music to boot.

⊙ **I Wonder Where You Are Tonight** (1967; Arhoolie). McCoury's first album was recorded just before he formed the Dixie Pals. Songs include "Hey, Hey Bartender" (a fun-lovin' nod to "Mule Skinner Blues"), a grassed-up version of Vernon Dalhart's "Prisoner's Song," and the standard "Roll In My Sweet Baby's Arms."

⊙ **High On A Mountain** (1972; Rounder). This was McCoury's first album released under the band name Dixie Pals (it was reissued on CD in 1995). McCoury's voice is sharp, high and strong, and the music (from hillbilly covers to originals by McCoury and Dick Staber) is classic in nature but altogether fresh.

⊙ **Classic Bluegrass** (1991; Rebel). An excellent anthology featuring 18 songs that McCoury and three different versions of the Dixie Pals recorded for Rebel between 1974 and 1984. Though McCoury's arrangements at this point of his career are not as fully charged as his '90s material, the songs are nonetheless beautiful, haunting and impeccably picked.

⊙ **A Deeper Shade Of Blue** (1993; Rounder). McCoury's version of the Jerry Lee Lewis hit "What Made Milwaukee Famous" is a standout on an album that garnered McCoury a much wider audience both inside and outside the bluegrass community. One of his best.

⊙ **The Cold Hard Facts** (1996; Rounder). As his voice gets stronger and his band even tighter, McCoury's recordings simply get better every time. This is easily one of his strongest albums to date. The material, the arrangements, the playing, the singing: it's powerful, innovative, and even at times mind-boggling.

⊙ **The Family** (1999; Cieli Music/DNA). What's to say except that THE FAMILY is yet another powerhouse, the instrumentation tightly screwed down and Del's voice sharp and bright. Songs include John Sebastian's "Nashville Cats," Bill Monroe's "Get Down On Your Knees And Pray," and Billy Smith and Ronnie McCoury's melancholy "On The Lonesome Wind."

Del McCoury

Bill Monroe

"He was a hard worker, Bill Monroe was. He didn't like lazy people."

—Del McCoury

No one disputes that Bill Monroe is the father of bluegrass. No one can, because Monroe is where bluegrass originated. It wasn't an old-time folk style passed through generations of Appalachian families; it was the music Bill Monroe developed with his band, the Blue Grass Boys. The young, inventive, hard-driven mandolin player didn't necessarily set out to forge an entire new musical genre, but that's exactly what had happened by the late 1940s and early '50s, when his amalgamation of traditional and modern styles—mountain-folk music, gospel, blues and jazz—was taken up and reinterpreted by countless up-and-coming musicians.

In the decades since, bluegrass music has gone in all sorts of wild new directions. Yet the shadow of Monroe hangs over every bluegrass artist to this day—in the high-lonesome vocals, intricate instrumental work, driving rhythms and mournful songs of rural life. And despite career ups and downs, not to mention country music's changing landscape (which knocked many a bluegrass artist off the traditional track), Monroe remained true to his music, maintaining a strict and steady approach for the duration of his career—guarding the music with his life, as it were. Because of his perseverence (and thanks to the support of numerous other players, fans and associates), bluegrass is as alive today as it was in its heyday—perhaps even more so.

William Smith Monroe was born on 13 September, 1911, and grew up on a 650-acre farm just outside Rosine, Kentucky, a small town in the western half of the state. The landscape is marked not by mountains, but by gentle rolling hills and scars from strip mine companies in search of coal. Monroe's father, James Buchanan "Buck" Monroe, made a living off his land—farming and selling coal and timber. His mother, Melissa Vandiver Monroe, kept herself busy caring for Bill and his five brothers and two sisters. Bill was the youngest of the bunch by eight years. He was a deeply lonesome child, and his sense of isolation was further aggravated by seriously poor vision.

Like many rural families of his day, Monroe's was musical. His father was a step dancer, and his mother sang old-time songs and ballads (Monroe has said his mother's singing was an inspiration for his high-tenor style) and played several instruments.

His brothers Birch and Harry played fiddle; Charlie and Bertha guitar. When Bill was eight or nine, he began playing mandolin. He might have prefered the fiddle or guitar, but he ended up with the mandolin because he was the youngest; his older siblings had already snatched up the more desirable instruments. It's an endearing story Monroe repeated many times during his lifetime.

Scholars have mapped out all sorts of influences on Monroe's musical development, but one of the key figures was his uncle, Pen Vandiver, a fiddler who lived nearby and who taught the young boy to play and sing. Several years later Monroe got his first taste of performing while accompanying Pen at local dances. Pen was not just a teacher, though. Monroe's mother died when he was just ten, and his father died six years later; because most of his siblings had moved away by then, Monroe went to live with his uncle who became his role model. Years later, Monroe memorialized his uncle in one of his most famous songs, "Uncle Pen"; he also recorded an entire album of his uncle's fiddle tunes.

Another teacher was Arnold Schultz, a local black man who worked in the coal mines and at night played guitar and fiddle at country dances—often with Monroe accompanying him. The church also played a significant role. Rosine's Baptist and Methodist churches often had visiting teachers leading "singing schools," and Bill and his siblings learned "shape-note" singing in these schools. Gospel quartet singing would eventually become an important aspect of Monroe's music.

In the '20s, Bill's brothers Birch and Charlie had moved to Detroit and Chicago in search of factory work. Such relocation was typical for young men from rural areas, and so when Bill turned eighteen in 1929, he joined his brothers, who at this point were in Whiting, Indiana. They began playing together and eventually won a regular gig on a Gary, Indiana radio station. When Birch dropped out, Charlie and Bill continued, calling themselves the Monroe Brothers and building up a healthy following. They stayed together through the better part of the '30s, recording some sixty songs (for the Victor label) and helping define the "brother duet" style popular during that time. But Charlie and Bill had a hard time getting along as musical and business partners, and in 1938 they parted ways.

On his own, Bill first organized a band in Little Rock, Arkansas, then moved to Atlanta, where he worked with guitarist and singer Cleo Davis. The pair played duets in a Monroe Brothers style, but Bill was determined to expand his sound beyond his past success. In 1939 Monroe hired two more players: fiddler Art Wooten and black-faced comedian Tommy Millard (comedians played an important role in the Blue Grass Boys, as Monroe never downplayed the "entertainment" aspect of his live shows). This group was the very first incarnation of the Blue Grass Boys, a name Bill gave to his group in honor of Kentucky, the Blue Grass State.

The year 1939 was significant for Monroe. He moved his group to Greenville, North Carolina for a better radio gig, and practised hard in a makeshift rehearsal space he'd rented in the back of a gas station. It's here—as well as during numerous small-time gigs in local schools and churches—that he first developed his own vocal and instrumental style (he wasn't used to singing lead or playing solos). He reworked songs like "Mule Skinner Blues" and "Footprints In The Snow"; he experimented with faster tempos and higher keys; he began emulating fiddle leads on his mandolin; he developed intricate harmonies and instrumental arrangements; and he gave his bandmembers solo breaks in the manner of jazz bands.

In October, 1939, Bill Monroe and the Blue Grass Boys were ready for the big time. They auditioned for the *Grand Ole Opry* and immediately won a spot. Monroe soon became a popular *Opry* attraction—and a popular touring act, especially throughout the Southeast, where he toured constantly during the week. (He couldn't travel much farther, since *Opry* members always had to return to Nashville for the Saturday night performance.)

The Jimmie Rodgers song "Mule Skinner Blues," a song Monroe played during his *Opry* audition, became his first signature tune. A hopped-up new version of an old favorite, it was marked by a speedy tempo and driving fiddle lines. "Monroe [did] to Rodgers' song what Elvis Presley would later do to 'Blue Moon Of Kentucky' in 1954," wrote Neil Rosenberg in his seminal book, *Bluegrass: A History*. After grabbing the attention of *Opry* audiences, "Mule Skinner Blues" became the first song Monroe recorded in 1940 during his first session as a solo artist, again for Victor. A second session for Victor was held in 1941.

Although his mid-'40s band with Flatt & Scruggs is considered the focal point—when all Monroe's musical ideas finally gelled and blossomed—the music Monroe and his band played during these early years was, in fact, "bluegrass." Monroe's mandolin may have only begun to show through in the mix—which was dominated then by fiddle and guitar—and the banjo may have been entirely absent (Monroe didn't incorporate a banjo player into his line-up until he hired David "Stringbean" Akeman in 1942), but a good deal of the music's fundamental characteristics had been developed in that Greenville gas station practice space and were now firmly in place: the speedy tempos, the virtuosic playing, the high-tenor vocals.

By the time of the first Victor session, Monroe's original bandmembers had left for various reasons. In their place he'd recruited guitarist Clyde Moody, fiddler Tommy Magness and bassist/comedian Willie Egbert Wesbrooks. Thus began a revolving-door bandmembership trend that would not only continue for the rest of Monroe's career, but would also become commonplace among bluegrass bands in general. Some of Monroe's players decided to strike out on their own (Moody, for instance, would later begin his own singing career). Others got drafted—and some of these draftees eventually returned (by law) to the band a few years later after they'd completed their service. All this makes it difficult to map Monroe's bandmembership in any sort of linear fashion.

The combination of World War II (which created a shortage of shellac as well as skilled workers) and a feud between record companies and the American Federation of Musicians (whose president, James Petrillo, claimed jukeboxes and radio DJ shows were putting musicians out of work) meant that record production was greatly diminished in the US from 1941–45. During this time, Monroe put a lot of energy into developing his live shows—even buying his own performance tent—turning a mere concert into a traveling outdoor extravaganza. As part of this, the Blue Grass Boys would often challenge local baseball players to a friendly game to drum up further interest in their shows.

In 1945, Monroe was signed to Columbia Records by producer Art Satherley. The band at this point included fiddler Chubby Wise, Wilene "Sally Ann" Forrester (who played the accordion and was one of the few female bluegrass musicians until the '60s), Howard Watts (aka Cedric Rainwater), Tex Willis, Curley Bradshaw, and Stringbean (David Akeman). The first session included "Kentucky Waltz," "Footprints In The Snow," "Rocky Road Blues," "True Life Blues," and the instrumental "Blue Grass Special."

The addition of two key players that year—guitarist and lead vocalist Lester Flatt and banjoist Earl Scruggs (they joined at separate times and didn't know each other previously)—proved the catalyst that allowed Monroe's music to truly explode. Flatt was a natural-born emcee for the show, and the twenty-one-year-old Scruggs' mind-blowing three-finger banjo style was an instant hit with audiences. Listening to the Blue Grass Boys' recordings from the period, the excitement is unmistakable, as Scruggs' banjo and Monroe's mandolin make smoke and fire out of the melody lines, and the songs shine with crisp intensity. Part of the power was certainly down to the skill of the individual players, but it was also the result of a strong collective energy. This was truly, as historian Alan Lomax later called it, "folk music with overdrive."

The group who recorded and played together from late 1945 through to early 1948—Monroe, Flatt, Scruggs, Wise, and Rainwater—was the most classic of all bluegrass bands. Songs from this period include "Heavy Traffic Ahead," "Blue Moon Of Kentucky," "Mother's Only Sleeping" (one of the first bluegrass songs to be copied stylistically), "Blue Grass Breakdown," "Molly And Tenbrooks" (which became one of the Stanley Brothers' first recordings), and "I'm Going Back To Old Kentucky."

In 1948, Flatt & Scruggs (and Rainwater) quit Monroe's band. It's pretty certain they'd figured out they could make far more money as headliners than as sidemen—a speculation that turned out to be true, as the pair soon enjoyed huge success on their own. Monroe was deeply bitter and felt betrayed, and he didn't speak to them for the next twenty years. Along with his split with his brother Charlie, it's one of the most famous feuds in bluegrass history.

Monroe, however, quickly regrouped. Among his new hires was banjoist Don Reno (who'd tried out for the position prior to Scruggs but had turned it down because he was about to be drafted). Columbia didn't record Monroe again until 1949; by this time Reno was gone, but Monroe had hired another up-and-coming star, guitarist/vocalist Mac Wiseman, who sang and played on the session. Wiseman stayed in Monroe's band less than a year.

In 1950, Monroe switched to Decca Records, chiefly because Columbia had signed the Stanley Brothers, and Monroe considered them rivals who were copying his music. (Soon, though, when Monroe realized they weren't out to steal from him but were actually developing a style of their own, his attitude mellowed and they became friends.)

Monroe's work in the '50s for Decca shows him further developing his sound and, in the process, writing and recording some of his most enduring (and autobiographical) classics, "Uncle Pen," "I'm On My Way To The Old Home," "When The Golden Leaves Begin To Fall," and "Memories Of Mother And Dad" among them. Even though his most famous band was long gone, the songs and the sound he'd honed during the '40s remained—and it's a good bet that the competition he felt from Flatt & Scruggs and the Stanley Brothers fueled his drive. Monroe's band during his first Decca sessions included fiddler Vassar Clements, soon to become an in-demand sideman, and singer/guitarist Jimmy Martin. Martin's voice was firm and strong, with an intensity that matched Monroe's; each inspiring the other to push harder, the pair created some of the Blue Grass Boys' best vocal work. Martin stayed with Monroe the better part of the early '50s before striking out on his own.

In 1954, the modern music world changed drastically when Elvis Presley hit town. An uptempo version of Monroe's "Blue Moon Of Kentucky" was on the B-side of his first single for Sun Records, but Presley had nothing but respect for bluegrass as its master; when he played the song on his one and only *Opry* appearance, he even apologized backstage to Monroe for changing the song. Monroe, well aware of the financial rewards of songwriting royalties, had no problem with Presley's version; he even re-recorded the song himself to capitalize on the young rock'n'roller's success.

Monroe recorded steadily during the '50s (Decca released his first long-play album, KNEE DEEP IN BLUEGRASS, in 1958), and except for one session when his brand-new label Decca tried

Bill Monroe

fitting him with an uptown sound—recording him in Nashville with a studio band, an experiment that ultimately went nowhere—his sound also remained as staunchly traditional as ever. Flatt & Scruggs may have been overtaking Monroe in terms of sheer popularity; and more importantly, rock'n'roll and rockabilly might have been grabbing the attention of America's teenagers and, in the process, digging deeply into the fan base of bluegrass and country music, but Monroe refused to play into these pop trends, remaining stubbornly true to his aesthetic—even if it meant his once-bright spotlight was shifting elsewhere.

When bluegrass music was discovered in the '50s and '60s by a new generation of urban folk revivalists—college students yearning for music that was "closer to the ground" (an expression used by *Opry* emcee George Hay)—the music found a new fan base. Earl Scruggs was the first bluegrass artist the revivalists latched onto; many of them knew little about Monroe. It wasn't until writer/promoter Ralph Rinzler came along that the tables began to turn. Rinzler published an interview with Monroe, who'd refused them up to that point, in the folk journal *Sing Out!*—the first time Monroe's life story had been told in print. A man who'd previously expressed himself only through music began emerging in a different light.

Rinzler became Monroe's manager in the early '60s, and he began booking him at festivals and college campuses. Monroe had also turned down significant live appearances such as Alan Lomax's Carnegie Hall concert of 1959, but in 1963 he made his first folk festival appearance at the University of Chicago. Later that year he played his first New York gig, performed at the LA folk club, Ash Grove, and appeared at the Newport Folk Festival. At the same time, Monroe's band—which had begun to wallow and lose its consistency—had picked up speed again when Del McCoury and Bill Keith joined the pack. Fans began paying careful attention once again to what the Blue Grass Boys were up to. In 1965, at the first multiday bluegrass festival in Roanoke, Virginia, Rinzler and promoter Carleton Haney put together a monumental tribute to Monroe called "The Story of Bluegrass," gathering past members of the Blue Grass Boys (minus Flatt & Scruggs) to take the stage with Monroe and illustrate how the music had developed over the years. Suddenly it was clear: Monroe was the undisputed "father of bluegrass." When Monroe was inducted into the Country Music Hall of Fame in 1970, his status was sealed.

Monroe performed on the *Opry* and toured regularly well into the '70s, '80s and '90s. Health

complications—cancer in 1981, heart surgery in 1991—did not stop him. He'd opened a country music park in Bean Blossom, Indiana in 1951, and when bluegrass festivals began appearing, he founded a festival of his own at Bean Blossom. He'd been inducted into the Nashville Songwriters Hall of Fame in 1971, and in 1988 he won a Grammy for Best Bluegrass Recording. In 1991 he became the charter inductee into the Bluegrass Hall of Honor. Two years later he was given a Lifetime Achievement Award at the Grammys. In 1996, after suffering a stroke, Monroe died on 9 September, four days short of turning eighty-five.

⊙ **Country Music Hall Of Fame** (1991; MCA). These 16 tracks are a carefully selected sampling of Monroe's recordings for Decca from the 1950s onward—a good choice for those not ready to invest in a box set.

⊙ **The Essential Bill Monroe And His Blue Grass Boys, 1945–1949** (1992; Columbia). A 2-CD box set of material from the most classic Blue Grass Boys period. The central focus of the collection are tracks Monroe recorded with Lester Flatt, Earl Scruggs, Chubby Wise, and Cedric Rainwater—bluegrass music's most famous band. The one drawback for serious fans, however, is that 16 of the songs here are (previously unreleased) alternate takes. Not exactly a big deal to casual listeners, but a surprising move considering the "essential" nature of the material.

⊙ **The Music Of Bill Monroe: From 1936 To 1994** (1994; MCA). A remarkable 4-CD box set that covers the entire breadth of Monroe's career. It starts with two Monroe Brothers songs, 3 from his early-'40s period, and 6 Columbia tracks; the rest of the collection, though, focuses on Monroe's prolific years with Decca (later MCA)—right up to a 1994 recording of "Boston Boy."

⊙ **16 Gems** (1996; Columbia). For those longing to hear the original recordings of the "essential" songs left off the 1992 box set—the versions commercially released by Columbia in the mid-'40s—here they are on one CD. An excellent, easy-to-digest starting point.

⊙ **The Essential Bill Monroe And The Monroe Brothers** (1997; RCA). It was a shame when RCA let its great collection of early-'40s Blue Grass Boys material, MULE SKINNER BLUES, fall out of print; thankfully they've rectified the situation, reissuing all 16 of those pre-Flatt & Scruggs songs (before there was a five-string banjo in the mix at all) in a package that also includes 9 Monroe Brothers numbers as a tasty bonus.

Bill Monroe

Banjo History And Styles

Responsible for the high-lonesome sound bluegrass fans adore, while at the same time relegated to the novelty ghetto by a host of uninformed listeners, the banjo plays a paradoxical role in country music history. Descended from West African stringed instruments that used gourds or drums, the "banjer" or "banza" was first introduced to the US by African slaves. Black singers and musicians who played this early four-string banjo were at first regarded with disdain by white audiences; however, black-faced minstrels who played the same instrument beginning around the early 1800s were embraced. These minstrels popularized the instrument in traveling shows; it was during this time, too, that the familiar fifth string was first added. Now standard, this string runs to a fifth peg halfway up the neck.

"In the early 1800s there were some very fine banjo makers," explains Larry Bowen, proprietor of Fifth String Music in Berkeley, California. "The banjo was played classically—like [one would play] the classical guitar—you're allowed to use all four fingers and thumb." In the late 1800s frets were introduced, allowing better control of tones above the fifth string. White southerners ultimately adopted the five-string banjo, while many black musicians moved on to the guitar, an instrument better suited to the blues. The four-string banjo remained an integral rhythmic accompaniment in dixieland and swing bands for a short period, but it's been largely unused since the '40s.

Most early banjoists used traditional techniques such as clawhammer or frailing. "Clawhammer and frailing are really close," says Donald Nitchie, editor of the Banjo Newsletter. "They're basically old-time down picking; you pick down." "In clawhammer playing the thumb is allowed to play any string, and the hand is held in the shape of a claw," explains Bowen. The similar frailing style is more restrictive, using the thumb only as a pivot on the fifth string. "The first finger, or sometimes you use the middle finger, will strike down on the string and that's followed by a brush [with the other fingers] and the thumb on the fifth."

In country music's earliest days, there were a handful of proficient players, such as Wade Mainer (who played his own unique two-finger style) and Snuffy Jenkins (a pioneer of three-finger playing). For the most part, though, the five-string banjo was perceived as a comic instrument, one commonly associated with enter-tainers like Uncle Dave Macon. It took Earl Scruggs' version of the three-finger style, popularized during his years in the Blue Grass Boys, to bring the banjo to the fore.

The three-finger style involves the thumb, index and middle fingers. The thumb plays the fifth string as a pivot note, a constant that the other notes race and fall around. This method of alternating different "banjo rolls" produces an almost inhumanly fast shower of notes, a sound that, when Scruggs first appeared on the Grand Ole Opry, thrilled and amazed bluegrass' newfound fans. Though he didn't invent the three-finger picking style itself (he picked it up as a boy from family members and from local players such as Jenkins), Scruggs' name has become synonymous with it. The style heard on popular songs like "Dueling Banjos" and "Foggy Mountain Breakdown," it's also one of the most distinctive sounds in bluegrass.

In the late-'50s, a new melodic or "chromatic" style of playing unrestricted by clawhammer or frailing techniques was developed by several players independently. It is most often associated with Bill Keith of Massachussetts and Bobby Thompson of Tennessee. Chromatic playing, often used in jazz, allows free movement of the picking hand and allows the player to hit any and all notes of a melody—as opposed to the more rhythmic plucking of other styles, which dance around the central melodic line.

"By chromatic you're virtually following the fiddle note for note as opposed to the three-finger style," says Bowen, "so you're able to play songs like the 'Sailor's Hornpipe.' The introduction to [television show] Hee Haw is played chromatically."

Some famed banjoists choose to follow their own muse. Bluegrass great Ralph Stanley, who started out playing clawhammer and then moved to a three-finger technique, now plays a style all his own, a straightforward series of banjo rolls that doesn't intersperse other patterns nearly as often as Scruggs-style. It's the perfect complement to his bluegrass laments and tales of lost love.

"Ralph is not what we call a true bluegrass banjo player," argues Bowen, "although he does do some of the bluegrass rolls and things like that. But like he says, his banjo playing is so easy, most people can't do it."

– Nick Tangborn

Lynn Morris

While women have been gaining more and more attention in bluegrass circles over the past few decades, strong female singers and bandleaders are scarcely an everyday phenomenon. And that's exactly why Lynn Morris is such an exciting and refreshing discovery: an artist as vocally soulful and musically genuine as Morris is a rarity in country music as a whole, let alone in bluegrass. Her sense of history is clear in her crisp acoustic arrangements, which are well-grounded in traditional bluegrass and country, but Morris also has a keen contemporary spirit that keeps her music vital and present. Listening to her firm, emotionally rich voice, it's no wonder she earned the Female Vocalist of the Year award from the IBMA in 1995. Obviously, that's just the beginning for this singer, bandleader, banjoist and guitarist who in a short amount of time has proven herself one of the major talents of bluegrass' current generation.

Morris grew up in west Texas, earned an art degree in Colorado, and has been playing professionally since graduating. Initially working as a banjo player, her talent won her awards and took her to festivals, military bases in the Pacific Rim (for the USO), and the *Grand Ole Opry*. She's also become a well-known music instructor. In 1988 she and bassist, songwriter and singer Marshall Wilborn (who'd soon become her husband) formed the Lynn Morris Band in Winchester, Virginia—a town about an hour west of Washington, DC that's also the birthplace of Patsy Cline. Wilborn grew up in Austin, Texas and played with Jimmy Martin and the Johnson Mountain Boys, among others, before joining up with Morris. Johnson Mountain Boys banjoist Tom Adams has also been a key player on all the group's recordings so far. The band released its self-titled debut on Rounder Records in 1990, following it up two years later with THE BRAMBLE AND THE ROSE and in 1995 with MAMA'S HAND.

⊙ The Lynn Morris Band (1990; Rounder). Together with Wilborn and Adams, Morris is joined by mandolinist Ronnie McCoury and fiddler Ray Legere on this debut. The songs are definitely wide-ranging, from Buck Owens and Bob McDill to Charlie Monroe, Carl Sauceman, and Hazel Dickens; there are also several originals by Morris, Wilborn, and Adams.

⊙ The Bramble And The Rose (1992; Rounder). This time the core group of Morris, Wilborn, and Adams is augmented by mandolinist David McLaughlin of Johnson Mountain Boys and Nashville Bluegrass Band fiddler Stuart Duncan, making this practically a bluegrass supergroup. Song choices run from Dolly Parton's "Coat Of Many Colors" to Mike Williams' "Blue Skies And Teardrops" and several by longtime bluegrass and country artist Jim Eanes.

⊙ Mama's Hand (1995; Rounder). Firmly rooted arrangements and skilful musicianship make this an exciting but also warm, soulful collection. The songs run from Wynn Stewart's "Wishful Thinking" (Morris' slowed-down arrangement emphasizing the song's inherent pathos, works surprisingly well) to John Lair's "Freight Train Blues" (with Wilborn taking the lead vocals and sounding not unlike Doc Watson) and Hazel Dickens' "Mama's Hand." The latter is clearly the album's centerpiece, and Morris' version has the makings of a contemporary bluegrass classic. Morris also wrote a couple of uptempo instrumentals that feature her banjo playing.

Nashville Bluegrass Band

"Just like any music, bluegrass has to grow to stay alive."

—Alan O'Bryant

With a penchant for a traditional bluegrass sound, a keen ear for standout song material, and a strong group-oriented ethic, the Nashville Bluegrass Band has, since forming in 1984, built itself into one of the top bands in modern bluegrass. The NBB's music is marked by gently flowing melodies with acoustic arrangements and decidedly bluesy overtones, their repertoire a deft mix of traditional bluegrass and country (Floyd Tillman, Bill Monroe, the Delmore Brothers, Bill Clifton), excellent contemporary songs (Gillian Welch and Richard Thompson), beautiful gospel numbers and a handful of originals.

The musicianship, too, is superb. Banjoist Alan O'Bryant (who's played bluegrass since he was a teenager, including sessions with Monroe and Doc Watson) and guitarist Pat Enright (founder of the West Coast band Phantoms Of The Opry) have been with the group since its inception, and the pair share the majority of the vocal duties. Fiddler Stuart Duncan (a popular session player) joined just after the band recorded its debut album, MY NATIVE HOME, for Rounder in 1985. The two other original members, mandolinist Mike Compton and bassist Mark Hembree (a onetime Blue Grass Boy), played with the group through two more albums, but quit in the wake of a serious bus accident while touring in 1988 (Hembree was badly injured). Since that time the NBB's line-up has settled on O'Bryant, Enright, Duncan, mandolinist Roland White (a member of the Kentucky Colonels during the '60s and, later, Country Gazette) and bassist Gene Libbea.

Since 1990 the NBB has recorded for Sugar Hill, and their music (and popularity) continues to strengthen and grow. Overall, the band creates a positive, life-affirming vibe that permeates the majority of their music, whether it's the silly "I Got A Date," the darkly humorous "The Fool," or more emotionally intense songs such as "Waitin' For The Hard Times To Go" or the gorgeous "Roll Jordan Roll," recorded with the Fairfield Four. In addition to their own albums, the NBB has played on releases by Doc Watson (1987's PORTRAIT) and backed up Peter Rowan on his 1988 album NEW MOON RISING.

⊙ **The Nashville Bluegrass Band** (1987; Rounder). Combines material from the group's first two albums, MY NATIVE HOME and IDLE TIME, including the Greg Brown song "The Train Carrying Jimmie Rodgers Home," which has become a favorite on the bluegrass circuit thanks to the NBB's arrangement.

⊙ **Home Of The Blues** (1991; Sugar Hill). The song selection includes a lively cover of Lee Hazlewood's "The Fool" (a hit for Sanford Clark in 1956), the Delmore Brothers' "Happy On The Mississippi Shores," and the uplifting gospel song "The First Step To Heaven," which features an excellent five-part vocal arrangement. The final treat is a collaboration with the gospel group the Fairfield Four on "Roll Jordan Roll."

⊙ **Waitin' For The Hard Times To Go** (1993; Sugar Hill). The NBB's reading of "Waltzin's For Dreamers" is likely one of the few bluegrass versions of a Richard Thompson song. The album won a Grammy, and thanks to stellar musicianship and song choices (including the excellent title cut by Jim Ringer) it's easy to see why. Easily one of the band's standout releases.

⊙ **Unleashed** (1995; Sugar Hill). Includes two songs by Gillian Welch: "Tear My Stillhouse Down" and "One More Dollar." There's also Bill Clifton's "Little White Washed Chimney," a great old-timey arrangement of "Boll Weevil," and another gospel song featuring the Fairfield Four, "Last Month Of The Year."

New Grass Revival

If for nothing else, the New Grass Revival will be remembered as the originators of the term "newgrass." But they were also one of the quintessential progressive bluegrass bands of the 1970s, a group that—like the Dillards, John Hartford, Clarence White, and the Nitty Gritty Dirt Band—was an important connection between the worlds of traditional bluegrass, folk and country-rock, both in terms of the music they played and audiences that showed up to hear it. The bandmembers did a fine job alienating many conservative bluegrass fans with their long hair, hippie attire and rock-loving rebel attitudes, not to mention their electric instruments. At the same time, however, the Revival-ists were talented, dedicated musicians who helped widen the scope of bluegrass and bring an entire new generation of fans into the fold.

It's hard, in some ways, to even justify calling New Grass Revival "bluegrass." Their instrumentation did include mandolin, fiddle and banjo, but the arrangements on the whole were far closer to country rock (even brushing dangerously close to prog rock) than the music of Monroe. Their music had a breezy, free-form country flair that appealed more to dancing hippies than dairy farmers and tractor drivers. And that was only the '70s; by the following decade, they'd pushed boldly through the pop-music threshold with songs like "What You Do To Me" and a version of Marvin Gaye's "Ain't That Peculiar."

New Grass Revival was formed in 1972 by Sam Bush, Courtney Johnson, Curtis Burch, and Ebo Walker. Bush, an accomplished mandolinist and fiddler, had first played in a band called Poor Richard's Almanac. He and banjoist Johnson later played in Bluegrass Alliance, which at that point included Walker on bass and traditionally minded fiddler Lonnie Peerce (guitarist and co-founder Dan Crary had already departed.) Guitarist Burch joined the increasingly modern-sounding Alliance in 1971, and when Pearce quit, the bandmembers renamed themselves New Grass Revival. John Cowan took over the bass position a year later, bringing his rock'n'roll background into the mix.

The band recorded mostly for Flying Fish during the '70s. Some called their bluegrass-inflected country-rock music refreshing, while others turned their backs, uninterested. In 1981, Johnson and Burch quit, and were replaced by Pat Flynn (formerly with Fresh Air) and banjoist Béla Fleck. They recorded for Sugar Hill before being signed to EMI in 1986, which released their best-selling material to date. Over the next three years, several of their songs made the charts, but in 1989 they finally called it quits. Bush is a popular session player these days; Fleck now fronts his own band, the Flecktones.

New Grass Revival

⊙ **When The Storm Is Over** (1977; Flying Fish). One of the band's earlier albums, it clearly illustrates what "newgrass" is all about by deftly mixing folk, bluegrass and country-rock styles. A little soft around the edges, and with a definite hippie vibe emanating from within, it's not for bluegrass fans who like their music traditional. The album has since been paired with 1976's FLY THROUGH THE COUNTRY and re-released on a single CD.

⊙ **Live** (1989; Sugar Hill). There are only 7 songs on this full-length album (recorded live in France at the Toulouse Bluegrass Festival in 1983), but one of them, "Sapporo," is drawn out to nearly 19 minutes—the band loved to indulge in extended instrumental jams, which is a major reason why a live New Grass Revival album makes good sense. The line-up at this point consisted of Sam Bush, John Cowan, Pat Flynn, and Béla Fleck; songs include a lively take on Townes Van Zandt's "White Freight Liner Blues" (an early staple of theirs) and Leon Russell's "One More Love Song."

Osborne Brothers

Along with Flatt & Scruggs, the Osborne Brothers were one of the biggest-selling bands in bluegrass. Though traditional when they began recording in the 1950s, in the decades that followed they showed themselves willing to experiment with such modern trappings as electric instruments, drums and a "commercial" country repertoire. This aggravated conservative fans but widened their audience considerably—"Rocky Top," released in 1968, was one of several Felice and Boudleaux Bryant songs they recorded during that time that were big hits for them. Yet despite all the arguments that ensued among bluegrass aficionados regarding their damaged authenticity (especially when they "went electric" in 1969), when the smoke and fire was gone, it was clear they'd managed to maintain their downhome integrity and bluegrass heart.

The Osborne Brothers are not only one of the biggest-selling bands in bluegrass, they're also a linchpin between the traditional bands of the '50s and the "progressive" bluegrass bands of the '60s and later. Bobby and Sonny Osborne began under the tutorship of the greats—Bill Monroe, the Stanley Brothers —and when they began recording together in the mid-'50s, they quickly gained respect as one of the classic outfits of that golden era. But they were also clearly aware of the changes taking place in country music, and when record companies decided that "old-fashioned" music was out, the Osbornes were quick to "experiment" with new sounds. And new audiences: they were the first bluegrass act, for instance, to play a concert on a college campus (Antioch College in 1960), which exposed them to a huge new audience of urban intellectuals and folk revivalists—one yet to be fully tapped. By that time, though, they'd already had an influence on young up-and-coming bands like the Country Gentlemen; John Duffey remembers listening to them religiously on WWVA's *Wheeling Jamboree* every Saturday night.

Bobby Osborne was born on 7 December, 1931, and Sonny Osborne on 29 October, 1937, in the mountainous countryside around Hyden, Kentucky. The family later moved to Dayton, Ohio, where their father worked for the National Cash Register Company. Bobby first played electric guitar in a local band, then teamed up with banjoist Larry Richardson. In 1949, the two friends joined the Lonesome Pine Fiddlers, an early bluegrass/country band, and cut four sides with them, including the original "Pain In My Heart" (which Flatt & Scruggs quickly covered).

Bobby hooked up with Jimmy Martin in 1951, recording a few songs for King, and then worked with the Stanley Brothers before he was drafted to serve in Korea. Sonny, meanwhile, had kept himself busy during this time: an excellent banjo player at an early age, he'd played and even recorded with Bill Monroe while only fourteen years old. In the early '50s, Sonny did some recordings for Cincinnati's Kentucky and Gateway labels—mostly straight bluegrass covers of Monroe and Flatt & Scruggs material, along with a few originals (one being "A Brother In Korea," written by his sister, Louise).

When Bobby returned, the brothers teamed up. They worked radio programs with Jimmy Martin in Knoxville and Detroit in the mid-'50s before moving to Wheeling, West Virginia and finally back to Dayton. There they hooked up with guitarist and singer Red Allen and, in 1956, won a record contract with MGM. "Ruby," their first release, is now a bluegrass standard. During this time they played around with a twin-banjo sound and some rockabilly material; their most significant development, though, was a vocal trio style that featured tenor Bobby, who had the highest voice (one of the brightest and purest in bluegrass), singing the lead melody. (Normally, the lead vocalist sings below the high tenor harmony part). By the end of the decade, the Osborne Brothers (Allen quit in 1958) were rearranging country songs to fit their vocal trio sound.

The brothers played the *Wheeling Jamboree* regularly and recorded with MGM until 1963, when they decided they needed a change. The Wilburn Brothers helped them get a new contract with Decca and appearances on the *Grand Ole Opry*, where they became members a year later. Though they'd been playing country material since the '50s, for this next decade, they began experimenting further with integrating bluegrass and modern country sounds. They wanted to widen their audience without losing their longstanding fans. They succeeded on the first count with a series of hit songs ("Up This Hill And Down," "Rocky Top") that featured such sacrilegious instruments as electric bass and piano. By the time they released "Tennessee Hound Dog" in 1969, their biggest hit so far, they'd "gone electric," which mostly involved adding pick-ups to their instruments. Traditionalists argued that they'd sold out, while the brothers claimed they were only trying to let their music be heard properly (especially at concerts) in an era ruled by electricity and volume. Whatever the case, their experimentation paid off in the eyes of the Country Music Association, who voted them Best Vocal Group in 1971. That same year, however, they traveled even farther afield; the song "Georgia Pineywoods" included an overdubbed string section.

A few years later, however, the Osborne Brothers put away their pick-ups and returned to a more traditional sound—thanks in part to the proliferation of bluegrass festivals, which gave the bands a good deal more concert work. The brothers also had several hits under their belts, allowing them more freedom to play music the way they wanted. They found their old fans hadn't completely abandoned them, and they have continued, in the years since, to maintain their trademark mix of bluegrass and country songs at festivals and concerts, on the *Grand Ole Opry*, and on a series of recordings for various labels (CHM, RCA, and Sugar Hill).

⊙ **From Rocky Top To Muddy Bottom** (1977; CMH). The 20 songs on what was originally a double-LP are all by master songwriters Boudleaux and Felice Bryant, many of which (including "Rocky Top") became chart hits for the brothers.

⊙ **Once More, Vols I & II** (1991; Sugar Hill). This CD (initially released on 2 separate LPs) compiles 24 recordings the Osborne Brothers made in the mid-1980s of some of their classic early MGM and Decca songs (thankfully avoiding overdone hits like "Rocky Top"). The arrangements are acoustic and traditional,

but the brothers' gorgeous harmonies—sounding in many ways stronger than ever—are the main event.

⊙ **Bluegrass 1956–68** (1995; Bear Family). An exhaustive (and expensive) box set of the Osborne Brothers' most classic material, recorded for both MGM and Decca. (A second Bear Family box, 1968–74, picks up where this one leaves off.)

Reno & Smiley

Don Reno, Red Smiley, and their band the Tennessee Cut-Ups were one of the most successful and popular bluegrass bands that formed in the wake of Bill Monroe. Reno's high tenor voice (which alternates between piercing and pretty) and Smiley's full, gentle and easygoing baritone made an excellent coupling. In addition, Smiley's even-keeled rhythm guitar-playing, combined with the instrumental prowess of banjoist/guitarist Reno, made their arrangements all the more intense and exciting. By the time they parted ways in 1964, they'd sold a respectable number of records for their longtime label, King, and in the process earned a well-deserved place in the pantheon of traditional bluegrass bands.

Reno was talented on a variety of instruments, but five-string banjo was his main choice, and he was the only serious rival—some say an equal—to the mighty Earl Scruggs. In fact, Reno came very close to following in Scruggs' shoes. In 1943 he auditioned for a spot in Monroe's Blue Grass Boys, but ultimately refused the job because he knew he was about to be drafted. Reno did take the job, however, in 1948 when Scruggs left Monroe's band (he stayed for a year), but who's to say how the development of bluegrass as a whole might have changed if Monroe's landmark mid-'40s Columbia sessions had featured anyone other than Scruggs on banjo—even a man of Reno's caliber.

Reno's talents didn't stop with his stellar three-finger banjo picking: he was also a skilled lead guitarist, a prolific songwriter, a strong singer, and he could play drums, steel guitar, bass, fiddle—practically any instrument put in front of him. On top of this, he often acted as the group's emcee and for a time even its manager, booking recording sessions and hiring sidemen. Born Donald Wesley Reno in Spartanburg, South Carolina on 21 February, 1926, he served an apprenticeship with the Morris Brothers and also worked with Arthur "Guitar Boogie" Smith, whom he would later

Osborne Brothers • Reno & Smiley

describe as a second father to him. Reno spent time in the Army unit known as Merrill's Marauders (made famous in a film by Sam Fuller), and after his discharge he played with Monroe, then joined Tommy Magness's Tennessee Buddies. It's here, in 1949, that he met Red Smiley.

Red-haired, friendly-faced Arthur Lee Smiley, Jr. was born on 17 May, 1925, in Asheville, North Carolina. He, too, played with the Morris Brothers, although not at the same time as Reno. His war duties included service in Sicily, where he was wounded and lost a lung. Upon his return to civilian life he, too, ended up in Roanoke, Virginia, playing with Magness.

Reno & Smiley recorded songs together for Federal (a King subsidiary) in 1951 as part of Magness's group, then left to work with Toby Stroud's Blue Mountain Boys before forming their own band, the Tennessee Cut-Ups, later that year. Signed to King, their first session as a duo was in early 1952. Though their debut single, "I'm Using My Bible For A Roadmap," was a hit, live gigs turned out to be scarce, and Reno & Smiley couldn't afford to maintain a full-time band. They disbanded the group and each man took a job. Reno ended up playing again in Arthur Smith's band, and his many credits during this time include co-writing and dueting with Smith on "Feuding Banjos"—a song that would later gain enormous popularity as the theme ("Dueling Banjos") to the movie *Deliverance*.

Despite the absence of a live band, Reno & Smiley did continue recording for King, thanks to steady record sales. The country music industry had been built around commercial recordings since its inception, but a band's longterm survival always depended on strong and frequent live performances. During the '50s, however, records were growing in popularity (as were radio programs featuring DJs instead of live bands). More and more people, both rural and urban, owned phonographs (for one thing, electricity was cheaper and more widespread), and records became the chief way they listened to music. Since Reno & Smiley weren't a live act in their earliest years, it was their steady output of recordings that solidified their reputation.

Between 1952 and 1954, the duo recorded some sixty gospel, instrumental and secular songs, many of them written by Reno. "Tally Ho," "I'm The Talk Of The Town," the uptempo banjo numbers "Limehouse Blues" (which even included a subtle drum part) and "Choking The Strings," and the gentle "It's Grand To Have Someone To Love You" are just a few of their hits from these sessions. In early 1955, Reno recorded all the instrumental and vocal parts for a cover of the Allen Shelton song "Home Sweet Home," which also became a substantial hit. Later that spring, after many requests for live appearances, the two men finally reunited as a performing group. They soon landed a steady stream of radio and TV work, including the *Old Dominion Barn Dance* on WRVA in Richmond, Virginia and a daily TV show in Roanoke. At each show, in addition to their music, they performed a comedy routine as Chicken Hotrod, Pansy, and the Banty Roosters.

During their fifteen years together, Smiley left most of the decisions regarding the group's musical direction to Reno. In a 1973 interview in *Muleskinner News*, Reno described Smiley as an honest, easygoing man and claimed that the two men never once bickered.

Except for a brief stint with Dot Records in 1957 (where Reno's pal Mac Wiseman was the country A&R man), and one record released on Grassound in 1961, Reno & Smiley recorded exclusively for King. By 1964, however, Smiley's health (he had diabetes) was failing. As well as being worried about his partner, Reno was restless to get out on the road on his own, and so the banjoist quit the group. Their last show together was at Temple University in February, 1965. Ironically, it was the first time the pair had played a college campus—a sort of venue that had, thanks to the folk revival, become a popular stomping ground for touring bluegrass musicians.

After the split, Smiley continued to perform on the *Roanoke* TV show, and longtime bassist John Palmer stayed with him. Smiley eventually called his new band the Bluegrass Cut-Ups, and they recorded several records for Rimrock and Rural Rhythm labels. The TV show was canceled in 1968, after which Smiley retired. He worked a few dates with Reno in 1970 and 1971, but died on 2 January, 1972.

As for Reno, he cut an album for Dot and recorded with fiddler Benny Martin (they had a minor hit with "Soldier's Prayer In Viet Nam") before hooking up with guitarist/mandolinist Bill Harrell—a key player on the Washington, DC bluegrass scene—in late 1966. Their partnership lasted ten years, and they recorded for King, Starday, and Monument, among other small labels. In 1973, when "Dueling Banjos" became a major hit, Reno and Arthur Smith sued for copyright infringement and won. In 1976, Reno moved to Lynchburg, Virginia, where he played regularly with his sons Dale, Don Wayne, and Ronnie. The boys have continued playing and working together following the death of their father on 16 October, 1984.

⊙ **A Variety Of Country Songs** (1959; King; reissued 1988). One of a handful of King albums that have been reissued on both LP and CD (complete with original artwork but, unfortunately, no explanatory notes or song credits), this collection is as worthwhile a starting place as any. Selections include the superb "There's Another Baby Waiting For Me Down The Line" and "Since I've Used My Bible For A Roadmap," a sequel to one of their most famous songs.

⊙ **1951–1959** (1993; Highland). A 4-CD box set that includes 115 of Reno & Smiley's most classic songs recorded for King and its subsidiary, Federal—presented in chronological order with an accompanying booklet.

⊙ **On The Air** (1996; Copper Creek). This collection captures Reno & Smiley on several radio and television appearances from the late '50s, when they were at their peak. Shows represented here include the *Old Dominion Barn Dance* and the *Don Owens TV Jamboree*, and there's plenty of music as well as some good old-fashioned promotional chatter.

⊙ **The Talk Of The Town** (1999; Westside). A collection of the pair's classic 1950s material on King—24 sides in all, including "I'm Using My Bible For A Road Map," "There's Another Baby Waiting For Me Down The Line," "Choking The Strings," and "Tally Ho."

Peter Rowan

S ince spending several years as lead singer and guitarist with Bill Monroe's Blue Grass Boys during the mid-1960s, Peter Rowan's been a contemporary beacon of traditional bluegrass. At the same time he was tagged early on as part of the progressive and country-rock end of the spectrum, thanks to his collaborations with Dave Grisman and his membership on the short-lived Grateful Dead spin-off band Old And In The Way. As a bandleader, singer and songwriter on his own, Rowan's starting point remains more or less in the realm of traditional bluegrass, though he also mixes various acoustic folk styles into the framework. He's got a decent tenor voice and is skilled on both guitar and mandolin; as for his songwriting, it has its ups and downs, as do his recordings in general. On the downside he can be precious and at times even hokey, but when's he's up (as on the 1988 Grammy-nominated album NEW MOON RISING, a collaboration with the Nashville Bluegrass Band), he's a hot player, fine songwriter and a confident showman.

Peter Hamilton Rowan was born on 4 July, 1942, in Boston, Massachusetts. He began pursuing music professionally during the '60s in the Boston area, where he played with banjoist Bill Keith, among others. Landing the position with Bill Monroe helped bring Rowan new-found attention and respect; in return, the presence of young, city-bred performers such as himself (and Keith and Del McCoury before him) helped bluegrass gain a new audience. Rowan next played with Earth Opera (which also included Dave Grisman) and the Bay Area-based SeaTrain before joining Jerry Garcia (banjo), Dave Grisman (mandolin), John Kahn (bass), and Vassar Clements (fiddle) in Old And In The Way. The group was a sort of back-to-his-roots project for Garcia, and to its credit the group's recordings do retain a hearty traditional feel. Among the mix of old-time favorites are a few Rowan originals, including "Panama Red," a catchy number that became a hippie-era standard of its own.

Since the mid-'70s Rowan has recorded in various folk styles and with all sorts of guests and collaborators, including his brothers Chris and Lorin (as the Rowans), guitarist Clarence White (under the name Muleskinner), Tex-Mex accordionist Flaco Jimenez (the Mexican Free Air Force), the Nashville Bluegrass Band, and contemporary Dobro master Jerry Douglas. Rowan recorded his first solo album under his own name,

PETER ROWAN, for Flying Fish in 1978. He lived
for a time in Nashville, where he concentrated on
country songwriting, but his heart appears to
remain closely tied to bluegrass.

⊙ **Old And In The Way** (1975; Grateful Dead;
reissued 1996; Arista). Culled from a series of live
recordings this short-lived group made in 1973, the
original OLD AND IN THE WAY album showcased Garcia's
banjo playing, the fiery fiddling of Vassar Clements, and
the songwriting talents of Rowan, who penned
"Panama Red," "Midnight Moonlight," and "Land Of
The Navajo." Two new and even more substantial
collections, THAT HIGH LONESOME SOUND and BREAKDOWN,
which further mine that same original series of live
recordings, have since been issued by Acoustic Disc,
the label owned by mandolinist Dave Grisman.

⊙ **New Moon Rising** (1988; Sugar Hill). Rowan's
voice has room to shine on this album, thanks in no
small part to the tight, bright arrangements from his
excellent backing group on this outing, the Nashville
Bluegrass Band. The song roster is packed with Rowan
originals such as "That High Lonesome Sound" and
"Meadow Green." Definitely one of his finest recorded
achievements.

⊙ **Dust Bowl Children** (1990; Sugar Hill). The songs
on this album center in concept around the Dust Bowl
days of the mid-twentieth century. It's a simple and
entirely solo acoustic album, and stylistically it's more
Woody Guthrie than Bill Monroe.

Mike Seeger

"I was determined to play the music I
wanted to, rather than trying to chase
the public."
— Mike Seeger

Though he's not a bluegrass picker per se, Mike
Seeger has, through most of his more than
four-decade music career, worked in close association with that genre—playing the same festivals
as many bluegrass artists during the 1960s, and
attracting a similar slice of the folk-revival audience.
He and the group he co-founded in the '50s, the
New Lost City Ramblers, played what they
referred to as "old-time" music—songs from the
'20s and '30s, the earliest decades of commercial
country (aka "hillbilly") music. In addition to
Seeger, the group's initial line-up included John

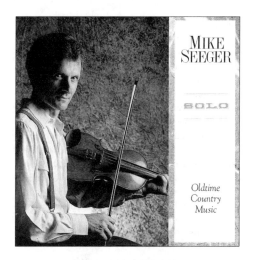

Cohen, a Yale-educated folk enthusiast, and Tom
Paley, a mathematician. Tracy Schwartz replaced
Paley in the early '60s. All of the members originally hailed from New York City, though the
group was based in Washington, DC. Together,
these eager young musicians played a significant
role in reviving popular interest in older rural music
styles, helping define "old-time" (a term used by
country people and record companies alike to
describe traditional hand-me-down folk songs from
years, even centuries, past) for future generations
of folkies. The group recorded quite a few albums
for Folkways beginning in the late '50s, many of
which became vital sources for old-time musicians
who came to the music later. Though they don't
play or record all that often, the Ramblers have
continued working together on and off through
the present day.

Seeger was born on 15 August, 1933, into one
of America's most famous folk-music families. His
father was a highly regarded musicologist, Dr
Charles Seeger, and his siblings included his half
brother Pete and sister Peggy, both folksingers in
their own right. When Mike was a child, his
parents were helping their good friends, musicol-
ogists John and Alan Lomax, assemble the Archive
of Folk Song at the Library of Congress in Washington, DC. With all that musical energy buzzing
around the house, it's no wonder that young Mike
gained such vast knowledge and respect for traditional American music.

Seeger himself is a skilled multi-instrumentalist
and decent singer, and in addition to his work with
the Ramblers he's cut numerous records and
toured under his own name since the '60s. Rather
than write songs himself, he's focused on digging
up older material and bringing it back to musical

Mike Seeger

life through contemporary recordings that are faithful to the original styles. In the process he's become one of the foremost authorities on old-time music. Although Seeger's scholarly approach tends to make much of his music a bit dry at times, on the other hand, his recordings are fascinating and extremely well rendered pieces that bring forgotten songs and styles to life like no history book ever could. They're also a refreshing counterpoint to the slick commercial sounds—be they the '50s folk of the Kingston Trio, the pop of Pat Boone, or the Nashville Sound country of Patsy Cline and Jim Reeves—that have dominated radio playlists since the days when Seeger first started performing.

New Lost City Ramblers

⊙ **The Early Years 1958–1962** (1991; Smithsonian/Folkways). A CD collection highlighting the group's first dozen albums, which were hugely influential on the old-time music revival movement. The line-up here is the original one of Cohen, Seeger, and Paley.

Mike Seeger

⊙ **Solo—Oldtime Country Music** (1991; Rounder). The instruments Seeger plays (dulcimer, autoharp, banjo, jaw harp, etc.) and the songs he covers are all over the rural-music map on this entirely solo outing. Scholarly, yes, but songs like the pretty "Wind And Rain" and the kooky "Ground Hog" (about a family hunting down and then cooking up a tasty groundhog for supper) ring with joy, sadness, and beauty.

⊙ **Southern Banjo Sounds** (1998; Smithsonian Folkways). The purpose of this CD is to showcase the huge variety of banjo styles that existed in the South during the nineteenth and early twentieth centuries— including clawhammer, frailing, and assorted two- and three-finger picking styles. Quite an invaluable collection for banjo pickers and scholars, not only for the variety of music included, but also for the extensive liner notes, which include detailed descriptions and histories of the playing styles, the songs and the instrument itself.

Strange Creek Singers

⊙ **Strange Creek Singers** (1972; Arhoolie; reissued 1997). Seeger was one of the five members of this short-lived group, which formed in the late 1960s out of friendship and mutual musical admiration. The others

include Ramblers member Tracy Schwartz, Seeger's wife at the time Alice Gerrard, Appalachian singer and songwriter Hazel Dickens (the only actual hill-country native of the bunch), and banjoist Lamar Grier. Rippling with warmth from the group's strong energy, the songs run from old-time standards "In The Pines" and "Sunny Side Of Life" to originals such as Schwartz's "Poor Old Dirt Farmer" and Dickens' stark and stunning "Black Lung," which she sings a cappella.

Seldom Scene

"The way we play resembles jazz, because for the most part it's free-form."

—John Duffey

John Duffey wanted a part-time band when he formed the Seldom Scene in 1971. But once word started spreading about this new band, it wasn't long before the Scene was on its way to becoming one of the most popular bluegrass bands of the '70s, both in its native Washington, DC area and beyond.

Mandolinist and tenor singer Duffey (a DC native) was a veteran of the Country Gentlemen, as was bassist Tom Gray; banjo player Ben Eldridge and Dobro player Mike Auldridge (one of the modern virtuosos on the instrument) had both played with Cliff Waldron in New Shades Of Grass, another popular DC-area bluegrass band. Rounding out the crew was John Starling, a doctor interning as an ear, nose and throat specialist who played guitar and sang lead.

The Seldom Scene became regular fixtures at local clubs and were soon favorites at festivals as well. They've recorded a large amount during their years with the Rebel and Sugar Hill labels, and like most contemporary bluegrass bands, their repertoire has been chock full of non-traditional numbers—Rick Nelson's "Hello Mary Lou" and Billy Joe Shaver's "Ride Me Down Easy"—planted alongside songs by Carter Stanley, Jimmy Martin, and Hank Thompson. They also wrote and arranged some originals written by various band-members. None of the members depended on the Scene for income, which freed them up to more or less play whatever and however they wanted.

The Scene's music has always retained a well-defined bluegrass streak in its instrumentation and arrangements, but its overall sound has, to varying degrees over the years, drifted rather far from traditional shores. Along with their far-reaching song choices (the Grateful Dead and even James Taylor sometimes made the set list), Auldridge's pedal-steel guitar and John Starling's smooth country baritone voice helped make this much more of a "modern" band—one geared toward urban and suburban tastes—than the Gentlemen had ever been. The Scene considered itself "sophisticated": no nasal voices, no rough and rural edges. Starling has even gone so far as to call Duffey "the father of 'newgrass.'"

The core instrumental line-up of Duffey, Auldridge, and Eldridge remained stable for twenty-five long years. Starling had quit in 1977 to pursue medicine, though he returned for a short while in 1991; he's since recorded solo albums that are more overtly country than the Scene ever was. Gray had left in 1987 and works for *National Geographic*. On December 31, 1995, however, fans at Washington's Birchmere Club witnessed Auldridge's final night with his longtime partners. He was quitting to pursue full-time his "side" project, Chesapeake (a more pop-flavored band that also records for Sugar Hill), taking bassist T. Michael Colman and guitarist-vocalist Moondi Klein with him. Duffey and Eldrige (a mathematician by profession), however, have since plowed ahead with new guitarist and singer Dudley Connell (of the excellent and far more traditional Johnson Mountain Boys), Dobroist Fred Travers, and bassist Ronnie Simkins.

⊙ **Live At The Cellar Door** (1975; Rebel). The band and its audience together create an extra-festive atmosphere on this live double album, recorded over two days in late 1974 at one of the Scene's regular DC haunts. The 22 songs include originals, instrumentals and assorted covers (including "California Cottonfields" and "Baby Blue"). A favorite among their fans.

⊙ **Act Four** (1979; Sugar Hill). Songs by Hank Thompson ("Girl In The Night"), Bob Wills and Carter Stanley, among others, give this album a well-balanced country-bluegrass flavor (as does Auldridge's pedal-steel playing). A bluegrass arrangement of Billy Joe Shaver's "Ride Me Down Easy" may sound odd, but it's a standout. Phil Rosenthal (who wrote three of the originals, including the superb "Leaving Harlan") is the group's new lead singer, replacing John Starling.

⊙ **Dream Scene** (1996; Sugar Hill). This is the first Scene album with the new line-up featuring Dudley Connell as guitarist and lead vocalist. He brings a bit of the Johnson Mountain Boys' traditional streak with him—along with top-quality songs like "Blue Diamond," a JMB favorite.

Larry Sparks

At a time when new bluegrass groups were shifting further away from a traditional acoustic sound, Larry Sparks proved the music was very much alive and worth exploring. From 1967—when he took the late Carter Stanley's place alongside Ralph in the Clinch Mountain Boys—to a solo career that's been going strong since 1969, Sparks has grown from a regional favorite to one of the top traditional bluegrass players on the circuit.

Sparks' material alternates between fired-up bluegrass numbers and slow-burning, mountain-tinged country ballads that are deeply lonesome and blue. He sings lead in a range similar to Lester Flatt or Carter Stanley, his voice etching an earthy, fireside warmth into every word. Like the great bluegrass singers before him, Sparks' voice is organic, rich and decidedly rural; he couldn't sing any other way, and we wouldn't want him to. Sparks is also an accomplished guitarist, and he knows his way around a mandolin, banjo, and Dobro as well. Over the years he's generally kept his band to a standard acoustic bluegrass instrumentation—fiddle, banjo, mandolin, bass, and Dobro—but he usually sings alone, only occasionally adding tenor harmonies.

In the '60s, Sparks was one of the new generation of up-and-coming bluegrass players who had been born and raised in the North—a growing trend, since so many Appalachian families had migrated out of the mountains in search of work, bringing their music with them. Sparks was born in 1947 in Lebanon, Ohio, a small town in the Miami Valley midway between Dayton (home base of the Osborne Brothers) and Cincinnati. His parents, who were from Kentucky, played old-time and bluegrass music, and by the age of ten Sparks was playing lead guitar in his brother-in-law's band, which emulated the Stanley Brothers' sound. In 1963 he met the Stanleys, who hired him for occasional gigs in the area.

Soon after Carter Stanley's death, Sparks became the new lead singer and guitarist in Ralph Stanley's new version of the Clinch Mountain Boys—difficult shoes to fill, but Sparks managed beautifully. He recorded five albums with Stanley before getting restless. In 1969 he formed his own band, the Lonesome Ramblers, which initially included David Cox, Joe Isaacs, Lloyd Hensley, and Larry's sister Bernice. Sparks was wedded to traditional bluegrass, but at the same time he struggled to find an original sound for his group; in the process he wrote lots of songs, arranged others to suit his style, and played with a succession of excellent musicians (including Ricky Skaggs, Mike Lilly, and Wendy Miller), both at festivals and on his albums—which were released over the years by labels such as Pine Tree, Old Homestead, June Appal, Starday-King, and Rebel. Over the next couple of decades he reached his mark, at least if testimonies on the back of his 1980 album, IT's NEVER TOO LATE, are any indication: "The pure stuff," wrote Ohio DJ Paul "Moon" Mullins. "Larry's feel for a song is just as deep as a Ralph Stanley, George Jones, or Hank Williams."

⊙ **Larry Sparks Sings Hank Williams** (1977; County). Sparks breathes fresh, honest country air into familiar songs like "I'm So Lonesome I Could Cry," "Mansion On The Hill," and "I Saw The Light." His band includes Ricky Skaggs on mandolin and onetime Monroe fiddler Chubby Wise.

⊙ **Classic Bluegrass** (1989; Rebel). An excellent compilation of material Sparks recorded during the 1970s and '80s for Rebel and other assorted labels. Standout tracks include the Keith Whitley gospel song "Great High Mountain," the gorgeous "Smoky Mountain Memories," and "John Deere Tractor," a deeply melancholy song that's unquestionably a high point of his career.

⊙ **Blue Mountain Memories** (1996; Rebel). After nearly three decades working on his own, Sparks continues to release superb albums of moving, innovative new material. Straight-up bluegrass numbers like "Ramblin' Pickin'" are quick on their feet, the a cappella "Gospel Train" is a spine-tingler, and country songs like "Stone Wall" and the title track are full-bodied but mellow. Why rush such soulful music?

Stanley Brothers

In 1947, Carter and Ralph Stanley and the Clinch Mountain Boys—which included original vocalist/mandolinist Pee Wee Lambert—became the first to cut songs modeled after the sound of Bill Monroe's Blue Grass Boys. Though they didn't necessarily know it at the time, their early recordings for Rich-R-Tone marked the birth of bluegrass as a style in and of itself—it was no longer the music of just one man. With their haunting, mountain-grown singing and sharp instrumental skills, the brothers brought soulful depth to a newly developed sound that was fresh, exciting and ripe for exploration.

The brothers' music is marked by the strong harmonies between Ralph and Carter, Ralph's banjo playing (which grew more confident each year), and Carter's steady guitar playing and lead vocals. In addition, Carter was one of the strongest songwriters the genre has yet seen. His numerous compositions are frequently covered by bands even today because they speak frankly and honestly of such intense, painful feelings as loneliness, lost love, and death, while at the same time echoing the pastoral beauty and lifestyle of his and Ralph's rural upbringing in Virginia's Clinch Mountains.

The Stanleys were also among the most traditional-sounding groups in bluegrass. They often included older folk and sacred material in their repertoire, and Carter's original songs frequently reflected these traditions in their structure and content. Where Monroe's music often focused on an instrumental ferocity intended to blow the listener's mind, the Stanleys tended toward slow-burning understatement. In the process they created beautiful, melancholic and deeply moving music that deftly balanced beauty and pain.

Pioneers of the music in its infancy, the Stanley Brothers grew to become one of the genre's strongest and most popular acts. Since Carter's death in 1966, Ralph has persevered with a regrouped version of the Clinch Mountain Boys, and he's revered today as an icon of traditional bluegrass. The brothers were born (Carter in 1925, Ralph in 1927) and raised on a farm near McClure in the rural southwestern panhandle of Virginia, a sliver of Appalachia squeezed between Kentucky and Tennessee. Their father sang, their mother played banjo, and they grew up attending the local Primitive Baptist Church, a hard, southern faith that would add a deeply religious edge to their music.

The boys were local entertainers early on, but when they finished high school they each got drafted to serve in World War II. Carter was discharged first and began playing on a radio show with local musician Roy Sykes. Here he met mandolin player Pee Wee Lambert and bassist Ray Lambert (no relation). When Ralph returned to civilian life in 1946, he linked up with Carter and formed the Stanley Brothers. Their new group, the Clinch Mountain Boys, included the Lamberts and fiddler Leslie Keith.

Their first significant break was a regular gig on WCYB, a new station in the Tennessee–Virginia border town of Bristol (where the Carter Family and Jimmie Rodgers were first recorded). The station could reach a wide area, which made it a sought-after gig (Flatt & Scruggs played on it, too, when they first started the Foggy Mountain Boys). The Stanleys quickly became a popular act on the *Farm And Fun Time* show, and one of their listeners was an eager young enterpreneur named Jim Stanton, who had just started Rich-R-Tone Records, an independent label based in Johnson City, Tennessee. Stanton signed the Stanley Brothers in 1947—barely six months after they'd formed the band—and they recorded fourteen songs for Rich-R-Tone over the next five years. These turned out to be significant recordings representing a transition between old-time mountain folk music and bluegrass (though the music wouldn't be given that name for another few years).

When the Stanleys first began playing, their biggest influences were Mainer's Mountaineers, the Monroe Brothers, and the Carter Family. Ralph played two-finger and clawhammer banjo styles, and the pair sang traditional old-time songs. Listening to their Rich-R-Tone recordings, however, you can almost hear the changes as they happen. From their first session (early 1947), "Death Is Only A Dream" is a straight gospel hymn, and the Carter Stanley original "Mother No Longer Awaits Me At Home" (an early taste of the sort of melancholy that would become a key element of his best songwriting) is a folk ballad in the brother-duet style. Their second session included "Little Maggie," which prominently features Ralph's two-finger banjo playing, and "Little Glass Of Wine" a tragic folk ballad that became a substantial regional hit. At their third session (in 1948), however, they shot through a version of Bill Monroe's "Molly And Tenbrook" complete with three-finger banjo (the first by Ralph on record), sharp, high tenor vocals (courtesy of Pee Wee Lambert, a Monroe fanatic),

strong fiddle work (by Art Wooten, a Monroe alumnus, who'd replaced Keith), and a speedy, exciting tempo. The Stanleys' "Molly And Tenbrook" (which beat Monroe's version to the stores) was the first copy of a song played in the manner of Bill Monroe's music.

Thanks largely to the popularity of "Little Glass Of Wine," RCA approached the Stanleys in 1948 offering a contract. It was Columbia's Art Satherley, though, who finally signed the group. The brothers recorded 22 songs for Columbia between 1949 and 1952. During this time, their instrumental and vocal work became tighter, and some superb (and now-classic) Carter Stanley originals emerged, including "The White Dove," "I'm A Man Of Constant Sorrow," and "The Fields Have Turned Brown." The subjects were often dark and painful—tragic death, betrayal and loss of either true love or an old way of life—delivered with a deep, heartfelt melancholy that has rarely been matched.

Carter and Ralph split for a short time in 1951, during which Carter played in Monroe's band—ironic considering that Monroe had quit Columbia in protest when the Stanleys were signed. But Monroe and Carter Stanley became friends, even writing songs together. In 1952, however, the brothers reunited, recorded one final session for Rich-R-Tone before signing with Mercury. It's on this label, where they stayed until 1958, that their bluegrass sound intensified and their confidence solidified. They recorded Monroe's "Blue Moon Of Kentucky" the same year as Elvis Presley, but standouts from the period also include "I Long To See The Old Folks," "Memories Of Mother," and "Angel Band." In 1958, the Stanleys switched labels to Starday and King, where they recorded a long string of albums well into the mid-'60s. The mature, enduring music they recorded during this time included "Rank Stranger," a dark, intense song that's one of the all-time classics of bluegrass. They also had their own TV show for a few years in Florida.

Like Monroe, the Stanleys refused to compromise their sound at a time when other bluegrass bands were adding electric instruments and playing more contemporary material, with the result that gigs became smaller and less frequent. It wasn't until the urban folk revivalists discovered bluegrass that circumstances began turning around (the Stanley Brothers, for instance, were invited to play the first Newport Folk Festival in 1959). Unfortunately, at this point, Carter Stanley's health took a downturn; he died on 1 December, 1966.

Carter's death left Ralph Stanley at a major crossroads. He'd always been the shy brother,

Stanley Brothers

concentrating on his banjo playing and vocal harmonies while Carter sang lead, wrote most of the songs and acted as the group's spokesman and emcee. The bluegrass world was therefore elated when Ralph announced he would take the reigns of the Clinch Mountain Boys and continue onward.

Since striking out on his own, Ralph's hazy, haunting tenor has grown into one of the most distinct voices in bluegrass, whether he's singing about "The First Step To Heaven" or the "Hills Of Home." His band—like Monroe's Blue Grass Boys—has become another nurturing center for up-and-coming players. Larry Sparks (who assumed lead vocal duties after Carter's death), Ricky Skaggs, Keith Whitley, Roy Lee Centers, and Charlie Sizemore are among the many who've cut their teeth in the ranks of the Clinch Mountain Boys. Other members such as fiddler Curly Ray Cline and bassist Jack Cooke would remain with Stanley for years to come.

Ralph's been incredibly proficient as a solo artist. Since the mid-'60s, he's recorded albums for King, Jalyn, Rebel (a relationship that lasted over twenty years), and Freeland (owned by Dick Freeland, who formerly ran Rebel), among other labels—leaving record buyers faced with a dauntingly huge variety of albums and collections to choose from.

Ralph hosts an annual Memorial Day weekend bluegrass festival at his family "home place" near McClure, Virginia. He was also given an honorary doctorate from Lincoln Memorial University and is regularly introduced on stage as "Dr Ralph Stanley." In 1992, the Stanley Brothers became the fourth artist or group inducted into the Bluegrass Hall of Honor in Owensboro, Kentucky, and a year later, the University of Illinois published John Wright's book *Traveling the Highway Home: Ralph Stanley And The Traditional World Of Bluegrass*. Ralph's 1993 collection SATURDAY NIGHT AND SUNDAY MORNING, featuring a huge list of guest artists including Monroe, George Jones, Patty Loveless, Vince Gill, Tom T. Hall, and Dwight Yoakam, opened many new eyes and ears to the world of bluegrass. It was also nominated for three different Grammys, Ralph's first time on that prestigious list. In 1999, Ralph repeated the guest-artist concept on another strong double-disc collection, CLINCH MOUNTAIN COUNTRY. You can hardly complain that Ralph's music, and legacy, isn't well documented. He also cut a duet album, I FEEL LIKE SINGING TODAY, with Nashville songwriter and longtime fan Jim Lauderdale.

⊙ **Long Journey Home** (1990; Rebel). The 16 songs on this collection, recorded in the 1960s, have a distinct old-time flavor.

⊙ **The Early Starday-King Years, 1958–1961** (1993; Highland). A 4-CD box set (with booklet) featuring material from a period when the Stanley Brothers' sound was full-bodied and mature. They were probably overrecorded during this time, and not enough care has been taken by King and/or Starday in re-releasing the best of this music in digestible form (ie a single CD as well presented and compiled as the Columbia and Mercury discs). This box, though, allows fans a chance to sift through 109 songs and find some true gems.

⊙ **Angel Band: The Classic Mercury Recordings** (1995; Mercury). On these mid-'50s sides, the duo's harmonies are tight and more fully developed than on their earlier work. It's an excellent starting point.

⊙ **The Complete Columbia Stanley Brothers** (1996; Columbia). On these 1949–1952 recordings, the brothers' vocal and instrumental skills were worlds away from their Rich-R-Tone years, but their sound was still earthy compared to their late-'50s work—and no less moving. Carter's voice is beautifully melancholy, with Ralph's high, thin tenor threading its way into the chorus like a spooky messenger from another world.

⊙ **Earliest Recordings: The Complete Rich-R-Tone 78s (1947–1952)** (1997; Rich-R-Tone/ Revenant). The recordings are crude, and much of the music has yet to gel into "bluegrass," but the mountain-folk harmonies and songs have a raw intensity that seems scraped from the earth itself.

Ralph Stanley

⊙ **Almost Home** (1992; Rebel). Twelve a cappella gospel quartet songs compiled from the previous couple of decades. It's intense, deeply traditional stuff that will raise the hairs on the necks of believers and atheists alike. Ralph's voice quivers like a snake in the hands of a Pentecostal preacher—reaching for heaven and getting mighty close.

⊙ **Saturday Night And Sunday Morning** (1993; Freeland). This is an incredible gathering of guest singers—from Dwight Yoakam and Vince Gill to Jimmy Martin and Alison Krauss—dueting with Ralph on 31 sacred and secular songs. Some are Stanley Brothers classics, others are by writers like Yoakam and Keith Whitley. A superb double-CD collection.

Stanley Brothers

⊙ **Clinch Mountain Country** (1999; Rebel). A double-disc sequel, at least in concept, to SATURDAY NIGHT AND SUNDAY MORNING. This time the impressive roster of guest artists sharing the mike with Ralph includes Junior Brown, Gillian Welch, Vince Gill, John Anderson, Porter Wagoner, Claire Lynch, and even Bob Dylan. Stanley songs are mixed with titles from the likes of the Louvin Brothers, Pee Wee King, George Jones, and the Carter Family.

Carl Story

North Carolina native Carl Story, the leading pioneer of bluegrass-gospel, has been playing country and bluegrass music with his band, the Rambling Mountaineers, since the 1930s. Yet despite this long career, he's often overlooked in the annals of bluegrass history because he's concentrated mostly (though not exclusively) on gospel material. His unadorned voice and rural gospel rhythms, however, ground his lofty subject matter in the earth and hills of the South. And while the fact that he's used banjo in his line-up since he first formed his band doesn't necessarily make his music "bluegrass," it does indicate he was dabbling right from the start with some of the same building blocks as Bill Monroe.

Story was born on 29 May, 1916 in Lenoir, North Carolina. His parents were both musicians and he was inspired by them, as well as by records and radio performances of such stars as Charlie Poole and Uncle Dave Macon. As a child, Carl learned the fiddle, guitar, and clawhammer banjo. He played fiddle on the radio as a teenager, and soon after hooked up with his boyhood pal, banjoist Johnnie Whisnant, to play with J.E. Clark and the Lonesome Mountaineers. By the time he was twenty, however, Story had formed his own band, the Rambling Mountaineers, with Whisnant and two guitarists, Ed McMahan and Dudley Watson. In the late '30s the group cut several songs for American Record Corporation, but these were unreleased and have since been lost (apparently, however, some home recordings from 1939 have survived). The group toured the South and played various radio stations, but by the early '40s the band's line-up began changing as members were drafted—players to pass through included guitarist Jack Shelton, banjoist Hoke Jenkins, and Dobro player Ray Atkins. In late 1942, Story joined Monroe's Blue Grass Boys as a fiddler before being drafted himself.

After he was discharged, Story reformed the Rambling Mountaineers and was soon signed to Mercury, with whom he recorded until 1953 (he briefly recorded for Columbia, but then rejoined Mercury in 1955). Story began playing guitar exclusively, and his line-up now centered around Dobro, mandolin, and bass. He sang both secular and sacred material, including some popular gospel quartets. At the time he was not playing Monroe-style bluegrass, but by 1957, when Story recorded his first session for Mercury-Starday (the two labels were briefly allied), his instrumentation had evolved again to include fiddler Clarence "Tater" Tate and banjo and mandolin players the Brewster Brothers. These were Story's first recordings with true bluegrass instrumentation, and among them was the instrumental "Mocking Banjo" (a version of the much-copied Don Reno-Arthur Smith duet "Feuding Banjos"). The session also marked a point when Story began mixing instrumentals with gospel material (he'd previously kept secular and sacred songs separate), an idea devised to help increase sales.

Story continued recording for Starday for many years as well as for a series of smaller labels such as Scripture and Spar. During the '70s he was signed to CMH, a then-new label co-owned by Arthur Smith (who also acted frequently as producer) that also signed Mac Wiseman, Don Reno, and the Osborne Brothers. In addition to radio shows, Story and his Rambling Mountaineers also did some TV work over the years, but when bluegrass festivals began taking off, that's where fans would most often find him. Gospel songs he became known for over the years include "Sweeter Than The Flowers," "I Heard My Name On The Radio," and "A Light At The River." By the '90s he was still recording and playing live, pushing his career in country music over the sixty-year mark. He died on 31 March, 1995.

⊙ **Mighty Close To Heaven** (1963; Starday; reissued 1994). Includes 12 songs with sacred content, including such familiar titles as "Amazing Grace," "Rank Stranger," and the Luke the Drifter (aka Hank Williams) recitation "A Picture From Life's Other Side."

⊙ **Early Years** (1982; Old Homestead; reissued 2000). These are some of Story's earliest recordings, made in the early-to-mid-1950s, a time before his sound had truly evolved into bluegrass as we know it.

⊙ **My Lord Keeps Record** (2000; Old Homestead). A double-CD collection that pulls together songs that Story cut for the Rimrock label in the '60s with the Brewster Brothers backing him up.

Joe Val

With every sharp, high-tenor cry, this Italian American from Massachusetts proved that you don't need Appalachian roots to have an authentic bluegrass soul. In fact, Joe Val was, like Bill Monroe, so proud of the region he was born and raised in—a place full of excellent opportunities to play and hear music—he decided to name his band after it: the New England Boys.

Born Joseph Valiante on 25 June, 1926 in Everett, an industrial town just outside of Boston, Val listened to cowboy yodelers, brother duets and hillbilly singers belt it out on the radio during the '30s and '40s. He was also taken with the songs of Monroe's Blue Grass Boys; it's this style of music that would finally get under his skin for good during the '50s, when the Lilly Brothers, Don Stover, and Tex Logan began playing together in Boston.

By 1952, the year the Lilly Brothers moved to Boston, Val had already played around town with the Radio Rangers and the Berkshire Mountain Boys. He'd started on guitar and banjo, but switched to mandolin, an instrument that allowed him to better concentrate on his singing. He had a bright voice that could reach the highest of high notes, but it was strong and full enough to carry the lead melody; it soon became the most distinguishing characteristic of his music.

Val played with the Lillys and Stover now and again, and later he also played and recorded with Bill Keith and Jim Rooney, two other up-and-coming Boston bluegrass artists. During the '60s he dabbled in the progressive end of the spectrum as a member of the Charles River Valley Boys, a Boston-area band that had, since the late '50s, centered around banjoist Bob Siggins—and which in 1966 released an album of Beatles songs in bluegrass style. But Val's heart was in the traditional stuff, and when he formed the New England Boys in 1969, that's where he hung his hat. The all-acoustic band featured crisp harmony vocals, excellent instrumentalists and crisp, moving arrangements of traditional material, both bluegrass and country (Roy Acuff, Grandpa Jones, the Louvin Brothers). But it was Val's soaring tenor voice—one in league with Monroe and Del McCoury—that stood out and quickly gained him his reputation as a new, exciting bluegrass talent.

First recording for Rounder in 1971 (ONE MORNING IN MAY, one of that Boston-area label's very first releases), Val and his band released a total of six albums for the label during the next decade

and a half. They also became a top-drawing live act on the New England circuit, and a favorite at festivals—at least, whenever Val could take time off from his day job as a typewriter repairman to play them. Inherently friendly, Val was well-loved as a musician, bandleader, and friend by those who knew him personally, and when he fell ill with cancer and passed away in the spring of 1985, the bluegrass world felt the loss deeply.

⊙ **Beatle Country (The Charles River Valley Boys)** (1966; Elektra; reissued 1995; Rounder). As a concept, an album of bluegrass-style Beatles songs is a novelty, indeed. When first released, it was a blatant attempt to capitalize on the then-raging Beatlemania. Despite that, the music inside turns out to be surprisingly strong and well-arranged, whether you're a staunch Beatles fan or not. The Boys (at this point consisting of banjoist Bob Siggins, guitarist Jim Field, mandolinist Val, and bassist Everett Lilly) ham it up on "Yellow Submarine" but give "Baby's In Black," "Ticket To Ride," "Paperback Writer," and other all-too-familiar numbers a hopped-up bluegrass spin that makes them sound fresher than they have in years.

⊙ **Diamond Joe** (1995; Rounder). This here's your best Joe Val starting point, an excellent 25-song compilation culled from 5 of the 6 albums he recorded for Rounder. His voice soars to incredible heights (of both the joyous and the deeply melancholy kind), his brilliant mandolin playing is placed front and center where it belongs, and his superb song choices and arrangements—Jim & Jesse's "Just Wondering Why," Monroe's "I Hear A Sweet Voice," and perhaps most especially the fiery, fast-paced traditional number "Diamond Joe"—make a strong case that Val's brand of traditional bluegrass is some of the strongest to have come down the pike in the past few decades.

Doc Watson

"People ask me what you have to do to play like that, and I say, 'You practice like the devil.'"

—Doc Watson

Arthel "Doc" Watson is one of country music's most inspirational performers, not to mention one of the most universally loved and respected—at least by those lucky enough to have become hooked on his music. He's not a bluegrass artist, but his old-time style comes out of a similar rurally bred, hand-me-down heritage; through the years, too, his music, both on record and during his many live appearances, has attracted many of the same audiences.

Doc Watson, San Francisco, 1986

Watson had been playing music all his life, around the house and with local bands, before he was "discovered" by folk revivalists in the early 1960s (when he was nearly forty years old) and given a brand-new, full-time career as a professional musician. His playing style was eye-opening and immediately accessible, and over the years it's helped bridge the gap between older Appalachian traditions and contemporary folk and country styles. What set Watson apart from his peers right from the start was not just his warm baritone voice (a fine instrument in its own right) but his flatpicking skills on his acoustic guitar—an instrument, unlike its electrified cousin, traditionally relegated to rhythmic roles rather than melodic leads and solos. Beginning with his intricate versions of fiddle tunes like "Black Mountain Rag," Watson exposed a new generation of eager musicians and fans, rural and urban alike, to an exciting new world of instrumental possibilities. His speed and dexterity was incredible, as was the fact that, on the same instrument, he maintained a steady rhythm throughout all that melodic action.

Watson's vast song knowledge, too, was staggering. His repertoire was based around volumes of traditional numbers (most credited as "arranged and adapted by Doc Watson") and songs by early hillbilly artists such as Cliff Carlisle, the Delmore Brothers, and Dock Boggs. Along the way, though, he also gathered plenty of excellent contemporary material by writers such as Jimmie Driftwood ("Tennessee Stud"), Townes Van Zandt ("If I Needed You"), John D. Loudermilk, Tom Paxton, and Bob Dylan. He recorded occasionally with Nashville studio musicians, but whether acoustic or electrified, his music always remained fundamentally tied—both structurally and spiritually—to the hills, and the cultural heritage of his youth.

Arthel "Doc" Watson was born on 3 March, 1923 near Deep Gap, a small town buried amidst North Carolina's Blue Ridge Mountains. He lost his sight due to illness very early in life. His family had a strong love of music, and young Arthel grew up listening to hillbilly artists like Riley Puckett (who was also blind) and the Carter Family, and learning to play harmonica, banjo, and finally the guitar. His parents were very encouraging, and they also taught him that his blindness need not debilitate him. He married, had a couple of children (including son Eddy Merle, named after country stars Eddy Arnold and Merle Travis), and began playing in local bands. He performed contemporary pop, rockabilly, and country material on electric guitar with local bandleader Jack Williams, but he also learned to flatpick fiddle tunes on his acoustic—the instrument that would eventually, once the folk revivalists got wind of him, become his stock and trade.

Doc continued playing old-time music with friends such as Gaither Carlton (a neighbor and the father of his wife, Rosa Lee) and Clarence "Tom" Ashley. While accompanying Ashley, a well-known traditional banjoist, Watson was eventually "discovered" by folklorists Ralph Rinzler and Eugene Earle, who were traveling through the area in 1960 looking for local musicians to record. Watson's skill as a guitar picker, his knowledge of traditional songs and styles, and his easygoing, intelligent manner stood out immediately. He never dreamed he could make a living playing the old-time songs he picked with friends and family around the house for fun, but there he was, on a New York City stage in 1961, playing for enthusiastic fans as the guitarist in Ashley's band. Later they were booked at festivals and for a run at LA's famous folk club, Ash Grove. Before long Watson was being billed as a solo artist, and his flatpicking skills were impressing youngsters such as Clarence White (of the Kentucky Colonels and later the Byrds).

Watson's initial recordings were released by Folkways. In 1964, the year he turned forty-one years old, he began a fruitful relationship with the folkie label Vanguard (home of the Weavers and Joan Baez), for whom he eventually recorded nine albums. That year he also began touring and recording with his son Merle, who'd learned guitar at home with his mother's help. Merle became Doc's accompanist and road manager, and he also wrote several songs for his father, including the Watson favorite "Southbound." His picking style was inspired not only by his father but also by blues greats like Mississippi John Hurt and contemporary rock artists like Duane Allman. Merle also added slide guitar to the Watson repertoire.

In 1971 Doc Watson joined the stellar line-up of traditional and contemporary country musicians that the Nitty Gritty Dirt Band assembled for their landmark album WILL THE CIRCLE BE UNBROKEN? His recording of "Tennessee Stud" was one of the highlights. On their own, Doc and Merle continued to tour all over the world and cut records for labels such as United Artists, Poppy, and Flying Fish. They won Grammy awards and also performed at the White House for President Jimmy Carter in 1980. The partnership was tragically cut short in 1985, however, when a tractor Merle was driving overturned and claimed his life.

Doc was, of course, devastated, but he's managed to persevere on his own. To honor the memory of his son, he organized MerleFest, a roots music festival held each spring in North Carolina that's become one of the country's biggest and best-known old-time and bluegrass gatherings. Doc's later recordings (most for the Sugar Hill label) include DOCABILLY; a jovial rockabilly collection that highlights the type of songs Doc first played in local dance bands as a young man; DOC AND DAWG, a virtuosic back-and-forth with mandolinist David "Dawg" Grisman; and MAC, DOC & DEL, a collaboration between Doc and bluegrass greats Mac Wiseman and Del McCoury. In 1995 Vanguard honored Watson by issuing a four-CD box set, THE VANGUARD YEARS. Watson doesn't tour so frequently anymore, but when he does appear, he's well worth catching. Not only are his picking and singing skills as sturdy as ever, he's simply one of the most inspiring and soulful performers, country or otherwise, working the music scene today.

⊙ **The Doc Watson Family** (1963; Folkways; reissued 1990; Smithsonian/Folkways). Collects many of the field recordings that Ralph Rinzler, Eugene Earle, Archie Green, and Peter Seigel made of Doc Watson and his family (including Doc's parents, his wife Rosa Lee and his father-in-law Gaither Carlton) during the early 1960s, showcasing Watson at his most raw and traditional. The CD reissue includes the original album's 15 songs, plus 11 previously unreleased recordings; a mix of solos, duets, and full group efforts, they're simple, pure, and utterly gorgeous.

⊙ **Bill Monroe And Doc Watson: Live Duet Recordings 1963–1980** (1993; Smithsonian/Folkways). As a public performer, Watson was still in his early years when he took the stage at the Ash Grove with Bill Monroe in 1963. As for Monroe, he was getting discovered for the first time by the folk revival crowd. Their two voices worked together beautifully in this low-key duet environment, as did Doc's guitar and Bill's mandolin. The songs on this charming and haunting collection are from that performance and mid-'60s collaborative shows, with one final song dating from 1980.

⊙ **The Best Of Doc Watson 1964–1968** (1999; Vanguard). At 23 songs, this is a substantial highlight of Doc's years with Vanguard—and far more affordable if you don't want to dish out for the 4-CD box set. Though not as raw as his Folkways recordings, songs like "Country Blues," "Tennessee Stud," and the intricate instrumental "Black Mountain Rag" are nonetheless very close to the earth. This is Doc during his "commercial" prime, when he was as genuinely thrilled to be playing as his audiences were to be listening.

Mac Wiseman

With warm eyes, a friendly face and a jolly, Burl Ives-like stature (he's portly and bearded), Mac Wiseman is one of the most endearing figures in bluegrass. His chief appeal is a mellow tenor voice that gently warms your insides like a

Mac Wiseman

Malcolm B. Wiseman was born on 23 May, 1925 in the small town of Cremora in Virginia's Shenandoah Valley. He grew up with traditional and gospel music, and also paid attention to commercial singers like Montana Slim and Bradley Kincaid. He took a course in radio at Shenandoah College, after which he worked as an announcer for WSVA in Harrisonburg. There, too, he started singing with Buddy Starcher, a popular radio singer in the region, before briefly working on his own and then landing a gig in Knoxville with Molly O'Day's Cumberland Mountain Folks. He recorded with her in 1946, worked with his own band again at WCYB in Bristol, and then with Flatt & Scruggs in 1947. Two years later he was a member of Bill Monroe's Blue Grass Boys, a job that lasted the length of 1949 and included playing guitar and singing on the master's final Columbia session. Wiseman sang lead on just one song, "Travelin' Down This Lonesome Road," but his voice was one of that song's strongest elements.

Wiseman was on his own again in the early '50s, and finally won a record contract with Dot, a new independent label. His recent work with bluegrass music's two biggest acts had had its effect, too: the instrumentation of Wiseman's band initially resembled that of both Monroe and Flatt & Scruggs. Wiseman, though, usually sang alone, with only minimal harmony vocals, and he soon began using twin fiddles—an idea that Monroe himself eventually adopted. And unlike most bluegrass bands, Wiseman didn't record instrumentals. But his updated renditions of early classics such as "I Wonder How The Old Folks Are At Home," "'Tis Sweet To Be Remembered" (which he used for years as his theme song), and Starcher's "I'll Still Write Your Name In The Sand" earned him a good deal of praise among bluegrass and country fans, who fell in love with his bright, warm singing.

Wiseman landed a regular slot on WRVA in Richmond, Virginia, in 1953, and his band, the Country Boys, included such notables as Eddie Adcock (later of the Country Gentlemen), Buck Graves, and Scott Stoneman. Wiseman's early songs were often successful on regional charts, but he finally made a more substantial dent in the Top 10 with "The Ballad Of Davy Crockett" in 1955.

summertime campfire. A longtime favorite at bluegrass festivals, Wiseman's also grown into the role of father figure and elder statesman for the genre, even acting as its spokesman, for instance, by narrating the 1992 bluegrass documentary *High Lonesome*—a role he performed with downhome charm and natural ease.

Wiseman played plenty of traditional bluegrass throughout his career, but has by no means limited himself to the genre. He's equally proficient as a country and folk singer, and he's performed and recorded these styles almost as often throughout his career. For Wiseman, bending his music in more contemporary directions was a matter of survival during the lean years of the mid-to-late '50s, when the popularity of traditional bluegrass was giving way to rockabilly on one hand and the Nashville Sound on the other. Diversification was Wiseman's tactic, and it helped him survive as a recording artist and performer.

Mac Wiseman

It was at this point, though, that Wiseman began turning his music more toward modern country and pop—certainly not an unheard-of move for a traditional act looking to survive in the wake of Elvis Presley. He disbanded the Country Boys in 1956; a year later he took a job as a country music A&R man for Dot Records (his signings included Reno & Smiley). He continued to cut his own songs for the label, but his direction was shifting away from traditional material. He even recorded a version of rocker Smiley Lewis's "I Hear You Knocking." Two years later he hit the charts again with "Jimmy Brown The Newboy," a Will S. Hays song the Carter Family had recorded.

Wiseman left Dot in 1962, signing up with Capitol. For five years beginning in 1965, he played on the WWVA *Wheeling Jamboree* in Wheeling, West Virginia. It was during the late '60s that bluegrass festivals began taking off, and Wiseman soon became a regular on the circuit. As for recordings, he jumped between several different labels during this time, depending on whether the mood was country or bluegrass: an album with the Osborne Brothers for Dot, a successful country single, "Got Leavin' On Her Mind," for MGM. In 1969 he signed with RCA and moved to Nashville. Songs he recorded then include "Johnny's Cash And Charlie's Pride" and "On Susan's Floor," but on the other hand, during

the early '70s he also made three far more straight-up traditional albums for RCA with Lester Flatt.

Throughout the '70s, and on into the '80s and '90s, Wiseman has continued to record and play traditional bluegrass and country, even flirting ever so gently with contemporary folk-pop (he made an entire album of Gordon Lightfoot songs for the CMH label). His bluegrass festival appearances were regular and consistently well received, and in 1993, he was inducted into the Bluegrass Hall of Honor.

⊙ **Classic Bluegrass** (1989; Rebel). This 22-song CD combines 2 albums (NEW TRADITIONS VOLS 1 & 2) that Wiseman recorded for Vetco in the mid-'70s. Though not as classic as Wiseman's Dot material, the songs and their acoustic arrangements are nothing short of traditional, the playing is crisp and warm, and Wiseman's voice is as smooth as ever.

⊙ **Early Dot Recordings, Vol. 3** (1992; MCA/County). County previously issued 2 other albums of Wiseman's Dot recordings from the 1950s, though they're not available on CD. Together or separately, these collections beautifully showcase the firm foundation of Wiseman's bluegrass-country soul—classic stuff no bluegrass fan should pass by. The songs are as lively as Wiseman's voice is warm and endearing; on top of that, VOL. 3's extensive liner notes (with song-by-song commentary from Wiseman) are excellent.

7

You Can't Catch Me: Rockabilly Busts Through the Door

Rockabilly was a marriage of blues and hillbilly styles that caused a ruckus in the country music community almost as soon as it hit the market. Coming fast and hard out of the South, this wild new music stole the limelight from the honky tonkers, crooners, and bluegrass pickers who'd been riding high throughout the previous decade. To staunch traditionalists this was an abomination; for those who "got it," however, rockabilly offered young and restless but still country-rooted performers a chance to stretch and cut loose musically in ways never previously imagined. As the *Opry* grew stronger and Nashville became the focal point of the country music industry, rockabilly—for a few white-hot, powerful years—widened the scope and gave the younger generation a music all their own.

Rockabilly ignited at the point where country and western merged with blues and R&B. Its roots can be traced decades back through jump blues, hillbilly boogie and western swing, but as a style in and of itself rockabilly was formally kicked off in the summer of 1954 with the arrival of **Elvis Presley**. Its chief foundations are right there for all to hear on either side of Presley's first Sun Records single: a hillbilly-triggered take on black R&B singer Arthur "Big Boy" Crudup's "That's All Right" backed with a hopped-up version of bluegrass daddy Bill Monroe's pastoral classic "Blue Moon Of Kentucky."

Given the intense, raw energy the music produced, the simplicity of it all is astounding. At rockabilly's core was the rhythm—a strong and steady beat made with just a guitar and a standup bass played in a slapping style. An electric guitar cut through like a sharp knife, and on top of it all was a hillbilly hepcat singer packing a punkish attitude and an assortment of lurid yelps, hiccups and raspy cries—not to mention swaggering dance moves—that gave the music the threat of danger, that made it *sexy*. There were no drums, at least at first, but the use of echo in the studio gave it a beefier illusion. As the music caught on, all sorts of instruments would be added, most commonly saxophone and piano, but at the core always were the two guitars and standup bass—simple, raw and rootsy. It was easy enough for any kid with a guitar, a sneer and an itchy hipbone to at least give it a try.

In the wake of the young and budding King, countless singers and bands followed his lead, each attempting their own version of the wild new musical style. Sun founder Sam Phillips was the guiding force behind a good many of these acts—

Carl Perkins, Jerry Lee Lewis, Billy Lee Riley, Sonny Burgess—as he had been behind his most famous protégé, Presley. Other singers emerged from towns all over the South and as far away as Texas (**Buddy Holly**, Sid King, Mac Curtis, **Ronnie Dawson**) and California (**Eddie Cochran**, the **Collins Kids**). Presley's success had told them they weren't alone anymore, that there were others fed up with the status quo. For some, then, rockabilly became a statement; for others it was simply a great way to meet girls. Whatever the inspiration, the music caught hold and stuck to the wall.

Early Rumblings

Hopped-up, guitar-focused dance rhythms had been around in country music since the days when honky tonk and western swing crossed paths. The Maddox Brothers and Rose, Moon Mullican, and the Delmore Brothers all played what became known as hillbilly boogie (see box p.133). When Rose Maddox and her brothers whooped things up on "George's Playhouse Boogie" and other high-energy, loosely structured dance songs; when western swing pianist Mullican greased up his instrument on the rollicking "Pipeliner Blues"; and when the Delmores sped up the folky pace of their "brother duet" style on "Freight Train Boogie," they were nudging country music in a new direction. Still, though, these innovations were within the genre's parameters—if not exactly safe for the whole family, at least acceptable as good-natured fun.

Elvis was by no means the first white hillbilly singer to take inspiration from black musicians. Dock Boggs, Frank Hutchison, Jimmie Rodgers, Bob Wills, Bill Monroe, and Hank Williams were just a few who were directly influenced by black artists, adopting elements of the blues into their style and repertoire. Nor did Elvis invent rock'n'roll per se. Pinpointing exactly who, or what, ignited this musical revolution is pretty much impossible, but it's fact that before Presley hit the scene the seeds had already been planted. Jackie Brenston and the Dominos had cut "Rocket 88" and "Sixty Minute Man" respectively, and these and other rocked-up R&B records were increasingly popular among white kids—something DJ Alan Freed was busy discovering up in Cleveland. And in 1953 Michigan native Bill Haley had made the national charts with "Crazy, Man, Crazy." That and earlier Haley recordings such as "Rock The Joint" do combine blues and country influences (Haley previously played western swing) into a hot-fired sound that moves within breathing dis-

tance of rockabilly, but there's a certain hick vibe that's missing—a flavor steeped in southern humidity and reeking of warm, wet soil.

While Elvis Presley was the talent that led the charge, Sam Phillips was the man behind the scenes who helped bring things together. Born in Alabama, Phillips worked as a DJ before starting the Memphis Recording Service in 1950 as a way to record the blues music that had thrilled him since he was a boy. He initially leased his recordings to labels such as Chess and Modern, then in 1952 started his own label, Sun. He hit paydirt with R&B singers Rufus Thomas and Junior Parker, then ventured into country music (Earl Peterson, Howard Serrat). It's at this point that Elvis Presley crossed his path—a shy, handsome hillbilly looking for a break.

The music that Presley and his "band"(guitarist Scotty Moore and bassist Bill Black) created at Sun—all under the watchful gaze of Phillips—was liberating. It broke through barriers, it communicated what mere words couldn't; it gave young people a new kind of confidence. Elvis yelped and moaned and shook his hips, the high school girls swooned, and their parents turned beet red with anger (or was it envy?). Yet Elvis never lost sight of or respect for the music he'd grown up with—country songs and sentimental ballads, too. He sassed things up on the wampus rocker "Baby, Let's Play House," but he also sang "I Love You Because," which Leon Payne had written a decade earlier for his wife. The latter is a part of the complete Presley picture, showing where he and so many other rockabilly singers were coming from—and what still lay buried in their hearts, beneath all the swagger and sweat and black leather.

Life After Elvis

After only five singles for Sun Records, Presley was signed over to RCA, and the rest is history. Phillips had other tricks up his sleeve, however, the three biggest being Johnny Cash, **Carl Perkins**, and **Jerry Lee Lewis**. Cash turned out to be far more of a straight country artist than the others, but early songs like "Get Rhythm" and "Hey Porter," cut with his back-up group, the Tennessee Two, do have shades of rockabilly in their arrangements. Perkins was a budding star who could have been an even bigger contender: his song "Blue Suede Shoes" hit the country, pop and R&B charts simultaneously in 1956 (vying for the top position with Presley's "Heartbreak Hotel"); unfortunately Perkins' career was halted by a car accident just at the height of his newfound fame, and after his recovery he never regained the momentum. As for Lewis, he caused quite a stir with "Whole Lotta Shakin' Going On" and "Great Balls Of Fire," but he shot himself in the foot when he married his thirteen-year-old cousin. Oh well, that's rock'n'roll.

There were other Sun artists, too, who made splashes in the charts, **Billy Lee Riley** ("Flying Saucers Rock'n'Roll"), Warren Smith ("Ubangi Stomp"), and Roy Orbison ("Ooby Dooby") among them. **Charlie Feathers** cut some decent country songs for Sun, but it was another Memphis label, Meteor, that released his bare-bones rockabilly sides "Tongue-Tied Jill" and "Get With It" in 1956. In yet another corner of Memphis, another rockabilly phenomenon was brewing in the form of the Rock And Roll Trio which featured singer/guitarist **Johnny Burnette**, his brother **Dorsey** on bass, and their pal Paul Burlison on lead guitar. The group's sound was amazingly simple, yet their recordings are among the genre's most definitive, with Burlinson's guitar cutting across the rhythm and Johnny's vocal yips keeping the edges ragged and rough.

Together with his crack band the Blue Caps, guitarist **Gene Vincent** from Norfolk, Virginia was one of rockabilly's top stars. He supposedly wrote "Be-Bop-A-Lula" while reading a *Little Lulu* comic during his journey to Los Angeles for a Capitol Records talent contest, which he won. In 1956 the song was a smash and Vincent's career as a leather-clad, sexually charged, hard-"boppin'" bad boy was giving Presley some competition. Vincent's friend Eddie Cochran is best known as the songwriter and original singer of "Summertime Blues," which years later became a hit for Blue Cheer, The Who, and even Alan Jackson. Cochran's heyday was the late '50s, a time when the genre was edging past its prime, but his songs still have a decent hillbilly growl.

A singer who took rockabilly to a place all his own was **Buddy Holly**. Born and raised in the Texas panhandle, Holly initially played country until he heard Elvis Presley, who gave him fresh inspiration. Like the classic Sun material, Holly's music was simply structured and highly rhythmic, but in many ways he refined and pared his sound down even further. It's music born in the wide-open spaces, and it breathes. There's an intense sort of quiet that sits patiently between the notes of songs like "Rave On," "Peggy Sue," and "Well ... Alright" (which were recorded with his band, the Crickets, at a small studio in Clovis, New Mexico).

These well-known artists are just the tip of the iceberg, because so much of rockabilly was about the one-hit guys—and in a few cases gals—who came and went in a flash but left some unforgettable gems. Some shot into the charts—Dale Hawkins with "Susie Q," **Janis Martin** with "Will You, Willyum," Ronnie Self with "Bob-A-Lena"—while most didn't make it past small regional labels like Meteor, Fraternity, and Saber. These recordings, some incredibly obscure, are what so many rockabilly collectors of the '70s and '80s would become rabid for: "Skull And Crossbones" by Sparkle Moore, "Rockin' Bones" by Ronnie Dawson, "Baby Doll" by Jimmie Dale. Countless more musicians were little more than after-school outfits making music in their parents' living rooms and garages and occasionally playing local dances. Some of these groups, if they had the money, ended up on "custom" pressings—records the artists paid for themselves and then sold at shows or gave away.

The Rest of the Country

During the mid- to late-1950s, rockabilly was a national sensation and, because it was tied at its roots to country music, it posed a very real threat to Nashville. Record companies turned their attentions to this raucous new music and struggled to meet the demands of the fast, young culture that had latched onto it. Other traditions suffered as a result. Fiddles and banjoes were suddenly deemed old-fashioned and outmoded, and even bluegrass music itself—from which rockabilly had gained much inspiration in terms of energy, speed and drive—came under threat.

Feeling the pinch and wanting to stay on top of current trends, many country artists jumped onto the rockabilly bandwagon. The results, as can be expected, were pretty mixed. Little Jimmy Dickens' "(I Got) A Hole In My Pocket" is full of fire, but Webb Pierce's "Teenage Boogie" feels stiff and contrived. George Jones, Leon Payne and Buck Owens each cut rockabilly songs under pseudonyms (Thumper Jones, Rock Rogers, and Corky Jones respectively), not wanting to alienate their country fans. **Wanda Jackson** felt no such shame; in fact she often satisfied her two audiences (country and rockabilly) by putting one song in each style on either side of a record. Marvin Rainwater was a country singer clearly inspired by rockabilly, as evidenced in songs like "Whole Lotta Woman" and the genuinely crazed "Hot And Cold." Others slipped a song or two into their sessions more as an experiment: Justin Tubb's "Rock It On Down To My House," Eddy Arnold's "Hep Cat Baby," Skeets McDonald's "You Oughta See Grandma Rock," and the Louvin Brothers' "Red Hen Hop" all demonstrate a rockabilly influence. The genre even got a nod from song parodists Homer & Jethro, who cut the spoofs "Hart Brake Motel" and "Two-Tone Shoes."

Still others such as Charlie Rich, Roy Orbison, Brenda Lee, and Conway Twitty began their careers singing rockabilly, but by the '60s had crossed over into mainstream country and pop. Rich, a pianist and one of country music's finest vocalists, played on assorted Sun sessions and had a minor hit with "Lonely Weekends," but his biggest hits were '70s countrypolitan smoothies such as "Behind Closed Doors." Interestingly, his true leanings were more toward jazz. Twitty hit the charts in 1958 with "It's Only Make Believe," and for a few years was a teen sensation; that didn't last, however, and he eventually wised up and switched fulltime to country. And the great Jerry Lee Lewis himself met success in Nashville with country songs like "What's Made Milwaukee Famous" and "Another Place, Another Time."

The End of an Era

By the time Elvis entered the Army in 1958, rockabilly was degenerating into formula, a dilution of its former spontaneous self. As the '60s arrived it was all but gone: Elvis turned his attention to movies, Perkins and Lewis struggled to regain their footing in country, and Holly, Eddie Cochran, and Johnny Burnette were killed one by one in plane, car, and boat accidents. The final straw was the "British Invasion" led by the Beatles (who, ironically, were deeply inspired by rockabilly artists such as Perkins and Holly, frequently covering their material). As the Beatles, the Stones, the Who and other groups grabbed the rock'n'roll spotlight, rockabilly was discarded as old-fashioned. Even Sam Phillips had pretty much abandoned his famous label; in 1969 he sold Sun to Nashville enterpreneur Shelby Singleton.

During the '70s, however, rockabilly was suddenly revived. The interest began in Europe: labels like England's Charly, Germany's Bear Family and Holland's White Label began compiling and

Anthologies

⊙ **The Sun Story** (1986; Rhino). The CD version has a whopping 8 fewer tracks than the original double LP—and some key R&B tracks got the axe—but this is still an ample round-up of classic Sun rockabillies, among them Presley, Perkins, Lewis, Riley, and Warren Smith.

⊙ **Get With The Beat: The Mar-Vel' Masters** (1989; Rykodisc). A collection of little-known, but highly charged hillbilly, swing and proto-rockabilly artists—Ginny Carter, Jack Bradshaw, Bobby Sisco—released by the tiny Mar-Vel' label during the 1950s.

⊙ **Get Hot Or Go Home** (1989; Country Music Foundation). Excellent compilation of late '50s rockabilly, most of it from the RCA vaults. Instead of the usual Sun stars we get the wiggy-voiced Joe Clay; Atlanta singer Ric Cartey (who wrote the Sonny James hit "Young Love"); and juicy tidbits from Janis Martin, Tommy Blake, Gordon Terry (a onetime Blue Grass Boy), and the Everly-like Sprouts. There are even cuts from Pee Wee King ("Catty Town"), Homer & Jethro ("Two-Tone Shoes"), and future countrypolitan star David Houston ("Sugar Sweet").

⊙ **Rockabilly Stars, Vol 2** (1990; CBS Special Products). Includes tracks by the Collins Kids, Little

Jimmy Dickens, Ronnie Self, Carl Perkins, Link Wray, Bob Luman, and Sleepy LaBeef. Hardly definitive, but a nice supplement.

⊙ **Rarest Rockabilly And Hillbilly Boogie/The Best Of Ace Rockabilly** (1991; Ace). An excellent compilation that clearly shows the ties between country and rockabilly. Many of the "rare" songs were vanity recordings for "custom" labels; others are more familiar. Artists include Jimmie Dale, "Rock Rogers" (aka Leon Payne), Bill Mack, Glen Glenn, and "Thumper" (George) Jones.

⊙ **Meteor Rockabillies** (1993; Ace). Compiles singles from the short-lived Meteor label based in Memphis. Charlie Feathers is about the best-known artist here, but that's just the point. Plenty of red-hot songs make it more than worthwhile.

⊙ **The Sun Records Collection** (1994; Rhino/BMG/RCA). A 3-CD box set that gives a much wider, and far better, picture of what Sun was all about. Includes blues (B.B. King), R&B (Rufus Thomas, Jackie Brenston), and country (Doug Poindexter, Onie Wheeler) as well as rockabilly.

reissuing original rockabilly songs, and concert promoters sought out the players themselves for festival appearances. In the process they gave new life to the careers of artists like Carl Perkins, Janis Martin, Billy Lee Riley, and Ray Campi, turning them into musical heroes. Eventually the fever spread to the US, culminating in the success of the Stray Cats.

Thanks to its raw energy and DIY spirit, rockabilly became a regular part of the punk-rock landscape. Revival artists like Shakin' Stevens and Robert Gordon cropped up during the '70s, and a decade later groups like the **Blasters** and singers like **Rosie Flores** played side-by-side with hardcore bands. Some punk outfits have latched firmly onto rockabilly sounds and styles—the Cramps, the Reverend Horton Heat, and an over-abundance of so-called "psychobilly" units. A rockabilly subculture was firmly in place by the mid-'90s (overlapping to some degree with the western swing revival) with groups like **Big Sandy And His Fly-Rite Boys**, **Ray Condo And His Ricochets**, and **High Noon** playing to clubs filled with dancing fans dressed in vintage threads. Charlie Feathers, Ronnie Dawson, Sonny Burgess, and **Sleepy LaBeef** recorded solid new albums during the '90s, and other onetime stars such as Wanda Jackson and the Collins Kids played the US nightclub circuit for the first time in decades.

Rockabilly:
The Artists

Hasil Adkins

Y ou'd be hard-pressed to find a musician more genuinely crazed from his pallid skin down to his brittle bones than West Virginia one-man-band Hasil Adkins. Playing guitar, banging drums and singing, all at the same time, his music isn't rockabilly in any pure or "classic" sense, but there's an undeniable energy about it—crude, maniac—that fits the bill, at least in spirit. Born in West Virginia in 1939, Adkins had a few of his songs released by small labels during the '50s ("Chicken Walk," "The Hunch"), but he cut most of his material himself at his home in the hills and stored it away for posterity. The Norton label has been Adkins' biggest champion, releasing his albums one after the other—some collections of his homemade tapes, others new studio recordings that are equally eccentric. As rotgut drunk and face-down gritty as some songs can get, it's clear that Adkins knows his country. Jimmie Rodgers was apparently a major inspiration, and he covers Jerry Lee Lewis, George Jones, and Bill Monroe songs with a skewed degree of reverence, alongside kooky originals like "Peanut Butter Rock'n'Roll" and "Gonna Have Me A Yard Sale."

⊙ **Out To Hunch** (1986; Norton). A collection of recordings from 1955–65 including "The Hunch," "Chicken Walk," and versions of "Rockin' Robin" and "High School Confidential" like you've never heard before. Start here and see how badly it scares you before moving on.

⊙ **What The Hell Was I Thinking** (1997; Fat Possum). The hip Mississippi blues label Fat Possum (home to R.L. Burnside) is responsible for this new batch of Adkins recordings, which show he's still crazy and out of bounds even in his sixties.

Big Sandy And His Fly-Rite Boys

W hen Big Sandy and the Fly-Rite Trio first formed in 1988, rockabilly was the clear musical focus. And while the music of Elvis Presley, Gene Vincent, Johnny Burnette, and other mid-'50s giants has since remained a substantial element of their repertoire, this well-traveled Anaheim, California band eventually stepped out of those rockabilly-retro confines and into broader territory that included swing, country and even a bit of Tejano and R&B. Dressed in vintage western outfits (not to mention driving the nation's highways in a beautiful 1949 tour bus), and attracting flocks of swing dancers to their live shows, the band has developed into a tight, well-seasoned, and quick-on-the-draw group of instrumentalists, and Sandy (aka Robert Williams) has emerged not only as a superb vocalist with a big, warm voice, but also as an excellent songwriter.

Their better-known records have all been released by HighTone, but Sandy and the Boys laid a lot of groundwork before they landed that contract. They recorded their first album, FLY RIGHT WITH BIG SANDY AND THE FLY-RITE TRIO, in bassist Wally Hersom's home studio, and released it on the small Dionysus label. They also toured constantly, building a loyal following among the burgeoning rockabilly-revival crowd. Their

second album, ON THE GO, was even more well-received than the first. When the band expanded its membership—taking on lead guitarist Ashley Kingman and steel player Lee Jeffriess—the name changed to the Fly-Rite Boys.

Released in 1994, the group's first HighTone album, JUMPIN' FROM 6 TO 6, remains one of their definitive works, partly because it's the most basic and straightfoward of their HighTone releases. It was produced by Dave Alvin and recorded live at Capitol Records Studio B in LA. The same might

Big Sandy's Top 5

"As far back as I can remember, I loved rockabilly," says Robert Williams, better known as **"Big Sandy,"** who with his Fly-Rite Boys has been tearing up the neo-rockabilly and western swing scenes since the late 1980s. "I was lucky enough to grow up in a household full of records. Elvis was the first thing I really latched onto, looking up the songs he covered and finding those records." Part Mexican-American, Sandy grew up in southern California; naturally he favors the West Coast swing flavor, but he melds rockabilly and hillbilly boogie as well (and on his 1998 solo record, DEDICATED TO YOU, he even threw some R&B and doo-wop into the mix). "I guess the first thing that really got me was when my dad found the Johnny Burnette Rock And Roll Trio's 'Train Kept A-Rollin'' at a thrift store. He and I listened to it, and that did it for me." The following are Big Sandy's five favorite rockabilly sides.

"Jumpin From Six To Six" by Al Barkle
"I found this record at a point where I was deciding what I wanted to do with the band. It sounded like a country artist who wanted to shift gears and step it up a bit. It's a country line-up with a steel guitar and another guitar that goes into orbit. That's the direction I decided to go with our band—I wanted to bring the hillbilly bop element to it."

"Run Baby Run" by Claude King
"King went on to have a hit with "Wolverton Mountain," but I'm into finding these earlier records. This is another style of rockabilly that I'm into—a rural sound with an overall acoustic feel. That's really what rockabilly is, with the prominent bass and guitar and a hot guitar solo. The guitar and bass get a great groove going. That's what I find to be missing in more recent attempts to re-create the music."

"That Ain't It" by Rock Rogers
"This is actually Leon Payne—the great songwriter—and it typifies the sound of records on Starday, my favorite label. It's an interesting record by a guy whose usual style is very reserved; on this one he's cutting loose. He was already established as a country artist, so he probably did it to cash in on the teenage market. It's just perfect—lines like, 'Don't come around here with that low down crud,' he's just having fun with it."

"Big Sandy" by Bobby Roberts
"People have asked if this is where I got the Big Sandy tag, and I explain no, but it's just a great, great, rockabilly record. Roberts worked alongside all the greats in Memphis, just down the street from Sun Studios. When I was younger, I thought, 'When I learn how to play the guitar, I want to sound like that.' It's a really searing solo. I met a guy who was related to him—his cousin—and he put me in touch with him. I want to do something with him and bring him back out. I feel a connection to him because of the name and also because my dad's real name is Bob Roberts."

"That's Why I'm Wicked" by Joe
"It just says Joe handwritten on an acetate. I picked it up in a thrift store so it's probably from California and it sounds like early 1950s—maybe 1953 or 1954—that transition period before rockabilly. It sounds like a western swing band fronted by a younger guy, the sort of thing I love. In talking to older musicians, they've said a lot of western swing bands would try to keep up with the times by having a younger singer come out and entertain the young people. Obviously the musicians are seasoned, but I have no idea who Joe is."

—Denise Sullivan

Big Sandy And His Fly-Rite Boys

western swing and country territory. Longtime Sandy fans might cite 6 To 6 as their favorite, but this album feels more mature, allowing greater room for Sandy's growing talents as a songwriter—the swinging "Too Late To Be True" and "Blackberry Wine," the Tejano-flavored "La Muchachita," the honky-tonkin' "You Say You Don't (But You Do)," the Tex Williams-style talking blues "My Sinful Days Are Over." The band, too, is leaner and meaner, in particular Jeffriess' steel and Kingman's guitar.

⊙ **Radio Favorites** (1999; HMG). Containing only 6 songs, it's a mere bite-size portion of new Fly-Rite Boys material, but the songs are finely crafted Sandy originals, and aside from his doo-wop solo album his voice has never sounded better.

be said of their follow-up, SWINGIN' WEST, which this time showed the Fly-Rite Boys maturing as players—tight rhythms and excellent guitar and steel work—and Sandy growing in huge leaps as a songwriter. He wrote about half the songs on 6 To 6, but on SWINGIN' WEST he was responsible for nearly all of them. The group's 1997 album FEELIN' KIND OF LUCKY was another beauty, their finest effort to date, confirming their predominant interest in western swing above purebred rocka-billy.

In 1998 Sandy and the band temporarily parted ways to explore even newer horizons. Sandy cut DEDICATED TO YOU, a tribute to classic Los Angeles doo-wop and R&B, which he'd grown up listening to alongside his beloved rockabilly, swing and country. As for the band, Jeffriess, Kingman, Hersom, drummer Bobby Trimble, and pianist Carl "Sonny" Leyland—the group's newest addition, who first guested on LUCKY—put together a hot-swinging (mostly) instrumental album titled BIG SANDY PRESENTS THE FLY-RITE BOYS. A year later they were back in the studio to record the six-song EP RADIO FAVORITES. They continue to tour regularly, though pianist Leyland and longtime bassist Hersom both left the group in 1999.

⊙ **Jumpin' From 6 To 6** (1994; HighTone). Their first album for HighTone bursts with jumping rhythms, lively melodies, hot instrumental work and Sandy's full-bodied vocals. Nine Sandy originals are interspersed with various country and R&B covers, including Frankie Miller's sassy "True Blue" and Hank Williams' tear-jerking "Weary Blues From Waiting."

⊙ **Swingin' West** (1995; HighTone). With this album, Sandy and the Boys veered their sound full-on into

The Blasters

"A breath of fresh air to start off the 1980s!"
—"Rockin'" Ronny Weiser

With a full-force swing and an urgent spirit, the Blasters brought rockabilly out of the past and right smack into the middle of the roots-conscious southern California punk-rock scene during the early 1980s. Fronted by Phil Alvin on vocals, guitar, and harmonica and his brother Dave on lead guitar, the group drew on surf, country, blues, and rock'n'roll to produce a loud, eclectic mix of styles they liked to call "American music." The term became the title of the first Blasters album, recorded in Ronny Weiser's garage and released in 1980 on his tiny Rollin' Rock label (only 2000 copies were originally pressed). Together with bassist John Bazz and drummer Bill Bateman, the Alvin brothers created a burly sound that paid tribute to '50s-era rockabilly but also made perfect sense to punk-rock ears. Performing alongside bands like X and the Circle Jerks, it turned out, wasn't that big a stretch, thanks to the Blasters' fast-paced, high-energy sound (and hot Dave Alvin originals like "Marie, Marie" and "American Music").

After AMERICAN MUSIC caused a stir, the Blasters were signed to Slash Records, the offshoot of an infamous punk fanzine and also the home of X, the Germs, and Los Lobos. Their 1981 album THE BLASTERS featured three new bandmembers—saxophonists Steve Berlin and Lee Allen, and pianist Gene Taylor—and received wide distribution via the Warner Brothers empire. The group recorded a live EP and two further studio albums, NON FICTION and HARD LINE, that featured both Alvin brothers. Songs such as "Border Radio" and "Long White Cadillac" are standouts. Dave Alvin quit the Blasters in the mid-'80s to pursue a solo career. He briefly joined the band X when original guitarist Billy Zoom left, playing on the albums POOR LITTLE CRITTER IN THE ROAD (credited to the Knitters, X's country alter-ego) and SEE HOW WE ARE, and in 1987 he released his first solo album, ROMEO'S ESCAPE. Dave has since gone on to a successful career as one of the finest singer-songwriters on the alternative country and roots-rock circuit (see separate entry p.555).

Phil Alvin has kept the Blasters alive on a sporadic basis since his brother's departure, and in 1986 he also recorded his own solo album, UN "SUNG" STORIES. By contrast to his brother's straightahead "American music" approach—songs that touch on blue-collar lives, failed romances, and scenes from American history—Phil Alvin's music is an eclectic mix of rock'n'roll, jump blues, vaudeville, and New Orleans jazz (STORIES featured both the Dirty Dozen Brass Band and the Sun Ra Arkestra). Good as it was, Phil didn't cut a follow-up until COUNTY FAIR 2000 in 1994. He continued to front Blasters shows throughout the '90s, and the band remains an on-and-off project to this day.

⊙ **American Music** (1980; Rollin' Rock; reissued 1997; HighTone). Raw and righteous, the music on the Blasters' debut album shows just how close punk rock at the time was to the purebred rockabilly of a quarter-century earlier. The 6 Dave Alvin compositions are mixed in with fresh, original takes on various country,

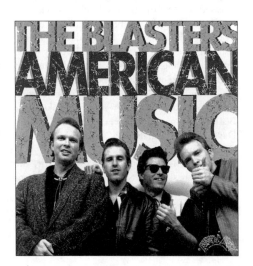

rock, and blues numbers. The garage spirit that permeates every song was never entirely revived on the group's Warner Brothers releases. This is some of the best rockabilly revival music on the market because it refuses to play by strict revivalist rules. The CD includes 6 previously unreleased tracks from the same original session.

⊙ **The Blasters Collection** (1990; Warner Bros.). A solid 20-song round-up of the group's material from their 1980s-era Warner Bros. albums, including re-recordings of "Marie Marie" and "American Music" (which originally appeared on AMERICAN MUSIC) and further tasty cuts such as "Border Radio," "Samson And Delilah," "One Red Rose," and "Long White Cadillac."

Johnny And Dorsey Burnette

While Elvis, Jerry Lee, and Carl Perkins were busying themselves with Sam Phillips at Sun Studios, another Memphis-based group of rock'n'rollers was working in another part of town on its own greasy, gritty mix of hillbilly and R&B. Johnny Burnette, Dorsey Burnette, and Paul Burlison—aka the Rock And Roll Trio—may not be as widely recognized in the annals of music history as the big-name stars at Sun Records, but as a group they operated right on that same cusp of rock'n'roll's development. As a result, their short-lived career has proven legendary and there's no doubt that their recordings are among the era's most definitive. Their music was packed with at least as much (if not more) raucous, gutsy energy as any rockabilly act on the market, past or present. Mid-1950s recordings such as "Honey Hush," "Rockabilly Boogie," "Lonesome Train (On A Lonesome Track)," and "Train Kept A-Rollin'" (written by Tiny Bradshaw and later revived by first the Yardbirds and then Aerosmith) are stripped-down gems of fuzz-toned glory.

The trio consisted of singer-guitarist Johnny Burnette (born 25 March, 1934 in Memphis, Tennessee), his brother Dorsey (born 28 December, 1932) on bass, and their friend Burlison (born 4 February, 1929 in Brownsville, Tennessee) on lead guitar. They met in Memphis in 1949 at a boxing match where Dorsey was competing. Johnny and Paul began playing together in the band of local musician Doc McQueen; Dorsey initially played

Johnny Burnette

chart hits: "Train Kept A-Rollin'" and "Tear It Up." In 1957 Dorsey left the group, apparently unhappy that his brother's name was taking top billing (they were often listed as Johnny Burnette and the Rock And Roll Trio). Dorsey was briefly replaced by Johnny Black, brother of Elvis's bassist Bill Black, but it wasn't long before the Rock And Roll Trio finally called it quits for good.

Johnny and Dorsey quickly made up and soon moved to California together. They began writing songs, and they each also had somewhat successful solo recording careers. Johnny began recording teen idol-type songs including "Sweet Baby Doll" and "You're Sixteen" (a substantial pop hit in 1960) for Liberty, Freedom, and other labels. Dorsey cut records for the Era label in the early '60s, and made a few dents in the pop market with "(There Was A) Tall Oak Tree" and "Hey Little One." During the '70s he found himself in the country charts with a string of mediocre hits, including "In The Spring (The Roses Always Turn Red)" and "Molly (I Ain't Gettin' Any Younger)."

Johnny Burnette's music career was cut short in 1964 when he was killed in a boating accident. Dorsey died in 1979 of a heart attack. As for Paul Burlison, he went into the construction business after the Trio split up, but in later years he began playing with a group of onetime Sun session men as the Sun Rhythm Section.

in a group with Scotty Moore and Bill Black (soon to be Elvis Presley's bandmates) before joining McQueen's outfit as well. Finally, in 1953, the three young men began gigging on their own as a trio. They played quite a bit of country music, but they soon discovered the crowd's enthusiasm when they picked up the pace and let things get more rough and ragged. After Elvis emerged with "That's All Right" and shook up the music world, the Rock And Roll Trio tried out at Sun Records but were turned down.

In 1956 the three young rockabillies headed for New York City in search of work, and within a few weeks they had stormed their way onto a local television program, the *Ted Mack Amateur Hour,* winning the talent show's contest three weeks in a row. This exposure led Decca to offer them a contract on their Coral subsidiary. They cut their first session in May, 1956, a second two months later, and a third in March of 1957. The first was held in New York, the last two in Nashville at Owen Bradley's studio (ironically one of the birthplaces of the Nashville Sound). Their music may be absolutely classic by today's standards, but at the time they only earned two minor

⊙ **You're Sixteen: The Best Of Johnny Burnette** (1992; Capitol/EMI). This collects 26 of Johnny's pop recordings from the late 1950s and early '60s, including "Dreamin'," "Cincinnati Fireball," "Little Boy Sad," "God Country And My Baby," and his big hit "You're Sixteen."

⊙ **Best Of Dorsey Burnette: The Era Years** (1994; Dominion Entertainment). This CD is really a re-release of Dorsey's 1960 Era album TALL OAK TREE with 5 previously unreleased tracks from the same period. Such songs as "Hey Little One," "Tall Oak Tree," and "I Got The Sun In The Morning" are unabashedly pop in structure, but rockabilly, country, and R&B influences are apparent in more than a few songs, including "Hard

Johnny And Dorsey Burnette

Rock Mine," "Hard Working Man," "Great Shakin' Fever" and "Big Rock Candy Mountain" (a hobo classic from the '20s written by Harry McClintock). At times resembling the great Charlie Rich, Dorsey's full-bodied voice works as well on the crooners as it does on the rock'n'roll material.

⊙ **Rockabilly Boogie** (1994; Bear Family). If you're looking for pure, unadulterated, bare-bones rockabilly, this collection of all the Trio's recordings for Decca in 1956 and 1957 just might be the Holy Grail. A few outtakes clutter the proceedings for casual fans, but overall it's a very worthwhile investment if your taste swings into ragged, fuzztoned rock'n'roll. "Train Kept A-Rollin'," "Honey Hush" and "Lonesome Train (On A Lonesome Track)" are purebred rockabilly—Dorsey's slap bass, Burlison's cutting lead guitar, and Johnny's excited vocal yips—but the Trio's country background is also within earshot, their take on the Delmore Brothers' "Blues Stay Away From Me" being a great example.

Eddie Cochran

Eddie Cochran

Though Eddie Cochran arrived at the tail end of rockabilly's golden era, a time when the music had lost much of its rural southern flavor and taken on a more formulaic character, songs like "C'mon Everybody," "Cut Across Shorty" and "Summertime Blues" still have vestiges of the music's hillbilly roots; they're also packed with a genuine youthful vigor that renders them appealing even decades later. If Cochran hadn't died at such a young age (he was only twenty-one), he'd likely have been a far bigger rock'n'roll hero. It's also possible he would have shifted back toward country, a music he dabbled in early on in his career.

Cochran was born on 3 October, 1938 in Minnesota and grew up in Oklahoma. During the early '50s his family moved to suburban Los Angeles, and it's here that Cochran's musical career began. When he was only sixteen he teamed up with future Nashville songwriter Hank Cochran ("Make The World Go Away") in a duo called the Cochran Brothers, although they weren't related. The rocked-up country and R&B material they recorded is interesting—Eddie's voice was the wild one, full of character-building yips and dips, while Hank's singing was more straightforward—but their songs failed to catch on commercially. With Eddie leaning more toward rock,

and Hank looking toward country, the pair eventually decided to split. Eddie then formed a partnership with songwriter Jerry Capehart, who also became his manager. He landed a deal with Liberty and in 1957 had his first national hit with "Sittin' In The Balcony," a song written by John D. Loudermilk. It's a halfway decent teen-crooner love ballad, though it's almost smothered by the heavy echo—a victim of the era's musical trends. Cochran also won roles in movies such as *The Girl Can't Help It*, *Untamed Youth* (in which he sang the cool, almost a cappella "Cotton Picker") and *Go, Johnny, Go*, which furthered his teen-idol credentials. In 1958 he and Capehart came up with the far wilder (and more resilient) "Summertime Blues." It was a smash hit at the time and has been a rock'n'roll standard ever since, revived a decade later by Blue Cheer and the Who (and in the '90s by Alan Jackson). The song also set a new tone for Cochran's music, one more firmly based in rockabilly.

Cochran's life was tragically cut short in 1960 while touring England when the taxi he and Gene Vincent were travelling in crashed. Vincent survived the collision.

Collins Kids

More than a mere novelty act, siblings Larry and Lorrie Collins were an exceptionally talented brother and sister team who gained respect as well as notoriety for the hot rockabilly material they recorded and performed during the late 1950s. Based out of the West Coast, they recorded for Columbia and appeared regularly on the popular Los Angeles TV show the *Town Hall Party*. Lorrie (born Lawrencine May Collins on 7 May, 1942) handled most of the lead vocals while her younger brother Larry (born Lawrence Albert Collins on 4 October, 1944) was a whiz on the guitar—often playing a double-necked monstrosity almost bigger than he was.

Both children grew up in Tulsa, Oklahoma. When Lorrie won a local talent contest, the show's host, steel guitarist Leon McAuliffe (once a member of Bob Wills' Texas Playboys), encouraged the family to move to California where professional prospects were more favourable. They took his advice, and after settling in Southern California both children began appearing on local radio shows. In 1954, they first began appearing on the *Town Hall Party*. Guitarist Joe Maphis was a mainstay on that television show, and he became Larry's mentor (Maphis also regularly played a double-necker). The Collins Kids signed with Columbia in 1955; they never had a true hit song, but did manage to record some excellent material ("Mercy," "Just Because," "Rock Boppin' Baby") that showcased Lorrie's crisp, sassy voice and Larry's sharp, fleet-fingered guitar leads. Lorrie married Johnny Cash's manager, Stu Carnell, in 1959, and the siblings broke up their act two years later when Lorrie had her first child. Larry recorded on his own after that, but he was better known as a songwriter, penning such popular hits as "You're The Reason God Made Oklahoma" and especially "Delta Dawn." Larry and Lorrie have since reunited several times for tours and special performances.

Ray Condo And The Ricochets

"I don't want to get rich. I just want a raise."

—Ray Condo

Vancouver, British Columbia, is an unlikely birthplace for a hardcore country and rockabilly band, but it's the town Ray Condo and his band The Ricochets call home. Ray is a singer and saxophonist with a sharp-edged voice, an untethered performance style, and a penchant for digging up obscurities—namely vintage honky-tonk, swing, R&B, boogie, and rockabilly songs. A native of Ottawa, Condo played with the rockabilly group the Hardrock Goners for eleven years before forming the Ricochets in 1995. Bassist Clive

Jackson, also a member of the Goners, joined him in his new venture, which soon included steel player Jimmy Roy, lead guitarist Stephen Nikleva, and drummer Steve Taylor. The last of the three members had previously played together in a group called the Five Star Hillbillies.

The Ricochets initially released their debut album, SWING BROTHER SWING, on a small Vancouver label, but soon after it was picked up and re-released by the San Francisco label Joaquin with several upbeat numbers replacing slower material. The result didn't adhere to any particular set of rules, however, and it would be wrong to label the band strictly "rockabilly," since the album, rather like their repertoire as a whole, contains a mixture of styles—western swing, jazz, rock, and R&B—all of which made perfect sense together. The power center of vintage rockabilly may well have been mid-'50s Memphis, but the energy and spirit of the music is scattered across multiple genres—and generations. Since their debut's release the Ricochets have toured all over Europe, Canada, and the US, and have released a follow-up CD, DOOR TO DOOR MANIAC.

⊙ **Swing Brother Swing!** (1996; Joaquin). On Condo's debut album, he and the Ricochets show that their tastes for vintage material are wide. In fact, the songs here are almost more western swing than rockabilly. Sure, Condo makes wild work out of rockabilly material like Lew Williams' "Something I Said," but more interesting are the swing songs—Hank Penny's "Hadicillin Boogie," for instance, and the Modern Mountaineers "Loud Mouth."

⊙ **Door To Door Maniac** (1998; Joaquin). The Ricochets rock a bit harder on their second outing— Glen Barber's "Shadow My Baby," Bill Ford's "Have You Seen Mabel," and Gene Vincent's "Jump Back, Honey, Jump Back" are tight, sleek and fast. But on the whole the album still reflects their diverse tastes in vintage swing, country, and boogie songs, including Bob Wills' "I'm Feeling Bad" and Billie Holliday's positively laid-back "Tell Me More."

Ronnie Dawson

Dallas, Texas-born guitarist Ronnie Dawson is a first-generation rockabilly artist who's improved with age—nearly forty years after his initial recordings as the "Blond Bomber," he rocks harder and sounds better than ever. He's

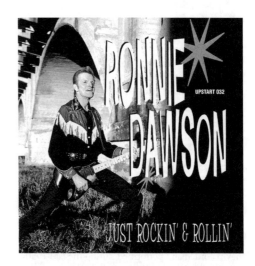

earned respect among revivalists, too, for his longtime commitment to the music, and this in turn has led to a more established musical career than the one he enjoyed as a youngster. Born in Texas in 1939, Ronnie cut records ("Action Packed," "Rockin' Bones") for Swan, Columbia, and assorted small labels during the '50s, earning his nickname the "Blond Bomber" for his flat-top haircut and boyish looks. He stuck it out in music during the next couple of decades (forming the country-rock band Steel Rails in the '70s) before rabid rockabilly revivalists in England got wind of his existence and brought him back to stage and studio. There's nothing all that unique about Dawson's recent rockabilly recordings except that they're completely solid and a great deal of fun—songs like "Down In Mexico," "Snake Man," and "Up Jumped The Devil" (showing shades of Jerry Reed) simply will not deteriorate anytime soon.

⊙ **Rockin' Bones: The Legendary Masters** (1996; Crystal Clear). A 2-CD compilation of Dawson's 1950s sides plus unreleased demos, alternate takes and other interesting tidbits.

⊙ **Monkey Beat!** (1994; No Hit). Kicks off with "Wham Bam Jam" and rocks solid from there on in with nuggets like "Down In Mexico" and "Snake Man." A great collection that shows exactly what Dawson's about. The CD also includes Dawson's first comeback album from 1988, STILL A LOT OF RHYTHM, as a bonus.

⊙ **Just Rockin' And Rollin'** (1996; Upstart). Dawson's rock is snazzier this time around, but the songs and arrangements are still in tip-top shape.

Charlie Feathers

"I loved bluegrass all my life, but I never did know how to play it."

—Charlie Feathers

Guitarist and singer Charlie Feathers is one of the great lesser-sung heroes of rockabilly, a man who was present at Sun Records during the mid-1950s, who cut some excellent recordings himself (including "Tongue-Tied Jill" for Sun competitor Meteor), but who didn't get his due as an artist for another twenty years, when the rockabilly revivalists rediscovered him. Despite some lean years, Feathers stuck with rockabilly and country out of sheer love for the music. He has always claimed that during his Sun years he wrote and arranged songs for Elvis Presley; the future King did make a national hit out of one of them, "I Forgot To Remember To Forget" (co-written with Stan Kesler). Like many of the details of Feathers' career, however, there's a cloudiness surrounding the facts of the song's actual source. Such ambiguities turn into petty discrepancies when you hear Feathers' own recordings, which are more emotionally tangled and raw around the edges than almost anything that came out of Memphis in the '50s. Feathers had a wild yip in his voice and a hillbilly-swamp sound that few in or out of rockabilly could ever hope to match.

Feathers was born on 12 June, 1932 in rural Mississippi. Growing up he was inspired by the bluegrass of Bill Monroe and the music of local bluesman Junior Kimbrough. He settled in Memphis about 1950, and within a few years had begun working for Sam Phillips. The exact nature of his role at Phillips' Memphis Recording Service is again unclear, but it likely included song arranging, demo recording and other session work. Phillips let Feathers record a single for his new label, Flip, then shifted the young man over to Sun, where he cut a series of hillbilly songs. Phillips supposedly wouldn't let Feathers do rock-type material, so Feathers jumped ship to another Memphis label, Meteor, which in 1956 released his first rockabilly single, "Tongue-Tied Jill" b/w "Get With It." Four months later Feathers was recording for Cincinnati-based King Records, an indie label well-established in the country field thanks to artists like the Delmore Brothers, Grandpa Jones and Moon Mullican. Feathers cut some of his firmest rockabilly sides for King, but by the '60s had shifted back to a series of smaller companies (including the short-lived Holiday Inn label).

Though he didn't find much fame during rockabilly's golden years, Feathers experienced a huge revival during the '70s, with fans fingering him as a member of the great Sun family who'd somehow become lost in the shuffle. During the '60s and '70s Feathers hadn't been sitting still: he'd continued to record (sometimes just at home) and to play gigs (mostly in and around Memphis). Now, however, he was being brought overseas for show dates and cutting studio sessions all over again. His health caused him trouble, but in 1990 he was able to play gigs and even record once more, doing so at Sam Phillips' Recording Service in Memphis. The resulting album, CHARLIE FEATHERS, was released on Elektra/Nonesuch's excellent American Explorer series (his only album on a major label), and it's an overlooked beauty. Feathers died in 1998.

⊙ **Charlie Feathers** (1991; Elektra/Nonesuch). Serious rockabilly fanatics might find this collection below par, but as gut-level country music it's a mighty achievement. Feathers' voice is almost more expressive than ever, and songs like "A Man In Love," "Pardon Me Mister," and "Oklahoma Hills" are thick with hillbilly soul.

⊙ **Tip Top Daddy** (1995; Norton). Acoustic demos from 1958 through to 1973, most of them cut by Feathers at home. The sound quality's not great, and some songs are crudely chopped short, but Feathers fans will find it interesting nonetheless.

⊙ **Get With It: Essential Recordings (1954–1969)** (1998; Revenant). This is the best Feathers compilation on the market, a one-of-a-kind double-CD that brings his early commercial recordings for Sun, Meteor, King, and other labels together with all sorts of demos and other rarities.

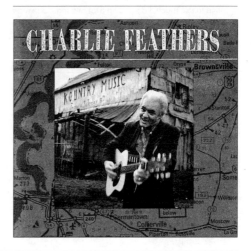

Sleepy LaBeef: Rules Of The Road

Every rockabilly fan should thank God for **Sleepy LaBeef** when they say their prayers at night. LaBeef, whose 1950s output included classic sides for Pappy Daily's great Starday label in Houston, is now virtually alone carrying the original rockabilly torch on a regular basis. He's a walking jukebox (though I'm not suggesting we call him the Rev. Jack van Impe of rockabilly), a guy familiar with every one of the musical ingredients that went into this great-tasting, boppin' soup and that has led it to be continually cooked and consumed over the past half century. During a typical night, LaBeef rips his way through a repertoire that runs from gospel and blues to country, swing, and early rock'n'roll and rockabilly standards. Now in his mid-sixties, LaBeef still keeps up an impressive schedule of some two hundred gigs a year, and his intensity, drive and distinctive baritone voice have never been stronger. What is it, then, that keeps him going?

"The love for it is the main thing. I grew up in south Arkansas where I had the chance to listen to all kinds of music. The biggest influences were the high-energy type—the foot-stomping, hand-clapping type of music. It was exciting and fun to do, so I've never lost that feeling through the years. It's like part of living and breathing. I especially liked Sister Rosetta Tharpe, Claude Ely, people like that. There was also Red Foley and Big Joe Turner.

"I first started doing medleys because I was a country boy raised on a little 40-acre farm, and I was kind of shy, kind of bashful, so when I got on stage I'd get all nervous 'cause I had stage fright. So that I didn't have to talk much, I'd just sing a lot of songs, one after the other." Later, he explains, he learned to enjoy the talking as well—but even so, the medleys continue to play a vital role. "I've always got a lot of songs to do."

Sleepy's adored by rockabilly fiends in America, Europe, and Australia but, perhaps ironically, he's about the last person who'd go to the trouble of re-creating, detail by meticulous detail, that famous mid-'50s Sun

DAVID REDFERN

Rockabilly veteran Sleepy LaBeef

sound—which explains his appeal to the rest of the population. He's so natural, so himself on stage, that you don't have to be a serious-minded rockabilly fanatic to enjoy cutting loose to his music.

"I don't think that a particular instrument or particular type of voice makes the music," he explains. "I think it's doing it with all honesty. It don't matter that we've got high singers and low singers out there, but you gotta be real about it. I think you should feel it. Some people I think perform because of the mode and method, and *learn* it, but it's much more fun if you really feel what you're doing and give it all you got. It's not a Scotty Moore lead guitar, it's not D.J. Fontana drums or Bill Black slap bass, it's a combination of who you got with you—and if they're doing the best they can do, I think the honesty shows up. It's what makes performing a joy, because you don't have to get into a stale rut, you don't have to hit the same old licks, you can ad-lib as you go along. You can live tonight—you don't have to imitate what you did yesterday." In other words, he says, "I try to keep the spontaneity there."

—Brian Gordon

Rosie Flores

R osie Flores isn't a straight rockabilly artist by any means, but the music has been a part of her sound since she began playing country–rock in West Coast nightclubs during the 1970s and '80s. She has survived on the fringes of country music ever since, but by the mid-'90s was focusing on rockabilly much more seriously. This was mainly as a result of her album, ROCKABILLY FILLY, a minor landmark that brought former rockabilly queens Wanda Jackson and Janis Martin back into action for several duet recordings.

Rosie Flores

Born in San Antonio, Texas, Flores moved with her family to San Diego when she was twelve. By the late '70s she had formed Rosie and the Screamers, a punk and rockabilly group that covered songs by Martin, Jackson and Gene Vincent among others. During the '80s she cut an album, FIESTA, with another cowgirl-styled group, the Screaming Sirens, then followed it with a solo album for Warner Brothers that was an attempt at straight-up country. It didn't get her far in Nashville, however. By the '90s she was making records for the indie label HighTone, including AFTER THE FARM, ONCE MORE WITH FEELING and 1995's hot-to-trot ROCKABILLY FILLY. Publicity for this last album involved touring the US with Jackson. In 1998 the Watermelon label released A LITTLE BIT OF HEARTACHE, a collection of country duets between Flores and rockabilly singer Ray Campi, one of her early inspirations, which they'd recorded eight years earlier.

⊙ **Rockabilly Filly** (1995; HighTone). A lively collection that pays tribute (mostly) to Flores' rockabilly influences. Includes songs by Butch Hancock and Lefty Frizzell, as well as Flores and guest singers Wanda Jackson and Janis Martin. Shows off Flores' lead guitar skills, too.

⊙ **Dance Hall Dreams** (1999; Rounder). Rosie's honky-tonk roots are not just showing, they're the main event here. Her voice and guitar playing are sharp and cool, and songs like "Little Bit More" and "This Ol' Honky Tonk" (a love song to those all-too-familiar bar-rooms) are among the finest she's written.

High Noon

A rockabilly revival group based in Austin, Texas, High Noon plays a pared-down brand of roots-based rock'n'roll. Their sound is modeled on Johnny Burnette and the Rock And Roll Trio, but they also throw in a healthy dose of honky tonk inspiration, a few boogie tunes, and even the occasional ballad for good measure. Bandmembers Sean Mencher, Shaun Young, and Kevin Smith are a stylish bunch in their vintage clothes and Brylcreemed coifs, but musically they keep things simple—standup bass, two guitars, and vocals—for an enticingly tight, spare sound.

Both rhythm guitarist (and lead vocalist) Young and bassist Smith hail from Denver, Colorado, where they played in a group called the Shifters. Lead guitarist Mencher is from Washington, DC, and has worked with Jimmie Dale Gilmore, among others. They formed High Noon in Austin in the late 1980s, and put out several releases—both on their own and via small European labels—before signing to Watermelon in the mid-'90s.

⊙ **Stranger Things** (1996; Watermelon). Spare arrangements, a straightforward approach and songwriting that jumps from classic rockabilly to hopped-up boogie-woogie keep the 15 original songs on this album wound up and ready to go.

⊙ **Live In Texas And Japan** (1997; Watermelon). Things get louder and rowdier on this CD, perhaps because it's a collection of live recordings. Twelve are from a 1989 radio performance on KUT-FM in Austin, Texas, while 8 others come from 1996 shows at Austin's Continental Club and Diamond Hall in Nagoya, Japan.

Buddy Holly

Singer, guitarist and songwriter Buddy Holly was one of the most influential and legendary figures in twentieth-century popular music. During his short-lived career in the 1950s, Holly wrote and recorded some of the rock'n'roll world's all-time classics, including "That'll Be The Day," "It's So Easy," "Well … All Right," and "Peggy Sue," each a firm nugget tightly packed with Holly's slightly frenetic, yet always well-controlled vocals—he loved to yip and yelp but he never roared or bellowed—sharp electric guitar leads, and lyrics about love, angst, anger, and desire. His music was built around a stripped-down and fairly standard rockabilly instrumentation of rhythm and lead guitar, bass, and drums, but the tension came with the restraint—Holly's songs were never lost in a fuzzy, noisy blur, making him the polar opposite of a cacophonous wild man like Billy Lee Riley ("Flying Saucers Rock'n'Roll"). Sure, Holly could cut loose when he wanted to ("Ready Teddy," "Rock Around With Ollie Vee"), but so many of his arrangements remained low-key in tone and sparse in structure. There was a surprising amount of space between the notes on songs like "Peggy Sue" and "Well ... All Right," for instance, but this only made the emotional content feel more tightly wound. Few power-rocking guitar bands of any generation have accomplished so much with so little.

Charles Hardin Holley (the original spelling of his name) was born on 7 September, 1936 in Lubbock, Texas. During the early '50s he played around Lubbock with his high school friend Bob Montgomery, and in 1953 they landed a regular show on the local radio station KDAV. They played a good deal of country (Hank Williams, Bill Monroe), but Holly was becoming more enamored with black blues and R&B. Hearing the music of Elvis Presley in 1954—and especially after meeting the King a year later when Buddy and Bob were the opening act for his Lubbock appearance—was exactly the justification Holly needed. He amped up the duo's sound (which they'd been calling "western bop"), and both his vocals and his guitar playing became sharper and edgier.

In early 1956, Holly (without Montgomery) was signed to Decca, and he cut his first sides in Owen Bradley's studio in Nashville with bassist Don Guess and guitarist Sonny Curtis (who later grew into a successful songwriter, penning "I Fought The Law" and "Love Is All Around," the theme to the *Mary Tyler Moore Show,* among many other hits). Decca sponsored two more Holly sessions in Nashville that year, but none of his singles ("Blue Days, Black Nights," "Modern Don Juan") sold very well, and towards the end of the year he was dropped from the label.

Earlier in 1956, Holly had traveled the one hundred miles from Lubbock to Clovis, New Mexico, where musician and songwriter Norman Petty had recently opened a small recording studio—and Petty charged by the song, not the hour, which was a boon for developing musicians like Holly. He subsequently spent a lot of time there over the course of several months honing his rockabilly sound (demos from that period later showed up on the 1983 album FOR THE FIRST TIME ANYWHERE). Freed of his Decca contract, Holly returned to Clovis in early 1957 with drummer Jerry Allison (who'd also played on some Decca sessions) and cut more songs with Petty manning the boards. Petty then shopped them around, eventually getting interest from a representative of Coral—a subsidiary, ironically, of Holly's former label, Decca. The record ("That'll Be The Day") actually ended up on another Decca subsidiary, Brunswick, and it was this time listed under a band name, the Crickets. To further complicate Holly's recording history, he was also signed under his own name to Coral. Either way, all the records from this time usually featured Holly on vocals and lead guitar, Allison on drums, Niki Sullivan on rhythm guitar, and Joe Maudlin on bass.

Released in May of 1957, "That'll Be The Day" shot straight to #1 on the *Billboard* pop charts. It was followed over the next year and a half by such now-classic recordings as "Not Fade Away," "Words Of Love," "Peggy Sue," "Everyday," "Well ... All Right," and "It's So Easy." All were cut at Petty's studio in Clovis, and most were written or co-written by Holly, with Petty's name often appearing on the song credits as well. It was an incredibly fertile and productive period, and both the songwriting and the arrangements were hugely innovative. Some were full-on rockers ("Oh Boy!") while others were about as tight, uncluttered and un-manic as anything on the rockabilly market ("Words Of Love," "Well ... All Right").

In 1958, Holly married Maria Elena Santiago, moved to New York City, and parted ways not only with Petty but also with his steady bandmates, who didn't want to abandon their homes and move east (Allison and Maudlin kept the rights to the Crickets name). Holly cut a new batch of songs in October that were marked by surprisingly lush and orchestrated arrangements. It's quite a change from the deliberately pared-down material he cut in Clovis, but once you get over the shock, songs like "True Love Ways" and "It Doesn't Matter Anymore" (written by Paul Anka) are actually rather pleasant. In January of 1959, Holly set off on a three-week package tour of the Midwest together with Ritchie Valens, J.P. Richardson (aka the Big Bopper), and Dion and the Belmonts. Backing Holly were guitarist Tommy Allsup, drummer Carl Bunch, and bassist Waylon Jennings—a fellow Lubbock native and the very same man who'd later shake up Nashville and make "outlaw" a household word. The group traveled mostly by bus, but during one stretch of the tour, Holly hired a private plane (which was named "American Pie") to fly him and his band to the next date. Jennings and Allsup, however, ended up giving their seats to Richardson and Valens. After taking off from Mason City, Iowa, the plane crashed in the early morning hours of 3 February, killing Holly, Richardson, Valens, and pilot Roger Peterson. The services four days later were attended by more than one thousand people, and Holly's body was buried at the Lubbock City Cemetery. He was only twenty-two years old, but already his impact on the pop-music world was immense.

A couple of months before his death, Holly recorded a series of demos in his New York apartment. (To date, the only place to hear the songs in their original voice-and-guitar format is on the six-LP, vinyl-only box set, THE COMPLETE BUDDY HOLLY, released by MCA in 1979). After his death, these recordings were overdubbed by Petty and others to become full-featured rock'n'roll numbers, and they were released on various collections throughout the '60s. Among the titles is one of Holly's best-known songs, "Peggy Sue Got Married."

⊙ **From The Original Master Tapes** (1985; MCA). A pretty decent single-disc collection covering most of Holly's classic Clovis recordings such as "Peggy Sue," "That'll Be The Day," "Well ... All Right," and "Words Of Love," as well as a few early Decca cuts and late-period New York recordings. It's basically a slimmed-down, less-expensive version of the double-disc BUDDY HOLLY COLLECTION.

⊙ **The Buddy Holly Collection** (1993; MCA). This 2-CD set does a great job covering the entire gamut of Holly's recorded output in what's still a fairly concise package. Running in chronological order, it begins with early garage tracks (which were posthumously overdubbed by Petty), moves through the Owen Bradley singles, spends plenty of time exploring the classic Clovis material, and concludes with 3 of his New York studio recordings and 4 of the overdubbed demos. It almost goes without saying that classic titles like "Not Fade Away," "Peggy Sue" and "Well ... All Right" are firm and tasty, but there are also beauties in each of the other periods—"Blue Days," "Don Juan," "Girl On My Mind," "Peggy Sue Got

Married," even the lush "True Love Ways." This is an extremely worthwhile investment for any rock or rockabilly fan.

Wanda Jackson

"I used to have so much fun singing, I would forget to get my money at the end of the night."

—Wanda Jackson

Oklahoma gal Wanda Jackson was one of the first major female rockabilly and country stars, and one of the first women to pursue a lifelong career in country music. While fellow rockabilly singer Janis Martin quit the business after getting married in her late teens, Jackson chose to keep working—though she did get the consent, and genuine support, of her husband, former IBM programmer Wendell Goodman, whom she married in 1961. Goodman has been her manager ever since.

Jackson mixed straight country material and hot-to-the-core rockabilly numbers almost right from the beginning, never feeling the need to hide one set of songs from the fans of the other (some country stars, including George Jones and Buck Owens, cut rockabilly material under pseudonyms). Songs like "Fujiyama Mama" and "Mean Mean Man" were hard and fast, giving her plenty of reason to shimmy around in her glamorous fringe dresses (designed by her mother), while "Tears Will Be The Chaser For The Wine" and the deeply bitter and vengeful "The Box It Came In" wept with genuine honky-tonk emotion.

Wanda Jackson was born on 20 October, 1937 in Maud, Oklahoma. Her father, also a musician, moved the family to California during the '40s. Encouraging her musical development, he bought her a guitar and took her to shows featuring the western swing bands of Tex Williams, Bob Wills, Spade Cooley, and others, which left a lasting impression on her. She was especially captivated, she later explained, by the "girl singer" in each band. By the '50s the family was back in Oklahoma City, which has been Jackson's home ever since. In 1952 she won a talent contest, resulting in her own show on a local radio station; this show led to her big break when bandleader Hank Thompson heard her on the air and asked her to perform with his band, the Brazos Valley Boys. She cut a few songs with the group, including "You Can't Have

TOM ERIKSON

Wanda Jackson, San Francisco, 1995

My Love," a duet with Thompson's bandleader Billy Gray that became a national hit. Jackson had wanted to sign with Capitol, Thompson's label, but was turned down, producer Ken Nelson explaining to her that "'girls don't sell records.'" So she signed with Decca instead.

After finishing high school, Jackson hit the road on her first tour (her father along as manager and chaperone), sharing the bill with Elvis Presley. The two hit it off and were even romantically involved. It was Elvis, in fact, who encouraged her to sing rockabilly. In 1956 Jackson finally signed with Capitol, staying with the label until the early '70s. From the '50s through to the early '60s she cut both rockabilly and country for the label, often putting one song in each style on either side of a record. And she had chart success with both: her version of "Let's Have A Party," which Elvis had cut earlier, was a pop hit for her in 1960 and became her signature song; she even began calling her band the Party Timers. A year later, she made the country charts with "Right Or Wrong" and "In The Middle Of A Heartache." She toured regularly, was twice nominated for a Grammy, and was a big attraction in Las Vegas from the mid-'50s through to the '70s.

Jackson's musical perspective shifted radically in the '70s after she and her husband discovered Christianity. She released one gospel album on Capitol in 1972, PRAISE THE LORD, before shifting to the religious labels Myrrh and Word. She spent more and more time on the gospel circuit, singing as well as giving religious testimonies. The landscape altered again, however, when rockabilly revivalists sought her out. She began playing rockabilly and country festivals in Europe during the '80s, and by the '90s American country artists such as Pam Tillis, Jann Browne, and Rosie Flores were singing her praises, too. Jackson even sang two duets with Flores on the latter's 1995 album ROCKABILLY FILLY and then embarked on a US tour with her. It was Jackson's first secular tour in the US since the '70s, not to mention her first time back on the nightclub circuit.

⊙ **Right Or Wrong** (1992; Bear Family). Four CDs of classic Jackson rockabilly and country from the first half of her career, for serious fans who can't get enough.

⊙ **Vintage Collection** (1996; Capitol). An excellent slice of Wanda's best from the late 1950s through the early '60s—20 cuts of both rockabilly ("Fujiyama Mama," "Mean Mean Man") and country ("Right Or Wrong," "The Window Up Above").

Wanda Jackson

Jerry Lee Lewis

> "Just gimme my money and show me where the piano is."
>
> —Jerry Lee Lewis

The creative energy that drives Jerry Lee Lewis is as pure, raw and untamed as any in country music. When he emerged from the depths of Louisiana in the mid-1950s he resembled a wild lion—his voice roaring with guttural urgency and youthful irreverence, his curly blonde hair whipping across his face, his fingers tearing at the piano keys as if they were fleshy bits of an animal he'd just killed. Much to the chagrin of the flag-waving, taxpaying, Eisenhower-supporting citizens of the time, Jerry Lee's music was an awesome and unstoppable power, one that unleashed the lust of a brand new generation that had only just been awakened by Elvis Presley's swirling hips. The concert halls Jerry Lee played in—even the radios and television sets he appeared on—pulsed, heaved, and throbbed with heated, animalistic energy. For anyone at the time whose blood was at all warm, he was a force difficult to resist.

If Jerry Lee had only ever recorded "Whole Lot Of Shaking Going On" and "Great Balls Of Fire," he'd still be one of the musical legends of the '50s. But between the worlds of Memphis and Nashville, rock'n'roll and country and western, Jerry Lee has sustained a long and impressive music career that has lasted more than four solid decades and reached into all corners of popular music. A decade after his rock'n'roll stardom, he re-emerged as a major Nashville hitmaker, scoring a string of Top 10 country hits that included "Another Place Another Time" and "What Made Milwaukee Famous (Has Made A Loser Out Of Me)." At the same time, though, he was still "the Killer," the mad musical genius with the untethered ego—busting through greasy rock and R&B material on stage, then turning around to quote biblical verse; flying as high as he could at every opportunity and still causing a ruckus no matter where or when he landed.

Jerry Lee's life and career make for an eye-opening and gripping story, and author Nick Tosches does a great job in his 1982 biography, *Hellfire*. Pulling together juicy anecdotes and sometimes dangerous scenarios with an eye for meaty detail, Tosches successfully conveys a sense of the demons, spirits, and forces both physical and otherworldly that drove—and still drive—one of rock'n'roll's most notorious wild men. The book is a highly recommended read not just for serious Lewis fans, but for anyone with a fascination for life's more bizarre creatures.

Jerry Lee was born on 29 September, 1935 in Ferriday, Louisiana. He was brought up in the Pentecostal faith, but he also learned piano early on, peering through the windows of clubs and beer joints to hear honky tonk and boogie-woogie blues. His rural southern childhood was a dichotomy between sin and salvation that would haunt him for the rest of his life. Growing up alongside Jerry Lee were two of his cousins, Mickey Gilley and Jimmy Swaggart, who were also talented pianists, and who would each go on to infamous careers of their own—Gilley as a country hitmaker and Texas clubowner (Gilley's, the "world's largest honky tonk") and Swaggart as a fire-and-brimstone television preacher (albeit one with a taste for New Orleans whores).

Lewis played his first public gig at a Ford dealership in 1949, then a year later he made it to Natchez radio station WNAT. That same year his parents enrolled him in a Bible college in Texas; ministerial aspirations may or may not have genuinely flashed before his eyes, but it wasn't long before he was kicked out. He knew he was blaspheming when he drank, boogied, and played the blues, but he simply couldn't help it. This was the tension that gave his music that rare and genuine fire.

In 1956 Lewis finally won the attention of Sun Records owner Sam Phillips. He moved to Memphis, began working at Sun as an accompanist, and was soon cutting his own records. His first record was a version of Ray Price's "Crazy Arms," but in early 1957 came "Whole Lot Of Shaking Going On," and through national radio and television exposure (which included a possessed Jerry Lee belting the song on the *Steve Allen Show*) the song quickly turned into a rock-'n'roll phenomenon. Next came "Great Balls Of Fire," and it was another smash; its flipside, a version of Hank Williams' "You Win Again," also did well. In December of that same year, however, Lewis made his famous, career-changing blunder: he married Myra Gale Brown, the thirteen-year-old daughter of his cousin, J.W. Brown (who was also the bass player in his band). Not exactly a well-thought-out decision, this was Jerry Lee's third marriage, his first taking place when he himself was a mere fourteen years old. The marriage was kept secret initially, but when Lewis embarked on a UK tour in the spring of 1958, he opted to bring Myra Gale with him, and suddenly the news

Jerry Lee Lewis

became very much public. The tour was quickly canceled, Jerry Lee's fans on both sides of the Atlantic turned against him, his performance fees fell from thousands of dollars per night to a couple of hundred, and his career headed straight for the toilet.

Jerry Lee never really hit bottom, however. True, the scandal halted his seemingly interminable rise to rock'n'roll superstardom, but killing the spirit and the drive of Jerry Lee Lewis wasn't going to be that simple. He didn't make it back to #1 again for another decade (with the country hit "To Make Love Sweeter For You" in 1969), but in the meantime he kept on playing and recording, almost as if nothing had happened, even denting the charts every now and again. He stayed at Sun through 1963, then he signed with Smash (a subsidiary of Mercury), and it's at this point that he began focusing more keenly on the country market. His early rock numbers remain his all-time classics, but a great deal of his Nashville material is excellent, high-proof honky tonk: "Another Place Another Time," "Would You Take Another Chance On Me," "She Even Woke Me Up To Say Goodbye," "She Still Comes Around (To Love What's Left

Of Me)," "Once More With Feeling," "What Made Milwaukee Famous (Has Made A Loser Out Of Me)," "Who's Gonna Play This Old Piano," "Mama's Hands," and "Honky Tonk Wine."

Lewis had his biggest country hits between the late '60s and early '70s, but he was actually on the *Billboard* charts fairly regularly right from his '50s beginnings through to the early '80s. He cut a huge variety of material during this time: country classics by Hank Williams, Floyd Tillman, Faron Young, and Jimmie Rodgers; rock'n'roll and R&B standards by Chuck Berry, Ray Charles, and the Big Bopper; and plenty of material by Nashville's new generation of songwriters—Tom T. Hall, Mickey Newbury, Kris Kristofferson, Paul Craft, Sonny Throckmorton, and Billy Joe Shaver. All the while, too, he kept up his reputation for carrying on—swallowing heaped helpings of booze and pills; 'accidentally' shooting a bandmember, Butch Owens, in the chest in 1975; appearing at the Graceland gates a year later with a loaded gun for a calling card; and working his way through a string of troubled marriages (two of his wives even wound up dead under strange circumstances).

Lewis records were released by Mercury proper during much of the '70s, but as the decade progressed his material became less interesting and more influenced by the Nashville Sound. In 1978 he jumped over to Elektra. The songs didn't bring him any #1 hits, but the sessions he cut in 1979 with guitarist James Burton and drummer Hal Blaine in Hollywood produced some beautifully re-energized material that blurred the lines between rock, soul, country, and blues. He next recorded briefly for MCA, then in the '90s he was picked up by Sire, which released YOUNG BLOOD in 1995, his first album in a decade. Amazingly enough, considering all "the Killer's" body and mind have been through during his long life and career, he's still out there, tearing it up on the road.

⊙ **18 Original Sun Greatest Hits** (1984; Rhino). The basics are here—"Shaking," "Great Balls Of Fire," "You Win Again," "High School Confidential," "Crazy Arms"—and they're all the casual fan needs to understand Jerry Lee's rockabilly roots. To stop here, however, without dabbling in the later Mercury/Smash material would be a shame.

⊙ **Classic Jerry Lee Lewis (1956–1963)** (1989; Bear Family). For the hardcore fans who really want it, the German label Bear Family has gathered 8 CDs' worth of Jerry Lee recordings from his rock'n'roll days, covering his complete output for Sun Records.

⊙ **Rockin' My Life Away** (1991; Warner Bros.). A 20-song compilation of recordings Jerry Lee cut for Elektra in 1979 and 1980. The Hollywood sessions produced the meatiest material Lewis had recorded in years, including Charlie Rich's "Who Will The Next Fool Be," Sonny Throckmorton's "I Wish I Was Eighteen Again," Bob Dylan's "Rita May," and Arthur Alexander's "Everyday I Have To Cry Some." The Nashville sessions were on the whole sweeter, but "Honky Tonk Stuff," "Thirty-Nine And Holding," and a surprisingly inspired version of "Somewhere Over The Rainbow" are worthwhile.

⊙ **All Killer, No Filler: The Anthology** (1993; Rhino). A 42-track, 2-CD compilation that brings his basic Sun tracks together with a healthy load of his Smash and Mercury material—titles such as "Another Place," "What Made Milwaukee Famous," "Would You Take Another Chance On Me," "She Even Woke Me Up To Say Goodbye," "Middle Age Crazy," and "Sometimes A Memory Ain't Enough." There's even a handful of Elektra tracks, including "Rainbow," "Thirty Nine," and "Rockin' My Life Away" (which is as good a theme song for "The Killer" as any). This is the kind of full-bodied, decades-spanning treatment that Lewis's long, diverse career more than well deserves.

⊙ **Killer Country** (1995; Mercury). A well-edited 20-track distillation of Jerry Lee's prolific Mercury/Smash output from the '60s and '70s. "The Killer" grew up in the Deep South with honky tonk all around him, so when he sings heartbreaking hits like "Another Place," "Milwaukee," "She Still Comes Around," and "The Hole He Said He'd Dig For Me," you better believe the pathos is real. Don't you fret, he also knows how to cut loose, as evidenced by "Me And Bobby McGee," the southern rock-inspired "Jack Daniels Old No. 7," and the crass Dan Penn composition "You're All Too Ugly Tonight."

Janis Martin

There weren't many female rockabilly artists during the music's heyday, but the few who did rise to the surface—Wanda Jackson, Brenda Lee, Bonnie Lou, Lorrie Collins, Jo-Ann Campbell, and Virginia native Janis Darlene Martin—possessed a mixture of gusto, courage, and youthful spirit that was as thrilling as it was admirable. Martin had a bright, vivacious voice and boisterous style that won her public attention via songs like "Ooby Dooby" and "Will You,

Willyum." Born in Sutherlin, Virginia on 27 March, 1940, she learned to sing and play guitar as a child, and by the time she was thirteen she'd become a cast-member of the *Old Dominion Barn Dance* in Richmond, Virginia. The song "Will You, Willyum," written by Richmond radio announcer Carl Stutz, was her breakthrough into what would be a brief but hot recording career. She cut a demo of "Willyum" in 1956, and when RCA executive Steve Sholes heard it he signed the teenager, making her the first female rockabilly singer to get major label-sized promotion. The song sold well, and Martin was dubbed the "Female Elvis" (she wasn't the only one, however: platinum-haired, thirty-year-old singer Jean Chapel had also been given the moniker). During the next few years Martin cut about two dozen songs, a mixture of rockabilly, country and pop material, including "Drugstore Rock'n'Roll," "Let's Elope Baby," "My Boy Elvis," "Ooby Dooby," "Love Me To Pieces," and "Bang Bang" (covered more than three decades later by Kelly Willis). She toured with her band, the Marteens—including a stint in Europe on a country package tour—and performed on pop programs like *American Bandstand* as well as country stalwarts such as the *Ozark Jubilee* and the *Grand Ole Opry*.

Family life, however, got in the way of Martin's music career. When RCA got wind that she'd been married since the age of fifteen, and especially after she had a child at the age of eighteen, they figured her feisty rockabilly image was irreversibly tarnished; that coupled with sagging record sales led to her being dropped in 1958. Two years later (and newly divorced) she recorded a handful of songs for the indie label, Palette. But about the same time she also remarried, and like so many women of her era she chose family over career (apparently it was an ultimatum handed her by her second husband). She briefly revived her career in the '70s, but Elvis Presley's death dulled her spirit. In the mid-'90s, though, Rosie Flores pulled Martin out of retirement to sing a couple of songs on her album ROCKABILLY FILLY.

⊙ **The Female Elvis: Complete Recordings, 1956–1960** (1994; Bear Family). A 30-song retrospective that pulls together all of Martin's recordings for RCA and Palette. Martin's voice was bright and attractive, but her singing came from the gut. The songs are a mixture of rockabilly, teen pop and country.

Carl Perkins

> "Someone once said that everything's been done before—and it has. It's just a question of figuring out a good mixture of it to sound original."
>
> —Carl Perkins

Carl Perkins had only one major hit ("Blue Suede Shoes") to Elvis Presley's multitude, but that doesn't mean he was simply a one-note rockabilly boy wonder. Songs he wrote over the years, including "Daddy Sang Bass," "So Wrong," "Dixie Fried," and "Everybody's Trying To Be My Baby" have endured, and his work has been covered by such artists as Johnny Cash, Jim Dickinson, Patsy Cline, and the Beatles. Perkins' guitar playing was also a major inspiration to up-and-coming players throughout the rock'n'roll era; and while many rockabilly one-shots burned out after a few years, his career continued to flourish. By the time of the rockabilly revival in the '70s, Perkins was considered a hero.

While he was a key element in the development of rock'n'roll, Perkins' edge has always remained close to his hillbilly roots. The best of his Sun singles (and some of his early Columbia material, too) have the swampy vibe of a true southern farm-bred boy. "Dixie Fried", in particular, burns as sweaty-hot and dangerous as the honky-tonk Saturday night ("he jerked out his razor but he wasn't shavin'") the song describes. Other songs captured elements of that raw country spirit, but none cut quite as close to the bone as that piece of work.

Carl Lee Perkins was born to a poor sharecropping family on 9 April, 1932 near Tiptonville, Tennessee. He learned guitar from another local sharecropper, and by his teens he and his brothers Jay and Clayton had assembled a band. Perkins soon developed to the point where he was sending his songs to various labels. Hearing Elvis on the radio in 1954 he headed for Sun Records in Memphis (where Elvis cut his first sides), figuring label head Sam Phillips would have an ear for the hybrid music he'd been playing. Like he'd done with Elvis, Phillips helped shape Perkins' bluesy hillbilly sound into full-fired rockabilly. His earlier singles tended more toward country, though his guitar licks still jumped right out at you. When Elvis was signed away to RCA in 1955, Phillips felt free to give Perkins a chance to record some rock'n'roll material. The result, "Blue Suede Shoes," a smart little ditty written by Perkins, shot to the top of the country, pop, and R&B charts in 1956, proving it wasn't just Elvis who spoke rockabilly's language. It was the biggest-selling Sun single to date.

It's hard to say how much more fruitful Perkins' early career would have been if he hadn't been involved in a serious car accident right in the midst of his "Blue Suede Shoes" success. Instead of singing his big hit on *The Perry Como Show*, as was planned, he was stuck in a hospital bed while Elvis whipped through the very same song on another TV show. By the time Perkins was back in business, there was no catching up on the King's phenomenal success.

Perkins was eventually signed (as was fellow Sun artist Johnny Cash) to Columbia Records in 1958. There he churned out further rockabilly-type songs, many of which are quite decent, though they lack the same loose, uninhibited energy of his Sun sides. None came anywhere close to his "Blue Suede Shoes" in terms of sales, and Columbia didn't hang onto him long. At this stage Perkins' personal life was deteriorating: he was frustrated by the opportunities he had missed, his brother Jay was dying from cancer, and he was firmly attached to the bottle. The Beatles cut a handful of his songs when they first started out, and that must have fueled his confidence, but for the most part the '60s were his darkest days.

Late in the decade, however, Perkins began touring as a guitarist and side attraction with Johnny Cash's entourage. He managed to beat his booze habit and stuck with Cash for a decade. As for his own recordings during this time, he label-hopped to Decca, Dollie, back to Columbia, and then on to Mercury and the English label Jet, among others.

Carl Perkins

Rockabilly Resources

As the new millennium takes off, the dedication and passion of rockabilly lovers raves on. It's no surprise, then, that fans have flooded the Web with countless sites about the music, the bands, the fanatics, and pretty near everything that bops. It would take months to navigate, much less list them all. So below are three different jumping-off points that work well for either the novice or devotee. All, too, have plenty more links to take you far deeper into the rockabilly cyberworld.

Rockabilly Central

(ⓦ www.rockabilly.net/index.shtml)
This site out of Chicago may be your first place to go for a couple of reasons. First, its comprehensive list of links to other sites is by far the best organized, logically divided into categories such as music, bands, labels, online record shops, merchandise, regional guides, booking and promotion, and so forth. The site also hosts well-written profiles on a number of current rockabilly bands. But for a treat, click on the name Billy Lee Riley, click "History," and suddenly you're brought to the Memphis City Guide, where you can go gaga taking a Webtour of Sun Records. (Or go directly to ⓦ www.memphisguide. com and immerse yourself in the rest of that city's musical history.)

Rockabilly Hall Of Fame

(ⓦ www.rockabillyhall.com)
This well-known, well-loved site out of England earns a bookmark with its up-to-date information regarding new CD releases and upcoming events, reviews, profiles, and tons of photos from the past along with others taken during recent gigs and festivals (for those who have only seen period photos of their favorite rockabilly stars, proceed with caution). The left-hand-side list of artists profiled on the site (and listed by first name—c'mon, all those Johnnies!) gives the impression it's a comprehensive listing. But where are Hasil Adkins, Deke Dickerson and ... hey, how could they leave out Herbie Duncan? Oh—click "Inductees List" under "I." All right, now you can find just about anyone who

recorded anything remotely connected to rockabilly; and sometimes there's a song list, too, and other times there are links to the artist's official Web site. I think I understand Lefty Frizzell's presence, but what are Fats Domino and Etta James doing here?

A Little Somethin' Rockabilly

(ⓦ www.teleport.com/~oricet/rockabilly/intro.html)
Whew. After getting lost in a gigantic site like the above, it's nice to find something compact—and endearing to boot. The lovely Orice Tanner hosts this site, which links current bands and best of all features photos of regular-type rockabilly lovers, with a variety of looks and attitudes, from all over the place. (Leah R., you gotta boyfriend?)

Okay, maybe now you're ready to dive deep into the **Rockabilly Ring** (ⓦ www.webring.org/cgi-bin/ webring?ring=rockabilly&id=57&list) for (at this writing) 306 links for bands, tour information and online mags— all randomly listed. Of course, there are some of us out there still without Web access. If that's you—or if your eyes are worn out from too much screen time—check out **Blue Suede News**, my favorite current 'zine on the 1950s, where rockabilly fits right in with other Fifties genres such as country and R&B. The writing can be sloppy, but each issue has more CD reviews than any Web site, along with proper attitude and plenty of photos. You can find them at ⓦ www.bluesuedenews. com or write them at Box 25, Duvall, WA 98019-0025, USA.

Finally, it's always worth your time seeking back issues of **Kicks** magazine. It was last published in 1992; since then, Billy Miller and Miriam Linna have spent most of the last eight years building their Norton Records empire. This mag is the greatest of them all, overflowing with passion, humor, rare photos, and invaluable information about your favorite rockabilly, R&B cat, surf band, or garage punker. They may still have some back issues in stock. Find them at ⓦ www.nortonrecords.com, or write them at: PO Box 646, Cooper Station, New York, NY 10276-0646, USA.

— Brian Gordon

His song "Restless" made a respectable impact in 1970, and a year later Cash turned Perkins' "Daddy Sang Bass" into a modern classic. When rockabilly was rediscovered during the '70s and '80s, Perkins attracted further attention, especially in Britain. In 1986 he cut THE CLASS OF '55 with Cash, Jerry

Lee Lewis, and Roy Orbison, and a decade later came GO CAT GO! (a sort of companion CD to a Perkins biography by David McGee) which paired Perkins with an assortment of star guests—Tom Petty, Paul Simon, George Harrison, and Willie Nelson among them. Perkins died in early 1998.

Carl Perkins

⊙ **Original Sun Greatest Hits** (1986; Rhino). These 16 sides from the 1950s are not only definitive rockabilly but a downright gritty, greasy thrill.

⊙ **Honky Tonk Gal: Rare And Unissued Sun Masters** (1989; Rounder). Perhaps more than any other rockabilly, with Carl Perkins the music's hillbilly roots are above ground and active. Just give a listen to the honky-tonk-inspired alternate takes of "Turn Around" and "Let The Jukebox Keep On Playing," or further obscurities like "What You Doin' When You Cryin'" and "You Can't Make Love To Somebody." An excellent companion CD to the GREATEST HITS collection.

⊙ **Restless: The Columbia Recordings** (1992; Columbia/Legacy). A selection of his '50s and '60s Columbia recordings. Not as classic as his Sun material, but that aside, songs like "Jive After Five" and especially "Hambone" are still dirty enough to entice.

⊙ **Definitive Collection** (1998; Charly). Two CDs, one of "Classic Tracks" (his Sun-era stuff) and another called "Diggin' The Vaults" (mostly demos and alternate takes).

Elvis Presley

"His music stands to the rest of rockabilly as genius does to talent."
—Greil Marcus

The roots of rockabilly may stretch back for decades, but the phenomenon itself—the music, the movement, the *revolution*—kicked off with the release of Elvis Presley's first Sun Records single in July of 1954: "That's All Right" backed with "Blue Moon Of Kentucky." Sam Phillips, Sun owner and '50s musical visionary, released a mere five Presley singles (ten songs total) before selling his contract for $35,000 to RCA a year later (though it doesn't seem like much to us today, at the time it was a mighty and altogether unprecedented sum, and it raised more than a few eyebrows). But those ten songs represent a serious chunk of modern rock'n'roll's foundations.

Presley is without a doubt a monumental musical figure. He's been embraced by multiple musical worlds—the glitzy popsphere of Las Vegas (where countless Elvis impersonators still haunt the casinos), the Rock and Roll Hall of Fame, and as of 1998 the Country Music Hall of Fame. He

attained a level of international stardom, popularity and success that will likely never be reached by any musician again. But as many songs as he recorded, and as bombastic as much of his music became, at the root of it all are those Sun singles. That's an easy fact to forget, given all the hype, but if you're ever in doubt of the King's worthiness, go back and give them a serious listen. Blues, country, pop, gospel, sentimental balladry, and teenage angst that borders on violence: it's all there—unadorned, yet deeply possessed, vibrating and even shining—in Scotty Moore's subtle but unpredictable guitar leads, Bill Black's rhythmic bass slaps, and Presley's amazingly expressive voice. So simple, yet what an emotional punch.

Elvis Aron Presley was born on 8 January, 1935 to a dirt-poor family in Tupelo, Mississippi. Later the Presleys moved to Memphis where the future King finished high school and got a day job. He cut some private acetates at Sam Phillips' Memphis Recording Service; his reason for doing so is still not clear. The woman at the desk, however, was paying attention. She was Marion Keisker, a local radio personality and Phillips' partner in the venture, and she told Sam about this young guy who'd impressed her. This led to an opportunity to cut a record at Sun. Phillips (who'd been on the look-out for a white singer who could sing in a black style) teamed Elvis with Moore and Black, two local musicians he'd worked with previously. After a few unsuccessful attempts at songs like "I Love You Because," Elvis started up with a crazy version of Arthur Crudup's "That's All Right," Moore and Black followed along, and rockabilly music stepped out into the light.

The Sun singles began as hits in the Memphis area, but when Elvis took to the road and showed the young folks how to shake and swing their hips in ways their parents never spoke of, generations' worth of polite southern respectability began to crumble. The revolution was now under way, and there was no turning around. The band picked up drummer D.J. Fontana in 1955, the same year Presley made the top of the national country charts with "I Forgot To Remember To Forget" and then the monumental "Mystery Train." By the end of the year, though, the whole machine was shifting gears and looking at the road through a brand new windshield. Elvis had picked up a new manager, Colonel Tom Parker, who'd previously guided the career of Eddy Arnold. One of the first things the Colonel did was move Presley to RCA. From that point on, Parker was at the wheel of the King's career.

Presley's RCA releases over the next couple of years—"Heartbreak Hotel," "Blue Suede Shoes," "Jailhouse Rock," "Hound Dog," and "Don't Be Cruel" among them—were huge hits at the time and are today his best known songs. They were as rocking, if not more so, as anything he'd cut before now, but they were a bit cleaner—having stepped ever so slightly away from the raw hillbilly/blues roots that had been the foundation of his Sun singles. At the same time, without the R&B-obsessed Sam Phillips in the control booth, Elvis was free to let his penchant for sentimental pop songs shine through more clearly (Dean Martin was one of his idols). Some songs such as "Love Me" and "Any-place Is Paradise" even included a background chorus, a typical feature of the Nashville Sound—which, ironically, was becoming the country establishment's "adult" answer to rockabilly's teen fury.

That's All Right: Elvis Presley

Elvis was drafted into the Army in 1958, and after his return to civilian life he concentrated on movies. His first few flicks (*Love Me Tender, Jailhouse Rock*, etc.) had appeared before his Army stint and worked as complements to his hit recordings, but during the '60s his roles in *G.I. Blues, Flaming Star, Viva Las Vegas, Clambake*, and many others were his main occupation. It's amazing how the career of this edgy rock'n'roll pioneer could become so soggy in such a short time.

Which only made his musical comeback all the brighter. It arrived in the form of an NBC-TV Christmas special in 1968, in which Elvis appeared in black leather before a live audience for the first time in years, sang rootsy, bluesy material, and generally showed himself capable of cutting loose and having a blast. (In the Elvis chapter of his book *Mystery Train,* Greil Marcus explains the excitement of this moment beautifully.) Reinvigorated, Presley returned to Memphis for a series of sessions at Chips Moman's American Studio, the result being the album FROM ELVIS IN MEMPHIS. His rockabilly days may have been long gone, but that album showed Elvis was paying attention again. The burly rhythms and gutsy sound (despite a somewhat overwrought production) have made it one of his finest efforts. His version of Mac Davis' "In The Ghetto" shot up the charts, and further songs from those Memphis sessions—

Percy Mayfield's "Stranger In My Own Hometown," Eddie Rabbitt's "Kentucky Rain," and the great "Suspicious Minds," his late-period signature number—continued to fuel the Elvis Presley fire.

In 1969 Elvis returned to live performing with a string of concerts in Las Vegas and then began touring the US. His band, centering around guitarist James Burton, included some of the finest players in the business. As the '70s wore on, however, and the crowds grew and grew, laziness set in all over again, and this time the rut was too big—and too lucrative—to escape. His presentation grew more and more wrapped up in rhinestones, white jumpsuits and over-the-top stage productions. To be fair, though, some of the live albums from this period are interesting, showing him messing around with the songs and the lyrics (consciously? purposefully? that's open to debate).

We all know where this path of excess led: 16 August, 1977, slumped on the bathroom floor at his gaudy Memphis homestead, Graceland, his body wrecked from too many prescription pills and fried peanut butter and banana sandwiches. Of course, the story of Elvis Presley doesn't really end there—it goes on and on, through countless tributes and TV specials and album reissues; and outside the gates of Graceland, the crowds of fans waiting to tour the place on any given day show no signs of thinning.

Elvis Presley

If you want a closer look at the King—whose story was no ordinary one—the best sources are Peter Guralnick's excellent biographies *Last Train To Memphis* and its sequel *Careless Love: The Unmaking Of Elvis Presley*. The aforementioned essay in Greil Marcus' *Mystery Train* is also insightful.

⊙ **The Million Dollar Quartet** (1990; RCA). A spur-of-the-moment event that happened when Elvis dropped by a 1956 Carl Perkins session and Sam Phillips had the wit to record it. Jerry Lee Lewis happened to be there as a session pianist, and Johnny Cash was called in (but supposedly didn't stay). The result is mostly fragmented, but loose and good fun.

⊙ **The King Of Rock'n'Roll: The Complete '50s Masters** (1992; RCA). A beautifully compiled 5-disc box set for those seeking the whole shebang of Elvis' formative years.

⊙ **Elvis 56** (1996; RCA). Collects all Presley's initial recordings for RCA, and it's a great companion to the Sun sessions. The raw hillbilly simplicity of the Sun recordings has pretty much dissipated, yet the songs are still rugged and quite thrilling.

⊙ **Sunrise** (1999; RCA). A 2-CD collection of Presley's Sun-era recordings. The Sun singles are absolutely essential, and they're packed together with loads of outtakes, alternate takes, and rarities—including live cuts from the *Louisiana Hayride* and the private acetate recordings he made before his sessions for Sun. Expands and updates RCA's earlier SUN SESSIONS CD and LP releases. Any one of these Sun-era collections is *the* place to start.

⊙ **Suspicious Minds** (1999; RCA). An expanded 2-CD collection centering around his superb 1969 album FROM ELVIS IN MEMPHIS, plus other Memphis sessions from the same period. Excellent players, excellent material ("In The Ghetto," "Kentucky Rain," "Long Black Limousine," "Stranger In My Own Hometown," "Suspicious Minds")—one of the essential Elvis albums. Previously issued on a single CD as THE MEMPHIS RECORD.

Billy Lee Riley

S inger and multi-instrumentalist Billy Lee Riley wasn't a national hitmaker, but he did leave a permanent mark on 1950s rockabilly history with two hot-fired numbers, "Red Hot" and "Flying Saucers Rock'n'Roll," both cut in Memphis for Sun Records. Riley and his band, the Little Green Men, created a raspy, rough-edged sound that was one of the craziest even on Sun. "Flying Saucers" is especially frenetic with its wild screams, otherworldly guitar riffs, and piano courtesy of Jerry Lee Lewis. As for "Red Hot"—a now-familiar R&B song by Billy "The Kid" Emerson built around the call-and-response lines "My gal is red hot/Your gal ain't doodly squat"—Riley made it a rockabilly standard.

Riley was born on 5 October, 1933 in Pocahantas, Arkansas. He played in a band with future producer Jack Clement and did session work at Sun before signing his own recording contract with the label. During the '60s Riley ended up in Hollywood, where he found lots of session work (playing harmonica and guitar) with the likes of the Beach Boys, Johnny Rivers, and Sammy Davis, Jr. He also continued to lead his own band and cut records, some of them enjoyable in the manner of LA pop-rock singer Rivers, but most hardly memorable (his 1972 version of Tony Joe White's "I Got A Thing About You Baby" is one funky exception). The rockabilly revival of the '70s rejuvenated interest in Riley's '50s recordings. In 1992 he cut the album BLUE COLLAR BLUES for the California label HighTone, though the bluesy sound has only tinges of his former rockabilly fury.

⊙ **Classic Recordings 1956–1960** (1990; Bear Family). A 2-CD set focusing on Riley's fertile rockabilly period, including songs cut on Sun and other Memphis labels.

⊙ **Red Hot: The Best Of Billy Lee Riley** (1995; AVI). A more down-to-earth single-CD collection of Riley's rockabilly that's probably more than plenty for most.

Gene Vincent

"**B** e-Bop-A-Lula" is one of the best-remembered songs of the 1950s, and though it was Gene Vincent's only real hit, the man who created that rockabilly sensation was far more than a mere one-shot wonder with a thrown-together garage band. Alternately guttural and sensual, Vincent's mid-'50s sides are some of the genre's most primal, and, at the same time, downright melodic. Vincent was also a character most didn't forget.

The rebellious Gene Vincent

equally raw and powerful, failed to chart anywhere near as high. His 1958 single "Lotta Lovin'" was the only other sizeable hit of his career. At about this time, though, Vincent was also downshifting his sound—the raw, primal energy that crawled all over his earliest sides had begun to dissipate, leaving smoother lines and gentler rhythms in its place. That's not to say, however, it was all throwaway stuff. He did bring standards like "Accentuate The Positive" and "Blue Eyes Crying In The Rain" into his repertoire, but on the other hand songs like "Crazy Times" and "Green Back Dollar" still showed an enthusiastic blend of R&B, country, and rock'n'roll.

Jerry Lee Lewis might have been the most insane, but Gene Vincent epitomized the bad boy image—his hair greased back, his lip curled into a sneer, and his gaunt frame wrapped up in black leather. If ladies truly do love outlaws, they definitely fell for Vincent, whose style was a lusty combination of raw rebellion and urgent sexuality. Vincent emerged onto the rockabilly highway directly in the backdraft of Elvis Presley, and together with his hot band, the Blue Caps, he tore up the pavement.

Vincent Gene Craddock was born on 11 February, 1935 in Norfolk, Virginia. He spent time in the Navy and later fell victim to a motorcycle accident, which left him with a permanent limp, a leg brace, and a good deal of pain that stayed with him his whole life. He began playing country music in various outfits around Norfolk, and he also cut some demos that eventually found their way to Capitol Records. Label executives there were looking for a strong rockabilly singer so they could capitalize on the selling power of Elvis Presley, and in 1956 they placed their bets on Vincent. They were immediately rewarded with "Be-Bop-A-Lula," Vincent's first single, which soared to the Top 10 in both the country and pop charts and earned him a good deal of notoriety. Follow-ups, however, such as "Bluejean Bop," "Race With The Devil," and "Crazy Legs," while

While the American market might not have latched onto his music as hoped, Vincent began to find new audiences overseas, and by the turn of the new decade he had already toured Europe, Australia, and Japan. During a British tour in 1960, however, he and his buddy, singer Eddie Cochran, were involved in a car accident that cost Cochran his life. Vincent parted ways with Capitol soon after that, eventually turning to smaller labels such as Challenge and Forever. Throughout the decade he concentrated much of his energy on Europe, but try as he might, his career never enjoyed a full-on revival. As time wore on he was also more and more plagued by his drinking, medical, and personal problems. Sadly, he died in 1971 at the young age of thirty-six, the victim of a ruptured stomach ulcer.

⊙ **The Screaming End: The Best Of Gene Vincent** (1997; Razor & Tie). Vincent recorded quite a lot for Capitol, and this single-CD compilation does a great job boiling his prolific output down to 20 of his choicest cuts. All his raw-powered mid-1950s gems are present, including "Be-Bop-A-Lula," "Woman Love," "Race With The Devil," "Crazy Legs," "B-I-Bickey Bi, Bo-Bo Go," and "Bluejean Bop."

Gene Vincent

8

It's Such a Pretty World Today: The Nashville Sound Arrives

During the 1950s, the country music industry was growing and strengthening into a powerful force, with Nashville—Music City USA—as its centerpoint. Rockabilly and rock'n'roll were a brief threat to the industry, stealing much of the youth market away, but the country establishment duly reacted with its own home-grown remedy—a smooth, pop-oriented style that became known as the Nashville Sound.

The idea behind the Nashville Sound was to give the music broader appeal in the pop as well as the country markets by softening country's twangier edges. Record producers **Chet Atkins**, Owen Bradley, Don Law, Ken Nelson, and later Billy Sherrill brought influences taken from the pop-music world into the Nashville recording studios. Goodbye fiddle leads, hayseed routines and nasal voices; hello string sections, background choruses and smooth, sophisticated singing. This country-pop blend—or 'countrypolitan' as it came to be known—worked like a charm, as far as record sales and radio listenership were concerned. "Many fans don't even know what they're enjoying," wrote Morris Duff in the *Toronto Daily Star* in 1964. Which was a good thing: if they'd thought it was "country," they'd probably have switched stations.

Warm, fireside crooners like **Eddy Arnold** and **Jim Reeves** were the countrypolitan team leaders, as was newly sophisticated country gal **Patsy Cline**, but ultimately the Nashville Sound affected far more than just a select group of artists. Even harder-edged singers like **Johnny Cash**, George Jones, Skeets McDonald, and Lefty Frizzell—who had each previously recorded in places like Memphis, Dallas, and LA—found their Nashville recordings infused with choruses and other crossover accoutrements.

Not that this was an entirely bad thing, as a number of beautiful recordings were made during this period. Reeves' "He'll Have To Go" and Cline's "Crazy" and "I Fall To Pieces," for instance, are true classics that ripple with emotional texture thanks in good part to their lush musical texture. Unfortunately, however, this wasn't always the case, especially as time wore on. With the same session players working record after record, and songs featuring more and more strings, choruses, lilting piano lines, and soft-lit arrangements, the Nashville Sound also led to what Bill Malone in his book *Country Music USA* called "the juggernaut of homogenization." By the '70s, even Chet Atkins himself was apologizing for it.

The Studio System

The Nashville Sound, however, was more than just a musical style; on a broader level it came to represent a method of making records that has had an impact on nearly every artist in Nashville, pop-oriented or not, from the late 1950s to the present day. By the '60s virtually every artist cutting songs in Nashville—be they **Don Gibson** or **Loretta Lynn**, Brenda Lee or Johnny Cash—was working amidst the growing network of producers, session men, song publishers, and high-tech recording facilities that had become the Nashville way of making records.

Nashville had been attracting attention as a country music center since the rise in national popularity of the *Grand Ole Opry*. The city's first recording facility, the Castle Recording Studio, opened in the mid-'40s in the Tulane Hotel, and nearly all the major record companies used it regularly (as did indies such as King and Bullet). In 1954, after several false starts in other locations, Decca producer Owen Bradley and his brother, session guitarist Harold Bradley, opened a recording studio in a Nashville neighborhood now known as Music Row. The Quonset Hut, as it was dubbed, was bought by Columbia in 1962; the label built its Nashville studio complex around it and used the facility for another two decades. Not long after the Quonset Hut began operating, RCA Records opened a Nashville recording facility nearby that became known as Studio B (it's now part of the Country Music Hall of Fame and Museum). Each of these studios became busy centerpoints of the burgeoning Nashville industry, booking many hundreds of sessions each year.

At the recording sessions themselves, precedents were established that are still firmly in place today. To begin with, producers became the guiding forces, often choosing the artist's material as well as shaping the arrangements and overall sound. Ralph Peer and Art Satherley pioneered the concept; in their footsteps came Decca's Paul Cohen, RCA's Steve Sholes, Columbia's Don Law, and Fred Rose of publishing company Acuff-Rose (the man in charge of Hank Williams' career and catalog). During the '50s and '60s, the main men in Nashville were Bradley, Atkins, and Law.

As the studio system grew, it attracted a sizeable group of top-notch session men who played primarily in the recording studios rather than on the road. These sidemen were, in many ways, the heart and soul of the Nashville studio system. Guitarist Zeke Turner and fiddler Tommy Jackson were among the first. When Atkins came to town he quickly became one of the most in-demand guitarists; Bradley, too, was a session regular. During the '50s and early '60s this system truly established itself, with players like guitarist Grady Martin, bassist Roy Huskey Jr., pianists Floyd Cramer and Hargus "Pig" Robbins, harmonica player Charlie McCoy, and drummer Buddy Harman showing up on the majority of records cut in Nashville. Though generally uncredited on records, they were consummate professionals, and their licks, fills, and rhythms frequently gave the songs additional flair—Martin's nylon-string guitar work on Marty Robbins' "El Paso" and Lefty Frizzell's "Saginaw, Michigan"; Cramer's slurred piano riffs on Hank Locklin's "Please Help Me, I'm Falling." The cream of this crop came to be known as the A Team, and they shifted freely between Decca, RCA, and other labels.

Finally, there were the Jordanaires and the Anita Kerr Singers, vocal groups who graced the backdrop of countless Nashville recordings. In addition to her singing duties, Kerr worked out the arrangements on numerous recordings and even did some producing for RCA (one of the first and only women allowed to perform such a task). Alongside Bradley and Atkins, she was an integral force in the Nashville Sound's development.

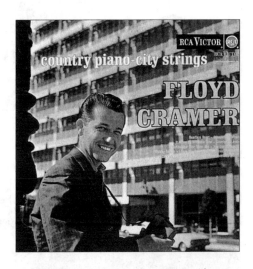

Another major new business venture in Nashville was the publishing house, whose job it became to supply the artists and producers with fresh song material. Acuff-Rose was Nashville's first, founded during the '40s; since then other companies like Cedarwood, Sure-Fire, and Tree popped up in town one by one, nabbing song catalogs (Acuff-Rose controlled Hank Williams'

songs, Cedarwood was home to Webb Pierce) and eventually signing professional writers to work for them exclusively. Felice and Boudleaux Bryant, Cindy Walker, Marijohn Wilkin, Don Robertson, Curly Putman, Harlan Howard, and Hank Cochran made professional careers out of songwriting almost exclusively. Others such as **Don Gibson**, Willie Nelson, **Roger Miller**, Mel Tillis, Mickey Newbury, and **Bill Anderson** were singing stars who first got their break through songwriting for the various publishing houses.

Pop Origins

The Nashville Sound took country music beyond the rustic image it had held since its commercial start four decades earlier, giving it a strong and decidedly contemporary edge intended to help it compete in the fast world of pop and rock'n'roll. In the process it became more geared toward middle-class listeners who lived in the suburbs, not just rural folks in the hills of Appalachia. Roughly from this point onwards, the country and western world has remained split between staunch traditionalists (who feel a countrypolitan compromise is a deal with the Devil) and fans who feel the music can and should change with the times.

The shift in the nature of country music was inevitable, however. The music has always appealed to a limited market radiating out from the South, while pop music spread over a vast, nationwide territory that, when conquered, meant far higher sales figures. And what country artist didn't aim to sell more records? So while the onslaught of rock'n'roll was certainly a motivation for change in the country music world, the move toward a pop-friendly sound was a trend that had been in place for years.

In fact, country's collusion with popular music trends may be traced back to some of the earliest commercial recordings. Jimmie Rodgers included Tin Pan Alley songs in his repertoire, as did many hillbilly artists of the period; and it was Vernon Dalhart, a wannabe opera singer with a formal New York approach to hillbilly songs, who recorded country's first million-selling record, "The Wreck Of The Old '97." Cowboy singers Gene Autry and Jimmy Wakely each had a voice as smooth as Bing Crosby's; Wakely, in fact, cut a series of duets with pop singer Margaret Whiting. And Eddy Arnold, one of the biggest-selling

Nashville's top vocal quartet, the Jordanaires

country artists of all time, had by the '50s turned from his down-home beginnings as the Tennessee Plowboy into a smooth sophisticate crooning "I Really Don't Want To Know" and "Make The World Go Away"—and winning a massive new audience in the process.

Country songs, too, had successfully crossed over into the pop-music ranks. Bing Crosby frequently recorded country and western material such as Al Dexter's "Pistol Packin' Mama" and Ernest Tubb's "Walking The Floor Over You." Other songs like Floyd Tillman's "Slippin' Around," Bob Wills' "San Antonio Rose," and Leon Payne's "I Love You Because" were covered by pop artists from the Dinning Sisters to Patti Page. By far the biggest crossover hit of all, though, was "Tennessee Waltz." Written and originally recorded by Pee Wee King and Redd Stewart, it was a multi-million-selling national success thanks to a 1950 version by Page. And in 1952, Tony Bennett took Hank Williams' "Cold, Cold Heart" to the top of the *Billboard* pop charts. By the time Chet Atkins and Owen Bradley hit the scene, then, it was quite clear that there was plenty of hillbilly money to be made in the world of pop music.

The Architects

Guitarist Atkins and pianist Bradley were the men at ground zero of the Nashville Sound's development. Settling in Nashville in 1950, Atkins played guitar on numerous sessions, recorded as a solo artist for RCA, and in his spare time led a laid-back group at the Carousel Club in a seedy downtown district called Printer's Alley. Many of Music City's future session stalwarts jammed with Atkins at the Carousel, including pianist Floyd Cramer, drummer Buddy Harman, and saxophonist Boots Randolph. Atkins was hired in 1952 as assistant to Steve Sholes at RCA; by 1960 he was head of A&R, in charge of a roster that included Eddy Arnold, Jim Reeves, and Don Gibson, and would soon take on Waylon Jennings, Charley Pride, and Dolly Parton, among many others.

Bradley worked for years in Nashville as a local bandleader and musical director at WSM radio (home of the *Grand Ole Opry*) before he was hired by Decca to assist producer Paul Cohen. He eventually ran the label's Nashville division, producing records at the Quonset Hut, the downtown studio he'd opened with his brother. Later, he opened another studio, the famous Bradley's Barn, located just outside of town (it burned to the ground in 1980 but was rebuilt on the same spot). As a producer, Bradley worked with a huge range of artists,

GLENN A BAKER ARCHIVES/REDFERNS

Nashville Sound progenitor Owen Bradley

including Red Foley, Kitty Wells, Webb Pierce, Bill Anderson, Conway Twitty, Loretta Lynn, and Bill Monroe. His most famous charge, though, was Patsy Cline, whom he turned from a brash honky-tonk wannabe into a smooth, hitmaking country stylist.

Both Bradley and Atkins regularly used background choruses, strings and horns on the country records they produced, ironing the twang out of the arrangements and giving the music an uptown sheen. Along with Arnold, Cline, and Reeves, other artists who successfully straddled this country-pop boundary include the **Browns**, **Sonny James**, Jimmy Dean, Marty Robbins, George Hamilton IV, and Ferlin Husky (whose hit song "Gone" was produced, ironically, by Ken Nelson, one of the architects of the Bakersfield Sound).

One of the landmark country-pop albums actually came from outside the genre. For his 1962 album MODERN SOUNDS IN COUNTRY AND WESTERN MUSIC, Ray Charles cut a series of country standards like "You Win Again," "I Love

Billy Sherrill

Bursting with Talent

Though the countrypolitan stylings of Reeves and Cline were hugely popular in the late 1950s and early '60s, this was by no means the only type of country music being made in or around Nashville. Bluegrass and honky tonk, for instance—traditional or 'hard' country, as older styles were being dubbed—never entirely disappeared. Bill Monroe and Ernest Tubb were major *Opry* figures, Hank Williams was still fresh in country fans' minds, and honky-tonkers like George Jones, Buck Owens, and Ray Price were having little trouble making the charts. Plenty more artists— Johnny Paycheck, Merle Haggard, Loretta Lynn, **Porter Wagoner**, Charlie Walker—maintained a harder edge to their brand of country, too.

If anything, Nashville during the '60s was a huge melting pot of singers and styles the likes of which Music Row hasn't seen (or you might say *allowed*) ever since. The town was bursting with talent, as eager young artists continually arrived on local doorsteps looking for work as songwriters, sidemen, or demo singers (used by publishing houses to shop songs to record companies). With the industry still relatively young and eager, and 'proper' channels of artistic introduction not yet fully established, there were more open channels (and open-minded attitudes) then than there are today. Country radio was growing fast, and record companies were continually searching for music to satisfy a hungry public that was not yet, at least as a whole, interested in choosing one musical style over another. Thus you had Reeves, who was killed in a plane crash in 1964, posthumously crooning "Blue Side Of Lonesome" at the same time that Haggard was busting out "Swinging Doors." And those were just two of the big hits: somewhere out in no man's land lay weirdos like Wagoner's "Rubber Room," Roger Miller's "You Can't Roller Skate In A Buffalo Herd," and Paycheck's "(Pardon Me) I've Got Someone To Kill"—a dark, deadly serious, and all-out frightening piece of work.

You So Much It Hurts," and "Born To Lose." The songs feature string and big-band arrangements that roam between playful, melancholy, and at times sweet—though they never entirely lose touch with the soul in Charles' veins. The massive popularity of this album and a follow-up second volume pulled country music further away from its hayseed trappings and into the mainstream of American popular culture.

The man who took the countrypolitan sound to its outer limits, however, was Billy Sherrill. A songwriter and onetime R&B bandleader, Sherrill came to Nashville in the early '60s and first made his name producing David Houston (including his big hit "Almost Persuaded"). Over the next couple of decades he went on to work with **Tammy Wynette**, George Jones, Johnny Paycheck, Tanya Tucker, and Charlie Rich, among others. Sherrill's highly orchestrated and frequently overdubbed arrangements almost made Jim Reeves sound quaint, yet at its best (Jones' "We Can Make It," Rich's "Behind Closed Doors") this sweeping, multilayered soundwash fit his artists, and the era, beautifully.

Female singers, too, were no longer a rarity. Kitty Wells had broken the ice a decade previously, but it was the boisterous Patsy Cline who truly changed the climate, winning a massive fan base and opening doors for up-and-coming singers in the process. Cline was killed in a plane crash in 1963, but in her wake came country legends Loretta Lynn, Tammy Wynette, and Dolly Parton—who were in turn just the cream of a diverse crop of female artists that included Jan Howard, Dottie West, Norma Jean, Connie Smith, Jeannie Seely, Liz Anderson, Bobbie Gentry, and **Jeannie C. Riley**.

Though singers like Lynn and Parton began with a (mostly) traditional country sound, they were also stellar songwriters who weren't shy about speaking their minds. Lynn songs like "The Pill" and "Don't Come Home A-Drinkin' (With Lovin' On Your Mind)" challenged country music's notoriously conservative status quo, as did Parton's "Dumb Blonde," and Gentry's "Fancy." The sassiest splash came from Jeannie C. Riley with her "Harper Valley P.T.A." (written by Tom T. Hall), not to mention the mini skirts she often wore—that is, until she became 'born again'.

As the modern world and all its cultural, social and political by-products—the Beatles, Bob Dylan, Vietnam, and Civil Rights, not to mention marijuana, amphetamines, and the sexual revolution—encroached further into country music territory, it was inevitable that these and other topics of thought and conversation would creep into the country vernacular. Before long hippies were even coming to Nashville to record and to play the *Opry*. A number of Nashville songwriters—among them Willie Nelson, Kris Kristofferson, and "Gentle On My Mind" songwriter John Hartford—found they had at least as much, if not more, in common with this younger generation than with the Nashville Sound's increasingly staid old guard. It's this creative restlessness, and a desire to regain personal artistic control of the recording process, that led to the so-called 'Outlaw' movement of the '70s.

Anthologies

⊙ **Columbia Country Classics, Vol 4: The Nashville Sound** (1990; Columbia). A substantial 26-song picture of Columbia's presence in Nashville during the 1960s and '70s. The range of artists is impressive, from Johnny Cash ("I Still Miss Someone") to Johnny Paycheck ("She's All I Got"); Stonewall Jackson ("A Wound Time Can't Erase") to Lynn Anderson ("I Never Promised You A Rose Garden"); David Houston ("Almost Persuaded") to George Jones ("The Grand Tour").

⊙ **From The Vaults: Decca Country** (1994; Decca). Sixty songs on 3 CDs that cover Decca's involvement in country music from the '30s through the end of the '60s (when the name was changed to MCA). The set is an impressive country and western history lesson. Tex Owens' "Cattle Call," Riley Puckett's "Short Life Of Trouble," and further classic songs by the likes of Bill Monroe, Red Foley, Kitty Wells, and Goldie Hill fill the first 2 discs. The third focuses on '60s-era artists such as Conway Twitty, Loretta Lynn, Warner Mack, Bill Phillips, the Wilburn Brothers, Jimmy Newman, and Patsy Cline.

⊙ **RCA Nashville Classics: The '60s** (1995; BMG). A German import CD that compiles 25 big-name RCA hits from the Nashville Sound heyday, including Floyd Cramer's "Last Date," Porter Wagoner's "The Carroll County Accident," Eddy Arnold's "Make The World Go Away," and Jim Ed Brown's "Pop A Top." For a bonus thrill there's even Sgt. Barry Sadler's "Ballad Of The Green Berets."

⊙ **Heroes Of Country Music, Vol 3: The Legends Of Nashville** (1996; Rhino). Mixes a good number of classic honky-tonk artists (Webb Pierce, Kitty Wells, Ray Price) with a few later pop-country stylists such as Patsy Cline, Marty Robbins, and Sonny James.

⊙ **Nashville 1928** (1999; Document). This ain't no Nashville Sound prototype. In fact, it's quite the opposite—field recordings made in Nashville in 1928 of early *Opry* performers and other regional hillbilly artists such as the Gully Jumpers, the Binkley Brothers, and the Dixie Clodhoppers. A curious glimpse into the local music 'scene' decades before the atmosphere became choked with rhinestones, stardust, and the ring of cash registers.

Nashville Sound: The Artists

Bill Anderson

"It [my college degree] bugged me in the beginning. When I first came to Nashville, I did everything but deny I'd ever been to college."

—Bill Anderson

Before his own recording career took off, "Whisperin' Bill" Anderson's stellar reputation as a songwriter was already fairly well established. His work has been covered by Ray Price ("City Lights"), Eddy Arnold ("The Tip Of My Fingers"), and Connie Smith ("Once A Day"), among many others; decades later Steve Wariner, Alabama, and Vince Gill were still covering his material. Though Anderson's gentle, whisperlight vocal style—often a mix of singing and recitation—is pretty enough, his sound is fairly safe and suburban. He did rack up numerous hit singles himself, but his greatest and most enduring talent is still as a songwriter. Much of his work tends toward the cute and/or sentimental ("Mama Sang A Song," "I Love You Drops"), yet there are some definite gems: "Bright Lights And Country Music" shows he's got honky tonk in his bones; "My Life (Throw It Away If I Want To)," cut in 1969, has a sassy anti-establishment attitude; and the desperately bleak "Three A.M." tells of a man on the verge of suicide ("in the news they'll say he couldn't even swim ...").

James William Anderson III was born on 1 November, 1937 in Columbia, South Carolina and raised near Atlanta, Georgia. He began writing songs while still in high school, and he wrote the classic "City Lights"—a big hit for Ray Price in 1958—when he was only nineteen. Anderson earned a degree in journalism from the University of Georgia and eventually landed a job with the *Atlanta Constitution*. At the same time he signed with Decca Records and began recording in Nashville with legendary producer Owen Bradley. As a singer he made his first splash with "Po' Folks," which led to an appearance on the *Grand Ole Opry*, and he's been a steady presence on the show ever since. "Still," "Mama Sang A Song," and the faster-tempoed "I Got The Fever" were further hits during the '60s.

Anderson's association with Bradley lasted until 1973, at which point he worked with producer Buddy Killen for a few more years. Some of his '70s songs not only flirted dangerously with disco beats, but attempted to give this suburban white boy a Mr Lovemaker persona. "Baby, when I want something I want it now," he growled on "I Can't Wait Any Longer." Calling it a poor man's version of Barry White's "Can't Get Enough Of Your Love, Babe" is being charitable. Still, you have to at least admire the man for trying something different.

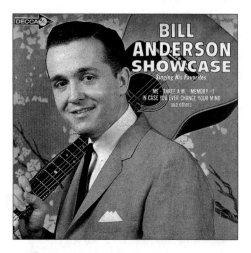

In addition to his solo recordings, Anderson also cut duets with Jan Howard, Mary Lou Turner, and even, in 1980, with David Allan Coe. Along with many singers of his generation he was active in the Association of Country Entertainers (ACE) during the '70s, a group motivated by the conviction that country music was losing sight of its heritage (see box p.436). Anderson's longtime label, MCA (formerly Decca), lost sight of its heritage, too, when it dropped him in the early '80s. He worked as a TV producer and even as a game show host, but it wasn't long before his songwriting talents were rediscovered by the next generation of Nashville stars—Gill, Wariner, Doug Supernaw, Ricky Skaggs, and Tracy Byrd are just a few of the artists who've covered his work. Nowadays, Anderson is still active on the *Opry* and also hosts the weekly show *Backstage At The Opry* for TNN (The Nashville Network). In 1998, Warner Brothers released his first album in eight years, FINE WINE—though it hardly compares to his best early material.

⊙ **Greatest Hits** (1996; Varese Sarabande). Eighteen original recordings, most of them highlights from his

Bill Anderson

1960s heyday such as "Po' Folks," "Still," "Three A.M.," "My Life," and "I Got The Fever" (the four '70s songs pale in comparison). A well-compiled overview of Anderson's prolific career.

Eddy Arnold

With over fifty years as a performer behind him, Eddy Arnold has proven himself one of the most popular and successful singers in all of country music. His long string of commercial smashes and crossover hit singles began in the 1940s, and four decades later he was still making the *Billboard* charts. Along the way he earned a respectable place in the Country Music Hall of Fame and racked up phenomenal record sales (in excess of eighty million, and counting).

Like Gene Autry and Red Foley, and pop stylists such as Bing Crosby, Tony Bennett, and Dean Martin, Arnold had a smooth, soft-edged voice innately suited to attractive pop melodies. In his heyday in the '50s and '60s, Arnold proved himself the ultimate Nashville Sound crooner—an artist who almost single-handedly defined the term countrypolitan. His musical approach was civil and gentlemanly—formal at times, but rarely stiff or stuffy. This was true whether he was singing about mother ("I Wish I Had A Girl Like You, Mother") romance ("That's How Much I Love You") lost love ("Bouquet Of Roses," "Make The World Go Away") or lonesome cowboys ("Cattle Call"). Early on Arnold had an almost folksy approach—on his records he was regularly billed as Eddy Arnold, the Tennessee Plowboy And His Guitar. Though he was hugely popular right from the start, stylistically he truly thrived in the age of the Nashville Sound, when his smooth voice was given state-of-the-art studio treatment and backed with various degrees of orchestration. Yet even as he took on a more sophisticated image during this second half of his career—trading in his cowboy hat and garbardine shirts for a tuxedo—the gentle, warm spirit of this onetime Tennessee farm boy remained a defining element of his personality.

Eddy was born Richard Edward Arnold on 15 May, 1918 to a farming family who lived near Henderson, Tennessee. As a child he sang in school, as well as at church and at home. His father died when he was young, and when the family farm was repossessed during the Depression, he brought in a few extra bucks here and there with his vocal talent. He also worked for an undertaker. After playing in bars and on radio, Arnold got his big break when he was hired as a vocalist in *Opry* star Pee Wee King's Golden West Cowboys. Having gained valuable experience and a growing fan base with the group, he stepped out on his own in 1943. WSM manager Harry Stone helped Arnold win a recording contract with RCA Victor—one he maintained, with only one brief break, for more than fifty years. One of his very first recordings, cut in December of 1944, was Tex Owens' "Cattle Call". The song became one of his signatures, and he re-recorded it more than once.

Arnold's popularity rose quickly thanks to songs like "It's A Sin," "I'll Hold You In My Heart (Till I Can Hold You In My Arms)," "Anytime," "Don't Rob Another Man's Castle," and "Bouquet Of Roses," all of which he first cut in the late '40s. He recorded a large amount of material during this time, but unfortunately it's not easy to track down. Because he re-recorded so many of his early hits as bigger, lusher production styles came into fashion, the original singles have rarely made it onto his many subsequent LP collections. But these early recordings are well worth hearing, with their simple, spare arrangements, and Arnold's gentle personality which was always right up front.

Eddy Arnold

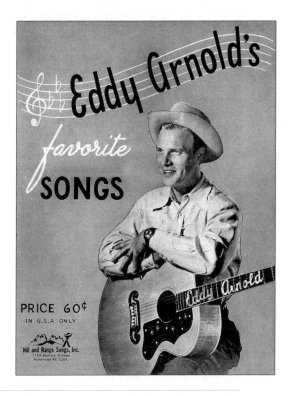

From the mid-'40s onwards, Arnold was a fixture in the country Top 10, and many of his songs crossed over into the pop charts as well. His manager for a time was Tom Parker, who'd later go on to lord over Elvis Presley's career. Arnold left the *Opry* in 1948, but he had plenty more media exposure through radio shows like the *Hometown Reunion*, films such as *Feudin' Rhythm* and *Hoedown*, and later his own television programs (*Eddy Arnold Time* and *The Eddy Arnold Show*). In 1953 he even played Las Vegas.

By the end of the '50s he had transformed himself from folky persona to sophisticated uptown stylist, the king of a countrypolitan lineage that grew to include Jim Reeves, Patsy Cline, Ray Price, and countless others. By the '60s Arnold was singing lushly orchestrated pop songs such as "What's He Doing In My World," "Make The World Go Away," and "Then You Can Tell Me Goodbye". He was pop-country personified, though on these and his many other recordings, his mellow-brewed voice (which had grown richer, deeper and more full-bodied) still retained its melancholy appeal.

In 1966 Arnold was elected to the Country Music Hall of Fame, and a year later he won the Country Music Association's Entertainer of the Year award—it was the first year the award was given, yet still it's an incredible feat for an artist who'd had his first hits two decades earlier. Arnold briefly jumped ship to record with MGM from 1973–75, but was soon back on RCA where he remained for another twenty years. He toured regularly through the '70s and into the '80s. By the '90s his voice sounded older and had more than a few quivers around its edges, but his mellow-gold tone was still largely intact.

⊙ **Cattle Call** (1963; RCA; reissued 1993; Bear Family). The title track, which he first recorded in the mid-1940s, has always been one of Arnold's signatures. The re-recorded version here features standard Nashville Sound treatment—as do the twelve other western-themed songs ("Cool Water," "Leanin' On The Old Top Rail," "The Wayward Wind," etc.). Yet the whole package is so smooth in sound and flows so beautifully it's hard not to fall under its spell. Bear Family has reissued the album on CD paired with his 1959 album THEREBY HANGS A TALE.

◉ **Standing Alone** (1970; RCA). Produced by West Coast pop-country innovator Lee Hazlewood (the man behind both Duane Eddy and Nancy Sinatra, not to mention his own line of warped solo material), this album strays into darker and more edgy territory than a

typical Arnold outing. The melancholy he brings to Steve Young's "Seven Bridges Road" is sweeping and dramatic, the individualism of Sonny Curtis' "My Way Of Life" is borderline brash, and the near-violent passion that Arnold exhibits in John Stewart's "July, You're A Woman" will knock you flat out.

⊙ **The Essential Eddy Arnold** (1996; RCA). A single-CD overview of Arnold's career, from his 1946 recording of "It's A Sin" all the way to 1990's "You Don't Miss A Thing". The first 4 songs are pre-1952—a rare treat for anyone who's tried to find his early hits on a CD collection—while the rest are from his countrypolitan glory days. All told, though, it's a respectable round-up.

⊙ **Strictly From The Hills** (1996; Bronco Buster). A great collection (one of two, in fact) that gathers 20 Brown radio transcriptions Arnold cut in 1950 with the Willis Brothers (then known as the Oklahoma Wranglers) and his frequent steel guitarist Little Roy Wiggins. The structure is loose, the overall feeling free-spirited, and the song roster includes catchy covers like Ted Daffan's "Worried Mind" and Jimmie Rodgers' "Never No Mo' Blues".

⊙ **The Tennessee Plowboy And His Guitar** (1998; Bear Family). If you're looking for Arnold's early singles in one package, this bulky 5-CD set is the place to find them, as all the songs here, hits and otherwise, were cut between 1944–50.

Chet Atkins

> "The Nashville Sound? That's just a sales tag."
>
> —Chet Atkins

If there was one single person most responsible for pushing country music in a more adult-contemporary direction during the 1950s and '60s, it was session guitarist, recording artist, producer, and RCA executive Chet Atkins. Along with Owen Bradley over at rival label Decca, Atkins bent country music away from its honky-tonk and hillbilly roots and into new suburban territory that was as influenced by contemporary pop as blues or old-time folk. Country had taken inspiration from pop music ever since the '20s, but with rockabilly having taken a huge bite out of the market Atkins felt (and rightly so) that for country to survive the battle it had to reconfigure itself as a more adult music. Thus the Nashville Sound was born.

Atkins was most influential as a producer, but he was also a successful recording artist himself and one of country's most outstanding guitarists. He has recorded thousands of songs and well over one hundred albums from the late '40s onwards, and much of the material is far more versatile than the polished, uptown sound with which his name is so closely associated. His influence as an instrumentalist has also extended beyond country to artists such as George Harrison and Mark Knopfler.

Charles Burton Atkins was born on 20 June, 1924 in Luttrell, Tennessee. He began playing guitar and fiddle as a child, and as a teenager he became enamored with the thumb-and-finger-picking style of guitarist Merle Travis. Venturing into the world of professional music, Atkins began playing fiddle with Bill Carlisle and Archie Campbell and later played guitar with Johnnie And Jack and then Red Foley. In 1946 he cut his first single for the indie label Bullet, and a year later he signed to RCA. After roaming from station to station and state to state, he finally moved to Nashville for good in 1950, where he played the *Opry* regularly as an accompanist with Maybelle Carter and the Carter Sisters. He also began doing session work, and was quickly assimilated into the growing roster of A-team studio musicians in Nashville.

Atkins had worked since his RCA beginnings with producer Steve Sholes, who began allowing the young guitarist to take on more responsibilities, including producing some sessions. In 1955, when RCA opened its own Nashville recording studio, Atkins was put in charge. It was about this time that rock'n'roll began to infiltrate the country market and steal away listeners, and so Atkins began polishing and softening the edges off the various acts he was recording. Thus, artists like Don Gibson and Jim Reeves turned from honky tonkers into crooners—and sold far more records than they'd ever done before. They were among a long list of artists that Atkins went on to sign, nurture, and produce over the next few decades.

As for his own recordings, Atkins had his first chart hit in 1955 with "Mr Sandman," but over

Frank Driggs/Archive Photos

Smoothing out the edges, producer Chet Atkins

the years very few of his songs made it into the *Billboard* Top 40. That's not to say he wasn't prolific—and popular. He cut song after song, album after album, on a regular basis through the '50s and '60s, and his recording career has continued up to the present day. Atkins' mostly instrumental albums freely mix jazz, blues, classical, pop, and country styles, with his fluid, easygoing, and deceptively simple picking style placed right in the forefront. In addition to his solo work, he has also cut full-fledged duet albums with such stellar pickers as Jerry Reed, Hank Snow, Doc Watson, and Merle Travis. Over the years he's won numerous CMA, ACM, and Grammy awards, and in 1973 he was elected to the Country Music Hall of Fame. Two decades later he was honored with a Lifetime Achievement Award from the National Academy of Recording Arts and Sciences. In the early '80s he left RCA for Columbia and surprised a few country stalwarts by recording a jazz album (STAY TUNED) with George Benson, Earl Klugh, and Mark Knopfler, and followed it up with further

Chet Atkins

jazz guitar albums. Atkins may not be as prolific a recording artist as he once was, but he's still a major presence in Nashville.

⊙ **Reflections (With Doc Watson)** (1980; RCA; reissued 1999; Sugar Hill). Chet Atkins and Doc Watson share easygoing styles and personalities that fit well together. A wholly enjoyable collaboration.

⊙ **The Essential Chet Atkins** (1996; RCA). This concise 20-song overview is a great place to begin exploring Atkins' long recording history with RCA. It includes a wide range of instrumentals, from hit country titles such as "Mr Sandman" and "Yakety Axe" to various pop covers ("Yesterday," "Snowbird," "The Entertainer").

The Browns

The Browns were a close-harmony brother and two sisters trio (Jim Ed, Maxine, and Bonnie Brown) who were stars of the early Nashville Sound era under the guidance of RCA producer Chet Atkins. The trio had several hits during the 1950s and '60s, and a steady fan base that kept their name alive well after they parted ways in 1967, but they're best remembered in history books and on compilation albums for their sole #1 hit, "The Three Bells," which topped the charts for ten weeks in 1959.

The three Brown siblings were born in the '30s and grew up together in Arkansas. While a teenager, Jim Ed won a spot on a radio show in Little Rock, and soon his sister Maxine was singing alongside him. By 1954 they were singing on the *Louisiana Hayride*, and that same year they cut their first single, "Looking Back To See," a lively ditty about the joys of flirtation written by the two siblings. The song was released on the Fabor label (run by Fabor Robinson, who also owned Abbott, home at the time to Jim Reeves and Johnny Horton), and it climbed to the Top 10 of *Billboard*'s country charts. A year later, Bonnie came on board, and as a trio their song "Here Today And Gone Tomorrow" was another hit. They next signed with RCA, and it's here that their career truly blossomed thanks to the lush uptown sound that producer Atkins gave them. Their most popular titles included "I Take The Chance," "I Heard The Bluebirds Sing," and especially "The Three Bells."

The Browns remained popular for the next decade, joining the *Grand Ole Opry* in 1963, scoring several more chart hits, and recording fairly prolifically. By the beginning of the '60s, Jim Ed was getting top billing on their records; unlike the back-and-forth duets of their Fabor years, the arrangements now featured Jim Ed's sweet baritone out in front while the harmony voices of sisters Bonnie and Maxine stayed mostly in the background. After the trio disbanded in 1967, Jim Ed continued as a solo artist. His recordings were many and ran from the nostalgic "How I Love Them Old Songs" and the sly "Broad Minded Man" to drinking songs such as "The Bottle Hasn't Been Made," the mournful "Bottle, Bottle," and the brilliant "Pop A Top," which even kicks off with the enticing sound of a beer can being "popped" open.

◉ **Looking Back To See** (1986; Bear Family). These 16 Fabor recordings are simpler and quirkier than the Browns' more famous RCA work. Romance is at the heart of most of the songs—some cute ("Looking Back To See"), others a little disturbing ("honey ... don't think" Jim Ed warns his lady in the Louvin Brothers composition "You Thought I Thought"). The oddest of all is the moonshiner song "Set The Dawgs On 'Em," one of several here that were previously unreleased. Pianist Floyd Cramer, guitarist Jimmy Bryant, and pedal-steel maestro Speedy West are among the studio musicians backing up Jim Ed and Maxine on these 1954 and 1955 sessions.

⊙ **The Essential Jim Ed Brown And The Browns** (1996; RCA). This 20-song overview of the Browns' long career begins with '50s-era hits like "Looking Back To See" and "The Three Bells" (but no "Bluebirds," which seems an odd omission) before moving into Jim Ed's solo material, including "Broad Minded Man," "Bottle, Bottle," "Southern Loving," and "Pop A Top"—the last song alone being almost worth the price of the entire collection.

Johnny Cash

"I never did an album that I wasn't proud of."

—Johnny Cash

The Man in Black, Johnny Cash, is an American legend and an international celebrity, an artist who needs little introduction but who deserves one anyway. He's a musical cross-breeder who, since his beginnings as a post-Elvis Sun Records

Uniting all generations—the legendary Johnny Cash

are some of the most classic country songs this side of World War II—many of which are as well-known, and as influential, as anything that came from the pen of Hank Williams. Hank is still, and probably always will be, the centerpoint of late-twentieth-century country music history, but Johnny Cash has certainly crossed greater musical boundaries, attracted a more diverse range of fans, and earned a wider international acclaim. Quite simply, Cash is one of the most important and influential figures in American popular music.

John R. Cash was born on 26 February, 1932 in Kingsland, Arkansas. He grew up on a 20-acre farm in the northeastern part of the state—a farm colony named Dyess that was set up by the Roosevelt administration during the Depression. He worked on the farm, absorbing all manner of country, blues and gospel music. His mother was a strict devotee of the Pentecostal faith, but she also encouraged her son's musical interests. Having graduated high school, Cash promptly left town, briefly working at an auto plant in Michigan before joining the air force. He was stationed in Germany, where he played music with fellow soldiers, and upon returning home he married Vivian Liberto, moved to Memphis, and began selling appliances. His brother Ray introduced him to a couple of mechanic friends who were also musicians—Luther Perkins and Marshall Grant. They became the Tennessee Two, playing lead guitar and bass respectively.

In 1954, the same year that Elvis Presley broke, Cash landed his first audition at the Memphis label Sun. It was Sun owner Sam Phillips who began calling Cash "Johnny." In early 1955 he was back in the studio with the Tennessee Two, and one of the songs they cut was "Hey Porter." Johnny Cash's first bona fide country hit

star in the mid-1950s, has earned respect from country, folk, gospel and rock'n'roll fans alike. He's a friend of Bob Dylan as well as Billy Graham; he's played in front of convicted criminals as well as a soon-to-be-pardoned President Nixon; and he's an inductee in both the country and rock and roll halls of fame. He has long used the Bible as his roadmap, which has certainly pleased his older fans, but at the same time he's always looked, and sounded, so incredibly cool that younger generations couldn't help but flock at his feet.

Cash's life story is studded with an impressive number of achievements, including his performances at San Quentin and Folsom prisons during the '60s; his popular TV show; his support of up-and-coming artists like Kris Kristofferson and the Statler Brothers; and his numerous gold records and awards. But at the foundation of Cash's career

Johnny Cash

arrived later that year when "Cry Cry Cry" charted in the *Billboard* Top 20. We all know Cash didn't really shoot a man in Reno "just to watch him die," but he did watch the movie *Inside The Walls Of Folsom Prison*, which was supposedly the inspiration for one of his most memorable songs, "Folsom Prison Blues." That song hit #4 in 1956, followed by Cash's first chart-topper, "I Walk The Line." These and other mid-'50s Sun recordings such as "Get Rhythm," "There You Go," and "Big River" made Cash one of the label's most successful artists. Many of the songs were his own compositions, but he also recorded others written by Jack Clement ("Ballad Of A Teenage Queen"), Charlie Rich ("The Ways Of A Woman In Love"), and Jimmie Skinner ("Doin' My Time"). In 1958 Cash signed with Columbia (and moved for a while to California), and out came further classics like "I Still Miss Someone," "Don't Take Your Guns To Town," "Tennessee Flat-Top Box," and especially "Ring Of Fire." The Columbia sessions were produced by Don Law instead of Phillips and/or Clement (who was an engineer at Sun as well as a songwriter). Law broadened the stripped-down Cash sound, which had remained fairly consistent at Sun, bringing piano, steel guitar, drums, and even background vocals into the mix.

The Columbia recordings evolved from hot singles into a series of concept albums that explored various aspects of the American experience. These included Songs Of Our Soil, Blood, Sweat And Tears, Mean As Hell, From Sea To Shining Sea and Bitter Tears. The last of these albums was the crowning achievement of the series, focusing on the Native American experience through songs written largely by Peter LaFarge. The best-known of these is "The Ballad Of Ira Hayes," which follows the tragic downfall of Native American and decorated World War II veteran Hayes, one of the soldiers to raise the famous flag during the Battle of Iwo Jima. The song was at first treated with trepidation by many DJs, who figured its content to be controversial, but Cash stood strong in support of both LaFarge's song and Hayes' memory. This in turn helped cement his growing reputation among the younger set—rock and folk music fans who were already attracted to Cash's music for its no-frills, down-to-earth style. In 1964, the same year that "Hayes" was released, Cash played the Newport Folk Festival.

Cash spent much of the '60s in a haze of pills and booze, but he eventually pulled himself out of the worst of it with the help of his soon-to-be-wife, June Carter (and more than a little boost from deep-welled Christian beliefs). June's mother, Maybelle, was one of the original Carter Family trio, and she and her two sisters had been touring as Mother Maybelle and the Carter Sisters since the '40s. Cash had already championed the Carter Family name for years, and he ultimately brought them into his touring show. As his first marriage crumbled and finally ended, his love for June grew. The two married in 1968 and have been living and touring together ever since. Their kooky and good-natured duet on "Jackson" was a hit for them in 1967 (though the definitive version belongs to Nancy Sinatra and Lee Hazlewood), as was "If I Were A Carpenter" in 1970.

One of the defining moments in Johnny Cash's career was the concert he gave at California's Folsom Prison in 1968. It was a truly rousing show, and the resulting live album hugely boosted his career. A year later he set up another show at San Quentin, and this one spawned the biggest hit of Cash's career, a live version of the Shel Silverstein song "A Boy Named Sue," complete with bleeped swearwords. Later that year he swept the Country Music Association awards: Cash was named Male Vocalist and Entertainer of the Year; "A Boy Named Sue" the Single of the Year; and Johnny Cash At San Quentin Prison the Album of the Year. Both Cash and "Sue" also won a Grammy each.

Then came the world of television. *The Johnny Cash Show* defined Cash's career between 1969 and 1971, but it also proved a great vehicle for Cash to introduce new blood into Nashville— artists who appeared on the show included Bob Dylan, Mahalia Jackson, Gordon Lightfoot, and even the Who. Dylan had been in and out of Nashville over the last few years cutting his albums Blonde On Blonde, John Wesley Harding and Nashville Skyline, and the last of the three featured Cash's vocals on the duet "Girl From The North Country." The two also cut a very informal session's worth of country standards; these have surfaced on bootleg albums and are great fun. Cash also boosted the career of newcomer Kris Kristofferson when he turned the budding star's composition "Sunday Morning Coming Down" into one of the biggest country singles of 1970.

Cash continued to record for Columbia through the '70s and into the '80s, and albums like Man In Black, The Junkie And The Juicehead, John R. Cash and Johnny 99 contain some solid new Cash songs as well as intriguing material by such writers as Billy Joe Shaver, Randy Newman, Bruce Springsteen, and Chip Taylor. At the same time, he clung fast to his religious principles and even played for President Nixon at the White House. Cash saw his autobiography, *Man In Black*, published in 1975, and in 1980 he was elected to the Country Music Hall of Fame (twelve years later he also made the Rock and Roll Hall of Fame). He joined his old Sun buddies Carl Perkins and Jerry Lee Lewis for the album THE SURVIVORS in 1982, and three years later he teamed with Kristofferson, Waylon Jennings, and Willie Nelson to record an album under the group name the Highwaymen. Two further Highwaymen albums surfaced over the following decade.

After twenty-eight solid years with Columbia, Cash parted ways with the label in 1986. He signed with Mercury, and stayed put into the early '90s, but his chart magic had disappeared by this stage. He continued to tour steadily, however, with a family group that included June, her sisters Helen and Anita, and son John Carter Cash. Then came yet another career turnaround when Cash signed with the American label and recorded the sparse, acoustic album AMERICAN RECORDINGS. A solo album featuring just himself and his guitar, it showcased some of the best songs he'd written in years. It wasn't exactly embraced by Nashville, but it did invite new attention and respect from rock'n'roll circles. A new generation of fans flocked to his shows and began digging though his older recordings. A follow-up album, UNCHAINED, featured innovative material by hip songwriters like Beck and Chris Cornell, as well as Tom Petty and the Heartbreakers as his backing band. The album won a Grammy in 1998. Cash the elder statesman was in the midst of enjoying his latest comeback when he fell ill with the obscure Shy-Drager syndrome, a disease of the nervous system that has (so far) halted his ability to perform. He has made brief and very limited public appearances, however, including stepping on stage during a 1999 all-star tribute show in New York that was later a television special. He also sang on June Carter Cash's 1999 solo album PRESS ON.

⊙ **Bitter Tears** (1964; Columbia; reissued 1994; Sony). The cover featuring Cash in a headband and mascara may seem campy at first sight, but the music inside is sincere and in no way dated. "The Ballad Of Ira Hayes" is now a classic, and it's clearly the centerpoint. Several further songs by Peter LaFarge, as well as a couple of Cash songs and a Johnny Horton composition ("A Vanishing Race"), make this concept

album (subtitled "Ballads Of The American Indian") a moving, spirited collection.

⊙ **At Folsom Prison** (1968; Columbia; reissued 1999; Columbia/Legacy). This is the album that brought Cash international stardom and set his career—which had been nearly derailed by substance abuse—right back on the fast track. The Man in Black is in ripe form, his voice as burly and full of growl as ever, and the crowd of 2000 inmates is chomping at the bit. The most recent CD reissue includes three previously unreleased cuts, presenting the concert in its entire, uncensored form.

◉ **Man In Black** (1971; Columbia). The song that gave Cash his nickname first appeared on this album, and in it he explains that his chosen color is more than just a fashion statement. "I'd love to wear a rainbow every day," he declares, but until the "poor" and the "beaten down" are better cared for, he'll stick to black to remind him of life's less-fortunate souls. Other songs have a spiritual and somewhat didactic bent to them, but at the same time they're fascinating, especially "The Preacher Said, 'Jesus Said,'" featuring the voice of Billy Graham.

⊙ **The Man In Black (1954–1958)** (1990; Bear Family). This 5-disc box set is the first in a 4-part (so far) series of Cash compilations released by Bear Family. Here his Sun years and very first Columbia recordings are presented in the deeper context they deserve, with assorted outtakes and demos riding alongside the familiar singles and album tracks. The only way to go for the serious Cash collector.

⊙ **The Sun Years** (1990; Rhino). A quick-fix way to explore Cash's musical foundation. The 18 tracks here (all original 1950s recordings) are stylistically the grittiest of his career, highlighted by spare shuffle rhythms and Cash's mighty voice. Titles like "Folsom Prison Blues," "I Walk The Line," "Guess Things Happen That Way," "Big River," and "Rock Island Line" are also among his most well-known.

⊙ **The Essential Johnny Cash (1955–1983)** (1992; Columbia/Legacy). This is the best overview of all the Cash offerings to date. It's a 3-disc set that runs from his Sun years through the whole of his Columbia career, covering all the highlights you'd expect and touching on a few you might not. You really can't go wrong.

⊙ **American Recordings** (1994; American Recordings). Cash's 1990s comeback album, produced by Rick Rubin, is as sparse as anything he's done since his Sun days. "Drive On" is one of the finest compositions he'd written in years, but he also makes beautiful work out of Nick Lowe's "The Beast In Me," Loudon Wainwright III's "The Man Who Couldn't Cry," and Kristofferson's "Why Me."

⊙ **Unchained** (1996; American Recordings). In his mid-sixties, and 41 years after his Sun debut, Cash was still creating some amazingly strong music. This time he is backed by Tom Petty and the Heartbreakers, and together they create amazing music with such untraditional material as Beck's "Rowboat," Chris Cornell's "Rusty Cage," and Josh Haden's "Spiritual." The title track, by Jude Johnstone, is of one Cash's most moving achievements on record.

Country Music Association

A trade organization consisting of promoters, radio professionals, record executives, song publishers, managers, and, yes, the artists themselves, the CMA's purpose was, and still is, to do just about all it can to get the music, and the industry surrounding it, as much notice as possible in the big wide world.

Unlike those of the *Grand Ole Opry*, the CMA's beginnings were not exactly humble or quaint. The group was founded by business professionals who, threatened by the onslaught of rock'n'roll, were acting out of a very real fear that their slice of the music-market pie was fast disappearing. The CMA was formed during the 1958 convention of the annual Country Music Disc Jockeys Association. Its two chief founders were Washington, DC promoter and broadcast executive Connie B. Gay (the CMA's first president) and music publisher Wesley Rose (of Acuff-Rose), who became the CMA's first chairman of the board. Radio executive Harry Stone (an early *Opry* innovator) was also on board that first year, but the person who wound up guiding the CMA through most of its significant developments was Jo Walker-Meador. She was initially hired as an office manager and later assumed duties as executive director, staying with the organization through to 1991.

The CMA was not about promoting traditional country music, or any other specific aspect of the genre. It was not an historical society, it was a business organization—a publicity machine—and its intentions were to show that country music was valuable commercial property. The CMA argued that country music reached millions of listeners, which meant it was a useful tool for advertisers; this in turn translated into greater revenue for the country music industry as a whole. In this regard, one of the CMA's initial tasks was increasing the number of fulltime country music radio stations. The group's success in this regard is reflected in the figures: from 81 all-country stations in the US in 1961 to more than 700 stations a dozen years later. As of 1996, the number had surpassed 2300.

What makes the CMA most visible to the general public is its annual awards ceremony. The concept was first initiated in 1967 (which, by the way, was two years after West Coast rival organization the Academy of Country Music instigated its own ceremony out in LA,

see box p.173). The CMA awards made it onto television a year later, and the show has since grown from less than an hour to more than three. Winning accolades from the CMA—especially the coveted Entertainer of the Year award—is one of the highest honors for a commercially oriented country artist. The CMA is also responsible for the annual Fan Fair, which has become a massive meet-and-greet session held each spring in Nashville (see p.516).

Benefits of being named Entertainer of the Year can certainly be read in increased record sales, but the single highest honor for country music professionals is induction into the Country Music Hall of Fame. This was another CMA idea, born in 1961—an aspect of the organization that kept it tied to the music's history and, in traditionalists' eyes, partially redeemed its commercial focus. Hall of Fame inductees include songwriters and executives as well as performers. The first three were Jimmie Rodgers, Hank Williams, and Fred Rose; a year later came Roy Acuff, the first living member. The number of inductees varies each year; more recent names include Merle Haggard (1994), Harlan Howard (1997) and Dolly Parton (1999). The bronze plaques honoring the Hall of Famers were displayed in the Tennessee State Museum until 1967, when the Country Music Hall of Fame and Museum was opened near Nashville's Music Row. It's a top tourist attraction in the city, housing Nudie suits, cars, guitars, and loads more memorabilia from stars past and present. Highly recommended.

The Hall of Fame and Museum is now operated by the Country Music Foundation (CMF), which was created in 1964 as a research and education branch of the CMA. Operating seperately from the CMA, the CMF truly *is* an historical organization, preserving the music and its traditions through its vast library of records, photographs, books, documents, and periodicals; its oral history and school educational programs; its record label and publication department; and the highly regarded *Journal of Country Music*. In 2000, the Country Music Hall of Fame and Museum was scheduled to move to a brand-new and much larger facility in downtown Nashville.

Roy Clark

For twenty-five years Roy Clark was the host of *Hee Haw*, and it's for this role—picking and grinning through skits and songs while sporting overalls, a stalk of alfalfa between his teeth, and fat sideburns—that he'll always be best remembered. But behind his success as a TV presenter, Clark is actually a hot guitar and banjo picker, a talented comic, a hit recording artist ("Tips Of My Fingers," "I Never Picked Cotton," "Thank God And Greyhound"), and a popular showman who played Vegas in the early 1960s and was among the first country artists to set up shop in Branson, Missouri. Both the CMA and the ACM (twice) have honored him as Entertainer of the Year.

Roy Linwood Clark was born on 15 April, 1933 in Meherrin, Virginia to a very musical family. As a teenager he toured with Grandpa Jones and began performing on television in the Washington, DC area. During the '50s he worked with rising TV (and recording) star Jimmy Dean, and Dean's manager Connie B. Gay helped get him further exposure, including appearances with George Hamilton IV. In 1960 Clark was hired to play guitar with Wanda Jackson—including a stint at the Golden Nugget in Las Vegas, as well as backing her up on "Let's Have A Party" and other classic recordings. Through Jackson's manager Clark managed to secure his own contract with Capitol (Jackson's label). His first album, THE LIGHTNING FINGERS OF ROY CLARK, clearly showcased his picking skills. In 1963 his recording of Bill Anderson's "The Tips Of My Fingers" made the country Top 10—a song that came complete with swelling strings and a soaring background chorus demonstrating that Clark could also handle pop ballads with the right amount of countrypolitan panache.

In 1967 he shifted from Capitol to Dot Records and soon had his second Top 10 hit with Charles Aznavour's "Yesterday When I Was Young." He had previously made occasional appearances on *The Beverly Hillbillies*, and in 1969 his TV career took off in earnest when he was tapped as co-host (with Buck Owens) of the new variety show *Hee Haw*. Although television now became his main occupation, he also continued his concert appearances as well as his recording. Further songs charted, including the sappy Felice and Boudleaux Bryant composition "Come Live With Me," Dorsey Burnette's "Magnificent Sanctuary Band," and the oddball "Lawrence Welk-Hee Haw Counter-Revolution Polka." He switched labels again to MCA in the late '70s, but by the early '80s his hit-making career had pretty much run its course. In 1983 he made the move to Branson, opening the Roy Clark Celebrity Theater, the first country music venue by a big-name entertainer to be built in that small Missouri town. He also joined the *Grand Ole Opry* in 1987.

⊙ **Greatest Hits** (1995; Varese Sarabande). Clark's picking takes (mostly) a back seat in favour of heavy string arrangements, and titles like "Tips Of My Fingers", "Come Live With Me," and "Yesterday When I Was Young" are predictable. But listen again: "I Never Picked Cotton" is a surprisingly frank nugget of brittle and vivid small-town anger, "Thank God And Greyhound" has a kooky turnaround twist that weirds it out, and "Right Or Left At Oak Street" is downright existential. Maybe this material isn't quite as pedestrian as it first appears.

Patsy Cline

> "You're not gonna run over Patsy. Not me or anybody else. She could handle things."
>
> —Charlie Dick

Though a honky tonker at heart and a rowdy, restless soul to boot, Patsy Cline possessed one of the most beautiful, powerful, and emotionally expressive voices in modern country music. The work she did with producer Owen Bradley is in many ways the epitome of all the good things about the Nashville Sound—the gently swaying melodies and smooth, silky arrangements that enhance the mood and allow the vocalist to shine.

The idea that women country singers could sell lots of records was proven during the early 1950s by Kitty Wells when she had her massive hit "It Wasn't God Who Made Honky Tonk Angels." The country music world as a whole, however, remained largely the domain of men, yet Cline wasn't about to let a little chauvinism stop the flow of her career. She swaggered her way past stereotypes and others forces of resistance, showing the men in charge—and the public in general—that women were more than capable of singing about such hard subjects as divorce and drinking as well as love and understanding. After years of struggle, Cline ultimately won a national reputation equal to (and in many eyes greater than) her male countrypolitan counterparts, Jim Reeves and Eddy Arnold. In the process, her aggressive, boisterous attitude opened doors for an entire generation of female singers, from Loretta Lynn to Dolly Parton and beyond. Sadly, Cline's career was cut short at its peak in 1963 when, returning from a benefit show in Kansas City, the plane she was riding in crashed, killing her along with fellow singers Cowboy Copas and Hawkshaw Hawkins and pilot Randy Hughes.

Cline was born Virginia Patterson Hensley on 8 September, 1932 in Gore, Virginia, a small town not far from Washington, DC. She grew up in nearby Winchester and early on developed an enduring fondness for the *Grand Ole Opry*. When she was sixteen she met *Opry* star Wally Fowler, who encouraged her singing and helped get her an audition on the show. Failing that audition, she continued to perform around Winchester, eventually landing a job singing with the local band Bill Peer and his Melody Boys. In addition to having a fling with young Virginia, Peer gave her the stage name Patsy. The new last name she picked up from Gerald Cline, whom she married in 1953 (four years later she divorced him and married Charlie Dick). In 1954 she was back in Nashville to appear on Ernest Tubb's *Midnight Jamboree* program (broadcast after the *Opry*), and she also cut her first recordings, including a version of Wells' "It Wasn't God Who Made Honky Tonk Angels."

Patsy Cline

Bill McCall, owner of Four Star Records (home to the Maddox Brothers and Rose and Webb Pierce, among others), got wind of Patsy's talent and decided to sign her in 1954. Paul Cohen, head of Decca's country division, began leasing these recordings from McCall, and he also arranged for Cline to record at the label's new Quonset Hut studio in Nashville, run by Owen Bradley. Cline worked with Bradley for the rest of her career, and the dynamic these two created is what ultimately led to the huge success of her later recordings. The

Four Star recordings yielded only one national hit, "Walking After Midnight." She stayed under contract with McCall through 1959 until Decca was able to sign her proper.

During her early career, Cline sang more straight-up honky tonk material full of steel guitar and fiddle. Titles like "A Church, A Courtyard, And Then Goodbye," "Honky Tonk Merry-Go-Round," and "Never No More" were sturdy enough, but they only hinted at the potential that lurked inside her. Bradley, however, sensed that potential early on, and so he began working to smooth out the arrangements and refine her voice into an instrument of torch-singing glory. Cline resisted at first but eventually succumbed, and the results—which didn't come quickly or easily—ultimately convinced her that this was the sort of music through which her talent shone best of all. By the early '60s this one-time cowgirl and denizen of countless honky-tonk stages had been transformed into a silky-voiced sophisticate playing the Hollywood Bowl.

Cline's first Decca release was 1961's "I Fall To Pieces," a song penned by Harlan Howard and Hank Cochran that Cline hated at first. Within months it had turned into a major pop-country crossover hit, her first since "Walking After Midnight." Cline was involved in a major car accident soon after its release, and her recovery time obviously cut into her touring and promotion schedule. Her follow-up song, however, "Crazy," written by Willie Nelson (and again Cline didn't like the song initially), brought her back with a bang and demonstrated she had staying power.

Cline's career and life came to a sad end on 5 March, 1963. The *Opry* put on a special tribute show to Cline, Copas, and Hawkins, and a couple of months later Decca released the double album THE PATSY CLINE STORY. The songs "Faded Love" and "Sweet Dreams," from her final sessions that February, became hits—in fact, like her countrypolitan compatriot Jim Reeves, who was killed in a plane crash a year later, Cline had songs on the charts for several years after her death. Even more amazing is the worldwide interest in her life story and the massive, enduring popularity of her music—she's remained one of the top-selling artists on MCA (formerly Decca) for decades. During the '80s "Always" made the charts, as did some electronically produced "duets" between Cline and Reeves. In 1985 the movie *Sweet Dreams,* starring Jessica Lange, brought her a vast new audience; the soundtrack, however, featured overdubbed versions of Cline's material—better to stick with the originals.

Further interest in Cline was generated when singer k.d. lang, in an overt attempt to re-create Cline's sound, recorded the album SHADOWLANDS with producer Owen Bradley. In 1973 Cline became the first individual female artist (the Carter Family had been honored as a group) inducted into the Country Music Hall of Fame. In recent years there's also been a controversial biography, *Patsy Cline: An Intimate Biography*; a couple of documentaries co-produced by Charlie Dick, *The Real Patsy Cline* and *Remembering Patsy*; and a successful stage musical, *Always … Patsy Cline* (originally starring up-and-coming country singer Mandy Barnett).

⊙ **The Patsy Cline Story** (1963; MCA). A single-disc, 24-track compilation that covers all the major bases—and packs in double the material of the more famous 12 GREATEST HITS package (which has sold a mighty four-million-plus copies since her death), making it a far better bargain and more substantial starting point.

⊙ **The Patsy Cline Collection** (1991; MCA). A 4-disc box set covering Patsy's entire recording career, from a couple of 1954 radio transcriptions, through to her 51 Four Star recordings (during which time she and producer Bradley experimented with pop, rockabilly and honky-tonk material), and finally basking in the magnificence of her classic Decca period. There are outtakes and live performances, too. Put together by the Country Music Foundation, this is a beautiful set that any serious Cline fan will fawn over.

⊙ **Live At The Cimarron Ballroom** (1997; MCA). Recorded in 1961 in Tulsa, Oklahoma, just after her car accident, this is an absolute gem of a document that gives us a much broader and more down-to-earth musical picture of Patsy Cline—one that stretches well beyond the studio beauty of her classic Nashville recordings. The repertoire runs from gutsy, playful numbers like "Stupid Cupid" and "Lovesick Blues" to her brand new (at the time) tearjerker "I Fall To Pieces," with lots of insightful stage gab in between. The recording quality isn't always perfect, but it wouldn't be as charming any other way.

⊙ **Walkin' After Midnight: The Very Best Of Patsy Cline** (1998; Collectibles). A 24-song collection of Cline's Four Star recordings cut during the late '50s. "Walkin' After Midnight" was the only hit of the bunch, but there are further interesting songs as well. Some ("Honky Tonk Merry-Go-Round") are hard-edged fiddle-and-steel country, while others ("Three Cigarettes In An Ashtray") foreshadowed her sophisticated sound that was soon to come.

Dick Curless

Like Dave Dudley, Maine native Dick Curless had a deep, rich voice and a catalog of hot truck-driving and highway-riding songs—"Big Wheel Cannonball," "Hard, Hard Traveling Man," and especially "A Tombstone Every Mile"—a 1965 country hit that was by far his best-known recording. But the road and its patrons were only part of this versatile singer's repertoire. His many albums for Tower and Capitol were crammed with songs speaking of love ("All Of Me Belongs To You"), farming ("Tater Raisin' Man"), hope ("Six Times A Day"), and even miracles ("Tears Of St Ann"). His voice was burly on the one hand, tender on the other, and it took center stage in nearly all his recordings. He could soar into the sky like a hawk, but just as easily the earth could open up and his voice drop right down inside, digging as deep as a mineshaft on songs like "Bury The Bottle With Me" (which must have hit uncomfortably close to home for Curless, who struggled with alcoholism most of his life) and the intensely quiet "Foggy, Foggy Dew."

Richard William Curless was born on 17 March, 1932 in Fort Fairfield, Maine, a small

The Soul of Dick Curless

town in the far north of the state. His family later moved to Massachusetts, but his Maine background remained in his blood, as well as in his music ("Tombstone," for instance, was about the perils of driving a particularly hairy stretch of highway in Maine). Curless learned guitar as a teenager, and in the late '40s he toured regionally with Yodeling Slim Clark and landed a radio show on a Massachusetts station. By the age of eighteen he'd earned the first of his nicknames: the Tumbleweed Kid (after a song he liked to play, "Tumbling Tumbleweeds"). During the '50s, when he was serving in the armed forces in Korea, he worked as a DJ and was dubbed the Rice Paddy Ranger. (Later still he'd be known as the Baron of Country Music, after a 1966 song of his, "The Baron.")

Curless first recorded in 1950 for the Standard label; after his military service, he cut further songs for Event and then Tiffany. He lived in Bangor,

Maine, where he played at the Silver Dollar and other local venues while also touring a little through New England and Canada, even winning Arthur Godfrey's *Talent Scouts* TV contest in 1957. During the early '60s, Dan Fulkerson, a radio station employee in Bangor, came to him with the song "A Tombstone Every Mile" and the two men formed the Allagash label to release it. When "Tombstone" began to catch on, the Capitol subsidiary Tower signed Curless and re-released it. "Tombstone" eventually reached #5 in the *Billboard* country charts in March of 1965. Over the next several years, three more of Dick's Tower recordings broke the Top 40, the true knockouts from this period (including "St. James Infirmary," "Foggy, Foggy Dew," and "Bury The Bottle With Me") remain buried on the several excellent albums released by the label. Tower had also purchased Curless' Event and Tiffany masters, and many of his Tower albums contained these recordings that he'd made during the '50s.

During the late '60s Curless joined Buck Owens' All-American Road Show, which also included Merle Haggard, Bonnie Owens, Kay Adams (with whom Curless cut the mediocre duet album A Devil Like Me Needs An Angel Like You), and Tommy Collins, among others. Curless also moved to Bakersfield for a short time. Beginning in 1970 his records were released on Capitol proper (Tower had folded), and he had several more hits, including "Big Wheel Cannonball," "Hard, Hard Traveling Man," "Drag 'Em Off The Interstate," "Sock It To 'Em J.P. Blues," and the hilarious "Loser's Cocktail." Capitol pushed his truck-driving material further out front, and in 1973 they even released an album, Live At The Wheeling Truck Driver's Jamboree—a true beauty that kicks off with a rollicking version of "Chick Inspector (That's Where My Money Goes)," which has to be one of the weirdest truck-driving songs ever recorded.

Curless stayed with Capitol until 1973, then departed after a falling-out with the label. The next several years saw major changes in his personal life. He finally quit drinking—which he later confessed was a serious problem—but unfortunately lost much of his stomach through surgery. He also found religion—rather than a crutch, it was more a means for him to feel at ease with his life. He recorded further material during the '80s, and in 1995 he finished what would be his final album, TRAVELING THROUGH. Sadly, Curless died of stomach cancer on 25 May, 1995 before the album's release.

⊙ **Traveling Through** (1995; Rounder). Recorded at Longview Farm in late 1994 and finished only months before Curless' death, this collection of blues, gospel and country was one of the most moving albums of the past decade. Songs like Chris Gaffney's "King Of The Blues," Hank Williams' "When God Comes And Gathers His Jewels," Lefty Frizzell's "I Never Go Around Mirrors," and Dick's own "I Don't Have A Memory Without Her" are stately and mature, but also easygoing, friendly and imbued with the calm of a person who's come to terms with life. The extensive liner notes are by Peter Guralnick.

⊙ **The Drag 'Em Off The Interstate, Sock It To 'Em Hits Of Dick Curless** (1998; Razor & Tie). A knockout 21-song collection of Dick's Tower and Capitol material. There are plenty of trucking songs, including "Big Wheel Cannonball," the sort-of title track and, of course, the great "Tombstone," but thankfully the compilers had the vision to include the downer of downers, "Bury The Bottle With Me," the catchy "Juke Box Man," and Curless' two great oddball numbers, "Loser's Cocktail" and "Chick Inspector (That's Where My Money Goes)."

Skeeter Davis

Kentucky singer Skeeter Davis has a clear, strong voice that's full of hillbilly texture—more akin to Loretta Lynn than the studio-smooth sound of Patsy Cline. During the 1960s, she enjoyed hits with songs like "Set Him Free," "Optimistic," and "The End Of the World" and also won a coveted spot on the *Grand Ole Opry*. Davis, however, had actually first earned her country recognition in 1953 with "I Forgot More (Than You'll Ever Know)" as half of the Davis Sisters. Sadly, her partner, childhood friend Betty Jack Davis (no relation), was killed a year later.

Davis was born Mary Frances Penick on 30 December, 1931 in Dry Ridge, Kentucky. She and Betty Jack began singing together in high school, eventually performing on radio stations throughout the region. They were signed to RCA in 1952, and a year later one of their recordings, "I Forgot More", went to #1. Later that year Betty Jack was killed, and Skeeter badly injured, in a car accident. After several years of mourning and indecision, Skeeter finally began focusing on a solo career; she moved to Nashville and hooked up again with RCA, this time with producer-guitarist Chet Atkins.

Her first solo hit came in 1959 with "Set Him Free." She also cut "Lost To A Geisha Girl" and "(I Can't Help You) I'm Falling Too," both answer songs to hits by Hank Locklin, "Geisha Girl" and "Please Help Me, I'm Falling" (these and other answer songs showed up on her 1961 album HERE'S THE ANSWER). Davis' 1963 hit "The End Of The World" is probably her best known recording. Later in the decade she recorded two albums of duets with Bobby Bare as well as a Buddy Holly tribute (1967's SKEETER DAVIS SINGS BUDDY HOLLY).

By the '70s she'd become something of a flower child on the *Grand Ole Opry,* wearing jeans and hippie hair; she was eventually suspended from the show in response to a public statement she made in defence of some Jesus freaks, who'd been hassled by the local cops (Davis herself was an outspoken Christian). She lost some favor with the boss men on Music Row, but she gained new footing in the mid-'80s when she cut the album SHE SINGS, THEY PLAY with NRBQ. A couple of years later she married the group's bassist, Joey Spampinato.

⊙ **The Essential Skeeter Davis** (1995; RCA). This decent hits collection starts with the Davis Sisters' "I Forgot More" before concentrating on Skeeter's 1960s hits like "Set Me Free" and "The End Of The World."

Jimmy Dean

Jimmy Dean, the popular singer from Texas, had big country hits with songs like "P.T. 109," "The First Thing Ev'ry Morning (And The Last Thing Ev'ry Night)," and especially with the self-penned signature song "Big Bad John". But Dean's television career was equally important to him, and during the late 1950s and mid-'60s he hosted a variety of TV programs, including *The Jimmy Dean Show.* Then, of course, there was the Jimmy Dean pure pork sausage, the chief product of his Jimmy Dean Meat Company, which he founded in 1968. Appearing regularly in TV ads wearing a big grin, he hawked the stuff to the point of parody—so much so that meat, not music, is what most folks remember him by today.

Born on 10 August, 1928 in Plainview, Texas, Jimmy Ray Dean served in the US Air Force in Washington, DC, and following his discharge stayed in the area to play with a band called the Texas Wildcats. He also began appearing on TV and radio, for which he was groomed by influential promoter Connie B. Gay. Dean cut some songs for the Four Star label in the early '50s, and one of them, "Bummin' Around," made the *Billboard* Top 5 in 1953. More importantly, though, Dean began hosting the local TV program *Town & Country Jamboree,* which led to his own *Jimmy Dean Show* in 1957. It didn't last long, but it placed Dean at the forefront of a trend in country and pop music—hosting one's own TV show—that was later followed by Roger Miller, Glen Campbell, Johnny Cash, and many others.

In 1961, freshly signed to Columbia, Dean struck it big with the #1 pop and country hit "Big Bad John," the tale of a hard-working and heroic coal miner. For subsequent recordings he continued with story songs ("P.T. 109") and also revealed a weakness for corny recitations (the thinly veiled anti-commie piece "Dear Ivan"). In 1963 Dean was back in the TV limelight with a new version of his old variety program, *The Jimmy Dean Show.* This time it lasted three years. Though television was increasingly the main focus of his career, he did continue recording, switching from Columbia to RCA in 1966 and charting several more times with songs like "Stand Beside Me" and "Slowly" (a duet with Dottie West). By the '70s, however, his hit streak had run out, while his career in front of the cameras showed no sign of slowing down. He was a regular on TV movies of the week, a frequent guest host for several different TV variety shows and, of course,

a familiar face and voice in households everywhere thanks to his famous sausages.

⊙ **Jimmy Dean's Greatest Hits** (1966; Columbia; reissued 1998; Columbia/Legacy). "Big Bad John" is the lead-off track, which is no surprise, and it's also the strongest and most memorable cut. Of the rest, recitations like "Dear Ivan" and "The Farmer And The Lord" are kitschy at best, and "P.T. 109" and his version of Tommy Collins' "Sam Hill" are toe-tapping but hardly out of the ordinary.

Roy Drusky

Georgia native Roy Drusky was a popular crooner during the 1960s whose smooth, mellow baritone voice was a dead ringer for Eddy Arnold's. In fact, unless you're deeply versed in either man's music, or make an effort to hear their songs side-by-side, you'll have a difficult time telling the difference. It's not just that Drusky appears to be aping Arnold vocally, he also worked the same stylistic territory—big productions, lush arrangements, and song choices that even go so far as to include Arnold favorites "The Tip Of My Fingers" and "Make The World Go Away". Comparisons aside, however, Drusky's work is pleasant enough if you like your music easygoing and rounded on every potential edge. He certainly racked up an impressive number of hits during the '60s although, on a creative level, he wasn't exactly breaking new ground. In the liner notes to his Mercury album MY GRASS IS GREEN, an anonymous writer descibes Drusky's style as clean and uncomplicated—a reflection of a simple, soulful nature. In truth, though, Drusky was about as suburban-sounding as country music got during the '60s.

Roy Frank Drusky, Jr. was born on 22 June, 1930 in Atlanta, Georgia. He didn't begin playing music seriously until he joined the Navy in the late '40s, during which time he taught himself guitar. After completing his service, Drusky studied veterinary medicine at Emory University, but he also played country music with a local group he assembled, the Southern Ranch Boys. He signed to Starday in 1953 (his first single was "Such A Fool"), and a few years later he recorded for Columbia, but none of his recordings turned many heads. Drusky worked a bit as a DJ, but he made further inroads in Nashville when Faron Young turned his compositions "Alone With You" and "Country Girl" into major #1 hits.

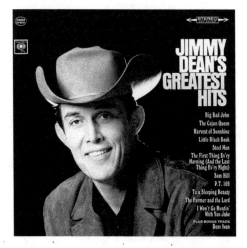

JIMMY DEAN'S GREATEST HITS

Big Bad John
The Cajun Queen
Harvest of Sunshine
Little Black Book
Steel Men
The First Thing Ev'ry Morning (And the Last Thing Ev'ry Night)
Sam Hill
P.T. 109
To a Sleeping Beauty
The Farmer and the Lord
I Won't Go Huntin' With You Jake
PLUS BONUS TRACK
Dear Ivan

Jimmy Dean • Roy Drusky

In 1960 Drusky finally had a hit of his own with "Another," a song he co-wrote that was released by Decca. There he worked with producer Owen Bradley, who helped nurture Drusky's crooner characteristics. Ironically, his first hit for Mercury (to which he switched in 1963) was a novelty number by Bill Anderson, "Peel Me A 'Nanner," though in truth the song was about disappointed romance—a subject that Drusky returned to more than once during his career. Ditto for cheating songs, the biggest of all being his 1965 hit "Yes Mr Peters," one of a series of duets Drusky cut with Priscilla Mitchell, a fellow Georgia native, onetime rock'n'roll singer, and the wife of Jerry Reed. During the '60s and into the early '70s, Drusky racked up an impressive number of Top 40 country hits, including songs by Liz Anderson ("Pick Of The Week" and "Strangers"), Kris Kristofferson ("Jody And The Kid"), Dennis Linde ("Long Long Texas Road"), and Neil Diamond ("Red Red Wine"). By the end of the '70s, however, Drusky's recording profile had faded from view.

⊙ **Songs Of Love And Life** (1995; Mercury/
PolyGram). The 13 songs on this Drusky package
maintain a fairly straightforward, soothing tone that's
pleasant and nice—though almost to the point of
making you feel dirty. Not exactly challenging stuff,
unless you're a big fan of Eddy Arnold, in which case
the vocal comparisons might be difficult to erase. Titles
include the big hits "Such A Fool," "Yes Mr Peters,"
"Peel Me A 'Nanner" and "Long Long Road," along
with two songs mined directly from the Arnold catalog,
"Tip Of My Fingers" and "Make The World Go Away".

Dave Dudley

When it comes to trucking songs, deep-voiced Dave Dudley is the leader of the pack. He's the man who put "Six Days On The Road" on the map as the most famous trucking song this side of "Convoy." And he had plenty more songs besides, including "Truck Drivin' Son-Of-A-Gun," "There Ain't No Easy Run," "Trucker's Prayer," "Listen Betty, I'm Singing Your Song," "Me And Ole C.B.," and "Rolaids, Doan's Pills, And Preparation H." He was even made an honorary member of the Nashville Teamsters (truck drivers') union. Eighteen-wheelers weren't the only output from this working man's poet: he covered a wide range of hardscrabble territory, from cowboys and miners to booze ("Day Drinking," a duet with Tom T. Hall, a frequent collaborator of Dudley's), patriotism ("Vietnam Blues," one of Kris Kristofferson's earliest compositions), and such universal subjects as romance and loneliness ("Lonelyville"). During his fifteen-year hitmaking career, from the early 1960s through the mid-'70s, he racked up thirty-three Top 40 country hits.

Dudley was born David Darwin Pedruska on 3 May, 1928 in Spencer, Wisconsin. He played semi-professional baseball, but after an arm injury eventually turned to music. A car accident in 1960 briefly set his burgeoning career back a few notches; he finally had his first taste of success with his 1961 single "Maybe I Do," released by the Vee label. Two years later another label, Golden Wing, released "Six Days On The Road." The song was written by Earl Green and "Peanut" Montgomery (a friend of George Jones who also penned one of the Possum's oddest numbers, "Unwanted Babies"), which was passed on to Dudley from fellow country artist Jimmy C. Newman. "Six Days" reached #2 in the country charts, and it's been a familiar road anthem ever since. Dudley was signed to Mercury after its release, and his career took off and remained successful for the better part of the '60s and '70s. He failed to make the charts very often in the '80s, but he did find he had a supportive fan base in Europe, and began concentrating his efforts on satisfying that market. Surprisingly, considering how successful he was in his heyday, few of his songs have made it onto CD. For vinyl junkies, however, his classic Mercury albums are well worth tracking down.

⊙ **Trucker Classics** (1996; Sun Entertainment). At only 12 songs it's slim pickings, but this CD does cover some of the major bases such as "Six Days On The Road," "The Pool Shark," "Two Six Packs Away," and "Me And Ole C.B." A proper Dudley retrospective has yet to be compiled.

REPRISE RECORDS

Don Gibson

Don Gibson

A long with Jim Reeves, Patsy Cline, and Eddy Arnold, singer, songwriter, and guitarist Don Gibson was one of the key players (and top stars) in the development of the Nashville Sound during the '50s and '60s. He not only possessed a smooth and gentle crooner's voice that fit the burgeoning style perfectly, he was also one of Nashville's premier songwriters, penning classics like "Oh Lonesome Me," "(I'd Be) A Legend In My Time," "Sweet Dreams," and "I Can't Stop Loving You." The latter, in particular, has been recorded many hundreds of times by countless country and pop singers; one of them, Ray Charles, included it on his landmark 1962 album MODERN SOUNDS IN COUNTRY AND WESTERN MUSIC.

Donald Eugene Gibson was born on 3 April, 1932 in Shelby, North Carolina. As a teenager he played with a group called Sons Of The Soil that took plenty of inspiration from western stalwarts Sons Of The Pioneers. They played a local radio show, and in 1949 Mercury Records brought them into the studio to cut four songs. One, "Why Am I So Lonely," was a Gibson original. Over the next several years Gibson struck out on his own,

recording further songs for RCA, Columbia, and MGM. He also signed on as a staff songwriter with the publishing company Acuff-Rose. Many of his songs from this period are more straightahead honky tonk—the fiddles and steel guitar up front in the arrangements, and the twang in Gibson's voice still intact. The best known of the bunch was definitely "Sweet Dreams" (later immortalized by Patsy Cline), which he cut for MGM in 1955; it made the Top 10, and a cover version by Faron Young did even better. Gibson was back on RCA in 1957, and his new producer, Chet Atkins, saw great possibilities in his voice and song style. He smoothed out the arrangements, cut out the fiddles, downplayed the steel, and turned Gibson into a hitmaking music star. This wasn't necessarily a crime, as many songs from this period—the hopped-up "Blue Blue Day," the rockabilly-inflected "Tell It Like It Is" and "Sweet Sweet Girl"—are solid and succinct.

Among Gibson's 1957 sessions for RCA were two songs that to this day are his signatures: "Oh Lonesome Me" and "I Can't Stop Loving You." While the latter is smooth and silky Nashville Sound pop at its most explicit, Gibson's wily voice on the rollicking "Oh Lonesome Me" sounds uncannily similar to soon-to-come country star Roger Miller. Surprisingly different stylistically—and, incredibly, both written in the same afternoon—they showed Gibson's versatility as a vocalist as well as a songwriter.

The late '50s and early '60s were a prolific time for Gibson, and he stayed at or near the top of the charts with hot-to-trot songs like "Look Who's Blue," "Just One Time," "Lonesome Old House," "Don't Tell Me Your Troubles," and "Big Hearted Me." These were all from his own pen, though he also recorded plenty of material from other writers such as Hank Snow, Mickey Newbury, and Felice and Boudleaux Bryant. Through much of the '60s Gibson had growing problems with drug addiction and missed engagements, which got him kicked off the *Grand Ole Opry* in 1963, and caused tensions with concert bookers as well as his record label. By 1970 he was determined to make a new start: he moved to Nashville (he previously been based out of Knoxville) and switched his contract to Hickory Records. Satisfaction came when he scored a hit with "Woman (Sensuous Woman)," a saucy Gary Paxton song that reflected Nashville's growing open-mindedness toward sexually charged subject matter ("release my body and let me live again"). He rejoined the *Opry* in 1975, and his classic songs came bursting back to life when Ronnie Milsap took "(I'd Be) A Legend In My Time" to #1 and Emmylou Harris and Reba McEntire each had a hit with "Sweet Dreams." In 1990 the Kentucky Headhunters made "Oh Lonesome Me" a chart hit once again. Gibson hasn't made it yet to the Country Music Hall of Fame, though he's a strong candidate, but he has been a member of the Nashville Songwriters Hall of Fame since 1973.

⊙ **A Legend In My Time** (1987; Bear Family). A single-CD, 26-track collection of Gibson's classic RCA recordings such as "Blue Blue Day," "Just One Time," a later version of "Sweet Dreams," "Don't Tell Me Your Troubles," and "Look Who's Blue."

⊙ **The Singer—The Songwriter** (1991; Bear Family). If you like Gibson's voice and songwriting, there's plenty of each on this power-packed 4-disc box set, which includes all the recordings from his formative years, 1949–60. It's also the only place to hear his early honky tonk recordings for Mercury (with Sons Of The Soil), MGM, Columbia, and RCA, many of which are excellent and much more raw than his Nashville Sound gems.

⊙ **Oh Lonesome Me** (1997; Collectibles/BMG). Includes the original 12 songs from Gibson's 1958 debut album ("Blue Blue Day," "Sweet Sweet Girl," "I Can't Stop Loving You") along with 4 bonus tracks.

Stonewall Jackson

Though Stonewall Jackson's 1959 hit "Waterloo"—not to be confused with the Abba song of the same name—kicked off a successful career for this onetime dirt-poor farmboy that lasted for well over a decade, these days Jackson's name isn't that well known. Which is a shame, because at his best he's actually a sturdy workaday honky tonker, making meaty work of songs like "I Washed My Hands In Muddy Water," "Don't Be Angry," and George Jones' "Life To Go." (At his worst he was crooning pap like the 1971 Lobo hit "Me And You And A Dog Named Boo").

Jackson was born on 6 November, 1932 in a railroad settlement near Tabor City, North Carolina. (His ancestry really does go back to the famous Confederate general of the same name). He started playing country music seriously while in the Navy, deciding to pursue a career once he got out. In 1956, with a few dollars and a decent pickup truck, he drove to Nashville, got an appointment to audition songs at Acuff-Rose the next day, and before he knew it he was singing on the *Grand Ole Opry*—which in turn got him a contract with Columbia. Jackson's is a seemingly fast and easy success story that's the fantasy of every budding country music singer, but in fact he was the only singer signed to an *Opry* contract without a hit to his name. In 1958, however, he secured one with "Life To Go," and a year later he was riding even higher on the million-selling success of "Waterloo." Over the next decade he had further hits—"B.J. The D.J.," "Blues Plus Booze (Means I Lose)," "Stamp Out Loneliness"—and became a regular fixture on the *Opry*. He stayed with Columbia through the early '70s, after which he cut records for MGM, the gospel label Myrrh, Little Darlin', and pedal-steel guitarist Pete Drake's label First Generation, among others.

● **The World Of Stonewall Jackson** (1972; Columbia). A double-album that's the best Jackson compilation to date.

⊙ **American Originals** (1989; Columbia). This CD series has never been the most substantial, but this selection does contain some of Jackson's highlights, including "Don't Be Angry" and, of course, "Waterloo."

⊙ **Classic Country** (1998; Sony/Simitar). A 14-song collection that pulls together some of Jackson's best titles, including "Waterloo," "I Washed My Hands In

Muddy Water," and "Blues Plus Booze (Means I Lose)."
"Me And You And A Dog Named Boo" is also on the
roster.

Sonny James

P ossessing a smooth, sweet voice and a penchant
for gentle love ballads, Sonny James (aka the
Southern Gentleman) was a ripe and ready candidate for the full-blown Nashville Sound
treatment. His successful blend of pop and country
styles led to a run of chart hits during the late 1960s
that's still one of the largest of any country singer.
The bulk of his songs, especially his later
recordings, blend into a pleasant but entirely
generic and often treacly mass, yet there is real
heart behind his best work, especially his '50s
Capitol material. These particular songs are
nowhere near as burdened with studio effects. The
arrangements on his 1957 album SOUTHERN GEN-
TLEMAN, in fact, are downright minimalist with
little more than steel and acoustic guitar, bass and
light drumbeats for accompaniment—beautiful
stuff that's ripe for reissue. There's even an a cappella gospel quartet, "My God And I," written by
James.

Sonny was a childhood nickname for James
Loden, born on 1 May, 1929 in Hackleburg,
Alabama. As a child he played fiddle and guitar,
sang in a family group with his sisters, and appeared
on shows like the *Big D Jamboree* and the *Louisiana
Hayride*. He served in the Korean War and after
returning from service he met Chet Atkins who
helped him get a contract with Capitol Records.
His first single was the self-penned "That's Me
Without You." This song and others like "I Forgot
More Than You'll Ever Know" and "For Rent"
were successful enough, but it was the song
"Young Love" that topped the country and pop
charts in 1957 and ultimately put young James on
the map. The song had a teen-idol flair to it that
prompted James to dabble in pop and rock styles
for a few years, briefly switching record labels in
the process. That experiment didn't fly far,
however, and by the early '60s he was back on
Capitol and singing country once again. For the
rest of the decade the hits came steady and strong:
"The Minute You're Gone," "Behind The Tear,"
"It's The Little Things," "Born To Be With You,"
"Only The Lonely," etc. During the early '70s
James moved to Columbia and continued to make
the charts, though his massive hit streak had slowed

somewhat. As a sideline he began producing other
artists' work, one song being the huge hit "Paper
Roses" for Marie Osmond. Later in the decade he
switched to Monument and then Dimension
Records, and by the '90s he'd retired back to
Hackleburg.

⊙ **Young Love: The Classic Hits Of Sonny James**
(1997; Razor & Tie). A 21-track compilation of James'
career highlights from "That's Me Without You,"
"Young Love," and the pop song "First Date, First Kiss,
First Love" to the 1970s hits "Empty Arms" and "Bright
Lights, Big City." His voice is certainly pleasant, and
songs like "I'll Never Find Another You" show an
interesting folk-revival influence, but the bulk are
lukewarm Nashville fare.

Loretta Lynn

> "Loretta sang what women were think-
> ing."
>
> —Minnie Pearl

A s a result of her song, "Coal Miner's
Daughter," and her autobiography and the
subsequent movie which both share the same
name, Loretta Lynn's rise from the woods of
Butcher Holler, Kentucky to the Country Music
Hall of Fame is one of the most well-known life
stories in modern music. She stands as a glowing
example of how honesty, raw talent, hard work,
and perseverance can pay off in terms of national
success. Throughout a long career of hit songs and
numerous awards, Lynn has maintained the same
spirit and integrity she exhibited from her earliest
years in the business. Nowadays she stands not just
as one of the top female artists of country music,
but as one of the music's top writers and singers.

With the hundreds of songs she's written and
sung since her singing career began in the early
1960s, Lynn has never backed away from a challenge. Whether her subject be drunken husbands,
sneaky women, faded love, or even the Pill, her
songs are as direct in their lyrics as they are in their
straightforward honky-tonk melodies. Compositions like "Don't Come Home A Drinkin' (With
Lovin' On Your Mind)," "Fist City" (in which she
physically threatens a woman looking to steal her
husband), "Your Squaw Is On The Warpath,"
"Who Says God Is Dead," and "Who's Gonna
Take The Garbage Out" (one of several duets with
Ernest Tubb) told it like it was. Her voice, too,

was a mixture of simplicity (complete with unabashed Kentucky twang) and confidence—it was pretty, yes, but not in the delicate sense. When she sang, she was up front and personal.

Men as well as women identified with Lynn's songs not only because of the strong, clear vocals, but also because of their honesty. Although committed to her marriage, she was never afraid to speak of its troubles and pains. Fed-up housewives heard "Don't Come Home A Drinkin'" and made it the first of her many #1 hits. Other songs such as "Dear Uncle Sam" (an anti-Vietnam War song from the point of view of a suffering wife), "Wings Upon Your Horns" (where an "angel" girl is seduced by a "devil" man), and, of course, "The Pill" challenged society's sexual and political boundaries. In general, her arrangements remained sturdy and traditionally sound—and this at a time when countrypolitan slickness was the dominant style.

Lynn was born Loretta Webb on 14 April, 1935 in rural Butcher Holler, Kentucky. She grew up in a deeply rural community with little formal education and by the age of thirteen had met and married the man with whom she would share her life: Oliver "Mooney" Lynn, Jr. Within a year, Loretta was pregnant with their first child, and the young couple had moved to Washington state. Mooney found work there, and Loretta produced a further three children by the time she was a mere eighteen years old. Encouraged by her husband, she began singing around the house; Mooney then bought her a guitar, and later set up an audition with a local group, the Penn Brothers. Before long, Loretta was singing at clubs and dance halls, and she even appeared on a Tacoma television program

(hosted by Buck Owens, who was on the brink of national fame himself). Canadian businessman Norm Burley spotted her and offered to finance her first recordings in Los Angeles in 1960. Burley's label, Zero, released Lynn's self-penned song "I'm A Honky Tonk Girl."

From the outset, Loretta and Mooney adopted a grassroots approach to promoting her new single, mailing out copies to DJs everywhere and even driving across the country, from town to town, distributing records to radio stations by hand. The effort paid off when "Honky Tonk Girl" reached #14 in the *Billboard* country charts. Traveling to Nashville, the Lynns knocked on publishing company doors until they eventually won the attention of Doyle and Teddy Wilburn (aka the Wilburn Brothers), who ran Sure-Fire. Pleased with what they heard, the brothers helped Loretta get a contract with Decca. In 1962, her recording of "Success," written by Johnny Mullins, became her first Top 10 single. During the first few years of her career, she sang regularly with the Wilburn Brothers on their television program and as part of their road show. She befriended Patsy Cline (writing a tribute to her, "This Haunted House," after she died), and she also cut a series of duets with Ernest Tubb, one of her longtime idols. With Tubb's encouragement, she became a member of the *Grand Ole Opry*.

For two straight decades beginning in the early '60s, Loretta made the *Billboard* charts on a regular basis. Her first big songs included "Before I'm Over You," "Blue Kentucky Girl," and "You Ain't Woman Enough," and in 1966 she finally reached #1 with the defiant "Don't Come Home A Drinkin'." (A year later Loretta's brother, Jay Lee Webb, recorded the dopey answer song "I Come Home A Drinkin' [To A Worn Out Wife Like You].") Not only was Loretta proving herself an excellent vocalist, most of her best songs came from her own pen: "Drinkin'," "Fist City," "Your Squaw Is On The Warpath," "The Pill," "Rated X," and "You're Looking At Country," among many others. She won the CMA's Female Vocalist of the Year three times (the award originated in 1967, and Loretta was the first recipient). In 1972 she also became the first woman to be nominated Entertainer of the Year. Further CMA awards came her way as half of a duo with Conway Twitty; the two had begun cutting songs together in 1970, releasing such titles as "After The Fire Is Gone," "Louisiana Woman, Mississippi Man," and the overly sentimental "As Soon As I Hang Up The Phone." They continued their musical partnership for years afterward.

Loretta Lynn

Loretta recorded her famous autobiographical song "Coal Miner's Daughter" in 1970. Six years later, the book of her life story, sporting the same title, hit the shelves. In 1980 came the movie starring Tommy Lee Jones and Sissy Spacek (who sang the songs herself and won an Academy Award for her performance). By now, Loretta was a bona fide legend—she even had her own tourist attraction, a sprawling ranch outside of Nashville that encompasses a tiny town called Hurricane Mills. She and Mooney bought it in 1967 as their home, and several years later they opened it as a campground, museum, and performance venue.

Legendary status aside, Lynn continued to make records, hitting the charts with titles like "When The Tingle Becomes A Chill," "Pregnant Again," "Out Of My Head And Back In My Bed," and "I Lie," although not as many of these hits were her own compositions. "Heart Don't Do This To Me" became her final Top 40 single in 1985, the same year a new country queen, Reba McEntire, was belting out "Somebody Should Leave" from the #1 spot. If Lynn's chart success had faded, she was still one of the most respected country singer-songwriters—she was named Artist of the Decade by the ACM in 1980, and eight years later was elected to the Country Music Hall of Fame. Her live shows, too, remained popular. Though she cut back on her recordings, in 1993 she did collaborate on the album HONKY TONK ANGELS with Tammy Wynette and Dolly Parton. Shortly afterwards, however, her husband Mooney fell ill, entered a long period of slow decline, and finally died in 1996. Although a major setback for Loretta—as was the death of her friend and partner Conway Twitty in 1993—she has persevered and continues to perform, albeit on a less regular basis.

⊙ **Country Music Hall Of Fame** (1991; MCA). On the one hand this is a great 16-song sampler of Loretta's tremendous output, hitting the highlights from "Success" through "Fist City," "Squaw," "Coal Miner's Daughter," and "The Pill." On the other, though, it may prove a tease, leaving you kicking yourself for not making the investment in the far more substantial box set.

⊙ **Honky Tonk Girl: The Loretta Lynn Collection** (1994; MCA). This 3-disc collection functions mainly as an extended 'best of' album—no demos or unreleased gems in other words, although two of her Zero recordings, "Honky Tonk Girl" and "The Whispering Sea," kick off the proceedings. But for pure Loretta it's

an excellent and very worthwhile overview, bulging with titles from the early 1960s on up to 1988's "Who Was That Stranger."

Roger Miller

To say Roger Miller burst onto the country music scene like a bat out of hell is almost an understatement. A well-regarded songwriter since the late 1950s, his singing career was much slower to come but finally did, as he slayed the charts in 1964 and 1965 with "Dang Me," "Engine Engine #9," "Do-Wacka-Do," and "King Of The Road," among others. He magically mixed tight, spare arrangements with a hot-fired country spirit, insanely clever wordplay, and a totally wacked-out sense of humor. His songs didn't always make sense ("My Uncle Used To Love Me But She Died"), but that was part of their beauty.

Miller's good-natured personality and superb wit were certainly a major part of his appeal, but his songs were far more than just novelties—inside each one of them were some very human situations and very real emotions. Some like "England Swings" and "You Can't Roller Skate In A Buffalo Herd" were unabashedly joyful; many others, though, including "Dang Me" and "Engine Engine #9," were actually quite down and out when pulled apart—it's just that Miller's wild and playful spirit gave them an uplifting spin. Some songs, however, were far from funny no matter how they were sung: "The Last Word In Lonesome Is Me," "A World So Full Of Love," "Husbands And Wives," and "One Dyin' And A-Buryin'" were actually quite devastating and revealed there was far greater depth to his talent than good yucks and clever soundbites would have indicated.

Roger Dean Miller was born on 2 January, 1936 in Fort Worth, Texas. His father died when he was a year old, and he grew up with his Uncle Elmer in Erick, Oklahoma. Elmer's daughter married Sheb Wooley, who was himself a budding singer soon to be famous for "The Purple People Eater," and he and young Roger forged a bond based on their musical aspirations. After serving in the Korean War, Miller played in an army hillbilly band in Atlanta, Georgia, where he met Bill Anderson, another soon-to-be singer-songwriting star. Once discharged from the Army, Miller moved to Nashville, where he got work as a bellhop. He eventually caught the attention of Minnie Pearl, who hired him to play fiddle, and

GEMS/REDFERNS

Do-Wacka-Do: Roger Miller cuts loose

year playing drums with Faron Young. Though his Decca records had all bombed, he was signed to RCA on the strength of his writing talent, and on this label he finally broke through as a singer with "You Don't Want My Love." Despite being a song about a jilted lover, it felt more silly than sad, thanks to Miller's clever wordplay and his kooky scat vocals, which from then on became his trademark. Further RCA recordings, including the slow and mournful "When Two Worlds Collide" (co-written with Bill Anderson) and "Lock, Stock And Teardrops," showed Miller had a sad and serious side to him as well.

Miller, however, didn't do well enough for RCA to hang onto him. Luckily, the Mercury subsidiary Smash Records was just starting up and looking for new talent. Miller had been contem-

George Jones; through Jones he won an audition with Don Pierce and Pappy Daily of Starday Records. This led to Miller's first recording session, where he cut the hard hillbilly weeper "My Pillow" and the rollicking "Poor Little John." He and Jones also wrote some songs together, including "Tall Tall Trees" (which Alan Jackson later covered).

While in Amarillo, Texas, Miller met honky-tonk star Ray Price, who hired him as a musician in his band, the Cherokee Cowboys. Price soon made a hit out of the Miller song "Invitation To The Blues." At this stage, Miller was signed as a songwriter with Tree Publishing, and his songs were beginning to make the charts, covered by the likes of Ernest Tubb ("Half A Mind"), Faron Young ("That's The Way I Feel"), and Jim Reeves ("Billy Bayou"). Such success put Miller in league with other budding songwriters like Anderson, Willie Nelson, and Harlan Howard. In 1958 he signed with Decca Records, and among the songs he recorded were a couple of honky-tonk duets with Johnny Paycheck (known at the time as Donny Young). He then spent a

plating a move to Hollywood and a film and/or TV career, but before he knew it he was back head-first in country music. This time he struck solid gold: in 1964, "Dang Me" shot to the top of the *Billboard* country chart and into the pop Top 10 as well. It was followed by "Chug-a-Lug" (cut at the same recording session) and "Do-Wacka-Do." All three played Miller's scat vocalizations to the hilt. The following year, if any doubts remained regarding his musical genius, they were entirely erased once "King Of The Road" hit the streets—a song that's still one of the all-time classics of country music. Miller earned his first five Grammy awards in 1965 and another six a year later.

His hit records had come quickly, one after the other for a couple years, but by 1966 things were already slowing down. Miller tried hosting his own television show that fall—he'd been a highly entertaining guest on assorted variety shows already—but it didn't last more than a few months. During the late '60s his writing slacked off, but he did cut excellent songs by hot young Nashville songwriters like Mickey Newbury ("Swiss Cottage

Roll, Truck, Roll

The truck: unfailing mover of commerce along America's highways. Its driver: often bleary-eyed and amped on caffeine or bennies, piloting that 18-wheeled beast along those seemingly endless asphalt ribbons. The trucking world has served as country music fodder since the 1930s, but the best songs in that genre concern more than just the rigs themselves—they're about simply attempting to stay sane. The man whose wife just left him can find comfort at the bar, and the guy in the clinker can usually find at least one iota of sympathy from the sheriff. That's not necessarily so for the truck driver, however. Between those all-too-infrequent truck stops, he remains alone and facing boredom, long hours, and random headlights (or the lack thereof). Despite the lingering effects of booze, pills, 100-mile cups of coffee, women, cholesterol, and cops, the truck driver rolls onward. His feelings are as naked and exposed as those of any other country-song character.

From that perspective come many of country music's trucking classics. Ted Daffan's 1938 "Truck Driver's Blues," acknowledged as the very first truck-driving song, provides the blueprint. Daffan's trucker is "feelin' kinda lonely" from his "head down to his shoes"; nonetheless, he's gotta "keep the wheels a-movin'." A handful of gems from the '50s up the emotional ante. Backed by a hot, crackling band, the trucker in Doye O'Dell's "Diesel Smoke" (the best rendition of this justifiably oft-covered ditty) is on the verge of cracking up due to exhaust, dangerous curves (asphalt and feminine), and beer. One worries he's in for a major wipe-out as soon as the song fades away. Lonnie Irving's unforgettable "Pinball Machine" tells of a trucker whose only friend, the almighty pinball machine, led to his wife and kids deserting him. All that remained, and quite insufficiently so, were his truck and the road (and more pinball). And then there's Red Simpson's "Roll, Truck, Roll," a recitation that's quieter in tone but depraved in its own right. The trucker in that song knows it's time to hang up his keys for good 'cause his son spends all day in school drawing pictures of trucks. Chicago doo-wop group Little Ben and the Cheers cut the rockabilly-ish "Roll That Rigg" [sic], a full-throttled B-sider about a trucker fighting bad weather and windy roads to get to his favorite truck stop and waitress. Passionate with a hint of paranoia, this wailer (released on the Laredo label) fits right into the pattern.

The '60s introduced the whole CB craze, which culminated in the unavoidable C.W. McCall hit "Convoy." But perhaps the most famous truck-driving song of all is still "Six Days On The Road," in which Dave Dudley (who took the song to #2 in 1963) sings of the boredom as well as (finally!) the relief and happiness of seeing his home town in the distance. But the upbeat nature of that song, combined with more interstates and fewer dangerous curves, have not quashed the genre's loneliness in more recent years. Townes van Zandt's "White Freightliner" and Terry Allen's juiced-up "Roll Truck Roll" (a different song than Simpson's) compare favorably with the older classics; and the folks at Diesel Only (the label behind the alt.country RIG ROCK JUKEBOX compilations) have admirably maintained the trucking song tradition to the present day. Yes, give it to me straight—for some of the most honest, direct country music, let's continue to hear from those singing truckers out there, who all too clearly remind us that you have to pay a price for the freedom of the road.

—Brian Gordon

Place") and Dennis Linde ("Where Have All The Average People Gone"), and he was the first to have hits with Bobby Russell's "Little Green Apples" and Kris Kristofferson's "Me And Bobby McGee." He also recorded the soundtrack for the western–comedy *Waterhole #3,* though he didn't write any of the songs.

Smash Records closed its doors in 1970, and Miller soon switched labels to Columbia. None of his recordings had the same fire, however, and he eventually slipped out of the country music spotlight. He stayed out until the mid-'80s, when he was tracked down and commissioned to write songs for the Broadway production *Big River,* a theatrical adaption of Mark Twain's *Adventures Of Huckleberry Finn.* It proved to be a hit, and Miller even won a Tony Award for best musical score. In 1991, however, he discovered he had throat cancer, and he died a year later on 25 October, 1992.

⊙ **Golden Hits** (1965; Smash). Miller's popular hits package from his mid-1960s heyday is now a budget-priced CD of 12 prime-period gems, including "Kansas City Star," "Dang Me," "King Of The Road," the peppy "England Swings," and the big-time downer "One Dyin' And A-Buryin'." Beware that some other hits collections include re-recordings of these same songs.

⊙ **King Of The Road: The Genius Of Roger Miller** (1995; Mercury). This 3-CD set is far more expansive. It focuses mostly on Miller's multitude of material, hits and otherwise, for the Smash label, but it also contains some of his early Starday, Decca, and RCA recordings—which are well worth hearing and have been largely overlooked ever since "Dang Me" fever struck—as well as a few later cuts, including two from BIG RIVER. It's a beautifully produced package (put together by the Country Music Foundation) with some cool demos, unreleased songs, live recordings, and assorted studio outtakes. Well worth the investment.

Dolly Parton

"If you want to know who I am, listen to my songs."

—Dolly Parton

Dolly Parton is easily among the best-known, and most universally adored, artists in all of country music. She's an international celebrity who's made the pop and country charts many times over, starred in hit movies, hosted television specials and series, and even opened her own tourist park, Dollywood, in Pigeon Forge, Tennessee, near her birthplace. She's an extremely savvy businesswoman who has always aimed for the top—and pretty much reached it, too. With all these accomplishments, however, it's easy to forget that Parton is at her very heart an incredibly talented songwriter ("I write every day ... it's kept me sane," she revealed in an interview in 1996) with a powerful mountain-bred voice and a bubbly personality that's packed with country charm and almost impossible to resist.

Dolly's is a true rags-to-riches story. She was born Dolly Rebecca Parton on 19 January, 1946 in a cabin in the Smoky Mountains near the town of Sevierville, Tennessee. She was one of twelve children in a musically inclined but dirt-poor Appalachian family; her song "Coat Of Many Colors"—about a girl ridiculed for the cherished coat her mother made her out of fabric scraps—is a vivid picture from her childhood. Parton gained much musical inspiration from singing in church, and also from an uncle, Bill Owens, on her mother's side. Owens encouraged her musical talent from a very early age and later helped her get settled in Nashville, working as her first manager.

Parton made her *Grand Ole Opry* debut as a teenager and cut her first single, "Puppy Love," for the tiny Goldband label in 1960. She spent time in and out of Nashville, working with the Tree publishing company, Mercury Records, and

cutting demos. She didn't, however, move to Nashville for good until she'd graduated from high school in 1964. A year later, she was signed to Monument Records. She and Owens wrote songs together, and one of them, "Put It Off Until Tomorrow," was a hit for Bill Phillips in 1966 (Parton sang harmony on the song, though she went uncredited). In 1967 Dolly finally gained the notice she deserved with "Dumb Blonde," a take-no-punches song about smashing sexist stereotypes. Like other songs soon to come ("Just Because I'm A Woman," "When Possession Gets Too Strong," "Down From Dover") it wasn't feminist per se, but it revealed a young woman unafraid to put forward a strong female perspective.

Dolly herself admits she never had a tough time as a woman breaking into male-dominated Nashville. She wasn't afraid to stand up to men—she had six brothers, after all—but she never had to actually go into battle. Her songs were all heart, but her approach was business right from the start. "I always said I look like a woman but I think like a man." She also figures she arrived at just the right time, when female singers (Patsy Cline and Loretta Lynn, among others) were breaking new ground in country music.

Dolly married Carl Thomas Dean in 1967, the same year she was invited to replace singer Norma Jean in Porter Wagoner's touring entourage and on his popular television show. This was her big break, as she suddenly had an audience of millions. She and Wagoner went on to record numerous songs together, beginning with "The Last Thing On My Mind" and including "We'll Get Ahead Some Day," "Tomorrow Is Forever," and "Daddy

Dolly Parton

Was An Old Time Preacher Man." Many of these were written by Parton, who also signed to Wagoner's label, RCA, as a solo artist and cut songs such as "Just Because I'm A Woman" and "In The Good Old Days When Times Were Bad." Her first big hit came in 1970 with a lively rendition of Jimmie Rodgers' "Mule Skinner Blues." After that she was on her way, hitting again and again with superb songs like "Joshua," "Coat Of Many Colors," "Touch Your Woman," "My Tennessee Mountain Home," and "Jolene."

One of the amazing things about these and other Dolly recordings from this period is that they maintained a traditional country sound at a time when countrypolitan strings and choruses were saturating the market. There were others besides Wagoner, evidently, who truly believed in her talent and heritage, and knew her Appalachian roots truly meant something.

Dolly left Porter's TV show in 1974, and though he continued producing her records for a time after that, by 1976 the pair had finally parted ways completely. The song "I Will Always Love You" was Dolly's tribute to her friend and colleague, who took their professional split very badly. (The song was a huge hit two decades later for Whitney Houston as the theme song to the film *The Bodyguard*.) Parton, though, needed to get out on her own—she needed to keep growing.

Despite winning the CMA's Female Vocalist of the Year award in 1975 and 1976, change was again in the air for Dolly. She was about as big as she was going to get in country music, and she wanted to try new markets—movies, pop music—without, she insists, losing touch with her Tennessee roots. In 1977 she did just that, jumping the fence into the pop market with the song "Here You Come Again." Despite its shiny, high-budget production values and the airplay it got on pop radio stations, it was still a country smash as well and earned Dolly the CMA's coveted Entertainer of the Year award. Her success as a pop-country crossover artist, however, was hardly surprising, as Kenny Rogers, Ronnie Milsap, Barbara Mandrell, and others were doing precisely the same thing. "Heartbreaker," "Starting Over Again," and "9 To 5" were among her hits from this period, the latter the theme song to her first movie. She also starred in the film *Best Little Whorehouse In Texas,* and in 1983 sailed her glitziest seas yet with the sappy Kenny Rogers duet "Islands In The Stream." A few years later she turned back in a traditional direction with the album TRIO, recorded with Linda Ronstadt and Emmylou Harris (a second volume, TRIO II, was released in 1999). In 1989

she again scored a few points with still-grumbling traditionalists when she hired Ricky Skaggs to produce her album WHITE LIMOZEEN, which included the snappy hit "Why'd You Come In Here Lookin' Like That."

Dolly's recording career kept on rolling throughout the '90s, but her hits dwindled as the decade wore on. She cut a collaborative album with Tammy Wynette and Loretta Lynn, HONKY TONK ANGELS—it's not bad but nothing monumental—and wrote her autobiography, *My Life And Other Unfinished Business.* Her 1996 collection of cover songs, TREASURES, was fairly bland, but in 1998 she cut one of her most pared-down albums in years, HUNGRY AGAIN. She followed it a year later with a full-on bluegrass album, THE GRASS IS BLUE. Though she won't ever give up songwriting and singing, she says, she did stop touring and playing regular concerts in order to focus more on her business ventures, including movies and television specials. In 1999 Dolly was inducted into the Country Music Hall of Fame.

⊙ **Coat Of Many Colors** (1971; RCA; reissued 1999; Buddha). The title song is one of Parton's most memorable creations; not just a beautiful melody, it's made all the more poignant in that it's basically a true story from her rural upbringing. The CD reissue has only the original 10 titles—slim in quantity, though thick with hard-country substance and spirit. In fact, further songs like the lusty "Traveling Man" and the disturbing "If I Lose My Mind" help make it one of Dolly's finest albums.

⊙ **The Essential Dolly Parton** (1995; RCA). A sampler focusing mostly on Dolly's late 1970s, early '80s pop-country hits—"9 To 5," "Heartbreak Express," "Islands In The Stream," etc. Start with VOL. 2 instead—in fact, you may want to skip this one entirely.

⊙ **The Essential Porter Wagoner And Dolly Parton** (1996; RCA). Dolly and Porter were one of the most outstanding duos in country music, cutting a long series of solid country songs together from the late '60s through the mid-'70s. This is a fine collection of their hits, which are all on the traditional side of the fence, before Dolly crossed over.

⊙ **The Essential Dolly Parton, Vol. 2** (1997; RCA). This is the true 'essential' CD to start with, as it focuses on Dolly's early RCA country period—classics like "Mule Skinner Blues," "Touch Your Woman," "Coat Of Many Colors," "Joshua," and the original recording of "I Will Always Love You."

Dolly Parton

⊙ **The Grass Is Blue** (1999; Sugar Hill). Bluegrass is a music Dolly has listened to and loved since childhood, and her voice and sometimes her songs have long hinted at its influence. Now she's cut her first full-on bluegrass album, and it's a very tasty one to boot. The instrumentation is acoustic and traditional (featuring pickers Jerry Douglas, Sam Bush, Stuart Duncan, Barry Bales, Jim Mills, and Bryan Sutton) and along with several entirely comfortable Parton originals (the title track is a haunting beauty) are songs from the likes of Lester Flatt, Hazel Dickens, and Johnny Bond.

Johnny Paycheck

"George Jones learned his style from Johnny Paycheck."

—Aubrey Mayhew

Johnny Paycheck is pure country, there's little doubt about it, but he's also proven himself a restless, and at times troublesome character—his career an untamed mix of the unpredictable, the tragic, and the downright fascinating. He had his biggest success as a hitmaker in the 1970s, most notably with the worldwide smash hit "Take This Job And Shove It," but his career stretches back two decades prior to that record's release, when he was honing his hard-edged honky-tonk sound in the service of such greats as Ray Price, Faron Young, and George Jones. Paycheck's strongest period on a creative level, however, was during the '60s, when he and his manager/producer, Aubrey Mayhew, created a series of outlandish, but thrilling country songs for the independent label Little Darlin', which they owned together. Some were twisted novelty numbers ("The Lovin' Machine"), others unabashedly dark and bitter anthems ("It Won't Be Long (And I'll Be Hating You)") but as a unit they were, and still are, among the most daring and original songs ever to have been cut within the city limits of Nashville.

Paycheck was born Donald Eugene Lytle on 31 May, 1938 in Greenfield, Ohio. He started playing guitar as a boy, and by his mid-teens had left home—riding trains, bumming around, playing songs wherever he could, until he eventually joined the Navy. While enlisted, Paycheck served his first sentence behind bars: he was court-martialed for slugging an officer and spent two years in a military prison. After his release in 1958 he drifted a bit more, but finally landed in Nashville, where his professional music career officially began. Under the stage name Donny Young, he signed with the publishing company Tree (home also to Roger Miller) and the record label Decca, for whom he cut a handful of singles. His solo career didn't exactly fly off the ground, so he accepted work playing with Ray Price (whose shuffle sound is echoed in some of Paycheck's recordings), Faron Young, Porter Wagoner, and George Jones. There's debate as to whether Paycheck's singing influenced Jones' late-period vocal work—his trademark vowel-stretching style—or vice-versa, but it's clear they had a lasting impact on each other's sound.

In the early '60s Paycheck cut a few songs for Mercury before beginning his partnership with Aubrey Mayhew. Mayhew was an executive at Pickwick Records (known for its budget-line reissues and album repackagings), and when he heard Paycheck's voice on demo, he was captivated. He convinced Donny Young to change his name to Johnny Paycheck, and then released several singles on the new Pickwick subsidiary, Hilltop. The first couple of releases tanked in the manner of Paycheck's earlier singles, but in 1965 he achieved a modest Top 40 hit with the Hank Cochran song "A-11". A year later, high on hopes that he had discovered a special talent, Mayhew quit his Pickwick job, and he and Paycheck went into partnership on a new label they called Little Darlin'. They set up an office in Nashville, with Mayhew as the president and Paycheck as the featured artist, and released "The Lovin' Machine", which became Paycheck's first Top 10 record. A debut album followed, JOHNNY PAYCHECK AT CARNEGIE HALL, which despite the title was a studio album cut, like the previous singles, at the RCA facility in Nashville.

The songs Paycheck and Mayhew created for Hilltop and Little Darlin' are really quite incredible. Some were silly to the point of psychotic ("Don't Monkey With Another Monkey's Monkey"), but titles like "The Ballad Of Frisco Bay," "(It's A Mighty Thin Line) Between Love And Hate," "Apartment #9"—which was a hit for its co-writer, Bobby Austin, as well as Tammy Wynette—"(Like Me) You'll Recover In Time," "If I'm Gonna Sink (I Might As Well Go To The Bottom)," and "(Pardon Me) I've Got Someone To Kill" are easily among the grittiest, darkest and most brutally forthright ever recorded in a Nashville studio, then or now. It's impossible to imagine any country star today tackling a song like "Someone To Kill," a dark-clouded masterpiece that takes the perspective of a man at a bar calmly explaining that he's about to go kill his wife and her new lover. "I know you'll excuse me if I say goodnight," he tells the stranger on the next stool, "but I've got a promise to fulfil." The subject matter may be wretched, but Paycheck's approach is remarkably matter-of-fact and non-judgemental—making the song all the more chilling, bold, and brilliant. Surreal subject matter aside, the arrangements are spare and well-grounded in '50s-era honky-tonk traditions; in particular, Lloyd Green's steel-guitar work is brilliant, sometimes piercing, at other times layering the somber mood with an additional spooky edge.

Several of the Little Darlin' releases did well on the *Billboard* country charts, but few were wholeheartedly embraced by the mainstream—which is no real surprise. Neither was Paycheck, who was a rowdy and restless spirit and hard to keep in line. In fact, by the end of the decade he was living on the West Coast, drinking hard, and heading straight for Hank-style oblivion. His ties with Mayhew were also straining, and when the hits failed to pile up Little Darlin' eventually went downhill. (Mayhew had signed a few other artists as well, including Jeannie C. Riley and Country Johnny Mathis, but none of them made any money for him either.) After Little Darlin' folded, Mayhew produced Paycheck's 1970 album AGAIN for the Certron Corporation, which included "Forever Ended Yesterday," "Living The Life Of A Dog," and the surprisingly tender "Julie," but soon after the two men had a final falling out.

By the early '70s, when Paycheck was living two steps from the gutter, he was tracked down and put in touch with producer Billy Sherrill. He cleaned up and dried out, and Sherrill signed him to Epic (also home to two other Sherrill clients, George Jones and Tammy Wynette). His first Epic single, "She's All I Got," was a winner, climbing to #2 in the country charts and winning a Grammy nomination. Sherrill's arrangements were denser than Mayhew's, and included more than a few Nashville Sound touches. That aside, though, quite a few songs from this period were excellent.

The '70s proved to be Paycheck's golden years, at least in terms of his popular appeal. He made the Top 40 on a regular basis each year until the early '80s with such songs as "Someone To Give My Love To," "Let's All Go Down To The River" (a duet with Jodi Miller), "For A Minute There," and the ubiquitous "Take This Job And Shove It," a blue-collar anthem written by David Allan Coe that became Paycheck's signature song (and even inspired a 1981 movie of the same name). Paycheck began the decade as a kind of redneck Valentino, singing songs like "Mr Love-

Johnny Paycheck: Don't monkey with his monkey

maker," "Loving You Beats All I've Ever Seen," "The Most Beautiful Girl," and "Slide Off Of Your Satin Sheets," while dressed in open-necked shirts and leisure suits. By mid-decade, however, he'd grown a beard, let his hair get shaggier, and more or less turned Outlaw with songs like "I'm The Only Hell (Mama Ever Raised)" and "11 Months And 29 Days". The latter was the title track of a gritty, blues-based 1976 album on which he (briefly) renamed himself Johnny Austin Paycheck, in an attempt to ally himself with the fringe element in Austin, Texas. Paycheck's star status peaked with "Shove It," and after it had come and gone his rebellious side resurfaced. "Me And The I.R.S." spoke of his battles with the feds, and "(Stay Away from) The Cocaine Train," "Drinkin' And Drivin'," and "Billy Bardo" (in which a bunch of stoners gun down a two-faced drug agent) weren't exactly subtle allusions to his recreational habits.

On the cover of his 1981 album, EVERYBODY'S GOT A FAMILY ... MEET MINE (on which the last three songs appear), he looked more like Charles Manson than any clear-minded country gal's idea of a latter-day Lovemaker.

Paycheck remained on the Epic roster through 1982, then he recorded for Mercury. He had a few more hits during the early '80s, one of the finest being "Old Violin," in which he faces old age with genuine trepidation. On the whole, though, the decade was probably one he'd rather erase. In 1985 he was carrying on a conversation at the North High Lounge in Hillsboro, Ohio with some local patrons—allegedly about the joys of eating wild game—when one patron brought up the subject of turtle soup. This somehow tipped the scales into territory offensive to the singer. "Do you see me as some kind of country hick?" he bellowed, drawing a pistol and pulling the trigger. Luckily the bullet only grazed the victim's shoulder. For that dirty deed, Paycheck was sent up the river for a seven-to-nine-year sentence in an Ohio prison (where he served only two years following the intervention of then-governor Richard Celeste, who incidentally was only a week away from retirement.) Celeste called Paycheck's sentence "unbelievably harsh," while prosecutor Rocky Coss disagreed: "He is a hoodlum, pure and simple." In any case, "The Only Hell Mama Ever Raised" was back on the streets.

During his time behind bars Paycheck quit drinking, smoking, and drug-taking, got his GED (the equivalent of a high school diploma), and generally turned his life around ... once again. Since his release, he's kept to the straight and narrow, preaching the good word of a drug- and alcohol-free lifestyle and touring small clubs and working-class towns across the US, trying to win back his dwindling fan base. In 1992 he released an excellent back-to-basics album, THE LAST OUTLAW, on Air Records, a tiny West Virginia label. It was only available at the time on cassette, but it's worth tracking down, as it includes a rousing duet with George Jones on the title track and such surly beauties as "Lefty Was Right" and "Big Bad Mama (On A Harley Hog)"—a statement of support for feminist empowerment as only Paycheck could sing it. The 1993 albums THE DIFFERENCE IN ME (Playback Records) and LIVE IN BRANSON, MO, USA (Laserlight) are less interesting, but we have the Country Music Foundation to thank for the excellent compilation THE REAL MR HEARTACHE: THE LITTLE DARLIN' YEARS—one of the most exciting country music CDs to hit the market in ages. Paycheck's emphysema has been causing him

health problems in recent years, but he continues to tour. In 1997 he joined the *Grand Ole Opry*, and there is talk of a new album on the horizon.

⊙ **She's All I Got** (1971, Epic; reissued 1998; Koch). This album marks the beginning of the second major phase of Paycheck's solo career—the fruitful hitmaking period after he hooked up with *über*producer Billy Sherrill. The title track was written by Jerry Williams (aka soul singer/producer Swamp Dogg), and it's one of the finest of Paycheck's 1970s-era recordings.

◐ **Slide Off Of Your Satin Sheets** (1977; Epic). This album directly preceded Paycheck's smash hit "Take This Job And Shove It," by which stage he was already beginning to reveal a burning restlessness and a fascination with Outlaw chic. Witness "I'm The Only Hell (Mama Ever Raised)," a fatalistic saga reminiscent of Merle Haggard's "Mama Tried," or Paycheck's own earlier gem "The Loser". The title track, in which his rich uptown woman can't get enough of his downhome loving, throbs with crude country lust, while "I Did The Right Thing" is colored by defeat—a cheating man returns, reluctantly and only out of a sense of duty, to his faithful woman. Talk about a stark scenario, that song (written by Bobby Braddock) spells it out plain.

⊙ **The Real Mr Heartache: The Little Darlin' Years** (1996; Country Music Foundation). Twenty-four examples of Paycheck's finest work, mixing a hardcore, no-bull honky-tonk approach with material that is so dark and off-the-wall, it's difficult to imagine it having even remote ties to Nashville (where it was, in fact, recorded). The "Ballad Of Frisco Bay" feels like a cold death-fog slowly, steadily descending. On the quirky "Jukebox Charlie," Lloyd Green's steel guitar is piercingly high and biting, yet used with spare and care; on "Touch My Heart" and especially "(It's A Mighty Thin Line) Between Love And Hate," the guitar is truly haunting. Paycheck's voice churns with bitterness on "A-11" and cries spooky tears on "Apartment #9," and then there's "The Cave," about a nuclear holocaust, and "(Like Me) You'll Recover In Time," which is set in an insane asylum. You won't be the same afterward.

⊙ **16 Biggest Hits** (1999; Sony/Epic). A no-frills, hits-oriented overview of Paycheck's dozen years on Epic. Liner notes are sorely missed, but the roster includes such worthy staples as "She's All I Got," "Someone To Give My Love To," "Slide Off Of Your Satin Sheets," "11 Months And 29 Days," "I'm The Only Hell (Mama Ever Raised)," "Me And The I.R.S.," and, of course, "Take This Job And Shove It."

Johnny Paycheck

Charley Pride

"I don't have skin hang-ups. I'm no color. I'm just Charley Pride, the man."

—Charley Pride

Though Charley Pride was by no means the first African-American to play and sing country music—black harmonica wizard DeFord Bailey was an *Opry* star as far back as the 1920s—he was certainly the most successful. From the '60s through the '80s he racked up long strings of serious Nashville hits including "All I Have To Offer You (Is Me)," "Is Anybody Goin' To San Antone," "She's Just An Old Love Turned Memory," and his biggest crossover single of all, "Kiss An Angel Good Mornin'." He had a smooth, warm voice and a genuine devotion to country music and its heritage, a combination that helped him win the hearts of even the most ardently conservative fans, despite the fact that prejudice on the whole was still rampant throughout the South. But Pride had grown up country, working the cotton fields and listening to the *Grand Ole Opry* with his father, and it showed—which is something people understood and appreciated.

Charley Frank Pride was born on 19 March, 1938 in Sledge, Mississippi. He was raised on a cotton farm where his parents were sharecroppers. He began playing guitar as a teenager, but he also loved baseball, playing with various professional and semi-professional leagues for several years, including a stint with the Negro American League team the Memphis Red Sox. He even tried out for the major leagues. During this time he lived all over the US, including an extended stay in Montana, where he also played music regularly. It was there, too, that Pride first heard encouraging words from Red Foley and Red Sovine, and soon he was trying his luck in Nashville. After struggling for a couple of years, he eventually caught the ear of producer Jack Clement, who in turn got Chet Atkins interested, and Pride was signed to RCA. His first single was "The Snakes Crawl At Night," a dark, tense song about a man who shoots his cheating wife. In promoting the song, the label called him "Country Charley Pride" but deliberately failed to send a photograph of the singer, so that DJs at first simply figured he was white. When he made his *Grand Ole Opry* debut a year later, he'd earned enough respect and enthusiasm for his music for his skin-color to be irrelevant.

Pride scored an amazing number of hits over the next couple of decades, twenty nine of them reaching #1. In 1971, the year of "Kiss An Angel Good Mornin'," he was named Entertainer of the Year by the Country Music Association. He also won Grammy awards for both secular and gospel recordings. He left RCA in 1986 but made further recordings for 16th Avenue Records and Honest Entertainment. During the '90s he finally officially joined the *Grand Ole Opry*, and he was also given a Pioneer Award from the Academy of Country Music.

⊙ **In Person** (1969; RCA; reissued 1998; Koch). A lively concert album recorded at Panther Hall in Fort Worth, Texas, in 1968. Includes, alongside Pride's early hits, a pair of loose and cool Hank Williams covers, one of which, "Kaw-Liga," eventually topped the charts as well.

⊙ **The Essential Charley Pride** (1997; RCA). Charley has a mellow, appealing voice that makes hits like "San Antone" and "Kiss An Angel" far more than mere passable pop. This collection covers the major bases from "Just Between You And Me," his first true hit in 1966, through 1979's "You're My Jamaica," although "The Snakes Crawl At Night" is oddly missing.

⊙ **From Where I Stand: The Black Experience In Country Music** (1998; Country Music Foundation/Warner Brothers). This excellent 3-CD set includes only four Pride hits, but it places them in context with other African-American country artists (Stoney Edwards, DeFord Bailey, Otis Williams) and singers such as Ray Charles, Etta James, and Ted Hawkins who either sang the occasional country song or were otherwise deeply inspired by the music. An excellent collection any way you look at it.

Jerry Reed

Jerry Reed was a hotshot guitarist who first earned his reputation as a session man before turning himself into a substantial hit singer and songwriter with a sassy hillbilly style. Songs like "East Bound And Down," "Amos Moses," the Grammy-winning "When You're Hot You're Hot," and the goofy "She Got The Gold Mine (I Got The Shaft)" were strong chart hits, just a few that made good ole boy Reed a regular presence in *Billboard*'s country Top 40 from the mid-1960s through to the early '80s. That's all well and good, but of course most folks probably remember Reed best of all thanks to his turn as a wiry-framed truck driver (and Burt Reynolds' sidekick) in the 1977 car-chase comedy *Smokey And The Bandit.*

Jerry Reed Hubbard was born on 20 March, 1937 in Atlanta, Georgia. A child prodigy on the guitar, he was first signed to Capitol Records during the mid-'50s while still a teenager. He also wrote songs early on, some of his biggest early successes being "That's All You Gotta Do" (a hit for Brenda Lee) and "Misery Loves Company" (Porter Wagoner). Later Elvis Presley recorded Reed's songs "Guitar Man" and "US Male." Reed recorded a bit for Columbia in the early '60s, married singer Priscilla Mitchell, and moved to Nashville, where he started playing on various studio sessions. Chet Atkins signed him to RCA in the mid-'60s, and he broke the country Top 20 for the first time in late 1967 with "Tupelo Mississippi Flash." His song "Amos Moses," a fast-talking tale of a ragged Cajun boy raised wild in the Louisiana bayou, made the pop Top 10 in 1970 and became Reed's first smash hit. Six months later came the sassy "When You're Hot, You're Hot," which topped the country charts for five straight weeks.

Reed's music was sizzling and sleek, with just the right amont of grit. His guitar picking was steeped in hot country and blues, a bit of rock'n'roll, and plenty of jazz, and his Georgia-bred hillbilly voice could handle ballads ("Georgia Sunshine") and country classics ("Wabash Cannonball," "Wayfaring Stranger") as well as the novelty songs for which he's best known. Atkins pretty much let Reed's talents speak for themselves; he didn't load up the arrangements with string sections, and in fact kept the atmosphere clean and full of breathing space. In the early '70s, Reed's guitar work and rising stardom eventually landed him a position on the *Glen Campbell Goodtime Hour* TV show, and his exposure there led to feature films. His first big role was in *W.W. And The Dixie Dance Kings* (1974), which starred Burt Reynolds, and that was followed by, among others, *Gator* and *Smokey And The Bandit* parts I, II, and III. The first Bandit flick featured the Reed hit "East Bound And Down," a rousing but fairly standard trucker's anthem. The title track to *Gator* was sort of a reprise of "Amos Moses," but was still swampy and dangerous (as was Reed himself, shotgun on his knee and mean squint in his eye, peering from cover of his 1976 album BOTH BARRELS, where "Gator" appeared).

Reed recorded steadily through the '70s and into the '80s, and songs like "I'm Just A Redneck (In A Rock And Roll Bar)," "Sugar Foot Rag," "Patches," and "She Got The Goldmine (I Got The Shaft)" continued to keep him in the country charts. But as often happens when stardom strikes—especially of the Hollywood variety—he wasn't writing as many songs anymore, and the quality of his recordings became spotty. He last made the Top 40 in 1983 with "Hold On, I'm Comin'," a duet with Waylon Jennings, after which his recordings tapered off. He left RCA for Capitol in the mid-'80s, though in 1992 he reunited with his onetime mentor Chet Atkins for the duet album SNEAKIN' AROUND. In 1999 Reed released the album PICKIN', and though the "picking" itself was enticing, the music lacked the fire of his earlier efforts. Still, Reed's presence on record store shelves once again was a welcome sight.

⊙ **The Essential Jerry Reed** (1995; RCA). Reed made his name with the biting yet good-natured novelty "When You're Hot, You're Hot" and the swampy "Amos Moses," and those two songs are, of course, included here, along with plenty more hits of his like "Lord, Mr Ford," "Alabama Jubilee," "East Bound And Down," and "The Crude Oil Blues." It would have been nice to see "Georgia Sunshine" included, but it's a solid Reed introduction nonetheless.

Jerry Reed

Del Reeves

Del Reeves is best known for the girl-watching novelty tunes "The Belles Of Southern Belle" and "Girl On The Billboard," both big hits for him in 1965, and the trucker's anthem "Looking At The World Through A Windshield." Although Roger Miller and Johnny Cash are two obvious influences, Reeves is actually a fine vocalist in his own right and capable of far more than just novelty numbers. Over a decade-long heyday his recordings ranged from a straightforward (and quite nice) Jim Reeves tribute album (no relation) to duets with Bobby Goldsboro and, finally, the stylized pop of songs like 1975's "But I Do." On these later hits, the bright horn section and lazy supper-club rhythm is more Dean Martin than Ernest Tubb (Tubb was one of Reeves' idols). How times had changed.

Del was born Franklin Delano Reeves on 14 July, 1933 near Sparta, North Carolina. He attended college, served in the Air Force, and during the '50s moved to California. He signed to Capitol in 1954, but first made his reputation as a master of ceremonies—a skill that landed him his own TV show. He later cut a few songs for Decca, Reprise, and Columbia as well, all of which made little impact. During the early '60s he headed back east to Nashville, where he eventually signed with United Artists. This time he hit the jackpot first with "Girl On The Billboard" and then with "The Belles Of Southern Belle." Reeves knew the value of a catchy phrase, and so he added a little "doodle-oo-doo-doo" to the vocal and guitar lines on both songs, a signature that earned him the nickname "The Doodle-Oo-Doo-Doo Kid."

Reeves joined the *Grand Ole Opry* in 1966 and has been a regular on the show ever since. He never quite broke free of the "Girl On The Billboard"-type songs that made him famous, but he did try experimenting with pop styles and even appeared in a few B-grade movies (*Forty Acre Feud*, *Sam Whiskey*). By the '80s he had disappeared from the United Artists roster and had moved to a succession of smaller labels. He remains a regular on the *Opry*, however.

⊙ **His Greatest Hits** (1994; Razor & Tie). This focuses entirely on Reeves' United Artists work, beginning with "Girl On The Billboard," running through "Windshield" and the barroom weeper "A Dime At A Time," and finishing off with "But I Do." Not bad, but not earthshattering, either.

Jim Reeves

"Put your sweet lips a little closer to the phone, let's pretend that we're together all alone," crooned "Gentleman" Jim Reeves on his smash hit "He'll Have To Go," a song about a man pining for his distant lover now spending time with someone new. A classic example of Reeves' winning Nashville Sound style, it's a truly beautiful song that's at once sweet and sad, romantic and melancholy. It's also one of the classics of the countrypolitan era, and it made Reeves—a Texas farmboy-turned-velvet-voiced crooner—an international sensation.

Reeves, like Patsy Cline, garnered a massive cult audience almost immediately after his death in 1964. He was at the peak of his popularity, and for many years after his death continued to top the country charts. The huge appeal he amassed among pop as well as staunch country fans both during his lifetime and after is, frankly, still an amazing phenomenon.

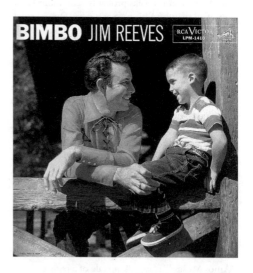

James Travis Reeves was born on 20 August, 1923 in Galloway, Texas and grew up loving music and baseball; his brief sports career, however, was cut short by an injury. During the '40s he began working as a DJ and announcer in east Texas. He occasionally played songs on the air, and in 1949 made some recordings for Macy's, a small honky-tonk label in Houston. In 1952 he was signed to

Del Reeves • Jim Reeves

Abbott, the label run by Fabor Robison that had also been home to both Johnny Horton and the Browns. Robison released more than three-dozen Reeves singles, including such memorable titles as the feisty "Red Eyed And Rowdy" and the silly "Beatin' On The Ding Dong." The songs as a whole are fairly straightforward honky tonk, much simpler than any of his later Nashville Sound recordings and definitely worth seeking out. "Mexican Joe" and "Bimbo", in particular, gained Reeves widespread attention from radio DJs and on the *Louisiana Hayride,* which he'd recently joined. Finally in 1955 Chet Atkins signed him to RCA.

Early RCA recordings like "Highway To Nowhere," "Waitin' For A Train" (the Jimmie Rodgers song), "According To My Heart," and Reeves' own "Yonder Comes A Sucker" retained a strong honky-tonk feeling with steel guitar and even prominent fiddles. The song that marked a turning point, however, was "Four Walls," a pop-country crossover hit in 1956 that made him a major Nashville star. By the late '50s he'd fully developed the slower-paced, lower-registered singing style that became his trademark. Further hits included "Blue Boy" and "Billy Bayou," and in 1959 he cut the song that became his signature, "He'll Have To Go," written by Joe Allison. From that point until his death, Reeves was a major recording and touring star.

The RCA album titles from the late '50s onward describe Reeves' pop sound perfectly: SONGS TO WARM THE HEART, THE INTIMATE JIM REEVES, A TOUCH OF VELVET. (Another one, TALL TALES AND SHORT TEMPERS, alluded to his notorious hot-headedness.) By this point Reeves sounded (and looked) more like Perry Como than Ernest Tubb, but somehow he still struck a chord with a huge portion of the country community, and fans continued to embrace him. His voice was smooth and creamy, the arrangements often quiet, cool, and moody—it felt more like late-night lounge music than anything hillbilly. Yet songs like "Throw Another Log On The Fire," Jimmy Work's "Making Believe," and Ned Miller's "Dark Moon" are absolutely beautiful.

Reeves developed a strong international following as well. He traveled to Europe frequently, charted regularly in the UK, and in 1962 toured South Africa. A year later he returned there to shoot the movie *Kimberly Jim,* which concerned a couple of gamblers and a diamond mine. Reeves was apparently quite popular in South Africa—so much that he cut an album entirely in Afrikaans, JY IS MY LIEFLING. His career, however, came to a tragic end when his private plane crashed (he was piloting it himself); he died on 31 July, 1964. His legacy lived on and prospered, however. In 1967 he was inducted into the Country Music Hall of Fame, and in 1969 the Academy of Country Music created the Jim Reeves Memorial Award, given annually to an artist who's contributed to country music's international recognition.

⊙ **Live At The Opry** (1987; Country Music Foundation). A great collection of Reeves performances from the *Grand Ole Opry* between 1953 (when he debuted on the show with "Mexican Joe") and 1960 that illustrates his transition from honky tonker to countrypolitan smoothie. It works for beginners as well as longtime fans; the song choices show a wide stylistic range, from "Yonder Comes A Sucker" to "Four Walls" and "He'll Have To Go," and the sound quality is consistently high.

⊙ **Four Walls—The Legend Begins** (1991; RCA). Collects 20 songs Reeves cut between 1953 and 1957 for Abbott and RCA, including "Bimbo," "Mexican Joe," "Am I Losing You," and "According To My Heart." This CD's more on the honky tonk side than the ESSENTIAL collection.

⊙ **Welcome To My World** (1994; Bear Family). The mother of all Bear Family box sets, this monster contains 16 CDs under one lid, plus the requisite bio-booklet and session details. Here you get every song Reeves recorded in his lifetime, from Macy's to Abbott to RCA, plus lots of previously unreleased demos and such, all presented with beautiful sound quality.

⊙ **The Essential Jim Reeves** (1995; RCA). A 20-track overview of Reeves' career, mostly culled from his later countrypolitan period. If you want smooth and creamy, this is the place to find it.

⊙ **Radio Days Vol. 1** (1998; Bear Family). A box set of radio transcriptions made for the *Country Music Time* program from the late '50s and early '60s.

Charlie Rich

"No matter what, Charlie Rich was going to tell you the truth."

—Sam Phillips

O ne of the finest voices in country music belonged to the late Charlie Rich, a versatile singer, songwriter and pianist who to this day has

Jim Reeves • Charlie Rich

never quite won the respect his talent cried out for and so rightly deserved. Critics have embraced his music, yes, but the general public still remembers him for his 1970s-era countrypolitan hits "Behind Closed Doors" and "The Most Beautiful Girl". Warm and tender as those songs remain—guilty pleasures, both of them, thanks mostly to Charlie's rich voice and soulful phrasing—they remain cheap and schmaltzy compared to the music he'd been making during the previous two decades.

Rich began his career in the '50s as a post-Elvis rockabilly artist, though he caught that musical whirlwind at the tail end of its heyday. But as much as he was capable of rocking out, blues and especially jazz were even more integral to his musical make-up—growing up he was a big fan of Stan Kenton, and also loved Miles Davis and Dave Brubeck. Rich really didn't get the freedom to indulge that side of his musical interests, at least on record, until the final years of his life. But that's not to say he was entirely stifled: during the first couple of decades of his recording career, he created a stunning and at-times brilliant mixture of musical styles that jumped back and forth (sometimes within the same song) between hopped-up rockabilly, late-night blues and jazz, crooner country, earthbound R&B, rich gospel, and honest-to-god soul.

Of any word that best describes his music, soul seems the most appropriate. "The material he does is very much his own personal brand of soul," wrote Peter Guralnick, "encompassing almost the entire spectrum of American popular music". As part of his 1971 book, *Feel Like Going Home*, Guralnick's essay on Charlie Rich is an unvarnished yet lovingly written and deeply moving read—as powerful as any profile of an American musician that's so far been written. Rich responded by titling a song after the book.

Rich was born on 14 December, 1932 in Colt, Arkansas, a small town not far from the Mississippi River and the city of Memphis. His family were Missionary Baptists, and he grew up in a strict religious environment, though one where gospel music was a regular presence. He played in a band while in the US Air Force during the early '50s, then worked as a farmer while also dabbling in supper club-style piano around Memphis. Sam Phillips signed him to Sun Records in 1957, but Rich worked initially as a songwriter and session pianist, never recording any solo sides for the label proper. Instead, he cut his first singles a year later for Phillips International, a Sun subsidiary. Only one

of them, the itchy and restless rocker "Lonely Weekends," dented the pop charts, but plenty more from this period—"Sittin' And Thinkin'," "Who Will The Next Fool Be," "Stay, Break Up"—are brimming with honest energy, vitality, and the kind of harmonic convergence (in a musical sense) that became his trademark.

For Rich, the mid-'60s offered a series of near-misses and dashed hopes—he tried over and over to gain a foothold in the industry, but never felt he was getting anywhere. At the same time, however, he created some truly thrilling music that burned with creative vitality. He signed with the RCA subsidiary, Groove, in 1963, and the label released such beefy, chewy fare as "Big Boss Man," "She Loved Everybody But Me," "Why, Oh Why," and "There Won't Be Anymore," all of which are among his finest work as both songwriter and song stylist. Other recordings, however, were buried in Nashville Sound overdubs. By 1965 Rich was on Mercury/Smash (which made him a labelmate of Jerry Lee Lewis), where he pushed even harder, working back and forth between songs that emphasized his raw boogie-woogie piano playing and others that showcased his soulful vocal work. The second notable hit of his career was the novelty number "Mohair Sam," but he failed to follow it up, and his career faltered. There were, however, plenty of standouts during his Smash years—a period Rich himself claimed was among the most satisfying of his career—as evidenced by "I Washed My Hands In Muddy Water," "Everything I Do Is Wrong," the soaring ballad "A Field Of Yellow Daisies "(written by his wife Margaret Ann), and the painful wail of "I Can't Go On".

Rich continued to work his mix of soul and country when he jumped to the Memphis label Hi; he cut some early compositions by Isaac Hayes and David Porter (including "When Something Is Wrong With My Baby"), as well as an album's worth of Hank Williams songs (CHARLIE RICH SINGS COUNTRY AND WESTERN) that had uptown, though nicely low-key arrangements. But it was his association with Epic Records and producer Billy Sherrill, which began in 1967, that turned Rich's talent into fame and made his name a household (and very bankable) word. It took five years for Sherrill's investment to pay off financially, but Rich's early Epic material is strong, sophisticated, and beautiful: the soothing "Nice And Easy," the mournful "San Francisco Is A Lonely Town," and the moving "Life Has Its Little Ups And Downs"—another Margaret Ann composition that's one of Charlie's finest, and most personally telling, recordings. The Epic material is marked by Sherrill's trademark lush production work, which sometimes drowns out Rich's finest assets (his piano playing, his soulful singing), but on the best numbers the songs and arrangements allow Rich's voice and fingers plenty of room to move.

Sherrill repackaged Rich as a straight-up country artist, which was a new persona for him, but it worked. In 1972, the Rich recording "I Take It On Home" made it to #6 on the *Billboard* country charts, and the tide began to turn. Six months later the gold came rushing in when "Behind Closed Doors" hit #1 and then became a major international smash—a song that spoke honestly of lust but never lost its sense of class, doing so with a melody that just about every housewife could hum. "The Most Beautiful Girl," another country smash, appeared a year later and was sweeter still. These and other silky-smooth hits from the mid-'70s ("A Very Special Love Song," a reconfigured "There Won't Be Anymore") put Rich in a whole new league: that of a pop-country crooner and hitmaking superstar. He was never quite comfortable in this new occupation, but played along as best he could. Nashville didn't exactly embrace Rich at first, either; when he landed the Male Vocalist of the Year award from the CMA in 1973, and a year later the coveted Entertainer of the Year, some *Opry* stalwarts figured him an inauthentic country artist—an outsider with a rock'n'roll background. Eventually, though, they came to acknowledge his musical (and personal) integrity.

As the decade progressed, Charlie's music fell deeper under the spell of Sherrill's sweeping productions, his powerful voice buried beneath string sections and background choruses. His personal problems, too, kept surfacing, most notably his drinking—a habit that had been nipping at his heels for many years. In 1975, while presenting the award for Entertainer of the Year during the televised CMA awards show, he opened the envelope, pulled out a lighter from his pocket, and set fire to the piece of paper as he announced the winner ("My good friend John Denver"). Its hard to know whether his moment of protest was motivated by booze, jet lag (he was supposedly exhausted from touring), or his increasing frustration with the pop directions not only of his own music, but country as a whole. He later apologized profusely, but in any case it was clear he'd reached saturation point.

Rich continued to chart regularly for the remainder of the decade, hitting #1 again with "Rollin' With The Flow" in 1977 and "On My Knees" in 1979 (a duet with Janie Fricke). He left Epic at the end of the '70s, and after moving to United Artists and then Elektra, his hit streak pretty much disappeared. He dropped into semi-retirement for the bulk of the '80s, choosing to stay at home in Memphis and to play music casually with friends. In the early '90s, he resurfaced with an excellent album on Sire, PICTURES AND PAINTINGS, which allowed him the freedom to indulge and explore his hard-to-categorize musical interests. Charlie's hitmaking days were well behind him and there were no industry pressures to hamper his creative energy. Sadly, the album was to be his swan song. He died on 25 July, 1995.

⊙ **The Fabulous Charlie Rich** (1969; Epic; reissued 1984; Koch). Rich's second Epic album (the first was SET ME FREE) collects some of his finest songs, including new and still-tight versions of the masterpieces "Sittin' And Thinkin'" and "Life Has Its Little Ups And Downs". The arrangements are not as raw as his earlier material, but the emotions are absolutely real.

⊙ **Pictures And Paintings** (1992; Sire). This is Rich's jazziest record by a long shot, though as is typical of nearly all his recordings, it's in no way a straightforward effort. Blues, country, gospel, and soul are important aspects of songs like "Don't Put No Headstone On My Grave," "Mood Indigo," "Feel Like Going Home," "Every Time You Touch Me (I Get High)". A mature, sturdy and beautiful record that stands among his finest work.

⊙ **Lonely Weekends: Best of the Sun Years** (1996; AVI). Rich wrote and first recorded many of his finest songs during his six-year association with Sun and

Charlie Rich

Phillips International. This compilation presents 25 of them in their original, undubbed form. Such Rich-penned songs as "Lonely Weekends," "Stay," "Sittin' And Thinkin'," "Who Will The Next Fool Be," "There Won't Be Anymore," and "Don't Put No Headstone On My Grave" are essential listening for anyone who gets chills and thrills when the worlds of country, soul, and rockabilly collide.

⊙ **Feel Like Going Home: The Essential Charlie Rich** (1997; Epic/Legacy). If you're looking for a neatly packaged overview of Rich's entire career, this is it. The 36 songs on 2 CDs begin with Sun-era singles like "Lonely Weekends" and "Who Will The Next Fool Be," and then move through a bunch of Groove, RCA, and Smash recordings before settling into and exploring Rich's long Epic association. The title song is included twice: once as it appeared on PICTURES AND PAINTINGS, the other a previously unreleased demo version (just Rich and his piano) that's this CD's crown jewel.

⊙ **Big Boss Man: The Groove Sessions** (1998; Koch/BMG). Contains 12 songs originally issued on the 1964 Groove album CHARLIE RICH, plus 5 bonus tracks. Nearly all were produced by Chet Atkins, and while his Nashville Sound touch is present, Charlie's soulful voice and fluid boogie-driven piano lines can't help but fly out of bounds. Songs like "Big Boss Man," "The Ways Of A Woman In Love," "She Loved Everybody But Me," and a surprisingly groovy "Ol' Man River" have a fire, funk, and spirit that no Nashville studio could fully contain.

Jeannie C. Riley

"I was ready to sock it to the entire world, which is what I did."

—Jeannie C. Riley

"Harper Valley P.T.A." was the smash hit that made Jeannie C. Riley an overnight sensation, and deservedly so: it's a hot piece of writing (by Tom T. Hall) that shot with a sly smile straight into the faces of conservative society, and Riley's voice had the right balance of small-town frustration, quick wit and sharp-tongued sass to make it work. Although she hadn't written the words, Riley really believed in what she was singing, making the song one of the most memorable, in any music genre, of the 1960s. In addition to putting its distributor, Plantation Records, on the Music Row map, the song was even made into a

film and TV series a decade later (both starring Barbara Eden). As for Riley, she was a very capable vocalist who enjoyed a chart career for several years afterwards, earning a place in country music as one of the strongest female voices at a time when Nashville was ripe for change.

Jeannie's beginnings were humble and her background deeply religious. She was born Jeanne Carolyn Stephenson on 19 October, 1945 in Anson, Texas. She married Mickey Riley while still a teenager, and the two moved to Nashville, where she found work as a secretary for songwriter Jerry Chesnut. After knocking on several record company doors, she finally landed a contract with Little Darlin', the independent label run by Aubrey Mayhew mostly as a vehicle for Johnny Paycheck (who was co-owner). The songs she cut didn't fly far, however (though the label eventually issued an album she recorded, SOCK SOUL). Riley's luck changed, however, when a demo of her voice found its way to Shelby Singleton. A one-time Mercury producer, Singleton was starting up his own Plantation label and looking for new talent. For his very first release, he matched a demo of a Tom T. Hall song he liked, "Harper Valley P.T.A.," to Riley's voice and suddenly had a massive hit on his hands. Released in 1968, it topped both the country and pop charts, sold millions of copies, and won both a Grammy and the CMA's Single of the Year award.

The song's lyrics centre on a woman, Mrs Johnson, who confronts a two-faced group of small-town P.T.A. mothers who've been talking trash about her behind her back. She does so in a mini-skirt, and so it made sense that this became Riley's look as well. At least, it made sense to her management team. As for Riley herself, she wasn't always comfortable with the sexy image, but she played along. She got to have her say musically, however, and several of her follow-up songs were equally sharp, tight, and radiating female frustration, including "The Girl Most Likely," "The Ballad Of Louise," and "The Back Side Of Dallas."

By the end of the '70s, Riley had decided to abandon the mini-skirts and Music Row manipulations to focus on her own gospel ministry. Her 1981 song "From Harper Valley To The Mountain Top" (and her autobiography of the same title) tells of her unhappiness with her pop stardom and her joy in renewing her faith.

⊙ **The Best Of Jeannie C. Riley** (1996; Varese Sarabande). The world wasn't always a pretty place in Riley's songs, as evidenced by the gritty and bitter "Back Side Of Dallas" (about a low-level prostitute), the tone of satisfied revenge in "The Girl Most Likely," and the frustrations of the lonely mistress in "Good Enough To Be Your Wife." Not to mention, of course, "Harper Valley P.T.A.," where hypocrisy is a daily ritual. These are Riley's best songs on this 15-song CD, but the nostalgic "Country Girl" and "There Never Was A Time" have an easygoing feel that's also appealing.

Connie Smith

The title of one of her mid-1960s albums, CUTE 'N' COUNTRY, doesn't really paint the full picture of this midwestern housewife-turned-Nashville star. With her sweet girl-next-door smile and long blonde hair, Smith was certainly attractive, but more importantly, she was a full-bodied vocalist and dynamic song stylist, and the evidence is clear in hits like "Once A Day," "Tiny Blue Transistor Radio," and "Cincinnati, Ohio" (three of a long list of songs penned by Bill Anderson, who jump-started Smith's professional career). These hits followed on the heels of Patsy Cline's massive success, just as women singers were beginning to get into their stride in the country mainstream. Smith's were definitely Nashville Sound recordings, but a prominent steel guitar and a firm voice gave the songs an edge that still feels sharp today.

Smith was born Constance June Meador on 14 August, 1941 in Indiana and raised in West Virginia and Ohio, where she began singing locally. She was already a happy housewife and mother by the time Anderson first heard her. With his help she was signed to RCA in 1964. "Once A Day," recorded during her first session, topped off at #1

and became one of the year's biggest songs; through the rest of the decade many more followed. Anderson wrote quite a few of her hits, but she also cut plenty of others by Dallas Frazier.

The pressures of the music business, however—touring, recording, promotion—led Smith to seek solace in both family life and, eventually, Christianity. She didn't give up her country career, but her popularity declined. She stayed with RCA until 1972 before switching to Columbia, for whom she cut the 1975 album CONNIE SMITH SINGS HANK WILLIAMS GOSPEL. After that she cut songs for Monument and, later, Epic. During the '90s she married neo-traditionalist country singer Marty Stuart. She's also remained a regular on the *Grand Ole Opry* since first joining in 1965.

⊙ **The Essential Connie Smith** (1996; RCA). A solid 20-song collection from Smith's 1960s and '70s tenure on RCA. "Once A Day," her self-penned "I'll Come Running," and Dallas Frazier's "If It Ain't Love (Let's Leave It Alone)" are great examples of her bold vocal style. The latter even has a fiddle running wild all over it, a rarity in Nashville at the time.

⊙ **Connie Smith** (1998; Warner Bros.). Smith co-wrote 9 of the 10 songs on this album, her first in years. Produced by Marty Stuart, it's solid fiddle-and-guitar country that's far gutsier than anything in the Garth-and-Reba mainstream.

Statler Brothers

Their popularity may have been overtaken by 'young country' fever during the 1990s, but for about a quarter-century before that the Statler Brothers were one of the most popular acts in country music. Songs like "Flowers On The Wall," "You Can't Have Your Kate And Edith, Too," "The Class Of '57," "How To Be A Country Star," and "Oh Baby Mine (I Get So Lonely)" were among their many hit songs spanning the mid-'60s through to the late '80s. They sang folk ("Billy Christian"), they sang country ("I Still Miss Someone"), they sang gospel ("How Great Thou Art"). Some songs were built around god-awful puns—"Edith," "Charlotte's Web," "We Got Paid By Cash" (meaning Johnny), and "Ruthless" (about losing a girlfriend named ... you get the picture)—while plenty more were mired in Baby Boomer nostalgia to the point of nausea ("Do You Remember These," "Child Of The Fifties,"

"Maple Street Memories"). On the whole, the Statlers' music was stuff your parents listened to—sort of an old-fashioned version of Alabama, and the kind that rock'n'roll was all about tearing apart. The fact can't be denied, however, that these four 'brothers' struck a chord with a huge number of fans craving a wholesome slice of Americana.

The group was originally formed as a gospel quartet, though one that also dabbled a little in country and pop music. Lew DeWitt, Philip Balsley, Harold Reid, and Joe McDorman began singing together in 1955 in their home town of Staunton, Virginia. In 1961 McDorman left and was replaced by Don Reid. They called themselves the Kingsmen at first, but because another group of the same name already existed (remember "Louie Louie"?), they became the Statler Brothers in 1964—a semi-serious moniker inspired by a popular brand of tissues. That same year they joined the road show of Johnny Cash, remaining with him into the early '70s. With Cash's support they landed a contract with Columbia, which released their first big hit "Flowers On The Wall." They cut several albums' worth of material for the label, but their barrage of hit songs wasn't fully unleashed until after they signed with Mercury in 1970. "Bed Of Rose's" made the Top 10 that year, after which the Statlers' singles kept on coming for two solid decades. Some were released under the name Lester "Roadhog" Moran and the Cadillac Cowboys, the Statler Brothers' hillbilly alter-ego.

In 1981, Lew DeWitt, whose health wasn't too good, quit the band; he died nine years later. His replacement was Jimmy Fortune, who was also a native of Virginia, although quite a bit younger than his new musical partners. With Fortune intact, the 'brothers' continued on their merry way. In 1991 they began hosting their own weekly variety show on TNN (The Nashville Network).

⊙ **Flowers On The Wall: The Essential Statler Brothers** (1996; Columbia/Legacy). This 18-track compilation covers the Statlers' years on Columbia during the 1960s. Hits like "Ruthless," "Kate And Edith," and the title track come alongside country standards such as "The Wreck Of The Old 97." Much of this early material has more of a folky, youthful vibe than their later Mercury recordings, showing off their strong vocal harmonies in a bare-bones manner that drifted away as their career progressed.

⊙ **A 30th Anniversary Celebration** (1994; Mercury). The Statlers are not for everybody—you'll either love and fully embrace their cute, catchy little melodies and safe-as-milk nostalgia, or you'll turn up your nose in disgust and go in search of some Aerosmith to get the bad taste out of your mouth. Blame it on the generation gap, but it's a sure bet that such wholesome fare as "The Class Of '57," "Whatever Happened To Randolph Scott" (a tribute to singing-cowboy era), "The Movies," "Child Of The Fifties," and "Maple Street Memories" aren't exactly geared toward the "young country" crowd. This 3-disc compilation includes a few Columbia singles but concentrates on the group's long Mercury association.

Mel Tillis

"Art is one thing, but you have to make a living."

—Mel Tillis

M el Tillis might be most famous for his stutter, which was the centerpoint of his downhome comic persona during his lifetime of concert and TV appearances, but as a singer he actually has a bold, clear (and completely unbroken) baritone voice. Tillis' most successful era was the 1970s, when he had a long string of Top 10 hits—including "I Ain't Never," "Good Woman Blues," and "Coca Cola Cowboy" (from the Clint Eastwood movie *Every Which Way But Loose*). He also won the Country Music Association's coveted Entertainer of the Year award in the same decade. But Tillis' career extended far beyond this period: he'd been recording since the late '50s, and continued to stay on the fringes of the country charts through the late '80s. And in addition to singing, he has built a strong reputation as a songwriter—which initially allowed him to establish a serious foothold in the music business during the late '50s. Along with fellow singer-songwriters from that period such as Willie Nelson, Roger Miller, Harlan Howard, and Bill Anderson, Tillis was part of a musical renaissance that helped pump new creative energy into Nashville at a time when homogeneity posed a very real threat.

Lonnie Melvin Tillis was born on 8 August, 1932 in Pahokee, Florida. His stutter developed during childhood, the result of a battle with malaria. After spending time in the US Air Force and working for the railroad, Tillis moved to Nashville to try his luck in the music business. His song, "I'm Tired", was a hit for Webb Piece in early 1957—followed by "Honky Tonk Song," "Tupelo County Jail," and others. Ray Price and Brenda Lee also charted with his material during this period. Tillis signed his own contract with Columbia in the late '50s, and over the next several years scored a few modest hits, including duets with Bill Phillips ("Sawmill") and Pierce ("How Come Your Dog Don't Bite Nobody But Me"). Other standouts from his Columbia days include "The Brooklyn Bridge," "Loco Weed," and "Walk On, Boy"—all worth tracking down.

During the mid-'60s Tillis switched to Kapp, and he cranked out an abundance of song material for his new label. Like his Columbia recordings, quite a few were strong—"Stateside" (which provided his band name, the Statesiders), "Let Me Talk To You," "All Right (I'll Sign The Papers)," and "Life Turned Her That Way" (which in 1988 climbed to #1 for Ricky Van Shelton)—though he had yet to achieve a breakthrough hit. If his day as star singer hadn't quite arrived, his songs still made headlines, thanks to the likes of Bobby Bare ("Detroit City"), Waylon Jennings ("Mental Revenge"), Charley Pride ("The Snakes Crawl At Night"), and Kenny Rogers and the First Edition ("Ruby, Don't Take Your Love To Town").

Tillis finally reached the Top 10 in 1969 with "Who's Julia". After that, the hits came one after another: "Heart Over Mind," "Commercial Affection," "Sawmill," "Midnight," "Me And The Blues," "Stomp Them Grapes," "Memory Maker," etc. He earned his first #1 in 1972 with "I Ain't Never," a big, burly, and thoroughly catchy number that had been a hit for Webb Pierce in 1959. Tillis cut most of the above titles for MGM, his label during the first half of the '70s. After that he jumped to MCA and then to Elektra and had further chart-topping success with "Heart Healer," "I Believe In You," "Coca Cola Cowboy," and "Southern Rains". Many of his '70s hits (most notably the MGM recordings) were based on sturdy honky-tonk traditions, though others took on more pop-oriented qualities that coincided with the glitzier trends of the era. This was, after all, the heyday of Kenny Rogers, Ronnie Milsap, and Barbara Mandrell.

In 1976, Tillis won the Entertainer of the Year award and was also inducted into the Nashville Songwriters Hall of Fame. By the '80s, however, although he continued to chart throughout the decade, his creative steam was on the wane. A curious 1981 duet album with Nancy Sinatra, for instance, was nothing special. By this stage, however, Tillis had built up an impressive financial empire, much of it as a result of investment in music-publishing companies (Sawgrass and Cedarwood, among others). He later wrote his autobiography (*Stutterin' Boy*) and built a theater

Mel Tillis

in Branson, Missouri, where he continues to perform. In 1998 he teamed up with Jerry Reed, Waylon Jennings, Bobby Bare, and songwriter Shel Silverstein for the collaborative album OLD DOGS. And the Tillis family legacy continues: his daughter, Pam Tillis, became a leading country artist in her own right during the '90s.

⊙ **The Memory Maker** (1995; Mercury/PolyGram). This 13-song collection highlights Tillis' MGM period, and not only is it easily the best hits collection of his work on the market, it's a thrill of a listen, top to bottom. Includes such substantial titles as "I Ain't Never," "Neon Rose," "Brand New Mister Me," "Midnight," "Me And The Blues," "Sawmill," and "Mental Revenge," all of them among his best-known songs—and for very good reason. The CD is part of Mercury's respectable American Essentials series.

Conway Twitty

"Women are special to most men, I think. They are to me. Men make most of the mistakes, in my opinion."

—Conway Twitty

Until his death in 1993, Conway Twitty had one of the longest and steadiest hit-making streaks of any country singer. During a career that ran from his mid-1950s days as a teenage rock'n'roll idol ("It's Only Make Believe" remained a life-long signature song) right into the '90s, he racked up a huge and steady number of Top 10 hits on both the pop and country charts. He earned forty *Billboard* country #1s alone, the most of any single artist (Merle Haggard is a close second). Where many country stars of his stature faded from the spotlight after a substantial run, Twitty's popularity continued to endure. Practically no other country star can claim such longevity.

Part of Twitty's secret was that he maintained an image of a citizen singer who gave his all for the fans—touring constantly and signing autographs. Always a keen businessman, he scoped his market carefully—conservative, yes, but with the sexual revolution heating America's nether regions, there were plenty of unspoken desires, too. These "forbidden places" Conway reached with his delicately dirty songs, showing that a world of fiery passion could and did exist beneath a veneer of southern respectability. His music was about love,

he would say—and he knew exactly how far he could push it. During the '50s he'd perfected a kinky, low-register growl in his voice that made his fans quiver. As the years rolled on, a repertoire of sensual song material emerged and, while never crude, it was just slippery enough to work its way under the skirts of Middle America. Titles like "You've Never Been This Far Before," "(I Can't Believe) She Gives It All To Me," "I'd Love To Lay You Down," and "I've Already Loved You In My Mind" aren't exactly subtle, but performed Conway-style they carry more than a touch of gentlemanly class.

Taken as a whole, Twitty's style can come off a bit bland. Yet at his core he was a pure country traditionalist, and a surprising number of his recordings—"Next In Line," "Fifteen Years Ago," "You've Never Been This Far Before"—are driven by a deep-welled honky-tonk energy. The best of all is "Play, Guitar, Play," which, built lyrically around a dark secret that's never revealed, burns with mystery and intrigue. It doesn't matter that the facts of the story remain elusive, because the tension and the shame in the singer's voice, and in the thick guitar riffs and chunky rhythm, are all that's needed.

The Twitty legacy began on 1 September, 1933 in Friars Point, Mississippi, with the birth of one Harold Lloyd Jenkins. As a child Harold listened every Saturday night to the *Grand Ole Opry*, and he also picked up some musical instruction from a black blues singer who lived next door. By the age of twelve he had his own radio show in Helena, Arkansas, where his family had settled. He was also seriously interested in baseball, but getting drafted into the Army halted his sports career. After

completing his service he decided he was more keen on pursuing music. Elvis Presley had captivated him, and in 1956 he cut a handful of sides for Sun Records. None was released, although one of them, "Rock House," was cut by Roy Orbison. Around this same time he adopted his stage name, derived from two nearby towns: Conway, Arkansas and Twitty, Texas. He cut a few wild-haired rockabilly songs for Mercury Records before settling at MGM, who released his massive hit single "It's Only Make Believe" in 1958. By this stage rockabilly had dissipated, but the single and other teen-idol numbers did have an obvious Presley influence; it also showed off Twitty's trademark growl and his penchant for melodrama, building slowly and steadily to a roaring climactic refrain. Stardom now in place, he cut lots more material for MGM and began appearing in rock'n'roll movies like *Platinum High School* and *Sex Kittens Go To College.*

Not exactly suited in temperament to rock music, Twitty eventually shifted to country. He'd included country songs in his repertoire and even written some himself; when Nashville songwriter Harlan Howard heard these, he brought Twitty into Rick Hall's studio in Muscle Shoals, Alabama, and had him cut a number of country demos. In 1963 Ray Price had a hit with one of them, "Walk Me To The Door." A year later Twitty made his escape from rock and pop music, deciding for good that country would be his future. Through Howard's help he was signed to Decca (soon to be known as MCA). It took a few years, but by the late '60s his country hit-making streak was off and running with "The Image Of Me," "The Next In Line," and "Fifteen Years Ago." These and other songs from this period are among the hardest, most honky-tonking of his career. His country stardom was sealed in 1970 with the recording of "Hello Darlin'," a song he'd written ten years previously. Over the next couple of decades, until his death, his name was never far from the charts. He also frequently cut duets with Loretta Lynn, the pair earning several #1 hits, as well as being nominated Vocal Duo of the Year by the CMA four times in a row.

Twitty maintained a control over the business side of his career few in country music (at least this side of Kenny Rogers and Garth Brooks) have ever managed. The empire of Conway and his Twitty Enterprises grew to include three song publishing companies, a chain of Twitty Burger restaurants, a resort in the Cayman Islands, and even the Nashville Sounds baseball team. And, of course, there was Twitty City, his personal residence-turned-tourist attraction, opened in 1982 in Hendersonville, Tennessee. It's since been bought out by a religious company—though a small shrine to Conway is maintained in the garden out back.

The secret of Conway's success lies in the fact that he hit upon a formula and stuck to it, which worked wonders for him at a time (the '70s) when Nashville was turning from the 'old-fashioned' sounds of Kitty Wells and Webb Pierce to the flash and glitter of Kenny Rogers and Barbara Mandrell. His appearance only changed a few times: when he switched from the pompadoured rock'n'roll idol to country singer in the mid-'60s, and a decade later when he dropped the slicked-back conservative hairstyle in favor of the 'modern' look of a god-awful perm. Whatever his motivation, though, it seemed to work, as his hits kept coming throughout the '80s (during which time he switched briefly to Warner Brothers, then back to MCA) and even into the '90s. On 4 June, 1993, after having just played a show at the Jim Stafford Theatre in Branson, Missouri, Conway collapsed on his tour bus from an abdominal aneurysm. He died the next day. The previous month he'd cut his final recording, "Rainy Night In Georgia," with Sam Moore (of Sam & Dave) for the RHYTHM COUNTRY AND BLUES album—a surprisingly soulful collection of duets on which the Twitty/Moore track is a standout.

⊙ **Silver Anniversary Collection** (1990; MCA). A single-CD hits collection that contains more than enough of Twitty's country material from the 1965 honky tonker "Guess My Eyes Were Bigger Than My

Conway Twitty

Heart" through to 1989's "She's Got A Single Thing In Mind"—though the exclusion of "Play, Guitar, Play" is a glaring mistake.

⊙ **Rockin' Conway: The MGM Years** (1993; PolyGram). Despite a meager 10 songs, and none of them true rockabilly, this set's still interesting. Alongside "Make Believe" it includes the sassy "Is A Blue Bird Blue" by Memphis soul man Dan Penn and "Lonely Blue Boy," which playfully shows off Twitty's trademark growl.

⊙ **The Conway Twitty Collection** (1994; MCA). A massive, at-times relentless 4-CD collection of Conway hit after Conway hit. The first disc, though, should be repackaged by itself, as it's a fantastic and quite succinct picture of Conway's journey from childhood days (a radio recording of "Cry Baby Heart"), through his rock'n'roll years ("Make Believe"), and on into his country heyday ("Hello Darlin'," "Fifteen Years Ago"). Along the way are some nice rarities, including the Sun recording "Rock House" and one of his demos produced by Harlan Howard, "Walk Me To The Door."

⊙ **Rock 'N' Roll Years** (1997; Bear Family). An impressive 8-CD set of all Conway's rock and pop recordings from the 1950s through the '60s, quite a few of them unreleased.

Porter Wagoner

The Thin Man from West Plains, Porter Wagoner, is probably more remembered as a TV star, *Grand Ole Opry* statesman, and the man who gave Dolly Parton her big break than he is as an innovative country recording artist and songwriter in his own right. The truth is, this Ozark Mountains native was a hitmaker from way back in the mid-1950s, when he first signed to RCA Victor, and his large repertoire has always been packed with such superb honky-tonk songs as "A Satisfied Mind," "Misery Loves Company," "Sorrow On The Rocks," and the cocky "Trademark" (one of his earliest compositions). He dressed in outlandish and wildly colorful Nudie suits, his blonde hair combed back in a puffy pompadour, but much of his music retained a well-grounded, hard-country feel.

And speaking of outlandish, during the '60s and '70s Wagoner concocted some of the most amazing story-songs of the period (with a series of eye-catching album covers to go with them),

including "The Cold Hard Facts Of Life," "Skid Row Joe," and the glorious "Rubber Room." Porter might protest, but many would cite the last song as among his crowning achievements; it's as off-the-wall as anything cut by a major country artist to date, a mindblower that simply has to be heard to be believed (you'll find it on the 1972 album WHAT AIN'T TO BE, JUST MIGHT HAPPEN).

Wagoner was born on 12 August, 1927 in Howell County, Missouri, and later moved with his family to the town of West Plains. He formed a bluegrass band during the '40s, and began his professional career broadcasting over a West Plains station out of a local butcher shop. He was hired in 1951 to appear on a Springfield, Missouri station, and a year later began his long recording association with RCA. His own records didn't sell right away, but "Trademark" became a big hit for Carl Smith in 1953. A year later Porter broke the Top 10 with the downhome and curiously eager ditty "Company's Comin'," and in 1955 he had his first #1 with "A Satisfied Mind," a classic country number written by Red Hayes. Porter played regularly on the popular TV show *Ozark Jubilee*, which was based out of Springfield, but in 1956 he made the move to Nashville. He joined the cast of the *Grand Ole Opry* in 1957, and that program has remained a huge part of his identity ever since.

The Porter Wagoner Show, which went on the air in 1960, was widely syndicated and became one of the decade's most popular music television programs. It mixed rural (and often cornball) humor with old-fashioned ads for medicinal products and

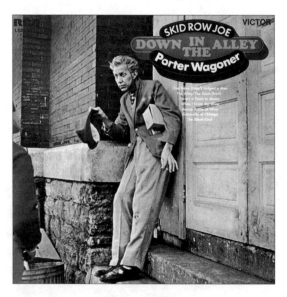

doses of hard-country music. The program show-cased not only Porter's music but also that of his associates, including comedian and fiddler Curly Harris and Porter's "gal singer" sidekicks Norma Jean and, later, Dolly Parton. The exposure on Porter's show helped launch the solo careers of both women. Parton came as close to a full-on partner with Wagoner as anyone, remaining on the program and as part of his touring show from 1967–75. Together they recorded a strong series of duet albums, many featuring Parton's compositions and Wagoner's arrangements. When Parton eventually left to pursue her a solo career—which included a jump into pop music—Porter was hurt and angry, to say the least, and legal action was even taken (their differences have since been resolved). It's no wonder, as by this point (the mid-'70s) Porter's brand of traditional country was long out of fashion and Parton's peppier and more youthful style showed a lot more staying power. Judging from the pop-oriented climate in Nashville at the time, it's very probable that Porter's solo career wouldn't have been as strong, and as long lasting, without Dolly's presence.

Throughout the '60s, Porter's own recordings remained fairly faithful to a solid-based honky-tonk style. Elements of the Nashville Sound did creep into his songs, but they never overwhelmed the proceedings, and most albums from this period are well worth a listen. Aside from his Dolly duets, Porter was also a regular presence in the *Billboard* charts as a solo artist throughout the '60s and into the mid-'70s. His hit titles included as "I've Enjoyed As Much Of This As I Can Stand," "Sorrow On The Rocks," "Cold Dark Waters," "Green, Green Grass Of Home," "The Cold Hard Facts Of Life," "The Carroll County Accident," and "Katy Did." He also helped create a series of

carefully crafted album covers that illustrated some of these specific songs and themes, and one of them, CONFESSIONS OF A BROKEN MAN, even won a Grammy for Best Album Cover in 1966.

Porter continued to be a visible country music presence after Dolly's departure, but during the mid-'80s he more or less retired from active recording and performing. His TV show finally went dark in 1981, and his last Top 40 hit, "This Cowboy's Hat," came in 1983. But that's not to say he entirely disappeared. In the '90s he co-hosted the pre-*Opry* TV show *Opry Backstage* with Bill Anderson, and he now enjoys the status as one of the *Opry*'s, and country music's, elder statesmen. He hasn't made it into the Country Music Hall of Fame as of this writing, but his induction is almost certainly on the horizon.

☉ **In Person** (1964; RCA; reissued 1998; Koch). This is a live album compiling songs Wagoner played over a two-night engagement in his old hometown of West Plains. It captures the spirit and style of live country music at the time, complete with between-song banter, comedy, and instrumental breaks along with titles like "Misery Loves Company," "Talk Back Trembling Lips," and "Foggy Mountain Top."

☉ **The Thin Man From West Plains** (1993; Bear Family). This solid four-CD box set covers Wagoner's early RCA recordings made between 1952–62. It's not the place to find greats like "The Cold Hard Facts Of Life" and "Rubber Room," but it is the place to look for his stone-straight (and sometimes cornball) country songs like "Headin' For A Weddin'," "Company's Comin'," "Eat Drink And Be Merry," "An Angel Made Of Ice," and "What Would You Do? (If Jesus Came To Your House)."

⊙ **The Essential Porter Wagoner And Dolly Parton** (1996; RCA). The focus here is on the duo's Top 10 hits, which isn't a bad way to go, as songs like "The Last Thing on My Mind" and "If Teardrops Were Pennies" are fine pieces of work indeed.

⊙ **The Essential Porter Wagoner** (1997; RCA). A straightforward 20-song retrospective of Porter's hit studio recordings from the '50s through to the mid-'70s. The major bases are mostly covered—titles like "A Satisfied Mind," "Company's Comin'," "Misery Loves Company," "Sorrow On The Rocks," "Skid Row Joe," "Green, Green Grass," "The Cold Hard Facts," and "Carroll County Accident". "Rubber Room" doesn't appear, however.

Wilburn Brothers

Teddy and Doyle Wilburn were a successful brother act whose heyday as recording stars lasted from the 1950s through to the early '70s. Their music was based on the close-harmony style of the Delmore Brothers, and during the '60s they helped bring the close-harmony sound into the modern era. To their credit, they pretty well managed to keep the traditional country sound of their earlier years alive on both their hit recordings and on their popular television program, *The Wilburn Brothers Show*.

The brothers were born a year apart in Hardy, Arkansas—Virgil Doyle in 1930 and Thurman Theodore in 1931. As children they sang with the Wilburn Family group (which also included their siblings Lester, Leslie, and Geraldine), even making an appearance on the *Grand Ole Opry*. They cut records for Four Star during the '40s, and by the end of the decade the four brothers were regulars on the *Lousiana Hayride*. There they met a then-unknown Webb Pierce; they gave his career a boost early on, and he in turn hired Doyle and Teddy to back him up on his first Decca session. In 1951 the two brothers were drafted, and after their service they began performing as a duo. They toured with Pierce, and in 1954 they landed their own Decca contract recording "Sparkling Brown Eyes" that year, a collaboration with Pierce that made it to #4 on the country charts.

The Wilburn Brothers joined the *Grand Ole Opry* in 1956, and for the next several years scored hits with songs like "I'm So In Love With You," "I Wanna Wanna Wanna," "Hey Mr Bluebird" (a duet with Ernest Tubb), "A Woman's Intu-

ition," and "Trouble's Back In Town." By the '60s they ventured into the business side of the music world setting up the publishing company Sure Fire and the booking agency Wil-Helm. They were instrumental in getting Loretta Lynn's career off the ground, first by signing her to Sure Fire and then by negotiating a recording contract for her with Decca. She also regularly performed with them on the road and on their television show, which first went on air in 1963.

Teddy and Doyle remained in the country charts through to the end of the '60s, and their biggest hits came during this decade, including "Roll Muddy River," "It's Another World," "Someone Before Me," and "Hurt Her Once For Me." Much of the time their arrangements remained simple and quiet, and their harmonies were still always the centerpoint of their recordings. Some songs, however, were filled out with steel guitar, piano flourishes, and the occasional background chorus (their 1961 album CITY LIMITS, for instance, was marketed as "Country Songs City Style"). To their credit, they never got entirely bogged down by the Nashville Sound; '60s recordings such as "Goody Goody Gumdrop" (which sounds sillier than it really is), "Blues Plus Booze (Means I Lose)," and "Santa Fe Rolls Royce" (about the joys of traveling by boxcar) showed how they'd chosen instead to develop a lively honky-tonk sound that was sharp, catchy, and bright. The brothers' hits tapered off during the '70s. Doyle died on 16 October, 1982; Teddy has since played the *Opry* on his own from time to time.

⊙ **Wilburn Brothers** (1998; Edsel). An 18-song British-issue CD bringing together many of their 1950s and '60s hit songs. Titles include "Sparkling Brown Eyes," "I Wanna Wanna Wanna," "Hey Mr Bluebird," "The Knoxville Girl," "Roll Muddy River," and "Hurt Her Once For Me."

Tammy Wynette

"All I was saying in the song was be understanding. Be supportive."

—Tammy Wynette

It would be difficult to picture Tammy Wynette without humming at least a few bars of "Stand By Your Man" in your head. Indeed, you can hardly talk about country music at all without that

Putting women's views into song: Tammy Wynette

song at least crossing your mind. Written by pro-ducer Billy Sherill (with help from Tammy herself) and turned into a worldwide country and pop sen-sation in 1968, it remains one of country music's strongest ballads—a song that arrived during the height of women's-lib fever and three decades later was still eliciting hot opinions as to just how fem-inist, or not, Wynette's (and Sherrill's) intentions actually were. Just ask Hillary Clinton, who caused a minor ruckus when she referenced the song during her husband's presidential campaign in 1992. "I'm not sitting here like some little woman baking cookies, standing by my man like Tammy Wynette," she fired off. Wynette wasn't pleased, of course, and Hillary later apologized.

Although "Stand By Your Man" remained Wynette's signature song throughout her career, it was just one of many hit songs from the mid-'60s onward that propelled this one-time hair-dresser into the country music pantheon. Like her contemporaries Dolly Parton and Loretta Lynn, Wynette created a solid female perspective on country radio that the listening public badly craved

(as record sales and chart figures quickly proved). In addition to "Stand By Your Man," she sang further songs urging support and forgiveness through troublesome times such as "I'll See Him Through," "He's Still My Man," and "Run, Woman, Run" (back to that man). But when the end of the road was reached, she also spoke plainly of the hard issues facing many modern-day couples—the most famous being "D-I-V-O-R-C-E," and we all know what that spells.

Frequently painted as the forgiving kind, Tammy could also be defiant—in "Your Good Girl's Gonna Go Bad," she announces her intention to hit the same bars as her philandering fellow; in "Sally Trash," she tells the man who can't appreciate a good thing at home to go back to his floozie and stop wasting her time. On the other side of the emotional coin, she wasn't afraid to get tender when the time was right ("He Loves Me All The Way"). But it was the vast and rocky worlds of romantic and domestic difficulties that were the regular, and favorite, song subjects for many of her fans. She returned to them again and again in the Grammy-winning "I Don't Wanna Play House," the deceptively quaint "Kids Say The Darndest Things," and others, which like most of her songs she rendered with that famous "teardrop" in her voice—as if each word, each breath, was going to break her up, start the waterworks flowing, and stop the show. Her style was melodramatic, yes, but underneath the goop ran a vein of unfettered emotional sincerity. It was a rare balance that few singers have ever achieved.

Tammy was born Virginia Wynette Pugh on 5 May, 1942 in rural Itawamba County, Mississippi to a sharecropping family. Her father died when she was only a year old, and her mother worked in a defense plant during World War II, leaving Tammy mostly in the care of her grandparents. As a child she worked in the cotton fields, but she also developed a love for music, especially gospel. In 1959 she married Euple Byrd, and to help make ends meet, went to beauticians' school. This meant that after their divorce she had a career to fall back on—though she still dreamed of being a singer, which she'd dabbled in while living in Memphis. In 1966 she moved to Nashville to pursue this dream, and her life soon began turning around.

Billy Sherrill was fast on the rise in Nashville during the mid-'60s, having recently produced several hits for David Houston including his nine-week #1 "Almost Persuaded." After moving to town, Wynette went to Sherrill's office to try pitching him some songs, and before she knew it she had a recording contract. Her first hit was a modest one, the somber "Apartment #9," written by Johnny Paycheck and Bobby Austin. But the sassy "You're Good Girl's Gonna Go Bad," released in the spring of 1967, shot all the way to the country Top 5. It set the tone for Tammy Wynette (her new stage name) as a woman who was going to tell it like it was. Ironically, Tammy was shy about her newfound fame—and was nowhere near as boisterous as Patsy Cline, for instance, or even as self-confident as Dolly Parton. That same vulnerability comes through in her songs, and it's part of what gives the emotions she was conveying such a genuine foundation.

After "Good Girl," Tammy's hit streak was unleashed and roaring. For the next decade, her name regularly made the top of the country charts, thanks to songs like "I Don't Wanna Play House," "My Elusive Dreams" (a duet with David Houston), "Stand By Your Man," "The Ways To Love A Man," "He Loves Me All The Way," and "Kids Say The Darndest Things." She won her first Grammy in 1967 for "I Don't Wanna Play

House," and beginning in 1968 she won the CMA's Female Vocalist of the Year three times in a row.

She was well on her way to earning her moniker as the "First Lady of Country Music" by this time, but that name really came about after she married the "President"—singer George Jones, in 1969, a man she had idolized for years. They sang such fetching duets as "We Go Together," "Take Me," "Golden Ring," and "We're Gonna Hold On," looking all the while like they were a match made in hillbilly heaven. It wasn't long, however, before the marital troubles began (George's drinking being one serious contributor). In 1975, Tammy was again singing "I Don't Wanna Play House," only this time to a divorce court. She married twice more before the decade was over, her final (and fifth) marriage was to songwriter-producer George Richey.

Wynette appeared here and there on the *Billboard* charts during the '80s with songs like "Cowboys Don't Shoot Straight (Like They Used To)," "Sometimes When We Touch" (a 1985 duet with Mark Gray), "Your Love," and "Beneath A Painted Sky." In 1992 she collaborated with the British dance-pop group KLF on the hit "Justified And Ancient," and in 1995 she rejoined her former husband and singing partner, George Jones, for the duet album ONE. Despite battles with illness that plagued her much of her life, she continued to tour on a regular basis. On 6 April, 1998, however, at only fifty-five years old, she died. An all-star memorial tribute was held at the Ryman Auditorium in her honor, and later that year she was inducted into the Country Music Hall of Fame. Asylum Records also released the tribute album TAMMY WYNETTE ... REMEMBERED featuring versions of her famous songs by the likes of Elton John, Melissa Etheridge, Emmylou Harris, Trisha Yearwood, and Brian Wilson.

⊙ **D-I-V-O-R-C-E** (1968; Epic; reissued 1997; Koch). Written by Curley Putman and Bobby Braddock, the title track of this early Tammy album (her third) is as tear-jerking as any country song before or since. It approaches parody, but stops just short thanks to the sincerity of Tammy's quivering voice. Most of the remaining ten songs are standard 1960s-era titles like "Honey," "Gentle On My Mind," "Yesterday," and "Lonely Street."

⊙ **Stand By Your Man** (1969; Epic; reissued 1999; Columbia/Legacy). This album was recorded not long after the success of D-I-V-O-R-C-E. The title track is the obvious standout, though further songs like

Tammy Wynette

"Joey" (written by her second, Don Chapel) and the Patsy Cline-ish "It Keeps Slipping My Mind" aren't shabby, either. This most recent CD version (Koch had re-released the album only two years earlier) includes two previously unreleased tracks from the same era, "I'm Only A Woman" and "There's Quite A Difference."

⊙ **Anniversary: 20 Years Of Hits** (1987; Sony). For the most part, Tammy's big hits remain her most visceral recordings, and to collect them in one place makes sense. Look to this 20-song disc for "D-I-V-O-R-C-E," "Stand By Your Man," "House," "Good Girl," "Kids Say The Darndest Things," "Run, Woman, Run," the Paycheck-Austin composition "Apartment #9," and a couple of duets with George Jones.

⊙ **Tears Of Fire: The 25th Anniversary Collection** (1992; Sony). For the serious Tammy fan, this 3-disc, 67-song box set is the place to start digging into her massive output. It stretches from the classic early hits to '80s and '90s duets with Vince Gill, Ricky Skaggs, Randy Travis, and the pop group KLF.

Tammy Wynette

9

Dreaming My Dreams:
The Outlaws Hit Town

The Nashville Sound was certainly revolutionary, broadening the country music audience beyond all expectation and creating a stable, reliable method of making hit records. 'Stable', however, became confused with 'formulaic' somewhere along the line, so that by the late 1960s and '70s much of what came out of Nashville suffered a dearth of creative inspiration. Some country singers like Loretta Lynn and George Jones were strong enough individualists to overcome any shortcomings in the recording process; and Merle Haggard and Buck Owens recorded (mostly) on the West Coast, where things were run a bit differently. The vast majority of country artists, however, were suffering the effects of an assembly line studio system. Streamlined production: that's what the Nashville Sound was all about—technical sophistication combined with cost-cutting efficiency. The result was a steady number of respectable hit songs that came in under budget, but for anyone with a burn in their soul and a touch of rambling fever, Nashville studios were hardly the environment to spark creative fires. "Are You Sure Hank Done It This Way?" belted **Waylon Jennings** in 1975, voicing frustrations that countless songwriters, singers, and pickers had most certainly wanted to express for years.

Much of the power in this Nashville Sound system lay in the hands of the producers. They picked the songs, assigned the session musicians, and lorded over the album's final mix. All a singer really needed to bring to a session was his or her

voice. And so it was really rather revolutionary when, instead of being told what to do and how to play, artists like Waylon Jennings, **Bobby Bare**, and **Willie Nelson** (each of them established and respected Nashville artists with hit songs dotting their resumes) decided it was high time *they* got to choose their own songs and play them their own way. On top of that, they insisted they should be allowed to use their road bands in the studio. Not that they didn't respect the technical prowess of the Nashville session men, it just seemed to make far greater sense to use pickers with whom they worked all year long on the road.

Terrified of causing offence, and frightened of losing the record-making formula that had proven so effective, the establishment had always been reluctant to change. But when singers like Jennings, Bare, and Nelson began producing their own records, it soon became clear that change, at least for these particular artists, was not such a bad thing after all. These artists possessed a certain ribald energy the stiff-collared industry lacked, and the proof was in their accelerating record sales. The 1976 concept album WANTED! THE OUTLAWS (featuring songs by Jennings, Nelson, **Tompall Glaser**, and **Jessi Colter**) became the first country album to officially sell a million copies. Suddenly, ironically—and perhaps inevitably—the Outlaw underground was emerging as the new mainstream, and both Nelson and Jennings were elevated to the status of bona fide country music superstars. In 1979 Nelson even won the CMA's prestigious Entertainer of the Year award.

Ladies Love Outlaws

The term 'Outlaw' more or less originated with a song by Lee Clayton, "Ladies Love Outlaws," that served as the title track of a 1972 Waylon album. Hazel Smith, publicist at Glaser Studios—a Nashville recording studio and all-around hangout spot run by Tompall, Jim, and Chuck Glaser that was better known as Hillbilly Central—began throwing 'Outlaw' around to describe the music of Jennings and Glaser. 'Country rock' and 'progressive country' were also in circulation, but when hip radio DJs and journalists picked up on the catchy Outlaw tag ("In Defense Of The Telecaster Cowboy Outlaws" was the title of one influential piece by Dave Hickey, published in *Country Music* magazine in 1974), it was as good as set in stone.

No matter how long Willie's hair grew, no matter how much turquoise jewellery and leather Waylon took to wearing, or how rowdily some of their hangers-on might have behaved on the tail end of a three-day drunken binge, the true objective of the Outlaw movement was creative control for the artists in the recording studio. And perhaps surprisingly for some, the kind of country they chose to play was often relaxed and spare, and it was firmly rooted in a hillbilly tradition. Jennings' albums mixed acoustic and steel guitars, a deep and steady rhythm, and his own full-bodied voice, which just happened to be one of the finest in the business. He wrote many songs himself, the rest coming from a mix of established writers (Roger Miller, Harlan Howard) and newcomers like **Billy Joe Shaver**, **Steve Young**, Bob McDill, and Billy Ray Reynolds. True, Waylon liked a steady bass beat, the odd Rolling Stones or Allman Brothers song, and an electric Telecaster sound that wasn't afraid to get scratchy, but what stood out most of all was how close to the earth the music remained. His rendition of Young's "Lonesome, On'ry And Mean" (something of a theme song for the new generation) had a rugged energy that had been sorely missing from country for far too long, while others (Mickey Newbury's "Frisco Depot," Dee Moeller's "Slow Movin' Outlaw") were dead-on somber and almost jarringly quiet.

Where the Nashville Sound had been directed at adults who couldn't understand rockabilly (or didn't care to), Outlaw music proved that country could appeal to young people once again—and do so without frightening off the older fans. Despite their ragged lifestyles and rock'n'roll associations, they retained an honest love and reverence for country music and its heritage. It showed in their music far more clearly than it did in the songs of, say, Olivia Newton-John, Dave And Sugar, or Kenny Rogers, who during the '70s came to represent a glitzier and more pop-oriented side of the Nashville fence.

While singers like Jennings, Nelson, Glaser, and **Kris Kristofferson** were friends, they and other so-called Outlaws weren't exactly an organized collective scheming to undermine the Nashville establishment. There was no Outlaw Manifesto, no book of rules, no elected leadership. "The only thing most of these guys have in common," wrote Hickey, "is that they were born on the west side of the Mississippi and often forget to go watery in the knees at the mention of Jeff Davis." (For those who don't remember their US history, Jefferson Davis was President of the Confederate States of America during the Civil War.) Still, by the mid-'70s a sizeable community of singers, songwriters, pickers, and assorted hangers-on had gathered in their wake.

The Songwriters

The creative control issue is the cornerstone of the Outlaw movement, but the roots of this fundamental change—and the air of freedom, independence and personal expression that came with it—go back to the late '50s and early '60s, when Nashville was building its now-strong community of songwriters. As publishing houses like Acuff-Rose, Cedarwood, and Tree cropped up to supply songs for the burgeoning studio system, songwriters who'd rolled into town on a whim and a dream suddenly found themselves with steady work. Harlan Howard, Dallas Frazier, Willie Nelson, Hank Cochran, and Mel Tillis were among the first wave, with Mickey Newbury, Tom T. Hall, and Bobby Braddock hot on their heels.

The subjects of the songs also reflected the changing times. Loretta Lynn's "The Pill," Bobbie Gentry's "Fancy," and Tom T. Hall's "Harper Valley P.T.A." (as sung by Jeannie C. Riley) and "Margie's At The Lincoln Park Inn" (sung by Bobby Bare) brazenly spilled sexual themes out into the open. **Tony Joe White**'s "Willie And Laura Mae Jones" spoke of the racial tension still alive in the south. And with "San Francisco Mabel Joy," Newbury bucked the system not only by writing a song about love between a Georgia farmboy and a city prostitute, but scrapped all by-the-book formulas and let it roll on for five and a half minutes.

Bare was a singer with an independent spirit who helped lay the groundwork for Outlaws to come. He'd established himself as a hitmaker in the early '60s with folk-tinged songs like "Detroit City" and "500 Miles Away From Home," even winning a Grammy in 1963. Later, he welcomed Billy Joe Shaver into the music business by signing him to a $50-a-week songwriting contract, then getting knocked-over drunk and throwing up in the young Texan's truck later that night. Ah, cowboy hospitality! Crude stories aside, however, Bare was actually a phenomenal singer and a supporter of new artists who helped Waylon get his RCA contract, championed the work of writers like Shaver and Hall, and who was also the first country star to voice his frustrations with the studio system and begin producing his own albums.

Roger Miller was another inspirational figure, not just for his own creations but, like Bare, because he gave support to up-and-coming songwriters. During the late '60s, when his own phenomenal songwriting juices ran dry, Miller recorded songs by Newbury and Dennis Linde; most notably, though, he was the first to cut "Me And Bobby McGee," a song by a young Rhodes Scholar, West Point graduate and Columbia Studios janitor named Kris Kristofferson, who was about to become one of country music's brightest new stars.

Kristofferson's arrival was the signal that change was at hand. "Bobby McGee," a song about a pair of carefree drifters, revealed he was superbly talented, but what pushed him into the Nashville spotlight was "Sunday Mornin' Comin' Down," an existential morning-after song that made poetry out of a beer-for-breakfast hangover. When Johnny Cash cut "Sunday Mornin'," it won Song of the Year honors at the Country Music Association awards in 1970. His peers showed up dressed in tuxedoes, standard outfits for such an event; Kristofferson, however, opted for black pants, turtleneck, and leather jacket. He was dazed and obviously liquored, though to what degree depends on who you ask. When his name was announced, he meandered to the stage, faced the wrong direction, and, when corrected, mumbled into the mike something about his respect for Merle Haggard (who was raking in the awards that year for "Okie From Muskogee"). Emcee Tennessee Ernie Ford wasn't amused and gave Kris a stern, disapproving glare. Too bad and too late: the new breed had arrived, and one of them had even sneaked past the gates.

Though Kristofferson did break into the charts as a singer, his writing was the thing that always stood out. Gems like "Casey's Last Ride," "Why Me," "Billy Dee," and "Help Me Make It Through The Night" (especially the sultry version by husky-voiced Sammi Smith) displayed his artful blend of literary imagery and gritty, ground-level emotions. Words like "sincere" and "real" cropped up regularly in critical reviews and during happy-hour conversations. Kristofferson gained further cachet when Janis Joplin turned "Me And Bobby McGee" into a rock'n'roll classic.

Honky Tonk Heroes

Waylon wasn't the first Nashville artist to break from the pack—making music according to the sounds in his head, not some studio rulebook—but he was the focal point of the Outlaw scene (ironically, he never cared for the term—if anything, he preferred 'hillbilly'). He'd been recording excellent material since the mid-'60s, but once he assumed greater artistic control his music truly blossomed. His 1973 album LONESOME, ON'RY AND MEAN was the first to feature his own production work; it was the subsequent collection, however, HONKY TONK HEROES, that became the Outlaw landmark and the first masterpiece of his career. Nine of the ten songs were written by Billy Joe Shaver, and the record's informal production and spare, simple arrangements brought the lyrics and melodies out into the open air in a refreshing way that country fans hadn't heard in ages. His second masterpiece, DREAMING MY DREAMS, was recorded at Hillbilly Central in 1975 and co-produced this time by the legendary "Cowboy" Jack Clement. The lead-off track alone ("Are You Sure Hank Done It This Way?") was hard to beat.

You could almost call Clement a father figure of the Outlaw scene, not only for his work with Glaser and Jennings, but because he'd spent the better part of two decades living and making records outside the norm. He'd gotten his professional start as an engineer at the renegade Sun Studios where he'd worked directly with artists such as Jerry Lee Lewis, Roy Orbison, and Johnny Cash. He'd also written quite a few songs, among them "Ballad Of A Teenage Queen" and "Guess Things Happen That Way" for Cash, "Miller's Cave" (a hit for Bobby Bare), and "Gone Girl" and numerous others for Tompall And The Glaser Brothers. During the '60s he was one of Nashville's only independent record producers, running his own studio and cutting songs for a wide variety of singers: mainstream hitmaker Charley Pride, Texas songwriter Townes Van Zandt, and the Glasers, a trio of wide-eyed Nebraska folkies whom Clement helped break into the country charts. One of

Clement's protégés was songwriter-producer Allen Reynolds, who wrote "Dreaming My Dreams" and helped Clement run his short-lived label, JMI Records, before going on to work with Crystal Gayle, Kathy Mattea, and, most notably, Garth Brooks (he produced nearly all Garth's albums from 1989 onward).

Like Jennings, Willie Nelson had not found much satisfaction with the status quo. He'd been a successful songwriter since coming to Nashville, penning "Crazy" (for Patsy Cline), "Hello Walls" (Faron Young), and "Night Life" (Ray Price) among many others, that cemented his country reputation for life. He also cut plenty of songs himself, but none ever took hold—something that is difficult to comprehend, given that he's now one of country music's finest and most universally loved vocalists. When Nelson's Nashville house burned down in late 1970, he took the opportunity to make a change, moving back to his home state of Texas, settling outside Austin. There he became the figurehead of an already burgeoning 'progressive country' scene peopled by the likes of Jerry Jeff Walker, Michael Martin Murphey, Kinky Friedman, and Ray Wylie Hubbard. Austin became the Outlaw outpost, a place where hippies and rednecks—both deeply attracted to this back-to-basics sound—mingled together, though not always comfortably, at clubs like the Armadillo World Headquarters.

At the same time, Nelson churned out excellent albums like PHASES AND STAGES and RED-HEADED STRANGER, both well-conceived concept albums. He'd argued for, and won, creative control, enabling him to keep the mostly acoustic arrangements sparse and quiet. His hair was longer than ever by this stage, and when he sang "Blue Eyes Crying In The Rain" on the CMA's awards show in 1975, he wore a headband and blue jeans (even Waylon had donned a tux) and insisted that his road band back him up. He was always gracious, though, and his fans loved him dearly no matter how he looked.

In many ways, Texas was the natural home for this kind of music. Jennings, Nelson, Shaver, and others had grown up in the state, as had many of their country heroes such as Ernest Tubb, Bob Wills, and Floyd Tillman. Texas had always enjoyed a spirit of personal freedom ever since the days of the Alamo and Sam Houston—it had something to do with the wide-open spaces, the do-it-yourself cowboy heritage, and the undying Lone Star pride among the state's residents.

In 1972, Willie Nelson performed at the first of several infamous outdoor music showcases in Dripping Springs, Texas. He liked the concept so much he began hosting the event himself, bringing singers like Tex Ritter, Tom T. Hall, Jennings, and Shaver together with an audience of farmers, suburbanites, and shirtless hippies for a rip-roaring good time. These Woodstock-like Fourth of July picnics also served as grass-roots promotion machines for Willie and Waylon, showcases for countrified rockers like Leon Russell, and launching pads for singer-songwriters like Shaver, **Guy Clark**, and—believe it or not—Jimmy Buffett, who in his early years showed traces of country learning.

Hillbilly Central

Back in Nashville, home base was Hillbilly Central, the Glaser brothers' recording studio, meeting hall, hang-out spot, and general focal point for all things Outlaw—a place where late-night recording sessions were as common as pinball competitions at the nearby Burger Boy (Waylon and Tompall both had a weakness for the game). By opening their own recording studio, Tompall, Chuck, and Jim Glaser had circumvented the studio system; they'd also started their own publishing company, and caused quite a stir when one of the songs they represented, John Hartford's "Gentle On My Mind," became a smash hit when recorded by Glen Campbell. The song mixed themes of free love and open-road rambling, and it went on to be one of the most recorded in Nashville history.

It's ironic that Tompall Glaser, the singer who most embraced the Outlaw moniker as a badge of honor, is the least remembered of his cohorts today. Not only a fine vocalist and songwriter ("Streets Of Baltimore," "Come Back Shane," "Charlie"), he was lord and master of Hillbilly Central, and with his strong business acumen could hold his own among Music Row's power elite—or at least make a good show of it. His 1973 solo album CHARLIE is a neglected classic, and the hillbilly-blues band he put together in the mid-'70s with guitarist Mel Brown and drummer Charles Polk (both from Bobby "Blue" Bland's band) was one of the era's hottest.

Glaser's most popular song was "Put Another Log On The Fire," a cute little number written by the late *Playboy* cartoonist, children's book author, and sometime singer Shel Silverstein, a prolific songwriter with an abundance of clever, humorous material. Glaser, Bare, Johnny Cash, and Dr Hook And The Medicine Show are among many artists who've covered Silverstein's songs. A good deal are corny and kooky—including the overplayed Cash hit "A Boy Named Sue"—but Silverstein was a versatile writer, as evidenced by such memorable gems as "If I'd Only Come And Gone" (Glaser), "Mama, I'll Sing One Song For You" (Dr Hook), and "One's On The Way" (Loretta Lynn).

The Rest of the Story

Ex-con singer David Allan Coe was tailor-made for the Outlaw scene, having spent much of his youth in an Ohio penitentiary. Songs like "Long-haired Redneck" and "Jack Daniels If You Please" were thick and tangled with country roots, but "humble" was not in his vocabulary. One of his songs even attempted to concoct a holy Outlaw triumvirate: "Willie, Waylon, And Me."

Hank Williams, Jr. also seemed right at home with the Outlaw moniker. For too many years he'd been groomed in the shadow of his famous father, and by the mid-'70s he was weary of it. The albums he recorded after this time—beginning with the refreshingly spare HANK WILLIAMS, JR. & FRIENDS and running more or less through his blustery early-'80s smash "Man Of Steel"—are his creative high point. Titles like "OD'd In Denver," "The American Way," and "Whiskey Bent And Hell Bound" are packed with braggadocio, but the hard-country excitement is at the same time difficult to ignore.

Johnny Paycheck also joined the club when he grew a beard and renamed himself "John Austin Paycheck" on his 1976 album 11 MONTHS AND 29 DAYS. This was in the wake of his attempt to fashion himself as a sensitive romantic on albums like MR LOVEMAKER and LOVING YOU BEATS ALL I'VE EVER SEEN. The hits that followed include "I'm The Only Hell (Mama Ever Raised)" and, of course, "Take This Job And Shove It."

Further singers and songwriters associated to varying degrees with the era include **Sammi Smith**, **Johnny Rodriguez**, **Jerry Jeff Walker**, and Guy Clark. Self-proclaimed "Texas Jewboy" **Kinky Friedman** wrote one of the finest songs of the era, "Sold American." But easily the most intense singer-songwriter to drift between Texas and Nashville was **Townes Van Zandt**, who in the late '60s and early '70s cut a series of excellent records in-between riding horses in Colorado and playing the coffeehouses around Houston. Two others, **Mickey Newbury** and Tom T. Hall, may have been clean-cut Music Row favorites for the '60s hits they'd written,

Anthologies

⊙ **Ned Kelly: Original MGM Motion Picture Soundtrack** (1970; United Artists; reissued 1998; Rykodisc). *Ned Kelly* was a film by Tony Richardson about a legendary nineteenth-century Australian outlaw. The soundtrack is packed with sturdy songs like "Shadow Of The Gallows" and "Stoney Cold Ground," most of them written by Shel Silverstein and performed by Waylon Jennings, Kris Kristofferson, Mick Jagger (who starred in the film), and Thom Gent. The music's great, the album more than just a curiosity.

⊙ **Wanted! The Outlaws** (1976; RCA; reissued 1996; RCA). This is a compilation of previously released songs by Waylon Jennings, Willie Nelson, Tompall Glaser, and Jessi Colter. It was the record company's concoction, and it hit stores at just the right time and made everyone involved lots of money. That aside, it's a decent (though by no means definitive) introduction to the mid-1970s Outlaw sound, especially since the reissued "20th anniversary" edition includes an additional 9 tracks from the period, plus 1 newly recorded Waylon and Willie duet (Steve Earle's "Nowhere Road").

⊙ **This Is Outlaw Country** (1998; Simitar). A budget collection that compiles a dozen of the era's significant Outlaw and hard-country tracks, including Waylon's "Ladies Love Outlaws," Freddy Fender's "Wasted Days And Wasted Nights," Jerry Jeff Walker's "Up Against The Wall Redneck Mother," Hank Jr.'s "Whiskey Bent And Hell Bound," and Gary Stewart's "She's Acting Single (And I'm Drinking Doubles)."

⊙ **Rebels And Outlaws: Music From The Wild Side Of Life** (1999; Capitol). Bad-ass country music wasn't just the providence of the Outlaw generation; the tradition stretched back decades, and this is the CD to prove it. Agendas aside, it's really just a great collection of hard country songs from some of country's best-known singers, like Tex Ritter ("Blood On The Saddle"), the Louvin Brothers ("Knoxville Girl"), Merle Haggard ("Branded Man"), Johnny Paycheck ("I've Got Someone To Kill"), Dick Curless ("Evil Hearted Me"), and Willie Nelson and Hank Cochran ("Ain't Life Hell").

but in terms of their own recording preferences (not to mention personal philosophies) they were more in line with the Outlaws. In 1969 Newbury became one of the very first Nashville artists to step outside the studio system, cutting his album LOOKS LIKE RAIN on a four-track system in a converted garage.

Gary Stewart, **Moe Bandy**, **Mel Street**, and **Gene Watson** also recorded some excellent honky-tonk material during the '70s, and while they were never considered Outlaw singers per se, they did share with Willie, Waylon, and the boys a hard-tack, back-to-basics approach. It was music that had far more in common with *Opry* icon Ernest Tubb than glitter-king Kenny Rogers, who by the late '70s was emerging as one of the biggest superstars Nashville had ever seen.

Getting Out of Hand

Ironically, however, once record executives figured out that Outlaws could still sell lots of records, they jumped on the opportunity and made the most of it. The culmination came in the form of the 1976 'concept' album WANTED! THE OUTLAWS, a compilation of previously released songs by Jennings, Nelson, Glaser, and Jessi Colter (aka Mrs Waylon Jennings).

For a few years in the early '70s, Waylon and Tompall were like brothers. Waylon kept office at Hillbilly Central, and pinball was just one of the habits they shared. Once the Outlaw craze became big business, however, the two stubborn singers had a huge falling-out. By this stage, however, and after the massive success of WANTED! THE OUTLAWS, the whole Outlaw schtick was fast becoming overused and stale. When Waylon was arrested for cocaine possession, he reacted by recording the song "Don't You Think This Outlaw Bit Done Got Out Of Hand?" Yeah, maybe it had. Some like Hank Williams, Jr. were still "Whiskey Bent And Hell Bound," but Willie, for his part, turned in the opposite direction and cut an album of pop standards, STARDUST. No one, it seemed, was going to pigeonhole ole Willie.

Outlaws: The Artists

Moe Bandy

"To hear Moe Bandy sing is to hear all that is right and good in country music."

—Nick Tosches

H e was certainly an anomaly, that Moe Bandy. To kick his way into Nashville's consciousness singing hard-line honky tonk at a time (the mid-1970s) when cuteness and glamour (Olivia Newton-John, Ronnie Milsap, John Denver) were the status quo—no one in their right mind would ever have put their money on Bandy's success. But succeed he did, pouring forth one Top 40 hit after another—more than three dozen in all—between 1974's incredible "I Just Started Hatin' Cheatin' Songs Today" and 1989's "Many Mansions." His old-school and entirely unadorned style was the antidote to all that pop-crossover madness: steel guitars and fiddles, his expressive, bar-room-bred voice, and a bushel of weighty titles ("Here I Am

Drunk Again," "Barstool Mountain," "She Just Loved The Cheatin' Out Of Me").

Moe was born Marion Franklin Bandy, Jr. on 12 February, 1944 in Meridian, Mississippi and raised in San Antonio. During the '60s and early '70s he released a string of singles on small labels like Satin, Gee Pee, and Footprint. Footprint was the first to release "I Just Started Hatin' Cheatin' Songs Today," a song that was then picked up by the slightly bigger indie label GRC (General

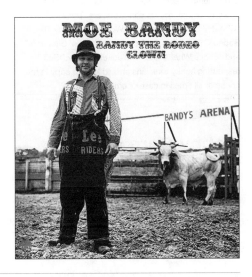

Moe Bandy

Recording Corporation) based in Atlanta, Georgia. It hit the country charts and set Bandy's career on its fifteen-year run. His GRC recordings remain his honky-tonk foundation, highlighted by such songs as "Bandy The Rodeo Clown" (written by Whitey Shafer and Lefty Frizzell), "Don't Anyone Make Love At Home Anymore" (Dallas Frazier), "I Sure Don't Need That Memory Tonight" (Eddy Raven), and "It's Always So Easy To Find An Unhappy Woman" (Shafer).

On the strength of those and other songs, Bandy was signed to Columbia, where he stayed until 1986. This stretch also included some truly solid pieces of work like "Hank Williams, You Wrote My Life," "The Biggest Little Airport In The World," and "It's A Cheatin' Situation" (which featured a then-undiscovered Janie Fricke). Beginning in 1979 Bandy cut a series of duets with Joe Stampley with titles like "Just Good Ol' Boys" and "Hey Joe (Hey Moe)"—not exactly cerebral stuff, but that wasn't the point. They even recorded a parody of Boy George called "Where's The Dress." Bandy began recording for MCA and then Curb in the late '80s, and his hit streak wound down about the same time his style shifted away from its traditional foundation. His 1988 hit "Americana" was marked by swelling strings and cheap sentimentalism for "people proud and free." Fans still high on the patriotic fumes of Lee Greenwood's "God Bless The USA" ate it up and made it Bandy's final gasp in the Top 10. Bandy has since opened a theater in Branson, Missouri.

⊙ **Honky Tonk Amnesia: The Hard Country Sound Of Moe Bandy** (1996; Razor & Tie). This 20-song compilation pulls together many of Bandy's best GRC and Columbia recordings and is proof of just how powerful and sturdy his songs still are. Titles include "Cheatin' Songs," "Unhappy Woman," "Bandy The Rodeo Clown," "Rodeo Romeo," "Cheatin' Situation," and "That's What Makes The Jukebox Play." Self-respecting honky tonk fans should keep a copy in the house at all times in case of emergencies.

Bobby Bare

In addition to releasing a string of excellent songs and albums during the 1960s and '70s, and possessing a smooth and unaffected voice that was among Nashville's finest, Bobby Bare was also a pioneer in terms of bringing smart new ideas, and self sufficiency, into that formula-laden town. He is not normally considered an Outlaw singer per se, but his efforts at gaining artistic control of his music, and also at helping new artists get their foot in the door, were significant. By the early '70s Bare had begun producing his own recordings and also cutting some of the genre's first concept albums—one being the Shel Silverstein collaboration LULLABIES, LEGENDS AND LIES. As a song publisher, Bare gave a dirt-poor Billy Joe Shaver his first weekly paycheck, and prior to that he'd helped Waylon Jennings get signed by passing a recommendation on to Chet Atkins at RCA (which was Bare's label at the time). And as for his own recordings, Bare has consistently been ahead of the game in terms of digging up and covering material by such adventurous songwriters as Mel Tillis, Ian Tyson, Tom T. Hall, Kris Kristofferson, Townes Van Zandt, and Rodney Crowell.

Robert Joseph Bare was born near Ironton, Ohio on 7 April, 1935. During the '50s he moved west to Los Angeles, where he became friends with such legendary musicians as steel guitarist Speedy West, honky-tonk bandleader Wynn Stewart, and songwriter Harlan Howard. He also cut some early singles for Challenge and Capitol. Before being shipped off into the army, he cut some informal demos, one being the song "All-American Boy." The record was eventually released by another indie label, Fraternity, although under the name of a friend of Bare's, Bill Parsons. Surprising to all, it turned into a pop hit. After his service, Bare recorded more songs for Fraternity, then in 1962 he joined the roster at RCA in Nashville.

Bare's first big hit (it made both the country and pop charts in *Billboard*) was "Detroit City," a Mel Tillis/Danny Dill composition about a lonely country boy stuck working in a Michigan auto plant and daydreaming of his southern home, Mama, and the girl next door. It won a Grammy and launched a career that was to remain strong and steady. Over the course of the next several years, he hit the charts again and again with songs like "500 Miles Away From Home" (another sad song about homesickness), the folk standard "Four Strong Winds" (written by Ian Tyson), "Just To Satisfy You" (an early Waylon composition), "The Streets Of Baltimore" (penned by Tompall Glaser and Harlan Howard), and "The Game Of Triangles" (a three-part collaboration with Norma Jean and Liz Anderson). Later in the decade he began mining the growing song catalogs of Tom T. Hall and Kris Kristofferson, and in the process he created the definitive versions of such now-classics as "(Margie's At) The Lincoln Park Inn" and "Come Sundown."

Bobby Bare

with Rosanne Cash) and "New Cut Road" (written by Guy Clark). He had his own TV series, *Bobby Bare And Friends*, on TNN in the mid-'80s, and also opened a tourist shop in Nashville, Bobby Bare Trap.

⊙ **The Mercury Years 1970–1972** (1994; Bear Family). This 3-CD set includes all Bare's Mercury recordings from the early 1970s. If you're willing to make the investment, it's highly recommended, as it catches Bare at a creative peak—at a point when he was both stripping down his sound and exploring the work of songwriters like Kristofferson, Hall, and Billy Joe Shaver. Includes the hits "How I Got To Memphis," "Come Sundown," and "Please Don't Tell Me How The Story Ends".

⊙ **The Best Of Bobby Bare** (1994; Razor & Tie). A substantial overview of the first decade of Bare's career that begins with "All-American Boy" and then runs through a 20-song line-up of such RCA hits as "Detroit City," "500 Miles," "Charleston Railroad Tavern," "Your Husband, My Wife" (a duet with Skeeter Davis), "God Bless America Again," and "(Margie's At) The Lincoln Park Inn."

⊙ **The Essential Bobby Bare** (1997; RCA). This Bare overview covers not only the singer's first tenure at RCA but also the period after he (briefly) returned in the mid-'70s. Thus we get not only such early hits as mentioned above but also "Marie Laveau," "Ride Me Down Easy," and the dopey but fun "Dropkick Me Jesus (Through The Goal Posts Of Life)".

Bare recorded for Mercury Records between 1970 and 1972, and many of these recordings are among his strongest. He then returned to RCA, staying with his old label for another few years. During that time he recorded LULLABYS, LEGENDS AND LIES in 1973, a concept album that brought together songs and stories about alleged American heroes—some old, some new, some sweet, some untrue. The songs all came from Shel Silverstein, including the #1 hit "Marie Laveau." Bare and Silverstein collaborated on further recordings, and in 1977 Bare also cut the album ME AND MCDILL, which featured songs by another Nashville song-writer, Bob McDill (who would later pen such hits as Alan Jackson's "Gone Country"). A further concept album was COWBOYS AND DADDIES, which included Texas-based songs like "Amarillo Highway" (Terry Allen) and "Up Against The Wall, Redneck Mother" (Ray Wylie Hubbard). Bare next switched to Columbia and then EMI, and he continued to chart into the early '80s with songs like "No Memories Hangin' Round" (a duet

Ed Bruce

As a country artist, Ed Bruce's greatest claim to fame is that he wrote "Mammas Don't Let Your Babies Grow Up To Be Cowboys," a #1 hit for Waylon and Willie in 1978. His pedigree as a reputable songwriter, however, stretched back more than a decade to when Tommy Roe cut "Save Your Kisses" (1962) and Charlie Louvin had a Top 10 hit with "See The Big Man Cry" (1965). Other notable numbers that bear Bruce's name include "The Man That Turned My Mother On" (Tanya Tucker), "Working Man's Prayer" (Tex Ritter), "The Price I Pay To Stay" (Jeannie C. Riley), and "Restless" (Crystal Gayle).

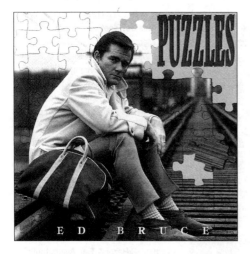

As a singer himself, Bruce has a rich, warm, and full-bodied baritone voice that's immediately striking. One listen to songs like "Puzzles" and "Blue Denim Eyes" will leave you wondering why he didn't achieve far greater fame as a recording artist in his own right. He did make his way, however, into the country charts quite a few times and even all the way to the top in 1981 with "You're The Best Break This Old Heart Ever Had." Bruce's voice has also graced the airwaves on commercials for the likes of McDonalds and John Deere, and he was a regular on the small screen—the series *Maverick*, for instance, and a variety of made-for-TV movies.

William Edwin Bruce, Jr. was born on 29 December, 1940 in Keiser, Arkansas. He grew up in Memphis, and in 1957 he went to see Jack Clement, who was at the time an engineer at Sun Records. Before he knew it he had Sam Phillips' attention and was laying down the rockabilly song "Rock Boppin' Baby" in the famous Sun studios. During the early '60s Bruce cut songs for RCA, Wand/Scepter (one being "See The Big Man Cry"), and other smaller labels. He had started in rockabilly, then tried pop music, and finally landed on his feet in the world of country. In 1966 he moved to Nashville and signed back up with RCA. Despite writing and recording such moving and

invigorating material as "Puzzles," "The Price I Pay To Stay," and "Lonesome Is Me," Bruce's songs didn't chart very high. He began making his money by singing on and narrating commercials. (For a time he even used to dress up Daniel Boone-style and travel the state of Tennessee as its mascot and spokesperson.)

Bruce next recorded for Monument, then after a brief hiatus in the early '70s he cut songs for United Artists, Epic, and MCA. It's during this time that he finally entered the country Top 40 under his own name. "Mammas Don't Let Your Babies" became his first sizeable success in 1975, and three years later Waylon and Willie cemented it in the public's consciousness. His biggest hit streak came in the early '80s and culminated with "You're The Best Break," a #1 country hit in 1981. Bruce was back on RCA during the mid-'80s, but reduced his output. In addition to his acting, he also hosted the TNN shows *Trucking USA* and *American Sports Calvacade*.

⊙ **The Best Of Ed Bruce** (1995; Varese Sarabande). An 18-song sampler of Bruce's smooth and finely honed recordings from the 1970s and '80s. Seventies-era influences are definitely present in these recordings, from a beefy Outlaw-driven undercurrent on some titles to the use of strings on others, but on the whole the material is solid and reliable.

⊙ **Puzzles** (1995; Bear Family). A great 29-song, single-disc collection of Bruce's 1966–68 recordings for RCA, after he "found himself" as a country singer. Some songs like "Blue Denim Eyes" are self-consciously poetic, but that was how things were then—and besides, his voice is so rich and strong that any sins of the lyric are quickly forgiven and forgotten. Other highlights include "Puzzles" (presented in three different versions, typical of Bear Family releases), "Lonesome Is Me," the early Kristofferson song "I'd Best Be Leaving You," and a version of "Last Train To Clarksville" slowed down so far it almost feels morose.

Johnny Bush

Houston, Texas native Johnny Bush will always be identified with "Whiskey River," a composition that his longtime friend, sort-of mentor, and one-time bandmate Willie Nelson covered so many times it became his theme song. A fine piece of work, the song certainly gave Bush's career—which saw only sporadic success on the country charts during the late 1960s and early '70s—a shot of juice that has kept him from disappearing entirely from view. Bush's tenor voice has a distinctive warble that bears a similarity to Ray Price's, though for some it's definitely an acquired taste; less arguable is his musical foundation, which is as solid as Texas bedrock and has always stayed true to fiddle-and-steel tradition, making Bush a decades-old favorite on the honky-tonk circuit.

Born John Bush Shin III on 17 February, 1935, Bush cut his teeth playing the clubs around Houston before joining the bands of first Nelson and then Ray Price during the '60s as both guitarist and drummer. By the end of the decade he'd begun working on his own, finally landing a recording contract with the Stop label. His song "Undo The Right" cracked the *Billboard* Top 10 in 1968 and was followed by the Marty Robbins composition, "You Gave Me A Mountain" a year later. Bush recorded further records for Stop and another label Million before signing with RCA in the early '70s. His version of "Whiskey River" made the charts in 1972, but it wasn't until Willie started performing the song during his live shows that the song's popularity grew. Willie finally recorded it later in the decade, though it failed to dent the Top 10. By that time, however, it was a staple of Nelson's repertoire.

As for Bush, his recording career suffered during the '70s as a result of throat problems. But he persevered and slowly rebuilt much of his voice—and his following. In the meantime he'd lost his RCA contract and begun recording for indie labels again, including Gusto and Delta. By the '90s, however, he was rediscovered as an original Texas honky-tonker. His 1994 release TIME CHANGES EVERYTHING featured both Nelson and Hank Thompson, and in 1998 the indie label Watermelon released TALK TO MY HEART, which won him new fans from the alternative country crowd.

⊙ **14 Greatest Hits** (1996; Power Play). A decent CD to start with, as it collects 14 of Bush's Stop and Million songs including "Undo The Right," "You Gave Me A Mountain," "Each Time," and "I'll Be There."

⊙ **Talk To My Heart** (1998; Watermelon/Sire). An album of straightforward material that'd be right at home in just about any roadside honky tonk. Songs include Whitey Shafer's "The Bottle, Your Memory, & Me," Justin Trevino's "Neon Nightmare," Willie Nelson's "A Moment Isn't Very Long," and Bush's own "The Cheatin' Line."

Guy Clark

"The best songs are always based on reality."

—Guy Clark

As the title of a 1995 compilation CD describes him, Guy Clark is a craftsman, a songwriter who approaches his life's work with a hands-on respect for both the material he's working with and its heritage. With an unhurried pace (one new album only every few years), yet strict attention to detail, Clark has produced an impressive catalog of timeless songs. He's the kind of songwriter young artists study and seasoned writers (and fans) admire. His style is more finely honed than the free-ranging imagery of his friend and sometime musical partner, the late Townes Van Zandt, but both men have elevated coffeehouse folksinging to an honorable Texas tradition.

STEVE GILLETT

Guy Clark

Clark has an attractive, dusty, Texas drawl, but as good as his recordings like "Better Days," "New Cut Road," and "She Ain't Goin' Nowhere" (with its stunning opening line, "Standin' on the gone side of leavin'/She found her thumb and stuck it in the breeze") are, he's never seen much commercial success as a singer. His songs, however, are another story. Over the years Rodney Crowell (who considers Clark not only a friend but a major inspiration), country supergroup the Highwaymen, and Ricky Skaggs have taken titles like "Desperadoes Waiting For A Train" and "Heartbroke" far up in the charts.

Clark was born on 6 November, 1941 in the West Texas town of Monahans. His mother worked and his father was in the army, and he was raised mostly by his grandmother who ran the local hotel. One of her resident guests was an oil-well driller who would later become the chief subject of "Desperadoes Waiting For A Train," one of Clark's best-known and most intensely moving songs. Other songs he's written also allude to his childhood—a community gathering to watch the train in "Texas 1947"; the philosophical musings of wood, sail and distant shores in "Boats To Build," inspired by a summer job he once held.

As a child, Clark first learned Spanish songs but his whole musical world opened up when he moved to Houston and began working the folk-music circuit. There he met blues singers Lightnin' Hopkins and Mance Lipscomb and fellow singer-songwriter Townes Van Zandt. Clark and Van Zandt were both getting their music careers off the ground, and they formed a strong friendship (often touring together) that lasted until Van Zandt's untimely death in 1997. It was in the musically rich atmosphere of Houston that Clark began developing his sturdy brand of folk- and blues-influenced country music.

During the late '60s Clark moved to California, living first in San Francisco (where he met and married his wife Susanna, a painter and songwriter) and then in Los Angeles, where he worked in the Dopera Brothers' famous Dobro factory. Tiring quickly of the area (sentiments he expressed in another classic song, "LA Freeway"), he and Susanna packed up and headed for Nashville. There he began writing songs professionally, and eventually also landed a recording contract with RCA, which released his debut album OLD NO.1 in 1975. By this time, Austin singer Jerry Jeff Walker had already had a progressive–country hit with "LA Freeway." That and other songs (including "Desperadoes") earned Clark a reputation as one of the most promising young writers among country music's new breed. His friends and songwriting support network in Nashville included Van Zandt, Mickey Newbury, and Rodney Crowell.

RCA released one more Clark album in 1976, TEXAS COOKIN'. He then switched to Warner Brothers for his next three albums, which were all released between 1978 and 1983. Three songs from this period actually sneaked into the high reaches of the country charts, including the catchy "Homegrown Tomatoes." And during the '70s and '80s several more had been picked up and recorded by singers from Johnny Cash and David Allen Coe to George Strait, Vince Gill, and Nanci Griffith. Bobby Bare hit with "New Cut Road" in 1982, that same year Ricky Skaggs took Clark's "Heartbroke" all the way to #1.

Clark was an established Nashville songwriter by now. He continued to work on his songs steadily, though he didn't record again until 1988's OLD FRIENDS, released by the indie label Sugar Hill. He then switched labels again to Asylum, where his 1992 album BOATS TO BUILD was released as part of the acclaimed *American Explorer* series (Jimmie Dale Gilmore and Charlie Feathers also had albums released in this series). Clark's eighth album was 1995's DUBLIN BLUES, and among its best moments was a new and far quieter version of one of his most personal songs, "Randall Knife," about the death of his father. Clark was back on Sugar Hill in the late '90s with the live album, KEEPERS, and in 1999 the stripped-down, acoustic affair COLD DOG SOUP.

⊙ **Old No. 1** (1975; RCA). Clark's debut album is still one of the era's finest collections of Texas-style country-folk songs. Clark didn't live in his home state when he cut this, but a Lone Star influence still ran thick in his blood on songs like "Texas 1947," "Desperadoes Waiting For A Train," and "She Ain't Goin' Nowhere."

⊙ **Old Friends** (1988; Sugar Hill). Simple, precise, low-key and honest, that's Clark's style, and he sticks to it beautifully on songs like Townes Van Zandt's "To Live's To Fly," "Come From The Heart," and the quiet title track (the latter two, by the way, co-written by Guy's wife Susanna). Not monumental, but certainly a pleasure.

⊙ **Boats To Build** (1992; Elektra/Asylum). After a five-year recording absence, songs like "Picasso's Mandolin," "Ramblin' Jack And Mahan," and the title track are a brilliant return to form.

Guy Clark

⊙ **Craftsman** (1995; Rounder). A 2-CD set that compiles Clark's 3 Warner Brothers albums—GUY CLARK, THE SOUTH COAST OF TEXAS and BETTER DAYS. After kicking off your Clark collection with OLD NO. 1, this is the next stop to begin digging deeper.

⊙ **Keepers** (1997; Sugar Hill). Recorded live at Nashville's Douglas Corner in 1996, this is Clark's first album with a full band in over a decade. It includes such Clark standards as "LA Freeway," "South Coast Of Texas," and "Homegrown Tomatoes," as well as a couple of new songs.

David Allan Coe

"I've always been in touch with my feminine side. I've never been afraid to show that. I'm genderless, more or less."
—David Allan Coe, 1997

David Allan Coe

He may be a lot of things, including an excellent vocalist, insightful songwriter, and mesmerizing personality, but David Allan Coe could never be described as subtle. Songs like "Longhaired Redneck," "Willie, Waylon And Me," and "If That Ain't Country" announced his presence with all the delicacy of an old Ford truck that's lost its muffler. Though steeped in traditional country, his style is about as bold and brazen as country music, Outlaw or otherwise, has yet experienced.

From the outset Coe proved himself eager to stage a scene. Driving a hearse, dressing in a cape and mask, and calling himself the Mysterious Rhinestone Cowboy, he parked himself outside the Ryman Auditorium (home of the *Grand Ole Opry*) and waited for attention to come his way. He also concocted a story about being on Death Row in the Ohio state penitentiary (he did do time behind bars, but for far lesser charges), which won him even more free publicity. He may have been slightly crazy and more than a little scary— he stood over six feet tall, wore dangling earrings, hung out with bikers, claimed to have multiple "wives," and was covered with hundreds of crude, prison-made tattoos—but set against a backdrop of conservative Nashville, he was also a thoroughly refreshing character.

All this would have amounted to little were it not for his talent as a songwriter. Bold honky-tonkers like "Living On The Run," "Jack Daniels If You Please," and "Take This Job And Shove

It" (the song that made its singer, Johnny Paycheck, a household name) were tangled thick with hillbilly roots and driven hard with a sturdy rhythm. At the same time, Coe showed sensitivity and emotional depth with ballads like "Would You Lay With Me (In A Field Of Stone)," "Now I Lay Me Down To Cheat," and "River," the latter a sympathetic song about the lonely prisoner's plight. Admittedly, Coe could get ugly—the ready-to-fight attitude he often carried on stage in the '70s, his half-loving, half-misogynist thoughts when the subject turned to women. He reached the pinnacle of crassness when he cut two X-rated "party" albums peppered with songs like "Fuck Aneta [sic] Bryant," "Cumstains On My Pillow," and "I Made Linda Lovelace Gag." As well as these, a rumor still circulates that he cut an album of seriously racist KKK material under a pseudonym, though its debatable whether the singer in question sounds much like Coe at all. He has, however, thrown around the word "nigger" often enough, including burying it in one of his better-known songs, "If

David Allan Coe

That Ain't Country." Maybe it's best not to dig too deep if you're afraid of what you might find.

Coe was born in 1939 in Akron, Ohio, an industrial city known as the rubber capital of the world. He was first institutionalized at the age of nine, and through his teens and twenties he was in and out of reform school and then prison. The charges were rarely serious—possession of burglary tools, car theft (it was supposedly a joyride), possession of obscene materials—which makes his death-row yarn all the more absurd. When later "clarifying" the tall tale, he explained that at one point he did spent time in a cell block technically designated "death row"—hence the truth-stretching.

After his release from prison in 1967, Coe headed for Nashville, determined to make it as a country singer. He began making his mark with the hearse and cape, hanging around the Ryman and/or nearby Tootsie's Orchid Lounge, where *Opry* stars took their whiskey. Record man Shelby Singleton, owner of Plantation Records (which released "Harper Valley P.T.A."), signed Coe to one of his other labels, SSS International. Coe's debut album, PENITENTIARY BLUES, is a raw, bluesy affair which, although interesting, lacks the depth of his later hard-country material. He kept on writing and singing, and by the early '70s other artists were picking up on his songs. His biggest break by a long shot came when teenage sensation Tanya Tucker recorded "Would You Lay With Me (In A Field Of Stone)." That led to Coe's signing with Tucker's label, Columbia.

Coe's early Columbia records are his best. The music was about as hard-edged as '70s country ever got, and the songs walked the line between shameless boasts and tender, sometimes self-deprecating confessions. "I've won every fight I've ever fought" he declares in the hard-country anthem "Longhaired Redneck", but he just as quickly turned and sang Guy Clark's "Desperadoes Waiting For A Train" and Mickey Newbury's "33rd Of August" with absolute sincerity.

While Waylon Jennings avoided using the term Outlaw, Coe embraced it, declaring himself the real thing and placing himself in the Holy Trinity with the song "Willie, Waylon And Me." That song was a decent hit, proving that Coe really could sing and that he had a genuine feel for the music. Steve Goodman's "You Never Even Called Me By My Name", the Coe-penned "Longhaired Redneck" and "If That Ain't Country" also made some waves. Coe's biggest marks in the country charts, however, came during the '80s with "The Ride," a song written by Gary Gentry about the

ghost of Hank Williams, and Coe's own "Mona Lisa Lost Her Smile," a weepy number with an infectious melody. The latter's arrangement was decidedly poppier, and it reflected the hugely toned-down, family-man image Coe was by this point projecting.

Coe remained with Columbia through the mid-'80s, after which time he released records on his own label, Tanya Montana (named after his daughter). He seemed to fade almost completely from the Nashville agenda, but he did tour steadily, especially in the Southeast. By the '90s he'd built a substantial following among not only grey-bearded bikers, but gin-pup fraternity boys and other wannabes attracted to his renegade past. His lifestyle nowadays isn't quite as outrageous, but his appearance is still rather warped—long beard and hair dyed blonde and braided with beads, tattoos freshly reinked. In 1997 Sony released his first major-label album in a decade, DAVID ALLAN COE LIVE! IF THAT AIN'T COUNTRY... His voice was almost as unhealthy as his appearance—'saggy' was the word used by writer Michael McCall—and no match when compared to his '70s heyday, but his fans haven't seemed to mind one bit.

⊙ **The Mysterious Rhinestone Cowboy** (1974; Columbia; reissued 1993; Bear Family). This is Coe's finest hour on record. The arrangements are hard as steel, and songs like Mickey Newbury's "33rd Of August" and Coe's own "Sad Country Song" and "River" are thoughtful and honest. The reissue comes packaged together with ONCE UPON A RHYME.

⊙ **Longhaired Redneck** (1976; Columbia; reissued 1993; Bear Family). As a renegade honky-tonker's bar-room anthem, the title track is hard to beat. The hard-driving "Living On The Run" is another standout. Bear Family has packaged REDNECK with the 1977 album DAVID ALLAN COE RIDES AGAIN, which includes "If That Ain't Country," the pretty "Greener Than The Grass We Laid On," and the boisterous "Willie, Waylon And Me."

⊙ **For The Record: The First Ten Years** (1985; Columbia). A solid collection top to bottom of highlights, hits or otherwise, from Coe's Columbia years. Titles include "You Never Even Called Me By My Name," "Longhaired Redneck," "If That Ain't Country," "Jack Daniels If You Please," "Stand By Your Man," and "Mona Lisa Lost Her Smile."

⊙ **Recommended For Airplay** (1999; Lucky Dog/Sony). "Song For The Year 2000" sounds like John Prine, but most of the tracks here are chunky and greasy. Coe's voice isn't what it once was, but like a beer gut on a biker, he ain't shy about letting it flop and fly as is. 'Pristine' has never been one of his trademarks, after all. And thank goodness for that, because this is an album you can *feel*. Some of today's 'young country' pretty boys could take a lesson or two in that department from ol' David Allan.

Jessi Colter

For the last few decades, singer and songwriter Jessi Colter has been known to most folks as Mrs Waylon Jennings, wife of the infamous Outlaw singer, whom she married in 1969. But Jessi (who took her stage name from a distant relative, outlaw Jesse Colter) has a strong voice in her own right, a warbly mixture of tearful and tangy. Waylon clearly was a boon to her career, but on her own she managed to cut a handful of hits during the mid-'70s. The best known of these by far was the self-penned "I'm Not Lisa," her signature song. With a voice as immediately pretty as her magazine-cover good looks, Jessi certainly had the potential to turn her music into the sweet pop-crossover sound so many of her contemporaries indulged in at the time. It's to her credit, then, that she kept some distance from the trends of the day; her background was actually gospel, and it's an influence that can be heard in more than a few of her compositions.

Colter was born Mirriam Johnson in Phoenix, Arizona on 25 May, 1943. She had a religious upbringing, and she sang and played piano in the church choir. Another Phoenix-based artist, Duane Eddy, produced her first recordings on Jamie, a local indie label co-owned by Lee Hazlewood that Eddy also recorded for. Eventually young Mirriam and Eddy married, and they moved to California, staying together until 1968. She met and married Waylon a year later, and it's through the soon-to-be Outlaw star that she made the move to Nashville and began her brief hitmaking career. She cut her first album for RCA (Waylon's label), but aside from a couple of duet recordings with her husband, she didn't truly break as an artist until her 1975 single "I'm Not Lisa," released by Capitol, hit #1. She followed it up with "Whatever Happened To Blue Eyes," but none of her subsequent recordings have come close to "Lisa"'s success. Colter did, however, achieve full-on 'Outlaw' knighthood when she was included on the 1976 compilation WANTED! THE OUTLAWS alongside Waylon, Willie Nelson, and Tompall

Glaser. Her composition "Storms Never Last" was a hit duet for her and Waylon in 1981, and since then she's been a regular member of his touring outfit, taking the stage for a song or two on her own.

⊙ **Jessi Colter Collection** (1995; Liberty). Built around a simple piano melody, Colter's biggest hit "I'm Not Lisa," is as sad in subject as it is sweet in tone. Colter's singing does have a soulful, husky quality—one more fully conveyed in songs like Tony Joe White's "That's The Way A Cowboy Rocks And Rolls" and the quiet "Here I Am." This CD covers Jessi's Capitol years, though at only 10 songs it's a paltry offering.

Stoney Edwards

Frenchy "Stoney" Edwards was the best-known African-American country singer to arrive in the wake of Charley Pride. But to mark him as such and leave it at that overshadows the fact that Stoney was a purebred country artist in his own right—and a lot less glamorous an entertainer than Pride—whose music fit neatly into the no-frills honky-tonk legacy of Hank, Lefty, and Merle. Stoney's rich, gentle baritone voice had an unabashed country twang and warble, his arrangements were rooted deep in country soil and colored by steel guitar, and songs he recorded such as "Mama's Old Quilt" (among many self-penned numbers) and "Dixie Boy" (written by John Schweers, whose work Stoney frequently covered) spoke plainly of his Oklahoma upbringing.

Edwards country career came late in life—he didn't begin playing or recording professionally until he was past forty. He was born near Seminole, Oklahoma on 24 December, 1929. His racial background was mixed (Irish and Native American as well as black), which made it hard for him to fit into any single community. He grew up illiterate and spent his teenage years as a bootlegger, helping his father and uncles sell the products of their stills. In 1950 he moved to California, eventually settling in Richmond, a blue-collar Bay Area town that had attracted large numbers of southern and midwestern immigrants—including many African-Americans—to work in the shipyards during World War II. He married, worked a series of odd jobs, and sang music on the side never taking it too seriously.

It was only after he suffered a debilitating accident in 1968—carbon-dioxide poisoning at a steel plant—that Stoney begin playing music more earnestly. He landed his Capitol contract in 1971, a few years in the wake of Charley Pride's success—which almost certainly helped him get signed. His songs, however, stood on their own, ringing with simple truths that were hard to deny ... or forget. "A Two Dollar Toy" was his debut single, about a guy who trips on his daughter's toy as he's busy leaving the family—then decides to stay. It sounds soppy, yes, but it's sung with such down-to-earth conviction—not to mention a hard-country arrangement—that any and all saccharine elements quickly vanish. Stoney went on to cut some five albums for the label over the next six years, though only three of his songs broke the country Top 40: "She's My Rock" (later covered by George Jones), "Hank And Lefty Raised My Country Soul," and "Mississippi You're On My Mind." When his Capitol association ended in the late '70s, Stoney continued to record for a series of small labels. He moved back to Oklahoma in the '80s, then fell victim to diabetes and finally cancer. He died in 1997.

⊙ **The Best Of Stoney Edwards: Poor Folks Stick Together** (1998; Razor & Tie). This CD pulls together 20 of Stoney's Capitol songs, from "A Two Dollar Toy" through to his 1975 single "Blackbird," a song written by Chip Taylor that was controversial for its use of the word "nigger" (albeit in context). In between are greats like "Odd-Job Dollar-Bill Man," "Mississippi You're On My Mind," the gospel-tinged "Jeweldene Turner (The World Needs to Hear You Sing)," and "I Bought The Shoes That Just Walked Out On Me," a Ray Price-like shuffle song.

Freddy Fender

Mexican-American singer and songwriter Freddy Fender didn't have what you'd call an easy path to stardom. But by the 1970s, after some twenty years of ups and downs—including a stint in the Marines that frequently landed him in the brig, and later a more serious prison sentence for marijuana possession—his music career began to turn around. "Before The Next Teardrop Falls" became a huge national hit, and another song he wrote fifteen years earlier, "Wasted Days And Wasted Nights," also gained him recognition as a Tex-Mex classic (among the song's most outspoken champions was Doug Sahm, who'd later work alongside Fender in the group Texas Tornados).

VIRGINIA LEE HUNTER

Freddy Fender

Fender was born Baldemar G. Huerta on 4 June, 1937 in San Benito, Texas. He originally recorded Spanish-language conjunto music during the '50s, and later moved toward rockabilly, adopting the name "Freddy Fender" as a means to attract wider white audiences. He first cut "Wasted Days And Wasted Nights" in 1959, and it was a regional hit around San Antonio; it was then re-released on Imperial and gained national attention as well. Just as the song was on the rise, however, Fender was busted for marijuana possession and was forced to serve three years in Angola prison, Louisiana. He cut some records while doing time, then after his release moved to New Orleans, where he played regularly in the local bar Papa Joe's.

In 1969 Fender moved back to Texas and eventually began working with producer and promoter Huey P. Meaux; among Meaux's previous production credits were early Sir Douglas Quintet (Doug Sahm) recordings, including the hit "She's About A Mover." Meaux brought Fender into a Houston studio, had him cut the ballad "Before The Next Teardrop Falls," and released it on his own Crazy Cajun label. It was picked up by ABC and became a massive #1 country and pop hit. Later that year "Teardrop" even landed Single of the Year honors from the Country Music Association. The song included a verse in Spanish, which actually added to its appeal; fans liked the Chicano flavor of Fender's quivering tenor voice, as it brought a fresh new sound and style to the mostly whitebread world of country radio.

Fender scored several more big hits over the next few years, including "Vaya Con Dios," "You'll Lose A Good Thing," and a remake of "Wasted Days." However, like so many rising stars thrust quickly and suddenly into the spotlight, Fender didn't handle the attention and fame all too well. Drug and alcohol abuse prompted a decline in popularity. He recorded a bit for Starflite and then Warner Brothers, but failed to achieve commercial success again until 1989, when he began working with Sahm, keyboardist Augie Meyers, and accordionist Flaco Jimenez in the Texas Tornados, an all-star band that mixed Tex-Mex, country, rock, blues, and other lively roots-music styles. They recorded their debut album in both Spanish and English, appealing to a far wider fan base than most American country bands are aware of. Two more albums followed while at the same time Fender enjoyed another revival of his solo career, playing gigs on his own when he wasn't touring with the Tornados. The four members parted ways a few years later, each returning to their own separate careers.

⊙ **Canciones De Mi Barrio: The Roots Of Tejano Rock** (1993; Arhoolie). If you want to hear Fender's roots in their raw, pure form, this 24-song CD collects original Spanish-language recordings from 1959 and 1964. They show the influence of Latin music but are stylistically more in line with rockabilly.

⊙ **The Best Of Freddy Fender** (1996; MCA). A collection of his original mid-1970s hit recordings made with producer Huey Meaux in Houston (the Warner Brothers-issued FREDDY FENDER COLLECTION, on the other hand, features re-recordings made in Nashville). "Teardrop" and "Wasted Days" are both on the roster.

The Flatlanders

One of the great 'lost' bands of modern country music, the Flatlanders were together for a mere two years and only recorded a single album with very limited distribution, but considering that Joe Ely, Jimmie Dale Gilmore, and Butch Hancock were the principle members—each of them with long solo careers ahead (see separate entries)—that short span was enough to earn the Flatlanders a legendary reputation.

Ely, Gilmore, and Hancock all grew up in the Texas Panhandle and had been friends since high school. After some youthful travels in various directions, in 1970 they each happened to be back in Lubbock, Texas. They began playing music together, and before long fiddler Tommy Hancock, musical-saw maestro Steve Wesson, bassist Sylvester Rice, and mandolinist Tony Pearson had jumped on board as well. In early 1972, with Kris Kristofferson's songs riding high in the charts and Waylon Jennings about to release "Ladies Love Outlaws," the Flatlanders secured a recording contract with maverick record-company executive Shelby Singleton (best known for his Plantation label, which released the smash hit "Harper Valley P.T.A.," and for buying Sun Records in 1969). The Flatlanders journeyed to Nashville that spring, cut their record, went home, and waited for their creation to hit the stores. Singleton mailed out promotional singles of the Gilmore-penned "Dallas" (still, by the way, his best-known song), but when it didn't catch on with DJs he decided to hold back the album's release. It eventually hit the shelves—but only on 8-track tape! By the end of the year, after a few casual gigs around Texas, the Flatlanders disbanded. Thankfully, Rounder Records dug up and reissued the album two decades later to great critical acclaim. Ely, Gilmore, Hancock, and other Flatlanders have occasionally reunited since for special events.

⊙ **More A Legend Than A Band** (1990; Rounder). A mix of acoustic folk, string-band, and country blues-type music. It's hillbilly music from another era

THE FLATLANDERS
featuring
JIMMIE DALE GILMORE
JOE ELY
BUTCH HANCOCK

More A Legend Than A Band

translated via Texas right to the fringes of 1970s Nashville. Includes songs written by lead-vocalist Gilmore ("Tonight I'm Gonna Go Downtown"), Hancock ("One Road More"), Willie Nelson ("One Day At A Time"), and the reclusive Al Strehli ("Keeper Of The Mountain").

Kinky Friedman

A self-declared "Texas Jewboy" (he's a Jew by heritage and a Texan by association) Kinky Friedman is one of a kind, an artist responsible for some of the progressive country scene's oddest material. Satire and smart social commentary ran heavy in songs like "The Ballad Of Charles Whitman" (about Austin, Texas' most famous sniper), "They Ain't Makin' Jews Like Jesus Any More," and the 'anti-feminist' anthem "Get Your Biscuits In The Oven And Your Buns In The Bed." He also wrote and recorded equally clever but far more serious material like "Rapid City, South Dakota", the surprisingly melancholy "Ride 'Em Jewboy," and the mighty "Sold American." The last of the three is a masterpiece—a tragic portrait of a washed-up country singer, it's one of the standout songs of its generation.

Kinky was born Richard Friedman in Chicago, Illinois on 31 October, 1944. He acquired true Texas roots while growing up in Austin, where he studied psychology at the University of Texas. After forming a band, the Texas Jewboys, he tried to market his music in LA but had little or no success. He turned next to Nashville, where Glaser Studios expressed some interest. Chuck Glaser produced Kinky's first record, SOLD AMERICAN, for the folk label Vanguard, which was released in 1973. The songs didn't chart, but they did earn Kinky a solid reputation among critics, along with plenty of notoriety for his unusual and seemingly touchy subject matter ("Biscuits" and "Jewboy" certainly turned some heads). The same was basically true for his follow-up albums, KINKY FRIEDMAN (released by ABC and featuring a couple of songs produced by Willie Nelson) and LASSO FROM EL PASO (Epic). The latter included a live version of "Sold American" taped while Friedman was on tour as a member of Bob Dylan's Rolling Thunder Revue.

Kinky may not have achieved mega-stardom, but the healthy following he has built up—especially in Texas—has sustained his music career ever since. In 1983 he released the album UNDER THE DOUBLE EGO, and in 1986 he ran for Justice of the Peace in Texas as a Republican (he lost). He also began writing mystery novels, the central character being a detective (and ex-country star) called the Kinkster. The books (sporting titles like *Armadillos And Old Lace* and *God Bless John Wayne*) sold well and quickly became his main occupation. He does still tour and record occasionally, however. In 1992 he was back on music store shelves with the CD OLD TESTAMENTS & NEW REVELATIONS, which included previously unreleased live versions of Friedman favorites like "Charles Whitman" and "Homo Erectus." A tribute album, PEARLS IN THE SNOW, appeared in 1999 featuring Kinky songs performed by Willie Nelson, Dwight Yoakam, Tompall Glaser, Lyle Lovett, Tom Waits, and several others.

⊙ **Sold American** (1973; Vanguard; reissued 1989). Kinky's debut album isn't your typical country record, Texan or otherwise. You'll laugh, you'll cry, you'll run in terror. Includes "Biscuits," "Ride 'Em Jewboy," "Charles Whitman," and the knockout title track.

⊙ **From One Good American To Another** (1995; Fruit Of The Tune). Like OLD TESTAMENTS, this is another oddball assortment of collectibles and rarities for hardcore Kinky fans; novices might just get confused. Treats include live radio recordings from the 1980s (reverent solo versions of country classics like "Old Shep" and "The Ballad Of Ira Hayes") and 1974 ("Amelia Earhart," "Rapid City"), and 3 songs from 1979 featuring Dr John and members of Dylan's road band.

Tompall Glaser

"In order to get goosebumps, you've got to strike a basic chord."
—Tompall Glaser

It's rather amazing that Tompall Glaser's name is not better remembered. The man was very much a country music star, after all, with hit records, a successful song publishing company, and even a popular recording studio all bearing his name. Of all the major Outlaw players, in fact (perhaps with the exception of David Allan Coe), Glaser showed the most enthusiasm when it came to exploiting the moniker. He titled one album THE GREAT TOMPALL AND HIS OUTLAW BAND, and was always dreaming up crazy Outlaw schemes to attract further publicity.

As for Tompall's music, it still stands tall on its own merits. He had a distinct and entirely pleasant husky-sweet voice, he wrote some enduring songs, and he simply had an honest feel for soulful country music. He cut a series of exciting records throughout the 1960s and '70s, both under his own name and with his brothers Chuck and Jim as Tompall And The Glaser Brothers. His debut solo album, CHARLIE, was a great (but amazingly overlooked) example of what Outlaw music was all about, and the Outlaw Band he subsequently put together, featuring blues guitarist Mel Brown, was a real sizzler.

Tompall Glaser was born on 3 September, 1933 in Spalding, Nebraska. With brothers Chuck and Jim, he formed the folk trio Tompall And The Glaser Brothers in the late '50s. Their tight harmony singing impressed Marty Robbins, who signed them to his own label and released their debut single, "Five Penny Nickel." In 1958 they moved to Nashville, where they signed with Decca. Here they also worked as session musicians, toured with Johnny Cash, cut a series of pretty folk songs that ended up on the Decca album THIS LAND, and joined the *Grand Ole Opry*.

Around the mid-'60s, the Glasers hooked up with producer Jack Clement, who helped steer their music away from the quaint folk-revival sound towards a contemporary-country direction. In 1966 the Glasers signed with MGM, and over the next several years they released a series of excellent albums. The music—still rooted to some degree in folk music—had a hip and lively flair that set it apart from typical Nashville Sound country. The harmonies were a definite highlight

and were dominated by the sturdy voice of lead singer Tompall. Throughout the rest of the decade and into the next, the brothers had a series of hits including "Gone, On The Other Hand," "Through The Eyes Of Love," "California Girl (And The Tennessee Square)," and the fantastically catchy "Rings." As well as producing, Clement wrote quite a few of their songs. Tompall also penned a few, and one of them, "Streets Of Baltimore" (co-written with Harlan Howard), is a minor classic that was covered by both Bobby Bare and, later, Gram Parsons.

In 1969 the brothers opened their own recording studio in Nashville. It soon took on the nickname Hillbilly Central and became a major focal point of the burgeoning 'underground' country scene in Music City—not only a place to make records when the right mood struck (which was sometimes in the dead of night), but also somewhere to simply hang out in laid-back comfort, safely walled off from the stiff, stale business vibe that buzzed up and down Music Row. Waylon Jennings recorded his classic DREAMING MY DREAMS album at Glaser Studios, and for a while he even kept an office in the building.

The Glasers also had their own publishing companies which enabled them to score their biggest coup of all. A young folkie songwriter named John Hartford came their way in the mid-'60s with "Gentle On My Mind," an easygoing song about a carefree ramblin' man that he'd had no luck selling. The Glasers snatched it up, and soon they had a taker in Glen Campbell, whose own singing career was just getting off the ground. In 1966 "Gentle On My Mind" was a smash country and pop hit, boosting the reputations of both its singer and its songwriter. It went on to become one of the most-covered songs in country music history.

Tompall And The Glaser Brothers had won all sorts of awards, including Vocal Group of the Year from the CMA and Vocal Group of the Decade from *Record World* magazine (they even named an album after that award). In 1973, however, they stopped playing and touring together. Tompall immediately began recording as a solo artist, and Outlaw became his badge of honor. His initial solo album, CHARLIE, showed Glaser at his creative peak, though it took a novelty song, "Put Another Log On The Fire" from his next album TOMPALL (SINGS THE SONGS OF SHEL SILVERSTEIN), to win him a spot in the country Top 40. In 1976, that song also became one of two Tompall recordings included on the compilation WANTED! THE OUTLAWS. That album may have sold a cool million, but the pompously titled album THE GREAT TOMPALL AND HIS OUTLAW BAND is more representative of what Tompall was all about musically. It marked a bold new sound centering around lead guitarist Brown and drummer Charles Polk, whom Tompall had hired from bluesman Bobby "Blue" Bland's band. Mixing black and white musical traditions (let alone players) was a bold step in conservative Nashville, but anyone who was paying attention knew that the Outlaw Band was one of the city's top outfits at the time.

As the '70s wound down, so did all the Outlaw excitement. Maybe one clear indication that things had changed came when Tompall and Waylon, who'd been close friends through much of the decade, had a major falling-out and parted ways. As for Tompall's career, in 1977 he recorded one more album with the Outlaw Band (with a slightly simpler title, TOMPALL GLASER AND HIS OUTLAW BAND) as well as a solo album, THE WONDER OF IT ALL. The latter was produced by soon-to-be Nashville bigshot Jimmy Bowen and yielded a minor hit with the honky-tonker "Drinking Them Beers."

The brothers reunited and signed with Elektra Records in 1980, and they had some success with the Kris Kristofferson song "Lovin' Her Was Easier (Than Anything I'll Ever Do Again)," the title of their reunion album. They split again in 1983, however, and Tompall returned to his Nashville recording studio. He released the solo album NIGHTS ON THE BORDERLINE for MCA Dot in 1986, but since then has largely remained out of the spotlight.

○ **Charlie** (1973; MGM). Tompall's best release as a solo artist or otherwise, CHARLIE is one of the true classics of Outlaw country. The mood is low-key and restrained overall, highlighted by deeply sad songs like "Gideon Bible," "Loneliest Man," and a knockout version of Kinky Friedman's bottomed-out cowboy lament "Sold American."

○ **Vocal Group Of The Decade** (1975; MGM). Released when the Glaser Brothers were in remission, Tompall's vocal handling of two early Jimmy Buffett songs ("The Christian" and "Tin Cup Chalice") alone makes this worth seeking out. The rest is icing on the cake. A superb Glaser Brothers collection.

○ **The Great Tompall And His Outlaw Band** (1976; MGM). The first of 2 albums to feature Tompall's hot new band showcasing lead guitarist Mel Brown. It's a tastefully restrained collection that mixes blues, R&B,

bar-room country and western swing influences with incredible skill and genuine soul.

⊙ **The Rogue** (1992; Bear Family). Tompall recorded a third album for ABC, UNWANTED OUTLAW, but the label folded before it was released. Here it is—no big surprises, but a few solid songs, among them Harlan Howard's "Like An Old Country Song" and Dennis Wilson's "The Man You Think To See." The CD also includes a group of country and pop classics ("I'll Hold You In My Heart," "My Pretty Quadroon") that Tompall cut during the 1980s and also never before released.

⊙ **The Outlaw** (1992; Bear Family). Packs together 2 albums Tompall cut for ABC during the late '70s, TOMPALL AND HIS OUTLAW BAND and THE WONDER OF IT ALL. Not as juicy as the previous MGM solo LPs, but it does include the standouts "Come Back Shane" and "Drinking Them Beers."

Tom T. Hall

T om T. Hall's songs have the casual feel of an afternoon chat at the corner drugstore, or a rambling, late-night story told over a cup of coffee or a bottle of bourbon. As Hall's songs unfold, he invites you to share the simple thoughts and day-to-day happenings of his own life and the lives of countless folks he's come to know during the course of his travels. He sings of a young hitchiker, a hog farmer, a coal miner, and a wounded veteran, and at first the anecdotes seem plain, nice, nothing out of the ordinary. But then it hits you: hidden inside these everyday experiences are moments of subtle but extraordinary insight.

Though his songs have an easygoing, conversational appeal, Hall has a literary, almost journalistic style which reveals itself in his sharp eye for detail—the "Dominicker chickens" in "A Trip To Hyden"; the "hot baloney, eggs, and gravy" in "A Week In A Country Jail"; the "little boy's bike" in "Margie's At The Lincoln Park Inn," a masterpiece of a song that speaks clearly of adultery between its lines. His songs are sometimes straight-up fun ("I Like Beer," "Subdivision Blues"), other times deeply sad ("Mama Bake A Pie," another stellar song, this time about a Vietnam vet's wounded homecoming). He sings about social issues ("The Man Who Hated Freckles") and local tragedies ("Trip To Hyden," about a coal-mine explosion), but just as quickly turns his pen inward ("I'm Forty Now"). Hall titled a 1970 album of

Tom T. Hall

unabashedly describe himself as one of Nashville's only democrats.

Hall himself signed to Mercury Records in 1967, making a small splash with "I Washed My Hands In The Morning Dew." A year later, however, when Jeannie C. Riley turned his song "Harper Valley P.T.A." into a massive pop and country smash, he was suddenly famous and began making the charts himself with songs like "Ballad Of Forty Dollars," "Homecoming," and "A Week In A County Jail." He went on to enjoy a healthy number of hits, in fact, throughout the rest of the '60s and all through the next decade, earning himself a reputation along the way as one of Nashville's most respected song-writers—and this despite his reluc-tance to steer clear of controversial subject matter ("Watergate Blues," "America The Ugly"). He also championed the work of new artists like Johnny Rodriguez and Billy Joe Shaver (whose hard-partying habits were the indirect subject of Hall's song "Joe, Don't Let Your Music Kill You"), and he honored blue-grass music by cutting THE MAG-NIFICENT MUSIC MACHINE in 1976 with Bill Monroe, Jimmy Martin, and other of the genre's greats.

Hall was inducted into the Nashville Song-writers Hall of Fame in 1978. His hitmaking days were drying up by the early '80s, but he did con-tinue to record now and again. Eventually, however, he moved toward a more reclusive lifestyle. It wasn't quite retirement, as he's con-tinued to write not only songs but also books, including the novel *The Laughing Man Of Woodmont Cove.*

his I WITNESS LIFE, and it's as good a phrase as any to sum up his frank, honest approach.

Born on 25 May, 1936 in Olive Hill, Ken-tucky, Hall wrote his first song at the age of nine, dropped out of school during his teens in order to work, formed a bluegrass band and, later, worked as a DJ. After a stint in the army (where he continued with his singing and songwriting), he moved to Virginia where he began writing courses at a local college. Friends encouraged his songwriting, and one of them brought a demo tape to Newkeys Music in Nashville. In 1963 Jimmy Newman became the first to cut a Hall song, "DJ For A Day." Hall moved to Nashville the following year, took a $50-a-week songwriting job at Newkeys, settled into a steady and incredibly disciplined nine-to-five writing schedule, and had further songs picked up by singers like Dave Dudley (who cut quite a few Hall songs over the years) and Johnny Wright. The latter hit #1 with "Hello Vietnam," which was sympathetic toward US foreign policy ("We must save freedom now at any cost") and is a surprising anomaly in the Hall oeuvre considering he would later

○ **In Search Of A Song** (1971; Mercury). The album title refers to Hall's penchant for driving around the South, meeting local folks in small country towns, hearing their stories and turning those tales into songs. The knockout "Trip To Hyden" is a perfect example.

○ **For The People In The Last Hard Town** (1973; Mercury). Nearly every one of Hall's 1960s and '70s Mercury albums contain excellent material and are worth seeking out. Besides the catchy title track, the true (and highly overlooked) standout here is "Pay No

Attention To Alice," a rambling story-song about "doing some drinking" with an army buddy and keeping tabs on the guy's alcoholic wife.

⊙ **Storyteller, Poet, Philosopher** (1995; Mercury). An excellent 2-CD, 50-song overview of Hall's long career. The focus is on Hall's '70s material (none of his '80s albums are represented), though it stretches as far back as "I Washed My Face in the Morning Dew" and includes a 1988 duet with Johnny Cash, "The Last Of The Drifters"—not to mention two unreleased tracks, "Give Her My Best" and "Levi Jones."

⊙ **The Essential Tom T. Hall: The 20th Anniversary Collection—The Story Songs** (1998; PolyGram). A solid collection not of Hall's biggest hits but of some of his most interesting and memorable stories. Includes "A Week In A County Jail," "Trip To Hyden," "Homecoming," and even "Pay No Attention To Alice."

⊙ **Real: The Tom T. Hall Project** (1998; Sire). A tribute album to Hall's songwriting genius, featuring Johnny Cash ("I Washed My Face In The Morning Dew"), Joe Henry ("Homecoming"), Freedy Johnston ("Coffee, Coffee, Coffee"), Iris Dement, Whiskeytown, Calexico, and eleven others.

Linda Hargrove

Linda Hargrove

"The music business nearly killed me."
—Linda Hargrove

Singer, songwriter and guitarist Linda Hargrove showed lots of promise as a strong young artist in Nashville during the mid-1970s. Her voice was earthy and soulful, her songs were a mixture of earthy country and laid-back rock'n'roll, and the arrangements on her albums like BLUE JEAN COUNTRY QUEEN were decidedly unglamorous. In terms of both musical and personal style, Hargrove aligned herself more with artists like Asleep At The Wheel (with whom she toured) and Willie Nelson than with anybody or anything remotely sophisticated—with her long straight hair and lack of heavy make-up, she was definitely an anomaly among female country artists at the time. Hargrove made the charts only briefly herself; she attained her biggest success as a songwriter, penning hits for Johnny Rodriguez ("Just Get Up And Close The Door"), Lynn Anderson ("I've Never Loved Anyone More"), George Jones ("Tennessee Whiskey"), and even Olivia Newton-John ("Let It Shine").

Hargrove was born on 3 February, 1949, in Tallahassee, Florida. She came to Nashville in 1970 and hooked up with steel guitarist Pete Drake, who became her mentor. Drake got her work on various studio sessions, and he also signed her to a publishing contract. West Coast country-rock artist (and former Monkee) Mike Nesmith helped Hargrove land a recording contract with Elektra, and her first album, MUSIC IS YOUR MISTRESS, was released in 1973, followed by BLUE JEAN COUNTRY QUEEN. After that Hargrove released further albums on Capitol and RCA. Even if she never had much chart success, she did tour regularly, worked up a steady following, and earned respect from such Nashvillians as Drake, Rodriguez, and Tom T. Hall.

By the end of the decade, however, she was burning herself out. During the early '80s she stepped away from the country music business and eventually turned to Jesus (who'd shown a presence on her albums already with songs like "The Only Man-Made Things In Heaven Are The Scars On Jesus' Hands"). She married Charlie Bartholomew

Linda Hargrove

and recorded a couple of Christian albums under her new name, Linda Bartholomew. In 1986, she contracted cancer, and she spent the next decade fighting the disease. She finally managed to beat it off, and by the late '90s was once again writing and singing.

◉ **Blue Jean Country Queen** (1974; Elektra). Unfortunately, Hargrove's mid-1970s recordings have yet not made it to CD, and her name isn't well remembered even among Outlaw country fans. Which is a shame, because this album (probably her finest) is a great mix of country, rock, soul, and even touches of western swing (mostly in Buddy Spicher's saucy fiddling). Hargrove can sing about love and nostalgia—and even show a positive outlook—without resorting to cheap sentiment, and without losing the edge in her down-to-earth arrangements.

Ray Wylie Hubbard

R ay Wylie Hubbard is yet another artist whose fame, at least in his formative years, was built around a single song. In his case it was the tongue-in-cheek sing-along anthem "Up Against The Wall, Redneck Mother," a rowdy parody of Texas good ole boy values that beautifully weaved together such subjects as pickup trucks, beer and anger toward young folks of the long-haired variety. "Redneck Mother" became Jerry Jeff Walker's theme song and it also gave Hubbard's solo career a much-needed boost. Since the 1970s, however, Hubbard has struggled to build a reputation beyond that song; by the '90s he was finally succeeding with such albums as LOCO GRINGO'S LAMENT, DANGEROUS SPIRITS, and CRUSADES OF THE RESTLESS KNIGHTS.

Born in Oklahoma on 13 November, 1946, Hubbard moved to New Mexico after graduating from college and eventually formed the band Ray Wylie Hubbard And The Cowboy Twinkies. Later he met Jerry Jeff and began writing songs with him. "Redneck Mother" came out of this period, and it's through Walker that the song gained its popularity—it appeared in 1973 on Walker's vibrant VIVA TERLINGUA album, and most self-respecting Texas country fans (at least the 'progressive' kind) knew it by heart. Hubbard's own albums, however, didn't fare so well, at least in terms of bringing him national fame. During the mid-'70s he and his band recorded for Atlantic and Warner Brothers, then Hubbard cut a solo album,

OFF THE WALL, for Willie Nelson's Lone Star label. Later, he worked with Walker's Lost Gonzo Band on the live album CAUGHT IN THE ACT. A few more records followed during the '80s and early '90s, but it really wasn't until Hubbard released LOCO GRINGO'S LAMENT on the Texas label, Dejadisc, that people began to take some notice of his work again. It's an open and honest record, reflecting a new attitude that was at least partly due to his kicking drugs and alcohol. Two further new albums have followed so far on the Philo label, and they all show Hubbard building a new audience with strong, confident material that's varied in subject matter and musical influences.

☉ **Loco Gringo's Lament** (1994; Dejadisc). Lloyd Maines and Brian Hardin co-produced this album of 12 new tracks, which alternate between low-key, introspective and largely acoustic-based songs, and others that wield a beefier, bluesier, and far more electrified sound. Hubbard's voice has a road-weary tone, which gives his singing an inviting lived-in quality.

☉ **Dangerous Spirits** (1997; Philo/Rounder). The 10 songs on SPIRITS take Hubbard into denser arrangements and musical territory that can get rather edgy and even dark. Love songs and a dose or two of good humor do exist ("Hey That's All Right" even brings to mind fellow Texas singer-songwriter Robert Earl Keen), but the spooky "Last Younger Son" is more the mood of the day. Lucinda Williams, Tony Joe White, and other guest artists make brief appearances.

Waylon Jennings

"There's nothing faddish or contrived or artificial about him. If he sings it, you can believe it."

—Chet Flippo, 1973

C ountry music in the 1970s—hell, country music ever since—would have been a whole different ballgame without the rich voice and bold presence of Waylon Jennings. He was a successful singer brave enough to demand creative control of his own records; when he got it, he turned out some of the era's strongest country albums and biggest hit songs, which in turn helped inspire a new perspective on country music. They called Waylon an 'Outlaw,' a name that originated with a song he cut in 1972 called "Ladies Love Outlaws," but he didn't take too well to being

called one himself—more often than not he prefered 'hillbilly.' Or cowboy. As for friends, they called him Hoss. Like it or not, however, Waylon was the movement's poster boy.

By the time of his landmark 1973 album HONKY TONK HEROES (composed almost entirely of laid-back cowboy-drifter songs by a fellow Texan, Billy Joe Shaver), Waylon was already a star. He'd been a professional musician since the '50s and a popular country hitmaker for close to a decade. He'd briefly played in Buddy Holly's band, but his rockabilly career ended when Holly was tragically killed in a plane crash (Jennings was supposed to be on that plane, too, but at the last minute gave up his seat to the Big Bopper). When Jennings started playing country seriously in the early '60s, his sound had a thick, steady rhythm that reflected his rock'n'roll background.

Many of Waylon's '60s recordings are excellent, but the music he created in the '70s demonstrated a far more confident approach. The songs, the arrangements and his full-bodied voice added up to some of the most deeply profound music that modern Nashville had yet experienced. The albums HONKY TONK HEROES, DREAMING MY DREAMS, and THIS TIME were instrumentally spare and almost jarringly low-key—quite the opposite of the lush, orchestral, and too-often predictable approach that Chet Atkins and other Nashville Sound producers had so finely honed. Songs like "Ride Me Down Easy," "Freedom To Stay," and "Are You Sure Hank Done It This Way?" harkened back to older country sounds, but they also revealed a hip, contemporary perspective. Whatever feathers were ruffled on Music Row, the truth soon became clear that Waylon was onto something. People both young and old were responding to his songs, and country music

as a whole, like they hadn't done since the onslaught of rockabilly twenty years previously. All of a sudden this bearded, shaggy haired, rough-and-tumble cowboy who preferred black leather to Nudie suits was turning into a superstar.

Waylard Arnold Jennings was born on 15 June, 1937 in Littlefield, Texas, a small town in the flatlands of the Panhandle. He started playing on a local radio station as a teenager with a band called the Texas Longhorns. In time this blossomed into a full-fledged career as a DJ, one he'd maintain on and off into the '60s. Working stations and playing country shows in Littlefield and nearby Lubbock, he met Buddy Holly, who got Waylon his first recording session in 1958 (the single "Jole Blon" was released by Brunswick) and then hired him to play bass in his band. Only a few months later, however, Holly was dead and Waylon found himself disillusioned and unsure where to turn. He eventually moved out to Phoenix, Arizona, continuing to DJ and also playing all sorts of honky tonks and bars. By the early '60s he'd earned a sturdy reputation in the region as a live performer, especially at a large Phoenix club called J.D.'s. Herb Alpert signed Waylon to A&M Records in 1963, but the two didn't quite mesh. Waylon figured himself a country singer, but many of the songs he recorded for that West Coast label seemed geared toward the urban folk crowd, including "Kisses Sweeter Than Wine" and Bob Dylan's "Don't Think Twice." The songs themselves weren't bad, but A&M wasn't much of a country label (it was probably best known for Alpert's own Tijuana Brass albums), and Waylon's records got little response.

Bobby Bare heard Waylon out in Phoenix and liked his style, even cutting two songs from Waylon's repertoire, Ian Tyson's "Four Strong Winds" and the Jennings original "Just To Satisfy You." He encouraged RCA's Chet Atkins to sign the young singer, and in 1965 Waylon was out of his A&M contract and on the RCA roster. When he first moved to Nashville he shared an apartment with a newly divorced Johnny Cash, but soon he was on the road. For years he kept up a grueling schedule of more than three hundred dates a year. His first RCA album was called FOLK-COUNTRY, showing that RCA, too, was trying to reach the younger generation. With his full-bodied voice and dark-eyed good looks, Waylon's appeal was strong right from the start. He played to mostly straight-laced country audiences, but younger fans were attracted as well. Songs like "Stop The World (And Let Me Off)," "Love Of The Common People," and Mel Tillis' "Mental Revenge" had a strong beat that showed his rockabilly influence and became a trademark of his sound. He also cut ballads such as "I'm A Man Of Constant Sorrow," Roger Miller's "Lock, Stock And Teardrops," and Harlan Howard's "Baby, Don't Be Looking In My Mind." He had a greased-back pompadour and spoke in a hipster's lingo, but he'd grown up pure country, and these roots were evident as soon as he started singing.

Waylon was very successful by the start of the '70s, but he was also growing restless. With all the touring and the recording sessions that were less and less inspired, it was time for a change. He'd worked well with Atkins, but other producers assigned to his records just didn't seem to get it. In 1970 he sidestepped Nashville and recorded an album in California, SINGER OF SAD SONGS, produced by Lee Hazlewood. His biggest and boldest step, however, came a couple of years later when he negotiated the rights to produce his own albums, pick his own songs, and use his touring band, the Waylors, in the studio. The first was LONESOME, ON'RY AND MEAN, and it brandished a deliberately spare, traditionally-minded approach that released Waylon from the creative confines of the Nashville Sound. No string sections, background choruses, or bullheaded staff producers to get in the way. To top off his new 'rebel' image, Waylon was now sporting long hair, a full beard and an entourage of leather-clad good ole boys only a fool would mess with.

The album that truly cemented Waylon's journey toward free expression was HONKY TONK HEROES. The cover alone caused a ruckus—a black-and-white photo of Jennings, Shaver, co-producer Tompall Glaser, and their rag-tag band of pickers drinking beer and laughing it up in RCA's hallowed Nashville Sound studio. The music inside, however, was near-impossible to argue with—fresh and inspired, subtle yet buzzing with life. It was thinking man's country, but it was also down-to-earth. Waylon continued along this path with THE RAMBLIN' MAN and the brilliantly quiet THIS TIME, and in 1975 he landed full on his feet with DREAMING MY DREAMS. This last album was produced by Jack Clement (who'd in a previous lifetime worked with Elvis Presley) at Glaser Studios, better known as Hillbilly Central. Bookended by the challenging "Are You Sure Hank Done It This Way?" and the reverent "Bob

Waylon Jennings

Wills Is Still The King," a tribute to one of Texas' musical heroes, it stands alongside HONKY TONK HEROES as a masterpiece of Waylon's career.

Some unjustly criticized Waylon's new sound as "going pop". They were probably responding to the fact that he had opened shows for the Grateful Dead, had played club dates in New York City, was getting written up in *Rolling Stone*, and had a new audience of long-haired, toke-friendly rock'n'rollers. Truth is, however, there was more sincere country soul on mid-'70s songs like "Mona," "Slow Moving Outlaw," "Let's All Help The Cowboys Sing The Blues," and "Old Five And Dimers Like Me" than almost anything he'd cut previously. Vocally and instrumentally, he never sounded better.

The hits began to mount up, proving that Waylon's experiments didn't waste anyone's time or money. Respect, however, was less easy to come by. Even when he won the CMA's Male Vocalist of the Year award in 1975, the establishment still considered him 'underground.' "They told me to be nice, I don't know what they meant," he joked when accepting his award. He even wore a tux (albeit without the tie) for the occasion—his pal Willie Nelson had opted instead for jeans.

Waylon and Willie had begun collaborating a few years earlier, and their musical partnership, not to mention friendship, has remained strong ever since. They recorded each other's songs and even cut duet albums together. Alas, the same can't be said of Waylon's association with Tompall

Glaser; the two were once inseparable Outlaw cohorts, with Waylon even keeping an office at Hillbilly Central, but they eventually had a huge falling-out, ostensibly over business matters.

The Outlaw schtick peaked with the 1976 release of the compilation album WANTED! THE OUTLAWS, which featured previously released songs by Waylon, Willie, Glaser, and Jessi Colter ("I'm Not Lisa"), who was also Waylon's wife. The album was more about marketing than making an artistic statement, and it hit at just the right time. It also marked the point where the Outlaw concept shifted from fresh-baked to burned-out.

Waylon had hit the charts throughout the Outlaw fever days with "I'm A Ramblin' Man," "Good-Hearted Woman" (a duet with Willie), "This Time," "Bob Wills Is Still The King," and many more. By the time WANTED! THE OUTLAWS was released he was one of country's biggest stars. His success continued hard and fast through the rest of the decade with the Austin homeboy favorite "Luckenbach, Texas (Back To The Basics Of Life)," the Ed Bruce classic "Mammas Don't Let Your Babies Grow Up To Be Cowboys" (again with Willie), and Bob McDill's "Amanda." He got boastful with "I've Always Been Crazy," but he also commented on the changing times with the poignant "Don't You Think This Outlaw Bit's Done Got Out Of Hand."

During the '80s he wrote and sang the theme to the TV show *The Dukes Of Hazzard*, cut an album of duets called WAYLON AND COMPANY, and began recording and touring with Willie, Johnny Cash, and Kris Kristofferson under the name the Highwaymen. All this, of course, happened in addition to his own solo recordings. None of his albums could match the genius and beauty of his earlier classics, but SWEET MOTHER TEXAS and WILL THE WOLF SURVIVE (the title track is a Los Lobos song) were two that held their own very well. The latter also marked Waylon's move after twenty years from RCA to MCA. Four years later, in 1990, he switched again to Epic.

His most recent chart hits were the early '90s recordings "Wrong" and "The Eagle." After that, his popularity finally gave way to changing times and tastes. "The new hats are here, it's increasingly clear, our time is slipping on by," he sang—in a voice more matter-of-fact than remorseful or angry—on the still-solid 1992 album TOO DUMB FOR NEW YORK CITY, TOO UGLY FOR LA. Since then he's continued to work with the Highwaymen, and he's recorded solo albums for the indie labels Justice (RIGHT FOR THE TIME) and Ark 21 (CLOSING IN ON THE FIRE). As of the late

'90s his concerts were still musically thrilling and, given the formulaic nature of much of contemporary country, as refreshing and vital as ever.

⊙ **Folk-Country** (1966; RCA; reissued 1998; Koch). On Waylon's debut album for RCA, producer Atkins let him bring his road band into the studio to play alongside the A Team. It's a much simpler and more innocent Waylon than the burly voiced 1970s incarnation, and entirely pleasant.

⊙ **Honky Tonk Heroes** (1973; RCA; reissued 1999; Buddha). Nine of the 10 songs are from the pen of Billy Joe Shaver, and Waylon's classic voice and spare approach helped make them anthems of the Outlaw age. An essential collection.

◉ **This Time** (1974; RCA). Produced by Willie Nelson, this album was as deeply quiet and moody as Waylon ever got. Songs like "Slow Moving Outlaw," "Mona," and "It's Not Supposed To Be That Way" simply shouldn't be passed up.

⊙ **Dreaming My Dreams** (1975; RCA). Waylon's career-topping achievement kicks off with the rocked-up anthem "Are You Sure Hank Done It This Way?" then shifts into a slower gear with beauties like "Let's All Help The Cowboys Sing The Blues" and the title track.

⊙ **The Journey: Destiny's Child** (1999; Bear Family). A 6-CD box set that covers the first decade of Waylon's career. Begins with his his initial 1958 single (produced by Buddy Holly) and includes his rare first album (WAYLON JENNINGS AT J.D.'S), his A&M sessions, and his RCA recordings through to 1968.

Kris Kristofferson

"Kris was everybody's idol in Nashville, all the street people's idol."

—David Allan Coe

The infiltration of Kris Kristofferson into the Nashville mainstream was a near-revolutionary landmark in modern country history. It wasn't just about opening the Music Row doors to laid-back cowboy attitudes, all-night parties and long hippie hair, it was about approaching the music itself from a new perspective. Songs like "Me And Bobby McGee," "Sunday Mornin' Comin' Down," and "Help Me Make It Through The Night" are today

Kris Kristofferson

event of the year—his stumbling onto the stage provoked a stern glare from host Tennessee Ernie Ford for all in TV land to see—but because the song was so different by the standards of the day. Johnny Cash had given "Sunday Mornin'" his stamp of approval by recording it, but turning a smoky Sunday hangover into poetry with lines like "the beer I had for breakfast wasn't bad so I had one more for dessert" was a concept many others found hard to swallow. However, with so much popular support behind that and other Kristofferson songs, all the folks on Music Row could do was wince in displeasure and brace themselves for the invasion.

Kristoffer Kristofferson was born on 22 June, 1936 in Brownsville, Texas. He studied creative writing at Pomona College in California, boxed, played football, and won a Rhodes Scholarship to Oxford, England. After a couple of years, however, he tired of academia and took up active duty in the Army, training as a helicopter pilot. While the Army had a career mapped out for him teaching English at West Point, Kris—who'd been writing songs and playing music on his own for years—was far more enamored with the music of Merle Haggard, Bob Dylan, and Johnny Cash. Through a friend he met songwriter Marijohn Wilkin ("Long Black Veil"), who ran a Nashville publishing company, Buckhorn Music. She liked Kristofferson's writing, and that was all the restless poet needed to hear. In 1965 he and his wife and daughter moved to Nashville.

such classics because they marked the transition between staid *Grand Ole Opry* traditions and a fresher, more open-minded approach—one that took into account Bob Dylan as much as Hank Williams. Some on Music Row may have disapproved, but the reality was that Nashville had been starved for songwriting that was this smart, down-to-earth, honest, and fearless.

Kristofferson's journey to Nashville is an amazing tale in itself. In his previous incarnation he was a Rhodes Scholar, Golden Gloves boxer, army helicopter pilot and budding novelist who dabbled in music on the side. To his military father's complete horror, he eventually chose the dubious path of songwriting over a solid gig teaching English at West Point. When in 1970 he walked on stage at the Country Music Assocation awards show to receive his trophy for writing "Sunday Mornin' Comin' Down," however, country music was never quite the same again.

That moment was significant not only because Kristofferson showed up sporting long hair, a hip black leather jacket, and a doper's gentle grin to what was (and still is) Nashville's classiest tuxedo

Kris cut a single but it went nowhere, and after that he struggled through some very lean years—living in a slum apartment, working as a janitor at Columbia Studios, bartending at the Tally Ho Tavern, and helicoptering oil workers out to the rigs in the Gulf of Mexico. In 1968 Roy Drusky cut one of his songs, "Jody And The Kid," but a bigger break came a year later when Roger Miller recorded "Me And Bobby McGee" and two other of Kris' songs. That deal was brokered by Mickey Newbury, a mutual friend and fellow songwriter. Kristofferson played songs with and picked up pointers from visiting folkies like Buffy Sainte-Marie, Joni Mitchell, and Graham Nash. He was already friends with Johnny Cash, and he wowed the Man in Black further by landing a helicopter

Kris Kristofferson

in his backyard to deliver a demo tape. In 1969 and at Cash's invitation, his performing career kicked off when he sang one song at the Newport Folk Festival. A year later Cash cut "Sunday Mornin' Comin' Down," which soared to #1 and resulted in Kristofferson's infamous CMA award.

Fred Foster had signed Kristofferson to his publishing company, Combine Music, in 1969 and given the budding writer much crucial support. In 1970 Foster's record label, Monument, released his first album, KRISTOFFERSON (later retitled ME AND BOBBY MCGEE). Though simple and unassuming, it's home to many of his best songs. Quite a few of these were picked up by other singers and shaken into big hits: Ray Price gave the slow-moving "For The Good Times" some country-politan class, Janis Joplin turned "Me And Bobby McGee" into a rock'n'roll anthem, and with her smoldering voice Sammi Smith made the sensual come-on "Help Me Make It Through The Night" impossible to resist. This last recording was quite scandalous by Nashville standards, as it not only implied that casual sex was nothing out of the ordinary, but was sung from a woman's point of view. These issues weren't *too* big a problem, however: it still won both the CMA's Single of the Year award and a Grammy in 1971.

Kristofferson has never been a pretty singer, but his deep, pockmarked voice was at the time entirely refreshing and honest. He made the pop and country charts several times over with songs like "Loving Her Was Easier (Than Anything I'll Ever Do Again)," "Jesus Was A Capricorn," "Josie," and the unabashedly introspective "Why Me" (his only country #1). These songs were taken from albums such as JESUS WAS A CAPRICORN, BORDER LORD, and THE SILVER TONGUED DEVIL AND I, released one after the other in the early '70s, all of them popular, and all also excellent showcases of his gut-level approach. He also cut three duet albums with singer Rita Coolidge, who became his second wife in 1973.

A strapping vision of manliness, it wasn't long before Kristofferson was shipped off to Hollywood. His first movie role was in Dennis Hopper's notorious *The Last Movie*, and this was followed by *Cisco Pike*, Sam Peckinpah's *Pat Garrett And Billy The Kid* (in which he plays an excellent Billy alongside James Coburn's Garrett), *Alice Doesn't Live Here Anymore*, *The Sailor Who Fell From Grace With The Sea* (a bodice-ripper co-starring Sarah Miles and promoted in *Playboy* with a steamy layout of "simulated" sex), *Convoy*, and *Heaven's Gate*. His shirtless publicity shot with Barbra Streisand for the 1976 film *A Star Is Born* may have

seemed like the peak of his run as a macho leading man, but today that photo, and the movie itself, are pure camp. Since that specific image is (unfairly) how most people remember him today, you could say it marked his career downturn—that, of course, coupled with the arrogance of fame and his increasing appetite for whiskey and dope (the *Star Is Born* storyline was barely fiction).

By the '80s Kristofferson had quit drinking (the drugs took a bit longer to shake), but musically his star was past its peak. His last big chart success as a solo performer, in fact, had been "Watch Closely Now" from the multimillion-selling *Star Is Born* soundtrack. That didn't matter so much, however, as he still worked in films (including Alan Rudolph's *Songwriter*), saw one of his songs ("They Killed Him") cut by Dylan, and became more involved in political issues such as protesting the US involvement in Nicaragua (see his 1986 album REPOSSESSED).

At the same time he teamed up with pals Johnny Cash, Waylon Jennings, and Willie Nelson under the name the Highwaymen. They released their first album in 1985 and have since recorded two more, HIGHWAYMEN II (1990) and THE ROAD GOES ON FOREVER (1995). In 1995 the Texas label Justice released Kristofferson's best album in years, A MOMENT OF FOREVER. By the late '90s he was busy making a strong comeback as an actor, proving his mettle in films like *Lone Star* (directed by John Sayles) and *A Soldier's Daughter Never Cries*. In 1999 Kristofferson re-recorded a bunch of his classic songs for his new label, Atlantic, with loads of special guests like Steve Earle, Matraca Berg, Vince Gill, and Alison Krauss. The results were released under the title THE AUSTIN SESSIONS.

⊙ **Me And Bobby McGee** (1970; Monument). Kristofferson's landmark debut album (originally entitled KRISTOFFERSON) was the turning point between old-fashioned Nashville values and a more adventurous age of country songwriting. It's packed from surface to core with Kristofferson's own beautifully raw, intensely soulful versions of "Casey's Last Ride," "Help Me Make It Through The Night," "Sunday Mornin' Comin' Down," and other modern classics.

⊙ **The Silver-Tongued Devil And I** (1971; Monument). More of the best of Kristofferson, including "Jody And The Kid," "The Taker," the overlooked "Billy Dee," and even a Billy Joe Shaver cover, "Good Christian Soldier."

⊙ **Singer/Songwriter** (1991; Sony). A great Kristofferson introduction and a smart concept: one disc is devoted to Kris' own recordings from 1970 through to 1986's "They Killed Him," while the other includes 19 of his songs in versions by Dave Dudley ("Vietnam Blues"), Sammi Smith ("Help Me Make It Through The Night"), Brenda Lee ("Nobody Wins"), and Hank Williams, Jr. ("If You Don't Like Hank Williams").

⊙ **Live At The Philharmonic** (1992; Sony). Recorded in New York City in 1972 but not released until two decades later, this 24-track disc showcases Kristofferson and his crack touring band (Donnie Fritts, Terry Paul, Stephen Bruton, etc.) in their prime. The impressive set list includes John Prine's "Late John Garfield Blues," the soul classic "Rainbow Road," and an updated "Okie From Muskogee."

⊙ **A Moment Of Forever** (1995; Justice). An impressive batch of new songs fills what's easily Kristofferson's best album in years. His voice is even rougher around the edges than it was two decades back, but the production (by Don Was) and Kristofferson's soul (dustier but wiser) intact.

Willie Nelson

"He was hot in Texas and that was the only place we could sell him."
—Chet Atkins

Few artists in country music have as long, broad, and stylistically diverse a musical history as Texas singer, songwriter, guitarist, and bandleader Willie Nelson. His reputation as an Outlaw icon and figurehead of the Austin, Texas music scene—a persona that emerged in the mid-1970s—is how most folks know him. And well they should: along with Johnny Cash, Nelson has been hugely successful in bridging the gap between the rock'n'roll counterculture and the country music mainstream, attracting fans on both sides of the fence with equal fervor. Throw in the pop standards on Nelson's 1978 album STARDUST, and his audience broadens even further to include fans from mainstream Middle America who had always steered clear of country music.

But Nelson had almost an entire career previous to all that activity. Arriving in Nashville in 1960, he became one of the era's most successful and highly regarded songwriters, penning such classics as "Crazy," "Family Bible," and "Hello Walls." As a recording artist he was prolific even then, though he rarely broke into the charts—and

creatively he felt stifled by the production methods of the time, and the fact that few on Music Row seemed to understand his approach. Willie's singing, for instance, was atypical—he had a style of phrasing that moved back and forth over the beat, landing just before and then just after it rather than squarely following the rhythm. Folks on Music Row tried to shape his sound into something they perceived as marketable, but it never quite worked. Still, the first half of Nelson's career remains an important part of who he is—and, frankly, there are some excellent songs and recordings from that period that many of his longtime fans have only barely explored.

The Willie as we know him surfaced on RED HEADED STRANGER and on a couple of mid-'70s albums just previous to it, SHOTGUN WILLIE and PHASES AND STAGES. These marked the turning point in his musical development, earning him the success as a recording artist that he'd long been craving. In the process they helped shift the direction of country music as a whole. Along with his pal Waylon Jennings, Willie had by that point become a leading figure in the so-called Outlaw movement, which was, at least in the beginning, about artists regaining creative control of their music in the studio. Willie fully achieved that control on RED HEADED STRANGER, which is exactly what makes it such a powerful record.

Willie Hugh Nelson was born on 30 April, 1933 in Fort Worth, Texas but grew up in the small town of Abbott. His family was musically inclined, surrounding him with gospel and country, though his interests soon deepened from honky tonk into western swing, polka, and even pop music. After serving in the Air Force and getting married (for the first time), Nelson began playing in country bands and also working as a DJ. One radio gig took him as far north as Vancouver, Washington, and it's here that he made his very first recordings ("No Place For Me" b/w "Lumberjack"), which he sold via his radio show. As the '50s progressed, he returned to Texas and continued to earn his stripes playing honky tonks and bar-rooms. His songwriting, too, was maturing. He wrote "Crazy" during this time as well as "Family Bible," and the latter he sold outright for a small sum—enough to pay for groceries for his family, but not even close to what that classic song was worth. When Claude Gray made it a Top 10 hit in 1960, Nelson wasn't even given a songwriter's credit. Still, it must have proven to him that he had what it took to write hit material.

Nelson moved to Nashville in 1960. He soon met another young songwriter, Hank Cochran,

Once a hippie, always a hippie: Willie Nelson

financial success by this time, thanks to songs such as "Crazy" (recorded by Patsy Cline), "Night Life" (Ray Price), and "Funny How Time Slips Away" (Billy Walker and pop singer Jimmy Elledge).

Nelson continued to make inroads into the Nashville establishment. In 1964 he joined the cast of the *Grand Ole Opry*, and was also a regular on Ernest Tubb's TV show. He recorded briefly for Monument (including an excellent version of the dark and bitter "I Never Cared For You," which resurfaced thirty-three years later on TEATRO), and then Chet Atkins signed him to RCA and tried his hardest to refashion him into a marketable country star. He attempted to add uptown elements such as swelling strings, he tried backing Nelson with Tubb's band the Troubadours, but nothing seemed to take hold. RCA released over a dozen albums between 1966 and 1972, but only seven singles cracked the country Top 40. Questionable production values aside, quite a few of these RCA recordings—titles like "My Own Peculiar Way," "Country Willie," "Blackjack County Chain," "Laying My Burdens Down," "Happiness Lives Next Door"—are excellent in their own right, as well as being an important part of the total Willie Nelson picture. He may have later have disowned them for failing to represent his true self and spirit, but many of the songs have remained in his repertoire.

Whatever successes Nelson enjoyed for his songwriting during the '60s, the fact remained he was frustrated as a recording artist. In December of 1970 fate intervened, allowing him the out he needed: his house in Nashville burned to the ground. At this point his marriage to Collie had collapsed, and so with two points of Nashville bedrock now crumbled, he opted to move to Austin, Texas. He'd always drawn large crowds during concert tours in his home state and in Austin was greeted like the prodigal son. He quickly realized it wasn't just rednecks and cowboys who were drawn to his brand of country but also the long-haired and the young. It was, in fact, a vastly diverse audience the likes of which Nashville label executives could never have understood at the time, but it was just the sort of open-minded attitude and spirit Nelson had been seeking.

who helped get him a weekly wage at the publishing company Pamper Music (co-owned by Hal Smith and Ray Price, in whose band Nelson would later play). There Nelson wrote "Hello Walls," which became a huge hit for Faron Young and brought Nelson his first major royalty check. The downtown bar Tootsie's Orchid Lounge became one of Nelson's favorite hangouts, where he drank and talked shop with the likes of Cochran, Harlan Howard, Roger Miller, and Mel Tillis. These men were among a new breed of literal-minded country songwriters whose work shot new energy into country music and helped keep the uptown countrypolitan sound from entirely dominating (and stifling) the genre. And in the process they were winning Nashville a reputation as a vital songwriters' town, a reputation it still holds today.

Nelson recorded quite a few demos during his time at Pamper (which was later bought by Tree, a company that was in turn ultimately bought by Sony), and he had cut some records back in Texas for D and other small labels, but his first major-label deal came when Liberty signed him in 1962. The label released two albums, and in 1962 the song "Touch Me" even broke the country Top 10. Only four of his Liberty recordings made a decent showing on the charts, however (including one duet with his second wife, Shirley Collie), and he was eventually dropped. Nelson was actually enjoying an amount of

Willie Nelson

This co-mingling of lifestyles and personal backgrounds eventually came to full fruition after Nelson began hosting his Fourth of July Picnics in the small town of Dripping Springs, attracting hordes of music-loving fans and a diverse roster of performers (Waylon Jennings, Tom T. Hall, Leon Russell, etc.)—and in the process attracting lots of national attention to himself. "That was one of the reasons that I put them on," he admitted in a 1977 interview in *Country Music* magazine, "to draw attention to myself." Of course, if reports are to be believed, the picnics were damn fine musical showcases as well.

It was after moving to Austin that Nelson's appearance began to change. He grew his beard and long hair and took on the laid-back, cowboy-hippie persona that he's maintained ever since. But it wasn't all about looks: his recording style was evolving, too. His 1971 album YESTERDAY'S WINE, for example, was more stripped down than many of his earlier recordings, and deserves a place near the top of his canon. In 1972, however, Nelson left RCA and signed to Atlantic, which had just started a country division. There he worked under the guidance of famed R&B and soul producer Jerry Wexler. SHOTGUN WILLIE was Nelson's Atlantic debut, and it was a rousing effort that included the funky title track, the Johnny Bush composition "Whiskey River," which came to be a theme song of Nelson's, and a faithful version of Bob Wills' "Bubbles In My Beer." The follow-up PHASES AND STAGES, a concept album about a divorcing couple, is another of his masterpieces.

In 1975, Nelson finally achieved commercial success as a recording artist with the album RED HEADED STRANGER—not only a great album in its own right but a pivotal work in the history of contemporary Nashville for the way it ignored formulas and gained country music wider audiences and new respect, especially among young people. Nelson cut RED HEADED STRANGER in a studio in Garland, Texas, and at first his new label, Columbia, was shocked by the sparseness of the acoustic arrangements. He managed to convince them to release the album as it stood, however, and it paid off in the biggest record sales he'd seen to date for his own recordings. He also earned his first country #1, "Blue Eyes Crying In The Rain," a Fred Rose composition from the '40s. In 1975 Willie and his band performed the song live on the Country Music Association awards show where he wore jeans, an embroidered shirt, and a headband. Like it or not, Music Row had to grin and bear it, because there was just no way to argue with success.

During the latter half of the '70s Willie continued to diversify. He cut a full-on duet album with his good friend Waylon Jennings simply entitled WAYLON AND WILLIE (which included the hit "Mammas Don't Let Your Babies Grow Up To Be Cowboys"); a pair of well-conceived tribute albums to Lefty Frizzell and Kris Kristofferson; and in what really turned heads among his stalwart fans, an album of pop standards, STARDUST. Released in 1978, STARDUST sold millions of copies, spawned further hit songs like "Georgia On My Mind" and "All Of Me," won Nelson Entertainer of the Year honors in 1979 from both the CMA and the ACM, and gained him a far wider audience than he'd ever known. By the time the '70s had come to a close, Nelson's stature as one of country music's biggest and best-loved stars was solidified.

If keeping track of Nelson's recordings and other accomplishments before RED-HEADED STRANGER was difficult, afterwards it became nearly impossible. All sorts of budget compilations and reissues of earlier recordings surfaced, and Nelson himself maintained a steady output of new material that jumped from concept to concept. He cut further pop-oriented collections like SOMEWHERE OVER THE RAINBOW and ALWAYS ON MY MIND, a concert album (the rousing WILLIE AND FAMILY LIVE), gospel (THE TROUBLEMAKER), and collaborations with Leon Russell (ONE FOR THE ROAD), Ray Price (SAN ANTONIO ROSE), and Merle Haggard (PANCHO AND LEFTY). He also began acting in feature films such as *The Electric Horseman*, *Barbarosa*, *Honeysuckle Rose*, and *Songwriter*, and these spawned soundtrack albums bearing his name. And then there was the Highwaymen, a supergroup consisting of Nelson, Jennings, Kristofferson, and Johnny Cash. Their eponymously titled debut album spawned the #1 hit "Highwayman" in 1985, and two further albums followed over the next decade.

Nelson's finances took a serious beating in the early '90s when he was chased down by the IRS (Internal Revenue Service) for millions in unpaid back taxes. One solution to repaying the massive debt was the release of the CD WHO'LL BUY MY MEMORIES, subtitled THE IRS TAPES, in 1991. For this, Nelson made twenty-five incredible solo acoustic recordings that slowed his music down to its bare minimum and were stunning for their stark, haunting beauty. Further albums from the '90s such as ACROSS THE BORDERLINE, SPIRITS, and TEATRO contained some excellent material and showed Nelson was still a vital and enthusiastic recording artist.

Willie Nelson

The Austin Oasis

The musical heritage in Texas is as big and wide as the state itself. For starters, it's been the home turf of such twentieth-century giants as Bob Wills, Lightnin' Hopkins, Ernest Tubb, and Buddy Holly. Melody and rhythm are everyday occurrences that drift through the air and permeate the soil. Influences cross state lines from all sides and swirl around inside—Cajun, cowboy, and R&B songs; German oom-pah music; New Orleans jazz; and conjunto and norteno melodies from down Mexico way. Tradition is firm, but innovation has always been important, too, the result being proud new strains of country, swing, blues, and rock'n'roll for all the world to marvel.

Cities like Houston, Dallas, San Antonio, Beaumont, and Lubbock have each earned musical reputations and experienced varying shades of activity, but at the center of it all is Austin, the state's capital city and cultural focal point. Located between Dallas to the north and the Alamo to the south, with LBJ's ranch an hour to its west and numerous dry towns stacked up to its east, Austin was and still is an oasis for free-thinkers in a state known for its traditional and often conservative values. The city, too, has long been a great place to hear live music, and during the 1970s, much of the local music scene's reputation revolved around the 'progressive country' sound—music that leaned noticably left of the Nashville mainstream. Willie Nelson arrived in Austin in 1971, and his presence—and his annual Fourth of July picnics—sparked local creativity and brought the region loads of national attention. The city's healthy musical climate was further boosted by the annual Kerrville Folk Festival (held in nearby Kerrville each year since 1972), the music show-cases at the local eatery Threadgill's (Janis Joplin was a regular performer), the progressive-minded DJs on radio station KOKE, and the eclectic psychedelic-cowboy shows at the Austin nightclub Armadillo World Headquarters.

Nelson and Jerry Jeff Walker were the kings of the Austin country scene throughout the '70s, but the region was also full of singer-songwriters who were almost as highly revered by local fans at the time. Many were picked up by national labels searching, in the wake of Outlaw (and country-rock) success, for a way to further exploit the progressive market. Few, however, made more than a minor dent outside the area.

Michael Martin Murphey was the town's premier "cosmic cowboy" (another moniker that was often attached to the progressive country sound), a suc-cessful songwriter and singer who was another of the region's top draws. A native of Dallas, Murphey initially based himself in LA where he met success as a song-writer ("Calico Silver" for the First Edition, "What Am I Doing Hanging Around" for the Monkees). In 1971, however, he moved back to Texas. He earned his country colors when he recorded Geronimo's Cadillac (1972; A&M), a raspy but warm and laid-back affair that showed off his dusty-golden voice, his naturally twangy style, and his skills as a songwriter—in particular "Back-slider's Wine" and the title track. Murphey's reputation as one of Austin's top acts was deserved at the time, though a few years later he cut the overly precious "Wildfire," a milky mainstream hit that gave away his soft-rock intentions. He recorded mainstream country albums during the '80s, and since then he's focused almost exclusively on cowboy material.

⊙ **Country Willie—His Own Songs** (1965; RCA; reissued 1999; Buddha). This was Willie's first RCA album, and it collected songs he'd written that had been turned into hits by others—"My Own Peculiar Way," "Night Life," "Darkness On The Face Of The Earth," "Hello Walls," and 8 more tracks. Stubborn 1970s-era Willie fans might find Chet Atkins' production inorganic, but truth is his hand is light, allowing the songs to speak for themselves.

⊙ **Shotgun Willie** (1973; Atlantic). This album's got grit, funk, and spirit. The soul influence of producer Jerry Wexler is evident in the horns that pop in now and again—a nice touch—but the music belongs to Willie. Knockout songs include the title track, "Slow Down Old World," and Johnny Bush's "Whiskey River."

⊙ **Phases And Stages** (1974; Atlantic). The concept here is the break-up of a relationship; side one is the woman's perspective, side two the man's. It was cut in Muscle Shoals, and the arrangements strip things right down to the bone. When Willie sings "It's Not Supposed To Be that Way," the emotions are raw and exposed, and the air around his voice echoes the pain.

⊙ **Red Headed Stranger** (1975; Columbia). This album is Willie at his creative peak; and it's also one of the penultimate Outlaw albums and, quite simply, one of the finest country albums of its time. The acoustic arrangements are bare and so low-key as to be shocking (at least to Music Row executives' ears). But the atmosphere allows Willie's warm, dusty-sweet voice room to truly breathe.

Willie Nelson

Not many artists release just one album in their lifetime (so far) and win as much critical acclaim as has Alabama native **Willis Alan Ramsey**. His eponymously titled 1972 record (first released on Leon Russell's label Shelter) contained simple, refreshing, and largely acoustic country, folk, and blues songs such as "The Ballad Of Spider John" (later recorded by Jimmy Buffett) and "Muskrat Love." The latter may have become insufferable after it was turned into a pop hit by the Captain and Tennille, but Ramsey's own droopy-eyed version is more like a stoner love song. A perfectionist who preferred tinkering in his home studio to bathing in public attention, Ramsey was notoriously reclusive even during the '70s. A decade later Lyle Lovett cited Ramsey as an influence, and this brought renewed attention to his infamous record. In 1999 Ramsey's album was reissued by Koch.

Gary P. Nunn was the guy who wrote "London Homesick Blues (Home With The Armadillo)," one of the definitive anthems of the era. The song later gained even more renown as the theme to *Austin City Limits*, the weekly public television musical showcase that first aired in 1976. "Home With The Armadillo" was Nunn's chief calling card, but not his only one. He was a talented instrumentalist, singer, and songwriter who cut numerous records of his own. Recent titles like TOTALLY GUACAMOLE and NOBODY BUT ME have come out on the Campfire label. **Ray Wylie Hubbard** wrote another popular Austin anthem, "Up Against The Wall Redneck Mother," and like "London Homesick Blues" it was first popularized by Jerry Jeff Walker on his 1973 album VIVA TERLINGUA. Though Hubbard made records and toured during this time, his solo career didn't really find its groove for another two decades, most notably with his 1994 release LOCO GRINGO'S LAMENT.

Other musicians associated with the local country-folk scene include singer-songwriters **Rusty Weir** and **Steve Fromholz**; self-proclaimed "Texas Jewboy" **Kinky Friedman**; western swing revivalists **Asleep At The Wheel**; and the late **Doug Sahm**, whose mixture of deep country blues, greasy R&B, honky tonk, and rock'n'roll epitomized the melting-pot nature of Austin's musical backdrop. Gentle-voiced **B.W. Stevenson** was based in Dallas but an Austin sympathizer to his quietly emotional, folk-friendly core; and **Bobby Bridger**'s Nashville-recorded album MERGING OF OUR MINDS (1972; RCA) is, considering the grittier-than-average tone of most Austin country music, surprisingly lush and pretty—his tenor voice more Glen Campbell than Willie Nelson.

Speaking of Willie, once he achieved superstardom, he didn't hang around the clubs and beer joints so often. The Austin music scene was still doing just fine, but eventually the big labels started looking elsewhere for money-making talents and trends, and Austin fever waned. Still, the city has retained its musical reputation—thanks in no small part to the annual South By Southwest Music and Media Conference—and a new generation of country artists has moved into the local spotlight, among them Joe Ely, Jimmie Dale Gilmore, Junior Brown, Robert Earl Keen, Dale Watson, and Kelly Willis. The Armadillo is long gone, but the city's live music scene is as alive and well as ever, thanks to such venerable venues as the hip Continental Club and the tried-and-true Broken Spoke; a wealth of pickers and singers who come to town looking for luck and can't seem to leave; plenty of fortifying barbecue and Tex-Mex joints; and a sturdy base of Texas-proud music lovers hollering like young dogs for more of those good country sounds.

⊙ **Who'll Buy My Memories** (1991; Sony). Dubbed THE IRS TAPES, these 25 songs are anything but throwaways. Nowhere is Nelson's voice as unadorned, pure and out in the open as it is here, where his only accompaniment is his own acoustic guitar. The songs are culled from his entire career and include stark and moving readings of "Yesterday's Wine," "Slow Down Old World," "Jimmy's Road," and "Pretend It Never Happened."

⊙ **A Classic And Unreleased Collection** (1995; Rhino). Longtime Willie fans who think they've heard it all have a treat in store if they haven't yet gotten their hands on this superb 3-disc box set. Includes his very first single, some Pamper Music demos, and a treasure trove of previously unreleased recordings: outtakes from the SHOTGUN WILLIE sessions, an unreleased 1974

concert, an album of country standards he called SUGAR MOON, and a Hank Williams tribute album. It actually works quite well, too, as an introduction to Willie's wide world.

⊙ **The Essential Willie Nelson** (1995; RCA). Yes it's true, many of the songs Nelson cut for RCA are burdened with strings and other Nashville Sound accoutrements, but that doesn't mean they should be discounted. Some, in fact, are more than merely palatable and are quite delicious. Titles like "Me And Paul," "Funny How Time Slips Away," "My Own Peculiar Way," and "Phases, Stages, Circles, Cycles And Scenes" (the precursor to his PHASES AND STAGES concept album) are among his finest creations.

Willie Nelson

⊙ **Teatro** (1998; Island). Willie gives a new spin to some awesome early material on this album, including "Three Days" (which Patsy Cline recorded), "My Own Peculiar Way," and a couple of his starkest titles: "Darkness On The Face Of The Earth" and "I Never Cared For You." Daniel Lanois produced the record, and the tracks were laid down in a converted Mexican movie theater.

Mickey Newbury

> "People have referred to me as a poet a number of times. I'm very satisfied with just being known as a songwriter."
>
> —Mickey Newbury

Along with Willie Nelson, Kris Kristofferson, and Tom T. Hall, Mickey Newbury was one of a new breed of songwriters who helped broaden the scope of country music during the 1960s and '70s. Newbury is often called a poet for his catalog of moody, introspective songs—"She Even Woke Me Up To Say Goodbye," "Poison Red Berries," "33rd Of August," "San Francisco Mabel Joy"— which were unlike anything country music was accustomed to when they first appeared. He boldly shunned Nashville formulas, writing songs instead that often ran to five or six minutes and allowing images to build slowly without needing to hammer the title into listeners' heads over and over. While country influences are definitely present, so are soul, blues, and folk; at their core his songs have more in common with Leonard Cohen than Roy Acuff. Despite his unconventional style, however, Newbury's compositions were hits in Nashville, picked up and recorded by such country heavies as Eddy Arnold, Kenny Rogers, Don Gibson, Roger Miller, and Jerry Lee Lewis. Pop stars Tom Jones, Andy Williams, Ray Charles, and Elvis Presley weren't far behind.

The bulk of Newbury's songs are marked by a profound melancholy and an intense, deep quiet—the woman crying for a lost lover in "How Many Times (Must The Piper Be Paid For His Song);" the drifter bemoaning his untenable solitude in "Frisco Depot." "When you're alone, there's nothing slower than passing time," Newbury sings in the latter song, one of the starkest visions of loneliness ever recorded. But as with the songs of his friend, the late and great Townes Van Zandt, to simply write off Newbury's music as "depressing" misses the point. Sadness is certainly part of the picture, but the feelings buried inside are far more complex—a mixture of spiritual malaise, honest insight, emotional epiphanies, and truly haunting beauty. This Newbury conveys with a gentle, dusty-edged tenor voice that's easily one of country music's most beautiful. It's incredible, in fact, that's he's not better known for his singing alone.

Part of the reason is that Newbury has, by choice, remained out of the spotlight for many years—he quit concert touring in the '70s and moved west to settle in Oregon, where his wife had grown up. Added to this, his catalog is largely out-of-print and/or available only in special (i.e. limited) editions. He's little known even by fans of Kristofferson and Van Zandt—ironically two singer-songwriters whose budding careers he boosted during the '60s. And that, simply said, is a downright shame, because his music is among the most innovative and inspired that Nashville has yet experienced.

Mickey Newbury was born on 19 May, 1940 in Houston, Texas. He spent his teens absorbing a wide range of music—classical, blues, country, rock'n'roll—and writing poetry. He read his work occasionally in local coffeehouses, but with folk music on the rise he soon turned to songwriting. At the same time he sang in a group called the Embers (they had a brief contract with Mercury) and hung out in Houston's black R&B and blues clubs. He even earned the nickname "The Little White Wolf" from bluesman Gatemouth Brown.

After a stint in the Air Force, a friend helped him land a songwriting job with the Nashville publishing house Acuff-Rose, and in 1963 he made the move to Music City. It's there that he met producer and song publisher Don Gant, whom he credits as a mentor not just to him but to plenty more budding songwriters. He also became friends with Roy Orbison, Roger Miller, Kristofferson, and Van Zandt. He later helped Kristofferson's career by passing "Me And Bobby McGee" on to Miller; brought Van Zandt, a fellow Texan, to Nashville and got his recording career off the ground; and also lent support to budding artists Guy Clark, Rodney Crowell, and David Allan Coe (who even dedicated his album THE MYSTERIOUS RHINESTONE COWBOY to Newbury).

Newbury's songwriting got off the ground in 1966, when Don Gibson had a hit with "Funny, Familiar, Forgotten Feelings." That kicked off a string of hits for a huge variety of pop and country artists, among them Kenny Rogers and the First Edition ("Just Dropped In"), Eddy Arnold ("Here Comes The Rain, Baby"), and Andy Williams ("Sweet Memories"). His popularity as a songwriter led to a record contract of his own. RCA signed him first, releasing his debut album, HARLEQUIN MELODIES, in 1968. The songs themselves are phenomenal, and Newbury's voice shines beautifully, but the production is heavy-handed. Today Newbury detests the album.

Newbury got out of the RCA contract, signed with Mercury instead, and began cutting records on his own terms. To emphasize this, he recorded his second album, LOOKS LIKE RAIN, in a small four-track studio run by studio engineer Wayne Moss in a converted garage. Cutting an album outside the Nashville studio system was a radical move back in 1969, making Newbury a country-music rebel several years before the term 'Outlaw' ever came into fashion.

LOOKS LIKE RAIN was a serious departure from the more straightforward presentation of HARLEQUIN MELODIES. It's a masterpiece of

Mickey Newbury

personal vision, with songs and sound effects (thunderstorms, wind chimes, lonesome train whistles) blended into a lush, gently swirling whole. All this helped make LOOKS LIKE RAIN feel like a single cohesive unit rather than a mere bunch of songs packaged together. It also contained initial versions of "San Francisco Mabel Joy" and "33rd Of August," two of his most enduring songs that he would return to on subsequent albums, each a slight variation on the last.

Mercury, however, didn't support the album, and so in 1970 Newbury switched to Elektra. There he continued his streak of superb albums with FRISCO MABEL JOY, HEAVEN HELP THE CHILD,

and the solo-acoustic LIVE AT MONTEZUMA HALL. The last of the three was packaged together with a re-release of LOOKS LIKE RAIN, the rights to which Newbury bought from Mercury and re-sold to Elektra. These albums contained such memorable Newbury songs as "Cortelia Clark" (about a blind street singer), the catchy "Mobile Blue" (a rarity for its fast tempo and sassy attitude), and the multifaceted "Heaven Help The Child." In 1972 Newbury actually made the charts with "American Trilogy," an arrangement of "Dixie," "Battle Hymn Of The Republic," and "All My Trials." Soon after the song became a standard in Elvis Presley's repertoire.

Newbury recorded two more albums for Elektra (I CAME TO HEAR THE MUSIC and LOVERS) and three for ABC/Hickory (RUSTY TRACKS, HIS EYE IS ON THE SPARROW, and THE SAILOR) before the '70s drew to a close. Though not quite as strong as his earlier efforts, all of them contain gems like the rocked-up "Dizzy Lizzy," the sweeping "Leaving Kentucky," and sly tale of "The Dragon And The Mouse." At this stage, however, Newbury had pretty much given up concert touring. As a performer he'd always considered himself more a folksinger (he never toured with a band), preferring coffeehouses to concert halls, but as time wore on he felt less need to play live. In 1980 he was inducted into the Nashville Songwriter's Hall of Fame, and during the following decade he only released two mediocre albums, AFTER ALL THESE YEARS and IN A NEW AGE. In 1994 he resurfaced with NIGHTS WHEN I AM SANE, an acoustic album recorded live in Nashville with guitarist Jack Williams. Two years later came LULLED BY THE MOONLIGHT, which he self-released under the label name Mountain Retreat, but it was only available by mail order as a limited edition. As of the late '90s, Newbury was spending his time writing songs, restoring the old farmhouse he lives in with his family in Oregon, and performing only a handful of live dates each year.

Mickey Newbury

Looks Like Rain (1969; Mercury). This is one of the great overlooked albums of the late 1960s, a masterpiece not only for the songs themselves ("33rd Of August," "She Even Woke Me Up To Say Goodbye") and Newbury's gorgeous singing, but for how it all holds so closely together, flowing from piece to piece in one gentle, mesmerizing gesture.

Frisco Mabel Joy (1971; Elektra). Another of Newbury's most fully realized collections packed with excellent but achingly sad songs such as "Frisco Depot," "How Many Times (Must The Piper Be Paid For His Song)," and "The Future's Not What It Used To Be." Luckily "Mobile Blue" and the lighthearted "How I Love Them Old Songs" are included to pep things up.

Live At Montezuma Hall (1973; Elektra). Where Newbury's studio albums are dominated by a sweeping melancholy, live he was a surprisingly jovial performer, as the between-song banter on this solo acoustic collection attests. Includes spare, almost naked-sounding versions of "Cortelia Clark," "Heaven Help The Child," "I Came To Hear The Music," and "San Francisco Mabel Joy." It's actually a double album, packaged with a re-release of Looks Like Rain.

⊙ **Nights When I Am Sane** (1994; Winter Harvest). Newbury recorded this collection live at the Hermitage Ballroom in Nashville, accompanied only by guitarist Jack Williams. His voice is still in fine form, and the songs include a handful of new titles along with spare, insightful versions of his classics.

⊙ **The Mickey Newbury Collection** (1999; Whistle Stop). So far, the only way to get any of Newbury's original albums on CD is this 8-disc collection, which includes all of his releases from 1969's Looks Like Rain to 1981's After All These Years (his early RCA recordings were left off). Contact: Whistle Stop, Box 888, Escanaba, MI 49829.

Johnny Rodriguez

"For some reason I can sing that shit-kicking stuff real easy."

—Johnny Rodriguez

Arriving on the scene a few years before Freddy Fender hit the big time with "Before The Next Teardrop Falls," handsome balladeer Johnny Rodriguez was actually the first country performer to infuse his music with Latin influences by singing some verses in Spanish. But Rodriguez was far more than a gimmick artist: he had a smooth, easygoing voice that was showcased especially well on songs like "Ridin' My Thumb To Mexico," "Poison Red Berries," and "That's The Way Love Goes," big hits for him that appeared on a strong series of albums he cut for Mercury during the 1970s. He was also an early protégé of Tom T. Hall, who gave Rodriguez his first break in Nashville and co-wrote nearly all the songs on the young artist's debut album, Introducing Johnny Rodriguez.

Juan Raoul Davis Rodriguez was born on 10 December, 1951 in Sabinal, Texas, a town about fifty miles west of San Antonio. There were originally ten children in his family, and so he grew up listening to all sorts of different music, but an early and serious inspiration was Merle Haggard. Rodriguez got into the country music business in a strange and very roundabout way, however. The story begins when he and some friends decided to steal some goats for a summer barbecue. They got busted, and since Rodriguez had just turned eighteen, he was sentenced to prison. A Texas Ranger, however, took pity on him and got him an early release—provided he take a job at Alamo Village, a tourist park owned by Happy Shaham where the movie *The Alamo* had been shot. There Rodriguez worked a variety of odd jobs including driving the stagecoach, re-enacting gunfights and singing in the cantina. It's in that capacity that Tom T. Hall and Bobby Bare, on vacation and passing through Alamo Village (they were friends with Shahan), first heard Rodriguez sing. Hall told him to look him up if he ever came to Nashville.

A year or so later, Rodriguez was in Nashville and on the phone to Hall, taking him up on his offer. The next day he was playing guitar in Hall's band. And within a year, Rodriguez had landed in the Top 10 hit with a recording of his very own, "Pass Me By (If You're Only Passing Through)." Hall collaborated with Rodriguez on his debut album, which also featured an early song by Billy Joe Shaver titled "Easy Come, Easy Go" (later retitled "Ride Me Down Easy"). After "Pass Me By" hurled Rodriguez into the spotlight, he followed up with a strong series of hit songs, including several #1s like "That's The Way Love Goes" and "Ridin' My Thumb To Mexico." Rodriguez wrote some of his own material (including "Mexico"), and he also recorded works by such progressive country songwriters as Linda Hargrove ("Just Get Up And Close The Door"), Mickey Newbury ("Poison Red Berries"), and the up-and-coming Shaver ("Texas Up Here Tennessee").

In 1979, Rodriguez signed with Epic and began working with producer Billy Sherrill. His hits by this point were not climbing as high in the charts, and he was also having some personal problems. He stayed with Epic through much of the '80s, then had his last Top 40 hit with Capitol before drifting into obscurity. In the mid-'90s, however, the indie label HighTone sought him out, brought him back into the studio, and released the album YOU CAN SAY THAT AGAIN. In 1998, however, Rodriguez found himself in yet another sticky situation. At his home in Sabinal, he accidently shot and killed a friend whom he claimed he'd inadvertently taken for a burglar. He was charged with murder, but a year later, a jury acquitted him, saying the shooting was justified as self-defense under Texas law.

⊙ **The Greatest Hits Of Johnny Rodriguez** (1976; Polygram; reissued 1993; Polygram). Though he was only in his twenties when he cut most of his early hits, Rodriguez's voice had a rich, mature tone that gave his songs an enduring quality. This hits package of his Mercury years covers most of the major bases including "Pass Me By," "Ridin' My Thumb," "Just Get Up And Close The Door," and "That's The Way Love Goes."

⊙ **You Can Say That Again** (1996; HighTone). Twenty years after his heyday, Rodriguez's voice doesn't sound as clean as it once did, but he still has full command of his material. Old-school honky-tonk songs like Whitey Shafer's "When It's Your Turn To Fall" fit nicely alongside more recent compositions by Robert Earl Keen ("Corpus Christi Bay") and Dave Alvin ("Every Night About This Time").

Billy Joe Shaver

"If the world is God's television set, Billy Joe Shaver is on Monday mornings at 3:00."

—Tom T. Hall

Even if Billy Joe Shaver never achieved the *Billboard* chart success or widespread recognition of his compatriots (and early benefactors) Waylon Jennings, Kris Kristofferson, Tom T. Hall, and Bobby Bare, he certainly gained a solid reputation as a standout songwriter among those who were paying attention. His voice wasn't exactly what most would call pretty, but it possessed a plain-spoken, heartfelt honesty. As for his songs, they were a mix of sensitive emotions, simple poetic images, and a bit of rough and ready cowboy attitude, all grounded in the east Texas soil ... and in Shaver's own life experiences. "I Been To Georgia On A Fast Train," in particular, is full of details from his growing-up years, and "Honky Tonk Heroes" brings to life the Green Gables, a honky tonk in Waco, Texas where his mother worked.

Shaver was born on 16 August, 1939 in Corsicana, Texas. His parents split before he was born, and his mother began working at Green Gables; so when he sings "my grandma's old-age pension is the reason that I'm standing here today," he's not kidding, as it's she who mostly raised him. As a young man he sang songs for the drunks at Green Gables, played football, did a restless turn in the Navy, got married (he would marry and divorce the same woman three times over the next few decades), and worked a series of day jobs. One was at a sawmill, where he lost part of his fingers in an accident, prompting him on a whim to hitchhike to Nashville and try to sell some songs. That was in 1966, but success didn't come until a couple of years later when he stopped by the office of singer Bobby Bare, who ran a small song publishing company, Return Music. Shaver had no tape to leave so he sang him "Restless Wind," and Bare gave him a $50-a-week writing job on the spot. The checks often bounced, but no matter, Billy Joe was in the door.

Shaver's songs began to see daylight in versions by Bare ("Ride Me Down Easy"), Kris Kristofferson ("Good Christian Soldier"), and Tom

T. Hall ("Willie The Wandering Gypsy And Me"). His real breakthrough, however, came in 1973 when Jennings recorded an album composed almost entirely of Shaver's songs, HONKY TONK HEROES. Shaver nearly came to blows with Waylon trying to get it cut, but his persistence definitely paid off. With its spare, simple arrangements and raw but easygoing sound, it was quickly marked out as one of the definitive Outlaw albums.

Shaver's own debut album was OLD FIVE AND DIMERS LIKE ME, produced by Kristofferson and released by Monument (Kristofferson's label) in 1973. Along with the title track, it contained the now-classic songs "Willie The Wandering Gypsy And Me" and "Georgia On A Fast Train." Shaver next cut a couple of songs for MGM, but again they failed to chart. "Raising hell" was, as he sang in "Fast Train," part of his lifestyle at the time, and coupled with some hard luck (both Monument and MGM folded while he was on the roster), it often got in the way of his career. With the support of Allman Brothers guitarist Dickey Betts, however, Shaver resurfaced in 1976 on the Capricorn label with the excellent WHEN I GET MY WINGS; he followed it up a year later with GYPSY BOY. Both had a much stronger electric sound than FIVE AND DIMERS and featured pickers like James Burton, Ricky Skaggs, Brian Ahern, Charlie Daniels, and Dickey Betts. Unfortunately, neither album sold very well, and strangely enough that label also folded (it's since been revived). Shaver did manage, however, to get his songs recorded by singers like Johnny Rodriguez, Johnny Cash, and even Elvis Presley. Both Cash and later John Anderson took a liking to "I'm Just An Old Lump Of Coal (But I'm Gonna Be A Diamond Some Day)," a song Shaver wrote just after he chose to give up his hard-partying lifestyle and turn to God for help. Since his debut album, religious references have cropped up in his songs (including "Chunk Of Coal" and the beautiful "Jesus Christ, What A Man"), but it's testament to his creative skill that they never dominate the emotions or otherwise get in the way.

In 1980 Shaver switched labels again, this time to Columbia, and recorded three more albums during the next decade, I'M JUST AN OLD CHUNK OF COAL ... BUT I'M GONNA BE A DIAMOND SOME DAY, BILLY JOE SHAVER and SALT OF THE EARTH. The last of these was produced by Shaver with his son, Eddy, who first played guitar with Billy Joe on OLD CHUNK OF COAL (he also played for a while in Dwight Yoakam's band). Billy Joe and Eddy began concentrating on touring and building their live act, and after a few years of this

they were ready to break on through. This time father and son recorded under the simple name of Shaver and found a whole new audience eager for their brand of earthy, soulful, but rocked-up country music. TRAMP ON YOUR STREET featured Eddy's hot-shot guitar work alongside Billy Joe's raspy but lovable voice; coming at a time when hunky hat acts were dominating Nashville, it was one of the hardest country records in years. Billy Joe and Eddy have been touring together regularly ever since. They cut a live album for Zoo, UNSHAVEN, but were dropped by the label a year later. Their next album, HIGHWAY OF LIFE, came out on Justice Records, after which they were signed to yet another indie label, New West. The acoustic country-gospel album VICTORY was followed by the burlier ELECTRIC SHAVER, an album dominated by blues-based rhythms and heaping helpings of Eddie Shaver's guitar.

⊙ **Old Five And Dimers Like Me** (1973; Monument; reissued 1996; Koch). A superb debut marked by spare, earthy, mostly acoustic arrangements of songs like "Bottom Dollar," "Jesus Christ, What A Man," and "Low Down Freedom." The CD reissue (from Koch) includes 2 bonus tracks, "Ride Cowboy Ride" and "Good Christian Soldiers."

⊙ **I'm Just An Old Chunk of Coal ... But I'm Gonna Be A Diamond Some Day** (1981; Columbia; reissued 1998; Koch). Of all the Columbia records, this one's the best, containing excellent lesser-known titles like "Ragged Old Truck," "(We Are) The Cowboys," and the quiet "Mexico."

⊙ **Tramp On Your Street** (1993; Zoo). With his son Eddy as his musical partner, Shaver boldly shot back into the country limelight with this searing, rocked-up collection. Includes hot new versions of "Georgia On A Fast Train" and "Old Chunk Of Coal" alongside a handful of new compositions. One of the high points of Shaver's recorded history.

⊙ **Honky Tonk Heroes** (1994; Bear Family). Compiles his MGM recordings with everything from his 2 Capricorn albums WHEN I GET MY WINGS (one of his best collections) and GYPSY BOY.

⊙ **Restless Wind: The Legendary Billy Joe Shaver, 1973–1987** (1995; Razor & Tie). An excellent sampler of Shaver's Monument, MGM, Capricorn, and Columbia recordings such as "Black Rose," "Lately I Been Leanin' T'ward The Blues," "Ride Me Down Easy," and the knockout "Ragged Old Truck."

Billy Joe Shaver

⊙ **Highway Of Life** (1996; Justice). While Tʀᴀᴍᴘ kept things electric and out front, Hɪɢʜᴡᴀʏ is quieter in tone and more introspective. "The First And Last Time," an acoustic demo cut in his kitchen, is among the most personal and intensely moving songs he's ever recorded.

⊙ **Victory** (1998; New West). For this album of all-spiritual material (including now-familiar titles like "Live Forever" and "If I Give My Soul"), Billy Joe spent a week in a studio with Eddy as his only accompanist on guitar and Dobro. The title refers to his mother, Victory Odessa Watson Shaver.

Sammi Smith

Sammi Smith was a strong vocalist with a husky, smoldering tone and a slow-burn delivery that was difficult to resist. She was best known for sexy come-on songs like Kris Kristofferson's "I've Got To Have You" and "Help Me Make It Through The Night," the latter a #1 smash in 1970 that put her name on the national radar. But Smith could convey pathos like nobody's business, and her talent shined brightest of all on down-and-outers such as "Saunders' Ferry Lane," a stark picture of winter loneliness, and "The Toast Of '45," a tear-jerking bar-room saga told from the perspective of a has-been starlet. Some of Smith's material did get bogged down with overeager string arrangements, but on the whole her songs—whether she'd written them herself or was covering the work of aces like Kristofferson, Mickey Newbury, or Troy Seals—were striking enough to transcend the often heavy-handed production work.

Jewel Fay Smith was born in 1943 in Orange, California but raised in Oklahoma. She started singing as a teenager around Oklahoma City and soon married a nightclub manager, but that didn't last. Through a friend she got a demo tape passed on to Johnny Cash, who loved her singing and soon had her in Nashville and signed to Columbia. Her next break was impressing Waylon Jennings, who hired her to tour with him and then recorded and even titled an album after a song she co-wrote, "Cedartown, Georgia." Smith's Columbia recordings aren't bad at all (nine are collected on the LP Tʜᴇ Wᴏʀʟᴅ Oꜰ Sᴀᴍᴍɪ Sᴍɪᴛʜ), but at the time they didn't make much of a splash. Before long she'd moved to Mega Records, a new Nashville indie label. Smith knew Kristofferson—then still a struggling songwriter just beginning to break—from her time at Columbia, and for her first album she jumped at the chance to record his song "Help Me Make It Through The Night" from a female perspective. The record company was hesitant to release it as the single, fearing its frank sexuality, but when DJs began testing it, public response was immediate and strong. The song won a couple Grammys and made stars out of both of them.

Smith had further successful singles with Mega including Merle Haggard's "Today I Started Loving You Again," her own lively love song "Kentucky," and Dallas Frazier and Whitey Shafer's "The Rainbow In Daddy's Eyes." As well as her friendship with Waylon she was also close to Outlaw hero Willie Nelson, and she was a regular at his infamous Fourth of July picnics in Texas. She eventually moved to Dallas and, later, out to Arizona where she became involved in Native American causes. She left Mega in 1975 (it went out of business soon after), switched to Elektra, and later recorded for Cyclone, Sound Factory, and Step One. By the late '70s and '80s, though, her sound was moving farther uptempo and uptown. Her Mega material definitely remains her finest.

◉ **Help Me Make It Through The Night** (1970; Mega). You'll have to seek out this LP (originally titled Hᴇ's Eᴠᴇʀʏᴡʜᴇʀᴇ until "Help Me Make It" hit big) for "Saunders' Ferry Lane," a song of deep sadness conveyed through the changing seasons ("summer drowned in the frozen lake as winter came to life") that's one of Smith's finest recordings.

⊙ **The Best Of Sammi Smith** (1996; Varese Sarabande). Fourteen of Smith's Mega highlights are included on this solid compilation, among them "Help

Me Make It Through The Night," "The Toast Of '45," "I've Got To Have You," and "Kentucky." A couple of Cyclone singles are thrown in for good measure, but they don't hold up to the rest.

Gary Stewart

"We just did what we wanted to do. And it ended up bein' on the edge of something."

—Roy Dea

Gary Stewart is living proof that country music can and will survive, popular trends of the day be damned. During the 1970s, such Stewart songs as "Out Of Hand," "Single Again," "Whiskey Trip," and "She's Actin' Single (I'm Drinkin' Doubles)" showed that bare-knuckled arrangements and cry-in-your-beer song material still attracted a sizeable audience. Stewart's vibrato-laden tenor voice was pure hillbilly, his guitar melodies defined by a powerhouse Telecaster sound. Some songs dripped with honky-tonk pathos, while others revealed the loud and proud influence of southern rock bands like the Allman Brothers. In either case, though—and at a time when questions were being raised about certain CMA award winners' country credentials—there was no doubt that the music Stewart and his producer, Roy Dea, were bringing to the table was out-and-out country.

Stewart was born on 28 May, 1945 in Letcher County, Kentucky. The family moved to Fort Pierce, Florida after Gary's father was in a mining accident, and the town has remained his home base ever since. He first recorded for the small Cory label in 1964, but he held a day job working in an airplane factory. He began writing songs with his friend Bill Eldridge, and during the late '60s they set their sights on Nashville. The pair got their songs cut by such singers as Nat Stuckey, Cal Smith, Warner Mack, Hank Snow, and Billy Walker, and Stewart later worked for a time with Owen Bradley at his Nashville studio, Bradley's Barn. He also recorded some material for Kapp, which surfaced on the MCA album YOU'RE NOT THE WOMAN YOU USED TO BE after he began making the charts.

Stewart got his break as a recording artist in the early '70s when RCA's Jerry Bradley took a chance on him. His first hit, "Drinkin' Thing," produced by Roy Dea, arrived in 1974; it was followed soon

after by "Out Of Hand" and "She's Actin' Single (I'm Drinkin' Doubles)," the latter of which became Stewart's first (and only) #1 hit. These appeared on his 1975 album OUT OF HAND, a brilliantly conceived chunk of country that stands as one of the finest honky-tonk records ever cut in Nashville. Follow-up albums like STEPPIN' OUT, YOUR PLACE OR MINE, and LITTLE JUNIOR, all released by RCA in the late '70s, contained further nuggets of glory like "Ten Years Of This," "Quits," "I Had To Get Drunk Last Night" (written by Rodney Crowell), "Whiskey Trip," and "Single Again"—a divorce song that scrapes so near the bottom it's borderline comedy.

Stewart earned about a dozen Top 40 hits between 1974 and 1981, but he never took the starmaking process all that seriously. He did work for a while as a member of Charley Pride's band, and in 1975 he appeared on the CMA award show playing "She's Actin' Single," but at the same time he wasn't exactly a poster-boy for responsible behavior. By the '80s his hits were drying up, though he continued to record. The album CACTUS AND A ROSE featured the Allman Brothers, and BROTHERLY LOVE was a duet with songwriter Dean Dillon (who wrote "Unwound" and other hits for George Strait). Stewart, however, eventually retreated back to Florida, choosing to work the local circuit and stay near home.

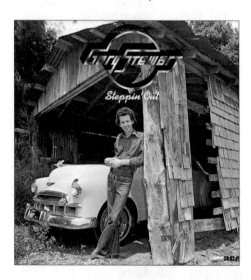

In the late '80s his career shifted back into gear when the California label HighTone brought him into the studio for a new album titled, appropriately, BRAND NEW. It included excellent songs like "Brand New Whiskey" and "An Empty Glass," which fit neatly alongside his classic mid-'70s recordings. HighTone also re-released his earlier albums and put together an excellent hits collection. Newly discovered by the alternative country crowd—some of whom saw him perform for the first time at the South by Southwest music conference in Austin—and finding his fans still remember him, Stewart was back on the road-house circuit (albeit only in Texas, a state he has a warm affection for). His voice was a bit wearier, but his music and spirit were still strong. During the '90s he released two more HighTone albums, BATTLEGROUND and I'M A TEXAN.

⊙ **Gary's Greatest** (1991; HighTone). This 17-song CD is a retrospective of Stewart's work from his mid-1970s classics through to 1990's "Let's Go Jukin'." It's also a rock-solid collection of dead-serious honky tonk—drinking and divorcing, loving and leaving, and then drinking all over again—stuffed with great titles like "Whiskey Trip," "Ten Years Of This," "Drinkin' Thing," "Single Again," and "She's Got A Drinking Problem."

⊙ **I'm A Texan** (1993; HighTone). Not as classic as his '70s material, this collection (his most recent studio album at the time of writing) demonstrates that Stewart still has what it takes in the honky tonkin' department. He only co-wrote one song ("It's True"); the rest come from the likes of Mickey Newbury ("Hand Me Another"), Billy and Jody Emerson ("I'm A Texan"), and Scotty Harrell and Eddie Hazelwood ("Honky Tonk Hardwood Floor").

Mel Street

M el Street was a honky-tonk singer from the heart of Appalachia who grew up on the music of George Jones and other classic honky tonkers before emerging during the 1970s to run up a string of Top 20 hits. "Borrowed Angel" was his first in 1972, but sadly, six years later, Street took his own life. His popularity was obviously still large in 1981 when a compilation on the Lakeshore label sold several hundred thousand copies, but by the '90s his legacy had substantially diminished. The name Mel Street hasn't survived as well as honky-tonk contemporaries like Moe Bandy—who turned to country-pop ("Americana") before opening his own theater in Branson—or Gary Stewart, who has gained new attention from the alt.country crowd.

King Malachi Street was born on 21 October, 1933 near Grundy, Virginia. As a teenager he

worked with radio entertainer Cecil Sturratt, who was based in nearby West Virginia. After getting married, however, he took a series of jobs (including high-line work as an electrician and more down-to-earth employment in an auto body shop) in towns like Wooster, Ohio and Niagara Falls, New York. He played a bit of music on the side, but didn't take it seriously again until after he and his family had moved to Bluefield, West Virginia. There he opened his own body shop and also began working with Sturratt again, this time on a local TV program, the *Country Jamboree*. He then graduated to hosting his own local show, *Country Showcase*.

Local DJ Joe Deaton helped Street record and release his first single, "Borrowed Angel," on the tiny Tandem label. It was eventually picked up by a slightly larger indie label, Royal American, which gave the song wide enough distribution for it to reach the country Top 10 in *Billboard* in 1972. He next recorded for Metromedia before signing with yet another indie, GRT, which released a series of albums during the mid-'70s that are packed with fiddle, steel guitar, and all sorts of sturdy honky-tonk material. Heartache was a frequent topic ("Strange Empty World," "You Cared Enough To Send The Very Best"), and cheating songs were rendered with the tension of a man recognizing the difference between stable and dependable love and raw, true passion ("Guilty As Sin," "You Make Me Feel More Like A Man"). "Forbidden Angel" is a sincere love song, though the object of affection is only seventeen years old—not exactly a topic any current Nashville star would dare touch, but it did make the Top 20 in 1974. Street also penned a couple of songs about his blue-collar past, "The High Line Man" and "Body Man," and he made great work out of the melancholy "Smoky Mountain Memories" (an early Earl Thomas Conley composition), Faron Young's "Wine Me Up," and even the John Fogerty tune "Green River." He signed to Polydor in 1977, but the label shut its Nashville division soon afterwards. Street inked a new deal with Mercury, but then tragedy struck six months later when he committed suicide on his birthday in 1978. At his funeral, George Jones sang "Amazing Grace."

⊙ **Mel Street's Greatest Hits** (1994; Deluxe). A great sampler of Street's Royal American, Metromedia, and GRT recordings, including "Borrowed Angel," "Don't Lead Me On," "Forbidden Angel," "Smoky Mountain Memories," "I Met A Friend Of Yours Today," and "You Make Me Feel More Like A Man."

James Talley

> "I'm not a missionary. I'm just someone that tells stories about our culture and tries to put them together in a craftsmanlike fashion."
>
> —James Talley

onsidering the compassion and genuine humanitarian spirit that are at the foundation of James Talley's songs—not to mention the occasional rearing of a social and/or political topic, be it about West Virginia miners or nuclear power plant employees in "Richland, Washington"—it's no surprise to discover that this Oklahoma-born singer-songwriter was once a social worker. It's also no surprise that his music was a favorite of President Jimmy Carter and his First Lady Rosalynn, who invited him to perform during their Inaugural Ball in 1977. In his music, Talley speaks clearly and without reservation about America and the world as he sees it; there are plenty of tears, a good amount of laughter, and even some anger, but what overrides all that is a feeling of perseverance—a willingness to keep on going, for better or worse.

Talley's work certainly shows the influence of folksinger Woody Guthrie, but the four albums that he cut for Capitol during the mid-'70s are also infused with his love of western swing, blues, and honky tonk. Talley was never the hitmaking type—none of his songs ever broke the country Top 40 in *Billboard*. But for those lucky enough to have heard his music, songs like the gentle and joyful "Alabama Summertime," the nostalgic "Deep Country Blues," the rousing "Tryin' Like The Devil," the straight-up honky-tonk love song "No Opener Needed," and the confrontational "Are They Gonna Make Us Outlaws Again?" (about the struggling underclasses, though it certainly echoed the sentiments of many Nashville artists as well) feel timeless. Fronted by Talley's warm, pleasant baritone voice, the largely acoustic-based arrangements are rich in spirit, low-key in tone, firmly planted in the soil but open enough on top to let in plenty of fresh air.

Talley was born on 9 November, 1943 in Mehan, Oklahoma, but spent much of his youth in New Mexico and Washington state. He went on to earn a degree in fine art and also worked toward a Ph.D in American Studies. Music was his calling, however, and he ended up in Nashville looking to ply his trade—and working for the city's health and welfare department in the meantime. He recorded one single for Atlantic, then decided to make the album he wanted to make with his own money. He pressed up a thousand copies of GOT NO BREAD, NO MILK, NO MONEY, BUT WE SURE GOT A LOT OF LOVE on his own Torreon label, and it was picked up by Capitol and re-released. Critics loved it, and he was able to continue recording for the label. TRYIN' LIKE THE DEVIL became his second album, followed by BLACK JACK CHOIR and then AIN'T IT SOMETHIN'. Talley nurtured a solid fan base (which included the Carters), and he grabbed headlines in the wake of the Inaugural Ball appearance, but in the late '70s he and Capitol parted ways. His music career slowly fell apart after that, and he eventually began selling real estate in Nashville. The German label Bear Family has since been busy keeping Talley's music alive and in print. They reissued his four Capitol albums, and they've also released a series of new collections: AMERICAN ORIGINALS (1985), LOVE SONGS AND THE BLUES (1989), THE ROAD TO TORREON (1992), and LIVE (1994).

⊙ **Got No Bread, No Milk, No Money, But We Sure Got A Lot Of Love/Tryin' Like The Devil** (1989; Bear Family). Talley's first 2 albums from 1975 and 1976 respectively are reissued here on a single CD. His music isn't the type to knock you over the head on first listen. Instead it's a pure, simple sort of beauty that slips inside quietly, and before you know it you're humming the melodies of "W. Lee O'Daniel And The Light Crust Doughboys" (a song about how Talley's parents met), "Forty Hours," "No Opener Needed," and "Are They Gonna Make Us Outlaws Again?"

James Talley

⊙ **Black Jack Choir/Ain't It Somethin'** (1989; Bear Family). Talley's third and fourth albums for Capitol, both originally released in 1977, are combined on this single CD. If you like what you heard on the first couple of albums, you're bound to also dig songs like "Nine Pounds Of Hashbrowns," "Poets Of The West Virginia Mines," "Alabama Summertime," and "Everybody Loves A Lovesong."

⊙ **The Road To Torreón** (1992; Bear Family). This is a project whose roots have been close to Talley's heart since his days living in Albuquerque, New Mexico in the 1960s. The songs are inspired by visits he took to small New Mexican villages and also from his experiences as a welfare worker in Albuquerque. The 11-song CD is accompanied by a softcover book of photographs by Cavalliere Ketchum documenting the life and people in rural New Mexico.

Townes Van Zandt

"Anybody who can't recognize the genius of Townes Van Zandt, I don't want to spend more than five minutes talking to them about music."

—Mickey Newbury

To call Townes Van Zandt a genius is not really an overstatement. How else can you explain the powerful and poetic draw of his songs? As inspired vocally as he was lyrically, the late and great Townes had the uncanny ability to reach deep into the recesses of the soul and touch places few songwriters, poets, or artists of any kind ever do. He could bring you down to a place so dark and sad you felt your soul was scraping the ground. Just as quickly, however, he could make you smile at the sparkle of a summer morning, or the eager look in a loved one's eyes. His approach was simple—usually just his own dusty-warm Texas voice and acoustic guitar. He was as adept at gentle love songs like "I'll Be Here In The Morning" as he was belting the hunger of "Dollar Bill Blues" or the devastating sadness buried inside "Waiting Around To Die." Pain and hurt are integral to his songs, but beauty is always present, even if just humming in the background or curling between the lines. As stark as his songs sometimes get, they never leave you entirely alone.

Townes was widely respected and admired as one of the greatest country and folk artists of his generation. He never once cracked the *Billboard* charts himself, but that's not what he was about. He recorded for small labels and plied his trade in coffeehouses and clubs all over the country, meeting and hanging out with all sorts of people and in the process, more often than not, raising a bit of hell and forgetting where he parked the car. A few of his songs brought him wider attention when covered by other singers; Emmylou Harris and Don Williams had a hit duet with "If I Needed You," and in 1983 Willie Nelson and Merle Haggard took "Pancho And Lefty" right to the #1 spot. Countless more singers, many of them excellent writers themselves, have covered his material simply for the joy of it: Doc Watson, Nanci Griffith, Jimmie Dale Gilmore, and Townes' longtime friend Guy Clark. Even the Cowboy Junkies and moody British band the Tindersticks have recorded his material.

John Townes Van Zandt was born on 7 March, 1944 in Fort Worth, Texas. His father was in the oil business, and the family frequently moved around—Montana, Colorado, Minnesota, Illinois, among other places. Townes spent a couple years in a military academy and a bit more time in college in Colorado, but he ultimately dropped out with the intention of becoming a folksinger. Colorado is a place that repeatedly crops up in his songs, and it's also a place of respite to which he often returned. He often talked fondly of entire summers he spent there alone in the mountains on horseback.

Townes next moved to Houston, where a folk music scene was growing during the mid-1960s. He played clubs like Sand Mountain and the Old Quarter (where in 1973 he recorded a live album that's one of his finest), and met singers Guy Clark, Jerry Jeff Walker, and blues legend Lightnin' Hopkins. Hopkins had a huge influence on Van Zandt, particularly on his guitar picking.

Another Texas songwriter, Mickey Newbury, heard Townes in Houston one night, and soon set him up with a recording gig in Nashville under the guidance of producer "Cowboy" Jack Clement. The sessions led to Townes' debut album, FOR THE SAKE OF THE SONG, released in 1968 on the small Poppy Records (distributed through MGM). The next five years were by far Townes' most prolific, as Poppy released the albums OUR MOTHER THE MOUNTAIN, TOWNES VAN ZANDT, DELTA MAMA BLUES, HIGH, LOW AND IN-BETWEEN, and THE LATE, GREAT TOWNES VAN ZANDT. Each album is filled with magnificent original songs—"To Live's To Fly," "Tecumseh Valley," "For The Sake Of The Song," "If I Needed You," "No Place To Fall,"

Townes Van Zandt

Townes Van Zandt, San Francisco, 1998

brought in a full range of pickers to back Townes, including guitarist Randy Scruggs, steel player Jimmy Day, pianist Spooner Oldham, and drummer Eddy Anderson. After this album, Townes didn't record again for nearly a decade, although he continued to tour. He moved back to Texas briefly before drifting once again back to Nashville, where he stayed put (as much as Townes stayed put anywhere) for the rest of his life.

In 1987 he was finally back in business as a recording artist, cutting his eighth studio album, AT MY WINDOW, for his new label, Sugar Hill. By this time Townes' clear, pretty voice had dropped to a lower register, but the weathered, somewhat road-weary tone was as honest and expressive as ever. The album was a beautiful return to form. Two years later Sugar Hill released LIVE AND OBSCURE (recorded in a Nashville club in 1985); two more live albums—the rough-sounding RAIN ON A CONGA DRUM and the far more crisp REAR VIEW MIRROR—also appeared in the early '90s. In 1990 Townes toured with the Cowboy Junkies, and he wrote a song for them, "Cowboy Junkies Lament," that made it onto the group's BLACK EYED MAN album. The Junkies in return wrote a song in his honor, "Townes Blues."

Sugar Hill released ROAD SONGS in 1994, on which Townes covers songs by Lightnin' Hopkins, Bruce Springsteen, the Rolling Stones, and others. At the end of that same year Sugar Hill released NO DEEPER BLUE, Townes' first studio album since AT MY WINDOW. In the late '80s he had been working on an ambitious project re-recording sixty of his songs for a planned career retrospective for Tomato Records. It has still not been released.

Despite his mindboggling talent for musical expression, Townes was a man pursured by personal demons no one else could quite see or understand. He battled with alcohol through much of his life, and it eventually wore him down. The musical world lost an angel and a hero when he died on 1 January, 1997. Almost immediately, songwriters and singers jumped to pay tribute to a singer-songwriter they'd considered a musical and poetic wonder, and a man many had called

"Pancho And Lefty"—which formed the core of his repertoire for the length of his career. They were as fresh and strong twenty years later as they were when first written.

Townes had been in and out of Nashville for years, but he finally moved there in 1976 with the encouragement of his new manager, John Lomax III. He signed a new deal with Tomato Records, which in 1977 released LIVE AT THE OLD QUARTER, HOUSTON, TEXAS, a double album and the first of several live recordings. It contained a wide range of his finest songs, and it was also the best recorded representation of his live shows. Alongside intense songs like "Kathleen" and "Tecumseh Valley" was a healthy dose of humor ("Talking Thunderbird Blues"), some clever storytelling ("Mr Mudd And Mr Gold"), and a couple of blues covers ("Cocaine Blues," "Who Do You Love").

His next album, FLYIN' SHOES, was produced by Chips Moman, who'd worked with Elvis Presley a decade earlier in Memphis. Moman

friend. Later that year Guy Clark, Emmylou Harris, Willie Nelson, Steve Earle, Townes' son J.T. Van Zandt, and several others performed at a special tribute to Townes taped for the TV show *Austin City Limits*.

⊙ **Our Mother The Mountain** (1969; Poppy; reissued 1994; WEA/Atlantic/Rhino). On Townes' second album, producer Jack Clement uses a wide assortment of instruments, including strings, flute, and drums, but it's never overbearing and actually works quite well. Townes' voice—gentle and sweet but eternally haunted—is always the focus, and songs like "St John The Gambler," "Kathleen," and the dark and bitter title track will last forever.

⊙ **Townes Van Zandt** (1970; Poppy; reissued reissued 1994; WEA/Atlantic/Rhino). Townes' voice is pure, honest, and sparkling on what is perhaps his finest studio achievement. As they were all his life, the songs on this album are a yin and yang between gut-wrenching ("Waiting Around To Die," "Lungs") and life-affirming ("Quicksilver Daydreams Of Maria," "I'll Be Here In The Morning").

⊙ **High, Low And In-Between** (1972; Poppy; reissued 1996; EMI). More classic Townes: "You Are Not Needed Now," "To Live's To Fly," and the humorous "No Deal." Speaking of deals, this one's a bargain, as the EMI reissue is packaged with his 1972 album THE LATE, GREAT TOWNES VAN ZANDT, which includes the original studio version of "Pancho And Lefty."

⊙ **Live At The Old Quarter, Houston, Texas** (1977; Tomato). This is an excellent place to start—a double album that's not only a superb live recording capturing him at his mid-1970s peak, but it serves as an excellent overview of his many classic songs. All are performed solo and acoustic, which is how he almost always presented them to his audiences.

⊙ **At My Window** (1987; Sugar Hill). Townes' voice was rougher at this point—"seasoned" is a better word—but he was still a sturdy singer and fine songwriter. This was his first studio recording in nine years, and it includes a new version of "For The Sake Of The Song," a true beauty, alongside new titles like "Snowin' On Raton."

⊙ **No Deeper Blue** (1994; Sugar Hill). Townes' first studio album since AT MY WINDOW. He plays guitar on just one song, but the Irish pickers who back him up (it was recorded in Limerick) are excellent. His voice has lost much of its sturdiness, but the album contains several excellent new songs. "A Song For" is a brutal opener ("You can't listen to it without throwing up blood," Townes once admitted), but "Katie Belle Blue" is a pretty lullaby for his daughter and the stunning "Marie" is one of the most intimate songs about homelessness ever written.

⊙ **Rear View Mirror** (1997; Sugar Hill). Originally released on a small label in Austin, Texas, this is the best live album since OLD QUARTER. Great sound quality, excellent song choices (including "Flying Shoes" and "Our Mother The Mountain"), and no joke songs like "Thunderbird" or between-song patter, which has been a major distraction all too often.

Jerry Jeff Walker

> "I wanted to have a band with the word 'Lost' in it."
>
> —Jerry Jeff Walker

As a songwriter, Jerry Jeff Walker will always be best known for "Mr Bojangles," a song he wrote at the beginning of his career that's now a pop classic. But good as a tune as "Bojangles" is, it hardly scratches the surface of Walker's long career as a laid-back singer and central figure in the 'progressive country' scene that was bursting with life in and around Austin, Texas. Since his arrival in the 1970s he's been a fixture in and around central Texas, drinking beer, raising hell, embedding songs by Guy Clark ("LA Freeway")

"it's a good night for singin'"

Jack Clement: Country Music Visionary

When Jack Clement was hired by Sam Phillips in 1956 as the Sun Studios engineer-in-training, the young Tennessee native already had something besides technical knowledge and a whole lot of curiosity. Jack was a musician and a free spirit, which at the time were unusual traits for a record producer.

Clement's career got off the ground at that famous Memphis label, where he worked the boards for the likes of Charlie Rich, Roy Orbison, and Johnny Cash. Perhaps most famously, Clement was the guy on hand when Jerry Lee Lewis first showed up at the studio. "This fellow told me he played piano like Chet Atkins plays guitar, I thought that was a neat idea, so I sat back and let him rip." Soon after that, Jack set up a recording date. One of the songs they first recorded was "Crazy Arms," which had been a Ray Price hit. "When I played that back for Sam, three measures into the thing he stops the tape and says, 'Now that I can sell.' We made a lacquer acetate right there in the control room and had it on the air that night." The phone started ringing off the hook, and Jerry Lee was on his way. So was Jack.

Clement left Sun in 1959 to pursue his own songwriting, then took Chet Atkins up on a job offer. Following a year of learning all he could from the then-reigning king of country music production, Jack moved to Beaumont, Texas, where he co-founded Gulf Coast Recording Studios. In 1965 he was living in Nashville, where he began working with up-and-coming singer Charley Pride. Jack paid for Pride's first demo session,

then spent the next seven years producing him. The resulting series of thirteen gold records cemented Jack's reputation as one of Nashville's most sought-after producers.

In 1969, Columbia Studios closed its doors to outside producers, and Jack saw an opportunity. He built Nashville's first 16-track recording studio, and it quickly became the busiest country studio in the nation. Around that same time, country artist Tompall Glaser—whose group, Tompall And The Glaser Brothers, Jack had produced during the 1960s and early '70s—also had a small studio downtown. "Hillbilly Central," as Glaser Studios was dubbed, was a refuge for country music outsiders who were tired of the city's conservative, button-downed sound and were aching to take the music somewhere new. "The Outlaw sound, as it was called, had more of a Memphis energy than a Nashville vibe," explains Jack. "It was a throwback to rock in its attitude and energy, people getting together and just getting crazy, trying new stuff out."

Jack found himself spending more and more time with the Outlaw bunch at Hillbilly Central, and so he eventually sold his own studio. In 1975, Jack and his old friend Waylon finally got it together and, sharing production duties, recorded Waylon's DREAMING MY DREAMS at Glaser Studios. The result was a collection of slow-tempoed, introspective originals. "Jerry Bradley [head of RCA Nashville] and them suits at the time didn't like that album, even though it made them some money. It was too different, they just didn't get it." The

and Ray Wylie Hubbard ("Up Against The Wall, Redneck") into the consciousness of every good ole boy in town, and holding court in the clubs and dance halls from Austin to his favorite tiny Texas burg, Luckenbach. Willie Nelson might have dominated the Austin spotlight when he pulled into town in 1972, but it was good-time guy Walker who—as frustrating and unreliable as he could be in the worst of times—remained the local hero.

Ironically, considering how close his association with Austin has been for nearly three decades, Walker is not a Texas native. He was born Ronald Clyde Crosby on 16 March, 1942 in Oneonta, New York. As a teenager he was smitten with the folk-music bug, and after high school he took off traveling, determined to see the country and to scratch out a living making music wherever he could. He drifted through Florida, Louisiana, and

Texas before moving to New York City. There he first recorded with the folk-rock group Circus Maximus (the band's original name was the Lost Sea Drifters), but the group split up after its second album. Walker recorded his solo debut, DRIFTIN' WAY OF LIFE, for Vanguard, then jumped to Atco (a subsidiary of Atlantic), which released his album MR BOJANGLES. He wrote the title song of the latter album after meeting a street singer named Bojangles in a New Orleans drunk tank. Walker's version never hit it big, but the Nitty Gritty Dirt Band hit the pop charts with it a few years later.

At the start of the '70s Walker lived briefly in Key West, Florida but soon found himself in Austin, where he settled and has remained ever since. After recording for Atco and Vanguard during his days in New York, he signed with MCA in 1972 and released a self-titled album, which included two songs by a then-unknown

album is still Jack's, and Waylon's, favorite, and it captures the best of both artists. Waylon's songwriting is direct and personal; Jack's arrangements are sparse, yet they convey a sense of space and mood. The performances are laid-back but delivered with urgency and passion, and as on many of Jack's recordings, the rhythm section is crisp and up front. The bass stands out, not only marking the tempo but helping shape the song's attitude and tone.

"The Outlaws were folks I could relate to," says Jack, "the kind of musicians who could pick up the tempo if the singer took it that way. For us there was nothing wrong to picking up the tempo if all of a sudden we felt like it. I guess that's an attitude that comes from rock. If Jerry Lee started in a bit faster, you best believe the drummer would get on up there. Today, few people play music, the music plays with them. Everybody today is trying to get it perfect with click tracks and computers. Music ain't supposed to be perfect, 'cause life ain't. I guess that's the Outlaw attitude."

"I produced tracks for Louis Armstrong, and I tell you, that's who I learned some things from. At the start of the session he'd go to the mic, and boy did that sound awful. The first stuff of the day, it was just no good, but what I learned was the value of warming up. During that time, he'd be playing with the song, checking it out, looking for an in. Today it's not that way, there's no sense of life or personality within the song. I heard there's a producer working today who makes the guitarist change the strings after every take. Today's producers don't even listen to what's going on, they watch it on their scopes. That's the exact opposite of what I'm after. I want the musicians in there together, without headphones, looking at each other and just letting it happen. Warm up, work it through, and then let it go, see where we get. These sessions today are run like corporate board meetings."

In the new millennium, Jack would like to just have country music start over. "There's too much stuff out there right now. We need to find a way into the new without forgetting what came before. But change is upon us, country sales are down, so things may soon be shifting." If that is true, Nashville may once again be looking to outsiders, misfits, and hillbilly visionaries like Jack Clement "to pick up the tempo."

—Mike Ryan

Guy Clark, "LA Freeway" and "That Old Time Feeling." The next year he cut what would be his best-known album, VIVA TERLINGUA, in the central Hill Country town of Luckenbach with his frequent musical partners, the Lost Gonzo Band. Again it contained some true modern Texas classics: Clark's "Desperadoes Waiting For A Train," Ray Wylie Hubbard's "Up Against The Wall, Redneck Mother," and Gary P. Nunn's "London Homesick Blues" (this last song is now the theme song to the TV show *Austin City Limits*). The rest was just pure gravy. The loose "gonzo" approach to album-making also set a precedent for further collections like 1977's A MAN MUST CARRY ON, a double album with a rowdy, rough-edged, good-natured vibe.

Walker was very fond of partying throughout much of his career (his friends called him "Jacky Jack"), and this wild and carefree lifestyle became part of his identity for many years. He's since cleaned up his act—in part thanks to his wife, Susan, whom he married in 1974—and he's continued to record steadily, hardly missing a beat. He released a couple of albums on Elektra/Asylum in the late '70s, but he remained mostly with MCA. That is, until his 1982 album COWBOY JAZZ, his last for any major label. In 1985 he showed the industry he could live without their help and released GYPSY SONGMAN, the first of a series of self-made cassettes he began selling through his huge mailing list. In 1987 Walker worked out a deal with Rykodisc to release his CDs, but he still sells the cassettes himself through his own company, Tried & True Music.

Walker may not be as unpredictable and out of control as he was years ago, but he hasn't slowed down. In the early '90s he hosted the weekly TV show *The Texas Connection* on TNN, and in 1993

Jerry Jeff Walker

he returned to Luckenbach for an anniversary recording that became the album VIVA LUCKENBACH! His birthday is a major celebration in Austin every March.

⊙ **Viva Terlingua** (1973; (MCA). An excellent Walker showpiece, cut live in Luckenbach, Texas with a hot as hell band on a damn good night. Two songs in particular, "Up Against The Wall, Redneck Mother" and "London Homesick Blues" (which opens with the line "I wanna go home to the Armadillo..."), have become standard Texas bar-room sing-alongs.

◉ **It's A Good Night For Singin'** (1976; MCA). Walker's voice is in its prime on this warm, easygoing collection that's packed with excellent songwriting. Tom Waits' "(Looking For) The Heart Of Saturday Night," Butch Hancock's "Standin' At The Big Hotel," Walker's own "Stoney," and Billy Joe Shaver's "Old Five And Dimers Like Me" are just the highlights.

⊙ **Best Of Jerry Jeff Walker** (1980; MCA). Though this comes up short with only 10 songs, it's an easy place to find Walker classics like "LA Freeway," "Mr Bojangles," "Desperadoes Waiting For The Train," and "Up Against The Wall, Redneck Mother."

⊙ **Lone Wolf: The Best Of The Elektra Sessions** (1998; Warner Archives). These 14 songs are from Walker's 2 Elektra albums, 1978's JERRY JEFF and 1979's TOO OLD TO CHANGE. Includes excellent songs by old friends and compatriots like Lee Clayton ("Lone Wolf"), Willis Alan Ramsey ("Northeast Texas Women"), Billy Callery ("Hands On The Wheel," also covered by Willie Nelson), and Mike Reid (the standout "Eastern Avenue River Railway Blues").

⊙ **Best Of The Vanguard Years** (1999; Vanguard). A healthy dose of Jerry Jeff's early recordings are found on this CD, which compiles 7 tracks from his 2 albums with Circus Maximus along with 11 from DRIFTIN' WAY OF LIFE. While the Maximus songs feel a bit precious and folky-sweet, the DRIFTIN' tracks are more like the Jerry Jeff we know—twangy and laid back. As a bonus, you also get acoustic demo versions of "Mr Bojangles" and "Louise."

Gene Watson

Along with Moe Bandy and Gary Stewart, Gene Watson was one of the few old-school honky tonkers to rise through the Nashville ranks during the 1970s. His songs were steady and reliable, and they showed his many years of experience in Texas honky tonks—he wasn't afraid of steel guitars or aching melodies, in other words. At the same time he had a rich, warm, and almost pretty voice that was like a cross between Merle Haggard and Glen Campbell. The result was that he could handle soulful ballads of romance and melancholy without resorting to syrup—from the sticky passion of "Love In The Hot Afternoon" to the mournful depths of "Farewell Party." At a time when Kenny Rogers and Ronnie Milsap were sweeping the awards shows, Watson amassed a respectable string of country hits, his music foreshadowing the back-to-basics sound of George Strait and John Anderson, who would soon make the neo-traditionalist sound bankable again.

Gary Gene Watson was born on 11 October, 1943 in Palestine, Texas. He began playing music as a teenager, and he gained loads of experience working the honky-tonk circuit—especially a joint in Houston called the Dynasty Club. While Watson was busy keeping the working men and women of southern Texas smiling (or crying as it may be, considering his penchant for down-and-outers), he also cut records for a variety of local labels during the '60s and early '70s. One of them was Wide World, which released his first album, GENE WATSON, a bare-bones honky-tonk affair that contains such firm, straightforward songs as "I Feel A Sin Coming On" and "I'm Not Strong Enough." Watson next recorded for Resco, and one of these songs, the lusty "Love In The Hot Afternoon," won him radio attention and eventually a contract with Capitol. The song reached #3 in the *Billboard* country charts and became the title track of his first album for his new label. Further Capitol hits of his included "Paper Rosie," "Farewell Party," "Should I Go Home (Or Should I Go Crazy)," and "Nothing Sure Looked Good On You". While with Capitol, his production took on more of a contemporary studio feel—background choruses entered the mix, for instance—but at the heart was the same sturdy guitar-and-steel foundation.

During the early '80s Watson switched to MCA, stayed true to his Texas-born sound, and enjoyed several more sizeable hits, even reaching #1 for the first time with "Fourteen Carat Mind." By the time he began recording for Epic in 1985, however (followed by a stint at Warner Brothers), his chart sucess was diminishing. During the mid-'90s he began recording for Step One, releasing such albums as UNCHARTED MIND, THE GOOD OLE DAYS, and JESUS IS ALL I NEED, and holding on tight to the soulful, no-frills style that's always been his trademark.

⊙ **Greatest Hits** (1985; MCA). Watson's MCA material was no less sturdy than his earlier Capitol sides. This CD is a thin one at only 10 cuts, but perhaps we should simply be thankful that it even exists, considering how fast mid-level stars like Watson (whose heyday was not really that long ago) are forgotten by the powers that be.

⊙ **Greatest Hits** (1990; Curb). Eleven of the 12 cuts here were originally released between 1975 and 1980 by Capitol, and all were Top 20 hits. It's the best Watson CD on the market so far, containing such enduring songs as "Where Love Begins," "Farewell Party," and "Love In The Hot Afternoon."

Tony Joe White

"If you have to explain it to them, you've lost it."
— Tony Joe White

Tony Joe White

Suited up in cowboy boots and a fringe-leather jacket, and sporting a handsome face framed by leg-of-lamb sideburns, Louisiana-raised singer and songwriter Tony Joe White was a swamp-stewed hipster with a sultry growl and a satchel of songs that spilled the South's underbelly out into the open air. As a songwriter, White (aka the Swamp Fox) ran up a impressive roster of accomplishments that included "Willie And Laura Mae Jones," "Rainy Night In Georgia," and "Polk Salad Annie"—the latter a Top 10 pop hit for White and a standard in Elvis Presley's post-Memphis repertoire. On his own recordings, White had a slow-simmering style that mixed country, rock, blues, and soul in no particular order. The arrangements were gutsy yet pared down—White's guitar tone was thick and untamed, and every once in a while a burst of horns punched through the humidity like a blast of southern refreshment. Carrying the melody was White's gutsy voice, which like Presley's was a tempting blend of saucy R&B and barbecued country.

White was born on 23 July, 1943 in Oak Grove, Louisiana. He performed locally before moving to Nashville in 1967 and securing a songwriting position with Bob Beckham's publishing company Combine Music. He also signed to Mon-

ument Records, which in 1968 released White's first few singles. "Soul Francisco" was the first to gain attention; it broke in France of all places, and it established his long-standing popularity in Europe. Next came the classic "Polk Salad Annie." Marked by White's swamp-gas grunts, wah-wah guitar, and an infectious, bad-ass melody, "Annie" told of a tough-skinned southern gal who kept her family fed by picking polk salad greens. Like many of White's songs, it was based on people he'd known growing up. "Annie" made the pop Top 10 in 1969 and established White's reputation. His follow-up singles, including "Roosevelt And Ira Lee" and "Save Your Sugar For Me," also made the charts.

Though he'd initially entered the business through Nashville, White was by no means a strict country artist. His records made the pop but not the country Top 40, and he wound up touring with rock acts like Creedence Clearwater Revival. He initially recorded in Nashville, but later he cut albums in both Memphis and Muscle Shoals,

Alabama. In 1970, White's song "Rainy Night In Georgia" became a hit for R&B singer Brook Benton. Other artists who covered his material have included Dusty Springfield ("Willie And Laura Mae Jones"), Tina Turner ("Steamy Windows"), Elvis Presley ("Annie," "I've Got A Thing About You Baby"), and Nat Stuckey ("Old Man Willis").

White recorded a handful of albums for Warner Brothers in the early '70s, after which he released albums on 20th Century, Casablanca, and Columbia. His popularity had dropped off in the US by the dawn of the '80s—and who could fault the public's apathy when Tony Joe was recording silliness like 1983's "Do You Have A Garter Belt"?—but he continued to release albums, and draw plenty of fans, in Europe. He hasn't entirely disappeared from the edges of the American music business, however. Tina Turner recorded some of his songs on a 1989 album; White's "Up In Arkansas" showed up on Waylon Jennings' 1994 album WAYMORE'S BLUES (PART II), and in 1998 White cut a new album of his own for Mercury, ONE HOT JULY. The Tony Joe White story, it appears, is not quite finished yet.

⊙ **The Best Of Tony Joe White** (1993; Warner Bros.). White's songs are soaked through with the complex people, places, and moods of the Deep South—the dirt-poor lifestyle of "Polk Salad Annie," the backwoods foolishness of "Roosevelt And Ira Lee," the anger that drives the "High Sheriff Of Calhoun County," and the racism that divides friends in "Willie And Laura Mae Jones." White can get melancholy, too, as in "Rainy Night In Georgia," "The Train I'm On," and "Ol' Mother Earth." Swampy, saucy, and delicious, this CD packs together 20 of his Monument and Warner Brothers recordings.

Don Williams

The king of the laid-back, smooth-voiced cowboys was Don Williams, a former folksinger (with the Pozo Seco Singers) who was a consistent chart topper during the 1970s and '80s. He earned the nickname "Gentle Giant" for his easygoing, golden-hued style and the fact that he was rather tall. On the whole Williams' songs are moody and nice, even if at times they don't ask a lot of hard questions or dig far beneath their pleasant, even-keeled surfaces. But in some ways their simplicity is deceptive. Ultimately, there's a

sincerity to Williams' music that's irrepressible, and it's that feeling that we carry away with us.

Williams was born on 27 May, 1939 in Floydada, Texas. In the '60s he helped found the Pozo Seco Singers, a vocal trio (with Susan Taylor and Lofton Cline) that made the charts with "Time" and other folk-pop hits. They broke up in 1969, leaving Williams to focus on starting a solo career. He eventually moved to Nashville, and there he signed with Jack Music, a publishing company owned by Jack Clement, former Sun Records engineer and soon-to-be 'Outlaw' producer-hero (at least in some folks' minds). Williams' debut solo album, DON WILLIAMS, VOLUME ONE, was released in 1972 on Clement's JMI label. Williams immediately made the country charts, first with his own composition "The Shelter Of Your Eyes" and then with a pair of Bob McDill compositions, "Come Early Morning" and "Amanda" (the latter was later also covered by Waylon Jennings). McDill was an up-and-coming Nashville songwriter who provided Williams with a substantial amount of material over the years, including "(Turn Out The Lights And) Love Me Tonight" and "Good Ole Boys Like Me." (Two decades later McDill was still at it, a cover version of his song "Gone Country" hitting #1 for Alan Jackson.)

Williams moved to ABC Records in the mid-'70s and then a few years later signed with MCA. All during this time he continued churning out hit songs on a steady basis. When the smoke cleared he had amassed an impressive total of 17 #1s, among them "Love Me Tonight," "Till The Rivers All Run Dry" (which Pete Townshend has covered), "I'm Just A Country Boy," and "I Believe In You." Williams recorded with Capitol in the mid-'80s (the label released his final #1 hit in 1986, "Heartbeat In The Darkness") and then signed to RCA, where he continued to make the Top 10 through the early '90s. All the while his style remained consistently warm, mellow, and downhome—a pleasant counterpoint to the flash and glitter of stars like Ronnie Milsap and Kenny Rogers, who were on the rise at the same time as Williams.

In addition to his consistent presence on the US country charts, Williams was very popular in Europe and especially England, and in 1980 he was even named Country Music Artist of the Decade by the British magazine *Country Music People*. When he wasn't touring or recording he dabbled in acting, appearing in the movies *W.W. And The Dixie Dance Kings* and *Smokey And The Bandit II* alongside Burt Reynolds, who was a fan

Don Williams

of his music. Williams continued to tour and record throughout the '90s. His 1998 album I TURN THE PAGE put him back on a major label (Giant) and proved he wasn't about to throw in any towels—or stray far from his familiar sound.

⊙ **20 Greatest Hits** (1987; MCA). Because of his frequent label-hopping, there is so far no entirely democratic overview of all Williams' hitmaking years on a single disc. But as best-of samplers go, this is a fine one, stretching (in chronological order) from the early 1970s JMI cuts "Amanda" and "Come Early Morning," through to his ABC-Dot years ("I'm Just A Country Boy") before running through his MCA years, winding up with his 1984 hit "Maggie's Dream." Nearly every song is typical of his mellow-minded, well-worn-in style.

Hank Williams, Jr.

> "I'm as gentle as a lamb and just as sweet as sugar; you don't have to be afraid of me."
>
> —Hank Williams, Jr.

There's no arguing that Hank Williams, Jr. is an artist full of macho attitude and southern braggadocio. It's a reputation that rustles unabashedly through songs of his like "Man Of Steel," "A Country Boy Can Survive," "The New South," and "All My Rowdy Friends Are Coming Over Tonight"—one that, for better or worse, he'll probably never shake. (Not that he's looking to do so anytime soon.) But as loud and boisterous as his music has become in recent years—he even bellows the theme song to *Monday Night Football* each week—that's not the entire Hank Jr. picture. Over a career that stretches back into the early 1960s, Hank has proven himself a talented musician and a deeply expressive vocalist and songwriter. When he's on form—alternately tender and playful, brutally proud and bitterly introspective—he reaches places that hard living cowboys like him usually never dare to explore. But because Hank Jr. has lived under the country music spotlight since the day of his birth, he's the kind of guy who's used to living his life in public view.

Hank recorded the bulk of his most enduring material between the mid-'70s and the early '80s. Ever since childhood, he'd been groomed to follow in his daddy's footsteps and it was at this point—when he was in his mid-twenties—that he finally busted free of other peoples' expectations of him and discovered his own style. It was also about this time that he had a near-fatal accident and took a long hard look at his mortality and the "Family Tradition" he was set to uphold. "I don't want to be the living proof," he moaned on his landmark album HANK WILLIAMS, JR. AND FRIENDS, and the cry for help seemed entirely genuine.

Hank Sr.'s first wife, Audrey, gave birth to Randall Hank Williams on 26 May, 1949 in Shreveport, Louisiana. His father died before he was even four years old and he grew up in the shadow of a man he never really knew. The younger Hank was raised in Nashville and directly under the country music spotlight. He performed on stage for the first time when he was only eight, and he made his first recordings at fourteen. At this point he was little more than a puppet performer, groomed by his mother as well as by producers at his record company, MGM (which had also been his father's label), to be the second coming of country's most hallowed figure. His recording life at this point was full of references to his father: he became the voice of his daddy on the soundtrack to the 1964 film *Your Cheatin' Heart*, a biopic on the elder Williams; he sang overdubbed "duets" with Hank Sr. on the 1965 album FATHER & SON (a trick he'd employ again decades later); and he cut a series of albums under the moniker Luke the Drifter, Jr.

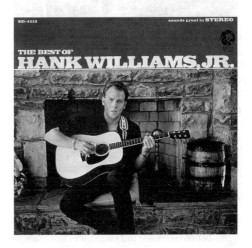

Hank made the charts now and again in these early years—and at least one early hit, the self-penned "Standing In The Shadows," revealed his weariness with all the Hank comparisons—but he didn't really come into his own musically until the '70s. Albums like ELEVEN ROSES and LIVING

Hank Williams, Jr.

PROOF showed him breaking from the mold and experimenting with new songs and new musical styles. His voice had also grown richer and deeper, and his songwriting was beginning to more directly reflect his personal experiences—life on the road in "Hamburger Steak Holiday Inn," his attempts to escape the pressures of life and career in "Montana Song." The latter appeared on his 1975 album HANK WILLIAMS, JR. AND FRIENDS, which marked his creative turning point and remains one of the finest albums of his career. Here Hank took full control of his music for the first time—instead of string sections or the Mike Curb Congregation, the stripped-down arrangements feature such guests as Charlie Daniels, Toy Caldwell (of the Marshall Tucker Band), and Chuck Leavell (of the Allman Brothers). Hank wrote most of the music himself—including the stark "Living Proof," which is among his finest and most emotionally naked songs—and also covered material by Shel Silverstein ("On Susan's Floor") and Caldwell ("Can't You See").

Another major turning point in his life came about the same time as the release of FRIENDS. In August, 1975, while hiking in Montana (the state was a favorite retreat of his), he fell face-first more than 400 feet down the side of a cliff. The accident left his face permanently scarred (hence the beard he grew afterward) and forced him into a long period of recovery. At the same time, however, it brought self-reflection and led, for one thing, to his autobiography, *The Living Proof*.

The FRIENDS album might have broken Hank out of his mold, but its 'Outlaw' nature (which didn't pay off in big hits the way Willie's RED HEADED STRANGER, for instance, did) didn't sit well with MGM. He quickly signed to Warner

Brothers and of his next couple of albums, 1977's THE NEW SOUTH was the standout, the title track a declaration of newfound pride and confidence. After these two releases Hank shifted labels yet again, this time to Elektra, where he worked with producer Jimmy Bowen. Together they created three strong albums in a row, FAMILY TRADITION, WHISKEY BENT AND HELL BOUND, and HABITS OLD AND NEW, which further reflected Hank's blend of Outlaw country and southern rock and blues traditions. The songs moved from macho ("The American Way") to reflective ("O.D.'d In Denver," "The Blues Man"); from rowdy ("I've Got Rights") to laid-back (the Gregg Allman song "Come And Go Blues"). And he was still talking about his daddy, only now from his own perspective ("Family Tradition")—and also with the help of friends like Kris Kristofferson (who wrote "If You Don't Like Hank Williams") and Waylon Jennings (who duets with Hank on "The Conversation").

During the '80s, Hank Jr. achieved true superstar status. His hits began piling up—among them the tough and bitter "A Country Boy Can Survive," the lonely "All My Rowdy Friends Have Settled Down," and the burly "Man Of Steel." Between 1986 and 1988 he won the Academy of Country Music's Entertainer of the Year award three times in a row, and the CMA gave him the same honors in 1987 and 1988. By this time he'd shifted away from the Outlaw-style country that defined WHISKEY BENT in favor of a louder and rowdier rock'n'roll sound. He was a one-man party machine and a favorite on the southern rock circuit right alongside Lynyrd Skynyrd. Hits like "Dixie On My Mind," "All My Rowdy Friends Are Coming Over Tonight" (he obviously found a new batch of them to keep the party going), "Born To Boogie," and "If The South Woulda Won" reflect this new attitude. He even stepped into the political arena with "Give Us A Reason," a message to Saddam Hussein cut during the Gulf crisis.

Follwing his '80s hot streak, Hank's songs didn't chart as high, although his fans remain rabid for his hard-boogie sound. He's obviously a talented musician, singer and songwriter, as his earlier albums have proven, but his '90s CD releases have so far failed to live up to those standards. Instead of "Old Habits" and "Family Tradition" we get "Fax Me A Beer," "Hollywood Honeys," "Hank Hill Is King" (about the lead character on the TV show *King Of The Hill*), "I'd Love To Knock The Hell Out Of You," and, of course, "All My Friends Are Coming Over For Monday Night

Football." I guess once Hank exorcized his demons, all he wanted to do was kick out the jams.

⊙ **Hank Williams, Jr. And Friends** (1975; MGM). This is a classic album that sits on the line between southern rock and Outlaw country and doesn't care which way the scales tip. Songs like "Stoned At The Jukebox" and "The Living Proof" are painful, while "Montana Song" feels like a breath of fresh air. With so much in its favor, it's a complete mystery why the album has never been released on CD.

⊙ **Whiskey Bent And Hell Bound** (1979; Elektra/Asylum; reissued 1995; Curb). The title track is not a party song but a stone-cold country downer, and like the bulk of the cuts on this tightly packed album, it's propelled by a beefy, confident rhythm. "Outlaw Women" and "Come And Go Blues" maintain a quiet edge, while the unusual "O.D.'d In Denver" cries out with remorse.

⊙ **20 Hits** (1995; Curb). Packing a thirty-year career onto a single 20-song CD will obviously result in some serious omissions—like, for instance, "Living Proof" and "A Country Boy Can Survive." But there's also lots to love here, from a couple of early Hank Sr. covers to "Whiskey Bent," "Old Habits," "Dixie On My Mind," and "All My Rowdy Friends Have Settled Down."

⊙ **The Complete Hank Williams Jnr** (1999; Curb). At only 45 songs on 3 discs, this is a long way from "complete." And while it's presented as a revamped and updated version of Curb's previous 3-CD set THE BOCEPHUS BOX (which is now out-of-print), the earlier set had not only far more interesting song choices but 17 more cuts overall. Here the focus is on Hank's '80s and '90s output, which should satisfy his boogie-rock fans but leave the rest frustrated.

Steve Young

"I can't say enough about Steve without starting to sound silly."

—Townes Van Zandt

Steve Young wrote one of the most enduring anthems of the Outlaw era, "Lonesome On'ry And Mean," a rambling-man song that Waylon Jennings covered in 1973. But that song was neither Young's first composition nor the last anyone heard of him: his career stretches from the 1960s, when he cut the album ROCK SALT &

NAILS (a record that featured Gram Parsons, Chris Hillman, and Gene Clark), all the way to the present, earning him accolades from critics (who have always loved his work) and his musical peers for his superb singing—a warm, dusty-edged baritone voice that can soar and sway—and guitar picking, which if anything has grown stronger over the years. During all those years in-between, Young wrote and recorded a healthy number of knockout songs, among them "Seven Bridges Road" (covered by both the Eagles and Eddy Arnold), "Montgomery In The Rain," and "Renegade Picker." The last of the three is the title track of a 1975 album that showed Young itching with raw talent and standing on the precipice of greatness—something he's achieved alone, despite the fact that Music Row, and much of the country music mainstream, has chosen not to pay him much attention.

Young was born on 12 July, 1942 near Newnan, Georgia, and he also spent part of his childhood in Texas and Alabama. All that gave him some serious southern roots, which run through the veins of many of his songs—and seem to tear at his soul as he struggles to figure out just what his legacy really is and where that leaves him. It certainly makes for songwriting that is at once stunningly beautiful, spiritual, and rippling with emotional turmoil. After graduating from high school in Beaumont, Texas, Young ended up in Montgomery, Alabama—a city that itself is marked by a diverse and rocky heritage as the onetime capital of the Confederacy and the site of some famous Civil Rights protests. It was also the birthplace of Hank Williams, which comes up in Young's song "Montgomery In The Rain," an intense piece of work about returning to a town that doesn't seem to want him around anymore.

Steve Young

Young played the bars and clubs around Montgomery before heading west to California. There he landed a recording contract with A&M, which released ROCK SALT & NAILS in 1969—a folk-tinged album that stands among the best of the West Coast country-rock genre. Young next signed with Reprise, which released the album SEVEN BRIDGES ROAD in 1972. When it disappeared quickly, the small New Mexico label Blue Canyon picked it up and re-released it. Along with the title track, which gained Young attention among West Coast artists like Bernie Leadon (of the Eagles) and Joan Baez, the album also included "Lonesome On'ry And Mean," which intrigued Waylon Jennings enough to record it as the title track of a 1973 album. This gained Young quite a bit of notoriety in Nashville (Jennings also regularly praised him in the press), and Young eventually moved there. In 1975 he cut the album HONKY TONK MAN for another small label, Mountain Railroad, and then he was signed by RCA. The label released RENEGADE PICKER in 1976, followed by NO PLACE TO FALL (another excellent album, the title track of which is a Townes Van Zandt song) two years later.

The RCA contract ended after that, and in the '80s Young was back on the independents. Rounder Records released TO SATISFY YOU in 1981, and at the same time they also released yet another version of SEVEN BRIDGES ROAD—this one featuring five cuts from the original Reprise release, four previously released cuts from the same sessions, and one new recording. It's an excellent introduction to Young's work—though unfortunately, like most of his earlier albums, it hasn't yet made it to CD.

Young toured extensively in the '80s and '90s, including stints in China and Mongolia on a US government-sponsored excursion. He also finally left Nashville and moved to Los Angeles, and that city has been his home base ever since. He released further albums in Europe during the '80s (LOOK HOMEWARD ANGEL and LONG TIME RIDER), and in 1991 the Texas-based label Watermelon signed Young and released SOLO/LIVE. Two years later came another typically fine album of new material, SWITCHBLADES OF LOVE.

⊙ **Renegade Picker** (1976; RCA). This is one of the great lost albums of the Outlaw period. The title track, though it appears to be about a musical rebellion, is actually an honest depiction of what Young himself was going through at the time—kicking drugs and alcohol. Other standouts include Guy Clark's "Broken Hearted People (Take Me To A Barroom)," Willie Nelson's "It's Not Supposed To Be That Way," and Rodney Crowell's "Home Sweet Home (Revisited)."

⊙ **Solo/Live** (1991; Watermelon). Recorded in Houston in 1990, this CD works well as an introduction to Young's music, containing several classic titles ("Seven Bridges Road," "Montgomery In The Rain," "Long Way To Hollywood") along with some great covers such as John D. Loudermilk's "Tobacco Road," Mentor Williams' "Drift Away," and "The Ballad Of William Sycamore," the words of which are a poem by Steven Vincent Benet.

⊙ **Lonesome On'ry And Mean** (1994; Raven). A 22-song compilation on a European label that includes such worthy titles as "Montgomery In The Rain," "Ragtime Blues Guitar," "Long Way To Hollywood," "Old Memories (Mean Nothing To Me)," "Rock Salt & Nails," and "That's How Strong My Love Is."

Steve Young

10

From Birmingham to LA: Bridging the Country-Rock Gap

A t the same time that Nashville's growing legion of musical renegades, Outlaw or otherwise, were busy shaking up the country music establishment, times were a-changin' on the other side of the fence as well. In the world of rock'n'roll that is, where enlightened flower children, curious hopheads, and budding folk-music scholars were discovering that country music was not so scary after all. When the hippies and hipsters cast aside their Nashville stereotypes, what they found was a vast legacy of honest, well-grounded music—songs that were actually quite easy for anyone to appreciate, no matter what length their hair or color of their neck.

Ever since rockabilly and the Nashville Sound spun off in different directions during the 1950s, country music's reputation among the younger set had suffered. Rock had become the domain of the edgy and free-spirited, while country was "old folks" music—conservative, corny, and more than a little backwards. The truth was that country had been a fundamental building block in the formation of rock'n'roll, but that was something many young people had forgotten less than a decade later.

Part of country's old-fashioned reputation was, to be fair, true—much of the music *had* grown stale. Even folk enthusiasts who loved bluegrass and old-time music found it difficult to cross the line and embrace straight country material, which they felt was bloated, impure, and creatively corrupt. Yet to write off the entire genre of contemporary country music was in itself an ignorant act, especially for a generation priding itself on its open-mindedness. In rejecting the rhinestone glitter and monotonous tone of the Nashville Sound, they were also discounting the artistry of Merle Haggard, Buck Owens, and Johnny Cash, whose songs were about as down-to-earth as any music of the period. Thankfully, it was only a matter of time before a handful of curious, adventurous rock'n'roll souls began to wake up and smell the morning dew.

Country and rock drifted into each others' yards in various ways throughout the '60s and '70s. The term 'country rock,' however, traditionally refers to a development in the music that took place in Southern California during the late '60s. This was a time when some musicians and fans, the ones who didn't quite make it "on the bus," were retreating from their electric Kool-Aid acid adventures to a more "back to basics" sound. **Gram Parsons**, **Chris Hillman**, **Gene Clark**, and Clarence White are among the genre's founding fathers; as pickers, singers, and songwriters they brought a strong country influence into the folk and rock music community via groups like The Byrds, the Flying Burrito Brothers, and bluegrass favorites Kentucky Colonels. As their music caught on, bands like the Grateful Dead, Creedence Clearwater Revival, and even the Rolling Stones picked up on the influences and began showing signs of a country habit.

Nashville Skyline

In 1966, Bob Dylan went to Nashville, a move that was not immediately understood or taken lightly. Only a year earlier he'd burst purists' bubbles with his anti-folk electric sound; now he was following the advice of his new producer, Bob Johnston, and recording his next album, BLONDE ON BLONDE, in Columbia's recently purchased studio on Music Row—the famous Quonset Hut facility opened in the '50s by Owen Bradley. The town was full of hot session pickers, after all, and had a seamless studio system with state-of-the-art equipment.

Dylan was no stranger to many in the country music world. His songs had already seeped into the repertoires of bluegrass artists like the Country Gentlemen and hip young singers like Waylon Jennings, but his BLONDE ON BLONDE sessions were something new—a significant step toward bridging the gap between country and rock, Nashville and the hip urbanites in LA and New York. It's a move that surprised more than a few of his fans—not to mention the old boys of Music Row—but at the same time it opened doors and broadened the horizons of listeners on both sides.

For BLONDE ON BLONDE, Dylan employed Nashville session stalwarts like Charlie McCoy, Wayne Moss, and Hargus "Pig" Robbins, but the songs themselves didn't really sound all that 'country.' His next two albums, however, JOHN WESLEY HARDING and NASHVILLE SKYLINE, unabashedly introduced a country vibe into the foreground, the latter album especially, which included "Lay Lady Lay" and "Girl From The North Country," a beautiful duet with Johnny Cash (the two giants had actually spent lots more time in the studio together, but the full session was never officially released).

By the late '60s, Cash was already a counter-cultural hero thanks to his sympathetic stance toward Native Americans (his BITTER TEARS album) and prisoners (the wildly popular JOHNNY CASH AT FOLSOM PRISON). He covered songs by Dylan and Peter LaFarge ("The Ballad Of Ira Hayes") and lent further support to the folk/rock cause by inviting left-of-center singers like Dylan, Joni Mitchell and

Buffy Sainte-Marie, and even the Who to perform on his popular TV show, which first aired in 1969. Sainte-Marie was a warbly-voiced Native American folk artist known for songs like "Universal Soldier" and "Until It's Time For You To Go." In the wake of Dylan's Nashville venture, she too decided to record in Music City. The difference was, however, that unlike Dylan, she entertained the notion of cracking the country music market. ("Going country" would become a trend among plenty more pop singers throughout the '70s.) Her resulting album, I'M GONNA BE A COUNTRY GIRL AGAIN, didn't cause many country fans to blink. Neither did folk duo Ian And Sylvia's NASHVILLE (1968) or ex-Beatle Ringo Starr's BEAUCOUPS OF BLUES (1970), to name two further cross-generation 'experiments' that made use of Nashville pickers and studio facilities.

This generous influx of new blood and fresh musical energy from the worlds of folk music and rock'n'roll, incidentally, occurred much to the delight of up-and-coming Nashville-based songwriters like Kris Kristofferson, who himself wasn't exactly being "understood" by the old guard quite yet.

Bluegrass and Byrds

As Dylan was exploring the wealth of the Nashville studio system, further crossovers between country, folk, and rock music were happening way out in Southern California. Los Angeles had become the centerpoint for much of the rock'n'roll industry, but the bands and artists who had settled in the area were quite a diverse lot—from folk-inspired janglers the Byrds to electrified wanderers Buffalo Springfield, orchestral popmeisters the Beach Boys, and crazy mixed-up hooligans the Mothers Of Invention. Glen Campbell was picking on numerous studio sessions and would soon emerge as a mighty pop-country star. Mixed in, too, was a sturdy community of progressive bluegrass groups led by the Kentucky Colonels, the Golden State Boys, and Ozark transplants the Dillards.

One important link in the country-rock chain was Chris Hillman. Early in the decade Hillman played mandolin in a bluegrass band with brothers Rex and Vern Gosdin (the latter of whom went on to a successful solo career in Nashville). The band was initially called the Golden State Boys, then later dubbed the Blue Diamond Boys, and, finally, the Hillmen. In 1964 Hillman took up the bass as a member of the Byrds, bringing his bluegrass background along for the ride.

Founded by Roger McGuinn, Gene Clark, and David Crosby, the Byrds were a centerpoint of the

The Byrds

folk-rock scene as a result of popular hits like "Mr Tambourine Man" and "Turn! Turn! Turn!" And as they evolved, an impressive number of influential folk- and country-oriented musicians passed through their ranks, including not only Hillman but guitarist Clarence White (formerly of the Kentucky Colonels) and singer-songwriter Gram Parsons.

Thanks to Hillman's presence, the Byrds' country roots were already in place by the time Parsons was hired in 1968. The two men had similar hillbilly inclinations—they were likely among the few West Coast hipsters who could sing along to Merle Haggard and Buck Owens—and Byrds founder Roger McGuinn, eager to explore new musical avenues and keep his group vital, gave a thumbs up to the new sound. Before long the Byrd boys were off to Nashville to cut what would be a landmark album in the evolution of country-rock, SWEETHEART OF THE RODEO.

Parsons was definitely the chief force driving that twang-infested album. He was a southern-born singer-songwriter who had idealistic (and naïve) visions of joining hands with the hippie folk-rockers in LA with those of upstanding citizens of Nashville. He'd been a devoted fan of country music for years already, and had developed a few country-rock chops with his short-lived group the International Submarine Band.

The Byrds not only recorded much of SWEET-HEART in Nashville, they debuted their new country sound as guests on the *Grand Ole Opry*. They sang Merle Haggard's "Sing Me Back Home" alongside the beautiful Parsons original "Hickory Wind," yet the reception they received from the *Opry* crowd was lukewarm at best. Even future Nashville rebel Tompall Glaser, on whose slot the group performed, was less than pleased (Parsons had boldly added "Hickory Wind" at the last minute). Afterwards, influential country-music DJ Ralph Emery gave the group a lot of grief about their *Opry* experience on his popular radio show; Parsons and McGuinn reacted to his wrath by writing "Drugstore Truck-Driving Man" in his honor.

Back home in California, Byrds fans weren't exactly dancing a jig over SWEETHEART either, at least not upon its release. Still buzzing off "Eight Miles High," they weren't sure whether to laugh or cry at songs on the album like Merle Haggard's "Life In Prison" and the Louvin Brothers' "The Christian Life." Parsons, however, wasn't joking. After quitting the Byrds, he continued on his country quest, honing his sound and style even further with the Flying Burrito Brothers (which Hillman also joined) and finally as a solo artist. Along the way Parsons proved himself to be a

DJ Ralph Emery

knockout songwriter with an attractive, rustic-pretty voice—skills that SWEETHEART only hinted at. In particular, the two albums he released under his own name, GP and GRIEVOUS ANGEL, are his crowning achievements. In his short life he helped a whole new generation of young folk and rock fans hear country music with new ears and appreciate and understand it for the very first time. Today he's revered as a founding father of the alternative-country scene.

One of those young people was **Emmylou Harris**, a budding but then-unremarkable folksinger whom Parsons first heard in a Washington, DC nightclub. He hired her to sing on both his solo albums, and her angelic harmonies give the songs incredible depth. Her experience with Parsons set Harris off on her own long and productive career, which began with the song "Boulder To Birmingham," a tribute to her former mentor. During the '70s her Hot Band earned a reputation as one of the best in the business and included such notables as James Burton, Ricky Skaggs, Rodney Crowell, and future MCA Nashville president Tony Brown.

Out on the Side

After the departure of Hillman and Parsons from the Byrds, McGuinn hired guitarist Clarence White, who'd formerly played bluegrass with the renowned Kentucky Colonels. White had also earned a reputation as a stellar session guitarist by this stage, and his presence allowed the Byrds their

final shouts of countrified glory. Like Parsons, White's life was also tragically cut short in 1973, but in this case it was a freak accident: he was hit and killed by a drunk driver while loading equipment.

As for Hillman, he stuck with the Burrito Brothers after Parsons' departure, and then went on to form the Desert-Rose Band. The latter was a well-rooted yet contemporary-minded country band that hit the mainstream during the height of late-'80s New Traditionalism. The group included another renowned West Coast guitarist, Herb Pedersen (who'd previously been a member of the Dillards, helping guide them in a country-rock direction on the albums WHEATSTRAW SUITE and COPPERFIELDS). Since the mid-'90s, Pedersen has kept himself busy fronting a bluegrass band, the Laurel Canyon Ramblers.

Gene Clark's solo career also had a deep country streak, and as a skilled singer and songwriter he is deserving of more serious scrutiny. A founding member of the Byrds, Clark wrote and sang some of the group's most classic songs before quitting in 1966 and jumping right into a solo career that's too-often overshadowed by his Byrd days. His first venture was a collaboration with the Gosdin Brothers that broadened his jangly past. His next two albums, however—both collaborations with bluegrass wizard Doug Dillard under the name Dillard And Clark—clearly indicated how comfortable he was singing and writing country material. His voice had a dusty, lived-in tone that seemed born for the music; and songs he's written over the years, including "Out On The Side" and "The Drifter" have revealed him to be one of the genre's strongest songwriters.

By the '70s, country melodies, riffs, and rhythms were a regular part of the rock'n'roll landscape. The Byrds retained a country feel, and groups like Creedence Clearwater Revival and even the Rolling Stones weren't afraid of a little twang. Further forays into country-rock territory came from former teen idol **Rick Nelson**, who had first ventured into the landscape with his 1966 album BRIGHT LIGHTS AND COUNTRY MUSIC; former Monkee **Michael Nesmith**, whose First National Band recordings are still overlooked and a far cry from "Last Train To Clarksville"; Lowell George, who played guitar with Frank Zappa before forming Little Feat in 1970 and cutting excellent hippie-twang road anthems like "Truck Stop Girl" and "Willin'"; the Grateful Dead, who regularly mixed blues and bluegrass into their rainbow stew; and the **Everly Brothers**, whose 1968 album ROOTS paid tribute to their deep country heritage. With hillbilly music seemingly coming from all directions, by the time Neil Young sang "Are You Ready For The Country?" on his 1972 album HARVEST, fans could actually answer yes.

By far the biggest name in California country rock—indeed, one of the most popular groups in all of modern popular music—was the **Eagles**. For it was this band that took the country-rock approach pioneered by men like Parsons and Hillman (co-founder Bernie Leadon had in fact been a member of the Flying Burrito Brothers) and translated it into mellow, radio-friendly hit songs. "Desperado" and "Take It Easy" are pleasant enough on the surface, but to call these and other Eagles hits "watered down" is not off the mark. The lack of sharp edges in the music gave way to the term 'soft rock' and came to define the West Coast sound during the '70s. **Poco** and **Linda Ronstadt** (with whom several Eagles members had previously played) traveled this same territory as well.

It's interesting, too, how long the Eagles' mellow-rock legacy has survived. Right into the new century, in fact, and not just in the world of rock'n'roll: the group has deeply influenced much of today's 'new country' sound probably as much as any single artist, country or otherwise. Brooks And Dunn, Little Texas, and the mighty Garth himself have probably cited the Eagles as a major influence more often than they have George Jones or Hank Williams. The enthusiasm displayed by singers like Alan Jackson, Vince Gill, Diamond Rio, and Trisha Yearwood on the 1993 Eagles tribute album COMMON THREAD is rather telling.

Will the Circle be Unbroken

The Byrds' attempt to bridge the gap between hippies and hardhats with SWEETHEART OF THE RODEO may have met with some success out west, but they didn't turn many heads in Nashville. Another group of young long-haired visionaries did, however: the **Nitty Gritty Dirt Band** with their 1972 album WILL THE CIRCLE BE UNBROKEN.

The group was best known at the time for its hit version of Jerry Jeff Walker's "Mr Bojangles." They'd mixed plenty of country into their repertoire by that stage, but for their album project they had a much broader and bolder vision. The idea was to bring country players both young and old into the studio together for an all-acoustic recording of traditional country classics like "Wildwood Flower," "Lost Highway," "The Precious Jewel," and "Tennessee Stud." Picking and

singing right alongside the Dirt Band members were such country legends as Roy Acuff, Doc Watson, Jimmy Martin, Merle Travis, and Maybelle Carter.

The result was a landmark recording project that brought traditional country music deep into the lives of a whole new set of fans. It was also a peace offering between the generations. Acuff for one was certainly skeptical and more than a little put off by the group's long hair and full beards (another infamous conservative, Bill Monroe, had declined to participate at all), but ultimately Acuff was thrilled by the fact that young people were appreciating his style of music—and playing it on acoustic instruments to boot. In the end he admitted the Dirt Band members were "very nice young boys."

Bluegrass banjo master Earl Scruggs, who had helped the Dirt Band assemble its all-star cast, was further bridging the generation gap with his own new group, the Earl Scruggs Revue, which included his longhaired sons Randy, Gary, and Steve. The group played songs by Dylan, Rod Stewart, and Shel Silverstein in a fairly straightforward country-rock style that was augmented by Scruggs' three-finger banjo and Josh Graves' Dobro. They even appeared at political rallies as well as festivals.

Austin

Nashville and LA were certainly country-rock hotbeds, but one of the most organic and naturally diverse musical melting pots of all was Austin, Texas. It's here that blues, honky tonk, conjunto, Cajun, western swing, and various other musical styles converged from all directions and crossed paths. The result was an incredibly rich musical scene that really took off during the 1970s. Country singers like Nelson and Jerry Jeff Walker were local heroes, as was tripped-out rock'n'roller Roky Erickson. The artist who epitomized this melting-pot vibe, however, was the late **Doug Sahm**. He worked alone and in various outfits during his lifelong music career, but it was his '60s and '70s group, the Sir Douglas Quintet, that most clearly bridged the gap between the San Francisco psychedelic scene, where the band spent several years in the 1960s, and the bars and dusty backstreets of San Antonio, where Sahm was born and raised.

This new 'progressive country' scene in Texas was proof of how well leather-faced cowboys could mix in close proximity with their country-groovin' hippie brothers and sisters. One place they often mingled was at outdoor music festivals such as

Willie Nelson's infamous Fourth of July Picnics, popular parties held annually in Dripping Springs, Texas during the '70s. Nashville compatriots like Waylon Jennings, Tom T. Hall, and Billy Joe Shaver regularly showed up, and the mix of music and free-spirited attitudes offered every evidence that fans of country music could no longer all be pigeonholed as a bunch of God-fearing, polyester-pantsuit-wearing conservatives.

Such harmonic co-existence between traditional country fans and curious folkies had actually been taking place at bluegrass festivals since the '60s, where Bill Monroe, Ralph Stanley, and Jimmy Martin often shared the bills with newcomers like the New Grass Revival. Scruggs, the Stanleys, and the Osborne Brothers had also been playing to young people on college campuses and at gatherings like the Newport Folk Festival. Kris Kristofferson debuted at Newport in 1969 between sets by rockabilly pioneer Carl Perkins and Cajun fiddler Doug Kershaw. And folk enthusiasts even managed to bring old-time legends like Jimmie Tarlton and Dock Boggs out of retirement.

The Future

During the '70s, country-rock spread out in various directions. The music of bands like the Allman Brothers, **Charlie Daniels**, the Marshall Tucker Band, and Lynyrd Skynyrd came under the heading of southern rock. They had real country in their souls, but theirs was a harder-edged sound bursting with Outlaw intentions and stadium-rock trappings. **Pure Prairie League** was on the softer side of the street, more in line with LA superstars the Eagles; .38 Special and Molly Hatchet, on the other hand, gave the music a raunchier and more redneck-riddled reputation. Hank Williams, Jr., in his quest to break free of his daddy's suffocating legacy, eventually found his personal space as an Outlaw-cum-southern rocker with songs like "Whiskey Bent And Hell Bound," "A Country Boy Can Survive," and "Man Of Steel." A decade later Steve Earle embraced the genre, too, with his burly, guitar-heaving joyride COPPERHEAD ROAD.

Another place where country and rock came together was in the early '80s LA punk scene, which spawned neo-honky-tonkers Rank And File, rockabilly group the Blasters, and cowpunks Rubber Rodeo, as well as hardcore bands like X, the Circle Jerks, and Fear. From that point it wasn't too big a step to Uncle Tupelo and the Jayhawks, hero bands of a burgeoning alternative-country movement known by such monikers as 'insurgent country,' 'No Depression' (in honor of an early Uncle Tupelo album), or simply 'alt.country.'

Anthologies

⊙ **Columbia Country Classics, Vol. 5: A New Tradition** (1991; Columbia). This 20-song compilation covers rather wide territory, from Johnny Cash in the 1960s ("Daddy Sang Bass") to his daughter Rosanne two decades later ("Seven Year Ache"). But it's a great opportunity to hear those and other relevant songs (from the likes of Merle Haggard, Jim & Jesse, David Allan Coe, and Rodney Crowell) alongside titles by Bob Dylan (the Nashville-recorded "I'll Be Your Baby Tonight"), the Byrds ("Hickory Wind"), Herb Pedersen ("Can't You Hear Me Calling"), and Poco ("Pickin' Up The Pieces").

⊙ **Heroes Of Country Music, Vol. 5: Legends of Country Rock** (1995; Rhino). Like all the compilations in Rhino's Heroes Of Country Music series, this CD is thoughtfully compiled and varied enough to be enticing for knowledgeable fans as well as beginners. The 18 songs include plenty of classics (the Everlys, the Flying Burrito Brothers, Linda Ronstadt) along with folks like the Lovin'

Spoonful, Dylan, Hearts And Flowers, Marshall Tucker, and Michael Nesmith.

⊙ **Best Of Country Rock** (1999; MCA). At only 10 songs, this CD is a rip-off in everything but its price (it's very much a budget collection). Shows the rockin' side of country music from Poco and Lynyrd Skynyrd on up through Steve Earle, Joe Ely, and Marty Stuart. Nowhere even close to definitive, but the songs themselves aren't half bad.

⊙ **Fallen Angels—Legendary Country Rock Recordings** (1999; BMG/Camden). The highlights for some on this European-issue CD are the two previously unissued International Submarine Band (i.e. Gram Parsons) demos, "November Nights" and "Just Can't Take It Anymore." But at 23 songs, it's a sturdy sampler in itself, also featuring songs by Michael Nesmith, the Everlys, southern rockers the Outlaws, and even honky-tonker Gary Stewart.

Country-rock: The Artists

Gene Clark

"We were all just a little bit ahead of our time."

—Gene Clark

With contemporary country stars stumbling over each other to pay tribute to the Eagles, and No Depression fans fawning over the tragic genius of Gram Parsons, the western-edged folk/country/rock recordings of the late Gene Clark have been too readily overlooked.

Most people familiar with the name know Gene Clark as an original member of the Byrds. Along with Roger McGuinn and David Crosby, Clark was one of the original members, and he wrote and sang some of their most memorable songs ("Eight Miles High," "Feel A Whole Lot Better"). As good as his work with the Byrds was, however, that aspect of his career has always over-shadowed his substantial creative achievements as a solo artist. Beginning with his 1967 album GENE CLARK AND THE GOSDIN BROTHERS and running until his sad death in 1991, Clark wrote and recorded an impressive body of moody, intro-spective songs—"Out On The Side," "In A Misty Morning," "One In A Hundred," "Gypsy Rider"—that drift effortlessly between the worlds of folk, psychedelic pop and country. His singing makes them that much more spellbinding, his voice a mixture of idealistic warmth, haunting melan-choly, spiritual wisdom, and worn-out despair.

Unfortunately, Clark the solo artist never had anything in the way of a hit record—he was always a step or two ahead of his time. Nor does his name carry the same caché in today's alternative-music circles as his fellow tragic-genius, Gram Parsons. Like Parsons, Clark was a pioneer in his blending of musical styles at a time when rock and country were on opposite sides of the fence, but he didn't champion the country-rock cause the way the Waycross, Georgia kid did—no *Opry* appearances, for instance. Like Parsons, Clark had addiction problems that led to his untimely death, although he didn't burn out in quite the same legendary blaze of glory. Nonetheless, his vision was among the strongest of his era, and the emotional power of his music endures decades later.

Clark was born on 17 November, 1941 in Tipton, Missouri. He grew up listening to country music and played in a few bands as a teenager. In 1962 the manager of folksinging troupe New Christy Minstrels heard him singing in a club and invited him to join the group. He stayed with them for a year and a half, but when he caught wind of the Beatles his musical inclinations were changed forever. In Los Angeles he met Jim (aka Roger) McGuinn and David Crosby, and in 1964 the trio formed the Jet Set, a name they soon changed to the Byrds. The group's debut single, Bob Dylan's "Mr Tambourine Man," was an immediate smash and made international stars of each of the Byrds. Clark stayed with the group through this early rise to fame, but in 1966 he left abruptly, claiming he was afraid to fly. Almost immediately, however, he formed a new group with Vern and Rex Gosdin (who'd earlier played in the bluegrass group the Golden State Boys with Byrds member Chris Hillman). Despite excellent songs and an all-star cast of West Coast musicians (Hillman, Clarence White, Glen Campbell, Leon Russell), the group's debut album failed to catch fire. Part of the problem was that Columbia released it the same month as the Byrds' YOUNGER THAN YESTERDAY and failed to promote it properly.

For his next venture, Clark partnered up with banjoist Doug Dillard, leader of West Coast blue-grass band the Dillards. Dubbing themselves Dillard And Clark, they cut two albums together for new label A&M, THE FANTASTIC EXPEDITION OF DILLARD AND CLARK (1968) and THROUGH THE MORNING, THROUGH THE NIGHT (1969). It's on these two albums that Clark's predilection for country music, hinted at in earlier recordings, fully broke through the surface, both in the excellent originals ("Out On The Side") and cover songs like "Rocky Top" (at that point still a new song and largely unknown outside bluegrass circles). "Kind of a contemporary bluegrass folk thing," is how Clark once described the music. Among the pickers were Hillman and Sneeky Pete Kleinow, both members of the Flying Burrito Brothers at the time, and soon-to-be Eagles co-founder Bernie Leadon. Clark and Leadon co-wrote the excellent "Train Leaves Here This Mornin'," which appeared both on FANTASTIC EXPEDITION and the Eagles' debut album.

At the time these albums were released, however, the country-rock craze that would soon sweep LA was not yet in place, and the Dillard And Clark albums were, unfortunately, ahead of their time. Once again, Clark had failed to achieve a hit. This was something that would elude and frustrate him throughout his career—not a big deal for a good many seasoned musicians, but very difficult for a man who'd tasted such huge fame with the Byrds just a few years earlier.

Gene Clark, San Francisco, 1990

Clark didn't splash down with another album until 1971, when A&M released his first full-on solo effort WHITE LIGHT (it's sometimes referred to simply as GENE CLARK). Containing such wonderfully haunting and introspective songs as "One In A Hundred" and "Spanish Guitar," the album established him as a moody but mature singer-songwriter. Though it again sold moderately, it did win him much-deserved critical acclaim, and it's among the most accomplished albums of his career.

In 1973, at the behest of Asylum Records, Clark rejoined his former Byrd mates McGuinn, Crosby, Hillman, and Michael Clarke for a reunion album. It sold very well, but on the whole the project never felt entirely organic—their hearts just weren't in it. The album did, however, include two Clark originals, "Full Circle" and "Changing Heart."

A year later, Clark was back in business with another excellent solo album, NO OTHER. Songs like "From A Silver Phial" and "The Strength Of Strings" (covered a decade later by British art-rock group This Mortal Coil) were treat enough, but as a bonus the album included a poster of Clark dressed like some sort of New Age transvestite—feathered hair, thick eye make-up, flowing shirt and satin bell-bottoms. Don't let the outfit scare you away from what's inside, though: the arrangements are lush, the songwriting masterful, and his voice as beautiful as ever. Curiously, a few years later, on the cover of his album TWO SIDES TO EVERY STORY, Clark's appearance had changed radically again to that of a woodsman, complete with a huge beard and red-checked wool coat.

Clark reunited once again with two of his Byrd bandmates, McGuinn and Hillman in 1978. The albums they cut together, MCGUINN, CLARK, AND HILLMAN and CITY, are not terribly exciting, but the reunion was a popular success—that is, until Clark abruptly quit once again. His next solo album was FIREBYRD, released on the Takoma label in 1984. It was more rock-oriented than any solo effort he'd released so far, highlighted by vibrant new takes on the mid-'60s Byrds hits "Mr Tambourine Man" and "Feel A Whole Lot Better."

In 1987 Clark teamed up with singer-guitarist Carla Olson from LA band the Textones to record what became his final studio album, SO REBELLIOUS A LOVER. It's a neglected jewel of an album that contains excellent duets between the two singers—not to mention one of Clark's finest achievements as both a writer and vocalist, the melancholy road song "Gypsy Rider." Clark had battled with alcohol and drug addition for years, but on 24 May, 1991 his body finally gave out. It was a sad end to a man who was one of the finest singers and songwriters of his generation, an artist who never in his lifetime won the recognition his work deserved.

⊙ **The Fantastic Expedition Of Dillard And Clark** (1968; A&M). The first of Clark and Dillard's collaborative albums is by far the better of the pair, and one of the finest of all Clark's creations, thanks to songs like "Out On The Side" and "Train Leaves Here This Mornin'." The UK label Demon has reissued both this and its follow-up, THROUGH THE MORNING, THROUGH THE NIGHT, but search for the version on Mobile Fidelity Sound Lab, which pairs the two onto a single CD.

Gene Clark

Tom Erikson

⊙ **White Light** (1971; A&M). As a solo artist, this is Clark's finest hour. Excellent originals ("Spanish Guitar," "With Tomorrow," "One In A Hundred"), a superb Bob Dylan/Richard Manuel cover ("Tears Of Rage"), and the Byrds-like title track are the highlights.

⊙ **Roadmaster** (1973; A&M; reissued 1992; Edsel). Originally released only in the Netherlands, this is a batch of outtakes and unreleased masters from several early-1970s A&M sessions featuring four different band line-ups. Two cuts ("One In A Hundred," "She's The Kind Of Girl") are with the Byrds, though they weren't all in the studio at the same time; on another he's backed by a post-Parsons line-up of the Flying Burrito Brothers. Despite its haphazard nature, it's an amazingly cohesive album, and the songs "In A Misty Morning," "Roadmaster," "She Don't Care About Time," and "I Remember The Railroad" are among his finest.

⊙ **No Other** (1974; Asylum). A splendid companion to WHITE LIGHT, with lush arrangements, excellent vocal work and great songs like "From A Silver Phial," "Life's Greatest Fool," and "Strength Of Strings."

⊙ **Two Sides To Every Story** (1977; RSO). An undervalued Clark album, the pared-down sound clearly takes a country-folk slant and includes such guest artists as Emmylou Harris, Doug Dillard, Byron Berline, and John Hartford.

⊙ **So Rebellious A Lover** (1987; Rhino; reissued 1992; Razor & Tie). Clark cut what turned out to be his final studio album with Textones singer Carla Olson. It's a gorgeous effort that's again largely undervalued. "Gypsy Rider" is one of Clark's finest songs, as is the haunting cowboy tale "Del Gato"—his voice dusty, trail-worn, and timeless. The reissue has 3 extra tracks.

⊙ **Silhouetted In Light** (1992; Demon). A live show of Clark with Carla Olson recorded in 1990 at McCabe's Guitar Shop in LA. They both sound great, and the repertoire includes older Clark songs as well as cool covers like John Prine's "Speed Of The Sound Of Loneliness."

⊙ **Flying High** (1999; PolyGram). A 2-CD set that covers Clark's recording career from Byrds days ("I'll Feel A Whole Lot Better"), through his Gosdin Brothers and Dillard And Clark recordings, and finishes with songs from WHITE LIGHT, NO OTHER, and TWO SIDES TO EVERY STORY. Also includes "American Dreamer," from the soundtrack to the obscure Dennis Hopper film *The American Dreamer*, and 7 previously unreleased tracks.

Commander Cody And His Lost Planet Airmen

This loose collective of hot pickers played a raucous, sometimes silly, but musically savvy mix of western swing, boogie, R&B, and honky-tonk music that made them country-rock favorites all through the 1970s, from California to Texas. Their best-known song was the novelty thrill ride "Hot Rod Lincoln," which earned them a decent FM radio following. Cody and the Airmen's repertoire, however, was actually much larger and more varied than that song implied, including country classics (Bob Wills' "San Antonio Rose"), trucker favorites ("Looking At The World Through A Windshield"), and assorted space-cowboy originals such as "Seeds And Stems," "Mama Hated Diesels," and the country-fried hippie-rock anthem "Lost In The Ozone."

Though associated during the '60s and '70s with the hippie crowd in San Francisco and the progressive country scene in Austin, Texas, Commander Cody And His Lost Planet Airmen actually came together in Ann Arbor, where various members were attending the University of Michigan. Cody is otherwise known as pianist and singer George Frayne, and he played in and around Detroit before hooking up with harmonica player Billy C. Farlow, guitarists John Tichy and Bill Kirchen, pedal steel player Don Bolton (aka the West Virginia Creeper), and other members of what became a large ensemble cast. In 1969 the group moved west to San Francisco, where they established a healthy following. Their debut album, LOST IN THE OZONE, came out in 1971 on the Paramount label and was quickly a favorite on the growing country-rock underground circuit. It also yielded their one big hit, "Hot Rod Lincoln." Their second album, HOT LICKS, COLD STEEL AND TRUCKERS FAVORITES, demonstrated their propensity to churn out 18-wheeler road anthems like "Truck Driving Man" and "Mama Hated Diesels." They cut two more albums for Paramount, including LIVE FROM DEEP IN THE HEART OF TEXAS (recorded in 1973 at the Armadillo World Headquarters in Austin), and then switched to Warner Brothers. After Tichy left the Airmen, Cody cut a solo album, MIDNIGHT MAN, in 1977 for Arista, and then reformed a new version of the group. They recorded a few more releases in the late '70s and '80s, and Cody has continued touring and recording with and without the Airmen moniker ever since. Guitarist and songwriter Kirchen has kept busy over the years as well—playing with his bands the Moon-lighters and Too Much Fun, touring with Nick Lowe, and releasing a series of solo albums beginning with 1994's TOMBSTONE EVERY MILE and running (so far) through 1999's RAISE A RUCKUS.

⊙ **Live From Deep In The Heart Of Texas** (1974; Paramount). The Airmen had a lot of friends in Austin, Texas, and so cutting a live album at the city's favorite Outlaw venue, the Armadillo World Headquarters, made perfect sense. The good vibes come across loud and clear via Johnny Horton's "I'm Coming Home," Buck Owens' "Crying Time," and the droopy-eyed stoner's anthem "Down To Seeds And Stems Again Blues."

⊙ **We've Got A Live One Here!** (1976; Warner Bros.). Another fine live collection, this time culled from a tour of England in early 1976. Tichy had by now departed, and the album acts as the Airmen's last great hurrah.

⊙ **Too Much Fun: The Best Of Commander Cody** (1990; MCA). Compiles 15 songs from the band's first four albums, including "Hot Rod Lincoln," "Seeds And Stems," "Beat Me Daddy Eight To The Bar," and the Tex Williams classic "Smoke! Smoke! Smoke! (That Cigarette)."

Charlie Daniels

The Charlie Daniels Band was one of the top southern-rock outfits during the 1970s, but more than any of their contemporaries in that genre (the Allman Brothers, the Marshall Tucker Band), when those southern fires died down, the CDB was able to slip past the gates and assimilate themselves into the world of country music. They've been ensconced on the fringes of the country circuit ever since, their hard-boogie sound augmented by a downhome, fiddle-friendly vibe that is a far cry from the mainstream but has proven consistently popular nonetheless.

As much as Daniels is a loud and proud boogie-woogie-bred country boy—and a guy who's not exactly shy about spouting his opinions, political or otherwise, during live performances—at the same time he's also a well-respected fiddler, guitarist, songwriter, and bandleader with a pedigree that stretches back to session work on Bob Dylan's NASHVILLE SKYLINE. The world

knows him best for his 1979 hit song "The Devil Went Down To Georgia," which revolved around a fiddle contest against the Devil himself. Long-haired country boys and girls, however, knew Daniels from several years previously for "Uneasy Rider," a talking blues from the perspective of an unassuming hippie trapped in a redneck bar. That song was Charlie's first notable hit, though perhaps in terms of its subject matter it was an anomaly: since then he's become more enamored with patriotic fodder such as "Let Freedom Ring" and libertarian anthems like "Long Haired Country Boy." "They call me a redneck, I reckon that I am," he admits on "Simple Man", the title song to his popular 1989 album, before going one step further on said LP and declaring "(What This World Needs Is) A Few More Rednecks"—meaning, he explains, "common folks" who respect "the Lord and the law and the working man."

Charles Edward Daniels was born on 28 October, 1936 in Wilmington, North Carolina. He played guitar from an early age, dabbling in rock'n'roll as well as rootsier music. During the '60s he moved to Nashville to work as a session guitarist, and it's in this capacity that he ended up playing on NASHVILLE SKYLINE, among other projects. He cut his first album, CHARLIE DANIELS, for Capitol in 1970, then the following year put together the Charlie Daniels Band. The group made its debut on the 1972 album TE JOHN, GREASE & WOLFMAN, which had a Dixie-fried sound full of blues, country, soul, and boogie that was obviously influenced by the Allman Brothers. "Uneasy Rider" showed up on 1973's HONEY IN THE ROCK, and it brought him his first Top 10 hit. Next came FIRE ON THE MOUNTAIN, which contained two more substantial hits, "Long Haired Country Boy" and "The South's Gonna Do It," and stands as one of the group's finest achievements.

"The Devil Went Down To Georgia," released in 1979, was a huge country and pop hit that also won Daniels a Grammy and a CMA award. It was the culmination of nearly a decade's worth of hard work and growing acclaim as a southern rock outfit with a stronger-than-average country flavor. Daniels had never been short on opinions or good ole boy ferment, but his popular success—coupled with the infiltration of Reagan-era right-wing politics into the American mainstream—added fuel to his political schtick. "In America," "Still In Saigon," and "The American Farmer" were some of the titles that followed. "Simple Man" was Daniels' last sizeable hit, but he's continued to tour and record on a steady basis. Most recently he's been recording for the Blue Hat label.

⊙ **Fire On The Mountain** (1974; Kama Sutra; reissued 1987; Epic). For instrumental execution and song choices alone, this album remains one of the CDB's finest. "The South's Gonna Do It" and "Long Haired Country Boy" are clear standouts, but other notable songs include "Trudy" and "Orange Blossom Special."

⊙ **A Decade Of Hits** (1983; Epic; reissued 1999; Sony/Epic). It's a slim package at only 10 songs, but at least this CD does bring all Daniels' early classics together in one place: "The Devil Went Down To Geogia," "The South's Gonna Do It," "Uneasy Rider," "Long Haired Country Boy," and "Still In Saigon."

⊙ **Simple Man** (1989; Epic). As crude, crass, and dubiously informed as are "Simple Man" and "A Few More Rednecks," this album remains a guilty pleasure. Admittedly, Daniels' colorful pinko-baiting lyrics ("I love them Rambo movies, I think they make a lot of sense") do lend the songs a disturbing element—believe me, this ain't about irony. But the arrangements are dirt-bred, downhome, and immediately appealing—refreshing qualities for an era lorded over by "hunks" like Ricky Van Shelton.

⊙ **The Roots Remain** (1996; Sony/Epic). A 45-song, triple-CD set that examines Charlie's career from the early 1970s through the early '90s. Includes a few live songs, B sides and previously unreleased cuts along the way.

Doctor Hook And The Medicine Show

This dazed and dusty outfit made its biggest splash in the early 1970s with the sing-along hit "The Cover Of *Rolling Stone*." That was just one of many good-time songs penned for them by songwriter, children's book author, and *Playboy* cartoonist Shel Silverstein. At their best, the members of Doctor Hook managed to squeeze out tears as often as they played their songs for laughs. "Sylvia's Mother" is a weeper so over-the-top it's almost comic, but songs like "Carry Me, Carrie" and "Mama, I'll Sing One Song For You" are catchy ballads presented with as much sincerity as the group (and songwriter Silverstein) could genuinely muster.

The two centerpoints of the band were Dennis Locorriere and Ray Sawyer, both of them operating as singers, songwriters, and guitarists. Each had a raspy, emotionally torn voice that worked like a crusty, crunchy coating on the twang-infused melodies. All the bandmembers had ragged hair and beards that belied their honest country soul, but it was Sawyer, with black eyepatch and scrunched-up cowboy hat, who became the focal point of the group.

Doctor Hook and the Medicine Show formed in the late '60s, when Alabama natives Sawyer and Billy Francis met Dennis Locorriere while playing bars and clubs around New Jersey. Through connections they won a chance to sing the theme for the 1971 Dustin Hoffman comedy *Who Is Harry Kellerman And Why Is He Saying Those Terrible Things About Me?* Silverstein was writing the film's music and was a hot product at the time following the smash success of "A Boy Named Sue," recorded by Johnny Cash. Doctor Hook soon landed a contract with Columbia, where they began their recording career cutting Silverstein's songs almost exclusively. Among these were "Sylvia's Mother" and "The Cover Of *Rolling Stone*." Both were sizeable pop hits, and Doctor Hook's first couple of albums sold in the millions.

After the group parted ways with Silverstein, further recordings failed to chart and they eventually went bankrupt. Switching to Capitol, they named their next album BANKRUPT and began a new career in more of a country-pop vein. Throughout the late '70s, songs like "Only Sixteen" (by Sam Cooke), "A Little Bit More," and "When You're In Love With A Beautiful Woman" made the charts in the US but fared even better in the UK, where Doctor Hook (they'd

Country Does Dylan

Country singers had begun picking up Bob Dylan songs even before the master himself stepped foot inside the Columbia studios in Nashville to cut BLONDE ON BLONDE. Many of the first to venture into his catalog were bluegrass musicians, which made sense, since the two worlds—folk and bluegrass—had been intertwining for years already. (Folk revivalists had shown interest in bluegrass and old-time country music since the late 1950s.) Of course, once Dylan did begin cutting his Nashville trilogy—and especially after he gained the endorsement of Johnny Cash—the situation evolved further. Rock musicians discovered the joys of recording in Nashville studios, and country singers (or their producers, as the case may be) figured out that Dylan's songs could be a valuable asset to their repertoires, lending a hip caché that just might sell them a few more records.

Johnny Cash, "It Ain't Me Babe"
Johnny was the first country artist not just to embrace Bob's music, but to forge a friendship with the man himself. Cash cut a memorable version of "Wanted Man" in 1970, but even better was his take on "It Ain't Me Babe," which appeared (along with two other Dylan songs) on his 1964 album ORANGE BLOSSOM SPECIAL. Cash's deep voice has the right amount of sarcasm and spit, keeping the song teetering on the edge between parody and true bitterness. A chorus of mariachi horns gives it extra punch.

The Dillards, "Walkin' Down The Line"
It's impossible to say which bluegrass band first added Dylan songs to their repertoire, but it is generally acknowledged that the LA-based progressive outfit the Dillards were the first to release one of his songs on an album (1964's LIVE!! ALMOST!!!). It's about a down-on-his-luck guy, but the Dillards give it a happy-go-lucky spin that works well. The song was suggested by the album's producer, Jim Dickson, who also was responsible for getting the Byrds to cut "Mr Tambourine Man."

Flatt & Scruggs, "Blowin' In The Wind"
If Lester Flatt had had his choice, he and Earl Scruggs would never have touched the Bob Dylan catalog. Flatt liked to keep things traditional—and besides, young Bob was a liberal. But during the '60s, this legendary bluegrass outfit was under pressure from their label, Columbia, to sell more

records and expand their appeal in the burgeoning folk-rock market. And so their new producer, Bob Johnston, had them cut some Dylan songs, five of which turned up on their 1968 album CHANGIN' TIMES. "Blowin' In The Wind" is notable because Flatt's vocals sound so unenthusiastic they verge on sarcasm. The duo split a year later.

The Hillmen, "Fare Thee Well"
Another band produced by Jim Dickson was the Hillmen, who cut two Dylan songs during their 1963–64 recording sessions (the album, however, wasn't released for another five years). The gentle and sad "Fare Thee Well" is a fairly straightforward song with an old-fashioned theme about a man taking off on a long and rambling journey and leaving his lover back at home. The band featured both Vern Gosdin and Chris Hillman.

Burl Ives, "I'll Be Your Baby Tonight"
Admittedly, the jolly folksinger wasn't a country artist really at all, but his oddly enthusiastic and almost hyperactive take on Dylan's "I'll Be Your Baby Tonight"—backed by a rollicking piano and some haunting fiddles—is just a curiosity that's worth noting. The song appears on Ives' Columbia album THE TIMES THEY ARE A-CHANGIN', which was produced by none other than Bob Johnston (one of Dylan's producers).

Waylon Jennings, "Don't Think Twice"
The song became the title track to Waylon's sole album on the A&M label, which compiled songs recorded in the mid-'60s, before he was signed to RCA and turned into a full-fledged country star. A&M was trying to market Waylon to more of a West Coast folk-rock audience, which didn't exactly suit either party. That aside, Waylon has a natural feel for Dylan's classic break-up song.

Leroy Van Dyke, "It's All Over Now, Baby Blue"
This is a big production full of heavy reverb, an acoustic guitar riff that won't quit, and a few background voices to boot, but it's Van Dyke's barnyard of a voice that really gives the song its deep, burly appeal. Van Dyke was best known for the songs "Auctioneer" and "Walk On By"; he cut this song later in his career, after he'd switched from Mercury to Warner Brothers.

dropped the Medicine Show half of their name) found a whole new audience. Capitol also released Sawyer's self-titled solo album in 1977 (it included several songs written by Glaser Studios publicist, Hazel Smith). While a few songs on Sawyer's album have a decent twangy appeal, it's nothing spectacular. None of the late-period Doctor Hook albums, in fact, have the same earthy, gritty sound that made their initial Columbia recordings so appealing. The group survived into the '80s, but it wasn't long before Sawyer and a sputtering version of Doctor Hook were flirting with the revival circuit.

⊙ **Doctor Hook And The Medicine Show** (1971; Columbia). Silverstein wrote nearly all the songs on the group's debut album, including the mock-serious weeper "Sylvia's Mother" and the rambling-man ballad "Mama, I'll Sing One Song For You." A great song that's frequently overlooked is "Judy," a Kafkaesque tale of the absurd about a humble cowboy-drifter who tries to stay out of people's way but still manages to annoy everyone he encounters—waitresses, cops, and churchgoers.

⊙ **Sloppy Seconds** (1972; Columbia). Another great collection of Silverstein-penned songs including the wacked-out "Freakin' At The Freaker's Ball," "Cover Of *Rolling Stone*," and the ballads "If I'd Only Come And Gone," (later cut beautifully by Tompall Glaser), "Carry Me, Carrie," and "Queen Of The Silver Dollar."

The Eagles

"We're never gonna fill their shoes, but we have a good time walking in their footsteps."

—Kix Brooks (of Brooks & Dunn)

The Eagles took the Southern California country-rock concept and turned it into a multi-million-dollar enterprise. Inspired by the music of artists like Gram Parsons, Chris Hillman, and Gene Clark, this soft-rock supergroup created a mellow-minded, country-tinged sound that had massive pop-radio appeal and sold records by the truckful. Songs like "Desperado" and "Peaceful Easy Feeling" are pleasant enough on the surface, yet that's about as far as they go—conspicuously missing is the soul, the fragile emotional edge, that emanates from such country-rock masterworks as Parsons' "A Song For You" or Clark's "Out On The Side."

Though they did have some crossover appeal, during their 1970s heyday the Eagles weren't a country group per se. Their focus instead was on the pop and rock market, which was far more lucrative. Yet by the early '90s, the soft-edged grooves of songs like "Take It Easy," "Tequila Sunrise," "Already Gone," and "Hotel California" turned out to have exerted a huge influence on a whole new generation of country music artists and fans. Thanks to the success of the Eagles tribute album, COMMON THREADS, the group's name is now as revered on Music Row as almost any of country music's classic singers.

The Eagles formed in 1971 when Glenn Frey, Don Henley, Bernie Leadon, and Randy Meisner, all members of Linda Ronstadt's backing band at the time, decided to strike out on their own. Each of them already had a wealth of professional musical experience. Nebraska native Meisner had been a founding member of Poco and later played in Rick Nelson's Stone Canyon Band. Minnesota-born Leadon had picked and sung as a member of the Flying Burrito Brothers and Dillard And Clark—in fact, a song he co-wrote with Clark, "Train Leaves Here This Mornin'," appeared on both the first Dillard And Clark album and the Eagles' debut. Michigan native Frey had played with J.D. Souther, among others, and Texas-born Henley had been a member of various groups including Shiloh.

With future record mogul David Geffen as their manager, the group signed to Asylum and released their self-titled debut album in 1972. They had immediate pop-chart success with songs like "Take It Easy" and "Witchy Woman." Their 1973 follow-up, DESPERADO, included the catchy "Tequila Sunrise," and their third album, ON THE BORDER, gave the band its first #1 hit, "Best Of My Love." This last album also marked the debut of their fifth bandmember, Don Felder. It was 1975's ONE OF THESE NIGHTS, however, that really made the Eagles the superstars they are today, with the title track, "Lyin' Eyes," and "Take It To The Limit" each climbing high in the pop charts. It also won them their first Grammy award.

Leadon left the band in 1975 (a few years later he joined the Nitty Gritty Dirt Band) and was replaced by Mr "Rocky Mountain Way," Joe Walsh. Another super-popular Eagles album arrived in 1976, HOTEL CALIFORNIA. It sold a million almost immediately, won them another Grammy, and the pop hit "New Kid In Town" crossed them over into the country charts. Later that year Meisner left the group and was replaced by Timothy B. Schmit, another former Poco member.

Country-tinged supergroup the Eagles

The Eagles' final studio album, at least on this leg of their journey, was THE LONG RUN, released in 1979. They won more awards, sold lots more records, released a live album (EAGLES LIVE), and then disbanded in 1982.

The next chapter began in the early '90s with COMMON THREADS, the infamous Eagles tribute album. It was a smash success and yielded several country chart hits—suddenly all sorts of Young Country stars were stumbling over themselves to say how much the Eagles had influenced whatever it was they were doing. Knowing a good business opportunity when they saw it, the Eagles reunited in 1994 for a massively successful concert tour and even released an album, HELL FREEZES OVER. Essentially an MTV *Unplugged* concert highlighting their past hits, it also included a handful of brand new songs. And, of course, it sold like hotcakes. The group hasn't recorded anything since then (at least so far), but they have played special engagements, such as a (very expensive) millennium concert in Los Angeles.

⊙ **The Eagles** (1972; Asylum). Start at the beginning and at least the Eagles sound is closer to its country-rock core. Includes the mildly pleasant "Take It Easy,"

the Jackson Browne song "Nightingale," and the Gene Clark/Bernie Leadon composition "Train Leaves Here This Mornin'."

⊙ **Their Greatest Hits (1971–1975)** (1976; Asylum). One of the biggest-selling albums of all time—well over 22 million copies so far. Chances are anyone who's interested in these overplayed '70s hits already owns a copy.

⊙ **Common Thread: The Songs Of The Eagles** (1993; Warner Bros.). With country stars like Vince Gill, Travis Tritt, Little Texas, and Alan Jackson showing where much of their creative inspiration originated—not in the hills of Appalachia but in the musical suburbs of 1970s LA.

Everly Brothers

Of all the close-harmony brother duets to have emerged in country music since the 1920s, the Everly Brothers were the most successful, broadening the style's popularity by bringing the delicate close harmonies and sweet, acoustic melodies into the pop arena. Right from the start, the Everlys straddled both musical worlds. They came directly out of an old-time folk music tradition, they were based during their early years out of Nashville, and many of the early classics came from the pens of country songwriting giants Felice and Boudleaux Bryant. Even so, songs like "Bye Bye Love," "Wake Up Little Susie," "All I Have To Do Is Dream," "When Will I Be Loved," and "Cathy's Clown" appealed directly to young pop and rock'n'roll fans. The Everlys' sound had an R&B underpinning, their lyrics often dealt with teenage angst, and their look was decidedly urban and hip.

Their harmonies, however, were what stood out most—simply rendered, delicately interwoven, and so pure and honest as to elicit tears. They recorded a good many excellent and innovative songs during their long career together, but nowhere else was quality so plain to hear than on SONGS OUR DADDY TAUGHT US, a 1958 album of old-time folk songs that showcased their gently twangy voices with very little accompaniment.

Isaac Donald Every was born on 1 February, 1937 in Brownie, Kentucky. His brother Philip was born in Chicago, Illinois two years later, on 19 January, 1939. Their parents, Margaret and Ike, were both musicians. Ike, in particular, was a renowned fingerpicking guitarist who left his mining job as a young man to pursue a career in music and radio, one that took him all over the Midwest. As a result, Phil and Don began singing with their family on radio shows at a young age. By the mid-'50s the family had landed in Nashville. There the brothers recorded briefly for Columbia, then in 1957 they signed with Cadence Records. Their first single, "Bye Bye Love," written by the Bryants, hit the country and pop charts in May that year and was a massive success. Their follow-up single, "Wake Up Little Susie," was equally popular. Like all their Cadence material, the songs were recorded in Nashville studios with some of the town's finest session pickers.

Over the next three years, the Everlys racked up a huge number of pop and country hits on Cadence. Many of their singles were geared toward a young rock'n'roll audience; rockabilly had, after all, just hit big-time and proven to many in the business that the teen market was where the real money lay. The Everlys still had plenty of country music in their systems, however, and in 1958 they cut SONGS OUR DADDY TAUGHT US, which remains one of their finest creations. They may have been pop stars, but they hadn't forgotten their roots. In 1960 they signed with Warner Brothers,

a West Coast company that was just then branching out from movies into the music business. The duo's initial recordings for the company such as "Walk Right Back" and "Cathy's Clown" were still, as before, cut in Nashville, and demonstrated further what a powerful and popular creative force the duo were.

About the time the Beatles arrived on US shores, however, the Everlys' popularity had peaked and was dropping off. They'd also split with their manager, Wesley Rose (the son of Fred Rose, Wesley ran the publishing company Acuff-Rose, which oversaw the Bryants' catalog among many others) and moved to California. To confound matters, both brothers were drafted into the military for a while. Despite all this change and turmoil, they continued to churn out a steady stream of singles and albums and remained popular in Europe. In 1968 they reconnected with their country past once again by cutting the album ROOTS, which turned out to be one of the pioneering country-rock albums of its day (it arrived the same year as the Byrds' SWEETHEART OF THE RODEO and Doug Dillard and Gene Clark's THE FANTASTIC EXPEDITION OF DILLARD AND CLARK). As successful as ROOTS was on an artistic level, it didn't sell very well. As for the brothers

Everly Brothers

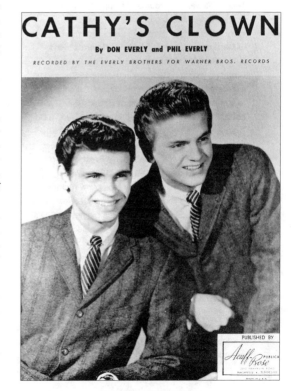

CATHY'S CLOWN
By DON EVERLY and PHIL EVERLY
RECORDED BY THE EVERLY BROTHERS FOR WARNER BROS. RECORDS

PUBLISHED BY
Acuff-Rose

themselves, they finally split up in 1973 in a cloud of professional and personal frustration. Don and Phil spent the next decade working as solo artists, but by 1983 things had cooled down enough that they could get back together. They've been touring and recording as a team again ever since.

⊙ **Songs Our Daddy Taught Us** (1958; Cadence; reissued 1989; Rhino). Phil and Don's harmonies shimmer with delicate beauty, and they're as immediately striking as any in the brother-duet canon. Even if you've heard songs like "Rovin' Gambler" and "Barbara Allen" played countless times, hearing the Everlys sing them—backed only with low-key acoustic arrangements—makes these timeless tunes seem new and fresh all over again. Other standouts include Gene Autry's "That Silver Haired Daddy Of Mine" and Karl and Harty's "I'm Here To Get My Baby Out Of Jail."

⊙ **Roots** (1968; Warner Bros.; reissued 1996). A decade after SONGS OUR DADDY TAUGHT US, the Everlys dipped back into the world of country music with ROOTS, reminding fans again of their country origins. In the process, they created one of the finest country-rock albums of the era, a solid, carefully arranged collection that mixed a pair of haunting Don Everly originals with classics like Merle Haggard "Mama Tried," Ray Price's "You Done Me Wrong," and Jimmie Rodgers' "T For Texas" (as well as a couple of snippets from a 1952 Everly Family radio broadcast).

⊙ **Cadence Classics: Their 20 Greatest Hits** (1987; Rhino). A reliable round-up of the Everly Brothers' years on Cadence in the late 1950s, and an excellent starter CD for the budding fan. It's the place to find the original recordings of classics like "Bye Bye Love," "Wake Up Little Susie," and "All I Have To Do Is Dream."

⊙ **Walk Right Back: The Everly Brothers On Warner Brothers, 1960–1969** (1993; Warner Bros./Archive). Devoted Everly fans know that their Warner Brothers years yielded more than a few excellent creations, and not just the big hits "Cathy's Clown" and "Walk Right Back." This 2-disc compilation digs into this period in some detail.

⊙ **Original British Hit Singles** (1994; Ace). The Everly Brothers were very popular in England right from their 1957 smash "Bye Bye Love," and this 22-song compilation pulls together their Cadence hits (which were released on the London label in the UK). It's another fine introduction to their classic early recordings.

Emmylou Harris

"The reason older people aren't buying [country] records is because nobody's speaking to them. So we have tribute records. I'm sorry, I don't want a tribute record."

—Emmylou Harris

We'll never know what would have happened to Emmylou Harris if she hadn't met Gram Parsons. Maybe she would have made it to Nashville anyhow, or maybe she'd be stuck playing Holiday Inns up and down the East Coast. Who knows. The fact remains, however that her career as we know it today was launched in large part by Parsons, who rescued her from folk-music obscurity to sing on his two solo albums. It wasn't just a one-sided favor—those Parsons records wouldn't have been the marvels they are today without Emmylou's harmonies. But as her own music career blossomed in the wake of her mentor's untimely death, Emmylou knew she'd never have gotten so far, so fast without Parsons' help. Right away she made a point of thanking him and doing what she could to promote his talent, which during the 1970s was still under-recognized.

Since striking out on her own in the mid-'70s, Emmylou has become one of the most universally loved and widely respected singers in country music. She's hit the top of the country charts many times over and won an assortment of Grammy and CMA awards. During the '70s her Hot Band was one of the finest in the business, including at various points such stellar pickers as James Burton, Ricky Skaggs, Rodney Crowell, and her producer-husband at the time Brian Ahern. During a period when mainstream country music was tending toward Gamblers and Rhinestone Cowboys, Emmylou kept her music firmly grounded and faithful to its roots. She hasn't written all that many songs herself, but over the years she's proven she has a knack for picking quality material and making it her own—whether it's an old Louvin Brothers song ("If I Could Only Win Your Love"), a jewel from the Gram Parsons archive ("Luxury Liner," "Sin City"), or a freshly written piece by Townes Van Zandt ("If I Needed You") or Gillian Welch ("Orphan Girl").

Emmylou's voice is a combination of pure and pretty—definitely more in a contemporary folk-inspired vein than the traditional mountain-bred style of Dolly Parton or Loretta Lynn. She's one of the finest harmony vocalists in all of country music, though on her own, her music is sometimes too pretty, often lacking a sharp edge; yet what saves it from being saccharine is a musical spirit that's obviously and absolutely genuine. Even on her less than successful albums, you can still feel her sense of adventure. The diversity of her sound over the years reveals a restless sort of energy continually driving her forward.

Emmylou Harris was born on 2 April, 1947 in Birmingham, Alabama. She grew up first in North Carolina then in Quantico, Virginia, a suburb of Washington, DC, where she got straight-As in high school and also began playing folk music. After a short college career studying drama in North Carolina and Boston, she opted instead for a musicical career and soon settled in New York City, the centerpoint of the folk music revival. There she played the clubs and met other up-and-coming artists like Jerry Jeff Walker. In 1970 the small label Jubilee released her first album, GLIDING BIRD, a collection of folksongs that she now generally ignores.

In 1971 she and her first husband, Tom Slocum, moved to Nashville, but a year later the two were separated and Emmylou was back in DC. It's at this point that Flying Burrito Brothers bandmembers Kenny Wertz, Rick Roberts, and Chris Hillman first heard her singing in a local folk-music club. Hillman told Parsons about her, and in the fall of 1972 she flew to California to sing harmony on Parsons' solo debut, GP. Her voice, angelic as it was, added a firm counterpoint to Parsons' own warm but fragile singing. She toured with Parsons in early 1973 and later that summer sang on his second album, GRIEVOUS ANGEL. By September, however, Parsons was dead from a drug overdose and Harris was left standing on her own.

Returning to DC, she put together a band and eventually negotiated a contract with Reprise Records, which had been Parsons' label. Her producer, Brian Ahern, had previously worked with the more pop-oriented Canadian singer Anne Murray, but he and Harris struck up a good relationship. He ended up producing and playing on her albums for nearly a decade and also became her second husband.

Emmylou's solo debut, PIECES OF THE SKY, was released in 1975 and featured guitarist James Burton and pianist Glen D. Hardin, two key players from Elvis Presley's band who'd also appeared on both of Parsons' solo albums. They became the cornerstones of the Hot Band, Emmylou's top-notch back-up group she maintained through the '70s and into the early '80s. PIECES

Emmylou Harris

OF THE SKY won immediate acclaim, and Emmylou was marked as a bright new star. She had risen out of the LA country-rock scene, but she was now accepted in Nashville circles as well—something Parsons himself always craved but never achieved. Before she knew it she even had a bona fide country hit with an old Louvin Brothers song, "If I Could Only Win Your Love." She followed that with a sweet version of Buck Owens' "Together Again," which in 1976 became her first #1. The album it appeared on, ELITE HOTEL, sold well and earned Emmylou her first Grammy. It also included three Gram Parsons compositions, "Sin City," "Wheels," and "Ooh Las Vegas." Continuing to pay tribute to her former mentor, she titled her third album LUXURY LINER, after another Parsons song.

Emmylou continued her steady stream of bright, well-grounded country recordings through the rest of the decade. She cut songs by the Louvin

Emmylou Harris

Brothers, Leon Payne, and Dallas Frazier on 1979's BLUE KENTUCKY GIRL, and her 1980 album ROSES IN THE SNOW had an acoustic bluegrass feel thanks to the influence of Ricky Skaggs, who'd joined her Hot Band in 1978 and was on the verge of country stardom himself. In 1980 Harris was named CMA's Female Vocalist of the Year.

Emmylou's final album with Ahern at the helm was WHITE SHOES, which reached into new territory with the Donna Summer song "On The Radio." After Emmylou and Ahern split she moved from LA to Nashville. For her next project she hooked up with singer-songwriter Paul Kennerly, the result being the 1985 album THE BALLAD OF SALLY ROSE. She and Kennerly were soon married as well. The 1987 album ANGEL BAND was a collection of acoustic country gospel songs. Also released in 1987 was TRIO, a collaborative recording featuring Harris, Linda Ronstadt, and Dolly Parton. Fueled by that album's success, Emmylou's label in 1990 released DUETS, a collection of previously released recordings. By 1992 her sound and style was back on the rootsy side with AT THE RYMAN, a live album cut at the former home of the *Grand Ole Opry* that featured an acoustic band she dubbed the Nash Ramblers.

In 1993 Emmylou moved from Warner Brothers to Asylum. The new label released her COWGIRL'S PRAYER in 1993, but it was the 1995 album WRECKING BALL that garnered her another sweep of critical acclaim and reached a whole new audience of alternative rock and country fans. WRECKING BALL was produced by Daniel Lanois, who'd previously worked with U2 and Bob Dylan, and it paired Emmylou's expressive voice with moody songs by Neil Young, Gillian Welch, Lucinda Williams, Steve Earle, and other contemporary artists. A few years later she was shifting directions again, recording her SPYBOY album live and even releasing it on her own label, Eminent. In 1999 she, Ronstadt, and Parton saw the release of their long-awaited follow-up effort, TRIO II.

⊙ **Pieces Of The Sky** (1975; Reprise). Emmylou's solo debut kicks off her winning 1970s streak that was marked by folky-sweet song material—some new, some traditional—excellent musicianship, impeccable production values and beautiful vocals. Includes "Boulder To Birmingham," Rodney Crowell's "Bluebird Wine," and a version of "Sleepless Nights," which she'd previously cut with Gram Parsons.

⊙ **Elite Hotel** (1976; Reprise). Her second album is another beautiful collection that feels slightly more confident. Includes a great version of the Burrito

Brothers' "Sin City," the Don Gibson song "Sweet Dreams" (made famous by Patsy Cline), and the traditional song "Satan's Jeweled Crown."

⊙ **Roses In The Snow** (1980; Warner Bros.). Ahern produced this record, as usual, but Hot Band member Ricky Skaggs exerted a powerful influence, giving the album a feeling of traditional bluegrass and Appalachian music. The players include Skaggs, Tony Rice, Albert Lee, and Jerry Douglas, with guest turns from Johnny Cash and Dolly Parton.

⊙ **Wrecking Ball** (1995; Elektra-Asylum). Producer Daniel Lanois creates a moody atmosphere that places Emmylou's pretty voice in a new context—one very different from the traditional orientation of her past efforts—and it works beautifully. It's not really a country record, but it is among her finest achievements.

⊙ **Portraits** (1996; Reprise Archives). A solid 3-CD overview of Emmylou's long career on Warner Brothers, beginning with several Gram Parsons duets and running through her early 1990s recordings. The handful of previously unreleased songs includes "Casey's Last Ride" (Kris Kristofferson), "Dimming Of The Day" (Richard Thompson), and "When I Paint My Masterpiece" (Bob Dylan).

⊙ **Spyboy** (1998; Eminent). After the studio splendor of WRECKING BALL, Emmylou decided to pare down and cut this album live. The band this time is lead guitarist (and co-producer) Buddy Miller, bassist Daryl Johnson, and drummer Brady Blade. Songs include "Love Hurts," "I Ain't Living Long Like This," and an updated version of "Boulder To Birmingham."

Chris Hillman

"I don't consider myself a solo artist; I consider myself a band or team guy."
—Chris Hillman

Chris Hillman was a major player in the development of country rock on the West Coast during the 1960s. If you weren't paying attention, however, you might have missed this fact, because Hillman wasn't one for the spotlight. He didn't work as a band leader or front man, but remained a behind-the-scenes figure instead—playing bass, singing harmony, writing and arranging songs, and generally helping guide the direction of two of the country-rock era's most influential groups, the Byrds and the Flying Burrito Brothers. Together with his friend and musical accomplice Gram Parsons, Hillman brought traditional country music to the ears of many folk-rock fans, and also into the repertoires of the region's top musicians—including Byrds leader Roger McGuinn, who would never have cut SWEETHEART OF THE RODEO of his own accord. After two decades of keeping his profile in the background, though, in the mid-'80s Hillman finally stepped into the spotlight as lead singer, songwriter, and guitarist with the West Coast country outfit the Desert Rose Band.

VIRGINIA LEE HUNTER

Chris Hillman (left) and Herb Pedersen

splitting up. Chris was next hired to play bass in the Byrds; he wasn't technically a founding member, but was there almost from the very beginning, playing on their debut album MR TAMBOURINE MAN. During his Byrds tenure, Hillman also wrote a few songs including "Time Between," "The Girl With No Name," and "So You Want To Be A Rock And Roll Star" (with McGuinn).

When Gram Parsons joined the Byrds in late 1967, Hillman suddenly had an accomplice—another musician who understood his lifelong love of country music. Hillman and Parsons turned McGuinn onto the beauty of Merle Haggard and Buck Owens, for instance, before guiding the Byrds headlong into country-rock territory with the landmark 1968 album SWEETHEART OF THE RODEO. Parsons quit soon after that album's release, and before the year was out, Hillman had followed suit. The two next formed the Flying Burrito Brothers, and Hillman co-wrote songs (with Parsons), contributed backing vocals, and played guitar on that group's 1969 debut album THE GILDED PALACE OF SIN. Even more so than the Byrds had done on SWEETHEART, the Burritos steeped themselves in the world of honky tonk—in the process bringing to the music a rock'n'roll sensibility that was all their own. "Cosmic American music," Gram liked to call it. SIN remains one of the seminal albums of the era.

Parsons left the Burrito fold after their follow-up album, BURRITO DELUXE. Hillman stayed on board for another few years, but after those first couple of albums the group had lost much of its originality and spark and was threatening to become another middle-of-the-road country-rock band. During the '70s Hillman played again briefly with the Byrds and then with Manassas (featuring Stephen Stills) and the Souther, Hillman, Furay Band. He cut his first two solo albums, SLIPPIN' AWAY and CLEAR SAILIN', in 1976 and 1977 respectively,

Hillman initially entered the Southern California music scene by way of bluegrass. A Los Angeles native (born on 4 December, 1944), he first played mandolin in a little-known bluegrass outfit the Scottsville Squirrel Barkers before joining the Golden State Boys, who were later renamed the Blue Diamond Boys and finally the Hillmen. That band also included banjoist Don Parmley (later of the Bluegrass Cardinals) and brothers Rex and Vern Gosdin (Vern would go on to be a mainstream country hitmaker). The Blue Diamond Boys recorded one album in 1963 and 1964 (it wasn't released until six years later) before

before heading back into the studio for another pair of records with two of his Byrds buddies under the name McGuinn, Clark, And Hillman.

Hillman's 1984 solo album, DESERT ROSE, served to promote his rebirth as a mainstream country bandleader during the height of the New Traditionalist era. About a year later, Hillman played a series of dates with guitarist/banjoist Herb Pedersen (who'd played on DESERT ROSE), bassist Bill Bryson, and guitarist John Jorgenson, and this led to his forming the Desert Rose Band. The group also included steel player Jay Dee Maness and drummer Steve Duncan. The quality of the musicianship was hard to beat, and the group earned a respectable string of Top 10 country hits between 1987 and 1990 that were marked (in the best of times) by a bright, twangy, and entirely refreshing sound. The first two albums, THE DESERT ROSE BAND and RUNNING, were the strongest. After their release the magic began to fade, bandmembers started leaving, and Hillman eventually called the whole thing off in 1994. He has since cut back on his musical projects, though he did record a duet album with Pedersen in 1996, BAKERSFIELD BOUND, and in 1998 he put together another solo album, LIKE A HURRICANE.

⊙ **The Hillmen** (1969; Together; reissued 1995; Sugar Hill). Solid, if somewhat uneventful, bluegrass with a traditional foundation (bass, guitar, mandolin, and banjo) but a progressive sensibility. Songs by Dylan, Pete Seeger, and the Gosdin brothers sit alongside old timers like "Barbara Allen." The clear harmony vocals and the picking are what make the music shine.

⊙ **Desert Rose** (1984; Sugar Hill; reissued 1990). For this solo album, Hillman brought on board such stellar pickers as James Burton, Herb Pedersen, Byron

Southern Rock

Though it's been said the South will rise again, it hasn't happened yet. But southern rock—a kissin' cousin to country and blues rock—did have its moment during the mid-1970s. Its linchpins were the **Allman Brothers** and Lynyrd Skynyrd, whose better aspects still resonate even today in the worlds of country and rock'n'roll. A number of the classic southern-rock bands were comprised of brothers or relatives. In further curious coincidences, most hailed from Georgia or northern Florida, and the majority of the major players from the era are no longer among the living.

The nexus for southern rock was Macon, Georgia, home to the Allman Brothers Band and Capricorn Records, known almost exclusively for its southern-rock pickings. The Allmans led the pack with a sound that was far more complex than the redneck boogie associated with the form. Two exceptional guitarists— Dickey Betts and Duane Allman—dueled on twin leads while the band jammed on country, blues, and jazz themes; the elements combined for exciting live improvisations.

Recorded just two years after forming, the original band was in peak form on 1971's THE ALLMAN BROTHERS BAND AT FILLMORE EAST. The album is frequently cited by critics as one of best live albums ever recorded— surely you haven't lived until you've heard "Whipping Post," "Statesboro Blues," and the LP-side-long "You Don't Love Me." Vocalist Gregg Allman is at his throaty, soulful best and brother Duane reigns on lead. Though they would follow with the substantial EAT A PEACH— which contained the sweet "Melissa" and country-rock "Blue Sky"—and BROTHERS AND SISTERS—which spawned a gigantic hit, "Ramblin' Man"—the death of guitarist Duane and bassist Barry Oakley (both in motorcycle accidents) after the release of FILLMORE EAST cast a long shadow over the band, from which they never quite recovered.

Next in the line came Jacksonville, Florida's **Lynyrd Skynyrd**. A rebel-rousing *three*-guitar group, they were the official hitmakers and Confederate flag–wavers of the genre—blame the redneck tag on them. Lyricist Ronnie Van Zant did have his sensitive moments ("Tuesday's Gone," "Free Bird," both from their debut PRONOUNCED LEH-NERD SKIN-NERD), but it was the shit-kicking numbers that were their signature. SECOND HELPING displayed a band so confident that Van Zant answered Neil Young's pejorative "Southern Man" with "Sweet Home Alabama." And he won: it was Skynyrd's biggest single to date. Yet it seems wherever they went, singer Van Zant and his bandmates found trouble, along with the proverbial liquor and drugs. The incident for which the fiery band is most remembered, however, was no fault of their own. In 1977, a plane crash killed Van Zant and new members Steve and Cassie Gaines, essentially forcing a hiatus while the rest recovered and regrouped.

Bluegrass and country artist **Charlie Daniels** served as an elder statesmen for the boys in southern rock when he and his band got swept into the fray with their toe-tappin' fiddle-tune "The South's Gonna Do It." The song namechecked the whole lot, and it was a big hit in 1975. There were also brothers Toy and

Chris Hillman

Berline, and Bernie Leadon. The songs run from Mickey Newbury's "Why You Been Gone So Long" to the Louvin Brothers' "I Can't Keep You In Love With Me," and the title track is a Hillman original that inspired his Desert Rose Band.

⊙ **A Dozen Roses: Greatest Hits** (1991; Curb). Contains the choicest cuts from the Desert Rose Band's first 3 albums; only serious fans will need to dig deeper. Hillman's voice was gentler, even sweeter, in tone than those of Steve Earle or Randy Travis, who were on the radio around the same time. But Hillman held his own just fine, thanks to his skills at writing catchy country melodies—and to the top-shelf musicians he'd hired to round out the organization.

⊙ **Like A Hurricane** (1998; Sugar Hill). After surviving 35 years in the music business, and having a hand in some landmark recordings along the way,

there's no reason at this point for Hillman to put together a record unless he wants to and the time is right. Rather than trying to break boundaries this time, HURRICANE shows Hillman reflecting on his past—confident, comfortable, and taking pleasure in the music for its own sake.

Rick Nelson

"Most of my early records were at least part country."

—Rick Nelson

R ick Nelson was one of the most popular singers of the 1950s and '60s, a onetime TV star (*The Adventures Of Ozzie And Harriet*) turned teen idol,

Tommy Caldwell of the **Marshall Tucker Band**, who with singer Doug Gray and their unusual use of reeds scored with the songs "Can't You See," "Fire On The Mountain," and "Heard It In A Love Song." Another band, the **Outlaws**, merged the dueling guitars of the Allmans with the harmony vocals of the Eagles and came up with a "Free Bird"-esque epic of their own in "Green Grass And High Tides." Former Outlaw Henry Paul then went on to head-up the contemporary southern rock outfit Blackhawk.

By the end of the decade, even smooth session men the **Atlanta Rhythm Section** ("So Into You") and experimentalists like the **Dixie Dregs** were flying under the southern rock banner. By then, however, imitators and hitmakers like **Molly Hatchet**, **.38 Special** (featuring Ronnie Van Zant's brother Donnie on vocals), and the **Rossington-Collins Band** (which was a

resurrected version of Skynyrd) were helping to usher out southern rock's halcyon days. None of these groups proved to have the staying power of the mighty Allmans or the original Skynyrd (though for a sampling of the best shots, you can try the Rhino compilation REBEL ROUSERS: SOUTHERN ROCK CLASSICS).

During the '80s, southern rock went underground while regional artists like R.E.M. and the B-52's did their best to stamp out the hellfire—and the South's redneck reputation. Concurrently, bands like **Drivin' 'n' Cryin'** and the **Georgia Satellites** brought a bit of the boogie back into their Atlanta-based, boot-stompin' rock'n'roll. By the '90s, southern rock was on the rise again thanks to the likes of **Travis Tritt** and the **Kentucky Headhunters** in country music, not to mention rock bands like the **Black Crowes**, **Widespread Panic**, **Blues Traveller**, and **Phish**, all of whom took cues from the Allmans when they introduced endless, improvisational jams into their new brand of boogie. Southern rock came full circle with the Crowes, who went so far as to recruit Allman keyboardist Chuck Leavell for their 1990 debut album SHAKE YOUR MONEY MAKER. Their follow-up, THE SOUTHERN HARMONY AND MUSICAL COMPANION, puts a modern spin on southern rock while it neatly incorporates gospel, blues, and glam rock.

As for the classic acts, at the end of the millennium reformed versions of the Allman Brothers Band and Lynyrd Skynyrd (with Johnny Van Zant on vocals) were still on the road, filling outdoor sheds during their annual summer tours. For better or worse, it looks like the South's gonna do it again.

—Denise Sullivan

Chris Hillman • Rick Nelson

who crooned and rocked his way repeatedly to the top of the pop charts. His music career was launched at what turned out to be the tail end of the rockabilly era, and he proved he could rock out when he wanted to—his pretty-boy looks, sweet voice, and suburban background be damned. During the mid-'60s, after he'd grown up a bit (he was only sixteen years old when he first recorded)— and also after his pop status had faded in favor of teen idols from British shores—he discovered the big, wide, wonderful world of country music. His 1966 album BRIGHT LIGHTS AND COUNTRY MUSIC didn't exactly revive his sagging career, but it did make him an early pioneer in the country-rock genre—coming a couple of years before the International Submarine Band's SAFE AT HOME and the Byrds' SWEETHEARTS OF THE RODEO.

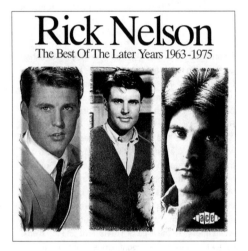

Ricky was born Eric Hilliard Nelson on 8 May, 1940 in Teaneck, New Jersey. His parents were bandleader Ozzie Nelson and singer Harriet Hilliard, known to millions of Americans during the '50s by just their first names, Ozzie and Harriet. As stars of the TV show *The Adventures Of Ozzie And Harriet*—along with sons Ricky and David— they became the quintessential Eisenhower-era suburban family. The show actually debuted on radio in 1949 before moving to television a few years later (it remained on the air into the '60s). Like many kids his age, Ricky was enamored with Elvis Presley, and soon wanted to try his hand at record making too. In 1957 a session was arranged for him by his father, and then an entire TV episode was written around his budding music career. This exposed him to a huge potential audience, and the concept worked like a charm.

The single ("I'm Walkin'") was released a couple of weeks after the episode, and before you could say "marketing strategy," it had sold in the hundreds of thousands.

Most of the young star's classic late '50s and early '60s sides for Imperial featured guitarist James Burton (a top West Coast session picker who would later gain fame as Elvis Presley's lead guitar man). Between 1957 and 1962, Nelson racked up a couple of dozen strong pop hits, including "Poor Little Fool," "Lonesome Town," and "Travelin' Man." Some songs were crooner-ish ballads, others rocked out harder, though never with the unvarnished verve of classic mid-'50s rockabilly. Nelson signed with Decca in 1963, but once the Beatles began to break in the US, his style of teen pop and rock was quickly overtaken by a new British Invasion. He was also wallowing musically, unsure of where to turn next for inspiration. The spark came when he took a suggestion from guitarist Burton and began digging into the world of country music. He was quickly hooked, and in 1966 he cut what became one of the very first country-rock albums, BRIGHT LIGHTS AND COUNTRY MUSIC. Nelson had made the country charts a few times during the '50s, but this album and its follow-up, COUNTRY FEVER, represented the first steps in a new direction for the former teen heart-throb—one he explored on and off for the duration of his career. In 1969 his country-rock experiments came to full fruition when he formed the Stone Canyon Band. The group included steel guitarist Tom Brumley, a former member of Buck Owens' Buckaroos and bassist Randy Meisner—who stuck around only for a short while before shooting off to join the Eagles.

The Stone Canyon Band gave Nelson a new identity, one fueled by the growing interest in country music among rock'n'roll fans—especially on the West Coast, where Nelson was based. The group's debut on album was 1969's LIVE AT THE TROUBADOUR; RICK SINGS NELSON was a strong follow-up, but it's the title track from the group's 1972 album, GARDEN PARTY, that remains the best known. On the one hand a song about the vapidity of celebrity, the lyrics also spell out in a very specific fashion Nelson's frustration at being labeled by his teen-idol past. ('Oldies' music was becoming a genre of its own at the time, much the way 'classic rock' came into being a decade later). "If memories were all I sang," Nelson sang, "I'd rather drive a truck."

In the late '70s Nelson signed to Epic and broke up the Stone Canyon Band (though Brumley stayed on). His later recordings are a mix of pop, soft country-folk, and neo-rockabilly—and his live shows even included a few of those "memories." Tragically, his life and career came to an end on 31 December, 1985 when the plane he, his fiancée, and his band were traveling in crashed near Dekalb, Texas. The following year, Nelson was inducted into the Rock and Roll Hall of Fame. His twin sons have since become rock-'n'roll idols themselves, touring and recording under the band name Nelson.

⊙ **Garden Party** (1972; MCA; reissued 1999). Nelson's country-rock explorations came to full fruition with the Stone Canyon Band. The title track here was by far their biggest single, and like most SCB recordings it's marked by a pleasantly laid-back quality that was typical of LA in the 1970s—though still retaining firm roots, thanks in no small part to Tom Brumley's steel guitar.

⊙ **The Best Of The Later Years 1963–1975** (1997; Ace). This tightly packed, 26-song CD highlights Rick's Decca years and demonstrates his versatility as a performer. On the first half he's charged up by such rock'n'rollers as Ray Charles' "I Got A Woman" and Dorsey Burnette's "Gypsy Woman." The second half is where the country starts, beginning with Terry Fell's "Truck Drivin' Man" and then graduating into Stone Canyon Band territory highlighted by Bob Dylan's "She Belongs To Me" and Rick's own "Garden Party."

⊙ **Stay Young: The Epic Recordings** (1993; Epic/Legacy). Nelson recorded for Epic during the late '70s, and the results were mixed, though not without some shining moments, such as "Wings" and Dylan's "Mama You've Been On My Mind." The latter is one of several previously unreleased songs produced by Al Kooper. Further rarities include tracks from his Memphis sessions that are restored to their original form for the first time (they were overdubbed for their initial release, much to Rick's chagrin).

Michael Nesmith

Despite his bubblegum past as a member of television pop group the Monkees, which too often overshadows his musical reputation, Michael Nesmith was an accomplished singer-songwriter with a distinct country flair. The records he made during the 1970s with his First National Band and as a solo artist are accomplished and quite beautiful, proof enough that his musical credentials were indeed genuine. Albums like ... AND THE HITS JUST KEEP ON COMIN' and LOOSE SALUTE are distinguished by Nesmith's reedy tenor voice, the steel guitar work of Red Rhodes, and bright-eyed original songs such as "Silver Moon," "Listen To The Band," and "Different Drum" (which had been a hit for Linda Ronstadt and the Stone Poneys).

In addition to his music, Nesmith was also an astute businessman. During the late '70s his media company, Pacific Arts, pioneered the concept of a music-video television program with a show called *Pop-clips*, which served as the inspiration for MTV. Thanks to his success in this field, Nesmith shifted his emphasis during the '80s from music to video publishing and film and TV production (his projects included the films *Tapeheads* and *Repo Man*). His business sense was no fluke: years earlier Nesmith's mother (Bette Nesmith Graham) had made a fortune after inventing typing correction fluid.

Michael Nesmith was born on 30 December, 1943 in Houston, Texas. Caught up in the urban folk revival, he played music in assorted groups, including some back-up work for Stax/Volt in Memphis. By the mid-'60s he'd landed in Los Angeles, where he played in a folk duo and cut a couple of singles. He also auditioned for a pop-music television show, and before he knew it he was a member of the Monkees. During his stint with the group, Nesmith led the crusade that allowed them to actually play on their records. He also wrote some songs for the group.

Nesmith (or Nez as his fans and friends call him) cut his first solo album, WICHITA TRAIN WHISTLE SONGS, for Dot Records in 1968, and a year later he quit the Monkees to go it alone. He formed the First National Band with bassist John London, drummer John Ware, and pedal-steel guitarist Red Rhodes, and they cut two records for RCA, LOOSE SALUTE and MAGNETIC SOUTH. The records yielded a couple of minor chart hits, "Joanne" and "Silver Moon." Two more albums followed with a slightly revised National Band line-up, 1971's NEVADA FIGHTER and 1972's TANTAMOUNT TO TREASON. After that, Nesmith recorded under his own name, switching in 1974 from RCA to his own music label, Pacific Arts. He recorded several more albums, but because of his film and video involvement, 1979's INFINITE RIDER ON THE BIG DOGMA was his last until he resurfaced in 1992 with TROPICAL CAMPFIRES. This last release was an acoustic affair with a tropical feel, and included the standards "Brazil" and "Begin The Beguine." Once again, it also featured

GLENN A BAKER ARCHIVES/REDFERNS

Michael Nesmith (center) with his First National Band

just another halfway decent band on the Southern California country-rock scene if not for one thing: WILL THE CIRCLE BE UNBROKEN? Their 1972 album was a musical landmark that helped turn a whole new generation of young fans and budding pickers onto the joys of traditional country music. Even today, many old-time and bluegrass players still sheepishly admit they first discovered the music thanks to CIRCLE (and/or the Grateful Dead offshoot OLD AND IN THE WAY). The album brought together country icons Roy Acuff, Earl Scruggs, Doc Watson, Merle Travis, Jimmy Martin, Vassar Clements, and Maybelle Carter to sing and pick alongside the NGDB on decades-old traditional favorites such as "Wildwood Flower," "Lost Highway," "Orange Blossom Special," "I'm Thinking Tonight Of My Blue Eyes," "Wabash Cannonball," and "Tennessee Stud."

Nesmith's longtime steel player, Rhodes. Nesmith now lives in New Mexico and tours only occasionally. In 1998 St Martin's Press published his first novel, *The Long Sandy Hair Of Neftoon Zamora*.

⊙ **... And The Hits Just Keep On Comin'** (1972; RCA). Compared with his First National Band material, this album is a more simple affair, with Nesmith and Rhodes playing all the instrumental parts. The song roster includes "Different Drum."

⊙ **The Older Stuff: The Best Of The Early Years** (1991; Rhino). An excellent collection of his early-1970s material with the First National Band.

⊙ **The First National Band Complete** (1993; Pacific Arts). A 2-CD set that includes MAGNETIC SOUTH, LOOSE SALUTE, and NEVADA FIGHTER in their entirely. The next place to turn if THE OLDER STUFF isn't enough.

Nitty Gritty Dirt Band

The Nitty Gritty Dirt Band first earned their musical reputation during the late 1960s and '70s playing a blend of contemporary folk, bluegrass, and novelty jug-band songs with a laid-back rock'n'roll sensibility. They also sported one of the most talented young musicians on the West Coast, John McEuen, a master on all sorts of stringed instruments. Still, the NGDB would be

The Nitty Gritty Dirt Band formed in the mid-'60s out of jam sessions at McCabe's Guitar Shop in LA, where Jeff Hanna and Bruce Kunkel began playing jug-band music together with Ralph Barr, Les Thompson, and Jimmie Fadden. Singer-songwriter Jackson Browne briefly played with this early incarnation of the group, too. The multi-talented John McEuen came to the NGDB through his older brother Bill, who was the group's manager and later their producer as well. They recorded a few albums for Liberty in the late '60s, had a minor hit with "Buy For Me The Rain," and went through a few more personnel shuffles before settling on a line-up of McEuen, Hanna, Fadden, Thompson, and Jim Ibbotson. They had a huge hit with the Jerry Jeff Walker song "Mr Bojangles," followed by WILL THE CIRCLE BE UNBROKEN? which they cut in Nashville instead of LA. It brought them a wealth of new attention in country, bluegrass, and rock circles alike.

After further line-up changes during the '70s, the group officially shortened its name to the Dirt Band and began heading in a more mainstream, country-pop direction. They continued to record and perform all through the '80s, and in 1989 cut WILL THE CIRCLE BE UNBROKEN, VOL. 2, a much less radical project that brought them together with the likes of John Denver, Ricky Skaggs, Roger McGuinn, and Bruce Hornsby, as well as Acuff, Johnny Cash, and Chet Atkins. The group continued performing together into the '90s, alternating between traditional acoustic and mainstream pop material.

⊙ **Uncle Charlie And His Dog Teddy** (1970; Liberty). The NGDB broke nationally thanks to "Mr Bojangles," "Some Of Shelly's Blues," and "House On Pooh Corner," hits that first appeared on this album.

⊙ **Will the Circle Be Unbroken?** (1972; United Artists). The recording project that proved traditional country music could cross the generation gap. It's a fun listen still, with Doc Watson's versions of "Tennessee Stud" a clear standout. It's also interesting for the between-song studio chatter, such as when Watson meets Merle Travis for the first time. Originally a triple LP, it's now on 2 CDs.

⊙ **Best Of The Nitty Gritty Dirt Band** (1987; EMI). A 16-song compilation covering their classic early years. Songs include "Buy For Me The Rain," "Mr Bojangles," "Some Of Shelly's Blues" (written by Michael Nesmith) and "Jambalaya."

Bringin' it all back home: the Nitty Gritty Dirt Band

Gram Parsons

"He redefined the possibilities of country music for me. If he had lived, he probably would have redefined it for everybody."

—Keith Richards

D uring his short lifetime, Gram Parsons created an incredibly resilient body of work that has not only survived but grown more appealing with age. To look at him, he was obviously a rock'n'roller; yet to hear him sing, his love for country music was honest and heartfelt. He was a Florida native transplanted to hip and trendy LA, a longhaired folksinger who wore Nudie suits emblazoned with marijuana leaves and adored Merle Haggard. And its in this mix of contradictory forces that he found his creative strength. With his band the International Submarine Band, as a member of the Byrds and the Flying Burrito Brothers, and in his otherworldly duets with Emmylou Harris, Parsons created music that breathed with grace, sadness, beauty, and wonder.

On the surface, Gram Parsons had everything—looks, talent, and plenty of money (his family owned a massive chunk of the Florida citrus crop). On the one hand he was full of confidence and drive—he spearheaded a major musical shift in the Byrds, which was no small feat considering they were one of the era's most popular bands, yet at the same time, he was restless and unsatisfied, not to mention misunderstood. Overriding all this was a tragic innocence, that of a boy genius corrupted by a deadly mixture of trust funds that were too deep, and rock'n'roll fantasies that were too grandiose. Considering the weight of all that unreality, it's no wonder he burned out at the tender age of twenty-six.

His strength was always in his music, however, and because of this his legacy has endured. In the context of songs like "Hickory Wind," "Sin City," "A Song For You," "She," and "Return Of The Grievous Angel," country music came to have real meaning for a whole new generation of fans, many of

GLENN A BAKER

Gram Parsons

whom were paying attention to it for the first time in their lives. And in the three decades since his heyday, the cult of Gram Parsons has shown no signs of drying up. The fusion of country and rock he pioneered in his own music may have been watered down by bands like the Eagles and Poco—something that annoyed Gram even during his lifetime—but at the same time he opened the doors of country music to other artists, including not only the Byrds but his buddies the Rolling Stones. And by the 1990s he'd become the godfather for a new generation of alt.country fans and the subject of a couple of tribute albums, COMMEMORATIVO and RETURN OF THE GRIEVOUS ANGEL.

Parsons was born Ingram Connor III on 5 November, 1946 in Winter Haven, Florida and raised both there and in Waycross, Georgia. His father, Coon Dog Connor, had married Avis Snively, whose family owned Snively Groves and was very wealthy. Gram's musical interests were encouraged early on, and to say he was pampered is probably putting it mildly. Not everything was fun and games, however—Grams' father, for instance, shot himself when Gram was barely a teenager. He picked up his last name when his mother remarried Robert Ellis Parsons.

Gram listened to and played all sorts of music as a teenager, and by high school he was flirting with folk music. In 1963 he joined the Shilos, a South Carolina folksinging trio. They spent a summer soaking in the Greenwich Village music scene in New York City, and even recorded once—a live college-radio broadcast of fairly straightforward folk material that's since been issued under the album title GRAM PARSONS: THE EARLY YEARS.

In the fall of 1965 Gram was a freshman at Harvard, but his college career barely lasted a semester. He was more interested in playing music and experimenting with drugs than completing his course work. The next spring he was living in the Bronx with a band he'd formed, the Like, and paying the rent out of his substantial trust fund. It's around this point that Gram began leaning his music toward country, thanks in part to the encouragement of his band's guitarist, John Neuse. He also wrote the songs "Brass Buttons" and "Luxury Liner" during this time. Wanting a hipper name, the Like became the International Submarine Band.

During a visit to California in 1966, Gram fell in love and also decided LA was a better place to launch his music career. He moved the band out west and set them up in a house in Laurel Canyon. In 1967 he convinced producer/singer/songwriter

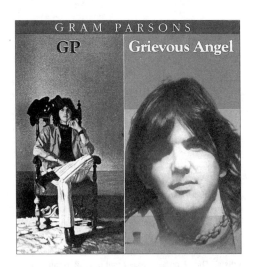

Lee Hazlewood ("These Boots Are Made For Walking") to cut an album by the band for his LHI label. Before SAFE AT HOME was even released, however, the Submarine Band had split up.

The following spring Gram joined the Byrds. He was hired as a keyboardist, but was soon exerting a strong country influence over the group (which had recently suffered the loss of founding members David Crosby and Gene Clark). The Byrds cut their next album partly in Nashville, where they also played as guests on the *Grand Ole Opry*. The result, SWEETHEART OF THE RODEO, was released in August of 1968 to mixed reactions, though today it's a classic against which subsequent California country-rock music is regularly judged. Gram wrote two of the songs, "Hickory Wind" and "One Hundred Years From Now," and originally sang lead on several other tracks—that is, until Hazlewood got wind of the project and threatened a lawsuit, feeling Gram had broken his earlier contract with LHI. McGuinn's voice was recorded over all but two of the songs.

Gram quit the Byrds in the summer of 1968, about the same time he entered the inner circle of the Rolling Stones entourage. He and Keith Richards became close friends for a time, Gram's influence eventually led to such countrified Stones songs as "Sweet Virginia" and "Honky Tonk Woman."

Chris Hillman also quit the Byrds in 1968, and he and Gram began writing songs together that became the basis for their new group, the Flying Burrito Brothers, which also included bassist Chris Ethridge and steel guitarist Sneeky Pete Kleinow. The band's debut album, THE GILDED PALACE OF SIN, came out on A&M in 1969 and is full of

Gram Parsons

excellent Parsons-Hillman originals like "Sin City" and "Wheels." The clear standout though is "Hot Burrito #1" (aka "I'm Your Toy"), a gorgeous, heart-wrenching ballad Parsons co-wrote with Ethridge.

Gram was deeply immersed in drugs and alcohol by this time. He cut one more album with the Burrito Brothers, BURRITO DELUXE, but was so drugged up that Hillman decided to kick him out of the band. He once again joined the European entourage that surrounded the Stones, but even they became tired of him, and by 1971 he was back in LA.

Gram first heard Emmylou Harris singing in a Washington, DC folk club at about this time. A year later, somewhat revitalized, and having won a new recording contract with Reprise, he flew Emmylou out to sing on the sessions. He also paid out of his own pocket to hire Elvis Presley band-members James Burton, Glen D. Hardin, and Ronnie Tutt to back him on the record. He tried to get Merle Haggard to produce, but Hag politely turned him down. No matter, the resulting album, GP, was a magnificent record and Gram's finest achievement to date. It was released in 1973, and that spring Gram assembled a road band he dubbed the Fallen Angels. Gram, Emmylou, and a gang of pickers toured the US (including a stop at the Armadillo World Headquarters in Austin, Texas) and even taped a radio concert in Long Island, which a decade later was released by Sierra Records as LIVE 1973. During the summer Gram pulled the same session pickers back in the studio for what would be his second and final solo album, GRIEVOUS ANGEL. Sadly, he never saw its release. Looking for a brief escape from his domestic anguish (his house burned down and a divorce was pending), he and a few friends drove out to Joshua Tree National Monument, a Mojave Desert park that was a favorite spiritual retreat of his. There he played pool, drank with the locals, and scored some heroin, which he slipped into his veins in Room 8 of the Joshua Tree Inn. He lost consciousness and eventually was rushed to a Yucca Valley hospital, where he was pronounced dead just after midnight on 19 September, 1973.

Gram Parsons' captivating life story is topped off by one final strange event. Two days after his death, his friends Phil Kaufman (aka the Road Mangler) and Michael Martin stole his body from the airport, where it was about to be shipped back to his stepfather in New Orleans. They then drove it out to Joshua Tree and burned it under the stars at a favorite spot of Gram's called Cap Rock. Gram had apparently confessed this wish to Kaufman a month earlier while the two were attending the funeral of their mutual friend, Clarence White. .

⊙ **Safe At Home** (1968; LHI; reissued 1991; Sundown). The one album Gram cut with his first country-oriented group, the International Submarine Band. It does include a few original songs ("Luxury Liner," "Blue Eyes"), but most are country standards like "A Satisfied Mind" and "Miller's Cave." Enjoyable, but not essential.

⊙ **Live 1973** (1982; Sierra). As the cult of Gram Parsons has grown larger over the years, this album has become more precious. You can hear the deterioration in Gram's voice, but the songs and overall musical energy are still vibrant and alive. It's got a grassroots feel that widens the scope of Gram's musical vision that little bit more.

⊙ **GP/Grievous Angel** (1990; Warner Bros.). Gram's two solo albums from 1973 and 1974, on the other hand, *are* essential listening. And packaged together on a single CD, they're also a bargain. The songs ("Return Of The Grievous Angel," "$1000 Wedding," "She," "A Song For You"), his warm but delicately quivering voice, the sturdy instrumentation, and the otherworldly harmonies from a young Emmylou Harris make these two records the creative pinnacle of Gram's short career.

⊙ **Warm Evenings, Pale Mornings, Bottled Blues 1963–1973** (1994; Raven). A decent 21-track compilation ranging over Gram's entire recording career, including his work with the Shilos ("Zah's Blues"), the Byrds, and the Burritos.

Poco

Poco traveled the same watered-down country-rock turf that their LA brethren the Eagles would later exploit. Despite coming together a few years before the Eagles, however, they were never anywhere near as popular or financially successful. The group was formed in 1968 by Jim Messina and former Buffalo Springfield member Richie Furay. They then hired Rusty Young (who'd played steel guitar with Buffalo Springfield), drummer George Gratham, and soon-to-be-Eagle co-founder Randy Meisner. Meisner didn't last long however, quitting before the group cut its debut. That album, PICKIN' UP THE PIECES, was released in 1969 on Epic, and clearly

Further Adventures In Country Rock

Plenty of rock'n'roll bands, especially during the early 1970s, played around with a country sound to varying degrees, though most only did so on individual songs—Creedence Clearwater Revival ("Lodi"), Little Feat ("Willin'"), and even the Rolling Stones ("Sweet Virginia"). Many more groups, however, spread the country-rock concept across entire albums. Some only dabbled in the genre, others were more inherently tied to it. The full-flowered classics of the country-rock genre are reviewed and discussed elsewhere in this chapter; below are ten more. Some you probably know, others you could easily have missed the first time around.

The Band, THE BAND (1969; Capitol). After serving as the backing band first of Ronnie Hawkins and then Bob Dylan, the five Band members collected their thoughts and ideas and began releasing records of their own. This was their eponymously titled second album, and it's soaked through with a genuine rural flavor that is refreshingly informal yet never reckless. It's also packed with classic Band titles like "Up On Cripple Creek," "The Night They Drove Old Dixie Down," and "Rockin' Chair."

Crosby, Stills, Nash And Young, DEJA VU (1970; Atlantic). Though this album isn't exactly 'country rock' per se, songs like "Teach Your Children" and "Helpless" did fit into the outer edges of a genre that at the time was finally becoming fashionable. More significantly, the album's huge popularity helped push the folk- and country-rock concept further into the mainstream.

The Grateful Dead, WORKINGMAN'S DEAD (1970; Warner Bros.). Jerry Garcia's background was in bluegrass and country, so it's natural that many of the Dead's songs retained a rural twang amidst all that psychedelic meandering. Though much more focused on their live shows, the Dead did occasionally put together a solid studio album. This is among their most cohesive and down-to-earth, an album that shows them exploring American roots music with studious, well-rehearsed intent. "Casey Jones" and "Uncle John's Band" are among the titles.

Mother Earth, MOTHER EARTH PRESENTS TRACY NELSON COUNTRY (1969; Warner Bros.). Tracy Nelson has a strong, soulful voice that adds real emotional power to this stellar collection of mostly country standards. Nelson was the lead singer of Mother Earth, a West Coast R&B band, so this was something of a musical experiment, but one that turned out beautifully. True, it wasn't exactly a best seller. But if more people heard it, more people would be knocked flat by Nelson's renditions of "I Fall To Pieces," "I'm So Lonesome I Could Cry," her own "Stay As Sweet As You Are Now," and even "Stand By Your Man."

Leon Russell, HANK WILSON'S BACK, VOL. 1 (1973; Shelter). Russell had a huge background in session work and songwriting ("A Song For You," "Superstar") before he began making records himself. He had grown up with country music, and so cutting an album of country favorites like Flatt

demonstrated the Buffalo Springfield influence. Within a couple of years, Messina also left Poco for greener pastures (joining the pop duo Loggins And Messina). By the early '70s Poco was sporting two new members, Timothy B. Schmit (later to be another Eagles bandmember) and Paul Cotton.

The band cut a series of albums in the '70s, some with a harder rock sound than others, but none ever sold in vast quantities. By the late '70s Young and Cotton were running the show—Furay, Gratham, and Schmit having all gone their separate ways—and it's this version of the group that finally broke into the mainstream with the song "Crazy Love" from their 1978 album LEGEND. In terms of chart success, the album was

by far the group's high point. They had a few more hits through the early '80s, but nothing too monumental, and in 1984 they split up. Five years later, however, the original five bandmembers reunited, and the result was the album LEGACY.

⊙ **Very Best Of Poco** (1975; Epic). A double LP now on a single CD, this 19-song collection covers their years on Epic Records from 1969–74.

⊙ **Crazy Loving: The Best Of Poco 1975–1982** (1989; MCA). This album picks up where the first hits collection leaves off and is highlighted by their major pop hit "Crazy Love."

Poco

& Scruggs' "Rollin' In My Sweet Baby's Arms," Hank Thompson's "A Six Pack To Go," and his friend George Jones' "The Window Up Above" wasn't so out of place. Russell's (aka Wilson's) quirky voice gives the familiar songs a tangy and strange flavor.

Ringo Starr, BEAUCOUPS OF BLUES (1970; Apple). This was Ringo's second album in the wake of the Beatles' break-up, and while it's more a country experiment than a true classic, it does have some fine moments. Pedal-steel maestro Pete Drake produced the affair, pulling in a huge assortment of Nashville's top studio musicians, including Jerry Reed, D.J. Fontana, Buddy Harman, Jerry Kennedy, and the Jordanaires. Ringo's hazy voice fits the mood of "Loser's Lounge," "$15 Draw," and the title track rather well.

John Stewart, CALIFORNIA BLOODLINES (1969; Capitol). Stewart is best known as a onetime member of the Kingston Trio and for writing the Monkees hit "Daydream Believer." But toward the end of the 1960s he ventured into a solo career, and this album is his crowning achievement. It was recorded with such Nashville A-team musicians as Charlie McCoy, Lloyd Green, and "Pig" Robbins, but its soul remains tethered to California. Sticklers might call it 'folk rock,' but songs like the haunting "Lonesome Picker," the surly "July You're A Woman," the twangy "Omaha Rainbow," and rousing "Never Goin' Back" clearly share sensibilities with the progressive side of country music. A forgotten classic worth tracking down.

Chip Taylor, CHIP TAYLOR'S LAST CHANCE (1973; Warner Bros.). "I Want The Real Thing" sings Chip Taylor on this album's lead-off track, and he proceeds to dish it right up. Real country, that is, cut with hot pickers and sung from the point of view of a guy who'd written one of the most classic rock'n'roll songs of all time, "Wild Thing." LAST CHANCE is an overlooked gem, the tone laid-back but Taylor's songs and voice full of juice. The album holds up today as beautifully as it ever did.

Neil Young, HARVEST (1972; Reprise). Country has been a part of Neil's music throughout his entire career—that raw, quivering twang is present on all his folkier stuff, be it Buffalo Springfield's "I Am A Child" or Neil's full-on country album OLD WAYS (1986). HARVEST remains one of his quintessential creations—stripped down and (mostly) acoustically based, it burned such laid-back country-hippie tunes as "Old Man" and "Heart Of Gold" into America's rock'n'roll consciousness. "Are You Ready For The Country?" You bet.

Steve Young, ROCK SALT & NAILS (1969; A&M). Before hooking into the Outlaw movement with his song "Lonesome On'ry And Mean," Steve Young had spent some time in LA in the early '60s playing folk and country material. This was his first solo album, and it was a strong piece of work that showed his deep southern roots, but at the same time it came out of a folk-rock sensibility. Gene Clark, James Burton, and Gram Parsons were among the musicians playing on the album. "Seven Bridges Road" first appeared here, too, which explains how the Eagles got hold of it.

⊙ **The Forgotton Trail 1969–1974** (1990; Epic). An expanded 2-CD collection of the group's tenure on Epic Records.

Pure Prairie League

The members of this Ohio-based country-rock outfit didn't exactly shatter any creative barriers during their 1970s flirtation with success, but at the same time their music made for a peaceful, easy listening experience. Their only widely memorable song was "Falling In And Out Of Love With You"/"Amie," a two-movement (but separately titled) anthem that was an FM radio hit in the mid-'70s. Their other claim to fame was that in 1978 they auditioned and then hired a young Vince Gill as their newest singer and songwriter, giving this future Nashville superstar his first shot at fame.

Pure Prairie League formed in Ohio in 1970, and earned their chops doing numerous gigs throughout the Cincinnati area. The band's lead singers, chief songwriters, and guitarists were George Powell and Craig Fuller; soon they were joined by bassist Jim Lanham, drummer Jim Caughlan, and, for their self-titled debut album, steel guitarist John David Call. It was their second album, BUSTIN' OUT, containing "Falling"/ "Amie," that broke the band nationally. The song took three years to hit, however, and by that time Fuller had quit. For the rest of the decade PPL enjoyed a decent following and released several albums on RCA—although the first two remain their most musically engaging.

The group also had a membership roster that seemed to be in continuous flux. By the late '70s Powell had quit as well, to be replaced by Gill. The bandmembers also moved their home base from Ohio to LA. Gill sang lead and wrote songs for the 1979 album CAN'T HOLD BACK and its follow-up, FIRIN' UP. The latter contained the pop hit "Let Me Love You Tonight," but after only a couple more mild hits Gill quit in 1983 to pursue a solo career, and soon after the group fizzled out.

⊙ **Bustin' Out** (1972; RCA). Includes "Falling In And Out Of Love"/"Amie" along with the thick soul-twang of "Leave My Heart Alone" and the far more wimpish "Angel." Not the most exciting stuff, but not offensive either.

Linda Ronstadt

Along with the Eagles (who worked for a time as her back-up band), Linda Ronstadt turned out to be one of the most popular exponents of the West Coast country-rock sound—and one of the top pop acts of the 1970s to boot. Her powerful voice—half pretty twang, half southwestern soul—took songs like "Poor Poor Pitiful Me" and "You're No Good" high on the charts, attracting further attention to the newly countrified music scene in Southern California. In the decades since then, she's branched out into pop standards, Spanish language folk songs, and even lullabies (her 1996 album DEDICATED TO THE ONE I LOVE), but her musical roots have always remained in the laid-back blend of folk, country, and rock that kicked off her career.

Ronstadt was born on 15 July, 1946 in Tucson, Arizona. At the age of eighteen she moved to Los Angeles where she formed the folk-rock group the Stone Poneys with Bob Kimmel and Ken Edwards. They signed with Capitol Records in 1966, and among

their recordings was the Michael Nesmith song "Different Drum," which became a staple in Ronstadt's repertoire. She cut her solo debut, HAND SOWN ... HOME GROWN, in 1969, followed by SILK PURSE (which she recorded in Nashville) and LINDA RONSTADT. These all showed her music moving away from folk-rock (as was much of the LA sound at the time) and into country-rock territory. Alongside contemporary material by Bob Dylan and Jackson Browne, she also demonstrated just how suited her voice was to classic country on songs like "Silver Threads And Golden Needles," "Lovesick Blues," "I Fall To Pieces," and Johnny Cash's "I Still Miss Someone." Her band during the early '70s included future members of the Eagles.

Ronstadt's commercial breakthrough album was 1974's HEART LIKE A WHEEL, which included such hit songs as "You're No Good," "When Will I Be Loved" (written by Phil Everly, recently split from his brother Don), and a cover of Hank Williams' "I Can't Help It (If I'm Still In Love With You)," which won Ronstadt a Grammy. From this point on into the early '80s, Ronstadt's music climbed high in the charts on a regular basis—"Love Is A Rose," "That'll Be The Day," and "Blue Bayou" were songs nearly any FM-radio listener could hum at the time. She made the country charts several times during the '70s and early '80s, but she found her biggest audience in the pop market.

Ronstadt branched out in various directions during the '80s—cutting Elvis Costello songs on

Linda Ronstadt

MAD LOVE, appearing in *The Pirates Of Penzance*, recording collections of pop standards, and exploring her heritage with the Spanish-language album CANCIONES DE MI PADRE. She's also continued to dip back into the country world. Most notable in this regard was her 1987 collaboration with Dolly Parton and Emmylou Harris, TRIO, which was a popular and award-winning success that spawned "To Know Him Is To Love Him" and other country hits. During the '90s she returned to the folk-rock fold with the albums FEELS LIKE HOME (1995) and especially WE RAN (1998). In early 1999 the sequel album TRIO II was finally released, and later that same year came a duet album between Ronstadt and Harris titled WESTERN WALL: THE TUCSON SESSIONS.

◉ **A Retrospective** (1974; Capitol). Ronstadt's country-rock recordings weren't exactly groundbreaking, but they did offer moments of true, soulful beauty. Her first several albums on Capitol remain the closest to the earth, and this double-LP collection did a great job pulling some of the finest tracks into a single package—reaching from her Stone Poney days up through HEART LIKE A WHEEL.

◉ **Heart Like A Wheel** (1974; Capitol). Ronstadt's commercial appeal skyrocketed after the release of this album, which marked the turning point from her early country-folk recordings into songs with a brighter and ultimately more pop-oriented feel. Along with belt-it-out hits like "You're No Good," she does a fine job with "Dark End Of The Street" and "Willin'."

◉ **Trio** (1987; Warner Bros.). It's not exactly 'traditional' in feeling or execution, but the initial collaboration between Ronstadt, Parton, and Harris is, at least relative to the country music world around them, fairly well stripped down. Includes a couple of old-time numbers ("Rosewood Casket") as well as some more contemporary material.

Doug Sahm

"[The Sir Douglas Quintet] did have a very unique sound. We always felt somebody would do it better; nobody ever did."

—Doug Sahm

More than any other progressive country artists hovering around Austin, Texas in the 1960s and '70s, San Antonio native Doug Sahm best represented the coming together of the state's vast musical heritage. The result is that during a career that lasted almost fifty years, he was able to incorporate a mind-bogglingly diverse array of styles and influences into his own music, be it the groovy psychedelic country of the Sir Douglas Quintet, the steamy roadhouse blues of the Last Real Texas Blues Band, or the lively Tex-Mex sounds of the Texas Tornados (a collaboration with Freddy Fender, Augie Meyer, and Flaco Jimenez). He and his various groups have won dozens of accolades over the years, but the true breadth of his musical talent has yet to be fully recognized. The fact is, there were few artists in any genre as well-versed in such a diverse range of music as Sahm.

Doug Sahm was born in San Antonio on 6 November, 1941 to Lebanese-American parents. Growing up, he experienced a wild mix of music around him—the western swing of Adolph Hofner, the electrified honky-tonk of Floyd Tillman, the blues of T-Bone Walker, and all sorts of Cajun, Mexican, and R&B bands. Sahm listened to as much of it as he could, and he understood something in just about all of it. As a child he started playing guitar under the name Little Doug Sahm, and he even once sat on Hank Williams knee during what turned out to be the Drifting Cowboy's final concert appearance.

As much as he had absorbed back-alley blues and honky tonk, however, Sahm also came of age alongside rock'n'roll. As a teenager he played with a group called the Pharoahs and cut a series of singles for regional labels like Sarg, Warrior, and Harlem. He was also constantly hounding local record mogul Huey P. Meaux (aka the Crazy Cajun) for a better deal, but it wasn't until the Beatles hit American shores that Meaux discovered a use for the pesky San Antone kid who never seemed to stop talking. To capitalize on the mania surrounding the British Invasion, Meaux concocted a fake Brit group, the Sir Douglas Quintet, and assigned Sahm the lead position. Sahm then pulled in keyboardist August Meyer, saxophonist Francisco Morin, bass player Harvey Kagan, and drummer Johnny Perez. Meaux's instincts were proven correct when the group's single, "She's About A Mover," was a smash success.

The British Invasion scheme could only work for so long before the group true origins were found out—although no one seemed to mind. Nonetheless, Sahm decided to abandon the group and his beloved Texas following a drug bust. His relocation to San Francisco wasn't entirely out of the blue, since like so many other free thinkers

Stoned faces don't lie: Doug Sahm

finally squared away his differences with the Texas authorities and moved back to San Antonio. His homecoming album was 1971's THE RETURN OF DOUG SALDAÑA, which he cut partly in Houston. The title alludes to his imagined Chicano roots—or at least those of the friends he had grown up with. Backing him up were some excellent regional players like saxophonist Rocky Morales, along with a couple of Quintet buddies, and songs like "Me And My Destiny," "Stoned Faces Don't Lie," and the Freddy Fender classic "Wasted Days And Wasted Nights" (Fender was wallowing in obscurity at the time, his career yet to be revived) show Sahm at his creative peak.

His next move was to sign with Atlantic Records, which had also nabbed yet-to-be-Outlaw Willie Nelson. Famed '60s soul producer Jerry Wexler had figured it was time Atlantic stepped into the progressive country game. In 1973, Atlantic released both Nelson's SHOTGUN WILLIE and Sahm's DOUG SAHM AND FRIENDS. The latter featured an all-star cast (including Bob Dylan, Dr John, and David Bromberg) on a roster of songs by Bob Wills, T-Bone Walker, Dylan ("Wallflower"), Nelson ("Me And Paul"), and Sahm. The clear standout track was "(Is Anybody Going To) San Antone," previously a hit for Charley Pride, only this time it was given a sharper treatment with the addition of twin fiddles, steel guitar, and Sahm's pleading voice. The follow-up album was entitled TEXAS TORNADO, which Sahm also briefly adopted as his new band name (Doug Sahm And The Texas Tornados). The progressive country scene around Austin, Texas was hot during the mid-'70s, and Sahm's 1976 album TEXAS ROCK FOR COUNTRY ROLLERS demonstrated he could write and sing some of the grooviest country music around. It's a forgotten classic of the period and another of the finest of his career.

During the '70s, Sahm also pulled together a new version of the Sir Douglas Quintet, but it lacked the creative spark that had driven the earlier

and long-haired dreamers of the time he was enamored with the groovy psychedelic scene blossoming in that West Coast city. In Frisco he assembled a band and cut the album HONKEY BLUES, then the rest of the original Quintet joined him out west and they recorded MENDOCINO. The latter album's title track became a psychedelicized country-rock hit. On the whole the Quintet's albums during this period (including TOGETHER AFTER FIVE and 1+1+1=4) are a glorious mix of psychedelic pop, wiry honky tonk, dirty blues riffs, and groovy rhythms. The music was serious, for sure, but it was packaged with a good-time vibe and some general freakiness thrown in.

Where "Mendocino" was a hippie joyride celebrating the California lifestyle, other songs like "Texas Me" and "Lawd I'm Just A Country Boy In This Great Big Freaky City" revealed that his home state was still on his mind. So after several years of living in San Francisco and assorted small towns to the north and south of the city, Sahm

incarnation. By the following decade he was channeling more energy into playing the blues. He cut albums such as JUKE BOX MUSIC (a smorgasbord of Texas blues and R&B) and THE RETURN OF THE FORMERLY BROTHERS (with Amos Garrett and Gene Taylor) and eventually pulled together a group he called the Last Real Texas Blues Band. In 1990 Sahm co-founded a new supergroup of sorts, the Texas Tornados, with Fender (who was at this point a reborn country star), Meyer, and accordionist Flaco Jimenez. The music was a catchy brand of Tex-Mex, and it caught on quickly in country circles as well as all over the Southwest. During their several years together, the Tornados toured regularly, cut four albums, hit the country album charts more than once, and won a Grammy. By the mid-'90s, however, the four compatriots had gone their separate ways. As the century neared a close, the ever-restless Sahm was still as busy as ever—cutting more albums under the Sir Douglas Quintet moniker, educating eager audiences on the history of Texas blues and roadhouse R&B (his concerts were like interactive seminars), and performing with friends like the Austin alternative-country group the Gourds. Sadly, Doug Sahm died on 18 November, 1999 in a hotel room in Taos, New Mexico, most likely from a heart attack.

⊙ **Texas Rock For Country Rollers** (1976; ABC/Dot; reissued 1997; Edsel). Sahm's easygoing country groove and saucy, good-time personality make this a joyride from start to finish. Songs like the silly "Cowboy

Peyton Place" and the monumental "Give Back The Key To My Heart" (later covered by Uncle Tupelo) will remain stuck in your head for maybe a lifetime.

⊙ **Texas Tornados** (1990; Reprise). The catchy "Who Were You Thinking Of" and Butch Hancock's "She Never Spoke Spanish To Me" are definite standout tracks on the Tornados' debut album, which sounds slightly brighter and fresher than the other three collections. They recorded a second version of this album entirely in Spanish.

⊙ **Best Of Doug Sahm And The Sir Douglas Quintet 1968–1975** (1990; Polygram). The best starting place, this 22-track collection is packed with great songs like "Texas Me," "Mendocino," "Catch The Man On The Rise," "Nuevo Laredo," "Michoacan" (from the movie *Cisco Pike*, which Sahm appeared in alongside Kris Kristofferson), "Be Real" (Sahm's most straight-up country song, cut in Nashville with producer Jerry Kennedy), and "Wasted Days And Wasted Nights." Many juicy ones are still missing; you'll have to seek out the original albums for them.

⊙ **Best Of Doug Sahm And Friends: The Atlantic Sessions** (1992; WEA/Atlantic/Rhino). The proliferation of special guests (most notably Dylan) on many of these Atlantic recordings from the 1970s gives them a feeling of being overrated. Still, "(Is Anybody Going To) San Antone" and "Texas Tornado" are excellent cuts, and if you don't get your expectations too high, chances are you won't be disappointed by the rest either.

Doug Sahm

11

These Are Not My People: 'Fifth Avenue' Country in the 1970s and '80s

"If Doris Day and Perry Como weren't available, then Glen Campbell and Crystal Gayle would have to do."

—Bill Malone, Country Music USA.

Let's face it: on a creative level, the period from the late 1970s through to the mid-'80s was one of the bleakest in country music history. The heyday of the Outlaws was over, and it would be another ten years before 'new traditionalism' became a buzzword. So while the pop music world was busy with disco, country buried its nose into assorted gaudy pop trends of its own—from bubble-gum sentimentalism (Debby Boone's "You Light Up My Life") to adult contemporary pap (**Ronnie Milsap**'s "Let's Take The Long Way Around The World"), watered-down cowboy music (**Johnny Lee**'s "Lookin' For Love"), and vastly overproduced Las Vegas-style schmaltz (**Kenny Rogers** and Dolly Parton's "Islands In The Stream"). After witnessing the "oceans and oceans of strings" at the 1978 CMA award show, *Washington Star* writer Boris Weintraub wondered if "perhaps it's time to find a new term to replace 'country.' Because, good or bad, there is precious little country left in today's country music."

Blame it on the lust for the greenback dollar. Like the fantasy visions of boundless fertile valleys that lured settlers to the American West, the vast pop music market has long been the Holy Grail for country artists, producers and executives seeking bigger, newer and more lucrative horizons. During the '50s, the Nashville Sound was developed specifically to broaden country's appeal. But the string sections and other countrypolitan touches marking the work of producers like Chet Atkins and, later, Billy Sherrill are endearing and homespun compared to the garish productions that passed for 'country' by the early '80s. Janie Fricke bounced through "He's A Heartache (Looking For A Place To Happen)" sounding like an annoyingly peppy aerobics instructor; wanting more than "The Gambler" was able to give, Kenny Rogers made a beeline for Lionel Richie (recording his "Lady") and then dueted with Sheena Easton on Bob Seger's "We've Got Tonight"; and **Barbara Mandrell** dressed herself in glitter and flashed her way across a Las Vegas stage in her 1983 production *The Lady Is A Champ*. Though a flashy song in its own right, Glen Campbell's "Rhinestone Cowboy" suddenly made too much sense.

Many of these songs were huge crossover hits, selling records to both country and pop fans by the millions—high sales figures, in fact, were the only reason many of these ditties existed at all. Though not a brand new phenomenon, the crossover song was becoming ever more lucrative as the music industry grew, which is why it became a major focus of country artists, producers, and label executives during the '70s. Pop artists, too, were discovering they could expand their market by adding a hint of country to their songs, and so the great crossover game began. The songs moved in both directions: Charlie Rich's "Behind Closed Doors" first topped the country and then the pop chart; **John Denver** crossed from pop to country with songs like "Back Home Again" and "Take Me Home, Country Roads"; and when she broke in the US, Australian singer **Olivia Newton-John** seemed to hit both markets at about the same time with the chirpy "Let Me Be There."

This also presented further problems for the country community's 'core' artists, who were increasingly upset that 'outsiders' were bullying their way into the country market. Things came to a head after the 1974 Country Music Association awards, when Newton-John took Female Vocalist of the Year honors and Ronnie Milsap (who at that point was brand new to country music and "hadn't paid his dues," as some folks felt) was named Male Vocalist of the Year. A group of traditionalists broke ranks with the CMA and formed their own group, the Association of Country Entertainers (ACE), dedicated, as one of their statements declares, to "the preservation of the type of country music that has been enjoyed by fans throughout the world for many years" (see box p.436).

Old and In The Way

These traditionalists felt threatened—and they were soon proven right, as more and more 'modern country' artists with pronounced pop sensibilities began winning awards and stealing top positions on the *Billboard* country chart. At the same time, country radio was booming, with more fulltime country stations than ever before—yet the popularity of these stations (or so the programmers felt) was largely based on the fact that they avoided the twangy stuff and concentrated on music with softer edges and, in many cases, a more polished sound. All this growth and change forced the country music industry to a turning point, ultimately splitting the community between staunch traditionalists (who felt the music sounded fine as it was) and those who preferred more 'modern' styles. (It's a gap that would continue to grow into the '90s, with 'young country' stars hogging the airwaves and record contracts and 'old-fashioned'

singers relegated to the stage of the *Grand Ole Opry*.) Whether you called it 'metropolitan,' 'Fifth Avenue,' or 'chicken' country, the crossover sound was the wave of the future.

And singers like Kenny Rogers rode that wave like nobody had before. One of the most popular country artists of the late '70s and '80s—of any decade, really—Rogers had, in fact, emerged from the world of popular music. He'd enjoyed a few hits with the folk-rock group First Edition, and some (like "Ruby, Don't Take Your Love To Town") had definite country leanings. He turned to Nashville as home base for his new solo career, making huge hits out of soft-country numbers like "Lucille" and "The Gambler." No sooner was the well-groomed singer a bona fide country superstar, however, before he was redefining his image again, this time working the adult contemporary market with even greater verve—punching out slick, schmaltzy hits like "You Decorated My Life" and "Don't Fall In Love With A Dreamer."

One of the decade's top-selling artists was a familiar face, Dolly Parton. She had impeccable country roots and had enjoyed a long, successful career singing hard country material, but in the late '70s she shifted from country to contemporary pop in an attempt to broaden her market. Her plan succeeded, although her music lost nearly all its homespun beauty (her 1999 bluegrass album, however, shows her reconnecting with those roots). But Parton's personality remained nothing short of genuine, and longtime fans, finding it impossible to be angry with her for very long, soon let her go her own way.

Barbara Mandrell was another singer who rose to superstar status during the '70s. Like Rogers and Parton, Mandrell was a savvy, calculating businessperson with high ambitions and a whole lot of drive. She'd had respectable country hits in the early part of the decade (including racy cheating songs that threatened to belie her pristine persona), but like Parton and Rogers she wanted a bigger market than Nashville alone could give her. By the beginning of the next decade she achieved her goal with a full-on, highly choreographed pop-country assault: a series of middle-of-the-road hits produced by Tom Collins (including "I Was Country When Country Wasn't Cool"); increasingly glitzy concert extravaganzas; and, to top it off, a flashy TV variety show with her sisters, Louise and Irlene.

Collins' highly polished (and sometimes bombastic) productions were a strong presence during this Vegas-infatuated period. At the same time he was working with Mandrell, Collins was busy sanding the Memphis edges off Ronnie Milsap. That pop trick boosted Milsap high in the charts, but it also erased the trickles of country soul he'd hinted at in his early material. By the early '80s, Collins was helming a series of disco-inflected, barely countrified hits by fresh-faced singer **Sylvia**.

Allen Reynolds is another star producer (famous in the '90s for his work with Garth Brooks) who came to prominence during the '70s, first through the pleasant, slow-poke country songs of Don Williams and, later, working with the pretty voice of **Crystal Gayle**. Reynolds' early work with Gayle sounds much closer to the music of Emmylou Harris, who was beginning to make it as a solo artist at about the same time. But after Gayle's "Don't It Make My Brown Eyes Blue" became a smash in 1977, she and Reynolds' musical direction shifted toward the uptown pop market and didn't look back.

And what were people thinking when they bought all those **Dave & Sugar** records? Chances are most current country fans wouldn't know a single tune by this saccharine trio if it hit them in the seat of their Wranglers, but Dave & Sugar (consisting of one-time Stamps Quartet singer Dave Rowland and a rotating roster of female Sugars) charted frequently during the late '70s. Think of them as a Nashvillian take on the Tony Orlando and Dawn concept and you're in the right ballpark.

Urban Cowboy

The biggest bombshell to hit Nashville, however—what became the roaring climax of country's love affair with pop—was the immensely popular 1980 movie *Urban Cowboy*. The film was based on a 1978 *Esquire* magazine article about Texas oil workers who spent their leisure time at Gilley's—the 'world's largest honky-tonk' in Pasadena, Texas presided over by singer Mickey Gilley—drinking up a storm and taking turns on the mechanical bull (a practice mechanism for rodeo riders that co-owner Sherwood Cryer had installed). Country music had been fast growing in popularity over the past several years, and this flick and its companion soundtrack album—which mixed songs by rock acts like the Eagles, Bob Seger, and Linda Ronstadt with others by Rogers, Gilley, and the Charlie Daniels Band—opened the floodgates, doing for country what *Saturday Night Fever* had done for disco. Nightclubs traded mirror balls for mechanical bulls (sold to them courtesy of Cryer); people who once danced the Hustle in platforms were now decked out in stiff leather boots and learning the Cotton-Eyed Joe; sales of pick-up trucks increased; and city department stores stocked cowboy hats, designer jeans, and Western shirts.

The *Urban Cowboy* soundtrack was, like the popular 1976 album WANTED! THE OUTLAWS— which compiled four Outlaw artists into one neat, easily digested package—a smart marketing move that hit at exactly the right time. By including an even-keeled mixture of pop, rock, and country, it exploited the crossover trends that had been growing over the past decade. Artists such as Daniels, Ronstadt, and Jimmy Buffett were already getting airplay on both rock and country stations. On top of that, none of the songs pushed too far in any single musical direction; David Allan Coe or Johnny Paycheck, for instance, were nowhere in sight. Instead we got the diluted pop-cowboy melody of Johnny Lee's "Lookin' For Love" (the *Urban Cowboy* theme song)—child's play compared to a song like Paycheck's "I'm The Only Hell (Mama Ever Raised)." Even respectable honky-tonker Mickey Gilley, one of the more substantial artists on the soundtrack, was showcased by the slow-dance soul classic "Stand By Me" (which became his biggest hit to date).

As the crossover hits accumulated during the late '70s, country record sales had grown higher than ever previously hoped for. When *Urban Cowboy* hit, however, the market became utterly saturated. It was only a matter of time, then, before casual fans—the type who drop trends as quickly as they buy into them—began to get restless for something new. Record sales that had only recently soared were now beginning a drastic downturn. By 1985, both the *New York Times* and *Time* magazine, among others, had published stories noting the serious decrease in country record sales (which sent Music Row executives into a tizzy). Many figured this meant the entire country music industry was headed for the scrap heap.

Which was far from the truth. Sales were down, but they were still higher than they'd been a decade earlier. And while the *Urban Cowboy* fad had run out of steam, country was still a music deeply ingrained in too many souls to die off that quickly. For one thing, there was **Alabama**. The band had busted its way into the charts the same year *Urban Cowboy* hit with such clean-cut, easy-to-swallow country-rock songs as "Mountain Music" and "Tennessee River," and there they remained for the better part of the '80s. Because they were able to balance the 'rebel' nature of southern rock with softer ballads—and because their image, too, was balanced: long hair that was very neatly trimmed—they had a huge appeal among young and old country fans alike.

Let's Go To Bed

Romantic love has been a staple subject in country since the music's earliest days, but for the most part the lyrics remained chaste. Most listeners were, after all, churchgoers. But when Floyd Tillman spoke of cheating in "Slipping Around," the ice began to break. By the turn of the 1970s, when the sexual revolution was in full swing, things got much more explicit. Smothering the act in double entendres was one thing, but songs like Kris Kristofferson's "Help Me Make It Through The Night" spoke much more freely of bedroom goings-on. This was a new era, one where singers weren't so afraid to "let their hair hang down," as Charlie Rich sang in "Behind Closed Doors." Here are some of the culprits:

Billy "Crash" Craddock Crash's manly voice punctuated his biggest hit, "Rub It In," with allusions to sex, yet the lyrics remained just abstract enough to allow his listeners' imaginations to run their own course.

Loretta Lynn With "The Pill," this country icon once again showed fearlessness toward controversial and up-to-now forbidden material—specifically that pertaining to female sexuality. "The feeling good comes easy now, since I've got the Pill," she sang on this 1975 hit, a line that's got to be the first overt reference to orgasm to make the country charts.

Barbara Mandrell Despite her well-maintained squeaky-clean image, Mandrell built much of her reputation on material that dealt directly with sex—from dirty late-night trysts ("The Midnight Oil") and randy bedroom anticipations ("Tonight My Baby's Coming Home") to lonely late-night longings ("Sleeping Single in a Double Bed").

Ronnie Milsap "I'm having day dreams about night things in the middle of the afternoon," sang Milsap on "Day Dreams About Night Things," his mid-1970s signature song. While not exactly explicit, it was the thought that counted, and Milsap's song successfully kept fantasies alive wherever AM radios were turned on.

Jeanne Pruett Pruett had already made her name with "Satin Sheets" (concerning a neglected wife for whom fancy bedroom accoutrements were no substitute for true lovin') before she moaned about a cheating husband coming home with "Honey On His Hands." A sad situation, yes, but oh what an image.

Charlie Rich Thanks to its massive success, Rich's hit "Behind Closed Doors"—where his woman "lets her hair hang down" and "makes me glad that I'm a man"—became one of the key songs opening country's door to more direct allusions to love and sex.

Margo Smith Where most singers concentrated on the dramatic sparks of love's initial fire, Smith fast-forwarded her subjects and instead focused on couples who'd been together for years. "Let's Make Love The Way We Used To" is one woman's plea to her complacent husband, while the protagonist in "Still A Woman" is proud of her sexuality despite the fact she's fast approaching forty.

Sammi Smith Kris Kristofferson's classic come-on song "Help Me Make It Through The Night" cut straight to the chase, and Smith's sultry voice pushed the song straight to the top of the charts, raising many eyebrows (and Lord knows what else) along the way.

Billie Jo Spears In "What I've Got In Mind," the husky-voiced Spears comes right out and says what she's thinking: "To tell the truth what I've got in mind is making love to you." A bold pronouncement, yes, but her fans, it seems, were ready for it. They turned it into a Top 5 hit.

Conway Twitty Maybe no country singer has gotten away with as much sexual material as Conway Twitty. Like Charlie Rich, Twitty maintained a stalwart reputation as a romantic—one who knew exactly where the borderlines of good taste lay. He could wend his way under the skirt of the everyday housewife with songs like "You've Never Been This Far Before," "I See The Want To In Your Eyes," and "I'd Love To Lay You Down," yet his image as respected family man and upstanding citizen was never questioned.

Dottie West When this Tennessee singer's career rose for a second go-round in the '70s, her material (and her persona) was much more overtly sexual. Witness "You Can't Get My Love Off The Bed," a sad tale of a failed relationship that makes good combination of the words "bed," "love," "get," and "off." Any allusion to stains in regards to love counts as explicit by most measuring sticks.

Alabama was also a (more or less) self-contained band—a concept previously rare in country music, which had been a star-singer-driven business since the early days of Roy Acuff. The popularity of Alabama (and of the **Oak Ridge Boys**, a one-time gospel group that had hit the country mainstream around the same time) set off a 'band' trend that continues to this day—for better or worse. But where Alabama was distinctly country, many of these up-and-coming groups continued the 'modern country' trend by styling their music around current Top 40 pop sounds. Among the worst offenders were **Exile** (who'd had a huge pop hit with "I Want To Kiss You All Over" before redefining themselves as country) and the Miami Vice-styled Sawyer Brown (who got their big break on TV's *Star Search*).

Many of these pop-country acts are, admittedly, easy targets, especially from ten or more years down the road. But too many of them represented a kind of music constructed more for its marketability than for—for lack of a better term—reasons of the soul. The fact that so much of the material doesn't hold up today is testament to its disposability.

All this is not to say pop influences don't have a significant role to play in country music. But in trying to be open-minded to contemporary trends—and in stepping all over themselves to rack up bigger and bigger sales figures—the majority of country music marketers went too far and greatly narrowed their focus. Record companies "streamlined" their rosters, dropping artists who couldn't achieve the same sales results; at the same time, country radio stations squeezed much of the old guard off their playlists with hardly a second thought. (This latter trend was augmented by the fact that many DJs and programmers came from pop backgrounds with little knowledge of country music's heritage.) The flip side of Nashville's financially successful story was that country music's half-century-old heritage was being trampled beneath all that showmanship and left to wither. Country had always stood for down-to-earth values, and for the industry to lose touch with this was a real tragedy.

Thankfully, the industry soon proved that it wasn't as hostile to classic singers, traditional roots, and solid, earthbound music as it may have seemed in the early '80s. George Jones, for instance, had bounced back into the spotlight with one of the biggest songs of his career, "He Stopped Loving Her Today." At the same time, singers like Ricky Skaggs, George Strait, and John Anderson were already making inroads onto the country charts, the first sparks of a back-to-basics sound that would eventually be dubbed 'new traditionalism.'

The 1970s and '80s: The Artists

Alabama

"I just like positive songs. I don't like sad endings."

—Randy Owen

If you can't hum the Alabama tune "Mountain Music" at the drop of a hat, then you didn't listen to much country radio during the 1980s. Written by lead singer/guitarist Randy Owen and released on the band's third album in 1982, the song quickly became one of their signatures (not to mention one of the most popular songs of the decade), helping propel this group of aw-shucks good-time guys into the stratosphere of country stardom.

If country summertime sing-alongs like "Mountain Music" were all that Alabama was about, they wouldn't be half bad. With three-part vocal harmonies (one of the band's trademarks), fiddle, guitar, and an easygoing country rhythm that takes inspiration from '70s-era rock bands like the Eagles, the song is inoffensive and almost likeable. Unfortunately, the group also has a penchant for trite, overproduced radio-ready ballads like "Old Flame" and "Love In The First Degree," and it's in this direction that cousins Owen, Jeffrey Cook, and Teddy Gentry—the group's core unit, who all share vocal duties—have steered much of Alabama's music for the bulk of their twenty-plus-year career.

Alabama are certainly closer to the soil than pop singers like Janie Fricke or Lee Greenwood—for starters they have genuine southern country roots—but despite the boys' long hair and beards (which are much neater than Waylon's or Willie's), and the hints of southern rock in songs like "Tennessee River," their music is squeaky-clean, safe, and germ-free. Gently blending pop and country into easily digestible formulas, their sound appeals across generations: they're just rebel enough for the young folks, but their parents also dig the boys' pretty harmonies, sentimental soft spots, and old-fashioned family values. And it's this huge and wide fan base that made them the most popular country group of the '80s.

'80s groovers, Alabama

They racked up twenty-one #1 singles, several of which crossed to the pop charts, sold many millions of albums, and won numerous music awards—including CMA's prestigious Entertainer of the Year award (they were the first group to do so) three years in a row, from 1982–84.

Owen and Gentry, who are first cousins, grew up on nearby cotton farms near Fort Payne, Alabama. They learned guitar and sang in church together, and during high school banded with another cousin, Cook, to form the group Young Country in 1969. A few years later (after Owen and Cook finished college) they renamed themselves Wildcountry and began touring around the Southeast. They also started writing songs, an early one being "My Home's In Alabama." In 1973 they moved to Myrtle Beach, South Carolina where they landed a regular gig at a bar called the Bowery.

The boys renamed themselves Alabama in 1977, the same year they secured their first record deal with GRT. The small label released a single, "I Wanna Be With You Tonight"; it got some attention, but GRT soon folded, and legal tangles kept Alabama from recording again for two years until they could buy out their contract. In 1980 they signed to MDJ Records, which released "I Wanna Come Over" and "My Home's In Alabama"; RCA Records took notice and quickly snatched up the band. By the end of the year, "Tennessee River," from their first RCA album, MY HOME'S IN ALABAMA, had become the group's first #1 single. From there Alabama's winning streak of non-stop hits continued well into the '90s.

Where the majority of country artists are singers and solo artists with different touring and studio musicians, the three cousins in Alabama are not only an actual band, but they accompany themselves as well (hardly a phenomenon in rock, this was actually somewhat rare in country at the time). Owen and Cook play guitar, and Gentry plays bass. A few different drummers passed through their ranks early on, but beginning in 1979 they found Mark Herndon, who introduced a stronger rock'n'roll influence just in time for their RCA contract—and helped keep the band's sound stable through their long succession of radio hits.

At a time when Nashville was infatuated with Vegas-inspired, overproduced pop, Alabama were at their best a smart, well-thought-out blend of country roots, breezy '70s-era rock, and teary-eyed downhome sentimentalism. The overriding problem with Alabama's music was that it always sounded as calculated as it likely was, and so it is today that they come off as nothing short of mediocre.

⊙ **Mountain Music** (1982; RCA). Their third album finds Alabama on the cusp of superstardom, just before they went overboard with the slick, "professional" production work. Be warned, though, that the album does have more than its share of schlock in "Close Enough To Perfect," "Take Me Down," and especially "Never Be One," a song Gentry wrote about his newborn's first birthday.

⊙ **Greatest Hits** (1986; RCA). This collection was a big seller right from the outset, which makes sense since it contains a bunch of their early big ones: "Mountain Music," "Old Flame," "Forty Hour Week," live versions of "Tennessee River" and "My Home's In

Alabama

Alabama," and "The Fans," a thank-you note to their millions of devotees.

⊙ **For The Record** (1998; RCA). A more substantial double-CD set of their most popular songs. Though the collection's subtitled "41 Number One Hits," only 32 actually made it to #1 on *Billboard*'s country charts (so far). Fans have reason to pay attention since, along with the aforementioned 41 hits, it includes the previously unreleased "Five O'Clock 500," "Keepin' Up," and "How Do You Fall In Love."

Bellamy Brothers

From the late 1970s through to the early '90s, Howard and David Bellamy were a hugely successful duo who sang a tame, pop-oriented brand of country-rock—unflashy, easily digested music that had more in common with the crossover California grooves of the Eagles and Poco than Waylon Jennings' tough-edged country or the glittery showmanship of Kenny Rogers. The Bellamy Brothers first made it big on the pop charts, hitting #1 in 1976 with the song "Let Your Love Flow." But it was the light-hearted, fun-sexy ditty "If I Said You Had A Beautiful Body Would You Hold It Against Me" (a song David wrote based on a quip by Groucho Marx) that better represents the type of music that made these two brothers so popular. Catchy and not entirely unpleasant, that song hit the top of the country charts in 1979 and kicked off their newfound (and far stronger) career in country music.

Howard and David both hail from Florida, and they played country-rock together around the South. They helped form the band Jericho in 1968, and after that group split they concentrated on writing songs as well as jingles. In 1975 David's song "Spiders And Snakes" became a hit for Jim Stafford; that same year the Bellamys (who had relocated to Los Angeles) were signed to Curb/Warner Brothers, for whom they recorded a series of pop songs including "Let Your Love Flow." Despite that song's success, their career took a few years to get off the ground, and it wasn't until "If I Said You Had A Beautiful Body" that the Bellamy Brothers settled comfortably into the country market. By the '80s their hits were coming regularly, from "You Ain't Just Whistlin' Dixie" to "Get Into Reggae Cowboy," the popular "Redneck Girl," "Kids Of The Baby Boom," and "Rebels Without A Clue." They occasionally

teamed up with the Forester Sisters on recordings, one such collaboration being John Hiatt's "Drive South" (an energizing number that Suzy Bogguss would later have a hit with). The brothers remained affiliated with Curb through the end of the decade. During the early '90s they began releasing albums on their own label, Bellamy Brothers Records.

❂ **Two And Only** (1979; Warner Bros./Curb). Containing the song "If I Said You Had A Beautiful Body," this was the album that kicked off the Bellamy Brothers' country career with gusto. Interesting that among innocuous pop-country ditties like "You Ain't Just Whistlin' Dixie" and "Wet T-Shirt" lies a cover of British folksinger John Martyn's "May You Never."

⊙ **Greatest Hits** (1982; MCA/Curb). A collection of early hits including "Let Your Love Flow," "Beautiful Body," "Get Into Reggae Cowboy," and "Redneck Girl."

John Conlee

"John Conlee will always be John Conlee; he's a great stylist."
—Rick Blackburn, CBS Records, 1986

A former mortician–turned–country singer, John Conlee was one of the few artists to emerge during the pop-oriented late 1970s/early '80s with an old-school sound. One of his earliest recordings, "Rose Colored Glasses," was a surprise hit that defined him as a traditionalist and—despite the swelling strings that dominated the chorus—put him more in league with modern-day honky tonkers Gene Watson and Moe Bandy than glamour-pusses like Ronnie Milsap or Kenny Rogers. (His roly-poly appearance, too, meant he'd never be much of a pin-up boy.) Follow-up releases such as "Backside Of Thirty" and "Friday Night Blues" proved Conlee's appeal wasn't just a fluke—his somewhat country-boy voice, penchant for steel guitars, and songs about drinking and losing in love still had appeal during those increasingly pop-oriented times.

As did his blue-collar persona. "I'm just a common man, drive a common van," Conlee sang on the Sammy Johns song "Common Man," in which he tells his date he'd rather eat at McDonalds and swill cheap beer than sip fine wine at swanky restaurants. It's a dopey song, but it's fun—and it

John Conlee

his arrangements and focused instead on the steel guitars and Conlee's rural-raised voice. BUSTED also contained "Common Man," and it kicked off Conlee's hot streak, when he had four #1 hits in a row: "Common Man," "I'm Only In It For The Love," "In My Eyes," and "As Long As I'm Rockin' With You." He switched to Columbia in 1986 and hit the top one more time with "Got My Heart Set On You." His recordings had tapered off by the '90s, though he still performed on the *Grand Ole Opry* (he's been been a member since 1981). He has also served on the board of Farm Aid as well as the Family Farm Defense Fund. In 1999 Conlee released LIVE AT BILLY BOB'S, recorded during a recent concert in Texas.

⊙ **Rose Colored Glasses** (1978; ABC). Ten songs ain't much, but when it comes to outdated artists, these days you've got to take what you can get. And at least a few of the songs here among Conlee's finest, including the title track and especially "Backside Of Thirty," a classic loser tune that leaves the singer wifeless ("she's gone back to mama"), dead drunk, and crying to himself in an empty apartment.

⊙ **20 Greatest Hits** (1988; MCA). Though out-of-print at the time of this writing, this is the CD to look for as, obviously, there are more songs for your money. In addition to "Backside Of Thirty" and "Rose Colored Glasses," notable titles include "Friday Night Blues," "Common Man," and a pair of fine Harlan Howard songs, "Busted" and "Nothing Behind You, Nothing In Sight."

obviously struck a chord with his fans, shooting all the way to #1 in 1983. Nashville Sound strings and choruses had been a part of Conlee's sound since the beginning, though, and by the mid-'80s he was drifting into more of a standard country-pop sound.

John Wayne Conlee was born on 11 August, 1946 and grew up on a farm near Versailles, Kentucky. After high school he worked for six years as a mortician, then he took a job as a radio announcer. He moved to Nashville in the early '70s, and in 1976 he signed with ABC/Dot. His song "Rose Colored Glasses" made #5 on the country charts in 1978, and within a year of that he'd reached the very top with both "Lady Lay Down" and the self-penned downer "Backside Of Thirty." In 1979 his records were released by MCA, which had absorbed the ABC label. Another working-class anthem, "Friday Night Blues," was a substantial hit in 1980; ditto for "Busted" two years later, the title track of a 1982 album that eliminated the unnecessary junk from

Dave & Sugar

S ome people called it "tuxedo country," but the thin pop of the singing trio Dave & Sugar—heard regularly on country radio from the late 1970s through to the early '80s—was far

more saccharine (and even less aurally appealing) than that moniker implies. With lightweight disco beats, smooth edges, and soft-focus melodies, Dave & Sugar songs such as "Golden Tears" and "Tear Time" were calculated, flashy, and devoid of much in the way of spirit or soul—like a cross between the Las Vegas pop of Tony Orlando and Dawn and the mawkish drone of Kenny G. But their success (at least in the eyes of their record company's executives) was undeniable: Dave Rowland and his revolving cast of Sugar singers (always women and always two at a time) enjoyed a string of chart-topping hits that helped give that period of country music its easy-listening veneer.

Like the women in Dawn and the men in the Pips, the singers in Sugar were nameless to most fans. The line-up did change regularly over the years, yet some of the women—Vicki Hackeman, Jackie Frantz, and Sue Powell among them—contributed substantially to the group's success (for one thing, they were often the lead singers). Unfortunately, they rarely gained individual credit—or even recognition—for their work. It's no wonder that they and subsequent Sugars began quitting at an increasingly rapid rate.

Dave & Sugar was, however, Rowland's idea. A California native, he moved to Nashville in 1970 to pursue his singing career. He joined the Stamps Quartet, and with them backed Elvis Presley; later he was (briefly) a member of the Four Guys. Rowland then worked as a singing waiter and formed a short-lived country-rock group. By 1975, however, he was singing back-up for Charley Pride with two women he'd recruited, Hackeman and Frantz. With a little help from Pride, the trio was

signed that year to RCA as Dave & Sugar. Their first single was Shel Silverstein's "Queen Of The Silver Dollar," and in 1976 they had their first #1, "The Door Is Always Open" (previously recorded by Waylon Jennings). Hits like "Tear Time," "I'm Knee Deep In Loving You," and "Golden Tears" followed, keeping them high in the charts for the next few years.

Tired of the road, Frantz quit the group in 1977 and was replaced by Sue Powell. A year later Hackeman also quit and Melissa Dean stepped in. Powell then quit in 1979 to pursue a solo career (she was signed to RCA and had a couple of hits in 1981). Jamie Kaye was her replacement—who soon left as well and in turn was replaced by Patti Caines.

In 1982, Rowland recorded a solo album, SUGAR FREE, for Elektra, but it wasn't terribly successful. He then regrouped Dave & Sugar, which led to further rounds of musical chairs for the various Sugars for most of the decade. The band's hit potential, however, had already dried up by that point. Today the group's pop sound is entirely dated, and for better or worse they've largely been forgotten.

⊙ **Anthology** (1998; Renaissance). If you've been missing your Sugar (and maybe Dave as well), here's a healthy serving—some 23 songs in all, from "Queen Of The Silver Dollar" through hits such as "Knee Deep," "New York Wine And Tennessee Shine," "Golden Tears," and "Gotta' Quit Lookin' At You Baby."

Mac Davis

The career of Scott "Mac" Davis was assured a respectable slot in the annals of pop songwriting after the native Texan wrote "In The Ghetto," a song Elvis Presley turned into a Top 3 pop hit in 1969. Davis himself recorded plenty of country-pop material during the '70s and '80s, racking up sizeable hits with such middle-of-the-road jingles as "Baby Don't Get Hooked On Me" and "Stop And Smell The Roses." His voice was thin and sometimes forced, his style was frequently cheesy—he was sort of a poor man's Tom Jones—yet in the best of times ("Texas In My Rear View Mirror," for instance) his music did have a laid-back appeal. Either way, it's his songwriting that has endured far longer than any of his own recordings.

Davis was born on 21 January, 1942, in Lubbock, Texas. He lived for a while in Atlanta, where he played rock'n'roll and began working for the Vee-Jay label as a regional manager. Later he worked for Liberty. At the same time, he was writing songs, and in 1968 "A Little Less Conversation" caught the ear of Elvis Presley. Soon after, Presley cut "In The Ghetto" during his Memphis sessions, followed by "Memories" and "Don't Cry Daddy." Around the same time, Davis' songs were also recorded by Bobby Goldsboro ("Watching Scotty Grow"), O.C. Smith ("Friend, Lover, Woman, Wife"), and Kenny Rogers and the First Edition ("Something's Burning"). As a solo artist, Davis was signed to Columbia in 1970, and two years later he topped the pop charts with "Baby Don't Get Hooked On Me." The song also crossed into the country charts, proving Mac's appeal to both audiences. Davis seemed drawn to overtly sexual come-on songs—not only the macho "Don't Get Hooked" but also the huffing and puffing "Naughty Girl" and the almost grotesque "Baby Spread Your Love On Me" ("wild and warm the way it used to be"). Today Mac's brand of bullish masculinity comes off as milky and silly, but at the time those and other songs helped fuel his hunky image (as did his role as a football star in the movie *North Dallas Forty*).

Davis earned the ACM's Entertainer of the Year award in 1974, and he also hosted his own TV variety show during the mid-'70s. He continued recording for Columbia ("Stop And Smell The Roses," "Burnin' Thing") through the end of the decade, then he switched to Casablanca, releasing further hit titles like "Texas In My Rear View Mirror" and "Hooked On Music." He

briefly recorded for MCA in the mid-'80s, but after that his chart hits disappeared. He co-wrote the 1990 Dolly Parton hit "White Limozeen," and that same year he soaked up the spotlight one more time when he performed in the title role of the Broadway show *The Will Rogers Follies*.

⊙ **Greatest Hits** (1979; Columbia). It's a sparse collection at only 10 songs, but they are Davis' best-known titles. Includes his versions of "In The Ghetto," "Friend, Lover, Woman, Wife," and "Something's Burnin'" along with his two 1970s-era blockbusters, "Stop And Smell The Roses" and "Baby Don't Get Hooked On Me."

⊙ **Very Best And More** (1984; Casablanca). Collects Mac's hits from his Casablanca days in the early 1980s such as "Texas In My Rear View Mirror," "Hooked On Music," and "It's Hard To Be Humble." The production is a little more laid back, which helps make these songs (most notably "Texas In My Rear View Mirror") among his best as a recording artist.

John Denver

John Denver was anything but a hard country singer, and he took a lot of flak for his smiling, soft-pop folksongs that were sincere to the point of cloying. Yet on another level, perhaps simply as a citizen and human being, he was also loved and respected. Even if you're one of millions who cringe every time "Sunshine On My Shoulders" comes wafting from your bedside clock radio, you have to admit the man was genuine, good-natured, and just plain nice. That might not be enough to make his music interesting (or even palatable) to non-believers, yet such qualities do count for something—as did Denver's earnest social, political, and environmental activism.

Denver didn't start out in country music. Inspired by the folk revival of the 1960s, he was originally an acoustic guitar-strumming pop singer and he released a couple of albums before his song "Take Me Home, Country Roads" went gold in 1971 and Nashville discovered just how lucrative his wholesome brand of music truly was. Throughout the rest of the '70s he was one of the nation's biggest-selling stars, topping the country and pop charts with songs like "Rocky Mountain High," "Annie's Song," "Back Home Again" (his first #1 country single), "I'm Sorry,"

John Denver

toward music. After high school he studied architecture at Texas Tech in Lubbock, Texas, but by that time was already engulfed in the folk revival, eventually dropping out of school and moving to California. He played in various clubs before landing himself a spot in the Chad Mitchell Trio, where he stayed from 1965–69. One of the first songs he wrote during this time was "Leaving On A Jet Plane," which Peter, Paul And Mary picked up and turned into a hit in 1969. That same year Denver signed to RCA and released his first solo album, RHYMES AND REASONS. By 1970 he and his first wife, Anne, were snugly settled in Aspen, Colorado.

Denver's 1971 album POEMS, PRAYERS AND PROMISES was the first to strike major gold with "Country Roads" and "I Guess He'd Rather Be In Colorado." After a string of even bigger hits, his popularity peaked in 1975 with the CMA Entertainer of the Year award and his *Rocky Mountain Christmas* TV special. After that time his chart hits were never quite so big. Denver was an international superstar by that point, however, and he recorded steadily well into the late '80s, including duets with Placido Domingo ("Perhaps Love"), the Muppets (the hit album A CHRISTMAS TOGETHER), Emmylou Harris ("Wild Montana Skies"), and the Nitty Gritty Dirt Band ("And So It Goes" from WILL THE CIRCLE BE UNBROKEN II). He also tried his hand at acting, appearing on the TV series *McCloud* and starring in the 1977 movie *Oh God!* with George Burns.

Throughout his career Denver (who was declared poet laureate of Colorado in 1974 by then-governor John Vanderhoof) was a popular live performer all over the world, and he was always active and outspoken regarding political and social causes. On 12 December 1997, however, Denver lost his life while flying a personal experimental aircraft over the Pacific Ocean near Monterey, California.

"Calypso," and "Thank God I'm A Country Boy." As well as scoring these hits, he also won the Country Music Association's Entertainer of the Year award in 1975—which caused quite a stir among many country stalwarts. During the CMA award ceremony, for instance, presenter Charlie Rich, upon opening the envelope that announced Denver as the winner, pulled out a cigarette lighter and torched the piece of paper, which burned and smoked as he read the name of "my good friend John Denver." (Denver was absent from the ceremony, by the way. It should also be noted that Rich, a well-loved and - respected man himself, later regretted the incident.)

Denver was born John Henry Deutschendorf, Jr. on New Year's Eve in 1943 in Roswell, New Mexico. His father was a pilot in the Air Force and the young Denver learned to love flying, but when his grandmother gave him a guitar he turned

○ **Aerie** (1971; RCA). Among a few early (and lesser-known) Denver originals are versions of John Prine's "Blow Up Your TV," Steve Goodman's "City Of New Orleans," and Kris Kristofferson's "Casey's Last Ride."

John Denver

⊙ **Back Home Again** (1974; RCA). Denver's first album to break big in country music markets features some of his best-known songs including "Thank God I'm A Country Boy," "Grandma's Feather Bed," "Annie's Song," and the title track.

⊙ **An Evening With John Denver** (1975; RCA). This double-live album has always been one of Denver's most popular collections, as it's packed with lively, family-friendly renditions of his wholesome favorites.

Exile

Slick, bland, and decidedly middle-of-the-road, the synthesizer-laden pop that Exile recorded after they "went country" in the early 1980s is a perfect example of the kind of "new directions" Nashville was infatuated with at the time. Exile was about as far from "rootsy" as a (supposed) country band can get, but their songs and albums sold extremely well; as far as the band's new label, Epic, was concerned, that was the bottom line—no matter that their music was barely distinguishable from the (so-called) "rock" they had been playing only a few years earlier.

At Exile's core is Kentucky-born singer/songwriter J.P. Pennington, who actually has impeccable country roots: his mother, Lily May Ledford, was a member of the hillbilly string band, the Coon Creek Girls, his father emceed the *Renfro Valley Barn Dance*, and his uncle was none other than *Grand Ole Opry* star Red Foley. But Pennington's tastes clearly bent toward rock'n'roll.

Exile actually dates back as far as 1963, when Pennington formed The Exiles. Ten years later he and the group renamed themselves Exile, and soon after that they hit the pop charts with "Try It On." Their career-making song, however, came in 1978—the disco-beating, high-school-dance favorite "Kiss You All Over." No follow-up single matched the million-selling success of that bombastic piece of pop, and Exile's career eventually dried up. They returned to Kentucky, playing bars around Lexington.

A few of their songs, however, began to be recorded by country acts like Dave & Sugar, Janie Fricke and Alabama. Taking notice of this, Exile's manager repackaged the band as 'country,' and landed them a Nashville deal with Epic Records and producer Buddy Killen. Both "Woke Up In Love" and "I Don't Want To Be A Memory" from their 1983 album, EXILE, reached #1, and

the band's new career was off and running. The hits—mostly bland, soft-rock numbers that passed for country at the time—came steadily, but by the end of the decade the band's line-up began to change. Lead singers Pennington and Les Taylor both quit to pursue solo careers (each releasing albums in the early '90s), and while Exile persevered on a new label, Arista, their huge chart success was now a thing of the past.

⊙ **Greatest Hits** (1986; Epic). Exile earned 10 #1 country hits during the 1980s, and many of their best-known singles lurk in the tepid shallows of this collection.

Donna Fargo

When this North Carolina country gal first wrote and recorded the ultra-cheery "Happiest Girl In The Whole USA," she was grading high school English papers in California. In 1972, however, the single was picked up by Dot Records and turned into a million seller, and the lives of Donna Fargo and her husband-producer-manager, Stan Silver, were instantly changed. The pair packed up and moved to Nashville, where Fargo was met with a slew of music awards, including a Grammy. Like wildfire in a breeze, her career was successfully launched.

Cheery, lighthearted songs were Fargo's trademark, from the cutesy "Funny Face" to the spirited, even sassy vibe of "Superman" (a peppy

ACE Up The Sleeve

As pop influences moved through Nashville at a blinding pace more than a few stalwart traditionalists found themselves feeling the pinch in terms of lagging record sales and radio airplay. When the industry's flagship organization, the Country Music Association (CMA), voted pop singer Olivia Newton-John Female Vocalist of the Year at its annual award show in 1974, two dozen country singers (among them Jim Ed Brown, Barbara Mandrell, Dolly Parton, Johnny Paycheck, Jeanne Pruett, Hank Snow, Conway Twitty, Porter Wagoner, Dottie West, and Faron Young) decided enough was enough. Gathering at George Jones and Tammy Wynette's house in Nashville one November night, just a few weeks after the CMA awards, they put their names on a letter that declared country music was "losing its identity" and there was now "a definite need for an organization that represents the interest of country music recording artists exclusively." At a second meeting a week later, the Association of Country Entertainers (ACE) was born.

The 1974 CMA awards were "the straw that broke the camel's back," remarked singer (and temporary ACE chairman) Bill Anderson at the time. The ACE members had simply become fed up with crossover artists such as Newton-John, Ronnie Milsap, and even Charlie Rich (whom many considered a rock'n'roller) taking the top country awards. Newton-John, who'd beaten out several of country's biggest names, ended up bearing the brunt of the attack. Not only was her music pop and her background British/Australian, she didn't even consider herself a 'country' singer at all. This was an outrage, according to ACE, and showed that the CMA awards weren't representing country music's heritage as they'd been designed to do.

As soon as the birth of ACE was announced, however, opinions began sailing back and forth, and the media had a field day. Some ACE members were guarded in what they said (fearing career damage), while others let rip. Some even implied that a conspiracy was taking place: "These people want to come in and take our music away," said Anderson in 1974. "These people came in and prostituted our business and watered down our music," echoed singer Billy Walker that same year. Walker's only definition of "these people" was "big money on the East and West Coast." George Morgan (ACE chairman until his death in 1975) commented that "the major problem in the industry is preserving our identity, because there seems to be a lot of infiltration."

ACE may well have been founded with the best of intentions, but it attracted a good deal of negative publicity right from the outset. "There's a bitter wind blowing in Nashville," wrote a New Jersey reporter in 1974. A mean-spirited image was less than helpful for an underdog group striving to establish a serious bargaining position in the country music industry. Its

song from her second album worth seeking for its wacky steel-guitar sound effects alone). These songs have plenty of pop appeal, but Fargo's also got a strong, rural voice, and she isn't afraid of her natural-born twang; at least on her early recordings, she bears more resemblance to Tammy Wynette than soft-pop crossover singers like Crystal Gayle. And for at least the first half of the '70s, when she first struck it big, Fargo's songs (many of which she wrote herself) were for the most part tastefully produced and low on schmaltz.

Fargo hails from Mount Airy, North Carolina, a region that's long been rich in traditional mountain music. Born Yvonne Vaughn, she sang a great deal as a girl, but instead of heading for Nashville, she became a teacher and settled in an LA suburb. There she met Stan Silver, her future husband and the man responsible for getting her music career off the ground. Fargo recorded for a few small labels during the '60s, including Ramco and Challenge, but songs like "Who's Been Sleeping On My Side Of The Bed" (too suggestive, claimed the DJs) and "Daddy" (which she would later re-record and turn into a hit) didn't catch fire. It wasn't until Dot Records picked up "Happiest Girl" that Fargo's career exploded. In just one year she turned into a star with a brand new life and career.

For the better part of the '70s, Fargo stayed high on the charts with songs like "Funny Face," "You Were Always There," "It Do Feel Good," "Mr Doodles," and remakes of "Walk On By" and "Mockingbird Hill." She briefly had her own TV special (produced by the Osmond Brothers), which ran for a year beginning in 1978, but that same year she was also diagnosed with multiple sclerosis. While the disease didn't halt her career, it did slow things down. She continued to perform and record throughout the following decade— including a 1981 gospel album (BROTHERLY LOVE), a minor-hit duet with Billy Joe Royal ("Members Only" from her 1986 album

Donna Fargo

success, however, lay in its ability to bring issues to both press and public attention. It also drew many singers together and allowed them an opportunity to air their views. "If we don't do anything but establish unity with ourselves," said Morgan at the time, "we've accomplished something."

By 1976, it was time to rein in the wild horses and re-focus ACE's priorities. To mark its two-year anniversary, the group held a press conference, at which vice-president Barbara Mandrell read a statement declaring ACE's new strategy. There'd be no more "striking out at symptoms," as ACE had done in the past, she read. "We do not hate Olivia Newton-John or John Denver [CMA's Entertainer of the Year in 1975]. We do not want to return country music to the sounds of the '40s. We do not object to Willie and Waylon and the so-called Austin Outlaws. We do not want to establish ourselves as censors of lyrics or instrumental arrangements. We do not object to newcomers or to innovations in sound and style." ACE, she said, extended a "sincere welcome to anyone sincerely understanding and respectful of country music."

What ACE did object to, she went on to say, were the "tight playlists" and "top-forty formula[s]" that dictated the programming on too many country music radio stations and often left out music by ACE artists that—they claimed—many fans wanted to hear. Such restrictive programming, Mandrell read, represented "the worst crisis country music as an art form has faced in twenty years." Tight playlists had long been an ACE complaint, but now radio was the group's chief culprit.

"We're criticizing the endless repetition of the same songs," is how ACE spokesperson Paul Soelberg put it.

Battling the entire country radio industry was no simple task, however. Radio programmers listened to ACE, but for the most part they made few or no changes. Radio was now a very big business and competition among stations was growing; and according to programmers at the time, tight playlists and Top 40 formats did work to keep ratings high. So even if ACE's membership roster hovered around 150 in the mid- to late '70s, and included some of country's biggest names (Merle Haggard, Roy Acuff, Roger Miller, Ernest Tubb), country-flavored pop songs still continued to waft from radios across America.

Then there was the issue of funding. A 1976 benefit at the *Opry* House sold 4000 tickets, and a series of family-oriented "Nashville Jubilee" concerts were also a success. Under the name Country's Travelers, ACE also put together group vacation packages with country stars acting as hosts (Jean Shepard, who became ACE chairperson in 1979, led the first trip to Hawaii). Yet despite all these and other noble efforts, it was becoming quite clear that ACE wasn't going to change the world. When the group's executive secretary ran off with $10,000 in 1979, it seemed an indication that momentum was waning. By the turn of the decade, when the *Urban Cowboy* soundtrack was high on the charts (and Mandrell herself was adorning herself in glitter), the organization had largely dissolved.

WINNERS), and the 1991 song "Soldier Boy," which referenced the Gulf War—though she jumped from label to label and her songs never quite caught fire. She did, however, survive a successful career in the music business with her integrity (both as a singer and strong, albeit underrated, songwriter) largely intact.

◉ **The Happiest Girl In The Whole USA** (1972; Dot). An under-appreciated songwriter, Fargo's material runs deeper than you might at first think (Dolly Parton was clearly a role model). "Funny Face" and the title track are certainly cute, but "Society's Got Us" is a biting satire of contemporary consumerism, and "The Awareness Of Nothing" stands out for its subtle threads of feminism.

◉ **Best Of Donna Fargo** (1995; Varese Vintage). Seventeen of Fargo's '70s-era Dot hits—from "The Happiest Girl" and "Superman" through "You're Not Charlie Brown (And I'm Not Raggedy Ann)" and

"Don't Be Angry"—are gathered on this overview CD, along with "Say I Do" from her 1981 album BROTHERLY LOVE.

Janie Fricke

A popular commercial-jingle and studio-background vocalist during the 1970s, Janie Fricke got her break as a solo artist when she was "discovered" as a standout background vocalist on a Johnny Duncan single. Fricke's music is closer to the kind of pop you'd hear during a gym workout than the country you'd sing while driving a tractor, but this was an era when lighthearted pop was peaking in popularity, and Fricke turned out to be right for the time. In many ways, she was the culmination of the country radio's mid-'70s crush on Olivia Newton-John.

Born 19 December, 1947 in South Whitney, Indiana, Fricke was first a college-coffeehouse folksinger before landing a job in Memphis singing radio promos and commercial jingles—work she successfully pursued around the country throughout the early '70s. Soon she was also a busy session background vocalist in Nashville, and it was her (uncredited) singing on several Johnny Duncan hits that finally won her a recording contract of her own. She signed to Columbia, and countrypolitan starmaker Billy Sherrill produced her first three (of a total that would eventually reach seventeen) albums.

Throughout her career, Fricke's sound shifted between country and pop, often depending on which producer she was working with (Sherrill, Jim Ed Norman, Bob Montgomery). Montgomery produced her 1982 album IT AIN'T EASY, which included the bouncy, fully aerobicized pop hit "He's A Heartache (Looking For A Place To Happen)" and the clean-cut love ballad "It Ain't Easy Being Easy," among others. By contrast, songs she cut in the mid-'80s with producer Noro Wilson gave her a bluesier and almost gutsy vocal sound.

In 1982 and 1983 Fricke finally won CMA's coveted Female Vocalist of the Year (for which she'd previously been nominated), among several other awards. And her hits continued through the mid-'80s. In 1986 she changed the spelling of her last name to "Frickie" (Elvis Costello had mispronounced it on a recent CMA award show), but later changed it back again. By the start of the '90s, however, she was being ignored by country radio. Columbia dropped her, and she switched to the indie labels Intersound and, later, Branson Entertainment. She also began selling a line of fashions based on her stage apparel.

⊙ **Anthology** (1999; Renaissance). The songs here are shining examples of pop music that doesn't hold up well over time. Fricke's voice is thin and overly clean on "He's A Heartache," an upbeat, post-disco sort of country song that almost feels like it's on 45 rpm, and "It Ain't Easy Being Easy" and "Tell Me A Lie" are formulaic love ballads. Still, if you're a confirmed Fricke fan, this CD ought to satisfy, as it packs 23 songs onto one disc.

Larry Gatlin

Larry Gatlin has an attractive, vibrato-tinged tenor voice that certainly shines when he works

it. It's a shame, however, that the majority of the material he sang during his late 1970s/early '80s heyday was so disposable. He may have demonstrated his creative potential early on—writing a bevy of pretty songs, singing tight-knit harmonies with his brothers Steve and Rudy—but once the smoke of his numerous chart successes dissipated by the mid-'80s, it was clear Gatlin was little more than a middle-of-the-road pop singer.

In some ways, Gatlin was like the slicked-down flip side of his one-time labelmate, ruddy-voiced Rhodes Scholar Kris Kristofferson. (The two even performed well together on the understated Gatlin-penned gospel-country song "Help Me," found on the back of Kristofferson's 1972 single "Why Me." It's one of Gatlin's best performances.) But while Gatlin was born with pipes that Kristofferson never dreamed of, he had nowhere near the same feel as a writer, nor the same grasp of the words and emotions he was singing.

Gatlin wrote much of his material, and a handful of his songs—generally those on his early Monument albums—are not bad. He was prolific and determined, and his success and popularity certainly can't be denied. He built his career out of pretty songs like "Broken Lady" (which won him a Grammy in 1976), the hook-laden "The Lady Takes The Cowboy Every Time," and the sexy come-on "What Are We Doing Lonesome". He and his brothers enjoyed a long string of chart hits that lasted into the early '90s.

Born in Texas, the Gatlin boys grew up with gospel music, an influence that's immediately apparent in their harmony singing. Larry sang with a gospel group, the Imperials, and while on tour he met Dottie West, who first recorded his songs and encouraged his career. Moving to Nashville, he sang back-up for Kristofferson before landing his own contract. THE PILGRIM, released in 1974, was his first album, and brothers Steve and Rudy were participants right from the outset. The brothers switched to Columbia in 1979, when they also began calling themselves Larry Gatlin And The Gatlin Brothers Band—and creating songs that were popular, though much slicker. By the end of the decade they were on Capitol; in 1992, however, they decided to quit touring, and instead built an entertainment center in Branson, Missouri.

◉ **Larry Gatlin With Family And Friends** (1976; Monument). Gatlin's third album consists of 10 songs, all penned by Gatlin, including the big hit "Broken Lady." Some call his lyrics crafty ("She's a broken lady waiting to be mended/Like a potter would mend a broken vase"), but these days they ring hollow. To his credit, though, the melodies are folksy and gently rambling—no more pop at this point than the Eagles. Inoffensive stuff.

☉ **The Best Of The Gatlins: All The Gold In California** (1996; Columbia Legacy). If you're looking for Gatlin hits from the 1970s and early '80s such as "Broken Lady," "Sweet Becky Walker," "Denver," "What Are We Doin' Lonesome," and "Houston (Means One Day Closer To You)," you've come to the right place.

Crystal Gayle

Although she's the younger sister of country legend Loretta Lynn, the pretty pop ballads Crystal Gayle is famous for are another breed entirely. Lynn's bright but earthy voice gave a hearty edge to gems like "Coal Miner's Daughter," "Fist City," and "Rated X." Gayle, on the other hand, made her reputation via the pop charts with tender songs like "Talking In Your Sleep" and "Don't It Make My Brown Eyes Blue." Two siblings have probably never sounded so far apart.

Bear in mind, however, that each is also a product of their time. Lynn's breakthrough came in the early 1960s, when a thick twang still meant something on country radio. Gayle jumped into the public eye in the mid-'70s, when a slicked-

down, pop-friendly sound was the country music industry's main focus. It's no wonder, then, that with her knockout good looks and sweet radio-friendly voice, Crystal Gayle made a picture-perfect pop-country star—one of the most successful and popular female singers of the late '70s and '80s.

Gayle's upbringing was also very different from her sister's. She was born Brenda Gail Webb in Paintsville, Kentucky in 1951, but only a few years later she and her family moved to Wabash, Indiana, a small town about two hours southeast of Chicago (and a long way from tiny Butcher Holler, Kentucky, where Lynn was raised). In this suburban environment, Gayle was exposed to a mix of urban and rural influences.

Crystal (a nickname given her by Loretta because of her supposed fondness for Krystal hamburgers) started in the music business under her big sister's shadow. She toured in Lynn's road show in the mid-'60s, which led to her first contract with Decca in 1970 and the single "I Cried The Blue Right Out Of My Eyes"—one of Lynn's songs. Quickly Crystal realized she needed her own voice and identity. Regular performances on Jim Ed Brown's TV show gave her a higher profile, and she soon signed a new contract with United Artists and began working with producer and songwriter Allen Reynolds (who was fresh from successful work with Don Williams). Reynolds was the man who helped Gayle develop the soft voice and mellow approach that have become her musical trademarks—and who also promoted her as a pop as well as country artist. A prolific songwriter (his hits include "Dreaming My Dreams" for Waylon Jennings and "Five O'Clock World" for the Vogues), Reynolds also wrote several of Gayle's early hits, including "Wrong Road Again" and "Somebody Loves You." (Reynolds would later achieve his biggest success as Garth Brooks' producer.)

Gayle's first two albums were both released in 1975, and her initial style was a pleasant, easygoing sort of country-folk blend—a close cousin to the music of Emmylou Harris, whose own solo career was getting started at the same time. From Gayle's second album came her first #1 country song, Richard Leigh's "I'll Get Over You." Leigh also wrote the 1977 hit "Don't It Make My Brown Eyes Blue," a song that boosted Gayle's career into the high reaches of the country and (most importantly) pop charts, making her a household name. It also won Grammy awards for both Gayle and Leigh.

Gayle's string of country and pop hits (and music awards) continued steadily through the '70s and well into the '80s. At the same time, her sound and musical direction turned more and more

toward showy, shiny pop material, leaving behind the gentle, spare country sound that spotted her early albums. In 1979 she switched to Columbia, bringing producer Reynolds with her; the subsequent album MISS THE MISSISSIPPI included the hits "Cold Shoulder" and "It's Like We Never Said Goodbye." (She later moved to Elektra, Warner Brothers, and finally, at the end of the decade, to Capitol.) Her career highlights during the '80s included working with Tom Waits on the soundtrack for Francis Ford Coppola's 1982 movie *One From The Heart*; a popular duet with Eddie Rabbitt, "You And I"; a performance at President Reagan's inauguration; and a string of Top 10 hit songs that refused to dry up until 1987. In 1993, her winning streak now faded, she re-recorded several early hits and standards for the Branson Entertainment label. Six years later she re-emerged with CRYSTAL GAYLE SINGS THE HEART & SOUL OF HOAGY CARMICHAEL (1999; Platinum), an orchestral project that places her pristine voice in a mature new jazz–pop context.

⊙ **Somebody Loves You** (1975; United Artists). Gayle's earliest albums are surprisingly down-to-earth, the songs drifting between spare, easygoing honky-tonk melodies and sentimental weepers. On this album, her second, the band include steel guitarist Lloyd Green and fiddler Buddy Spicher, with Janie Fricke contributing background vocals. Gayle's self-titled debut album was also released in 1975, and both were produced by Allen Reynolds. .   .

⊙ **Classic Crystal** (1979; EMI Manhattan). This greatest hits collection has the best-known songs from Gayle's early career, including "Ready For The Times To Get Better" and of course "Don't It Make My Brown Eyes Blue," all produced by Reynolds.

⊙ **Crystal Gayle** (1994; MCA). Originally issued in 1978 under the title I'VE CRIED THE BLUE RIGHT OUT OF MY EYES, this 10-song collection contains Crystal's earliest recordings, three of which were written by Loretta Lynn (and one, "Too Far," by Marty Robbins). Crystal's voice has an appealing country twang, songs like "M.R.S. Degree" are cute, and Owen Bradley's Nashville Sound production is typically lush, but she's a greenhorn here, still operating from under her sister's shadow.

Mickey Gilley

By the end of the 1970s, Mickey Gilley was already a chart-topping, award-winning country singer and honky-tonk pianist with a solid, consistent style, but when the 1980 movie *Urban Cowboy* hit the screens and turned into a blockbuster, his career shot into the mainstream. Gilley's Club, the Texas honky-tonk Mickey had owned for ten years, was the setting for the film, and so it was that Gilley—along with his house band led by guitarist Johnny Lee—ended up as a focal point of the movie's soundtrack. Gilley's thick, bluesy, but easy-to-digest brand of honky-tonk was perfect stuff for the stiff-booted newcomers who were looking for a flavorsome country sound, but one light enough on the twang, moan, and warble so as not to turn their suburban stomachs. Gilley's piano playing was lively and sometimes full of bluster—a style similar to that of his cousin, Jerry Lee Lewis. He was a respectable musician, one remarkably consistent throughout his career: His voice was neat but not overly pretty, and his songs and albums mostly avoided the schlocky trappings that plagued so many album productions of the '70s and '80s.

Gilley was born in 1936 in Natchez, Mississippi, just across the Mississippi River from Ferriday, Louisiana, where his cousin Jerry Lee hails from. Gilley, Lewis, and their other cousin Jimmy Swaggart played piano together as children, both boogie-woogie and gospel, but Gilley didn't consider music as a profession until cousin Lewis hit the charts in the mid-'50s. Gilley cut a few singles in the late '50s, played sessions in New Orleans for producer Huey Meaux (best known for his work with the Sir Douglas Quintet), did some lounge work around the South, and eventually, during the '60s, built a strong local following at the Nesadel Club in Houston. The Paula label released Gilley's album, DOWN THE LINE, in 1967, and he charted for the first time with "Now I Can Live Again" a year later.

In 1970, in a Pasadena, Texas, joint that had formerly been called Sherry's Club, Gilley (along with partner Sherwood Cryer) opened his famous "world's biggest honky tonk." In 1974, a song he'd recorded for fun, "Room Full Of Roses" (a one-time hit for George Morgan), gave Gilley his first #1 hit, and was the first of many old songs he'd remake as his own. Gilley signed to Playboy Records and over the next several years had further hits, including the Bill Anderson song "City Lights," George Jones' "Window Up Above," Sam Cooke's "Bring It On Home," and good-time party tunes like "Don't The Girls All Get Prettier At Closing Time" and "The Power Of Positive Drinkin'." Gilley signed to Epic in 1978 when Playboy folded, and his hits continued well into the mid-'80s—boosted, certainly, by the success of *Urban Cowboy* (the soundtrack of which featured Gilley's slow-dance country take on the soul standard "Stand By Me"). By 1987, however, he'd quit Epic and signed to Airborne (which soon folded) and dissociated himself with Gilley's Club—which went out of business two years later. Gilley then turned his attention to Branson, Missouri, where he became one of the

first to build a theater in that soon-to-be boom town.

⊙ **Ten Years Of Hits** (1984; CBS). There's plenty of substantial Gilley-style honky tonk on this one-stop hits collection, including "Room Full Of Roses," "City Lights," "Window Up Above," "The Power Of Positive Drinkin'," and the rollicking "Don't The Girls All Get Prettier At Closing Time."

Lee Greenwood

In many ways, Lee Greewood represents the worst elements of the country music industry's infatuation with glitzy showmanship—synthesized, syrupy instrumentation and cheap flourishes of soft-rock melodrama. If singers like Kenny Rogers and Barbara Mandrell opened Nashville's door to these kinds of pop-crossover trappings, then it's folks like Greenwood who stepped on through and took full advantage of the moment. Not only did the smoky-voiced singer have a penchant for plasticized pop that goes back to his days playing Las Vegas lounges, he also turned out to be a superb spokesman for über-patriots, honing in on the conservative undercurrent of America's Reagan years with his rousing self-penned anthem "God Bless The USA." That song may well be a source of aggravation these days, but at the time of its release in 1984 it tingled the spines of more than a few flag-wavers—and sent Greenwood's already popular singing career soaring. The success Greenwood has achieved is frightening, but it's also a clear example of just how far into the abyss of adult-contemporary pop country singers (and listeners) were capable of wandering.

Born 27 October, 1942 on a farm near Sacramento, California, Greenwood grew up playing the saxophone and singing pop and country (including stints with Del Reeves and Mel Tillis). Eventually, young Lee and his band at the time, Apollo (later the Lee Greenwood Affair), found themselves in Las Vegas; after the group split up, he worked as a blackjack dealer and lounge performer (in 1973 he was lead singer in the revue Bare Touch of Vegas). In 1979, Larry McFaddan (Tillis' bandleader) encouraged Greenwood to turn his attention to Nashville—perfect timing, as the country industry was smack in the middle of its Vegas-pop infatuation. By 1981 he had a contract with MCA.

Mickey Gilley • Lee Greenwood

Hot on the heels of Kenny Rogers (an obvious influence in terms of his vocal tone and phrasing), Greenwood hit the country charts that year with the Jan Crutchfield song "It Turns Me Inside Out." Formulaic soft-pop ballads like "Ring On Her Finger, Time On Her Hands" and "I.O.U." (which crossed over to the pop charts) followed; by 1984 he'd twice won CMA's Male Vocalist of the Year and picked up a Grammy, among other awards.

Greenwood's chart success continued throughout the '80s, and following the release of "God Bless The USA" his stage show became more red, white, and blue; by 1992 the song, more alive than ever, was a favorite among Gulf War supporters. That year he also released the album AMERICAN PATRIOT, perhaps in reference to the numerous honors he'd been receiving: the Congressional Medal of Honor Society's Patriot Award, the AMVET Silver Helmet Award, and the VFW Americanism Gold Medal, among others. Greenwood even became the mascot of a US aircraft carrier. In 1996 the Lee Greenwood Theater, part of a large retail and entertainment complex, opened in the Smoky Mountain town of Sevierville, Tennessee.

☉ **Greatest Hits** (1985; MCA). All Greenwood's major early-1980s hits are here, including "It Turns Me Inside Out," the sickly sweet "I.O.U.," and the show-stopping "God Bless The USA". Those who regularly complain of the trite, banal qualities of '90s-era 'young country' will re-adjust their perspective by listening to this stuff, which is closer to the insipid pop of Michael Bolton than nearly anything that's ever before passed as 'country.'

Johnny Lee

In a way you can't fault Johnny Lee. However empty his brand of country may have felt, and however annoying his hits may have become, all the guy really did was grab a career opportunity handed to him on a silver platter and run with it as far as he could.

Lee was the guitarist in the house band at Gilley's, the Pasadena nightclub featured in *Urban Cowboy*, and his composition "Lookin' For Love" not only appeared on the multimillion-selling soundtrack, but was chosen as the movie's theme. Talk about overnight success: the song's smooth-voiced melody made him a household name, but

he had more than one hit up his sleeve— "Cherokee Fiddle" and "One In A Million" among them. His easygoing brand of good-time, bar-room country-rock was never overtly offensive, yet it was tailored to radio tastes at the time, and these days it lacks creative sparkle.

Raised on a Texas dairy farm, Lee didn't have an easy childhood—his father left the family shortly after he was born (they wouldn't meet again until Johnny was nineteen). He later joined the Navy and spent time in southeast Asia, then wound up back in Texas and working in Mickey Gilley's band. When Gilley opened his famous club in 1970, Lee began fronting the house band. He recorded a little during the '70s, including a countrified version of Rick Nelson's hit "Garden Party" entitled "Country Party." When he landed a part in *Urban Cowboy* in 1980, however, his life was transformed. In 1981 he quit Gilley's group and formed his own Western Union Band, and he even opened his own club, Johnny Lee's. His hit "Lookin' For Love" almost singlehandedly defined the slicked-up country-rock of the *Urban Cowboy* era. The formula worked well for him over the next several years, as he hit the charts again and again with songs like "Pickin' Up Strangers," "Cherokee Fiddle," and "You Could've Heard A Heart Break." By the mid-'80s, however, his hitmaking potential (not to mention his marriage to *Dallas* TV-star Charlene Tilton) had dried up and his label decided to drop him. He eventually signed with Curb in 1989 and released NEW DIRECTIONS, but the album failed to make waves. He also wrote an autobiography, *Lookin' For Love*, and later released the album WOODS AND WATER through TV marketing. By the '90s he was back to playing the clubs.

☉ **Greatest Hits** (1983; Warner Bros.). The one album to get if you can't live without Johnny Lee hits like "Lookin' For Love," "Cherokee Fiddle," "One In A Million," and "Hey Bartender."

Barbara Mandrell

"When I got to Hollywood, I wanted control."

Barbara Mandrell

Barbara Mandrell was 'the Princess of Steel' (a prodigy on steel guitar) when she first stepped onto a stage as a girl, but by the time she was barely thirty years old she'd turned herself into one of the reigning queens of country music. Her huge popularity in the 1970s and '80s was based not only on hit records (though she had those, too), but also on her glamorous television series and glitzy concert extravaganzas.

At the peak of her career Mandrell was far more than a musician—she was a celebrity, a star, and she played the part to the hilt. Yet she wasn't frivolous about her celebrity status; like fellow superstar Dolly Parton, Mandrell was a smart businesswoman who calculated her every move. A strong work ethic had been instilled in her as a child, and she almost never gave herself a moment's rest. At the same time, she drove herself so hard and fast that she almost burned out from exhaustion.

Mandrell was born in Houston on Christmas Day in 1948. Raised by musical parents, Barbara was the eldest of three girls (Louise and Irline, who'd later star with her on TV). As a child she learned steel guitar and assorted other instruments (including accordion, saxophone, and banjo); by the time she was twelve she was playing steel on stage with guitarist Joe Maphis in Las Vegas and on the *Town Hall Party* program, as well as performing with several other country stars. A few years later, Mandrell, her sisters, and her parents— mother Mary Ellen and father Irby (who'd later become her manager and a driving force behind her career)—formed the Mandrell Family Band together and toured the US and Asia. Mandrell's future husband, drummer Ken Dudley, was also in the band, and after she finished high school the pair were married, with Mandrell planning to become a housewife.

When Dudley was drafted and shipped overseas, however, Mandrell changed her mind; she moved to Nashville with her parents and embarked on her mission to become a country star. With Irby now her manager, she was signed to Columbia in 1969 and had some minor hits over the next few years. Her first producer was Billy Sherrill, who at the time was also busy with Tammy Wynette, Tanya Tucker, and Charlie Rich. Mandrell stayed with Columbia until 1975, during which time she recorded a good deal of colorful, spirited country soul. "Treat Him Right," "Do Right Woman—Do Right Man," "The Midnight Oil," and "Tonight My Baby's Coming Home" are just a few of the highlights from what's easily her most interesting (and enduring) period. The songs weren't exactly all roots and downhome twang, but they were certainly closer to the ground (and the soul) that any of her later, more suburban material.

The subjects of many of Mandrell's songs were also racy for the time, dealing openly with such topics as lust ("Tonight My Baby's Coming Home"), sexual loneliness ("Sleeping Single In A Double Bed"), and late-night love trysts ("The Midnight Oil"). "I'll feel kinda dirty," she moaned in that 1973 cheating song, "because I'll have the midnight oil all over me." What's ironic about her subject matter is that Mandrell herself—a devout Christian, mother, and wife—always maintained an impeccably clean, family-oriented profile.

In 1976, Mandrell switched to the ABC/Dot label, where she began working with producer Tom Collins (who was also working with Ronnie Milsap and would later turn his attention to Sylvia). With this new pop-minded producer, her career took off from the respectable countrypolitan foundation she'd established with Sherrill and shot into new, broader territory. "Sleeping Single In A Double Bed" became her first #1 in 1978, and more hits followed. Mandrell dove head-first into schmaltz ("Years"), sniffed at bubble-gum ("Love Is Thin Ice"), diddled with disco ("Crackers"), and made a weak attempt to maintain her roots ("I Was Country When Country Wasn't Cool"). Collins churned out frightfully slick and garish productions, but Mandrell thrived in her new environment. "Just because my roots are in country," she told *Chicago Tribune* writer Jack Hurst, "doesn't mean my branches can't go elsewhere." She donned fancy clothes, surrounded herself with bright lights, and won numerous awards—including, in 1980, prestigious Entertainer of the Year awards from both the Country Music Association (which she won again in 1981) and the Academy of Country Music.

Mandrell's career climaxed when she and her sisters hosted a network variety show in the early '80s, *Barbara Mandrell And The Mandrell Sisters* (produced by Sid and Marty Krofft, who'd earlier given the world surreal kids shows like *Lidsville* and *H.R. Puff'n'Stuff*). Though gaudy to the point of being camp, the shows proved hugely popular. Barbara, however, ended the series less than two years later due to exhaustion. Despite this, she continued touring and also shunned her last vestiges of humility by performing in Las Vegas in the glitzy stage extravanganza *The Lady Is A Champ* (which was made into a cable TV special). Her career, however, abruptly halted in 1984 when she and two of her children were involved in a head-on car collision. They survived, but Mandrell was hospitalized for a year. She rebounded with a few small hits, but by the late '80s Nashville was hot on neo-traditionalism, and her chart success tapered off. Refusing to be beaten, she continued performing and acting, wrote an autobiography (*Get To The Heart: My Story*), and opened the Mandrell Country museum in Nashville. In 1997, however, she shocked her fans by declaring she was quitting country music in favour of her acting career.

⊙ **The Midnight Oil** (1973; Columbia). Mandrell's early-1970s albums with producer Billy Sherrill contain her best material. Though unfortunately out-of-print, she brings a lively, soulful spirit and a less-inhibited country twang to songs like "Tonight My Baby's Coming Home," "Jamestown Ferry," and the title track. Vocally Mandrell sounds closer to Tammy Wynette or even Sammi Smith than the glam queen she became a few years later; and Sherrill's production, while hardly "subtle," never overwhelms his subject.

⊙ **The Best Of Barbara Mandrell** (1979; MCA). This CD collects the bigger of Mandrell's mid-'70s singles—the cheating song "Midnight Angel," the bouncy hit "Sleeping Single In A Double Bed"—from the period after she switched to MCA from Columbia.

⊙ **Super Hits** (1997; Columbia). Collecting many of Mandrell's early Columbia songs (all produced by Sherrill), this budget-priced CD includes "Treat Him Right," "Do Right Woman—Do Right Man," "The Midnight Oil," and "Tonight My Baby's Coming Home."

Ronnie Milsap

Appalachian-born song stylist Ronnie Milsap spent his formative years performing soul, blues, rock, and piano-lounge pop before hitting the big time as a Nashville star in the mid-1970s, and it was his ability to coalesce these influences into radio-ready material that defined his style and gave him mainstream appeal. He crooned soothing ballads ("A Legend In My Time"), soared down the lost-love highway ("Smoky Mountain Rain"), smoothed the bitter edges of hard-tack honkytonk ("I Hate You"), and stimulated the libidos of many a midwestern housewife ("Daydreams About Night Things"). Ultimately, though, he was wooed by the polished showroom glamour that infiltrated Nashville in the late '70s, and by the new decade his sights and sounds were focused on pleasing the pop market.

Blind from birth, Milsap (who hails from rural North Carolina) discovered music as a child, playing classical music on violin and piano, but he also listened to country, bluegrass, and, later, rock'n'roll. During the '60s he formed his own groups, played in J.J. Cale's band, signed with Scepter Records, and had an R&B hit single, "Never Had It So Good." He moved to Memphis in 1969, where his work with producer Chips Moman included playing keyboards on Elvis Presley's "Kentucky Rain." He also played regularly at a local club. Moman signed Milsap to his Chips label, which led to Milsap's pop hit "Loving You Is A Natural Thing." In 1971 he won a contract with Warner Brothers and recorded his first album.

Two years later, however, Milsap moved to Nashville. There he hooked up with producer Tom Collins (soon to make his reputation with Sylvia and Barbara Mandrell as well as Milsap), and won a new contract with RCA. The Dan Penn/Leroy Daniels song "I Hate You" was his first single, followed by Eddie Rabbitt's cutesy "Pure Love," Kris Kristofferson's "Please Don't Tell Me How The Story Ends," and the Don Gibson weeper "(I'd Be) A Legend In My Time." His smooth vocal style, coupled with undercurrents of Memphis soul and tastefully tailored sexuality ("Daydreams About Night Things"), helped win him a huge following; he hit the top of the charts many times over the next ten to fifteen years and regularly won trophies—including several Grammys—at the top awards shows.

Milsap's earlier recordings revealed his soulful background much more distinctly. But the twangsoul of "I Hate You" is a far cry from his work in

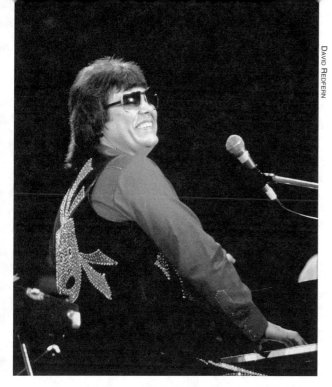

Ronnie Milsap

the 1970s and '80s, thanks to recordings like "Snowbird," "He Thinks I Still Care," "Just Another Woman In Love," and "Could I Have This Dance" (which appeared on the *Urban Cowboy* soundtrack). Her alto voice is rich, complex, and soulful, and she can handle romantic and dangerously sentimental material without—at least in the best of times—resorting to saccharine trappings or an overly sanitized tone. Earlier songs like "He Thinks I Still Care" and "Danny's Song" do have a discernible country edge—the steel guitars are given a respectable presence—but for the most part her music has more in common with pop and lightweight soul. Still, the presence of strings hadn't bothered Nashville audiences before, and so she maintained an appeal to country fans throughout her career.

Morna Anne Murray was born on 20 June, 1945 in Springhill, Nova Scotia. She grew up in coal-mining country and earned a college degree in physical education. After a year of teaching, she began singing on a Canadian TV program, the *Sing-Along Jubilee*, in the late '60s. The musical director was Brian Ahern (later Emmylou Harris' producer and husband), and he ended up producing Murray's first album, WHAT ABOUT ME, released on a Canadian label in 1969. After that she signed with Capitol, and in 1970 her recording of the Gene MacLellan song "Snowbird" crossed into the US market and landed her in the country Top 10 (a feat that surprised her at the time—she hadn't been much of a country music fan while growing up). Further exposure for her in America came via the *Glen Campbell Goodtime Hour*, on which she was a regular. Her 1973 version of Kenny Loggins' "Danny's Song" was her second Top 10 country hit, and a year later she landed her first #1 with "He Thinks I Still Care" (previously a hit for George Jones). At the same time, she had an AM radio hit with the Beatles song "You Won't See Me," proving her double-edged appeal to pop as well as country audiences.

Though she maintained her home base in Canada, Murray was a very strong musical presence in the US throughout the 1970s and '80s. She racked up 11 country #1s during this time—songs like "I Just Fall In Love Again," "Blessed Are The Believers," "Nobody Loves Me Like You Do" (a CMA award–winning duet with Dave Loggins), and "Now And Forever (You And

the '80s, when his songs and albums turned far slicker, his performances and arrangements more sweeping and bombastic. Milsap did fit the times properly—snug up against the pace and tone set by Kenny Rogers, Milsap helped create the sheen of Las Vegas sophistication that intoxicated Nashville during that era—and he certainly sold plenty of records, but his music never ventured far from the middle-of-the-road. His voice remained pleasant enough, but whatever adventurous promise he'd shown early on with his more soulful work had long since disappeared.

⊙ **Greatest Hits** (1980; RCA). Milsap's bigger hits from the 1970s are collected here, and they run the gamut from decent songs like "I Hate You" and "(I'm A) Stand By My Woman Man" to bland but palatable numbers like "Daydreams About Night Things" and all the way down to hard-to-stomach pap like "Back On My Mind Again" and "What A Difference You Made In My Life."

Anne Murray

Canadian singer Anne Murray was a hugely popular country-pop crossover artist during

Me)." On top of that, she met success in the pop market with "You Needed Me" (a 1978 Grammy winner) and with remakes like the 1961 Everly Brothers song "Walk Right Back" and the Monkees' 1967 hit "Daydream Believer." She continued recording in the '90s, but by that point her impressive streak of *Billboard* chart hits had run its course.

◉ **Country** (1974; Capitol). Collecting assorted country singles that Murray released early in her career, this is actually a very cohesive album that shows her and producer Brian Ahern's ability to creat an appealing mix of steel guitars and strings. Her strong voice makes great work out of such crafty, catchy material as "Snowbird," "She Thinks I Still Care," Gordon Lightfoot's "Cotton Jenny," Chip Taylor's "Son Of A Rotten Gambler," John D. Loudermilk's "Break My Mind," and Scott McKenzie's peppy "What About Me."

⊙ **Now And Forever** (1995; EMI Music Canada). This 3-CD collection is packed with enough live tracks, unreleased songs, and alternate takes of familiar works (as well as standard studio cuts) to keep Murray fans happy for ages to come.

Juice Newton

When she first splashed onto the country scene in the early 1980s, Juice Newton was more of a pop rocker than a country singer. There's little twang in her big, full voice, and only a hint in the blustery melodies of songs like "Love's Been A Little Bit Hard On Me" and "Angel Of The Morning"—but then again twang was long out of fashion in 1981, the year that latter song (written by Chip Taylor and a hit for Merrilee Rush in 1968) made Newton a major new player in the country music market.

Though her early material with the group Silver Spur is wonderfully strong and bluesy, Newton's more popular solo albums are unfortunately on the bland and overproduced side of the tracks. To her credit, however, she occasionally chooses decent song material—a reminder of her varied musical background. And while the rough, earthy edges of her voice—traits reminiscent of Bonnie Raitt, an early influence on Newton—have been sharply toned down on her commercial hits, she does belt the songs straight from her gut. Newton wins points for vocal strength and energy, but unfortunately, these

qualities aren't fully exploited or even emphasized enough. Like so many country artists of her generation, her best-known music was marred by slick pop-oriented production and unwieldy flourishes of melodrama.

Born on 18 February, 1952 in New Jersey and raised in Virginia, Judy Kay Newton was first attracted to R&B before the folk revival grabbed her attention while she was attending college in California. She played the coffeehouse circuit, and here met fellow singer-songwriter Otha Young, who became her longtime musical partner (and boyfriend). They first fronted a rock band called Dixie Peach, then, in 1973, formed the country-rock outfit Silver Spur. Newton proved herself capable of handling a wide range of material, and her powerful vocals took center stage on the recordings the group did for RCA and Capitol during the mid-'70s. When they disbanded, Newton continued recording on her own (still often using Young's material), and songs like "It's A Heartache" (also a huge hit for Bonnie Tyler) and "Until Tonight" jumped between the country and pop charts—a trend that would continue for years to come. Newton's career finally hit the big time in 1981, when Richard Landis took over production duties and gave her the smash "Angel Of The Morning" and a hit album, JUICE.

Newton had several substantial hits during the '80s, including "Queen Of Hearts" and "Hurt." Her albums often featured songs by Young as well as assorted '60s R&B and pop material. She won a Grammy, played for President Reagan, and had a hit duet with Eddie Rabbitt ("Both To Each Other"). As the '80s wound down, so did her chart success, and her last studio album was 1989's AIN'T GONNA CRY.

◉ **After The Dust Settles** (1976; RCA). The loose country-rock on Newton's Silver Spur albums allows her the room she needs for her powerful, earthy voice to really shine. The material here could use a stronger focus, but Newton proves herself the star attraction, ripping through an amalgamation of folk, rock, country, and blues with abandon.

⊙ **Anthology** (1997; Renaissance). "Angel Of The Morning" is a decent song, and Newton's 1981 hit version of it is certainly among the best of her solo recordings. In too many cases, however, the songs are overproduced, and Newton's voice sounds toned down and caged—chomping at the bit for a chance to gallop. This is a substantial career overview that includes all her major hits.

Juice Newton

Olivia Newton-John

At a time when many of Nashville's old guard were already grumbling that pop trends were invading their territory—and stealing valuable radio space from "real" country singers—blond-haired, bright-eyed vocalist Olivia Newton-John popped her pretty voice onto the country charts. And if that wasn't enough, in 1974 her success was widespread enough to earn her one of Nashville's most coveted awards—the Country Music Association's Female Vocalist of the Year award. If she'd only known the controversy her popularity would stir up in the country music community—the reaction included strong defensive words from the newly formed Association of Country Entertainers (ACE)—she (and her management) just might have steered clear.

The controversy, however, wasn't really Newton-John's fault. Crossover trends were proving lucrative during the '70s, and her country chart success was simply the product of a scheme to expand her sales market by promoting her music to both pop and country audiences. When she began getting Top 10 country singles, and then when she won that CMA award, it was obvious the plan had worked. Too bad, though, that Newton-John didn't consider herself a country singer (and said so publicly, which didn't help matters) and also made a massive *faux pas* when she announced she'd love to meet Hank Williams someday (not knowing he'd been dead for two decades).

The irony is that many Nashville singers who were initially outspoken about the pop trends she represented would later plow the same fields looking for larger markets. A decade after Newton-John's heyday, for instance, onetime ACE vice-president Barbara Mandrell would take country glamour over the top with her glitzy Las Vegas stage extravaganza. As Mary A. Bufwack and Robert K. Oermann note in *Finding Her Voice: The Illustrated History Of Women In Country Music*, the truth in many ways was that Mandrell and other glam-oriented singers (Crystal Gayle, Lynn Anderson) were country insiders, and Newton-John was an outsider.

Born in Cambridge, England in 1948 and raised in Australia, Newton-

John first recorded folk songs—one of her earliest singles was a traditional number, "Banks Of The Ohio," and her first UK hit (in 1971) was a Dylan song, "If Not For You." Soon, however, she turned to pop music, and a few years later she was known all over the world for peppy numbers like "Let Me Be There" (her first major hit on the pop and country charts in 1973) and sugar-saturated ballads such as "I Honestly Love You" and "Have You Never Been Mellow." After the CMA fiasco, she nodded a bit more toward country with "Please Mr Please," "Every Face Tells A Story," and "Let It Shine" (the latter written by Linda Hargrove)—and even recorded in Nashville for the first time—but in reality she simply wasn't built to sing country. She hit the country charts a few more times during the '70s, but by the turn of the decade she was back to belting disco-inflected pop songs like "Physical" (her biggest hit to date), as well as concentrating on film roles, including *Grease* and *Xanadu*.

⊙ **48 Original Tracks, 1971–1975** (1994; EMI). This British-issue double-disc collection the folk-tinged recordings Olivia made for Festival Recordings International. Titles include "Banks Of The Ohio," "If Not For You," "Angel Of The Morning" (recorded nearly a decade before Juice Newton's hit version), "The Air That I Breathe," and "Have You Never Been Mellow."

Olivia Newton-John

Oak Ridge Boys

The Oak Ridge Boys have a long history that stretches back into the 1940s and includes more than a few membership changes. However, the incarnation of the group that tore up the country charts in the '80s with pop-country hits like "Y'All Come Back Saloon" and "Elvira" is far different stylistically from the original, which focused exclusively on gospel material. Founded in 1945 as the Oak Ridge Quartet, the group was initially led by vocalist, gospel promoter, and *Opry* star Wally Fowler. The Quartet had grown out of Fowler's country outfit, the Georgia Clodhoppers, but quickly overtook that group in popularity. Smitty Gatlin took over in 1956 and led the Quartet for many years after that. By this point, the Quartet was an entirely new group, and in the early '60s the named changed to the Oak Ridge Boys—though the musical focus was still on sacred material.

Alabama native William Lee Golden joined the Oak Ridge Boys in 1965, and it's after he joined—together with Duane Allen a year later—that the group began its transition from gospel to mainstream country. The Oak Ridge Boys recorded for various labels during the '60s and '70s, inching their way into secular music territory with commercially oriented songs, flashy stage shows, and increasingly long hair, which discouraged many of their old-time fans. During their Columbia tenure in the mid-'70s they recorded songs like "The Baptism Of Jesse Taylor," "Why Me," and "Loves Me Like A Rock." At this point the band membership was based around Golden, Allen, Richard Sterban, and Joe Bonsall, and it was this particular quartet that became massive country-pop hitmakers from the late '70s through to the early '90s.

Signing with ABC/Dot, the Oak Ridge Boys had their first big success when their single "Y'All Come Back Saloon" shot to #3 in the country charts in 1977. Despite the 'saloon' reference, the subject matter was extremely tame. They hit #1 a year later with the sappy "I'll Be True To You," after which they began pouring out a steady stream of big chart hits (most released on MCA, which absorbed ABC in 1979). The biggest titles from their first few years at MCA included "Sail Away," "Leaving Louisiana In The Broad Daylight" (a Rodney Crowell tune that Emmylou Harris had also covered), and "Trying To Love Two Women," but the mightiest of all was 1981's "Elvira." That song had been written and recorded fifteen years earlier by onetime Bakersfield resident Dallas Frazier; already rather dopey, the Oak Ridge Boys turned it into a household melody that as many listeners despised as adored.

The Oak Ridge Boys stayed at or near the top of the country charts through the '80s with the help of songs like "Bobbie Sue," "American Made," "Touch A Hand, Make A Friend," and "It Takes A Little Rain (To Make Love Grow)." Golden left in 1987, and his replacement was Steve Sanders, a former gospel music star. The band continued to chart through the early '90s, around which time they switched to RCA. By the mid-'90s they were on Capitol, and in 1996 Sanders resigned from the group and Golden returned. Their heyday as million-selling hitmakers is over, but the Oak Ridge legacy continues via their hits collections and ongoing live performances.

⊙ **Greatest Hits** (1980; MCA). The Oak Ridge Boys' hitmaking heyday has been split into three individual hits collections, each sporting a meager 10 titles (although the price for each remains relatively low). On this first volume you'll find "Y'All Come Back Saloon," "Leaving Louisiana," "I'll Be True To You," and "Trying To Love Two Women." VOLUME 2 is home to "Elvira" and "American Made"; the third installation captures "Bobbie Sue," "Touch A Hand," "Gonna Take A Lot Of River," and "Take Pride In America."

Mary Kay Place

Best known for her role in the well-loved 1970s TV sitcom *Mary Hartman, Mary Hartman*, in which she played wannabe-country-queen Loretta Haggers (and won an Emmy for the part), Mary Kay Place turned out to be a decent country singer herself—in real life and under her own name. Place's music may have been on the lighter side of honky tonk, but her voice was relaxed and pleasant, and her spirit was nothing short of genuine—refreshing qualities during a decade when Marie Osmond and Debby Boone were lighting up the charts.

A native of Tulsa, Oklahoma, Place moved to Los Angeles to work in the entertainment world. She wrote scripts for shows like *M*A*S*H* and *The Mary Tyler Moore Show*, and landed some acting roles, but her biggest break came through Norman Lear, for whom she'd worked as a secretary. He initially gave her a spot on *All In The Family* singing her song "If Communism Comes Knocking On Your Door, Don't Answer It," and this led to her role on *Mary Hartman*.

As Haggers, Place sang self-penned novelty numbers like "Vitamin L" and "Baby Boy," and it's songs like these that ended up on her first album, TONIGHT! AT THE CAPRI LOUNGE: LORETTA HAGGERS, released in 1976. The songs may have been cute and funny, but where Haggers was a hack, Place was serious. Produced by Brian Ahern (Emmylou Harris' longtime producer and second husband) and featuring Harris and her Hot Band, Dolly Parton, and Anne Murray, among other guests, Place's album won the praise of critics and fans, and it was even nominated for a Grammy.

For her second outing, Place broke free of the Haggers role. "The one thing I was determined not to do," she told *New York Times* reporter John Rockwell in 1976, "was make a silly record, a write-off you'd play only one time." The country on AIMIN' TO PLEASE was much more straight and serious than on her debut. Once again it featured the work of Ahern and Harris' Hot Band along with guests Nicolette Larson, Leon Russell, and Willie Nelson. Place's duet with Nelson on the Bobby Braddock song "Something To Brag About" even made the charts.

Place made a total of three records before the film and television world eventually sucked her back in. She'd already appeared in the films *Bound For Glory* and *New York New York*, and during the '80s she landed a substantial role in *The Big Chill*, among others. By the '90s she'd also directed episodes of TV shows like *Friends* and appeared in the mini-series *Tales Of The City* and the excellent but short-lived teen drama *My So-Called Life*. Her music career may be largely forgotten these days, but for the curious, her albums are still out there.

○ **Tonite! At the Capri Lounge: Loretta Haggers** (1976; Columbia). Two Haggers favorites from *Mary Hartman*, "Vitamin L" and "Baby Boy," highlight Place's debut, but this isn't a comedy album. Place also sings "Settin' The Woods On Fire," the Louvin Brothers' "Get Acquainted Waltz," and Dolly Parton's good-time song "All I Can Do" with the enthusiasm of someone who knows her country.

Jeanne Pruett

"I could probably sing 'Stardust,' but it ain't nearly as pretty to me as 'Wild Side Of Life.'"

—Jeanne Pruett

"**S**atin Sheets" was Jeanne Pruett's career hit, a 1973 #1 that was far more country-sounding than most songs coming out of Nashville at the time. It was her biggest hit by a long shot, but not her only one—she made a respectable chart showing several more times during the '70s with songs like "I'm Your Woman," "You Don't Need To Move A Mountain," and (in 1980) "Temporarily Yours." Her twangy voice had a pleading (and sometimes piercing) tone, and her attitude was nurturing in titles like "Hold On To My Unchanging Love" and "A Poor Man's Woman," but she also evoked the wisdom of someone who knew what she wanted—her declarations of love, fidelity, and longing came from a place of strength.

Jeanne was born Norma Jean Bowman on 30 January, 1937 near Pell City, Alabama. She and her husband, Jack Pruett, moved to Nashville in 1956, and he landed a job playing guitar with Marty Robbins. She first recorded for RCA in 1963, worked as a songwriter for Robbins' publishing company, then in 1969 she signed with Decca (which became MCA shortly thereafter). Pruett made small waves with her 1971 single "Hold On To My Unchanging Love," broke the Top 40 soon after with "Love Me" (a self-penned song that Robbins also covered), then finally topped the charts in 1973 with "Satin Sheets." The song's southern-rooted twang wasn't an anomaly, as Pruett cut further deep-country songs such as "A Poor Man's Woman" and especially the cheating song "Honey On His Hands." As for hits, she made the country Top 10 a few more times, but during the early '80s (by which time she'd left Decca for the indie label IBC) her chart success was fading. By that point, however, she was a regular on the *Grand Ole Opry*, and she later began hosting a cooking show on TNN as well as publishing a series of cookbooks under the title *Feedin' Friends*.

⊙ **Greatest Hits** (1998; Varese Sarabande). A 16-song overview of Pruett's career (minus the early RCA singles). All her Decca/MCA hits are included, along with her debut Decca single, "Hold On To My Unchanging Love," and her 1975 recording of "Honey On His Hands," a minor hit but one of her strongest recordings. The 3 IBC hits here demonstrate that, even in the early '80s, she still retained her hard-country sound—pop trends never quite had their way with Jeanne. Two 1983 duets with Marty Robbins close out the collection.

Eddie Rabbitt

New Jersey native Eddie Rabbitt was a successful songwriter ("Kentucky Rain" for Elvis Presley, "Pure Love" for Ronnie Milsap) and, later, a hit artist himself, breaking into the country Top 10 repeatedly during the 1970s and '80s with such songs as "Drinkin' My Baby (Off My Mind)," "Every Which Way But Loose" (the title track to the 1978 Clint Eastwood movie), and the smash "I Love A Rainy Night." His style was smooth and tailored enough to give him pop appeal, but at the same time he wasn't—at least all the time—a glitzy show off. Early songs like "Drinkin' My Baby," "Rocky Mountain Music," and "Two Dollars In The Jukebox" showed he had a country soul, but at the same time they were cool and easy-going with a gentle beat and pleasant, contemporary vibe.

Edward Thomas Rabbitt was born on 27 November, 1941 in Brooklyn, New York and raised in East Orange, New Jersey. During the '60s he cut singles for 20th Century and Columbia, and he moved to Nashville in 1968, where he had some success as a songwriter. George Morgan and Roy Drusky cut his songs, and then in 1970 Elvis Presley turned "Kentucky Rain" into gold. Rabbitt signed to Elektra in 1974, and he first made #1 in the *Billboard* country charts two years later with "Drinkin' My Baby (Off My Mind)." The self-penned song showed that Rabbitt had the ability to forge the proper balance between country and pop—never veering too far in either direction, at least when he was being careful. This made him quite an appealing figure in Nashville at the time, and his hits came hard and steady for the next fifteen years. Some songs like "I Just Want To

Love You" dipped shamelessly into schlocky arrangements, but "I Love A Rainy Night"—which topped both the country and pop charts in 1980—was a bouncy and slightly chunky country-rock ditty.

Rabbitt shifted to Warner Brothers in 1983 and then RCA two years later, but despite the changes, the hits just kept on coming: "You And I" (a duet with Crystal Gayle), "The Best Year Of My Life," "B-B-B-Burnin' Up With Love," and a remake of Dion's "The Wanderer." He last made the Top 40 in 1990 with "American Boy," recorded for Capitol. Like many stars of his country-pop era, Rabbitt's popularity faded after the arrival of hat acts like Garth Brooks and Clint Black, though he continued to record and tour. He died of cancer in 1998.

⊙ **All Time Greatest Hits** (1991; Warner Bros.). Rabbitt is yet another victim of third-rate CD compilations, though this 10-song disc does compile a few of his tastier cuts such as "Rocky Mountain Music" and "Two Dollars In The Jukebox." "I Love A Rainy Night" is, yes, included, in case you were wondering, though "Every Which Way But Loose" is strangely absent.

Kenny Rogers

Thanks to his penchant for glitzy, Las Vegas-style productions and schmaltzy, adult-contemporary songs, Kenny Rogers grew to symbolize some of the most troubling, pop-infatuated directions country music was taking during the late 1970s and early '80s. Along with Barbara Mandrell, Rogers led the pack of Nashville singers who set their musical sights on crossover success in the pop music market—and made the most of the celebrity status that came with it.

On the other hand, when the silver-haired singer did get his hands on decent material (by such writers as Don Schlitz, Alex Harvey, or Mickey Newbury)—and when he kept his arrangements casual—he was a moderately appealing countrypolitan stylist. His middle-of-the-road voice was more gruff than pretty, and his range was limited, yet he possessed a soothing tone that wrapped itself around the edges of his lyrics with paternal warmth. Decorating his words with a gentle, endearing growl (a stylistic trick reminiscent of Conway Twitty, who in many ways is Rogers' role model) was just icing on the cake.

Rogers, however, was first and foremost a businessman—one of the most (financially) successful singers to ever pass through Nashville. And his business acumen didn't just play out in the form of his chain of chicken restaurants, Kenny Rogers' Roasters (another reference to Twitty, who founded a chain of drive-in restaurants), it also helped guide the various directions this musical chameleon would take over the years. During a career that dates back to the late '50s, Rogers has—as a solo artist and with an assortment of bands—dipped his toes into rockabilly, jazz, revivalist folk, psychedelic rock, country, pop, and easy-listening balladry, adapting his voice and persona to match the style of the moment. It makes sense, then, that his career path would lead not only to crooning MOR schmaltz from the stages of Nevada casinos, but also to a collaboration with '70s-pop icons the Bee Gees.

Though he accumulated huge wealth during his prime, Rogers was born (in 1938) and raised in a poor section of Houston. As a high school senior he played in a rockabilly band, the Scholars, who released a few singles. He later appeared on *American Bandstand*. By 1959, however, he was playing jazz with the Bobby Doyle Three, who released one album. Rogers then jumped to the Kirby Stone Four, but didn't last long with them, either. He landed a solo contract with Mercury, but the label only released a few dud singles before dropping him. In 1966 he joined the folk revivalist singing group New Christy Minstrels. A year later he and fellow Minstrels Mike Settle, Terry Williams, and Thelma Lou Camacho (along with drummer Mickey Jones) formed the pop-rock

group the First Edition, who won a contract with Reprise in 1967.

The First Edition's early material showed a mix of influences, from wacky psychedelic folk to bouncy pop and Beatles-influenced rock. Their first single was the Mickey Newbury song "Just Dropped In (To See What Condition My Condition Was In)"; rife with kooky non-sequiturs, it matched the spirit of the times and gave the First Edition a pop hit. Even though rhythm guitarist Settle wrote most of the group's original material, and the members all shared singing duties (especially on earlier albums), Rogers—who's described as "ruled by his head, not his heart" on the back of the band's second album, as well as "a good money manager"—eventually emerged in the leadership position. By the end of the decade the group was billed as Kenny Rogers and the First Edition, with Rogers soon sharing production duties alongside Jimmy Bowen (a pop producer who would become one of the most powerful figures in Nashville during the '80s).

The First Edition enjoyed a few more hits, including "Ruby, Don't Take Your Love To Town" (a Mel Tillis song that foreshadowed Rogers' country leanings) and Mac Davis' "Something's Burning." Writer Alex Harvey contributed a significant portion of the band's later material, such as "Tell It All Brother" and "Ruben James." The latter was only a minor hit for the First Edition, but a few years down the road this pleasant, catchy number became one of the strongest (and most enduring) in Rogers' repertoire. The group left Reprise in 1973 for Kenny's new Jolly Rogers label, but soon broke up, leaving Rogers out of business and in debt. But the suave singer quickly recovered, signing as a solo act with United Artists and, with the help of producer Larry Butler, fashioning himself into a well-groomed pop-country performer—one tailor-made for contemporary radio.

Rogers' crossover success came like a flood. It started with "Lucille," which hit #1 on the country charts in 1977 and the Top 5 on the pop charts. The song boasted modest arrangements and a true country flavor, but its seemingly casual melody, coupled with Rogers' seemingly casual vocals, were at the same time thoroughly calculated to win the hearts of a wide range of listeners. The mainstream appeal Rogers enjoyed with this song and others with a similar soft-country feel—"Daytime Friends," "Coward Of The County," and especially the Don Schlitz song "The Gambler"—sealed Rogers' superstar status and in the process virtually defined the focus the country music industry would adopt over the next several years. There was obviously far more money to be made in pop music than crossover-seeking producers like Chet Atkins or even Billy Sherrill had previously realized.

By the end of the decade, Rogers was setting his sights almost entirely on the pop market. He had revived '60s singer Dottie West's career in 1978 with a series of hit duets, including "Every Time Two Fools Collide" (his association with her would last several years), and in 1980 he paired up with Kim Carnes for "Don't Fall In Love With A Dreamer." He had proved his might as a bombastic balladeer on "You Decorated My Life" in '79, and the following year he boosted the pop quotient further with the Lionel Richie song "Lady." By 1983 he was dueting with Sheena Easton on Bob Seger's "We've Got Tonight" and working with the Bee Gees on EYES THAT SEE IN THE DARK, his first album for new label RCA. Produced by Barry Gibb, it gave him one of the biggest songs of his career, "Islands In The Stream"—a duet with another crossover artist (albeit one with deep and entirely authentic country roots), Dolly Parton. Rogers went on to perform and record frequently with Parton, including a popular Christmas album. Continuing his star associations, his 1985 album THE HEART OF THE MATTER was helmed by Beatles' producer George Martin.

By the mid-'80s, however, with the new traditionalist era of Randy Travis, Ricky Skaggs, and George Strait bringing harder country sounds back onto the radio, Rogers' chart success began to dwindle. At that point it didn't really matter, however; his financial investments were sound, and his popularity was sealed as one of the public's favorite singers of all time. His acting career was also alive and well (never mind that his biggest screen fame has been on a TV mini-series based on "The Gambler," which has seen far too many sequels). By the '90s he was still recording, performing and doing charity work. He also published his autobiography, *Making It With Music*, in 1993, and hosted the cable TV program *The Real West*.

⊙ **Ten Years Of Gold** (1977; United Artists). This collection was hugely popular when first released, helping define Rogers as a major hitmaker. It's pre-"Gambler," but it does contain such career-defining numbers as "Lucille," "Ruby, Don't Take Your Love To Town," "Reuben James," and "Daytime Friends," most of which retain a warm, nostalgic appeal similar to that of old Dean Martin records.

⊙ **The Gambler** (1978; United Artists). Here's the album (and the song) that first comes to mind when you think of Rogers. Don Schlitz wrote the title track (he went on to pen hits for Randy Travis and the Judds, among many others), but several others are by Alex Harvey, a frequent First Edition composer. Rogers' version of "San Francisco Mabel Joy" holds nothing to songwriter Mickey Newbury's own (Newbury is a far more skilled and soulful vocalist), but it's interesting.

⊙ **Kenny Rogers And The First Edition: Greatest Hits** (1996; Hip-O/MCA). Early First Edition albums feature original material written by Mike Settle that mixes psychedelic folk and bouncy 1960s pop-rock; the songs are borderline kooky, though they never stray far from the accepted musical boundaries of the era. This overview CD collects 16 of the First Edition's best-known cuts, including "Something's Burning," "Ruby," "Ruben James," and the trippy "Just Dropped In."

T.G. Sheppard

With a repertoire divided almost evenly between country-tinged rock songs and schlocky pop love ballads, T.G. Sheppard was a singer ripe and ready for the *Urban Cowboy* era. He wasn't on the movie soundtrack when it smashed its way onto the album charts in 1980, but he did win himself a streak of hits from the mid-'70s through to the early '80s that fit neatly alongside that flash-in-the-pan format. Sheppard's music wasn't too distinct (he was neither a hardcore honky-tonker like Gary Stewart nor a glitzy balladeer like Kenny Rogers), but his voice had a fairly sturdy foundation. And his better songs like "Last Cheater's Waltz" and "Do You Wanna Go To Heaven" do have a decent rhythmic undercurrent and an easygoing appeal despite the unnecessary strings and choruses (Nashville Sound leftovers) present in the arrangements.

Sheppard (his stage name supposedly came about after someone suggested he call himself the German Shepherd) was born William Browder in Humbolt, Tennessee; his uncle was *Grand Ole Opry* comedian Rod Brasfield. He toyed with recording and record promotion work in the '60s and early '70s before cutting the song "Devil In A Bottle" (by Bobby David). After many failed attempts, he finally licensed it to Motown, which was trying to break into the country market with its new label Melodyland (later renamed Hitsville). Released in 1974, the song made it to #1 and even briefly crossed over to the pop charts. Sheppard stayed with the label until 1977, then switched to Warner/Curb, and the hits started flying: "You Feel Good All Over," a re-make of the Turtles' "Happy Together," "Last Cheater's Waltz," "War Is Hell," "Slow Burn," a particularly unbearable version of the Harry Nilsson hit "Without You," and many more. In 1984 he sang a duet with Clint Eastwood, "Make My Day," for the *Sudden Impact* soundtrack, as well as a duet with Judy Collins, "Home Again." The following year he signed with Columbia, and while he had a few more hits, singers like George Strait and Randy Travis were bringing traditionalism back into fashion, making Sheppard's brand of country-pop less market-friendly. He has, however, continued to tour regularly with his band, Slow Burn. He also has his own theater in Pigeon Forge, Tennessee.

⊙ **The Best Of T.G. Sheppard** (1992; Curb). A decent representation of Sheppard's original recordings from the late 1970s and early '80s, including numbers like "War Is Hell," "Do You Want To Go To Heaven," and "Last Cheater's Waltz" as well as "Make My Day."

Margo Smith

Ohio kindergarten teacher Margo Smith was already a successful singer by the time she emerged in the late 1970s with a sexy new image and heated up kitchen radios across the country with thirtysomething love songs like "Still A Woman" and "Make Love The Way We Used To." These and other hits dealt frankly with sex, specifically between middle-aged couples who'd been together for years (Margo herself had long been married to banker Ken Smith and didn't even begin singing professionally until she was in her mid-thirties). Few singers spoke so unabashedly of attempting to reinvigorate love's fading fires, especially from a woman's perspective. In addition to her lyrical boldness, this country everywoman-turned-spokesperson for passion even began posing seductively on her album covers: 1979's A WOMAN showed her in a pink satin nightgown revealing some serious cleavage, and on 1980's DIAMONDS AND CHILLS she wore another revealing outfit with a plunging neckline. Ironically, only a few years later Smith had reverted to an entirely wholesome image, and was safe and snug once again as a sweet smalltown Christian gal.

Margo Smith was born Betty Lou Miller in Dayton, Ohio in 1942. She'd been singing since childhood, and when she took up teaching she often wrote songs to use in her lessons. In 1975 she was signed to 20th Century Records and her song "There I Said It" made the charts. The label shut down its Nashville division, however, and in 1976 Smith switched to Warner Brothers. Working with producer Norro Wilson, she had some sizeable hits over the next couple of years, including "Save Your Kisses For Me," "Love's Explosion," and two songs that hit #1 on the country charts: "Don't Break The Heart That Loves You" (a song written by Benny Davis and Ted Murray that Connie Francis had had a hit with in 1962) and "It Only Hurts For A Little While" (a song previously covered by the Ames Brothers).

In 1979 Smith's single "Still A Woman" made the Top 10 and boldly asserted her sexy new persona. She spoke openly of sex in interviews, her stage show was increasingly flashy (with spandex and satin outfits galore), and her fan club grew larger. She also left her husband and in 1982 married Richard Cammeron (who became her manager and founded Cammeron Records, for which Margo later recorded). Soon after, however, she dropped her glam-queen image and turned homespun once again—even going so far as to call her sexy image a "mistake." In the mid-'80s she released THE BEST OF THE TENNESSEE YODELER, which paid tribute to one of her favorite singers from childhood, Bonnie Lou. Later she began singing gospel with her daughter, Holly. More recently, Smith contributed vocals to THE LITTLEST STAR: A MUSICAL STORY, a children's

CD released in 1999 that is designed as a companion to a yet-to-come picture book.

● Don't Break The Heart That Loves You (1978; Warner Bros.). This album contains Smith's two #1 hits, the title track and "It Only Hurts For A Little While." The production as a whole is heavy on the strings, and too many songs sink in sappiness, but "Ode To A Cheater" is one clear standout.

● A Woman (1979; Warner Bros.). For this album and a few others that followed, Margo transformed herself into a middle-aged sexpot. Though largely forgotten nowadays, the song "Still A Woman" (co-written by Smith, producer Norro Wilson and Mac David) was a decent hit for her, thanks in part to the frankness of its subject matter.

Billie Jo Spears

Though Billie Jo Spears had her biggest hits during the 1970s, she was far more earthy and grounded than most singers passing for 'country' during the decade. Songs like "Never Did Like Whiskey" had little in common with "Happiest Girl In The Whole USA" or syrup-sodden "You Light Up My Life," yet at the same time Spears wasn't exactly an Outlaw—there was too much of an old-school quality about her deep country style. Her voice was husky, strong and confident—sort of a combination of Loretta Lynn twang and the swampy soul of Bobbie Gentry.

Spears was born on 14 January, 1937 in Beaumont, Texas. She cut her first single while still a teenager, the cutesy novelty song "Too Old For Toys, Too Young For Boys," and it was released by the indie label Abbott (the onetime home of both Johnny Horton and Jim Reeves) under the name Billie Jean Moore. She also performed on the *Louisiana Hayride*. Taking encouragement from producer/songwriter Jack Rhodes (who'd written "Too Old For Toys"), Spears moved to Nashville in the early '60s. She signed briefly with United Artists before moving to Capitol, where she stayed through the early '70s. Her 1969 single "Mr Walker, It's All Over" reached #4 in the *Billboard* country charts. Sassy and full of spark, the song told of a secretary who was fed up with discrimination on the job and not afraid to say so. For Capitol, Spears also cut straight-up versions of such popular hits as "Ode To Billie Joe," "Harper Valley P.T.A.," and "Games People

Play," and she dabbled in novelty songs like "Get Behind Me Satan And Push," which played up her vocal similarities to Loretta Lynn. More interesting were "Home-Loving Man" (one of several Rhodes compositions on her debut album, THE VOICE OF BILLIE JO SPEARS) and the dark and tortured "Stepchild," written by Dallas Frazier.

Spears had her biggest success on the country charts after she returned to United Artists in the mid-'70s. "Blanket On The Ground" hit #1 in 1975, and it was followed by a hefty string of hits over the next six years, including the rocking come-on song "What I've Got In Mind," the melancholy "Misty Blue," and the bold and carefree "Never Did Like Whiskey." She'd had some difficulties with her vocal chords a few years earlier, but her singing actually sounded more distinct and confident than it had during her Capitol years. In 1976, the ACM (Academy of Country Music) named her the year's Most Promising Female Vocalist. Spears maintained a presence on the country charts through the mid-'80s, and to her credit—at least on her best material—she steered (mostly) clear of the pop trends of the day, the arrangements allowing her full-bodied, rural voice plenty of space. Since her heyday, however, she's been a bigger star in England than she has on her home turf.

⊙ The Best Of Billie Jo Spears (1994; Razor & Tie). The top singles of Spears' late-1970s tenure on United Artists make up the majority of the songs here. "Blanket On The Ground," "Silver Wings And Golden Rings," "Never Did Like Whiskey," and several others soar with fire and spirit yet never lose touch with the rich, rural qualities of Spears' voice.

Sylvia

By the early 1980s, glitzy disco-inspired pop music had made dangerous inroads into the Nashville establishment. Thankfully, this trend wouldn't last, but for a few years glam queens like Crystal Gayle, Barbara Mandrell, and a newly redecorated Dolly Parton had a firm grip on the country charts; not far behind was Sylvia, a fresh-faced young woman from Kokomo, Indiana who had a pop sensibility, youthful good looks, and loads of ambition.

Sylvia (last name Kirby, though she never used it professionally) came to Nashville determined to break into the industry. She started as a secretary at a publishing company (working for her soon-to-be producer Tom Collins) and soon became a demo singer as well as a back-up vocalist for the likes of Mandrell and Janie Fricke. She auditioned for a spot in the glam-country group Dave & Sugar but didn't get the part; the audition did, however, bring her to the attention of RCA, and she was eventually signed. Early songs included "You Don't Miss A Thing" and "Tumbleweed" (a strange blend of disco and western), but it was 1981's "Drifter" that finally hit #1. The even-more-pop-encrusted "Nobody" from her 1982 album JUST SYLVIA crossed over to the pop charts and became the biggest song of her career. In many ways, Sylvia's youthful vigor and bouncy, chirpy style—which had large appeal among young girls—fore-shadowed the late-'80s success of adolescent pop singers like Debbie Gibson and Tiffany.

A picture-perfect long-haired beauty, Sylvia was also ready-made for the video age, which was just coming into fashion, and her songs "Snapshot" and "The Matador" were among the first country music videos. Sylvia's chart success began to peter out by the mid-'80s, and she finally quit touring due to stress. A few years later she was guest hosting TNN's *Crook And Chase* show as well as her own *Holiday Gourmet* cooking special.

⊙ **Anthology** (1997; Renaissance). Sylvia's Top 40 hits from the 1980s are collected on this 24-track CD, which also includes 4 songs from a never-released album titled KNOCKIN' AROUND. Among the album's tracks is a cover of the Association's "Never My Love."

Tanya Tucker

Tanya Tucker

"I have a whole audience that really doesn't know my music. They know me as a celebrity, a tabloid queen."

—Tanya Tucker

When it comes to teenybopper country stars, LeAnn Rimes has nothing on 1970s starlet Tanya Tucker, who also made her major label recording debut at the age of thirteen. Rimes wowed fans with her Patsy Cline-styled voice, but Tucker's husky Texas twang was sassy, sexy, and full of youthful fire. Her producer at Columbia, Billy Sherrill (whose other charges included George Jones, Tammy Wynette, and Barbara Mandrell), wasn't afraid to load her up with songs not generally geared towards (or much understood by) kids: "Delta Dawn," "Why Me," "The Man That Turned My Mama On," "Blood Red And Goin' Down," and the David Allan Coe composition "Would You Lay With Me (In A Field Of Stone)." She wasn't even sixteen years old when she belted these and other songs to the top of the country charts in the early '70s, and plenty of folks felt she was being exploited. But young Tanya also had enough wisdom to know what she was singing about—and to know that the combination of her young age and mature material was a tremendous boost to her appeal.

Unlike many a teen star, Tucker's career has endured well beyond her growing-up years—albeit with many ups and downs along the way. She grew famous as much for her love affairs and partying habits as for her music, and her wild-child lifestyle (especially her brief engagement to Glen Campbell) kept the tabloids busy. But at the same time, her fans continued to adore her, and she remained a strong and resilient hitmaker through the '80s and even deep into the '90s. By the turn of the millennium, and still not even forty years old, she was one of the most seasoned female country singers

Tanya Tucker

in Nashville, having lived the majority of her life in the public eye and on the *Billboard* charts.

Tucker was born on 10 October, 1958 in Seminole, Texas, but did much of her growing up out west in Arizona (she lived for several years in Willcox, which was the hometown of cowboy star Rex Allen), Utah, and Nevada. Even as a child she had a powerful voice, and she began performing with visiting country stars. Tanya's father put together a demo tape of her singing that eventually found its way to Nashville and into the hands of Epic/Columbia producer Billy Sherrill. Sherrill signed her in early 1972, when she was only thirteen years old. Her first single was "Delta Dawn," and it charted in the country Top 10 that summer (a year before Helen Reddy's pop version of the song). Though he was the king of the countrypolitan sound and famous for smoothing edges and building 'walls' of string arrangements, Sherrill frequently kept Tucker's music more spacious, choosing to play up the hillbilly twang in her full-bodied and very adult-sounding voice. On top of that, the concept of a teenager singing such grown-up material as "What's Your Mama's Name" (her first #1 in 1973), "Blood Red And Goin' Down" (in which a girl waits in the car while her daddy exacts murderous revenge), and "Would You Lay With Me In A Field Of Stone" (which basically said 'come to bed with me,' although Tanya defended it as a noble and sweet love song) made for quite an intriguing package.

Tucker stayed at Columbia and under Sherrill's guidance until her sixteenth birthday in 1974, when she signed a lucrative contract with MCA. She continued to meet success on the charts with songs like "Lizzie And The Rainman," "San Antonio Stroll," and "It's A Cowboy Lovin' Night." Her 1978 album T.N.T. was widely promoted, and it also pushed her image as a saucy sex symbol (she was featured on the cover in tight black pants with the mike chord snaking between her legs). Unfortunately, most of the music inside—slickly produced attempts at pop-rock crossover—was as cheesy as the cover and did little to push her creative edge. She did, however, manage to win the attention of plenty of male suitors, one of whom was Glen Campbell (who was twice her twenty-two years). After several duet recordings and lots of coverage from the tabloids, their relationship came to a stormy end just short of marriage. Later Tucker claimed Campbell had abused her physically.

Tucker switched to Arista and cut CHANGES in 1982, but her career was hitting a slump at this point. In 1986, however, she was signed to Capitol

and back on the charts with songs like "I'll Come Back As A Woman" and "Strong Enough To Bend." Though her sexy voice and bold style were still the main attractions, the production on songs like "Just Another Love" (#1 in 1986) was more pop-oriented than the classic material she'd cut with Sherrill. The songs did, however, put her right back at the top of the country charts and keep her there for the next nine years. In 1991 she won the CMA's Female Vocalist of the Year award, and that honor arrived the very same night as her second child (who like her first was born out of wedlock— something the always-hungry tabloids latched onto with glee). At that point she was nearly a twenty-year veteran in the country music business—and only in her early thirties. She stayed on the charts through a good part of the '90s and continued to record throughout the decade. Her last studio album of the century was COMPLICATED, released by Capitol in 1997, the same year her autobiography *Nickel Dreams: My Life* hit the bookstores.

⊙ **Greatest Hits** (1975; Columbia). Tucker's early Columbia recordings cut under the guidance of producer Sherrill are still her most appealing. Her voice is fresh and full of tension, and the songs themselves are lusty and strong—"Blood Red And Goin' Down," "Delta Dawn," "The Jamestown Ferry," "The Man That Turned My Mama On." Only 10 tracks, but enough to get you started.

⊙ **Greatest Hits** (1989; Liberty). If you're after more recent Tucker material, this hits collection pulls together 10 of Tucker's big late-1980s hits cut for Capitol and its subsidiary, Liberty, including "Strong Enough To Bend," "Just Another Love," and "It Don't Come Easy." Though most are overproduced, the lead-off track, "Daddy And Home," is a sweet Jimmie Rodgers composition that she handles with gentleness and care.

⊙ **What's Your Mama's Name/Would You Lay With Me (In A Field Of Stone)** (2000; Collectibles). This is more like it, two of Tucker's early-'70s Columbia albums on a single 24-track CD. WHAT'S YOUR MAMA'S NAME (her second album) is the strongest, packed with songs like "Blood Red And Goin' Down," "California Cottonfields," and the Johnny Rodriguez hit "Pass Me By." The production on "Would You Lay With Me" is heavier on the strings, but further songs from this album—"Why Me Lord," "The Baptism of Jesse Taylor," "The Man That Turned My Mama On"—are excellent. "Delta Dawn" and "Love's The Answer" are included as bonus tracks.

12

Wild and Blue: Traditionalism Makes a Comeback

Maybe it was the harmonic convergence, or perhaps it was just plain circumstance, but 1986 turned out to be a knockout year in country music. Never mind that pop-oriented singers like Janie Fricke and Lee Greenwood were still topping the country sales charts: this was the year that 'new traditionalism' came of age in Nashville. **Steve Earle**, **Randy Travis**, **Lyle Lovett**, **Dwight Yoakam**, and the **O'Kanes** were the artists that clinched the deal, thanks to an impressive debut album released by each of them that year. It's true that new albums arrive on the scene all the time, but what made these so significant was how solid they sounded. These were strong, highly individualistic visions from some of the most offbeat country artists to come hollerin' down the Nashville pike in years. Finally, after a decade rife with middle-of-the-road pap, Music Row was showing a willingness to take chances with edgier artists—singers who cut against the grain. Maybe there was hope after all.

Too often, a new artist's debut album is little more than an assortment of songs (and styles) tossed against the wall in order to see which one sticks. Each of these five artists, however, came to the table with their musical approach—what they wanted to play and how—already honed and ready to roll. They weren't basing their songs on contemporary trends, marketing statistics, or potential crossover appeal. They weren't just singers begging for a break. They played music as it came to them from somewhere deep inside, and this is exactly what showed.

It's also significant that none of them sounded alike. Earle's rock-influenced twang on GUITAR TOWN was the closest thing to hard-bitten Outlaw country that most folks had heard in a decade. On his self-titled debut, Lyle Lovett added a lively Texas swing to his laid-back, front-porch folksongs. The O'Kanes filled their eponymous debut with catchy songs that were deliberately spare and simple. By the time of Dwight Yoakam's debut, GUITARS, CADILLACS, ETC. ETC., he'd rejected Nashville for the West Coast and was steeped in the Bakersfield honky-tonk tradition of his hero Buck Owens. And when **Randy Travis**, who would soon become one of the most popular singers of the decade, came bursting into the spotlight with STORMS OF LIFE, he did so with a rich, pure voice that conjured the country music of decades past—and brought him endless comparisons to George Jones and especially Merle Haggard, two of his heroes.

What bound each of these artists together was their unabashed embrace (to varying degrees) of traditional country music styles and influences—in the voices, the instrumentation, the arrangements—the sort of feet-on-the-ground, ear-to-the-past elements that had been fading from mainstream country music ever since the advent of the Nashville Sound. Once they were tagged with the 'new traditionalist' moniker, it was a sign the industry recognized its newest trend. As a result, by the start of the following decade clean-cut, cowboy-hatted singers would be pouring from radio and video programs by the truckload and some guy named Garth Brooks would be proclaimed as the industry's new messiah.

Setting the Stage

This mid-'80s traditionalist turn, however, didn't just happen out of the blue. The story actually begins several years earlier courtesy of three entirely different artists: **George Strait**, **John Anderson**, and **Ricky Skaggs**. Strait, a Texas cowboy-turned-country singer with a refreshing no-frills style, hit the airwaves in 1981 with the pure-bred honky tonker "Unwound." Over the next few years he shifted from Haggard-esque ballads like "Fool Hearted Memory" to a stronger western swing influence (even titling his third album RIGHT OR WRONG, after the Bob Wills standard). Anderson made an initial splash with his version of the Billy Joe Shaver song "I'm Just An Old Chunk Of Coal (But I'm Gonna Be A Diamond Someday)"—bridging the gap between '70s Outlaws and '80s new traditionalists—before hitting the big time two years later with the hugely popular "Swingin'." And Skaggs, who sported some of the most impressive credentials of any Nashville newcomer in ages (he'd spent the '70s playing with Ralph Stanley, the Country Gentlemen, and Emmylou Harris, among others), began his decade-long string of hits with "Don't Get Above Your Raising," an old Flatt & Scruggs tune that he adroitly updated.

When Strait, Skaggs, and Anderson (and **Rosanne Cash**, whose "Seven Year Ache" was nothing to sneeze at) first appeared on the radar, the urban cowboy trend (the movie, the clothes, the dance steps) was in full swing. The popular *Urban Cowboy* soundtrack became the apex of a decades-long trend away from a traditional country (fiddles, steel guitars, twangy voices) in favor of contemporary pop elements (streamlined vocals, flashy productions, lush arrangements). By jumping into the pop market, country record sales and radio listenership grew dramatically. The downside,

however, was declining support for anything that sounded old and in the way.

Major national trends rarely last long, and so it was for urban cowboy. Not long after loading up on boots, jeans, and Johnny Lee albums, fans grew bored with the redundancy. This is where Strait, Anderson, and Skaggs entered the picture. And when songs like Strait's "Unwound" and Anderson's "Swingin'" turned into hits, the labels moved. Columbia picked up **Rodney Crowell**, the O'Kanes, and **Ricky Van Shelton**; Warner Brothers signed Randy Travis; RCA took on the **Judds** and **Keith Whitley**; and MCA nabbed Earle, Lovett, **Reba McEntire**, and Texas folkie **Nanci Griffith**. (Interestingly, MCA at the same time dropped country-rocker **Joe Ely**—only to snatch him back a few years later when they realized his appeal hadn't disappeared). Perhaps it was the warbling voice of Austin favorite **Jimmie Dale Gilmore** (a friend and former bandmate of Ely's) that kept him from being signed as well; instead Gilmore wound up on the West Coast indie label HighTone (temporary home to Ely), which in the long run was probably best for his musical development.

Yoakam entered through a side door: signed to Reprise in Los Angeles, he made his way onto the country charts in 1986 with the old Johnny Horton hit "Honky-Tonk Man"; since then he's become one of contemporary country's most popular 'outsider' (non-Nashville) artists, and one of its most vital. Reprise also signed **Rosie Flores**, another LA-based singer whose self-titled debut (produced by Yoakam cohort Pete Anderson) won her a Best New Female Vocalist nomination from the Academy of Country Music. Sire (home at the time to the Smiths and Talking Heads) signed Canadian singer **k.d. lang**. It took a while for Nashville to warm to this talented lesbian/vegetarian activist, but her reverence for Patsy Cline eventually (if only briefly) won them over.

Obviously, the time was right for these artists, and the proof is that their songs did make the charts. One who was honestly amazed at his success was Kieran Kane, whose band the O'Kanes hit #1 in 1987 with "Can't Stop My Heart From Loving You." "I'm very proud of the work," he said, "but the fact that [our records] were accepted commercially is phenomenal." He explains it by way of the waning urban cowboy trend: "Record companies' sales started falling off, and they needed something else to satisfy the public ear, and so the door opened up." Even Warner Brothers' signing of Randy Travis was, says Kane, "at the time a fairly radical move to make. His first single barely charted, but he went on to become a huge success."

Though she's become the biggest and most garish show queen of '90s country, Reba McEntire—a powerhouse vocalist with seemingly unstoppable drive—is regularly lumped in with new traditionalism, which isn't entirely accurate. The rodeo-riding daughter of an Oklahoma cattle rancher, she first recorded in the '70s, but much of her early material was unfocused. When she switched from Mercury to MCA in the mid-'80s and recorded the album MY KIND OF COUNTRY, she was allowed to let her roots shine, and the result was a more traditional approach in the song choices and arrangements. But this proved an illusion: by the time of her follow-up, WHOEVER'S IN NEW ENGLAND—the title track of which clinched her superstardom—her style had coalesced into something far more polished, showy, and emotionally manipulative. And despite the Oklahoma twang that still thrives in her vocal work, she's moved in a pop-oriented direction ever since.

The Judds—mother Naomi and daughter Wynonna—were another superstar outfit with wide appeal, but the small-town country roots they brandished early on remained a healthy part of their image. Between their acoustic-based arrangements and Wynonna's powerful voice, many of their singles have a pleasant downhome vibe that's hard to resist. Even as their music grew increasingly tailored for radio play, the Judds at the same time never lost touch with this. By the end of the decade they'd become a hugely popular and extremely well-loved group, which in turn made their 1991 farewell tour (Naomi quit due to illness) one of the most tearful events in modern country history. As a solo artist Wynonna has, like Reba, embraced pop to a greater extent than she and her mother ever did—and in the process become one of country music's superstars.

From Greenwood to Scaggs

Despite this newfound fuss over traditionalism, the NashVegas holdovers—the Greenwoods, Frickes, and Mandrells—didn't simply disappear. On the contrary, these crossover crooners continued to sell in the millions. The Kenny Rogers/Dolly Parton duet "Islands In The Stream," for instance, hit top of the country charts the same year as Anderson's "Swingin'"; three years later Travis' "Diggin' Up Bones" preceded Exile's "It'll Be Me" in the #1 slot. What this chart-sharing demonstrated was that the country industry had expanded to a point where it was no longer based around a single style—or a single community. It

could easily accommodate pop- and rock-oriented artists like Kenny Rogers and Alabama on the one hand, and rootsier artists like Anderson, Travis, and Yoakam on the other. "I don't think it's a return to a more traditional country sound," producer and then-MCA executive Jimmy Bowen told the *Journal Of Country Music* in 1986, referring to the popularity of Skaggs, Strait, and the Judds. "I think it's a return of a more traditional sound that takes its place alongside several other sounds in country music. Some people have a hard time believing, seeing, or wanting country music to be other than one thing. It's healthy that you go from Greenwood to Skaggs."

Bowen was an LA pop producer (Dean Martin, Frank Sinatra, Kenny Rogers, and the First Edition) who came to Nashville in the '70s and has since done as much to boost the country music industry's growth as perhaps any single person could (at least in the days before Garth Brooks). He was a master at building the bottom line and making profits soar. When taking over operations of the flagging MCA in 1984, within a year he'd practically turned the label around. Part of the process, however, often included shaking down label staffs and cutting artist rosters, tasks that made him as hated by some on Music Row as he was loved by others. In addition to his business skills, Bowen also knew how to make hit records, and as producer he did so for Strait (DOES FORT WORTH EVER CROSS YOUR MIND), McEntire (WHOEVER'S IN NEW ENGLAND), Hank Williams Jr., Conway Twitty, and many others. At the end of the decade he jumped over to Capitol Nashville (which he renamed Liberty, though it's since changed back) just in time for the ascendance of the mighty Garth.

Bowen had a knack for hits, but it was Tony Brown—who began his long-running career at MCA when Bowen hired him away from RCA—who became the biggest booster for the label's rootsier, edgier artists. A onetime session pianist and touring musician (he played with the Oak Ridge Boys, Elvis Presley, Emmylou Harris, and Rodney Crowell among others), Brown grew to become one of the most influential producers and A&R men of the '80s and '90s. He helped shape the breakthrough MCA albums of Earle, Lovett, and Griffith and later worked with **Patty Loveless**, **Kelly Willis**, Marty Brown, Wynonna Judd, and Reba McEntire. (He also continued to produce his old friend Crowell even though the singer was at the time on rival label Columbia.) Brown has since become MCA Nashville's president, though he continues to produce; and his support for the emerging Americana radio format (and his signing of left-field singers like Chris Knight and Alison Moorer) show he's still adamant about keeping an edge to his label's roster. Because of this, he enjoys a healthy respect both in and out of the mainstream—something few major-label producers (not to mention executives) seem able to achieve.

As the '80s wore on, new traditionalism came closer and closer to being the industry's new norm. By 1987 Randy Travis was one of country music's most popular artists. That year also saw the emergence of another soon-to-be superstar,

Ricky Van Shelton. For many, this hunky specimen in a cowboy hat and white tank-top (the look he sported on his debut album cover) was the postcard-perfect embodiment of new traditionalism. Not only did he look just like an ordinary working Joe stretched out on the couch and ready for the weekend (the polar opposite of Kenny Rogers' Vegas flash), his voice was pleasantly burly, and many of his hits were updated covers of older material such as "Statue Of A Fool" (Jack Greene) and "From A Jack To A King" (Ned Miller). But there's a slickness in

The Road Goes On Forever

Something about this decade, the 1980s, when Nashville was buckling under some stylistic, neo-trad changes—and further ideas were bubbling in from Texas and other points west—proved fertile for tunes about facing the highway of life.

Terry Allen, "Amarillo Highway"
The highway has never been so sizzling and dangerous as it is in Allen's paean to asphalt spittle and Chrysler cowboys. "Gonna stuff my hide behind some power glide," he sings, "an' get some southern fried back in my eyes." Hand me another Lone Star, son.

Rosanne Cash, "Runaway Train"
"The curves around midnight aren't easy to see," warns Cash in this tale of a love affair roaring headstrong down a rocky road (or, in this case, a pair of steel rails) and tempting disaster.

Rodney Crowell, "Leaving Louisiana In The Broad Daylight"
Southern small-town values get a kick in the pants as a restless young woman decides to leave home—and Papa ain't too happy about it.

Steve Earle, "Someday"
One of the minor hits on Earle's debut album GUITAR TOWN was this stark, lonesome song about a small-town guy dreaming of leaving his filling-station job, hitting the road, and finding the happiness awaiting him out in the big wide world.

Butch Hancock, "Two Roads"
The "poet laureate of West Texas" (which is how some folks refer to Hancock) presents us with a typically absurd parable. His hero faces two roads: which leads

to life, which to ruin? Is there a right answer? And do we cry about it, or do we just have a laugh?

Lyle Lovett, "Farther Down The Line"
The song unfolds through the voice of a rodeo announcer—oh that Lyle, he's a clever one—yet even though it's a smooth country melody, it's actually a love song, not just a paean to road-weary cowboy culture.

Kathy Mattea, "Leaving West Virginia"
Mattea's semi-autobiographical coming-of-age saga is not just founded on genuine feeling, it's got a substantial melody and arrangement to back it up.

George Strait, "Amarillo By Morning"
Another rodeo song, only this time the protagonist is the rider himself, who hasn't been home in quite a while, it seems, and has pretty much lost everything "along the way"—his wife, his saddle, his money. Still, he doesn't want to stop—after all, he feels, personal freedom's worth loads more than a fat bank account.

Randy Travis, "Storms Of Life"
How does a good ole boy mend a broken heart? With a pickup truck, a working radio, a "six pack on the front seat," and "a box of chicken wings." It's just such little details that make this number (penned by Troy Seals and Max D. Barnes) so evocative and powerful.

Dwight Yoakam, "South Of Cincinnati"
Instead of leaving, the protagonist here is the one left behind. Sad, nostalgic and pretty, it's an early Yoakam song that's still among his most masterful.

Shelton's music that's missing from the better songs of Earle, Strait, and even Travis. Shelton's songs sound overly clean, a bit too smooth around the edges. It was like he'd been tailored to fit the genre. So instead of taking new traditionalism a few steps further, he was the cement poured around its shoes that kept it locked in place. One of his achievements, however, still reverberates throughout Nashville: his cowboy hat and T-shirt were the inspiration for the 'hunk' look of the '90s.

Shelton was also the bridge between the class of '86 (Earle, Travis, Yoakam) and the rising stars of the next decade, among them Clint Black, Alan Jackson, and Garth Brooks. By this point the term 'new traditionalism' had lost its edge—nearly every new singer who stepped into a music video was wearing a wide-brimmed hat, starched shirt, and Wranglers and giving thanks to God, Mama, and Georges Strait and Jones. The new hats had definitely arrived, and country music would never be the same again.

New Traditionalism: The Artists

Terry Allen

"Today's rainbow is tomorrow's tamale."
—Terry Allen

One of the list of brilliant musical visionaries to emerge out of the plain, sprawling Texas Panhandle town of Lubbock was tall, brawny-voiced Terry Allen. Slightly older than his fellow Lubbockites Jimmie Dale Gilmore, Butch Hancock, and Joe Ely—with whom he's collaborated and is often associated—Allen was actually an early inspiration to that dazzling trio. As a songwriter and singer, his richly textured, lyrically complex songs are studded with social commentary, dark humor, and a good amount of smart-ass attitude and unrepentant vitriol. Sarcasm might surface frequently, but the bottom line in his work is really human compassion. Allen writes songs and stories about characters on the fringes of society—the "remains," he calls them. Good, bad, or in-between, they're the kind of people overlooked, or, worse, run over, in the blinding race for power, glory, and salvation.

Allen is one of country music's most insightful songwriters—and one hell of a performer when he chooses to step out (believe it or not, he can be shy on stage). His voice is brawny and scratched, his Texas drawl is as thick as summer humidity, and his honky-tonk piano playing is rugged but passionate. He's a long way from Nashville, but his music is as country as the Texas dirt he's walked upon for much of his life. A few of his songs have reached toward a wider audience, most notably "New Delhi Freight Train" (made semi-famous by Little Feat) and "Amarillo Highway" (covered by Bobby Bare, Joe Ely, and Robert Earl Keen).

If anything, Allen has earned a wider reputation for artistic endeavors outside the world of music. He's recorded on and off since the mid-1970s, but he's also created a substantial body of work as a visual and multimedia artist. His work includes sculpture, photography, painting, poetry, performance, and film. He's earned NEA grants and even a Guggenheim fellowship. And in 1994, he collaborated with his wife, Jo Harvey Allen, on the stage play *Chippy*, which was commissioned by the American Music Theater Festival in Philadelphia.

Allen was born on 7 May, 1943 in Wichita, Kansas, and he grew up in Lubbock. His mother played jazz piano, and his father was a booking agent who brought Elvis Presley and Little Richard to town. Allen left for LA in the early '60s to study art, and he received a BFA from Chouinard Art Institute. He recorded his first album, JUAREZ, in 1975, which grew out of a larger conceptual vision involving paintings and drawings. The story focused on four characters and the concept of Mexico as an ultimate escape. Allen has called JUAREZ a soundtrack to a film that doesn't exist, and years later he adapted it for the stage. The album is basically Allen solo with a little instrumental help along the way. He recorded it in San Francisco, and it was released on Fate Records, a label he co-founded. The project has stayed in his mind ever since. One of the standout songs, the fiery and near-raging "There Oughta Be A Law Against Sunny Southern California," showed up

Terry Allen

on his 1983 album BLOODLINES, and "What Of Alicia" resurfaced on HUMAN REMAINS.

Allen's next project was even more ambitious—a double-album opus titled LUBBOCK (ON EVERY-THING) that was about growing up in, leaving, and ultimately coming to terms with that town. It was ambitious—like crazy bits of dreams and memories strung together—but it worked, and it stands as the masterpiece of Allen's musical career. The album was cut in Lubbock, which forced Allen to face the hometown demons he long ago figured he'd left behind. Ironically, he felt more at home there than he ever expected. The musicians assembled for the project were dubbed the Panhandle Mystery Band, and they included Joe Ely, guitarist Jesse Taylor, fiddler Richard Bowden, accordionist Ponty Bone, and brothers Lloyd, Kenny, and Donnie Maines. Pedal-steel maestro Lloyd Maines was also a producer at Caldwell Studios, where the album was cut. LUBBOCK included two of Allen's best-known songs, "Amarillo Highway"—one of the hottest road songs ever written—and "New Delhi Freight Train."

Two further albums surfaced on Fate during the next few years, SMOKIN' THE DUMMY (1980) and BLOODLINES (1983), with the Panhandle Mystery Band again congregating at Caldwell Studios. The latter album included a reworking of "Sunny Southern California" (from JUAREZ) and a divinely twisted tale called "Gimme A Ride To Heaven Boy," in which an unwitting driver picks up a hitchhiking Jesus—who drinks his beer before pulling a gun and then stealing his car. It's funny as well, and it certainly gives new meaning to the phrase "God damned."

During the early '80s, Allen wrote the score for *Amerasia*, a film by German director Wolf-Eckart Buehler; the Thai band, Caravan, were employed as musicians. Later in the decade, the San Francisco-based Margaret Jenkins Dance Company commissioned Allen to write two new musical pieces, *Pedal Steal* and *Rollback* (they were subsequently released together on a single CD). Allen also contributed songs to the David Byrne film *True Stories*. And in the early '90s he worked with his wife on the play *Chippy* (which included songs and performances by such Texas notables as Butch Hancock, Jo Carol Pierce, Robert Earl Keen, and Wayne Hancock). Allen's first non-soundtrack album in many years was HUMAN REMAINS, released in 1996. Three years later came SALIVATION.

⊙ **Lubbock (On Everything)** (1979; Fate; reissued 1995; Sugar Hill). Attacking closed-mindedness from small-town Texas to the big cities of Nashville and LA, the 22 songs on LUBBOCK are a picture of survival—it's sometimes pretty, but it's also funny, caustic, raunchy, touching, and sad. "Amarillo Highway" is a dangerously enticing road song, "The Great Joe Bob" is a tragic tale of a fallen high school hero, and "Truckload Of Art" pokes good fun at hifalutin cultural attitudes. Taken individually, these songs are amazing; as a unit, they're pure brilliance.

⊙ **Human Remains** (1996; Sugar Hill). Allen writes superb character-driven songs, and this album takes us deep into the often-rocky lives of folks who've stepped into the big bad world from all over the map—the Mexican teenager in "What Of Alicia," the dysfunctional couple in "Room To Room" (one of three duets with Lucinda Williams). "Gone To Texas" is biting and sarcastic—and a total crack-up.

⊙ **Salivation** (1999; Sugar Hill). Allen's music is still full of fire and spit, but at the same time, there's a twisted sense of humor that curls from the edges of his brawny voice. He's still obsessed with Jesus—and all manner of religious fallout—and with people on the underbelly of society, the folks who always seem to be running away, getting into trouble, having a laugh, and maybe, if they're lucky, discovering something about themselves they didn't know before.

John Anderson

Along with George Strait and Ricky Skaggs, Floridian John Anderson was one of the first country artists in the early 1980s to kick Nashville in its urban cowboy ass and get things moving back toward a more traditional sound. Early singles such as "1959," "Wild And Blue," and the immensely popular "Swingin'" set Anderson in motion as a neo-traditionalist innovator with a strong, individualistic style. His smooth, slightly nasal-toned tenor voice has a distinct Lefty Frizzell influence, and his music (like his Outlaw-era predecessors) mixes firm traditional country influences with a rock'n'roller's perspective. He's definitely one of the overlooked greats of the early '80s.

Anderson was born John David Alexander in Apopka, Florida on 13 December, 1954. He played in rock bands as a teenager, and listened to the likes of the Stones and Alice Cooper, but thanks to his songwriting sister Donna he eventually discovered country singers like George Jones and Merle Haggard. He moved to Nashville in the early '70s, taking odd jobs (including working on the roof of the *Grand Ole Opry* before it opened in 1974), and eventually he landed a writing gig with a local publishing company. The small Nashville label Ace of Hearts (not to be confused with the Boston punk label of the same name) released Anderson's first single, "What Did I Promise Her Last Night," in 1974. A few years later he was signed to Warner Brothers, who released several singles including "Your Lying Blue Eyes," "Low Dog Blues," and "She Just Started Liking Cheatin' Songs" followed, in 1980, by Anderson's first album. Despite some leftover Nashville Sound elements in Norro Wilson's production, Anderson's solid traditional approach cut through and marked him as an artist to watch. The song "1959" became his first Top 10 single, and he followed it up with an updated version of Billy Joe Shaver's "I'm Just An Old Lump Of Coal (But I'm Gonna Be A Diamond Someday)."

Anderson's fame was cemented in 1982 when he hit the coveted #1 spot with "Wild And Blue." With its strong fiddle lines, punchy rhythm and sexually charged lyrics, it's among the best songs of Anderson's career. The album of the same name also included "Swingin'," a catchy rock-inflected number that proved even more popular (it reached #1 in 1983, crossed over to the pop charts, and eventually was named CMA's Single of the Year and won Anderson the CMA's Horizon Award). The song is one of several Anderson co-wrote with Lionel Delmore whose father, Alton, was half of the Delmore Brothers.

Further Anderson hits from this period include "I Just Came Home To Count The Memories" (from the 1981 album of the same name), "Would You Catch A Falling Star," and "Black Sheep."

This last album, co-written by filmmaker Robert Altman and actor Danny Darst, was another sturdy, neo-trad rocker that became Anderson's third #1. But by the mid-'80s, conflicts between Anderson and Warner Brothers led to a slow decline in his record sales, and he eventually left the label for MCA Nashville. He recorded two albums for MCA with producer Jimmy Bowen (many of whose tracks were later compiled on the 1994 release YOU CAN'T KEEP A GOOD MEMORY DOWN). But while the songwriting and arrangements were square-on country, they couldn't revive his waning popularity, and Anderson continued sliding toward the black hole of obscurity (watching his contemporary George Strait still shining on the charts must have been thoroughly frustrating).

After a brief flirtation with the short-lived Universal label, Anderson finally signed with another new label, BNA, in 1992. Suddenly his name was back in lights as the single "Straight Tequila Nights" shot to #1 and the album from which it came, SEMINOLE WIND, also became hot property. The title track, one of Anderson's finest songs, also made the Top 10. Anderson has since enjoyed a few more hits (including "Money In The Bank" from his 1993 album SOLID GROUND), and his status as a neo-traditionalist pioneer has solidified. Who says justice in the music industry is never done? Admittedly it took actual chart hits to gain Anderson the respect due him—but at least he eventually got it.

⊙ **John Anderson** (1980; Warner Bros.). The sentimental "1959" (written by Gary Gentry) is Anderson's only hit from his debut, but "Havin' Hard Times" (co-written by Anderson and Delmore), which opens the album, is actually the strongest song and should have been a contender. Other notables include "She Just Started Liking Cheatin' Songs" (the other side of the coin from Moe Bandy's '70s hit "I Just Started Hating Cheating Songs Today") and the weepy "Girl At The End Of The Bar." Norro Wilson's production mixes strong beats and prominent pedal steel lines with leftover Nashville Sound choruses and strings, which are vastly out of place. Thankfully, Anderson's voice is strong enough to overcome such disturbances.

⊙ **Wild & Blue** (1982; Warner Bros.). This is the standout album of Anderson's early career. The title track, written by John Scott Sherrill, holds up as one of the era's best songs (the Mekons have even covered it). A more overlooked gem is "Disappearing Farmer" (written by Sandy Pinkard and James Cowen), which speaks of farm troubles and stubborn men. And, of course, the pull of "Swingin'" is hard to resist.

⊙ **Greatest Hits** (1984; Warner Bros.). An all-in-one package of many of Anderson's choice cuts from the early '80s. Overall it's a far better starting place than the 1996 collection on BNA, or even the 1998 ESSENTIAL collection, both of which concentrate on his later material.

⊙ **Seminole Wind** (1992; BNA). Anderson's comeback album was a welcomed breather among an overabundance of Garth-inspired droners. "Straight Tequila Night" is an average bar-room down-and-outer; better is Bobby Braddock's "Look Away," a poignant take on Dixie, the region and the song. But best of all is the moving title track—written by Anderson, it tells of the disappearing Seminole culture as Florida's Everglades are drained—which stands as one of his finest achievements as both a singer and songwriter (Sally Timms of the Mekons recorded an excellent cover of this song, by the way).

Carlene Carter

As the daughter of June Carter and 1950s honky-tonk star Carl Smith—making her the third generation of the Carter Family—Carlene Carter's got a serious country pedigree. Luckily for her, it wasn't such a battle to live up to the charge as it was a struggle to figure out how to best express herself. Since she first started recording on her own in the late '70s, Carter's straddled the fence between new wave rock and peppy country—who knows, she might have played even more rock'n'roll if it weren't for her famous bloodline. Yet by 1990, when she released the album I FELL IN LOVE, she seemed to have settled more or less into her newfound role as a bona fide country singer.

Carlene was born Rebecca Carlene Smith on 26 September, 1955 in Madison, Tennessee. Her parents divorced when she was only two, and her mother married Johnny Cash ten years later. As a child she and her stepsister, Rosanne Cash (Johnny's daughter from his first marriage), toured and sang with the Carter Family. When she was only fifteen Carlene married her first husband, Joe Simpkins, and had a daughter, but the pair divorced soon after. At nineteen she married Jack Routh and had a son with him, but again the marriage didn't last long. By this point, however, her solo

Carlene Carter

career was on the move. Her first album, CARLENE CARTER, was produced by Brinsley Schwarz and Bob Andrews, and her band included further members of Graham Parker's Rumour along with Carter's soon-to-be-husband Nick Lowe. But it was her 1980 album MUSICAL SHAPES, again produced by Lowe, that finally won her critical praise.

By now Carter was living in London and playing with the likes of Lowe and Paul Carrack (Squeeze). Her follow-up records, BLUE NUN (a British-only release) and C'EST C BON, failed to catch on commercially, and she eventually took a break from recording that lasted for the rest of the decade. Her marriage to Lowe also broke up during this time.

Carter's 1990 album I FELL IN LOVE was a true comeback effort and a very pleasant surprise. She'd returned to the States in the late '80s, hooked up with old friend Howie Epstein (a member of Tom Petty's band), and Reprise eventually signed her. The resulting album was produced by Epstein and featured such top-drawer West Coast studio musicians as Benmont Tench, Jim Keltner, James Burton, and Albert Lee. (The background singers alone were an all-star line-up that included Dave Edmunds, Jim Lauderdale, Kevin Welch, Kiki Dee, Nicolette Larson, and Levon Helm.) Much more distinctly country than her earlier releases, I FELL IN LOVE gained Carter the attention she needed, and she even landed a couple of bona fide country hits ("I Fell In Love" and "Come On Back"). Three years later her LITTLE LOVE LETTERS album, another pepped-up country affair, also was well received. That album was released by Giant, as was her 1995 follow-up, LITTLE ACTS OF TREASON.

◐ Musical Shapes (1980; Warner Bros.; reissued 1991; Demon). This album won heaps of critical praise upon its release, but its mixture of rockabilly, country, and new-wave rock'n'roll feels uneven today. "Cry" is a lively rocker, and her duet with Dave Edmunds ("Baby Ride Easy") holds up fine, but her new-wave take on "Ring Of Fire" is virtually unlistenable. Overall Carter's at her best when she sticks close to the country, as on the A.P. Carter song "Foggy Mountain Top" and "To Drunk (Too Remember)." As a bonus, the CD reissue includes her 1981 album BLUE NUN.

☉ I Fell In Love (1990; Reprise). Like most of the songs on this record, Carter's big breakthrough into the country market, the title track is catchy, bright, and bursting with energy. Her voice is full of bounce, and at her best (such as her cover of Leon Payne's "You Are The One") she exhibits a captivating spirit. Coming on the cusp of the 'young country' era, the record's peppy twang is invigorating and still fresh.

☉ Hindsight 20/20 (1996; Warner Bros.). Compiling familiar tracks from Carter's hit 1990s albums as well as a handful from her earlier days, this collection is a fine overview of her recording career to date.

Rosanne Cash

Growing up under the shadow of the Man in Black on his rise to international fame, Johnny Cash's daughter, Rosanne Cash, definitely accumulated her share of teenage angst, drug habits, emotional restlessness, and rebellious attitude. Along the way, however, she made a pretty serious mark as a country singer and songwriter during the 1980s. Not only did she record excellent material like "Seven Year Ache" and "Runaway Train," she was also one of the decade's most popular country artists, racking up a strong series of hits, including eleven #1s. She experimented with pop, new wave, and rock'n'roll styles—female-empowering songs like "Hold On" just might strike a chord with Shania Twain's fans—but classic country music, including the songs of her father, also remained a major influence (one of her top hits was a faithful version of Johnny's "Tennessee Flat Top Box"). Rosanne's sound wasn't always 'neo-traditional,' but albums like SEVEN YEAR ACHE (produced, like

nearly all her records at the time, but then-husband Rodney Crowell) helped give back to country music the edge that had been lost during the *Urban Cowboy* era.

Cash was born in Memphis, Tennessee, on 24 May, 1955—a time when her father was just getting his music career off the ground. Rosanne grew up mostly in Southern California, and her parents divorced while she was still young. After graduating high school, she worked as a crewmember and back-up singer with her father's road show. She recorded her debut album for the German label Ariola, though it was never issued in the US.

During the late '70s, Cash met Rodney Crowell (a hip young songwriter and member of Emmylou Harris' Hot Band), and the two married in 1979. That same year, Crowell produced Cash's second album (and first for Columbia), RIGHT OR WRONG. It included her father's "Big River," Gary Nunn and Karen Brooks' "Couldn't Do Nothin' Right" (previously cut by Jerry Jeff Walker), and four songs written by Crowell, including "No Memories Hangin' Round." The last song was a duet with Bobby Bare and her first Top 20 country hit. If RIGHT OR WRONG signaled her rising talent, Cash's next album, SEVEN YEAR ACHE, was the one that pushed her over the edge into stardom. The title track (an infectious song written by Rosanne) made it to #1, as did "My Baby Thinks He's A Train" and "Blue Moon With Heartache." SOMEWHERE IN THE STARS came next, followed by RHYTHM AND ROMANCE. The latter was almost new wave—right down to her orange hair, the bright pink lettering all over the album cover, and the peppy production by David Malloy. Still, she continued to make the country charts yet again with songs like "I Don't Know Why You Don't Want Me" (which won her a Grammy) and the Tom Petty/Benmont Tench song "Never Be You."

Crowell was back in the producer's seat for 1987's KING'S RECORD SHOP. One of the showcase tunes on that collection (and one of its four #1 hits) was "Tennessee Flat Top Box," written and recorded by father Johnny back in 1961. At the end of the '80s, Columbia released a collection of Rosanne's hit songs, and it showed just how powerful a country force she'd been throughout the decade. Her relationship with Crowell, however, was coming unraveled by this point. Her songs had always had an autobiographical nature, and so it was with her 1990 album INTERIORS, which chronicled much of what she was going through in the break-up of her

Rosanne Cash

Following in daddy's footsteps: Roseanne Cash

marriage (they finally divorced in 1992). INTE-RIORS was critically acclaimed at the time, and it still stands among her finest work, but it didn't yield any serious hits of the sort she was accustomed to. Her musical output slowed down considerably after this; only two albums have (so far) followed, THE WHEEL (1993) and 10-SONG DEMO (1996). The latter was produced by her new husband, John Leventhal, and released by Capitol Records. Rosanne also published a collection of short stories entitled *Bodies Of Water*. At the end of the decade she was living in New York City with her husband and three daughters.

⊙ **Seven Year Ache** (1981; Columbia). The title track (written by Rosanne) is her best-known hit for good reason, its melody as catchy and appealing as any in her repertoire. "My Baby Thinks He's A Train" is another foot-tapper, with some fine electric-guitar work vying for attention alongside Cash's voice; and her thick and twangy version of Merle Haggard's "You Don't Have Very Far To Go" is just as bold in its honky-tonk arrangement.

⊙ **King's Record Shop** (1987; Columbia). After the big pop-rock attitude of RHYTHM AND ROMANCE, this album (thankfully) took a few steps back down to earth. "Tennessee Flat Top Box" was a reverent cover of Johnny Cash's early classic, but the contemporary energy in songs like "If You Change Your Mind" and the delicious "Runaway Train" showed Rosanne was

still a modern girl. Her singing is bold and bright ("Rosie Strikes Back"), yet it's also emotionally fragile (the bare-bones "Why Don't You Quit Leaving Me Alone")— and the dichotomy is what's so damn appealing.

⊙ **Interiors** (1990; Columbia). The pain of Rosanne's break-up with husband Rodney Crowell is right out in the open on this finely crafted album, her strongest to date. The lead track "On The Inside" takes us right into her world (and does so with yet another infectious melody), and the remaining songs, most penned by Cash, never let up. The production (also by Cash) is more low-key than almost any of her work to date, making for an album that's stark in tone yet absolutely compelling.

Earl Thomas Conley

Former steel worker Earl Thomas Conley had a long string of chart hits in the 1980s, but he's never been as closely associated with neo-traditionalism as his contemporaries John Anderson, Ricky Skaggs, and George Strait have been. This is partly because he also had a soft spot for syrupy schlock and seemed to grow fonder of it as his career progressed. Listening to early hits like "Fire And Smoke" and "Somewhere Between Right And Wrong," however, is a different story, as

Conley has a strong voice and a firmly grounded, soul-styled approach to honky tonk.

Conley was born in 1941 in Portsmouth, Ohio, a small town on the banks of the Ohio River. He listened to country music and the *Grand Ole Opry* as a child, but also loved the music of Elvis, Roy Orbison, and the Beatles. After a stint in the Army he worked in Ohio steel mills and began writing songs. In 1970 he moved to Huntsville, Alabama, where he worked factory jobs, played in local clubs, and recorded a demo and eventually some singles for the local Prize label. There he also became familiar with the Muscle Shoals music scene. Eventually he moved to Nashville, where he began scoring hits as a songwriter: Mel Street recorded his "Smokey Mountain Memories" (as did bluegrass singer Larry Sparks), and Conway Twitty had a big hit with "This Time I've Hurt Her More (Than She Loves Me)," which Conley had co-written with Mary Louise Larkin (whose husband, Nelson, had first recorded Conley in Huntsville). Conley soon signed a recording contract with GRT, and his first single, "I Have Loved You Girl (But Not Like This Before)," was even a minor chart hit. He later signed to Warner Brothers and recorded further singles (and also began using his middle name); then he switched to Sunbird, Nelson Larkin's new label. Here he finally hit with his songs "Silent Treatment" and "Fire And Smoke." Both made the Top 10 in 1981 and were included on his 1981 album debut on Sunbird, BLUE PEARL. RCA quickly jumped on Conley and bought his contract, and the hits became frequent and steady for the better part of the decade.

FIRE AND SMOKE, Conley's first album for RCA, was a success, but it was his 1982 album SOMEWHERE BETWEEN RIGHT AND WRONG that really took off—as did the 1983 follow-up, DON'T MAKE IT EASY FOR ME (which yielded four #1 country hits, at the time a record-breaking feat), and 1984's TREADIN' WATER. He wrote or co-wrote many of his early hits, one of his regular writing partners being Randy Scruggs, son of the legendary banjoist Earl Scruggs. Conley's material shifts between the honky tonk of "Fire And Smoke" and "Heavenly Bodies" and the more adult-contemporary sound of "Honor Bound" and "Nobody Falls Like A Fool." As the years (and the hits) rolled on, however, his sound grew slicker, with new-wave beats frequently replacing country shuffles; vocally, Conley began to sound more in Kenny Rogers' camp than George Jones' (with whom Conley had been compared). By the end of the decade, his music was virtually drowning in pop-influenced saccharine.

Though he released the well-received YOURS TRULY in 1991 (which included a duet with Keith Whitley, "Brotherly Love"), Conley's hitmaking streak was pretty near wrapped up at this point. A new era of country music had dawned, and it was more radio-hit driven than ever before. One result was that even chart-topping artists like Conley lost much of their name recognition in the shuffle, as fans were inundated with one new singer after another. Which is too bad, since a healthy portion of Conley's songs, especially his earlier material, are worth more than a distant memory.

⦿ **Fire And Smoke** (1981; RCA). Side one of this album contains Conley's most honky-tonking songs: "Too Much Noise (Truckers Waltz)," "Smokey Mountain Memories," "This Time I've Hurt Her More (Than She Loves Me)," and the title track. This straight-up country stuff is great, while the rest represents the (often unbearable) pop influences that are the other side of the Conley coin. The band includes Randy Scruggs and steel maestro Lloyd Green.

⊙ **The Essential Earl Thomas Conley** (1996; RCA). A decent overview of Conley's RCA recording career, it begins with strong songs like "Fire And Smoke," "Somewhere Between Wrong And Right," and "Heavenly Bodies" before dipping far too deeply into schlock ("I Can't Win For Losing You," "Honor Bound"), which pretty near ruins the show.

Rodney Crowell

"He's got the best ear for songs of anybody in the world. About songs for a specific person."

—Rosanne Cash

What makes Rodney Crowell such a standout artist of the 1980s is not just his own recordings—as good as some of them are—but the fact that he's proven himself a talented guitarist, producer and songwriter as well. He first honed his guitar chops professionally as a member of Emmylou Harris' Hot Band, a highly prestigious gig for an up-and-coming musician during the '70s. The following decade his production work on his then-wife Rosanne Cash's albums such as SEVEN YEAR ACHE and KING'S RECORD SHOP helped her win critical respect and a string of hits. And throughout his career Crowell's seen his songs recorded by the likes of the Oak Ridge Boys

Earl Thomas Conley • Rodney Crowell

("Leaving Louisiana In The Broad Daylight"), Crystal Gayle ("Till I Gain Control Again"), and even Bob Seger ("Shame On The Moon").

As a solo artist Crowell has recorded plenty of excellent material himself, beginning with his star-studded 1978 debut AIN'T LIVING LONG LIKE THIS (which featured Harris, James Burton, Ry Cooder, Ricky Skaggs, Willie Nelson, and many others) and continuing through two decades and three different record labels—Warner Brothers, Columbia, and MCA. Much of his music mixed a traditional country vibe with rock'n'roll elements, though Crowell sometimes tried too hard to be different (hiring Ramones producer Craig Leon for BUT WHAT WILL THE NEIGHBORS THINK, for instance, and Booker T. Jones for his country-soul album STREET LANGUAGE). Yet for all his offbeat experimentation, he always walked away with his integrity intact. It wasn't until he hired his former piano player Tony Brown to produce his Columbia albums DIAMONDS AND DIRT and KEYS TO THE HIGHWAY (interesting since Brown was a staffer at MCA at the time) that Crowell finally achieved the major chart success he'd long ago deserved.

Crowell was born into a musical family in Houston, Texas on 7 August, 1950. He played in bands growing up, and in the early '70s moved to Nashville, where he first met Guy Clark, Townes Van Zandt, and Mickey Newbury, three men who are about the best inspirations any aspiring song-writer could hope to have. Jerry Reed was the first to record one of Crowell's songs, "You Can't Keep Me Here In Tennessee," and he also signed the budding writer to his publishing company. In 1975 Crowell moved to Los Angeles to play guitar with Harris, and soon she was covering his songs as well ("I Ain't Living Long Like This" and "Leaving Louisiana In The Broad Daylight" among them).

Crowell eventually quit Harris' band and formed his own group, the Cherry Bombs. He was soon signed to Warner Brothers and his debut album, AIN'T LIVING LONG LIKE THIS, appeared in 1978. About that same time he produced Rosanne Cash's debut RIGHT OR WRONG. After its release the two married, and Crowell went on to produce the majority of Cash's hit songs throughout the '80s.

Crowell had some minor hits of his own during his early career, as well as attracting wide critical acclaim, but it was his 1988 album DIA-MONDS AND DIRT that broke him on country radio, giving him an unprecedented streak of five #1 singles including "She's Crazy For Leavin'" (co-written with Guy Clark), "It's Such A Small World" (a duet with Cash), and "After All This Time," which won him a Grammy for Best Country Song. Crowell's popular success continued with his follow-up album, KEYS TO THE HIGHWAY. In 1992 he and Cash divorced, and Crowell's next release, LIFE IS MESSY, reflected emotions from that split (it was also in some ways a response to Cash's own break-up album INTE-RIORS). Brown finally brought Crowell onto the MCA roster in 1994, and the first record was LET THE PICTURE PAINT ITSELF. The follow-up, JEWEL OF THE SOUTH, included a variety of special guests, among them Vince Gill (who had briefly played guitar in Crowell's band), Kim Richey, Béla Fleck, and the Mavericks' Raul Malo. Crowell has never repeated the chart run he enjoyed after DIAMONDS AND DIRT, but he continues to meet success and garner respect from his ardent fans both on and off Music Row.

○ **Ain't Living Long Like This** (1978; Warner Bros.). Crowell's debut features several of his best-known songs such as the excellent "Leaving Louisiana In The

Rodney Crowell

STEVE GILLETT

Broad Daylight," "Voila, An American Dream," and the title track. Overall the album is solid, and even Crowell's version of "Elvira" (recorded before the Oak Ridge Boys got hold of it) sounds great. On top of all this, the band—James Burton, Albert Lee, Ry Cooder, Ricky Skaggs, Jim Keltner, Willie Nelson, and Emmylou Harris among them—is unbeatable.

⊙ **The Rodney Crowell Collection** (1989; Warner Bros.). This compilation picks out the better tracks from his first three albums for Warner Brothers, Ain't Living Long Like This, But What Will The Neighbors Think, and Rodney Crowell.

⊙ **Diamonds And Dirt** (1988; Columbia). This is the album that made Crowell a #1 star—five times over, in fact, thanks to "It's Such A Small World," "I Couldn't Leave You If I Tried," "She's Crazy For Leavin'," "After All This Time," and "Above And Beyond." It remains a solid listen.

⊙ **Greatest Hits** (1993; Columbia). Taken from his years on Columbia in the late 1980s and early '90s—the peak of Crowell's run on the charts—this is a well-sequenced hits collection that moves. The song choices include "She's Crazy For Leavin'," "Even Cowgirls Get The Blues," "After All This Time," and "Talking To A Stranger" (a duet with Mary Chapin Carpenter).

Steve Earle

"If he'd stuck it out in Nashville I think he would have inherited what Travis Tritt has now."

—John Lomax

More than any other country singer who came to prominence during the 1980s, Steve Earle had the raw sound, physical appearance and no-bullshit attitude of a modern-day Outlaw. From the bold twang of his debut album, Guitar Town, to the thunder that echoed across Copperhead Road—not to mention the knockout acoustic picking on his post-rehab comeback Train A Comin'—Earle has established himself as a guy who does things his own way, the status quo (and other peoples' rules) be damned.

At the same time, however, Earle is a thoughtful artist steeped in the legacy of his songwriting heroes, Townes Van Zandt and Guy Clark. His blue-collar sentiments and midwestern rock'n'roll arrangements have long invited comparisons to Heartland singers like Bruce Springsteen and John Cougar Mellencamp (though maybe Waylon Jennings is a better benchmark). But as much as he kicks out the jams, he also maintains connection with the heart and soul of his subjects, writing about small-town angst ("Someday"), disappearing farmers ("The Rain Came Down"), drug-running 'Nam vets ("Copperhead Road"), and even the death penalty ("Billy Austin") from a very personal perspective. Like Van Zandt, Earle's songs often take us into regions of intense darkness, yet he's also able to touch home base with a love song like "You Belong To Me" and inspire optimism with "It's All Up To You." For a guy who's been in and out of jail cells, hard-drug habits and rehab programs—not to mention several marriages—it's all the more satisfying that he's survived his hard times and continues to pump out strong material.

Steve Earle was born on 17 January, 1955 in Fort Monroe, Virginia, but soon after his family moved back to Texas, eventually settling near San Antonio. He quit school after the eighth grade, and drifted in and out of trouble, but he also started playing guitar. He traveled the state playing music throughout his teens, eventually settling in Houston and marrying for the first time. It's here that Earle first met Townes Van Zandt. Soon after that he moved to Nashville, where he met Guy Clark and Rodney Crowell, among others, and got an education playing at picking parties. He moved back to Texas but then returned again to Nashville and eventually found some work as a songwriter. Carl Perkins, Zella Lehr, and even Johnny Lee ("When You Fall In Love," a hit in 1982) all recorded his material. One of the songs Earle wrote during this early period was "The Devil's Right Hand," which had the air of a classic almost immediately (Waylon Jennings would later record it, though Earle's Copperhead Road version is the definitive one). By this point Earle was married for the third time and had a son (Justin Townes).

Publishers Roy Dea and Pat Clark signed Earle and released four of his songs as an EP titled Pink And Black. This got him attention from Epic, who signed him and released a few singles (they've since been re-released on the album Early Tracks). In 1985 producer/A&R man Tony Brown brought Earle onto the MCA roster, a move that resulted in his debut album, Guitar Town. This proved his breakthrough: the album's pared-down sound won him the support and attention of critics and fans on both sides of the country-rock fence—it was simply the most hard-edged country record to emerge from

Steve Earle

Nashville in years. Incredible as it may seem today, several songs (including "Someday" and "Guitar Town") even charted respectably. Earle it seemed was strolling the garden path toward country stardom.

His follow-up, EXIT 0, came out a year later. Like GUITAR TOWN, Earle recorded it with his touring band the Dukes—a move that Waylon Jennings had fought for a decade back but one that was still out of the ordinary by Nashville standards. Again a few songs made the charts, but it was also becoming clear Earle was restless in the role of burgeoning Nashville hitmaker. For his next project, he moved from MCA's country roster to its LA-based pop-rock division. The folks there likely had a much better sense when it came to marketing the big sound contained on COPPERHEAD ROAD (which this time was recorded in Memphis at Ardent Studios). From the kick-off title track onward, this intense creation thundered like a hillbilly hot rod on a heavy-metal highway, taking no prisoners and holding nothing back. Molly Hatchet, however, it was not: though Earle obviously loved to let the guitars rip, his music was even here as much about songwriting as volume. And for added flavor he'd brought some impressive musical pals on board: the Pogues backed him up on the rousing "Johnny Come Lately," and Telluride (Sam Bush, Jerry Douglas, Mark O'Connor, Edgar Meyer) played on the album-closer "Nothing But A Child" (songwriting royalties of which were donated to a homeless children's charity). From start to finish, the energy remains firm and the musical vision as succinct as anything he's done. Country radio ignored it, of course, but album sales pushed half a million (a trend impeded when Uni, the MCA subsidiary that released it, fizzled out shortly after).

By the time COPPERHEAD ROAD was released, however, it was obvious Earle had some serious private demons he could no longer keep locked up. Not only had his handsome bad-boy appearance turned into something out of a biker nightmare (long hair and headband, ragged beard and ripped shirtsleeves), his personal life was more and more streaked with complications and controversy. In one notorious incident he landed in jail after punching a Dallas cop (who minutes before had had him in a billy-club stranglehold)—and this was after one of his own concerts. He'd also divorced and married a couple more times, and his drug and alcohol problems were getting ugly again. Few at the time likely knew the full extent of his habits, but Earle would later admit to first dabbling in heroin as a teenager.

Steve Earle

His fourth album THE HARD WAY wasn't as fully realized as COPPERHEAD ROAD, but it still contained shades of greatness. The chief problem was that, like EXIT 0, it more or less reprised the sound and style of its strong-willed predecessor. Because of this it remains Earle's most underrated album. Stellar moments like "The Other Kind" and "Billy Austin" (about a guy on death row, it gave Earle a platform on which to speak out against the death penalty, which he frequently did at concerts) make it a sleeper worth seeking.

Because of his increasingly unpredictable behavior, MCA decided it couldn't deal with Earle any longer. The label released the live album SHUT UP AND DIE LIKE AN AVIATOR (which was packed with Dixie-fried braggadocio) and then allowed his contract to expire. During the early '90s Earle and the Dukes toured all over the world, sometimes as the opening act for Lynyrd Skynyrd (Earle even flirted with the idea of joining that band), but as the years rolled forward his fast and dirty lifestyle was taking its toll. He played some solo acoustic performances (which came off brilliantly), but plenty more signs pointed toward a hard crash and early demise. In 1994, when he faced a year in jail for drug possession charges, he wound up in a drug rehabilitation center instead. It's here that he finally met his devils head-on.

Steve Earle

Miraculously, Earle did clean out his closets and straighten up. When news spread that he was back in the world and even recording again, his fans tossed off their mourning clothes and cheered him on. He brought Norman Blake, Peter Rowan, and Roy Husky into the studio to support him on his all-acoustic comeback album TRAIN A COMIN'. When he took that group on his first post-rehab tour, folks saw first-hand that he was a changed man who was ready again to rock'n'roll. He signed to Warner Brothers (staying out of the Nashville loop even though it was still home) and started his own record label, E-Squared. His next album he titled (appropriately) I FEEL ALRIGHT, and it garnered him further attention and acclaim. A gutsy, honest rock'n'roll album, this was the Steve Earle folks had been waiting for. Earle was also outspoken about the state of country music (among other topics) as ever, and as a result found himself the new hero of the growing alternative-country movement.

Earle is now a full-fledged, fulltime musician all over again, not only making his own music but also lending a hand to others (he produced the one new Waylon and Willie cut for the anniversary reissue of WANTED! THE OUTLAWS, for instance, as well as albums by E-Squared artists Cheri Knight and the V-Roys). He released EL CORAZÓN in late 1997, and THE MOUNTAIN in 1999 (a bluegrass collaboration with the Del McCoury Band), and he continues to tour on a regular basis.

⊙ **Guitar Town** (1986; MCA). It's hard to go wrong with Earle's debut, thanks to such great songs as "Someday," "Hillbilly Highway," and "Guitar Town." The production (by Tony Brown and Emory Gordy, Jr.) and arrangements are sharp and spare, as is the writing, thanks to Earle's keen, hard-eyed perspective. Perhaps more country than rock'n'roll this time around, Earle's musical range is nonetheless incredibly diverse, and it's obvious he speaks both languages (as well as blues and folk) with inherent ease.

⊙ **Copperhead Road** (1988; MCA). Earle crossed to the bad side of the tracks with this hard-rock (but still twang-infested) opus—and made one hell of a solid record. It'll be hard for him to ever top the raw power he created on the title track, which gives a post-Vietnam spin to a tale of hillbilly bootleggers. The rousing "Johnny Come Lately," with the Pogues backing him up, has further vestiges of post-war trauma, and the powerful "Devil's Right Hand" will knock you flat.

⊙ **The Hard Way** (1990; MCA). Earle's most underrated album retains the hard edge of COPPERHEAD ROAD on songs like "The Other Kind," but slows down for his haunting anti-death-penalty ballad "Billy Austin" (which foreshadows "Ellis Unit One," his contribution to the *Dead Man Walking* soundtrack).

⊙ **Train A Comin'** (1995; Winter Harvest). This all-acoustic album marked Earle's return to recording after beating the devils from his life. The songs include originals he wrote over the last twenty years ("Hometown Blues," "Nothing' Without You," "Sometimes She Forgets") alongside covers such as "The Rivers Of Babylon" and Townes Van Zandt's "Tecumseh Valley." The excellent band features guitarist Norman Blake, mandolinist Peter Rowan and bassist Roy Huskey, and Emmylou Harris pipes in on two cuts.

⊙ **El Corazón** (1997; Warner Bros./E-Squared). The melancholy "Christmas In Washington" makes a beautiful opener to an album that's Earle's strongest in a decade. The music runs from acoustic bluegrass ("I Still Carry You Around" featuring the great Del McCoury Band) to the full-frontal rock'n'roll of "Taneytown" and the gritty "N.Y.C.," and the writing is solid throughout. Further guests include Emmylou Harris, gospel artists the Fairfield Four, and punk band the Supersuckers.

Steve Earle And The Del McCoury Band

⊙ **The Mountain** (1999; E-Squared). Using the Del McCoury Band, one of the tightest and most revered outfits in contemporary bluegrass, as his backing outfit this time was a brilliant move on Earle's part. His singing adds a rock'n'roll edge to the proceedings, as usual, but the songs (Earle penned all of them) and arrangements are reverent to traditional bluegrass. Far from a mere experiment, the music moves and grooves throughout.

Joe Ely

J oe Ely is a burly voiced, highly charged singer with firm country roots and a musical approach (and attitude) that's part free-spirited troubadour, part roadhouse rock'n'roller. Though he does it rarely, he can play and sing beautifully alone, with just his own acoustic guitar as accompaniment. But put a band behind him and his louder sensibilities come thundering down the line. Yet even at his most blustery, his country soul remains visible—maybe it's an inherent part of his Texas heritage, but roots like his can't be completely buried. Much of Ely's music has a macho aura about it, too, yet it's exactly this energetic vibe and pronounced confidence that enable this guy to take a decent song—whether he wrote it or not—and make it snap.

Signed as a solo artist to MCA in 1977, at the tail end of the Outlaw era, Ely was tagged as one of a new breed of singers sticking to traditional country styles and giving the genre fresh hope. Yet despite a string of excellent albums (not to mention his 1973 debut with the Flatlanders), Ely proved himself the restless kind—too individualistic to become a country hitmaker. After dabbling in rock'n'roll (he'd toured the UK with the Clash and come back a changed man) and then turning to a high-tech sound for 1984's HI-RES, MCA finally dumped him. Funny, then, that he spun around and recorded one of the best (and most honky tonk) albums of his career, 1987's LORD OF THE HIGHWAY, released on the indie label HighTone. A few years after that MCA changed its mind again and re-signed him. MCA Nashville president Tony Brown proudly hung onto Ely the way a child clings to a favorite blanket—a smart move, because being an artist with a strong, deliberate voice (not to mention genuine Texas roots, which automatically adds clout), Ely's music burns with a built-in fever few contemporary artists would dare pretend to. Too bad for both parties, then, that Ely got dropped once again in the late '90s, a victim of bottom-line cuts in the wake of further label mergers.

Ely was born on 9 February, 1947 in Amarillo, a medium-sized town in the Texas Panhandle that's a long way from pretty much everything. By the time he was twelve his family had moved two hours south to Lubbock, another isolated town but one with surprisingly rich musical roots (Buddy Holly, for instance, was born and raised there). Ely's been closely associated with the place ever since. As a teenager he played rock'n'roll in local clubs, but by the age of seventeen he left town for Dallas and later Houston. After that he traveled, often by hopping trains, writing and playing music the whole way. LA, New York City, New Mexico, and Europe were all stopping points before he landed again in Lubbock, where he hooked up with his old friend Butch Hancock and another singer, Jimmie Dale Gilmore. The trio became the nucleus of the Flatlanders, a short-lived band that recorded one acoustic-based album in 1972—an album that's since taken on legendary status (see separate entry p.353).

After that band split up, Ely formed his own band (which included such Texas regulars as Lloyd Maines, Ponte Bone, and Jesse "Guitar" Taylor) and built a strong local following. MCA eventually got wind and signed him, bringing him to Nashville to record. His self-titled debut album came out in 1977, and he was immediately singled out as a strong new original. His debut also included songs by his old pals, Gilmore and Hancock (their songs, especially those of Hancock, have continued to show up on Ely albums ever since). Ely's follow-up, the equally excellent HONKY TONK MASQUERADE, was even named one of the top albums of the decade by *Rolling Stone*. For his third album, DOWN ON THE DRAG, he recorded in Seattle with a new producer, Bob Johnston.

Ely's tour of the UK with the Clash in the late '70s inspired his next project, LIVE SHOTS, recorded in three London clubs. By this point his acoustic country streak was fading in favor of a louder electric sound; he switched from MCA's Nashville to its pop (LA) roster and in 1981 released MUSTA NOTTA GOTTA LOTTA, which was basically a rock 'n' roll record.

His 1984 album HI-RES was probably the last straw for MCA, which had patiently awaited a hit from this powerhouse performer. Like Neil Young's TRANS, HI-RES was a digital album in a pre-digital era, and it didn't catch on. MCA

MICHAEL WILSON

Joe Ely

Joe Ely

dropped Ely soon after. The California indie label HighTone knew an opportunity when they saw it, however, picked up the renegade artist and released LORD OF THE HIGHWAY, which today stands as one of Ely's most enduring records. Ely followed it with DIG ALL NIGHT before MCA executives realized the error of their ways and re-signed the singer in 1990, bringing him back with a bang by releasing the album LIVE AT LIBERTY LUNCH. Two years later came LOVE AND DANGER, co-produced by Tony Brown, which featured two songs, "Whenever Kindness Fails" and "The Road Goes On Forever," by fellow Texan Robert Earl Keen. Since then the latter song has practically become the new state anthem, boosting Keen's career in the process. In 1994 Ely was one of several Texans who contributed songs and sang on the soundtrack to the play *Chippy* (written by fellow Lubbockian Terry Allen and his wife Jo Harvey Allen). More recently Ely has focused on a southwestern theme with LETTER TO LAREDO and TWISTIN' IN THE WIND. On these, the raw approach that marked his early work has been traded for a newfound complexity that's immediately apparent in his singing, writing and arranging. A new Ely album is planned for release on an independent label in 2000.

⊙ **Joe Ely** (1977; MCA). Ely busts out of the chute with a strong debut that's not exactly Outlaw, but fits somewhere between Austin's country-rock and Nashville's soon-to-come neo-traditionalism. His versions of Hancock's "Tennessee's Not The State I'm In" and "If You Were A Bluebird" are clear standouts, as are Gilmore's "Treat Me Like A Saturday Night" and Ely's own "I Had My Hopes Up High." Thankfully, producer Chip Young allows the band its rough edges, maintaining a raw feeling that also contributes to the music's warmth.

⊙ **Honky Tonk Masquerade** (1978; MCA). Another top-notch, western-flavored country album (produced again by Young) that's easily one of Ely's finest. Not only are many individual songs superb ("Boxcars," "Tonight I Think I'm Gonna Go Downtown"), the whole album maintains a consistent vibe despite its mood swings between high-energy material ("Cornbread Moon") and melancholy musings ("Because Of The Wind").

⊙ **Lord Of The Highway** (1987; HighTone). The title track (another Hancock gem) and "Me And Billy The Kid" (written by Ely) help make this one of Ely's strongest collections to date. It's also a straight-up honky tonk album that brought him back to Earth (i.e.

Texas soil) after his dabblings in rockabilly (MUSTA NOTTA) and synthesizers (HI-RES).

⊙ **Letter To Laredo** (1996; MCA). Marked by the beautiful, distinctive flamenco strumming of European guitarist Teye, Laredo is a mostly acoustic record with a strong southwestern flavor. It's a strong record and marks a broadening of Ely's musical direction.

⊙ **Twistin' In The Wind** (1998; MCA). TWISTIN' picks up where LAREDO left off, but this time Ely's approach is more electric. A few of the songs stand out, but it's the musicianship that makes this album among Ely's most solid. For one thing, TWISTIN' features five guitarists Ely has worked with over the years: Jesse "Guitar" Taylor, Lloyd Maines (a pedal-steel whiz who's another Lubbuck mainstay), Teye, David Grissom, and Mitch Watkins.

Foster & Lloyd

During the late 1980s, Radney Foster and Bill Lloyd developed a hook-filled country style that combined rockabilly rhythms, jangly guitar licks, and a hip, alternative-rock sensibility. Their sound was more country-rock than either the Judds or the O'Kanes, two other duos who were popular around the same time. The strength was in their dichotomy: Foster had a stronger country music background, while Lloyd was a big Beatles fan. This blend of influences made their early singles enticing, though after several years it also drove them in separate musical directions.

Lloyd was born on 6 December, 1955 in Fort Hood, Texas but raised in Kentucky. He moved to Nashville in the early '80s, worked as a song-writer for the MTM Music Group, and released a solo rock'n'roll album, FEELING THE ELEPHANT, on the Throbbing Lobster label. Foster was also born in Texas, in the border town of Del Rio on 20 July, 1959. His background was more steeped in country music, but his tastes also ran from Tejano to rock. After college, he, too, moved to Nashville and ended up at MTM, where he met Lloyd. The two began writing and playing music together, and one of their songs became a hit for Sweethearts Of The Rodeo. The two singer-songwriters eventually won the attention of RCA's Joe Galante, who signed them in 1987. Foster & Lloyd's single "Crazy Over You" made the country Top 10, and over the next several years they had further hits—including "Sure Thing,"

"Texas In 1880," and "What Do You Want From Me" from the pair's debut album, FOSTER & LLOYD.

Their debut album was their strongest collection of songs, and their popularity as a unit slowly waned with each of their two follow-up releases FASTER AND LLOUDER (1988) and VER-SIONS OF THE TRUTH (1989). They parted ways in 1990, each pursuing a solo career. Lloyd shifted into a power-pop direction, and that's what you'll find all over SET TO POP (1994; East Side Digital) and STANDING ON THE SHOULDERS OF GIANTS (1999; Koch). Foster remained tied to Nashville, and his 1992 album for Arista, DEL RIO, TX 1959,

Lubbock: More A Legend Than A City

Maybe it's the city streets that stretch from the middle of town straight to the distant horizon; or the flat terrain, heat and isolation; or the wind that seems to blow all night and all day. Or maybe it's the myriad UFO sightings—the most famous being the so-called Lubbock Lights, photographed in 1951. Whatever it is, Lubbock, Texas is one of those places where things just ... converge.

And take off. Music, for instance. Lots of it, certainly more than you'd expect from a plain-Jane, medium-sized city—nothing flashy, nothing quaint— out in the West Texas plains some 350 miles west of Dallas. The name **Buddy Holly** needs mentioning first of all. Holly was born and raised in Lubbock, and his rock'n'roll spirit will forever haunt the town's cultural heritage. **Waylon Jennings** soaked up some of that Lubbock energy, too, though he was only passing through, working as a DJ before joining Holly's band. And then there was the **Flatlanders**. A more recent creation, they have gained the city a whole new audience of fringe-friendly alternative country fans. As the group's CD title states, the Flatlanders were MORE A LEGEND THAN A BAND—their actual time together in the early 1970s was short-lived, yet their influence has been felt for decades afterward.

Before conceiving the group, founding members **Jimmie Dale Gilmore**, **Butch Hancock** and **Joe Ely** had each already experienced the classic Lubbock irony: each left town soon after high school, yet each also found himself drawn right back inside almost before they knew what was happening. It's almost as if the town had some mystical pull—though the value of that explanation depends on who you ask. **Terry Allen** might scoff at the mention of mystical forces, yet he, too, has experienced that same pull. He escaped Lubbock in the early '60s with his wife, playwright and actress Jo Harvey Allen; the town, however, continued to haunt him. Finally in the late '70s he was drawn back to record an album—which he titled, appropriately, LUBBOCK (ON EVERYTHING).

Of that Flatlander trio, Ely was the first to land a solo recording contract. He was signed to MCA, yet his first few albums are like snapshots of his hometown's musical landscape. Hancock's songs (and a couple of Gilmore's) are all over the roster; and the pickers include such Lubbock stalwarts as guitarist **Jesse Taylor**, steel player **Lloyd Maines** and accordionist **Ponty Bone**. These musicians also doubled as members of the Panhandle Mystery Band, Terry Allen's backing outfit on his Lubbock-recorded albums. And they've shown up on albums by Gilmore and Hancock as well. For a town that everyone seems to want to leave, there sure is a lot of love in the air.

Maines is the rare Lubbockite in that he's chosen to plant roots and stay put. And why shouldn't he? Since producing Allen's LUBBOCK album at the local Caldwell Studios, he's gained regular work behind the glass for such left-of-center country artists as Wayne Hancock, Richard Buckner, Ray Wylie Hubbard, Robert Earl Keen, and Uncle Tupelo. He's a busy man both as a producer and also as an instrumentalist: he's one of the finest pedal-steel players in contemporary country music, and ever since he made his debut on Ely's first album, his picking has shown up on countless recordings. He also has performed and recorded with his siblings as the Maines Brothers. Oh, and his daughter? That's Natalie Maines, lead singer of the Dixie Chicks.

The list of musicians hailing from Lubbock, however, doesn't stop with the Flatlanders, Allen, or even Maines. Singer-songwriter **David Halley** ("Rain Just Falls") hails from the city, as do blues-based artists **Delbert McClinton** and **Angela Strehli**. **Jo Carol Pierce** is another of Lubbock's musical offspring. Her chief brainchild has been the performance piece BAD GIRLS UPSET BY THE TRUTH (1995; Dejadisc), but she also had nineteen of her songs compiled on ACROSS THE GREAT DIVIDE (1994; Dejadisc) in versions sung by Ely, Allen, Kris McKay, Michael Hall, and Gilmore, among others. And speaking of Gilmore, he and Pierce were once married.

As sick and fed up as they appear to be with the subject, the truth is, Lubbock boys Ely, Allen, Gilmore, and Hancock can't seem to stop talking about their onetime hometown. They're as perplexed by its strange energy—its "mystique"—as anyone. As Ely once remarked, "It's a hard place to stay, but in some ways, a harder place to stay gone from."

Foster & Lloyd

won him new acclaim and a handful of hits, including "Just Call Me Lonesome" and "Nobody Wins." He later released a couple more albums for Arista, LABOR OF LOVE (1994) and SEE WHAT YOU WANT TO SEE (1998).

⊙ **The Essential Foster & Lloyd** (1996; RCA). This 20-song collection pulls a decent selection of songs from their 3 albums. All the big hits are here, from the rockabilly-inspired "Crazy For You" to the beefier "Texas 1880" and the pleasantly jangly "Fair Shake."

Radney Foster

⊙ **Del Rio, TX 1959** (1992; Arista). The sound here is twangier than any of Foster & Lloyd's material, though a rock'n'roll edge does remain in the 'young country' rhythms that drive songs like "Nobody Wins" and "Hammer And Nails."

Jimmie Dale Gilmore

"Most of my real audience ... they're kind of eclectic people. They're not the kind that judge by the categories, you know?"

—Jimmie Dale Gilmore

More than any Austin-based artist of the 1980s and '90s, Jimmie Dale Gilmore has come to represent that Texas town's country music scene the way Willie Nelson and Jerry Jeff Walker did during the cosmic cowboy era of the '70s. Gilmore's warbling tenor voice renders him immediately recognizable as a singer, and his warm, folky manner is tinged by a personal spiritualism he neither hides nor feels the need to shout about in public. If Austin had an ambassadorship, Gilmore would be a natural for the job.

Jimmie Dale's popularity has only grown so strong since the late '80s, when he released his first two solo albums, FAIR AND SQUARE and JIMMIE DALE GILMORE. His musical history, however, stretches back much further. Austinites have witnessed his talents since he settled there at the start of the decade, and as one of the Flatlanders he was a legend to the few familiar with

that band's short life. Gilmore's first two albums, then, allowed the rest of us to catch up. They're definitely his most honky tonking to date; since then he's drifted into a more ambiguous territory that exists between country, folk and rock'n'roll. Altogether he's wound up in a place far different from the blustery rock of his Flatlander bandmate Joe Ely, and equally so from the West Texas folk songs of his good pal (and sometimes performing partner) Butch Hancock.

Gilmore was born on 6 May, 1945 and spent his initial years in Tulia, Texas, a small town in the Panhandle between Amarillo and Lubbock. His father played lead guitar in a local country band. When Gilmore was in grade school his family moved to Lubbock, a town that's nurtured a surprising number of musicians. Here he met Butch Hancock (they've been friends since 1957, he boasts) and, later, Joe Ely. It was Ely who turned Gilmore on to Townes Van Zandt—a revelatory moment, Gilmore says, because of the way Van Zandt so seamlessly integrated the worlds of folk and country music. It was another Lubbock native, though, Terry Allen, whom Gilmore credits with giving him the inspiration to write his own songs. (One of his first, "Treat Me Like A Saturday Night," is now one of his best known; it first appeared on Ely's debut album.)

Gilmore began playing guitar at sixteen. He and Ely formed the T. Nickel House Band and played around Lubbock before Gilmore took off for Austin during the mid-'60s. Upon returning

Jimmie Dale Gilmore

to Lubbock he hooked up again with Ely and Hancock (who'd each also done some traveling), and the trio formed the Flatlanders (see separate entry p.353). The group recorded one album in Nashville in 1972 that mixed acoustic folk, string-band country and country blues; the album also included what's still Gilmore's best-known song, "Dallas." By the end of the year, however, the band had split up.

Gilmore was already enamored with Eastern philosophy, and during the rest of the decade he pursued these spiritual interests more seriously. He studied under the guru Maharaji and moved to Denver, playing music only as a hobby. (Gilmore's songs did, however, show up on Ely's solo albums.) In 1980, he returned to Austin where he began playing regular gigs and building a strong local following. Finally, in 1988—when he was well into his forties—Gilmore released his debut solo album, FAIR AND SQUARE, on HighTone, a West Coast indie label that at the time was Ely's home. This and especially his 1989 follow-up, JIMMIE DALE GILMORE, had a more straightforward honky-tonk style than anything Gilmore has done previously or since. Together these albums helped place him at the forefront of a new generation of alternative country artists—just as Austin itself was becoming noticed again as a musical hot spot.

In the wake of this newfound attention, Rounder Records dug up the Flatlanders album and released it under the appropriate title MORE A LEGEND THAN A BAND. That same year Virgin Australia put out TWO ROADS, a duet album that features Gilmore and Hancock trading songs during the pair's Australian tour. Gilmore was soon signed to Elektra-Nonesuch, which released AFTER AWHILE in 1991 as part of the label's American Explorer series. The album retained a country feeling but was less honky-tonk in nature, and it won Gilmore even more acclaim as a distinct and wholly original voice in country music. Nashville showed little interest, but *Rolling Stone* critics voted Gilmore Country Artist of the Year in both 1991 and 1992.

Gilmore's next album, SPINNING AROUND THE SUN, again featured a mix of contemporary and traditional country-flavored songs (including two by Hancock and one Hank Williams cover) and a fuller instrumental sound fronted by Gilmore's rich, warm voice. His 1996 release BRAVER NEWER WORLD, however, showed him leaning further away from a country sound and more towards the kind of hard-to-pin-down contemporary arena shared by fellow Texan Lyle Lovett. For instance, where Ely produced

Gilmore's debut and recorded it in Texas, BRAVER NEWER WORLD was produced and recorded by T-Bone Burnett in LA. The situation changed all over again, however, when Elektra dropped Gilmore in the late '90s. He toured a little during the intervening years (and even appeared in the Coen Brothers movie *The Big Lebowski*), but in 2000 he finally released another excellent collection, ONE ENDLESS NIGHT, on the independent Windcharger label (with distribution through Rounder).

⊙ **Jimmie Dale Gilmore** (1989; HighTone). Gilmore's follow-up is tighter than his debut, and it sports a traditional sound that's more visceral and earthy than anything he's done since. Songs include a new version of "Dallas," the rousing "That Hardwood Floor," and an excellent but infrequently performed Hancock song "When The Nights Are Cold."

⊙ **After Awhile** (1991; Elektra Nonesuch). Gilmore's third album is still traditional-sounding and definitely country, but the hardwood-floor honky-tonk has been toned down. The result is not only a more introspective tone, but a more personal approach. The instrumentation shifts between acoustic and electric, and the song roster features two Gilmore classics: "Tonight I Think I'm Gonna Go Downtown," from the Flatlanders album, and "Treat My Like a Saturday Night." One of Gilmore's best efforts to date.

⊙ **Braver Newer World** (1996; Elektra). T-Bone Burnett produced this album, which spins Gilmore's music even further away from his honky-tonk roots. It's a sophisticated album full of sensual, textural beauty, and it has a heavier emphasis on rhythm and percussion than previous releases. Gilmore's delicate moods and phrasings are intact, however, and his warble keeps the experience grounded: when he sings, you can't help but envisage the West Texas plains stretching into forever. Highlights include two deeply quiet songs written by A.B. Strehli, the reclusive brother of blues singer Angela Strehli.

⊙ **One Endless Night** (2000; Windcharger/Rounder). After the sonic experimentation of BRAVER NEWER WORLD, Gilmore comes back to basics on this release, his first on an indie label in over a decade. He co-produced it with guitarist Buddy Miller, known for his 'living room' approach to record making. While many of the arrangements are full of fiddle, steel, organ and electric guitar (such as the rollicking version of Townes Van Zandt's "No Lonesome Tune"), the overall feeling is comfortable and contemplative. Another gem.

Jimmie Dale Gilmore

Nanci Griffith

Texas-born singer-songwriter Nanci Griffith came to country from a folk-music background, and she's kept a sweet-voiced, acoustic-based tone to her music throughout her career. She's a hard-working and dedicated artist who toured all over and released a series of independent albums before ever getting national attention and a Nashville recording contract. Though she wasn't a rocked-up honky tonker like Steve Earle, she did sign with Earle's (and Lyle Lovett's) label at the time, MCA, in 1987. Her songs on the whole have been more successful in the country charts when covered by other artists—Kathy Mattea with "Love At The Five And Dime," Suzy Boggus with "Outbound Plane"—but her reputation has continued to grow, and twenty years after he recording debut, her popularity was stronger than ever.

Griffith was born on 16 July, 1954 in Seguin, Texas and grew up in Austin. She attended the University of Texas in Austin, and after college she briefly taught kindergarten. She'd been singing folk music since her teenage years, however, and she eventually chose to pursue music fulltime. Her first album, THERE'S A LIGHT BEYOND THESE WOODS, came out on a local label, BF Deal (it was reissued by Philo). Griffith had won acclaim at the annual Kerrville Folk Festival in Kerrville, Texas—the closest to a Texas music lovefest since the demise of Willie Nelson's summertime picnics—and over the next several years she toured festivals, coffeehouses and clubs constantly. During the early '80s she cut the albums POET IN MY WINDOW (1982), ONCE IN A VERY BLUE MOON (1985), and THE LAST OF THE TRUE BELIEVERS (1986). These showcased her literary lyrics and story songs (she emphasized her bookish quality by posing on album covers holding tomes by such authors as Eudora Welty, Carson McCullers, and Truman Capote), her sweet girlish voice, her penchant for small-town values and her gentle, folk-infused arrangements. TRUE BELIEVERS contained "Love At The Five And Dime," which became Kathy Mattea's first Top 10 hit in 1986 and gained Griffith attention in Nashville.

MCA's Tony Brown signed Griffith in 1986, and her major label debut, LONE STAR STATE OF MIND, was released a year later. The title track

became the first of only two in Griffith's career that made the Top 40. It was her most commercial (and country-sounding) record to date—her tried and true folk style was now pepped up with Lloyd Green's steel guitar, Béla Fleck's banjo, and other tastefully layered instrumental elements. LITTLE LOVE AFFAIRS (1988) repeated the country formula (though the liberal use of James Hooker's synthesizer gets in the way) and gained her one more Top 40 hit, the sad and sentimental "I Knew Love." ONE FAIR SUMMER EVENING (also 1988) captured a live show in Houston, while for STORMS (1989) she was shifted to MCA's pop division in LA, and the album was recorded with rock producer Glyn Johns at the helm. Her final MCA album was LATE NIGHT GRAND HOTEL (1991).

Griffith next signed with Elektra and released one of her most acclaimed albums, OTHER VOICES, OTHER ROOMS, a collection of cover songs by Townes Van Zandt, John Prine, Kate Wolf, Bob Dylan, and others. Five years later she cut a sequel, OTHER VOICES, TOO (A TRIP BACK TO BOUN-

SENOR McGUIRE

Nanci Griffith

TIFUL), and it included songs by Richard Thompson, Guy Clark, Sandy Denny, and Sonny Curtis (the list of guest singers on the album was equally large and impressive). In between she cut the more pop-oriented FLYER (1994) and BLUE ROSES FROM THE MOONS (1997). The latter included guest appearances from the Crickets and a duet with Darius Rucker of Hootie and the Blowfish. In 1999, Griffith recorded THE DUST BOWL SYMPHONY with the London Symphony Orchestra; it was an ambitious project that featured lushly arranged versions of songs from her twenty-year-old catalog like "Love At The Five And Dime," "Late Night Grand Hotel," and "Trouble In The Fields."

⊙ **Last Of The True Believers** (1986; Philo). For Griffith fans, "Love At The Five And Dime" is the showpiece here, as it virtually reeks of her biggest musical trademarks: bittersweet romanticism, small-town sentimentalism and literary allusions. The title track is a lively and memorable number, and instrumentalists such as Béla Fleck and Mark O'Connor give the arrangements a newgrass vibe.

⊙ **Lone Star State Of Mind** (1987; MCA). Griffith's folk style has always tended toward the precious and sweet. Here, however, on her first MCA album, the bigger production (especially the prominent pedal-steel guitar) gives songs like "Trouble In The Fields," "Ford Econoline," and the title track a beefier quality. "From A Distance" is mired in sap, while Robert Earl Keen's "Sing One For Sister" is another standout.

⊙ **Other Voices, Other Rooms** (1993; Elektra). Ironically, considering she's such an applauded songwriter, one of Griffith's most popular albums is this collection of folk songs written by others. But her reverence for the works of Townes Van Zandt ("Tecumseh Valley"), John Prine ("Speed Of The Sound Of Loneliness"), Woody Guthrie ("Do Re Mi"), and others is clear in her easygoing versions. A bit pretty at times, but overall enjoyable.

⊙ **The MCA Years: A Retrospective** (1993; MCA). This 18-track sampler is not a bad way to introduce yourself to Griffith, as it includes some of her best-known titles: "Trouble In The Fields," "Love At The Five And Dime," "Outbound Plane," "From A Distance" (a Julie Gold song later made into a pop hit by Bette Midler), and the sentimental "Gulf Coast Highway," which has become one of her signatures.

Butch Hancock

Butch Hancock is a Lubbock, Texas–born folksinger with a sharp dry wit, a talent for clever (and often kooky) wordplay, and loads and loads of engaging melodies that are built around a simple foundation of acoustic guitar and his own raspy, Dylanesque voice. Along with his longtime Lubbock pals Jimmie Dale Gilmore and Joe Ely, Hancock was a founding member of the Flatlanders in the 1970s. Since then he has grown into one of the finest—and most prolific—songwriters to emerge from the sprawling Texas horizon in recent decades. Songs like "West Texas Waltz," "If You Were A Bluebird," "Boxcars," "She Never Spoke Spanish To Me," and "Standin' At The Big Hotel" are a mix of the mystical and the absurd, and as a whole they relay a good-natured attitude toward life and all its foibles. These and other titles have been covered by such artists as Jerry Jeff Walker, the Texas Tornadoes and Emmylou Harris—and, of course, Gilmore and Ely, who rarely let an album go by without at least one Hancock song on it. Hancock's own recordings, however, have never gained much national attention beyond regional and underground country-folk circles. Perhaps that's partly because he's taken such a do-it-yourself approach, publishing his music himself and releasing nearly all his albums on his own Rainlight label. He's got loads of ambition and drive, however—check out his 14-cassette series, No 2 Alike, which documented a six-night stint at Austin's Cactus Cafe in 1990. During that extended showcase, Hancock played 140 of his own songs, and he never repeated a single one.

Butch was born George Norman Hancock on 12 July, 1945 in Lubbock, Texas. He studied architecture, but he was ultimately more drawn to music and songwriting. He met Gilmore in junior high, and the two have been close friends ever since—touring and recording together, and generally performing each others' songs (and singing each others' praises) whenever possible. Their initial collaboration was during the '70s in the short-lived band the Flatlanders (see separate entry p.353). After that, Hancock eventually settled in Austin. Joe Ely recorded a bunch of Hancock's songs on his first few albums (they were later compiled on a British release titled MILKSHAKES AND MALTS); by the late '70s, Hancock finally decided it was high time he began recording himself.

His first solo album was WEST TEXAS WALTZES & DUST-BLOWN TRACTOR TUNES (1978), which he released on his own label, Rainlight. The title track is a funny, rambling paean to dancing, milkshakes, silly dogs, and good loving, and it's one of Hancock's signatures. Further albums followed over the next decade, including THE WIND'S DOMINION, FIREWATER (SEEKS ITS OWN LEVEL), and YELLA ROSE (with Marce

Lacouture). All were released on Rainlight, and all possess a loose, spontaneous quality. The British label Demon compiled a double album's worth of these songs on the 1989 release OWN AND OWN; it also included four new songs recorded with a band that Butch dubbed the Sunspots. The US label Sugar Hill has also issued two CD compilations of Hancock's recordings, OWN AND OWN and OWN THE WAY OVER HERE. In the mid-'90s, Hancock recorded his most full-blown studio effort to date, EATS AWAY THE NIGHT, produced by onetime Lucinda Williams collaborator Gurf Morlix. In addition to songwriting, Hancock is a prolific photographer, and for several years during the '90s he owned a gallery and performance space, Lubbock Or Leave It, in downtown Austin. He continues to release albums on Rainlight, and he's also reissued some of his early solo albums onto CD for the first time.

Naomi and Wynonna Judd

⊙ **Own And Own** (1991; Sugar Hill). This is almost a straight reissue of the double-LP Demon collection (two songs, "Leo And Leona" and "Split And Slide," are missing), and it's a great introduction to Hancock's world. Includes "West Texas Waltz," "Firewater," "Bluebird," "The Wind's Dominion," "Like A Kiss On The Mouth," and a dozen more.

⊙ **Eats Away The Night** (1995; Sugar Hill). Hancock cut this full-blooded studio album with three musicians from Lucinda Williams' backing band—guitarist Gurf Morlix, bassist John Ciambotti, and drummer Donald Lindley—who spice up the proceedings nicely. "To Each His Own" and "Junkyard In The Sun" show he's not afraid to rock, while "Pumpkineater" and the title track are acoustic and quiet. Including new versions of "If You Were A Bluebird," "Boxcars," and "Welcome To The Real World Kid."

The Judds

"If it wasn't for music, I would have been one screwed-up kid."
—Wynonna Judd

When Naomi and Wynonna Judd disbanded their immensely popular mother-and-daughter duet act in 1991, it was one of the most tear-filled events in country music history. To their loyal and longstanding fans, losing the Judds was like losing Princess Diana. They were royalty—one of modern country music's most popular and universally loved acts. And it's easy to see why. Their songs had the feel of old-time folk music, yet they were charged with vibrant arrangements, pretty harmonies and Wynonna's gutsy lead vocals. Mother Naomi was the guiding force, infusing the music with folky southern charm and spiritual wisdom, and embellishing her family's rags-to-riches history with sentimental details (and this at a time when America was obsessed with "family values"). Daughter Wynonna, on the other hand, was often sullen and moody—though it was her voice that was the duo's lead instrument. Being a Judd, however, wasn't always pretty. They quarreled often, placing their dinner-table confrontations in full view of their public; but they also sang each others' praises. Their fans, of course, ate it up. And when the time came for this country family to say goodbye, everybody shed real tears.

Naomi's original name was Diana Ellen Judd, and she was born on 11 January, 1946 in Ashland, Kentucky. She married Michael Ciminella and had her first daughter, Christina (born 30 May, 1964), the same year she finished high school. The young family moved to Los Angeles, where their second daughter, Ashley (who's since gone on to Hollywood stardom), was born. When the marriage broke up, Diana and her daughters began a Gypsy-like odyssey that took them from Southern California to Berea, Kentucky (where Diana attended nursing school), back to California (Marin County this time), and finally to the outskirts of Nashville. Along the way she worked odd jobs, became enamored with New Age ideals, and tried to make some Hollywood connections. She also changed her name to Naomi, her daughter Christina

The Judds

became Wynonna, and the three of them reverted to Naomi's maiden name, Judd.

Wynonna, meanwhile, was developing into a powerful singer, and Naomi encouraged her musical interests, which included both old-time folk music and more contemporary singer-songwriters like Bonnie Raitt and Joni Mitchell. After moving to Nashville, Naomi began a long process of pitching them as a mother-daughter duo to the suits on Music Row. She initially met with little success, though she did land them a spot on Ralph Emery's morning TV show, which gave them some exposure. Naomi also passed a tape to someone at the hospital where she worked, who, as it turned out, had connections in the business. In classic Cinderella fashion, the tape made its way to the right person, and Naomi and Wynonna were allowed to audition for RCA executives, who were knocked out by their strong harmonies and folk-infused style. The Judds were signed in 1983, and soon after they had made the country charts with "Had A Dream (For The Heart)," a Dennis Linde song that had been a pop hit for Elvis Presley. Producer/engineer Brent Maher and guitarist/bandleader Don Potter became important collaborators in the development of the Judds' sound.

"Had A Dream" was one of six songs on the Judds' debut "Mini LP" (a short-lived marketing concept), released by RCA in 1984. The same disc also housed their next single and one of their most memorable songs, "Mama He's Crazy." Marked by prominent steel guitars and Wynonna's gutsy lead voice, the song hit the top of the country charts in the spring, becoming the first of the fourteen #1 hits they clocked up during their career. Later that year, RCA released the Judds' first full-length album, WHY NOT ME, the title track of which won the the CMA's Single of the Year award in 1985. Over the next several years, the Judds also won a handful of Grammys and a streak of CMA and ACM awards for both Vocal Group and Vocal Duet Of The Year. Their sound grew noticeably slicker as the years rolled forward, and while record sales did trail off a bit toward the end, their popularity held steady and strong.

The Judds seemed to be an unstoppable musical force, but in the fall of 1990, Naomi Judd called a press conference and tearfully announced her retirement from performing due to chronic hepatitis. The duo then embarked on a massive 124-date 'farewell' tour that climaxed in late 1991 with a televised concert special. After some intense soul-searching and plenty of professional encouragement, Wynonna ultimately broke out on her own with a polished but still gutsy, blues-based sound that turned her into one of the top female solo artists of the '90s. Naomi didn't stay completely out of the business, however. She published her autobiography, *Love Can Build A Bridge* (which had also been the title of the final Judds album), and helped direct Wynonna's career.

On New Year's Eve 1999, Naomi and Wynonna reunited for a concert in Phoenix, Arizona. Fueled by the positive response—and Naomi's announcement that she had won her battle with hepatitis—mother and daughter made plans for a multicity reunion tour that spring. They also recorded four new songs together that were packaged as a bonus disc with Wynonna's 2000 album NEW DAY RISING.

⊙ **Greatest Hits** (1988; RCA). At their best, the Judds mixed the simplicity of old-time folk music with a contemporary approach that was bright and exciting. Their sound eventually grew much slicker—becoming mired in sentiment and melodrama—but early songs such as "Mama He's Crazy," "Grandpa (Tell Me 'Bout The Good Old Days)," and "Why Not Me" spoke of old-fashioned values and personal empowerment in a plain, straightforward style.

⊙ **Greatest Hits, Volume 2** (1991; RCA). A companion collection that pulls together 10 songs from the entire length of the Judds' career, including "John Deere Tractor" (a beautifully melancholy song that was previously recorded by bluegrass singer Larry Sparks), "Let Me Tell You About Love" (their final #1 hit from 1989), and "Love Can Build A Bridge."

Robert Earl Keen

"My favorite songs, the ones that work out best for me, come from a real snap in my head."

—Robert Earl Keen

Texas singer-songwriter Robert Earl Keen has a sharp wit, a laid-back cowboy style, and an eye for detail, all of which combine in songs that are as easy on the ears as they are packed with insight. Humor defines much of Keen's early songs, and he's often funny, as in "Copenhagen," a song about chewing tobacco and the folks who use it, or "Merry Christmas From The Family," about a nightmarish holiday gathering. His comedy can be dark at times (the vengeful "Whenever Kindness Fails"), and he can also be serious and introspective, as on the melancholy "Rolling By," the sad tale of "Mariano," and "Corpus Christi Bay," the last about two oil-worker brothers that's among his finest efforts. Beneath the surface of everything he writes, however, is a sincere understanding of the human condition, both the warts and the smiles, that shows through in his vivid characters and situations.

Born on 11 January, 1956 in Houston, Texas, Robert Earl Keen, Jr. (he originally recorded under his full name, then dropped the "Jr.") attended Texas A&M University where he began writing songs both on his own and with his friend Lyle Lovett. "I'm not sure how much either one of us had to do with what the other was doing," Keen said in a 1989 interview, "but we were both kind of doin' it at the same time." Their best-known collaboration is still "The Front Porch Song" (aka "This Ole Porch"), which appeared on each man's debut album.

Keen moved to Austin and played local clubs and festivals for several years, and he recorded his debut, NO KINDA DANCER, for Philo. The independent label was also home at the time to Nanci Griffith, who sang on Keen's album and also cut one of his songs. At the instigation of Steve Earle, Keen moved to Nashville in 1985, trying to get his foot in the door of the country music business, but he didn't feel comfortable there, and only became frustrated watching the careers of friends like Lovett and Earle soar. After a couple of years he returned to Texas, where he's remained ever since.

It was back in his home state that his reputation for singing and writing clever, neo-cowboy songs began to develop. He signed with Sugar Hill and cut another couple of albums, THE LIVE ALBUM (1988) and WEST TEXTURES (1989), but his big break came when Joe Ely cut two of his songs, "Whenever Kindness Fails" and "The Road Goes On Forever," on his 1992 album LOVE AND DANGER. Both were the standout tracks on Ely's album, and the latter in particular became a modern-day anthem that everyone in Austin, like it or not, seemed to know by heart. Later, country supergroup the Highwaymen made it the title track of their third album in 1995. Keen has since become a leading artist on the Texas alternative-country scene. He signed with the newly formed Arista Austin label, releasing the overambitious rock'n'roll effort PICNIC in 1997 and the more down-to-earth WALKING DISTANCE a year later.

He also formed a hot band of Austin pickers that's one of the state's finest.

⊙ **No Kinda Dancer** (1984; Philo; reissued 1995; Sugar Hill). Some of Keen's perennial favorites were first planted here, "The Front Porch Song" and "Rolling By" among them. Humor abounds on an effort that's more cowboy folk than honky tonk. Both in terms of the songwriting and Keen's somewhat rumpled but still compelling voice, the music here is low-key, never flashy, a bit silly at times, but cool and accomplished.

⊙ **A Bigger Piece Of Sky** (1993; Sugar Hill). The darkness and the light come together with a full, wind-whipped force on this tightly packed album, Keen's finest to date. Perhaps reacting to his reputation as a jokey songwriter, there are streaks of mean, and a few moments of violence, in songs like "Whenever Kindness Fails," "Jesse With The Long Hair," the bitter "Blow You Away" (a Pogues-ish song featuring Maura O'Connell on vocals), and the brooding "Here In Arkansas." Vivid and intense.

⊙ **No. 2 Live Dinner** (1996; Sugar Hill). Keen's second live album is a great showcase of his strong, tight-at-the-seams road band and his wide range of material. He goes for laughs on "Merry Christmas From The Family" and "Five Pound Bass," gets moody and nostalgic on "Rollin' By," and kicks out the jams on Terry Allen's "Amarillo Highway" and, of course, the party-on anthem "The Road Goes On Forever." It's close to a 'hits' collection as any of his releases so far.

---

k.d. lang

Canadian singer k.d. lang was definitely an atypical sort for a country artist—from her strangely lowercased initials to her campy song style and, of course, the fact that she was a lesbian (something she announced officially well after everyone seemed to know it), not to mention an outspoken vegetarian and anti-meat crusader (which ticked off more than a few beef eaters in the music industry). Yet lang's rich, soaring voice—clearly conjuring the spirit of her mentor, Patsy Cline—was able to, at least in the early half of her career, transcend generations and even genres. Her album SHADOWLAND was produced by Nashville Sound stalwart Owen Bradley (who'd also been Cline's producer), and a couple of lang's songs—"I'm Down To My Last Cigarette" and "Full Moon Full Of Love"—landed in the *Billboard* country charts during the late 1980s. lang has since gone on to explore smoky pop and torch music, but country music remains a part of her identity.

k.d. was born Kathryn Dawn Lang on 2 November, 1961 in Consort, Alberta. While attending college, she discovered Patsy Cline's music, and she was immediately smitten. She formed a band, k.d. lang and the reclines, and released TRULY WESTERN EXPERIENCE on an independent Canadian label. lang next signed to Sire, and her 1987 album, ANGEL WITH A LARIET (produced by Dave Edmunds), won her some attention in Nashville—which was more open-minded at the time toward newer, edgier country material. She cut a hit duet with Roy Orbison, "Crying," and then in 1988 she recorded SHADOWLAND with producer Owen Bradley. That album sold fairly well, and the song "I'm Down To My Last Cigarette" even dented the country charts—though it failed to ignite for her a fulltime Nashville career. By this point, however, she had gained substantial popularity with hip young audiences, mostly from the rock'n'roll side of the fence. Her 1989 album, ABSOLUTE TORCH AND TWANG, won her a Grammy for Best Female Country Vocal Performance (Lyle Lovett also won that year). On her 1992 album, INGENUE, however, lang shifted away from country and into a torch-song style. Further albums from the '90s include the soundtrack to the Gus Van Zant movie *Even Cowgirls Get The Blues*, the pop album ALL YOU CAN EAT, and the cigarette-obsessed DRAG.

⊙ **Shadowland** (1988; Sire). k.d. lang showed she could closet her campy style when she wanted to on this lush, finely crafted piece of work. Owen Bradley's production casts a 1960s-era shadow over the proceedings, as does the cast of folks lending a hand—legendary pickers like Buddy Emmons and some very notable guest vocalists (Kitty Wells, Loretta Lynn, Brenda Lee). Songs include Roger Miller's "Lock Stock And Teardrops" and Harlan Howard's "I'm Down To My Last Cigarette."

⊙ **Absolute Torch And Twang** (1989; Sire). As the title announces, the twang factor here is turned up much higher than on SHADOWLAND—though not without a bit of 'torch' to keep the emotional intensity simmering. Songs include "Big Big Love," "Wallflower Waltz," and "Big Boned Gal."

Patty Loveless

> "I've never been one to carry a banner of traditional country. But that is what happened with me; and I do think that I do the traditional style well."
>
> —Patty Loveless

Kentucky singer and sometimes songwriter Patty Loveless was another of Tony Brown's signings at MCA in the mid-1980s, when new traditionalism was burning its way through Nashville. Loveless' style isn't exactly rootsy—you'd never mistake her for Kitty Wells—nor is she as rocking as Steve Earle or even as folky as Nanci Griffith. On the whole, in fact, Loveless sounds rather mainstream. But her strong voice is full of Appalachian-bred inflections, her song choices are adventurous (Lucinda Williams' "The Night's Too Long," Steve Earle's "A Little Bit In Love," Claire Lynch's "Some Morning Soon"), and even her poppier songs have a sense of depth beneath their catchy appeal. If one single virtue stands out most, however, it's Loveless' belief in what she's singing—honest emotion and a sense of conviciton come through clearly no matter whether she's singing an honorable duet with George Jones or ditties like "I'm That Kind Of Girl" and "Timber, I'm Falling In Love."

Loveless was born Patricia Ramey on 4 January, 1957 in the Appalachian town of Pikeville, Kentucky. She grew up singing with her brother, and as a teenager she was hired to sing with the Wilburn Brothers. She wound up marrying the Wilburns' drummer, Terry Lovelace, and moving with him to North Carolina. She sang rock and pop music around the Charlotte area for the better part of a decade before the marriage began to crumble. In 1985 she moved to Nashville, modified her last name to Loveless, began distributing a demo tape, and was soon signed to MCA. She recorded several singles for the label, and in 1987 these were collected for her first album, PATTY LOVELESS. It was an inspired and respectable effort, but her second album, IF MY HEART HAD WINDOWS, gained her more attention, mostly because the title track, a George Jones hit from 1960, took her into the Top 10 for the first time. She followed that success a few months later with "A Little Bit In Love," written by fellow MCA artist Steve Earle. In 1989 Loveless married Emory Gordy, Jr., who'd co-produced her first two albums (and would continue to do so for years to come).

During this rise to fame, Loveless developed a friendship with George Jones, whose songs she's covered more than a few times. She sang on his award-winning "I Don't Need Your Rocking Chair," and a later duet with the Possum, "You Don't Seem To Miss Me," was named Vocal Event of the Year by the CMA in 1998. She seems to have a knack for that particular award, as she won it again the very next year for "My Kind Of Woman/My Kind Of Man," a duet with Vince Gill (another singer with whom she's often collaborated.) The song appeared on Gill's album THE KEY as well as on Loveless' second hits collection, CLASSICS.

Patty Loveless

⊙ **On Down The Line** (MCA, 1990). In the rush to praise Loveless' hit albums like HONKY TONK ANGEL and WHEN FALLEN ANGELS FLY, this effort gets overlooked. It's really quite a good balance between her mountain-bred roots (there's more twang in her voice here than on later albums) and contemporary approach. Thus she does a fine job sassing things up on Matraca Berg's "I'm That Kind Of Girl," but at the same time "Some Morning Soon" (written by bluegrass singer Claire Lynch) shows that traditional material comes just as naturally to her. Further standouts include Lucinda Williams' "The Night's Too Long" and "You Can't Run Away From Your Heart."

Loveless scored her first #1 hit in 1989 with "Timber, I'm Falling In Love," a silly but undeniably catchy song penned by Kostas, a Greek immigrant who—thanks in large part to the success of "Timber"—has gone on to be one of Nashville's most bankable songwriters, sort of the Harlan Howard of the '90s. The song appeared on Loveless's third album, HONKY TONK ANGEL, along with further hits such as "Chains" and "Blue Side Of Town." She cut two more albums for MCA, ON DOWN THE LINE (1990) and UP AGAINST MY HEART (1991)—both of which hold up very well—before switching to Epic. She had a brief setback in 1992 when she underwent surgery on her vocal chords, but by the following year she was back in business. Her Epic tenure began with ONLY WHAT I FEEL (1993) and WHEN FALLEN ANGELS FLY (1994). This latter album won her a CMA award for Best Country Album, and her next release, THE TROUBLE WITH THE TRUTH (1995), landed her Female Vocalist of the Year honors from both the CMA and the ACM.

⊙ **Greatest Hits** (1993; MCA). Though it doesn't dig too deep, this CD is still a decent starting place. It packs together 10 of Loveless' best-known songs from the first half of her career, including "Timber," "Chains," "Jealous Bone," "On Down The Line," and "If My Heart Had Windows."

⊙ **Classics** (1999; Epic). The dozen songs here are culled from Patty's albums on Epic, which if a little more polished than her earlier material, have been even more successful in terms of chart figures and trophies. Her duet with Jones, "You Don't Seem To Miss Me" (written by Jim Lauderdale), is an obvious standout, well deserving of all its praises. Other big hits you'll find here are "You Can Feel Bad," "I Try To Think About Elvis," and the Gill collaboration "My Kind Of Woman/My Kind Of Man."

Patty Loveless

Lyle Lovett

> "I like my audience. I always feel when up on stage performing that I could enjoy having a cup of coffee with any one of them."
>
> —Lyle Lovett

Lyle Lovett may be a Texan right down to his custom-made boots, and country will probably always be an integral part of his eclectic sound, but don't try to pin the guy down. Since his recording debut in 1986, Lovett has brought a healthy taste for jazz, swing, pop, and blues right alongside his respect for contemporary Texas folksingers and good old-fashioned honky tonk. Lovett's debut album had a laid-back, down-to-earth country feel that lumped him in with fellow New Traditionalists Steve Earle and Dwight Yoakam; he even made the country charts a few times. Yet he was never quite at home in Nashville. By record number three (the Grammy-winning LYLE LOVETT AND HIS LARGE BAND), he was belting out R&B and swing numbers like "Here I Am" and Clifford Brown's "The Blues Walk," showing that his music had always been as much about saxophones as steel guitars. No wonder, then, that he eventually switched from the Nashville division of his label, MCA, to a new home base in LA. That doesn't mean that country ever left his bones. Just listen to 1996's THE ROAD TO ENSENADA or the Texas singer-songwriter collection STEP INSIDE THIS HOUSE, in which he pays tribute to such influences as Townes Van Zandt, Eric Taylor, and Willis Alan Ramsey.

Lyle Pearce Lovett was born on 1 November, 1957 in Klein, Texas, a small town founded by a very distant grandfather that's a suburb of Houston these days. He attended Texas A&M University, studied both German and journalism, gained inspiration from the folk-music scene thriving around Houston and Austin (which included such notables as Van Zandt, Ramsey, Guy Clark, and Nanci Griffith), and started writing songs. After spending some time in Europe, he recorded a demo tape in Arizona of all places. Guy Clark helped pass it on to the right people in Nashville—namely MCA producer Tony Brown, who signed Lovett in 1986 (around the same time Brown also signed Earle and Griffith).

Lovett's self-titled debut album (consisting of those Arizona recordings with some overdubbing and remixing) featured such memorable songs as "This Old Porch" (co-written with Robert Earl Keen), "Further Down The Line," "God Will," and "Cowboy Man." Five of the album's songs charted, and "Cowboy Man" became Lovett's one and only bona fide Top 10 country hit. His next album, PONTIAC, included the gentle "If I Had A Boat" and the bitter and brash "She's No Lady." Two songs, "She's No Lady" and "I Loved You Yesterday," did make a small impact on the country charts, but the album was more enthusiastically embraced outside of Nashville. If country audiences weren't biting, it didn't matter, because Lovett was developing a secure following among adventurous fans on the outskirts of the pop and rock market. His third album, LYLE LOVETT AND HIS LARGE BAND, featured the jazzed-up and R&B-infused road band he'd assembled for his PONTIAC tour. The album was evenly divided between swing and country material, showing Lovett could operate within multiple musical worlds without flinching. One of the album's highlights was his version of "Stand By Your Man"—so straightforward that it can't help but drip with irony—and it was featured in the film *The Crying Game*.

At the turn of the decade, Lovett moved his musical focus to Los Angeles, where he recorded

Lyle Lovett

his fourth album, JOSHUA JUDGES RUTH, during 1991 and 1992. Instead of Tony Brown at the helm, the album was produced by George Massenburg (along with Lovett and his regular collaborator, Billy Williams). During that same period he also made his Hollywood acting debut in Robert Altman's *The Player*. Lovett has also appeared in Altman's *Short Cuts*, *Pret-a-Porter*, and *Cookie's Fortune*—as well as *The Opposite Of Sex*—but what really turned him into a Hollywood conversation piece was his marriage to actress Julia Roberts, whom he'd met during the filming of *The Player*. Their marriage only lasted a couple of years, but it made him a household name among the supermarket crowd.

Lovett released I LOVE EVERYBODY in 1994, and it was another critically acclaimed album. He followed it with THE ROAD TO ENSENADA, a somewhat more country-sounding collection that won him a well-deserved Grammy in 1996 as Best Country Album. Two years later, he revisited his Texas folk-music roots with STEP INSIDE THIS HOUSE. In 1999 Lovett released the concert album LIVE IN TEXAS, which brought together songs from throughout his thirteen-year career.

⊙ **Lyle Lovett** (1986; MCA). Lovett has a clever, dry wit that's punched with irony yet also steeped in bleak introspection. This album is among his simplest and most straightfoward, but all his quirks and contradictions are in place: the stabs and humor and sarcasm as well as moments that are stark-naked and black. Songs like "This Old Porch" and "Further Down The Line" give the album an overriding western-folk flavor, but his eclectic musical instincts do show through.

⊙ **The Road To Ensenada** (1996; MCA). There's something bright and simple yet wholly engaging about the songs on this album, Lovett's fifth. At the same time, it's as emotionally complex as anything he's done. Steel guitar sneaks under the curtains now and again, "I Can't Love You Anymore" has a rural road-song vibe, and "That's Right (You're Not From Texas)" feels like western swing, but it's still not really a 'country' album per se (even though it was declared so at the Grammys).

⊙ **Step Inside This House** (1998; MCA). This 2-disc set is Lovett's homage to the Texas singer-songwriters whose work he grew up listening to and admiring. The largely acoustic arrangements are simple and low-key, yet it's a marvel of a collection. Even though Lovett didn't write any of the songs here (they came instead from Townes Van Zandt, Guy Clark, Robert Earl Keen,

Walter Hyatt, Vince Bell, and several others), he gives them an incredible sense of life. This is not just a history lesson or an admirable nod to his influences, it's a pure joy of a listen—and one of Lovett's finest achievements.

Kathy Mattea

Though her music skirted the outer reaches of new traditionalism—thanks in large part to her folksy acoustic collection WALK THE WAY THE WIND BLOWS—West Virginia-born singer Kathy Mattea comes off as far less adventurous than many artists who came of age during that era. She did cover songs by Nanci Griffith ("Love At The Five And Dime"), Larry Cordle ("Lonesome Standard Time"), and Tim O'Brien ("Walk The Way The Wind Blows"), and over the years she's developed a serious interest in Scottish folk music. Yet as artistically well-intentioned as she might be—and as decent a vocalist as she generally is—the majority of her music has landed squarely in the middle of the road.

More interesting, perhaps, is Mattea's activism, most notably her role in AIDS awareness on Music Row (she wore a red ribbon to the CMA award show in 1992, even speaking about it during the ceremony when specifically told not to), and was motivator behind the RED, HOT & COUNTRY compilation in 1993 (proceeds of which went to AIDS research). And as one of the most popular female artists of the early '90s, Mattea deserves accolades for her no-frills approach: no big hair or cutesy, country-bumpkin persona. Even if her music was mainstream, she herself was honest, unadorned and sincere.

Mattea was born on 21 June, 1959 in Cross Lanes, West Virginia. As a child she loved folksingers like Joni Mitchell, James Taylor, and Buffy Sainte-Marie, and her brand of country has always retained a folky sound at its core. She first played in a bluegrass band, Pennsboro, at West Virginia University, and later ended up in Nashville. There she began singing demos, a gig that led, in 1983, to a recording contract with Mercury with Allen Reynolds (Crystal Gayle, Garth Brooks) as her producer. Her first couple of albums lacked clear direction, and it wasn't until her third, WALK THE WAY THE WIND BLOWS, that she gained serious attention thanks to the chart success of "Love At The Five And Dime." Her first #1 hit, "Goin' Gone" (another Griffith tune), came from her follow-up album UNTASTED HONEY, as did "Eighteen Wheels And A Dozen Roses," which has proven the biggest hit of her career. Other hits include "Come From The Heart," "Burnin' Old Memories," and "Where've You Been" (co-written by her husband, Jon Vezner).

Mattea's won several awards over the years, including the CMA's Female Vocalist of the Year in both 1989 and 1990 and a Grammy for "Where've You Been." Her hits continued into the mid-'90s, and she's also recorded a gospel album (GOOD NEWS) and pursued an interest in Scottish folk music with singer Dougie McLean. Throughout her career she's proven herself willing to work with songwriters and players from the fringe territories, and her 1997 album LOVE TRAVELS included songs by Gillian Welch, Jim Lauderdale, Janis Ian, and Cheryl Wheeler.

⊙ **Walk The Way The Wind Blows** (1986; PolyGram). This acoustic album includes Nanci Griffith's "Love At The Five And Dime," which was Mattea's first major hit. Like much of Griffith's work, however, the song's got integrity yet suffers from heavy syrup content. "Leaving West Virginia" (written by Mattea), focusing on a melancholy moment of leaving home and small town behind, is the clear standout— one of the best of Mattea's career. The title track is by Tim O'Brien, who also guests on the record (one of several known entities including Vince Gill, Don Williams, and Béla Fleck). Overall Allen Reynolds' production is thankfully restrained—not exactly traditional, but certainly subtle compared with other pop-country artists of the period.

⊙ **A Collection Of Hits** (1990; Mercury). An all-in-one collection of Mattea's best-known songs, including "Eighteen Wheels And A Dozen Roses," "Goin' Gone," and "Where've You Been."

Reba McEntire

"I think country music is getting out of the cornfield, which is what I want to do."

—Reba McEntire

One of the most well-loved country entertainers of the 1980s and '90s, Reba McEntire has come a long way. From small-town roots in Oklahoma, she's grown into a superstar performer who practically defines the term 'show queen'—

a woman whose powerhouse voice has no trouble filling coliseums as she belts out hit after hit with dramatic flair. She worked hard to achieve her position as a top-selling artist, and for her perseverance and smart business sense alone she deserves respect. Yet it's also noteworthy that no matter how high her star has climbed, Reba has also always maintained a charming public persona; and instead of erasing her country roots to gain pole position on the charts (as was the trend during the '70s and '80s), she's flaunted her twang as proudly as her (once-massive) head of red hair.

Before the name Shania Twain ever passed any radio DJ's lips, Reba was also the major female voice in country music during the early '90s. "To me, she's a mixture of Dolly Parton and Tammy Wynette," remarked Tony Brown in a *Journal Of Country Music* cover story on Reba. "She's a mixture of Dolly's business savvy and work ethic, and Tammy's ability to record songs that strike home with females." Reba is also regularly lumped in with new traditionalist singers like George Strait, Ricky Skaggs, and Randy Travis. Much of her early material was slick and lacked focus, but when she switched from Mercury to MCA and recorded the album MY KIND OF COUNTRY—which celebrated her country roots—the result was a more traditional style fronted by her enormously energetic voice.

On the whole, however, the majority of her music lands in the categories of overproduced, melodramatic, formulaic, and even bombastic. MY KIND OF COUNTRY might have reflected her rootsy side, but even by the time she recorded her next album, WHOEVER'S IN NEW ENGLAND, her music was pushing into heavy-handed and at times saccharine territory (though at the same time it shot up the charts and boosted her career even further). A true country heart might beat inside, but her glamorous pop-country veneer is impossible to ignore.

Reba was born on 28 March, 1954 in Chockie, Oklahoma and raised on a cattle ranch by her rodeo-riding father and singing mother. As a child she competed in the barrel races at rodeos and also formed the Singing McEntires with her brother Pake (who became a recording artist himself and released two albums on RCA) and two sisters. The group sang locally and even recorded for the indie label Boss in the early '70s. When Reba was invited to sing the national anthem at a rodeo in Oklahoma City, country artist Red Steagall, who was performing that day, found himself smitten with her voice; he helped her record and shop a demo, and this eventually led to a contract with Mercury.

Reba's first single was "I Don't Want To Be A One Night Stand," and it was followed by a steady stream of medium-sized hits. (During this period she also graduated from Southeastern State University and married rodeo rider Charlie Battles.) Reba herself, though, admits she wasn't always pleased with the music she was making at the time (too many low-energy ballads for one thing). She scored her first #1 in 1983 with "Can't Even Get The Blues," but it wasn't until after she jumped from Mercury to MCA Nashville in 1984 that she truly came into her own. Her first MCA album JUST A LITTLE LOVE was produced by Norro Wilson and still didn't quite gel; her follow-up, however, MY KIND OF COUNTRY, was her most cohesive-sounding release to date and a key turning point in her career. On the cover she stood smiling, dressed in Wranglers and her National Finals Rodeo Belt Buckle against a backdrop that included the American flag and "God's Beautiful Mountains," as she described them in the liner notes. "That leads us inside," she continued, "to where the music comes from the past and the present." Produced by Harold Shedd, the album eschewed strings (at Reba's insistence) for a bigger fiddle and pedal-steel sound, and it nudged her away from pop and into the growing neo-traditionalist camp. Thanks to the encouragement of newly appointed MCA executive Jimmy Bowen, Reba was able to pick her own songs, too. Her first #1 from that album, "How Blue," had a bluegrass feel and is still one of the rootsiest songs she's ever recorded.

For her next album, WHOEVER'S IN NEW ENGLAND, Reba and new co-producer Bowen took her neo-trad sound and shifted it back toward the mainstream. For example, while "Somebody Should Leave" from MY KIND OF COUNTRY is weepy, it exhibits tasteful restraint; the production on "Whoever's In New England" is bigger and the sentimentalism far more obvious, even manipulative. Reba and Bowen knew what they were doing, however, as the latter song became her most popular to date, pushing her over the edge into the big time. The album went gold, the song won her a Grammy, and at the end of 1986 Reba was honored as the CMA's Entertainer of the Year. As her hits continued to add up, her stage show also grew—from merely standing on the floor to, ultimately, flying from coliseum rafters and belting songs with supercharged enthusiasm.

Reba's star shone brightly throughout the rest of the decade and deep into the next. By the time she arrived at 1990's RUMOR HAS IT, her sound and production were almost entirely pop-oriented. Her 1995 release STARTING OVER was an all-covers album paying tribute to her musical influences, yet it was packed with such pop songs as "Talking In Your Sleep," "Please Come To Boston," "On My Own," and "By The Time I Get To Phoenix."

Divorcing Charlie Battles in 1987, Reba later married Narvel Blackstock, her steel player and road manager. Smart businesspeople, the couple eventually took control of the McEntire machine, from selling T-shirts to making records. They formed Starstruck Entertainment—which includes publicity, artist management, and even dabbles in film deals—and it's housed in a big new office building on Music Row (complete with recording studio). In 1990 Reba debuted on the big screen as a gun-toting survivalist in the kooky horror film *Tremors*, and she later had a role in Rob Reiner's film *North*. Her autobiography, *Reba*, was published in 1994.

Reba is one of few contemporary country artists (George Strait being another) who can claim anything resembling career longevity. Like Dolly Parton, she's proven herself savvy on the business front, and the ethic of hard work and responsibility instilled in her since childhood seems to have paid off big time. Her music may have suffered in recent years, but her skills as an entertainer—a term she uses proudly—are some of the strongest in the industry.

⊙ My Kind Of Country (1984; MCA). The string sections of her earlier recordings are thankfully missing on what's easily the most down-to-earth and traditional-sounding album of her career. From "How Blue" onward, it's packed with guitars, fiddles and sparse arrangements, resulting in a back-to-basics feeling she'll likely never match again.

Reba McEntire

⊙ **The Best Of Reba McEntire** (1985; Mercury). Not the most comprehensive overview of Reba's early years on Mercury, as it entirely ignores her 1970s recordings (she signed with the label in 1975). It'd be nice to hear her development, especially since those early records are long out-of-print. Still, there are glimpses that show her searching: "Only You (And You Alone)" carries the influence of Patsy Cline, and "Today All Over Again" almost cops the Tammy Wynette 'teardrop' style, while on "Can't Even Get The Blues" (her first #1), Reba gets to cut loose a bit—a mark of things to come.

⊙ **Whoever's In New England** (1986; MCA). The title track—a tear-jerking, heartstring-tugging, emotionally manipulative ballad—clinched Reba her stardom. The whole album, in fact, is surprisingly melodramatic considering the kind of country she was touting just two years earlier. Even Reba's gutsy voice and thick Oklahoma twang can't displace the heavy-handed arrangements on hits such as "Better Days," "Little Rock," and of course "Whoever's In New England."

⊙ **Greatest Hits** (1987; MCA). These hits come from Reba's initial MCA years (1984–'86) and include "How Blue," "Somebody Should Leave," "Whoever's In New England," and What Am I Gonna Do About You."

⊙ **For My Broken Heart** (1991; MCA). In 1990, several members of Reba's band were tragically killed in a plane crash. This album speaks of the loss and honors their memories.

⊙ **Greatest Hits Vol. 2** (1993; MCA). This hits package picks up in the late '80s and brings Reba into the next decade, her stardom growing larger with each leap and bound. Songs here include "Is There Life Out There" and "For My Broken Heart." The latter was the title track to a 1991 album that paid tribute to her bandmembers, several of whom were tragically killed in a plane crash a year earlier.

The O'Kanes

"I'm very proud of the work, but the fact that [our records] were accepted commercially is phenomenal."

—Kieren Kane

Though these days they have fallen by the wayside of country music history, the O'Kanes were a popular country duo during the mid- to late-1980s—and among a significant group of artists reclaiming traditional sounds and styles in mainstream country music at the time. The music created by singer-songwriters Kieren Kane and Jamie O'Hara was based around sparse, mostly acoustic arrangements and pretty, folk-styled harmonies; their music, in fact, was close in feel to brother duets like the Louvins or the Everlys. It wasn't strictly old-time music, however. At the time they hooked up, both artists were established Nashville songwriters, and each had proven his contemporary appeal with hits for singers like the Judds, John Conlee, and Alabama.

Toledo, Ohio native O'Hara (a former football player) and New Yorker Kane (a session guitarist and songwriter who'd worked most of the '70s in LA) first began writing and recording songs together in 1985. O'Hara was fresh from writing "Grandpa (Tell Me 'Bout The Good Old Days)" for the Judds (it won him a Grammy in 1986) and Ronnie McDowell's #1 hit "Older Women." Kane had penned Alabama's "Gonna Have A Party" and John Conlee's "As Long As I'm Rocking With You." Kane had also cut a solo album for Elektra in 1982, and songs from that album (as well as a couple of Warner Brothers singles) had even charted.

Calling themselves the O'Kanes, the two men signed with Columbia in 1986, collected their demo recordings made during the past year, and released them as their self-titled debut album. They co-wrote nine of the ten songs together, produced the recordings on their own, and their efforts paid off better than expected: four of the songs hit the country Top 10, and "Can't Stop My Heart From Loving You" even reached #1. The label loved them, and let them make another album that, like the first, was recorded entirely on their terms ("Basically we'd record an album and turn it in finished," says Kane, "and the first time the label would hear anything was when it was done".) Released in 1988, TIRED OF THE RUNNIN' earned them two more chart hits ("One True Love" and "Blue Love") and, as a bonus, even won a Grammy for Best Album Package.

By the end of the decade, however, the O'Kanes concept was running out of creative steam, and the duo ultimately split up, both continuing their songwriting careers. Columbia released a third O'Kanes album in 1990, IMAGINE THAT, but it didn't attract much attention. In 1993, O'Hara released his debut solo album, RISE ABOVE IT, on RCA; marked by mature songwriting and straightahead production, it's a solid and enjoyable record if you can still find it. Kane recorded another solo record (FIND MY WAY HOME) for Atlantic that same year, though like O'Hara's it didn't sell very well. Six months after its release, Kane was dropped. His answer? Start his own label. With his friends and country-music cohorts Kevin Welch, Harry Stinson, Tammy Rogers, and Mike Henderson, Kane founded the collectively owned Dead Reckoning in 1995. The label's first release was Kane's solo album DEAD REKONING (sic). Records by the other label co-owners have followed, along with a group album, A NIGHT OF RECKONING, under the name Dead Reckoners. Kane's second solo album for Dead Reckoning, SIX MONTHS, NO SUN (1998), was another impressive collection that mixed laid-back, late-night songs ("Kill The Demon"), cool covers (Johnny Bond's "I Wonder Where You Are Tonight"), and upbeat, urban-drenched material.

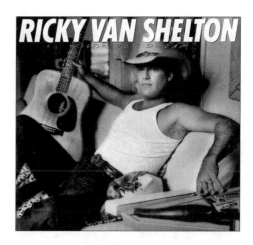

⊙ **The O'Kanes** (1986; Columbia). The duo's debut consisted of the songs they recorded as demos during the previous year. The acoustic arrangements (mandolin, fiddle, accordion) and vocal harmonies are the main focus, giving it a bluegrass feel at times. An underrated and overlooked (these days at least) album.

Kieran Kane

⊙ **Dead Rekoning** (1995; Dead Reckoning). A richly textured but still relatively low-key affair—Kane's music has always been more about the songs themselves than any flashy coating. His writing is tight and crafty—in a more perfect world, the catchy "This Dirty Little Town" would have been a sizeable radio hit. Nice covers, too, of Hank ("Ramblin' Man") and Buck ("Love's Gonna Live Here").

⊙ **Six Months, No Sun** (1998; Dead Reckoning). Kane's fourth album as a solo artist is another impressive collection that mixes moody, late-night songs ("Kill The Demon"), cool covers (Johnny Bond's "I Wonder Where You Are Tonight"), and edgy, character-driven material ("Table Top Dancer").

Ricky Van Shelton

One of the most popular country acts to emerge in the late 1980s, Ricky Van Shelton was the bridge that linked new traditionalists like George Strait, John Anderson and Steve Earle with the 'new country' hat acts who stormed the scene at the turn of the decade. Shelton sang in a honky-tonk style (and made much of his reputation covering classic country hits by the likes of Ned Miller and Jack Greene), but his approach had a much more contemporary vibe than, for instance, that of fellow traditionalist Randy Travis. Shelton's music was easy-to-swallow, in large part thanks to his handsome baritone voice, and his fans ate it up like candy. To top matters off, he debuted on the cover to his first album, WILD-EYED DREAM, dressed in a white muscle T-shirt, jeans, and cowboy hat—a look that, like it or not, tagged him as country music's first 'hunk.'

On the one hand Shelton's working-man image was a refreshing antidote to the Vegas flash of Ronnie Milsap and Kenny Rogers—and a pleasant listen at that. Ultimately, however, Shelton's music lacked the emotional depth that marked the classic work of singers like Charlie Rich (whose song "Life's Little Ups And Downs" Ricky covered) and George Jones—and for that matter, Randy Travis. Shelton's brand of traditionalism was just too picture-perfect.

Ricky Van Shelton was born in Grit, Virginia on 12 January, 1952. His father sang gospel, and Ricky grew up singing it, too, though he also loved pop music. At fourteen he started singing country in his brother's band. In the early '80s, when his then-girlfriend (and later his wife) Bettye got a job in Nashville, he went with her. Eventually, through friends (notably Tennesseean columnist Jerry Thompson) he managed to win a record deal at Columbia and with Thompson as his manager. As this was the peak of the new traditionalist era, Ricky's debut album WILD-EYED DREAM couldn't have met better timing, and it immediately yielded him several big hits. By the end of the year he'd won the ACM's New Male Vocalist of the Year award; a year later he nabbed the CMA's Horizon Award.

Ricky Van Shelton

Hits from Ricky's subsequent albums LOVING PROOF (1988) and RVS III (1990) kept him on the charts and in the public eye for several more years. Though most of his work was pop-oriented in production and performance, the song choices were sometimes interesting—Ned Miller's "From A Jack To A King," Jack Greene's "Statue Of A Fool," Mickey Newbury's "Sweet Memories" (a duet with Brenda Lee)—and showed Ricky did have an ear for the classics. Most of his albums from this period went platinum, and even his Christmas album, RICKY VAN SHELTON SINGS CHRISTMAS, and his gospel collection, DON'T OVERLOOK SALVATION, sold well. At the same time Shelton began writing a series of children's books, the first two titles being *Tales From A Duck Named Quacker* and *Quacker Meets Mrs Moo*.

By the time Shelton released A BRIDGE I DIDN'T BURN in 1993, however, his popularity was tapering off. After the release of LOVE AND HONOR a year later he quit Columbia, saying he was fed up with the label. He also admitted he'd had a serious drinking habit but that he was now clean and sober. In 1997 he was back in business with the album MAKING PLANS, only this time he financed the project himself and worked out a deal to distribute it (at least initially) only in Wal-Mart stores.

☉ **Wild-Eyed Dream** (1987; Columbia). Shelton's debut is far less substantial and rough-edged than it might appear. Despite his attractive voice and plenty of decent material—Harlan Howard's "Life Turned Her That Way," Buck Owens' "I Don't Care," Merle Haggard's "Working Man's Blues"—the passion feels more fabricated than truly heartfelt.

☉ **Greatest Hits Plus** (1992; Columbia). Despite his penchant for overproduction, a handful of Shelton's songs can make for pleasant listening if placed in the right context. This collection is the proof: it cuts out the chaff and leaves some of his catchiest numbers such as "I Am A Simple Man," "Living Proof," and "Wild Man."

Ricky Skaggs

"The cycle comes back around, if you just stand still."

—Ricky Skaggs

Turning a Flatt & Scruggs song into a #1 hit at the height of the urban cowboy craze was a feat no one could have predicted. But that's just what Ricky Skaggs did in 1982 with "Crying My Heart Out Over You," kicking off a decade-long run on the charts—a run that, in addition to coloring his own records gold, helped jumpstart a healthy resurgence of traditionalism in mainstream country music.

One of Nashville's most traditional artists, Skaggs managed to turn decades-old songs by Webb Piece and Cindy Walker ("I Don't Care"), Mel Tillis ("Honey [Open That Door]"), and even Monroe himself (a lively rendition of the master's classic "Uncle Pen")—along with contemporary numbers by the likes of Texas songwriter Guy Clark ("Heartbroke") and bluegrass artist Larry Cordle ("Highway 40 Blues")—into widely popular hits. The video for Skaggs' 1985 song "Country Boy" (a song by '70s guitarist Albert Lee written during his days with Heads, Hands, And Feet) even featured Monroe along with New York City mayor Ed Koch. The folks at Epic (Skaggs' label from 1981–1991 and owned by CBS) might have been skeptical of his ability to sell records when they first considered signing him, but CBS chief Rick Blackburn must have been down on his knees thanking the Lord each night that he didn't balk, as Skaggs went on to rack up thirty-one *Billboard* Top 40 hits—eleven of them #1 singles.

Skaggs was born on 18 July, 1954 in Cordell, Kentucky. His father, Hobart, bought him a mandolin at the age of five, which inspired Hobart to pick up guitar again; soon the family was playing gigs together and Ricky was gaining a reputation as a child prodigy. Once, at a local concert, he was invited on stage with Bill Monroe to play an Osborne Brothers tune. The Skaggs Family (as they billed themselves) toured regularly around the region, and for a time moved to the Nashville area, hoping to get Ricky a spot on the *Grand Ole Opry* (that failed, but he did get to play on Flatt & Scruggs' TV show). Throughout his childhood, Ricky worked on his mandolin skills; later he picked up guitar and fiddle as well. He had had a love for bluegrass and country music since early childhood—particularly the haunting harmonies of the Stanley Brothers—and when he met guitarist and fellow Stanleys fan Keith Whitley at a local talent contest, the two teenagers quickly became friends and musical partners. Their career break came soon after: when Ralph Stanley heard the pair playing Stanley Brothers songs at a local club, he invited them both on tour with him. Skaggs was only fifteen when he joined Stanley's Clinch Mountain Boys in 1970.

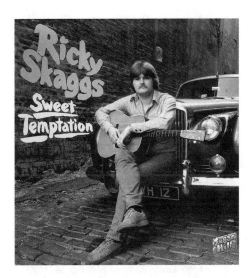

Skaggs recorded several albums with Stanley and two with Whitley before he quit the group and moved to Washington, DC. There he joined the Country Gentlemen (as their fiddler) and later played with another progressive bluegrass group, J.D. Crowe And The New South. He eventually formed his own band, Boone Creek, which played both bluegrass and pop. That group recorded two bluegrass albums before Skaggs quit to take a spot in Emmylou Harris' Hot Band in 1978 (his first time with a full-on electric band). He played on several Harris records, but it was his work on 1980's ROSES IN THE SNOW—he sang and helped with the arrangements—that gained him wide attention. During this time he also toured occasionally with Buck White and the Down Home Folks, and he recorded his first solo album, SWEET TEMPTATION, along with a duet album with Tony Rice, SKAGGS AND RICE (both for the independent bluegrass label Sugar Hill).

After a decade of hard work, by which time he'd developed a solid reputation as a serious player and budding bandleader (and remember he was still in his mid-twenties at the time), Skaggs finally felt himself ready for the big time, and he sought out a major label contract. It was a struggle convincing Music Row that a traditional act could still fly, but Skaggs persevered. He was halfway though recording his second solo album for Sugar Hill, DON'T CHEAT IN OUR HOMETOWN (which would eventually be released in 1984), when he began simultaneously working out a deal with CBS in Nashville. He was signed to CBS subsidiary Epic, even winning the right to produce his albums himself—a move that, if it had been denied, would likely have radically altered his sound (and

certainly affected the course of modern country music history). His first single for Epic, an uptempo version of Flatt & Scruggs' "Don't Get Above Your Raising," made it to the Top 20 and proved his inclinations were right. By mid-1982 he'd racked up two #1 hits and had even joined the *Grand Ole Opry* as its youngest member. The awards started coming, too: Male Vocalist of the Year and the Horizon Award from the CMA, and best New Male Vocalist from the ACM.

The beauty of Skaggs' success is that he didn't compromise his music to win his chart success. Nearly all the songs on WAITIN' FOR THE SUN TO SHINE, his first album for Epic, were traditional country and bluegrass numbers (by the likes of Carter Stanley, Monroe, and Merle Travis), and all featured a lively mixture of acoustic and electric playing (and nary a hint of strings or uptown choruses). Skaggs arrangements were the key, allowing the music to speak in an '80s language (smoothing lines and picking up tempos, for instance); yet Skaggs was careful never to pave over the music's original spirit. His voice, too, retained a gentle creaky tone that was old-fashioned yet entirely pleasant. Skaggs won the CMA's prestigious Entertainer of the Year award in 1985, by which time he'd also received honors for his touring and instrumental work several times over.

Skaggs married singer Sharon White on 4 August, 1981 and went on to produce and play on albums for her family's group, the Whites (both Sharon and her father, Buck, with whom Skaggs had toured during the '70s, performed on Skaggs' albums, too). A duet between Sharon and Ricky, "Love Can't Ever Get Better Than This," won the pair a CMA award for Vocal Duo of the Year in 1987. In the early '90s Skaggs joined the likes of Vince Gill, Marty Stuart, and Steve Wariner to play in fiddler Mark O'Connor's project the New Nashville Cats. The group (more than fifty players in all) wound up winning CMA and Grammy awards and even landed a hit with the Carl Perkins song "Restless."

Skaggs continued to chart on his own well into the early '90s. His final album for Epic, however, was 1991's MY FATHER'S SON. SOLID GROUND, released in 1995, became his first album for his new label, Atlantic. Two years later he released the country record LIFE IS A JOURNEY on Atlantic and BLUEGRASS RULES! on Rounder— the latter his first all-bluegrass album in well over a decade. It also marked a shift Skaggs was making musically: "I'm going to do bluegrass from now on," he told journalist Jon Weisberger in 1997. He'd made that promise a year earlier, after spending many hours with Bill Monroe during the bluegrass founder's final days. He's since greatly increased his bluegrass dates. And with country radio having shifted its attentions to newer and younger stars, it's a move that makes perfect sense.

There's no denying that Skaggs' earlier recordings are, by and large, the most interesting and enduring of his catalog today. But even at his most mainstream, there's an integrity that shines through Skaggs' work. And the fact that in 1997 he felt the call back to bluegrass shows his connection to the rich rural music he grew up with is still honest and intact.

⊙ **Sweet Temptation** (1979; Sugar Hill). Skaggs' first solo album is packed with bluegrass and country songs by Carter Stanley ("I'll Take The Blame"), Bill Monroe and Lester Flatt ("Little Cabin Home On The Hill"), Dolly Parton ("Put It Off Until Tomorrow"), and others. The all-star band includes Tony Rice, Jerry Douglas, Emmylou Harris, Tony Brown, and Albert Lee. It's a great album that shows Skaggs emerging as a strong lead vocalist and bandleader.

⊙ **Waitin' For The Sun To Shine** (1981; Epic). This album sort of picks up where SWEET TEMPTATION left off and once again features stellar playing and a roster of classic songs. Highlights are the feisty update of Flatt & Scruggs' "Don't Get Above Your Raising" and great renditions of Webb Pierce and Cindy Walker's "I Don't Care," Johnny Bond's "Your Old Love Letters," and Ralph Stanley's "If That's The Way You Feel." Ironically, it's the tender title track (written by Sonny Throckmorton and the album's only contemporary number) that stands out strongest.

⊙ **Highways & Heartaches** (1982; Epic). Skaggs' career really took off with this album. Standouts include Guy Clark's "Heartbroke" (the first by the Texas songwriter to hit #1). Larry Cordle's "Highway 40 Blues," Jim Eanes' "I Wouldn't Change You If I Could," and Shake Russell's "You've Got A Lover." This and WAITIN' FOR THE SUN TO SHINE are among Skaggs' most enduring albums.

⊙ **Bluegrass Rules!** (1997; Rounder/Skaggs Family). Skaggs finally decided it was time to return to bluegrass. Here he offers reinterpretations of such classics as "Little Maggie," "Rank Stranger," and "Rawhide." While not essential Skaggs, it's definitely worthwhile and fun.

⊙ **Country Gentleman: The Best Of Ricky Skaggs** (1998; Epic Legacy). This 2-disc set is culled from the country material Skaggs recorded for Epic Records

between 1981 and 1991. Although it concentrates on the hits (it doesn't even include "Waitin' For The Sun To Shine," for instance), it's still very well put together and reveals Skaggs' development during that period quite clearly. The program begins with "Don't Get Above Your Raising" and runs through a decade's worth of songs, wrapping things up with "From The Word Love" from Skagg's 1991 album MY FATHER'S SON. Until a collection rolls around that encompasses his work outside the mainstream (during the '70s, for example), this stands as his most comprehensive collection to date.

George Strait

"George looks as cool and hip as any of these young twenty-year-old cats. He just takes care of himself. He's a very aware individual."

—Tony Brown

C lean-cut, soft-spoken George Strait is hardly the picture of a rebel, but when his song "Unwound" first hit the airwaves in 1981, its traditional arrangements and Strait's Haggard-esque drawl went directly against the grain of mainstream country. Which is exactly why it sounded so good. This was the peak time for suburban-slick country—urban cowboy everything was hot, and Barbara Mandrell was the CMA's reigning Entertainer of the Year (an honor she'd pick up again by the end of 1981). Strait, however, opted for a back-to-basics minimalist approach. His music was free of such detritus as synthesized strings, and what poured forth from his debut album, STRAIT COUNTRY, was some of the honkiest, tonkiest music Nashville had produced in eons.

Strait has since gone on to enjoy one of the most enduring careers of any contemporary country performer—still headlining coliseum shows and selling records well into the late '90s (this in an era when singers come and go as frequently as the weather and few 'older' artists get any radio airplay at all). Many new country stars now give thanks to Strait as often as they do to Haggard and Jones. It's true that a good deal of Strait's latter-day material sounds middle-of-the-road, but the low-key Texan has at the same time always maintained a respectable degree of integrity in his music.

Strait was born on 18 May, 1952 in Poteet, Texas and raised in Pearsall, a town southwest of San Antonio. His father taught school but also ran

George Strait

STRAIT COUNTRY came out in 1981, followed a year later by STRAIT FROM THE HEART, and both have a more up-front honky-tonk sound than anything Strait's recorded since. They also showcase several songs co-written by Frank Dycus and Dean Dillon ("Unwound," "Down And Out," "Friday Night Fever," "Marina Del Rey"); Dillon in particular was a young songwriter and singer who wrote or co-wrote numerous hits for Strait. Other notable tunes from this time include "Fool-Hearted Memory" (his first #1 hit), "Heartbroke" (a Guy Clark song that Ricky Skaggs ran to the top), the beautiful "Amarillo By Morning" (a Terry Stafford song that's one of Strait's all-time greats), and "A Fire I Can't Put Out" (written by Darryl Staedtler, a Texas songwriter who first shopped Strait's demo around Nashville in 1977).

For his third album, however, RIGHT OR WRONG, Strait switched producers (from Blake Mevis to Ray Baker) and brought a western swing element into the arrangements—most notably in the title track, which had been a hit for Bob Wills. Wills' fiddler, Johnny Gimble, even played on the session. On DOES FORT WORTH EVER CROSS YOUR MIND (for which he switched producers again, to Jimmy Bowen) Strait's new dance-hall sound fell into place even more succinctly. By the time he'd racked up another handful of hits from this album—which also won Album of the Year awards from the CMA and ACM—it was clear Strait was headed for superstardom.

Throughout the rest of the decade his career soared, as he continued to record strong material (including the eternal "All My Ex's Live In Texas") and win awards. He was named the CMA's Male Vocalist of the Year in 1985 and 1986, and in 1989 and 1990 he was given their top honor: Entertainer of the Year. What's amazing, too, is that even as the age of Garth Brooks was dawning, Strait's popularity didn't fade out. It was singers like Brooks and Alan Jackson, in fact, who began acknowledging Strait as a major influence. Many also copped his cowboy-in-a-starched-shirt look, which soon led to an epidemic of cookie-cutter 'hat acts' wearing wide-brimmed Stetsons and crowing about Merle and Mama and the red, white and blue. Titling his 1992 album HOLDING MY OWN, Strait seemed to be nodding back in these young bucks' direction with a gentle good-luck grin.

One of the most consistent singers in modern country, Strait hasn't wavered much from the style

the family's ranch, where George spent many weekends. He played music in high school, after which he spent a couple of months at Southwest Texas State University before dropping out to marry his high-school sweetheart, Norma. Later he joined the Army, where he began playing country music. After that he enrolled back in Southwest Texas State in an agricultural program. At the same time he joined a band of university students (Ron Cabel, Terry Hale, Tommy Foote, and Mike Daily, grandson of Pappy Daily) and played locally under the name Ace In The Hole, a band name Strait has maintained ever since. They recorded a few sides during the late '70s for D Records (a small Dallas label founded in 1958 by Pappy Daily and then run by his sons Bud and Don). Strait also took a couple of trips to Nashville that didn't pan out. After finishing school he managed a ranch and played music at night. He was on the verge of taking a job designing cattle facilities when he gave Nashville one more shot. This time, a friend at MCA (Erv Woolsey, who'd later become Strait's manager) helped get him an ear at the label, and a chance to record; the strength of his take on "Unwound" won him a deal. The song became Strait's first single and jumped right to the Top 10.

George Strait

he developed at the start of his career. The good side of this is that the no-frills nature of his sound has remained intact—no crossover pop hits à la Kenny Rogers, no forty-piece orchestral arrangements. Neither did his starring role in the 1992 movie *Pure Country* sully his laid-back cowboy image; instead, it helped it grow (the soundtrack alone sold four million copies, his biggest seller to date). Yet at the same time, much of Strait's music—especially in these later, more settled years—has wound up feeling overly conservative and less than exciting. Such is the price of consistency, no doubt. His 1996 album BLUE CLEAR SKY was a respectable effort (the title track one of his finest singles in recent years), but few of his late-'90s singles have jumped out the way such beauties as "Amarillo By Morning," "The Cowboy Rides Away," or "All My Ex's Live In Texas" once did.

Whether or not Strait achieves a spot in the Country Music Hall of Fame (it seems inevitable down the road), he deserves respect for his ability to sustain a hyge career over two solid decades of change. And besides, support from his fans seems in no short supply even in the twenty-first century. He's still headlining national concert tours, still making the *Billboard* charts. For a laid-back cowboy bent on keeping things simple, that ain't no small potatoes.

⊙ **Strait Country** (1981; MCA). There's no denying "Unwound" is an excellent song, but the honky-tonk foundation behind that and "Friday Night Fever" (the flipside of John Conlee's 1980 hit "Friday Night Blues") is balanced on this album by such sentimental numbers as "If You're Thinking You Want A Stranger (There's One Coming Home)." Even that song, though, has little of the modern sheen of a Lee Greenwood or Ronnie Milsap. The album is ultimately uneven, but it helped mark Strait as a cowboy to pay attention to.

⊙ **Does Fort Worth Ever Cross Your Mind** (1984; MCA). The title track is a Strait classic, as is "The Cowboy Rides Away," one of his loveliest ballads that remains tastefully sentimental. Overall on this album, Strait's sound has gelled. Neither glossy-smooth nor old-time crunchy, his brand of country is easygoing and highly accessible—a style he's maintained with dignified consistency throughout his career.

⊙ **Greatest Hits** (1985; MCA). If you want just a sampler, these 10 songs (from STRAIT COUNTRY, STRAIT FROM THE HEART, and RIGHT OR WRONG) are an excellent representation of Strait's early work—and they're still some of his best. "Fool Hearted Memory" is immediately catchy—with obvious Haggard inflections

in Strait's voice—and "Amarillo By Morning" stands as one of the most beautiful tunes he's ever recorded. Further nuggets include "Down And Out," "Let's Fall To Pieces Together," and the hot-dance classic "Right Or Wrong."

⊙ **Ocean Front Property** (1987; MCA). "All My Ex's Live In Texas" is probably Strait's best-known (and loved) song. It's got a gentle western-swing feeling, but the melody is simple, smooth and entirely catchy. The title is another career standout, and master songsmith Hank Cochran's contribution as a co-writer may have something to do with it.

⊙ **Strait Out Of The Box** (1995; MCA). This 4-CD set re-examines Strait's career from top to bottom. It includes his major hits as well as quite a few rarities, but well put together, for the casual fan it's probably too much at once.

Marty Stuart

"I love being a renegade, I love being a little bit to the left."

—Marty Stuart, 1992

As a child, Marty Stuart was a prodigy on the mandolin and guitar, touring with bluegrass legend Lester Flatt while barely a teenager and with Johnny Cash while in his early twenties. With that kind of musical pedigree, it's no wonder he grew into one of the best neo-traditional singers in Nashville during the 1990s. Throughout his career, Stuart has mixed his love of classic honky tonk and bluegrass with a streak of youthful rebellion and the unabashed energy of a hillbilly-bred rock'n'roller. The combination made him appealing to both traditional and contemporary audiences—his excitement for country music is contagious. But whether making the charts or lurking just outside Top 10 stardom, he's continued to show consistent levels of artistic integrity, musical craftsmanship and genuine enthusiasm.

Stuart was born on 30 September, 1958 in Philadelphia, Mississippi. He was an instrumental talent by the time he was twelve, and it's at this age that he began touring with a streak of country legends: the gospel-bluegrass Sullivan Family, bluegrass bandleader Lester Flatt (with whom Stuart performed until Flatt's death in 1979), fiddler Vassar Clements, and guitarist Doc Watson. Stuart also played with Johnny Cash for six years in the early

'80s. His first two solo records were on independent bluegrass labels: WITH A LITTLE HELP FROM MY FRIENDS (1978; Ridge Runner) and BUSY BEE CAFE (1982; Sugar Hill). As the decade progressed, however, his style moved away from bluegrass. In 1986 he signed with Columbia and released MARTY STUART, which had a stronger rockabilly feel—though his style wasn't quite settled in place yet. A couple of songs made the Top 40, but overall the album didn't sell too well. Stuart recorded a follow-up for Columbia, LET THERE BE COUNTRY, but the label held it back (it was finally released in 1992).

Stuart's commercial breakthrough came in 1989, when he signed with MCA and released HILLBILLY ROCK. Again, the rockabilly influence was prominent, mixed in with nods to honky tonk (Johnny Cash's "Cry Cry Cry") and songwriters from outside the mainstream (Joe Ely's "Me And Billy The Kid"). The punchy Paul Kennerly song "Hillbilly Rock" made the Top 10, and Stuart was finally earning a reputation as a viable commercial entity as well as a devoted neo-traditionalist. His next MCA album, TEMPTED, was another hot slice of contemporary country-rock, and it produced further hits in "Burn Me Down," "Little Things" and "Tempted."

In 1991 Stuart co-wrote a song with fellow rising star Travis Tritt, "The Whiskey Ain't Workin'," and the two recorded it as a duet on Tritt's 1991 album IT'S ALL ABOUT TO CHANGE. Tritt returned the favor and sang on Stuart's 1992 hit "This One's Gonna Hurt You (For A Long, Long Time)," which was also the title track of Stuart's third MCA album. Between 1991 and 1992, the two long-haired country boys also hit the road

together on what they dubbed the 'No Hats' tour—'hat acts' being the trend of the day among the mainstream-minded in Nashville. The friendship didn't stop there, and Tritt and Stuart have since contributed songs and vocals to each others' albums.

As Stuart's star status climbed, he never lost his enthusiasm for the classic music he grew up with. He was, and still is, a country music fan. He wears elaborate Nudie suits (and some stitched by Nudie protégé Manuel) on album covers and in performance; he travels the country in a tour bus that once belong to Ernest Tubb; he collects and plays guitars formerly owned by Hank Williams, Clarence White, Maybelle Carter, Lester Flatt, and other legends; he's written articles about and published photographs on country artists for various magazines; and he joined the board of the Country Music Foundation in 1991 (more recently he has served as board president) and the *Grand Ole Opry* in 1993. During the '90s Stuart continued to record for MCA, releasing LOVE AND LUCK (1994)—which included covers of the Gram Parsons/Chris Hillman song "Wheels" and Billy Joe Shaver's "If I Give My Soul"—HONKY TONKIN'S WHAT I DO BEST (1996), and THE PILGRIM (1999). In 1997 Stuart married '60s-era country hitmaker Connie Smith, and he co-produced and co-wrote most of the songs on her 1998 comeback album.

⊙ **Hillbilly Rock** (1989; MCA). Stuart had been a recording artist for over ten years by the time he cut this album, his MCA debut. It's a solid one, too, with Stuart's 'hillbilly rock' style firmly in place all the way through. The title track is a hot standout, as are "The Wild One" (a Merle Kilgore/Tillman Franks song),
"Western Girls," and the brilliantly catchy "Easy To Love (Hard To Hold)."

⊙ **This One's Gonna Hurt You** (1992; MCA), Stuart's third MCA album kicks off with a bang—"Me And Hank And Jumpin' Jack Flash"—but again invokes the spirit of classic country, which has always been his guiding light. Tritt duets with Stuart on the title track, and Stuart's old boss, Johnny Cash, lends his voice to "Doin' My Time," a bluegrass standard written by Jimmie Skinner.

STEVE GILLETT

Marty Stuart

Marty Stuart

⊙ **Marty Party Hit Pack** (1995; MCA). Fun-lovin'
package of Marty's MCA hits—"Burn Me Down,"
"Hillbilly Rock," "Now That's Country," "Tempted," etc.
It also includes an Elvis tribute ("Don't Be Cruel"), a
version of the Band's "The Weight" with the Staples
Singers (from the 1994 compilation RHYTHM, COUNTRY &
BLUES), his duet with Travis Tritt on "The Whiskey Ain't
Workin'," and a couple of previously unreleased tracks.

⊙ **The Pilgrim** (1999; MCA). This is Stuart's most
musically ambitious and emotionally complex project to
date—the crowning achievement of his twenty-year (so
far) recording career. The concept surrounds a love
triangle and concerns marriage, deception, suicide and
redemption. The songs (some of them spoken word
pieces) are haunting, deeply moving, and bursting with
musical vibrancy. They dance, they cry. The album's
chock full of special guests, too, including Cash, Ralph
Stanley, Emmylou Harris, Earl Scruggs, and George
Jones.

Randy Travis

Of all the singers who emerged in the 1980s,
Randy Travis had the voice that could knock
them all flat—a rich, full-bodied baritone brimming
with laid-back southern charm. In terms of style
and tone, Travis clearly took his cues from Merle
Haggard (who in turn copped from Lefty Frizzell)
and a few more from George Jones—both of
whom have remained major musical heroes of his.

Releasing his debut album, STORMS OF LIFE,
in 1986—a time when traditionalism was coming
back into fashion—Travis quickly turned into one
of country's most popular artists. He crossed the
generation gap with little trouble, wowing older
fans with his deep-rooted love of traditional sounds
(he completely avoided strings and other Nashville
Sound overtones, playing "nothing but good
country music," as he described his style in early
interviews), yet winning the hearts of young fans
with his easygoing approach and incredible voice
(of course his tremendous good looks didn't hurt
matters either). By the end of the year STORMS
OF LIFE had produced four major country hits; by
1987 it had sold a million copies, the first debut
country album to do so within a year of release.
Travis' follow-up album, ALWAYS AND FOREVER,
sold even better.

Travis grew up listening to honky tonk, and
when he sang it his background showed—the
emotions seemed to emerge from a place inside

himself over which he had little control. When he
sang of love gone awry on songs like "Diggin' Up
Bones" and "Storms Of Life," the music was so
full of genuine soul it was hard to believe he was
only in his mid-twenties at the time they were
recorded. By the end of the decade he was one of
country music's biggest draws, a position he would
finally relinquish only after the emergence of the
new hats—artists such as Clint Black, Alan Jackson,
Vince Gill, and, ultimately, Garth Brooks.

Travis was born Randy Traywick on 4 May,
1959 in Marshville, North Carolina, a small town
near Charlotte. Randy's father encouraged his six
children to learn music, and in the process instilled
in Randy a deep affection for singers like Hank
Williams, Gene Autry, and Ernest Tubb. Randy
first played in a country band with his brother, but
by age of fourteen he was singing solo in local
nightclubs. At about the same time, however, he
developed a rowdy streak, and regularly got into
trouble with the law. He dropped out of school
in ninth grade, and he'd likely have landed in
prison had it not been for Charlotte nightclub
owner Lib Hatcher. Randy had won a talent
contest at her club Country City USA, and at one
point, when he was facing some serious jail time,
Hatcher convinced the judge to release him into
her custody. Almost overnight Randy cleaned up
his act and began taking his music career seriously.
He worked in the kitchen at Hatcher's club, and
she became his manager—a business relationship
that's lasted throughout his career (to top it off,
and after years of speculation, the pair got married
in 1991).

In 1981 Hatcher sold Country City and she
and Randy moved to Nashville, eventually

Randy Travis

settling at a tourist-oriented nightclub called the Nashville Palace. She managed the place and Randy worked in the kitchen and sang in the evenings. Demo tapes of his songs circulated Music Row to no avail, but Randy did release a live album under the name Randy Ray. In 1985, however, Warner Brothers finally figured they needed a traditionalist to match the success other labels were enjoying with George Strait and Ricky Skaggs, and so Randy was finally signed—and given yet another name change, this time to Travis.

Released in 1986, Travis' debut album, STORMS OF LIFE, was quickly recognized as a monumental achievement. Travis was naturally gifted with a voice that could turn heads and melt hearts, and the songs he sang (by such top-notch writers as Don Schiltz, Paul Overstreet, Troy Seals, and Max D. Barnes) tapped emotional depths few contemporary singers would even dare explore. STORMS also turned into one of the most popular albums of the year, eventually winning Travis a handful of CMA, ACM, and Grammy awards.

Travis followed STORMS a year later with ALWAYS AND FOREVER. Though not quite as stunning as his debut (it mined pretty near the same territory), it was still very substantial in the song department, and it sold even better than the first. By the time his third album, OLD 8x10, hit the stores in 1988, Travis was one of country music's biggest acts. He also had established a pattern of smooth-minded traditional material that showcased his gorgeous voice—a pattern he would, unfortunately, rarely deviate from through the bulk of his career. Yet such a conservative approach had its pluses, as no matter how popular he became Travis always retained the natural honky-tonk feel he'd staked out from the beginning.

By the early '90s new stars were emerging and Travis' popularity began to dip. At the same time, exhausted from the heavy tour schedule he'd endured for years, he opted to take a break from the road—though he continued to release records and make the charts on a regular basis. By this point he'd also started acting, and he's since landed roles in a growing list of TV movies and feature films (among them *Maverick* and *Black Dog*).

After releasing the album FULL CIRCLE in 1996, Travis decided he was unhappy with Warner Brothers and quit the label. The following year, he signed on with the brand-new Nashville division of the DreamWorks label. In early 1998 his album YOU AND YOU ALONE became Dream-Works' first country release.

⊙ **Storms Of Life** (1986; Warner Bros.). From "On The Other Hand" (Travis' first #1, written by Paul Overstreet and Don Schlitz) and continuing through "Diggin' Up Bones," "1982," and "Storms Of Life" (one of Travis' strongest and most enduring songs, written by Troy Seals and Max D. Barnes), this collection of unpretentious, no-frills honky-tonk proves itself pretty near timeless thanks to the superb songwriting, arrangements and vocal work. Albums this good simply don't come around very often.

⊙ **Always And Forever** (1987; Warner Bros.). Not as much of a knockout as Travis' debut (mostly because it was so stylistically similar), this is still a solid record thanks to such songs as "Forever And Ever, Amen," "Too Gone Too Long," and the excellent but underrated "What'll You Do About Me."

⊙ **Greatest Hits Vols. 1 & 2** (1992; Warner Bros.). These are actually 2 separate discs, although they were released at the same time and might as well have been sold together. They contain many of the hightlights of Travis' career to date; in addition, each sports two new songs.

Keith Whitley

"If I'm going to have to be compared to someone, I'd rather it be Lefty than anyone I know of."

—Keith Whitley

From his bluegrass beginnings playing with Ralph Stanley's Clinch Mountain Boys to the #1 country hits of his final solo albums, the late Keith Whitley proved himself a hard-country holdout at a time when pop still dominated radio playlists and sales charts. Whitley developed a no-nonsense edge to his music, tightening his sound when others were going soft. There's heavy doses of Merle Haggard (and by turn Lefty Frizzell) in Whitley's voice, which almost makes songs like "Brother Jukebox" and "I'm No Stranger To The Rain" sound like they emerged from a time machine. When Whitley died at the age thirty-four of alcohol poisoning, it was immediately clear Nashville had lost a major talent—one who had finally hit his stride.

Whitley has since become an icon of neo-traditionalism in Nashville, a guy the industry can point at as someone able to marry good ole honky-tonk sounds with contemporary hitmaking energy (and what record executive wouldn't have time for an artist who racked up several #1s in a short period and then continues to sell records from beyond the grave?). But as has happened with so many rock'n'roll icons, the attention verges on overkill. He was a troubled man, something perhaps reflected in his ongoing stylistic struggle—one he only began to settle during his last few years (for one thing, he complained in interviews of being confined by the bluegrass reputation he'd earned as a teenager). The upswing, however, is that many of his songs are undeniably solid and well deserving of their accolades.

Jessie Keith Whitley was born on 1 July, 1954 in the small town of Sandy Hook in eastern Kentucky. He started playing music as a child, and at the age of eight he appeared on Buddy Starcher's Charleston, West Virginia TV show. During his early teens he worked on his guitar and vocal skills, and eventually he formed a bluegrass band, known as the Lonesome Mountain Boys (among other names). The group included his new pal Ricky Skaggs (whom he'd met at a local talent contest) on fiddle, Whitley's brother Dwight on banjo and Skaggs' father, Hobart, on rhythm guitar.

Whitley got his career break when Ralph Stanley heard him (and Skaggs) playing Stanley Brothers songs at a local gig. He ended up hiring the pair for his band, the Clinch Mountain Boys, when Whitley was still only fifteen. Whitley worked with Stanley on and off over the better part of the decade, recording several albums and earning himself a decent bluegrass reputation along the way. By the late '70s, feeling Stanley's band too constraining, he joined the more progressive outfit J.D. Crowe And The New South (Skaggs had also been a member). He played with Crowe for three years, contributing vocals to the group's most straight-up country album to date, SOMEWHERE BETWEEN (including a version of "I Never Go Around Mirrors," a song Whitley re-recorded on his third solo album).

Thanks to SOMEWHERE BETWEEN, Whitley finally won attention from Nashville. RCA signed him and released his first solo record, HARD ACT TO FOLLOW, in 1984 (it was a six-song "mini" album, a regular treatment for debut artists at RCA at the time; the Judds debuted in the same fashion). This and Whitley's next album, LA TO MIAMI (both produced by Norro Wilson), got a respectable response, including some chart success with the sentimental "Miami, My Amy." This re-fueled the singer and helped him push even further with his third album, DON'T CLOSE YOUR EYES. Co-produced this time by Garth Fundis and Whitley, much of the pop sentimentalism

that marred his early vocal work was left behind. As a whole the album was also much more cohesive. Whitley scored his first #1 with the title track, another sentimental number but one rife with steel guitar and piano. It was followed by "When You Say Nothing At All" and his superb rendition of the Sonny Curtis/Ron Hellard song "I'm No Stranger To The Rain" (which won Single of the Year from the CMA in 1989).

By this point Whitley had married Lorrie Morgan, who would soon be enjoying a major singing career herself. Unfortunately, in tragic honky-tonk fashion, he'd also developed a nasty drinking habit—one that eventually ended in tragedy on 9 May, 1989. He didn't even live long enough to see the release of his fourth album, I WONDER DO YOU THINK OF ME, which he'd recently finished recording. Even if Whitley's untimely death hadn't brought the album all the added attention, it would still be his crowning achievement.

Whitley's fame didn't slow down in the '90s. Morgan recorded a "duet" with her late husband for the 1990 hit "Til A Tear Becomes A Rose," an electronic creation that was named Vocal Event of the Year by the CMA. A duet between Whitley and Earl Thomas Conley released a year later was also quite popular. Soon after the Whitley packages began to appear: a greatest hits album; a collection of unreleased recordings, KENTUCKY BLUEBIRD (which includes songs with his first band, the Lonesome Mountain Boys, and a portion of "You Win Again" that he sang on Starcher's TV show as a child); an album Whitley and Skaggs recorded with Stanley in 1971 (SECOND GENERATION BLUEGRASS); and a 1994 collection KEITH WHITLEY: A TRIBUTE ALBUM that featured Alan Jackson, Alison Krauss, Mark Chesnutt, and others.

⊙ **Don't Close Your Eyes** (1988; RCA). Whitley's third album was the first where he finally stepped confidently and with both feet onto the hard-country terrain he knew and loved so well. "I'm No Stranger To The Rain" is one of the finest songs he ever recorded, and his update of Lefty Frizzell's "I Never Go Around Mirrors" shows off his vocal talent like nothing else. The slow, sad moan of a desperate and dying man, perhaps Whitley could relate to that song's pathos a bit too closely.

⊙ **I Wonder Do You Think Of Me** (1989; RCA). On Whitley's final studio album, his hard-country style is fully in place and engaging from start to finish. The title track is a great Haggard-esque weeper, "Talk To Me

Keith Whitley

Texas" has an optimistic swing despite its lonely lyrics, and "Tennessee Courage" and the excellent "Brother Jukebox" lay the truth on the line with a no-bull, back-to-the-basics foundation. If you want Whitley at his most hearty, here you are.

⊙ **Greatest Hits** (1990; RCA). This best-of package draws mostly from Whitley's last 2 albums, DON'T CLOSE YOUR EYES and I WONDER DO YOU THINK OF ME. It also includes the "duet" with Morgan, "Til A Tear Becomes A Rose," and an unreleased demo, "Tell Lorrie I Love Her." It's a more focused collection than RCA's subsequent package THE ESSENTIAL KEITH WHITLEY, which spends too much time mining Whitley's first couple of albums.

Kelly Willis

Considering her expressive voice, striking looks, and how much money and energy MCA put into promoting her, it's surprising that Kelly Willis didn't make a bigger dent in the commercial country market. Born on 1 October, 1968 in Lawton, Oklahoma, and raised in Virginia, Willis began singing as a teenager in a band with drummer and songwriter Mas Palermo (whom she later married). The pair moved to Austin, Texas, formed a new group, Radio Ranch, and began winning local acclaim. Willis was signed to MCA by Tony Brown, and her debut album, WELL TRAVELLED LOVE (1990), featured Radio Ranch as her backing band and several songs penned by Palermo.

For Willis' follow-up album, BANG BANG (1991), producer Brown brought several Nashville pickers into the studio with the Radio Ranch members. The result was yet another sturdy effort that walked the line between honky tonk and rock'n'roll—a mix quite familiar to the Austin crowd. On a national level, however, sales failed to pick up. Willis recorded one final album for MCA without her band, KELLY WILLIS, but after that she was dropped. Over the next few years, alternative-country fans (and not just her Austin regulars) began paying her some attention. She sang a duet with Son Volt's Jay Farrar on the RED HOT & BOTHERED compilation (a Townes Van Zandt song), and in 1996 she released a four-song EP on A&M, FADING FAST, that showed her in a more relaxed atmosphere. Critics and fans were then ready and waiting with open ears when Willis finally released her fourth full-length album, WHAT

I DESERVE, on Rykodisc in 1999. The album confirmed Kelly's step away from the mainstream and into country music's fringe territory, where she's found a far more receptive and enthusiastic audience.

⊙ **Well Travelled Love** (1990; MCA). Willis' debut arrived just as the new traditionalist era was giving way to Garth and company, which perhaps accounts for her unsuccessful attempts at blending into the mainstream. Commercial concerns aside, songs by such notables as Steve Earle, Paul Kennerley, Monte Warden, and John Hiatt make a fine showcase for Kelly's singing.

⊙ **What I Deserve** (1999; Rykodisc). Kelly Willis moves in even hipper circles this time around, singing material by Paul Westerberg, Chuck Prophet and Dan Penn, Nick Drake, and Bruce Robison (her new husband), among others, as well as songs she co-wrote with the Jayhawks' Gary Louris. The players, too, include Prophet, Robison, Mark Spencer, and pedal-steel favorite Lloyd Maines. Willis has an attractive, soulful voice that's hard not to like, though to be honest she falls short of the complexity that divides artists who sound good from those who can truly command their material. But if not a full-on knockout, this is still an enjoyable album—her best to date and, perhaps, a signal of good things to come.

Kelly Willis

Dwight Yoakam

"We're certainly country-rock with a hyphen. It's what I've always felt about my music."

—Dwight Yoakam

Dwight Yoakam is living proof that a mainstream country music singer can, if he or she has the right mix of talent, drive, and gumption, survive and even thrive outside the confines of contemporary Nashville. Yoakam grew up in Ohio, and while he did briefly try selling himself in Nashville, for the majority of his career he's been based out of Los Angeles, where he felt there was a more open-minded attitude toward both country music and rock'n'roll. Yet even though he didn't enter the country world through tradi-

Dwight Yoakam

tional channels, he quickly worked his way onto the charts to become a multiplatinum success story.

Not to mention one of the finest country singers and songwriters of our time. From the rousing neo-traditionalist sound of his debut, GUITARS, CADILLACS, ETC., ETC. to more experimental 1990s-era efforts like GONE, Yoakam (working in collaboration with his longtime producer/guitarist Pete Anderson) has kept his music fresh and adventurous. He initially hit at a time when traditionally minded singers like George Strait and Ricky Skaggs were the current rage, but instead of riding coattails, he honed his own style with Telecaster guitar leads and sharp, rock-flavored rhythms. Yoakam's voice has a classic hillbilly twang that's appealing in its own right, but

his musical influences have come from all directions—pop, punk, soul, swing, and honky tonk. He's unafraid to bring in strings, horns, or an organ—or to pare down the arrangements until there's little left but his quivering voice. But whatever his music has turned out to be, the bottom line is he's done it all on his own terms.

Yoakam was born on 23 October, 1956 in Pikeville, Kentucky. He did most of his growing up in Columbus, Ohio, where he listened to a wide variety of music—the Byrds, the Stones, Buck Owens, the Supremes. He graduated high school in 1974, briefly attended Ohio State University, and played in local bands. He tried knocking on some doors in Nashville during the late '70s, but he didn't get much response, so he headed west to Los Angeles, where he's lived ever since. He was drawn to Southern California not only because it had been the home base of one of his chief heroes, Buck Owens, but also because, as he later put it, the West Coast offered "an environment that was more conducive to the expansion of the perimeters." Country-rock music—and, in particular, Emmylou Harris and her Hot Band—had been thriving there during the '70s, resulting in records that appealed to Yoakam's wider musical sensibilities.

In LA, Yoakam hooked up with guitarist Pete Anderson, and the two have been musical partners ever since—Anderson producing and playing guitar on all Yoakam's releases to date. Yoakam landed one song ("I'll Be Gone") on the alternative country compilation A TOWN SOUTH OF BAKERSFIELD, which Anderson produced. He played rock-'n'roll clubs more often than country bars, which actually made sense, since there was a thriving roots-rock scene in postpunk LA at the time, headlined by bands like the Blasters, Rank And File, and Los Lobos. In 1984 Yoakam's first record, a six-song EP titled GUITARS, CADILLACS, ETC., was released by the indie label Oak. Two years later, Reprise picked it up and re-released it with four additional tracks (and a modified title; GUITARS, CADILLACS, ETC., ETC.). When the single "Honky Tonk Man," a Johnny Horton composition from the '50s, soared onto the country Top 5, Yoakam was suddenly a hot country property. The song was an appealing blend of a traditional honky tonk structure, hot Bakersfield-inspired guitar licks, and a sassy rock'n'roll attitude. It hit the charts when country fans were ready for a change, and it helped Yoakam become one of the top stars of the New Traditionalist era.

He immediately proved that his success was no fluke. His follow-up single, "Guitars, Cadillacs," was equally popular, as was his second album, HILLBILLY DELUXE. Like his debut, DELUXE reached the top of the *Billboard* country album charts. It also yielded four Top 10 hits in "Little Sister" (an Elvis Presley hit from 1961), "Little Ways," "Please, Please Baby," and "Always Late With Your Kisses" (a classic Lefty Frizzell composition). In 1988, Yoakam took his reverence for classic country music one big step further by pulling Buck Owens out of retirement to sing with him on "Streets Of Bakersfield." The song was an overlooked Owens composition, and it became Yoakam's first #1 single. It also fueled an Owens revival: Buck not only toured with him that summer, he also began recording and playing shows again on his own.

Yoakam finished the decade with a hits collection (JUST LOOKIN' FOR A HIT) and then cut IF THERE WAS A WAY in 1990, which included the single "It Only Hurts When I Cry," which he'd co-written with another country legend, Roger Miller (who died two years later). The album that pushed Yoakam's career to even greater heights, however, was THIS TIME, released in 1993. It was full of infectious singles like "Pocket Of A Clown," "A Thousand Miles From Nowhere," and the Grammy-winning "Ain't That Lonely Yet," and it has sold the best of any Yoakam album so far—more than three million copies. The beauty of it was that he had lost none of his country-rock edge—in fact, his songs were, if anything, sharper and tighter than they'd ever been.

Yoakam had dabbled in acting years earlier, but during the early '90s he began taking it more seriously. It's a second profession that he's remained dedicated to ever since. Peter Fonda directed Yoakam in an LA theater production in 1993, and a year later he appeared in a short scene opposite Nicolas Cage in the John Dahl film *Red Rock West*. His role as the mean-tempered boyfriend in Billy Bob Thornton's 1996 hit film *Sling Blade*, though, gave him his greatest screen exposure to date. Since then he's had roles in films such as *The Newton Boys* (1998) and *The Minus Man* (1999), and he's even stepped into the role of director and screenwriter on the movie *South Of Heaven, West Of Hell*, due for release in 2000.

His music hasn't fallen by the wayside, however. In 1995, Yoakam released both a solid live collection, DWIGHT LIVE, and another hit studio album, GONE. The latter showed him experimenting a bit more with his sound—from the R&B groove of "Nothing" to the moody and minimally arranged "This Much I Know." Less interesting was his 1997 album UNDER THE COVERS, a mixed-bag collection of cover songs like the Clash's "Train In Vain," the Kinks' "Tired Of Waiting" (performed in a brash and overbaked swing-band style), and "Playboy," a song cut back in 1961 by Wynn Stewart, another Bakersfield icon. In 1998 Yoakam released the album A LONG WAY HOME, and a year later came a second hits collection (LAST CHANCE FOR A THOUSAND YEARS: GREATEST HITS FROM THE '90S) and a book (A LONG WAY HOME: TWELVE YEARS OF WORDS) containing the lyrics to all his songs so far.

⊙ **Guitars, Cadillacs, Etc., Etc.** (1986; Reprise). Yoakam's debut is one of the classics of its time, a stripped-down honky tonker that takes just as much of its sensibility from the wild side of rock'n'roll. "Honky Tonk Man" updates Horton's song for modern ears while still remaining wholly reverent; further songs like "South Of Cincinnati," "Miner's Prayer," and "It Won't Hurt" show Yoakam isn't just a pretty voice but a deep and introspective songwriter as well.

⊙ **Looking For A Hit** (1989; Reprise). All Yoakam's albums have redeeming qualities and are worth a listen, but some folks just want the cream of the crop. And so comes this 10-song CD, containing such familiar chart hits as "Little Sister," "Honky Tonk Man," "Streets Of Bakersfield," and "I Sing Dixie" along with curiosities like "Sin City" (a duet with k.d. lang).

⊙ **This Time** (1995; Reprise). Yoakam's transition into the 1990s couldn't have come more beautifully than this finely crafted album. His sound was still his own, but it moved with the times—big and bright on one hand, yet still simple and grounded all the way through. Titles like "A Thousand Miles From Nowhere," "Ain't That Lonely Yet," and "Try Not To Look So Pretty" are among his best to date.

⊙ **Last Chance For A Thousand Years: Greatest Hits From The '90s** (1999; Reprise). Yoakam was so successful during the '90s that he earned a second hits collection. This one has titles culled from IF THERE WAS A WAY, THIS TIME, GONE, and the UK-only release LA CROIX D'AMOUR along with three new tracks: "Thinking About Leaving" (co-written with Rodney Crowell), Waylon Jennings' "I'll Go Back To Her," and the cute Queen ditty "Crazy Little Thing Called Love."

Dwight Yoakam

Hunks, Hat Acts, and Young Country Darlings: Nashville in the 1990s

It was almost like someone had flipped a switch: at the beginning of the 1990s, the popularity of country music exploded like it never had before—out of the hillbilly ghetto and into the fast lane of the American mainstream. Vestiges of country's past were still present—twangy voices, steel guitars, fiddles, and more than a few nods to God, Mama, and Merle Haggard—but this 'new country' sound was a far cry from oldies music. The stars themselves were now a lot younger—hunks in hats, pretty gals in boots, and bright-eyed, freshly scrubbed faces everywhere you turned. And more often than not fans now got their first glimpse of these folks via a splashy music video, rather than a *Grand Ole Opry* appearance.

As the hillbilly edge was trimmed off and the music watered down with more pop-friendly elements, Nashville opened itself up to a whole new audience. Country fans had traditionally been southern and rural, but now they came from all persuasions and backgrounds. Even baby boomers brought up to despise the sound of a pedal-steel guitar felt it was safe to embrace the music. The melodies were as infectious as anything on MTV—and those boys and girls were just so cute. How could you turn your back on **Clint Black**, **Faith Hill**, or **Clay Walker**? And who for goodness

sake could take their eyes off that bellybutton on **Shania Twain**?

The driving force behind this Nashville 'revolution' was album sales. Where only a decade earlier a country record was a major success when it went gold (500,000 copies sold), sales now reached platinum status (over a million) on a regular basis. And Nashville hasn't been the same since. Hoping to capitalize on this 'young country' concept, new acts were signed in greater numbers than ever before. And in the process, onetime superstars faded into the background. Commercial radio picked up on this trend with little trouble—after all, country stations had been rejecting 'classic' artists and 'old-fashioned' sounds for decades already, all in the name of higher ratings and a bigger share of the pop market. But by the '90s, tune into your local mainstream country station, and it was suddenly a rarity to hear even the likes of Haggard, Waylon Jennings, Tammy Wynette, or George Jones. Jones' 1980 recording "He Stopped Loving Her Today" had been a megahit, sure, but only a decade later it was ancient history.

The World According to Garth

Country music's popularity had actually been building over the previous decade, thanks to the popularity of singers like Randy Travis, George Strait, Reba McEntire, and Ricky Van Shelton. But there's a good reason why at the turn of the decade album sales and media attention seemed to accelerate very suddenly. In 1991 *Billboard* began using a technology called SoundScan to tally music sales for its weekly charts. Instead of relying on retailers to tell them which songs and albums were selling best—a very unscientific system open to all sorts of corruption and uncertainty—chart figures were now based on actual sales. And country music turned out to be one of the big surprises: the week it was instigated, **Garth Brooks**' album NO FENCES jumped from #16 to #4. The biggest coup of all was that Garth's next album, ROPIN' THE WIND, debuted at #1 on the pop album charts. Both records went on to sell well over ten million copies. For the first time ever a country music singer was in the megasales league with the likes of Michael Jackson and Billy Joel. Such sky-high album sales immediately redefined success in an industry that had only seen its first platinum album, the compilation WANTED! THE OUTLAWS, a scant fifteen years earlier.

Brooks was a combination of elements that proved hard to beat. He wore a cowboy hat and jeans, hailed from Oklahoma, and carefully maintained a visage of small-town humility. Everything he did was "for the fans." Yet shy he was not. He was a charismatic showman, his concerts extravagant affairs packed with light shows, complex stage sets, and Brooks himself flying from the rafters on cables, headset mike strapped across his face. He was also responsive to the media, embracing it at every opportunity. In interviews he spoke frankly (confessing his extramarital affair, supporting his lesbian sister), well aware how publicity translated into album sales. He had been a business major in college, after all.

As for his music, Brooks' combined the old with the new and in the process redefined the Nashville Sound standard. His debut album hit stores in 1989 when neo-traditionalist singers like Travis and Strait were still high in the charts. And while he shared their honky-tonk inclinations, he also brought in outside elements—most notably the arena-rock traits of '70s artists like the Eagles and Journey, and the saccharine sentiments of singer-songwriters like James Taylor. These were artists whom he had grown up listening to right alongside classic traditionalists like Haggard and Jones. Brooks' albums thus became a mix of barroom honky tonkers ("Friends In Low Places"), darkly tinged power anthems ("The Thunder Rolls"), and syrupy, heart-tugging ballads ("The River," "The Dance"). He even went so far as to cover a Billy Joel song (the aptly titled "Shameless") on ROPIN' THE WIND.

The New Hats Are Here

Garth wasn't working alone, though. A new generation of singers such as Clint Black, **Alan Jackson**, **Travis Tritt**, and **Vince Gill** were breaking on the horizon as well. Most of these newcomers were also rooted in neo-traditionalism—to a greater degree than Brooks, in fact—and kept their music close to the ground. At the same time they were generally well-scrubbed and clean-shaven—image was more important than ever in this age of music videos and traditional family values—and more often than not they were topped off with a cowboy hat to signify their roots (a trend unintentionally inspired by onetime rancher George Strait) and separate them from such schmaltzy, adult-contemporary country singers as Kenny Rogers and Lee Greenwood. Hence the term 'hat acts.'

One of the best of the new breed, and a guy who helped kick things off, was Clint Black. His first album, KILLIN' TIME, was released in the spring of 1989—the very same time as Brooks' self-titled debut—and proved immediately popular. For about a year, Black was the hitmaker to bet on, thanks to the runaway success of his debut single, "Better Man," a Haggard-esque number with a thick-cut guitar riff and a huge, deep hook. KILLIN' TIME led the charge into the '90s, and it remains one of the era's finest.

Travis Tritt was a burly voiced Georgia native who appeared at the tail end of 1989 with a Top 10 single "Country Club." His sound was a mix of blue-collar sentiments ("Lord Have Mercy On The Working Man") and gut-level honky tonk ("Here's A Quarter [Call Someone Who Cares]"), but he was really more embroiled in the southern rock legacy of the Allman Brothers and Lynyrd Skynyrd (and for that matter, Hank Williams, Jr.). Though Tritt could get blustery, his understanding of and respect for country music's roots is genuine. He knows his history for one thing: his second album, IT'S ALL ABOUT TO CHANGE, included a rocked-up version of "Don't Give Your Heart To A Rambler" by Jimmie Skinner, a midwestern singer most country fans under fifty had probably never even heard of.

Garth's second album, NO FENCES, was the one that made him a superstar, in large part thanks to "Friends In Low Places," a song about a country boy who causes a scene at a snobby black-tie party—presumably his ex-girlfriend's wedding.

Curiously, it showed up at the same time on NO FENCES and on TOO COLD AT HOME, the debut album from **Mark Chesnutt**, one of the finest honky-tonk stylists to grace Nashville during the '90s. The two versions of "Low Places" had surprisingly different tones: where Brooks turned it into a rowdy sing-along anthem, complete with party-hardy whoops and hollers, Chesnutt created a more somber and lonely mood—when his protagonist escapes to the bar with his buddies, it truly feels like a drowning of sorrows. Either way, the song itself (written by Dewayne Blackwell and Earl Bud Lee) gave the middle finger to arrogant uptowners everywhere—an anthem of rebellion that became a theme song for the whole new country era.

Chesnutt's "Low Places" may have been completely overshadowed by Brooks' version, but other songs he recorded like "Too Cold At Home" and "Brother Jukebox" did break this young Texas singer onto the charts. Chesnutt's never achieved superstar status, but he has maintained a steady presence throughout the decade—album after album shows he has a keen sense of what makes country music tick.

Jackson was another newcomer who shot to the forefront with his 1990 singles "Chasin' That Neon Rainbow," "Wanted," and "Here In The Real World." His personality was reserved and country-humble, though being tall, blonde, and strappingly handsome certainly got him noticed in an age when hunks and hats were all the rage. Jackson's songs have a simple, even-keeled honky-tonk foundation that's as refreshing as it is predictable. But his appeal is wide, and he's remained one of Nashville's top-selling artists and one of the contemporary industry's most dependable songwriters.

Marty Stuart entered the '90s with some impressive musical credentials. A child prodigy, he'd played guitar and mandolin with Lester Flatt when he was barely a teenager and picked guitar for years behind Johnny Cash. During the '80s he developed a hot-fired country style of his own that took a long, strong look back at the '40s and '50s. He cut his first album in 1982, but he didn't really break into the mainstream until his 1991 album TEMPTED. Like his buddy Travis Tritt, Stuart was enamored with country music's heritage—he even bought Ernest Tubb's tour bus. He and Tritt also rebelled against Nashville uniformity by playing shows together under the banner "The No Hats Tour".

With country music selling like never before, the labels were predictably jumping all over each other to sign new stars and capitalize on the situation. As a result, within a few short years the market was saturated with almost indistinguishable boy singers wrapped up in Wranglers and topped off by Stetsons. Country music's heritage—the mountain-bred harmonies of the Carter Family, the lonesome hillbilly hollers of Hank Williams—seemed farther away than ever before.

Still, for all the rampant homogeneity, a number of singers from the early '90s did stand out in terms of both personality and song material. **Doug Stone** was one who made great work of some serious down-and-outers like "I'd Be Better Off (In A Pine Box)" and "Ain't Your Memory Got No Pride At All." Like Steve Earle a decade earlier, **Mark Collie** brought a gritty, introspective, and at times dark edge to such rooted songs as "Another Old Soldier" and "Trouble's Comin' Like A Train." As a bonus, his debut album, HARDIN COUNTY LINE, even featured guitarist James Burton. Listen to **Sammy Kershaw** sing hits like "Anywhere But Here" or "Cadillac Style" and he's almost a dead ringer for George Jones. And Larry Boone, with his deep and hefty voice, sounded like a refreshing throwback to the golden age of the '40s and '50s—though vocally his closest comparison might be Austin honky tonker Dale Watson.

Like George Strait, **Chris LeDoux** had authentic cowboy credentials that earned him his right to a hat—he was a rodeo champ during the '70s. He'd also already cut nearly two dozen albums on his own label before Garth Brooks mentioned his name in a song ("Much Too Young To Feel This Damn Old") and Liberty signed him in 1990. One guy who truly did appear "much too young" was **Tracy Lawrence**. But his debut album STICKS AND STONES (helmed by Clint Black's producer, Jeff Stroud) had enough solid songs to earn him recognition as more than just a hat-act clone. The same was true for **Tracy Byrd**, another young buck with a Strait fixation who squeezed his way into the Nashville line-up with a cover of Johnny Paycheck's 1970s hit "Someone To Give My Love To" and the catchy "Heaven In My Woman's Eyes"—sturdy songs that sound like they're coming from a guy twice Byrd's age.

Beyond the Cowboy Horizon

Not every singer and band who emerged during this period adopted a cookie-cutter Haggard-and-Jones style. Blackhawk (featuring guitarist Henry Paul from country rockers the Outlaws) and the Kentucky Headhunters were steeped in southern rock—the latter cutting whooped-up cover versions of songs like "Oh Lonesome Me" and "The

Ballad Of Davy Crockett." The **Mavericks**, led by singer-songwriter Raul Malo and his Orbison-esque voice, built a strong following in Miami before signing to MCA and achieving platinum success with their 1994 album WHAT A CRYING SHAME. Though Nashville's support proved limited, the Mavericks have managed to nurture and build upon their substantial grassroots following.

If LeDoux and Strait earned their credentials on horseback, **Aaron Tippin** earned his "Working Man's Ph.D." in the blue-collar world as a welder, pilot, and farmhand (not to mention a body builder). "Ph.D." and "I Got It Honest," though they bristle with macho attitude, are sturdy and proud; others, however, like "Country Boy's Toolbox," lean too hard on novelty. And speaking of novelty we come to **Tim McGraw**, who ram-rodded his way into Nashville with the 1994 song "Indian Outlaw," the crassest piece of work since George Jones' "Poor Chinee." Another of McGraw's songs, "Refried Dreams," played on further cultural stereotypes. His fans, however, didn't seem to mind—the album that contained both songs, NOT A MOMENT TOO SOON, sold millions and turned McGraw into one of Nashville's top stars.

Crooner Vince Gill has an undeniable taste for saccharine material—but just as undeniable is the quality of his tenor voice, which is as sweet and pretty as it is pure and soaring. Luckily not everything he does is drowned in overdubbed string sections—he brings his substantial bluegrass and country-rock background (he spent a few years singing with Pure Prairie League) into play just as frequently.

And who can forget the line dance craze? The idea was built around group spirit—no partners necessary, everyone lines up and moves through the steps together. Just like "The Hustle." In country music, the big breakthrough line dance number was the "Achy Breaky," choreographed by Melanie Greenwood and based on the 1992 **Billy Ray Cyrus** smash hit. Cyrus was a Kentucky-born singer who'd been struggling for years before his debut single, "Achy Breaky Heart," shot to the top of both the country and pop charts. It's a big-beat, thick-headed song that's as dumb as any in country, though that was part of its charm. As were Billy Ray's bulging muscles (he was the ultimate 'hunk' singer) and his mullet haircut. The poor guy, though, has spent years since trying to erase the critical backlash that erupted in the wake of that song's success.

Another popular line dance song was the "Boot Scootin' Boogie," which came courtesy of

Brooks & Dunn, the decade's most popular duo by a long shot. Kix Brooks and Ronnie Dunn had each struggled as songwriters and singers on their own, but their careers finally got off the ground in 1991 when they teamed up and cut the album BRAND NEW MAN. "Boot Scootin' Boogie" was just one of several high-energy singles from that album.

Ladies' Choices

Make no mistake about it: male artists dominated the country music industry in the early 1990s—just as they had throughout the music's history. But that doesn't mean there weren't strong female singers and songwriters out there making some serious waves.

The one singer who throughout the '90s came closest to matching Garth Brooks in terms of ambition, flash and drive is Reba McEntire. She had already established her star power during the '80s, years before Garth's name turned to gold. She'd toyed with new traditionalism but eventually found her niche with slicker, more pop-inspired ballads and belters. The same was true for Wynonna Judd, who also built her career during the '80s as half of the mother-daughter group the Judds, but who as a solo artist turned toward a more pop-oriented sound—and gained new ground in the process.

Of the newcomers, one of the most successful has been **Trisha Yearwood**, a onetime demo singer who made a big splash with her full-bodied voice and catchy debut single "She's In Love With The Boy." With the help of Garth Brooks (she opened for him on his 1991 tour), Yearwood's career was soon off and running. Much of her music is streaked with her unfortunate penchant for sentimental schmaltz, but songs like "Wrong Side Of Memphis," "XXX's And OOO's (An American Girl)," and "Oh Lonesome You" are marked by a genuine go-get-'em spirit. When Yearwood really cuts loose, it feels like freedom.

Mary Chapin Carpenter was a coffeehouse singer-songwriter for years before she landed on the country music charts. She's got folk music in her blood, which lends her music a more traditionally rooted quality than the average Reba McEntire power ballad. Another Nashville singer who began her career with a spare, down-to-earth sound was **Suzy Bogguss**. Songs such as Rodney Crowell's "Guilty As They Come" and the Patsy Montana classic "I Want To Be A Cowboy's Sweetheart" from her overlooked 1989 debut SOMEWHERE BETWEEN are a breath of fresh country air from days gone by.

Other singers who emerged during this time include **Pam Tillis**, Lorrie Morgan, Martina McBride, Terri Clark, and Sara Evans. **Faith Hill**'s bright voice and peppy song style (not to mention her golden good looks) have kept her star shining since her 1993 debut "Wild One," but her career soared even higher in 1998 thanks to her sunny, infectious, radio-tailored single "This Kiss." McBride first made a splash with the award-winning video to her 1994 hit "Independence Day" (which dealt frankly with spousal abuse), and by the late '90s she, too, was well on her way to pop-crossover success. Too bad the same story isn't true for Jann Browne, Kelly Willis, Matraca Berg, **Joy Lynn White**, and Bobbie Cryner, all of whom showed artistic promise but never found much footing on the charts.

Among the latest crop of rising female stars, perhaps Missouri native Sara Evans shows the most promising signs of marrying honky-tonk roots with mainstream success. Her 1997 debut, THREE CHORDS AND THE TRUTH, was produced by Pete Anderson and maintained a sturdy country foundation (she comes off like a female Dwight Yoakam), yet she was successfully marketed to mainstream audiences, who were drawn to her powerful voice and hook-filled songs. No wonder legendary songwriter Harlan Howard has spoken so highly of her, and stars like Vince Gill and Alison Krauss lent vocal support to her follow-up, NO PLACE THAT FAR.

Deana Carter ("Strawberry Wine") and teenage powerhouse vocalist **LeAnne Rimes** ("Blue") were two major country sensations who emerged midway through the decade, just as the market was getting desperate for new blood. Rimes was only thirteen when she cut "Blue," a song three decades old that was supposedly written for Patsy Cline—at least that was the story fed to the press. Why Rimes followed what was a halfway substantial song with a cover of the insufferable Debby Boone hit "You Light Up My Life" is impossible to understand.

Rimes and Carter sold plenty of records, but by far the biggest post-Garth blockbuster of an artist, man or woman, to smash onto the charts was Canadian singer Shania Twain. Teaming with producer (and now husband) Robert John "Mutt" Lange (whose previous clients include Def Leppard and Michael Bolton) for her 1995 album THE WOMAN IN ME, the pair created songs that were sharp, sassy, sexy, and clearly modeled to attract the MTV generation. Of course Twain's fashion-model looks, skin-tight outfits, and frequently bared midriff didn't hurt matters. The package worked—

both THE WOMAN IN ME and its follow-up, COME ON OVER, have each topped ten million in sales.

Changing Times

By the time Twain hit, the times had been a-changin' on Music Row. Garth's albums had walked out the door in previously unfathomable numbers, but in truth there were few artists who could even come close to that kind of selling power—especially as the market became saturated with crooning cowhands and watered-down balladeers. How many Clay Walkers, Lila McCanns, David Kershes, and Kenny Chesneys could the average music fan keep straight at one time anyhow?

Twain was obviously a singer who could sell in large numbers, and in many an executive's eye she was a saving grace—more vital to the future market than even Brooks himself. Rimes and Carter also sold in respectable numbers, and further newcomers like Mindy McCready, Jo Dee Messina, and boyish crooner Bryan White showed decent promise on the country futures market.

The **Dixie Chicks**, however, were the only actual sensation to hit Nashville in the late 1990s. Cute, funny, and rippling with charm and spirit, the three Chicks are a difficult act to resist even without hearing a lick of their music—which, by the way, is as sassy and perky as you'd imagine. Everyone loves the Dixie Chicks. Their 1998 album WIDE OPEN SPACES brought them numerous CMA and ACM awards and at the turn of the millennium it had surpassed the eight million mark in sales. Though they seemed to appear out of nowhere, the Dixie Chicks (albeit with a different vocalist) had actually been touring and recording their lively mix of cowgirl folk and rootsy country since the early '90s. Their new sound is much slicker and less grassroots, but when it shows up on commercial country radio it is deeply refreshing.

The Dixie Chicks aside, by the end of the decade the major Music Row labels were signing fewer new artists. And the handful who had made it in the door and were under tremendous pressure to deliver the goods or find themselves back on the street. Artistic development (allowing an artist a few years to find his or her legs) is a concept that Music Row has shown little interest in lately. In 1998, brand-new MCA hopeful **Allison Moorer** (who happens to be an excellent singer and songwriter) landed an Academy Award nomination for her song "A Soft Place To Fall" from the Robert Redford film *The Horse Whisperer*. She got to stay on the roster for another round, while Decca artist **Chris Knight**—whose 1998 debut album was one of the finest to come out of Nashville in ages—was dropped. Nothing personal, just business. In fact, the whole Decca imprint got the axe after parent company MCA came under the umbrella of its new parent company, Seagram's. Knight wasn't the only MCA casualty: Bakersfield group Big House, Texas powerhouse Joe Ely, and even George Jones—one of the icons of the entire '90s generation—were each served walking papers as well. And, of course, MCA was by no means the only Nashville label growing anxious over financial statements and trimming its roster to meet the bottom line. By the late '90s it was a trend among nearly every major Nashville record company.

The Fringes: The Future?

As record companies trim the fat, and mainstream country radio still refuses to play anything but the safest of sounds, life on the fringes of the country music world grows steadily stronger ... and more vital. Artists like Marty Brown and Kelly Willis have already wound up on indie labels HighTone and Rykodisc respectively. **Mandy Barnett**, touted as the second coming of Patsy Cline, has switched from Nashville-based Asylum to LA-based Sire. Matraca Berg, a respected and very

Anthologies

⊙ **Rhythm, Country & Blues** (1994; MCA). The producers of this compilation did an excellent job pairing up country and R&B stars on 11 classic tunes from both camps. Little Richard and Tanya Tucker tear their way through "Somethin' Else"; Al Green and Lyle Lovett are a groovy match on "Funny How Time Slips Away"; B.B. King and George Jones pull off a particularly bombastic version of "Patches"; Clint Black gets funky with the Pointer Sisters on "Chain Of Fools"; and Conway Twitty (his last recording before his death) pairs with Sam Moore for a moving take on "Rainy Night In Georgia." Lots of surprises and thrills.

⊙ **Keith Whitley: A Tribute Album** (1994; RCA). When honky-tonker Keith Whitley died in 1989, Nashville snapped to attention and showered him with a surprising amount of attention and acclaim. This tribute album showed up several years later, and it's full of 1990s-era star power: Alan Jackson ("Don't Close Your Eyes"), Tracy Lawrence ("I'm Over You"), Joe Diffie ("I'm No Stranger To The Rain"), Mark Chesnutt ("I Never Go Around Mirrors"), and Alison Krauss ("When You Say Nothing At All").

⊙ **Harley Davidson Country Road Songs** (1996; Capitol). Admittedly it's a dumb packaging concept, but the music inside of this "road songs" sampler is actually pretty cool—a selection of Outlaw country (David Allan Coe, Hank Jr., Willie Nelson) juxtaposed with the work of 1990s stars like Alan Jackson, Mark Chesnutt, Lee Roy Parnell, Clay Walker, Trace Adkins, and Tanya Tucker. Thirty songs are spread across 2 discs, so it's certainly a substantial collection.

⊙ **Traveller: Music From The Motion Picture** (1997; Asylum). This is a fun soundtrack—that is, if you're drawn to the idea of Randy Travis singing "King Of The Road," Jimmie Dale Gilmore running through the Lefty Frizzell classics "If You've Got The Money" and "I Love You A Thousand Ways," and Mandy Barnett crooning "Dark Moon" and "Dream Lover." We could do without Bryan White's bouncy "Rocking Robin," but fellow Nashville newcomer Lila McCann's twangy take on "Please Help Me I'm Falling" is surprisingly strong.

⊙ **The Horse Whisperer** (1998; MCA). This CD—the soundtrack to a Robert Redford film—has a distinct western feel, and it's perhaps more an Americana sampler than anything mainstream country radio would normally play. Technicalities aside, it's a great way to sample the work of edgier artists such as Allison Moorer (her Academy Award–nominated "Soft Place To Fall"), Lucinda Williams ("Still I Long For Your Kiss"), Don Walser ("Big Balls In Cowtown"), and Iris Dement ("Whispering Pines")alongside stars like George Strait ("Red River Valley"), Dwight Yoakam ("Cattle Call"), and the Mavericks ("Dream River"). And former Flatlanders Joe Ely, Jimmie Dale Gilmore, and Butch Hancock sing together on the gentle "South Wind Of Summer." Beautiful.

⊙ **Cryin' Lyin' Lovin' & Leavin'** (1998; Rebound). The concept here is pretty much self-explanatory. Artists include Mark Chesnutt ("Too Cold At Home"), Vince Gill ("I Never Knew Lonely"), the Mavericks ("My Secret Flame"), Suzy Bogguss ("Cross My Broken Heart"), Tracy Byrd ("Holdin' Heaven"), and Michelle Wright ("Take It Like A Man").

successful songwriter (her work's been cut by the likes of Trisha Yearwood, Faith Hill, Deana Carter, and even Dusty Springfield), saw her 1997 album released on the Nashville imprint Rising Tide (though that label has since folded). And the Nashville indie label Dead Reckoning is forging ahead thanks to the music and hard work of artist/owners Kieran Kane, Kevin Welch, Tammy Rogers, Mike Henderson, and Harry Stinson.

Can success happen from these fringe territories? Alison Krauss is a perfect example that it is possible—her albums have sold millions, even though she's largely a bluegrass artist and has remained with indie-label Rounder. Yet despite her popularity and sales figures to back her up, country radio still won't play her songs.

Jim Lauderdale is another highly respected singer-songwriter who's worked on the fringes of the mainstream for years. He writes good songs and has a fine voice, though he can be a bit too sincere—at least by commerical radio standards. The same lack of mainstream success is true for Berg, Moorer, Knight, Joy Lynn White, Junior Brown, and honky-tonk bar band **BR5–49**. Even the Mavericks, despite a string of chart hits, have had more success in the long run working on a grassroots level—touring and supporting themselves outside industry circles. And they've built quite a strong following that way—as have Steve

Earle, Jimmie Dale Gilmore, Lucinda Williams, Dale Watson, Robert Earl Keen, and Guy Clark. They might be variously tagged as alternative, neo-traditional, retro, folk, or progressive, but these days they're as much a part of the big, wide, wonderful world of country music as any multiplatinum Nashville star.

If country music is hoping to move in new directions and garner some real excitement once again, it's going to have to look to these and other artists—if not actually bringing Freakwater and/or Dale Watson into the fold, then perhaps taking some inspiration from them. The hat act schtick has long ago proven tired and overbaked. Garth and Shania can't carry the marketing load forever, even with the help of multiplatinum stars like Jackson, McGraw, Hill, and Rimes. And a band like the Dixie Chicks spicing up the country roster every couple of years isn't enough to keep the industry vibrant, let alone afloat. Many insiders and label executives agree that change is inevitable, perhaps even desperately needed if the country music industry is going to remain financially fruitful. Shake-ups have happened before—honky tonk in the '40s, Outlaws in the '70s, new traditionalists in the '80s. What it will sound like this time, though, and where it will come from, remain a mystery. But isn't that just the beauty of it?

Young Country: The Artists

Mandy Barnett

"To me, where country comes from is what makes it great."

—Mandy Barnett

Crossville, Tennessee native Mandy Barnett (born 28 September, 1975) certainly has a fine set of pipes, and she can sing Patsy Cline like nobody's business—which she did for a couple of years in the starring role of the stage production *Always … Patsy Cline*. Barnett was still a teenager

when she landed that gig, and it seemed like a perfect launching pad into the world of Nashville. Before she was twenty-one she had a record deal with Asylum. Yet as proud (if at times overproduced) an effort as it was, and as many critical praises as it received, her much-hyped debut album, MANDY BARNETT, didn't exactly burn up the country charts. Apparently, her renditions of songs like Willie Nelson's "Three Days" and Jim Lauderdale's "Planet Of Love" were just too substantial for mainstream tastes.

Barnett is a strong, confident vocalist and a budding country visionary, much more so than her studio-shiny debut album indicates. Her penchant for classic country songs and styles comes across far more clearly in her second effort, I'VE GOT A RIGHT TO CRY. Ironically, for this album she switched from Nashville label Asylum to the LA label Sire, which significantly enough is home to k.d. lang, another Cline-conjuring vocalist. What's even more noteworthy is that RIGHT TO

Mandy Barnett

CRY, like lang's 1988 album SHADOWLAND, featured production work by Owen Bradley, one of the chief creators of the Nashville Sound in the '50s—and the man who produced Patsy Cline. In the hands of Barnett, Bradley, and his brother Harold (co-producer on the album and a longtime studio session guitarist), the Nashville Sound is transformed from the mindless formula it became during the '60s into a wonderfully lush country style that feels absolutely classic. Barnett's album was Bradley's final project as a producer before his death in 1998.

⊙ **Mandy Barnett** (1996; Asylum). Cline's influence is out front on Willie Nelson's 1962 classic "Three Days" and the Kostas/Richard Bennett song "I'll Just Pretend." Though the production is at times crowded with strings and syrup, a few songs do suggest that great things are yet to come—Barnett's delicate handling of Jim Lauderdale's "Planet Of Love," for example, and her unhurried take on the traditional "Wayfaring Stranger."

⊙ **I've Got A Right To Cry** (1999; Sire). A lavish, sweeping production that fills the room and feels entirely classic, this album allows Barnett more creative space and freedom. She covers great songwriters like Don Gibson ("Give Myself A Party") and Mickey Newbury ("Funny Familiar Forgotten Feelings"), and her versions of Porter Wagoner's "Trademark" and Russell Brown and Pat McLaughlin's "The Whispering Wind (Blows On By)" are especially strong.

Clint Black

If Garth Brooks hadn't happened along at the exact same time, Texas honky tonker Clint Black might have climbed to even greater heights. Black's bold neo-traditionalist sound makes him a more rightful heir to the throne of 1980s honky tonker George Strait than the more pop-oriented Brooks—not to mention that Black shot right out of the chute with one of the era's strongest albums, KILLIN' TIME, and a single that is still almost impossible to beat, "Better Man." With a warm, Haggard-inspired baritone voice and a straight-shooting style that nods to rock'n'roll but always keeps the Texas roadhouse in sight, Black proved himself a consistent hitmaker thanks to such solid material as "Killin' Time," "Burn One Down," "Good Run Of Bad Luck," and "No Time To Kill." If these and other songs weren't exactly based on personal experience, the emotions definitely felt real. Even as Brooks rose to the top with mind-boggling speed, and began selling albums by the tens of millions, Black remained a popular and vital participant in the world of contemporary country music—a singer and songwriter with no shortage of creative integrity and genuine honky-tonk spirit.

Black was born in 1962 in New Jersey, where his father was working on a temporary job, but his family quickly moved back to Texas, making Clint a Texan by all but the most technical definitions. He was raised most of his life in Katy, a suburb of

Mandy Barnett • Clint Black

Houston, and he grew up singing and writing songs, often performing with his brother Kevin. In the early '80s he landed a regular gig at Benton Springs Club in Houston, and it's there that he met Hayden Nicholas, who's been his friend and frequent songwriting partner ever since. Together they penned "Better Man" and five other songs on KILLIN' TIME. He also met ZZ Top's manager Bill Ham, who eventually took Black on as a client and helped get him signed to RCA in 1988. Black's debut single was "Better Man," and it shot to #1 in the spring of 1989, making him an instant star. The album KILLIN' TIME eventually gave Black

Clint Black

three more country chart toppers, "Killin' Time," "Nobody's Home," and "Walkin' Away," and by late 1990 had sold more than two million copies. PUT YOURSELF IN MY SHOES, his follow-up album, the title track of which was a lazy-tempoed song about lost love reminiscent of Haggard's flirtations with Dixieland, was also a huge seller. By this point Black was touring regularly and winning awards for his albums, songs and vocal skills. In 1991 he married TV star Lisa Hartman (*Knots Landing*).

Black's third album, THE HARD WAY, released in 1992, showed he was still in top form as a singer and songwriter (he even co-produced it this time with James Stroud), but the string of hits he'd seen from his first album proved near impossible to match. Besides, Garth Brooks was now soaking up much of country music's national spotlight. Black was a bigger draw in concert than he'd ever been, however—his show had expanded from a straightahead, no-frills song showcase into an arena-sized, rock'n'roll-styled extravaganza, complete with smoke machines and a stage set designed after a Utah desert landscape (where his video "We Tell Ourselves" had been shot). But with the ups of stardom come the downs, most notably a series of lawsuits stemming from a falling out with his manager, Ham, over publishing rights and other financial concerns.

In 1993 Black toured with Wynonna Judd, sang a hit duet with her (the schmaltzy "A Bad Goodbye"), contributed "Desperado" to the massively popular Eagles tribute album COMMON THREADS, and kept his name in lights with another respectable collection of his own material, NO TIME TO KILL. In 1994 he landed a role in the movie *Maverick*, and "A Good Run Of Bad Luck" made it onto the soundtrack. After his fifth album, ONE EMOTION, and a collection of Christmas songs, Black took a break from the road for a couple of years. He was back in business, though, after the release of his 1997 album NOTHIN' BUT THE TAILLIGHTS. Sales weren't as high as his earlier albums, but TAILLIGHTS did yield him another round of hit singles. The following year Black and Hartman co-produced and co-starred in the TV movie *Still Holding On: The Legend Of Cadillac Jack*, about rodeo star Cadillac Jack Favor, who was wrongly imprisoned for murder. Black had earlier penned a song about Favor, "Cadillac Jack," that appeared on his GREATEST HITS collection. After filming he was back on the touring circuit again. In 1999 he released D'LECTRIFIED, an album that carried the curious cautionary statement, "Warning: No Electric Instruments Used In This Recording." Among the acoustic arrangements and almost swing-sounding set of tunes is a remake of a 1975 Waylon Jennings hit that Black has retitled "Are You Sure Waylon Done It This Way."

⊙ **Killin' Time** (1989; RCA). Top to bottom, and song for song, this is one of the finest country records to come out of Nashville in the last couple of decades.

⊙ **The Greatest Hits** (1996; RCA). Collects Black's biggest hits from his 5 previous albums along with 4 new songs (including "Cadillac Jack"), his schmaltzy duet with Wynonna ("A Bad Goodbye"), and a live version of his Eagles cover "Desperado." Not a bad overview, but Killin' Time is still a better introduction.

⊙ **Nothin' But The Taillights** (1997; RCA). This time Clint collaborates not only with Hayden Nicholas but a host of other songwriters, including Steve Wariner, Kostas, and Matraca Berg. He also brings in such duet partners as Alison Krauss and Union Station ("Our Kind Of Love"), Martina McBride ("Still Holding On"), and guitar hotshots Chet Atkins, Wariner, and Mark Knopfler ("Ode To Chet"). Overall, though, Taillights is less edgy than most of his past efforts.

Suzy Bogguss

"Her voice sparkles like crystal water."

—Chet Atkins

ROBERT M ASCROFT

Suzy Bogguss

S uzy Bogguss kicked off her Nashville career with a folk-inspired, traditionally-minded country album, SOMEWHERE BETWEEN, that even included a cover of Patsy Montana's 1935 classic "I Want To Be A Cowboy's Sweetheart." Not typically the stuff that transforms newcomers into platinum stars, though the album did garner the her substantial respect among critics—and as a bonus, a pair of Top 40 hits, "Cross My Broken Heart" and "My Sweet Love Ain't Around," the latter a Hank Williams composition. Bogguss has since gone on to earn her share of hits and hot albums, most notably 1991's ACES, which yielded a two Top 10 hits, "Outbound Plane" and the title track.

Bogguss was born on 30 December, 1956 in the small Illinois town of Aledo. After majoring in art at Illinois State University, she came to Nashville in the mid-'80s and found work as a demo singer, among other odd jobs. During this period she met her husband-to-be, Doug Crider, and he's been involved as a songwriter and/or producer on all of her albums to date. Bogguss had recorded a self-released album a few years earlier, and this eventually helped land her a contract with Capitol Records, where she stayed put through most of the '90s. She earned the CMA's Horizon Award in 1992. Since her debut, Bogguss' arrangements have been streamlined to more closely fit desires of country-pop radio, but her roots-minded integrity shows through nonetheless. She cut a duet album with Chet Atkins, SIMPATICO, in 1994,

and her song choices have always revealed a respectable sense of adventure: John Hiatt's "Drive South" (which hit #2 in 1992), Jimmie Rodgers' "In the Jailhouse Now" (with Atkins), and Julie Miller's "Take Me Back." Her 1998 album NOBODY LOVE, NOBODY GETS HURT was one of her finest collections, but it turned out to be her last for Capitol. A year later she released SUZY BOGGUSS on the new label Platinum.

⊙ **Somewhere Between** (1989; Liberty). It's not as if this album is a milestone, but it's immediately striking and truly enjoyable, basking in the glory of neo-traditional—at times almost hillbilly-sounding—country music. Songs such as Rodney Crowell's "Guilty As They Come," Merle Haggard's "Somewhere Between," and the Patsy Montana classic "I Want To Be A Cowboy's Sweetheart" are a very pleasant revival of days gone by.

⊙ **Nobody Love, Nobody Gets Hurt** (1998; Capitol). This album (produced by Bogguss and Crider) has an edge that some of Bogguss' mid-'90s material was

Revvin' it up: BR5-49

lacking. Standouts include "Just Enough Rope," "Somebody To Love," and "Take Me Back," the last song written by alt.country singer-songwriter Julie Miller and featuring background vocals by Garth Brooks. The title track (penned by Bobbie Cryner) is proof that emotionally tender content need not don the saccharine trappings of so many Nashville ballads.

BR5-49

Part kitschy throwbacks, part bar-room crowd pleasers, but possessing a genuine affection for American roots music, the neo-hillbilly group BR5-49 (the name comes from a Junior Samples routine in Hee Haw) are an anomaly, to say the least, in Nashville music circles. How many groups playing classic country songs in downtown Nashville bars, after all (in this case Robert's Western World), land themselves a major label record contract? That's just what happened with BR5-49, who were signed to Arista in 1995 after consistently drawing big crowds to Robert's and winning accolades from the mainstream and alternative press for their honky-tonk and hillbilly-boogie music, good-natured stage manner and grass-roots appeal.

The group first formed in 1994 when Las Vegas native Gary Bennett and Missourian Chuck Mead began playing together at Robert's, a combination bar and western-wear store. With Bennett and Mead sharing the lead vocal and guitar duties, BR5-49 eventually solidified with a five-man line-up filled out by multi-instrumentalist Don Herron (steel, fiddle, etc.), bassist "Smilin'" Jay McDowell and drummer "Hawk" Shaw Wilson. Their first release was a six-song EP titled LIVE FROM ROBERT'S that included originals like "18 Wheels And A Crowbar" alongside the murder ballad "Knoxville Girl" (made famous by the Louvin Brothers) and "Ole Slewfoot," a whopper of a bear story that Johnny Horton and Buck Owens, among others, have recorded. BR5-49's first proper full-length album came out several months later to more fanfare and praise. Their cover of Moon Mullican's "Cherokee Boogie" landed them a Grammy nomination, but there were no Billboard hit singles—then again, that wasn't what BR5-49 was exactly aiming for. Since then they've released BIG BACKYEAR BEAT SHOW (1998), another rollicking showcase, and the band's third full-length collection, COAST TO COAST, was due in the spring of 2000. BR5-49 may not be single-handedly transforming country music's future, but they are producing some refreshing toe-tappers that bring the past back into the present with wit, charm, and hep-cat style.

⊙ **BR5-49** (1996; Arista). BR5-49's full-length debut is catchy, lively and tastefully produced. The 11 songs consist of Bennett and/or Mead originals (the hopped-up "Even If It's Wrong," the mournful "Lifetime To Prove") and several cool honky-tonk classics, among them Moon Mullican's "Cherokee Boogie," Mel Tillis and Webb Pierce's "I Ain't Never," and Gram Parsons' "Hickory Wind."

Brooks & Dunn

Kix Brooks and Ronnie Dunn aren't brothers; neither are they a close-harmony outfit in the style of the Everlys, Louvins, or even the Judds. They are, however, one of the most successful duos in the history of country music. Ever since their 1991 debut album BRAND NEW MAN, which spawned the high-energy hit "Boot Scootin' Boogie" (and a silly line dance to go with it), Brooks & Dunn have been regulars on the *Billboard* charts, sold albums by the millions, and swept the Vocal Duo honors at the major country music awards shows.

The key to their success is not only that they work well together—writing songs, putting up with each others' company on long concert tours—but that they have such different personalities. Sporting a classic cowboy hat and mustache, Brooks (born 12 May, 1955 in Shreveport, Louisiana) is the excitable good ole boy—running up and down the stage during the duo's quick-paced, high-production live shows. Dunn (born 1 June, 1953 in Coleman, Texas), on the other hand, is the tall dark stranger. He has a quieter, more brooding personality—not to mention a goatee and penchant for black clothing. Before hooking up in 1991, Brooks worked for nearly a decade as a songwriter (his "I'm Only In It For The Love" was a #1 for John Conlee in 1983), and in 1989 he recorded a self-titled solo album for Capitol. As for Dunn, he studied theology and then spent years playing the clubs and recording for an independent label. Dunn came to Nashville after winning a talent contest, and at the urging of Arista Nashville president Tim DuBois, he paired up with Brooks.

The duo's debut album, BRAND NEW MAN, was a smash success, selling some five million copies. They won their first Vocal Duo of the Year honors from the ACM in 1991 and the CMA a year later, and they retained a monopoly on that category throughout the decade. Brooks & Dunn's next album, HARD WORKING MAN (1993), was nearly as successful as their first, containing further hits such as the stadium shouter "Rock My World (Little Country Girl)"—with a guitar riff that seems lifted straight off an AC-DC album—and the power ballad

GLENN WEINER

An unlikely combination: Brooks & Dunn

Brooks & Dunn

"That Ain't No Way To Go." On Waitin' On Sundown (1994) and Borderline (1996), they've continued down this pathway of success. But if the formula hasn't changed too much—hard and fast party anthems mixed with melodramatic ballads—they've managed to write, and find, enough splashy material to prevent them from growing stale: the redneck rocker "Little Miss Honky Tonk," the saucy "Mama Don't Get Dressed Up For Nothing," B.W. Stevenson's laid-back love song "My Maria."

In 1996, the CMA named Brooks & Dunn its Entertainer Of The Year (the ACM did the same in both 1995 and 1996). By the end of the decade, the pair were still going strong. Their fifth studio album, If You See Her (1998), included a schmaltzy duet with Reba McEntire on the title track as well as a boisterous version of Gary Stewart's "Brand New Whiskey" and a faithful take on "Husbands And Wives," a song written three decades earlier by Roger Miller.

⊙ **Brand New Man** (1991; Arista). The production isn't quite so big and tall on Brooks & Dunn's debut album. The country flavor, too, runs deeper and wider, from the title track right through the dopey smash hit "Boot Scootin' Boogie." The sound isn't exactly rural, but honky tonkers like "I've Got A Lot To Learn" and "I'm No Good" are surprisingly down-to-earth.

⊙ **The Greatest Hits Collection** (1997; Arista). At 19 songs, this is a substantial compilation, containing most of the duo's big hits from their first 4 albums together. They show their quiet side plenty of times ("You're Gonna Miss Me When I'm Gone," "Neon Moon"), but it's the rocked-up party songs that have always been Brooks & Dunn's trademarks: "Little Miss Honky Tonk," "Rock My World (Little Country Girl)," and "Hard Workin' Man."

Garth Brooks

"I don't ever have a problem with people who say my stuff isn't country. Everybody's got their own opinions."

—Garth Brooks

There are a handful of country singers—Jimmie Rodgers, Hank Williams, Elvis Presley—who've had a major influence not just on the music but on the direction the industry itself has taken. Like it or not, Garth Brooks belongs on that list as well. From the point when he first hit the charts

in 1989, and especially after his album Ropin' The Wind debuted in Billboard at #1, the country music market opened up like it never had before, and sales shot through the roof. Garth's success made it absolutely clear that country was a music that could speak to anyone and everyone—good ole boys in Oklahoma, suburbanites in California, even a few hundred thousand folks in New York City, who turned out for his Central Park concert in 1997.

It's true that the business side of Garth Brooks quickly became a driving force. The man has sold some 80 million albums and counting, so obviously there are many people making money out of him—and they want to continue doing so. But the Garth revolution really was, at least at first, about the music. Garth was on one hand a neo-traditionalist singer, his music a natural progression from the back-to-basics, mid-'80s sound of George Strait, John Anderson, Randy Travis, and Ricky Van Shelton. Garth's self-titled debut album, released in 1989, was full of steel guitars, fiddles, honky tonk rhythms, and Garth's Oklahoma twang. But he brought something else to country music—namely, his penchant for '70s rock and pop music. In addition to obvious country influences like Strait and Jones, Garth has admitted many times over how much a fan he was of bands like the Eagles, Journey, and Kansas, and singers like James Taylor and Billy Joel. And the influence is there on each and every one of his albums—melodramatic power anthems, slickly produced

Garth Brooks

party tunes, and soaring, sentimental ballads that border on maudlin. He then mixed these elements with a brighter, bolder honky-tonk sound—one fired with loud guitars and his hyperactive brand of showmanship.

The response was amazing—it was like he'd pressed all the right buttons at the same time, and the public just started salivating on cue. Was this the result of spontaneous creative inspiration? Or was it calculated? Probably a mixture of both. But whatever the case, Brooks was, before he was thirty years old, an unstoppable commercial powerhouse and the biggest-selling artist in the history of country music. (In 1998 he made further history, becoming the top solo artist in US album sales, out-stripping Elton John, Billy Joel, and Elvis Presley.)

Troyal Garth Brooks was born on 7 February, 1962 in Luba, Oklahoma into a musical family: his father played a little guitar and mandolin, and his mother, Colleen Carroll, had actually recorded for Capitol in the '50s. Garth played sports and attended Oklahoma State University in Stillwater partially on an athletic scholarship (for javelin). He majored in advertising, picking up business pointers he'd later put to good use. He also played the local nightclubs. After graduating he made one failed attempt at cracking the Nashville market but turned for home after only one day; regrouping, he tried again in 1987 as a member of a band called Santa Fe. The band split up but Garth kept at it, singing on demo sessions and getting his name out wherever he could. In 1988 he signed with a prestigious management company, and this led to a record deal with Capitol. His debut was released in April of 1989—the very same week as Clint Black's debut album, KILLIN' TIME.

Almost from the outset Garth's star potential was clear. His first single, "Much Too Young (To Feel This Damn Old)," made the Top 10, and in December its follow-up, "If Tomorrow Never Comes," hit #1. "Not Counting You" and the tearjerking ballad "The Dance" were also big hits. A year later, after the release of NO FENCES, Garth's career shot out of orbit. The biggest impetus was the megahit "Friends In Low Places," a bar-room sing-along that quickly became an audience favorite. Further hit singles followed ("Two Of A Kind, Workin' On A Full House," "The Thunder Rolls"), and by the middle of 1993 the album had sold an almost incomprehensible ten million copies. The awards quickly began piling up, too: the Academy of Country Music wasted no time, naming him Entertainer of the Year in 1990 (and for several years afterwards); the Country Music Association

followed suit, tapping him for the Horizon Award in 1990 and, finally, Entertainer of the Year for the first time in 1991.

When it was released in September of 1991, Brooks' third album, ROPIN' THE WIND, made history as the first country album to debut at #1 in the Billboard pop album charts. Like NO FENCES it also went on to sell over ten million copies. One of the album's biggest singles was "Shameless," a bombastic piece of work written by none other than Billy Joel. It's still one of Garth's biggest numbers in concert. And speaking of which, Garth's live shows had transformed into amazing mega-spectacles of lights, sound, complex stage sets, and brash, rock'n'roll-styled fury. Sometimes, when fancy struck, he even smashed his guitar into bits. All this begged the question, first asked by Waylon Jennings two decades back: would Hank have really done it this way?

Next in line came THE CHASE followed by IN PIECES, and while each outsold nearly every other country release on the market, neither came close to the sales figures of Garth's previous two releases. No one dares call albums that sell five or six million "disappointments," but from a marketing perspective, a fifty percent drop in sales is what's known as the "wrong direction." Save for his 1994 collection THE HITS (a "limited" release that happened to sell nine million), none of Garth's subsequent albums have matched his early '90s sales figures.

This obviously troubled Brooks and after releasing FRESH HORSES in 1995, he even had the audacity to refer to himself as an "underdog." Such a term, frankly, was entirely wrong, as Garth was still a massive commercial force. Just ask the four million fans who bought FRESH HORSES (arguably his worst album to date); the hundreds of thousands who turned out in Central Park to see him perform in 1997; or the audiences who've tuned into his numerous TV concerts and specials over the years. Or ask Scott Hendricks, former Capitol Nashville president who was "replaced" in the wake of a feud between Brooks and the label surrounding the release of his 1997 album SEVENS. And then consider that Brooks pulled off one of the most brazenly commercial moves in country music history: re-releasing his first six albums in a box set titled THE LIMITED SERIES. Granted, there were six new songs inside, and the price was affordable, at least relative to other box sets (as low as $24 at certain outlets). But that still wasn't enough to keep it from smelling like a swindle.

Could Garth top a move like that? Indeed. With SEVENS he'd discovered a new tactic, labeling the initial CD run as the First Edition (a gimmick Music Row has since picked up on with other artists). For his 1998 collection DOUBLE LIVE, he went a step further, not only releasing a First Edition, but printing up a different CD booklet for each million sold (different photos, different liner notes). Though the music was exactly the same, you know that more than a few fans bought each and every one of them.

In 1999, Garth branched out into a couple of brand new areas. First up was a seven-week stint playing spring-training baseball with the San Diego Padres. Later that year came the pop-rock album IN THE LIFE OF CHRIS GAINES, produced by Don Was. It's a fictional 'greatest hits' collection of a fictitious singer—who happens to be the lead character in *The Lamb*, a film that Garth is co-producing (and starring in). The film project, though, is still in the planning stages. As for the CHRIS GAINES album, it didn't prove all that popular, and it left some fans wondering if their hero was abandoning

country music for a pop career. Garth insists it was only a "chapter" in his development, not a new direction. Meanwhile, the Academy of Country Music named Brooks their Artist of the Decade, which placed him alongside such notables as Alabama (1980s), Loretta Lynn (1970s), and Marty Robbins (1960s). And at the very end of 1999, Garth mentioned during a television interview that he was considering an early retirement. "Music is not the first thing in my life anymore," he said; instead, he wanted to focus more time and energy on raising his three daughters. So far he hasn't explained what "retirement" would mean exactly. As the old adage goes, only time will tell.

⊙ **Garth Brooks** (1989; Capitol). Garth's debut is as innocent as his music gets. "I've Got A Good Thing Going" and "Much Too Young (To Feel This Damn Old)" are straightforward, even likeable, as is the Jack Clement song "I Know One," which is as easy to swallow as a Glen Campbell melody. But the album's

Fan Fair

Fan Fair, the annual meet-and-greet sponsored by the *Grand Ole Opry* and the Country Music Foundation, wasn't always the mega-festival that it is today. The event grew out of the fan club parties that the International Fan Club Organization (IFCO) hosted at the Country Music Disc Jockey Convention held in Nashville every October. Five thousand people attended the first Fan Fair, which took place at Nashville's Municipal Auditorium in April of 1972. The following year, organizers moved the event to June and the attendance doubled. After a decade of steady growth, Fan Fair relocated to the Tennessee State Fairgrounds, where it has been since 1982, and where it now draws 20,000 or more people each year.

Many of country's biggest names turn out for the festivities, and not just to make cameo appearances. Reigning superstars such as Trisha Yearwood and Vince Gill, as well as young hopefuls—and legends like George Jones and Kitty Wells—spend at least a day or two at the fairgrounds. Most sign autographs (Garth Brooks signed for twenty straight hours in 1996); host fan club parties (Alan Jackson rented out the Ryman Auditorium for his six-hour party in 1997); and play record label showcases for crowds of up to 15,000 at the Nashville Speedway (adjacent to the fairgrounds). The event is also host to the annual Grand Masters Fiddling Championship.

The people who attend Fan Fair are very much a breed apart: compared with rock and pop audiences, who seem ever in search of the next big thing, their

loyalty is patently unhip. Most years they brave severe weather—thunderstorms or sweltering heat, and often both—to see and touch, even have their picture taken with, their favorite stars. Most make no bones about waiting in line for hours, or about being herded around livestock barns to obtain the ultimate fan momento: an autograph.

Some commentators view the proceedings as little more than the mass flowering of trailer-park kitsch. And to be sure, with its surfeit of cheesy, overpriced memorabilia and its dozens of overzealous fans decked out like human billboards, the event isn't without its tacky side. But to reduce the largely suburban fairgoers to caricature is not only unfair, it misses the point: Fan Fair exists to celebrate the deep and abiding kinship between the people who make country music and those who listen to it.

Seemingly without parallel (no such gathering takes place in the limo and Leer jet world of Hollywood or rock'n'roll), the artist-fan relationship in country music stems from the fact that, historically, singers come from the same rural, blue-collar stock as their fans. To cite two recent examples: Alan Jackson used to sell used cars, and Trace Adkins worked as a derrick man and pipe-fitter in Louisiana. Granted, most singers eventually leave their humble beginnings behind. But in country circles, the unwritten rule is "don't get above your raisin'." In other words, no matter how big you get, you'd best not act like you're any better than your fans.

—Bill Friskics-Warren

Garth Brooks

not without its burden of melodrama: "If Tomorrow Never Comes" and especially the Tony Arata song "The Dance" show Garth's penchant for schmaltz was in place right from the start.

⊙ **No Fences** (1990; Capitol). As his career takes off, the barstool traditionalism begins fading into the backdrop. The rousing nature of "Friends In Low Places" is hard to deny, as is the goofy and good-natured honky-tonk vibe of "Two Of A Kind, Workin' On A Full House." "The Thunder Rolls" was an important cut, but the production makes it sound like something from a late-period Journey album.

⊙ **Ropin' The Wind** (1991; Capitol). The kick-off track has an almost rootsy appeal—no wonder, as it was written by bluegrass artist Larry Cordle. It's 180 degrees, however, from one of the album's most popular tracks: Garth's cover of "Shameless." Capping off the record is "The River," another entry in the catalog of maudlin ballads that are hugely popular among his fans.

⊙ **In Pieces** (1993; Liberty). A bit more back-to-basics than The Chase, his previous effort. Here you'll find the simple-minded "American Honky Tonk Bar Association," the rock'n'roller "Ain't Going Down (Til The Sun Comes Up)," and "One Night A Day," which sounds like a cross between Don McLean (another 1970s hero of Garth's who even appeared with him onstage in Central Park) and Gerry Rafferty.

⊙ **Double Live** (1998; Capitol). If big is what you want, this 26-song album won't disappoint, from the hoarse bombast of "Shameless" to an audience sing-along version of "The Dance." Along the way comes the extended version of "The Thunder Rolls" (in which the wife takes revenge on her cheating hubby) and a sentimental Dylan song "To Make You Feel My Love" (also one of the six new songs from his box set). It's a curious creation, too—not a straight live album at all, but a digital mish-mash where pieces of songs from more than 300 (!) shows have been edited into a seamless whole and even layered with newly recorded studio overdubs.

Junior Brown

"People will label you 'quirky,' and I hate that word. I'm totally serious about my humor."

—Junior Brown

Junior Brown

Hearing Junior Brown's powerfully deep voice and thick guitar leads, you just might lay your bets that this suit-and-tie-wearing Texan was a honky-tonk troubadour caught in a time warp. Or at least a throwback to bygone roadhouse days and nights. But just when you thought you had him pegged, Brown rips out a finger-bleeding solo on his custom-made "guit steel" (a double-necked combination of electric and steel guitars), and suddenly you're immersed in a free jazz-cum-acid rock haze. Brown's country foundation is solid—one of his best-known songs is called "My Baby Don't Dance To Nothing But Ernest Tubb," which is as reverent as it is humorous—but his adventurous mind is very much open to the lure of rock'n'roll, surf, blues and jazz (he once cut a version of Hoagy Carmichael's "Hong Kong Blues").

Jamieson "Junior" Brown has Texas written all over him, but he originally hails from Cottonwood, Arizona, where he was born on 12 June, 1952. He learned guitar at an early age, and as a teenager began his long career as a gun for hire in assorted bands of all shapes and styles. He mostly worked around the Southwest before landing in Austin, Texas in the late 1970s. During the mid-'80s he put together a honky-tonk combo with his wife, Tanya Rae, and they began to attract attention at local club appearances. In 1990, the

Junior Brown

British label Demon issued Brown's debut album, 12 SHADES OF BROWN, a brilliant showcase of clever wordplay, beefy guitar leads and musical styles that run from Tubb and Bob Wills to Speedy West and Jimi Hendrix (whose name was invoked in Brown's concert reviews almost as often as Tubb's).

Incredible, considering the conservative nature of most Nashville country music, Brown was signed to Curb, and in 1993 the label reissued 12 SHADES in the US. Curb also released Brown's second album, GUIT WITH IT, another knockout showcase that included concert favorites like "Highway Patrol" (a Red Simpson gem), "Party Lights," and "My Wife Thinks Your Dead." Thankfully, Brown's Curb signing hasn't altered his mix of both funny and serious songs, or his wild-man guitar playing. Country radio hasn't played him much, but his word-of-mouth following is strong, and it easily criss-crosses the boundaries between mainstream and alternative fans. In what might be considered a minor coup, Brown even won a CMA award in 1996 for Music Video of the Year for his song "My Wife Thinks You're Dead" (earlier in the decade the award had gone to such big-name stars as Alan Jackson, Martina McBride and Garth Brooks). Brown has released four full-length CDs to date on Curb—the most recent being SEMI-CRAZY (1996) and LONG WALK BACK (1998)—and one EP, JUNIOR HIGH (1995).

⊙ **12 Shades Of Brown** (1993; Curb). The beauty of Brown's music is that he's unafraid to roam the outer limits—and he has a damn fun time in the process. "My Baby Don't Dance To Nothin' But Ernest Tubb," "Too Many Nights In A Roadhouse," and "Broke Down South Of Dallas" are still some of his finest—a deft mixture of clever words, mind-blowing guitar work, and a surprisingly self-reflective attitude. More serious titles like "Don't Sell The Farm" and "A Way To Survive" add balance to the batch.

⊙ **Semi-Crazy** (1996; Curb). Brown's third full-length release doesn't exactly move beyond the territory already covered on his earlier records, but his stylistic trademarks are certainly intact: his deep voice (which rivals the pipes of both Tubb and Dick Curless), outstanding guitar playing (the wind-whipped "Surf Medley"), and catchy, good-humored songs built around clever and self-deprecating one-liners ("Venom Wearing Denim," "Gotta Get Up Every Morning"). The title track (about a pair of truck drivers) is a duet with Red Simpson, who wrote "Highway Patrol," a standard in Brown's repertoire.

Marty Brown

Marty Brown is a genuine country boy from Maceo, Kentucky with a honky-tonk heart and a strong hillbilly twang that resembles the raw singing of Hank Williams himself. Brown (born on 25 July, 1965) moved to Nashville with little more than a guitar and some big dreams, but he ended up getting nationwide exposure and a subsequent contract with MCA when the TV show *48 Hours* focused on the story of his attempt to make it in modern-day Music City. His debut album, HIGH AND DRY (1991), had a stone-cold honky-tonk sound that was, ultimately, far too thick and unsophisticated for most contemporary country fans to digest. The critics raved, but the album didn't sell too well—at least in the numbers expected of a major-label artist. Brown took a novel approach to promoting the album by touring Wal-Mart stores from coast to coast; this brought him further attention, but radio programmers still refused to bite. He also toured with Austin country artist Jimmie Dale Gilmore, whose fringe-country audience was much more suited to Brown's no-frills sound.

Brown's second album, WILD KENTUCKY SKIES (1993), was broader in scope and bigger in production; he was trying to please contemporary ears while still holding onto his traditionalist values. Songs like "No Honky Tonkin' Tonight" and the haunting "Gone" are memorable, but once again, the album failed to produce any notable radio hits. MCA gave Brown one final shot with CRYIN', LOVIN', LEAVIN' (1994), but it, too, failed to meet target sales figures, and Brown was eventually dropped. Two years later he was signed to the Oakland, California label HighTone (home at

varying times to Gilmore, Joe Ely, and Dale Watson). Brown's fans anticipated this move away from Nashville would result in an uninhibited jewel of an album that was free of commercial constraints; what they got, however, was HERE'S TO THE HONKY TONKS (1996), a mediocre affair that, while containing enjoyable moments ("The Day The Bootlegger Died," "Behind Bars"), took no new chances and lacked the sense of honky-tonk adventure he'd exhibited earlier. Brown's recording career has since faded from view—a situation that hopefully is only temporary—though his song "I'm From The Country" ("and I like it that way") did end up as the title track of Tracy Byrd's 1998 album.

⊙ **High And Dry** (1991; MCA). The knockout title track sounds like Hank Williams brought back to life. But while hardcore honky tonk is Brown's forte, his excellent debut album—his best effort by a long shot—also contains rockabilly songs ("Don't Worry Baby"), ballads ("I'll Climb Any Mountain"), a touch of swing ("Ole King Kong"), and brilliant pop nuggets like "Every Now And Then." At a time when Nashville was crawling with clean-cut 'young country' conformists, this was one album that gave traditionalists a reason to get up in the morning.

GEORGE HOLZ

Tracy Byrd

Tracy Byrd

O f all the Nashville hats, Tracy Byrd has one of the finest voices—a rich, easygoing baritone that shifts and shapes the words with confidence and downhome sincerity—and sounds far more mature than Byrd's boyish-faced appearance would suggest. He grew up listening to singers like Ray Price and George Strait, and his healthy respect for straight-up honky tonk ripples through every one of his albums to date. He's recorded some great covers such as "Someone To Give My Love To" and "She's All I Got," both 1970s hits for Johnny Paycheck (the latter written by soul singer Swamp Dogg), but contemporary songs like "Heaven In My Woman's Eyes" (written by Mark Nesler, who was also once Byrd's lead guitarist) and "Big Love" (the title track of his 1996 album) are equally compelling.

Byrd was born in 1966 in Vidor, Texas, a small town near Beaumont and Port Arthur in the state's southeast corner. It's an area that's been home to many musical greats past and present, including George Jones, Janis Joplin, and Mark Chesnutt; another young Nashville cat,

Clay Walker, was a classmate of Byrd's in high school. Byrd played nightclubs in the region for several years before MCA Records got wind of the young singer and signed him up. His self-titled debut album hit the stores in 1993 and got a decent reaction for the single "Someone To Give Me Love To" and especially "Holdin' Heaven." It was his second album, however, NO ORDINARY MAN, that really shot him to stardom, thanks to such big-time hits as the dopey novelty number "Watermelon Crawl" and the slightly soggy but hugely popular love song "The Keeper Of The Stars," named Song of the Year by the Academy of Country Music. So much for the sophomore slump. Byrd, though, has said in retrospect it's his least satisfying release because it strayed farthest (though not that far) from his traditionalist roots. His next couple of albums, LOVE LESSONS (1995) and BIG LOVE (1996) brought him back around to a more clear-cut honky-tonk approach—and also produced further hits ("Big Love," "She's All I Got"). "Heaven In My Woman's Eyes," from LOVE LESSONS, is a sincere, no-frills beauty, and it'll likely prove one of the hallmarks of his career.

Byrd has never felt the urge to move to Nashville, preferring to stay rooted to the area

Tracy Byrd

he grew up in, and that says something about his musical approach as well. He clearly speaks in a language contemporary audiences can understand, yet his is a sturdy, no-nonsense style that always keeps its honky-tonk roots within earshot.

⊙ **Love Lessons** (1995; MCA). "Heaven In My Woman's Eyes" is the clear standout, but the Bill Anderson song "You Lied To Me" and the swampy "Down On The Bottom" (co-written by Nesler and Byrd) are also worthwhile.

⊙ **I'm From The Country** (1998; MCA). Less compelling than earlier collections, COUNTRY is still an enjoyable listen. The title track was co-written by Marty Brown (who'd originally planned it for his own album).

⊙ **Keepers/Greatest Hits** (1999; MCA). A well-rounded retrospective that includes his novelty hits ("Watermelon Crawl," "Lifestyles Of The Not So Rich And Famous"), honky-tonk cover songs ("Someone To Give My Love To," a sturdy version that nearly tops Paycheck's own), the radio-hit version of "The Keeper Of The Stars," and such neo-traditionalist gems as "Heaven In My Woman's Eyes" and the good-natured "I'm From The Country."

Mary Chapin Carpenter

F ull-throated singer-songwriter Mary Chapin Carpenter first gained her musical pedigree as a coffeehouse folksinger before moving on to Nashville and transforming herself into a hitmaking (and award-winning) commercial country star. Carpenter's upbringing wasn't exactly rural: she was born in Princeton, New Jersey on 21 February, 1958 and attended Brown University. After college, she played the coffeehouse circuit around Washington, DC, often with guitarist and songwriter John Jennings (who would eventually become her producer). Columbia showed an interest and signed Carpenter, and her debut album, HOMETOWN GIRL, was released in 1987. The album gave her progressive, folk-inspired songs slightly more radio-friendly arrangements, though it wasn't until her second album, STATE OF THE HEART, that she finally broke into the Top 10 with "Quitting Time" and "Never Had It So Good."

Carpenter was named New Female Vocalist of the Year by the ACM in 1989, a promising pat on the back that paid off after she released SHOOTING

STRAIGHT IN THE DARK in 1990. Her third effort produced the Cajun-flavored, dance-friendly hit song "Down At The Twist And Shout," among others, and bumped her up to platinum status. The next album, COME ON COME ON, was even more successful, thanks to hits like "Passionate Kisses" (a Lucinda Williams song that earned a pair of Grammys), "He Thinks He'll Keep Her," and "I Feel Lucky." Both the ACM and CMA awarded her Female Vocalist of the Year in 1992, and the CMA repeated the honor in 1993. Carpenter (who around this time stopped hyphenating the Mary-Chapin half of her name) continued to record hit albums such as STONES IN THE ROAD (1994) and A PLACE IN THE WORLD (1996), though sales didn't quite match the glory days of the triple-platinum COME ON. Carpenter has been active in political causes such as AIDS awareness, environmentalism, and the Pro-Choice movement, and she's also written a selection of children's books.

⊙ **Shooting Straight In The Dark** (1990; Columbia). Carpenter's breakthrough album was still a folkie collection at its core, but the songs were presented with a contemporary (albeit still tasteful) production, and it contained enough hooks to keep casual listeners interested. "Down At The Twist And Shout" is the standout party cut, featuring the Cajun band Beausoleil, while other songs—"Going Out Tonight," "The More Things Change"—are more introspective.

⊙ **Party Doll** (1999; Columbia). A greatest hits album, sort of. Carpenter's popular 1990s titles are here, but not always in their original form—"Twist And Shout" is a rowdy version from a 1997 Super Bowl pre-game performance, and "Stones In The Road" is an acoustic version recorded live in London. All this, plus a few new titles, makes PARTY DOLL (the title comes from a Mick Jagger song she covers) not exactly the most straightfoward of introductions, but certainly an interesting and enticing collection, especially for her fans.

Mark Chesnutt

"Don't put me in Branson yet, because I can still rock'n'roll with the best of them."

—Mark Chesnutt

M ark Chesnutt has a straight-shooting, neo-traditional style that has remained among the most down-to-earth and beautifully consistent of all the new hats who first broke ground in the early 1990s. Though he's got a knack for choosing great song material, Chesnutt rarely writes his own; from an early age he chose instead to concentrate on singing. His is an impressive voice, too—well-rounded and easygoing, simple yet full of depth and small-town warmth. Though basic ham-and-eggs honky tonk has been Chesnutt's forte since the beginning, he's also proven himself adept at a range of material—whether it's the lost-love balladry of "Too Cold At Home" (his debut single and first hit); the bar-room self-pity of "Brother Jukebox"; a classic cover song like "Rainy Day Woman" (a duet with Waylon Jennings); or the working-man's anthem "It Sure Is Monday." He even brings a level of respectability to such bombastic material as "Almost Goodbye" and, more recently, "I Don't Want To Miss A Thing." Over the years Chesnutt may not have sold anywhere near as many records as Alan

MARK CHESNUTT
Almost Goodbye
D-10851

Jackson or Garth Brooks—or for that matter George Strait, a man who was one of Chesnutt's major influences—but he's proven himself to be a steady hitmaker and, most importantly, one of the most consistently enjoyable performers of the past decade.

Chesnutt was born on 6 September, 1963 in Beaumont, Texas. George Jones, Tracy Byrd, and Clay Walker are among the many musicians who also hailed from the area (Byrd was at one

point a member of his band). Chesnutt started singing professionally while in his teens, and for the next decade he steadily worked the clubs around Beaumont and throughout southeast Texas. Among the many songs that he cut for assorted regional labels, "Too Cold At Home," written by Bobby Harden also proved to be his ticket into Nashville. A tape of the song found its way to the desk of MCA's Tony Brown who flew to Beaumont to hear Chesnutt sing, and who promptly offered the newcomer a record deal.

Chesnutt's MCA recording of "Too Cold" was an immediate chart hit, and soon afterwards he made it to #1 with his version of Paul Craft's "Brother Jukebox" (a classic cry-in-your-beer song that Keith Whitley had cut just before he died). Chesnutt's debut album, TOO COLD AT HOME—produced, like nearly all of his subsequent albums, by Mark Wright—also included a dour take on "Friends In Low Places," released just before Brooks' sing-along version. Chesnutt spent the better part of the following year on the road, and his second album didn't hit the stores until 1992. Titled LONGNECKS AND SHORT STORIES, it's one of the most succinct neo-trad nuggets of the period. "Old Flames Have New Names" (co-written by Bobby Braddock), "I'll Think Of Something," "Old Country," and "Bubba Shot The Jukebox" (which is, thankfully, not as stupid a song as the title implies) were all hits that helped cement Chesnutt's reputation for honest and unflashy country music. In 1993 he topped the charts again with the undeniably catchy "It Sure Is Monday"—not quite "Take This Job And Shove It," but certainly a feeling everyone could relate to. Later that year he picked up the Horizon Award from the Country Music Association.

Chesnutt's albums have more or less hit the mark ever since—WHAT A WAY TO LIVE (highlighted by the lonesome ballad "Down In Tennessee"), WINGS (produced by Tony Brown), and THANK GOD FOR BELIEVERS, a back-to-basics album that featured Chesnutt as co-writer on about half the songs. In 1999 Chesnutt demonstrated he could still hit high on the charts with "I Don't Want To Miss A Thing," a Diane Warren power ballad previously covered by Aerosmith on the *Armageddon* soundtrack. Though it was by far the schmaltziest song on his album of the same name, it obviously revealed that Chesnutt was more open to commercial pop material than he'd been previously. You can't blame the guy for wanting to widen his musical scope—thankfully he achieves that goal not just with "Miss A Thing" but with a dose of western swing ("That's The Way You Make An Ex") and a good deal of rock'n'roll-flavored numbers. As for Chesnutt's next move, a new album is in the works and scheduled for a fall 2000 release.

⊙ **Too Cold At Home** (1990; MCA). A smart debut that's full of impressive material such as "Brother Jukebox," "Broken Promised Land," and Chesnutt's down-and-out take on "Friends In Low Places"—a more emotionally complex take on the song than Brooks' party-on version.

⊙ **Long Necks And Short Stories** (1992; MCA). A modest but solid showcase of what 1990s neo-trad country was all about. Along with hits like "Old Flames Have New Names" and "Bubba Shot The Jukebox" it included a duet with George Jones ("Talking To Hank"), a Steve Earle weeper ("I'm Not Getting Any Better At Goodbyes"), and a twang-and-steel-infused version of Charlie Rich's "Who Will The Next Fool Be."

⊙ **Greatest Hits** (1996; Decca). A mixed bag of Chesnutt songs, it includes true gems like "Too Cold At Home" and "It Sure Is Monday" along with lesser (though still interesting) songs like "Goin' Through The Big D" and "Blame It On Texas."

⊙ **I Don't Want To Miss A Thing** (1999; MCA). Don't let the commercial sheen of the title track scare you away, because this album is actually quite varied—from guitar-heavy honky tonk ("I'm Gone") to western swing ("That's The Way You Make An Ex"), with a little Tex-Mex flavor ("Jolie") and a few straight-up honky tonkers thrown in for good measure.

Mark Collie

"I think every country artist today is influenced by rock'n'roll."
——Mark Collie

Mark Collie was one of many second-tier country artists who emerged in the early 1990s with a handful of decent songs. Songs like "Trouble's Coming Like A Train" and "Hardin County Line" (the title track to his debut album) mix neo-traditional country and hot-fired rock'n'roll in the manner of Steve Earle, who was clearly an influence. But on that same debut album Collie showed he could wear several hats, including that of a straight-up balladeer ("Let Her Go"), a clever tunesmith with an ear for catchy melodies ("Something With A Ring To It"—a song Garth Brooks later covered), and a guy able to reach across generations and pay his respects without resorting to cheap sentiments ("Another Old Soldier").

Collie was born in Waynesboro, Tennessee in 1956. He played in bands and toured around a little before moving to Nashville in the early '80s. There he wrote songs and played more nightclubs before being signed by Tony Brown to MCA in 1989. Brown and Doug Johnson produced HARDIN COUNTY LINE, which was released the following year. "Ring To It" didn't even crack the Top 40, which is surprising considering its clever lines and undeniable melodic hooks, but Collie finally won his first sizeable hit with "Let Her Go." A few more followed from his second album, BORN AND RAISED IN BLACK AND WHITE, but his biggest was "Even The Man In The Moon Is Cryin'," a catchy and tastefully restrained weeper that appeared on his 1993 album MARK COLLIE. Collie released one more album on MCA, UNLEASHED, before he switched to Giant for the 1995 album TENNESSEE PLATES. Few of the songs on these later albums, however, hold up as well as "Hardin County Line" and "Man In The Moon."

⊙ **Hardin County Line** (1990; MCA). Collie wrote or co-wrote all the songs on his debut, and most show him to be full of promise. The title track is edgy and mysterious, and it connects the dots right back to Steve Earle. "Another Old Soldier" and "Deliver Me" are further highlights on an album that's consistently enjoyable. As a bonus, James Burton plays guitar and the Fairfield Five add vocals to "What I Wouldn't Give."

⊙ **Even The Man In The Moon Is Crying** (1998; MCA). A decent but short (10 songs) budget-line compilation of Collie's MCA material including the title track, "Calloused Hands," "Hardin County Line," and "Something With A Ring To It."

Billy Ray Cyrus

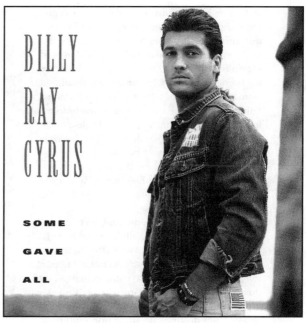

There's very little middle ground when it comes to Billy Ray Cyrus: you either love the guy or think he's an utter fool. He's best known for his smash hit "Achy Breaky Heart" (written by Don Von Tress), a song that made line dancing a national phenomenon for the first time since "The Hustle." It broke struggling singer Cyrus into the mainstream overnight—the album surrounding it, SOME GAVE ALL, topped the Billboard charts for over a month in 1992 and sold nine million copies—but being about as dumb as they come, the song also exposed Cyrus to endless ridicule. His decidedly unfashionable haircut and his Chippendales-style stage moves didn't improve matters much either. Travis Tritt caused a stir when he criticized Cyrus for turning country music into an "ass-wiggling contest" (he later apologized).

"Achy Breaky" is something this Flatwoods, Kentucky native has since worked hard to overcome. He's hasn't quite managed that yet, though you have to give him credit for trying. Cyrus' two follow-up albums, IT WON'T BE THE LAST and STORM IN THE HEARTLAND, didn't sell too well, and offered little musically beyond the trite '70s rock that had marked his debut—a mix of Eagles, James Taylor, and watered-down Mellencamp. His 1996 album TRAIL OF TEARS, however, is a different story—a noble attempt at musical redemption with its rootsy, grittier arrangements and the personal mood of songs like "I Am Here Now" and "Need A Little Help" (co-written with Von Tress). For the title track's video, Cyrus and his posse followed the route of Cherokee Nation's infamous Trail of Tears march (during which more than 2000 people died) ... except they did so on Harley Davidsons, not on foot. On the whole, though, the album was a surprisingly sincere effort. Cyrus attempted to keep on this straight and narrow musical path with his fifth studio album, SHOT FULL OF LOVE, but while it featured the fine guitar work of Mike Henderson, many of the songs were unfortunately mired in the same '70s-rock trappings. It also failed to produce any sizeable hits. Billy Ray's fans may still be willing to stand by their man, which is perhaps why, despite indications that his career is flagging, Music Row is still willing to bankroll him. In early 2000 Cyrus signed a new recording deal with Monument (a division of Sony), and a new album was planned for a summer release.

⊙ **Trail Of Tears** (1996; Mercury). Before all the Cyrus naysayers begin their diatribes against the Mullet King, they need to at least listen to this album, his most personal and musically down-to-earth collection to date. Some songs (such as "Tenntucky," co-written with Mark Collie) are mediocre Heartland rock, but the title track is surprisingly subtle, the mandolin lead giving it a bluegrass feel. His sincerity's on his sleeve as he sings Merle Haggard's "Sing Me Back Home," but his bluesy, laid-back take on J.J. Cale's "Crazy Mama" is the best song he's recorded yet.

⊙ **The Best Of Billy Ray Cyrus: Cover To Cover** (1997; Mercury). Compiles songs from his first 4 albums, from "Achy Breaky Heart" to "Trail Of Tears," with more than enough overproduced treacle ("Cover To Cover," one of 3 new tracks) and rock'n'roll bombast ("Storm In The Heartland") in between.

Joe Diffie

"There's a line there. You go too far and it's really stupid."

—Joe Diffie

Joe Diffie arrived on the Nashville scene when the hat acts were just getting off the ground and a neo-trad sound was very much in vogue. He had dabbled in Haggard-esque honky tonk, but ultimately grew more comfortable with a high-energy sound that had more to do with rock'n'roll than honky tonk. Country, however, has been part of his background since childhood. Born on 28 December, 1958 in Tulsa, Oklahoma, Diffie played gospel, rock, country and bluegrass in Oklahoma before moving to Nashville in 1986. He first won acclaim as a demo singer, his voice gracing countless cassette tapes used to shop songs to labels and artists. This eventually led to his own recording contract with Epic Records in 1990; amazingly enough, his debut single, "Home," shot to #1.

Many of Diffie's songs do exhibit a traditional country foundation, especially material from his first couple of albums, A THOUSAND WINDING ROADS (1990) and REGULAR JOE (1992). His third release, HONKY TONK ATTITUDE, contained the novelty hits "John Deere Green" and "Prop Me Up Beside The Jukebox (If I Die)," and it also showed him drifting into more pop- and rock-influenced territory. This shift became clearest of all on his fourth album, THIRD ROCK FROM THE SUN, his most popular to date. Diffie still included some dumb redneck numbers for which he was gaining a reputation—"Pickup Man" and "Junior's In Love" (written by Dennis Linde)—along with straight-up rockers ("Third Rock From The Sun") and tender ballads ("So Help Me Girl"). THIRD ROCK was followed by a Christmas album in 1995, MR CHRISTMAS, which, along with standards like "Let It Snow" and "O Holy Night," included "Leroy The Red Necked Reindeer." Guess which one made the Top 40. His other 1995 release, LIFE'S SO FUNNY, was highlighted by yet another hit novelty tune, "Bigger Than The Beatles," but that album and its follow-up, TWICE UPON A TIME, didn't sell as well as his previous efforts. Diffie's hits have slowed down, but he continues to record. In 1999 he released A NIGHT TO REMEMBER, which included "I'm The Only Thing (I'll Hold Against You)," a Diffie-penned song that Conway Twitty recorded just before his death in 1993.

⊙ **Greatest Hits** (1998; Epic). A dozen of Diffie's hits are collected here, though the selection is heavily weighted in favor of novelty numbers like "John Deere Green," "Prop Me Up," "Third Rock," and "Bigger Than The Beatles." Earlier cuts like "Home" and especially "Ships That Don't Come In" make an attempt to balance things out.

Dixie Chicks

Who doesn't like the Dixie Chicks? That seemed to be the question in Nashville during the late 1990s, when the peppy, happy-sounding Chicks came (seemingly) out of nowhere with their multiplatinum sensation of an album, WIDE OPEN SPACES. The truth is, however, that the Chicks had been around (albeit with a different line-up) since 1989, singing cowgirl songs (their debut album was titled THANK HEAVENS FOR DALE EVANS) as well as bluegrass, swing, and more standard country fare. Initially, the group was built around fiddler Martie Erwin, her banjo- and Dobro-playing sister Emily, bassist Laura Lynch, and vocalist/guitarist Robin Lynn Macy.

As teenagers in Texas, the Erwin sisters played together initially in a bluegrass outfit called Blue Night Express, while Macy fronted the Dallas bluegrass band Danger In The Air. After releasing DALE EVANS in 1991 (on the Crystal Clear label), the initial Dixie Chicks slowly began to win attention—positive reviews in Texas papers and appearances on the *Grand Ole Opry* and even Garrison Keillor's radio program *A Prairie Home Companion*. For a Christmas single, "Home On The Radar Range," the Chicks hired Lubbock, Texas steel-guitar maestro Lloyd Maines to play on the record, a twist of fate that led to their connection with his daughter (and the Chicks' soon-to-be lead singer), Natalie Maines.

The original Chicks recorded a couple more albums together, LITTLE OL' COWGIRL and SHOULDN'T A TOLD YOU THAT. Macy left during this time owing to stylistic differences and a need to play more straight bluegrass. Lynch briefly took over the lead vocal slot, but she, too, hit the trail, tiring of the constant touring. The Erwin sisters then hired Natalie Maines in the lead vocalist role, and their current incarnation was born. Instigating a complete makeover, the girls ditched their cowgirl dresses for flashier outfits and a more deliberately styled look, and the western and bluegrass songs took the back burner to a slicker, pop-oriented sound. They were signed to the revived Monument label (now a division of Sony), and in 1998 they released WIDE OPEN SPACES, which updates their traditional country sound with bright production and peppy rhythms. The album appealed to pop as well as country fans, and it's (so far) racked up more than eight million in sales—a mighty feat at a time when country album sales were on the downslide and Music Row was suffering a creative slump. The toast of the town, the

Loveable cowgirls: the Dixie Chicks

Dixie Chicks immediately earned a streak of CMA, ACM, and Grammy awards. Their follow-up album, FLY, has turned into yet another multi-platinum pop-crossover success.

⊙ **Wide Open Spaces** (1998; Monument). If their overall sound is polished and modern, this cute trio's arrangements are still based around fiddle, banjo, Dobro, and guitar, making them far more traditional-sounding than, say, fellow Nashville bombshells Faith Hill or Shania Twain. The balance between new and old is precisely the Chicks' appeal: they employ hot vocals, rock-driven rhythms, and lyrics that deal with female empowerment, but they aren't afraid of the twang factor, which gives them a refreshing edge in an increasingly pop-oriented landscape.

Vince Gill

"I never stopped believing in him, because that voice of his, I'm telling ya, it's like ... like ...."

—Tony Brown

Vince Gill has a sweet, warm tenor voice that's one of the prettiest in Nashville. He leans toward material that shows it off, which means many of his songs are sweet and pretty as well. Gill's a crooner, for the most part, not a honky tonker or hillbilly or jaded bar-room picker (though he is an accomplished guitarist). Traditional sounds and styles are in his blood—he studied and played bluegrass for years before arriving in Nashville—and he does incorporate elements of hillbilly, a dose or two of twang, and more than a few bluegrass arrangements into his overall presentation. But much of his music is marked by heart-wrenching balladry, sensitive-guy melodies, and an overabundance of strings. No matter what this award-winning, platinum-selling superstar sings, however, or how slick some of his material can get, the pristine quality of his voice—and his impeccable musicianship—is impossible to ignore.

Vincent Grant Gill was born in Norman, Oklahoma on 12 April, 1957. Growing up he learned guitar and banjo and played a lot of bluegrass—which makes sense, as his tenor voice is perfectly suited to the music's high-lonesome sound. After high school, Gill played with Sam Bush and Dan Crary in Bluegrass Alliance, a 'new-grass' band that recorded one album together, KEN-TUCKY BLUE, in 1975. Later he moved to LA and joined the group Sundance with fiddler Byron Berline. Hearing that the country-rock band Pure Prairie League was looking for a lead singer, he

Vince Gill

auditioned and got the job in 1979. He stayed with them through three albums.

Gill's next move was Nashville focused. He joined Rodney Crowell's band the Cherry Bombs, and through ex–Bombs pianist Tony Brown (at this point an A&R man for RCA), he won his first solo recording contract with RCA. His debut record was a six–song EP, TURN ME LOOSE (a format RCA tried with other first-time signees such as the Judds), released in 1984. "Victim of Life's Circumstance" was his first Top 40 hit, and

Vince Gill

his chart success only got bigger from there. Two full-length RCA albums followed, THE THINGS THAT MATTER and THE WAY BACK HOME, which contained such hits as "If It Weren't For Him" (a duet with Rosanne Cash), "Cinderella," and Everybody's Sweetheart."

Gill's biggest commercial breakthrough, however, came after he signed with MCA (where his friend and supporter Brown was now employed) and released WHEN I CALL YOUR NAME. The 1989 album was produced by Brown and went platinum, thanks to such hits as the title track and "Never Knew Lonely." Ballads became his forte, a style that's kept him at the top of the charts ever since. He won his first of several Male Vocalist of the Year awards from the CMA in 1991, and he's been similarly honored by the ACM. He's also won further awards (including several Grammys) for songs such as "I Still Believe In You," "When Love Finds You," and "Go Rest High On That Mountain." In 1993 and 1994 the CMA named him Entertainer of the Year, and he has since hosted their annual awards ceremony several times. In 1996 Gill explored his musical roots, from bluegrass to blues, on HIGH LONESOME SOUND. Two years later his album THE KEY continued his hot streak of popular, as well as critical, acclaim. A new studio album was due for release in early 2000, and a Vince Gill box set is also in the works.

⊙ **The Way Back Home** (1987; RCA; reissued 1999; Buddha). The lead-off track "Everybody's Sweetheart" is a hopped-up number with a pared-down arrangement, but the overall tone here leans toward heart-tuggers like "The Way Back Home" and "The Radio." That these last two songs are still appealing despite their saccharine arrangements is testament to Gill's vocal prowess.

⊙ **When I Call Your Name** (1989; MCA). Gill's voice is in top form on the title track, an aching ballad that even jaded listeners might have a hard time dismissing. Other songs like "Oklahoma Swing" (a duet with Reba), "Ridin' The Rodeo," and Guy Clark's "Rita Ballou" have a rootsier country feel, which is a refreshing break from all that emotional outpouring.

⊙ **The Essential Vince Gill** (1995; RCA). Collects Gill's RCA hits from the 1980s, beginning with "Victim Of Life's Circumstances" and running through songs like "I've Been Hearing Things About You," "Oklahoma Borderline," "The Way Back Home," and Cinderella." It's a decent overview of Gill's first few years in Nashville.

⊙ **Souvenirs** (1995; MCA). The songs on this hits package represent the Vince Gill that everyone has come to know and love. SOUVENIRS collects his MCA hits from the late '80s through the mid-'90s, including "I Still Believe In You," "When I Call Your Name," "Don't

The Black Country Music Association

You wouldn't know it from country music's lily-white face, but African Americans have been listening and making their own contributions to the music at least as far back as 1926, when harmonica ace DeFord Bailey debuted on the *Grand Ole Opry*. Black men tutored Hank Williams and Bill Monroe, two of country's greatest innovators; and since the end of World War II, thirty-two African Americans, including Ray Charles, Charley Pride, Stoney Edwards, O.B. McClinton, Ruby Falls, Big Al Downing, Dobie Gray, and Cleve Francis, have placed singles on the country charts. Yet with the exception of Pride—who among RCA artists was once second only to Elvis Presley in record sales—the achievements of these singers remain largely unrecognized. Most people don't even know about the African origins of the banjo.

The Black Country Music Association (BCMA), a Nashville-based, non-profit outfit, is hoping to change that. The organization educates people about the role that country music has played, and still plays, in the lives of African Americans. (According to a recent survey, 17 to 24 percent of the nation's black population listens to country music.) The BCMA is also working to open Music Row's doors to more black singers, songwriters, producers, and executives.

"You can't shake the music tree and, in seventy-five years, have only one black man fall out who can sing country music," claims singer Cleve Francis, co-founder, with Nashville songwriter Frankie Staton, of the BCMA. "As someone who loves country music, I'm ashamed of the way the industry has used Charley Pride as a poster boy to prove that it's not racist. Until Music Row's hierarchy questions the moral wisdom of what it's doing, things aren't going to change."

Strong words, perhaps, but the statistics bear Francis out. As this book goes to press, only one African American (Trini Triggs) has a record deal with a Nashville major label (Curb). Just as disturbing, a survey of Music Row turned up scarcely a dozen black musicians and back-up singers, only a handful of a black songwriters, and no high-ranking black record executives.

"I sent demos out all over Nashville and got a lot of good responses," says country hopeful Kandy Lee. "It was always funny to see the looks on people's faces when they finally met me, 'cause I never told anybody I was black. They'd come out to meet me in the lobby—they'd seem really excited to talk to me—and they'd go, 'Oh ... *you're* Kandy.' I've even had people ask me to sing on the spot to prove that it was my voice on the demos." It's hard to imagine that anyone ever put Tim McGraw or Shania Twain through such a trial.

BCMA leaders know that gaining entry to Music Row will be difficult, especially since it's tough for aspiring artists of any race to gain the industry's attention. The BCMA is also aware that, as outsiders, black entertainers may have to work twice as hard and be three times as good as the non-black competition if they hope to land record deals.

More than just bemoaning the situation, however, BCMA has organized showcases of promising black talent, as a result of which, two acts, Wheels and Cynthia Talley, signed with major labels (although the imprint in question, Asylum Records, has since dropped both). The BCMA has also joined the CMA and rented booths at Fan Fair—the annual Nashville meet-and-greet hosted by the *Grand Ole Opry* and the CMA. Says Staton: "We have to prove that there's a market for blacks singing country music—that, and that there's enough black talent out there to break to country radio."

—Bill Friskics-Warren

Let Our Love Start Slippin' Away," "Liza Jane," and a duet with Dolly Parton on "I Will Always Love You."

Faith Hill

1998 was Faith Hill's year, thanks to the song "This Kiss," which streaked to the top of the charts, won her numerous CMA and ACM awards, and turned her third album, FAITH, into a multi-platinum success. This doe-eyed, blonde-haired beauty from Star, Mississippi is now one of the most popular singers in contemporary country music. "This Kiss" is peppy in spirit and all about hooks—nothing too deep, which is exactly the point. Hill's light and bright style has been in place, actually, since she first hit the Nashville scene in 1993 with "Wild One," another hook-laden #1 smash. Her debut album, TAKE ME AS I AM, also yielded "Piece Of My Heart," a song Janis Joplin had twisted into a piece of gutsy, bluesy soul twenty-five years earlier. Imagine Linda Ronstadt singing it, straighten out whatever kinks are left, and you get the picture of what Hill's version is like.

Faith Hill

Faith Hill

well outside the typical Nashville circuit. She's also been chosen as a model for Cover Girl cosmetics, which means her face now graces the covers of magazines like *Glamour* as well as *Country Weekly*.

⊙ **It Matters To Me** (1995; Warner Bros.). If one Hill album stands out slightly from the rest, it's this one, thanks to a healthy dose of Reba-styled rock and twang ("Bed Of Roses," "You Will Be Mine") and the harsh realities of "I Can't Do That Anymore" (an Alan Jackson song) and especially the dark and violent "A Man's Home Is His Castle." Produced by Hill and Scott Hendricks, who was at one point her fiancé.

⊙ **Faith** (1998; Warner Bros.). Hill's third album is her glossiest affair yet, clearly showing the influence Shania Twain has had on the country market. It's heavily produced, yes, but at least it's honest about being a pop album. Includes songs by Bekka Bramlett and Billy Burnette (the vaguely husky "Better Days"), Gretchen Peters (the almost down-to-earth "The Secret Of Life"), and rock artists Aldo Nova ("I Love You") and Sheryl Crow ("Somebody Stand By Me").

That's not to say Hill isn't a fine vocalist. She has a decent (if somewhat limited) set of pipes, not to mention a knack for catchy tunes that stick in your craw and don't dislodge easily. Her debut was a bit shrill, but on her second album, IT MATTERS TO ME, her voice sounded more lived in (she'd had throat surgery just before recording it), the songs slightly more diverse. "Let's Go To Vegas," a Reba-styled rocker about getting hitched on the fly, was the first big single, followed by the schlocky title track. Hill also included an upbeat gospel song ("Keep Walkin' On," a duet with Shelby Lynne) and tackled spousal abuse for a second time on "A Man's Home Is His Castle." Written by Ariel Caten, the latter was surprisingly visceral—much more so than "I Would Be Stronger Than That," her first take on the subject (written by Gary Burr, who co-produced TAKE ME AS I AM).

In 1996 Hill married country singer Tim McGraw, creating one of the most fawned-over country music couples since the heyday of George Jones and Tammy Wynette. Hill and McGraw won a CMA award for their predictably schmaltzy 1997 duet "It's Your Love," and a year later Hill returned to the spotlight on her own with the album FAITH and the runaway hit "This Kiss." Hill is now a major crossover success: Both FAITH and its equally shiny follow-up, BREATHE (1999), have soared on the pop as well as country charts, sold in the millions, and brought her to the attention of listeners

Alan Jackson

"I've always just kinda been consistent, I guess."

—Alan Jackson

Alan Jackson is the most straightforward honky tonker of the young country generation, a singer rooted in a spare 1950s-era style and cut very much in the no-frills George Strait mold. His neo-traditional spirit feels honest and true—he and his longtime producer Keith Stegall have built his sound around steel guitars and fiddles and kept it that way. Jackson's personality is warm and humble to the point of innocence, and then there's the matter of his tall frame, big smile, and handsome features, which have made him a hunky poster boy for the hat-act generation. With a sturdy voice and a bushel of hit albums to his credit (twenty million in sales and counting), the guy seems nothing less than truly blessed.

There's an uncomplicated feeling about many of Jackson's songs: the summertime fun of "Chattahoochee" (one of his biggest hits to date) and "Mercury Blues"; the honky-tonk urge driving "Chasin' That Neon Rainbow"; the simple dreams behind "Livin' On Love." Even "Don't Rock The Jukebox" feels more like a rousing anthem à la "Friends In Low Places" than a weeper that would land you face down on the tavern floor. Jackson does sing plenty of songs about heartache and pain ("Here In The Real World," "Someday," "Tonight I Climbed The Wall"), and he's a prolific and very dependable songwriter, it's just that on the whole, his material lacks the depth of Hank, Haggard, or George Jones—who are clearly his heroes. Still, in the long run we can overlook many of Jackson's shortcomings because his spirit is so genuine. At roots level his music is very easy to like—the melodies are just so relaxed, friendly, wholesome and catchy. The same thing may be said for his stage personality, as anyone who's seen his live show will vouch for. He's the kind of singer who inspires undying loyalty among his fans, in the manner of country stars of years gone by. And his support of 'real' country music, on record and in interviews, has only grown stronger over time.

Alan Eugene Jackson was born on 17 October, 1958 in Newnan, Georgia. As a child he loved cars, and collecting classic automobiles (and Harley Davidsons) is a "hobby" he's maintained ever since. While in his twenties he started writing songs and sitting in with local country bands, and then in 1985 he and his wife Denise up and moved to Nashville. One lucky break came when Denise met Glen Campbell in the Atlanta airport; this led to Jackson working as a staff songwriter for Campbell's publishing company, Seventh Son Music. In 1989 he became the first act signed to the new Nashville branch of Arista Records. His debut album HERE IN THE REAL WORLD, produced by Keith Stegall, was released in 1990, and he quickly hit the charts with the singles "Chasin' That Neon Rainbow," "Wanted," and "Here In The Real World." The simple structure of the songs coupled with Jackson's pleasant voice and friendly demeanor made him an immediate winning package.

HERE IN THE REAL WORLD was a platinum success, and his follow-up album, DON'T ROCK THE JUKEBOX, was even more popular. The title track paid tribute to George Jones, an icon among the hat-act generation, and its lively barroom beat (despite the supposedly down-and-out pretext) has helped it remain one of Jackson's signature songs. It was his third album, however, A LOT ABOUT LIVIN' AND A LITTLE 'BOUT LOVE, that fired him into superstar status. It contained the self-penned hits "Tonight I Climbed The Wall" and the hugely popular "Chattahoochee" along with the K.C. Douglas/Robert Geddins song "Mercury Blues." All helped increase his album sales to more than six million units—by far his biggest-selling collection to date.

His fourth album, WHO I AM, was also a smash hit highlighted by Rodney Crowell's "Song For The Life," his country-boy update of the Eddie Cochran rocker "Summertime Blues," and "Gone Country," a song written by Nashville veteran Bob McDill about pop singers who switch to country music as a money-making trend (few on Music Row, of course, are complaining when it's the other way around). In an ironic twist of sorts, several years later Jackson was advertising trucks to a bastardized version of the song, bellowing the chorus "Ford Country" from TV screens across the nation.

The success of WHO I AM on the heels of two very popular albums proved that Jackson had more than enough staying power. Though his sales figures have never approached the levels of Garth Brooks or Shania Twain, he's remained one of Nashville's top acts—even if his next couple of albums, EVERYTHING I LOVE and HIGH MILEAGE, showed him straying very little from the same safe, clean, and at this point predictable path. He's a country artist you can depend on for a decent tune that carries you through the workday but also reminds you that what you're hearing is, indeed, *country* music—and in contemporary Nashville that actually means quite a lot.

⊙ **Here In The Real World** (1990; Arista). A strong collection that set Jackson's pattern: steel guitars, fiddles, spare honky-tonk arrangements and his own warm voice. You'd have a hard time not liking this.

⊙ **A Lot About Livin' And A Little 'Bout Love** (1992; Arista). If his 1991 album DON'T ROCK THE JUKEBOX turned him into a superstar, this album set his career in stone. "Chattahoochee" and "Mercury Blues" are simple summertime fare, while "Tonight I Climbed The Wall" and "(Who Says) You Can't Have It All" are more introspective, maintaining a balanced mood.

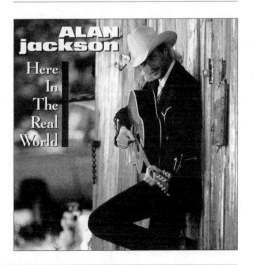

Alan Jackson

⊙ **Who I Am** (1994; Arista). "Summertime Blues" is almost a throwaway, as is "All American Country Boy." The big hit "Gone Country" is decent, but the real gems are the Rodney Crowell-penned "Song For The Life" and the confessional title track.

⊙ **Greatest Hits** (1995; Arista). A 20-song collection of his biggest hits—"Chattahoochee," "Gone Country," "Don't Rock The Jukebox," "Midnight In Montgomery," "Dallas," "Wanted," etc.—this is a substantial package and a great place to get a picture of why Jackson's been so successful.

⊙ **Everything I Love** (1996; Arista). More of the same from a guy who's nothing if not consistent. The lead-off track "Little Bitty" was written by Tom T. Hall—cute and catchy, nothing more, and that's just fine. "Buicks To The Moon" is another harmless novelty song, "A House With No Curtains" has a by-now-familiar subject of love that's drifted away. "There Goes" is a downer with a melody that's hard to resist, but it's "Between The Devil And Me" that feels truly touched by darkness—a welcome intensity in Jackson's world.

⊙ **Under The Influence** (1999; Arista). A collection of classic (and in some cases, lesser-known) country songs that have had an impact on Jackson over the years, this album shows his honky tonk spirit is in the right place. The ultimate version of "Pop A Top" still belongs to Jim Ed Brown (he cut it in 1967), but Jackson's take on this classic bar-room downer is a lot of fun. Further covers here include "Kiss An Angel Good Mornin'" (a massive Charley Pride hit), "Revenooer Man" (a Johnny Paycheck composition), and Merle Haggard's "My Own Kind Of Hat."

Wynonna Judd

W ynonna Judd was half of one of country music's most popular duos when, in the early 1990s, she was thrust into a solo career after her mother and musical partner, Naomi, quit the business due to chronic hepatitis. Wynonna (her fans know her just by her first name) was not quite prepared to stand alone under the spotlight, but with lots of encouragement, she finally emerged with her solo debut, WYNONNA, and a fistful of Top 10 hits that helped her grow into one of the most popular country singers of the '90s.

Wynonna was born Christina Claire Ciminella in Ashland, Kentucky on 30 May, 1964. Her parents divorced in 1972, and she grew up mostly under her mother's care. They moved (with her sister Ashley) between California and Kentucky before settling in Tennessee, where the Judds became a musical phenomenon during the '80s (see separate entry p.479). Naomi had spent a lot of time and energy educating her daughters about traditional folk and country music, and this was the foundation of the Judds' sound. But since her adolescence, especially during her California years, Wynonna had become enamored with rock and blues music as well—singers from Bonnie Raitt to Joni Mitchell. So when it came time for her solo career, she headed further away from folkish country, turning more seriously toward pop, R&B, and blues-based rock'n'roll material.

On Wynonna's self-titled debut album (for her new label, Curb/MCA), producer Tony Brown allowed her pop-rock sensibilities room to move, backing her up with electric guitars and bigger (and shinier) arrangements. Material ranged from the soft Dave Loggins number "She Is His Only Need" (her first solo #1 in 1992), to "No One Else On Earth," which showed she knew how to rock. The album went on to sell a stunning five million copies. Her sound was by no means all guts and glory, though: "Only Love" and "Is It Over Yet," for instance—both from her follow-up album, TELL ME WHY (1993) —were sentimental ballads built around strings, acoustic guitars and gentle percussion. In 1996 Wynonna released a third album, REVELATIONS, and a year after that came THE OTHER SIDE (as well as her hits package the WYNONNA COLLECTION). On New Year's Eve, 1999, she joined her mother for a Judds reunion concert in Phoenix, Arizona. The duo recorded four new songs together, and these were packaged as an additional disc inside initial limited edition copies of Wynonna's new solo album, NEW DAY DAWNING, which was released in the spring of 2000.

⊙ **Wynonna Collection** (1997; Curb/MCA). Collects hits from Wynnona's first three solo albums. Her voice is a powerful instrument that's deserving of admiration, but songs like the bouncy "I Saw The Light" and the sentimental "Is It Over Yet" are pretty pop—even by 1990s new country standards. She comes off much stronger on gutsier material like "No One Else On Earth," "Rock Bottom," and "Girls With Guitars" (the latter a Mary Chapin Carpenter song).

⊙ **New Day Dawning** (2000; Curb/Mercury). Recorded at studios in both Nashville and the Bahamas, and with three different producers, a lot of time, money, and effort has gone into what is something of a comeback album for Wynonna (it's her first release in three years).

It's not that radical a departure from her earlier material, but she does sound much bolder, and more confident than ever. As for the Judds tracks, they're energetic ("Stuck In Love"), silly ("Big Bang Boogie"), sentimental (Jesse Winchester's "That's What Makes You Strong"), and even a little preachy ("The '90s Were The '60s Turned Upside Down").

Sammy Kershaw

"Think about it. Why should I be mad if they want to compare me to the greatest country singer that ever lived?"

—Sammy Kershaw

Sammy Kershaw sounds like George Jones, and there's little he or anyone else can do about it. But where lesser artists might have cowered in fear of being labeled copycats, Kershaw bravely embraced the parallel—give a listen to the vocal slurs and curls on his 1991 single "Cadillac Style" and see if you don't agree. He's sung plenty of Jones songs from the stage, and he even went so far as to bring Jones himself on board for a duet, "Never Bit A Bullet Like This," on his 1994 album, FEELIN' GOOD TRAIN. ("That was scary," he admitted in a 1997 interview. "We were a foot away from each other, looking at each other, singing into the same microphone.") But his music is the ultimate test, and over the years songs like "Anywhere But Here," "Haunted Heart," and the melancholy "Yard Sale" have proven grounded enough to give this Louisiana good ole boy a honky-tonk identity of his own.

Kershaw was born in 1958 in Kaplan, Louisiana, a small town southwest of Lafayette and right in the heart of Cajun country. One of his distant cousins is fiddler Doug Kershaw, known best for his Cajun-styled country hit "Louisiana Man." During his teens Sammy played alongside a local musician, J.B. Perry, which enabled him to learn about and meet all sorts of country artists. One was singer Mel Street, who was a powerful influence on him. In his twenties Sammy played the clubs and cut some independent singles, and in 1991 he was signed to Mercury. His debut was "Cadillac Style," a frisky, good-natured number that climbed high in the charts and immediately marked him as a Jones stylist. "Don't Go Near The Water," "Yard Sale," and "Anywhere But Here" quickly followed, but it's "Cadillac" that has remained his signature song. All of these tracks were taken from his debut album, DON'T GO NEAR THE WATER, released in 1991.

Kershaw's follow-up, HAUNTED HEART, was released two years later, and it spawned the #1 hit "She Don't Know She's Beautiful," the campy "Queen Of My Double Wide Trailer" (penned by Dennis Linde), and the moody title track. His third album FEELIN' GOOD TRAIN maintained his hitmaking streak, beginning with "National Working Woman's Holiday," a play on the typical working man's anthem, where Sammy shows he's man enough to stand up for his woman's rights on the job. "Everyone likes a little time and a half, but we both know you're worth more than that," he declares. Like "Cadillac Style" and "Double Wide," it's basically a novelty song, though it's got enough substance to keep it interesting. Kershaw's hitmaking streak tapered off at this point, and his next album POLITICS, RELIGION, AND HER attempted a more serious route forward—though it also contained a cover of the '70s hit "Chevy Van." By the time LABOR OF LOVE was released in 1997, Kershaw's honky-tonk roots were giving way to a more soulful vocal style and a shinier production, even on a song as seemingly straightforward as "Honky Tonk America." He was also singing in a slightly lower register, which meant the Jones comparisons were less pronounced. Both albums featured a new producer, Keith Stegall, who took over from the team of Buddy Cannon and Norro Wilson. The formula is obviously working, as LABOR OF LOVE sold a respectable half a million copies. His 1999 release MAYBE NOT TONIGHT showed him moving even further away from the traditional sound of his early days.

⊙ **The Hits/Chapter 1** (1995; Mercury). Kershaw's material really grows on you. He has an attractive voice that plays well whether the song is upbeat and wrapped around a hook ("Cadillac Style," "National Working Woman's Holiday") or down and out ("Yard Sale," "I Can't Reach Her Anymore"). This is a fine overview of the hits from his first three albums, which are, so far, still his finest efforts.

Chris Knight

"I wouldn't know how to go about polishing a song."

—Chris Knight

A native of Slaughters, Kentucky, Chris Knight wasn't a typical Stetson-wearing, radio-slick young country singer when he debuted on Decca

when there's Nashville cash involved—rather they're a talent that's in his blood and won't be disappearing anytime soon. Though it's a mystery where, it's a near certainty that he will eventually land on his feet.

⊙ **Chris Knight** (1998; Decca). Knight's songs are straight-shooting and dead-honest portraits of farmers, truck drivers, lovers, and losers—most down on their luck and desperate, but each searching for a spot of truth in life, something to hope for beneath all the hardship and superficiality. It's a knockout debut album that moves between full-on, twang-infused rock'n'roll and stark acoustic performances. It's proof that stellar music does indeed bubble up through the Nashville system from time to time.

Chris Knight

Records in 1998 (Decca was at that point a subsidiary of MCA). He turned heads instead with songs and melodies that were unadorned, gritty, and at times brutally frank. Vince Gill he wasn't: he had much more in common with the likes of Billy Joe Shaver, Steve Earles, and John Prine, all songwriters who aren't afraid to speak the truth and get their hands dirty. Knight knew what both hardship and hard work were about. He'd grown up in a tiny coalmining town, and before Nashville showed any interest in him he'd spent five years with the Kentucky Department for Surface Mining Reclamation and Enforcement.

Frank Liddell of Bluewater Music and, later, Decca recognized the rugged beauty of Knight's music when he heard him sing at a songwriters' night in Nashville; he signed him to a publishing deal with Bluewater, which in turn led to his record deal with Decca. MCA Nashville president Tony Brown also believed in Knight, and he promoted him as the label's leading entry in the hopefully soon-to-be-burgeoning Americana radio market. As far as intentions go, all this was well and good. But the Americana dreams failed to materialize fast enough, at least by corporate standards, and a year later Knight lost his contract—falling under the same axe that felled the entire Decca subsidiary.

Like the characters and the landscapes in his songs, however, Knight's music is far stronger than that. It's obvious from just a few listens that songwriting and singing are not something he does only

Jim Lauderdale

Jim Lauderdale has landed more than a few songs on records by such mainstream stars as George Strait, Patty Loveless, Kathy Mattea, and Mark Chesnutt. The fact that several have turned into radio hits has made Lauderdale a hot commercial property in Nashville. But that's as a writer. His own recordings are a different story. He's consistently received positive critical attention for his voice and tight, bright style, which fits somewhere between Bakersfield edginess and Nashville accessibility. Lauderdale's records, however, haven't sold anywhere near the number that mainstream labels demand. Luckily, the right people on Music Row seem to like him, ensuring a fairly steady release of albums since his 1991 debut PLANET OF LOVE.

Born on 11 April, 1957 in Troutman, North Carolina, Lauderdale first launched his professional career in New York City, singing in musicals such as *Diamond Studs* (opposite an as-yet-undiscovered Shawn Colvin) and *Pump Boys And Dinettes*. He later moved to Los Angeles, where he played the club circuit, often with his good friend Buddy Miller. Pete Anderson (known best as Dwight Yoakam's producer and guitarist) included one Lauderdale cut, "What Am I Waiting For," on the West Coast country compilation A TOWN SOUTH OF BAKERSFIELD, VOLUME II. In 1987, Anderson produced Lauderdale's debut solo album for CBS Records, a peppy, neo-twang affair, but it was never released. Four years later, however, Lauderdale did finally make record store shelves with PLANET OF LOVE, which was produced this time by Rodney Crowell and John Leventhal (the latter co-wrote many of the songs). The sound is a bit slicker, but songs like "Where The Sidewalk Ends" and especially "Wake Up Screaming" are excellent.

Lauderdale jumped to Atlantic for PRETTY CLOSE TO THE TRUTH and EVERY SECOND COUNTS, then signed with the indie Upstart for 1996's PERSIMMONS. The Nashville label BNA released his next effort, WHISPER (1997), though it was hardly a mainstream effort—Lauderdale's rootsy influences, from Buck Owens to Ralph Stanley (who plays on one cut), still showed through quite clearly. In 1999 he released both a solo album, ONWARD THROUGH IT ALL, and a full-on duet album with Stanley and his Clinch Mountain Boys, I FEEL LIKE SINGING TODAY.

⊙ **Persimmons** (1996; Upstart). There's not a huge difference in style between Lauderdale's albums, but don't let that stop you from listening to a variety of them. When it comes to writing (and recording), this guy knows what he's doing. Here like on all his records, he churns out a steady stream of tight little beauties, with blues rockabilly and country balladry all factoring into his musical equation.

⊙ **Onward Through It All** (1999; RCA). Even though he's on a big Nashville label, Lauderdale shows little concern here for modern-day trappings or mainstream trends. And thank goodness for that. Not to say that country radio shouldn't be paying attention, as Onward is yet another respectable showcase for Lauderdale's tight voice and arrangements—and one that is typically packed with his myriad rootsy influences, from the West Coast to the Appalachians.

⊙ **I Feel Like Singing Today** (1999; Rebel). Ralph Stanley is one of the few remaining direct connections to bluegrass music's golden era. Lauderdale and Stanley share vocal duties on this traditionally minded bluegrass collection, which features Lauderdale originals as well as a few old gems.

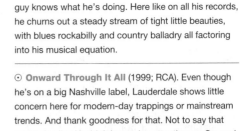

Tracy Lawrence

Scarcely in his twenties when he made his recording debut in 1991 with STICKS AND STONES, Tracy Lawrence (born 27 January, 1968 in Atlanta, Texas) showed tremendous promise as an up-and-coming neo-traditionalist in an already hats-heavy scene. Nashville, however, nearly proved fatal to the young star, when, in 1991, just after completing the album, he was shot during a holdup in a Music Row parking lot. Thankfully, he quickly recovered, and later that same year the song "Stick And Stones" became his first of many #1 hits.

STICKS AND STONES, in fact, produced four Top 10 hits in all for this young artist with the full-bodied, honky-tonk voice. An impressive feat, yet Tracy's follow-up album, ALIBIS, topped that achievement with four straight #1s. Lawrence's success came early (in addition to high sales, he was named Best New Male Vocalist by the ACM in 1992) and his career seemed to be increasing in strength, but his personal life hasn't been without its complications. Ironically, the same year that his song "Renegades, Rebels And Rogues" (from the movie *Maverick*) hit the Top 10, Tracy was involved in another firearm incident—only this time he did the firing (he was allegedly spooked by a group of teenagers). He was arrested but released on probation. His chart success contin-

Jim Lauderdale

Jim Lauderdale • Tracy Lawrence

ued throughout the decade—I SEE IT NOW and TIME MARCHES ON produced more hits, and his 1997 album THE COAST IS CLEAR was critically acclaimed as his most mature work to date. Unfortunately, however, Lawrence's run-ins with the law were to continue. In 1998 he was convicted of spousal abuse—and his recording contract was put on hold. A new album was finally scheduled for release in early 2000 with the appropriate (and hopeful) title of LESSONS LEARNED. Time will tell.

⊙ **Sticks And Stones** (1991; Atlantic). Lawrence's debut has a strong honky-tonk flavor, thanks in part to tasteful board work by James Stroud (who had produced Clint Black's debut just two years earlier). Lawrence's drawling voice is a typical Haggard/Strait/Jones mix, but songs like "Somebody Paints The Wall," the silly "I Hope Heaven Has A Honky Tonk," and especially "Sticks And Stones" make the collection as a whole an appealing first effort.

⊙ **Live And Unplugged** (1995; Atlantic). Instead of a traditional best-of collection, the 10 'hits' compiled here were cut live during a recent concert tour. The titles are taken from his first 3 albums and include "Sticks And Stones," "Today's Lonely Fool," and "If The Good Die Young" (as well as "Renegades, Rebels And Rogues" from the *Maverick* soundtrack).

⊙ **The Best Of Tracy Lawrence** (1998; Atlantic). The number of songs has increased to 14 from the LIVE AND UNPLUGGED's 10, and a handful of newer songs such as "Time Marches On" and "Stars Over Texas" bring the collection more up-to-date. There's also one previously unreleased track, "Her Old Stompin' Ground," though perhaps the title's a bit dangerous and unwise considering Tracy's conviction this same year.

Chris LeDoux

Before he came to the attention of Music Row, Chris LeDoux was a bronc-riding champion, rancher, and a country singer with a stunning twenty-two self-released albums to his credit. His big Nashville break came after he was mentioned in a song by Garth Brooks, "Much Too Young (To Feel This Damn Old)," which appeared on Garth's 1989 debut album. A year later Garth's label, Liberty (now Capitol), signed LeDoux. He's only made a few waves on the charts since then (his biggest single being a duet with Brooks, "Whatcha Gonna Do With A Cowboy"), but

more importantly he's earned accolades for his super-high-energy live shows, which are full of loud, rock-edged country material and often climax with fireworks and flashpots. Beneath all that excitement, however, is dusty-voiced LeDoux and his cowboy pedigree, a welcomed breeze of authenticity on a country music landscape overpopulated with hat-act singers who've never looked a horse in the eye or spat on the ground.

LeDoux was born in 1948 in Mississippi and later moved with his family to Texas. He was a rodeo rider from the age of fourteen, and his winning streak peaked in 1976 when he was named World Champion bareback bronc rider. His music emerged out of this lifestyle—songs like "Bareback Jack" and "Getting By A Quarter At A Time" about small-town cowboys, rodeo bums, and the folks who love them. Some of these songs were definitely amateur, even cheesy, while others had a homespun charm that won him a decent following. By the time he quit rodeo riding in 1980, he'd already released more than ten albums on his own label, billing himself as "The Singing Bronc Rider." He spent the '80s tending his ranch in Wyoming, raising his family, playing music and cutting more records. His following grew steadily, but it wasn't until the day he heard that Brooks song on the radio that his career took a new, dramatic turn. He signed to Liberty, and the label promptly re-released not one, but nearly all of LeDoux's previous recordings. Next came his first Nashville-produced collection, WESTERN UNDERGROUND (named after his touring band), but it was his second Liberty album, WHATCHA GONNA DO WITH A COWBOY, that gained him the most attention, thanks to his duet with Brooks on the title track. He's since released several more albums including LIVE!, a 1997 collection that showcased his hot-fired cowboy rock'n'roll, and 1998's ONE ROAD MAN, which included duets with both Charlie Daniels and Jon Bon Jovi.

⊙ **Live** (1997; Capitol). Can you imagine an entire song about chewing tobacco? Try "Copenhagen" on for size. Clearly foolish (as is its companion piece, "Copenhagen Angel"), it's one of 17 songs that rock the house and fire up the crowds on this rousing live collection, a mixture of old ("Bareback Jack") and new ("Gravitational Pull," "This Cowboy's Hat") LeDoux. Though he's pushing fifty here, this collection shows him to be as tightly wound and excitable a performer as any artist half his age.

Chris LeDoux

⊙ **20 Greatest Hits** (1999; Capitol). A substantial round-up of LeDoux's Capitol/Liberty material—both chart hits and fan favorites—that updates and replaces the 1994 collection BEST OF CHRIS LEDOUX. Many of the songs do remain the same, including his happy-go-lucky Garth Brooks duet "Whatcha Gonna Do With A Cowboy" and hopped-up material like Joe Ely's "For Your Love" and LeDoux's own "County Fair." But we also get his version of Springsteen's "Tougher Than The Rest," the invigorating cowboy saga "Stampede," and his Bon Jovi duet "Bang A Drum."

The Mavericks

"You can always tell what the Mavericks are listening to because it comes out in our records. God help us if we ever got hold of a polka album."

—Paul Deakin

It's the hooks in the Mavericks' "Mr. Jones," the lead track on FROM HELL TO PARADISE, the Miami band's second album (and first for major label MCA), that pull you in off the street. And it's the soaring tenor of Cuban-American lead vocalist (and songwriter) Raul Malo, and the tight package of the group's instrumental foundation—bassist Robert Reynolds, drummer Paul Deakin and guitarist David Lee Holt—that keeps you riveted all the way through this intriguing song, an underrated piece that's one of their finest. Malo's lyrics deal with revisiting his childhood home and facing the inevitable changes that have occurred, and it's full of complex emotions—haunting and reflective on one hand, but sung and played with passion and urgency. When Malo sings the tag line "There's nothing left inside, Mr Jones"—a neighbor's remark regarding Malo's once-proud family house—memories that have existed for years, even decades, inside his head are in an instant knocked right out of place.

But there are many more songs where this came from: "This Broken Heart," "What A Crying Shame," the honky-tonk shuffle "There Goes My Heart," the lush "I've Got This Feeling." As well as a monumental songwriter, Malo is a knockout vocalist whose closest comparison is the great pop-country stylist Roy Orbison. Malo's talent—and that of his fellow bandmembers, strong musicians all of them—has carried this band from the clubs of Miami to streets of Music Row. On a musical level they combine elements of rock, blues, Latin pop, soul and honky tonk; on an immediately visceral level, they know how to craft a melody—both on record and on stage—that won't let go.

The band formed in Miami in the late 1980s, when Malo, Reynolds, and Deakin realized their mutual interest in rockabilly and vintage country music. In 1990 they released an album on the small Y&T label, and it garnered enough attention (as did their energetic live shows) to land them a deal with MCA. Guitarist Holt was brought on board at this point, and the band entered a Miami studio and put together FROM HELL TO PARADISE. Critics raved, but country radio didn't bite, and so the band honed a sharper, more focused country sound for its next effort, WHAT A CRYING SHAME (1994). They also replaced Holt with new lead guitarist Nick Kane, who's remained with them ever since. This time, radio programmers perked up, and three of the album's songs showed up on the country Top 40. The Mavericks' reputation as an exciting live act soared, too, and it's this aspect that, over the course of time, has helped the group sell more albums than any of their hit singles or radio airplay. "Here Comes The Rain," from the 1995 album MUSIC FOR ALL OCCASIONS, earned the Mavericks a Grammy, and in both 1995 and 1996 they were named

Chris LeDoux • The Mavericks

ANGELA LUBRANO

Frontman Raul Malo of the Mavericks

Vocal Group of the Year by the CMA. Their fifth album, TRAMPOLINE (1998), was their most musically eclectic, and adventurous, project to date. In 1999, MCA released SUPER COLOSSAL SMASH HITS OF THE '90S, which compiled earlier material and threw in four new tracks as a bonus.

⊙ **From Hell To Paradise** (1992; MCA). "Mr Jones" leads off a strong collection that also boasts the Buck Owens classic "Excuse Me (I Think I've Got A Heartache)," the mournful ballad "This Broken Heart," and the painfully personal title track, about Malo's family's immigration from Cuba to the US. An album that will last a long while.

⊙ **What A Crying Shame** (1994; MCA). The title track is a jewel, the guitar-driven melody built around hooks so delicious they'll almost make you cry. Malo wrote that and others—the classic-sounding shuffle "There Goes My Heart," the sing-along weeper "Memory"—with Greek-born hitmaking songwriter Kostas, and the collaboration paid off in a handful of Top 40 hits. The

beauty of the Mavericks' success is that they never felt the need to compromise their honky-tonk integrity to achieve their platinum status.

⊙ **Trampoline** (1998; MCA). The punch of horns and the warble of a B-3 organ—not to mention some extravagantly orchestral string passages—are tastefully blended with the guitars, bass and drums on this wide-open musical landscape of an album. Chart hits are no longer a concern, which frees the band to stretch out stylistically and take chances the way few groups—country or otherwise—dare to do.

Tim McGraw

> "I'm a redneck and I admit it."
>
> —Tim McGraw

Tim McGraw first smashed his way onto the country charts, and into the Nashville spotlight, in 1994 with "Indian Outlaw," a beefy song pumped up with crude references to wig-wams, tom-toms, peace pipes, and "buffalo briefs" that's the biggest slice of crass since George Jones announced that "bow-wow" makes good "chow-chow" in "Poor Chinee." Protests were raised against McGraw's soon-to-be signature ditty, but that didn't stop his growing legion of fans from pulling out their credit cards: the album "Indian Outlaw" appears on, NOT A MOMENT TOO SOON, has since sold to the tune of five million copies. As for McGraw—well, he grew into one of the top-selling artists in contemporary country music.

The son of baseball hero Tug McGraw, Tim was born on 1 May, 1967 in Delhi, Louisiana. He grew up as Tim Smith (he was born out of wedlock, the product of a summertime fling) and didn't get to know his father until his teenage years. Tim moved to Nashville in 1989, and within a couple of years he landed a contract with Curb Records. His early hits (collected on his 1993 debut album TIM MCGRAW) were minor, but the following year came NOT A MOMENT TOO SOON. From that point onwards, McGraw's career soared. The rowdy "Indian Outlaw" was the song that broke him, but the album included a couple of sugar-coated ballads—the title track and "Don't Take The Girl"—that showed he liked to croon as well as party.

McGraw picked up a couple of awards from the Academy of Country Music, and then continued his streak toward superstardom with his

1995 album ALL I WANT and further big hits "I Like It, I Love It" and "Can't Be Really Gone." In 1996 he married fellow rising star Faith Hill, creating a new First Couple in country music—the most fawned over since the ill-fated bond between George Jones and Tammy Wynette. Hill dueted with her new hubby on "It's Your Love," which appeared on McGraw's fourth album, EVERYWHERE. The song was so unabashedly sweet it made you cringe, yet it also shot to #1 and won the newlyweds a CMA award for Vocal Event Of The Year. The album was brimming with love songs, in fact, including the title track and the happy-go-lucky "Just To See You Smile." Save for his debut, McGraw's albums—including his 1999 release A PLACE IN THE SUN—have all topped the *Billboard* charts and sold well past the platinum level.

⊙ **Not A Moment Too Soon** (1994; Curb). McGraw lets his hair down on party anthems like "It Don't Get Any Countrier Than This" and, of course, "Indian Outlaw." But he shows equal weakness for schmaltz on "Don't Take The Girl," which is still one of his most popular songs. Where later albums are far slicker, McGraw does allow his honky-tonk influences ("Give It To Me Strait" he pleads in one fetching number) more space here.

⊙ **Everywhere** (1997; Curb). The fiddle intro on the lead-off track, "Where The Green Grass Grows"—coupled with McGraw's thick Louisiana vocals and the song's pastoral imagery—give hope that McGraw hasn't completely lost touch with his roots and given himself over to big, brassy productions. The song is unique among the collection, however, as the album is mostly built around tender ballads like "It's Your Love" and "One Of These Days."

John Michael Montgomery

> "I get picked on by the critics a bit because I don't sing about politics or whatever. The only answer I can give anybody is I want the youngest person and the oldest person to like it and understand it."
>
> —John Michael Montgomery

Kentucky native John Michael Montgomery was a classic mid-'90s hat act. He had handsome, clean-cut features, a snappy black cowboy hat, and a pleasant voice that mixed the twangy with the tender, all of which added up to multiplatinum sales and the #1 position (more than once) on both the country singles and album charts. But Montgomery's slick pop-rock sound, though not too frilly, wasn't all that innovative either—in fact, whether he was rocking out or getting sweet, it was pretty middle-of-the-road. Hits like "Be My Baby Tonight" and "I Swear" are not entirely unpleasant, and they certainly have their share of hooks. But taken as a whole, Montgomery's music is fairly predictable and lacks much real excitement.

Born on 20 January, 1965 in Danville, Kentucky, Montgomery played with his family's band—and later with his brother—before signing to Atlantic in 1991. Right from the start he had a hit with "Life's A Dance," the title track of his debut album; that release and his next two albums, KICKIN' IT UP and JOHN MICHAEL MONTGOMERY, each sold tremendously well. Montgomery earned a hot streak of big hits throughout the mid-'90s that included

Tim McGraw

"I Love The Way You Love Me," the MOR shit-kicker "Be My Baby Tonight," the slow and sappy "Rope The Moon," and the #1 smash "I Can Love You Like That," which was also a pop hit for the group All-4-One. Probably Montgomery's biggest hit from this period was "I Swear," which won him Single Of The Year honors in 1994 from both the Academy Of Country Music and the Country Music Association. The CMA also lauded him with its Horizon Award. By 1997 Montgomery had racked up enough serious singles to justify a GREATEST HITS collection. LEAVE A MARK (1998) and HOME TO YOU (1999) followed, though neither one showed him straying very far from the formulas that earlier made him such a multiplatinum success.

⊙ **Kickin' It Up** (1994; Atlantic). This is home to "I Swear," among other hits. Montgomery can conjur a cool, tough-guy vocal tone when he wants to, as on "Full Time Love" and "She Don't Need A Band To Dance." And fiddle and steel are featured in his arrangements, alongside Brett Mason's twangy electric leads. But in terms of song material, Montgomery's second album predictably flutters back and forth between working-man rock anthems ("Friday At Five") and tender balladry ("Ropin' The Moon").

⊙ **Greatest Hits** (1997; Atlantic). For the one-stop shopper, 14 of Montgomery's biggest hits are crammed onto this collection, including "Sold (The Grundy County Auction Incident)," "I Swear," "No Man's Land," "Life's A Dance," "I Love The Way You Love Me," and "Beer And Bones."

Alison Moorer

Allison Moorer

Alabama native Allison Moorer is one of the freshest new singers, and one of the most remarkable new songwriters, to debut on a Nashville major label in a long time. Her voice is rich, soulful and slightly dusty around the edges—a beautiful match to songs that alternate between sad longing and warm desire. Moorer's songs are more rooted in tradition than the Teflon pop material typical of big stars like Faith Hill and Shania Twain; she has yet to break into mainstream radio, but when her song "A Soft Place To Fall" landed an Academy Award nomination (she performed it in Robert Redford's *The Horse Whisperer*), her fame escalated. Moorer's performance of the song was a highlight of the 1999 Oscar ceremony; the Oscar connection also helped her get a Best New Female Vocalist nomination that year from the Academy of Country Music.

Allison Moorer was born in Mobile, Alabama on 21 June, 1972, the younger sister of country singer Shelby Lynne. Her background was very musical, but the family also endured a terrible tragedy when their father shot their mother during an argument, and then himself. Moorer attended college in Mobile before moving to Nashville where she sang back-up for her sister. Although she'd been singing since she was a child, she didn't start writing songs until she moved to Nashville—and after meeting songwriter Doyle "Butch" Primm, whom she later married. Moorer's first appearance on record was singing harmony on the album THINGS FALL APART by alt.country singer Lonesome Bob. Her own career gathered momentum after she and Primm met producer Kenny Greenberg. A demo they put together found its way into the hands of MCA Nashville president Tony Brown. He signed Moorer, and he also sent a tape of her music to Robert Redford (MCA was handling the *Horse Whisperer* soundtrack), who flew her out to perform in the film. Moorer's debut is traditional on the one hand, fresh and contemporary on the other. It's full of spare and subtle tones and delicate, complex emotions, but don't simply file it away as a fringe record—in fact, it's easy to picture songs like the uptempo "The One That Got Away," the lovely "Alabama Song," and even the honky-tonk-infused "I Found A Letter" wafting from the car radio. And you never know, it's a place Moorer just might be before long. Two years after her debut, Moorer's as-yet-untitled sophomore

album was scheduled for release in the fall of 2000.

⊙ **Alabama Song** (1998; MCA). "A Soft Place To Fall" is a clear standout, but not every song is brimming with such melancholy. "The One That Got Away" shows she's comfortable to rock'n'roll, while "I Found A Letter" and "Easier To Forget" are tied at their roots to honky tonk—a style Moorer's voice fits beautifully. The arrangements, too, are tastefully spare, shifting to fit the mood but never getting in the way.

Lee Roy Parnell

The best of Abilene, Texas native Lee Roy Parnell's music is based around his hot, boogie-influenced lead (and slide) guitar playing and beefy

The Jewel Of Middle America: Branson

Branson, Missouri, the booming Ozark sanctuary for commercially disenfranchised country and pop stars, is a shrine to all things square in the entertainment business. More than thirty-nine theaters line the town's so-called Strip, always crowded with an endless parade of bumper-to-bumper recreational vehicles that bring millions of retirees and rednecks out to shake some toe-tapping senior-set action.

Branson has actually been a popular tourist spot since the late nineteenth century, when tours of the nearby Marvel Cave began to lure visitors, and three adjacent lakes cemented the areas appeal for hunting, fishing, and watersports enthusiasts. The town first took a turn towards country music in 1967, with the grand opening of Presley's Jubilee Theater, presenting an old-timey cracker barrel full of tried-and-true formulae. Perennial Jubilee headliners, the Baldknobbers (named for a nineteenth-century band of brigands) found that their corny hillbilly schtick wowed the midwesterners. It was a swell racket, one that steadily grew and grew. By the late '80s, Branson was established as a haven for tourists seeking old-school country entertainment, and the Chamber of Commerce was trumpeting some staggering attendance figures.

As press coverage of the midwestern Mecca filled Sunday supplements and airwaves, more and more performers began to appear there, and back in pre-Garth Nashville, a small blister of resentment formed. Self-made hobo Boxcar Willie reigned supreme in Branson, and a tide of erstwhile country

hitmakers like Glen Campbell, Mel Tillis, Mickey Gilley, and Charley Pride surged into town as well. But many top artists, like Johnny Cash and Merle Haggard (both of whom spent a miserable season of sit-down, three-shows-a-day grind) soon discovered that unless one actually owned and operated a Branson venue, it was virtually impossible to make any real money.

Soon, the town magnetically drew in an impressive roster of dead-in-the-water pop fossils—the Osmonds, Bobby Vinton, Tony Orlando, and Wayne Newton all began to operate there. The last two entered a joint venture that quickly soured, first through sexual harassment allegations brought against Orlando by two of his back-up singers, then by an ugly feud that culminated in the partners locking each other out of the theater.

Branson remains a solid tourist spot. As Bobby Vinton recently said: "Where else in the world could you find a place where there are twenty theaters with sold-out matinees on a Tuesday afternoon? It's unbelievable ..." Not quite as unbelievable as the surreal vision of Vinton himself—picture, if you will, a reptilian mask of cosmetic surgical procedure, hair dyed a rich russet tone, belting out "Blue Velvet" to an adoring house full of retirees. Forget David Lynch and Dennis Hopper: Branson is altogether bizarre, a last bastion of molded plastic Americana the likes of which can be found nowhere else.

—Jonny Whiteside

Allison Moorer • Lee Roy Parnell

R&B rhythms—which come courtesy of his band, the Hot Links. If much of Parnell's material seems tailored for a bar-room Saturday night crowd, that's no coincidence. Before his Nashville career picked up during the early 1990s, Parnell (born 21 December, 1956) was based out of Austin and spent many years touring around Texas. He moved to Nashville in 1987, where he initially landed a publishing deal and, a couple years later, a recording contract with Arista. His debut album, LEE ROY PARNELL, was released in 1990 and revealed him busting hard and strong through songs—many of them originals or co-writes—that had been heavily dosed with blues, soul, rock'n'roll and R&B. His roadhouse past was all over the place, from the saucy "Oughta Be A Law" (a song by Gary Nicholson and Memphis mainstay Dan Penn) to the horn-infused soul number "Let's Pretend" (which Parnell co-wrote with Cris Moore).

Parnell's commercial breakthrough came with the release of his second album, LOVE WITHOUT MERCY. And it's no wonder, as his first Top 10 chart single, "What Kind Of Fool Do You Think I Am," had a more focused, mainstream-country sound. He also hit with the title track and "Tender Moment." Still, while Parnell's blustery boogie-blues sound was toned down a little, it hadn't entirely disappeared. Since the album's release, he's managed to find a friendly balance between blow-out R&B songs and straightforward ballads—gritty-ass guitar riffs and tender melodies—and it's a balance that kept his name in the charts through much of the '90s. Arista released the Parnell compilation HITS AND HIGHWAYS AHEAD in 1999, and in the spring of 2000, Lee Roy embarked on a European tour with the Texas Tornados, filling in for the late Doug Sahm.

⊙ **Lee Roy Parnell** (1990; Arista). This is blues-based Texas rock'n'roll, but it's also got a deep and serious streak of Memphis and/or Muscle Shoals soul and R&B. The horns and saxophones alongside Parnell's beefy lead guitar place the songs more in line with Delbert McClinton (or the late Doug Sahm on a blues-heavy night) than George Jones. It's Parnell's rowdiest, rawest, and gutsiest album to date.

⊙ **Love Without Mercy** (1992; Arista). Parnell seems to have reached the conclusion that if he holds back on the horns, turns up the steel guitars, and throws in a few ballads, he might just sell some records. And he has. But a handful of songs are still red-eyed and

rowdy. "Road Scholar" in particular—no surprise, since it's a duet with fellow Texas roadhouse rocker Delbert McClinton.

⊙ **Every Night's A Saturday Night** (1997; Arista). The compromise Parnell made back in 1992 between country commercialism and his natural-born roadhouse attitude is pretty refined on his fifth album. The title track is full of guitar-driven fire, while "All That Matters Anymore" is a quiet and touching (albeit rather introspective) ballad. Trisha Yearwood guests on the overly sweet "Better Word For Love," Guy Clark pops in for a lively version of his song "Baton Rouge," and Parnell gets down and dirty with Merle Haggard's "Honky Tonk Night Time Man."

LeAnn Rimes

"I would love to sing every kind of music anyone would let me sing, because I've grown up listening to everything."

—LeAnn Rimes

Having a #1 country album at the age of thirteen is a pretty tough act to follow, but teenage singing sensation LeAnn Rimes has managed, at least so far, to keep her name on the charts, her full-bodied voice on the radio, and her fans happily lapping up her (sometimes questionable) CD releases. Rimes' breakthrough hit "Blue," written by Bill Mack and originally intended for Patsy Cline (at least according to press bios), gained her the kind of widespread national acclaim that is difficult to repeat. Only time will tell how all this attention may settle in Rimes' psyche—perhaps it will even give her string-sodden music the edge it so sorely lacks right now. So far, however, she has proven a reliable commercial property, and this despite being saddled with such schlocky material as "Looking Through Your Eyes" and "You Light Up My Life."

Rimes was born on 28 August, 1982 in Jackson, Mississippi. Her parents encouraged her singing as a child, and before LeAnn was ten she was performing on stage and winning talent contests, including the TV show *Star Search*. Rimes recorded her first album, ALL THAT, in 1994 for the Nor Va Jak label. She was next signed to Curb, and her album BLUE hit stores in 1996. Talk about 'young country': Rimes was only thirteen at the time, which invited comparisions with saucy '70s startlet Tanya Tucker and, as far back as the '50s, pre-pubescent rockabilly-cum-country singer Brenda Lee. Rimes' voice was uncannily rich and powerful as she worked her way through such mature material as the mournful title track and Deborah Allen's "My Baby" ("my baby is a fulltime lover, my baby is a fullgrown man"). The album sold more than three million copies, leading Curb to reissue ALL THAT under the new title UNCHAINED MELODY: THE EARLY YEARS. Next came YOU LIGHT UP MY LIFE: INSPIRATIONAL SONGS, which showed off her voice on pop songs like the title track and "The Rose." It also left many wondering why on earth she was singing "God Bless America" and—most curious of all—the "Star-Spangled Banner." SITTIN' ON TOP OF THE WORLD (1998) was almost worse, full of gooey, string-laden material like Carol Bayer Sager and David Foster's "Looking Through Your Eyes" and further pop curiosities such as Prince's "Purple Rain." In 1999, with a newer, sassier look, Rimes was back on the charts with her fifth album, LEANN RIMES.

⊙ **Blue** (1996; Curb). No matter what you think of Rimes' music as a whole, it's hard not to agree she has a set of pipes that are rich far beyond her meager years. The title track is the clear standout here, a throwback to the Nashville Sound era. "My Baby" is a standard 'young country' rocker, while her version of "Cattle Call" (a duet with Eddy Arnold, who made the song famous fifty years earlier) is fair and reverent.

Doug Stone

It's almost as if Doug Stone is schizophrenic. Half his reputation was established with self-deprecating downers like "I'd Be Better Off (In A Pine Box)," but then he'd just as easily turn around with a schmaltzy love song like "Too Busy Being In Love." The fact that the latter made #1 in the country charts is a frightening reminder that fans of such saccharine kings as Lee Greenwood and Kenny Loggins are still among us. Yet as godawful a song as "Too Busy" is, it's hard to dismiss an artist who at the same time could churn out "Pine Box," "Ain't Your Memory Got No Pride At All," and "Warning Labels" —stone-cold weepers that harken back to honky tonk's glory days of barstool pity and face-down shame. Stone's voice is higher and sweeter than that of Merle Haggard, a singer he's been compared to more than once, but arrangements tinged with steel guitar and fiddle keep the songs grounded in neo-traditionalist turf. Though Stone didn't wear a hat, he fit into the early 1990s country scene very snugly.

Stone was born in Newnan, Georgia in 1956. He landed his first record contract in 1988 with Epic, and his debut single, "Pine Box," made the charts two years later, even nabbing him a Grammy nomination. He had a string of hits over the next several years, among them "Fourteen

The Luscious LeAnn

LeAnn Rimes • Doug Stone

Minutes Old" (1990), "In A Different Light" and "A Jukebox With A Country Song" (1991), and "Warning Labels" and "Too Busy Being In Love" (1992). In April of 1992, Stone, who was only in his mid-thirties at the time, underwent quadruple bypass heart surgery. Ironic, isn't it, that the album he released that year was titled FROM THE HEART. In 1993 and back in action, Stone's MORE LOVE featured a new producer (James Stroud, the man behind Clint Black) and a much beefier sound on songs like "Addicted To A Dollar" that lend welcome substance to Stone's sometimes too-sweet voice. Several songs here were included in the film *Gordy*, in which Stone also acted.

☉ **From The Heart** (1992; Epic). "Ain't Your Memory Got No Pride At All" is as close to Haggard as Stone gets, while "The Workin' End Of A Hoe" brings to mind John Anderson. "Warning Labels" is also worthwhile, but be sure to skip "Too Busy Being In Love" and "Why Didn't I Think Of That," stomach-churning pap that will repeat on you for days.

☉ **Pure Country** (1997; Sony). Though some of the big hits are missing (most notably "Pine Box"), this budget CD does bring some of stone's sturdier material together, including "The Workin' End Of A Hoe," "Addicted To A Dollar," "Leave Me The Radio," and "A Jukebox With A Country Song."

Pam Tillis

S he may be the daughter of legendary singer and songwriter Mel Tillis, but Pam Tillis earned star status of her own during the 1990s, thanks to her passionate, sharp and brazen country voice that earned her such hits as "Shake The Sugar Tree," "Don't Tell Me What To Do," "Mi Vida Loca (My Crazy Life)," and "Cleopatra, Queen Of Denial." These and other songs presented distinctly female points of view that were brimming with emotional empowerment. "If you take my love for granted, I'll shake the sugar tree," sings Tillis. "I've got to raise some commotion before you show me some real emotion."

Born on 24 July, 1957 in Plant City, Florida, Tillis debuted on the *Opry* as a child and began performing on her own as a teenager. After some experimental years spent performing in a San Francisco band and writing songs and singing on demo tapes in Nashville, Tillis was signed to Warner Brothers in 1983. Her debut

album was titled BEYOND THE DOLL OF CUTEY, a pop-oriented affair that wasn't hugely successful. In 1989 she signed with Arista, and it's at this point that her country career fell into place. Her first Arista album, PUT YOURSELF IN MY PLACE, yielded several hits including "Don't Tell Me What To Do," "One Of Those Things," and "Maybe It Was Memphis." That and follow-up albums such as HOMEWARD LOOKING ANGEL and SWEETHEART'S DANCE sold well and established Tillis as a reliable commercial artist. The CMA backed her up by naming her Female Vocalist of the Year in 1994. Through her hitmaking career, Tillis has retained her country integrity, for the most part avoiding what could be an easy drift into saccharine territory. She's also taken an active role in shaping her career, from writing songs to producing her own albums, including her 1998 release EVERY TIME.

☉ **Greatest Hits** (1997; Arista). Pam Tillis is not afraid to give her music a deep country shine. Her sharp, high voice is always in control of the melody, and though she beefs up her arrangements with fiery rock rhythms, the moan of the steel guitar is an ongoing presence in her arrangements. Songs like "Mi Vida Loca," the sassy "Cleopatra," the empowering "Sugar Tree" are infectious, and the neo-realistic "All the Good Ones Are Gone" (meaning decent single men) is sad but not cheaply sweetened.

Aaron Tippin

P ensacola, Florida-born singer and songwriter Aaron Tippin has a strong voice that's compelling, if also somewhat strange—on the one hand bold and blustery, but on the other high and almost reedy. It gives an interesting edge to his blue-collar brand of honky tonk, and he uses it to full effect on such day-job anthems as "Working Man's Ph.D." and "I Got It Honest." "If you check out my paycheck you'll see that there ain't that much on it/But every single penny I made, I got it honest," sings Tippin. It's rousing stuff—tough as steel, full of country pride, and, taken one song at a time, downright refreshing. Tippin goes overboard at times with novelty songs like "Many, Many, Many Beers Ago," "There Ain't Nothing Wrong With The Radio" (the car barely runs but country streams out of the speakers just fine), and "Country Boy's Toolbox" (don't mess with it, ladies—it's sacred territory). After several albums you do start to wonder how many times this onetime farmer, machinist, pilot, and bodybuilder can dish out the same working man's rhetoric. Luckily, Tippin has other songs up his sleeve—including stark ballads of loneliness ("Cold Chill") and introspection ("The Man Who Came Between Us [Was Me],") as well as full-on love songs ("You Are The Woman"). One of his finest moments is with the Al Anderson song "Without Your Love." Generally speaking, Tippin's a sturdy singer and respectable songwriter, and since the release his 1990 debut album, YOU'VE GOT TO STAND FOR SOME-THING, he's held a steady course through burly, blues-inflected, but always honky-tonk-grounded territory. By 1998 that was becoming a precious musical commodity: he was even moaning "What this country needs is a little more steel guitar" on the title track of his 1998 album WHAT THIS COUNTRY NEEDS, and he certainly wasn't far off the mark. We can only hope his own music continues to dish it up as well.

⊙ **Lookin' Back At Myself** (1994; RCA). A blustery but thoroughly enjoyable album of blue-collar honky tonk, highlighted by "I Got It Honest," the rousing "Mission From Hank," and the goofy but fun "Country Boy's Tool Box."

⊙ **The Essential Aaron Tippin** (1998; RCA). Sixteen cuts, including the hits "Working Man's Ph.D.," "There Ain't Nothing Wrong With The Radio," "Many, Many Beers Ago," "Call Of The Wild," and "I Wouldn't Have It Any Other Way." Not a bad introduction at all.

Travis Tritt

"If you're in the music business and you're not capable of carrying a guitar in one hand and a briefcase in the other, then you're making a serious mistake."

—Travis Tritt

Since running up the charts with his 1989 single "Country Club," Georgia-born country star Travis Tritt has created a "rough and rowdy" image for himself as a modern-day Outlaw-cum-Southern renegade. On songs like "Here's a Quarter (Call Someone Who Cares)" and "Back Up Against The Wall," he has a loud and brazen Southern-rock style that's equal parts honky tonk, bar-room blues and corn-fed rock'n'roll. He can bust through anthem's like "Looking Out For Number One," "Bible Belt" (a duet with Little

Feat), and "Blue Collar Man" (this last song written in collaboration with Lynyrd Skynyrd's Gary Rossington), and he's succeeded in tapping into the same fan base—good ole boys and girls raised on red-dirt farms and ripened with Jack Daniels—that has propelled the likes of Skynyrd,

STEVE GILLETT

Travis Tritt

Charlie Daniels, and Hank Williams Jr. to country-rock stardom.

But Tritt is a bigger man than his denim-and-leather exterior would indicate. As much as he's embraced the Outlaw schtick, he is actually a varied stylist—a talented singer and songwriter who can't be so easily pinned down. He's recorded more than his share of ballads ("Worth Every Mile," "Nothing Short Of Dying"), and plenty more of his songs are straightahead, no-frills honky tonk ("It's All About To Change,"

Travis Tritt

"Where Corn Don't Grow"). More so than the average hat act, Tritt has also shown his knowledge of, and genuine affection for, country music's heritage. How many of his chart-topping contemporaries, for instance, would choose to cover a '40s-era song by Jimmie Skinner ("Don't Give Your Heart To A Rambler")—let alone even know who Skinner was? So if Tritt's Southern-rock posturing (he's been known to ride out onto stage on a Harley hog), big-man arrangements, and burly, even brassy voice can at times be overbearing, his hillbilly heart and soul are in the right place.

James Travis Tritt was born on 9 February, 1963 in Marietta, Georgia. He sang gospel and picked up guitar as a child, and during the '80s he played the nightclubs around Atlanta. Warner Brothers soon became interested in him, and in 1988 he was signed to the label's Nashville division; he's remained on their roster ever since. His first album, COUNTRY CLUB (1990), included a string of hit songs, with "Help Me Hold On" becoming his first #1. His follow-up, IT'S ALL ABOUT TO CHANGE, contained "The Whiskey Ain't Workin'" (a duet with his friend and frequent collaborator Marty Stuart) and the brash "Here's A Quarter (Call Someone Who Cares)." The album wasn't all thunder and lightning, however, as it also included gentler material like "Nothing Short Of Dying" and "Anymore." The "Whiskey" collaboration won Tritt and Stuart both Grammy and CMA awards, and they embarked on their celebrated "No Hats" tour together during 1991 and 1992. The two have a neo-traditionalist streak and a strong sense of individualism that sometimes runs against the grain of contemporary Nashville—they're sort of the Waylon and Willie of the '90s generation. They've continued working together on and off ever since, including further duets "This One's Gonna Hurt You (For A Long, Long Time)," "Honky Tonkin's What I Do Best," and "Double Trouble."

Since his debut album (which has sold more than three million copies so far), Tritt's earned a place as one of contemporary country music's top male artists. He was honored with the CMA's Horizon Award in 1991, and subsequent albums such as T-R-O-U-B-L-E (1992), TEN FEET TALL AND BULLETPROOF (1994), and THE RESTLESS KIND (1996) all produced hit songs and sold in respectable numbers. His 1998 album, NO MORE LOOKING OVER MY SHOULDER, however, didn't fare so well, which led to Tritt and Warner Brothers parting ways at the end of the decade. By early 2000 he'd inked a new deal with Sony.

⊙ **Greatest Hits—From The Beginning** (1995; Warner Bros.). All Tritt's albums to date have their share of positive and satisfying material, be it hardline honky tonk, tender balladry, or blustery Southern-rock ferment. This collection works fine as a Tritt introduction—plenty of power ballads that you can take or leave, but it also pulls together such rousing titles as "Country Club," "Here's A Quarter," and "Ten Feet Tall And Bulletproof."

⊙ **The Restless Kind** (1996; Warner Bros.). Tritt brings Don Was on board as producer, but the result, while solid, isn't radically different from his previous efforts. "Restless Kind" (penned by Mike Henderson) is proud and strong, "Back Up Against The Wall" is more bad-boy braggadocio, "Double Trouble" is another fun-loving duet with Stuart, and the final song, "Where Corn Don't Grow" is one of Tritt's most memorable, and meaningful, honky-tonk ballads to date.

Shania Twain

"It's easy to rhyme—kids can write rhymes. The hard part is saying what you want to say and making it musical."

—Shania Twain

The biggest new sensation to hit Nashville since the advent of Garth Brooks was a beautiful and spunky singer from Ontario named Shania Twain. For many, Twain represents everything that's wrong with contemporary country music—from the commercial-pop trappings in her arrangements to the sexual flash of her music videos. But she's also a hugely popular singer—her 1995 album THE WOMAN IN ME and its follow-up, COME ON OVER, have each sold more than ten million copies.

Twain didn't just fall into stardom; music had been a part of her life since she was a child singing in taverns around the town of Timmins, Ontario, where she grew up. She was born Eileen Edwards on 28 August, 1965 in Windsor, Ontario. Her father deserted the family when she was a child, and her mother remarried, taking the name Twain. When she was twenty-one, her mother and stepfather were both killed in a car crash, and Shania (a new first name she adopted) was left in charge of her four younger brothers. She made ends meet by singing at a resort until her brothers were old enough to move out on their own. After that she circulated a demo tape, and this led to her signing with Mercury Nashville. Her first album, SHANIA TWAIN, was

© Dan Dion Photography

The irrepressible Shania Twain

Shania was named the CMA's Entertainer of the Year, and at the turn of the millennium, COME ON OVER was still active on the charts, having sold more than sixteen million copies.

⊙ **The Woman In Me** (1995; Mercury). If the idea of jumpy, vaguely country melodies coated with a MTV-styled sheen borrowed from rock'n'roll is an appealing concept, you're in for a treat. For the rest of us, Twain may not be our cup of tea, but at least she's brazenly honest about the commercial nature of her material.

⊙ **Come On Over** (1997; Mercury). The twang is almost entirely missing from her third album, and the lyrics are almost embarrassingly trite on their own ("We're gonna rock this country ... right out of this world"; "If you wanna touch her, ask!"), but packaged in Lange's big productions and presented with Twain's powerful voice these 16 songs obviously made sense to a lot of people.

Clay Walker

released in 1993, but while the music was pretty, any distinctive features were almost entirely lost in the 'young country' shuffle.

The sassy pop style that's become her trademark came about after she met British rock producer Robert John "Mutt" Lange, whose previous clients had included Def Leppard, AC/DC, Michael Bolton, and the Cars. Twain and Lange began writing songs together, and he helped her update and brighten her sound. By the time her second album, THE WOMAN IN ME, hit the stores they were also married. During its first year of release the album spawned a handful of #1 hits and sold millions. It was a fast breakthrough, and amazingly enough it came without tour support—her promotion was based largely on her series of sexy music videos. Her follow-up album, COME ON OVER, raised speculation that she wouldn't be able to maintain such a serious selling streak, but two years later that album, too, had broken the ten million mark. She'd also mounted her first major tour, which met with great success. Two years after its release, COME ON OVER was still producing hit singles such as "That Don't Impress Me Much" and "Man! I Feel Like A Woman!" In 1999

B eaumont, Texas native Clay Walker hit the country scene running in 1993 with two back-to-back #1 hits, "What's It To You" and "Live Until I Die." He wasn't going to win any awards for lyrical content ("I just want to live until I die," he sang, "how 'bout you?"), but he had loads of youthful energy on stage, a golden Texas twang, and, of course, plenty of boyish good looks (even at thirty he still looks like a teenager fresh off the family farm). Born on 19 August, 1969, Walker hails from a corner of Texas that's also been home to George Jones, Mark Chesnutt, and Tracy Byrd. He studied business in college and also regularly played local clubs such as the Neon Armadillo. Producer James Stroud helped Walker secure a contract with Giant Records, which released his self-titled debut album in 1993. The two #1 hits helped the album go platinum, a feat Walker repeated with his next couple of releases, IF I COULD MAKE A LIVING (1994) and HYPNOTIZE THE MOON (1996).

Walker's success came quickly, but he maintained his place in the country charts—and in his fans' eyes—throughout the decade. In 1996, he announced he had multiple sclerosis, yet the disease has so far had little effect on his career. Songs like "She's Always Right," "Cold Hearted," and the title track from his 1999 album LIVE, LAUGH, LOVE showed that, as Walker entered his third decade, he was matur-

Shania Twain • Clay Walker

ing into a consistent and reliable artist. Ultimately, his music is still relatively tame, but to his credit, his Texas bar-room roots remain clearly visible in his voice and songs.

⊙ **Greatest Hits** (1998; Giant). Walker's Top 10 successes are the main event of this 14-song collection, which rounds up highlights from his first four albums, including such #1 biggies as "What's It To You," "Dreaming With My Eyes Open," and "This Woman And This Man." His voice is warm and golden-hued, and while he can get as sappy at times as the next hat-wearing cowboy singer, he also maintains a decent neo-traditionalist style.

Joy Lynn White

J oy Lynn White has a bold, strong voice that exudes depth, complexity, and promise. Her songs proudly mix neo-traditionalism and West Coast spirit with a taste for blues and soul—which places her more in league with gutsy singers like Tracy Nelson or Bonnie Raitt than any of Nashville's recent crop. Maybe that's why she's never climbed very high on the country charts—there's too much going on in her music than a two- or three-minute murmur on an afternoon radio program can accurately convey.

Born on 2 October, 1961 in Turrell, Arkansas and raised in Indiana, White got her start singing in bar bands and recording commercial jingles. In 1982 she moved to Nashville, where she eventually got work as a demo singer. She cut two albums for Columbia in the early '90s, BETWEEN MIDNIGHT & HINDSIGHT and WILD LOVE (1994), but none of her songs even made the country Top 40, and she was eventually dropped. A couple of years later she was picked up by Little Dog, a label affiliated with Mercury but founded and run by Pete Anderson, producer/guitarist with Dwight Yoakam. Anderson produced White's 1997 album THE LUCKY FEW. Country radio, however, still wasn't interested—even though Yoakam showed up to duet with her on "It's Better This Way." LUCKY FEW is a solid record, and critics were quick to sing White's praises; it even made a respectable showing on *Gavin*'s Americana chart. But all that wasn't enough to boost sales and keep the label interested. White is currently without a recording contract, though she does a lot of session singing and plays around the Nashville area.

She also joined singer-guitarist Walter Egan (the very same guy who wrote the Gram Parsons song "Hearts On Fire"), steel player Buddy Cage, and other Nashville musicians in a group called the Brooklyn Cowboys, who released the album DOIN' TIME ON PLANET EARTH, in 1999.

⊙ **The Lucky Few** (1997; Little Dog). White's powerhouse voice is the standout instrument on her third album, produced by Pete Anderson and Dusty Wakeman. Among the consistently strong roster of songs are two titles penned by Lucinda Williams ("I Just Want To See You So Bad," "I Think I Lost It") and three by Jim Lauderdale (his ripe and restless "Try Not To Be So Lonely" is one of the immediate standouts).

Hank Williams III

"He's got something, I think."

—Merle Kilgore

W hat's a boy supposed to do? When he grows up to find that not only his Dad, but his Gandpappy as well, are super-duper country legends, there just seems no way out of at least making a go of it. And so we have Shelton Hank Williams, or just Hank Three for short, the latest incarnation of country music's infamous honky-tonk legacy. Shelton was born the son of Hank Williams, Jr. and his second wife, Gwen; his parents divorced when he was young, and he grew up with his mother and her new husband, having minimal contact with his father. He was initially enamored with hard rock and punk music (the Dead Kennedys, the Misfits), but upon hearing Texas honky tonker Wayne Hancock he began turning back toward country. Hancock's voice and style bears an uncanny resemblance to the first Hank Williams, and this got Shelton thinking that possibilities still existed for making gutsy, down-to-earth country music.

After graduating high school, he played punk rock and took gigs where and when he could get them. During the mid-1990s he participated in a project for Curb Records called THE THREE HANKS that, with the help of digital manipulation, brought together the voices of all three Hank Williamses. This opened doors, helping Hank III win a recording contract of his own, and his debut album, RISIN' OUTLAW, was finally released in 1999. It's a hard-edged honky-tonk affair, showing the influence of Wayne Hancock (Shelton covers three of Hancock's songs), '70s Outlaw hero Waylon Jennings, and grandpa Hank Williams himself. It's not exactly selling in droves, and country radio—for the time being at least—has no interest in giving it any airplay. Even Hank III himself has vehemently talked it down in interviews, saying it sucks because it's overproduced. Yet it's captivating fans of old-school honky tonk, and the fact that it's being at least marginally supported by a major Nashville label seems encouraging—though how long Curb will put up with an artist talking trash about his own record remains to be seen.

As for Shelton himself, he claims he's still interested in blending his punk/metal past with his hard-country legacy, so only time will tell what he comes up with. In the spring of 2000, he embarked on a national tour opening for Beck, and his band featured lead guitarist Duane Denison of the punk outfit Jesus Lizard.

⊙ **Risin' Outlaw** (1999; Curb). Hank III's album doesn't exactly break any new ground, but on a purely visceral level it's loads of fun and it'll sure get your boots tapping in the dirt. The songs and arrangements are steeped in thick, unabashed honky tonk (the southern boogie rock of his father is nowhere to be heard), though in attitude Shelton seems eager to align himself with Outlaw heroes like Waylon Jennings (hence the album title). Or Wayne Hancock, a 1990s outsider whose old-school music is clearly a major influence—after all, Hancock wrote three of the songs and gets a big thank you in the credits.

Trisha Yearwood

"I've had to say to myself, well, if I passed Emmylou Harris on the street, would I be able to hold my head up?"

—Trisha Yearwood

Much of the 'Young Country' hoopla in the early 1990s boom period surrounded the new male singers. But Georgia native Trisha Yearwood cut herself a serious niche among them with the hook-laden song "She's In Love With The Boy," which topped the country charts in 1991. The song's lively country-pop melody and Yearwood's full-bodied voice allowed her to stand out from the growing crowd of hat acts. A little boost of encouragement from Garth Brooks (they were demo singers together in the late '80s), and Yearwood's career has soared ever since.

Make no mistake about it, though: Yearwood clearly stands on the country-pop side of the fence. She occasionally gets twangy with songs like "Wrong Side Of Memphis," and she definitely rocks up her tempos when the need arises ("That's What I Like About You"); her second album, in particular, HEARTS IN ARMOR, is packed with instrumental virtuosity that keeps the South within sight. But the majority of her music, especially her later material, is big-production stuff that leans toward overbaked tenderness (for example, the 1997 single "How Do I Live" from the movie Con Air). Maudlin balladry aside, however, Yearwood's music on the whole is strong and confident—much of it revealing a strong female perspective running through the songs she chooses.

Yearwood was born on 19 September, 1964 in Monticello, Georgia. She attended Belmont College in Nashville, where she was a business major with an eye on music management. An internship on Music Row led to her short but strong career as a demo singer, and it's in this capacity that she first met Brooks, who was also just getting started in the music business. After signing on with Brooks' management company, Yearwood won a recording contract of her own with MCA Records. Her self-titled debut album and the hit song "She's In Love With The Boy" came speeding onto the charts in 1991 and this was followed by a tour with Brooks. Playing large arenas (Brooks was at that time riding high on his NO FENCES success) was quite a leap for Yearwood, still a relatively unknown singer, but she came out on top. All eyes were feasted upon her when she released her second album,

Hank Williams III • Trisha Yearwood

HEARTS IN ARMOR, which must have been painfully stressful, but in the long run it proved even more popular, containing such enduring songs as "Wrong Side Of Memphis" and "Walkaway Joe."

Yearwood has never matched the massive sales of someone like Brooks, but she has always sold respectably enough to keep her label interested. In 1993 she was even the subject of a biography, *Get Hot Or Go Home*, in which author Lisa Guberick explored the various forces vying for control of Yearwood's budding career. Yearwood has produced a steady string of hits ever since, from "The Song Remembers When" in 1993 (the title track to her third album) to "How Do I Live," "In Another's Eyes," and "Perfect Love," three new recordings included on her 1997 hits collection SONGBOOK. In 1997 Yearwood was named Female Vocalist of the Year by the Country Music Association, and her song "How Do I Live" (which also appeared in the movie *Con Air*) won a Grammy. After a break from the spotlight, Yearwood was back in action in the spring of 2000 with REAL LIVE WOMAN, an album she'd been working on since May of 1999. The album features members of Yearwood's road band as well as a guest turn from Emmylou Harris.

⊙ **Trisha Yearwood** (1991; MCA). While she often tends to the sappy side of country, this debut album on the whole contains well-written and well-crafted songs that ring with the genuine twang of steel guitars.

⊙ **Hearts In Armor** (1992; MCA). The Matraca Berg/ Gary Harrison song "Wrong Side Of Memphis" is a

grand, semi-twangy kick-off to what's easily Yearwood's strongest, most musically vibrant collection. "Walkaway Joe" is sympathetic without being entirely sappy, and the O'Kanes song "Oh Lonesome You" gives Yearwood's hot studio band (including guitarist Brent Mason, fiddler Stuart Duncan, and steel player Weldon Myrick) plenty of room to cut loose. Her backing vocalists include Vince Gill, Garth Brooks, and Emmylou Harris.

⊙ **Songbook: A Collection Of Hits** (1997; MCA). If you can step in-between pop dross like "How Do I Live," "Down On My Knees," and "In Another's Eyes" (her hit duet with Garth Brooks) you'll discover a handful of lively and likeable songs as "XXX's And OOO's (An American Girl)," "Wrong Side Of Memphis," "She's In Love With The Boy," and "Perfect Love."

14

Settin' the Woods on Fire: Alternative Country in the 1990s

ike any genre, country music has its mainstream acts and its 'alternatives'—it's just that no one bandied around the term 'alternative country' until recently. That moniker was actually a product of the rock'n'roll world, where 'alternative' had become a musical category and marketing buzzword of its own during the 1980s and '90s, thanks to the success of bands like R.E.M., the Smashing Pumpkins, and Nirvana. Once struggling on independent labels and college radio stations, these and other bands of their ilk rose from nightclub stages to the heights of the *Billboard* charts, turning yesterday's underground into the mainstream of the '90s.

Alternative, however, while it appears to have meaning, is actually a pretty vague term, not easy to wrap a definition around. In country, the genre (if it even deserves such categorization) has come to mean a whole lot of things—from the hearty punk-rock twang of the Waco Brothers and Uncle Tupelo to the Appalachian-styled melodies of Gillian Welch, the Telecaster country of Bakersfield Sound aficionados the Derailers, and the truck-stop honky tonk of Dale Watson. The thread binding them together is that each of these artists has been consistently ignored by the mainstream country music

industry. "If you're not played on mainstream country radio, you're alt.country," wrote *Billboard* columnist Chet Flippo in 1996, and that's as good a definition as any.

Much of the driving force behind this whole alt.country movement was, ironically, punk rock, as a generation of rock'n'rollers who'd grown up on bands like Black Flag, the Clash, the Meat Puppets, and the Replacements began branching out musically, looking backward as well as forward. In the process, many discovered country music. After all, punk rock had been about taking music back down to a grassroots level; you didn't have to know all the chords, you just had to want to play. Similarly, traditional country and old-time folk music was about creative and emotional expression that was simple, honest, and direct. Like punk, its heritage was built on a do-it-yourself spirit, and its history was peopled with singers and pickers who were amazingly expressive musicians despite being a lack of professional training. Looking at it that way, the connection between the two worlds wasn't so tenuous after all.

"To us, punk rock and folk music are very similar," says Jeff Tweedy, co-founder of Uncle Tupelo and, later, Wilco. "Maybe not sonically, but in terms of where it's coming from. It's people who don't feel they've been treated very good, trying to be direct and honest about how they feel."

So while mainstream country artists looked to such acts as the Eagles, Neil Diamond, and even Journey for inspiration, Uncle Tupelo, the **Blood Oranges**, Freakwater, and other indie-rock adventurers began exploring the raw power of traditional country and old-time music—taking their inspiration from Hank Williams, the Louvin Brothers, Merle Haggard, and Loretta Lynn as well as the Minutemen, the Velvet Underground, and the Rolling Stones.

Where There's No Depression

The alternative-country wave that rushed its way through the 1990s more or less started with Uncle Tupelo, a trio of high-school buddies from Illinois. On their 1990 debut album NO DEPRESSION, Tweedy and his singing and songwriting partner Jay Farrar went back and forth between fast, rough-cut punk rock and slower, twangier ballads that were clearly country inspired. The title track was an obscure Carter Family song from the Depression days of the '30s ("I'm going where there's no depression/to a better land that's free from care/I'll leave this world of toil and trouble/my home's in heaven, I'm going there"). Few of the fans who turned up at Uncle Tupelo's club shows likely had any idea who the Carter Family was—they were much better versed in the catalogs of Dinosaur Jr., Hüsker Dü, Mudhoney, and other indie-rock darlings. For that matter, if Uncle Tupelo's fans had known "No Depression" and other of their songs were actually country tunes, they might have scowled in disgust and fled for home. Uncle Tupelo, however, wasn't a country band—they played rock'n'roll and spoke a language of gritty guitars and midwestern angst. Whatever twang they happened to throw in the mix, their punk credentials were solid.

As Uncle Tupelo grew in popularity, an Internet fan club-cum-chat folder popped up on America Online, and it was named No Depression in honor of the band's first album. In 1995, the chat group evolved into a bimonthly magazine, also called No Depression. It featured articles and reviews on all sorts of alternative country music, placing Uncle Tupelo in context with other indie bands and artists such as the Waco Brothers, Blue Mountain, Lucinda Williams, the Blood Oranges, Robbie Fulks, and Go To Blazes. By this point fans were even using the term 'No Depression' to describe the music itself.

No Depression, though, wasn't the only buzz-word. Country singer-songwriter Kevin Welch

had tried to promote the term Western Beat, which he'd picked up in Europe, even titling his 1992 album after it. That term didn't stick, but in trying to coin a catchy moniker for the huge range of music that skirted the edges of country, folk, and rock, Welch was definitely onto something. In 1994, the independent Chicago record label Bloodshot released a CD compilation titled FOR A LIFE OF SIN: A COMPILATION OF INSURGENT CHICAGO COUNTRY, which included groups like Freakwater, the Bottle Rockets, and Robbie Fulks—artists whose take on country was definitely way outside the mainstream. And the college-radio publication *The Gavin Report* began tracking a new radio format they called Americana. These and other terms like alt.country (a reference to the Internet's role in the music's popularization, on the No Depression site as well as a newsgroup called Postcard2), twangcore, the silly y'alternative, and even 'country and Westerberg' (Replacements founder Paul Westerberg is one of indie rock's golden boys) have come to describe a whole world of artists who have a penchant for country but who don't fit into the current Nashville mainstream.

Not the First Time

At the foundation of the No Depression, insurgent, or whatever-y'all-choose-to-call-it movement is music that blurs the lines between country and rock. Not that such a concept is anything new—after all, Elvis Presley's first Sun Records single included a hopped-up cover of Bill Monroe's "Blue Moon Of Kentucky." Elvis and the rockabillies of the 1950s were about giving hillbilly music a rock'n'roll booster shot; a decade later, country-rock artists like Gram Parsons, Gene Clark, and the Nitty Gritty Dirt Band did the opposite, bringing traditional country influences into rock'n'roll circles. Albums like the Byrds' SWEETHEART OF THE RODEO, the Flying Burrito Brothers' THE GILDED PALACE OF SIN, and the Dirt Band's WILL THE CIRCLE BE UNBROKEN gave country music a contemporary spin, opening ears and minds to a world that was for many young people very foreign. "When we came across the Flying Burrito Brothers," noted Tweedy about Parsons' late-'60s band, "it opened a door in a way a lot of other stuff hadn't. It's very much country music, but [Parsons] is writing from his perspective, his world."

Parsons has become the No Depression movement's figurehead—it's "unholy ghost," as the *No Depression* manifesto calls him, "minister to the shotgun wedding of country music and rock'n'roll, long before the Eagles crashed the reception." Neil

Young is another inspiration, as are country singers like Waylon Jennings and Willie Nelson, who attracted more than a few rock'n'rollers during their '70s Outlaw days. What sets Parsons apart, though, is that he was a rock'n'roller with genuine Nashville aspirations; one who, despite his steel-guitar melodies and *Grand Ole Opry* fantasies, was never accepted or embraced by Music Row—always an outsider looking in. It was a fate many '90s-era bands and singer-songwriters could relate to.

And by no means was Uncle Tupelo even the first punk band to incorporate country into their sound. The Southern California punk-rock scene of the '80s, for instance, had been a fertile ground for all sorts of musical experiments and hybridizations. Country-inspired bands like Rank And File, the Beat Farmers, and Lone Justice ('cowpunk' was the unfortunate term of the day) frequently played the same LA clubs, and shared some of the same fans, as roots-rock groups Los Lobos and the Blasters, psycho-blues bands Tex and the Horseheads and the Gun Club, and even hardcore acts like Black Flag and Fear. Gram Parsons-devotees, the Long Ryders, bounced between the cowpunk scene and another sub-genre called the Paisley Underground. There were even a few bona fide country singers, among them Dwight Yoakam, who was just getting started at the time. "It was a fascinating time to be part of the musical community," Yoakam noted a decade later. "We were embraced and able find an audience through the clubs, which were showcasing a very eclectic mix of bands."

All this country and western activity in and around Los Angeles was really little surprise: the music had a long history in the region, from cowboys movie stars to western swing bands to the Telecaster sound popularized by Buck Owens and Tommy Collins. So when Social Distortion sang "Ring Of Fire" and X released a full-on country album, POOR LITTLE CRITTER ON THE ROAD, under the name the Knitters, fans took such moves in their stride.

Back east, another '80s country-punk act, **Jason And The Scorchers**, got its start in of all places, Nashville. This rowdy outfit mixed loud, brash guitar rock with slow-paced, twangy material—and covers of songs by Leon Payne and Bob Dylan thrown in for good measure. They built a solid following from the ground up (and in total defiance of the slick Kenny Rogers and Dolly Parton hits then churning out of Music Row), drawing huge crowds and eventually getting signed to EMI. By the end of the decade, however, they'd pretty much disintegrated, which meant they

missed alt.country's glory days by only a few years. They did regroup and even recorded again, but the results weren't nearly as thrilling.

Never Been This Far Before

When it comes to No Depression and other 1990s version of alt.country, however, the arrow of inspiration still points to Uncle Tupelo, as it was in the wake of their growing popularity that an actual community of alt.country fans coalesced. One of the chief turning points was their much-lauded third album MARCH 16–20, 1992, a pared-down, all-acoustic recording that mixed originals with traditional old-time folk and country songs like "Satan Your Kingdom Must Come Down" and the Louvin Brothers' "Great Atomic Power." With this album, there was no denying that country music was stuck in their soul. Indie-rock fans and critics agreed: the album's back-to-basics sound was entirely refreshing.

Ironically, some of these alt.country bands sounded far more traditional than the average Nashville act on country radio. At the top of that heap was Freakwater, an acoustic group that took much of its inspiration from classic artists like the Carter Family and Bill Monroe. Catherine Irwin and Janet Bean were high-school buddies who learned to harmonize on old-time country tunes at the same time they were hanging out in the punk-rock scene of Louisville, Kentucky. Bean later moved to Chicago and co-founded the indie-rock band Eleventh Dream Day, but she and Irwin maintained a musical partnership and eventually began recording as Freakwater. Their cover songs (from Conway Twitty's "You've Never Been This Far Before" to Bill Monroe's "Little Girl And The Dreadful Snake") as well as Irwin's excellent originals retain an Appalachian allure—though often touching on contemporary class and gender issues as well as traditional country themes like failed love and death.

"Country music has such a great sense of melody," says Bean, "it's not about fancy chords, or how many different parts you can put into a song." She credits her bandmate Irwin—who grew up listening to artists like the Greenbriar Boys, Tammy Wynette, and Bill Monroe—for turning her on to country music. "Because someone I appreciated and respected didn't find [country music] embarrassing, it let me listen to it in a different way." Which is probably how many indie-rock fans felt about it: if onetime punks like Freakwater were into country, it must be OK.

Another Louisville singer and songwriter, **Will Oldham**, working under his own name, that of his band Palace (aka Palace Songs and/or the Palace Brothers), or his sometime alter-ego Bonnie Prince Billy, has also toyed with Appalachian and old-time styles. There's a hillbilly sensibility in much of what Oldham does, but it's by no means 'authentic' in the manner of an old-time revivalist: his voice quivers and cracks, his lyrics are often twisted up and borderline nonsensical, and the instruments wander freely back and forth across the melodies. The first Palace Brothers album, THERE IS NO-ONE WHAT WILL TAKE CARE OF YOU, came off like overindulgent backwoods schtick. Yet it wasn't that simple, as the songs at the same time were haunting and entirely mesmerizing. Such an achievement's not easy to pull off—witness the over-the-top trailer-trash schtick of bands like Southern Culture on the Skids and the Chickasaw Mudpuppies.

Minneapolis band the Jayhawks have a groovy style that mixes jangly melodies with a pastoral, country-informed sound. They first recorded in the '80s, but it was their 1992 album HOLLYWOOD TOWN HALL that broke them out of the indie-rock underground. The group also backed up their friend Joe Henry on his 1992 album SHORT MAN'S ROOM, which is filled with acoustic story-songs that aren't country or folk per se, but nonetheless nod to that heritage. The Jayhawks later shifted to a more pop-oriented sound after the departure of singer, songwriter, and guitarist Mark Olson, who now records with his wife, singer-songwriter Victoria Williams, as the Original Harmony Ridge Creek Dippers.

Bluegrass has also been an inspiration to bands like Austin's the Bad Livers and Boston's the Blood Oranges. The latter group was fronted by singer and mandolinist Jimmy Ryan and mixed his electrified, bluegrass-tinged rock'n'roll with the haunting melodies of singer and bassist **Cheri Knight**. After the band drifted apart in the mid-'90s, Knight has blossomed on her own with a pair of excellent solo albums.

By mid-decade, the indie-rock landscape was scattered with an impressive variety of alt.country bands: the dark and introspective songs of singer-songwriter **Richard Buckner**; the curiously lush sound of the Nashville-based band **Lambchop**; the gutsy, country-tweaked rock'n'roll of **Go To Blazes**; the introspective meanderings of the Scud Mountain Boys; the heat-scarred western rhythms of Calexico. **Whiskeytown** was one of the more blatant Uncle Tupelo-influenced bands, though their second album STRANGER'S ALMANAC showed singer-songwriter Ryan Adams growing up and finding his own voice. As for Uncle Tupelo itself, the band had by 1994 split in two, with Farrar fronting **Son Volt** and Tweedy the more rock'n'roll-oriented **Wilco**.

Alternative to What?

But alternative country was not entirely made up of reformed punks digging for roots and grazing the fields; as it shaped into a genre of sorts, a world unto itself, it came to include artists and singer-songwriters who truly were born-and-bred on country music but had not yet found outlets for their music via standard Nashville channels.

Labels, of course, are problematic: plenty of artists figured alt.country to be a ghetto categorization and ultimately limiting. And for some, it didn't quite seem the right moniker. There's nothing 'alternative' about the kind of country that Dale Watson plays, for instance—it's as straight-up as Hank, Lefty, or Johnny Paycheck. But Music Row, obsessed as it was with hat acts and 'young country' stars, had simply grown too tight and conservative to allow Watson and his music—or that of fellow Texas honky tonker Wayne Hancock, introspective country-folk artist **Iris DeMent**, or spiritualized Texas singer Jimmie Dale Gilmore—a room at the inn. So they were relegated to the sidelines—urban nightclubs instead of the annual George Strait Country Music Festival; the pages of *No Depression* instead of *Country America*; and indie labels like HighTone and Rounder instead of the Nashville divisions of MCA or Sony.

One guy who Nashville didn't quite know how to handle was Steve Earle. He first shot up the charts in the '80s with his debut album GUITAR TOWN, but pretty quickly it was clear Earle wasn't going to play by Nashville's rules. His domain was a widening netherworld between country and rock. But after a bout with drug addiction and a series of albums that distanced him from mainstream country, he's found his niche—on the top of various Americana stations' playlists and running his own record label, E-Squared. Unafraid to speak his mind, and still boasting a substantial fan base, he's become an unofficial spokesman for all things alt.country.

Right alongside Earle on those Americana radio playlists is Lucinda Williams. She's a Southern-bred rock'n'roller with a firm footing in folk, country, and the blues, and her self-titled 1988 album—which contains such beauties as "Side Of The Road" and "Passionate Kisses" (the latter a Grammy winner and a country chart hit for Mary Chapin Carpenter)—is one of the focal points of the alt.country scene.

Dale Watson is no hybrid country-rocker—his music is based firmly in the honky-tonk

The Dead Reckoners: (left to right) Tammy Rogers, Harry Stinson, Kieran Kane, Kevin Welch, Mike Henderson

tradition of Hank, Merle, and Johnny Paycheck, classic singers he's constantly referring to in songs like "Nashville Rash" and "A Real Country Song." Watson's adopted home state of Texas, in fact, is a whole country and western world unto itself. On his 1995 debut album THUNDERSTORMS AND NEON SIGNS, Wayne Hancock sang with a voice as honest and lonesome as that of Hank Williams. **Alejandro Escovedo** comes from a diverse musical background (the Nuns, Rank & File, the True Believers), and today he writes and sings deeply personal songs that are hooked around a moody country vibe. Another Austin-based artist, **Kelly Willis**, was actually signed to MCA for three albums during the early '90s, but since being dropped she's come more into her own, working with the likes of Jay Farrar (of Son Volt) and guitarist Chuck Prophet. The latter was formerly with LA's Green On Red (another of those Paisley Underground bands), and he now lives in San Francisco and writes and plays music with his wife, Stephanie Finch.

Nashville itself is a tough town to crack, as Robbie Fulks attests in his song "Fuck This Town," a true story about the two years he lived there trying to write mainstream country hits for a local publishing company. He eventually fled back to Chicago, where he became a darling on that city's curiously strong alt.country scene (rallied together in part thanks to local label Bloodshot Records).

Five artists who've managed to make their peace with Nashville are Kieren Kane, Kevin Welch, Mike Henderson, Tammy Rogers, and Harry Stinson. All work or have worked with major labels in the past: Kane, Welch, and Henderson had recording contacts themselves; Stinson is a producer and professional backing vocalist; and both Rogers (as a fiddler) and Henderson (as a guitarist) are in-demand session regulars. Feeling the need for stronger creative control of their own material, they decided one night over a bottle of whiskey (it's good to find that cowboy-style business methods are still alive) to form their own record company, Dead Reckoning. Since 1995 the five owner-artists have run it as a collective, touring together, performing on each others' records and sharing business duties. They're not making bucketloads of money this way, but the scheme has managed to keep their music in public view.

"The Nashville way of selling music is through hits," says Kane. "The concept of career development doesn't exist. Whoever sticks to the wall, that's who they go after." Kane recorded a solo album for Atlantic in 1993, FIND MY WAY HOME, but when it failed to sell high and fast enough, he was dropped—and this despite the fact that he'd had bona fide hits as half of the O'Kanes during the mid-'80s. Dead Reckoning, on the other hand, is *all* about artistic development. "Success for me is finishing an album and being able to listen to it and go, 'yeah, it works.'"

In addition to onetime Nashville signees like Kane and Welch, Kelly Willis and Marty Brown—and artists like Chris Knight, BR5-49, and Junior Brown, who exists on the far fringes of the mainstream—the alt.country community has grown to embrace entire generations of older country artists—singers and pickers who've found themselves ignored by the industry ever since 'young country' became the operating buzzword. Johnny Cash's two mid-'90s albums got more attention from the rock press than anywhere else; Merle Haggard and Tom T. Hall were two artists honored with tribute albums, TULARE DUST and REAL respectively, that included singers like Dave Alvin, Iris Dement, Joe Henry, Calexico, and Whiskeytown; and Ralph Stanley, Don Williams, Hank Thompson, Townes Van Zandt, and Hazel

Dickens have all been given feature-length treatments inside the pages of *No Depression* magazine. At the same time that mainstream country radio stations were routinely chucking Merle Haggard and George Jones from their playlists, many alt.country fans were more and more interested in exploring the music's history, its roots. Who's buying those classic country reissue CDs? It's more likely to be an indie-rock fan than a Garth or Reba disciple.

So the question remains, where do things go from here? Can the mainstream open up just enough to accommodate artists like Lucinda Williams, Dale Watson, and Son Volt? Many alt.country artists and fans continue to harbor such hopes, that one of their songs will break on through to the other side, just as Nirvana's "Smells Like

Anthologies

⊙ **Commemorativo: A Tribute To Gram Parsons** (1993; Rhino). This Gram tribute arrived a few years before the No Depression scene co-opted his aura, and it's a nice collection. Highlights include Uncle Tupelo ("Blue Eyes"), Joey Burns and Victoria Williams ("Return Of The Grievous Angel"), Bob Mould and Vic Chesnutt ("Hickory Wind"), and the Mekons ("$1000 Wedding").

⊙ **For A Life Of Sin: A Compilation Of Insurgent Chicago Country** (1994; Bloodshot). This compilation, the first release by Chicago indie label Bloodshot, is the source of the term 'insurgent country.' Includes songs by Jon Langford, Freakwater, Robbie Fulks, the Handsome Family, the Sundowners, and many others—some steeped in tradition but others rough-edged and ready to rumble.

⊙ **Nashville: The Other Side Of The Alley** (1996; Bloodshot). You have to wonder whether the average Music Row executive knows that Lambchop, Paul Burch, Hayseed, Tom House, Greg Garing, and Duane Jarvis even exist. All this CD's artists are or were based in Nashville and show that the town has a surprisingly active music scene operating on its ground level.

⊙ **Rig Rock Deluxe** (1996; Diesel Only/Upstart). Did someone say truck stop? This is the third CD is a series of truck-themed compilations from New York label Diesel Only. Includes quite a diverse crew:

Son Volt, Cheri Knight, Kelly Willis, Red Simpson and Junior Brown, Kay Adams and BR5-49, and the great Buck Owens singing "Will There Be Big Rigs In Heaven."

⊙ **Straight Outta Boone County** (1997; Bloodshot). A tribute to the *Boone County Jamboree*, a radio barn dance that ran over the WLW airwaves out of Cincinnati beginning in 1939. The artists are contemporary (Whiskeytown, Hazeldine, Sally Timms, Waycross) while the songs are period classics by artists who regularly played the Jamboree. A clever concept and good fun at that.

⊙ **Uprooted: The Best Of Roots Country Singer-Songwriters** (1998; Shanachie). Collects songs that fall more on the folk and roots side of the fence sung by Dale Watson, Robbie Fulks, Tom Russell and Iris Dement, Kelly Willis, Wayne Hancock, Paul Burch, and others. Well-sequenced and a beautiful listen.

⊙ **Mile Marker 383** (1999; Starbucks/Universal). Strange as it may seem, one of the strongest and most diverse alt.country CD overviews to date comes courtesy of the heinous corporate enterprise known as the Starbucks Coffee Company. Peter Blackstock of *No Depression* contributes liner notes, and songs run from Lyle Lovett and Lucinda Williams to Cheri Knight and Belfast, Ireland's Bap Kennedy.

Teen Spirit" did in 1991. In the short term, the gates of Music Row probably won't be swinging wide anytime soon. But ultimately there's no reason why such a coup couldn't happen, if the forces were right and the planets properly aligned. That's how new traditionalism came to be in the mid-'80s, when artists like Steve Earle and Lyle Lovett sneaked past the guards at the gate. And if such a breakthrough does happen, well then there'll be another alternative to the alternative cropping up somewhere down the line to give country music a run for its money one more time.

Alternative Country: The Artists

Dave Alvin

Since leaving the Blasters (see separate entry p.265) in 1986 to go his own way, guitarist and songwriter Dave Alvin has added "singing" to his list of credentials and really taken off as an artist. He may have begun with a voice that was limited in range and tone, but over the course of several albums, and many years of playing solo and/or fronting his rock band the Guilty Men, he's learned how to transform those limited resources into a fine, expressive instrument. He can wail, shout, and moan, but he can just as deftly pull things back to barely a whisper, edging his way around the words on acoustic story-songs like "King Of California."

As well as a top-notch guitarist—one of LA's hottest, and few would argue— Alvin was already an impressive song-writer during his Blasters days, having penned much of the group's material including favorites like "Long White Cadillac" and "Border Radio." But where the Blasters stayed focused on gut-level rockabilly, as a solo artist, Alvin's songs branch out stylistically and bring all sorts of blues, country, and folk influences into his rock'n'roll mix. He often focuses on life in Southern California—the kids lighting fireworks in "Fourth Of July," the pavement and cement in "Dry River," and the countless lost souls stuck all over town ("Thirty Dollar Room," "Wanda And Duane"). Alvin even has a

couple of poetry books to his credit, *Any Rough Times Are Now Behind You* and *The Crazy Ones.*

Alvin claims he was nervous and drunk when he recorded his first album, 1987's ROMEO'S ESCAPE (released in England under the title EVERY NIGHT ABOUT THIS TIME), and so the vocals came off rough. Songs like "Fourth Of July" and "Every Night About This Time," however, are real beauties—X covered the former, Joe Ely the latter, and Alvin himself came back to both on his first all-acoustic album, KING OF CALIFORNIA (1994). Before CALIFORNIA, there was BLUE BLVD (1991), and it's this album that finally showed he wasn't just a roots-rock spin-off act, but actually an insightful singer-songwriter with a distinct point of view. Songs like "Haley's Comet" (about the death of Bill Haley) and the title track—not to mention "Dry River," one of his finest creations—

STEPHEN W SMITH

Dave Alvin

Dave Alvin

jump out with bold, gritty imagery. MUSEUM OF HEART (1993) followed, and then came KING OF CALIFORNIA, on which he stripped away the noise, turned down the guitars, and boldly let his country-inflected voice and songs stand on their own. His 1996 album INTERSTATE CITY was a live and loud collection that showed off his hot touring band, the Guilty Men. But he seems increasingly enamored these days with the stripped-down format, and so in 1998 he turned out yet another excellent acoustic collection, BLACK JACK DAVID.

⊙ **Blue Blvd** (1991; HighTone). Alvin's personal masterpiece starts with a lonely downtown drive at 3 AM, brings us face-to-face with a rock'n'roll legend during his sad, final days ("Haley's Comet"), and spins further tales of doomed relationships, dying soldiers, riverbeds that have been paved with cement ("I used to stand in that dry river and dream that I was soaking wet"). It's got guts and loads of urban soul, and the songs will last long into the night and many nights to come.

⊙ **King Of California** (1994; HighTone). On his first all-acoustic collection, Alvin revisits songs from his past ("Fourth Of July," "Border Radio," "Every Night About This Time") as well as a few covers (Tom Russell's "Blue Wing") and several new titles. By this point he's a confident, seasoned singer.

⊙ **Black Jack David** (1998; HighTone). The title track is a traditional number that's been traced back to medieval days (see Nick Tosches' book *Country*). The album is a rich and varied lot, from vivid story songs like "California Snow" (co-written with Tom Russell) and "1968" (with Chris Gaffney) to the sad and lonely "From A Kitchen Table."

Blood Oranges

The Boston-based Blood Oranges were country and punk-rock influences before No Depression ever became an indie-rock craze. The band was founded by Jimmy Ryan, a mandolinist and bluegrass aficionado who'd previously picked at festivals and played in an assortment of rock and country bands, including the new wave group Decentz in Burlington, Vermont. Much of the Blood Oranges' music showed Ryan's bluegrass influence—quick-paced melodies, prominent leads on his solid-body electric mandolin, and his reedy tenor voice. But all that was balanced out on one side by a rock'n'roll energy that could get loud and fuzzy, and on the other by the melancholic songwriting and beautiful, mournful singing of bassist Cheri Knight. Knight creations such as "The Crying Tree," "All The Way Down," and "Shadow Of You" ring with autumnal sadness and deep, spiritual longing, and they're some of the group's most memorable works.

Ryan, Knight, guitarist Mark Spencer and drummer Ron Ward formed the Blood Oranges in the late 1980s (drummer Keith Levreault joined in 1991). They played around Boston and up and down the East Coast, and in 1990 released their debut album, CORN RIVER. The follow-up was only a five-song EP, LONE GREEN VALLEY, but it hinted at the greatness that arrived two years later with THE CRYING TREE. Featuring some of their finest songs, THE CRYING TREE is definitely a crowning achievement not only of the band's shortlived career, but of the alt.country scene as a whole. It was produced by guitarist Eric "Roscoe" Ambel, who became something of an alt.country guru for his work with the Oranges as well as Go To Blazes, Blue Mountain, and the Bottle Rockets, among others.

The Oranges split up in 1995, partly due to the bandmembers' various outside projects. Ryan had formed the acoustic bluegrass outfit the Beacon Hill Billies in 1991 with John McGann, and they released three records on East Side Digital. Later Ryan, Spencer, and Levreault hooked up again and recorded a CD under the band name Wooden Leg. The group has since toured with a new line-up. Ryan also keeps busy playing with the Celtic band Sunday's Well and the Pale Brothers, a collaboration with Mark Sandman of Morphine. Spencer, who also produced the debut Wooden Leg CD, had been keeping busy himself, playing guitar with singer-songwriter Freedy Johnston, among others. As for Knight, she's blossomed and branched out as a strong singer, songwriter, and guitarist, releasing a couple of excellent solo albums.

⊙ **Corn River** (1990; East Side Digital). An impressive debut that shows the band finding their groove in a mix of lively bluegrass, unrepentant rock'n'roll and sad-eyed country.

⊙ **Lone Green Valley** (1992; East Side Digital). Short, but very worthwhile, the standout track on this 5-song EP is the Knight song "All The Way Down," which is one of the high points of the band's entire catalog.

⊙ **The Crying Tree** (1994; East Side Digital). This was the culmination of the band's short career, showing a full-bodied maturity in the singing, playing, and songwriting. Songs like "Hinges" and "Hell's Half Acre" are fired up and verging on unruly, while ballads like "Bridges" (written and sung by Spencer) and "Shine" are equally impressive. The heartstoppingly beautiful title track, written and sung by Knight, is a masterpiece.

Blue Mountain

Oxford, Mississippi is a modest college town soaked in southern tradition, surrounded by gently rolling countryside and frequently blanketed by thick, southern humidity. It's the heart and soul of Faulkner country, where the famous author grew up and then wrote many of his classic novels. This setting, both literary and pastoral, is also home to Blue Mountain, a country-informed rock'n'roll band that's been making music there since forming in 1993. The group is centered around the husband and wife team of singer-guitarist Cary Hudson and bassist Laurie Stirratt, both of whom had previously played with Laurie's twin brother John Stirratt (now bassist with Wilco) in a punk band called the Hilltops. Drummer Matt Brennan joined Cary and Laurie for Blue Mountain's recording debut, a self-titled album released on their own label.

Blue Mountain next signed with the punk label Roadrunner, which released their second record, DOG DAYS, in 1995. Produced by Eric Ambel (Bottle Rockets, Blood Oranges), the project featured new drummer Frank Coutch. It was a fairly laid-back affair, with a southern country flavor spread all over its fourteen songs, but at the same time the band was not afraid to let the guitars ring forth with gusto. HOMEGROWN followed in 1997, a self-produced album recorded at a local studio. Cary and Laurie also started their own label, Black Dog, which reissued the Hilltops' 1991 album BIG BLACK RIVER as well as new projects by bands such as the Gimme Caps (John Stirratt's side project), Marah (the brilliant LET'S CUT THE CRAP AND HOOK UP LATER ON TONIGHT), and the Continental Drifters. Blue Mountain's fourth album, TALES OF A TRAVELER (1999), was produced by Dan Baird, formerly of the Georgia Satellites.

⊙ **Dog Days** (1995; Roadrunner). This is a pleasant, mesmerizing album that moves in long, loose-limbed strides. A mixture of acoustic and electric guitars colors the edges, generating enough heat to steam the windows, but Hudson's voice has a cool tone and an undeniably country twang, and the overall mood is casual and unhurried.

Bottle Rockets

The Bottle Rockets make a big stink about the fact that they hail from Festus, Missouri, a small Mississippi River town just south of St Louis. And with a name like Festus, why shouldn't they play it up? It sure adds color—the small-town variety—to their hard-boogie, guitar-driven, country-informed rock'n'roll sound. There's as much Lynyrd Skynyrd and Bad Company in their music as Buck Owens or Merle Haggard. But for all the southern swagger that singer, guitarist and chief songwriter Brian Henneman may conjure from the stage, his songs are worlds away from the average redneck party anthem. Instead of embracing the Confederate flag—an emblem splattered across pickup truck windows and bumpers all over the South—Henneman confronts its racist undertones in "Wave That Flag" ("Maybe being a rebel ain't no big deal/But if somebody owned your ass, how would you feel?"). He paints a humorous yet ultimately sobering blue-collar picture in "Sunday Sports," and takes a jab at the "angry fat man on the radio" (Rush Limbaugh, we presume) on the neo-Guthrie folksong "Welfare Music." Don't presume, however, that Henneman and his bandmates are averse to having a good loud time. Check out "Radar Gun," a thundering, metallic blast of a song about overeager cops and their shiny new toys.

The Bottle Rockets formed in 1992 out of a Missouri-based punk-rock band called Chicken Truck that featured Henneman, drummer Mark Ortmann, guitarist Tom Parr, and bassist Robert Parr. When Chicken Truck more or less dissolved, Henneman took a job on the road crew with Uncle Tupelo; that band's two singer-songwriters, Jeff Tweedy and Jay Farrar, had also grown up in a small town just outside of St Louis. Henneman sometimes played with Tupelo as well, and he was a featured instrumentalist on Tupelo's album MARCH 16-20, 1992. With the help of Tweedy and Farrar he put together a demo tape and landed a record deal with the (once proud but now defunct) indie label East Side Digital. He brought Ortmann and Tom Parr back on board and added new bassist Tom Ray. Calling themselves the Bottle Rockets, they cut their self-titled debut album in 1993. It won instant attention for its rurally driven songs that married a thick country sensibility with loud guitars and insightful lyrics. The Rockets' follow-up, THE BROOKLYN SIDE (1994), was even stronger—louder all in the right places, but overall more musically varied and betraying a far more confident approach.

Fueled by Uncle Tupelo's popularity and the growing attention to anything alt.country, Atlantic signed the Bottle Rockets and reissued the THE BROOKLYN SIDE. Affiliation with a major label, however, wasn't exactly a blessing for the band. The Bottle Rockets churned out a third album, 24 HOURS A DAY, and while it was technically released in 1997, Atlantic put very little energy into promoting it. Unless you were paying close attention to the band's every move, you'd never have known it even existed. A year later the Rockets parted ways with Atlantic and signed with Texas-based Doolittle. They released LEFTOVERS in 1998, a seven-song EP of previous recordings that didn't make the 24 HOURS A DAY album. One of the songs on that album, "Get Down River," also featured in the PBS television series *River Of Song*, about music along the Mississippi River (a companion CD was also issued by Smithsonian Folkways). In 1999 came BRAND NEW YEAR, a collection of all new Bottle Rockets recordings. Like THE BROOKLYN SIDE, it was produced by Eric "Roscoe" Ambel (Blood Oranges, Go To Blazes), and it featured the band's new bassist, Robert Kearns.

⊙ **The Brooklyn Side** (1994; East Side Digital; reissued 1995; Atlantic). The folkish strains of "Welfare Music" fit and the gentle "Pot Of Gold" fit just fine beside the thunder of "Radar Gun" and "Sunday Sports." Henneman takes redneck cops, cheap cars, conservative radio hosts and television sports programs to task, but he and the band have a blast busting out some of the burliest southern boogie rock this side of Macon, Georgia.

Richard Buckner

For a few short years in the 1990s, Richard Buckner worked his way from playing for tips on San Francisco streets to recording a couple of albums for MCA, touring the country many times over, and earning rave reviews as one of the most creative singer-songwriters working the fringes of the alt.country and indie-rock circuits. Buckner writes and sings moody, introspective and often dark songs that frequently invite comparisons to the late, great Townes Van Zandt, one of his musical heroes. But he's also a restless soul who's rarely, it seems, satisfied with the plate in front of him and always searching for a different sound or approach. This has led him from the folkish, pedal-steel-infused songs of his debut album, BLOOMED, through the more adventurous rhythms and sonic textures that marked his next two releases, DEVOTION & DOUBT and SINCE.

Buckner was born in 1964 in Fresno, California, but he grew up in various towns up and down the San Joaquin Valley. He studied English at Chico State University, then during his mid-twenties set out for Atlanta, Georgia. He was looking for a change of pace, and it's there that his songwriting began to take real shape. Returning to California, he settled in San Francisco. He first strummed and sang on the streets, but before long he was playing local clubs both as a solo artist and with a band he formed, the Doubters. His sound was steeped in Texas-style country and folk music—Butch Hancock was not only an influence but also a fan—so it made sense that Buckner traveled to Lubbock, Texas to record BLOOMED, with pedal-steel ace Lloyd Maines spinning the knobs. It was largely a solo affair, recorded quickly (four days) and with a few local musicians Maines pulled in to help out. Originally released in 1994 on Germany's Glitterhouse, the Texas label Dejadisc picked it up (five years later it was reissued again by Rykodisc with five extra tracks).

During the next couple of years, Buckner's life saw some major changes. He'd married before BLOOMED, and after touring to support the album he and his wife removed themselves from the spotlight to an isolated cabin on an Indian reservation near Bellingham, Washington. It's here, however, that their marriage fell apart, and Buckner fell into a state of haunted darkness and despair. Personal trauma aside, the experience (says Buckner) proved fertile ground for his songwriting, and enabled him to emerge with a chunk of the songs for his second album, DEVOTION & DOUBT. He never speaks of divorce directly, but you can hear it in-between the lyrics, as more than one song deals with people coming undone—drifting apart, sinking and dragging bottom.

For DEVOTION & DOUBT, Buckner opted for an entirely new approach to his debut. He was now signed to MCA, and the label gave him a surprising amount of freedom and resources to do what he wanted. Buckner and his new producer, J.D. Foster, hired Joey Burns and John Convertino, who are the rhythm section of Tucson, Arizona's Giant Sand and also the co-leaders of their own desert-brewed outfit, Calexico. Buckner had been enamored with

Richard Buckner

Giant Sand's 1994 album GLUM, and he'd wanted to work with Burns and Convertino since hearing it. The resulting collaboration led to an album that's both haunting and adventurous, unafraid to explore the dark little corners and toy with the unknown. It's quiet and sombre, but it's also rich with sonic texture—from a chord organ and a Mexican *vihuela* right down to a cricket that happened to be in the studio during one song ("On Travelling").

Buckner spent the next year more or less on the road, touring to publicize DEVOTION & DOUBT. During this time he wrote more songs that eventually wound up on his third album, SINCE. Again he

Richard Buckner, San Francisco, 1998

worked with producer J.D. Foster, and guest musicians this time included Syd Straw and John MacEntire (Tortoise). SINCE is another subtle but multilayered adventure in words, rhythm, texture, and melody—intriguing, though Buckner's label, MCA, didn't quite see it that way. Perhaps wondering what happened to the alt.country honor student they thought they'd signed—anything 'country' in Buckner's music had dissipated into something that was no longer so easy to categorize—the label finally dropped him in 1999. Which is perhaps just as well for both parties. Buckner's next project is a song cycle based on the *Spoon River Anthology*, a collection of poems and monologues written by Edgar Lee Masters. He plans to record and release the album on a small Arizona label, Convent, some time in 2000. As for his once-tumultuous personal life? Things have since settled down. He's now remarried and living in Edmonton, Alberta.

⊙ **Bloomed** (1995; Dejadisc; reissued 1999; Rykodisc). Much of the music on Buckner's debut album is quiet and sad, his songs tastefully flavored with pedal steel, mandolin, fiddle and accordion, thanks to the keen ears of producer Lloyd Maines. Coming back to this album after several years, what's interesting is that—whether Buckner's singing about a "Gauzy Dress In The Sun" or the sadness of love disappeared in "Blue And Wonder"—there's a poetic innocence, an almost idealistic quest for truth and beauty, that shows through and will likely never be repeated.

⊙ **Devotion & Doubt** (1997; MCA). Emotional interrogation and a haunting quiet pervade much of this album, about half of which was written fresh in the wake of Buckner's marital break-up. "He said, 'I'll pull you down'/She said, 'Yeah, I know you will,'" he sings in the very first song, "Pull." You can hear the midnight winds shifting and the hallucinations stepping out of the darkness. It's also an adventure, however, in the texture of sound and the playfulness of rhythm.

⊙ **Since** (1998; MCA). You could say that SINCE is Buckner's most 'rock' sounding record to date, but it's also the kind of album that won't let itself be pinned down too easily. At times just an acoustic guitar accompanies Buckner's mournful and sometimes fragile voice, while on other songs the drums and the guitars rumble forward with urgency. Unraveling this one may take some time, but the ground rule seems to be that nothing is as straightforward as it seems.

Paul Burch

One of a new generation of country artists based in Nashville yet working well outside the mainstream, Paul Burch has genuine feel for the traditional side of the music. His voice is bright, warm, and clear, and his acoustic-based arrangements are seasoned liberally with fiddle and pedal steel. As well as the classic honky tonk and western swing clearly running through his veins—he does a great job with Webb Pierce's "Drifting Texas Sand"—his music really shows a wide range of influences, from Buck Owens to the Beatles.

Burch was born on 29 January, 1966 in Washington, DC. His parents were art and music lovers, and the family spent some years living on the Arthur Godfrey Farm, an artists' compound near DC. After attending Purdue University Burch moved to Boston, where he started playing professionally, and then in 1994 he headed for Nashville. He first gained notoriety as part of a revitalized Nashville music scene that also included Greg Garing and BR5-49. Burch began playing regular gigs in Garing's band at Tootsie's Orchid Lounge, and though the group attracted lots of attention and seemed to be onto something with their traditional country sound, it didn't last. After several months Burch and Garing parted ways.

Hooking up with steel player Paul Niehaus (who'd also played in Garing's band), the two began performing on their own and also as members of Lambchop, a loose and sprawling Nashville-based group. From there Burch formed his own group, the WPA Ballclub (which includes members of Lambchop). His first record, PAN AMERICAN FLASH, was initially released on the French label Dixiefrog Records; Checkered Past picked it up and released it in the States, followed soon after by his fine sophomore effort, WIRE TO WIRE. Burch plays guitar, drums, and vibraphone on his own records; he also continues to play the vibes as a member of Lambchop. His third album with the WPA Ballclub, BLUE NOTES, was scheduled for release by Merge Records in the summer of 2000. Most recently, he's been writing songs based on a novel by Tony Earley, *Jim The Boy*.

⊙ **Wire To Wire** (1998; Checkered Past). The overall mood on Burch's second album is bright and peppy, even when the tempo is gentle and the subject matter down and out (as on "Borrowed And Broke"). Fun, well-crafted and unflashy, the album shows Burch is a talent to keep you eyes on.

Iris DeMent

"Iris has a voice I like a whole lot."

—John Prine

Iris DeMent has a warm, warbly voice and an inviting country-folk style that has more in common with the old-time songs of the Carter Family than any contemporary Nashville artists. In an era that worships music videos and flashy production work, DeMent's music is immediately refreshing, which partly explains why she won acclaim almost immediately after her 1992 debut album, INFAMOUS ANGEL, was released. The chief reason for her success, however, is that she's a heartfelt songwriter with a simple, honest approach who's not afraid to speak her mind and take a few chances when she feels like it. Many of her songs have an autobiographical nature, bringing to life her close-knit family, their small-town values, their love of music and their deep religious beliefs. DeMent grew up attending church (the Assemblies of God) often several times a week, but by the age of sixteen she had become disillusioned with organized religion and turned her back on it for good. Old-time gospel music, however, was so much a part of her childhood that it couldn't help but manifest itself in her music, giving it a sincerity that could never have been manufactured. This quality shows through no matter what her subject, be it the simple day-to-day lifestyles of "Our Town," the lonely Idaho housewife in "Easy's Getting Harder Every Day," or the crying fathers, mothers and sons in the disturbing "Wall In Washington."

DeMent wrote extensive liner notes to INFAMOUS ANGEL that describe her personal background, the knowledge of which adds a rich character to the songs. She was born on 5 January, 1961 in Paragould, Arkansas. Her parents were farmers, and besides taking their religion very seriously, they also instilled a love of music in their children (Iris was the youngest of fourteen). They listened to country artists like Johnny Cash and Loretta Lynn (although usually they only bought their gospel releases) and sang regularly around the house and in church. DeMent has forever cherished this experience. "No voice has inspired me more than my mother's," she proclaimed on INFAMOUS ANGEL; she even featured her mother, Flora Mae DeMent, on the final track, "Higher Ground."

Iris did most of her growing up in Southern California, where the family moved when she was only three. Hard times had struck, and they needed to uproot from their corner of northeast Arkansas (a region her family had lived in for generation) to find work. At the age of seventeen, Iris left home, got her GED (the equivalency of a high school diploma), and worked a series of odd jobs. She eventually landed in Topeka, Kansas, where she wrote her first song at the age of twenty-five. She began focusing more intensely on music; she

MARK TUCKER

Iris DeMent

of her songs, "No Time To Cry," on his album 1996. DeMent fans seemed to come from all corners: Pop singer Natalie Merchant sang DeMent's song "Let The Mystery Be" on her *MTV Unplugged* showcase (with David Byrne as her duet partner), and "Our Town" was featured on the final episode of the TV show *Northern Exposure*.

For her third album, THE WAY I SHOULD, DeMent wanted a different sound, so she hired producer Randy Scruggs (son of banjo legend Earl Scruggs, who plays on the record) and put together an album that at times feels like rock—she wasn't afraid of electric guitars or even drums. It also showed that she was just as adept at speaking her mind on political as well as personal issues. "Wasteland Of The Free," in particular, angrily railed against modern America's conservative agenda and corporate-infected lifestyle. It was a bold step, and DeMent took some flack for it—though most fans identified with her sentiments completely, just as they had with "Our Town," "Childhood Memories," or "Mama's Opry." Her feelings and opinions were, after all, as honest and genuine as they'd ever been.

moved to Kansas City, learned guitar, wrote more songs and gained enough courage to start singing in public, initially just at open-mike nights at local venues. Sometime around 1990 she moved to Nashville, hoping to give her songs more exposure. The strategy worked. She signed with Philo, a division of Rounder that also was home to Nanci Griffith at the time, and released INFAMOUS ANGEL in 1992.

The album met with almost immediate critical acclaim, enough to attract Warner Brothers, which signed DeMent a year later and reissued her debut. By this point she'd moved back to Kansas City to be with her boyfriend, Elmer; soon afterwards the two were married. John Prine was an early fan and frequently praised her work, and she toured with Nanci Griffith, an opportunity that helped increase her fan base. In 1994 she released MY LIFE, another inspiring and moving collection dedicated to her father that like its predecessor featured rich, acoustic arrangements. That year Iris also sang "Big City" on the Merle Haggard tribute album TULARE DUST, and Merle himself was impressed. He not only talked about her in interviews, but cut one

Since the release of her third album, DeMent has been touring regularly, and she's also made quite a few guest appearances on various recording projects. Among them are the Jimmie Rodgers and Tom T. Hall tribute albums, a couple of Tom Russell releases, Steve Earle and the Del McCoury Band's THE MOUNTAIN, and John Prine's IN SPITE OF OURSELVES. She's also working on another collection of her own.

⊙ **Infamous Angel** (1992; Philo; reissued 1993; Warner Bros.). Family, love, small-town values and organized religion are among the subjects on DeMent's charming and entirely moving debut. "Mama's Opry" tells of her mother's love of country music's greatest radio program, while "Let The Mystery Be" gently pushes away the hardline religious "rules" she grew up with.

⊙ **My Life** (1994; Warner Bros.). "No Time To Cry" (about the death of her father) and "Easy's Getting Harder Every Day" (about a fictional housewife whose

Iris DeMent

life has become routine and sad) are two of DeMent's all-time masterpieces, and they give this powerful collection a deep, quietly introspective tone. DeMent may have been writing songs less than ten years at this point, but she reaches places few artists do in a lifetime.

⊙ **The Way I Should** (1996; Warner Bros.). The production is a leap in a new direction—much more plugged in—and it may take stalwart folk fans by surprise. As will DeMent's bold, haunting, and at times angry lyrics on songs like "Wall In Washington" (about the Vietnam veterans' memorial) and "Wasteland Of The Free." In similar fashion, she spits out the words on "I'll Take My Sorrow Straight," her most country-sounding song to date. But her desire to broaden her sound and approach is exactly what makes DeMent's music so strong and genuine. Dig deep, there's a lot here.

The Derailers

T his straight-up country revival band has a sincere sound that's part rockabilly, part swing and part honky-tonk. The bandmembers are big fans of Buck, Merle, and the Bakersfield sound, which is immediately obvious in their high-strung, Telecaster-driven melodies and the friendly twang of their two-part harmonies. They also know how to get a crowd out onto the dance floor. The Derailers are based out of Austin, Texas, but have their roots in Portland, Oregon, where vocalist/guitarist Tony Villanueva and lead guitarist Brian Hofeldt grew up and first played music together. After moving to Texas in 1993, they officially formed the Derailers. A strong regional following and a 1995 album on local label Freedom (LIVE TRACKS) led to their signing with Watermelon Records and the release of the acclaimed JACKPOT a year later. When Watermelon entered into a partnership with Sire, the Derailers remained on the roster; this meant that their 1997, REVERB DELUXE, enjoyed greater distribution and gained them more widespread recognition. In 1999 they released FULL WESTERN DRESS, another Telecaster-savvy collection that not only referenced vintage rockabilly and the Bakersfield sound all over again, but this time featured guest vocals from Buck Owens himself.

⊙ **Jackpot** (1996; Watermelon). The Buck Owens comparisons hit you immediately and often on the band's second album, produced by Dave Alvin. Their honky-tonk sound is reverent, refreshing and fun— can't argue with that—but in the long run the songs lack distinction.

⊙ **Reverb Deluxe** (1997; Sire/Watermelon). Again a fine honky-tonk effort, the group widening their scope slightly with the easygoing ballad "Can't Stop A Train" (something they pull off quite well), the Rick Nelson-inspired "Pawnshop Wedding Rings," and the fiddle-heavy "I Don't Believe I'll Fall In Love (Today)."

Alejandro Escovedo

"I like those contrasts, you know. Dissonance, and beauty, and melody, and dissonance."

—Alejandro Escovedo

C oming from a large and very musical family, it's no wonder that Alejandro Escovedo has spent his lifetime exploring various styles and shapes of music—from punk in the 1970s (the Nuns) to country (Rank & File) and roots rock (True Believers) in the '80s and, more recently, a deep and dark blend of acoustic folk and guitar-driven rock'n'roll released (beginning with 1992's GRAVITY) under just his own name. His acoustic-driven Alejandro Escovedo Orchestra has played around his current home town of Austin, Texas since the late '80s; when he goes on the road, however, he often strips his accompaniment down to a minimum. Whatever the line-up, it's the contrast between electric guitars and strings (usually cello and violin) that's at the center of his sound. In terms of subject matter, Alejandro's songs can get intense and almost painfully introspective, but it's this very quality that drives him—he's not out to write the great three-minute rock'n'roll classic or a country tune with a radio-friendly melodic hook. Escovedo is not to everyone's taste—his arrangements and especially his lyrics can take on a lofty air—but when he strikes, he hits deep. The editors of *No Depression* magazine obviously felt it; in 1998 they honored Escovedo with the weighty title "Artist of the Decade."

Escovedo was born on 10 January, 1951 in San Antonio, Texas. There were twelve children in his family, and several of them pursued music professionally—most notably his half-brother Pete Escovedo, who played drums with Santana and later became a key figure on the Latin jazz scene in the San Francisco Bay Area (Pete's daughter, by the way, is pop star Sheila E.). Alejandro grew up first in Texas and then Southern California, where he was turned onto punk rock. He formed the Nuns in San Francisco in the mid-'70s, then in 1979 he joined Chip and Tony Kinman (formerly of the Dils) in the cowpunk band Rank & File. They settled in Austin and eventually signed to the LA punk label Slash, which placed them in league with fellow roots-oriented outfits such as the Blasters, the Long Ryders, and Lone Justice.

Rank & File, however, was more the Kinmans' creation; Escovedo played on the group's 1982 debut album, SUNDOWN, before quitting to pursue his own interests. The Kinmans cut two more Rank & File albums without him, then formed the experimental pop outfit Blackbird and, more recently, the cool, western-tinged Cowboy Nation. As for Escovedo, he turned around and founded the True Believers with his guitarist brother, Javier. Together with third guitarist Jon Dee Graham, the group signed with EMI and cut its debut album, TRUE BELIEVERS, in 1985, with legendary Memphis producer Jim Dickinson at the helm. They began winning a substantial following

around Austin, but their fire and energy was quashed when their record company failed to release their follow-up album. Spirit broken, they finally split up in 1988. Alejandro began playing with the loud and loose garage-rock band Buick MacKane, but he also started doing solo shows around Austin for the first time. He experimented with a quieter, folky style, eventually bringing cello and violin into the mix alongside electric guitars and drums. For special occasions he assembled what he called the Alejandro Escovedo Orchestra, a group that ranged as high as thirteen members.

Escovedo's first solo record, GRAVITY, was released in 1992 by the Texas label Watermelon. Much of the attention he received for GRAVITY, however, centered around the intensity of its subject matter—and, more specifically, on a recent tragedy in Escovedo's life. His relationship with his wife and longtime companion, Bobbie Levie, had been deteriorating for some time; the couple separated, and in 1991 Bobbie killed herself, which thrust heavy and blatant meaning on Escovedo songs like "She Doesn't Live Here Anymore," "Last To Know," and "Tell Me Why." The songs weren't necessarily all about her suicide, but it was unavoidable that his relationship with Bobbie rang through much of that album and Escovedo's 1993 follow-up, 13 YEARS.

TODD WOLFSON

He didn't sell a huge amount of records, but, fueled by positive response to his songs and live shows, Escovedo's solo career did gain momentum. He signed to Rykodisc and released his third album, WITH THESE HANDS, in 1996; Willie Nelson even added vocals on the song "Nickel And A Spoon." Rykodisc had also issued a True Believers' CD, HARD ROAD (1994), which included that group's debut album along with the follow-up that had been languishing in obscurity. In 1997 Rykodisc also issued a Buick MacKane CD, THE PAWN SHOP YEARS. As a solo artist, however, Escovedo jumped over to Bloodshot. That Chicago indie label released the acclaimed live album MORE MILES THAN MONEY in 1998, followed by BOURBONITIS BLUES a year later.

Alejandro Escovedo

The latter includes Escovedo originals like "I Was Drunk" along with covers such as Lou Reed's "Pale Blue Eyes," the Gun Club's "Sex Beat," and Jimmie Rodgers' "California Blues."

⊙ **Gravity** (1992; Watermelon). This album really is the foundation of Escovedo's solo career, containing such deep, dark, and at times devastating material as "Gravity/Falling Down Again" (still a centerpiece of his live shows), "Broken Bottle," "Five Hearts Breaking," "Last To Know," and "Paradise." Escovedo's poetic soul is out in the open, and the arrangements—shifting between electric and acoustic—maintain a refreshing simplicity.

⊙ **More Miles Than Money: Live 1994–1996** (1998; Bloodshot). Escovedo is more seasoned as a solo artist by this point, and while he sounds comfortable and confident, the arrangements (guitars, strings, bass and drums) are still simple and low-key. The live recordings are taken from various locations, and there's minimal crowd noise or even applause, which allows the songs more room to breathe. It's also a chance to hear him shift from the quiet of a song like "Broken Bottle" into the rock'n'roll fury of "I Wanna Be Your Dog," a concert favorite of his.

Freakwater

> "If I'd gone to seventh grade and carried my Statler Brothers tapes with me, I probably would have been ostracized."
>
> —Janet Bean

Since forming in the 1980s, Freakwater has made some of the most traditional-sounding acoustic music in or out of Nashville. That much of it has been original material written and recorded by a couple of punk-rock gals from Louisville, Kentucky is ironic—though not entirely surprising. While mainstream country stars busied themselves rifling through the Eagles catalog for inspiration, Catherine Irwin and Janet Bean were harmonizing on songs by Bill Monroe, the Louvin Brothers, and the Carter Family. In the process they've helped open the eyes of a new generation of indie-rock fans—who make up their core audience despite material that's old-time and acoustic—to the wide world of traditional country music. It's not that huge a leap, after all: the back-to-basics nature of Freakwater's country sound, and their fascination with themes of death and unrequited

love, have built-in appeal to punks and rock-'n'rollers seeking wider musical horizons.

Irwin and Bean knew each other from their high school days growing up in Louisville, Kentucky, and it's there during the '80s, amidst a burgeoning punk-rock scene, that they first began singing together. From the start, through, it was never a fulltime musical venture. For one thing, Bean moved to Chicago in 1989, where she and her husband, Rick Rizzo, pursued their indie-rock dreams with their band Eleventh Dream Day. But the distance between the two women didn't stop Bean and Irwin from maintaining their musical relationship.

Bringing bassist David Gay on board, Freakwater cut its eponymous first record in 1989 for Amoeba, a tiny (and now defunct) label that was also home to Eleventh Dream Day's early albums. That record and its follow-up, 1991's DANCING UNDER WATER, had a tentative feeling, as Irwin and Bean found their footing as singers and songwriters. UNDER WATER sported only five Irwin originals, but it did include interesting cover songs such as Bill Monroe's "Little Girl And The Dreadful Snake" and the Stanley Brothers classic "Rank Strangers" that betrayed Freakwater's leanings toward the dark and strange side of country music—something they've nurtured ever since. Their third album, FEELS LIKE THE THIRD TIME, appeared on the Chicago indie label Thrill Jockey and won them wider attention. That and its follow-up, OLD PAINT, revealed a newfound confidence in both singing and songwriting. "My Old Drunk Friend," "Waitress Song," and the shiveringly vivid suicide song "Gone To Stay" were respectful of classic Appalachian and hillbilly styles, yet at the same time they spoke a

Freakwater

contemporary language of romantic confusion, working-class frustration and personal despair. Their harmonies were the main event, blending beautifully alongside shimmering acoustic arrangements and aching melodies.

Freakwater never toured much in their early days, but as they became more popular they overcame their stage fright and expanded their line-up: in addition to Irwin, Bean, and Gay, the 1997 album SPRINGTIME featured multi-instrumentalist Max Johnston, a former member of Uncle Tupelo and Wilco. Freakwater came close to signing with Steve Earle's E-Squared label during the mid-'90s, a move that might have brought them greater visibility, but ultimately they chose to stick with Thrill Jockey. The group's 1999 album, END TIME, showed them now playing with a drummer and turning up the volume a bit—more of a '70s-style country-rock outing than an old-time affair. Some stalwart fans were disheartened, but most were captivated by the group's bold move into new (albeit still very genuine) musical territory.

⊙ **Dancing Under Water** (1991; Amoeba; reissued 1996; Thrill Jockey). Not as sturdy as their later work, but definitely a pleasant album to come back to and explore. "Your Goddamn Mouth" is a bitter, amusing Irwin original, and the covers of Bill Monroe, Leon Payne, Merle Travis, and others illustrate their musical upbringing.

⊙ **Feels Like The Third Time** (1993; Thrill Jockey). Their breakthrough album is kicked off by the catchy "My Old Drunk Friend," one of Irwin's finest songs. Also includes cool covers of Conway Twitty's "You've Never Been This Far Before" and cowboy singer Red River Dave's "Amelia Earhart."

⊙ **Old Paint** (1995; Thrill Jockey). Irwin's songwriting skills really shine on songs like "Gone To Stay," "Waitress Song," and "White Rose," making this the band's best to date and one of the finest albums of the alt.country generation as a whole. The vocal harmonies, too, are more confident and strong.

⊙ **Springtime** (1997; Thrill Jockey). Though OLD PAINT was a tough act to follow, this is another solid collection that definitely grows on you. Again it's marked by strong harmonies and enticing acoustic arrangements.

⊙ **Endtime** (1999; Thrill Jockey). Freakwater moves out of the Carter Family-inspired landscape that's long been their home turf and stakes a claim in bright new

territory—employing electric guitars and a full drum kit. This, by the way, is good news: Irwin and Bean were more than ready, and in fact needed to push their sound out of its acoustic-driven safety zone. The tone on "Cloak Of Frogs" and "Sick, Sick, Sick" is no less stark than their best early work, while others ("Cheap Watch," "Queen Bee") buzz with newfound energy.

Robbie Fulks

"Robbie's just an amazing songwriter, idomatic issues aside."

—Steve Albini

Sharp-tongued country artist Robbie Fulks does have a mouth on him. If you have any doubts, cue up his anti-establishment rant "Fuck This Town," found on his second album SOUTH MOUTH. It's a catchy little ditty about his failed attempt to take a seat at the Nashville songwriters' roundtable and he's not afraid to tell it like it was.

With smart-alecky lyrics and a feisty city-boy attitude, many of Fulks' songs do smack of novelty. Yet there's more going on beneath the surface of his albums than wisecracks and clever wordplay. Fulks is an accomplished singer and songwriter, who can touch the heart and move us to tears with genuine down-and-outers like "Barely Human" and "South Richmond Girl."

Fulks was born on 25 March, 1963 and grew up in Pennsylvania, Virginia, and North Carolina before attending Columbia University in New York City. He moved to Chicago and then toured for a couple of years with the Special Consensus Bluegrass Band. Back in Chicago, Fulks became a regular fixture in local clubs before a friend working for Acuff-Rose in Nashville convinced him to come south and try his luck writing country hits. When that experience led nowhere, Fulks resettled in Chicago. His luck changed, however, when he landed a track ("Cigarette State") on Bloodshot Records' first 'insurgent country' compilation FOR A LIFE OF SIN. The follow-up compilation, HELL-BENT, included his song "Took A Lot Of Pills (And Died)," a sassy number that caused heads to turn and earned him a contract of his own with Bloodshot. He cut two albums for that Chicago label before being snatched up by Geffen. The big label released LET'S KILL SATURDAY NIGHT, and while it took him in a deeper, heavier rock'n'roll direction, for longtime Fulks fans, a certain charm from his earlier recordings was lacking. And besides, Fulks just wasn't the type of artist who was going to sell in large quantities. Parting ways with Geffen, he was back on Bloodshot in 1999 with the sarcastically titled CD THE VERY BEST OF ROBBIE FULKS—which was actually a collection of live cuts, previously shelved recordings and other Fulks-y curiosities.

⊙ **Country Love Songs** (1996; Bloodshot). Includes the infamous "She Took A Lot Of Pills (And Died)" and other shots of silliness, but clear standouts are "Barely Human" (a total downer) and "The Buck Starts Here," a neo-classic honky-tonk tune that's thick with steel guitar and twisted country remorse.

⊙ **South Mouth** (1997; Bloodshot). Many of the songs here ("I Told Her Lies," "Fuck This Town") are hyperactive city-twangers that border on novelty, but when Fulks isn't sassing up and mouthing off, other well-crafted tunes like the edgy "Cold Statesville Ground" and Louvin Brothers-esque "South Richmond

Girl" show us he's got more than one color in his parachute.

⊙ **Let's Kill Saturday Night** (1998; Geffen). This album is surprisingly heavy on the guitars—at least compared to his first two twangfests—and unashamed to get loud. Yet it also takes Fulks a step or two forward—beyond the No Depression city limits and out into the open range. Taken as a whole, it's his most exciting album to date.

⊙ **The Very Best Of Robbie Fulks** (1999; Bloodshot). Fulks the smart-ass lyricist doesn't let his fans down on this odds and sods collection of previously unreleased material—the unabashedly crass "White Man's Bourbon," the spot-on tribute to "Roots Rock Weirdos." Typically, his songs are built around catchy phrases like "May The Best Man Win" and "Parallel Bars," the latter a duet with Kelly Willis, but he also throws in a few ballads of the gentler sort: the *faux*-torch song "I Just Want To Meet The Man" and the sincere tributes to "Jean Arthur" and "That Bangle Girl."

Americana

Who would have thought that George Jones, a singer who has charted more than one hundred and fifty country singles in his career, would find himself labeled too country for country radio? Or that the roots rock of singer-songwriter Lucinda Williams would be dubbed too twangy for rock radio? As hard as it is to believe, such was the state of American popular radio in the mid-1990s. Enter Rob Bleetstein, then an editor at *Gavin*, a weekly San Francisco-based trade publication. In hopes of gaining more exposure for country-influenced artists whose music didn't fit into radio's increasingly narrow and compartmentalized formats, Bleetstein instituted the *Gavin* Americana chart on 20 January, 1995.

Forty-seven radio stations from across the United States reported to *Gavin* during the chart's first week, and within four years this number had doubled. This means that at the end of the century, 96 stations were playing at least twelve hours of alternative country music each week (the minimum number required to qualify as a reporting Americana station). Approximately two-thirds of these are commercial stations, including many whose main format is "hot new country" music (from the likes of Garth Brooks and Shania Twain). The remainder broadcast as public radio affiliates or college stations. To put this into perspective, more than 2500 US signals broadcast mainstream country music.

The music that gets played on Americana stations is remarkably diverse, running from singer-songwriter folk, Tex Mex and bluegrass to honky tonk, western swing and punk-bred country-rock. Recently, for example, the five most added records one week were those by Texas singer-songwriter Lyle Lovett; newgrass banjoist Béla Fleck; Country Music Hall of Famer Willie Nelson; alt.country poet Kevin Welch; and bluegrass-bred folkie—and Tom T. Hall protégé—Nancy Moore. None of these artists, except for Nelson, has ever enjoyed commercial success to match that of country megastars Brooks and Twain. Whereas Lovett might sell 50,000 to 100,000 copies of his latest disc (terrific numbers by Americana standards), Twain's latest album has moved well in excess of ten million units.

Yet despite the Americana chart's negligible impact on the conglomerate-dominated record industry, the format has nevertheless named and given expression to a grassroots movement—otherwise known as 'no depression,' 'insurgent country,' 'twangcore,' or 'y'alternative'—that has gained momentum among disenfranchised listeners. Although she acknowledges it's a long shot, Jessie Scott, the new Americana editor at *Gavin*, believes the format could yet be a catalyst in mainstream country circles, much as the new traditionalist movement was during the mid-'80s.

—Bill Friskics-Warren

Robbie Fulks

Go To Blazes

Philadelphia-based Go To Blazes churned out half a dozen albums and a handful of singles in their twelve-year lifespan, and while none of their songs ever made anyone rich, they did earn the band a solid reputation in Europe and well as the US for their thick and juicy, country- and blues-inflected brand of rock'n'roll. It was music born of long days in basement practice rooms and red-eyed nights working bars and clubs up and down the East Coast—hard work that paid off in tight playing and some amazingly insightful songwriting.

Lead guitarist Tom Heyman, rhythm guitarist and lead singer Ted Warren, bassist Christopher Horner, and drummer Keith Donnellan formed Go To Blazes in 1987 in Washington, DC. A year later they relocated to Philadelphia, settling in a run-down, crime-ridden neighborhood that seemed to suit their temperament just fine. The band's self-titled debut album came out on Skyclad in 1988, followed by LOVE, LUST AND TROUBLE two years later on the French label Skyranch. Both had a raunchy bar-band feel punctuated by elements of gritty blues, Outlaw country, and 1960s-era garage punk. They also landed songs on RIG ROCK JUKEBOX and RIG ROCK TRUCKSTOP, two indie-rock compilations released by the trucker-obsessed label Diesel Only.

The Go To Blazes sound had matured tremendously by the time of ANYTIME ... ANYWHERE. This third album was released in 1994 by East Side Digital, featured new bass player Ted Papadapoulos, and was produced by Eric "Roscoe" Ambel, who also worked with the Blood Oranges and the Bottle Rockets. The songwriting (by Heyman and Warren) was stronger and more grounded, the playing more focused. The standout was "Bloody Sam," a tribute to filmmaker Sam Peckinpah (*The Wild Bunch*) penned by Heyman that brings fiddle and acoustic guitar into the mix. The song spins the saga of a man-to-man road trip to Mexico with Peckinpah in the driver's seat, actor Warren Oates "riding shotgun," "cocaine on the switchblade" and "a quart of Johnnie Walker" between them, and twenty-five years' worth of Hollywood spite on their minds.

In 1995, the Blazes recorded an all-acoustic album, GO TO BLAZES AND OTHER CRIMES, for the German label Glitterhouse, on which they covered songs by Lou Reed, Lee Hazlewood, Kinky Friedman, and Hank Williams Jr., among others, as well as a couple from their own catalog. It was a loose affair recorded live to two-track,

with not a whole lot of planning behind it, but that casual approach proved to be its charm. One final album came out in the US, WAITING AROUND FOR THE CRASH, and though the band's acclaim seemed to be growing in alternative country and indie rock circles, a year or so later they decided to call it quits. Heyman has since moved to San Francisco, where he fronts a new band, Triple Shiner.

⊙ **Anytime ... Anywhere** (1995; East Side Digital). From the raunchy edges of "Messed Up Again" to the Flamin' Groovies' "Yesterday's Numbers" and the raunchy saga of "Bloody Sam," the band sifts through the corners of a roadhouse garage for a gutsy sound that's as down-to-earth as it is dangerous. Warren's voice is greased with an urban bar-room twang, while Heyman's guitar bristles with energy.

⊙ **Go To Blazes And Other Crimes** (1995; Glitterhouse). They didn't set out to make a masterpiece, just to have a good time with some of their country and rock'n'roll favorite songs, and the result is an immensely listenable slice of Americana's underbelly. The Blazes do a proud version of Kinky Friedman's down-and-out classic "Sold American," along with Hank Jr.'s "OD'd In Denver," Lee Hazlewood's "She Comes Running," Lou Reed's "Underneath The Bottle," and Gene Clark's "Out On The Side."

⊙ **Waiting Around for the Crash** (1996; East Side Digital). A companion piece to ANYTIME in that it's another strong collection of songwriting and playing that shifts from rough-hewn country to straight-up rock'n'roll. "No Mercy" pulls at the seams between memory and reality, and "Why I Drink" pulls no punches, while the brilliantly catchy "New Morning Sun" ponders the bleak consequences of yet another day-job hangover.

Wayne Hancock

"Ain't nothing like a warm bed when it's coming down in buckets outside."

—Wayne Hancock

Possessing one of the thickest nasal twangs of any contemporary singer, Wayne "The Train" Hancock is the genuine article, a proud son of Texas who brings the sounds of old-school honky tonk and hot hillbilly swing right into the twenty-first century. Born on 1 May, 1965 in Dallas, Hancock grew up listening to all sorts of pop, swing and country music, but he remembers Hank Williams (whom his voice most resembles) and Ernest Tubb as two big early influences. During his teen years Hancock earned his chops playing in bars and clubs throughout East Texas. After graduating from high school, he joined the Marines on a six-year stint and was stationed in Hawaii (hence the Hawaiian

shirts he often wears on stage). He moved to Austin in 1991, and it's here that his musical career took off in earnest. He landed a gig touring with Asleep At The Wheel, recorded some demos for Elektra, and was briefly courted by Warner Brothers. In the process, he learned that Nashville was not the place he wanted to hang his hat.

Hancock's real breakthrough was his appearance in *Chippy*, a theater piece written and produced by Jo Harvey Allen and her husband Terry Allen. He appeared in the play along with fellow Texans Joe Ely, Robert Earl Keen, Jo Carol Pierce, and others, and two of his recordings (including the mournful "Thunderstorms And Neon Signs") were included on the soundtrack. He was signed to the Texas indie label Dejadisc, and his debut album, THUNDERSTORMS AND NEON SIGNS, was released in 1995. The album immediately stood out for its sparse arrangements—guitars, bass, and steel (no drums)—Hancock's bold and confident nasal voice, and a bunch of compelling original songs. Hancock has become a big hit with the rockabilly and swing crowds, who love his vintage sound and hot dance tunes, yet at the same time he's not just retro chic—his music feels original and fresh. When Dejadisc folded, Hancock signed with Ark 21, and that label has released two further collections, THAT'S WHAT DADDY WANTS (1997) and WILD, FREE & RECKLESS (1999).

⊙ **Thunderstorms And Neon Signs** (1995; Dejadisc). Lubbock legend and pedal-steel ace Lloyd Maines produced Hancock's debut, an almost dangerously stripped-down affair that's as hot as an East Texas rail yard in July ("Juke Joint Jumping," "Double A Daddy"). The title track is the biggest knockout of them all, and "Cold Lonesome Wind" ("It's after two and it just started to rain") will take you to a faraway place you might not want to return from.

Wayne Hancock

MICHAEL DIETZ

Joe Henry

"I certainly find myself dictated to by songs rather than any kind of club that I'm supposed to belong to."

—Joe Henry

Joe Henry's music doesn't stay in one place for long. He's let the rock'n'roll sparks fly plenty of times, but he's also toyed with bare-bones acoustic arrangements and steel-guitar country. Two of his 1990s albums, SHORT MAN'S ROOM and KINDNESS OF THE WORLD, leaned toward country and won him a good deal of new attention, both for their spare acoustic arrangements and Henry's keen narrative sense—as a songwriter, he retains what he calls "a healthy respect for mystery," working his way around the edges of a story, setting the scene with glimmers and nods. But just when you think you have the guy pegged as some sort of (god forbid) "singer-songwriter" type with an English degree, he messes up the picture, pulling in drum machines and turning up the guitars. But that kind of playful, adventurous spirit only makes his music all the more fascinating.

Henry was born on 2 December, 1960 in Charlotte, North Carolina, but he grew up in Georgia, Ohio, and Michigan. His father was a big Doc Watson fan, but in Michigan (where Henry spent much of his teenage years) he also discovered the joys of Iggy and the Stooges. He eventually began gigging around the state, and earned enough notoriety to land a deal with Profile Records, who released his debut album, TALK OF HEAVEN, in 1986. Next stop was New York City. He signed to A&M, and the result of that deal was his most rock'n'roll album to date, MURDER OF CROWS. Produced by Anton Fier (Golden Palominos) and featuring Mick Taylor on guitar, it proved an unsatisfying experience for Henry—he lost all stylistic control to the record label—and a less-than-satisfying listen.

Henry reacted to CROWS by cutting his follow-up album, SHUFFLETOWN, live to two-track and using all acoustic instruments—including trumpet played by jazz legend Don Cherry. Produced by T-Bone Burnett (who's remained a friend and collaborator ever since), it's a pleasant, intimate record that luxuriates in its simplicity and is in no hurry to go anywhere. A&M, however, didn't know what to do with it, and before long Henry was dropped. Which is just as well, because he wound up stepping out of the major-label circus ring and cutting one of the finest records of his career, SHORT MAN'S ROOM. Released by Mammoth Records in 1992, the record was packed with brilliantly written songs like "Diving Bell," "King's Highway," and the title track, all propelled by low-key arrangements that shifted his music in a distinct country-folk direction. His friends, the Jayhawks, were his backing band on the album—which was initially only planned as a series of demos (as was, ironically, the Jayhawks' own breakthrough album BLUE EARTH)—and that Minneapolis group lends an easygoing country-rock vibe that carries Henry's voice and lyrics but never gets in the way. A year later came KINDNESS OF THE WORLD, which wasn't quite as deliberately rural but still seemed informed by a country sensibility. Like SHORT MAN'S ROOM it was cut quickly—eight days in Daniel Lanois' New Orleans studio (Henry's wife manages Lanois' career).

Henry really outdid himself with his 1996 album, TRAMPOLINE. Stylistically it was a deliberate departure—very much a studio-crafted album (Henry even built a studio in his garage) and more about drum loops than steel guitars. His lyrics—his sense of storytelling, knack for character development and eye for detail—were as compelling as ever, but until now he'd never paid so much attention to the way a record sounded. It was far thicker and more texturally complex than anything he'd done to date. Henry continued his recording-studio adventures on his 1999 release FUSE. Drummer Carla Azar (who first played on TRAMPOLINE) is again his foundation, while T-Bone Burnett pops in as his spiritual guide.

⊙ **Short Man's Room** (1992; Mammoth). A proud collection of rurally-driven narratives—some dark and lonely, others funny and strange—that come to life with

Joe Henry

a spare country-rock sound courtesy of the Jayhawks. Without trying too hard, Henry created a real gem.

⊙ **Kindness Of The World** (1993; Mammoth). More superb songwriting and arrangements that again feature a couple of Jayhawks—along with guest singer Victoria Williams. Henry says he wrote "She Always Goes" as a type of song George Strait might cover (we're still waiting), and for added color he throws in a beautifully sincere version of Tom T. Hall's "I Flew Over Our House Last Night."

⊙ **Trampoline** (1996; Mammoth). An adventurous, edgy, and absolutely engaging new direction for Henry, with a heavier emphasis on rhythm. It's a very textural album, too, with ghostlike murmurs and other sonic mysteries drifting in from every corner. Hypnotic and addictive.

Tom House

When Nashville-based poet, songwriter and singer Tom House saw his first CD released in 1997, he was in his mid-forties—a late start in a business that is so focused on youth, but that doesn't seem to bother him much. Born on 18 February, 1949 in Durham, North Carolina, House has actually been a published poet since his teens; he just never got around to writing songs until he was well into his twenties. All that life experience, however, has enabled him to build a repertoire of fascinating material that, while clearly showing the influence of Appalachian folk and old-time hillbilly music, is definitely more twisted than the songs you hear at the average folksingers-in-the-round showcase. "I'm In Love With Susan Smith," for instance, about the woman (Smith) who was in the news during the '90s for drowning her child, is a dark and bitter song that takes society to task for damning her so blindly; "I Got Neighbors" is a disturbing vision of spousal abuse; and "White Man" speaks about the great American tradition of looking the other way. An abundance of mandolin, fiddle, and guitar keep his music grounded in tradition, but House's voice is so full of cracks and quirks that he can't help but meander off the road now and again. He never crashes, though; he knows too well what he's doing. Play House's music alongside that of old-time masters like Dock Boggs or Roscoe Holcomb, and his strange style begins to make far more sense—it's surprisingly direct, in fact. House put together a couple of

cassettes on his own before signing to the new Chicago-based indie label Checkered Past, which released his first two CDs in the late '90s. Since then, he has shifted over to another Chicago label, Catamount (founded by Eric Babcock, who was also the founder of Checkered Past). House's third album, 'TIL YOU'VE SEEN MINE, was released in early 2000.

⊙ **The Neighborhood Is Changing** (1997; Checkered Past). House's debut album is quirky, yes, but don't let that scare you off, because it's a solid, mesmerizing achievement that beautifully mixes House's offbeat lyrics and voice with broad strokes of downhome music. Songs like the lively "C'mon Through Carolina," the dark "I Got Neighbors," and the disturbing "I'm In Love With Susan Smith" creep beneath your skin before you know what happened.

⊙ **This White Man's Burden** (1998; Checkered Past). Slightly more melodic and rhythmically focused than his debut, House speaks honestly of human experiences, issues, and follies against a backdrop of old-time acoustic music that takes us back to the good ole days while at the same time facing us directly forward.

Mike Ireland

Before hitting the trail as a solo artist, Missouri native Mike Ireland spent the first half of the 1990s as bassist/vocalist for the Starkweathers, a Kansas City alt.country band that showed lots of promise, then split up in 1995 before breaking very far out of midwestern obscurity. During their short lifespan they only released a handful of singles and one five-song EP; songs like "Little White Trash Boy" (on the Bloodshot Records compilation HELL-BENT: INSURGENT COUNTRY VOLUME 2) and the 1996 Sub Pop single "Do You Like To Be Lied To" (b/w "Town Of Shame") are well worth searching for. Since the Starkweathers' break-up, Ireland has fronted a new group he dubbed Holler, which includes Michael Lemon on guitar, steel and mandolin, and drummer Paul Lemon (both former Starkweathers) along with guitarist Dan Mesh. In 1998, the band released its first full-length CD on Sub Pop, LEARNING HOW TO LIVE. Songs like the dark and bitter "House Of Secrets," the morose "Graveyard Song," and the self-deprecating "Cold Cold Comfort" deal with per-

CHRIS TOLIVER

Mike Ireland (second from right) and Holler

sonal losses Ireland suffered in recent years—not only the disintegration of his band but his marriage as well. Perfect fodder for country music, of course, but Ireland's songs are not about novelty; the melodies and the emotions are honest and natural.

⊙ **Learning How To Live** (1998; Sub Pop). Ireland's debut album is country top to bottom, though the styles vary—from guitar-oriented honky tonk and gently swaying hillbilly songs (including a cover of the murder ballad "Banks Of The Ohio"), to thick, countrypolitan-style arrangements replete with swelling strings.

Jason & The Scorchers

One of the first bands to create a raw blend of 'country' and 'punk' music was Jason & The Scorchers, which was formed in Nashville by Illinois native Jason Ringenberg in 1981. His bandmates included guitarist Warner Hodges, bassist Jeff Johnson, and drummer Perry Baggs, and the group (initially known as Jason & The Nashville Scorchers) gained a strong local following. They

were all about rock'n'roll played hard and fast, but at the same time Ringenberg felt tied to the country music he'd grown up with. There was a twang in his voice no matter how fast or loud the band played, and when they slowed things down, they proved they could play a hillbilly number as straight as nails.

The Scorchers' initial recording was a four-song EP entitled RECKLESS COUNTRY SOUL, released in 1982 on the indie label Praxis. A year later came another EP, the six-song FERVOR, and this led to a major label recording contract with EMI. The new label reissued FERVOR, and in 1985 came the Scorchers' first full-length proper album, LOST & FOUND, which earned more critical praise. Sales figures, however, were another story. Two albums later, and eight years after they'd been in business, the band split up.

That was only the first chapter, however. Ringenberg first took a shot at the mainstream with his 1991 album ONE FOOT IN THE HONKY TONK, released on Liberty (Garth Brooks' label), but country radio wasn't biting. Ironically, the Scorchers had bitten the dust just as the whole alt.country was getting off the ground. All four original members reunited in 1993, began touring again, and recorded the albums A BLAZING GRACE (1995) and CLEAR IMPETUOUS MORNING (1996)

Mike Ireland • Jason & The Scorchers

Tony Mottram/Retna

Jason & The Scorchers

with R.E.M. as Gram Parsons, with the grungy guitars of Neil Young and Crazy Horse hovering in the background. The Jayhawks came out of a rock'n'roll community that included such legendary groups as Hüsker Dü, the Replacements, and Soul Asylum, and in some ways their folk-inspired sound was the antidote to the visceral punk energy that defined the music scene in that cold, flat, northern city. Their melodies rippled with melancholy, their lyrics rang with references to liquor stores, cups of coffee, falling snow, broken windows, and "winos and office girls in the park." That these images were often more urban than pastoral may have contributed to their appeal with the punk-rock crowd.

The Jayhawks formed in 1985 when guitarist Mark Olson hooked up with bassist Marc Perlman, drummer Norm Rogers, and guitarist Gary Louris. Olson, Louris, and Perlman remained the core of the group through most of their releases. The band's self-titled debut album, released in 1986 on Bunkhouse (a label started by their manager), was a compelling start, and despite limited release it gained them critical attention. It was on their follow-up, however, BLUE EARTH, that the Jayhawks sound coalesced into something poetic and mesmerizing. The latter album was released by the local indie-rock label Twin/Tone, and it featured a new drummer, Thad Spencer. The Jayhawks were by this point more than a local secret, and before long they'd inked a deal with Def American, home of Slayer, the Black Crowes (who were big fans of the band), and, later, Johnny Cash. The result was HOLLYWOOD TOWN HALL, produced by George Drakoulias, who'd previously worked with the Crowes. The production was bigger and louder than any of their previous efforts, but the songs were still moody, introspective, touched by folk and country influences. They toured with the Black Crowes, made MTV videos, and generally exposed themselves to a much wider audience. They also backed up their friend, Joe Henry, on his albums SHORT MAN'S ROOM and KINDNESS OF THE WORLD, and Louris and Olson played on records by artists such as Maria McKee and Victoria Williams (whom

for the Mammoth label. Both albums showed their country-punk aesthetic had changed little since the group's inception. On the one hand, they'd remained dedicated to their sound; but on the other, their music hadn't grown much—it was just the same as it ever was. The band did, however, begin to win new attention as early alt.country innovators, and their initial releases were also reissued. In 1998 Mammoth released a two-CD live album, MIDNIGHT ROADS & STAGES SEEN. At this point the band was still in its original form save for bassist Kenny Ames, who had only recently replaced Johnson.

⊙ **Both Sides Of The Line** (1996; EMI). A reissue of the complete FERVOR EP and the LOST AND FOUND album on a single CD. Their unfettered version of Dylan's "Absolutely Sweet Marie" kicks off a collection that's consistently fast and raucous all the way through. The only points where the Scorchers let up are on the country songs, which are slow, sad, and surprisingly straightforward. In retrospect, it's these tracks that actually sound less dated.

The Jayhawks

"I'm very impressed."

—Johnny Cash

Minneapolis band the Jayhawks created a country-rock sound that was laid-back yet jangly—they seemed to have as much in common

Olson would later marry). Louris also spent quality time with his side project, Golden Smog, an indie-rock supergroup that included members of the Replacements, Run Westy Run, Soul Asylum, and, later, Wilco.

The Jayhawks edged their way further in the direction of rock and pop music on their fourth album, TOMORROW THE GREEN GRASS, released in 1995. Soon after that, however, Olson quit the band and moved with his new wife, Victoria Williams, to a cabin in the desert near Joshua Tree, California. There they've struck up a new musical collaboration they call the Original Harmony Ridge Creek Dippers, and they've self-released three albums to date. Louris and Perlman have kept the Jayhawks name and released one further album so far, SOUND OF LIES. This time the sound was shinier and almost pure pop, though rather nicely done. The band has continued to tour and record, and their sixth album was scheduled for a May 2000 release on Columbia.

⊙ **Blue Earth** (1989; Twin/Tone). Olson wrote most of the songs here, which were originally just demos the band had recorded over the previous couple of years when they were deciding whether to stay together or split up. With some remixing and overdubbing, the resulting album is a shimmering beauty—melodically laid-back, yet also possessing an overcaffeinated edginess. The guitars can get raw and grungy, but there's lots of open space in the arrangements.

⊙ **Hollywood Town Hall** (1991; American). The amps are turned up a few extra notches, but the mood on the Jayhawks' third album is still loose and comfortable. The melodies and lyrics are as meandering and curious as ever, and Olson and Louris' voices weave in and out of each other like flies in a windowless porch. Both the writing and playing, in fact, are tighter than ever on songs like "Waiting For The Sun," "Two Angels" (a remake of a BLUE EARTH song), "Nevada, California," and the glorious "Wichita."

Cheri Knight

Cheri Knight first made herself known to the music world as bassist, singer, and song-writer with the Blood Oranges. Her voice—sturdy, earthy and at times haunting and mournful—was a highlight of the group, as were songs she wrote such as "The Crying

Tree" and "All The Way Down." When the Oranges split up in 1995, Knight began working on material she released a year later on her first solo album, THE KNITTER. For that album she switched to playing guitar, and the songs showed her maturity and newfound confidence as a singer, songwriter and bandleader. THE KNITTER was produced by Eric Ambel, who also worked with the Blood Oranges, the Bottle Rockets, and others, and it earned Knight further well-deserved acclaim. After that she was signed by Steve Earle's label E-Squared, which released her excellent second effort, THE NORTHEAST KINGDOM, in 1998. Former dB's drummer Will Rigby played with her on both records, and KINGDOM also featured her former Blood Oranges bandmates Jimmy Ryan and Mark Spencer. In addition to maintaining her music career, Knight continues to live and work in the farming community of Hatfield, Massachusetts, and her rural, earthbound lifestyle definitely informs her music.

⊙ **The Knitter** (1996; East Side Digital). Knight stakes her claim as a solo artist with strength and confidence on her debut album. Whether she's playing ballads ("Last Barn Dance" is so gorgeous you'll weep with joy) or power chords ("The Knitter" shows she has no fear of rock'n'roll), the songs retain a rural flavor that keeps her music thoroughly grounded.

⊙ **The Northeast Kingdom** (1998; E-Squared). Her follow-up album is equally excellent, her writing and singing only improving with time. The arrangements, too, are fuller this time around and quite tasty. As on her debut, Knight mixes strong, guitar-friendly material with country-driven melodies and ballads that are as melancholy as they are mesmerizing. Co-producer

Cheri Knight

TOM ERIKSON

Cheri Knight (right) with Jimmy Ryan, San Francisco, 1998

Steve Earle lends some instrumental support as well, and Emmylou Harris makes a superb duet partner with Knight on "Crawling" and "Dar Glasgow."

Lambchop

Not many alt.country bands would claim Nashville Sound producer Billy Sherrill as a major inspiration, but then again, Lambchop isn't your typical country band—alternative or otherwise. With a membership that usually hovers somewhere between nine and fourteen players, depending on who's available and taking into account any friends that might have dropped by, Lambchop is almost more of a music collective than a 'band' in the typical sense of the word. Leader of the pack is Kurt Wagner, who writes most of the songs, plays guitar and sings lead in a voice that's so laid back it's borderline morose. His songs are moody and lush (hence the Sherrill comparison), but they're also peppered with a quirky sense of humor and never entirely devoid of irony. Titles like "All Smiles And Mariachi," "Your Fucking Sunny Day," "The Scary Caroler," "Soaker In The Pooper," and "Your Face My Ass" are hardly the stuff on which Nashville was built.

The instrumentation is quite stunning—keyboards, a string section, the punch of horns, saxophone, a tin whistle, oddball percussion that includes "open-end wrenches" and a "lacquer-thinner can," and plenty of guitar. The music can get wacky and even loud, and Wagner is certainly not afraid of naughty words ("I Sucked My Boss's Dick" is one song on the 1995 EP HANK) and cryptic, off-the-wall lyrics that border on non sequitur. But for the most part Lambchop's sonic aura remains cool and even a little spooky—and surprisingly subdued, considering the number of instruments and players involved.

Wagner hails from Nashville, and he formed Lambchop there in the late 1980s as an informal get-together amongst musically inclined friends. It eventually evolved into a band that little by little began to take itself more seriously. Other regulars who've stuck with the program over the years include bassist Marc Trovillion, saxophonist Deanna Varagona, steel player Paul Niehaus, and organist John Delworth. Niehaus, and Varagona now also play with Paul Burch and the WPA Ballclub, and Burch in turn plays drums and vibes for Lambchop. Lambchop cut a quirky debut album for Merge in 1994, I HOPE YOU'RE SITTING DOWN aka JACK'S TULIPS, but it was their second offering, HOW I QUIT SMOKING, that showed Wagner and company settling into a smoother, moodier and more string-laden style. The band's never been entirely rooted in country, however, and later albums show them toying with R&B and Muscle Shoals-type soul. They've also collaborated with singer-songwriter Vic Chesnutt, backing him up on his album THE SALESMAN AND BERNADETTE and cutting an excellent single under the name A Loose Confederation Of City States. In early 2000 they released NIXON.

Lambchop

⊙ **How I Quit Smoking** (1996; Merge). On Lambchop's second album, the guitars and strings add depth to the arrangements, while they're balanced out by Farfisa organ, a tin whistle, and an assortment of horns and percussion. Despite occasional bouts of craziness, it's a beautiful, engaging record.

⊙ **Thriller** (1997; Merge). Lambchop drifts slowly away from their lush country sound on this album and into darker territory, though they never get entirely out of control—Wagner's moody voice and vibe are still intact. "Your Fucking Sunny Day" is a punchy standout, and three songs are written by F.M. Cornog (aka the quirky indie-rock artist East River Pipe).

⊙ **What Another Man Spills** (1998; Merge). Where will Lambchop take us this time? Away from the countrypolitan mood that defined them two years earlier and into a funkier, more soul-inflected landscape. There's even a Curtis Mayfield cover, "Give Me Your Love (Love Song)."

Buddy And Julie Miller

"Some people put it all together better than others, and Buddy is definitely one of those people."

—Gurf Morlix

Guitarist Buddy Miller didn't record an album of his own until 1995's YOUR LOVE AND OTHER LIES, but considering the experience he logged since he began playing country and bluegrass in the late '60s, it's amazing it took him so long. In a similar fashion, Julie Miller emerged seemingly out of nowhere as a mesmerizing harmony vocalist and compelling songwriter on Buddy's debut album—and two years later was the star of her own knockout delight, BLUE PONY. This talented husband-and-wife team, however, have been playing music together on and off since they first met in Austin, Texas in the '70s.

Buddy was born in Fairburn, Ohio in 1952, Julie in Dallas, Texas in 1956. They met while auditioning for guitar and vocal spots in some local Austin bands, married in 1981, and have been working together—and following each other around the country—ever since. They lived in New York for a short time around 1980, where Buddy met country singer and songwriter Jim Lauderdale, who quickly became both a friend and musical collaborator. The Buddy Miller Band at the time also featured a young Shawn Colvin on lead vocals. After New York, the Millers moved back through Texas then on to San Francisco and Los Angeles, where Buddy took a gig playing guitar with Lauderdale, who was a rising talent among that Southern California city's then-burgeoning roots-music scene. While Buddy and Jim were doing their country gigs, Julie recorded her first of several Christian albums for the Myrrh label.

The couple finally moved to Nashville in 1993, where Buddy set up a home recording studio that's been his and Julie's musical base ever since. Buddy has a warm voice with a gentle twang, his style is bright and well-grounded in arrangements that are friendly and easygoing. He and Julie frequently

write songs together, and several of her (secular) compositions showed up on Buddy's debut album, YOUR LOVE AND OTHER LIES, released by HighTone in 1995. Julie also won a recording contract with HighTone, which allowed her to shift back into secular musical territory. Her 1997 album BLUE PONY showed off not only her songs but her girlish voice, a mixture of innocence, playfulness, and soul-stirring beauty. Victoria Williams comes to mind, which is not entirely a coincidence, as the two are good friends.

YOUR LOVE AND OTHER LIES raised Buddy's visibility and acclaim in the country music community. In the wake of her WRECKING BALL success, Emmylou Harris tapped him as lead guitarist in her touring band (the album itself featured a song written by Julie). He's stuck with her ever since, even co-producing her 1998 album SPYBOY. Buddy also co-produced Jimmy Dale Gilmore's 2000 album ONE ENDLESS NIGHT. Both Buddy and Julie have continued releasing solo albums. Buddy's 1997 album POISON LOVE was marked by sharp, bright vocals and stellar picking courtesy of fiddlers Tammy Rogers and Sam Bush, steel guitarist Al Perkins, drummer Brady Blade, and bassist Daryl Johnson from Emmylou's band. In 1999, HighTone released Buddy's third album, CRUEL MOON, along with Julie's second, BROKEN THINGS. Buddy and Julie Miller may not be household names to mainstream country fans, but their songs might ring some bells, as their work has been recorded by such stars as Lee Ann Womack, Brooks & Dunn, Suzy Bogguss, and the Dixie Chicks.

Buddy Miller

⊙ **Your Love And Other Lies** (1995; HighTone). Kicking off with the punchy "You Wrecked Up My Heart," Miller's warm voice, tastefully restrained guitar playing, and spare but lively arrangements lead the way across a wide-open field of love and loneliness. Miller wrote or co-wrote 7 of the album's 13 tracks and recorded the majority of them right in his Nashville living room. As a result, the album feels more like a gathering of friends (an impressive group that includes Lucinda Williams, Dan Penn, Emmylou Harris, and Julie Miller) than a formal session.

⊙ **Cruel Moon** (1999; HighTone). At times moody and stark, at other times lively and bright, this is Buddy's most intense, and musically complex, album to date, one that will have a lasting impact. He's got to be one of the hardest-working musicians in Nashville: that he can create an album this soul-stirring while still working

Julie Miller, San Francisco, 1988

mentation is (largely) acoustic, and the nasal voice of lead singer and songwriter Mike Coykendall quivers and creaks like a coffee pot simmering on an old Franklin stove (his singing, by the way, is a dead ringer for that of folk-rock artist John Stewart.) As for the songs, they're timeless pieces crammed with melancholy and wonder—moody, haunting, and in no hurry to get anywhere. Though the band was formed in San Francisco, Coykendall himself hails from Norwich, Kansas, and it's this combination of modest, small-town upbringing, rock'n'roll awareness (between 1985 and 1991 he played in a psychedelic punk outfit called Klyde Konnor), and easygoing West Coast attitude that gives the Old Joe Clarks such depth and appeal. Not to mention, of course, the tight, warm textures created by bandmembers such as his wife, onetime avant-garde musician Jill McClelland-Coykendall, and multi-instrumentalist Kurt Stevenson.

Mike and Jill left Kansas for San Francisco in 1991 and formed the Old Joe Clarks a year later. The first bandmember they recruited was Stevenson, and the trio became the core of the Clarks' debut album, TOWN OF TEN. The band initially released it themselves in 1996, but about a year later it was picked up and reissued by the

as a guitarist, producer and bandleader with folks like Emmylou, Jimmie Dale, Lauderdale, and Steve Earle is almost mindboggling.

Julie Miller

⊙ **Blue Pony** (1997; HighTone). The first entirely secular album from Julie Miller is full of such fresh, genuine spirit it just might blow you away. Her wonderful voice has an endearing, almost childlike tone—similar to that of her good friend Victoria Williams—but don't let that fool you, as Miller's an assertive, confident singer. Her songs move through blues, Appalachian folk, and rock-inflected country with a daring, adventurous determination.

⊙ **Broken Things** (1999; HighTone). "Magic" is not a work to be used lightly, but Julie's songs and her voice, too, fit the description—the sort of soulful spirit that's impossible to explain, yet is immediately moving. There's a stronger, sometimes heavier sound here than on her debut, the guitars and drums enhancing the powerful vibe of songs like "All My Tears" ("When I go don't cry for me") and "I Need You" ("I need something like an asylum 'cause I go wild".)

Old Joe Clarks

There's a taste of Appalachia in the music of the Old Joe Clarks—the band name itself, after all, is derived from an old fiddle tune. The instru-

The Old Joe Clarks
Metal Shed Blues

Chicago indie label Checkered Past. Their second album, METAL SHED BLUES, arrived in early 1999; where the folk elements stood out more on the debut, this time the songs were marked by subtle, moody textures that enhanced the melancholy atmosphere surrounding Coykendall's voice and lyrics. Live, the band (which had added a few more players by this point) was sharp and tight—a mesmerizing experience. Later that year, however, Mike and Jill decided to move to Portland, Oregon; the band has so far maintained a long-distance working relationship, playing shows in both cities. In March 2000, Coykendall and his same crew of players from METAL SHED BLUES were scheduled to re-enter the studio to record the third Old Joe Clarks album.

⊙ **Metal Shed Blues** (1999; Checkered Past). Though the instrumentation tends toward the acoustic—fiddle, banjo, Dobro, and guitar—and the melodic sentiment leans in the direction of country and folk music, this is less about old-time traditions than it is about creating moods and atmospheres to fit Coykendall's introspective, bare-bones songs. Keyboards, clarinet, and electric guitars drift in and out of the mix, adding a bit of fuzz around the edges. It's a melancholy creation, but it glows. Definitely an album to lose yourself in.

Old 97's

"We've never pretended to be a country band. Well, not for the most part."

—Ken Bethea

Texas quartet the Old 97's—singer-guitarist Rhett Miller, bassist Murray Hammond, guitarist Ken Bethea, and drummer Philip Peeples—earned their reputation playing smart, crafty songs that mixed Bakersfield honky tonk, Memphis rockabilly, and punk-rock attitude. The group formed in Dallas in 1993 and cut their debut album HITCHHIKE TO RHOME for the local label Big Iron. Bloodshot Records signed them soon afterwards and released WRECK YOUR LIFE. Miller's bright voice and smart lyrics on that album gained the group a new round of attention on the then-burgeoning alt.country scene, and before they knew it they had stepped up to the big leagues, signing with Elektra for their 1997 album TOO FAR TO CARE, which showed them turning up the rock'n'roll a few notches. The result was a welcome change—hard-edged, but still-twangy.

By the time of the group's 1999 album, FIGHT SONGS, however, the guitars were grungier and the country elements that were the foundation of their early sound had slipped father out of the picture. Longtime Old 97's fans were a bit miffed, but the band's popularity has surged—the new approach having won them a wider audience on the alternative-rock circuit. Club shows have been packed, and they've even received some radio play. In the fall of 1999, the band joined X/Knitters member John Doe on "Cryin' But My Tears Are Far Away," a track recorded for the Knitters tribute album, POOR LITTLE KNITTER ON THE ROAD.

⊙ **Wreck Your Life** (1995; Bloodshot). The majority of the material here is lively, good-natured and well-crafted—"Victoria" is undeniably catchy, and "Old Familar Steam" has a cool lonesome feeling. These days, this kind of country-punk blend is commonplace; nonetheless, WRECK YOUR LIFE shows the Old 97's were on the ball before alt.country was an overused term.

⊙ **Fight Songs** (1999; Elektra). The country has slipped much further out of the picture on this album; the band seems to be searching for something different but hasn't quite yet found it. The guitars are grungier and the mood heavier on "Jagged" and "Crash On The Barrelhead," and that's promising; but too many others fall into nondescript alternative-rock territory.

Palace (aka Will Oldham)

"There's no difference between any activity of the day and a song, though the song is what gives activity meaning."

—Will Oldham

It seems Will Oldham just doesn't like being pinned down, so keeping track of his plentiful recordings under numerous names—Palace, Palace Songs, Palace Brothers, his alterego Bonnie Prince Billy, or sometimes plain old Will Oldham—isn't exactly an easy task. His music, while low-key and sometimes desperately quiet, isn't what you'd call straightforward—it's a mixture instead of absurd hillbilly murmurs, rambling alone-in-the-apartment poetry, and unshowered (perhaps even unrehearsed) garage-band jams. His fascination with Appalachian

Old 97's • Palace (aka Will Oldham)

music shows most clearly on the Palace Brothers' first album, THERE IS NO-ONE WHAT WILL TAKE CARE OF YOU. Since then, Oldham's style has developed into one marked by sometimes indecipherable stream-of-consciousness lyrics, a threadbare and frequently broken vocal style, and melodies that are playful as they are disturbing. Whether it comes off as pretentious or intensely moving, there's little question that Oldham's an intelligent and talented musician, even if he's not very forthcoming in interviews—and even if he isn't the most compelling performer (he reportedly hates playing live).

Oldham was born on 16 August, 1969 and grew up in Louisville, Kentucky. Early on he dabbled in acting, his most notable role being the child preacher in John Sayles' 1987 film *Matewan*. He also briefly attended Brown University before meandering into the indie-rock world first with a band called Box of Chocolates. He then formed the Palace Brothers with musicians who included his brother Ned and Brian McMahan from the rock bands Slint and Squirrel Bait. In 1993 they cut their first single, "Ohio River Boat Song," for the Drag City label, and then the album THERE IS NO-ONE WHAT WILL TAKE CARE OF YOU. The follow-up, PALACE BROTHERS (aka DAYS IN

THE WAKE), took the mood and sonic aura down even a few more notches, until the bones of Oldham's songs were poking through their melodic skin. It wasn't entirely a solo record, but it did place Oldham clearly at the center of the Palace picture. Goodness knows how many singles, EPs, and albums have followed—the guy is nothing if not prolific. He rocked things up on VIVA LAST BLUES (produced by Steve Albini), toyed with a drum machine on ARISE THEREFORE, and cut an excellent version of David Allan Coe's "In My Mind" (a single released on his own Palace Records imprint). The only constant seems to be his fans, who mop up his music like Sunday gravy. By the time we get to the Bonnie Prince Billy album I SEE A DARKNESS, the hillbilly schtick he was playing back in 1993 has long disappeared—yet the songs themselves still carried that same unmistakable Oldham mystique.

⊙ **There Is No-One What Will Take Care of You** (1993; Drag City). A loose ramble of a record that flirts with old-time country, blues, and gospel, and leaves listeners wondering as to the sincerity of it all, yet haunted at the same time by the enchanting (and often meandering) melodies—not to mention Oldham's broken voice, which moves cautiously from word to word. Songs such as "(I Was Drunk At The) Pulpit" and "Idle Hands Are The Devil's Playthings" take on traditional themes of family, religion, sin, and isolation, twisting them into a mesh of corruption and guilt.

⊙ **Lost Blues And Other Songs** (1997; Drag City). A collection of singles, B-sides and other assorted rarities—plus five previously unreleased tracks—that's as much as a Palace "career" retrospective as exists at this point. Includes "Ohio River Boat Song," "Trudy Dies," "Little Blue Eyes," "Stable Will," "Horses," and "Gulf Shores," among others.

⊙ **Joya** (1997; Drag City). This was released under

EDIE VEE

Will Oldham

Will Oldham's name, and on a visceral level alone, it's his most hypnotic album to date. The rhythmic grooves carry you effortlessly from song to song, and Oldham's voice, though still parched and quivering as usual, maintains a steady, slow pace.

Pernice Brothers

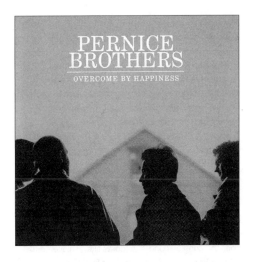

After quitting the Scud Mountain Boys in 1997, singer, songwriter, and guitarist Joe Pernice formed the Pernice Brothers with his brother Bob and assortment of friends and musical associates (including Peyton Pinkerton from the New Radiant Storm Kings). Where the Scuds were more focused on acoustic country music, the Pernice Brothers are more about mellow-minded pop songs. Pernice's gentle, whispery voice will certainly be familiar to Scud Mountain Boys fans, and the low-key tempos and tones do keep both bands in the same ballpark. But on their debut album, the Pernice Brothers songs are far more lush, thanks in large part to the 'orchestra' of strings and horns that accompanies the six core players.

In 1999, Joe Pernice and several of his Pernice Brothers bandmembers (including Pinkerton, Thom Monahan, Laura Stain, and Mike Belitsky) recorded a new album under yet another band name, Chappaquiddick Skyline. While the sound was basically the same, the reason for the name change was the absence of Joe's brother Bob. Another full-on Pernice Brothers record, however, is in the works and planned for release in the not-too-distant future.

⊙ **Overcome By Happiness** (1998; Sub Pop). With strings, guitars, horns, and gentle, lilting melodies, the Pernice Brothers' music feels like an indulgence, a guilty pop pleasure, but the songs and arrangements are so finely crafted, so gorgeously rendered, that once sinking into your psyche the music stays put and you begin calling for more. Go with the feeling.

⊙ **Chappaquiddick Skyline** (2000; Sub Pop). Another crafty bunch of songs from Joe Pernice and most of his Pernice Brothers bandmates. The subject matter's as down and out as ever ("I hate my life," sings Joe Pernice at the start of the first track, "Everyone Else Is Evolving"), but as is typical of Pernice's best work, it's also mesmerizing and beautiful. Includes a cover of New Order's "Leave Me Alone."

Scud Mountain Boys

Initially a punk-rock band that answered by the name the Scuds, this Northampton, Massachusetts-based quartet earned a respectable local following during the early 1990s. However, bandmembers Joe Pernice, Stephen Desaulniers, Bruce Tull and Tom Shea soon found they were more enthusiastic about the acoustic-country music they'd play at home around the kitchen table after gigs. Finally, they came up with the idea to actually bring their acoustic guitars and even the kitchen table to a show, and the Scuds were reborn as the Scud Mountain Boys.

The band had a slow, whisperlight, acoustic-based sound that could be plenty melancholy—you probably had no idea just how haunting the Olivia Newton-John hit "Please, Mister, Please" really was. They weren't a traditional hillbilly-type band: stylistically they were more tied to the '70s in terms of both their easygoing melodies and introspective songwriting. The band's recording career was short but sweet: their debut album was PINE BOX, released first on cassette then later pressed on vinyl by the local label Chuck. DANCE THE NIGHT AWAY followed that same year (1995), and a year later the band was signed to Sub Pop. Their third album, MASSACHUSETTS, gained them much wider attention. Touring in the wake of MASSACHUSETTS, the bandmembers admitted they had enough songs for a fourth album, but Sub Pop chose instead to re-release the first two albums on a single CD. Unfortunately, the players' enthusiasm waned; Pernice quit the band in 1997, and before the year was out the Scud Mountain Boys had disbanded for good. Pernice now fronts a new outfit, the Pernice Brothers, and Desaulniers and

Shea have since recorded with the Ray Mason Band on the album CASTANETS.

⊙ **The Early Year** (1997; Sub Pop). A double-CD reissue of the band's first 2 albums, PINE BOX and DANCE THE NIGHT AWAY, both originally released by Chunk Records in 1995. Includes '70s pop-country covers such as "Please, Mister, Please," "Gypsies, Tramps And Thieves," and "Where's The Playground, Susie" that, surprisingly enough, are quite mesmerizing.

⊙ **Massachusetts** (1996; Sub Pop). The crowning achievement of the band's short career, the songs on their third album are again country in tone and built on a spare, acoustic structure. It retains the same kitchen-table spirit of their first two albums—success didn't spoil the band's sound. Standouts like "Knievel" and "Liquor Store" may seem fragile at first, but they're actually quite sturdy and down-to-earth.

Son Volt

Son Volt

When Jay Farrar quit Uncle Tupelo in 1994, his new band Son Volt more or less picked up where Farrar and his former bandmate, Jeff Tweedy, had left off. Like Uncle Tupelo's final album ANODYNE, Son Volt's 1995 debut TRACE half consisted of restless, guitar-gritty punk rock; the rest was dark, brooding, and largely acoustic-driven country. Such a comparison makes sense not only because of Farrar's musical inclinations, but because TRACE (as well as its follow-up, STRAIGHTAWAYS) was produced by Brian Paulson, who also manned the boards on ANODYNE.

Of the two Tupelo front men, Farrar definitely had the strongest country inclinations, and his full-bodied, minor-key-friendly voice wound beautifully around the band's slower, more melancholic songs. The same is true of his work with Son Volt. And it's the slower acoustic songs that really allow Farrar's voice (one of the band's most appealing features) to shine: beneath a quiet melody or the cry of a steel guitar, the wind and the road and the midwestern rivers and towns of his youth come alive and settle into the back of your mind. The opening track, "Windfall," is a near-perfect rendering of the moods, feelings, and pastoral dreams at the core of the No Depression scene. Son Volt's follow-up albums, STRAIGHTAWAYS and WIDE SWING TREMOLO, haven't broken the formula Farrar and his bandmates (onetime Uncle Tupelo drummer Mike Heidorn and brothers Jim and Dave Boquist)

established on TRACE. But the musicianship is firm and strong, and Farrar's songwriting is deadly serious and substantial. He could benefit from taking a few more chances in his music, but for now we'll just enjoy the moods and the view out the car window as the midwestern landscape rolls on past.

⊙ **Trace** (1995; Warner Bros.). Produced by Brian Paulson (who also produced ANODYNE), the 11 songs are an up-and-down ride between the acoustic folk of "Windfall" and the roughed-up and fully electrified "Drown." This is the album to start with, and it may be all you need. "Tear Stained Eye," "Ten Second News," and "Windfall" show Farrar and the band at their moodiest best, and subsequent recordings have yet to match that high-water mark.

⊙ **Straightaways** (1997; Warner Bros.). Even Jay Farrar admitted that this album was "an extension of the last one." To Son Volt's credit, though, STRAIGHTAWAYS is a worthy sequel as it contains a healthy dose of haunting, darkly edged songs like "No More Parades," "Creosote," and "Cemetery Savior."

⊙ **Wide Swing Tremelo** (1998; Warner Bros.). After the low-key moods of STRAIGHTAWAYS, Farrar steps up the pace slightly on Son Volt's third outing. Once again, though, the band's musical formula of midwestern guitar-rock and late-night twang is well in place.

Souled American

"If life was great for everybody, there wouldn't be a need for Souled American."

—Chris Grigoroff

To describe Souled American as 'country' is as lackadaisical as saying they're just another Chicago indie-rock band with a cult following—though both are part of the story. It's the slow pace that first strikes you—like homegrown psychedelic-hillbilly music played at half speed—but as one critic aptly wrote, they're "slow but not lazy." It takes plenty of strength and conviction, in fact, to give these loping melodies such warm, rich textures. The drums are minimal, the electric bass often takes the lead, and the twangy, crackling vocals curl around the lyrics with lonesome clarity. This is music that seeps into your pores.

Bassist Joe Adducci and guitarist Chris Grigoroff both grew up in Charleston, Illinois with a love of old-time country music. They met in 1983 and formed Souled American soon after—well before 'alt.country' and 'No Depression' were buzzwords. They were joined by guitarist Scott Tuma and drummer Jamey Barnard. The band signed with the indie-rock label Rough Trade and recorded three albums between 1988 and 1990: FÉ, FLUBBER, and AROUND THE HORN. They gained some critical attention and even toured a bit, but unfortunately the American branch of Rough Trade went bankrupt not long after the release of AROUND THE HORN. This meant the band's records were suddenly difficult to find (they weren't reissued until almost a decade later). AROUND THE HORN hadn't sold very many copies

to begin with, and the band couldn't land another American contract. Instead, they turned their attention to Europe, recording their fourth album, SONNY, for the European division of Rough Trade (which was still in business).

By this point, however, the handful of Souled American fans remaining in the US began to think the band had dissolved. They were surprised when rare copies of SONNY showed up in import bins, followed by two further collections, FROZEN and NOTES CAMPFIRE, these released by the German label Moll. Jamey Barnard had left by the time of these European records, and the band's sound (a drummer-for-hire was brought in only sporadically) had grown even slower and murkier. In 1997 they played shows in Chicago and San Francisco and drew enthusiastic crowds that were much larger than anyone could have anticipated. In 1998, Checkered Past gave FROZEN and NOTES CAMPFIRE distribution in the US for the first time, and a small San Francisco label tUMULt has taken responsibility for repackaging and re-releasing (in two-for-one packages) the first four Souled American albums. A new album is reportedly in the works as well.

⊙ **Fé/Flubber** (1998; tUMULt). The first two Souled American albums are probably the most immediately accessible of their recordings, with more pronounced rhythms and song structures that tie them, and however tenuously, to artists like the Band, Neil Young, and Camper Van Beethoven.

⊙ **Around The Horn/Sonny** (1998; tUMULt). With AROUND THE HORN, Souled American slowed things down to a crawl, pulling the songs apart and taking things almost one note at a time. It's haunting and hypnotizing stuff, as is SONNY, a collection of cover songs.

Uncle Tupelo

"I like to tell people, 'Jay and I used to stand in line to get INXS tickets.' When we were doing that, we would think: 'We're country pioneers going to see INXS.'"

—Jeff Tweedy

You can blame the term No Depression and its ensuing scene on Uncle Tupelo, a trio of

Souled American • Uncle Tupelo

UNCLE TUPELO - ANODYNE

rock'n'roll kids from Belleville, Illinois (just across the Mississippi River from St Louis) who gave their debut album that very name—it was an obscure Carter Family song from the 1930s that they'd worked up. Uncle Tupelo were by no means the first rock band to load country into their repertoire—or even the first bunch of punks to sing with a twang—but it was a unique touch that stood them out from the crowd and made lots of sense. It wasn't just a novelty to gain attention, it was entirely organic: singer-songwriters Jeff Tweedy and Jay Farrar approached their music under the influence of Buck Owens, George Jones, and Neil Young as well as Black Flag and the Clash, and they drove it all home with a grassroots energy built on teenage angst and small-town frustration that made sense to '90s indie-rock ears. What was amazing about the response was that most of their nightclub fans probably knew little, if anything, about Owens, the Carter Family, or even Hank Williams.

Tweedy and Farrar formed Uncle Tupelo in 1987 with drummer Mike Heidorn. The three had previously played all-out punk-rock together in a high-school band they called the Primitives, which also included Farrar's brother Wade. The newly christened trio was still loud and proud, but they'd also become more enamored with country which, like punk, was traditionally a do-it-yourself kind of music. And when the bandmembers discovered the music of '60s country-rock hipster Gram Parsons, they knew they were onto something. The band built a sturdy midwestern following, and in 1989 they signed with the small indie label Rockville, which released their debut album, NO DEPRESSION. The album spoke of small-town life—the frustrations and anxieties—in a plain, immediate style that shifted from the thrashing

punk of "Graveyard Shift" to the moaning, late-night country strains of "Whiskey Bottle." The follow-up album, STILL FEEL GONE, showed that their songwriting skills and instrumental prowess were improving further.

The milestone album for Uncle Tupelo was on a technical level their simplest, MARCH 16–20, 1992, cut over those dates with producer Peter Buck. It was all-acoustic this time—originally not so much a stylistic decision as a move intended to keep the proceedings uncomplicated—and included some fascinating covers that revealed the band exploring the territory of traditional country and old-time folk music more seriously. The album won Uncle Tupelo wider attention, and before long they were signed to Sire. At this point Heidorn had left and drummer Ken Coomer had replaced him. For their major-label debut, ANODYNE, they also brought multi-instrumentalist Max Johnston and bassist John Stirratt on board, with Lloyd Maines stepping in on pedal steel. The album proved to be their finest achievement—thanks to excellent songwriting and masterful arrangements that blended their country and rock'n'roll influences into an almost seamless whole—but it was also their swansong. After eight months touring in support of the album, and winning new fans with every show, Farrar abruptly quit the group in May of 1994. He formed Son Volt later that year, pulling Heidorn back into the drummers' slot. Tweedy also launched his own group, Wilco, with Coomer, Johnston, and Stirrat remaining on board.

⊙ **No Depression** (1990; Rockville). The debut album is rough in spots, moving in fits and starts between angst-ridden punk of "Screen Door" and "Graveyard Shift" and the country strains of "Whiskey Bottle," "Life Worth Livin'," and the title track. It's an invigorating ride and still sounds fresh.

⊙ **Still Feel Gone** (1991; Rockville). Another back-and-forth between country and punk, with well-crafted songs like the fiery "Gun" and the twangier "True To Life" showing Tweedy and Farrar maturing as writers and singers.

⊙ **March 16–20, 1992** (1992; Rockville). Entirely acoustic, the arrangements pared down but still vibrant and rich, this proved Uncle Tupelo's breakthrough album in terms of national recognition. It's a great one, too, with fascinating cover songs (the traditional "Satan Your Kingdom Must Come Down," the Louvin Brothers' "Great Atomic Power") mixed in-between outstanding originals written and recorded in a similar style.

⊙ **Anodyne** (1993; Warner Bros.). The band's crowning achievement for its almost seamless blend of country influences within a sturdy rock'n'roll framework. Songs like "Slate," "Acuff Rose," the Doug Sahm song "Give Back The Key To My Heart" (on which Sahm himself appears as guest vocalist), and the gorgeous title track are masterful achievements, the arrangements highlighted by the addition of steel guitar, fiddle, Dobro, and mandolin.

Waco Brothers

The players may all be seasoned rock'n'roll veterans, but there's nothing tight and shiny about the Waco Brothers, and that's exactly the point. This well-lubricated, loosely structured outfit takes great pride in digging through the roots of American roots music and chewing it up with a toothy punk-rock grin. Sure, the Waco Brothers can get rowdy, sometimes even reckless ("wasted swing" they once called their music). But for all that, they're not out to make fun of anyone or to rip the genre apart. The Wacos' music spills over with the bandmembers' love of merry-making and their deep reverence for music, country and otherwise, of all shades and colors, just as long as it's sincere.

Leading the Waco pack is Jon Langford, best known as the co-founder of and main instigator behind the punk-rock group the Mekons. That British-born band first got off the ground in Leeds in 1977, and as they grew up musically, Langford and his bandmates became increasingly enamored with American country music—albums such as FEAR AND WHISKEY and END OF THE WORLD. Several of the bandmembers relocated to Chicago around the end of the '80s, and they've been mainstays on the Chicago indie rock/country scene ever since. Timms has cut a series of western-flavored albums that showcase her lovely voice (1999's COWBOY SALLY'S TWILIGHT LAMENTS FOR LOST BUCKAROOS is a real beauty). As for Langford, he's dipped into a wide assortment of musical projects, among them his neo-punk band Skull Orchard and album-length tributes to Johnny Cash and Bob Wills under the band name Pine Valley Cosmonauts. And, of course, the Waco Brothers.

The Wacos center around Langford, but the membership also includes guitarist Dean Schlabowske, mandolin player Tracey Dear, pedal-steel player Mark Durante, bassist Alan Doughty,

and drummer Steve Goulding. Assembling the band wasn't exactly a premeditated affair. Under the group name Hillbilly Lovechild, Langford had contributed a track to the Bloodshot Records 'insurgent country' compilation FOR A LIFE OF SIN in 1994, and Bloodshot co-founder Nan Warshaw suggested he turn that experiment into a full-blown album. Thus were the Waco Brothers born. Their debut album, ...TO THE LAST DEAD COWBOY (1995), was a rumbling and ragged creation of original material, songs that were as much inspired by Hank Williams as the Clash. The band is not a fulltime venture for any of its members, and they don't tour all that often, but so far they've survived through three additional albums: COWBOY IN FLAMES (1997), DO YOU THINK ABOUT ME? (1997), and WACO WORLD (1999). Even though the songs do employ pedal steel and sometimes mandolin, and there are hints of a Hank and Lefty twang underneath the grinding guitars, don't expect 'country' in the classic sense. After all, these are just a bunch of punk socialists playing for beer money. Good thing they're seasoned professionals who know what they're doing.

⊙ **Cowboy In Flames** (1997; Bloodshot). The Wacos do a buzzsaw cover of Roy Acuff's "Wreck On The Highway" that captures the song's aggressive spirit, and a handful of steel-tinged, twang-infested numbers ("Dollar Dress," "Dry Land"), but it's Langford's song "The Death Of Country Music" that's the crowning achievement—digging up bones, spilling a little blood, and having a party, yet demonstrating throughout the group's deep reverence for all that's made country tick over the past century.

Dale Watson

"My songs come directly from my life, as I see it and feel it. I don't write songs through a Nashville board room committee. I'm ashamed of what popular music has become."

—Dale Watson

Texas-based singer, songwriter, and guitarist Dale Watson is among the finest contemporary ambassadors of country music's hard-edged, honky-tonkin' side—a world populated by truck drivers, beer joints, and classic country radio stations. Watson's music has the feel of 1950s and '60s honky tonk—the kind popularized by greats like Buck

ANGELA LUBRANO

Dale Watson

Dale Watson

early on, and after graduating from high school spent the next seven years honing his country music skills in the bars and honky tonks around Pasadena. In 1988 he moved to LA partly to be closer to the Bakersfield sound, but also at the encouragement of his friend and fellow musician, Rosie Flores. He played guitar in the house band at the Palomino Club during their weekly barn dances, and even landed a small acting role in the River Phoenix picture *Thing Called Love*. He cut two songs for Curb Records in 1990, "One Tear At A Time" and "You Pour It On," and he also had a song included on volume three of A TOWN SOUTH OF BAKERSFIELD, a CD series compiling Southern California country artists.

Watson moved to Nashville in 1992 and landed a songwriting job with the publishing company Gary Morris Music, but he soon moved back home to Texas, settling this time in Austin. He's been a fixture on that city's country music scene ever since. The West Coast label HighTone signed Watson and released his debut album in 1995. Since then, he and his band, Lone Star, have continued to burn up the tour circuit, spreading the honky-tonk gospel all over Texas and in clubs from New York to California—not to mention throughout England, Germany, Australia, and other international locales. The CMA has yet to acknowledge his existence, but Watson has been honored at the British Country Music Awards. After three albums on HighTone, a collection of truck-driving songs (THE TRUCKIN' SESSIONS), and a European-only release (PEOPLE I'VE KNOWN, PLACES I'VE SEEN), Watson has signed with a major label, Sire, and looks forward to even wider recognition.

Owens, Merle Haggard, Johnny Paycheck, and George Jones, all of whom he pays tribute to in songs like "Nashville Rash," "A Real Country Song," and "I Hate These Songs." As much as Watson admires the past, however, he's no simple throwback: his gritty-edged, hot-fired spirit is firmly planted in the present day. He's not winning any popularity contests on Music Row—"Help me Merle I'm breaking out in a Nashville rash, it's lookin' like I'm falling in the cracks," he sings on "Nashville Rash," a song on his debut CD CHEATIN' HEART ATTACK—but his deep Texas drawl and excellent repertoire of no-nonsense material have won him critical acclaim and a strong following along country music's fringe—which these days is actually a fairly substantial territory.

Watson was born in Alabama on 7 October, 1962, but his family later moved to Pasadena, Texas, where he spent the majority of his teenage years. He began playing guitar and writing songs

⊙ **Cheatin' Heart Attack** (1995; HighTone). Watson's debut is one of the finest and most classic-sounding country records of the past decade, thanks to catchy songs like "List Of Reasons" and the title track (which in a more perfect world would've been clear country hits), the weeper "You Lie," and the bitter but amusing "Nashville Rash."

⊙ **Blessed Or Damned** (1996; HighTone). The kick-off track "Truckin' Man" is another hopped-up beauty, and the rest of the album falls into place behind it,

584 **Settin' the Woods on Fire: Alternative Country in the 1990s**

Dale Watson grew up in Pasadena, Texas where country music was all he heard. "It wasn't 'til I moved to LA in 1987 that I found out Jerry Lee Lewis was better known for his rock tunes than his country," Watson explains. "I had never even heard of rockabilly or Gram Parsons 'til then." Since his 1995 debut album, CHEATIN' HEART ATTACK, Dale Watson has amassed a large body of compositions that work from deep within the heart of the traditional honky-tonk sound without sounding retro. Here he talks about the songs that have most influenced him.

"Ring Of Fire," Johnny Cash
"The guitar sound of Luther Perkins, that's what really made me want to play country guitar. That guitar sound conveys an attitude and it's got swagger, that's what I'm after in my guitar playing."

"Love's Gonna Live Here," Buck Owens
"The whole West Coast sound opened my ears to how a song can be arranged around the guitar. The way that big bottom note on the guitar just jumps out at you, in the Bakersfield Sound the guitar is right up front with the voice."

"San Antonio Rose," Bob Wills
"I grew up with Bob Wills music in my pores, it permeated everything in Texas. I play beer joints mostly, and those kinds of mid- to fast-tempo good-time songs go over best. You can hear the honesty in every note, there's nothing fake, yet the music is always fun."

"Silver Wings," Merle Haggard
"The melody, the lyrics, the arrangements are beyond any specific time period. It's what I call classic in that it's timeless and undated. Writing that timeless song is my goal. Being emotional without being sentimental, being timeless without being retro."

"Mama Tried," Merle Haggard
"Merle, Kris Kristofferson, Willie, Roger Miller, they wrote songs about crime, suicide, murder, interracial marriages, you can hear the honesty in those songs, they don't pull punches. In today's country, they've got to keep it light; it can't have real grit or real emotion, because then you'd evoke emotion, and that's too scary for the suits."

—Michael Ryan

---

continuing the sturdy honky-tonk pattern he established on his debut.

⊙ **I Hate These Songs** (1997; HighTone). Watson fans will find few surprises here, but there are far worse things in the world than another collection of purebred, hard-bitten country songs. His songwriting and arrangements, in fact, are as tight and appealing as ever on songs like "Jack's Truck Stop & Café" and "Ball & Chain." And the title track, which namechecks a series of country classics ("Silver Wings," "Oh Lonesome Me," "He Stopped Loving Her Today") that break up Watson every time—"I sit in my car and I bathe in their sorrow," he moans—hence his "hatred."

⊙ **The Truckin' Sessions** (1998; Koch). Watson spends much of the year on the road, and so an album of songs about trucks and truck drivers made sense. It's a fun collection that gives his brand of honky tonk a specific focus this time. Originally a cassette-only release of 10 songs that Watson and his band cut in one day, the CD version adds 4 additional cuts.

Gillian Welch

Singer-songwriter Gillian Welch has a talent for dark, sobering songs that deal with rural hardship. The fact, however, that she was born in New York City (2 October, 1967) and grew up in the suburbs of Los Angeles—as opposed to the Appalachian hills—has raised the hackles of some stubborn hillbilly music fans. Welch sings about cotton farming and being an orphan on "God's highway" with apparent sincerity, though personally she's probably never seen her stillhouse torn down or been reduced to only "five cold nickels" in her pocket. Yet does that really matter? Because the bottom line remains that Welch has an attractive, moody voice and a knack for writing compelling, lyrical story songs and character sketches in the tradition of old–time mountain-folk music and bluegrass. The passion and sincerity in her music is undeniable. And she's certainly not the first city-bred gal to find inspiration in the songs of the Carter Family or the Stanley Brothers.

Dale Watson • Gillian Welch

Welch's partner in crime is guitarist David Rawlings, whom she met in Boston while attending the Berklee School of Music in the early 1990s. They began performing together after moving to Nashville, and it was there, while opening a show for Peter Rowan, that producer T-Bone Burnett first heard them. He brought the pair out to Hollywood to cut what became Welch's debut album, REVIVAL. Two years later Burnett also produced Welch's follow-up, HELL AMONG THE YEARLINGS—perhaps even more spare and bittersweet than its predecessor. Since its release in 1998, she and Rawlings have toured on a regular basis.

⊙ **Revival** (1996; Almo Sounds). Welch's debut is a strong collection of originals (many co-written with Rawlings) that beautifully showcase her spare, traditional style. Some such as "Orphan Girl" (covered by Emmylou Harris on WRECKING BALL) are almost dead quiet and feature just Welch and Rawlings; on others, producer T-Bone Burnett brought in some heavy-hitting accompanists, including guitarist James Burton and drummer Jim Keltner—though their star power never outweighs the simple power of Welch and Rawlings' music.

⊙ **Hell Among The Yearlings** (1998; Almo Sounds). In terms of writing and execution, the songs here are a step forward for Welch and Rawlings. Except for the near-rockabilly diversion "Honey Now," the overall mood is more in line with the banjo-inflected "Rock Of

Ages" and the drugged-out "My Morphine"—quiet, haunting and mesmerizing.

Whiskeytown

"There's nothing better than making yourself feel great about expressing the fact that you feel like shit."

—Ryan Adams

At first you might want to discount Whiskeytown as a rip-off. Any self-respecting Uncle Tupelo fan who takes a quick spin of Whiskeytown's debut album, FAITHLESS STREET, would certainly recognize the raspy, slightly broken voice of chief singer and songwriter Ryan Adam as a dead ringer for that of Jeff Tweedy (once of Tupelo and now of Wilco)—not to mention Whiskeytown's penchant for mixing a grungy guitar sound with a southern backyard twang on songs that search, round and round, for the soul of small-town life. But then those songs just get under your skin—the love-wrecked loser in "Drank Like A River," the picture of Jesus that hangs above the sink in "Mining Town," the forgotten love letters that "smelled of her ancient perfume" in "Houses On The Hill." They might not be masterpieces, but there's a passion in Adams' bourbon-laced voice that keeps the music running back and forth in your head—and makes you want to hear that song about small-town angst and drinking one more time.

Whiskeytown first formed in Raleigh, North Carolina in 1994, just after Adams' former punk band, the Patty Duke Syndrome, broke up. Adams hooked up with drummer "Skillet" Gilmore and then slowly pulled together guitarist Phil Wandscher, fiddler Caitlin Cary, and bassist Steve Grothmann. They cut an EP for the North Carolina label MoodFood, then in 1995 the label released FAITHLESS STREET. The album and subsequent live shows (including a well-attended 1996 showcase at the South By Southwest music conference in Austin) gained the group plenty of attention at a time when alt.country bands were the hot new thing

TOM ERIKSON

Gillian Welsh (foreground) and David Rawlings

Gillian Welch • Whiskeytown

alt.country quintet Whiskeytown

among frustrated indie-rock patrons. Whiskeytown signed with Outpost (a division of Geffen) and cut the album STRANGER'S ALMANAC. By this point Grothmann and Gilmore had departed, and bassist Jeff Rice and drummer Steve Terry were brought on board.

STRANGER'S ALMANAC was far more low-key than their debut, even tender at times, and it became another critic's favorite. Adams was clearly the center of the picture, thanks to his whiskey-soaked voice and moody songwriting—talents he was really still only developing, being barely over twenty-one years old at the time. He was also, however, proving himself something of a problem child to work with. Save for Cary, who's remained loyally in place, all of Whiskeytown's original bandmembers—and quite a few who succeeded them as well—have quit or been fired. And live shows, well, they've always been a gamble. On good days the band has proven wildly brilliant, Adams the polite and gracious host; other times the show has dissolved into a drunken, embarrassing mess. Still, Adams' talents are undeniable, and so far Outpost has continued to support the band. ALMANAC proved enough of a success for the label to pick up and reissue FAITHLESS STREET in what was supposedly its original song order (with extra tracks thrown in). At the same time, MoodFood released RURAL FREE DELIVERY, a compilation of more early recordings, and Bloodshot issued some Whiskeytown singles. A new Whiskeytown album was recorded in 1999, but in

the wake of the PolyGram/Universal merger, both Geffen and Outpost were phased out of the corporate picture, leaving the band without a record company. This bump in the road, however, hasn't stopped the prolific Adams from writing loads of new songs. In late 1999 and 2000, he showcased his latest batch of brilliant (and deathly quiet) new material at a series of solo acoustic shows—during which he appeared brooding, yet relatively polite—and the concept of an Adams solo album was also on the drawing board.

⊙ **Faithless Street** (1996; MoodFood; reissued 1998; Outpost). At times delicately arranged, but still dirty and burned around the edges, FAITHLESS STREET proves an exciting debut that pulls you in with catchy melodies and virile Southern-rock spirit. The reissued version drops "Oklahoma" from the original but brings in 9 additonal tracks. Two ("16 Days" and "Excuse Me If I Break My Own Heart Tonight") are early, rougher versions of songs that showed up later on STRANGER'S ALMANAC.

⊙ **Stranger's Almanac** (1997; Outpost). Adams may have a rough voice, but he's an expressive and passionate singer; as for his songwriting, it seems to only get better with time. A few songs are rowdy ("Waiting To Derail"), but the standouts are quiet, haunting beauties like "16 Days," "Houses On The Hill," and "Dancing With The Women At The Bar."

Whiskeytown • Wilco

Wilco

> "Before you formulate where you're going, I think it's important to see where people have been. I personally can't understand how you can think you're creating something new and fresh without hearing what you're supposedly springing off from."
>
> —Jeff Tweedy

Wilco's Jeff Tweedy

You could argue that Wilco has almost entirely dropped country music from its agenda—as the band's grown and progressed, Jeff Tweedy and company have shown far more interest in 1970s rock'n'roll, hooks and all, than anything honky tonk or hillbilly. But the connection is there, and not only because singer, songwriter and guitarist Tweedy was a founding member of Uncle Tupelo. Since forming Wilco in 1994, in the wake of Uncle Tupelo's demise, Tweedy and his bandmates (initially John Stirratt, Ken Coomer, and Max Johnston; now Stirratt, Coomer, and guitarist Jay Bennett) have shown they can't quite shake the twang out of their mix—listen to songs like "Forget The Flowers" (from BEING THERE) and "Passenger Side" (from A.M.). Still, though, the more guitar-oriented direction makes perfect sense as Tweedy was the stronger rock'n'roll influence even in his Tupelo days (songs like "Gun" and "Screen Door" were his creations). All this, of course, is just fine, as the excellent BEING THERE attests. Since that album's release in 1996, Wilco has stepped out of the No Depression pigeonhole and into a world they find brighter and more promising.

⊙ **A.M.** (1995; Sire). Wilco's debut finds Tweedy and company searching for a more rock-edged sound to call their own. Much of the music feels only partway there, which isn't surprising for a band just finding its legs. Yet there is plenty to like here, and songs like "Box Full Of Letters," "Passenger Side," and "Too Far Apart" show the band can be fun as well as pensive.

⊙ **Being There** (1996; Reprise). This double album is chock full of gritty rock ("Monday") and catchy pop ("Outtasite [Outta Mind]") songs that have a welcomed 1970s-era familiarity. Don't worry, it's not derivative—the music has a fresh, contemporary energy that belongs entirely to Wilco. It's a fun ride, but it has its moody, edgy side, too, thanks to songs like

"Misunderstood," "Someone Else's Song," and "Sunken Treasure."

⊙ **Mermaid Avenue** (1998; Elektra). These aren't straight Woody Guthrie cover songs, they're actually a collaboration: British singer Billy Bragg and Wilco took lyrics to unfinished Guthrie songs and created music to go with them. It's an inspired idea that works most of the time.

⊙ **Summer Teeth** (1999; Reprise). A brighter and somewhat lighter take on the pop hooks and rock'n'roll riffs they explored so well on BEING THERE.

Lucinda Williams

> "The worst thing would be to sell out. I've got such an innate fear of that happening that my defenses go up if I even think something's headed in that direction."
>
> —Lucinda Williams

As a singer and songwriter who virtually obliterates the lines between rock, blues, and country, Lucinda Williams has garnered an immense amount of respect and adulation from critics, fellow musicians and fans alike. Most of that reverence is deserved, as she's written some incredible songs that have proven their endurance decades later—"Sharp Cutting Wings," "King Of

Hearts," "Passionate Kisses," "Side Of The Road," "Pineola." But in the process she's also gained an unfortunate reputation as a prima donna thanks to her quest for artistic perfectionism—she's only released five albums in twenty-some years for an assortment of record labels, making fans wait four, six, and even eight years for her next project. She's spun the story as that of a lonesome artist fighting the endless fight for creative control and artistic integrity, and to her credit she's so far managed a strong payoff each time. Her albums are consistently solid on a musical level, her voice a rough-edged kind of pretty that's inherently soulful, and the songs more often than not deeply personal—her music is her own, it feels and sounds like that of no one else.

Williams was born on 26 January, 1953 in Lake Charles, Louisiana. Her father is Miller Williams, a respected poet and English literature professor, and Lucinda grew up in intellectual surroundings and in an assortment of locales where her father traveled for work—from the American South all the way to Santiago, Chile. She was inspired early on by Joan Baez and Bob Dylan, then later discovered Hank Williams and Delta blues artists like Robert Johnson, Howlin' Wolf, and Skip James. Further musical growth came during the '70s, when she traveled the country with her guitar, settling for a short time first in Austin (where the progressive country scene was in full swing) and then Houston (where singers like Townes Van Zandt and Nanci Griffith were establishing themselves in local coffeehouses). Feeling the time was ripe to make a statement herself, in 1978 Williams stepped into a Jackson, Mississippi recording studio and cut her first album, RAMBLIN' ON MY MIND, a collection of blues and country covers. She followed this with HAPPY WOMAN BLUES, which she recorded in Houston with a full band. All the songs on that album were Williams originals, and they're an excellent bunch from top to bottom—in fact, titles like "Lafayette," "King Of Hearts," "Sharp Cutting Wings (Song To A Poet)" are among the finest of her career. It's a crime that she generally ignores them when she plays live.

Williams' first two albums had far more of an acoustic country and blues feel, but by her third album, LUCINDA WILLIAMS, she'd developed a firm and very much plugged-in rock'n'roll sound. That record didn't hit stores until eight years after its predecessor, during which time Williams had moved back and forth between Texas and Los Angeles and been courted by various record labels. She was determined to maintain creative control of her music, and it's the indie-rock label Rough

Trade that eventually heard what she was saying. The resulting album still had a twang, but it also wasn't afraid to get loud, expanding her audience into the world of rock'n'rollers, though without losing her country integrity: songs from the album such as "The Night's Too Long" and "Passionate Kisses" went on to be country chart hits for Patty Loveless and Mary Chapin Carpenter respectively, with the latter even winning a Grammy. Playing guitar on the album and co-producing it with Williams was Gurf Morlix, a buddy from her Houston days who used to play with B.W. Stevenson. Morlix remained Williams' close musical partner for nearly a decade. The band also included drummer Donald Lindley and bassist John Ciambotti, and both stuck with her for years as well (Lindley died in 1999).

Rough Trade released a five-song EP in 1989, PASSIONATE KISSES, and then Williams signed with RCA and began cutting a record for that major label. But the creative-control issue reared its head again, and Williams, unhappy with what the RCA and its production team were doing with her

© DAN DION PHOTOGRAPHY

Lucinda Williams

Lucinda Williams, San Francisco, 1999

music, quit the label and shifted to another indie, Chameleon. The ensuing album was SWEET OLD WORLD, and though it had by that point been four years since LUCINDA WILLIAMS, anticipation had been steadily building, and it was extremely well received. Whatever travails she'd been through with RCA, SWEET OLD WORLD seemed to prove that Williams' instincts regarding production issues were correct.

Despite her newfound respect both in and out of the industry, Williams still found it difficult to get her artistic desires to synch up with the recording process. She next signed with American Recordings (owned by Rick Rubin, who also released Johnny Cash's AMERICAN RECORDINGS and UNCHAINED albums); however, the label didn't survive long enough to follow through with the release of Williams' next album, 1998's CAR WHEELS ON A GRAVEL ROAD which was ultimately released by Mercury (ironically, both Rough Trade and Chameleon had gone out of business as well). What took so long this time? During that six-year gap between albums, Williams had been in and out of the studio time and again, recording the songs over and over and running through a series of musicians and producers in an attempt to get the sound "right." She hired Steve Earle as a producer but then dropped him; later she even fired her longtime guitarist Morlix. For many watching the process unfold, it moved past the point of comedy into the realm of frustration and disbelief; how much of what she was complaining about was actually true? And how long could she carry on like this?

Once again, however, she survived, even triumphed. Despite the stories of her nitpicking studio behavior that had filtered into the press ("Lucinda Williams Is In Pain" was the sarcastic title of a 1997 *New York Times Magazine* article), and the mounting impatience of even her staunchest fans, Williams emerging in 1998 with another album that both bowled over the critics and won her an ever larger fanbase. CAR WHEELS was proclaimed one of the best albums of the year (it went on to win a Grammy), and her shows were attracting bigger audiences than ever before. Late in 1998 she even shared the bill on a short tour with Bob Dylan and Van Morrison. As a bonus, by this point Williams' stage presence had improved immensely: ten years earlier she'd been stiff and uncomfortable, but in the years since she'd slowly warmed up, and touring in support of CAR WHEELS she actually seemed to be enjoying herself.

Whether Williams can ever break into the mainstream as a performer—something she seems

on the verge of doing but has always eluded her—is still up in the air. Just how long it'll take her to release her next album, and whether the fans will survive another six-year waiting game, are questions equally shrouded in mystery.

⊙ **Ramblin'** (1978; Folkways; reissued 1991; Smithsonian Folkways). A well-crafted, enjoyable collection that pays tribute to the great songwriters Lucinda grew up on—Robert Johnson, Memphis Minnie, Hank Williams, the Carter Family. The instrumention is simple, just Williams and guitarist John Grimaudo. The original full title was RAMBLIN' ON MY MIND.

⊙ **Happy Woman Blues** (Folkways, 1980; reissued 1990; Smithsonian-Folkways). Williams' first collection of original material is steeped in country and blues and filled with beautiful semi-acoustic arrangements, this time featuring a full band. In all the fanfare over her later releases, it's also amazingly overlooked—which is weird, because it's the strongest collection of her career, thanks to the quietly beautiful "Sharp Cutting Wings," the joyous "Lafayette," the wild and restless "Maria," and the intense and painful plea for romantic reciprocation, "King Of Hearts."

⊙ **Lucinda Williams** (1988; Rough Trade; reissued 1998; Koch). The album that broke Williams in both rock and country circles, thanks to her singing—as earthy and visceral as it is at times delicate and sweet—and songwriting. Titles like "Changed The Locks," "Passionate Kisses," and "Side Of The Road" are classics. The reissue on Koch includes includes 5 songs from her 1989 EP PASSIONATE KISSES and one previously unreleased song, "Sundays."

⊙ **Sweet Old World** (1992; Chameleon). "Pineola" is a powerful standout on what is yet another strong Williams collection. That song's not the only emotional knockout, however: Other notables include "He Never Got Enough Love," "Something About What Happens When We Talk," and the title track.

⊙ **Car Wheels On A Gravel Road** (1998; Mercury). Despite all the critical attention it received upon its release, this album is not the godsend it was touted to be. The songwriting, the arrangements, and the singing are certainly fine—much of it moving, some of it even profound—but the material also feels overworked. No one can tell Lucinda how long she should take to make an album, but it's hard to listen to CAR WHEELS and not wonder why on earth it took so long.

Lucinda Williams • Stephen Yerkey

Stephen Yerkey

TOM ERIKSON

Steve Yerkey

Stephen Yerkey is one of the greatest, little-known song-writers and singers west of the Mississippi. He can moan a gritty blues, growl hard-bitten country from a place deep inside his gut, or whisper the warmth of hope. His voice alone is an amazing instrument—full of quirks and kinks, but at its core always sturdy, creamy, and full-bodied. When Yerkey conjures up visions of cowboys, drunks and other desperate dreamers, his voice curls and ripples around the words, which jump in all directions but ultimately give in to Yerkey's control, easing to the ground and laying flat out. Behind him a steel guitar cries as the music shifts down low and the night moves onward into early dawn.

Yerkey's first band was Nonfiction, which he formed in San Francisco in the 1980s with Chris and Lance Campbell. They put out one record on the English label Demon, and while people in the know practically worshipped the thing, it never made Yerkey (the band's lead vocalist and song-writer) much of a living. He worked the clubs in San Francisco for a few years as a solo artist, often teaming up with other local artists like Chuck Prophet, Stephanie Finch, and Patrick Win-ningham. He cut songs for an album that was never released, including the awesome "Texas Is A Big Thing To Have In The Back Of Your Mind," then moved to Austin, Texas. After a year, however, he was back in Frisco, his momentum renewed once again. He recorded a new selection of songs that became his one and only solo album, CONFIDENCE, MAN, and this time it saw the light of day on the local label Heyday (it was also reissued in Europe by the German label Moll). Yerkey now lives in Grass Valley, California. He's currently without a deal, but he does perform occa-sionally and he continues to write songs.

⊙ Nonfiction (1988; Demon). The song "Dead Into West Virginia," Yerkey's spooky but rousing vision of the final hours of Hank Williams, should by all rights be a classic. Other songs like the moody "If I Do Dream Of You (Don't Wake Me Up)" and the whip-smart "Lightning Rod" prove this guy wasn't just fooling around—he's a songwriter and singer to be reckoned with.

⊙ Confidence, Man (1994; Heyday). Yerkey tried to veer somewhat away from his country inclinations on this record toward a bigger, wider production. However, songs like "Maker's Mark," "Where Cash Is King," and "I Just Haven't Laid Down Yet" prove his roots are firm and planted.

Stephen Yerkey

Directory of Bands and Artists

This is primarily a directory of bands and artists who have been assigned an individual entry in the book. These artists appear in plain type and the page reference indicates where an entry begins. Entries in italics are important individuals, institutions, or events featured less extensively—for example, Grand Ole Opry, or Country Music Association. The word 'The' has been ignored in alphabetizing the entries: thus The Blasters appear under 'B'.

A

Academy Of Country Music, The 173
ACE 436
ACM 173
Acuff, Roy 103
Adams, Kay 169
Adkins, Hasil 263
Alabama 428
Allen Brothers 8
Allen, Rex 49
Allen, Terry 461
Allman Brothers 410
Alvin, Dave 555
Anderson, Bill 292
Anderson, John 462
Arnold, Eddy 293
Asleep At The Wheel 74
Association of Country Entertainers 436
Atkins, Chet 294
Austin, Bobby 169
Autry, Gene 50

B

Bandy, Moe 343
Bare, Bobby 344
Barnett, Mandy 508
BCMA 527
Bell, Delia And Bill Grant 208
Bellamy Brothers 430
Big Sandy And His Fly-Rite Boys 263
Black Country Music Association 527
Black, Clint 509
Blasters, The 265
Blood Oranges 556
Blue Mountain 557
Blue Sky Boys 8
Boggs, Dock 10
Bogguss, Suzy 511
Bond, Johnny 170
Bottle Rockets 557
Boyd, Bill And Jim 75
BR5-49 512
Brooks & Dunn 513

Brooks, Garth 514
Brown, Junior 517
Brown, Marty 518
Brown, Milton And His Musical Brownies 75
Browns, The 296
Bruce, Ed 345
Bruner, Cliff 77
Bryant, Jimmy 201
Buckner, Richard 558
Burch, Paul 559
Burnette, Johnny And Dorsey 266
Bush, Johnny 346
Butler, Carl And Pearl 106
Byrd, Tracy 519

C

Cagle, Buddy 171
Campbell, Glen 171
Carlisle, Cliff 11
Carman, Jenks "Tex" 174

Robison, Carson 37
Rodgers, Jimmie 38
Rodriguez, Johnny 372
Rogers, Kenny 450
Rogers, Roy 61
Ronstadt, Linda 420
Rowan, Peter 246
Russell, Tom 58

S

Sahm, Doug 421
Scud Mountain Boys 579
Seeger, Mike 247
Seldom Scene 248
Shaver, Billy Joe 373
Shelton, Ricky Van 489
Shepard, Jean 195
Sheppard, T.G. 452
Simpson, Red 196
Skaggs, Ricky 490
Skillet Lickers 40
Skinner, Jimmie 144
Sleepy LaBeef 272
Smith, Carl 145
Smith, Connie 327
Smith, Margo 453
Smith, Sammi 375
Snow, Hank 147
Son Volt 580
Sons Of The Pioneers 62
Souled American 581
Sparks, Larry 249
Spears, Billie Jo 454
Sprague, Carl 64
Stanley Brothers 250
Statler Brothers 328
Stewart, Gary 376
Stewart, Wynn 197
Stone, Doug 541
Stoneman, Ernest "Pop" 42
Story, Carl 253
Strait, George 492

Street, Mel 377
Stuart, Marty 494
Sylvia 454

T

Talley, James 378
Texas Ruby And Curly Fox 148
Thompson, Hank 87
Tillis, Pam 542
Tillman, Floyd 149
Tills, Mel 329
Tippin, Aaron 542
Travis, Merle 198
Travis, Randy 496
Tritt, Travis 543
Tubb, Ernest 151
Tubb, Justin 153
Tucker, Tanya 455
Turk, Nathan 194
Twain, Shania 544
Twitty, Conway 330
Tyler, T. Texas 200
Tyson, Ian 65

U

Uncle Tupelo 581

V

Val, Joe 254
Van Zandt, Townes 379
Vincent, Gene 284

W

Waco Brothers 583
Wagoner, Porter 332

Wakely, Jimmy 66
Walker, Clay 545
Walker, Jerry Jeff 381
Walser, Don 67
Watson, Dale 583
Watson, Doc 254
Watson, Gene 384
Welch, Gillian 585
Wells, Kitty 153
West, Speedy 201
West, Speedy And Jimmy Bryant 201
Wheeler, Onie 155
Whiskeytown 586
White, Joy Lynn 546
White, Tony Joe 385
Whitley, Keith 497
Whitman, Slim 156
Wilburn Brothers 334
Wilco 588
Williams, Don 386
Williams, Hank 157
Williams, Hank Jr. 387
Williams, Hank III 546
Williams, Lucinda 588
Williams, Tex 89
Willis, Kelly 499
Wills, Billy Jack 90
Wills, Bob And His Texas Playboys 92
Wills, Johnnie Lee 96
Wiseman, Mac 256
Wood, Smokey 97
Work, Jimmy 161
Wynette, Tammy 334

Y

Yearwood, Trisha 547
Yerkey, Stephen 591
Yoakam, Dwight 500
Young, Faron 162
Young, Steve 389